COOK'S CONTINENTAL TIMETABLE

COOK'S CONTINENTAL TIMETABLE

A new edition of the August 1939 issue of Cook's Continental Timetable with enlarged type and introduction by J. H. Price

DAVID & CHARLES
Newton Abbot London North Pomfret (Vt)

This book is a new edition with enlarged type of the
August 1939 issue of Cook's Continental Timetable

British Library Cataloguing in Publication Data

Cook's continental timetable
1. Transportation – Europe – Timetables
– History – 20th century
I. Thomas Cook Limited
380.5′22′094 HE 242

ISBN 0-7153-9113-5

Printed in Great Britain
by Butler and Tanner, Frome and London
for David & Charles Publishers plc
Brunel House Newton Abbot Devon

Published in the United States of America
by David & Charles Inc
North Pomfret Vermont 05053 USA

INTRODUCTION

to Reprint of 1939 Cook's Continental Timetable
by J H Price

Cook's Continental Time Table was first published in March, 1873. At first it appeared four times a year, but it became a monthly publication in January 1883, designed as a handy pocket-sized alternative to the bulky *Bradshaw's Continental Railway and Hotel Guide.* Whereas Bradshaw tried to include every line of railway, Thomas Cook's editor John Breddall knew which routes and destinations interested the tourist and business traveller and which did not, and produced a one-shilling timetable which met 95% of the travel trade's requirements in only one-third of Bradshaw's space. The formula was successful and although the Continental Bradshaw has long since disappeared, the *Thomas Cook Continental Timetable* is still doing well, appearing every month though no longer at one shilling, the price which applied from 1873 to 1918. It rose to 2s.6d. in 1919 and to three shillings in 1937, but publication was suspended from September 1939 to the summer of 1946.

The edition of August, 1939, was therefore the last to appear before the wartime suspension of publication (when many Thomas Cook staff served in Royal Engineers Movement Control) and the last to appear in the original 1873 format. It was also the last issue to include air schedules and overseas shipping services. When publication was resumed in 1946, the ocean shipping services were transferred to *Cook's Ocean Sailing List* and Cooks' staff used *Bradshaw's Air Guide* for air services. The postwar Continental Timetable was therefore considerably thinner than the 1939 edition, but was also larger in page size for easier reading.

This David & Charles reprint of the August 1939 *Cook's Continental Time Table* has been produced in a larger size than the original (216mm by 138mm, instead of 183mm by 127mm) so as to be easier to read. The 1939 typeface was rather small and also subject to heavy wear by direct-impression letterpress printing, which caused it to thicken with use. The reprint includes all the timetable and text pages and nearly all the advertisements, except for a few hotel announcements omitted to make way for this new introduction. However, we must admit that the 1939 timetable was harder to use than its present-day namesake, because the tables were referred to by page numbers instead of table numbers, and this made it impracticable to repeat the numbers on the maps. At a time when nearly all international travel was by train and ship, constant practice kept travel clerks familiar with the book's contents and many of them knew the numbers off by heart.

The 1939 timetable began with 48 pages of general travel information on train accommodation, steamer cabins, currency regulations, passports and visas, a glossary of useful phrases in six languages, a list of Cooks' offices, and some less likely ones such as a list of golf courses on the Continent. Then follow the international express trains operated by Thomas Cooks' associate the Wagons-Lits Company, which are given pride of place over other trains, each one (including the Orient Express and the Golden Arrow) having a table to itself. This section is followed by the long-distance international through routes and services.

The most interesting pages for the transport historian may well be 138 to 148. Eleven pages were all that Cooks needed to show Europe's international air services in 1939, yet there were already nearly 100 services to, from and in Europe including Imperial Airways' Empire Route flying-boat services from Southampton Water to Sydney and Durban. The Australian service took ten days, with nine intermediate stops where passengers stayed overnight at hotels and the flying-boat was anchored nearby. There was already an hourly service between Croydon and Paris (Le Bourget), but aircraft did not yet have sufficient range to fly the Atlantic. Some of the flights to northern Europe left from Heston aerodrome in Middlesex. The most extensive route network in 1939 was that of Deutsche Lufthansa. The new Airways Terminus near London Victoria had just opened, but the limousine for Air France passengers still left from the Dorchester Hotel in Park Lane.

The bulk of the timetable, pages 149 to 343, consists of rail timetables for each country of Continental Europe, North Africa and the Middle East. Comparison with present-day timetables shows that most train services were both slower and less frequent than they are today, except on routes such as Berlin–Vienna and Berlin–Munich where political boundaries have changed. You could for instance go from Poland to Romania in 1939 without crossing any Russian territory. Most trains were steam-hauled, but several countries had begun to electrify some of their main lines, especially in mountainous regions, and there were already some fast diesel railcars in Germany. Some of the place names used in 1939 may be unfamiliar today, such as Fiume for Rijeka, Gravosa for Dubrovnik, Danzig for Gdansk, Breslau for Wroclaw, Antivari for Bar (but Constantinople had already become Istanbul).

Pages 348 to 481 are for the shipping historian. Until 1939, *Cook's Continental Time Table* also served as a guide to all the world's shipping lines except for those in Cooks' North Atlantic Sailing List. They include many famous names; some such as the Pharaonic Mail Line, Cowasjee Dinshaw, Chargeurs Réunis, Fabre & Fraissinet and Hamburg South America Line did not survive the war, but the others re-started their services when peace returned and carried on until the growing airline industry left the shipping companies dependent on the car ferry and cruising trades. River steamers shown in the pages included the Volga, the Yangtze River Line, the Irrawaddy Flotilla and Cooks' own cruise ships on the Nile.

The cover of the 1939 Continental timetable was orange, as was every issue from 1873 to 1975 except the centenary issue of March 1973. The present flame red cover dates from September 1975.

Extract from page 38 of August 1939 Continental Timetable:

'Passengers must always be present at the Custom House Examinations, and hand their keys to the examining officer. The Customs' Examination is one of the greatest drawbacks to the pleasures of foreign travel, but passengers will do well to remember that civility costs nothing, and may purchase much, and that the Custom House Officers are merely performing a duty perhaps as disagreeable to themselves as to the traveller.'

SEVENTH YEAR. AUGUST, 1939.

COOK'S CONTINENTAL TIME-TABLE

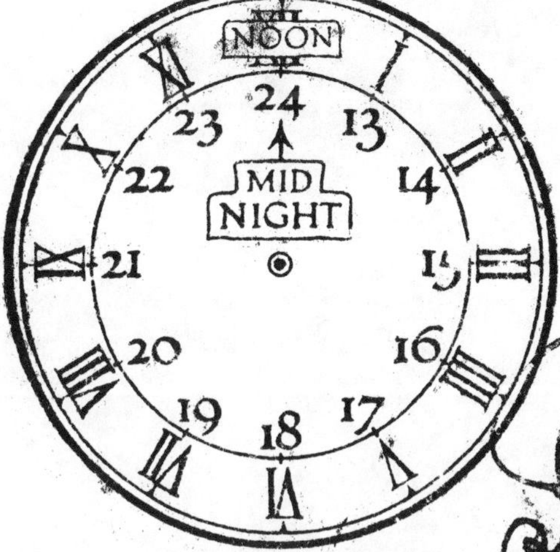

STEAMSHIP AND AIR SERVICES GUIDE

Based on the 24-Hour System

WITH TEN SECTIONAL MAPS

PRICE 3/

(POST FREE 3s. 3d.)

OFFICES OF THOS. COOK & SON, LTD.—*continued.*

GIBRALTAR, MALTA, EGYPT, SUDAN.

Gibraltar—56, Main Street (P.O. Box 190). (C).
Malta—25, Strada Mezzodi, Valletta. (C).
Alexandria—2, Rue Fouad I. (P. O. Box 185). (C).
Aswan—Grand Aswan Hotel (C). (Nile season only.)
Cairo—Near Shepheard's Hotel. (C).
Khartoum—Grand Hotel. (Nile season only.) (C).
Luxor—Near Winter Palace Hotel. (Nile season only.) (C).
Port Said—15, Rue Sultan Hussein. (C). Ticket Office in Station. (E)

PALESTINE AND IRAQ.

Baghdad—Al Rashid Street (opposite Maude Bridge) (P.O. Box 12.) (A).
Jerusalem—Julian's Way (P.O. Box 500). (A).
Haifa—British Sailors' Society Building, Palmers Gate (P.O. Box 273). (A).

INDIA, BURMA, CEYLON AND MALAYA.

Bombay—Hornby Road (P.O. Box 46) (A); also in Taj Mahal Hotel.
Calcutta—4, Dalhousie Square East (P.O. Box 26). (A).
Colombo—Lloyds Building, Prince Street (A); also in Grand Oriental Hotel (opposite the landing jetty).
Delhi—Oriental Building, Queensway, New Delhi. (A).
Sub-Office in Delhi: Kashmir Gate. *Winter only.*
Karachi—Finlay House, McLeod Road (P.O. Box 94). (A).
Lahore—46, The Mall (P.O. Box 179).
Madras—1/4-5, First Line Beach, George Town (P.O. Box 171). (A). Also in Connemara Hotel.
Rangoon—102, Phayre Street (P.O. Box 78). (A).
Simla—The Mall (P.O. Box 8). (Summer only.) (A).
Singapore—39, Robinson Road (A).

CHINA AND JAPAN.

Hong Kong—Queen's Building, opposite Star Ferry Pier (P.O. Box 38). (A).
Kobe—Oriental Hotel (P.O. Box 398). (A).
Peking—Grand Hotel de Pekin. (A).
Shanghai—119, Nanking Road (P.O. Box 519). (A).
Tientsin—63, Victoria Road. (A).

AUSTRALIA AND NEW ZEALAND.

Adelaide—National Mutual Building, 91, King William Street. (A).
Auckland—N.Z. Insurance Co.'s Buildings, Queen Street, C.1 (Box 24). (A).
Brisbane—Hibernian Building, Adelaide St. (A).
Christchurch—158A, Hereford Street (145). (A).
Melbourne—269, Collins Street. (A).
Perth—22, Forrest Place (Box L.907).
Sydney—National Mutual Building, George Street (Box 3590 S). (A).
Wellington—Bank of New Zealand Building, Lambton Quay, C.1. (A).

SOUTH AND EAST AFRICA

Bulawayo—Lonsdale House, Main Street (Box 961). (A)
Cape Town—30, Strand Street (Box 12). (A).
Durban—Mercury Lane, West Street (Box 33). (A).
Johannesburg—Corner of Fox and Loveday Streets (P.O. Box 4569). (A).
Mombasa—Opposite Kilindini Post Office (Box 515). (A).
Nairobi—Stanley House, Hardinge Street (Box 1241). (A).
Salisbury—Stanley House Stanley Avenue (A)

CANADA AND UNITED STATES.

Atlanta, Ga.—First National Bank Building. (A).
Baltimore (Md.)—305, N. Charles Street (A).
Beverly Hills (California)—9463 Wilshire Boulevard. (A).
Boston—360, Boylston Street. (A).
Chicago—16, North Michigan Avenue. (A).
Los Angeles—520, West 6th Street. (A).
Montreal—Dominion Square Building, 1241, Peel Street. (A).
New York—587, Fifth Avenue. (A).
221, Broadway (Tels.: Cooktravel).
Waldorf-Astoria Hotel (Tels.: Cookwaldof)
Philadelphia—1621, Walnut Street. (A).
Pittsburg, Pa.—Union Trust Building, Arcade (No. 145). (A).
San Francisco—318, Stockton Street. (A).
Toronto—68, King Street West. (A).
Vancouver (B.C.)—Granville Street.
Washington (D.C.)—812, Fifteenth St. N.W. (A).

COOK'S SPECIAL CORRESPONDENTS (not staffed by Cook's, nor under their control).
Hamburg—Weltreisebureau Union, G.m.b H., 7, Alsterdamm. Tels.: Coupon.
Munich.—Amtliches Bayerisches Reisebureau, 12, Ritter von Epp-Platz. Tels.: Weltreisen.

(A) Telegrams: **COUPON.** (C) Telegrams: **COOK.**

WAGONS-LITS/COOK OFFICES

Head Office (Administration only): 40, RUE DE L'ARCADE, PARIS (E)

ABBAZIA, Italy—Bagno Savoia, Corso Vittorio Emanuele III. (*Summer only.*) (**D**).

ADELBODEN, Switzerland — Dorfstrasse. (Winter Sports Season only.) (**D**).

AIX-LES-BAINS, France — Square du Temple de Diane. (*Summer only.*) (**D**).

Agence Generale, E. Caola and S. Jarrier, 2, Rue Davat. (*Winter only.*) Telegrams: Generagenc.

ALEPPO, Syria—Rue Gul Ab. (**D**)

ALEXANDRIA, Egypt—At the Station. (**E**).

ALGECIRAS, Spain—Puerto. (**D**).

ALGIERS, Algeria—61, Rue d'Isly. (**D**).

AMIENS, France—29, Rue de la République. (**D**).

AMSTERDAM, Holland — 10, Vijgendam (*Postbus No.* 706), Amsterdam C. (**D**). Amstel Hotel.

ANKARA, Turkey—Bankalar Caddesi No. 1. (**D**).

ANTWERP, Belgium—3, Place Teniers. (**D**).

ARAD, Roumania — Palatul Minoritilor, Bulevardul Regina Maria. (**D**).

ASWAN, Egypt—Sudan Government Railways Building. (**E**).

ATHENS, Greece—7, Place de la Constitution. (**D**).

BARCELONA, Spain—8-10, Paseo de Gracia (**D**).

BASLE, Switzerland—7, Centralbahnplatz (**D**).

BEIRUT, Syria—Rue Allenby (B.P. 85). (**D**).

BELLAGIO, Italy—Ticket Office, Lungo Lario. (*Summer only.*) (**D**).

BEOGRAD (Belgrade), Yugoslavia—1, Rue Kolarceva (**D**). Ticket Office in the Station.

BERLIN, Germany—
35, Unter den Linden, W 8. (**C**).
40, Unter den Linden, N.W.7. (**D**).
17, Kurfuerstendamm, W 50. (Tels.: Zoosleep.)

BERNE, Switzerland—2, Spitalgasse. (**D**).

BIARRITZ, France—1, Villa Larralde. (**D**).

BILBAO, Spain—8, Calle Hurtado de Amezaga. (**D**).

BLANKENBERGHE, Belgium — Casino Municipal Digue de Mer. (*Summer only.*) (**D**).

BORDEAUX, France—28-30 Cours de l'Intendance (**D**); and Place Gabriel (Palais de la Bourse).

BRASOV, Roumania—61, Strada Regele Carol I. (**D**).

BRATISLAVA, Slovakia—Sturova ulica c, I rohnam. Andreja Hlinky. (**D**).

~~**BRINDISI, Italy**—Hotel International.~~ (**D**).

BRUSSELS, Belgium—
17, Place de Brouckère. (**D**).
Grands Magasins "Au Bon Marché" (opp. Nord Station). (Tels.: Bonsleep.)
155, Rue de la Loi. (Tels.: Resleep.)
53, Avenue Louise. (Tels.: Lousleep.)
Ticket Office in Gare du Midi.

BUCHAREST, Roumania—Calea Victoriei 39. (**D**).
23, Strada Lipscani. (Tels.: Lipscasleep.)
Hotel Athénée Palace, Rue Episcopiei 1-3.

BUDAPEST, Hungary—Vörösmarty-ter 5, Budapest V. (**D**)

BUENOS-AIRES, Argentina—602, Florida. (**E**).

CAEN, France—128, Boulevard des Allies. (**D**).

CAIRO, Egypt—Rue Ibrahim Pacha, Shepheard's Building (**D**).

CANNES, France—1, Promenade de la Croisette. (**D**).

CASABLANCA, Morocco—Rue de l'Horloge. (**D**).

CERNAUTI, Roumania—1, Str. Iancu, Flondor. (**D**).

CHAMONIX, France—Avenue de la Gare, near the Casino (15th June to 15th Oct. and 18th Dec. to 28th Feb. only). (**D**).

CHISINAU, Roumania—Boulevardul Regele Carol II, No. 69. (**D**).

CLUJ, Roumania—18, Piata Unirei. (**D**).

COLOGNE, Germany—1, Domhof. (**D**). Ticket Office in Central Bahnhof. (**E**).

CONSTANTINE, Algeria—13, Rue Georges Clémenceau. (**D**).

CONSTANZA, Roumania—11, Piata Independentei. (**D**).

COPENHAGEN, Denmark—
1, Vesterbrogade. Palais de l'Industrie. (**D**).
Central Station: *Kiosque G.*
Ticket Office in Hotel d'Angleterre, 34, Kongens Nytorv. (Tels.: Angsleep.)
Ticket Office in Tivoli Gardens (*Summer only*).

CRACOW, Poland—12, Rue Slawkowska. (**D**).

DIJON, France—21, Place Darcy. (**D**).

EFORIA, Roumania—(*Summer only*).

ELISABETHVILLE, Belgian Congo—Avenue Royale. (P.O. Box 223.) (**D**).

(**A**) Telegrams: **COUPON.** (**C**) Telegrams: **COOK.** (**D**) Telegrams: **SLEEPING.**
(**E**) Telegrams: **WAGOLITS.**

WAGONS-LITS/COOK OFFICES—*continued.*

ESTORIL, Portugal—Estoril Parc. (D).
FEZ, Morocco—122, Boulevard Poeymirau. (D).
FLORENCE, Italy—7, Via Tornabuoni. (D). Ticket Office in New Station.
FRANKFURT-ON-MAIN, Germany—27, Kaiserstrasse. (D).
GALATZ, Roumania—38, Strada Domneasca. (D).
GDYNIA, Poland—7, Rue Br. Pierackiego. (D).
GENEVA, Switzerland—
4, Rue du Mont-Blanc. (D).
Ticket Office: Gare de Cornavin. (F).
GENOA, Italy—Palais de l'Hotel Colombia, Via Balbi. (D). Maritime Station—*Tickets only, on arrival and departure of Steamers.*
GHENT, Belgium—30, Place d'Armes. (D).
GRANADA, Spain—5, Plaza del General Franco. (D).
GRENOBLE, France—6, Place Victo Hugo. (D).
GSTAAD, Switzerland—Ticket Office in Station (*Winter Sports Season only*).
THE HAGUE, Holland—17, Hoogstraat (D).
HAMBURG, Germany — Cook's Special Correspondents: Weltreisebureau Union G.m.b.H., 7, Alsterdamm. (A).
HARBIN (Kharbine), Manchukuo—
Harbin Pristane—Information Office, 132 Kitaiskaya Street. (D).
Harbin New Town—6, Soongary Prosp. (D).
Harbin Foudziadiane—20, Cheng Yang Gué
INNSBRUCK, Germany—Hotel Tyrol. (D)
~~**INTERLAKEN, Switzerland**~~—Höheweg (D)
IRUN, Spain—Ticket Office in the Station.
ISTANBUL, Turkey—Galata: Köprubasi. (D). Ticket Office: 259, Istiklal Caddesi, Bevoglu.
IZMIR, Turkey—Boulevard Ataturk (Birinci Kordon 144. (D).
JASSY, Roumania—Strade Lapusneanu No. 49. (D).
JUAN-LES-PINS, France—Banca Commerciale Italiana, Boulevard Wilson (*Summer only*).
KANTARA EAST, Egypt—M. le Contrôleur des Wagons-Lits. (E).
KARLSBAD Germany— 16, Mühlbrunnenstrasse. (D)
KATOWICE, Poland—9, Rue Dyrekcyjne. (D). Ticket Office in Station (open from 19.0 to 0.0).
KAUNAS, Lithuania—55 Laisvies Al ee. (D), Ticket Office in the Station.
KNOCKE-SUR-MER/LE ZOUTE, Belgium—115, Digue de Mer. (*June 8 to Sept. 15 only.*) (D).
LAUSANNE, Switzerland—
2, Avenue du Theâtre. (D).
Ticket Office in the Station.
LE TOUQUET, France—88, St.Jean. (*Summer only.*) (D).
LIEGE, Belgium—19, Rue du Pont d'Avroy (D).
LILLE, France—78, Rue Nationale. (D).
LIMA, Peru—801, Jiron Union. (E).
LISBON, Portugal—87c, Rua do Carmo. (D).
~~**LOBITO, Angola**—Post Box 187.~~ (E).
LODZ, Poland—68, Rue Piotrowska. (D).
LOURDES, France—61, Rue de la Grotte (*Summer only*). (D).
LUCERNE, Switzerland—1, Haldenstrasse. (D).
LUGANO, Switzerland—27, Quai Vincenzo Vela. (D).
LUXOR, Egypt—At the Station. (E).
LWOW, Poland—15, Place Halicky. (D).
LYONS, France—Place Bellecour. (D). Bureau du *Nouvelliste* 14, Rue de la Charité. Tels.: (Nouvelliste). Information Office in Terminus Hotel.
MADRID, Spain—27, Calle de Alcalá. (D). Also in Palace Hotel.
MALAGA, Spain—20, Calle de Strachan. (D).
MARSEILLES, France—67, La Canebière. (D). Ticket Office in Gare St. Charles.
MEGEVE, France—Ticket Office at P.L.M. Motorbus Station (*Winter Sports Season only*). (Tels.: Autogare.)
MEMEL, Germany—Hermann Göring Strasse 24. (D).
MENTONE, France—22, Av. Felix Faure. (D).
METZ, France—3, Rue Gambetta. (D).
MEXICO CITY—1, Ave. F. Madero. (E).
MILAN, Italy—6, Via Manzoni. (D). Ticket Office in the Station.
MONTE CARLO, France—Avenue de Monte Carlo (between Casino and Post Office). (D).
MONTREUX, Switzerland—Arcades du National, Bon Port (C.P. 284). (D).
MULHOUSE, France—4, Rue du Sauvage. (D).
MUNICH, Germany—Cook's Special Correspondents: Amtliches Bayerisches Reisebureau, 12, Ritter von Epp-Platz. (Tels.: Weltreisen.)
MURREN, Switzerland—Ticket Office in Palace Hotel. (*Winter Sports Season only*).
NANTES, France—7, Place Royale. (D).
NAPLES, Italy—19-22, Via Partenope. (D). Ticket Office in Stazione Centrale. Stazione Marittima, Molo Luigi Razza (Tickets only, on arrival and departure of steamers).
NICE, France—
5, Promenade des Anglais. (D).
Ticket Office: 13, Place Masséna. (Tels.: Massleep.) Ticket Office in the Station.

(A) Telegrams: COUPON. **(C) Telegrams: COOK.** **(D) Telegrams: SLEEPING.**
(E) Telegrams: WAGOLITS. **(F) Telegrams: GARSLEEP.**

WAGONS-LITS/COOK OFFICES—*continued.*

OPORTO, Portugal—Palacio da Nacional, Praca da Liberdade. **(D).**

ORADEA, Roumania—2, Bulev. Regele Ferdinand. **(D).**

ORAN, Algeria—8, Rue d'Alsace Lorraine **(D).**

OSLO, Norway—Continental Building, 24-26, Stortingsgaten. (P.O. Box 745.) **(D).**

OSTEND, Belgium—43, Promenade Albert Ier. **(D).**

OUDJDA, Morocco—Ticket Office in Gare d'Oudjda de Voyageurs. (*Summer only.*) (Tels.: Hotel Terminus).

PALERMO, Italy—445-449, Via Roma. **(D).**

PALMA, Majorca—5-7, Paseo del General Franco. **(D).**

PARIS, France—
2, Place de la Madeleine. **(A).**
14, Boulevard des Capucines. **(D).**
118, Avenue des Champs-Elysées. (Tels.: Champsleep.)
62, Rue du Bac. (Tels.: Gausleep.)
Hotel Moderne, 8 bis, Place de la Republique (Tels.: Repsleep.)
Maison de France, 127, Avenue des Champs-Elysées.
Ticket Offices: Grand Hotel, Gares de l'Est du Nord, d'Orsay, de Lyon.

PAU, France—Agence Générale, 42, Rue Louis Barthou. (Tels.: Massignac.)

PLOESTI, Roumania—6, Strada M. Cogalniceanu. **(D).**

PONTRESINA, Switzerland — Kurverein. (*Winter Sports Season only*).

PORT SAID, Egypt—Ticket Office in Station **(E).**

POZNAN, Poland—12, Bronislawa Pieracikiego. **(D).**

PRAGUE, Bohemia—26, Prikopy **(D).**

RABAT, Morocco—In Station (Ville). **(D).**

RIGA, Latvia—Kalku Iela 4. **(D).** Ticket Offices in Gares Russe Internationale.

RIO DE JANEIRO, Brazil—52, Avenida Rio Branco.

ROME, Italy—9-11, Via Vittorio Veneto. **(C).**
93, Piazza San-Silvestro. **(D).**
Ticket Office in Terminus Station.

SAINT - ETIENNE France—Bureau de Voyages du Mémorial, 12 Rue Gérentet. **(D).**

SAINT-JEAN DE LUZ, France—82, Rue Gambetta. (*Summer only.*) **(D).**

ST. MORITZ, Switzerland—Hauptstrasse, 65. (Banque Populaire Suisse) **(D).**

SAN CARLOS DE BARILOCHE, Argentina—Edificio Baur Hermanos. (*Jan.* 1—*Feb.* 28 *only*).

SAN REMO, Italy—2, Via V. Emanuele **(D).**

SAN SEBASTIAN, Spain—2, Calle Andia. **(D).**

SANTIAGO, Chile—1058, Agustinas. (Casilla 1534). **(E).**

SAO PAULO, Brazil—4, Praça Patriarca, Caixa Postal No. 2793. **(E).**

SEVILLE, Spain—12, Avenida de la Libertad. **(D).**

SIBIU, Roumania—13, Str. Regina Maria **(D).**

SOFIA, Bulgaria—Kniaz Boris, 2. **(D).**

STOCKHOLM, Sweden—16, Gustav Adolfs Torg. **(D).**

STOLPCE, Poland—In the Station. **(D).**

STRASBOURG, France—30, Place Kleber. **(D).**

TALLINN, Estonia—Mundi 1, Raekojaplats **(D).**

TANGIER, Morocco—Rue du Statut (Consulat Général de France). **(D).**
Ticket Office on Wharf.

TAORMINA, Italy—108, Corso Umberto. **(D).** (*Winter only*).

THESSALONIKI, Greece—1, Rue Roi Constantin. **(D).**

TIMISOARA, Roumania-Bulevardul Regele Ferdinand, Pal. "Bancile Banatene Unite." **(D).**

TOULON, France—27, Avenue Vauban. **(D).**

TOULOUSE, France — Voyages de la Dépêche, 42 bis, Rue d'Alsace Lorraine. **(D)**

TRIESTE, Italy—2, Piazza Malta. **(D)**; also in Gare Maritime on arrival of steamers.

TUNIS, Tunisia—65 Av. Jules Ferry. **(D).**

TURIN, Italy—2, Via S. Teresa (Piazza San Carlo). **(D).**

VALENCIA, Spain—Av. Nicolas Salmeron No. 7. **(D).**

VARNA, Bulgaria—8, Boulevard Slivnitza. **(D).**

VENICE, Italy—Piazzetta dei Leoncini. (P.O. Box 760.) **(D).**

VENTIMIGLIA, Italy—Kiosk in Station.

VICHY, France—At the Casino. (*Summer only.*) **(D)**

VIENNA, Germany—Kärntnerring 11. **(D).**

VILLARS, Switzerland—Banque Cantorale Vandoise. (*Winter Sports Season only*).

VIRBALIS, Lithuania-Contrôleur des Wagons-Lits (in Station). **(D).**

WARSAW, Poland—Hotel Bristol, Krakowskié Przedmiescie, 42 44, Warszawa I. **(D).** Kiosk in the principal Station.

WENGEN, Switzerland — Ticket Office, Hotel Metropole. (***Winter Sports Season only.***)

WIESBADEN, Germany — Ticket Office Verkehrsamt, Wilhelmstrasse, 24-26. (*Summer only*).

ZAGREB, Yugoslavia—Jelatchitchev Trg., 13. **(D).** Ticket Office in Station.

ZURICH, Switzerland—42, Bahnhofstrasse. **(D).**; also in Central Station.

(A) Telegrams: **COUPON.** **(C)** Telegrams: **COOK.** **(D)** Telegrams: **SLEEPING.**
(E) Telegrams: **WAGOLITS.**

INTRODUCTION

A PUBLICATION which for sixty-six years has made its appearance month by month without a break, even during the long months of the War, when it was the only Foreign Time Table appearing in this Country, stands in no need of recommendation here. The ample and varied character of the Miscellaneous Information for travellers will be seen from the table of contents, while amongst the many special features which distinguish this work are the Through Services from London to all Continental towns, in Section II; the elaborate Steamship Services in Section III, and the many Sectional Maps.

THE TWENTY-FOUR HOUR SYSTEM OF EXPRESSING TIME.

This was the first English publication to adopt the twenty-four hour system for all the Railway Services of the Continent.

Users of Time Tables published on the Continent are already familiar with the sytem, but for the benefit of the uninitiated we subjoin a few examples.

The Hours are numbered consecutively from 1 to 24, starting from Midnight, as shown on the dial on the cover, the letters a.m. and p.m. being abolished. A Train arriving or departing at 1.10 p.m. is shown as 13.10; at 5.15 p.m. as 17.15; at 9.30 p.m. as 21.30, and so on. The figures "24.0" indicate a train arriving at Midnight, but a departure at that hour is shown by "0.0."

Arrivals or departures at any time between Midnight and 1 a.m. are expressed by "0.1" to "0.59."

Every care has been taken to render the Time Tables correct in accordance with the latest advices, but changes are constantly being made by the Companies concerned, and the publishers cannot hold themselves responsible for the consequences of either changes or inaccuracies.

THOS. COOK & SON, LTD.

Sixty-seventh Year. August, 1939.

COOK'S

Continental Time Table

STEAMSHIP AND AIR SERVICES GUIDE

A simple Guide to the Principal Rail, Road, Steamship and Air Services of Europe (also of Siberia, Syria, Egypt, Algeria, etc.) with Ocean Steamer Services to all parts of the World.

BASED ON THE TWENTY-FOUR HOUR SYSTEM.

EDITED AND COMPILED BY C. H. DAVIES, F.R.G.S.
FOR

THOS. COOK & SON LTD.

Originators of the Tourist and Excursion Systems

ESTABLISHED 1841.

General Foreign Passenger Agents Pennsylvania Railroad.

Head Office: BERKELEY STREET, LONDON, W. 1.

COOK—WAGONS-LITS

World Travel Service.

350 OFFICES THROUGHOUT THE WORLD.

CONTENTS.

PAGES.

List of Cook's and Wagons-Lits Offices, with Telegraphic Addresses ... ... 1 to 5
General Index of Stations and Ports ... ... 10 to 30

Section I.—Useful Information for Travellers.

Calendar 31
List of Ambassadors and Consuls ... ... 32 & 33
Passports, Visas ... ... 34 to 37
Custom House Regulations ... ... 38 & 39
Baggage, Registered Baggage ... ... 39 & 40
Foreign Moneys, Travellers' Cheques ... ... 41 to 49
Weights and Measures 50
Postal and Telegraphic Information 51
Public Holidays on the Continent 52
Temperature 53
Useful Phrases ... ... 54 & 55
Other Useful Information ... ... 56 to 59
Variation of Time in Different Countries ... 60

Section II.—Continental Time Tables.

PAGES

Through Routes from London ... ... 62 to 64
General Continental Routes ... ... 65 to 74
Special Accommodation, Sleeping Cars, Etc.... ... 75 & 76
Private Cabins on Channel Steamers ... ... 77 & 78
Pullman Car Trains and Trains de Luxe ... ... 79 to 85

TIME TABLES: Railway, Air and Inland Steamers—

British Railway Services ... ... 88 to 110
Through Services to and from Europe 111 to 137
Air Services ... ... 138 to 148
General Continental Services

- Belgium ... ... 149 to 154
- Holland ... ... 155 to 160
- Germany, and Hungary ... ... 161 to 215
- Poland ... ... 203 to 205, 226 to 229, 331
- Bohemia, Moravia and Slovakia ... ... 206 to 207A
- Lithuania, Latvia and Estonia... 208
- Denmark, Sweden and Norway ... ... 216 to 224
- Finland 228
- Union of Socialist Soviet Republics ... ... 230 to 235
- France ... ... 236 to 277
- Switzerland ... ... 278 to 297
- Italy ... ... 298 to 320

Section II.—Continental Time Tables (continued).

	PAGES
SPAIN AND PORTUGAL, INCLUDING BALEARIC ISLES	321 to 329
ROUMANIA	330 & 331
YUGOSLAVIA	332 to 332B
BULGARIA	332 to 332B
TURKEY	333 & 334
PALESTINE, SYRIA, HEDJAZ, IRAQ AND IRAN	334 & 335
GREECE	336 & 337
EGYPT, SUDAN AND CYPRUS	338 to 340
ALGERIA, MOROCCO AND TUNIS	340 to 342B
OVERLAND ROUTES TO MALTA	343

Section III.—Steamship Services.

Map shewing Mediterranean Steamer Routes.. between pages	338 & 339
Information for Passengers	344
Index to Companies	346 & 347
Tables of distances between Principal Ports in England, Scotland and the Continent, and Principal Ports in the Mediterranean and Black Sea	348 & 349
Summary of Services from England to the Mediterranean	350
Summaries of Services from Alexandria, Beyrout, Brindisi, Genoa, Haifa, Marseilles, Naples, Piræus, Port Said, Istanbul, Trieste, Venice	351 to 356
Summary of Services between the United Kingdom and Scandinavia	401
Summary of Services, England to Continental Ports	401
TIME TABLES, with full Itineraries, Names of Steamers, Gross Tonnage, and particulars of Passenger Accommodation, etc.	357 to 481
PART I.—United Kingdom and Continent, Ports north of Gibraltar to the Mediterranean, Black Sea, and via Suez Canal to Ports east of Suez	357 to 369
PART II.—Services in the Mediterranean and Black Sea, and from the Mediterranean to Ports east of Suez	371 to 400
Egypt (Nile Steamship Services)	370
PART III.—United Kingdom to the Continent, Ports North of Gibraltar, Norway, Denmark, Sweden, U.S.S.R., etc.	402 to 412
PART IV.—Local Steamship Services between Continental Ports north of Gibraltar; Scandinavia and U.S.S.R.	413 to 430
PART IVa.—Special Supplement showing Norwegian Fjord Steamer Services. SUMMER ONLY	431 to 441
PART V.—United Kingdom and Continent to Africa (via West Coast), and South America, Canada, Canary Islands, Australia (via The Cape), etc., etc.	442 to 468
PART VI.—Colonial and Miscellaneous Services, etc.	469 to 481

Sectional Maps.

	BETWEEN PAGES		BETWEEN PAGES
Belgium, Holland, and Northern France	113-114	Switzerland	279-280
Northern Germany	162-163	Northern Italy	298-299
Sth. Germany, and Hungary	190-191	Southern Italy	312-313
Norway, Sweden and Denmark	217-218	Spain and Portugal, including Balearic Isles	321-322
Southern France	257-258	Mediterranean	338-339

GENERAL INDEX

Of Stations, Ports and Towns shown in the Railway, Steamship, Air and Diligence Tables.

Aabenraa, 419
Aachen, 80, 128, 137, 151, 165, 166, 240
Aalborg, 215A, 404, 419
Aalen, 186
Aalesund, 224A, 414, 415, 418, 420 421, 428, 439, 440, 468
Aandalsnaes, 219, 221 439
Aarau, 282, 283
Aardal 225
Aardalstangen, 435, 436, 437 438
Aarhus, 214, 215, 215A, 419
Aarosund, 214
Abancourt, 238, 242
Abano, 320
Abbazia, 305, 375, 376
Abbeville, 237
Aberdeen 92 to 97, 105 to 107
Abergavenny, 98, 99
Abidjan, 147
Abisko, 218
Abo 142, 228, 404, 414, 416, 421, 423, 472
Abonema, 447
Abu Simbel, 370
Acajutla, 450, 458
Accra, 147, 445 to 448, 452, 456A, 472
Achladocampos, 336
Acqui, 300
Ada, 452
Adana, 83, 144, 333, 334
Adapazari, 333
Addis Ababa, 143
Adelaide, 146, 363, 365, 366, 382, 442, 450, 458, 463, 468, 471, 473, 476
Adelboden, 296
Aden, 357, 358, 359, 363 to 367, 369, 382, 383, 384 385, 389, 390, 470
Adrianople (see Edirne)
Aedipso, 378
Æghion, 336, 371B
Afarnes, 439
Affreville, 341
Affroun, 341
Afyon, 334
Agadir, 147, 392
Agay, 263, 264
Agen, 249, 252
Aghia Nicolao, 378
Agram (see Zagreb)
Agrigento, 314, 315
Agrinion, 336
Agulo, 465
Ahwaz, 368, 472
Aigle, 280, 290, 291
Aillevillers, 268, 271, 272
Ain Ghrasesia, 342B
Ain Sefra, 342
Ain Temouchent, 342
Airolo, 287, 296
Aix, 263
Aix-les-Bains, 82, 121, 122, 138, 265, 267
Ajaccio, 138, 254, 376, 387, 392
Akcaabod, 375
Akhissar, 334
Akrata, 336
Akstafa, 231
Akureyri, 414, 418, 421
Akyab 145, 147
Al, 219
Alanya, 375
Alaschir, 334
Alassio, 81, 299
Albacete, 323
Albbruck, 180, 212
Albenga, 299
Albertville, 121, 122, 265
Alcamo-Calatafimi, 315
Alcazar, 85, 323 to 325
Alcazarquivir, 342A
Alcudia, 138, 328, 399
Alderney, 405, 407
Aldesago, 292
Aleksandrovo, 380
Aleksinac, 332
Alencon, 111, 241
Aleppo, 83, 334, 335
Aleppy, 382
Alès, 254
Alessandria, 118, 300 to 303
Alexandretta, 333, 362, 371B, 375, 386, 388
Alexandria, 143, 145, 146, 338, 361, 367, 369, 371, 371B, 372, 378, 381, 382, 386, 387, 388, 393, 397, 473, 443
Alexandrople, 333, 337, 372
Alexandrov (U.S.S R.), 230
Alexandrovo (Pol.), 226
Alexandrovsk (C. Asia), 233
Alexisbad, 167
Alexishafen, 470
Alf (Bullay), 210
Algeciras, 85, 325, 328 371, 399
Alghero, 143, 395, 397A
Algiers, 138, 142, 340 to 342, 342B, 359, 361, 364, 369, 377, 391, 393, 394, 398 448, 454, 455, 464
Algoa Bay, 463, 467
Algodor, 323
Algoz, 328
Alhucemas 399
Alibunar, 330
Alicante, 142, 323, 325, 368, 399, 464, 465, 468
Allahabad 145, 146, 147
Allinge, 417
Almelo, 131, 159
Almeria, 324, 368, 399, 465
Alimssa (see Omis)
Almoraima, 325
Almorchon, 323
Alor Star, 145, 146
Alora 324
Alp Grum, 289
Alphios, 337
Alpnachstad, 281, 289, 293
Alsasua, 321, 322
Altafjord, 428
Altdorf, 295
Altenbeken, 165, 166
Alt-Munsterol (see Montreux-Vieux)
Altona, 81, 130, 132, 161, 162, 169
Alula, 384
Alirk, Nor. 221
Alvesta 215A
Alvik, 438
Alzo, 318
Amalfi, 320, 391
Amapala, 450, 458
Amberieu, 266
Ambriz, 457
Amelie-les-Bains, 117
Amersfoort, 131, 132, 156, 159
Amfiklia, 336
Amiens, 123, 124, 237, 238, 242
Amlabukti, 435, 438
Amman, 335
Amrum,
Amoy, 470, 471, 474, 475
Amsteg-Silenen, 287
Amsterdam, 79, 80, 84, 129 131, 139 to 142, 146, 154, 156 to 159, 163, 178, 358, 363, 364, 405, 406, 450, 452, 456
Amstetten, 187, 197
Anamur, 375
Ananalave, 390
Anapa, 393
Ancona, 118, 144, 309, 312, 313, 361, 371B 372, 376, 384, 385, 397A, 456A
Andaman Islands 469
Andeer 295
Andelot, 267
Andermatt, 287, 291, 296
Andernach, 176, 177, 209,
Andoya, 428
Andros
Ange, 218
Angermünde, 205
Angers, 111, 247
Angoche, 471
Angola, 446
Angon, 275
Angora (see Ankara)
Angoulême, 115, 116, 248
Angra dos Reis, 479
Angvik, 222
Ankara, 83, 144, 333, 334
Annecy, 121, 122, 267, 275
Annemasse, 121, 122, 265, 267
Ansbach, 184, 188, 189, 194
Antalaya 371B, 375, 390
Antibes, 264
Antigua, 449, 452, 466, 472
Antilles, 466
Antivari (Bar) 380
Antofagasta, 450, 454, 456 458, 462, 463, 474
Antung, 470
Antwerp, 79, 80 130, 131 139, 142, 149 to 154, 165, 359, 360 362, 363, 365, 368, 369, 377, 402, 403, 405, 407, 409, 410, 416 to 418, 420, 423, 425, 445 to 448, 450, 452, 453 456, 458, 459, 463 466, 468
Aoba, 470
Aosta 296, 300, 320
Apapa, 446, 447, 452, 472
Apeldoorn, 131, 159
Apollonia, 397
Appenweier, 126, 127, 181 to 183
Appenzell, 285
Arad, 84, 203 274, 330, 331
Aragona-Caldare, 314, 315
Aranjuez, 323, 324
Arbe (see Rab)
Arcachon, 115, 116 247
Arco, 308
Ardalstangen, 435, 436
Are, 218
Arendal, 142, 219 to 222, 413, 418, 424
Arezzo, 303
Argegno, 317
Argeles, 251
Argentan, 244
Argentière, 253
Argos, 336, 337
Argostoli, 371B, 378
Arica, 450, 454, 456, 458 462, 463, 474, 478
Arifiye, 333
Arkhangelsk, 230
Arles, 259 to 262

Arlon, 149
Armentières, 236
Armudlu, 375
Arnhem, 129, 155 to 157, 159 209, 210
Arnoldstein, 199
Arona, 119, 120, 302, 318
Arosa, 291
Arras, 238
Arrecife, 465
Arroyo, 325
Arta (Balearic Is.), 328
Arth, 289, 294
Arth-Goldau 287, 289
Aruba, 456. 474
Arvant, 254
Arvika, 215A
Ascension, 369
Asch, 192
Aschaffenburg, 77, 188, 189
Aschen, 84
Aschersleben, 167
Asciano, 309
Askhabad, 231
Askvoll, 434
Asmara, 143
Asprochom., 337
Assab, 382, 383, 384, 398
Assens, 214, 419
Assinie, 446, 448
Assisi, 309, 320
Assiut, 80, 82, 338, 370
Assling, 199, 269, 332A
Assmanshausen, 209
Assuan, 82, 338
Astafjord, 440
Astara, 233
Asti, 300, 301
Astoria, 449
Astrabad, 233
Astrakhan, 233
Aswan (see Assuan)
Asyut (see Assiut)
Atbara, 339
Ath, 149
Athens (see also Phaleron Bay and Piræus), 83, 141 to 147, 274, 332A, 333, 336, 337.
Atrani, 391
Attnang, 187, 196
Aubigny, 236
Auckland, 459, 460, 463, 472, 476, 477, 479
Augsburg, 186 to 189, 194
Aulnoye, 137, 238, 239, 240 271
Aurisina, 200, 305, 307
Aurland, 435, 436
Aussig, 195, 196, 209
Aversa, 310
Avezzano, 311
Avignon, 79, 113, 114 255, 259 to 263
Avila, 85, 321, 322
Avlona (see Valona)
Avonmouth, 449
Avranches, 245
Ax, 251
Axim,
Ax les Thermes, 117
Ayamonte, 327
Ayancik, 375
Ayasoulouk (Ephes), 333
Ayat, 338
Aydin, 333
Ayer, 296
Ayerbe, 326
Azbarren, 321
Azores, 445, 448, 455 (See also Caes do Pico Corvo, Fayal, Flores, Graciosa, Lages do Pico Sao Jorge, Ponta Delgada, Santa Maria and Terceira).
Azua Barahona, 466
Baalbek (see R's-Bal-b'k)
Bacharach, 176, 17 209
Backnang, 184
Badajoz, 323
Bad Aussee, 196
Bad Brambach, 130, 192
Bad Elster, 130, 192
Bad Ems, 169, 175 to 177
Baden (Switz.), 212, 282, 283
Baden-Baden, 127, 182, 183, 212, 273
Baden-West, 81, 126, 131, 182, 183, 273
Badgastein, 197, 199, 269
Bad Griesbach, 181
Bad Harzburg (see Harzburg)
Bad Homburg, 171
Bad Kissingen (see Kissingen)
Badkleinen, 162
Bad Nauheim, 170
Badrashein, 338
Bad-Reichenhal (see Reichenhall)
Bad Schandau, 195
Bad-Schwalbach, 171
Bad Tölz (see Tölz)
Baeza, 324, 325
Baghdad, 83, 141, 143, 145, 146, 147 334, 368, 472
Bagnara (Calabria),
Bag-de-Bigorre (see Bigorre)
Bag-de-Luchon (see Luchon)
Bahamas, 462. (See also Nassau).
Bahia, 444, 445, 451, 453, 454, 455, 456, 457, 461, 464 479
Bahia de Caraquez, 458
Bahrein, 145, 471
Baie Benier, 390
Baiedes Tortues, 390
Baisieux, 127, 149
Bakar, 332B, 381
Bakhmatch, 230
Bakke, 432, 433
Baku, 231, 233
Balboa, 449, 462, 474, 478, 479
Bâle, 80, 81, 83, 85, 123 to 127, 129, 131, 137, 138, 142 149, 174, 178 to 183, 197, 237, 266, 268 to 270, 278, 279, 281 to 284, 286 to 288, 299, 330
Balestrand, 435 to 438
Balholmen (see Balestrand)
Bali, 146, 475, 476
Baliana 338
Balik-Papan, 146, 475
Bellenstedt, 167
Balsfiord, 440
Baltimore, 459 468
Bamako, 147
Bamberg, 185, 188 to 192
Bandak, 221, 225
Bandaksli, 221
Bandirma, 334, 375
Bandoeng, 146
Bandol, 264
Bangkok, 145 146, 147, 360, 445, 470, 471, 476, 479, 480
Bangui, 142
Banjoewangi, 469, 471
Banningville 147
Ban Sot, 480
Bar (see Antivari)
Bar-le-Duc, 272
Baranowicze, 226, 227
Barbados, 449, 450, 452, 466, 472
Barca d'Alba, 322, 327
Barcelona, 113, 114, 117 142, 251, 255, 322, 325, 326, 363, 365, 368, 369, 382, 397A, 399, 448, 454, 456A, 464, 468
Bari, 143, 310, 311, 313, 361, 371B, 372, 374, 382, 383, 397A
Barletta, 313 374
Barmen (see Wupperthal-Barmen)
Barnsley, 88 to 91
Barnstaple, 102, 104
Baroe, 146
Barra do Dande, 457
Barreiro, 327, 328
Barranquilla, 481
Basingstoke, 135
Baska, 379, 381
Basra, 83, 143, 145, 334, 384 471, 472
Bassac, 480
Bassano, 306
Bassein, 475
Basse-Terre, 466
Bastia, 254, 376, 387, 395
Bata, 446, 465
Batavia, 145, 146, 358, 362, 364-368, 385, 445, 447, 469, 470, 475, 476, 480
Bath, 98, 99
Bathurst, 447, 452, 456A
Batna, 341
Battipaglia, 311, 312
Batumi, 231, 233, 393
Baveno, 119, 120, 280, 302, 318
Bayeux, 243
Bayonne, 85, 115, 116, 250 to 253
Bayreuth, 188 to 19
Bayrischzell, 194
Bear Island, 428
Beatenberg, 289
Beatenbucht, 289, 292, 294
Beatushohlen, 292
Beaulieu, 79, 81, 82, 113, 114, 264
Beauvais, 238
Beauvallon 263
Bebra, 165, 70 to 173, 194
Bechar, 341
Beckenried, 293
Bedeau, 342
Bedej, (Eil),
Bedous, 252
Beiarn, 424
Beira, 145, 359, 363, 382, 444 446, 448, 452, 457, 467, 471, 472, 474, 476, 479
Bekescsaba, 203
Belawan Deli, 360, 362, 364, 365, 368, 476, 479, 480
Belem, 479. (See also Para)
Belet Uen, 143
Belfast, 88 to 97, 459
Belfort, 83, 123 to 125, 266, 268, 271
Belgard, 205
Belgrade, 83, 84, 141 143, 144, 199, 200, 201, 211, 269, 274, 330, 332, 332A 332B, 333, 337
Belikesir, 334
Belize, 456 472, 481
Bellagio, 317
Bellano, 317
Bellavista, 317
Bellegarde, 121, 122, 265 to 267
Bellingham, 449
Bellinzona, 81, 124, 125 270, 284, 287, 295, 302, 318
Bellovo, 332
Belluno, 306, 308
Belmez, 323
Belmont, 123
Benderi, 30
Bender Kassim, 384
Bender Shahpour, 384
Benevento, 310
Bengasi, 143, 396 397
Benguellr 457
Bengueria, 342A
Benha, 338
Beni-Mançour, 340
Beni-Ounif, (see Figuig)
Benito, 446
Bentheim, 130 132
Bentschen, 128, 205, 240
Beuthen, 81, 204
Ben-Zireg, 342
Berbera, 384 470
Berchtesgaden, 187, 212, 213
Bergamo, 304, 318
Bergen, 142 219, 221, 403, 413 to 415, 418, 420, 421, 424, 425, 428, 433 to 435, 437 438, 459

Bergen-op-Zoom, 155
Bergün, 286
Berkak, 219, 221
Berlin, 81, 128, 130, 132, 137, 139 to 141, 144, 152, 157, 159, 163, 164, 166, 168 to 174, 185, 190 to 193, 195, 202, 203 to 205, 206A, 207, 208, 214, 215A, 216, 226, 227, 232, 240
Bermuda, 449, 462, 472
Berncastel, 210
Berne, 83, 85, 119, 120, 123 to 125, 127, 138, 142 174, 178, 268, 269, 278, 279, 281, 282, 288, 292, 299
Bernina-Hospice, 289
Berrechid, 342A
Berrouaghia, 341
Berwick, 105 to 107
Besançon, 253, 267
Beslan, 231
Bestwig, 165
Béthune, 238
Bevers, 286, 291
Bex, 280, 290
Beyrout, 147, 334, 335, 361, 362, 367, 369, 371, 371A, 371B, 377, 378, 381, 386, 388, 389, 390, 392, 393, 443, 454, 455
Beuel, 175
Bezdair, 211
Béziers, 255, 117
Bhamo, 475
Bialystok, 227
Biarritz, 85, 115, 116, 135, 142, 250, 253,
Biasca, 287
Biberach, 180
Biberbrucke, 287
Bicocca, 314, 315
Bideford, 102, 104
Bielefeld, 163, 164
Bienne (Biel), 123 to 125, 278, 282, 283
Biessenhofen, 190
Bietigheim, 184 to 186, 274
Bigorre, 115, 116, 252, 253
Bigossowo, 140, 208, 230
Biharkeresztes, 331
Bilali, 336, 337
Bilbao, 321, 322, 363, 368, 464
Bingen, 176, 177, 209, 210
Bingerbruck 176, 177, 179, 275
Binz, 420
Biograd n/m 375, 379, 381
Bir-bou-Rekba, 342B
Birkenhead, 92 to 99
Birmingham, 92 to 99
Birdum Creek, 146
Birkeland, 224
Bisceglie, 373, 374
Bischofshofen, 197, 199
Biskra, 341
Bissau, 446, 457
Bistrica, 332A
Bitoli, 337
Bitterfeld, 166, 172, 173
Bivio 5,825 ft. (Switz.), 295
Bivio Aurisina, 305
Bizerta, 342B, 394
Bjerke, 440
Bjorgo, 221
Björkelo, 224A
Blackpool, 92 to 97
Blandain, 127, 149
Blankenburghe, 153, 239
Blankenburg, 167
Blansko, 207
Bled-Jezero, 332A
Bleiburg, 198
Blida, 341
Blois, 248
Bluff, 460
Bludenz, 197
Bo Nor, 223
Bobadilla, 85 324, 325
Boche di Cattaro, 455
Bockfjord, 428
Bockstein, 199
Boden, 218
Bodenbach, 195, 196, 209
Bodmin, 102, 104
Bodo, 142 415, 422, 424 428, 433
Boeleleng, 476
Bogazkoprn 333, 334
Boghari, 341
Bogliaco, 318
Bogumin, 194, 202 to 204, 206A, 207, 207A, 227, 228, 331
Bois-le-Duc (see Hertogenbosch)
Boissum, 166
Bokhara, 231
Bol,
Bolama, 457
Bolkesjo, 223
Bolladore, 320
Bollnas, 218
Bologna, 83, 118 to 120, 174, 178, 193, 196, 270, 300, 303, 306 to 308, 313
Bologoe, 230
Bolzano, 198, 306, 307, 319
Boma, 446
Bombay 357, 361 363, 365, 367, 369, 382, 384, 385, 469, 471, 473, 478
Bona, 142, 340, 342, 342B, 391, 394, 398
Bonaire, 456
Bonifacio, 376, 397A
Bonigen, 294
Bonn, 175 to 177, 209, 210
Bonny, 448
Bontheim, 159
Boppard, 176, 177, 209
Boram, 470
Borca, 306
Bordeaux, 85, 111, 115, 116, 135, 138, 142, 245, 246, 248, 250 to 252, 255, 321, 377, 405, 407, 418, 445, 452, 466
Bordighera, 81, 113, 114, 299
Borgholm, 425
Borgo S. Lorenzo, 312
Borlange, 216, 217
Bormes les Mimosas, 263
Bormes, 263
Bormio Bagni, 319
Bornholm 416 417, 426
Boroy
Bosa, 395, 397A
Boschpol, 205
Boston (U.S.A.), 443, 454 455, 459, 468, 472, 473 480
Bougainville, 470
Bougie, 340, 398
Bouira, 340
Boulogne, 79, 82 to 85, 112, 115 to 126, 237, 259 to 262, 270, 330, 343, 406, 444, 446, 449, 450, 451, 456, 459, 461
Boulogne-Tintelleries, 237
Bou Medfa, 341
Bourbonne-les-Bains, 268
Bourg, 121, 122, 266
Bourg St. Maurice, 121, 122, 265
Bourg St. Pierre, 296
Bourgas (see Burgaz)
Bourges, 249
Bournemouth, 101, 103
Boussens, 251
Bouveret, 265, 288 293
Bovallstrand 416
Boxtel, 155, 157
Böyum, 222
Bozen-Gries (see Bolzano)
Brac, 381
Biacke, 218
Bradford 88 to 91, 108
Braila, 80, 330, 360, 372
Brain le Compte, 239
Bramminge, 214
Brasso, 202, 331
Brassus 279
Bratislava, 84, 130, 141, 202, 206A, 207, 207A, 211
Braunlage, 167, 168, 212
Brava, 384
Brazzaville, 147
Breauté-Beuzeville, 242
Breclava, see Lundenburg
Breda, 129, 155, 156
Bredannaz, 275
Bregenz, 187, 197, 269, 273, 285, 294
Breifon, 223
Breil, 299
Bremanger, 434
Bremen, 128, 130, 132, 161, 164, 169, 174, 362, 363, 365, 402, 405, 406, 407, 414, 422, 445, 446, 450, 452, 453, 458, 459
Bremerhaven, 164, 406, 422, 451
Brennero, 82, 83, 193, 198, 307
Brenzone 318
Brescia, 304, 305, 318, 319
Breskens, 427
Breslau, 81 140, 141, 144, 203, 204 207
Bressanone, 307
Bressuire, 246
Brest (Fr.), 245, 246
Bretten, 184
Brevik, 6, 220
Briançon, 263
Bridlington 105 to 107
Brienz, 281, 289, 294, 426
Brigue, 83, 119, 120, 123 to 125, 269, 280, 288, 291, 296
Brimnes 438
Brindisi, 118 to 120, 123 to 125, 143 to 145, 270, 310, 311, 313, 371A, 371B, 372, 373, 374, 378, 382, 383, 384, 385
Brioni, 372, 373, 376, 381
Brioude, 254
Brisbane, 145, 146, 365, 366, 368, 382, 442, 444, 450, 458, 460, 463, 469, 470, 473, 476, 478, 479
Brissago, 318
Bristol, 98, 99, 362, 449
Brive 117, 247, 249
Brno, 195, 202, 206A, 207
Brocken, 167
Brod (Yugoslavia), 332, 332B
Broken Hill, 145, 147
Bromberg (see Bydgoszcz)
Brønnøysund, 142, 433
Broome, 469
Brottem, 225
Bruchsal, 182 to 184
Bruck a/Mur (Aus.), 84, 196, 199, 200
Bruck (Tyrol), 213
Bruckneudorf, 128, 200, 274
Bruges, 150, 153, 239
Brugg, 282, 283
Brunig, 281
Brunnen, 287, 293
Brunswick, 132, 166 to 168
Brussels, 79 to 81, 84, 127, 128, 130, 131, 139, 149, to 154, 178, 236, 330
Bryansk, 230
Bryyga, 437
Bubaque, 446
Bucharest, 80, 81, 83, 84, 128, 139, 141, 143, 144, 202 to 204, 211, 227, 230, 274, 330 to 331, 332B
Büchen, 168, 169
Buchloe, 187
Buchs, 83, 123 to 125, 197, 269, 285, 286, 295

Budapest, 83, 84, 128, 132, 141, 143, 144, 200 to 203, 207A 211, 227, 269, 274, 307, 330, 332A
Bude, 102, 104
Budel, 153
Budua, 380. 398
Budweis, 196
Buena Ventura, 450, 456, 458, 463, 474, 478
BuenosAires, 146, 444, 445, 449, 451, 453 to 456, 457, 458, 461, 462, 464, 468, 479
Buerat, 397
Bulach, 284
Bulawayo, 145
Bulle, 279, 290
Bunder Abbas, 471
Burdujeni, 204
Burg-Fehmarn, 424
Burgaz, 332B, 361, 372, 377
Burgenstock, 289
Burgos, 85, 115, 116, 140, 321, 360, 384, 385
Burnie, 365, 366
Burton-on-T'nt, 88 to 91
Burutu, 447, 472
Burma, 480. (See also Mandalay, Prome, and Rangoon)
Bursa, 375
Bushire, 146, 147, 471
Bushman's Bay, 470
Busigny, 236, 239
Busreh (see Basra)
Butzow, 162
Buxton, 88 to 91
Buzau, 80, 204, 330, 331
Bygdin, 222, 225
Bygdisheim, 222
Bygland, 221, 224
Byglandsfjord, 219, 221 224, 225
Bygstadt, 434
Bykle, 221
Byske, 426

Cabinda, 457
Cabo Blanco, 465
Cabo Juby, 465
Cabrera, 399
Cacak, 332
Caceres, 325
Cadca, 207A, 227
Cadenabbia, 317, 320
Cadenazzo, 287
Cadiz, 324, 325, 328, 368, 454, 464, 465, 468
Caen, 241, 243, 245, 422
Caes do Pico, 448
Cagliari, 143, 315 395, 397A
Cahors 117
Caineni, 331
Cairns, 469 to 471, 473
Cairo, 80, 82, 145, 146, 334, 335, 338, 339, 370
Cajueiro, 444
Calabar, 446, 447 to 448, 452
Calais, 79, 81 to 85, 112 to 128, 149, 236 to 238, 259 to 262, 265, 270, 271, 330, 343
Calalzo, 306, 308
Calamata (see Kalamata)
Calasetta, 397A,
Calcida, 372
Calcutta, 145, 146, 147, 359 361, 363, 369, 385, 469, 471, 474 479
Caldare, 314
Calimno, 373, 374
Callao, 450, 454, 456, 458 462, 463, 474, 478
Caltagirone, 315
Caltanissetta, 314
Calvi, 254, 376
Cambodge, 480
Cambodia, 480
Cambrai, 236
Camedo, 292
Camelford, 102, 104
Cameroons (North),
Caminreal, 326
Camooweal, 146
Campanha, 327
Campfer, 295
Canary Isles (see Las Palmas, Teneriffe, and Palma, Canary Is.; for inter-island service, including other local ports, see p. 465).
Canazei, 319
Cancello, 311
Candia, 371B, 378
Canea, 371B, 378
Canfranc, 252, 326
Canicatti, 314, 315
Cankiri, 334
Cannakale, 375
Cannes, 79, 81, 82, 113, 114, 138, 201, 259 to 264, 299, 454
Cannero, 318
Cannobio, 318
Canterets, 251
Canton, 470, 474
Cap d'Ail, 79, 81, 82, 264
Cape Coast, 446, 447, 472
Cape Haitien, 453, 466
Cape Mount, 452
Cape Palmas, 446, 447
Cape Town, 145, 363, 369, 382, 442, 444, 446, 447, 448, 452, 456A, 457 458, 460, 463, 467, 468, 472, 474, 476, 479
Capellen-Stolzenfels, 176, 177
Capolago, 287-317
Capraia, 395
Capri, 391
Capua, 311
Carate, 317
Carbonin, 212, 306
Carcagente, 325
Carcassonne, 252
Cardiff, 98, 99
Carezza, 319
Carinena, 326
Carlisle, 88 to 97
Carlsbad (see Karlsbad)
Carlotorte, 397A
Carlovassi, 371B. 378
Carlsruhe, 81, 84, 126, 127, 129, 131, 140, 174, 178, 180, 182 to 184, 186, 212, 273, 274
Carmarthen, 98, 99
Carmen Sylva, 80
Carnaro Islands,
Carnavon, 469
Cartagena, 323, 368, 450, 453, 456, 465, 466, 474, 481
Carupano 456, 466
Casablanca, 85, 142, 342A, 360, 362, 363, 369, 374, 382, 392, 445, 448, 454, 456A, 457, 460, 464, 466, 468
Casamozza, 254
Caserta, 310, 311
Casetas, 322, 326
Caspe, 326
Cassala, 143
Cassarate, 292
Cassel, 130, 132, 165, 170 to 173
Cassino, 311
Castasegna, 295
Castejon, 322
Castel Bolognese, 313
Castelsardo, 397A
Castellammare, 315
Castellammare Golfo, 395
Castelletto d Brenzone, 318
Castellon, 325
Castelnaudary, 252
Castelrosso, 147, 374
Castelvetrano, 315
Castillejo, 323, 324
Castillejos, 342A
Catabangan, 473
Catakolo, 337, 371B
Catalagzi, 334
Catalca, 333
Catania, 82, 143, 314, 315, 361, 363, 371B, 372, 377, 382, 384, 385, 396, 397A
Catanzaro, 311
Cattaro (see Kotor)
Caudebec, 423
Cauterets, 115 116
Caux, 291
Cavalla, 372
Cavalaire, 263
Cavalière, 263
Cavigliano, 292
Cayenne, 466
Ceara, 444, 458
Cebu, 362 473, 475, 479, 480
Cecina, 301
Cefalu, 314
Ceklis, 202, 207
Celerina, 286
Celje, 332A
Celldomolk, 201
Centrale (Vesuvius Railway), 300
Cephalonia (see Argostoli)
Cerbère, 114, 117, 255, 326
Cercy-la-Tour, 254,
Cerkesköy, 333
Cernauti, 81, 204, 331
Cernavoda, 80
Cernobbio, 317
Cervignano, 305
Ceska Trebova, 207
Ceske Budejovice, 206
Cetinje, 398
Cetinkaya, 334
Cette (see Sete)
Ceuta, 342A, 368, 397A, 399, 454, 465
Ceylon (see Colombo)
Chabarovsk 232
Chagny, 254, 259 to 262
Chalchis, 337, 378
Châlons-sur-Marne, 84, 123 to 124, 268, 270, 272
Châlon-sur-Saone, 259 to 262
Chambery, 82, 118, 121, 122, 257, 265
Chamblet Neris, 250
Chamonix, 121, 122, 253, 267
Champerico, 450, 456, 458
Champery, 288, 290
Champex-Lac, 296
Chanaral, 474
Changchun (see Hsinking)
Changsha, 470
Charbar, 471
Charleroy, 152, 240
Charleville, 145
Charlottenberg (Sweden), 215A
Chartres, 244, 246
Chasse, 257, 259 to 262
Châteaux d'Oex, 290, 296
Châteaudun, 247
Châteauroux, 117, 240
Château Thierry, 272
Châtelard Ville, 253
Chaudfontaine, 152
Chaumont, 83, 85, 123 to 251, 268, 270
Chaux-de-Fonds, 278
Chefoo, 362, 470, 474
Chelmsford, 110
Cheltenham, 98, 99
Chemnitz, 141, 192
Chêneé, 152
Cherbourg, 243, 403, 404, 406, 407, 450, 459, 461
Cherso, 374
Chersonisso, 378
Chesières, 290
Chester, 92 to 99

Chesterfield, 88 to 91
Chiasso, 81, 123 to 125, 174, 178, 270, 287
Chiavari, 301
Chiavenna, 212, 295, 304
Chienli, 470
Chilivani, 315
Chinchilla, 323
Chinde, 467, 471
Chinkiang, 470
Chios, 371B, 378, 385
Chisinau, 330
Chittagong, 469
Chiusa, 307
Chiusi, 303, 309
Chivasso, 298, 300
Chojnice, 227
Chosen (see Corea)
Christianssand, 139, 142, 215A, 219, 222, 223, 224, 410, 413, 416, 418, 423, 424, 428
Christiansund, 142, 223, 224, 414, 415, 418, 420, 421, 439, 440, 468
Chungking, 470
Chur (see Coire)
Chust, 207A
Churwalden, 295
Ciboure, 253
Cierfs, 295
Cieszyn Zach, 227
Cittanova, 381
Ciudadela, 399
Ciudad Real, 323, 324
Ciudad Trujillo, 453, 464, 466
Ciuinita, 80
Civitavecchia, 118, 301, 395
Clarens, 280, 293
Clavadel, 296
Clavières (see Ulzio-Clavières-Sestrières)
Cleres (Fr.), 241, 242
Clermont, 237
Clermont Ferrand, 247, 254
Cleves, 131, 156
Cloncurry, 145, 146
Cluj, 331
Cobh, 404, 406, 407, 409, 459
Coblence (Germany), 126, 132, 169, 171, 175 to 177, 181, 209, 210, 275
Coblence (Switzerland), see Koblenz
Cocanada, 471
Cochem, 181, 210
Cochin, 358, 359, 366, 367, 382, 385, 390
Cochin China, 480
Coimbra, 85, 327
Coire, 83, 85, 123 to 125, 127, 174, 178, 269, 285, 286, 288, 291, 295
Colchester, 110
Col de Voza, 253
Colico, 304, 317
Colle Isarco, 307, 319
Colmar, 181
Cologne, 80, 81, 84, 128, 129, 131, 132, 137, 139, 140, 141, 150, 151, 155 to 157, 161, 163 to 166, 175 to 183, 188, 189, 209, 210, 240, 330
Colomb Bechar, 342
Colombo, 358 to 369, 382, 385, 389, 390, 445, 471, 473, 474, 478, 479, 480
Colon, 449, 454, 467 to 458
Comana, 331
Como, 123 to 125, 270, 287, 304, 317, 320
Compiegne, 239
Conakry, 147, 445, 446, 447, 448, 456A, 472
Conegliano, 308
Congo River
Constance, 126, 131, 180, 184, 212, 284, 285, 294
Constantine, 142, 340, 341
Constantinople (see Istanbul)
Constantza, 80, 202, 204, 274, 330, 331, 360, 361, 372, 377, 388, 392, 393
Contonou, 446, 452
Contrexeville, 271, 272
Cook Islands, 481
Copenhagen, 81, 130, 132, 136, 139, 140 to 142, 143, 162, 204, 214 to 216, 404, 405, 407, 410, 416 to 421, 422, 425 to 427, 460
Coppet, 293
Coquilhatville, 147
Coquimbo, 456, 474
Cordova 85, 323 to 325
Corea, 478
Corfu, 147, 372, 373, 374, 378, 380
Corinth, 336
Corinto, 450, 456, 458
Coromandel Coast Ports, 471
Corral, 456, 458, 463
Corsica (steamship services, see Ajaccio, Bastia, Calvi and Ile Rousse; train services, see p. 254)
Corte, 254
Cortina, 83, 319, 306
Corunna, 321, 368, 445, 450, 461, 462, 464 to 466
Corvo, 448
Cos, 373, 374
Cossack Roads, 469
Cossonay, 267, 278
Costesti, 331
Cotonou, 147, 445, 447, 472
Cottbus, 204
Courtrai, 149, 239
Courmayeur, 300, 320
Coutras, 248 250
Cowes, 101, 103
Coutances, 245
Cracow, 81 203, 204, 207, 227, 228
Crailsheim, 184, 186, 274
Craiova, 83, 330, 331
Cranenburg, 156
Crefeld, 130, 156
Creil, 237 to 239
Crewe, 92 to 99
Crikvenica, 375, 379, 380 381, 398
Cristobal, 450, 454, 456 to 458, 462, 463, 464, 466, 474, 479, 481
Crotone, 311
Croydon, East, 111
Croydon (Airport), 138, 139, 140
Csap, 201, 202, 207
Cumana, 456
Cuba (see Havana)
Cuddalore, 471
Cuio 457
Culemborg 419
Culoz, 118 121, 122, 265, 266
Cuneo, 299
Cuprija, 332
Curaçao, 450, 453, 456, 457, 459, 462 to 464, 466, 474, 479
Curtici, 84 203, 331
Curzola, 374, 379, 380
Cutch Mandvie, 471
Cuxhaven, 420
Cyprus (see Larnaca, Limassol, Famagusta and Nicosia)
Czegled, 202
Czernowitz (see Cernauti)

Dahme, 424
Dairen, 232, 360, 362, 363, 365, 369, 470, 471 475, 479
Dakar, 147 382, 445, 447, 448, 452, 454, 456A, 460, 464, 472
Dalarö,
Dalen 221, 223
Dalheim, 153
Dalni (see Dairen)
Dalsfjord, 434
Daly Waters, 146
Domanhour, 338
Damascus, 141, 147, 335
Damesme 342
Danilov, 230
Dante, 382, 384, 463A
Danzig, 140, 144, 205, 226, 227, 369, 407, 409, 410, 419, 423, 427
Dar-es-Salaam, 359, 363, 364 382, 463A, 389, 471, 476, 479
Darlington, 105 to 107
Darmstadt, 81, 174, 176, 177, 182, 183, 185, 188, 189, 212
Dart, 390
Dartmouth,
Darwin, 145, 146, 470, 473
Daugavpils, 208
Davao, 478, 479 480
Davoli, 143
Davos Platz, 85, 123 to 125, 127, 269, 286, 296, 319
Dax, 85, 115, 116, 250, 251
Deauville, 148
Deblin, 227
Decebal (see Curtici)
Dedeagatch (see Alexandrople)
Delagoa Bay (see Lourenço Marques)
Delemont, 123 to 125, 268, 278
Delfi (see Gravia)
Delft, 129, 158
Delhi, 479
Delle, 83, 85, 123 to 125, 268, 269, 278
Demerara, 452, 456, 466 472
Demir Kapija, 332A
Denham 469
Den Pasar, 146
Denzlingen 184
Depienne, 342B
Deraa, 335
Derbesiye, 334
Derby (England), 88 to 91
Derby (Australia), 146, 469
Dermulo, 306
Derna, 143, 397
Desenzano, 305, 318
Dessau, 171
Deva, 321
Devdelija, 332A
Deventer 159
Devonport, 102, 104
Diablerets, 291, 296
Diakofto, 336, 337
Diano Marina, 299
Diarbekir, 334
Diedenhofen, 181
Diego-Suarez, 377, 389 390
Dieppe, 111, 241
Diez, 169
Dijon, 113, 114, 118 to 122, 138, 259 to 263, 265 to 267
Dilly Timor (see Timor)
Dinair, 333
Dinan, 244 245, 426
Dinant, 138, 210, 271
Dinard 148, 244, 245, 426
Dinkelsbuhl, 194
Dire Daua, 143
Dirschau (see Tczew

Disentis, 288, 291
Divaccia, 305, 307
Divonne-les-Bains, 121, 122
Djama, 341
Djankoi, 230
Djask, 147, 146
Djederda, 342B
Djelfa, 341
Djerbah (see Gerba)
Djibouti, 143, 359, 360, 377, 382, 383, 384, 385, 388, 390, 445, 470
Djulfa (see Dzhulfa)
Dobbiaco, 83, 198, 306
Doboj, 332B
Doebele (Latvia), 208
Dodoma, 145
Dogana Italiana (Domodossola-Locarno), 292
Dokka, 220, 221
Dol, 244, 245
Dôle, 266, 267
Domazlice (see Taus
Dombaas, 219
Dombuhl, 194
Dominica, 449, 452, 472
Domma, 470
Domodossola, 83, 119, 120, 269 280, 288, 292, 302
Donaueschingen, 180
Donauworth, 194
Doncaster, 142
Dorchester, 98, 99, 101, 103
Dordrecht, 129 154 to 156, 416, 419
Dorgali, 395, 397A
Dortmund, 130, 139, 140, 163, 164
Dörtyol, 333
Douai, 236, 238
Douala, 147
Dover, 79, 80, 112 to 116, 119 to 127, 237, 363, 365 450, 452, 453, 456
Dragutinovo, 332A
Drama, 337
Drammen, 219, 220 224
Dreiannen Hohne, 167
Dresden, 128, 130, 132, 140, 141, 144, 163, 164, 166, 168, 169, 172, 173, 190 to 192, 195, 196, 202, 204, 206, 209, 240
Dreux, 244
Drvenik 381
Duala, 445 to 448 452, 456A
Dubai, 471
Dublin, 92 to 97, 459
Dubrovnik (Ragusa), 332, 332B, 375, 379, 380, 398, 455
Dubrovnik 2 (Gruz), 361, 373, 374, 379, 380, 381, 398
Duisburg, 130, 131, 163, 164, 210
Duingt, 275
Dulcigno (see Ulcinj)
Dunaburg (see Daugavpils)
Dundee, 92 to 97, 105 to 107, 407
Dunedin (N.Z.), 460 479
Dunkerque, 137, 236, 238, 363 377, 410, 418, 452, 466
Durango, 321
Durazzo, 144, 373, 374, 380
Durban, 145, 359, 363, 382, 442, 446, 448, 452, 456A, 458, 463, 468, 471, 472, 474, 476, 479
Duren, 151
Durham, 105, 107
Durlach, 182, 183, 186
Dusseldorf, 128, 129, 131, 132, 139, 157, 161 163 to 166, 209, 210 209, 210
Duvivier, 340
Dyranuten, 221
Dyrkorn, 439
Dzhulfa, 231
Dziedzice 203

East London (Africa), 363, 382, 444 446, 448, 452, 456A, 463, 467, 472, 474, 476, 479
Ebenhausen, 185
Ebensee, 196
Eberbach, 185
Eboli, 311
Edessa, 337
Edinburgh, 88 to 97 105 to 107
Edirne, 332, 333
Eforia, 80
Eger, 84, 128, 130, 188 to 190, 192, 195, 196, 274
Egersund, 413
Egge (Nor.), 224A
Egirdir, 333
Eglisau, 284
Ehrenbreitstein, 175
Ehrwald Zugspitzbahn 193
Eibsee, 192
Eichenberg, 170, 171
Eidanger, 220
Eide, 224A, 225
Eidevik, 434
Eidfjord, 223, 432, 433, 438
Eidsbugaren 225
Eidsfoss, 225
Eidsora, 222
Eidsvold, 219, 225
Eigerwand, 289
Eikefjord, 434
Eikesdal, 225
Eikesdalsvatn, 222
Eilsleben, 168
Eina, 218, 220
Eindhoven, 155, 158
Einsiedeln, 287
Eisenach, 132, 172, 173
Eisfelder-Talmühle, 167
Eismeer, 289
Ekern, 225
El Berd, 341
El Guerrah, 340, 341
El Kantara (Alg.), 341
El Obeid, 339
El Wedj, 477
Elaziz
Elbeuf-St.-Aubin, 241
Elbing, 205
Elbingerode, 167
Eleusis, 336
Elizabethville, 147
Elne, 117
Elsinore, 1 6, 214, 216
Elsterwerda, 195
Eltville, 175, 209, 210
Elvas, 323
Elveseter, 224
Elzach, 184
Embrun, 263
Emden, 175
Emmerich, 84, 131, 132, 157, 209, 210
Empalme (Majorca), 328
Empalme de Barcelona, 326
Empoli, 309
Ems (see Bad Ems)
Enfidaville, 342B
Engelberg, 290
Engelhartszell, 211
Engelholm, 216
Engelien, 225
Enkhuizen, 422
Entebbe, 145
Entroncamento, 85, 325, 327
Enzeli (Iran), see Pechlevi
Eoisheim, 223
Epernay, 272
Epi, 390
Epinal, 271, 272
Eregli, 334
Eremo (Vesuvius Railway), 300
Erfurt, 132, 172, 173, 185
Ergani
Eriksrud, 225
Ermezinde, 327
Ermidas-Sado, 328
Erquelines, 240
Ersekujvar, 202
Ervalla, 217
Erzingen, 180
Esbjerg, 136, 214, 215, 404, 406, 418
Eschweiler, 151
Escorial, 85, 321
Eskefjord, 414
Eskisehir, 333, 334
Esmeraldas, 458
Espeluy, 324
Esschen, 79, 130, 154
Essen, 130, 139 to 141, 163, 164
Estoril, 85, 327
Esztergom (Gran), 211
Etang, 254
Etaples, 112, 237
Etne, 223
Ettal, 213
Ettlebruck, 152
Etzwilen, 284, 285
Eu, 238
Evian-les-Bains, 121, 122, 293
Evpatoria, 393
Evreux-Embranch., 243
Exeter, 98, 99, 102, 104
Exmouth, 102, 104
Eydehamn, 413
Eydtkau, 81, 130, 205, 240
Eydtkuhnen (see Eydtkau)

Faaborg, 419
Fabriano, 312
Faenza, 312, 313
Fagernaes, 220, 222
Faisi, 470
Falconara, 312, 313
Faleide, 434
Falkenberg, 166, 195, 204
Falköping, 216
Falmouth, 98, 99
Falun, 216, 218
Famagusta, 340, 361, 362, 367, 371B, 378, 386
Farafangana, 377, 390
Faroe Islands, 418
Farsala, 336
Farsund, 413
Fasana, 381
Fasano Riv., 318
Faskrudsfjord, 414
Faro, 328
Fastov, 230, 231
Fatsa, 375
Faurei, 80, 331
Fayal, 448
Fayet, 267
Fécamp, 242
Fedala, 342A
Fedj-et-Tame ur, 342B
Fehmarn, 424
Feignies, 239
Felanitx, 328
Feldkirch, 197, 269
Feltre, 319
Femunn, 225
Fénérive, 390
Feodosia, 230, 393
Fernando Po, 447, 457, 465
Ferrara, 308, 309
Fetesti, 330 331
Feutersoey, 296
Fevzipasa, 334
Fez, 342A
Fidenza, 303
Fiera di Primiero, 212
Fiesch, 291
Fiesole, 320
Figuig, 342
Fiji, 472
Filisur, 286
Finhaut, 253
Finschafen, 470
Finse, 219
Finsnes, 415, 428
Fionnay, 296
Fishguard, 98, 99

Fiume, 144, 200, 201, 305, 361, 371A, 371B, 372 to 376, 380, 383, 384, 385, 397A (See also Sušak)
Fjaera, 223, 438
Fjaerland, 435
Fjällbacka, 416
Flaa, 225
Flaam, 435 to 438
Flatmark, 219
Fleetwood, 92 to 97
Flekkefjord, 222, 413
Flemma, 222
Flensburg, 162, 424
Flers, 244
Flims, 296
Flims-Dorf, 295
Florence, 81 to 83, 118 to 120, 143, 174, 178, 185, 193, 196, 201, 270, 301, 303, 307 to 309, 312, 313, 320
Flores, 448
Florianopolis, 451
Florina Ville, 337
Floro, 414, 415, 421, 428, 434
Fluelen, 287, 293, 295
Flushing, 129, 130, 155, 156, 427
Foggia, 118, 270, 310, 311, 313
Foix, 251
Folden, 424
Foligno, 309, 312
Folkestone, 79, 112, 119 to 122, 125, 126, 137, 237, 343
Folligny, 244
Fondo, 306
Fontainebleau-Avon, 256, 259, 261, 262
Font-Romeu (see Odeillo)
Foochow, 363, 470, 474
Forbach, 179
Forcados, 448, 472
Forde, 224A, 434
Fordefjord, 434
Formentera, 399
Formia, 310
Fornovo, 300
Fortaleza, 479
Fort Bayard, 475
Fort Dauphin, 377, 390
Fort-de-France, 457, 466
Fort Lamy, 147
Fortezza, 83, 198, 307
Fortun, 224
Fossano, 298
Fossheim, 224
Fossli, 221
Fowey, 363
Frankfurt (Main), 81, 84, 126, 128, 129, 132, 139, 140, 141, 164, 170 to 179, 181 to 183, 185, 188, 189, 275, 330
Frankfurt (Oder), 203, 204, 205
Franzensbad, 130, 190, 192, 196
Franz-J. Hohe, 213
Frasne, 119, 120, 267
Frauenfeld, 285
Fredericia, 214, 215, 215A, 419
Frederikshavn, 215A, 418, 420
Fredrikshald (see Halden)
Fredrikshalds Canal, 225
Fredrikstad, 216, 423, 431
Freetown, 446, 447, 452, 456A, 472
Freiburg, 126, 127, 131, 140, 141, 180, 182 to 184, 212
Freilassing, 187
Fréjus, 264
Fremantle, 363, 365, 366, 368, 382, 442, 444, 463, 468, 469, 471
Fresvik, 436, 437
Freudenstadt, 180, 212
Fribourg, 279
Friedrichsfeld, 182, 183
Friedrichshafen, 129, 146, 180, 184, 186, 285, 294
Fronningan, 435, 436, 437, 438
Frose, 167
Frouard, 275
Fruitigen, 288, 296
Fuente S. Esteban, 322
Fuentes d'Onoro, 85
Fugleberget, 415
Fulda, 172, 173, 194
Funchal (see Madeira)
Funchiera, 328
Funicolare, 300
Furka, 296
Fürth, 188, 189
Furth-im-Wald, 188, 189, 206
Fusan (see Husan)
Fuschertorl, 213
Fussen, 190, 212, 213
Gabela, 332B
Gabès, 342B, 387
Gaboon Congo, 448
Gafour, 342B
Gafsa, 342B, 387
Gagri, 393
Galanta, 202, 207A
Galatz, 80, 211, 330, 360, 372, 377, 393
Gallarate, 302, 318
Gallipoli, 313
Galveston, 479
Galway, 406, 407, 459
Gan, 207A
Gandia, 399
Gandria, 295
Gannat, 250, 254
Gao, 147
Gap, 263
Garda, Lake of, 318
Gardone, 318, 319
Gargnano, 318
Garnes, 219
Garmisch Partenkirchen, 192, 193, 212, 213, 319
Gavle, 216, 217, 426
Gaza, 146, 335
Gavutu, 470
Gastaad, 80
Gdansk (see Danzig)
Gdynia, 141, 144, 205, 226, 369, 407, 409, 410, 416, 419, 427, 449, 459, 468
Gebeit, 339
Gedaref, 339
Gedser 130, 132, 162, 204, 214
Geiranger, 224, 439, 440
Geldermalsen, 156
Gelibolu, 375
Gemlik, 375
Gemunden, 188, 189, 194
Generoso, 317
Geneva, 119 to 122, 127, 138 to 141, 144, 174, 250, 259, 261, 262, 265 to 267, 278 to 280, 282, 283, 288, 293
Genoa, 81, 82, 118 to 120, 123, 124, 127, 142, 143, 174, 178, 201, 264, 269, 270, 287, 288, 299 to 302, 343, 359 to 363, 364, 365, 368, 371A, 371B, 372, 377, 382, 383, 384, 385, 387, 393, 395, 397A, 398, 443, 448, 454, 455, 456A, 464, 468, 473
Gera, 130
Geraldton, 469
Gerardmer, 271
Gerba, 397
Gernrode, 167
Gerona, 326
Gersau, 293
Gerze, 375
Gessenay (see Saanen)
Ghardimaou, 340, 342B
Ghent, 80, 149, 150, 154, 405, 410
Chephyra, 336
Ghisonaccia, 254
Gibraltar, 325, 357, 358, 361 to 369, 371, 374, 443, 454, 455, 456A, 464
Gien, 256
Giessbach, 281
Giessbach Falls, 294
Giessen, 165, 169 to 171
Gijon, 321, 368, 462, 464, 466
Giovo Pass, 319
Giresun, 375
Girgenti (see Agrigento)
Gisors, 241
Giswil, 281
Giurgiu, 211, 331
Givet, 271
Givors, 257
Gizo, 470
Gjedser (see Gedser)
Gjeilo, 219
Gjemnes, 222, 439
Gjovik, 218, 221, 225
Gladbach, 153, 165
Gladstone, 45
Glarus, 286
Glasgow, 88 to 97, 105 to 107, 368, 403, 407, 459
Glashutte, 212
Glatz, 195
Gleiwitz, 144, 204
Gletsch, 291, 296
Gletscher, 289
Glion, 291. (See also Territet)
Glomfjord, 428
Glos Montfort, 241
Gloucester, 98, 99
Glovo Pass, 213
Gmund, 195, 196, 206
Gmunden, 196
Goch, 156
Gödesberg, 176, 177, 209, 210
Godoysund, 433
Goes, 155
Goeschenen, 123 to 125, 287, 291
Göhren, 426
Göhren-Bürckó, 426
Gol, 222
Gold Coast
Golfo Aranci, 397A
Gomagio, 212
Gonaives, 453, 466
Gondjeli, 333
Gondo, 296
Gönyü, 211
Gooie, 405
Görele, 375
Gorinchem, 419
Gorizia, 308
Gorky, 231, 233
Görlitz, 204
Gornergrat, 280, 288
Gornia-Orehovitza, 332B
Goslar, 166, 167
Gossau, 282, 283, 285
Gotha, 130, 172, 173
Gothenburg, 132, 136, 1[illegible] to 142, 162, 215A, 21[illegible] 218, 221, 369, 408, 41[illegible], 416, 418, 420, 425, 456, 459, 463, 468
Gottingen, 170
Gouda, 157, 159
Gracac, 332B
Graciosa, 448
Grado, 381
Gradsko, 332A
Graiba, 342B
Grainru-Bad, 192
Gran (see Esztergom)
Granada, 324, 325
Grand Bassa, 446
Grand Bassam, 382, 447, 448, 456A, 472
Grand Canary (see Las Palmas)
Grand Cess, 446
Grand Lahou, 448, 452, 456A
Grand Popo
Granheim, 224
Granollers, 326
Gran Tarajal, 465
Granville, 244
Granvin (Eide), 220, 224, 432, 433, 438
Grasse, 113, 114, 263
Gratzen, 196

Gravarne, 416
Gravesend, 136, 402
Gravia, 336
Gravosa, 373, 375
Graz, 143, 196, 199, 200, 201
Great St. Bernard, 296, 300, 320
Grebbestad, 416
Greenock, 88 to 91, 459
Grein, 211
Grenada, 449, 452, 472
Grenoble, 121, 122, 257, 259, 263
Griesbach Bad, 181
Griesen, 193
Grigore Ghica Voda (see Oraseni)
Grimmenthal, 185
Grimsby, 404, 406
Grimsel Hospiz, 296
Grimstad, 222, 413
Grinde, 435, 437
Grindelwald, 281, 292
Grodno, 227
Groesbeek, 156
Grömetz, 424
Grong, 220
Groningen, 129, 131, 159
Gross-Boschpol, 205
Grosswardein (see Oradea-Mare)
Grosseto, 301
Grotli, 222, 224
Grovane, 219
Grund, 296
Gruz (see Dubrovnik 2)
Gstaad, 290, 296
Gsteig, 296
Guadeloupe, 464
Guadix, 324
Guanta, 456
Guarda, 327
Guayaquil, 449, 450, 456, 458, 463, 474
Gudvangen, 224, 224A, 435 to 438
Gudhjem, 417
Guelma, 340
Guercif, 342A
Gueret, 250
Guernsey, 135 136, 405, 407
Guerrah (see El Guerrah)
Guethary, 250, 253
Guevgeli, 83, 332A, 336
Guillarey, 321, 327
Gulbene, 208
Gulsvik, 219, 225
Gumligen, 281
Gunten, 294
Güsten, 171
Gütergluck, 166, 171
Guttal Post, 213
Guttannen, 296
Gwadur, 145, 471
Gwalior, 145
Gyékényes, 201, 332B
Gyoma, 203
Gyor (Raab), 200, 201, 211
Gythion, 371B
Haapamaki, 228
Haarlem, 79, 129, 131, 158
Habaniyeh, 145
Haderslev, 419
Hadsund, 419
Hagen, 132, 165
Hagenau, 169
Hagenow, 169
Hague, The, 79, 80, 129, 131, 154, 157 to 159, 178
Hertenstein, 293
Haifa 143, 146, 334, 335, 361, 362, 365, 367, 369, 371, 371A, 371B, 377, 378, 381, 386, 388, 392, 393, 443, 454, 455
Haiphong, 445, 390, 470, 475, 479
Haiti, 453, 456, 462, 466
Haiya Junction, 339
Halberstadt, 166 167
Halfa (see Wadi-Halfa)
Halifax (N.S.), 459, 472, 480, 481
Halle, 139 to 141, 166 to 168, 171 to 173, 191, 204
Hallsberg, 215A, 216, 217
Halmstad, 216, 410
Halmeu 202
Hälsingborg, 136, 215A, 216, 410, 420, 422, 425
Haltern, 161
Hama, 335
Hamadan, 83, 334
Hamar, 219, 225
Hameln, 166
Hamburg, 81, 128, 130, 132, 139, 141, 142, 159, 161, 162, 169, 170, 174, 194, 204, 205, 214, 215, 215A, 216, 240, 359, 360, 362, 363, 365, 369, 402, 403, 405, 407, 409, 410, 414 to 416, 421, 424, 443, 446, 447, 450 to 453, 458 459, 468
Hamm, 163 to 165, 175
Hammam Meskoutine 340
Hammelburg, 188, 189
Hammerfest, 415, 419 428
Hamont, 153
Hanau, 172, 173, 185
Handeck Falls, 296
Hangö (see Hanko, Fin.)
Hanko (Fin.), 228, 417
Hankö (Norway), 431
Hankow, 470
Hanoi, 147
Hanover, 81, 128, 130, 132, 137, 139 to 141, 163, 164, 166, 168, 170, 194
Hansweert, 416
Haparanda, 218
Harbin, 232
Harburg, 161, 170
Hardanger, 432, 433
Harfleur, 242
Hargarten-Falk, 126
Harlingen, 405, 427
Harmanger, 217
Harmanli, 332
Harnosand, 217, 426
Harrogate, 88 to 91 105 to 107
Harstad, 142 415, 424, 428, 428, 433, 440
Harwich, 110 129 to 132, 136
Harzburg, 167, 212
Harzgerode, 167
Hasle, 417
Hasselfelde, 167
Hasserode 167
Hassleholm 215A
Hatvan, 202
Haugesund, 142, 222, 413 to 415 418, 420, 421 425, 433, 438
Haukeliseter, 223
Hauptbahn, 162
Hausach, 126, 180
Hauderes, 296
Haugastol, 219, 221, 438
Havana, 450 454, 458, 462, 463, 464, 466, 468, 474, 479, 481
Havernes, 225
Havre, 111, 242, 377, 402 to 404, 409, 418, 422, 423, 443 to 445, 453, 456, 459, 462, 466
Hawaii (see Honolulu and Hilo)
Haydarpasa, 83, 333, 334
Hazebrouck, 150, 236, 238
Hedemora, 217
Hegyeshalom, (see Nickelsdorf)
Heidelberg, 174, 176, 177, 180, 182 to 184, 191, 212, 273
Heiden, 289
Heilbronn, 184, 185
Heiligenblut, 213
Hel (Pol.), 226
Helder, 427
Heligoland, 407, 420, 422
Hell (Nor.), 220
Helland, 439
Hellesylt 222, 223, 439, 440
Helmstedt, 168
Helsingborg (see Hälsingborg)
Helsingfors, 140 142, 228, 404, 414, 417 423, 424, 425, 427
Helsingor (see Elsinore)
Helsinki (see Helsingfors)
Henchir-Souatir, 342B
Hendaye, 85, 116, 135, 248, 250, 251, 253, 321
Hengelo, 130 to 132, 155, 156, 159
Henjam, 471
Herbesthal, 80, 84, 128, 151
Hereford, 98, 99
Hercegnovi, 332B, 374, 379, 380, 398
Herenthals, 153
Heringsdorf, 426
Herisau, 285
Hermigua, 465
Herrljunga, 216
Hertogenbosch, 155 to 158
Herzberg, 200
Hessleholm
Hestmanoya, 415
Heudeber, 167
Heydebreck, 203, 204
Heysham, 88 to 97
Heyst, 153
Hidasnemeti, 202
Hierapolis (see Gondjeli)
Hildesheim, 166
Hillerod, 214
Hilo, 478
Hilterfingen, 294
Hindenburg, 204
Hinterrhein, 295
Hintersee, 212
Hirson, 137, 238, 271
Hirtshals, 215A, 416
Hjandal, 223
Hjelle, 222, 225
Hjeldnesset, 440
Hjuksebo, 219, 220
Hobart, 366, 460, 473
Hobro, 419
Höchst, 173
Hodeidah, 384, 470
Hodonin, 206A
Hof, 185, 190 to 192, 195
Hog Harbour, 390
Hohenschwangau, 212
Hoihow, 470, 479
Hokksund, 219, 220, 224
Holmsund, 426
Holsen, 224A
Holstebro, 214
Holtenau (see Kiel-Holtenau)
Holyhead, 92 to 97
Holzkirchen, 194
Holzminden, 166
Homburg, Bad (see Bad Homburg)
Homburg (Saar), 275
Homs (Libya), 397
Homs (Syria), 335
Honefoss, 219, 220
Honfleur, 243, 422
Hong-Kong, 145 358, 360, 362 to 365, 367, 369, 382, 385, 389, 460 to 473, 474, 475, 476, 478 to 481
Honnef, 209
Honningsvaag, 415
Honolulu, 456, 472, 473, 477, 478
Hook of Holland, 131, 132, 156, 158, 159, 419
Hopa 375
Horb, 184
Horgen, 293
Hornberg, 180
Hornindal, 225
Horni-Dvoriste, 196
Hörnum, 420

Horsens, 419
Horten, 220, 405
Hospenthal, 296
Hotel Schneefernerhaus (Zugspitzgipfel), 192
Hougsund (see Hokksund)
Houlgate, 243
Houston.
Houx, 210
Hovden, 221, 224
Høyanger, 435
Hranice, 207
Hrusky, 206A
Huddersfield, 92 to 97
Husan, 232
Hudiksvall, 217, 426
Hué, 480
Huelva, 324, 368
Huesca, 326
Hull, 88 to 91, 105 to 107, 368, 402, 404, 405, 406, 407, 410, 421, 460
Hum, 332B
Hun, 210
Hunnebostrand, 416
Husavik, 414, 421
Husum, 426
Huy, 240
Hvar, 374, 379, 380
Hvideseid, 224
Hyeres, 79, 113, 114, 259 to 263
Hyvinkaa, 228

Ialta (see Yalta)
Iasi, 330
Ibiza, 399
Ibo, 471
Iceland Ports, 414, 418, 421, 427
Ichang, 470
Igls, 198
Igney Avricourt, 272
Ijmuiden, 450 452
Ikang, 447
Ikaria, 378
Ilanz, 288, 296
Ilawa, 227
Ile-Rousse, 138, 254, 376
Ilfracombe, 98, 99, 102, 104
Il Fuorn, 295
Ilo-Ilo, 473
Ilowo, 226
Immendingen, 180, 184, 284
Immensee, 287, 294
Immenstadt, 187, 212
Imperia, 371B, 397A
Imst, 197, 213
Inca, 208
Indherred, 440
Indra, 208
Indre Kvaroy, 433
Inebolu, 375, 377
Ingolstadt, 191, 194
Inhambane, 467
Innertkirchen, 296
Innichen, 198
Innsbruck, 82, 83, 123 to 125, 129, 193, 197, 198, 269, 286, 307, 319, 330
Inoi, 337
Insterburg, 205, 208
Interlaken, 80, 83, 85, 119, 120 123 to 125, 127, 174, 178, 269, 279, 281, 290, 292, 294
Intra, 318
Inverness, 92 to 97, 105 to 107
Ipswich, 110
Iquique, 454, 462, 463, 478
Irkutsk, 232
Irmak, 334
Irun, 85, 115, 135, 250, 321, 322, 327
Isafjord, 414, 418, 421
Ischl, 196, 198
Iselle, 296
Iseltwald, 294
Iseo, 318
Iskenderun (see Alexandretta)
Ismailia, 338
Isola (Lake of Orta), 318
Isola Bella, 318
Isola (Trieste), 381
Isoire, 254
Istanbul, 83, 84, 141, 144, 274, 332, 333, 360, 361, 369, 371B, 372, 375, 377, 388, 392, 393, 454
Isternia,
Istria (Coasting Service), 376
Itea,
Ivory Coast, 452
Ivrea, 300
Izmir, 144, 333, 334, 360, 361, 371B, 372, 374, 375, 388, 393
Izmit, 334

Jablonowo, 225
Jaca, 252, 326
Jacksonsville, 468
Jacmel, 453, 466
Jaen, 324
Jaffa, 335, 361, 362, 367, 369, 371A, 371B, 378, 382, 386, 388, 443
Jagerndorf, 195
Jagstfeld, 185
Jamaica (see Kingston
Jaren, Nor., 218
Jaroslaw, 226, 228
Jasina, 207A
Jask, 471
Jassy (see Iasi)
Java, 146, 469 to 471, 475, 476
Jeddah, 384, 470, 477, 481
Jelgava, 208
Jelsa, 379, 381
Jemelle, 149
Jena, 191
Jenbach, 197
Jerapetra, 383
Jerbah (see Gerba)
Jerez, 324, 325
Jersey, 135, 136, 405, 409
Jerusalem, 146, 335
Jerxheim, 166, 168
Jesenice (see Assling)
Jesselton, 480
Jeumont, 240
Jibuti (see Djibouti)
Jimera, 325
Jimbolia, 83, 331, 332A
Jodhpur, 146, 147
Johannesburg, 145
Jolster, 225
Joniskia, 208
Jönköping, 216, 221
Jostedal, 224
Juan-les-Pins, 113, 114, 264
Juba, 370
Julier Hospice, 295
Jungfraujoch, 289

Kabakca, 333
Kabul, 141
Kagan, 231
Kairouan, 342B
Kalaa-Djera, 342B
Kalaa Srira, 342B
Kalaat-es-Senam, 342B
Kalamata, 336, 337, 371B, 372
Kalambaka, 336
Kalavrita, 337
Kaldenkirchen, 129, 157
Kalinin (Tver), 230
Kalinovka, 230
Kalisz, 226
Kalmar, 420, 425, 427
Kalonero, 337
Kaltbad, 289
Kamaran, 470
Kamenz, 195
Kandersteg, 123 to 125, 269, 288
Kanizsa (see Nagykanizsa)
Kansk-Eniseiski, 232
Kantara, 335, 338
Kaolack, 147
Kaplitz, 196, 206
Kaprije 381
Karabuk 334
Karachi, 145, 146, 147, 357, 361, 363, 369, 384, 385, 471, 479
Karaklis, 231
Karatsu, 478
Karditza, 336
Karikal, 471
Karjaa, 228
Karlsbad, 84, 128, 130, 188, 189, 195, 196, 274
Karlshamn, 425
Karlskrona, 425
Karlsruhe (see Carlsruhe)
Karlstadt, 215A, 216
Karungi, 218
Karymskaya, 232
Kaspichan, 332B
Kassa, 202, 207A
Kassala, 339
Kastel, 173
Katha, 475
Katowice, 81, 203, 204, 228
Katrani, 335
Katrineholm, 216
Kaufbeuren, 187, 190
Kaunas, 128, 140 208
Kautenbach, 159
Kavassila, 337
Kavieng, 470
Kayseri, 333, 334
Kazalinsk, 231
Kazan, 233
Kazatin, 230, 231
Keelung, 364, 475, 479
Kehl, 84, 126, 182, 183, 272 274
Kehrsiten, 289, 293
Keizyo, 232
Kelantan, 480
Kelebia, 200, 332A
Kellenbusen, 424
Kemi Fir, 142, 228
Kempen, 156
Kempten, 186, 187, 193
Kenadza 342
Kenali, 337
Kermanshah, 83, 334
Kesteren, 156
Keswick, 92 to 97
Keta,
Khanikin, 83, 334
Kharbin (see Harbin)
Kharkov, 230, 231
Khartoum 143, 145, 339, 370
Khartsisk, 231
Kherson
Khios (see Chios)
Khong, 480
Khone Nord, 480
Khone Sud, 480
Khoramshahr, 384, 471, 472
Kiel, 130, 162, 424, 426
Kiel-Holtenau, 417, 449
Kiev, 204, 227, 230, 231
Kil, 215A, 216, 218
Kilindini, 359, 471
Kilindire, 375
Killini, 337
Kilwa, 471
Kimberley, 145
Kineshma, 233
Kingisepp, 206
Kingston (W.I.), 449, 453, 455, 456, 459, 460, 462, 463, 472, 474, 481
Kinn, 434
Kinsarvik, 221, 438
Kirkenes, 419, 424, 428
Kirku, 334
Kirov, 232
Kirtenesset, 434
Kiruna, 218
Kis-Körös, 200
Kisimajo, 382, 383, 384
Kissingen, 185, 188 to 190
Kitzbühl, 83 197
Kiukiang, 470
Kiwerce, 227
Kjendalen, 225
Klagenfurt, 143, 196, 198, 199

Klaipeda (see Memel)
Klausenburg (Kolozsvar), see Cluj
Klein-Bettingen, 127, 149
Klein-Reifling, 197
Kleven, 413
Klosters, 286
Knocke, 148, 153, 239, 427
Kobe, 358, 360, 362 to 365, 367, 369, 385, 389, 468, 471 to 473, 474, 478 to 480
Coblence Koblenz (Germany), see
Koblenz (Switz.), 283, 284
Kochel, 194, 212, 213
Koepang, 145
Kogo, 446
Kohlfurt, 204
Kokkola, 228
Koko, 447, 472
Kolambugan, 473
Kolding, 214
Kolin, 195
Kolozsvar (see Cluj)
Koluszki 203
Komarom, 200
Komiza, 379, 380
Komotau, 196
Kongsberg, 219, 223, 224
Kongsvinger, 215A
Konia, 334
Königsberg, 140, 205, 227
Königswinter, 175, 209
Konin, 226
Konitz (see Chojnice)
Konotop, 230
Konstantinovka, 231
Konstanz (see Constance)
Kopervik, 413
Kopmanholmen, 426
Korčula (see Curzola)
Kornsjö, 216
Korsœr, 215
Kosice, see Kassa
Köslin, 205
Kosseir, 384 481
Kostolany, 207A
Kosti, 339, 370
Kostroma, 233
Kotka, 414, 423, 453
Kotonou (see Cotonou)
Kotor, 373, 374, 379, 380, 398
Kotoriba, 201, 332A
Kouvola, 228
Kovno (Lit.), see Kaunas
Koweit, 145, 471
Kowel, 227
Kragero, 219, 222, 413
Kraljevica (see Portore)
Kralovo, 207A
Krasno, 204
Krasnovodsk, 233
Krasnoyarsk, 232
Kratie, 480
Kreiensen, 166, 170, 171, 194
Kreminica, (see Ke li)
Krems, 211
Kreuznach 179
Kribi, 447, 452
Krimice, 206
Krionery, 336
Kristiansand, see Christianssand
Krk (see Veglia)
Kroderen, 220, 225
Kroekja Bro, 221
Kroken, 224
Kronstadt (see Brasso
Krossbu, 224
Kroubs, 340, 341
Krustpils, 206
Krykjebo, 438
Krylbo, 217, 218
Kuantan, 480
Kudat 480
Kufstein, 82, 198, 213
Kuibishev, 231, 233
Kukas, 143, 206
Kunovice, 206A
Kurrachee (see Karachi)
Kursk, 230 231
Kus Adasi,
Küssnacht, 287, 293
Kustendje (see Constantza)
Kutchuk-Cekmece, 333
Kutno, 226
Kuty, 207
Kvenangfjord, 440
Kvisvik, 223, 224 440
Kviteseid, 223
Kwan Tchai Wan, 481
Kyparissia, 337
Kyrnica, 203
Kyrping, 223, 438
Kysak, 207A

La Barre, 253
La Baule-Escoublac, 135, 247
La Bourboule, 249
La Comballas, 296
La Croix de Cavalaire, 263
La Encina, 323, 325
La Foux, 263
La Guayra, 450, 453, 454, 456, 464, 466, 474
La Lécherette, 296
La Libertad 450, 454, 456, 458, 462, 466, 478
La Linea, 328
La Macta, 342
La Maddelena, 397A
La Madeleine, 236
La Palma (Can. Is.) see Palma (Can. Is.)
La Plata, 479
La Point à Pitre (see Pointe-à-Pitre)
La Puebla (Balearic Isles), 328
La Reunion, 377, 389, 476
La Rochelle 111, 135, 246, 418, 462
La Roche-sur-Foron, 121, 122, 267
La Roche-sur-Yon, 111, 135, 246
La Roda, 324, 325
La Seyne Tamaris, 264
La Thuile, 212
La Tour de Carol, 117
La Union, 450, 456, 458
Labuan, 480
Lae, 470
Laerdal, 222, 435 to 438
Lages do Pico, 448
Lagos (Portugal), 328
Lagos (Nig.), 446 to 448, 452, 456A, 472
Lagosta, 373 to 375
Lahour, 446
Laibach (see Ljubliana
Laigle, 111, 241, 244
Lakehurst, 146
Lamalou les Bains, 117
Lamballe, 245
Lamia, 337
Lamothe, 247, 250
Landau, 181
Landeck, 85, 197, 213, 291, 295, 319
Landen, 151, 152
Landerneau, 245, 246
Landquart, 85, 123 to 125, 269, 286, 288
Landshut, 190
Landskrona, 425
Landwarow, 208, 227
Langara, 216
Langeac, 254
Langen, 197, 213
Langwies, 291
Langnau, 279
Langogne, 254
Langres, 268, 271
Langsele, 218
Lannion, 245
Laodicea (see Gondjeli)
Laon, 83 to 85, 123, 124, 236 to 238, 270
Lapovo, 332
Lappi, 228
Laqueuille, 247, 249
Larache, 363
Larengau, 470
Larissa, 336
Larnaca, 361, 371A, 371B, 378, 386, 388
Laroche, 259 to 262
Larvik, 215A, 217, 220, 413 420
Las Casetas (see Casetas)
Las Nieves, 465
Las Palmas, 369, 442, 446 to 448, 451, 454, 455, 456A, 457, 458, 461, 462, 464, 465, 467, 468, 472
Laskowice, 226
Lasva, 332B
Latakia, 371B, 386
Lathuille, 275
Lauda, 185
Laugszargen, 208
Launceston (England), 102, 104
Laurana
Laurium 336
Lausanne, 83, 119, 120, 138, 142, 267, 278 to 280, 282, 283, 292, 293
Lauterbrunnen, 281, 292
Laval, 244
Laveno, 304, 318
Lawoczne, 201
Laxa, 215A, 216
Le Bourget, 140
Leamington, 98, 99
Lecce, 313
Lecco, 304, 317
Lech, 213
Le Canadel, 263
Le Chable, 296
Le Creusot, 254
Le Croisic, 247
Le Fayet (see Fayet)
Le Lavandou, 263
Le Locle Ville, 267
Le Mans, 111, 241, 244, 247
Le Mont Dore (see Mont Dore)
Le Pont, 279
Le Rayol, 263
Le Sepey, 296
Le Touquet, 138
Le Trayas, 264
Le Treport (see Treport)
Le Zoute, 139
Leeds, 88 to 91, 108
Leer, 175
Leeuwarden, 129, 131, 159
Leghorn, 118, 301, 309, 360, 361, 363, 371B, 372, 376, 377, 382, 383, 384, 385, 395, 397A, 443, 454, 456A
Lehrte, 163, 164, 168, 170
Leicester, 88 to 91, 109
Leiden, 129, 131, 158
Leikanger, 435, 437, 438
Leipsic, 81, 128, 130, 132, 140 to 141, 163, 164, 166, 168, 169, 172, 173, 190 to 192, 195, 204
Leirvik, 437
Leith, 407, 421
Leitmeritz, 209
Leixoes, 444, 445, 451
Leksand, 217
Lemberg (see Lwow)
Lenggries, 194
Leninakan, 231
Leningrad, 208 228, 230, 408
Lenkoran, 233
Lenk, 290
Lenno, 317, 320
Lenzerheide, 295
Leoben, 82, 196, 198, 199
Leominster, 98, 99
Leon, 321
Leopoldov, 206A, 207A
Leopoldville, 147
Lerida, 322
Lermoos, 193
Leros, 274, 373, 374
Lervik, 432, 433
Les Arcs, 113, 114, 264
Les Aubrais, 115, 116, 248, 249
Les Avants, 290
Les Cayes, 466
Les Houches, 253
Les Lecques, 263
Les Mosses, 296
Les Sables d'Ol, 111, 246

Les Salins (Tunis), 342B
Les Salins d'Hyeres, 263
Les Tines, 253 ierres)
Les Verrieres (see Ver-
Lesce Bled, 199, 332A
Lesina (see Hvar)
Leskovac, 332A
Leucade, 380
Leuk, 119, 120, 280
Leukerbad, 290
Levanger, 440
Levanto, 301
Levico, 306
Leysin, 291, 296
Lianokladi, 336, 337
Libau (see Liepaja)
Liberia, 452 (See also
Libourne, 248 Monrovia)
Libreville, 147, 445, 456A
Licata, 315
Lichtenfels, 191
Lido (Venice)
Liege, 80, 81, 128, 151, 152, 158, 240
Liegnitz, 204
Lienz, 198, 213, 319
Liepaja, 208, 409, 427
Liesta, 282
Lifou, 390
Likhoslavl, 230
Lille, 79, 127, 137, 149, 236, 238, 239
Lillehammer, 219, 225
Lillesand, 222, 413
Limassol, 361, 362, 371B, 378, 386
Limburg, 169, 171
Limoges, 117, 249, 250, 252
Limone, 318
Lindau, 129, 180, 186, 187, 197, 212, 273, 282, 283, 285, 294
Linderhof, 213
Lindi, 382, 471
Linga, 471
Linköping, 215A, 221
Linthal, 286, 295
Linz (Aus.), 84, 187 to 189, 196, 206, 211
Linz (Germany), 175, 209
Lisbon, 85, 115, 116, 138, 140, 142, 144, 250, 322, 323, 325, 327, 328, 359, 360, 363, 368, 403, 410, 443 to 446, 448, 450, 451, 455, 457, 461, 468
Lisieux, 243
Lison, 243, 245
Litochoron, 336
Little St Bernard, 212, 300
Littoria, 310
Lividia, 336
Liverpool, 88 to 99, 142, 357, 358, 360 to 363, 368, 406, 407, 410, 442, 444, 447, 448, 453, 457, 459, 460, 462, 468
Livingston, 450
Lixouri, 371B, 378
Llandudno, 92 to 97
Ljubljana, 144, 200, 332A
Loanda, 446, 457
Loano, 299
Lobito, 369, 446, 457, 467
Lobositz, 195, 206
Locarno, 125, 270, 287, 292, 318, 319
Locle, 279
Lodingen, 415, 424, 428, 440
Lodz-Kal, 226
Loèche (see Leuk)
Loèche-les-Bains (see Leukerbad)
Loen, 223, 224A, 225, 434
Loevenstein, 419
Lofer, 319
Lofoten, 415, 428
Loftus, 223, 432, 433, 438
Lohne, 163, 164
Lokken, 221
Lokoshaza, 84, 203, 331
Lom, 211
Lombrum, 470
Lome, 445, 446 447, 448, 452, 456A
London, 79 to 85, 88 to 99, 101 to 132, 135 to 140, 142, 145, 150, 155, 156, 185, 236 to 238, 241, 242, 259 to 262, 265, 330, 343, 358 to 362, 364 to 369, 402, 403, 404, 405 to 410, 442, 444, 447, 448, 453, 455, 457, 459 460 to 462, 467
Longpre, 237
Longreach, 145, 146
Longueau, 137, 238
Longuyon, 126, 137 271
Longyear City, 428
Lord Howe Island, 469, 470
Lorient, 246
Los Angeles, 444, 449, 450, 453, 454, 456, 458, 460, 462, 466, 468, 473, 477 to 480
Losonc, 202
Loughborough, 88 to 91
Lourdes, 115 116, 251, 252
Lourenço Marques, 145, 359, 363, 382, 444, 446, 452, 456A, 457, 463, 467, 471, 472, 474, 476, 479
Lourtier, 296
Louvain, 151, 152
Lovere, 318
Lovinobana, 202
Lowestoft, 110
Lowiez, 226
Loyalty, Islands, 390
Lozovaya, 230, 231
Luanda (see Loanda)
Lübeck, 132, 161, 162, 168, 205, 416, 420, 424
Lublin, 226, 227
Lucca, 309
Lucerne, 80, 123 to 125, 127, 131, 174, 178, 212, 270, 279, 281, 282, 284, 287, 290, 293, 302
Luchon, 117, 249, 251
Ludd, 335
Luderitz Bay, 446
Ludlow, 98, 99
Ludvika, 216, 218
Ludwigshafen, 176, 177, 181 to 183, 209, 273, 275
Ludwigslust, 169
Lugano, 81, 123 to 125, 174, 290, 292, 295, 302, 317, 319, 320
Luganville, 390
Luino, 125, 270, 287, 302 317, 318
Luka Sipanska, 379
Lulea, 218, 426
Lulubourgas, 333
Lunde, 219, 221
Lundenburg, 203, 206A, 207
Lunderskov, 214, 215
Luneburg, 168, 170
Luneville, 272
Lungern, 281
Lure, 268, 271
Lussino, 144
Lussinpiccolo, 373, 375, 376, 381
Luttre, 152
Luxembourg, 80, 127, 148, 149, 152, 158, 178, 179, 181, 271 275
Luxor, 80, 82 145, 338, 339, 370
Luz-St. Sauveur, 115, 116, 251
Lwow, 81, 201, 204, 226 to 228, 331
Lydda, 146
Lymington, 101 103
Lyngenfjord, 428, 440
Lyngor, 413
Lynton, 102, 104
Lyons, 174, 250, 255 to 257, 259 to 262, 264 to 266
Lysekil, 416
Lyttelton (N.Z.), 459, 460 479
Maaloy, 414, 415, 421, 428
Maan, 335
Maastricht, 158, 178
Macassar, 362, 447, 469, 475, 476, 480
Maccagno, 318
Maceio, 479
Machatch-Kala, 231
Macon, 113, 114, 259 to 262, 266
Madang, 470
Maddalena 395
Madeira, 442 to 448, 451, 454, 456, 457, 458, 461, 462, 467, 468, 472
Maderno, 318
Madonna di Campiglio, 319
Madras, 359, 361, 363, 369, 385, 390, 469, 471, 474, 479
Madrid, 85, 115, 116 140, 144, 248, 250, 321 to 326
Magallanes, 458, 462
Magadino, 318
Magdeburg, 132, 163, 164, 166, 168 to 171
Magenta, 298
Maghagha, 338
Maglie, 313
Magnesia (see Manisa)
Mahé, 476
Mahanoro, 390
Mahomerah (see Khoramshahr)
Mahon, 399
Maintirano, 390
Mainz, 129, 131, 175 to 177, 179, 181 to 183, 188, 189, 209, 210, 273, 275
Maiori, 391
Maison Carrée, 340, 341
Majunga, 377, 389, 390
Makalla, 470
Makambo, 470
Makarska, 374, 379, 380 381
Makassar, 146
Makena, 480
Malacca 360, 480
Malaga, 144, 324, 325, 328, 368, 397A, 399, 454, 464, 465, 468
Malakal, 145
Malangen, 428, 440
Malatya, 334
Malaunay, 241, 242
Malaya (Coasting Service), 480
Malcesnie, 318
Maldeghem, 427
Male, 306, 319
Malfors, 221
Mali, 381
Malines, 150 to 153
Malles, 212, 306
Malinska, 379, 381
Malmo 132, 139 142, 162, 204, 215A, 216, 217, 408, 410, 420, 422, 425
Malo, 470
Maloja, 295
Mals, 295, 306
Malta, 143, 343, 357, 300, 359, 361, 362, 366 to 367, 386, 387, 388, 393, 395 to 396, 397A
Malvern, 98, 99
Malzaga, 321
Manacor, 328
Manakara, 377, 390
Mananjary, 377 390
Manaos, 444, 458
Manchester, 88 to 99, 109, 367, 368, 406, 407, 449
Manchouli, 232
Mandal, 222, 415
Mandalay, 475

Mandello, 317
Mangalia, 80
Mangrole, 471
Manila, 358, 360, 362, 363, 365, 369, 382, 447, 468, 469, 472, 473, 476, 478 to 480
Manisa, 334
Mannheim, 81, 129, 140, 174, 176 to 178, 182 to 183, 210
Manningtree, 110
Manresa, 322
Manta, 458
Mantes, 242, 243
Mantyluoto, 414
Manzanares, 324
Manzanillo, 478
Maracaibo, 453, 456
Maranham, 444, 458
Marasesci, 330
Marburg, 170
Marchegg, 206A
Marchena, 325
Marco, 327
Mardine, 334
Margonia, 315
Mariager, 419
Maribor, 200, 332B
Mariehamn, 416, 421
Marienbad, 84, 188, to 190, 195, 206, 274
Marienburg, 205, 227
Marifjoeren, 224
Maristuen, 222
Markt Oberdorf, 190
Marktredwitz, 190
Marmagoa, 471
Marnia, 342
Marrakech, 342A
Marron Ampuero, 321
Marsala, 315 395
Marseilles, 79, 81, 82, 113, 114, 138 to 140, 142, 143, 146, 147, 174, 252, 254, 255, 257, 259 to 264, 266, 299, 343, 357 to 369, 371, 371B, 372, 375 to 377, 382, 384 to 394, 397A, 398, 443, 445, 448, 449, 454, 456A, 457, 460, 464, 468, 473
Marstrand,
Marshall, 446
Martigny, 119, 120, 253 271, 280, 289, 296
Martinique, 449, 464
Martinsbruck, 295
Mary (Merv), 231
Mascara, 342
Maslinica, 381
Massalubrense, 391
Massaua, 359, 382, 383, 384, 385, 481
Mastouta, 340, 342B
Matadi, 456A
Matlock Bath, 88 to 91
Matsamudu, 389
Maubeuge, 140, 239
Mauritius, 389, 457, 467, 476
Mauisset, 221
Mayotte 389
Mazara del Vallo, 395
Mazagan, 363
Mazatlan,
Mbeya, 145
Méchéria, 342
Medan, 146
Medea, 341
Medina (Spain), 85, 115, 116, 321, 322, 327
Medina (Syria), 335
Meersburg, 294
Megalopolis, 337
Megara, 336
Megaspilion, 337
Mehamn, 419
Meheli, 389
Meilen, 286, 293
Meiningen, 185
Meiringen, 281, 296
Meitene, 208
Mejillones, 462
Meknes, 342A
Melbu, 415, 428
Melbourne, 146, 357 363, 365 366, 368, 382, 442, 444, 450, 458, 460, 463, 468 to 471, 473, 476 to 479
Melchthal, 296
Melilla, 144, 368, 399
Melitopol, 230
Melk, 211
Mellerud, 216
Memel, 205, 208, 409, 417, 426
Menado, 475, 478
Menaggio, 295, 317, 320
Menerville, 340
Mengen, 184
Menthon, 275
Mentone, 79, 81, 82, 113, 114, 259 to 262, 264, 299
Merano, 193, 198, 295, 306, 307, 319, 320
Mercier Lacombe,
Mergui, 471
Merida, 323
Merka, 382, 384, 456A
Merligen, 292
Merok, 222, 223
Merrey, 271
Mersa Matruh, 146
Mersin, 333, 362, 371A, 375, 386
Merv, (see Mary)
Messina, 82, 118, 312, 314, 337, 361, 363, 371B, 372, 377, 382, 383, 388, 396, 397A, 456A
Meshedesser, 233
Mesocco, 295
Metaponto, 311
Metkovic, 332B, 374, 380, 381
Metlaoui-Philippe-Thomas, 342B
Metz 126, 127, 137, 179, 181, 271, 275
Mezieres-Charleville, 126, 137, 271
Mezimosti-Veseli, 196, 206
Mezzocorona, 306, 307
Middelburg, 155
Middelfart, 419
Middlesbrough, 105 to 107
Miike, 478
Mikindani, 471
Mikonos, 378
Milan, 81 to 83, 118 to 120, 123 to 125, 127, 138, 139, 141, 142, 144, 174, 178, 185, 193, 201, 269, 270, 280, 284, 287, 288, 295, 298, 300 to 305, 307, 313, 318
Mimmemhausen-Neufrach, 180
Minden, 163, 164
Mindresunde, 222, 225
Minehead, 98, 99
Mineralnye Vodi, 231
Minia, 80, 338
Minori, 391
Minsk, 230
Miranda de Ebro 85, 115, 116, 321, 322
Miri, 480
Miramonte, 306
Mirecourt, 271
Miskolc, 201, 202
Missolonghi, 336
Misurata, 397
Misurina, 212, 306, 319
Mittenwald, 193, 212, 213
Mitylene, 372, 378
Mjolby, 215A, 217
Mjosa, 225
Mo (see Rana)
Mocimboa, 471
Modalen, 225
Modane, 82, 118, 265
Modena, 303
Modica, 315
Moel, 225
Mogadiscio, 143, 382, 383, 384, 456A
Mogador, 363, 392
Mogan, 465
Mohaes, 211
Mohamerah (see Khoramshahr)
Mohilany, 227, 231
Moirans, 257
Moji, 364, 369, 471, 473, 478, 479
Moka,
Molde, 142, 222, 414, 415, 421, 428, 439
Moldova, 211
Molretta, 373, 374
Moll, 153, 224
Molle (Kullen), 422
Mollendo, 450, 454, 456, 458, 462, 463, 474, 478
Mombasa, 359, 363, 369, 382, 384, 389, 471, 474, 476, 479
Monaco, 79, 113, 114, 264
Monastero (see Munster, Grisons)
Monastir (see Bitolj)
Mondane, 298
Mondsee, 198
Monfalcone, 305
Monforte, 321
Monopoli, 373, 374
Monrovia, 147, 446, 447, 452, 456A
Mons, 239
Montalto, 301
Montana, 287
Montargis, 256
Montauban, 117, 249, 252
Montbeliard, 266
Montbovon, 290
Montchanin, 254
Mont Cenis, 118
Mont-de-Marsan, 253
Mont Dore, 247, 249
Montebelluna, 306
Monte Bré, 292
Montecatini, 309
Monte Carlo, 79, 81, 82, 113, 114, 264
Monterolier, 242
Monte Spluga, 212
Monte Video, 444, 445, 449, 451, 453 to 456, 457, 461, 462, 464, 468, 479
Monthey, 288, 290
Monti, 315
Montlucon, 249, 250
Montmelian, 257, 265
Mont Pelerin, 280
Montpellier, 255
Montreal, 459, 472
Montréjeau, 117, 249, 251
Montreux, 119, 120, 280 290, 291, 293
Montroc, 253
Montserrat (Spain), 326
Montserrat (W.I.), 452, 472
Monza, 304
Mopti, 147
Morcenx, 115, 116, 250, 253
Morecambe, 88 to 91
Moreda, 324
Moret, 256, 259, 261, 262
Morez, 267, 279
Morges, 279, 293
Mori, 308
Morlaix, 245
Moroantsetra, 390
Morombe, 390
Moroni, 389
Mortara, 302
Morteau, 267
Morundava, 390
Moscow, 128, 142, 208 226, 227, 230 to 233
Mosjoen, 422, 433

Moss, 142, 216, 413
Mossamedes, 457
Mossel Bay, 363, 444, 452, 474, 476, 479
Mostaganem, 398
Mostar, 332, 332B
Mosty Slaskie, 227
Mosul, 83, 334
Motala, 217, 221
Motril, 368
Motteville, 242
Mouchard, 266
Moulins, 250, 256
Moulmein, 469, 471, 480
Mouscron, 149, 239
Mouslimie, 334
Moutier, 278
Moutiers Salins, 121, 122, 265
Moville, 459
Mozambique, 145, 359, 363, 382, 456A, 457, 471, 476
Mudanya, 375
Muhlacker, 184, 186, 273
Mühlen, 295
Mukden, 232
Mulhouse, 123 to 125, 181 266, 268 to 270
Mulenen, 288, 292
Mundal, 222
Munich, 82, 84, 126, 127, 129, 132, 139 to 141, 144, 180, 184 to 193, 194, 197 to 199, 212, 213, 272, 282, 283, 285, 319, 330
Munkacs, 201
Munster a/S. (Ger.), 179, 275
Munster (Westph., Ger.), 161, 175
Munster (Furka, Switz.), 291
Munster (Grisons, Swit.), 295, 319
Muntok, 475
Murakcresztur, 201
Muravera, 397A
Murcia, 323
Mureen, 292
Murnau, 193, 213
Muscat, 471
Musel, 368
Mycenae, 336
Myli, 336
Myrdal, 219
Mytho, 480

Nabeul, 342B
Nabresina (see Aurisina)
Naes, 225
Nagasaki, 472, 478, 479
Nag-Hamadi, 338
Nagoya, 362, 363, 364, 473, 478, 479
Nagykanizsa, 201
Nairobi, 145
Nakskov, 419
Namsos, 220, 224, 421, 422
Namur, 127, 149, 210, 240, 271
Nancy, 137, 268, 271 to 273, 275
Nanking, 232, 470
Nantes, 111, 135, 246, 247
Naphone, 480
Naples, 82, 118, 143, 147, 270, 300, 301, 303, 310 to 312, 314, 320, 361, 363, 364, 365, 371A, 371B, 372, 377, 382, 383, 384, 385, 386, 388, 391, 393, 395 to 397, 397A, 443, 454, 455, 456A, 473
Narbonne, 113, 114, 117, 252, 255, 326
Narva, 208
Narvik, 218, 415, 424, 428, 440
Nassau, 462, 472, 481
Nassjo, 215A, 216, 217
Natal, 369, 444, 457, 467
Natschen, 291
Nauders, 212, 319
Nauheim, 175
Naumburg, 172, 173
Nauphlia, 337, 371B
Naye (see Rochers-de-Naye)
Neckarelz, 185
Negapatam, 471
Negoreloje, 81, 128, 226, 227, 230, 232
Negresse, 115, 116, 250
Neisse, 195
Nelaug, 220
Nesflaten, 223, 431
Neslandsvatn, 219
Nestren, 219
Neu Bentschen, 205
Neubrandenburg, 162
Neuchatel, 119, 120, 278, 279, 282, 283
Neudietendorf, 172, 173, 185
Neuenahr, 176, 177
Neuenmarkt-Wirs, 191
Neufchâtel, 241
Neuhausen 180, 284
Neumunster, 162
Neuss, 129, 156, 157, 165
Neustadt, 180 181
Neustrelitz, 204
Neuveville, 278
Neuwied, 175, 209, 210
Nevers, 254, 256,
Nevis, 452, 472
New Alesund, 428
New Caledonia, 457
Newcastle (England), 105 to 107, 148, 403 to 405, 408, 409
Newcastle (Australia), 450 473
Newchwang, 470
Newhaven, 111, 241
New Hebrides, 390
New Orleans, 454, 464, 468, 481
Newport, Mon. (Great Britain), 98, 99,
Newport (Curaçao), 453
Newport News, 468, 480
New York, 443, 445, 447, 449, 454 to 456, 459, 446, 463, 468, 472 to 474, 479, 480, 481
Nexo, 417
Niamy, 147
Nice, 79, 81, 82, 113, 114, 174, 201, 259 to 264, 299, 364, 376, 388 454 (see also Villefranche)
Nickelsdorf, 84, 200
Nicolae Titulescu (see Halmeiu)
Nicolas, 378
Nicosia, 146, 340
Nicotera, 312
Niederlahnstein, 175, 209
Niedernhausen, 171
Niederried, 281
Niesen-Kulm, 292
Nieuwediep, 427
Nigde, 333
Nikitovka, 231
Nimes, 113, 114, 254, 255
Nimule, 370
Ningpo, 470
Niort, 245, 246
Nisch, 83, 84, 274, 332, 332a
Nishni-Novgorod (see Gorky)
Nisiro, 374
Nisser, 225
Nogara, 307
Nong Keo, 480
Nor, 225
Nordagutu, 219, 220
Norddeich, 175
Nordeide, 435, 437
Nordendon, 215
Norderney, 422
Nordfjord, 414, 440
Nordfjordeid, 223, 434
Nordhausen, 167, 168 171
Nordlingen, 186, 194
Nordmaling, 426
Nordmore, 439
Nordsisfjord, 434
Nordsjo, 225
Norfolk (U.S.), 459
Norfolk Island, 470
Norheimsund, 221, 224, 432, 433
Normanton, 146
Norrkoping, 215A, 410, 423, 425
North Cape, 415, 428
North Cape (Can.) 481
North Helgeland, 424
Northallerton, 105 to 107
Northeim, 170
Norsholm, 215A, 221
Norsup, 390
Norwich, 110
Nossi-Bé, 377, 389, 390
Nottingham, 88 to 91, 109
Noto, 315
Notodden, 220, 221, 223
Noumea, 390, 457, 476
Novara, 270, 287 298, 302
Nova-Zagora, 332B
Noveant 275
Novi, 379
Novo Redondo, 457
Novi-Sad, 211, 332A
Novorossisk, 372, 393
Novosibirsk, 232
Nowy Targ, 203
Nuremberg, 84, 128, 132, 138, 140, 141, 184 to 191, 194, 206, 274
Nusaybin, 83, 334
Ny-Alesund, 427
Nyborg, 215, 419
Nykjöbing, 419
Nykobing (Den.), 214
Nykoping (Sw.), 215A
Nymegen, 129, 131, 155 156, 159, 210
Nynashamn, 420
Nyon, 279, 293
Nystuen, 222
Oakland, 453
Obbia, 384
Obeliai, 208
Obera Ipsee, 291
Oberammergau, 193, 212 213
Oberarth, 289
Oberau, 213
Oberbarmen, 165
Obercassel, 175
Oberdorf, Markt, 190
Obergurgl, 213
Oberhausen, 132, 157, 161, 164
Oberhof, 185
Oberhofen, 294
Oberkotzau 191, 192
Oberlahnstein, 209
Obermodern, 179
Oberstdorf, 187, 212
Oberwald, 291
Obrovac, 381
Oceania (Inter-insular Service), 390
Odda, 223, 224, 432, 433, 438
Odeillo-Font-Romeu, 117, 251
Odense, 214, 215, 419
Oderberg (see Bogumin)
Odessa, 204, 230, 372, 388, 393
Odnes, 220, 221
Oebisfelde, 163, 164
Oetzthal, 197, 213
Of, 375
Ofenburg, 295
Offenburg, 126, 127, 131, 180, 182 183
Ogulin, 332B
Oie, 222, 223, 440
Oil Rivers, 456A
Oissel, 242
Okehampton, 102, 104
Øksfjord, 415, 419
Olden, 223, 224A, 225, 434
Oldenzaal, 130, 132, 159
Old Sennar Junction, 339
Olen, 222, 223, 432, 438
Olten, 281 to 283
Olib, 381

Ollon, 290
Olomouc, 207
Olympia, 337, 449
Omegna, 318
Omis, 379, 380, 381
Omišalj 379
Omsk, 232
Oneglia, 299, 397A (see also Imperia)
Onsaker 225
Onslow, 469
Oostvoorne-on-Sea, 419
Opdal, 219, 223, 439
Opobo, 447
Oporto, 85, 322, 327, 403, 410, 443, 444
Oppenau, 181
Opstryn, 225
Oradea 83, 202, 331
Oran, 142, 341, 342, 377, 391, 392, 393, 394, 398, 399, 448, 464
Orange, 259 to 262
Oraseni, 81, 227, 331
Orbetello, 301
Ordu, 375
Orduna, 322
Orebic, 379
Orebro, 216, 217
Orehoved, 216
Orehovo, 211
Orel, 230, 231
Orenburg, 231
Oristano, 315, 395, 397A
Orleans, 115, 116, 248, 249
Orléansville, 341
Ormara, 471
Örnsköldsvik, 426
Orosei, 395, 397A
Orotava (see Teneriffe)
Orsera, 381
Orsha, 230
Orsières, 289, 296
Orskog, 439, 440
Orsova, 211, 331
Orta, 318
Orte, 303, 309, 312
Ortello, 318
Ortisei, 319
Orvieto, 303, 320
Osaka, 362, 363, 364, 473, 474, 478, 479
Oscarshamn, 425
Ose, 221, 224, 225
Oschersleben, 166
Osen, 225, 431. (See also Suldalsosen)
Osijek, 201
Oslo, 132, 139 to 142, 162, 204 215A, 216, 218, to 220, 222, 223, 224, 369, 405, 410, 413, 414 416, 418, 423, 424, 431, 438, 448, 459, 463, 468
Osnabruck, 130, 132, 159, 161, 163
Ospedaletti, 81, 113, 114, 299
Ostarije, 332B
Ostend, 80, 81, 84, 127, 128, 148, 150, 178, 239, 330, 445
Osterburken, 185
Ostersund, 218
Ostrow, 226, 230
Oswiecim, 228
Otranto, 313
Otrokovice, 206A
Otchemtchiri,
Otta, 219, 224
Ottignies, 149
Oudjda, 342, 342A
Ouchy, 293
Oued-Sarrath, 342B
Oued-Kébérit, 342
Oued-Zem, 342A
Ouistreham, 422
Ouled Rhamoun, 340
Oulu, 142, 228
Oumache, 341
Overaas, 225
Oystese, 221, 224, 432, 433
Pachia Ammo, 378
Padong, 476
Padborg, 162, 215
Padstow, 102, 104
Padua, 305, 306, 308, 320
Paestum, 312
Pag, 381
Pagny-sur-Moselle, 271, 275
Pago Pago, 477
Paita, 456, 462, 474
Pajegiai (see Pogegen)]
Pakanbaroe, 146
Pakhoi, 470, 475, 479
Paksane, 480
Pakse, 480
Palau, 395, 397A
Palembang, 145, 146, 476
Palencia, 321, 322
Palermo 82, 118, 143, 314, 315, 361, 363, 377, 384, 388, 395, 397, 397A, 455
Pallanza, 302, 318
Palma (Africa),
Palma (Canary Is.), 458, 465, 468
Palma (Majorca), 143, 328, 368, 397A, 398, 399
Palmi, 312
Pampatar, 456
Pampilhosa, 85, 327
Pamplona, 322
Panama Canal, 444, 445, 447, 448, 453, 456, 459, 460, 463, 479, 480
Panama City, 448, 453, 456, 459, 479
Pantelleria, 395
Paola, 312
Papeete, 457
Paphos, 386
Para, 444, 458, 479
Paramaribo, 456
Pardigon, 263
Pardubice, 207
Parenzo, 381
Paris, 79, 81 to 85, 111 to 122, 125, 126, 137, 138, 140 to 143, 145, 152, 154, 197, 205, 237 to 252, 254 to 257, 259 to 262, 264 to 275, 279, 280, 288, 321, 322, 330, 332, 333, 343, 392, 394
Parkanynana, 202
Parkeston Quay (see Harwich)
Parma, 300, 303
Parnahyba, 444, 458
Parndorf, 200
Pärnu, 423
Partinico, 315
Pasajes 363, 368
Pascani, 204, 330, 331
Pasewalk, 162
Pasni, 471
Passau, 84, 128, 132, 188, 189, 195, 196, 211, 330
Patmos, 373, 374
Patras, 336, 337, 361, 371B, 372, 378, 380, 455
Pattburg, 162
Patti, 314
Pau, 85, 115, 116 248, 250 to 252
Pavia, 302
Payas, 371B, 375
Pazar, 375
Pazardjik, 332
Pechlevi, 233
Pécs, 201
Peiping (see Peking)
Peking, 232
Penang, 358, 360, 362 to 365, 367, 385, 445, 447, 469, 471, 474, 476, 478 to 480
Penzance, 98
Pepinster, 128, 151, 152
Perigueux, 247, 249, 250
Perim, 470
Perkovic-Slivno, 332B
Perledo-Varenna, 304
Pernambuco, 146, 444, 445, 451, 454, 455, 456, 461, 464, 479
Perpignan, 117, 255
Perrégaux (Alg.), 342
Perrentruy, 125
Perth (Scotland), 92 to 97, 105 to 107
Perth (W. Australia), 146
Pertuis, 263
Perugia, 309, 320
Pescara, 311, 313
Peschiera, 305, 318
Peskopeja, 143
Petit Croix, 268
Petit Goave, 466
Petitjean, 342A
Petrovitz, 203
Petrovsk, 233
Pfaffikon, 287
Pforzheim, 186, 273
Pfronten-Reid, 193
Pfunds, 295
Phaleron Bay, 454, 455
Philadelphia, 468
Philippeville, 340, 391, 394, 398
Philippine Islands, 360, 476. (See also Manila)
Philippopolis (see Plovdiv)
Piacenza, 118, 300, 303, 313
Piatra-Olt, 331
Piedicolle, 332A
Pierrefitte, 115, 116, 251
Pilatus-Kulm, 289
Pillau, 417, 426
Pillon, 296
Pimental 456
Pinerolo, 298
Pinhal-Novo, 328
Piræus, 336, 337 360 to 369, 371, 371A, 371B, 372, 373, 374, 377, 378, 380, 381, 382, 386, 388, 393, 443
Pirano, 381
Pirna, 209
Pirot, 332
Pirovac, 381
Pisa, 82, 118, 300, 301, 309
Pisco, 478
Piscopi, 374
Pistany, 141, 206A, 207A
Pistoia, 309
Pitea, 426
Pitesti, 331
Plata (Argentina), see La Plata
Plata (S. Domingo), see Puerto Plata
Plati, 337
Plattling, 188, 189
Plauen, 130, 192
Pleinfeld, 187, 191
Pleven, 332B
Ploesti, 80, 84, 331
Plombières, 271
Plouaret, 245
Plovdiv, 332B
Plymouth, 98, 99, 102, 104, 358, 359, 361, 362, 365, 367, 404, 407, 409, 444, 448, 450, 451, 456, 466
Plzen, 188, 189, 195, 196, 206
Pnom-Penh, 480
Podwoloczyska, 204
Pogegen, 208
Poggio Rusco, 307
Pointe Noire, 147, 445, 382, 446, 456A, 457
Pointe-à-Pitre, 457, 466
Poitiers, 115, 116, 245, 246, 248
Pola, 144, 307, 371B, 373, 376, 381
Polath, 333
Policastro, 312
Poljud, 381
Poltava, 231

Pompeii, 311, 320
Pondicherry, 390, 471
Pondo, 470
Pons, 245
Pontarlier, 119, 120, 279, 443, 445, 455
Ponta Delgada (see Azores)
Ponte Leccia, 254
Ponte-Tresa, 290, 317
Pont l'Eveque, 243
Pontoise, 241
Pontorson, 245
Pontresina, 286, 289
Poprad-Velka, 202, 207A
Pordoi Pass, 319
Porebunder, 471
Porlezza, 317, 320
Pornichet, 247
Porquerolles, 376
Porrentruy, 123, 124, 268
Porsgrund, 219
Portimao, 328
Port Alma, 444, 473
Port Amelia, 359, 363, 382, 471
Port au Prince, 453, 456, 466
Port Bell, 145
Port Blair, 469
Port Bou, 113, 117, 255, 326
Port Bouet, 445, 446, 447, 448, 452, 456A, 472
Port Chalmers, 459
Port Cros, 376
Port Darwin (see Darwin)
Port d'Atelier, 268, 271
Port de Paix, 466
Port Dickson, 480
Port Elizabeth, 382, 444, 446, 448, 452, 456A, 467, 472, 474, 476, 479
Port Etienne, 147
Port Gentil, 147, 445, 456A
Port Harcourt, 446 to 448, 452, 472
Port Hedland, 469
Port Holland, 473
Port Kembla, 473
Port Limon (see Puerto Limon)
Port Lincoln, 146
Port Louis, 377, 479
Port Lyautey, 342A
Port Marshall, 447
Port Moresby, 470, 476
Port Natal, 457. (See also Durban)
Port of Spain, 453
Port Okha, 471
Port Olry, 390
Port Pirie, 473
Port Royal, 463
Port Said, 146, 335, 338, 357 to 369, 371B, 377, 378, 382 to 385, 388 to 390, 393, 445, 455, 473
Port Samson, 469
Port Sandwich, 390
Port Stanley, 462
Port Sudan, 339, 357, 358, 359, 361 to 363, 366, 369, 370, 383, 384, 386, 456A, 470, 477, 481
Port Swettenham, 360, 362, 365, 469, 471, 480
Port Vendres, 117, 255, 391
Port Vila, 457, 476
Portland, 448 to 450, 453, 454, 458, 466, 480
Porto-Alexandre, 457
Porto Amboim, 457
Porto Bardia, 397
Porto Cabello (see Puerto Cabello)
Porto Ceresio, 302, 317, 318
Porto Cristo, 328
Porto Empedocle, 315
Porto Lago (see Lero)
Porto Maurizio, 397A
Porto Novo, 471
Porto Rico, 453, 456, 464, 472
Porto Santo, 448
Porto Sucre, 456
Porto Torres, 395, 397A
Porto Vecchio, 254, 376
Portoferraio, 395
Portofino, 320
Portogruaro, 305
Portore, 381
Portorose, 381
Portovesme, 397A
Portsmouth, 101, 103
Poschiavo, 289
Posen (see Poznan)
Positano, 320, 391
Postumia, 83, 200, 201, 307, 332
Potenza, 311
Poti, 393
Potsdam, 168
Pougues-les-Eaux, 256
Poulo-Condore, 475
Pozante, 333
Poznan, 81, 128, 141, 205, 220, 226, 240
Pozzuoli, Solfatara, 310
Pragersko, 200
Prague (see Praha)
Praha, 84, 130, 132, 141, 144, 188 to 190, 195, 196, 202, 203, 206, 206A, 207, 207A, 274, 331, 332B
Praia, 446, 457
Praia di Rocha, 328
Prastion, 340
Prato, 303, 309
Predeal, 331
Preko, 379, 381
Prerov, 203, 206A, 207, 331
Presov, 207A
Pre St. Didier, 300, 320
Pressburg (see Bratislava)
Preston, 92 to 97
Prevesa, 372, 380
Prickule, 208
Prigradica, 379
Prilep, 337
Primolano, 306
Principe, 457
Probstzella, 191, 193
Prome, 475
Propriano, 376
Przemysl, 226, 228
Przeworsk, 228
Pskov, 230
Puchov, 207
Puck, 226
Puerto Barrios, 450, 456, 464, 481
Puerto Cabello, 450, 453, 456, 464, 466, 474
Puerto Cabras, 465
Puerto Colombia, 450, 453, 454, 456, 462, 464, 466, 474
Puerto Cortez, 456, 481
Puerto Limon, 450, 454, 464, 466, 481
Puerto Mexico, 450
Puerto Montt, 462
Puerto Plata, 453, 454, 466
Puerto Rico (see Porto Rico)
Pugliano, 300
Puigcerda, 251
Pukow, 232
Puntarenas, 450, 454, 456, 458
Puyoo, 115, 116, 251
Pyrgos, 337
Pyrmont, 166
Pythion, 332, 333

Quebec, 459
Quedlinburg, 167
Queenstown (see Cobh)
Quelimane, 467, 471
Quevy, 239
Quimper, 246
Quimperlé, 246
Quinhon, 390
Quittah (see Keta

Raab (see Györ)
Rab, 375, 379 380, 381, 398
Rabat, 342A, 363
Rabaul, 470, 473, 476
Radolfzell, 180, 294
Radviliskis, 208
Raegefjord, 413
Rafa, 335
Raftsund, 415, 428
Ragaz, 286
Ragusa (see Dubrovnik I)
Raiatea, 457
Rajajoki, 228
Rakek, 200, 201, 332A
Rakvere, 206
Rambang, 145
Rana (Mo), 433
Randers, 215A 419
Randsfjord, 225
Rangoon, 145, 146, 147, 358, 362, 369, 385, 469, 471, 474, 479
Rapallo, 301, 320
Rapperswil, 286, 287, 293
Ras-Baalbeck, 335
Ras El Ein, 335
Ras-el-Ma-Crampel, 342
Ras Hafun (see Dante)
Rastatt, 180, 182, 183
Rattvik, 217, 218
Raumanzach, 180
Raumo, 414
Raureni, 331
Ravenna, 309, 312, 313, 371B, 374
Rayak, 335
Razdelnaya, 230
Rea, 218
Realp, 296
Redon, 246
Regensburg, 188 to 190, 195
Reggan, 142
Reggio, 311, 312
Reichenau, 286, 288, 294, 295
Reichenbach, 192, 195
Reichenberg, 141
Reichenhall, 187, 212
Reil, 210
Reims, 123, 124, 237, 268, 270 to 272
Reinsvold, 218
Relizane, 342
Remagen, 176, 177, 209, 210
Rena, 219
Rennes, 135, 244 to 246
Resia, Pass of, 212, 3[illegible]
Ressen Bemmel, 156
Restinga, 465
Rethymo, 371B, 378
Reunion (see La Reunion)
Reus, 326
Reutte, 187, 193, 213
Reval (see Tallinn)
Reydarfjord, 414
Reykjavik, 414, 418, 419, 421
Rheims (see Reims)
Rheine, 130, 159, 163, 175
Rheinfelden, 283
Rheydt, 157
Rhilane, 342B
Rhine Steamers, 209
Rho 298
Rhodes, 141, 143, 371A, 371B, 372, 373, 374, 388 454, 455
Rhone Glacier (see Gletsch)
Riffelalp, 288
Riffelberg, 288
Riga, 81, 128, 130, 132, 140, 205, 208, 227, 230 240, 409, 419, 423, 425
Rigi Klosterli, 289
Rigi Kulm, 289
Rigi Staffel, 289
Rijeka (see Fiume)

Riihimaki, 228
Rimini, 309, 312, 313
Ringebu, 219
Ringkobing, 214
Ringoy, 223, 432, 433
Rio Benito (see Benito)
Rio de Janeiro, 146, 444, 445, 449, 453 to 455, 456, 457, 458 461 462, 464, 479
Rio de Oro, 465
Rio Grande do Sul, 451, 453, 457, 479
Riom, 254
Ripon, 105 to 107
Riposto, 397A
Rise, Nor., 220
Risor, 413
Ristovac, 332A
Ritupe, 206, 230
Riva, 308, 319
Riva Citta, 318
River Cess, 446
River Congo, 472
Rives 257
Rize, 375
Rjukan, 220
Roa, 218
Roanne, 256, 257
Robinson Crusoe Island, 462
Roccapalumba, 314, 315
Roccella Ionica, 311
Rochefort, 246
Rochers-de-Naye, 291
Roderau, 195
Rodriguez, 476
Roermond, 153, 158
Rogoznica, 381
Roisheim, 224
Rolandseck, 176, 177, 209
Rolle, 279, 293
Roman, 330
Romanshorn, 186, 285, 294
Rome, 81, 82, 118 to 120, 127, 138, 139, 140, 143, 144, 146, 174, 178, 185, 193, 196, 201, 270, 300, 301, 303, 307 to 312, 314, 320, 343
Romont, 279
Romsdal, 439
Roncegno, 306
Ronco, 318
Ronda, 85, 325
Rönne, 416, 425, 426
Ronnebyredd, 425
Rorvik, 421, 433
Röros, 219
Rorschach, 187, 282, 283, 285, 289, 294
Rosales, 324
Rosario, 462, 479
Rosenbach, 199
Rosendaal (Holl.), 79, 80, 129, 130, 154 to 156
Rosendal (Nor.) 433
Rosenheim, 187, 198
Roskilde, 214, 215
Rosslau, 166, 171
Rost, 428
Rostock, 162, 204
Rostov, 231
Rotenboden, 288
Rothenburg, 188, 189, 194
Rothkreuz, 284
Rothorn-Kulm, 289
Rotterdam, 80, 129, 131, 136, 139, 142, 154 to 159, 163, 209, 210, 359, 360, 362, 365 368, 369, 403, 405 to 410, 414, 416, 419, 423, 446, 447, 450 452, 453, 455, 458, 459, 462, 468
Roudnice, n. Lab, 206
Rouen, 111, 241, 242, 423
Roussé, 211, 331, 332B
Rovaniemi, 228
Rovato, 304, 305
Rovereto, 307, 308
Rovigo, 308
Rovigno, 381
Rowne 227
Royan, 111 245
Royat, 247, 254
Roykenvik, 225
Rozwadow, 226
Rübeland, 167
Rudesheim, 175, 209 210
Rudkjöbing, 419
Rugby, 92 to 97
Rugen, 426
Rungsted, 214, 215
Rustœn, 225
Rutbah, 145
Ruva Bay, 471
Rybinsk, 233
Ryde, 101, 103

Saalfeld, 191
Saalfelden, 197
Saanen, 290
Saarbrücken, 126, 141, 179, 275
Saarburg, 179, 272, 273
Saargemund, 179
Saas-Balen, 296
Saas-Fee, 296
Saba, 456
Sabang, 362, 364, 368
Sablé, 111, 247
Sabuniyah, 334
Säckingen, 180
Saebo, 221, 440
Saetersdalen, 225
Saffi, 363, 392
Sagan, 204
Sagunto 326, 368
Saida, 342
Saigon, 384, 385, 389, 390, 445, 475, 476, 479 to 480
St. Agata Militello, 314
St. Amour, 266
St. André le Gaz, 257
St. Antioco, 395, 397A
St. Anton, 197
St. Auban, 263
St. Barbe du Tlèlat, 341, 342
St. Barthelemy, 466
St. Bernhardin, 295
St. Blasien, 212
St. Brieuc, 245
St. Candido, 83, 198
St. Cergue, 279
Ste Croix (Switz.), 287
St. Croix (W.I.), 449
St. Etienne, 256, 257
St. Euphemia, 312
St. Eustatius, 456
St. Florent, 376
St. Gallen, 142, 282, 283
St. Germain-des-Fosses, 250, 254, 256, 257
St. Gervais, 121, 122, 253, 267
St. Gilgen, 198
St. Gingolph, 265, 293
St. Giovanni di Medua, 373
St. Goar, 176, 177, 209
St. Goarshausen, 175, 210
St. Gotthard Hosp., 296
St. Helena, 369, 467
St. Hilaire St. Nazaire, 257
St. Jean de Luz, 85, 115, 116, 250, 253
St. Jean-de-Maurienne, 265
St. Johann (Tirol), 197
St. John (New Brunswick), 459
St. John's (Newfoundland), 459
St. Just, 257
St. Kitts, 449, 452, 456, 466 472
St. Laurent, 466
St. Lo, 245
St. Lorenz, 198
St. Louis, W.A. 147
St. Lucia, 449, 452, 466, 472
St. Malo, 135, 244, 245, 405, 409, 426
St. Marc, 453 466,
St. Margrethen, 282, 283, 285
St. Maria (Switz.), 295
Sainte Marie, 390
St. Martin, 456, 466
St. Martin-Sail-les-Bains, 256
St. Maurice, 119, 120, 280, 288
Ste. Maxime, 263, 376,
St. Michael (Aus.), 199
St. Michael's (Azores) 443, 448
St. Moritz, 85, 123 to 125, 127, 178, 213, 269, 285, 286, 289, 291, 295, 319
St. Nazaire, 247, 466
St. Nicholas, 288
St. Omer, 236
St. Pierre d'Albigny, 265
St. Pierre-des-Corps, 115, 116, 248
St. Pietro de Carso, 200, 305, 307
St. Quaranta, 372, 373, 374, 378, 380
St. Quentin, 236, 239, 240
St. Rambert d'Albon, 257, 259 to 262
St. Raphael, 79. 82, 113, 114. 263, 264, 376
St. Rhemy, 320
St. Stephano, 300
St. Sulpice Laurière, 249
S. Teresa G., 395. 397A
St. Thomas, 449, 456, 460, 466
St. Valentin, 187
St. Veit a. d. Glandorf, 199
St. Vincent (C.V.), 444, 446, 457, 461
St. Vincent (W.I.), 452, 472
St. Wolfgang, 198
Saintes, 111, 245, 246
Salamanca, 85, 115, 116, 322 327
Salamaura, 470
Salaverry, 456, 474
Saldus, 208
Salerno, 311, 320
Salgotarjan, 202
Sali, 381
Saligny, 330
Salihli, 334
Salisbury (England), 102, 104
Salisbury (Rhodesia), 145
Sallom Junction, 339
Salo (Lake Garda) 318
Salonica, (see Thessaloniki)
Salsomaggiore, 303
Saltpond, 446, 447
Saltsjobaden, 217
Salvador, 458
Salvore, 381
Salzbergen, 159, 163
Salzburg, 83, 84, 123 to 125, 127, 129, 142, 144, 186, 187, 197 to 199, 269, 274, 319
Samach, 335
Samaden, 286, 291
Samarai, 470, 473, 476
Samarang, 362, 364, 368, 445, 469, 470, 475, 476
Samarkand 231
Sambava, 390
Sami, 378
Samsun, 333, 372, 375, 377
San Antonio, 456, 458, 462, 463
San Candido (see Innichen)
San Carlos, 465
San Dalmazzo di Tenda, 299
San Diego, 456
San Fernando, 324
San Francisco, 448 to 450, 453 454, 456, 458, 460 466, 468, 473, 477 478, 480
San Gavino, 315
San Gimignano, 320
San Jeronimo, 323, 324

San Jose de Guatemala, 450, 454, 456, 458, 466
San Juan, 453, 454, 464, 466, 474
San Leonardo, 320
San Marino, 309
San Martino di Castrozza, 319
San Michele, 306
San Nicolas, 465
San Pedro de Macoris, 448, 453,
San Remo, 81, 82, 113, 114, 264, 299
San Salvadour, 263
San Salvatore, 290
San Sebastian (Canary I.), 465
San Sebastian (Spain), 85, 115, 116, 321
San Vicente, 326
San Vito di Cadore, 306
Sand, 224, 224A, 431
Sandane, 224A, 434
Sandakan, 473, 474, 476, 480
Sanden, 225
Sandifjord 220
Sandnaes, 413, 421
Sandnessjoen, 142, 415, 422, 428, 433
Sandown, 101, 103
Sandvika, 223
Sangerhausen, 171
Santa Comba, 327
Santa Cruz de la Palma (see Palma, Canary Is.)
Santa Cruz de Tenerife (see Teneriffe)
Santa Fe, 479
Santa Isabel, 446, 452, 465
Santa Margherita (Rapallo), 301, 320
Santa Margherita (Lugano), 317
Santa Maria (Azores), 448
Santa Maria (Bal. Is.) 328
Santa Maria Maggiore, 292
Santa Marte, 456, 481
Santander, 321, 322, 363, 368, 462, 464, 466
Santany, 328
Santarem, 327
Santhia, 298
Santiago de Cuba, 466, 481
Santo Domingo (see Ciudad Trujillo)
Santos, 444, 445, 449, 451, 453 to 456, 457, 461 462, 464, 468, 479
Sao Jorge, 448
Sao Thomé, 446, 457
Sapele, 447, 472
Saragossa, 144, 252, 322, 326
Sarajevo, 332, 332B
Sarande (see St. Quaranta)
Saraniovo, 332
Saratov, 233
Sargans, 83, 85, 123 to 125, 269, 285, 286

Sark, 405, 407
Sarmettes, 390
Sarnen, 296
Sarnico, 318
Saronno, 304
Sarpsborg, 423 brucken)
Sarrebruck (see Saar-
Sarzana, 300, 301
Saseno, 373
Sassandra, 445, 446, 448
Sassnitz, 130, 132 162, 204, 215A, 216 426
Satoraljanjhely, 201
Sauda, 223, 413, 431
Saudesjoen, 413, 431
Sauland, 223
Savannah, 468, 480
Savannakek, 480
Savenay, 246
Saverne, 272
Savognin, 295
Savona, 298 to 300, 371B 397A
Savsoona, 377
Sazaire, 457
Sbeitla, 342B
Scalanova (see Kus Adasi)
Scarborough, 105 to 107
Schafbergspitze, 198
Schaffhausen, 180, 184, 185, 284, 285, 287, 294
Schaftlach, 194
Schandau, 209
Scharding, 188, 189, 196
Scharnitz, 193
Scheidegg, 289, 292
Scheveningen, 131
Schiedam, 158, 402
Schierke, 167, 212
Schifferstadt, 181
Schio (see Chios)
Schleswig, 162
Schliersee, 194
Schnabelwaid, 190
Schneidemuhl, 205, 206,
Scholastika, 212
Schonau, 212
Schuls, 295
Schuls-Tarasp, 213, 291, 295
Schwandorf, 190
Schwarzach, 197
Schwarz St. Veit, 199
Schweinfurt, 185, 188 to 191
Schwerte, 165
Schwyz, 287
Schynige Platte, 292
Sciacca, 315
Scio (see Chios)
Seaton, 102, 104
Seattle, 444, 448 to 450, 453, 454, 456, 458, 462, 466, 473, 478
Sebenico (see Sibenik)
Sedan, 271
Sedrun, 291
Seefeld, 193
Seem 225
Seesen, 166
Seelisberg, 292
Segni, 311

Segond Channel, 470
Segou, 147
Seinajoki, 228
Seishin, 477
Selbusjoen, 225
Selestat, 181
Selinunte, 315
Selje, 434
Seljord, 223, 224
Sellin, 426
Selzach, 278, 282, 283
Selzthal, 196, 197, 199
Semarang, 145, 146, 447, 480
Sembrancher, 296
Semlin (see Zemun)
Semmering, 199, 200
Senj (see Zengg)
Sennar Junction, 339
Sennar Town, 339
Sens, 259, 261, 262
Senta, 332A
Seoul (see Keizyo)
Sepoy, 291
Sered, 207A
Seregno, 304
Serqueux, 241, 242
Serquigny, 241, 243
Serres, 337
Sestri Levante, 301
Sestrieres (see Ulzio) Clavieres-Sestrieres)
Sete, 113, 114, 252, 255, 392, 398, 456A
Sétif, 340
Setubal, 410
Sevastopol, 230, 393
Seven Sisters, 415
Seville, 144, 323 to 325, 327, 328 368, 397A, 398, 465
Sevlus, 207A
Seychelles, 471
Seydisfjord, 414, 421
Sfax, 342B, 387, 396
Shanghai, 232, 358, 360, 362 to 365, 367, 369, 382, 385, 389, 447, 468, 470 to 473, 474, 475, 476, 478, 480
Shanklin, 101, 103
Sharjah, 145, 471
Shasi, 470
Sheffield, 88 to 91, 109
Sheher, 470
Shellal, 82, 338, 339, 370
Shendi, 339
Shepetovka, 227, 231, 233
Sherbro, 446, 447
Shimidzu, 473, 478, 479
Shmerinka, 204, 230
Shrewsbury, 98, 99
Shuster, 472
Siam (West Coast), 480
Siangtan, 470
Sibari, 311
Šibenik, 332B, 373, 375, 379, 380, 381, 398
Sibiu, 331
Sidi bel Abbès, 342
Sidi-el-Aidi, 342A
Sidmouth, 102, 104
Siedlce, 226
Siena, 309, 320

Sierra Leone, 448
Sierre, 119, 120 280, 287 296
Siglufjord, 414, 418, 421
Sigmaringen, 184
Sigmundsherberg, 196
Sihlbrugg, 284, 289
Sihwald, 289
Sikea, 426
Silba, 379
Silkeborg, 215A
Siljord, 225
Sils Maria, 295
Silvaplana, 295
Simlenes 436, 43
Simi, 373, 374
Simonsdorf, 227
Simplon, 119, 120, 296,
Sinelnikovo, 230
Singapore, 145, 146, [illegible] 360, 362 to 365, 367 to 369, 379, 382, 384, 385, 389, 390, 445, 447, 469, 470, 471, 473 to 476, 478 to 480
Singen, 126, 180, 184, 284
Siniscola, 395, 397A
Sinkat, 339
Sinob, 375
Sinoe, 446
Siofok, 201
Sion, 119, 120, 280, 296
Sirdal, 225
Sirkedji, 83
Sirmione, 318
Sirte, 397
Sita, 208
Sitges, 117, 326
Sitia, 378
Sittard, 158
Sivas, 333, 334
Sjoholt, 224A
Skanevik, 223, 432, 438
Skanderborg, 215A
Skei, 225
Skelleftehamn, 426
Skern, 214
Skien, 219 to 221, 423
Skiensfjord, 424
Skierniewice 203
Skjervöy, 419
Skjolden, 435 to 438
Skjoldevik, 222
Skoplje, 83, 141 332A
Skoppum, 220
Skradin, 381
Skrljevo, 201, 332B
Skrunda, 208
Slata, 342B
Slatdoly, 141
Slinde 435 to 438
Sliten, 397
Smolensk, 230
Smyrna (see Izmir)
Snaasen, 225
Sniatyn Zalucze 227
Snyten, 217
Sob, 202
Sochi, 393
Socoa, 253
Sódartälje, 425
Soderhamn, 217, 426

Soerabaya (see Sourabaya)
Soest, 130, 165, 166
Sofia, 83, 84, 144, 274, 331, 332, 332B, 333
Sogndal, 224, 435 to 438
Sohag, 80, 338
Soissons, 238
Solda (Sulden), 319
Solenzara 254
Soller, 328
Solothurn, 282, 283
Solsnes, 435
Solvorn, 436
Soma, 334
Sombor, 332A
Sommerfeld, 204
Somovit, 211
Sonceboz, 278
Sönderborg, 419
Sondmore, 439
Sondrio, 304
Sorge, 167
Sorrento, 320
Sorum, 221, 225
Souellaba (see Duala)
Souk Ahras, 340, 342
Soumain, 238
Sourabaya, 145, 146, 362, 364, 368, 445, 447, 469, 470, 475, 476, 479, 480
Sousa (see Susa)
Sousse (see Susa)
Southampton, 101, 103, 111, 135, 242, 357, 359, 360, 363 to 368, 402 to 407, 442, 443, 446, 450, 451, 452, 457, 459 to 461, 463, 466, 467
South Shields, 105 to 107
Spa, 128, 151, 152, 240
Spalato (see Split)
Spanish Guinea, 448
Sperillen, 225
Spezia, 300, 301, 395
Spielfeld, 200
Spiez, 123 to 125, 269, 281, 288, 290, 294
Spisska-Nova, 141
Spittal, 198, 199
Spitzbergen 427, 440
Split, 144, 196, 332B, 371B 373 to 376, 379 to 381, 384, 385, 398, 454, 455
Splugen, 295
Spoleto, 312
Spondigna, 306, 319
Stäfa, 293
Stainach-Ird, 196, 197
Stalden, 288, 296
Stalheim 224, 224A
Stalingrad, 233
Stamora-Moravica, 330
Stampalia, 374
Staffelhohe, 289
Stanislawow, 227
Stankov, 206
Stanleyville, 147
Stans, 290
Stansstad, 290, 293
Stansserhorn, 290
Stari-grad, 379, 380
Stargard, 205
Starnberg, 193
Starogard, 227
Stathelle, 222,
Stavanger, 142, 148, 403, 413 to 415, 418, 420, 421, 425, 431, 433, 459
Stavoren, 422
Stein, 294
Steinach (Germ.), 188, 189, 194
Stein-Sackingen, 283, 284
Stelvie Pass, 319, 320
Stendal, 163, 164, 169
Stenkjaer 220, 224, 440
Stentsch (see Neu Bentschen)
Sterpenich, 127, 149
Sterzing (see Vipiteno)
Stettin, 140, 162, 205, 417, 418, 420, 423, 426
Stiege, 167
Stillida, 372
Stirling, 92–97, 105–107
Stockholm, 130, 132, 136, 139, 140, 142, 162, 204 215A, 216, 217, 218, 221, 408, 410, 416, 417, 420, 421, 423 425 to 427
Stockton, 105 to 107
Stokmarknes, 415, 428
Stolberg, 151
Stolp, 205
Stolpce, 81, 226, 227, 230, 232
Ston, 381
Stören, 219
Storlien, 218, 220
Storvik, 218
Stradella, 300
Stralsund, 162, 204
Stranda, 439, 440
Stranraer, 92 to 97
Strasbourg, 80, 84, 126, 127, 137, 141, 149, 162, 178, 179, 181 to 183, 250, 266, 272 to 274, 330
Strba, 207A
Stresa, 119, 120, 269, 280, 302, 318
Strengen, 221
Strömstad, 416
Struer, 214
Stryn, 224A, 225, 434
Stryj, 201
Stuttgart, 84, 126, 127, 129, 140, 141, 182 to 186, 193, 194, 273, 274, 284, 285
Stylis, 337
Suakin, 339, 477
Subotica, 332A
Suchdol, see Zauchtel
Sucurac, 381
Suez, 338, 357, 359, 363 to 365, 369, 382, 383, 384, 385, 386, 389, 390, 456A, 473, 477, 481
Sukhomi, 393
Suldal, 225
Suldalsosen, 224. (See also Osen)
Sulgen 285
Sulima, 446
Sulina, 211, 360, 372, 377, 393
Sulmona, 311
Sumartin, 381
Sumatra, 480
Suna, 318
Sundal, 433
Sunde 432, 433
Sundsvall, 217, 218, 426
Sunderland, 105 to 107
Sundvolden, 225
Sunfa, 332
Sunnan, 225
Sunndalsora, 223, 440
Supetar, 380
Suphelle, 222
Surdon, 244
Surinam, 466
Sürmene
Surna, 224, 440
Sursee, 282
Sus, 296
Susa, 342B, 387, 396, 460
Sušak, 201, 332B, 361, 374, 379, 380, 381, 398
Sutivan, 380, 381
Su-u, 470
Suva, 457, 460, 463, 472, 477
Suvigliana, 292
Svalbard (see Spitzbergen)
Svaneke, 417
Svangstrand, 225
Svendborg, 419
Svenes, 224
Sverdlorsk 232
Svilengrade, 83, 332, 333
Svolvaer, 415, 424, 428 433
Svorkmo, 224
Swanage, 101, 103
Swansea, 98, 99, 363, 410 449, 462
Swatow, 470, 474
Swinemünde, 417, 426
Sydenden, 225
Sydney, 146, 363, 365, 366 368, 382, 390, 442, 444, 450, 458, 460, 463, 468 to 473, 476, to 478, 479
Sylte (la Valldall Sylte)
Syra, 378
Syracuse, 82, 118, 143, 314, 315, 343, 371A, 384, 387, 396
Szeged, 202
Szenc, 202, 207
Szentgotthard, 201
Szolnok, 203
Szombathely, 201
Tabeditt, 342B
Tabia, 342
Tabor, 206
Tabou 445, 446, 448
Tacoma, 449, 458
Tahiti (see Papeete)
Tai, 306
Tailfer, 210
Takoradi, 446 to 448, 452, 456A, 472
Taku, 362
Taku Bar, 360
Talara, 463, 474
Talavera, 325
Talcahuano, 456, 458, 462, 463
Tallinn, 139, 140, 208, 409, 418, 423, 424
Talloires, 275
Tamaris (see La Seyne-Tamaris)
Tamatave, 377, 389, 476
Tamerna, 341
Tammerfors (see Tampere)
Tampere, 142, 228
Tampico, 450, 454, 458
Tananarive, 147
Tanga, 359, 363, 471, 476, 479 364
Tangier, 85, 142, 342A, 359, 363, 366 to 369, 374, 392, 397A, 399, 460
Tangoa, 470
Tanna, 390
Tanne, 167
Tantah, 338
Taormina, 82, 118, 314, 388
Tapa, 208
Tarakan, 146
Taranto 310, 311
Tarare, 256
Tarascon, 113, 114, 252, 255, 259 to 262
Tarbes, 115, 116, 251 to 253
Tarnopol, 204
Tarnow, 228
Tarragona, 325, 326, 363, 368, 397A, 399, 464, 465, 468
Tarsus, 333
Tartu, 208
Tarvisio, 82, 196, 199, 308
Tashkent, 231
Tasucu, 375
Taunton, 98, 99
Taus, 188, 189, 206
Tavistock, 102, 104
Tavoy, 471
Tawao, 479
Taza, 342A
Tbilisi, 231
Tcherkeskeny, 333
Tchirpan, 332
Tczew, 205, 226, 227
Tebessa, 342, 342B
Tebouk, 335
Tegernsee, 194, 212, 213
Teheran, 83, 141, 233, 334
Teius, 202, 331
Tela 481
Telemarken Lakes, 225
Tel Aviv, 335, 361, 362 371B, 386
Tel Kotchek, 83, 334
Tellsplatte, 293
Telokbetong, 447
Teluk Anson, 480
Temesvar (see Timisoara)
Tempi, 336
Tenby, 98, 99

Teneriffe (Santa Cruz), 369, 442, 446 to 448, 452, 454, 457, 464, 465, 467, 468, 472
Teplitz, 196
Terceira, 448
Terezin-Bohusovice, 206
Tergnier, 236, 237, 239, 240
Termini, 314
Termoli, 311 313
Termonde, 150 154
Terneuzen, 427
Terni, 309, 312
Terontola, 303, 309
Terranova, 315, 395, 397A
Territet, 119, 120, 280, 291, 293
Terschelling, 427
Teruel, 326
Tetschen, 209
Tetuan, 144, 342A
Teulada, 397A
Texel, 427
Tezze, 306
Thakkek, 480
Thale, 167
Thalwil, 284, 286, 293
The Hague (see Hague)
Thebes, 336
Theodosie (see Feodosia)
Thessaloniki, 83, 143, 144, 274, 332A, 333, 336, 337, 360, 361, 372, 378
Thionville, 126, 169, 179, 275
Thonon-les-Bains, 121, 122, 265, 293
Thorn (see Torun)
Thorshavn, 414, 418, 427
Thouars, 246
Thourout, 150, 239
Thun, 281, 288, 292, 294
Thursday Island, 469, 470, 473, 478
Thusis, 286, 295
Tiefencastel, 286, 295
Tientsin, 232, 470, 474, 479
Tighina, 230, 330
Tijesno, 381
Tiko, 446
Tilburg, 129, 155, 156
Tilsit, 132, 205, 208
Timbuktu, 147
Timisoara, 83, 330, 331
Timor (Dilly) 473
Tinglev, 215
Tingvoll, 223, 224
Tinnoset, 220, 225
Tinnsj (Lake), 225
Tinos, 378
Tirana, 143
Tirano, 289, 304, 319, 320
Tiraspol, 230
Tirebolu, 375
Tirins, 337
Tirlemont, 151, 152
Tiszaujlak, 207A
Titisee, 126, 180, 212
Tivat, 379
Tivoli, 311
Tizi, 342
Tlemcen, 342
Toblach (see Dobbiaco)
Tobruk, 397
Tocino, 323
Tocopilla, 454, 462, 463, 474
Todalsoren, 440
Todi, 320
Todtmoos, 212
Tokle, 232
Toledo, 323
Tolga, 341
Tölz, 194, 212, 213
Tommerup 214, 215
Tonkin, 475
Tonnere, 259 to 262
Tonsad, 225
Tonsberg, 220, 431
Tonsasen 220
Toprakkale, 333, 334
Tor, 477
Töreboda, 221
Torghatten, 415
Tornea (see Tornio)
Tornio, 218, 228
Torquay, 98, 99
Torre Annunziata, 311
Torre das Vargens, 323, 325
Torre Gaveta, 312
Torre Pellice, 298
Torrevechia, 397A
Torrington, 102, 104
Tortoli, 395, 397A
Tortona, 300, 302
Tortosa, 325
Torun, 226
Totland Bay, 101, 103
Touggourt, 341
Toul, 272
Toulon, 79, 82, 113, 114, 259, 260, 261 to 264, 365, 376
Toulouse, 117, 142, 249, 251, 252, 255
Tourane, 390, 445
Tour-de-Carol, 251
Tournai, 79, 149, 236
Tours, 115, 116, 245 to 248
Townsville, 145, 444, 469, 470 471 473
Tozeur, 342B
Trafoi, 295, 319
Trapani, 315, 395
Trarbach 210
Trau (see Trogir)
Traunkirchen, 196
Travemünde, 417, 424, 426
Trebizond, 372, 375
Treib, 292, 293
Trelleborg, 130, 132, 162, 204, 215A, 216
Tremezzo, 317, 320
Trencianska-Tepla, 206A
Trengereid, 219, 24
Trengganu, 480
Trento, 306, 307
Treport, 238
Tretten, 219
Treuchtlingen, 187 to 189, 191, 194
Treungen, 220, 225
Treviglio, 304, 305
Treviso, 306, 308
Triberg, 126, 131, 180, 212
Trient (see Trento)
Trier, 126, 179, 181, 210, 275
Trieste, 83, 118 to 120, 123, 124, 144, 196, 199 to 201, 270, 274, 305, 308, 331, 332, 332A, 361, 371A, 371B, 372 to 385, 397A, 454, 455, 456A
Trikala, 336
Trinidad, 449, 450, 452, 453, 456, 466, 472
Tripoli (Libya), 143, 393, 395 to 397
Tripoli (Syria), 83, 334, 335, 361, 371B, 378, 386, 388, 392
Tripolis, 336
Trogir, 375, 379, 380, 381
Troisdorf, 165, 175
Trois-Ponts, 152
Troistorrents, 290
Trollfjord, 415, 428
Trollhättan, 216, 221
Tromsö, 142, 415 428, 440
Trondheim, 142, 218 to 221, 223, 224, 414, 415, 418, 420 to 422, 424, 428, 433, 439, 440
Troppau, 195
Trouville, 243, 422
Troyes, 125, 268
Trpanj, 381
Trstenik, 379
Trzebinia, 203, 228
Tsingtau, 362, 365, 470, 474, 479
Tsuruga, 477
Tua, 327
Tuarse, 393
Tuddal, 223
Tula, 230, 231
Tulagi, 470
Tulcia, 211
Tulear, 390
Tulkeram, 335
Tulln, 196
Tumaco, 458
Tunis, 138, 143, 340, 342B, 343, 367, 387, 391, 393, 394, 395, 396, 397
Turenne, 342
Turgi, 282, 283
Turin, 82, 118, 138, 144, 265, 280, 288, 298 to 303, 305, 313, 343
Turku (see Abo)
Turmont, 227
Turn-Severin, 211, 331
Tuschkau-Kosolup, (Czecho), 190, 195, 206, 274
Tuticorin, 359
Tutzing, 193, 194
Tvedestrand, 222
Tveitsund, 223, 224
Tyin, 222, 225
Tyinholmen, 225
Tynset, 219
Tyrifjord, 225
Tyssedal, 432
Tzaribrod, 83, 332

Uddevalla, 416
Udine, 82, 199, 308
Ueberlingen, 180 294
Uelzen, 169, 170, 194
Uetliberg, 289
Uj-Domovar, 201
Ujina, 479
Ulcinj, 380
Uleaborg (see Oulu)
Ulefos, 221
Ulianovsk, 233
Ulm, 184, 186, 193, 273, 274
Ulvenæs, 225
Ulvik, 224, 224A, 432, 433 438
Ulvö Harbour, 426
Ulvön, 426
Ulzio (Clavieres-Sestrieres), 82, 118, 298, 320
Umago, 381
Umea, 426
Unterschachen, 295
Unterwasser, 295
Ünye, 375
Uppsala, 217, 218
Uriage, 257
Urigen, 295
Urnerboden, 295
[illegible] 334
Uskoplie, 332B
Usk[illegible] (see Skoplje)
Ussel, 247
Utaker, 438
Utne, 432, 433
Utrecht, 129, 131, 132, 155 to 159
Utrera, 324, 325
Utvik, 434
Uzice, 332
Uzunkopru, 333

Vaagyjoid, 440
Vaasa, 142
Vadheim, 224A, 435, 437 438
Vadsö, 415, 419, 428
Vadstena, 221
Værene, 424
Vakarel, 332
Vakfikebir, 375
Vaksvik, 440
Valea Visului, 207A
Valenca, 327

Valence, 257, 259 to 262
Valencia, 252, 323, 325, 326, 363, 368, 397A, 399, 448, 464, 465, 468
Valenciennes, 236, 238, 271
Valka (Est.), 208
Valka (Lat.), 208
Valladolid, 321, 322
Valldall Sylte, 221, 439, 440
Valle, 224
Vallegranrey, 465
Vallehermoso, 465
Vallorbe, 83, 119, 120, 267, 279
Vallorcine, 253
Valognes, 243
Valona, 373, 374, 380
Valparaiso, 450, 454, 456, 458, 462, 463, 474, 478
Vals, 296
Valsavoja, 315
Valverde, 465
Vancouver, 444, 448 to 450, 453, 454, 456, 458, 460, 462, 466, 472, 478
Vannes, 246
Vao 390
Varberg, 216
Vardö, 415, 419, 428
Varenna, 317. (See also Perledo-Varenna, 304)
Varese, 302, 304, 318
Varna, 332B, 360 to 361, 372, 377
Vassenden, 224A, 225
Vastervik 425
Vassijaure, 218
Vastanfors, 217
Västerås, 425
Vathy (Aulis), 337
Vathy, (Samos), 371b, 378
Vatin, 330
Vatomandry, 377, 390
Vaxholm
Veglia 379
Vejle, 419
Velaluka, 379, 380, 381
Velden, 198, 199
Veles, 332A, 337
Velesin, 206
Velestino, 336
Velika-Kikinda, 332A
Vendome, 247
Venice, 82, 83, 118 to 120, 123, 124 127, 138, 140 to 144, 193, 196, 199, 201, 212, 270, 298, 303, 305 to 309, 313, 319, 361, 371A, 371B, 372, 373, 374, 375, 376, 379, 380, 381, 382, 383, 384, 385 397A, 398, 454, 455, 456A
Venlo, 129, 130, 155 to 157
Venta de Banos, 85, 321
Ventnor, 101, 103
Vera Cruz, 450, 454, 458, 464, 466, 468
Verawal, 471
Verselli, 298
Vereiorova, 331
Verma, 219
Vernayaz, 253, 280
Vernet-les-Baires (see Villefranche-V.-les-B.)
Vernex Montreux (see Montreux)
Vernon, 242
Verona 82, 193, 198, 303, 305, 307
Verres, 300
Verrières, 119, 279
Versailles, 244
Versegères, 296
Verviers, 151, 152
Vesoul, 266, 268, 271
Vesteraalen, 424, 428
Vestfossen, 225
Vestmanno, 414, 418, 421
Vestnaes, 224A, 439
Vesuvius Rly., 300
Vetlefjord, 224A, 435, 437
Vevey, 119, 120, 280, 293
Veynes, 26
Veyrier, 275
Veytaux-Chillon, 280
Vianna do Castello, 327
Viareggio, 301
Viatka (see Kirov)
Vicenza, 305
Vichy, 138, 254, 256
Vicosoprano, 295
Victoria (Brazil), 464, 479
Victoria (British Cameroons), 446, 447, 452
Victoria (B.C.), 449, 472, 473
Victoria Point (Burma), 471
Videseter, 222
Viege (see Visp)
Vienenburg 167
Vienna, 82 to 84, 123 to 125, 127 to 129, 132, 139 to 141, 143, 144, 186 to 189, 195 to 204, 206, 206A, 211, 269, 274, 286, 308, 330 to 332, 332B
Vienne, 259 to 262
Vientiane 480
Viersen, 130
Vierzon 117, 249
Vieuxport, 423
Vigevano, 302
Vigo, 321 327, 368, 445, 450, 461, 462, 464, to 466
Vigo di Fassa, 319
Viipuri, 142, 228, 423
Vik(Viken), 224A, 435, 437
Vikesund, 220
Vila, 390, 470
Vilani, 206
Villa Literno, 310
Villa Real de S. Antonio, 327
Villa S. Giovanni, 312
Villach, 82, 196, 198, 199, 269
Villalba, 321, 322
Villagarcia, 368, 465
Villar Formoso, 85, 322, 327
Villars s./Bex, 290
Villefranche, 264, 359, 364, 365
Villefranche s./Saone, 259 to 262
Villefranche-Vernet-les-Baines 117, 251, 255
Villeneuve, 280, 293
Villingen, 180
Vilna (see Wilno)
Vinh, 480
Vinkovci, 83, 331, 332, 332A
Vintimille, 81, 82, 113, 114, 174, 201, 259 to 262, 264, 299
Vipiteno, 319
Vire 244
Virieu le Grand, 266
Vis, 379, 380, 381
Visby, 420
Vise, 158
Visnæs 223
Visp, 119, 120, 123, 124, 280, 288
Viterbo, 320
Vitoria, 321
Vittoria, 315
Vitry-le-François, 270, 272
Vitrey-Vernois, 268
Vittel, 271
Vitznau, 289, 293
Vizagapatam, 359
Vladimir, 231
Vladivostock, 232, 476
Vlieland, 427
Vlodrop, 153
Voghera, 300, 302
Vohemar, 390
Vohwinkel, 165
Voiron, 257
Voitersreuth, 192
Volo, 336, 360, 361, 372, 378
Volochisk, 204, 230
Vordingborg, 214
Vologda, 230
Voss, 219, 220, 224, 224A, 438
Vostica, 380
Vraa, 225
Vraaliosen, 225
Vranany, 206
Vrbnik, 381
Vrboska, 381
Vrsac, 330
Vrutky, 202, 207A
Vukovar, 211
Vyazma, 230

Wabern, 170
Wadebridge, 102, 104
Wadenswil, 287, 293
Wadi Halfa, 145, 339, 370
Wad-Medani, 339
Waldhaus-Flims, 295
Waldkirch, 184
Waldshut, 180, 212, 283
Walfish Bay, 382, 446, 472
Wallis Islands, 390
Walkenried, 168
Wallisellen, 282, 283
Walsoorden, 416
Wangerooge, 422
Wanhsein, 470
Wanne, 161
Warburg, 130, 165
Warnemunde, 130, 132, 162, 204, 214, 417, 426
Warri, 447, 472
Warsaw, 81, 128, 140, 141, 202, 203, 205, 207, 208, 226, 227, 232 240, 274, 331
Wasa, 414, 426
Wasserbillig, 181
Wasta, 338
Waterloo, 152
Weesen, 286
Wegeleben, 167
Weggis, 293
Weiden, 190
Wei-hai-wei, 470
Weilheim, 193
Weimar 130, 172, 173
Weinfelden, 285
Weisau, 190
Weissenburg (Fr.), 181
Weissenburg (Switz.), 290
Weissenfels, 172, 173
Weissenthurm, 176, 177
Welikije Luki, 140
Wellington, 459 460, 463, 476, 479
Wels, 187 to 189
Wemeldinge, 416
Wengen, 292
Wernigerode, 167, 214
Wesel, 157, 161, 210
Weseli (see Mezimost Veseli)
Westerland, 420
West Hartlepool, 105 to 107
Wetzlar, 169
Wewak, 470
Weymouth, 98, 99, 101, 103, 135, 136
Whitby, 105 to 107
Wiborg (Fin.), see Viipuri
Widdin, 211
Wiebelsbach, 185
Wiesbaden, 128, 129, 131, 171, 173, 176 to 178, 273, 275
Wiesbaden-Biebrich, 209, 210
Wil, 282, 283
Wildbad 186, 273
Wilderswil, 281, 292
Wildungen, 170
Wilhelmshaven, 164, 422
Willinstad, 453
Wilno, 227
Windermere, 92 to 97
Winklern, 213
Winneba, 446, 447
Winterthur, 282 to 285
Wirballen, 81, 128, 130, 208
Wisby (see Visby)
Wittenberg, 166, 172
Wittenberge, 169

Wloclavek, 226
Wolfertschen, 289
Woloczyska (see Volochisk)
Wolverhampton, 92 to 99
Woodlark Island, 470
Worcester 98 99
Wörgl, 197, 198
Worms. 176, 177, 209, 273, 275
Wuhu, 470
Wupperthal-Barmen, 165
Wupperthal-Elberfeld, 165
Wurzburg, 128, 129, 132, 185, 188 to 191, 194
Wyndham, 146

Xanthi, 337

Yalta, 393
Yambo, 477
Yambol, 332B
Yangtsze Gorges, 470
Yarmouth (I.W.), 101, 103
Yarmouth (Norfolk), 110
Yaroslavl, 233
Ybbs, 211
Yenice, 333, 334
Yerevan, 231
Yerkoy, 334
Yeovil, 98, 99, 102, 104
Yochow, 470
Yokkaichi, 473, 478, 479
Yokohama, 358, 360, 362 to 365, 367 to 369, 468, 472, 473, 478 to 480
Yolcati, 334
York, 88 to 91, 105 to 107
Ypres, 150
Ystad, 425
Yuki, 477
Yule Island, 470
Yverdon, 278, 287
Yvetot, 242
Yvoire, 293

Zabkowice, 203
Zacharo, 337
Zafra, 323
Zagreb, 141, 144, 196, 199 to 201, 331, 332, 332A, 332B
Zaira, 397
Zakopane, 203
Zamboanga, 473, 479
Zante, 371B, 378
Zanzibar, 359, 363, 382, 471, 474, 476, 479
Zara, 144, 373 to 375, 381, 382
Zaragoza (see Saragossa)
Zauchtel, 196, 203, 206
Zbaszyn, 128, 226
Zdolbunow, 227
Zebrzydowice, 203, 228
Zeebrugge, 131, 153
Zeilah, 470
Zelenika, 332B
Zell-am-see, 85, 197, 213
Zemgale, 208, 227
Zemun (Semlin), 332A
Zengg, 379, 380
Zerbst, 166
Zermatt, 119, 120, 123, 124, 280, 288, 291
Zernez, 291, 295, 319
Zevenaar, 84, 132, 157
Zevgolatio, 336, 337
Zibeftch (see Ristovatz)
Zidani Most, 200, 332A
Ziegelbrucke, 286
Ziegenhals, 195
Zielkowice, 226
Zijpe, 416
Zile, 333
Zilina, 202 206A, 207 207A, 227
Zilupe, 206
Zinal, 296
Zinder, 147
Zinnowitz, 426
Zirje, 381
Zlarin, 379
Zlatidol, 332
Zlin, 141, 206A
Zofingen, 282
Zollino, 313
Zomobolja (see Jimbolia)
Zonguldak, 334
Zoppot, 205, 226 417, 426
Zuara, 397
Zuera, 252, 326
Zug, 284 287, 294
Zugspitzgipfel, 192
Zumarraga, 321
Zuoz, 291
Zurich, 80, 83, 85, 123, 125, 127, 131, 138, 139, 140 to 144, 174, 178, 180, 184 to 187, 197, 212, 269, 282 to 287, 289, 293
Zurs, 213
Zutphen, 129, 130, 155, 156, 159
Zweilutschinen, 281
Zweiselstein, 213
Zweisimmen, 290
Zwolle, 129, 159

CALENDAR, 1939/40

JULY

S	M	T	W	T	F	S
-	-	-	-	-	-	1
2	3	4	5	6	7	8
9	10	11	12	13	14	15
16	17	18	19	20	21	22
23	24	25	26	27	28	29
30	31	-	-	-	-	-

AUGUST

S	M	T	W	T	F	S
-	-	1	2	3	4	5
6	7	8	9	10	11	12
13	14	15	16	17	18	19
20	21	22	23	24	25	26
27	28	29	30	31	-	-
-	-	-	-	-	-	-

SEPTEMBER

S	M	T	W	T	F	S
-	-	-	-	-	1	2
3	4	5	6	7	8	9
10	11	12	13	14	15	16
17	18	19	20	21	22	23
24	25	26	27	28	29	30
-	-	-	-	-	-	-

OCTOBER

S	M	T	W	T	F	S
1	2	3	4	5	6	7
8	9	10	11	12	13	14
15	16	17	18	19	20	21
22	23	24	25	26	27	28
29	30	31	-	-	-	-
-	-	-	-	-	-	-

NOVEMBER

S	M	T	W	T	F	S
-	-	-	1	2	3	4
5	6	7	8	9	10	11
12	13	14	15	16	17	18
19	20	21	22	23	24	25
26	27	28	29	30	-	-
-	-	-	-	-	-	-

DECEMBER

S	M	T	W	T	F	S
-	-	-	-	-	1	2
3	4	5	6	7	8	9
10	11	12	13	14	15	16
17	18	19	20	21	22	23
24	25	26	27	28	29	30
31	-	-	-	-	-	-

JANUARY

S	M	T	W	T	F	S
-	1	2	3	4	5	6
7	8	9	10	11	12	13
14	15	16	17	18	19	20
21	22	23	24	25	26	27
28	29	30	31	-	-	-
-	-	-	-	-	-	-

FEBRUARY

S	M	T	W	T	F	S
-	-	-	-	1	2	3
4	5	6	7	8	9	10
11	12	13	14	15	16	17
18	19	20	21	22	23	24
25	26	27	28	29	-	-
-	-	-	-	-	-	-

MARCH

S	M	T	W	T	F	S
-	-	-	-	-	1	2
3	4	5	6	7	8	9
10	11	12	13	14	15	16
17	18	19	20	21	22	23
24	25	26	27	28	29	30
31	-	-	-	-	-	-

APRIL

S	M	T	W	T	F	S
-	1	2	3	4	5	6
7	8	9	10	11	12	13
14	15	16	17	18	19	20
21	22	23	24	25	26	27
28	29	30	-	-	-	-
-	-	-	-	-	-	-

MAY

S	M	T	W	T	F	S
-	-	-	1	2	3	4
5	6	7	8	9	10	11
12	13	14	15	16	17	18
19	20	21	22	23	24	25
26	27	28	29	30	31	-
-	-	-	-	-	-	-

JUNE

S	M	T	W	T	F	S
-	-	-	-	-	-	1
2	3	4	5	6	7	8
9	10	11	12	13	14	15
16	17	18	19	20	21	22
23	24	25	26	27	28	29
30	-	-	-	-	-	-

	1939	1940	1941	1942
Ash Wednesday	Feb. 22	Feb. 7	Feb. 26	Feb. 18
Easter Sunday	Apl. 9	Mar. 24	Apl. 13	April 5
Whit-Sunday	May 28	May 12	June 1	May 24

	1939	1940	1941	1942
Bank Holiday	Aug. 7	Aug. 5	Aug. 4	Aug. 3
Advent Sunday	Dec. 3	Dec. 1	Nov.30	Nov.29
Xmas Day, Dc.25	Mon.	Wed	Thur	Friday

For Public Holidays on the Continent, see page 52.

SECTION I.

USEFUL INFORMATION FOR TRAVELLERS.

ADDRESSES OF AMBASSADORS AND CONSULS IN LONDON.

For Passport requirements of Foreign Countries, *see pages* 34-37.

Country or Republic.	Embassy or Legation, London.	Consul in London.	Office hours of Consulate.
AFGHANISTAN	31, Prince's Gate, S.W.7.	31, Prince's Gate, S.W.7.	—
ALBANIA	—	—	—
AMERICA (U.S.) ..	~~4, Grosvenor Gardens, S.W.~~	1, Grosvenor Square, W.1.	9-1, 2-4. Sat. 9
ARGENTINE REP'BC	11, Lowndes Square, S.W.1.	12, South Place, E C.2.	10 30-1.
BELGIUM	103, Eaton Square, S.W.1	10, Belgrave Place, S.W.1.	10-1,3-5. Sat. 10-1
BOLIVIA..........	Westminster Bank Building	1A, Grosvenor Gardens	—
BRAZIL	19, Upper Brook St., Mayfair	Aldwych House, Aldwych, W.C.2.	1-5. Sats. 11-1
BULGARIA	24, Queen's Gate Gardens S.W.7.	17A, Onslow Gardens, S.W.7.	10-1 (Not Sats.)
CHILI	3, Hamilton Place, W.1.	76, Victoria Street, S.W.1.	10-1, 3-5
CHINA	49, Portland Place, W.		10-12.30, 2-4
COLOMBIA	18, Grosvenor Crescent, S.W.1.	12 Cadogan Place, London, S.W.1	9.30-5
COSTA RICA	—	33, King William St., Lon. Bdge, E.C.	11-4, Sats. 11-1
CUBA	30, York Terrace, Regent's Park, N W.1.	~~329, High Holborn, W.C.~~ (273 Bank Chambers)	9.30-12.30, 2-4
DENMARK	29, Pont Street, S.W.	Passport and Visa Office, 29, Pont Street, S.W.1.	10.30-1.30
DOMINICAN REP'BC	67, Eaton Place, S.W.1.	78, Fleet Street, E.C.4.	10-4
ECUADOR REP'BC	—	21, Cavendish Square, W.	1-5
EGYPT	75, South Audley St., W.1.	26, South Street, Mayfair, W.1.	11-1 Sats., 11.0-12
ESTHONIA	167, Queen's Gate, S.W.7.	167, Queen's Gate, S.W.7.	10-1
FINLAND	37, Smith Square, Westminster	37, Smith Square, Westminster.	10-1, 2-4 Sats. 10-1
FRANCE	~~Albert Gate House, S.W.1.~~	~~51, Bedford Square, W.C.1.~~	10-4
GERMANY	9, Carlton House Ter., S.W.	18, Belgrave Square, S.W.	10-12, 2-4 Sats., 10-12
GREECE	51, Upper Brook St., W.1.	7, Park Lane, W.	10-1 Sats. 10.30-12.30
GUATEMALA	—	11, Queen Victoria Street, E.C.4.	2-5
HAYTI	11, Queen Victoria St., E.C.4.	4, Denmark Street, W C.2.	10-5. Not Sats.
HONDURAS	—	15, Union Court, Old Broad St., E.C.2	—
HUNGARY	46, Eaton Place, S.W.1	46, Eaton Place, S.W.1.	11-1
IRAN (PERSIA)....	50, Kensington Court, S.W.8	Consular Business transacted at Legation.	10-1. Sats. 10-1
IRAQ	22, Queen's Gate, S.W.7.	22, Queen's Gate, S.W.7.	[illegible] 10-1 Sats., 10-12 noon
ITALY	4, Three Kings Yard, W.1.	68, Portland Place, W.1.	10-12, 2.30-3.30, Sats. 10-12
JAPAN	37, Portman Square, W.	15, St. Helen's Place, Bishopsgate, E.C.3.	10-1, 2.30-5.0 Sat., 10-1.
LATVIA	87, Eaton Place, S.W.1.	87, Eaton Place, S.W.1.	10-1
LIBERIA..........	37, Pont Street, S.W.1	410, Mansion House Chambers, Queen Victoria Street, E.C.4	11-4 (except Sat)
LITHUANIA	19, Kensington Palace Gardens, W.	19, Kensington Palace Gardens, W.	10.30-12.30 Sats., 10.30-12.(
LUXEMBOURG .... (DUCHY OF)	—	Moorfields House, Tenter Street, Moorgate, E.C.2.	10-1,2-4, Sat.10-1
MEXICO	48, Belgrave Square, S.W.1.	8, Halkin Street, S.W.1.	9-3, Sat. 10-1.

ADDRESSES OF AMBASSADORS AND CONSULS IN LONDON—continued.

Country or Republic.	Embassy or Legation in London.	Consul in London.	Office Hours of Consulate.
MONACO	—	38/39, Bruton Street, W.1.	—
NETHERLANDS....	21A, Portman Square, W.1.	28, Langham Street, W.1.	9.30-12.30, 2-4, Sat. 9.30-12.
NICARAGUA	—	15, Union Court, Old Broad St., E.C.	10-5.
NORWAY..........	21, Cockspur Street, S.W.	26/7, King Street, Cheapside, E.C.2.	10-3.
PANAMA..........			11-1, 2-4, Sat. 11-1.
PARAGUAY........	12, Russell Square, W.C.1.	51, Cornwall Gardens, S.W.7.	10.30, 4-30 (except Sat.)
PERSIA (See IRAN)	—	—	—
PERU	59, Sloane Gardens, S.W.1.	59, Sloane Gardens, S.W.1.	11-1.30, 2.30-4, Sat. 11-1.
POLAND	47, Portland Place, W.1.	63, Portland Place, W.1.	9-12, 2-3, Sat. 9-12.
PORTUGAL........	11, Belgrave Square, S.W.1	8, Strathearn Place, Hyde Park Square, W.2	11-1, 2-4, Sat. 11-1.
ROUMANIA........	4, Cromwell Place, Kensington, S.W.	4, Cromwell Place, Kensington, S.W.7.	10-1.
SALVADOR	—	7, Union Court, Old Broad Street, E.C.	2-5, Sat. 11-1.
SAUDI-ARABIA	—	115, Ebury Street, S.W.1.	—
SPAIN	24, Belgrave Square, S.W.	21, Cavendish Square, W.1.	10.30-1 Sat. 10.30-12 no.
SWEDEN..........	27, Portland Place, W.	63 New Cavendish St W.1 ~~Bank Cham., 329, High Holborn, W.C.~~	10-3, Sat. 10-1.
SWITZERLAND	18, Montagu Place, Bryanston Square, W.1.	18, Montagu Place, Bryanston Square, W.1.	11-1, 2-4, Sat. 11-1.
THAILAND (SIAM)	23, Ashburn Place, South Kensington, S.W.	23, Ashburn Place, S.W.7.	10-1, 2-5,
TURKEY	69, Portland Place, W.1.	18 Cadogan Gardens ~~10, Lower Sloane Street, S.W.1.~~	10-2, Sat. 10-1.
UNION OF SOCIALIST SOVIET REPUBLICS	13, Kensington Palace Gardens, W.8.	3, Rosary Gardens, S.W.7.	10-1 (closed on Thursdays).
URUGUAY	53, Harrington Gardens, Kensington, S.W.7.	55, Harrington Gardens, S. Kensington, S.W.7.	10-4, Sat. 10-12.
VENEZUELA	50, Pall Mall, S.W.1.	~~Victoria House, Southampton Row, W.C.1.~~ 50 Pall Mall, S.W.1	10.30-12, 2.30-4.30 Sat. 10.30-12.
YUGO-SLAVIA	195, Queen's Gate, S.W.	195, Queen's Gate, S.W.	11-1

1 Palace Gate, W.8.

BRITISH CONSULS ABROAD.

CONSULS, or Vice-Consuls, are stationed at all important towns, and will readily assist travellers in case of difficulty or misunderstanding with foreign officials. English travellers in Oriental Countries are recommended to leave their cards at the British Consulates in places they may visit, not only as complimentary to H.M.'s representative, but as a precautionary measure in the contingency of Consular assistance being required.

PASSPORTS.

Travellers requiring Foreign Office Passports can obtain them through any office of Thos. Cook and Son, Ltd., together with the necessary Visas of Foreign Ambassadors or Consuls in London, for travelling on the Continent. Passports issued prior to July, 1929, are invalid and new documents must be procured.

EXTRACTS FROM PASSPORT REGULATIONS.

1. Application for Foreign Office Passports must be made on special form which will be supplied by Thos. Cook & Son, Ltd., upon application. Husband and wife, and children under 16, can be included on one Passport if travelling together.

2. Passports are issued in London between the hours of 10 and 4 (Saturdays, 10 to 1), and in Liverpoo between the hours of 9.30 and 4 (Saturdays, 9.30 to 1). The Passport Offices are closed on Sundays and Public Holidays (except in London between the hours of 10 a.m. and noon for cases of special emergency only). Applications should, reach the Passport Office not less than four days before that on which the Passport is required.

3. Foreign Office Passports are granted—
   (i) To natural-born British subjects, and to British subjects by naturalization in the United Kingdom, in the British Dominions or Colonies, or in India.
   (ii) To the wives and widows of the above persons.
   (iii) (*a*) To married women who were British subjects at the time of their marriage and have not, by reason of marriage to an alien, acquired the nationality of their husbands.
   (*b*) To married women whose husbands have, during the continuance of the marriage, ceased to be British subjects, unless by reason of the acquisition by their husbands of a new nationality they also have acquired that nationality.

4. Passports are available for five years, in the first instance, unless otherwise stated. They may be renewed from time to time for further consecutive periods of one to five years from the date of expiry, provided the total period of validity of ten years from the original date of issue is not exceeded.

5. (*a*) British Passports are not available beyond ten years from the original date of issue. Thereafter, or if at any time the Passport contains no further space for Visas, a new Passport must be obtained.
(*b*) A Passport including particulars of the holder's wife is not available for the wife's use when travelling alone.
(*c*) Children who have reached the age of 16 years require separate Passports. When applying for a Passport they should send with their application the written consent of father or other legal guardian.

6. (i) The Passport declaration of the applicant must be verified by a declaration made by a member or official of any *Banking Firm* established in the United Kingdom, or by a ***Mayor, Magistrate, Provost, Justice of the Peace, Minister of Religion, Barrister-at-Law, Notary, Solicitor, Physician, Surgeon, etc.,*** resident in the United Kingdom and being himself a British subject. The applicant's Certificate of Birth and other evidence may also be required. Applicants serving in His Majesty's Forces may have their declarations verified by their Commanding Officer.
(ii) In the case of children under the age of 16 years requiring a separate Passport, a declaration must be made by the child's father or other legal guardian in a Form (B) to be obtained upon application to Thos. Cook and Son, Ltd.
(iii) In the case of persons naturalized in any of the British self-governing Dominions, a recommendation should be produced from the High Commissioner or Agent-General in London of the State concerned. Persons naturalized or ordinarily resident in any of the Crown Colonies may be required to obtain a letter of recommendation from the Colonial Office.

7. If the applicant for a Passport be a British subject by naturalization, the Certificate of Naturalization must be forwarded to the Passport Office with the declaration or letter of recommendation. British subjects by naturalization will be described as such in the Passports.

8. British Passports are only available for travel to the countries named thereon, but may be endorsed for additional countries. The possession of a Passport so endorsed does not, however, exempt the holder from compliance with any immigration regulations in force in British or foreign countries, or from the necessity of obtaining a Visa where required.

9. Passports endorsed as valid for the British Empire are also available for travelling to territory under British protection or mandate, not, however, including Palestine or Transjordan, for which the Passport must be specially endorsed, or the Aden Protectorate for which both an endorsement and a visa are needed.

10. A Passport cannot be issued or renewed by the Foreign Office on behalf of a person already abroad; such person should apply, in a foreign country, to the nearest British Mission or Consulate, or, within the British Empire, to the nearest Passport-issuing authority.

11. Persons resident in Ireland (except Northern Ireland) should make application for Passport facilities to the Ministry of External Affairs, Dublin.

PASSPORTS—continued.

CHARGE FOR PASSPORT .. .. 17s. 6d.

(Including procuration fee).

PASSPORT REQUIREMENTS OF FOREIGN COUNTRIES

WITH CHARGES FOR VISAS.

Cook's fee for obtaining Visas, where possible, 2s. 6d. each Visa.

Compiled from information supplied by the Foreign Office.

FOR ADDRESSES OF AMBASSADORS AND CONSULS IN LONDON, SEE PAGES 32 AND 33.

(The *visa* fees quoted are liable to fluctuation according to rates of exchange.)

In certain countries free or reduced rate VISAS are granted in connection with special events, and full particulars of these can be had on application.

s. d.

Argentine.—Obtainable also at Liverpool, Cardiff, Newport (Mon.), Southampton, Glasgow, Newcastle, Manchester and Dublin. Personal attendance is necessary and two forms and two photos required. In the case of Tourists' *visas*, 1 photograph, Letter in duplicate from applicant, and letter from Steamship Company. 20 0

Belgium.—No *visa* required for British subjects.

Belgian Congo.—Passengers must obtain *visa* from Belgian Consul of their place of residence before starting their journey.

Two application forms and two photographs necessary. Medical certificate and good conduct certificate required in certain cases, which documents must be legalized by a Belgian Consul.

Cost of *visa* 16 8

Legalization of medical and good conduct certificates .... each 23 9

Bolivia.—Personal attendance is necessary, also two letters of reference. Medical certificate, vaccination certificate, and one photograph. Decree of Government of Bolivia requires persons entering Bolivia to be provided with *visa* of Bolivian Consular Officer in London and at Antofagasta, Arica, Puno Laquiaca, Corumba, Brazilia, as the case may be, reporting themselves to Police on arrival 6 0

Brazil.—Applicants for *visas* must produce two letters of recommendation from responsible persons or business houses on headed paper.

Medical and vaccination certificates required, also forms and photograps. Forms must be filled in in Portuguese.

s. d.

Obtainable also at Liverpool, Southampton, Manchester, Glasgow, Cardiff and Dublin. Personal attendance necessary. In the case of bona fide tourists special facilities are available for the obtaining of *visas* without personal attendance 22 0

Bulgaria.—Passengers must report to the Police within 24 hours of arrival.

Visa only valid 45 days from date of issue, and for one journey only 20 4

Transit *visa*, valid 45 days, for one journey only 20 4

Transit *visa*, valid three months, for two journeys 40 8

Passengers remaining longer than seven days must obtain identity cards supplying three photographs.

Chile.—Personal attendance is necessary, three forms, three photographs and two letters of reference required and vaccination certificate. In the case of Tourists, *visas* can be granted without personal attendance.

Obtainable also at Liverpool, Glasgow, Cardiff, Hull and Dublin 30 9

China.—Two forms required 13 4

Transit *visa* 4 0

Columbia.—Personal application should be made if possible. Two forms required, also two photographs, letter of reference and health certificate.

Obtainable also at Liverpool 8 5

Costa Rica.—Vaccination and health certificates required 12 0

Cuba.—One form required. Letter of reference required 8 8

s. d.

Danzig.—British subjects entering by sea do not require *visas*. Entering or leaving overland, Polish *visa* necessary (see Poland).

Denmark.—No *visa* required for Britis subjects.

Dominican Republic 8 4

Ecuador.—*Visas* may be obtained also at Liverpool, Glasgow, and Southampton.

Documentary evidence, vaccination and health certificates required 12 6

Egypt.—One form necessary.

Obtainable also at Liverpool.

Passengers landing in Egypt during stay of vessel (for a few hours only, and not making a journey) need not obtain *visa* 13 4

Transit 1 4

Special seven days *visa* 1 0

Special Cruise *visa* 1 0

Arrival and departure cards to be filled up.

Esthonia.—*Visa* valid one journey, but given for one year repeated journeys in special cases 13 4

Transit 1 5

Ethiopia.—An Italian *visa* is required.

Finland.—One form and photograph required.

If passport bears a previous *visa* given by the Finnish Consul in London, it is not necessary for form or photograph to be submitted. Passengers should state reason of journey and length of stay however. *Visa* valid up to one year 8 0

Transit, allowing five days' stay 0 10

France.—No *visa* required for British subjects.

French Colonies (except Syria).—No *visa* required, but a special declaration form in duplicate must be filled in 8 6

Transit *visa* 1 2

Return transit *visa* 2 4

One form required.

Tourists visiting France, staying more than two and not exceeding six months, can obtain a tourist card (Carte de Tourisame) from a French Consul of their place of residence, free of charge. Personal attendance necessary. Persons proceeding to France to take up employment must be provided with a "Contrat de Travail," and medical certificate, which must be *visaed* by a French Consul.

Germany.—Entry *visa*, single journey, valid three months 2 0

Entry *visa*, repeated journeys, valid three months 3 6

Transit *visas* valid for 6 weeks from date of issue.—

Transit *visa*, single journey 2 0

Return transit *visa* 3 6

Entry *visa*, valid for 12 months, repeated journeys, (one form required 13 6

Persons proceeding to Germany to take up employment must obtain permit from German authorities before departure.

Greece.—For stay of more than 30 days a sojourn permit must be obtained from the Police. Passengers in transit must leave at the first opportunity, otherwise they will be called upon to pay double fee for consular *visa* when leaving.

s. d.

Summer Tourist *visa* (June to September) 7 4

Visa valid one year, repeated journeys (reason of journey to be stated) 14 3

Transit *visa*, valid three months, one journey 1 6

Guatemala.—*Visas* granted on request, four forms, four photographs. Personal attendance 12 0

Hayti.—*Visa* now necessary, which must be obtained in country of departure 13 0

Honduras.—Applicants for *visa* must, before applying to Consul, obtain a consular stamp for $10 from the National City Bank of New York, 36, Bishopsgate, E.C. 5

Hungary.—Until Sept. 30th, 1939, the Hungarian *visa* for holders of British passports issued in Great Britain, Northern Ireland, Irish Free State, and all other parts of the British Empire will not be required.

Iran (Persia).—Certain formalities are necessary before leaving Iran concerning which a British Consul should be consulted. Two forms and two photographs required 13 4

Transit 1 6

Iraq.—*Visa* valid for one year 10 0

Transit *visa* valid for one journey 1 1

One form required.

Reason of journey to be stated.

Italy.—No *visa* required for British subjects.

Visa required for Italian Colonies. Persons visiting Italy must, within three days of arrival register with the Police 13 5

Japan.—One form required. Obtainable also at Liverpool 8 0

Transit *visa* 0 10

Persons will not be allowed to land in Japan unless passports are in order.

Latvia.—Bona fide business travellers may be granted *visa* on a letter of reference from firm representing. *Visa* valid for repeated journeys during one year for business people, and one month one journey pleasure visits 14 7

*Transit *visa* allowing three days' stay in Latvia granted on production of *visa* of country of destination.

Transit 1 5

Liberia.—Obtainable also at Liverpool, Manchester and Glasgow. In addition to *visa* an alien declaration is necessary 4 2

Alien declaration 9 4

Lithuania.—Valid up to one year 14 10

In transit 1 6

One form required.

Passports to be stamped by Police within 24 hours of arrival. Transit *visas* can be issued by Frontier Police on train, but such *visas* do not allow break of journey.

Luxembourg.—No *visa* required for British subjects.

	s.	d.
Mexico.—Personal attendance necessary. Obtainable also at Liverpool, Glasgow, Hull, Cardiff, Birmingham and Newcastle. Permit to enter Mexico necessary before applying for *visa*; nine photographs necessary; six full-face and three in profile. In the case of tourists, six full-face photographs are required.		
Cost of Passport *visa*	13	10
Visa of Vaccination Certificate	4	8
Tourist Card	4	8
Identity Card	4	8
Netherlands.—No *visa* required for British subjects. *Visas* are not required for travelling to Netherlands Colonies.		
Nicaragua.—*Visa* valid for one year	16	0
Valid for one month	6	0
Norway.—No *visa* required for British subjects.		
Panama.—Transit or entry	25	0
Paraguay.—*Visas* may also be obtained at Manchester, Liverpool, Birmingham, Bradford, Glasgow, Cardiff and Southampton. One photograph, vaccination certificate and letter in support required	8	0
Persia.—*See* Iran.		
Peru.—Personal attendance necessary	8	0
Poland.—One form required. For Danzig (*see* Danzig).		
Visa valid for one journey only	20	10
Visa valid 12 months for repeated journeys, each journey not exceeding two to three months' stay in Poland	33	4
Single transit	2	1
Return transit *visa*	4	2
Persons must report to the Police within 24 hours of arrival in Poland and effect registration with authorities within eight days. Passengers landing in Gdynia while steamer is in port for day or half-day do not require *visa*.		
Portugal.—No *visa* required for British subjects. *Visa* required for Portuguese possessions, one form required	14	9½
Or if more than one person mentioned on passport	21	9
Roumania.—Persons must report to Police within 24 hours of arrival, and if staying more than eight days must obtain a permit from Police authorities.		
Visa valid for one year for repeated journeys. One form required	14	8
Transit *visa*	2	8
Salvador.—*Visas* may also be obtained at Liverpool and Birmingham, 2½ dollars	11	0
Saudi Arabia	*gratis*	
Spain and Spanish Morocco. — Three forms, three photographs, two references and guarantee are required. Personal application should be made. British subjects travelling to and or through Spanish Morocco should communicate with British Consul at Tangier, Fez, Rabat, etc.		
Sweden.—No *visa* required for British subjects.		
Switzerland.—No *visa* required for British subjects visiting Switzerland. If proceeding to Switzerland for the purpose of taking up employment special *visa* must be obtained. Personal application necessary to Swiss Consul. *Visas* may also be obtained at Liverpool, Manchester and Glasgow.		
Thailand.—Two forms required	8	0
Transit *visa*	0	10
Letter to be submitted stating reason of journey, etc., if business letter from firm representing.		
Turkey.—One journey, valid two months	7	7
Transit valid two months allowing 15 days' stay	3	10
Return *visas* valid 2 months	15	2
,, ,, ,, 4 ,,	22	10
,, ,, ,, 6 ,,	30	5
One form and two photographs required.		
United States of America. — Personal attendance necessary, also signed letter from responsible firm or individual addressed to the American Consul-General and vouching for the character, health and financial ability of traveller.		
Visa is available for any number of journeys to the United States within a period of 12 months from the date of *visa*, provided that the passport to which it is affixed continues valid for that period.		
Passengers travelling through the United States *en route* to another country, may obtain a transit *visa*. No letter ot recommendation required.		
Application for *visa* must be made to the American Consular Office of the district in which the holder of the passport is usually resident.		
United States authorities require on a passport the photographs of all persons mentioned therein, including children under 16 years of age	10 dollars	
Temporary visitors:		
Entry *visa*	2 dollars	
Transit *visa*	20 cents.	
Limited entry certificates—valid for 10 days stay in U.S.A. Passengers must enter and leave by same steamer	*gratis*	
Uruguay.—Personal attendance necessary at Consulate four days before departure	22	6
Union of Soviet Socialist Republics.—Georgia, Ukraine, White Russia, Transcaucasia and Russia.		
Three application forms to be filled up and three signed photographs required	15	2
Application forms each	0	3
Transit visa	1	6
Venezuela.—Certificates of vaccination, good health, birth, good conduct, etc., documentary evidence required, personal attendance essential	*gratis*	
Yugoslavia.—One form required		
Transit *visa* valid single journey, 30 days	1	3
Return transit *visa* valid 60 days	2	6
Visa valid for one year, repeated journeys	26	0
Tourists visiting Yugoslavia can obtain a special *visa* valid for three months, *aller et retour*, providing that they stay a minimum of three days in one place in Yugoslavia. Cost of special *visa*	1	0

CUSTOM HOUSE REGULATIONS.

Custom House Regulations.—Examinations are generally made at the station nearest the frontier. Thus, in the case of travellers from France to Spain, baggage is examined at Irun, and at Hendaye in the reverse direction. Passengers must always be present at the Custom House Examinations, and hand their keys to the examining officer. The Customs' Examination is one of the greatest drawbacks to the pleasure of foreign travel, but passengers will do well to remember that civility costs nothing, and may purchase much, and that the Custom House Officers are merely performing a *duty*, perhaps as disagreeable to themselves as to the traveller.

Hand baggage is examined by the Customs at the port of entry into a country and at every frontier. As a general rule, passengers have to descend from the train at the frontier and go through the Customs' House, but in the case of a number of express trains it has been arranged that the examination shall take place in the train. This facility is on the increase.

At Calais, Boulogne and Dieppe, licensed facteurs can be engaged to assist in passing hand baggage, etc., through the Customs at a fixed charge per package.

List of stations at which baggage is generally examined :—

Aachen (Ger.)
Bale (Switz.)
Bentschen (Pol.)
Bettembourg(Lux.)
Blandain (Belg.)
Bentheim (Ger.)
Bielo-Ostrov (Rus.)
Bogumin (Od'rb'rg Slovakia)
Brennero (It.)
Brigue (Switz.)
Buchs (Switz.)
Cerbère (Fr.)
Charlottenberg (Nor. & Swed.)
Chiasso (Switz.)
Constance (Baden)
Cranenburg (Ger.)
Dalheim (Ger.)
Delle (Fr.)
Domo d'Ossola (It.)
Elten (Ger.)
Emmerich (Ger.)
Erquelinnes (Belg.)
Esschen (Belg.)
Eydtkuhnen (Ger.)
Flushing (Holl.)
Furth, I.W. (Ger.)
Friedrichsh'fn(Wt)
Frederikshald (Norway)
Feignies (Fr.)
Fiume (Italy)
Geneva (Switz.)
Gmünd (Ger.)
Goch (Ger.)
Haparanda (Sweden)
Hendaye (Fr.)
Herbesthal (Belg.)
Irun (Spain)
Iselle (Italy)
Jeumont (Fr.)
Kaldenkirchen (Germany)
Kaplitz (Ger.)
Kehl (Ger.)
Kornsjo (Norway and Sweden)
Liebenau (Bohemia)
Lindau (Bav.)
Lobositz (Bohemia)
Luino (Italy)
Lundenburg (Ger.)
Malmö (Sweden)
Modane (France)
Mouscron (Belg.)
Nickelsdorf (Hungary)
Nymegen (Holl'd)
Oldenzaal (Holl'd)
Padeborg (Den.)
Paris (Fr.)
Pontarlier (Fr.)
Porrentruy (Switz.)
Port Bou (Spain)
Quévy (Belg.)
Rajajoki (Fin.)
Rosendaal (Holl'd)
St. Margrethen (Switz.)
Schaffhausen (Switz.)
Singen (Bad.)
Splugen (Switz.)
Storlien (Norway and Sweden)
Suchdol (Moravia)
Tarvisio (Italy)
Terezin-Bohusovice n. O (Bohemia)
Tornio (Fin.)
Troisvierges (Belg.)
Tuschkau-Kosolup (Bohemia)
Valenciennes (Fr.)
Vallorbes (Switz.)
Vassijaure (Nor. and Swed.)
Venlo (Holland)
Vintimille (Italy)
Zevenaar (Holland)

Letter *c* in tables signifies that Customs' examination usually take place at stations indicated.

Prohibited Articles.—The following are some of the principal articles that travellers are prohibited from bringing into Great Britain :—False money, gold, jewellery under 18 carat, extracts of coffee, chicory, tobacco stalks stripped of the leaf, tobacco stalk flower, copyright books reprinted abroad, articles with marks or names imitating those of British manufacturers.

For Registered Baggage, see table on page 40.

DUTIABLE ARTICLES.

The principal articles subject to Customs' Duty in various countries are as follows :—

BELGIUM.—New wearing apparel, wines, liqueurs, perfumed spirits, tobacco, cigars, cigarettes, sugar, gold and silver-plated ware ; *prohibited*, saccharine.

Ten cigars, or 20 "cigarillos," or 25 cigarettes, or 50 grammes of tobacco are allowed to enter this country free of duty (if declared). Duty on cigars or cigarettes is 12 fc. per kilo.

CUSTOMS REGULATIONS—continued.

DUTIABLE ARTICLES—continued.

FRANCE.—New wearing apparel, linen, silks, lace, embroideries, curtains, carpets, knick-knacks, ivory, tortoise-shell, jewellery, typewriters, sewing machines, perfumery, spirits, tobacco, tea, soap, candles, provisions; *prohibited*, cartridges, matches, cards, medicines.

The duty on tobacco entering France is 200 fcs. per kilo, on Turkish tobacco 280 fcs., cigars (Havana) 520 fcs. per kilo; other kinds, 320 fcs. per kilo; cigarettes, 320 fcs. per kilo. Male adult passengers entering France are allowed to take with them not more than 10 cigars or 20 cigarettes, or 40 grammes of tobacco free, (ladies, 20 cigarettes) provided the same be declared. If not declared it is liable to seizure and the owner is liable to a fine of five times the duty.

TEA.—The duty on Chinese and Japanese teas entering France is 6.55 fcs. per kilo; India and Ceylon teas 9.80 fcs. per kilo, plus 7% *ad valorem*.

GREAT BRITAIN.—Practically all articles are liable to duty on entry into the United Kingdom. Exceptions: Used wearing apparel and articles that have been in owner's possession abroad for a period of one year or over, or were originally taken from this country.

GERMANY.—New wearing apparel, knick-knacks, toys, soap, cigars and cigarettes, tobacco, confectionery, wood and bronze ware; *prohibited*, preserved meats.

ITALY.—New wearing apparel, silk, lace, embroideries, carpets, tea, tobacco, liqueurs, perfumery, sweetmeats; *prohibited*, drugs and medicines, saccharine, tobacco in leaf, tobacco manufactured over 2 lb.., firearms and gunpowder are only allowed importation subject to special permission.

TOBACCO.—Only 10 cigarettes or 2 cigars, or an equivalent weight of tobacco, are allowed to be taken into Italy by any one traveller, duty free. Passengers found in possession of more than this quantity are liable to a fine anywhere in Italy, unless they can prove that duty has been paid. Duty 100 gold lire per kilo on tobacco, 130 gold lire on cigars and cigarettes.

SWITZERLAND.—New wearing apparel, hats and bonnets, tea, coffee, provisions, soap, salt, sugar, confectionery, wines and spirits, perfumery, tobacco, stationery, jewellery, candles.

The following are the duties on tea and tobacco entering Switzerland:—Tea, 0.75 fcs. per kilo (about 2 lb.); cigarette tobacco, 12 fcs. per kilo; pipe tobacco, 7 frs. per kilo; cigars, 10 frs. per kilo; cigarettes, 15 frs. per kilo.

Passengers are usually allowed free about 2 oz. tobacco or about 40 cigarettes, or about 10 cigars.

The above rates, and those on previous page, are given from latest tariffs, but are liable to alteration without notice, and the publishers cannot accept responsibility for them.

BAGGAGE.

As the conveyance of luggage forms an important item in the expenses of a Continental tour, travellers should condense their luggage as much as possible. *It should be borne in mind that a passenger cannot claim more space for his hand baggage than the space in the netting overhead.* As a rule, the seat space does not exceed 22 inches in width. On the mountain railways there are frequently no racks for hand baggage. All baggage should be marked with the owner's name and place of destination in full and fastened with case locks. Padlocks and straps are objectionable, being liable to damage or removal. Canvas coverings are also undesirable, their removal often leading to the loss of the package. Jewellery and other valuables should not be placed in registered luggage.

Charges and Free Allowance.—Free allowance on ordinary tickets in France, 30 kilos (66 lb.) In Belgium, Holland, Switzerland, Germany, Austria, Hungary, and Italy *all* luggage is charged for, there being no free allowance except for small packages carried in the hand. In Italy, handbags or parcels conveyed free with passengers must not exceed 20 kilos in weight, or 18″ × 9″ × 12″ in measurement.

Baggage and Freight Department.—Arrangements can be made with THOS. COOK AND SON, LTD., for the collection of PASSENGER'S BAGGAGE from any address and for its conveyance to the steamer by which the passenger is booked, or for shipment as FREIGHT. BAGGAGE, EFFECTS, MERCHANDISE, LIVE STOCK, etc., can be despatched through Cook's to any part of the world at lowest rates, or warehoused if desired. Full particulars may be obtained from their Shipping and Forwarding Department, Berkeley Street, London, W.1, or Branch Offices. OMNIBUSES can be engaged to convey passengers and baggage between hotels and stations or *vice versa* in London and Paris by giving twenty-four hours' notice.

Baggage Insurance.—As the robbery of baggage and pilfering of trunks occasionally happens, travellers using COOK'S tickets are strongly recommended to have their luggage insured, which may be done by the payment of a small premium at any of their Offices. The insurance covers articles insured, by sea and land, and in all places and situations against the risk of their being lost, against theft and pilfering, and against the risk of damage by fire or sea water. Insurance can be effected for amounts of £25 and upwards. Jewellery can also be covered by this insurance, provided it is not placed in the registered baggage. Full particulars can be obtained at any Cook's Office.

BAGGAGE—continued.

REGISTERED BAGGAGE.

Holders of through tickets can register their luggage from London to almost any of the principal cities in Europe, and there is usually a free allowance of 66 lb. in this case, except in Holland, Germany, Switzerland and Italy.

BAGGAGE REGISTERED OUTWARDS.

Baggage Registered to	Via	Will be examined at
Paris (Nord)	Calais, Boul'gn or Dunkerque	Paris
Paris (St. Lazare)	Dieppe or Havre	Paris
Brussels	Calais Ostend	Brussels
Other Belgian destinations	Calais	Blandain
Antwerp, Liege, Spa, Verviers, Ghent, Bruges, Ostend and Louvain	Ostend	Ostend
Biarritz	Bo'logne Calais or Dunkerque	Biarritz
French Stations (except Riviera 11.0 service)	Calais or Bo'logne	French Port
Marseilles, Hyeres, St. Raphael, Cannes, Antibes, Nice, Beaulieu, Monaco, Mentone, Vintimille	A	Respective destinations
Juan-les-Pins and Grasse	A	Cannes
Cap d'Ail	A	Beaulieu
Monte Carlo	A	Monaco

Baggage Registered to	Via	Will be examined at
Other French Stations	Dieppe, Havre, or Dunkerque.	French Port
San Remo	A	Destination
Other Italian Stations	A	Vintimille
Dutch destinations	Fl'shing or Hook	Dutch Port
North German Stations	Fl'shing or Hook	Bentheim
South German Stations	Fl'shing or Hook	Cleves, Emmeric or Kaldenkirchen
Any German Station (via Aix-la-Chapelle)	Calais or Ostend	Aix-la-Chapelle
Any Austrian Station (via Aix-la-Chapelle)	Ostend	Passau
Bale (via Luxemburg)	Ostend	Bale¶
Swiss destinations (via Laon or Hirson)	Calais and Bale	Bale¶
Swiss destinations	Dieppe	Swiss ¶ frontier
Swiss Stations	Dunkerque & Bale.	Bale¶
Swiss Stations	Dunkerque & Delle	D'nkerque and Porrentruy¶
Piestany	All thro' routes	On arrival in summer Frontiers in winter

A—By 11.0 through service *via* Calais.

¶ Or at destination when Custom House exists, *e.g.*, Interlaken, Lugano, Lausanne, St. Moritz, etc.

Baggage registered for Brussels or any place not beyond Verviers, when unclaimed by owners, will be found at Brussels Entrepôt, about two miles out of the city; and for any place beyond Verviers, at Herbesthal. There will be a trifling expense for Customs' formalities.

Baggage registered through from London or from Paris to any of the chief Italian cities, and not examined at the Italian frontier, is sent to destination in bond at owner's cost, great trouble and delay being occasioned thereby.

Baggage being conveyed from the East, *westward*, and destined for *Belgium*, is examined at Herbesthal. Baggage *passing through* Belgium for either France or England is not examined at all by the Belgian Customs.

In returning from the Continent to London *via* Dover, hand baggage is examined at Dover. Baggage registered from the Continent to Victoria *via* Calais, Boulogne, or Dieppe, is examined at Victoria, all other baggage at English port.

FOREIGN MONEYS.

Foreign money may be bought or exchanged at any of Cook's Offices, which will also arrange for remittances by mail or telegram. The safest and most convenient means of carrying funds is afforded by Cook's Travellers' Cheques, which are cashed at Cook's Offices and Banks all over the world.

¶ See note at bottom of page 49.

Approximate Value. ¶ £ s. d.

ARGENTINE.

Monetary Unit=

	£	s.	d.
Peso (paper) .. .. (Nominal)		1	0
Nickel, 20 „		0	2½
„ 10 „		0	1½
„ 5 „		0	0⅝
Copper, 2 „		—	
„ 1 „		—	
Gold, 5 Peso, Argentine	1	13	0

Notes are issued by the Republic for 50 centavos, 1, 5, 10, 50, 100, 500 and 1,000 Pesos.

AUSTRIA.

From March, 1938, Austria became a Province of Germany and accounts are now kept in German currency. The former Austrian money s converted at a rate of 1½ Austrian Schillings equal 1 German Mark. As from May 1st, 1938, travellers domiciled outside German Reich territory may use Travel Marks in former Austrian territory.

AUSTRALIA.

The Commonwealth issue gold, silver and bronze coins for the same denomination as Great Britain, excepting silver coins of 2/6.

The notes hitherto issued by the six Federated States have been taken over by the Common wealth Government, and for a time remained in circulation with a printed notice across them to that effect. These have now been replaced by notes issued by the Commonwealth Government in denominations of 10/-, £1, £5, £10, £20, £50, 100 and £1,000.

English notes are at a premium of 25%.

BAHAMA ISLANDS.

English notes and coinage circulate.

Approximate Value. ¶ £ s. d.

BELGIUM.

Monetary Unit=

	£	s.	d.
1 Franc of 100 centimes		0	1
Bronze, 1 centime		—	
„ 2 centimes		—	
Nickel, 5 „		—	
„ 10 „		—	
„ 25 „		—	
„ 50 „		0	0¾
„ 1 Franc		0	1⅝
„ 5 Francs		0	8¼
Silver, 20 „		2	9
„ 50 „		6	10¾

Notes are issued by the National Bank for 50 100, 500, 1,000 and 10,000 Francs.

The zinc fractional coinage, issued during the War, has now been withdrawn.

The 1, 2, 5, 20 Franc National Bank notes are now withdrawn from circulation.

On October 26th, 1926, a new unit of currency was introduced termed the "Belga," 1 Belga gold = Fcs. 5 paper.

BERMUDA.

English money is the legal tender, but United States Dollars are freely accepted.

BRAZIL.

Monetary Unit=

	£	s.	d.
Milreis (paper)		0	2¾

Although nominally on a gold basis the circulating medium is chiefly paper.

	£	s.	d.
Nickel, 100 Reis		0	0⅜
„ 200 „		0	0¾
„ 400 „		0	1¼
Silver, 500 „		0	1½
„ 1,000 „		0	3
„ 2,000 „		0	6

Notes are issued by the Republic, also by the Banco do Brazil for 1, 2, 5, 10, 20, 50, 100, 200, 500 Milreis.

Old notes are gradually withdrawn by discounting them on a percentage basis over a given period.

FOREIGN MONEYS—continued.

¶ See note at bottom of page 49.

Approximate Value. ¶ £ s. d.

BRITISH EAST AFRICA—*See Kenya Colony.*

BRITISH WEST AFRICA.

English Notes and coin circulate in the Colonies grouped under this heading, although the West African Currency Board have an issue of their own as follows:—

	£	s.	d.
Bronze, 1/10th Penny		—	
„ ½d.		—	
„ 1d.		—	
Silver, 3d., 6d., 1/- and 2/		—	
Notes, 1/-, 2/-, 10/-, £1 and £5		—	

BRITISH HONDURAS

Monetary Unit=

	£	s.	d.
1 Dollar of 100 Cents.		4	2
Copper, 1 Cent.		0	0½
Nickel, 5 Cents.		0	2½
Silver, 10 „		0	5
„ 25 „		1	0½
„ 50 „		2	1

Notes are issued by the Government of British Honduras for 2, 5, 10 Dollars.

BULGARIA.

Monetary Unit=

Bulgarian Leva present value about ⅛d.

	£	s.	d.
Leva of 100 Stotinkis		0	0⅛
Copper, 50 Stotinkis		—	
Nickel, 1 Leva		0	0½
„ 2 „		0	1
„ 5 „		0	2½
„ 10 „		0	5
Silver 20 „		0	10
„ 50 „		2	0
„ 100 „		4	0
Gold, 10 „ Pre-War		11	6
„ 20 „	1	3	0

Notes are issued by the Bulgarian National Bank for 500, 1,000 and 5,000 Levas.

All notes prior to 1922 are now valueless.

CANADA.

Monetary Unit=

	£	s.	d.
Dollar of 100 Cents.		4	3
Bronze, 1 Cent.		0	0½
Nickel, 5 Cents.		0	2½
Silver, 5 „		0	2½
Silver, 10 Cents.		0	5
„ 20 „		0	10
„ 25 „		1	0¾
„ 50 „		2	1½
„ 1 Dollar Jubilee Coin		4	3
Gold, 5 Dollars	£1	15	0
„ 10 „	£3	10	0

Notes are issued by the Government for 25 Cents, $1 $2, $5, $500 and $1,000, and by the various Banks of Canada for $5, $10, $20, $50 and $100.

CANARY ISLANDS.

Spanish money is the currency in use. (See Spain).

CEYLON.

Monetary Unit=

	£	s.	d.
Rupee of 100 Cents.		1	6½
Silver, 50 Cents.		0	9
„ 25 „		0	4½
„ 10 „		0	2
Nickel, 5 „		0	1
Copper, 1 Cent.		—	
„ ½ „		—	

Currency notes are issued of 1, 2, 5, 10, 50, 100 and 1,000 Rupees.

CHILI.

Monetary Unit=

Peso of 100 Centavos (gold) .. .. —

Formerly the gold basis was 1/6 per gold Peso, but recently a new gold standard has been set up approximately to the present value of paper.

1 Peso paper approximately 0 2

Coins:—

	£	s.	d.
20 Peso, gold (Condor)	1	10	0
10 „		15	0
5 „		7	6
50 „ (1926)	1	5	0
1 Silver (new)		0	4
Silver, 50 Centavos		0	2
„ 20 „		0	1
„ 10 „		—	
„ 5 „		—	
Copper, 2½ „		—	
„ 2 „		—	
„ 1 „		—	
„ ½ „		—	

Notes are issued by the Government for 1, 2, 5, 10, 20, 50, 100, 500 and 1,000 Pesos.

CHINA.

1 Silver Dollar 0 8½

On April 6th, 1933 the Chinese Government announced that in future all public and private transactions must be made in terms of Silver Dollars in order to complete the abolition of the former Tael.

On November 1st, 1935, China departed from the Silver standard and called in all silver.

Coins:—

	£	s.	d.
Silver, 1 Dollar		0	8½
„ 50 Cents.		0	4[illegible]
„ 20 „		0	2[illegible]
„ 10 „		0	1

Notes are issued by the Central Bank of China payable in dollars.

In March, 1938, The Federal Reserve Bank of China' took over all Bank Notes circulating in North China and issued new notes for use in that territory.

FOREIGN MONEYS—continued.

¶ See note at bottom of page 49.

COLUMBIA.

Monetary Unit—	Approximate Value. ¶ £	s.	d.
Silver, 1 Peso		2	0½
„ 50 Centavos		0	10
„ 20 „		0	5
„ 10 „		0	2½
Nickel, 5 „		0	1
„ 2 „		0	0½
„ 1 „			—

Old notes prior to 1909 which are not convertible into gold are worthless.

Notes are issued by the Bank of the Republic for 1, 2, 5, 10, 25, 50 and 100 Peso oro.

COSTA RICA.

Monetary Unit—	£	s.	d.
Colon of 100 Centavos		1	0½
Silver, 50 Centavos			—
„ 25 „			—
„ 10 „			—
„ 5 „			—
Bronze, 10 „			—
„ 5 „			—
Nickel, 2 „			—
Copper, 1 „			—
Gold, 20 Colons	1	18	0
„ 10 „		19	0
„ 5 „		9	6
„ 2 „		3	10

Notes are issued for 1, 2, 5, 10, 20, 50 and 100 Colons.

CRETE.

The currency is the same as for Greece, but notes are issued, also Silver and Copper coins of equal value to the Greek currency.

CUBA.

Notes are issued by the Republic of Cuba in denominations of Peso 1, 2, 5 and 10, and have replaced the former Spanish and U.S.A. currencies, although U.S.A. currency is still accepted. Silver coins are issued for 10, 20, 40 cents silver and 5 cents nickel.

CZECHOSLOVAKIA.

Monetary Unit—	£	s.	d.
Czecho Kronen		0	1¾

Note.—In October, 1938, certain districts in the Sudeten Area were taken over by Germany and during the transition period, a rate of 12 pfennigs was paid for each Kc. 1. In future German currency will be used in the districts affected.

On March 16th, 1939, Bohemia and Moravia became German Protectorates by proclamation. The Slovak State has also been placed under Reich Protection.

DENMARK.

	Approximate Value. ¶ £	s.	d.
Monetary Unit—Krone of 100 Ore		1	1
New Coinage			
Aluminium Bronze, 2 Kroner		2	2
„ „ 1 „		1	1
„ „ ½ „		0	6½
Nickel, 25 Ore		0	3¼
„ 10 „		0	1¼

Bank Notes are issued for 5, 10, 50, 100 and 500 Kroner. Notes of 1 Kroner issued during the War are now withdrawn. Prior to 1914 the coinage of Denmark, Norway and Sweden was interchangeable, but at present each country only accepts its own money.

ECUADOR.

Monetary Unit—	£	s.	d.
Sucre of 100 Centavos		0	10½
Silver, 1 Sucre		0	10½
„ 50 Centavos		0	5¼
„ 20 „		0	2
„ 10 „		0	1
„ 5 „		0	0½
Copper, 2 „			—
„ 1 „			—
„ ½ „			—
Gold, 10 Sucres (1 Condor)	1	6	0

English gold is legal tender at 10 Sucres=£1.

Notes are issued by the local Banks but all notes, except those issued by the Banco del Ecuador, are being withdrawn.

EGYPT.

Monetary Unit—	£	s.	d.
Egyptian Pound of 100 Piastre	1	0	6
Silver, 20 Piastre		4	1¼
„ 10 „		2	0½
„ 5 „		1	0¼
„ 2 „		0	5
„ 1 „		0	2½
Nickel, 10 Milliemes		0	2½
„ 5 „		0	1¼
„ 2 „		0	0½
„ 1 „		0	0¼
Bronze, ½ „		0	0⅛
„ ¼ „		0	0 1/16
Gold, 100 Piastre or E£1	1	13	0
„ 50 Piastre or E£½		16	6

The National Bank of Egypt issues notes E£1, E£5, E£10, E£50 and E£100.

English notes are sometimes accepted as 97½ Piastres, but are generally at a small discount.

ESTONIA.

From January 1st, 1928, a new monetary unit was established. The Kroon, or Krone, of 100 Sents (Cents) new gold parity=18.159 per £1. 100 old Marks=1 Kroon.

Present exchange 17½-18½.

FOREIGN MONEYS—continued.

¶ See note at bottom of page 49.

FINLAND.

Monetary Unit=

	Approximate Value. ¶ £	s.	d.
Markkaa of 100 Pennia		0	1
Copper, 5 Pennia			—
" 10 "			—
Nickel, 1 Markkaa		0	1
" 50 Pennia		0	0½
" 25 "		0	0¼
Aluminium Bronze, 20 Markkaa		1	8
" " 10 "		0	10
" " 5 "		0	5

Notes are issued by the Finlands Bank for 20 50, 100, 500 and 1,000 Markkaa.

FRANCE.

Monetary Unit=

	£	s.	d.
1 Franc of 100 Centimes		0	1½
Copper, 1 Centime			—
" 2 Centimes			—
Nickel, 5 "			—
" 10 "			—
" 25 "			—
" 5 Francs		0	6¾
Jetons 50 Centimes		0	0¾
" 1 Franc		0	1½
" 2 Francs		0	2¼
Silver, 10 "		1	1½
" 20 "		2	3

Notes are issued by the Bank of France for 50, 100, 500, 1,000 and 5,000 Francs.

Local notes were issued by the Chamber of Commerce in many towns, but these have now been demonetized.

Formerly, Gold and Silver coins of France, Belgium and Switzerland were current in each of these countries, but this is no longer entirely the case, and in fact both in France and in Belgium Gold and Silver coins have ceased to circulate. New coins (Jetons), aluminium bronze, have recently been put into circulation for 50 Centimes, Fcs. 1 and Fcs., 2 each.

GERMANY.

Monetary Unit=

	£	s.	d.
1 Reichsmark of 100 Pfennig		1	8
Silver, 5 Reichsmarks		8	4
" 2 "		3	4
Nickel, 1 " 1933		1	8
" 50 Reichspfennig		0	10
Aluminium Bronze, 10 Rentenpfennig		0	2
" " 5 "		0	1
Copper, Reichspfennig			—
" 2 "			—
" 1			—

All pre-war coin ogether with the many war issues in Nickel, Iron, Zinc and Aluminium, are demonetized.

Notes are issued by the Reichsbank for R. Marks, 10, 20, 50, 100 and 1,000; also by the Renten Bank for 10, 50, 100, 500 and 1,000 Renton Marks.

Reichsmarks and Renten Marks have the same value.

GIBRALTAR.

English money circulates freely.

Notes are issued by the Government of Gibraltar for 2/-, 5/-, 10/-, £1 and £5.

New notes, dated October 1st, 1927, have bee issued by the Government of Gibraltar.

GREECE.

Monetary Unit=

	Approximate Value ¶ £	s.	d.
Drachma of 100 Lepta		0	0½
Nickel Bronze, 20 Lepta			—
" " 50 "		0	0¼
" " 1 Drachma		0	0½
" " 2 Drachmas		0	1
Nickel, 5 "		0	2½
Silver, 10 "		0	4½
" 20 "		0	9

Formerly both French and English Gold was freely accepted, but the present currency is almost entirely paper.

Notes are issued by the Bank of Greece for 50, 100, 500, 1,000 and 5,000 Drachmas.

One and 2 Drachmas notes ceased to be legal tender after December 31st, 1926.

In 1922 and 1926, in order to raise a forced loan, all notes in circulation were cut in half. The left hand portion circulating for half the face value in 1922, and for 75% of the face value in 1926.

These cut notes are now withdrawn from circulation.

GUATEMALA.

By Act of November 26th, 1924, a new unit of currency was introduced, namely, the Quetzal of 100 Centavos based on U.S.A. currency.

New Quetzal notes have been issued for 1, 2, 5, 20 and 100 Quetzal, printed by Messrs. De La Rue & Co. Ltd., London. These replace the former debased paper Pesos.

	£	s.	d.
Gold, 1 Peso (old)		5	0
" 5 " "	1	5	0

HAITI.

Monetary Unit=

	£	s.	d.
Gourde of 100 Centimes		0	10

American currency circulates freely and has a fixed basis of conversion of 5 Gourdes=one Dollar, U.S.

Notes are issued by the National Bank of the Republic.

FOREIGN MONEYS—continued.

¶ See note at bottom of page 49.

HOLLAND.

Monetary Unit=

	Approximate Value. ¶ £ s. d.
Gulden of 100 Cents	2 3
Bronze, ½ Cent	—
„ 1 „	—
„ 2½ Cents	—
Nickel, 5 „	0 1½
Silver, 10 „	0 2½
„ 25 „	0 6½
„ 50 „	1 1½
„ 1 Gulden	2 3
„ 2½ „	5 7½

Notes are issued by the Netherlands Bank for 10, 20, 25, 40, 60, 100, 200, 300 and 1,000 Guldens. Zilverbons issued by the Government for 1 and 2½ Guldens are withdrawn.

HONDURAS (Republic).

Monetary Unit=

	Approximate Value. ¶ £ s. d.
Peso of 100 Centavos	Nominal 4 0
Silver, 1 Peso	Nominal 2 0
„ 50 Centavos	Nominal 1 0
„ 25 „	Nominal 0 6

Notes are issued for 1, 5, 10, 20, 50 and 100 Pesos.

HONG KONG.

	Approximate Value. ¶ £ s. d.
Silver, 1 Dollar (Mexican)	1 3
„ 50 Cents	0 7½
„ 20 „	0 3
„ 10 „	0 1½
„ 5 „	0 0¾
Copper, 1 „	—

Notes are issued by the European Banks for 1, 5, 10, 25, 50, 100 Dollars.

HUNGARY.

Monetary Unit=

	Approximate Value. ¶ £ s. d.
Pengoe of 100 Filler	0 10
Copper, 1 Filler	—
„ 2 „	—
Nickel, 10 „	0 1
„ 20 „	0 2
„ 50 „	0 5
Silver, 1 Pengoe	0 10

Notes were first issued in the new currency in 1926 and replace the former Kronen notes on the basis of 12,500 old Kronen = 1 Pengoe.

New notes have been issued for 5, 10, 20, 50, 100 and 1,000 Pengoes.

The stabilized value is 27,825 Pengoes equals £1.

INDIA.

Monetary Unit=

	Approximate Value. ¶ £ s. d.
Rupee of 16 Annas	1 6
Bronze, ¼ Anna	
„ ½ „	—
Nickel, 1 „	0 1½
„ 2 Annas	0 2¼
Silver, 4 „	0 4½
„ 8 „	0 9
„ 1 Rupee	1 6

Notes are issued by the Government of India for 5, 10, 20, 50, 100, 500, 1,000 Rupees.

Prior to 1920 the standard value of a Rupee was 1/4, nominally based on the gold Mohur of 15 Rupees, and sovereigns were legal tender at 15 Rupees to the £, but in 1920 the value rose to 2/10 and an effort was made to stabilize it on the basis of 2/- or 10 Rupees to the £. The Rupee has now been stabilized at 1/6.

A Lak or Lakh equals 100,000 Rupees.
100 Lacs = a Crore.

A Pie is the 12th part of an Anna, or 192nd part of a Rupee.

IRAN (Persia).

Monetary Unit=

1 Rial of 100 Dinars.

Formerly the unit was the Toman of 100 Kran, but by a decree of March 13th, 1932, both the Toman and Kran will cease to be legal tender after September 23rd, 1932.

For purpose of conversion 1 Kran is equal to 1 Rial, and 100 Rial equals 1 Pahlevi = £1.

Notes formerly issued by the Imperial Bank of Persia must be withdrawn by September 23rd, 1932, and they will be replaced by a new issue by the National Bank of Persia in denominations of 5, 10, 20, 50, 100 and 500 Rials.

IRAQ.

Monetary Unit=

Formerly Indian currency circulated, but from 1st April, 1932, a new currency was introduced, the unit being the Dinar of 1,000 Fils. This currency is linked to Sterling, one Dinar being equivalent to 20 Shillings.

Notes are issued by the Currency Board for the Government of Iraq in denominations of 250 and 500 Fils, also 1, 5, 10 and 100 Dinars.

	Approximate Value. ¶ £ s. d.
Silver, 50 Fils	1 0
„ 20 „	0 5
Nickel, 10 „	0 2½
„ 4 „	0 1
Copper, 2 „	0 0½
„ 1 Fil	0 0¼

FOREIGN MONEYS—continued.

¶ See note at bottom of page 49.

ITALY.

Monetary Unit—

	Approximate Value. ¶ £ s. d.
1 Lira of 100 Centesimi	0 2½
Bronze, 5 Centesimi	—
„ 10 „	—
Nickel 20 „	—
„ 50 „	0 1¼
„ 1 Lira	0 2½
„ 2 Lire	0 5
Silver 5 „	1 1
„ 10 „ } Cease to be legal tender	2 2
„ 20 „ } after Dec. 31, 1937.	4 4

Only notes issued by the Banca d'Italia now circulate, notes issued by the Banca di Sicilia and Banca di Napoli are now valueless.

Notes are issued for 10, 50, 100, 500 and 1,000 Lire.

Notes of Lire 1 and 2 were withdrawn in 1923. Lire 25 notes ceased to have any value on June 30, 1928, and Lire 5 and 10 notes ceased to be legal tender after December 31st, 1928. A new Lire 10 was issued in 1935.

JAMAICA.

English notes and silver are current, but in addition local notes for £1, £5 and £10 are issued by Barclays (D., C. & O.) Bank, Bank of Nova Scotia and Royal Bank of Canada. Currency notes for 5/- and 10/- are issued by the Island Government.

Local Coin, Nickel, 1 Penny.
„ „ „ ½ „
„ „ „ ¼ „

JAVA.

The currency value is the same as in Holland, but local notes are issued by the Java Bank for 5, 10, 20, 25, 30, 40, 50, 60, 100, 200, 300, 500 and 1,000 Gulden.

There is also a local issue of coinage identical in value with that of Holland.

JAPAN.

Monetary Unit—

	£ s. d.
Yen of 100 Sen	1 2
Bronze, 1 Sen (1922 issue)	0 0¼
Nickel, 5 „	0 1
„ 10 „	0 1¾
Silver, 50 „	0 7
Gold, 5 Yen	12 11
„ 10 „	1 5 10
„ 20 „	2 11 8

Notes of 10, 20 and 50 Sen are now withdrawn. Notes are issued for 1, 5, 10, 20 and 100 Yen.

JUGOSLAVIA (Greater Serbia, Serbes, Croates and Slovenes).

Monetary Unit—

	Approximate Value. ¶ £ s. d.
1 Dinar of 100 Para	0 1
Nickel, 50 Para	0 0½
„ 1 Dinar	0 1
„ 2 „	0 2
Silver, 10 „	0 10½
„ 20 „	1 9
„ 50 „	4 5

Notes are issued by the National Bank for 100 500 and 1,000 Dinar. Present Exchange approximately 210/220 per £1.

KENYA COLONY (Formerly British East Africa).

Monetary Unit—

E. African Shilling of 100 Cents .. 1 0

At the close of the War the currency in circulation was the Rupee of 100 Cents in British and Geman East Africa, and the unit was changed to Florin on the formation of the present Kenya Colony to be succeeded by the East African Shilling.

All notes of the former Rupee and Florin issues are withdrawn and now valueless.

Notes are issued by the East African Currency Board for 5, 10, 20, 100, 200 and 1,000 Shillings.

KOREA.

Notes are issued by the Bank of Chosen, but Japanese notes and coin circulate.

LATVIA.

Monetary Unit—

1 Lat = 100 Santimes. Gold parity, 25/22.
50 Roubles, old currency = 1 Lat Gold.

	£ s. d.
Copper, 1 Santime	—
„ 2 Santimes	—
„ 5 „	0 0½
Nickel, 10 „	0 1¼
„ 20 „	0 2¼
„ 50 „	0 4½
Silver, 1 Lat	0 9

Notes are issued by the State for 5 and 10 Lats, and by the Latvian Bank for 20, 50, 100 and 500 Lats.

LITHUANIA.

Monetary Unit—

1 Lit of 100 Cents.

	£ s. d.
Nicks, 5 Cents	0 0¼
„ 10 „	0 0½
„ 20 „	0 1
„ 50 „	0 2½
Silver, 1 Lit	0 5
„ 2 Lits	0 10

Notes are issued by the Lithuanian Bank for 1, 2, 5, 10, 50 and 100 Lits. Stabilized valued 48/00 Lits per £1.

MALTA.

A special issue of local Treasury notes was authorized in 1914, but these were withdrawn in 1915, and only English notes and coin circulate.

FOREIGN MONEYS—continued.

¶ See note at bottom of page 49.

Approximate Value. ¶ £ s. d.

MAURITIUS.

Monetary Unit=

	£	s.	d.
Rupee of 100 Cents		1	5⅞

Government notes are issued for 5, 10 and 50 Rupees.

MEXICO.

Monetary Unit=

	£	s.	d.
Dollar or Peso of 100 Centaves		1	0
Silver, 50 Centavos			—
Copper, 20 „			—
„ 10 „			—
„ 5 „			—
„ 2 „			—
„ 1 Centavo			—

The notes issued by the Provisional Government during the Revolution are now worthless, and the present medium of exchange is paper. Certain notes issued by Banks before the War have a nominal redeemable value.

MONACO.

French currency only is in circulation, but gold coins of F. 20 and F. 100 have been issued.

MOROCCO.

Monetary Unit=

	£	s.	d.
1 Real or Dollar Silver		0	7

Notes.—Only notes issued by the Moroccan Government now circulate.

	£	s.	d.
1 Real or F. 5		0	7
4 Reals or F. 20 and		2	4
20 Reals or F. 100		12	0

NEWFOUNDLAND.

Canadian currency is used.

NEW ZEALAND.

Until 1934 only English coin circulated together with notes issued by the Bank of New Zealand, the National Bank of New Zealand and certain Australian Banks.

From August 1st, 1934, the Reserve Bank of New Zealand became the sole Bank of issue and notes of 10/-, £1, £5, £10, £20, £50 and £100 are in circulation.

After Feb. 1st, 1935, English silver ceased to be legal tender and at present special coinage for New Zealand is in circulation.

	s.	d.		s.	d.
Silver	2	6	Silver	0	6
„	2	0	„	0	3
„	1	0			

English Bank notes are at a premium.

NIGERIA.—*See British West Africa.*

NORWAY.

Monetary Unit=

Krone of 100 Ore. *New Coinage.*

	£	s.	d.
Nickel, 1 Krone		1	0
„ 50 Ore		0	6
„ 25 „		0	3
„ 10 „		0	1¼

These new coins are all perforated with a hole in the centre.

Bank Notes are issued for 5, 10, 50, 100, 500 and 1,000 Kroner. Notes of 1 and 2 Kroner ceased to be legal tender after July 1st, 1926.

PALESTINE.

From November 1st, 1927, the Egyptian currency formerly in use was replaced by a new Palestine currency, the unit of which is the Palestine Pound of 1,000 Mils.

	£	s.	d.
Silver, 100 Mils		2	0
„ 50 „		1	0
Nickel Bronze, 20 Mils		0	4⅘
„ „ 10 „		0	2⅖
„ „ 5 „		0	1⅕
Bronze, 2 Mils		0	0½
„ 1 Mil		0	0¼

Notes are issued by the Currency Board for 500 Mils, 1, 5, 10, 50 and 100 £P.

PARAGUAY.

Monetary Unit=

	£	s.	d.
Peso of 100 Centavos		0	1

The currency is chiefly a depreciated paper one, notes being issued for 1, 2, 5, 10, 20, 50, 100, 200, and 500 Peso.

PERSIA.—*See Iran.*

PERU.

Monetary Unit=

	£	s.	d.
Sol Silver or Paper		1	0
Gold, 1 Libra = 10 Sols	1	12	0
„ ½ „ = 5 „		16	0
„ 1/5 „		6	5

Prior to 1914 there were no notes in circulation, but the Bank of Peru now issue notes for 5, 10, 50, and 100 Soles Oro.

PHILIPPINE ISLANDS.

Monetary Unit=

	£	s.	d.
Peso of 100 Centavos		2	1
Nickel, 5 Centavos		0	1¼
Silver, 10 „		0	2½
„ 25 „		0	6¼
„ 50 „		1	0½
„ 1 Peso		2	1

Bank Notes of Peso 1, 2, 5, 10, 20, 50 and 100; Treasury Notes are issued for 2 Pesos and upwards, U.S. Gold and Notes circulate freely at 50 Cents U.S. = 1 Pesos Philippine.

POLAND.

Monetary Unit=

	£	s.	d.
1 Zloty of 100 Groschen		0	9
Bronze, 1 Groschen			—
„ 2 Groschens			—
„ 5 Do.		0	0¼
Nickel, 10 „		0	0½
„ 20 „		0	2
„ 50 „		0	4½
„ 1 Zloty		0	9
Silver, 2 „		1	6
„ 5 „		3	9
„ 10 „		7	6
Gold, 10 „	Not in Circulation.		
„ 20 „	Not in Circulation.		
„ 50 „	Not in Circulation.		
„ 100	Not in Circulation.		

Notes in the new currency were first issued in 1924, although the first issue was dated 1919, and are in denominations of 1, 2, 5, 10, 20, 100, and 500 Zloty.

The 1, 2, 5, 10 and 20 Zloty notes first issue are withdrawn from circulation.

FOREIGN MONEYS—continued.

¶ See note at bottom of page 49.

Approximate Value. ¶ £ s. d.

PORTUGAL.

Monetary Unit=
1 Escudo of 100 Centavos, which replaces the old Milreis of 1,000 Reis.

		£	s.	d.
Copper,	1 Centavo			—
„	10 Centavos			—
Nickel,	50 „			—
„	1 Escudo			—
„	50 Escudos			—
Silver,	2 „			—
„	5 „			—
„	10 „			—

Gold is at a premium and not in general circulation. The only gold coins are the old Mil Reis issue and their value is as follows:—

		£	s.	d.
Gold,	1 Mil Reis		4	5
„	2 „		8	10
„	5 „	1	2	2
„	10 „	2	4	4

Notes are issued by the Bank of Portugal for the following denominations:—20, 50, 100, 500, and 1.000 Escudos.

Escudo Paper 0 2¼

PORTUGUESE COLONIES.

The Banco Nacional Ultramarino issue local notes for each of the following Colonies:—

Lorenco Marques, St. Thome, Cape Verde, Guiana — In Milreis as formerly used in Portugal.

The Bank of Portugal issue notes for use in the Azores and 100 Mil Reis Azores paper=80 Escudos Portuguese.

Sterling notes for £1, £5 and £10 are issued by the Banco Nacional Ultramarino for use in Lorenco Marques and district. These are now at a considerable discount as compared with Sterling.

Nova Goa.—The Banco Nacional Ultramarino issue notes payable in Rupees for use in Portuguese India.

RHODESIA.

Until October 12th, 1931, notes and coin of the Union of South Africa were freely accepted, but on that date Rhodesia departed from the Gold Standard and established her own currency.

In 1932 a special issue of coinage was minted, for use in Southern Rhodesia, the denominations being the same as for Great Britain.

Notes are issued by the Standard Bank of South Africa and Barclay's Bank (D.C. & O.), for 10/- £1 and £5.

ROUMANIA.

Monetary Unit=
Leu or Ley 0 0⅓

The former Gold parity was 25/22 per £, but present exchange approximate 660 per £.

Notes are issued by the National Bank of Roumania for 500 and 1,000 Lei, all other denominations are withdrawn.

Coinage.—Most of the coins issued prior to 1929 are withdrawn and demonetized. Present coinage, Lei 100 Silver, Lei 20, 10 and 5 Aluminium Bronze, Lei 2 and Lei 1 Nickel. Bani 50 and 25 Aluminium.

RUSSIA.

In 1924, Russian currency was stabilized on a gold basis, the new unit being the Chervonetz 10 Roubles with a theoretical gold value of £1 1s. 1½d. per gold Chervonetz, but travellers were compelled to pay in their own foreign currency. From January 1st, 1936, payments in foreign currency were abolished and a new external value of the Rouble fixed at 1 Rouble=3 French Francs, or approximately 25 Roubles per £1. Amended in Oct. 1936 to 4¼ French Francs=1 Rouble, 24¾ Roubles=£1.

The State Bank of the Union of Soviet Socialist Republic issue notes for 1, 3, 5, 10 and 25 Chervonetz; also for Roubles, 5, 3 and 1. Notes and coin of the old regime are no longer current, and all notes, whether Romanoff Kerensky, or early Soviet issues are now worthless.

New copper and silver coins bearing the hammer and sickle sign are now in circulation.

SALVADOR.

Monetary Unit=
Peso of 100 Centavos 2 0

Notes are issued by the Banco Occidental Banco Agricola Commercial and Banco Salvadorino in denominations of 1, 2, 5, 10, 25, 50, 100 and 500 Pesos.

The value of the Peso varies with the Price of Silver. Old notes issued by the Banco Nacionale are worthless.

SERBIA.—*See Jugoslavia.*

SIAM.—*See Thailand.*

SPAIN (Since July, 1936, Nominal).

Monetary Unit=

		£	s.	d.
Peseta of 100 Centimos				—
Bronze,	5 Centimos			—
„	10 „			—
Silver,	50 „			—
„	1 Peseta			—
„	2 Pesetas			—
„	5 „			—
Gold,	20 „			—
„	25 „ (Alphonso)			—

Notes of 25, 50, 100 and 1,000 Pesetas are issued by the Bank of Spain.

Gold is at a premium and is not in general circulation.

All silver coins prior to 1869 are demonetized. (*See Canary Islands*).

STRAITS SETTLEMENTS

		£	s.	d.
Copper,	1 Cent		0	0¼
Silver,	5 Cents		0	1¼
„	10 „		0	2¾
„	20 „		0	5½
„	50 „		1	2
„	1 Dollar		2	4

Notes are issued by the Government for 1, 5, 10, 50, 100 Dollars, also for 10 and 25 Cents.

FOREIGN MONEYS—continued.

¶ See note at bottom of page.

SWEDEN.

Monetary Unit=Krona of 100 Ore

	Approximate Value.¶ £ s. d.
Bronze, 1 Ore	0 0⅛
„ 2 „	0 0¼
„ 5 „	0 0⅝
Silver, 10	0 1¼
„ 25 „	0 3
„ 50 „	0 6
1 Krona	1 0
2 Kronor	2 0
Gold, 5 Kronor	5 6
„ 10 „	11 0
„ 20 „	22 0

Bank Notes are issued for 5, 10, 50, 100 and 1,000 Kronor. Notes of 1 Krona are withdrawn.

Danish and Norwegian coin which formerly circulated throughout Scandinavia is no longer accepted outside their respective countries.

SWITZERLAND.

Monetary Unit=

	Approximate Value.¶ £ s. d.
Franc of 100 Centimes	0 11½
Bronze, 1 Centime	—
„ 2 Centimes	—
Nickel, 5 „	0 0½
„ 10 „	0 1
„ 20 „	0 2¼
Silver, 50 „	0 5½
„ 1 Franc	0 11¼
„ 2 Francs	1 10½
„ 5 „	4 8½

Notes are issued by the Swiss National Bank for 20, 50, 100, 500 and 1 000 Francs.

Silver coins bearing the figure of Helvetia in a sitting position are demonetized.

Foreign Gold and Silver coins no longer circulate.

SYRIA.

Notes were first issued by the Banque de Syrie in August, 1919, in denominations of 1, 5, 10, 25, 50, 100, 500 Piastres and £10. £25 and £50 Syrian.

	Approximate Value.¶ £ s. d.
100 Piastre=One Pound Syrian	2 3
1 „ =20 Centimes French	—

THAILAND (Siam)

A new unit has recently been introduced, the Baht, divided into 100 Satangs. The par of Exchange is fixed at 11 Baht=£1.

Notes are issued by the Government for 1, 5, 10, 20, 100 and 1,000 Ticals.

TURKEY.

Monetary Unit=

	Approximate Value.¶ £ s. d.
Piastre of 40 Paras	—
Nickel, 5 Paras	—
„ 10 „	—
„ 20 „	—
„ 40 „	—
„ 25 Piastres	—
Aluminium Bronze, 10 Piastres	—
„ „ 5 „	—
„ „ 2½ „	—

		Approximate Value.¶ £ s. d.
Gold, ¼£T 25 Piastres	Pre-War	7 0
„ ½£T 50 „	Pre-War	14 0
„ 1£T 100 „	Pre-War	1 8 0

In 1927 new notes were issued by the Republic for 1, 5, 10, 50, 100, 500 and 1,000 T.

All old type notes were finally demonetized on June 5, 1928. Gold is at a considerable premium and not in general circulation.

	Approximate Value.¶ £ s. d.
£T1, Paper=100 Piastres	3 0

UNION OF SOUTH AFRICA.

The currency is on a Sterling basis, although subject to exchange which varies from time to time. Notes issued by the National Bank of S. Africa, The Standard Bank of S. Africa, The Natal Bank, The Nederlandsche Bank of S. Africa, still circulate, but these Bank Notes are gradually being replaced by notes issued by the South African Reserve Bank.

Notes issued are in denominations of 10/-, £1, £5, £10, £20 and £50. Both English Silver and the old Kruger Silver still circulate, but in 1923 a new Silver coinage was minted specially for use in S. Africa. (See also Rhodesia).

UNITED STATES.

Monetary Unit=

	Approximate Value.¶ £ s. d.
Dollar of 100 Cents	4 3
Copper, 1 Cent	0 0½
Nickel, 5 Cents	0 2½
Silver, 10 „	0 5
„ 25 „	1 0¾
„ 50 „	2 1½
„ 1 Dollar	4 3
Gold, 1 „	7 0
„ 2½ Dollars	17 6
„ 5 „	1 15 0
„ 10 „ (Eagle)	3 10 0
„ 20 „	7 0 0

Notes, Silver Certificates, National Bank Notes and Federal Reserve Notes are issued in amounts of 1, 2, 5, 10, 20, 50, 100, 500 and 1,000 Dollars.

URUGUAY.

Monetary Unit=

	Approximate Value.¶ £ s. d.
Peso of 100 Centesimes	1 7
Nickel, 1 Centesimo	0 0¼
„ 2 Centesimes	0 0½
„ 5 „	0 1
Silver, 50 Centesimes	0 9½
„ 1 Peso	1 7

Bank Notes are issued in the following denominations:—1, 5, 10, 50, 100 and 500 Pesos.

VENEZUELA.

Monetary Unit=

	Approximate Value.¶ £ s. d.
Bolivar of 100 Centimos	1 0

Notes are issued for 5, 10, 20, and 100 Bolivars.

Since Great Britain went off the Gold Standard on Sept. 21st, 1931, all other currencies based on Gold are liable to constant change, consequently the values shown are given with all reserve.

WEIGHTS AND MEASURES.

The following is a summary of the chief weights and measures in use on the Continent and in the East :—

Belgium, Denmark, France, Germany (including Bohemia and Moravia), Greece, Holland, Hungary, Italy, Jugoslavia, Norway, Portugal, Poland, Roumania, Slovakia, Spain, Sweden, Switzerland and U.S.S.R. use the metrical system as follows:—

Metrical and English Weights and Measures.

Mètre = 39·3708 in. = 3·281 ft. = 3 ft. 3⅜ in. = 1·0936 yard.
Square Mètre (mètre carré) = 1 1-5th square yard = 1·196).
Are (or 100 sq. mètres) = 119·6 square yards.
Cubic Mètre (or Stere) = 35⅓ cubic feet.
Centimètre = 2-5ths inch.
Kilomètre = 1093 yards = ⅝-mile.
10 Kilomètres = 6¼ miles.
100 Kilomètres = 62 1-10th miles.
Square Kilomètre = 2-5ths square mile.

Hectare = 2½ acres (2·471).
100 Hectares = 247·1 acres.
Gramme = 15½ grains (15·432).
10 Grammes = ⅓-oz. Avoirdupois.
15 Grammes = ½-oz. do.
Kilogramme = 2 1-5th lbs. (2·204) Avoirdupois.
10 Kilogrammes = 22 lbs. Avoirdupois.
Metrical Quintal = 220½ lbs. do.
Tonneau = 2,200 lbs. do.
Litre = 0·22 gal. 1¾ pint.
Hectolitre = 22 gallons.

English and Metrical Weights and Measures.

Inch = 2·539 centimètres = 25·39 millimètres.
2 inches = 5 centimètres nearly.
Foot = 30·47 centimètres.
Yard = 0·9141 mètre.
12 yards = 11 mètres nearly.
Mile = 1,609 kilomètre.
Square foot = 0·093 mètre carré.
Square yard = 0.836 mètre carré.
Acre = 0·4046 hectare = 4003 sq. mètres nearly.
2½ acres = 1 hectare nearly.
Pint = 0·5679 litre.

1¾ pint = 1 litre nearly.
Gallon = 4·5434 litres.
Bushel = 36·347 litres.
Oz. Troy = 31·103 grammes.
Pound Troy (5760 grains) = 373·121 grammes.
Oz. Avoirdupois = 28·349 grammes.
Pound Avoirdupois = (7,000 grains) = 453·592 gram.
2 lbs. 3 oz. = kilogramme nearly.
100 lbs. = 45·359 kilogrammes.
Cwt. = 50·802 do.
Ton = 1016·048 do.

BURMA.—1 Pulgat = 1 inch; 1 Tha = 154 in.; 1 Tain = 1069·44 yds.; 1 Dain = 2·430 miles. 1 Solay = 1 pint; 1 Sali = 1 gallon; 1 Teng = 1 bushel; 1 Viss = 3·6 lbs.

CHINA.—1 Tsun = 1·41 in.; 1 Chek = 14·1 in.; 1 Li = 486·176 yds.; 1 Po = 3 miles; 1 Tau = 1·15 galls.; 1 Kin = 1·333 lbs.

EGYPT.—1 Kirat = 1·125 in.; 1 Draa = 27 in.; 1 Gasab = 3 yds.; 1 Feddan = 1·1019 acres; Ardab (Cairo) = 4·9246 bushels; 1 Dirhem = 47·661 Tr. grns.; 1 Kantar = 98·046 lbs.; Oka = 2·723 lbs.

INDIA.—1 Moot = 3 in.; 1 Guz = 1 yd.; 1 Coss = 2000 yds.; 1 Beegah = 1600 square yards; 1 Seer = 2·20462 lbs.; 1 Seer = 1·76195 pints. Bombay: 1 Guz = 27 in.; 1 Beegah = 3927 sq. yds.; 1 Seer = 7 lbs.; 1 Maund = 82 lbs.

IRAN (Persia).—1 Babriz or Meshedman = 6¼ lbs. 1 Seistanman = 13 lbs.

JAPAN.—1 Sun = 1·1931 in.; 1 Shaku = 11·931 in.; 1 Ri = 2·44034 miles; 1 Sai = 0·03176 pint; 1 To = 3·703889 gallons; 1 Koku = nearly 5 bushels.

MALAYA.—Avoirdupois Weights—1 Tahil = 1⅓ ozs.; 1 Kati = 1⅓ lbs.; 1 Pikul = 133⅓ lbs.; 1 Koyan = 533⅓ lbs. Lineal Measures—1 Chhun = 1 19/40 inches; 1 Chhek = 14¾ inches. Measure of Capacity—"Liquid Measures."—1 Pau or Quarter Chupak = 2 Gills; 2 Pau or Half Chupak = 1 Pint; 1 Chupak = 1 Quart; 1 Gantang = 1 Gallon; 63 Gantangs = 1 Hogshead; 126 Gantangs = 1 Pipe; 252 Gantangs = 1 Ton. Measure of Capacity—"Dry Measure."—1 Pau or Quarter Chupak = 2 Gills; 2 Pau or Half Chupak = 1 Pint; 1 Chupak = 1 Quart; 1 Gantang = 1 Gallon; 2 Gantangs = 1 Peck; 8 Gantangs = 1 Bushel; 64 Gantangs = 1 Quarter.

TURKEY.—1 Pike = 27¼ in.; 1 Agatsch = 3·1159 miles; 1 Cantar = 1·417 gallons; 1 Cantar = 124·08 lbs.

POSTAL INFORMATION.

Letters.—It is safest, where possible, to direct letters (prepaid) to the care of Cook's Office, or to the care of an hotel or banker, otherwise letters and parcels should be addressed "Poste Restante." Travellers on the Continent are advised to *see* that their letters, etc., are weighed and properly stamped.

Registered Letters sent care of "Poste Restante" are usually only delivered to applicant on production of Passport.

Late Fee Letters.—At many head Post Offices and at some other Post Offices, letters for despatch by the Provincial Night Mails may, on payment of a special late fee, be posted after the ordinary hours of collection. Letter-boxes for the receipt of late letters bearing an extra ½d. stamp are affixed to all Mail Trains to which Sorting Carriages are attached. Letters for Continental Post may be posted in London at General Post Office between 6.0 p.m. and 7.0 p.m., with Late Fee of 1d.

Postage.—Imperial & Foreign :—To Aden, Australia, Bahrein, Banks Islands, Basutoland, Bechuanaland, Brunei, Burma, Ceylon, Cook Islands Dubai Egypt, Fanning Island, Fiji Islands, Friendly Islands, Gilbert and Ellice Islands, Hong Kong, India (British and French), Kenya, Labuan, Malay States (Federated and Unfederated), Mauritius, Muscat, Nauru, New Guinea (Mandated Territory), New Hebrides, New Zealand, Norfolk Island, North Borneo, Northern Rhodesia, Nyasaland, Palestine, Papua, Samoa (Territory under British Administration), Sarawak, Seychelles, Solomon Islands, Southern Rhodesia, South West Africa, Straits Settlements, Sudan (Anglo-Egyptian), Swaziland, Tanganyika Territory, Tibet, Tonga, Transjordan Uganda, Union of South Africa and Zanzibar; LETTERS, 1½d. per ½ oz.; POST CARDS, Single 1d.; Reply 2d. (Letters and post cards for these countries are despatched by air as the normal means of transmission). To other parts of the British Empire, H.M. Ships abroad, and U.S.A.: LETTERS, 1½d. first oz. and 1d. each additional oz.; POST CARDS, Single 1d.; Reply 2d. To all other places, LETTERS, 2½d. first oz., 1½d. each additional oz.; POST CARDS, Single 1½d.; Reply 3d. (Letters and post cards for all European countries, except Gibraltar, Malta, Portugal and Spain, prepaid at the above mentioned rate of 2½d. first oz. and 1½d. each additional oz. (post cards 1½d.) are despatched by air or by surface transport, whichever offers quicker delivery.

Printed Papers (including newspapers and books), to all destinations abroad, ½d. per 2 oz. COMMERCIAL PAPERS, to all destinations abroad, ½d. per 2 oz., with a minimum charge of 2½d. SAMPLES, to all destinations abroad, ½d. per 2 oz., with a minimum charge of 1d. The limit of weight for letters is 4 lb., for printed papers and commercial papers 5 lb. (Empire destinations) and 4 lb. (foreign destinations) and for samples 5 lb. (Empire destinations) and 1 lb. (foreign destinations). For the definition of printed papers, commercial papers and samples, see the *Post Office Guide*. The return postage varies. For example, letters from Belgium frcs. 1.75; France frcs. 2.25; from Holland 12½ cents., Italy lire 1 25, Switzerland 30 cents., Spain 50 cents. for first 20 grammes; Germany, R. Mks. 0.25 for 20 grammes; R. Mks. 0.15 for every additional 20 grammes. Post Cards are: from Belgium frcs. 1.00: France frs. 1.25; Italy 75 cents; 20 cents. from Switzerland; 7½ cents. from Holland, R. Mks. 0.15 from Germany. Newspapers are 45 centimes (France), 2½ cents. (Holland) for 50 grammes; R. Mks. 0.05 from Germany. If a letter be insufficiently prepaid, the surcharge collected from the addressee is double the deficiency. English stamps, etc., can be used only in the United Kingdom; in Germany, German stamps must be used, and so on; but International Reply Coupons (6d. each) are exchangeable in any country for stamps representing the postage on a single rate letter from that country, and Imperial Reply Coupons (3d. each) are similarly exchangeable in any country in the British Empire. For Registered Letters 3d. extra is charged. Newspapers are not allowed to be sent through the post in Russia.

Air Mail.—Surcharged air mail services are available to most countries to which letters and postcards are not forwarded by air in ordinary course. For full particulars of air postage rates, etc., see the Air Mail Leaflet, obtainable free of charge at Post Offices.

Money Orders can be obtained for most places abroad at a commission of 6d. for every £1 or fraction up to £3; thence 3d. for each additional £1 up to maximum amount. See *Post Office Guide*. For equivalent amounts see Money Table. Postal authorities on the Continent require absolute proof of identifications before payment can be made. Sometimes local business or official witnesses are required. Telegraphic or Postal remittances can be made through Cook's Offices.

Poste Restante.—Letters for the Continent should be addressed very legibly, particularly the Christian and Surname, the latter of which should be UNDERLINED, omitting "Esquire," "Bart.," or other title, which officers of foreign Post Offices are apt to take for a name. As they often find great difficulty also in reading English writing, and in the pronunciation of English names, persons applying for letters should present their cards with their names written plainly, or a photograph with a clearly addressed envelope. **N.B.**—Letters for posting found among passengers' baggage at the French or English Custom Houses, subject the sender and bearer to the risk of penal consequences.

Telegrams.—Alternative routes exist to certain places, but the sender of a telegram need not specify a route unless he wishes to do so. The main routes are "Govt. Cable," "Govt. Wireless," "Imperial Cable," "Imperial Wireless," "Western Union," "Commercial" and "Northern." In some cases the "Wireless" routes are cheaper than the other routes. The ordinary charge per word (including name and address) from the United Kingdom is as follows:—Algiers, 3d.; Belgium, 2½d.; Denmark, 2½d.; Egypt, 1st region, 9d., 2nd region, 10d.; 3rd region, 1/1; France, 2½d.; Germany, 2½d.; Gibraltar, 2½d.; Greece, 4d.; Holland, 2½d.; Hungary, 3½d.; Italy, 2½d.; Yugoslavia, 3½d.; Malta, 3d.; Norway, 2½d.; Portugal, 3d.; Roumania, 4d.; Russia, 5d.; Spain, 2½d.; Sweden, 2½d.; Switzerland, 2½d.; Turkey, 5½d.; Brazil, 1/7, and upwards; China, 2/9; Japan, 2/9; Java, 3/2; Madeira, 7½d. and 8½d.; United States, from 9d. upwards. Ordinary telegrams may be sent to any part of the British Empire at a rate not exceeding 1/3 per word.

European Letter Telegrams may be sent to most European countries at half the ordinary rates, the minimum charge being as for 25 words.

Other services available to most extra-European countries are: Deferred Service at half the ordinary rates, Night Letter Telegram and Daily Letter Telegram services at about one-third of the ordinary rates. For these two latter services there are minimum charges as for 25 words.—See *Post Office Guide*.

International Telephone Services.—Telephone service is available between Gt. Britain and Ireland and all Continental countries with the exception of Albania. The following are typical charges for calls of 3 minutes' duration from any exchange in England and Wales (beyond the first 3 minutes the charge per minute is one-third of the unit charge). Paris, 6/-; Marseilles, 9/-; The Hague, 7/6; Lucerne, 8/-; Cologne, 8/-; Berlin, 10/-; Vienna, 11/-; Copenhagen, 11/-; Rome, 13/3; Stockholm, 14/-; Moscow, 17/6. At night (7.0 p.m.—8.0 a.m.) charges are reduced to approximately three-fifths of the day rates.

(SEE PAGE 31 FOR CALENDAR).

PUBLIC HOLIDAYS ON THE CONTINENT 1939

There are no "BANK HOLIDAYS" in the countries named below, but the dates given are observed as Public Holidays (Fêtes Légales), and business is suspended, museums and galleries closed.

BELGIUM.—New Year's Day, Jan. 1; Easter Monday, April 10; Ascension Day, May 18; Whit-Monday, May 29; National Fête, July 21; Assumption, Aug. 15; All Saints' Day, Nov. 1; Armistice Day, Nov. 11; Christmas Day, Dec. 25.

BOHEMIA, MORAVIA AND SLOVAKIA.—Epiphany, Jan. 6 (closed from noon); Easter Saturday, April 8 (closed from noon); Easter Monday, April 10; Labour Day, May 1; Ascension, May 18 (closed from noon); Whit-Saturday, May 27 (closed from noon); Whit-Monday, May 29; Corpus Christi, June 8 (closed from noon); SS. Peter and Paul, June 29 (closed fron noon); SS. Cyril and Methode, July 5 (closed from noon); John Hus Fête, July 6; Assumption, Aug. 15 (closed from noon); S. Venceslas, Sept. 28; National Fête, Oct. 28; All Saints, Nov. 1 (closed from noon); Immaculate Conception, Dec. 8 (closed from noon); Christmas Day, Dec. 25; Boxing Day, Dec. 26 (closed from noon).

DENMARK.—New Year's Day, Jan. 1; Maundy Thursday, April 6; Good Friday, April 7; Easter Monday, April 10; Prayer Day, May 5; Ascension Day, May 18; Whit-Monday, May 29; Christmas Day, Dec. 25; Boxing Day, Dec. 26.

FRANCE.—New Year's Day, Jan. 1; Shrove Tuesday, Feb. 21; Mid-Lent, Mar. 16; Easter Monday, April 10; Ascension Day, May 18; Whit-Monday, May 29; National Fête, July 14; Assumption, Aug. 15; All Saints' Day, Nov. 1; Armistice Day, Nov. 11; Christmas Day, Dec. 25.

GERMANY.—New Year's Day, Jan. 1; Good Friday, April 7; Easter Monday, April 10; Ascension Day, May 18; Whit-Monday, May 29; Corpus Christi, June 8 (Catholic places only); All Saints' Day, Nov. 1 (Catholic placos only); Day of Atonement, Nov. 22; Christmas Day, Dec. 25; Boxing Day, Dec. 26.

GREECE.—New Year's Day, Jan. 1; Epiphany, Jan. 6; Carnival, Feb. 20; Independence Day, March 25; Good Friday, April 7; Easter Monday, April 10; St. George's Day, April 23; Labour Day, May 1; Ascension Day, May 18; St. Constantin, May 21; St. Esprit, May 29; SS. Peter and Paul, June 29; National Holiday, Aug. 4; Assumption, Aug. 15; St. Dimitrius, Oct. 26; Christmas Day, Dec. 25; Boxing Day, Dec. 26.

HOLLAND.—New Year's Day, Jan. 1; Good Friday, April 7; Easter Monday, April 10; Ascension Day, May 18; Whit-Monday, May 29; Queen's Birthday, Aug. 31; Christmas Day, Dec. 25; Boxing Day, Dec. 26.

ITALY.—New Year's Day, Jan. 1; Epiphany, Jan. 6; S. Joseph, March 19; Foundation of Rome, April 21; Ascension Day, May 18; Corpus Domini, June 8; SS. Peter and Paul, June 29; Assumption, Aug. 15; Fascisti March on Rome, Oct. 28; All Saints' Day, Nov. 1; Victory Day, Nov. 4; Conception, Dec. 8; Christmas Day, Dec. 25. In addit on, the day of Patron Saint of each city is recognized by the Government as a local holiday.

NORWAY.—New Year's Day, Jan. 1; Maundy Thursday, April 6; Good Friday, April 7; Easter Monday, April 10; Constitution Day, May 17; Ascension Day, May 18; Whit-Monday, May 29; Prayer Day, Nov. 3; Christmas Day, Dec. 25; Boxing Day, Dec. 26.

SPAIN.—

SWEDEN.—New Year's Day, Jan. 1; Epiphany, Jan. 6; Annunciation Day, Mar. 25; Good Friday, April 7; Easter Monday, April 10; Labour Day, May 1; Ascension Day, May 18; Whit-Monday, May 29; Midsummer Day, June 24; Christmas Day, Dec. 25; Boxing Day, Dec. 26.

SWITZERLAND.—New Year's Day, Jan. 1; Good Friday, April 7; Easter Monday, April 10 (not Lucerne); Ascension Day, May 18; Whit-Monday, May 29 (Protestant places only); Corpus Christi, June 8 (Catholic places only); Assumption Day, Aug. 15 (Catholic places only); Jeune Genevois, Sept. 7 (Geneva only); Patrons' Day (Lucerne), Oct. 2; All Saints' Day, Nov. 1; Immaculate Conception, Dec. 8; Christmas Day, Dec. 25; and Dec. 26 (Zurie Canton); Dec. 31 (Geneva only).

Name of Place.	Jan.	Feb.	Mar.	Apl.	May	June	July	Aug.	Sept.	Oct.	Nov.	Dec.	Rain-fall Inches
Algiers	53·2	58·1	60·8	63·9	68·5	74·2	76·9	76·8	73·7	71·1	61·2	62·0	—
Athens	46·4	47·8	52·6	59·1	67·9	75·9	80·6	80·0	73·2	65·8	57·8	50·1	—
Auckland	66·2	65·9	66·3	65·5	57·7	53·3	51·3	52·4	54·2	56·2	58·5	59·8	43·03
Barcelona	51·8	50·5	53·0	53·4	58·8	63·6	72·1	74·6	70·3	65·6	59·7	51·8	—
Bergen	34·2	33·6	35·4	42·1	48·9	55·0	57·9	57·6	52·7	45·1	38·5	34·7	78·74
Berlin	36·6	32·2	39·9	49·1	55·3	66·0	63·3	61·6	56·4	48·9	37·0	32·6	30·30
Bombay	74·5	74·8	78·0	82·1	84·6	82·4	79·5	79·4	79·4	80·7	79·3	76·4	67·
Boston	27·0	28·0	35·0	45·3	56·6	65·8	71·3	68·9	62·7	52·3	41·2	31·6	43·38
Brussels	36·3	38·8	42·4	49·3	55·9	62·6	65·1	64·4	59·2	51·4	43·0	37·9	28·78
Buenos Aires	74·4	73·6	70·6	63·3	57·4	52·2	51·2	51·6	57·4	61·2	67·2	72·2	—
Cairo (Egypt)	54·1	56·1	62·4	69·8	76·0	82·1	83·0	82·0	78·3	73·4	65·3	57·0	1·2
Calcutta	65·2	70·2	79·3	85·0	85·7	84·5	83·0	82·4	82·6	80·0	72·4	65·3	61·81
Capetown	69·3	69·7	68·0	63·1	59·8	55·5	54·8	55·6	57·0	60·7	64·2	67·3	—
Christchurch, N.Z.	60·8	58·7	60·0	57·6	47·8	44·9	40·7	44·8	48·9	51·8	55·1	55·7	25·45
Cologne	43·8	39·4	46·4	55·6	58·0	68·0	68·5	70·2	60·7	54·5	46·1	36·3	28·30
Colombo	79·0	79·8	81·2	83·0	82·9	81·9	80·9	81·2	81·3	80·0	79·7	79·3	78·24
Copenhagen	32·7	32·3	34·7	42·4	51·8	59·7	62·6	60·8	54·8	46·7	39·2	34·3	—
Dresden	31·5	33·5	38·3	46·9	55·0	61·4	64·4	62·6	57·0	47·6	39·1	31·1	22·34
Dunedin	57·1	57·7	59·5	53·8	48·0	43·7	41·7	45·8	46·0	50·6	51·0	51·2	37·06
Florence	47·8	45·8	49·2	53·8	68·0	72·0	74·0	72·6	61·4	59·6	51·6	47·6	—
Geneva	30·2	34·8	40·0	48·2	55·7	62·2	65·8	64·2	58·4	49·8	40·2	37·6	—
Hongkong	59·8	58·9	63·1	70·3	77·1	81·0	82·0	81·7	80·6	76·2	69·4	62·9	85·16
Istanbul	41·2	37·4	47·4	58·0	62·4	71·8	76·2	72·4	67·0	64·6	51·4	43·2	—
Jerusalem	45·2	50·8	53·3	60·3	67·3	71·7	74·7	75·7	71·8	71·0	57·2	46·8	—
Khartoum	69·4	71·4	80·9	83·3	90·0	91·4	85·8	86·7	88·0	87·3	79·8	72·3	6·66
Kobe	40·1	40·3	45·3	55·8	63·5	70·3	77·5	80·4	73·8	63·3	53·4	44·2	53·37
La Paz	53·2	52·3	54·7	50·4	47·8	45·3	45·3	47·3	48·9	52·5	54·0	53·2	—
Lima	73·4	74·7	73·6	70·2	65·8	62·5	61·2	60·8	61·2	63·0	65·6	69·5	—
Lisbon, Estoril	53·92	57·82	57·95	60·72	66·40	66·80	70·8	68·87	68·93	65·63	58·04	55·60	—
London	42·7	42·3	46·0	48·5	56·4	60·3	60·5	62·2	60·3	55·3	44·4	46·5	20·0
Los Angeles	54·3	55·1	56·9	59·4	62·5	66·7	70·4	71·6	69·5	64·6	60·3	56·5	15·49
Luxor	64·0	65·0	76·0	—	—	—	—	—	—	—	—	—	—
Madeira	61·2	60·0	61·6	62·3	64·8	67·2	70·9	72·4	72·2	70·3	65·6	65·9	—
Madras	75·1	76·7	80·0	84·0	86·7	86·4	84·5	83·3	83·0	80·6	77·5	75·5	49·02
Madrid	40·8	49·7	49·2	54·3	58·1	70·9	74·9	76·6	67·4	56·3	48·9	41·9	—
Malaga	54·1	55·9	59·5	63·0	65·3	73·6	77·4	75·0	73·9	68·0	60·0	55·9	—
Malta	52·5	57·7	60·0	67·2	72·2	75·2	79·3	85·4	83·2	70·0	58·2	53·2	25·
Manila	76·1	77·0	79·3	82·0	82·8	81·9	80·2	80·4	79·9	79·3	78·1	76·8	77·27
Melbourne	67·5	67·2	64·7	59·6	54·1	50·3	48·5	51·0	53·9	57·5	61·3	64·5	25·60
Merano	40·0	45·0	51·0	54·0	60·0	65·0	68·0	66·0	61·0	57·0	45·0	38·5	3·4
Mexico	53·8	56·7	60·4	64·0	64·6	63·7	62·4	61·9	62·1	58·5	55·6	53·4	—
Miami, Florida	66·5	69·5	70·2	72·8	76·4	80·0	81·0	81·4	80·1	77·0	71·8	68·0	—
Milan	32·9	37·8	45·5	54·0	62·5	74·0	74·2	71·6	65·1	54·7	43·4	35·5	—
Munich	28·1	23·4	38·2	45·6	54·4	60·8	64·1	62·8	56·1	47·1	37·8	26·1	43·30
Naples	44.6	46·4	48·4	54·4	66·2	71·4	74·0	74·0	68·0	64·6	53·6	45·4	—
Nelson, N.Z.	64·3	64·0	64·8	61·8	52·7	48·8	46·6	48·7	52·2	54·1	56·8	58·6	—
New Orleans, La.	53·5	57·3	63·4	68·6	74·8	80·6	82·6	81·8	78·0	70·3	60·8	54·8	—
New York	30·0	31·0	38·0	49·0	60·0	69·0	74·0	73·0	66·0	55·0	44·0	34·0	—
Nice	46·1	48·0	51·0	57·0	58·0	68·0	71·0	69·0	69·0	61·0	52·0	48·0	—
Oslo	24·10	24·10	29·50	39·90	50·90	59·90	62·6	60·60	52·7	41·9	32·20	25·50	23·
Palermo	50·3	51·4	54·3	58·5	64·0	70·6	76·0	76·7	73·0	67·0	59·4	53·4	—
Palma	52·7	53·4	55·2	58·4	63·5	70·8	75·3	77·0	71·7	63·5	58·0	53·0	—
Paris	36·0	39·6	44·2	50·2	57·2	62·6	65·8	65·2	60·0	52·0	43·6	38·2	—
Peiping	23·0	30·2	41·0	57·2	68·0	75·2	78·8	77·0	68·0	54·5	39·2	28·4	23·38
Rangoon	74·7	77·3	81·2	85·0	82·2	79·5	78·8	78·7	79·1	80·0	78·3	75·6	—
Rio de Janeiro	78·4	78·7	77·2	74·6	71·4	69·2	68·4	69·2	69·8	71·2	74·0	76·7	—
Rome	43·3	46·0	50·8	55·0	68·0	73·0	77·0	80·0	73·4	66·4	56·1	52·0	—
San Diego, Calif.	54·3	55·1	56·7	58·5	60·8	63·9	67·2	68·7	67·1	63·7	59·7	56·0	—
San Francisco	49·5	51·3	52·7	53·7	55·5	57·0	57·3	58·0	59·3	58·4	55·5	50·9	22·7
Santiago	69·3	68·2	64·6	59·2	53·2	46·7	48·1	50·5	53·5	58·3	63·4	67·3	—
Shanghai	37·7	39·4	46·3	56·3	65·7	73·5	80·7	80·6	73·0	63·3	52·2	42·4	44·78
Sofia	29·0	31·3	41·5	50·3	59·0	64·7	68·7	68·0	60·7	51·4	39·9	32·5	—
Stockholm	27·0	26·4	29·8	38·1	47·8	57·2	62·2	59·5	52·5	43·2	34·7	28·8	—
Sydney	73·0	73·5	69·8	65·3	57·77	53·6	53·9	55·6	59·9	65·9	67·3	70·1	57·70
Tokyo	37·4	38·8	44·2	54·7	61·7	68·7	75·4	77·9	71·6	60·8	50·9	41·4	61·58
Venice	38·6	37·8	45·2	53·6	60·8	73·8	75·8	77·8	64·6	59·6	47·2	38·2	—
Vienna	28·1	31·6	39·2	49·3	58·8	64·6	68·0	66·7	59·5	49·6	38·7	31·3	—
Wellington, N.Z.	62·1	60·2	62·7	61·4	53·9	50·7	48·4	49·2	51·5	53·7	56·0	57·4	—
Yokohama	39·2	40·3	45·1	55·2	62·6	69·1	75·9	78·3	72·3	61·9	52·3	43·2	68·79

THERMOMETER, see page 58.

USEFUL

Loth's "Tourist's Conversational Guide" in English, French, German and Italian, of Foreign Languages for Travellers, with Phonetic

English.	French.	Spanish.
How? How much?	Comment? Combien?	Como? Cuanto?
What? When? Where?	Quoi? Quand? Où?	Qué? Cuando? Adonde?
Why? Who?	Pourquoi? Qui?	Porqué? Quien?
Now, always, late, early	Maintenant, toujours, tard, de bonne heure.	Ahora, siempre, tarde, temprano
That is too much	C'est trop	Es demasiado
Yes. No. Have you? I have	Oui. Non. Avez-vous? J'ai	Si. No. Tiene usted? Yo tengo.
Go quickly. Go slowly	Allez vite. Allez lentement	Vé deprisa (vé lijero). Vé despacio.
I want— Give me—	J'ai besoin de— Donnez-moi—	Yo quiero— Deme usted—
Sunday, Monday, Tuesday	Dimanche, Lundi, Mardi	Domingo, Lunes, Martes
Wednesday, Thursday, Friday, Saturday	Mercredi, Jeudi, Vendredi, Samedi	Miércoles, Jueves, Viernes, Sábado
1, 2, 3, 4, 5, 6, 7	Un, deux, trois, quatre, cinq, six, sept.	Uno, dos, tres, cuatro, cinco, seis, siete.
8, 9, 10, 11, 12, 20, 100	Huit, neuf, dix, onze, douze, vingt, cent.	Ocho, nueve, diez, once, doce, veinte, ciento.
First class. Second class	Première classe. Deuxième classe	Primera clase. Segunda clase
Where is my luggage?	Où est mon bagage?	Adonde está mi equipaje?
Register my baggage to—	Enregistrez mon bagage pour—	Facture mi equipaje para—
Single ticket. Return ticket	Billet simple. Billet d'aller et retour.	Billete de ida. Billete de ida y vuelta.
Bring me— Make haste	Apportez-moi— Dépêchez-vous	Tráigame— Aligere usted
Waiter!	Garçon!	Mozo!
I want a bedroom	Je désire une chambre à coucher	Yo quiero un cuarto de dormir
Good morning! Good evening!	Bonjour! Bonsoir!	Buenos dias. Buenas tardes
Do you speak English?	Parlez-vous Anglais?	Habla usted Inglés?
Where is my room?	Où est ma chambre?	Adonde está mi cuarto?
Cold, warm water	De l'eau froide, chaude	Agua fria, agua caliente
A towel. Soap	Un essuie-main. Du savon	Una toalla. Jabon
A cup of tea, coffee	Une tasse de thé, café	Una taza de té, café
When do we start?	Quand partons-nous?	Cuando vamos?
When shall we arrive?	Quand arriverons-nous?	Cuando llegaremos?
Here is something for you	Voici un pourboire	Tome usted (una propina)
The Custom House	La Douane	La Aduana
Here are my keys	Voici mes clefs	Aqui están mis llaves
I have nothing liable to duty	Je n'ai rien à déclarer	No tengo nada a declarar
Where is the train for—?	Où est le train pour—?	Adonde está el tren para—?
Drive me to Hotel—	Conduisez-moi à l'Hôtel—	Lléveme al Hotel
At what time does the train start?	A quelle heure le train part-il?	A que hora sale el tren?
Do we change carriages for—?	Changeons-nous de voiture pour—?	Cambiamos de coche para—?
Please tell me the way to—	Pour aller à—, s'il vous plait?	Tenga la bondad de dirigirme a?
If you please. Thank you!	S'il vous plait. Je vous remercie!	Si usted quiere. Muchas gracias!

In SPANISH j and g before e and i are pronounced like ch in loch (German ch) and ll is pronounced something like the French ill in fille.

PHRASES.

price 1/6, will be found very useful, as also will Marlborough's "Self-Taught Series Pronunciation"

Italian.	German.	Esperanto.
Come? Quanto?	Wie? Was kostet's?	Kiel? Kiom?
Che cosa? Che? Quando? Dove?	Was? Wann? Wo?	Kia? Kiam? Kie?
Perchè? Chi?	Warum? Wer?	Kial? Kiu?
Adesso, ora, sempre, Tardi, di buon'ora.	Nun jetzt, immer, spät, zeitig, früh	Nun, Ĉiam, Malfrue, Frue.
Questo é troppo	Das ist zu viel	Tio estas tro multe.
Si. No. Avete? Io ho	Ja. Nein. Haben Sie? Ich habe	Jes. Ne. Ĉu vi havas? Mi havas.
Camminate presto. Andate più adagio.	Gehen Sie schnell. Gehen Sie langsam.	Foriru rapide. Iru malrapide.
Ho bisogno— Dàtemi	Ich brauche— Geben Sie mir	Mi bezonas— Donu al mi.
Domenica, Lunedì, Martedì	Sonntag, Montag, Dienstag	Dimanĉo, Lundo, Mardo.
Mercoledi, Giovedi, Venerdi, Sabato	Mittwoch, Donnerstag, Freitag, Samstag (or Sonnabend).	Merkredo, Jaŭdo, Vendredo, Sabato
Uno, due, tre, quattro, cinque, sei, sette	Eins, zwei, drei, vier, fünf, sechs, sieben.	Unu, du, tri, kvar, kvin, ses, sep.
Otto, nove, dieci, undici, dodici, venti, cento.	Acht, neun, zehn, elf, zwölf, zwanzig, hundert.	Ok, naŭ, dek, dekunu, dekdu, dudek, cent.
Prima classe. Seconda classe	Erster Klasse. Zweiter Klasse	Unua klaso. Dua klaso.
Dov'é il mio bagaglio?	Wo ist mein Gepäck?	Kie estas mia pakaĵo?
Voglio registrare il mio bagaglio per—	Ich möchte mein Gepäck nach—aufgeben.	Rekomendu mian pakaĵon al—.
Biglietto di corsa semplice, Biglietto di andata e ritorno.	Einfache Fahrkarte. Rückfahrkarte.	Bileto por iro. Bileto por iro kaj reveno.
Portatemi. Fate presto	Bringen Sie mir—. Beeilen Sie sich	Alportu al mi. Rapidu.
Cameriere	Kellner (more frequently: "Ober").	Kelnero.
Voglio una camera da letto	Ich möchte ein Zimmer	Mi bezonas litĉambron.
Buon giorno. Buona sera	Guten Morgen. Guten Abend	Bonan tagon. Bonan vesperon.
Parlate Inglese?	Sprechen Sie englisch?	Ĉu vi parolas la lingvon anglan?
Dov'é la mia camera?	Wo ist mein Zimmer?	Kie estas mia ĉambro?
Acqua fredda, calda	Kaltes, warmes wasser	Malvarma, varma akvo.
Un asciugamani. Sapone	Ein handtuch. Seife	Viŝilo. Sapo.
Una tazza di té (caffé)	Eine Tasse Tee (Kaffee)	Taso da teo.
Quando partiamo?	Wann fahren wir ab?	Je kioma horo ni forlasos.
Quando arriveremo?	Wann werden wir ankommen?	Kiam ni atingos.
Prendete, questo è per voi	Hier ist Ihr Trinkgeld	Jen estas trinkmono.
La dogana	Das Zollhaus	La dogano.
Ecco le chiavi	Hier sind die schlüssel	Jen estas miaj ŝlosiloj.
Non ho niente di dazio	Ich habe nichts zu verzollern	Mi havas nenion imposteblan.
Dov'é il treno per—?	Wo ist der Zug nach—?	Kie estas la vagonaro por—?
Conducetemi all'albergo—	Fahren Sie mich nach Hotel—	Konduku min al hotelo—
A che ora parte il treno?	Wann geht der Zug ab?	Je kioma horo la vagonaro foriros.
Si cambia carozza per—?	Müssen wir nach—umsteigen?	Ĉu ni ŝangas vagonojn por—?
Scusi, per audare a—?	Bin ich auf dem Wege nach—bitte?	Mi petas vin direkti min al—.
Per favore, Grazie	Bitte. Ich danke Ihnen	Mi petas. Mi dankas vin.

In ESPERANTO letters have the following sounds—ĉ as ch in church; j as y in boy; ĵ as s in pleasure; aŭ as ow in now; ŝ as sh in she; ĝ as g in gem; c as ts; g as g in go; aj as y in my.

OTHER USEFUL INFORMATION.

Bicycles.—Travellers taking bicycles to the Continent should become members of the National Cyclists' Union or Cyclists' Touring Club.

Buffets.—There are buffets at nearly all the stations mentioned in these tables; the principal are marked *b*.

Cabs are generally cheap abroad, more especially in Italy. The tariff will be found inside the cab and, in addition, it is usual to give the driver a gratuity.

Children.—

CHILDREN'S FARES FOR LOCAL BOOKINGS ARE AS FOLLOWS:—

	Free.	Half Fare.	Full Fare.
Great Britain	Under 3 years	Between 3 and 14 years	Over 14 years
Ireland	„ 3 „	„ 3 „ 14 „	„ 14 „
Algeria	„ 4 „	„ 4 „ 10 „	„ 10 „
Belgium	„ 4 „	„ 4 „ 10 „	„ 10 „
Bulgaria	„ 4 „	„ 4 „ 10 „	„ 10 „
Denmark	„ 4 „	„ 4 „ 10 „	„ 10 „
Egypt	„ 4 „	„ 4 „ 10 „	„ 10 „
Finland	„ 4 „	„ 4 „ 10 „	„ 10 „
France and Corsica	„ 4 „	„ 4 „ 10 „	„ 10 „
Germany	„ 4 „	„ 4 „ 10 „	„ 10 „
Greece	„ 3 „	„ 3 „ 7 „	„ 7 „
Holland	„ 4 „	„ 4 „ 10 „	„ 10 „
Hungary	„ 4 „	„ 4 „ 10 „	„ 10 „
Italy	„ 4 „	„ 4 „ 10 „	„ 10 „
Jugoslavia	„ 4 „	„ 4 „ 10 „	„ 10 „
Morocco	„ 4 „	„ 4 „ 10 „	„ 10 „
Norway	„ 4 „	„ 4 „ 10 „	„ 10 „
Palestine and Syria	„ 4 „	„ 4 „ 10 „	„ 10 „
Poland	„ 4 „	„ 4 „ 10 „	„ 10 „
Portugal	„ 4 „	„ 4 „ 10 „	„ 10 „
Roumania	„ 4 „	„ 4 „ 10 „	„ 10 „
Spain	„ 3 „	„ 3 „ 6 „	„ 6 „
Sweden	„ 4 „	„ 4 „ 12 „	„ 12 „
Switzerland	„ 4 „	„ 4 „ 12 „	„ 12 „
Tunisia	„ 4 „	„ 4 „ 10 „	„ 10 „
Turkey (Oriental Rly.)	„ 4 „	„ 4 „ 10 „	„ 10 „
Turkey (State Rly.)	3 „	„ 3 „ 7	„ 7 „

Children's Through Bookings.—In connection with through international bookings, the age limits for children's tickets vary in some cases from those shown above. Particulars may be obtained from any office of Messrs. Thos. Cook & Son and Wagons-Lits. Children travelling at reduced rate are usually allowed only half the weight of free luggage granted for adults.

Church Services Abroad.—Church of England Services are mostly supplied by the *Society for the Propagation of the Gospel*, 15, Tufton Street, Westminster, S.W. (who have more than 250 Chaplaincies), and the *Colonial and Continental Church Society*, 9, Sergeants' Inn, London, E.C. (who have about 115 Chaplains), at various places on the Continent. It is a rule with these Societies to celebrate the Holy Communion every Sunday. A few regular Embassy and Consular Chaplains are appointed by the Foreign Office. All Foreign Chaplains are licensed either by the Bishop of London or the Bishop of Gibraltar, the latter diocese including the Mediterranean coast and islands. In the chief cities there are also Presbyterian, Wesleyan, and other churches.

Clothing.—For an ocean passage, the tourist should provide for all kinds of weather. Clothing should be sufficient to guard against chills, and outside wraps, overcoats and rugs will be found useful. Ladies will find serge or woollen dresses the best. Gentlemen are recommended to have warm clothing throughout, with an overcoat, so that no discomfort is felt on deck. In visiting countries at seasons when rain may be expected, a mackintosh is a most important accessory. Gentlemen will find a light felt hat the best.

Coupes on Continental railways are of various descriptions, and are charged for at supplementary rates. See pp. 75-76.

Couriers.—Thos. Cook & Son, Ltd., have first-class Couriers available to relieve the traveller of the many difficulties so often inseparable from independent travel, such as transfer of passenger and baggage between station, steamer, and hotel, payment of tips, arrangements for sightseeing, etc. The services of our Couriers, who speak fluently the language of the countries visited, are of great assistance to business men travelling on the Continent. The Couriers are men of good appearance, who, by long experience, have obtained an intimate knowledge of the principal cities of Europe. They are *not in uniform*, being quite distinct from our uniformed staff in attendance at railway stations, ports, etc. Particulars can be obtained from any of Cook's Offices.

Dogs (not accepted unless muzzled).—One Passenger is not allowed to take more than two dogs by the Southern Rly. Co.'s Passenger Boats. Dogs going to or from the Continent, in batches of three or more, will be conveyed by Cargo Boat. Stringent regulations are in force with regard to the admission of dogs into England, and particulars of the restrictions may be obtained at any of Cook's Offices.

The following are the charges for conveyance of Dogs by passenger trains and steamers:—
(Subject to alteration without notice).

London to	Calais (accompanied)	5s. 3d.*
„	Paris *via* Dieppe	9s. od.†
„	Hook of Holland	10s. 6d
„	Antwerp	10s. 6d.
„	Flushing	10s. 6d.
Calais to	Paris	30 fcs.
„	Bale	72 fcs.
Paris to	Biarritz	77 fcs.
„	Cannes	102 fcs.
„	Hyères	92 fcs.
„	Ventimiglia	108 fcs.
Paris to	Marseilles	83 fcs.
„	Mentone	108 fcs.
„	Nice	105 fcs.
„	Monte Carlo	107 fcs.
„	Modane	68 fcs.
„	Pau	79 fcs.
„	Bale	51 fcs.
„	Strassburg	49 fcs.
„	Geneva	60 fcs.

*Dogs (unaccompanied) forwarded by the Grande Vitesse Service, or by the Mail Service, are charged by weight at double the parcels rate. †For dogs not exceeding £2 in value.

Expenses.—Thos. Cook & Son, Ltd., will be pleased to give an inclusive estimate for any tour or journey, covering travel, hotels, with (if required) private sitting rooms and bath rooms, excursions, guides, sightseeing, etc., in fact, every necessary expenditure with the exception of drinks and gratuities.

Fees.—At many hotels on the Continent a special charge (of approximately 10% of bill, is made in lieu of tips. Porterage of luggage is not included in the bills.

Golf.—See pages 58 and 59.

Guide Books.—Cook's publish a concise, reliable, and inexpensive series of Handbooks to London, Paris, Switzerland, Holland, Belgium, Rhine and Black Forest, Normandy and Brittany, Rivieras of France and Italy, Florence, Venice and Venetia, Rome, Naples, Milan and the Italian Lakes, Northern and Central Italy, Southern Italy, Spain and Portugal, Norway, Sweden and Denmark, North Africa, Palestine, Syria and Iraq, Egypt and the Sudan. They are on sale, together with a selection of other publishers' Guide Books, at all Cook's Offices A condensed list of Guide Books, etc., will be found on page 86.

Hotel Accommodation.—To be able to select and reserve before leaving home the particular accommodation desired is an advantage which needs no emphasizing. Thos Cook & Son, Ltd., can secure in advance accommodation at any class of hotel in any part of the world, from single bedrooms to suites of apartments, on any floor, with whatever aspect may be desired. They also arrange "En Pension" terms for an extended stay in one place.

Hotel Coupons.—Cook's have evolved a new system of Hotel Coupons designed to provide the maximum of help to motorists and others travelling on the Continent without pre-arranged stopping places. All that a traveller has to do is to purchase a supply of the coupons before starting on his journey, and use them in various multiples as payment for accommodation at various grades of hotel. Thus, for a night's stay at a modest country hotel three or four coupons may be sufficient, while at a first-class hotel seven or eight may be needed. The scheme includes hotels of six separate grades, clearly set out in a list which is supplied to purchasers of the coupons. For full particulars of the scheme, see special brochure obtainable at Cook's Offices.

Interpreters in Cook-Wagons-Lits uniform meet principal trains and steamers at following places, and assist holders of their tickets free of charge:—Alexandria, Algeciras, Algiers, Amsterdam, Antwerp, Athens (and Piræus), Auckland, Bale, Barcelona, Bergen, Berlin, Beyrout, Biarritz (Summer only), Bombay, Boulogne, Brindisi, Brisbane, Brussels, Bucharest, Budapest, Buenos Aires, Cairo, Calais, Calcutta, Cannes, Cape Town, Cherbourg, Coire (Winter only), Cologne, Colombo, Copenhagen, Dieppe, Delhi, Dover, Durban, Florence, Folkestone, Frankfort, Geneva, Genoa, Gibraltar, Hague, Haifa, Hamburg, Havre, Hendaye, Hong-Kong, Innsbruck, Interlaken (Dec.-March and June-Sept.), Irun, Istanbul, Jerusalem, Kantara, Karachi, Karlovy-Vary (Summer only), Kobe, Lausanne, Lisbon (not steamers unless specially advised), Liverpool, London (Liverpool Street, St. Pancras, Euston, Tilbury, Victoria and Waterloo), Lucerne (Summer only), Lugano (Summer only), Lyons, Madras, Madrid, Malta, Marseilles, Melbourne, Mentone (Winter only), Milan, Monte Carlo, Montreux, Naples, Newcastle, Newhaven, New York, Nice, Oslo, Ostend, Palermo (Winter only),

Palma, Paris, Peiping (Peking), Perth (Fremantle), W.A., Port Said, Praha (Prague), Rangoon, Riga, Rome, Rotterdam, St. Malo (Summer only), Shanghai, Singapore, Southampton, Stockholm, Suez, Sydney, Syracuse, Tientsin, Toulon (Orient Line arrivals and departures only), Trieste, Tunis, Turin, Venice, Vichy (Summer only), Vienna, Vigo, Vintimille, Warsaw Wiesbaden (Summer only), Yokohama, Zurich.

The Interpreters are not usually on duty on Sundays except by special arrangement.

London (Tilbury Docks).—Cook's Baggage Clerk is in attendance on the arrival of ocean liners at Tilbury, to arrange the clearance and forwarding of passengers' baggage.

Letters for persons travelling on the Continent should, if possible, be sent to hotels previously arranged, at fixed dates, in preference to the Postes Restantes. Travellers transacting business with Messrs. Cook can have their mail sent to the care of their Offices. Letters, etc., should be clearly addressed, and "Mr." should be used instead of "Esq." Writing should be distinct and initials and other capital letters should be printed, thus B.

Motor Car Tours.—Travellers wishing to hire a private motor car for any journey or tour, at home or abroad, are invited to consult Thos. Cook & Son, Ltd., who maintain a special Motoring Department. Cook's are prepared to quote inclusive charges for everything that may be required—the hire of car and chauffeur for any period and any itinerary, hotel accommodation of any grade, and special sightseeing in any places visited. In all cases they provide for full running expenses, including chauffeur's board and lodging and garage charges.

Cook's are equally at the disposal of motorists who wish to tour at home or abroad in their own cars.

Pickpockets.—Travellers are warned against pickpockets and train thieves.

Pillows.—A down pillow is a great comfort in travelling, and will frequently make a night's railway journey endurable, or even comfortable. On the Express and "Rapide" Trains on the Region Sud-Est and other railways in France and Italy, pillows can be hired at the rate of four francs for the journey.

Smoking Carriages are attached to all trains. Carriages in which smoking is not permitted are labelled to that effect, viz.: "Nicht Raucher," "Non Fumeurs," "Nietrooken," or "Non Fumare."

Thermometer.—While the Fahrenheit scale is generally used in England, the Centigrade scale is in vogue on the Continent. The following Table shows the comparison between the Fahrenheit Centigrade and Réaumur scales:—

	Fahrenheit. England	Centigrade.	Réaum.
Boiling	212	100	80
	203	95	76
	194	90	72
	185	85	68
	176	80	64
	167	75	60
	158	70	56
	149	65	52
	140	60	48
	131	55	44
	122	50	40
	118	45	36
	112	45	36
Fever	104	40	32
Blood.	98	37	29
	95	35	28
	86	30	24
	77	25	20
Summer	76	24	19
	68	20	16
	59	15	12
Temperate	55	13	10
	50	10	8
	41	5	4
	39	4	3
	37	3	2
	35	2	1
	33	1	0·8
Freezing	32	0	0·0
	23	5	·4
	14	·10	·8
	5	·15	·2

To convert
Cent. into Fahr. multiply by 9, divide by 5, and add 32.
Réaum into Fahr. multiply by 9, divide by 4 & add 32.
Fahr. into Cent. deduct 32, multiply by 5, divide by 9.
Fahr. into Réaum, deduct 32 multiply by 4, divide by 9.
Cent. into Réaum, multiply by 4, divide by 5.
Réaum into Cent., multiply by 5, divide by 4.

GOLF.

The following is a list of the principal Links:—

Algeria.—Algiers (Mustapha Superieur) (9).

Belgium.—Antwerp (Capellen (18), Brussels (Tervueren) (18), Brussels (Waterloo) (18 and 9), Ghent (Les Buttes Blanches) (18), Hainaut (nr. Mons) (9), Knocke (3 courses of 18 holes), Lombartzijde and Westende (18), Ostend (Coq-sur-Mer) (18), Spa (18).

Bulgaria.—Sofia (9).

Canary Islands.—Las Palmas (9).

Corsica.—Lozari (4 miles from Ile Rousse) (18).

Cyprus.—Nicosia (9).

Denmark.—Copenhagen (Springforbi) (18), Elsinore (9), Esbjerg (9), Fanö (Esbjerg) (9), Odense (9).

Egypt and Sudan.—Alexandria* (18), Assuan† (9), Cairo (Gezira Sporting Club)* (18), Mena House* (Jan.-Aug.) (9), Heliopolis† (18), Helouan† (18), Maadi† (18), Port Said† (18), Port Sudan† (9), Suez† (9), Khartoum† (9 and 9). Haifa† (9). * Laid on grass. † Laid on the desert.

France.—Aix-les-Bains (18), Aix en Provence (in preparation), Amiens (Allonville (18), Antibes-Juan les Pins (9 and 9 in preparation), Arcachon (Gironde) (9) (18 in preparation, Argeles Gazost (18), Avignon (9),Bagnoles-de-l'Orne (9),Beauvallon (9),to be extended to 18,Biarritz (18, ladies 9),Biarritz (Chiberta) (18), Brides-les-Bains (9), Bordeaux (18), Boulogne s/Mer (Wimereaux) (18), Cannes (Mandelieu (18 and 9), Cannes (Country Private Club) (18), Carcassonne (18) in preparation, Chamonix (18), Chantilly (36), Chevreuse (18) in preparation, Chateauneuf de Grasse (AM) (in preparation), Combloux (6), Compiegne (18), Coutainville (9), Dampierre s/le Doubs (9), Dax (in preparation), Deauville (18), New Deauville (18), Dieppe (18 and 9), Dinard (St. Briac) (18), Dives-Houlgate (18), Divonne (18), Elisabethville (Paris) (18), Etretat (18), Evian-les-Bains (18), Fontainebleau (18), Font Romeu (9), Fourqueux (36), Granville (18), Hardelot (18), Harve (18), Hendaye (18), Hossegor (18), Hyeres (18), Hyeres (Costabelle) (18), La Baule-le Pouliguen (18), La Bourboule (9, and 9 in preparation), Lamorlaye (18), Le Mans (9), Le Puy (9), Le Touquet (18), (9), Luchon (9), Lyons (18), Lys-Chantilly (18), Marly (18), Marseilles (Les Milles) (12), Monte Carlo (Mont-Agel) (18), Mont Dore (9), Megeve (9), Mentone (Sospel) (18), Morfontaine (18), Nantes (Noelles) (9), Nice (Cagnes) (18), Montbeliard (9), Nancy (9), Ormesson (S. and O.) (18), Ozoir-la-Ferriere (30), Paris (La Boulie, Versailles) (18 and 9), Pau (18, and ladies 9), Nouveau-Pau (18), Pen Guen (St. Cast) (18), Pornic (9), Pougues les Eaux (9), Rheims (9), Rouen (18), Royan (18), Royat (9), Sables d'Or-les-Pins (18), St. Jean de Luz (La Nivelle) (18), St. Jean de Luz (Ste. Barbe (9), St. Jean de Luz (Chantaco) (18), St. Cloud (18).(18), St. Germain en Laye (18), (9), St. Honoré les Bains (9), Salies-de-Béarn (9), Sart (Flers Breucq) (18), Saumur (9), Selestat (9), Strasbourg (9), Superbagueres (9), Tours (9), Thorene (18), Uriage-les-Bains (9), Valenciennes (Nord) (9),Valescure St. Raphael (18),Vichy (18),Vittel (18),Villard-de-Lans (9) in preparation.

Germany.—Aachen (9), Aschau (near Bad Ischl, Salzkammergut) (9), Baden-Baden (18), Bad Eilsen (9), Bad Nauheim (9), Bad Reichenhall (Hotel Axelmann, Stein) (9), Bad Saizbrunn (18), Berlin-Nedlitz (18), Berlin (Wannsee) (18), Berlin (Westend) (9), Bremen (9), Breslau (9), Brunswick (9), Chemnitz Plaune-Flöha (18), Cologne (18), Constance (9), Crefeld (15), Darmstadt (9), Dellach am Woerthersee (9), Dresden (9), Ems (18), Feldafing (Upper Bavaria) (9), Frankfort a/M. (18), Freudenstadt (9), Hamburg (Gross-Flottbek) (9), Hamburg (Reinbeck) (9), Hamburg (Falkenstein) (18), Hanover (9), Heiligendamm (9), Homburg v.d. Hohe (11), Igls (near Innsbruck) (9), Karlsbad (9), Kiel (Kitzeberg) (9), Kissingen (9), Leipzig (Gaschwitz) (9), Madgeburg (9), Mannheim (9), Marienbad (18), Merseburg-Leuna (9), Munich (9), Munster (6), Norderney (9), Oberhof i Th. (9), Partenkirchen (9), Pertisau am Achensee (9), Rostock (9), Saarow (Berlin-Scharmutzelsee (9), Salzbrunn Sch. (18), Schwalbach (9), Semmering (9), Stuttgart (9), Travemuende (18), Vienna (Krieau) (18), Vienna (Lainz) (18), Villingen (9), Wiesbaden (9), Wildungen (9), Wuppertal (9).

Greece.—Athens (Gleefada), 30 minutes by car (9).

Holland.—Amsterdam (Duivendrecht) (18), Arnheim (9), Breda (9), Domburg (9), Deventer (9), Eindhoven (18), Enschedé (9), The Hague (18), Hattem (9), Hertogenbosch (9), Hilversum (18), Huister Heide (near Utrecht) (18), Hummelo (9), Noordwijk (18), Rockanje (18), Rotterdam (9), Zandvoort (18).

Hungary.—Budapest (Szechenyi Hill) (18), Balantonfoeldvar (near Lake Balaton) (9).

Iraq, Baghdad.—Royal Golf Course (9), two miles ; Railway Golf Course (9), 1½ miles.

Italy.—Abbazia-Laurana (9), Bordighera)9), (Nov.-April), Brioni Islands (18), Cadenabbia and Menaggio (18) (Mar. 15-Nov. 15), Carezza (Karersee) (June-Sept.) (18), Clavieres (9) (Aug.-Sept.), Florence (Ugolino) (Sept. 15-June 15) (18), Gardone Riviera (9) (Sept.-June), Lido (Venice) (9), Madonna di Campiglio (9) (June-Sept.), Mendola (9) (June-Oct.), Merano (9), Milan (Monza) (May-Sept.) (9), Palmero (Mondello) (Nov.-April) (9), Pallanza (18), Rapallo (9), Rhodes (Ægean Islands) (9), Rome (Acquasanta) (Nov.-May) (18), San Remo (Oct. 15-May 15) (18), Stresa (9) (April-Oct.), Turin (9), (Mar.-Sept.), Varese (9), Villa d'Este (18) (Mar. to Nov.).

Malta.—Marsa (Nov.-April) (18). *Morocco.*—Fedhala (9), Tangier (9).

Norway.—Oslo (Bogstad) (18). *Poland.*—Warsaw (Siekierki) (9), Powsin (County Club) (9).

Portugal.—Estoril (18), Espinho (near Oporto) (18), Lisbon (Ajudo) (9), Vidago (9).

Rhodes Island.—Bodi (9). *Roumania.*—Bucarest (Baneasa) (18), Constanza (9) in construction, Sinaia (9). *Syria.*—No golf courses.

Slovakia.—Piestany (9), Starv Smokovec (9).

Spain.—Algecircas (The Rodes) (9), 20 minutes from Hotel Reina Cristina (open to Hotel visitors only), Barcelona (Pedralbes) (9), Bilbao (Neguri) (-), and San Ougat del Valles (18), Comillas (Santander) Oyambre) (9), Gibraltar (Campamento) (9), Madrid (Puertade Hierro) (18), Malaga (Torremolinos) (9), San Sebastian (Lasarte) (9), Santander (Pedreña) (27), Seville (Tablada) (9), Sitges (9), Zarauz (Guipuzcoa (9), Balearic Islands (Puerto Alcudia) (9).

Sweden.—Links at Bastad (18), Djursholm (18), Falsterbo (18), Gothenburg (Hofas) (18), Halmstad (18), Halsingborg (Viken) (9), Kristianstad (18), Lidingö (18), Malmö (9), Saltsjöbaden (9), Stockholm (Kevinge) (18), Ystad (9).

Switzerland.—Aigle (Montreux Territet, Caux) (9), Axenfels-Brunnen (9), Axenstein (9), Bale (9), Berne (Gurten (9), Burgenstock (9), Crans sur Sierre (18), Flims-Waldhaus (9), Geneva (18), Gstaad (9) (July, August and September), Interlaken (Einigen-Thun) (9), Lausanne (18), Les Rasses-Ste-Crois (9), Locarno (Ascono) (9), Lucerne (Dietschberg) (18), Lugano (Magliaso) (9), Maloja (9), Montana S'Sierre see *Crans*, Neuchatel (9), Ragaz (9) (April 15 to October 15), Samaden (for CelereinaPontresina) (18), St. Moritz-Spa (San Gian) (9), St. Moritz (Kulm Hotels) (9), Schinznach (9), Thun (9), Villars-sur-Bex (9), Vulpera-Tarasp (9) (July 1 to September 20), Zurich Dolder (9), Zurich (Waltikon) (18).

Tunisia.—La Soukra (Tunis, 15 minutes trams) (9).

Turkey.—Istanbul (Mashlak) (18).

This table has been specially revised by Prof. W. W. Campbell, Director, Lick Observatory, California.

TIME.—Variation of Time in different Countries. The following COMPARATIVE TIME TABLE will be found useful:—

Trains in Great Britain, France, Belgium, Luxembourg and Spain run on Greenwich (West European) time; in Switzerland, Italy, Denmark, Norway, Sweden, Germany and Jugoslavia, on Mid-European time (one hour fast of Greenwich); in Holland, Amsterdam time (20 minutes fast of Greenwich); in Roumania, Bulgaria, Egypt, and part of Turkey, on East European time (two hours faster than Greenwich); in Eastern States of U.S.A. on Eastern standard time (five hours slower than Greenwich), and in Western States on Pacific standard time (eight hours slower than Greenwich).

WHEN IT IS 12 0 AT	Meantime of	IT IS THE FOLLOWING LOCAL TIME AT																										
		Amsterdam	Athens	Auckland	Berlin	Berne	Brussels	Budapest	Cairo	Cologne	Copenhagen	East European time	Greenwich	Jerusalem	Madras	Melbourne	Mid-European time	Munich	New York	Oslo	Ottawa	Paris	Rome	Petrograd	Stockholm	Sydney	Trieste	Vienna
Amsterdam ..	..	12 0	1315	2320	1234	1210	1140	1257	1346	12 8	1231	1340	1140	14 1	17 1	2120	1240	1227	6 45	1223	6 38	1150	1230	1342	1253	2145	1236	1246
Athens	Greece ..	1045	12 0	..	1119	1055	1043	1141	1230	1053	1115	1225	1025	1246	1546	20 5	1125	1112	5 29	11 8	..	1034	1115	1226	1137	2029	1120	1130
Auckland	N. Zeal'd	..	1 56	12 0	..	..	..	..	..	..	..	2 21	0 21	..	..	1130	1 21	..	..	..	..	..	..	..	..	..	..	..
Berlin	..	1126	1241	..	12 0	1136	1124	1223	..	1134	1157	13 6	11 6	..	..	..	12 6	1153	6 11	..	..	1116	1156	13 8	1219	..	12 1	1212
Berne.......	..	1150	13 5	..	1224	12 0	1148	1246	..	1158	1221	1330	1130	..	..	..	1230	1217	6 35	..	..	1140	1220	1331	1242	..	1225	1236
Brussels......	..	1220	1317	..	1236	1212	12 0	1259	..	1210	1233	1343	1143	..	..	..	1243	1229	6 47	..	..	1152	1235	1344	1255	..	1238	1248
Cairo	Egypt ..	1014	1130	2134	1048	1025	1012	1111	12 0	1023	1045	1155	9 55	1216	1516	1935	1055	1041	4 59	1038	4 52	10 4	1045	1156	11 7	20 0	1050	11 0
Cologne......	Rhine ..	1152	13 7	..	1226	12 2	1150	1248	..	12 0	1222	1332	1132	..	..	..	1232	1219	6 36	..	..	1142	1222	1333	1244	..	1227	1238
Copenhagen ..	..	1129	1245	..	12 3	1139	1127	1226	..	1138	12 0	1310	1110	..	..	..	1210	1156	6 14	..	..	1119	12 0	1311	1222	..	12 5	1215
Dublin	Ireland ..	1245	14 0	..	..	..	..	..	..	..	..	1425	1225	..	..	..	1325	..	..	..	..	..	..	..	..	..	..	..
East European time	see above	1020	1135	2139	1054	1030	1017	1116	12 5	1028	1050	..	10 0	1221	1521	1940	11 0	1046	5 4	1043	4 57	10 9	1050	12 1	1112	20 5	1055	11 6
Jerusalem	Palestine	9 59	1114	2118	1033	10 9	9 57	1055	1144	10 7	1029	1139	9 39	12 0	15 0	1919	1039	1026	4 43	1022	4 37	9 48	1029	1140	1051	1944	1034	1045
Lisbon	Portugal	1256	1412	..	1330	13 6	1254	1353	..	13 5	1327	1437	1237	..	..	..	1337	1323	7 41	..	..	1246	1327	1438	1349	..	1332	1342
Greenwich ..	England	1220	1335	2339	1254	1230	1217	1316	14 5	1228	1250	14 0	12 0	1421	1721	22 0	13 0	1246	7 4	1243	6 57	12 9	1250	14 1	1312	22 5	1255	13 6
Istanbul	..	1024	1139	..	1058	1034	1022	1120	..	1032	1054	12 4	10 4	..	..	..	11 4	1051	5 8	..	..	1013	1054	12 5	1116	..	1059	1110
Madras	India	..	..	..	..	..	..	..	..	..	..	8 39	6 39	..	12 0	..	7 39	..	..	..	..	..	..	..	..	..	..	..
Madrid	..	1234	..	..	13 8	1245	1232	1331	..	1243	13 5	1415	1215	..	..	..	1315	13 1	7 19	..	..	1224	13 5	1416	1327	..	1310	1320
Melbourne ..	Victoria ..	..	..	..	..	..	..	..	..	..	..	4 20	2 20	..	..	12 0	3 20	..	..	..	..	..	..	..	..	..	..	..
Mid-European time	see above	1120	1235	2239	1154	1130	1117	1216	13 5	1128	1150	13 0	11 0	1321	1621	2040	12 0	1146	6 4	1143	5 57	11 9	1150	13 1	1212	21 5	1155	12 6
Moscow	..	9 49	..	..	1023	9 59	9 47	1046	..	9 58	1020	1030	9 30	..	..	..	1030	1016	4 34	..	..	9 39	1020	1131	1042	..	1025	1035
Munich	..	1133	..	..	12 7	1443	1131	1230	..	1141	12 4	1314	1114	..	..	..	1214	12 0	6 18	..	..	1123	12 4	1315	1226	..	12 9	1219
New York ..	U. States	5 16	..	..	1749	1726	1713	1812	..	1724	1746	1856	1656	..	..	..	1756	1742	12 0	..	..	17 5	1746	1857	18 8	..	1751	18 1
Oslo	Norway ..	..	1252	..	..	..	..	..	..	..	..	1317	1117	..	..	..	1217	..	..	12 0	..	..	..	..	..	..	..	..
Ottawa	Canada ..	..	..	..	..	..	..	..	..	..	..	19 3	17 3	..	..	..	18 3	..	..	..	12 0	..	..	..	..	..	..	..
Paris	France ..	1210	..	..	1244	1220	12 8	13 7	..	1219	1241	1351	1151	..	..	..	1251	1237	6 55	..	..	12 0	1241	1352	13 3	..	1246	1256
Petrograd	Russia ..	1018	..	..	1052	1029	1016	1115	..	1027	1049	1159	9 59	..	..	..	1059	1045	5 3	..	..	10 8	1049	12 0	1112	..	1054	11 4
Rome........	..	1130	..	..	12 4	1140	1128	1226	..	1138	12 0	1310	1110	..	..	..	1210	1157	6 14	..	..	1119	12 0	1311	1222	..	12 5	1216
S. Francisco ..	California	2029	2145	1949	21 3	2039	2027	2126	2215	2038	21 0	2210	2010	2231	1 31	5 50	2110	2056	1514	2053	15 7	2019	21 0	2211	2122	6 15	21 5	2115
Stockholm ..	..	11 7	..	..	1141	1118	11 5	12 4	..	1116	1138	1248	1048	..	..	..	1148	1134	5 52	..	..	1057	1138	1249	12 0	..	1143	1153
Sydney	N.S.W. ..	..	..	..	..	..	..	..	..	..	..	3 55	1 55	..	..	10 0	2 55	..	..	..	..	..	..	..	..	12 0	..	..
Vienna	..	1114	1230	2234	1148	1124	1112	1211	13 0	1122	1145	1255	1055	1315	1615	2034	1155	1141	5 59	1137	5 52	11 4	1144	1256	12 7	2059	1150	12 0

SECTION II.

CONTINENTAL TIME TABLES

WITH PRACTICAL INFORMATION

ON

Through Routes, Special Accommodation, Sleeping Cars, Trains de Luxe, Private Cabins on Channel Steamers, etc.

CONTENTS.

	PAGE
THROUGH ROUTES FROM LONDON	62 to 64
GENERAL CONTINENTAL ROUTES	65 „ 74
SPECIAL ACCOMMODATION ON TRAINS	75 „ 76
SLEEPING CARS	
LITS-SALONS	
COUCHETTES	
RESTAURANT AND DINING CARS	
TRAINS DE LUXE AND PULLMAN TRAINS	
PRIVATE CABINS ON CHANNEL STEAMERS	77 „ 78
EXPLANATIONS OF THE TABLES	87
TIME TABLES	88 „ 343
AIR SERVICES	138 „ 148

THROUGH ROUTES FROM LONDON

ALPHABETICALLY ARRANGED.

(NOTE.—Page numbers from 79 to 85 and 111 to 132 refer to tables showing the through services; numbers above 132 refer to tables showing full particulars of each section of the route.)

Figures in italics and brackets show the minimum time occupied *in hours* unless otherwise specified: these times are by rail and steamer; by air the journeys would be quicker.

To AJACCIO	*(40h.)*	via Marseilles or Nice, thence by steamer of Fraissinet Co.	376
To ALEXANDRIA (Egypt)	*(5d.)*	via Marseilles (see Marseilles), thence to Alexandria by M.M.	388
Do.	*(6d.)*	via Marseilles (see Marseilles), thence Pharaonic Mail Line	386
Do.	*(4d.)*	via Brindisi (see Brindisi) thence by Adriatica	371A
Do.	*(5d.)*	via Genoa, thence by Adriatica Co's. Express steamer	371A
Do.	*(5d.)*	via Naples, thence by Adriatica Co.'s Express Steamer	371A
Do.	*(5d.)*	via Genoa, thence by Misr Line.	387
To ALGIERS	*(44h.)*	via Marseilles (see Marseilles), thence Transatlantique	394
Do.	*(44h.)*	via Port Vendres, thence by Cie Nav. Mixte	391
To AMSTERDAM ..	*(11¼h.)*	via Harwich, Flushing, 129, or 155 to	158
(Holland)	*(11½h.)*	via Harwich, Hook of Holland	131, 158
To ATHENS (Greece) ..	*(72½h.)*	via Brindisi (see Brindisi), thence by Adriatica to Piræus)	371B
Do.	*(68½h.)*	via Calais, Paris, Simplon, Belgrade and Nisch, Simplon-Orient Express ..	85
Do. ..	*(3d. 16½h.)*	via Brindisi (see Brindisi), thence to Piræus by Hellenic Line	378
Do.	*(5d.)*	via Marseilles and M.M. Steamer ..	388
To BAGHDAD	*(6d. 17h.)*	via Simplon-Orient and Taurus Exp. 83,	334
To BALE (Switzerland) ..	*(15h.)*	via Calais or Boulogne, Paris 125, 268,	269
Do.	*(18½h.)*	via Newhaven, Dieppe to Paris, page 111, thence	268
Do.	*(12½h.)*	via Calais (Boulogne), Laon 123 or 237,	270
Do.	*(19h.)*	via Dover, Ostend and Brussels, p. 127, on from Brussels	149, 179
Do.	*(18h.)*	via Dover, Dunkerque, Lille ..	137
Do.	*(23h.)*	via Flushing, Cologne	129
Do.	*(21h.)*	via Hook of Holland, Cologne ..	131
To BALEARIC ISLDS.	( )	via Barcelona, thence Trasmediterranea S.S. Co.	399
To BARCELONA (Spain)	( )	via Paris, Toulouse, Pt. Bou 117, 249,	252
To BERLIN	*(18½h.)*	via Calais and Nord Exp.	81
Do.	*(18½h.)*	via Ostend, Brussels, Cologne (luxe)	128
Do.	*(21½h.)*	via Harwich, Flushing 130, 155, 159,	163
Do.	*(20h.)*	via Harwich, Hook of Holland, 132, 159,	163
To BORDEAUX (France)	*(14¾h.)*	via Paris, 115, or to Paris, 111, 112 or 137 thence	246, 248
Do.	*(21h.)*	via Dieppe Le Mans	111

To **BRINDISI** (Italy) ..	(*42h.*)	via Paris, Simplon, 119, 111, 112, or 137, 269,	280, 313
Do.	(*45h.*)	via Paris, Mt. Cenis, Turin, 118 or 265, 298,	301, 310, 313
Do.	(*39½h.*)	via Calais or Boulogne, Laon, Bale, St. Gothard to Milan, p. 123, thence pp.	287, 313
To **BRUSSELS** (Belgium)	(*6½h.*)	via Dover, Calais, Lille ..	127, 149, 236
Do.	(*7h.*)	via Dover, Ostend ..	127, 128 or 150
Do.	(*12¾h.*)	via Harwich-Antwerp	131, 153
Do.	(*12½h.*)	via Harwich, Zeebrugge ..	131, 153
Do.	(*12½h.*)	via Dover, Dunkerque, Lille	137
To **BUCHAREST** (R'mania)	(*55¾h.*)	via Trieste and train de luxe ..	83
Do.	(*50½h.*)	via Nord Exp. to Berlin, thence Cracow	81, 204
Do.	(*46½h.*)	via Strasbourg and train de luxe ..	84
Do.	(*46½h.*)	via Ostend, Vienna and Budapest (luxe)	84
To **BUDAPEST** (Hungary)	(*30¼h.*)	see routes to Vienna, thence ..	200
To **COLOGNE** (Prussia)	(*11½h.*)	via Dover, Calais	81, 128, or 112, 149, 151
Do.	(*11¾h.*)	via Dover, Ostend ..	80, 128, or 150, 151
Do.	(*13h.*)	via Harwich, Flushing	129 or 155, 157
Do.	(*14¾h.*)	via Harwich, Hook of Holland,	131 or 156, 157
Do.	(*20¾h.*)	via Harwich, Antwerp, Brussels ..	131, 151
To **COPENHAGEN** (Denmark)	(*29½h.*)	via Calais or Ostend to Hamburg, p. 81, thence .. .. pages	162, 204, 216
Do.	(*32h.*)	via Harwich, Flushing	130, 216
Do.	(*34½h.*)	via Hook of Holland	132 or 162, 216
Do.	(*31¾h.*)	via Harwich and Esbjerg ..	136, 214
To **DRESDEN** (Saxony)	(*23¼h.*)	via Calais or Ostend to Cologne, p. 128; thence .. .. pages	163, 168
Do.	(*23½h.*)	via Harwich, Flushing	130, or 155, 159, 168
Do.	(*23¼h.*)	via Hook of Holland	132 or 159, 168
To **GENEVA** (Switzerland)	(*18¼h.*)	via Paris	121 or 266
To **GIBRALTAR** ..	( )	via Paris, Madrid, Cordova,	115, 248, 250, 321, 324, 325
Do.	(*4d.*)	via Peninsular and Oriental Steamer	366
Do.	(*4d.*)	via Orient Line	365
To **HAMBURG** (Germany)	(*18h.*)	via Calais (or Ostend), Cologne (luxe),	81, 128, 161
Do.	(*20¼h.*)	via Harwich, Flushing	130 or 155, 161
Do.	(*19⅛h.*)	via Harwich, Hook of Holland,	132 or 159, 161
To **INTERLAKEN** ..	(*17½h.*)	via Boulogne, Laon, Delle,	123, 268, 270, 281
To **IRKUTSK** (Siberia) ..	(*7d. 8½h.*)	via Warsaw, Moscow, thence Omsk,	132, 232
To **ISTANBUL**	(*65½h.*)	via Calais, Paris and train de luxe	83, 332
Do.	(*65½h.*)	via Ostend, Vien'a, Budap't (luxe)	84, 123, 200
Do.	(*8d.*)	via Marseilles (see Mars'les) & M.M. Str.	388
Do.	(*7d.*)	via Trieste (see Trieste) and Adriatica Str.	371B
To **LISBON** (Portugal) ..	(*50h.*)	via Salamanca, 85, or to Paris, 111, 112 or 137, thence	248, 250, 321
Do.	( )	via Madrid (see Madrid), thence ..	325
To **MADRID** (Spain) ..	( )	via Dover, Dunkerque, Paris, 85 or 137,	248, 250, 321
Do.	( )	via Dieppe to Paris, 111 or 241, thence	248, 250, 321
To **MALTA**	(*58h.*)	Calais, Paris, Rome	343
Do.	(*75h.*)	by Marseilles and Pharaonic Mail Line	343

THROUGH ROUTES FROM LONDON—continued.

To MARSEILLES (France)	(26h.)	via Calais or Boulogne, Paris 82, 113, 259
Do.	(21h.)	via Dieppe, Paris 111, 259
To MILAN (Italy) ..	(23¾h.)	via Mt. Cenis 118, or to Paris 111, 112 or 137, thence 265, 298
Do.	(24½h.)	via Paris, Bale, St. Gothard, 111, 112, or 125, 137 and 270, or 268, 287
Do.	(22h.)	via Paris, Lausanne, Simplon (luxe), 83 119
Do.	(20½h.)	via Calais or Boulogne, Laon .. 123 or 237, 270, 287
Do.	(27h.)	via Ostend, Luxemburg to Bale 127 or 149, 287
To MOSCOW	(50¼h.)	via Calais or Ostend, Berlin, Warsaw (luxe) 81, 205, 227
Do.	(63h.)	via Harwich, Hook, Berlin 132, 205, 208, 227
To MUNICH (Bavaria) ..	(22h.)	via Ostend, Cologne, Nuremberg, 128, 150, 175, 176, 188
Do.	(22½h.)	via Flushing to Cologne .. } 129 or 132,
Do.	(24h.)	via Hook to Cologne .. } 175, 176, 188
Do.	(18½h.)	via Calais and Strasbourg (luxe service) 84
To NAPLES (Italy) ..	(34¼h.)	see routes to Rome, thence .. 310
To OSLO (Norway ..	(42¼h.)	via Newcastle and Bergen 403, 219
Do.	(42¾h.)	via direct steamer Fred Olsen Line .. 405
To PARIS (France) ..	(6½h.)	via Dover, Calais, or Folkestone, Boulogne, 112, 237
Do.	(7¾h.)	via Newhaven, Dieppe .. 111, 241
Do.	(12¾h.)	via Southampton, Havre .. 111, 242
Do.	(11h.)	via Dover, Dunkerque 137
To PRAGUE .. .. (Bohemia)	(25h.)	via Calais, Chalons & Strasbourg (luxe), 84, 272 to 274
To ROME (Italy) ..	(29½h.)	via Calais, Paris, Mt. Cenis 82, 265, 301
Do.	(29¾h.)	via Calais or B'logne, Lausanne, Simplon 119
Do.	(29¾h.)	via Paris, Bale, Milan .. 111, 112, or 137, 268, 270, 301, &c.
Do.	(27¼h.)	via Laon, Bale, Milan 123, 270, 303
Do.	(33¾h.)	via Luxemburg, Bale, Milan 117, 287, 303
To STOCKHOLM (Sweden)	(56¼h.)	via Bergen and Oslo .. 403, 218, 219
Do.	(46¾h.)	via Svenska Lloyd Steamer from London or Newcastle, 408 ; to Gothenburg and thence by rail 217
Do.	(39¼h.)	via Harwich, Esbjerg .. 136, 217
Do.	(43½h.)	via Harwich, Hook, Berlin, Sassnitz, Trälleborg 132, 204, 217
To STUTTGART (Wurt.)	(15½h.)	via Paris .. 84, 111, 112, or 137, 273
Do.	(21¾h.)	via Cologne, 128 129 or 131 thence 182, 184
To TEHERAN	(7d. 5h.)	via Simplon-Orient and Taurus Exp., 83, 334
Do.	( )	via Berlin, Shepetovka Baku, 231, 233
To TRIESTE (Italy) ..	(28¼h.)	via Calais, Paris, Milan (tr. luxe) 83, 119, 305
To VENICE (Italy) ..	(25¾h.)	via Paris, Milan (tr. luxe) .. 83, 119, 305
To VIENNA (Germany) ..	(25¼h.)	via Cologne .. 84 or 128, 150, 188, 330
Do.	(25¼h.)	via Calais and trains de luxe 84, 128, 330
To WARSAW (Poland)	(26½h.)	via Calais or Ostend, Berlin and train de luxe, 81, 128
To ZURICH Switzerland)	(15½h.)	via Calais, Laon, Bale .. 123, 283
Do.	(18¾h.)	via Calais, Paris, Bale .. 125, 283
Do.	(23h.)	via Brussels, Luxemburg, 127 or 149, 150, 283

GENERAL CONTINENTAL ROUTES.

(For Deep Sea Steamship Services see pages 345 to 481).

PAGE

Aachen, Cologne 151
Aachen, Elberfeld, Cassel, Bebra .. 165
Aachen, Magdeburg, Berlin .. 166
Aachen, Liege (Antwerp), Brussels 152
Adrianople, Edirne, Istanbul, &c. .. 333
Agen, Perigueux, Limoges, Paris .. 249
Agen, Tarbes 252
Air Services .. .. 138 to 148
Aix-les-Bains, Annecy (Geneva), Chamonix-Mt. Blanc 267
Alexandria, Cairo 338
Algeciras (Gibraltar), Bobadilla, &c 325
Algerian, Moroccan and Tunisian Railways .. .. .. 340 to 342B
Alicante, Alcazar, Madrid 323
Alpnach, Vitznau, Lucerne (Stmrs.) 293
Alpine Routes (Diligences) .. 295 to 297
Altona (see Hamburg)
Amiens, Boulogne, Calais, London 237
Amiens, Lille, Valenciennes (Calais) 238
Amiens, Laon (Reims) 237
Amiens, Paris 237, 238
Amiens, Rouen (Havre) 242
Amsterdam, Arnhem, Emmerich, Cologne 157
Amsterdam, Boxtel, Venlo, Cologne 157
Amsterd'm, Nymegen, Cleves, Cologne 156
Amsterdam, Rosendaal, &c. .. 154
Amsterdam, Salzbergen (Osnabruck, Hamburg, Berlin) 159
Amsterdam, The Hague, Rotterdam 158
Amsterdam, Maastricht, Liége .. 158
Amsterdam—Through Services :—
England via Flushing 129
England via Hook of Holland .. 131
England Air Service 139
Belgium and Paris 154
Germany via Cleves 156
Germany via Emmerich or Venlo 157
Germany via Salzbergen.. .. 159
Switzerland and Italy 178
Ancona, Foligno, Rome 312
Angers, Le Mans (Paris) 247
Annecy Lake Steamers 275
Antwerp, Brussels (Paris) .. 154
Antwerp, Ghent (Ostend) .. 150
Antwerp, Gladbach 153
Antwerp, Herenthals, M. Gladbach 153
Antwerp, Rosendaal, Rotterdam (Amsterdam) 154

PAGE

Antwerp, Liége, Aix, Cologne .. 151
Antwerp—Through Services :—
England via Harwich 131
England via Flushing 130
England via Ostend 150
Holland via Esschen 154
Aosta, Chivasso, Turin 300
Arcachon, Bordeaux 247
Arlberg Route .. 123, 197, 269, 286
Arnhem, Breda, 156 ; Zwolle, Hengelo, &c. 159
Arona, Milan ; Arona, Novara .. 302
Arth-Rigi Railway 289
Arth, Zug (Steamer) 294
Aschaffenburg, Mayence, Cologne 177
Aschaffenburg, Wurzburg, Munich 188
Astrakhan,Nishni-Novgorod(St'mers) 233
Athens, Corinth, Patras 336
Athens, Laurium (for Cape Sunium) 336
Attnang, Ischl, Stainach-Irdning .. 196
Augsburg, Nuremberg 187
Avranches, Lison (Caen) 245
Ayasoulouk (Ephesus), Izmir .. 333
Baden-Baden, Bale & Heidelberg 182, 183
Baghdad via Simplon and Taurus Express 83, 334
Baku, Tiflis, Batumi ; Baku, Rostov 231
Bale, Appenweier (Strasbourg),Baden, Carlsruhe, Heidelberg (Mannheim, Mainz), Frankfort 183
Bale, Colmar, Strasbourg, Neustadt, Mainz, Frankfort 181
Bale, Delle (or Mulhouse), Belfort, Chaumont, Troyes, Paris.. .. 268
Bale, Neuchatel, Lausanne, Geneva 278
Bale (via Berne), Lausanne, Geneva 279
Bale, Olten, Lucerne 282
Bale, Olten, Berne, Thun, Interlaken 281
Bale, Schaffhausen, Constance and Winterthur 284
Bale, Schaffhausen, Constance and Lindau 180
Bale, Zurich (Coire, &c.) .. 283, 286
Bale—Through Services :—
England via Laon or Paris 124, 126
England via Luxemburg.. .. 127
England via Flushing 129
England via Hook of Holland .. 131
England via Dunkerque .. 137
England—Air Service 138
Belgium via Luxemburg.. .. 149

Bale—Through Services :—
Cologne, 178 ; Berlin, &c. .. 174
Innsbruck Vienna, &c. (Arlberg) 197, 269
Italy via St. Gothard .. 270, 287
Barcelona, Paris .. 114, 117, 251, 255
Barcelona, Port Bou (Narbonne), 255, 326
Barcelona, Tarragona, Saragossa, Madrid 326
Bari, Taranto, Reggio 311
Basra via Baghdad 83, 334
Batumi, Tiflis, Baku 231
Bavarian Motor Services .. 212, 213
Bayonne, Irun ; Bordeaux, Paris 250
Bayonne, Pau, Toulouse (Paris) .. 251
Belgian Railways .. 37 to 42, &c.
Belgrade, Zagreb, Vienna 200
Belgrade, Bucharest 330
Belgrade, Nisch, Sofia, Istanbul .. 332
Bellegarde, Annemasse, Bouveret .. 265
Bellegarde, Culoz (Lyons), Macon (Paris) 266
Bergen, Voss, Oslo 219
Berlin, Bremen .. .. 164 or 169
Berlin, Breslau (Oderberg, Vienna), Cracow, Lemberg, Bucharest .. 204
Berlin, Cassel and Frankfort :—
Via Erfurt, Eisenach 173
Via Nordhausen, Eichenberg .. 171
Via Kreiensen, Gottingen .. 170
Berlin (Danzig), Eydtkuhnen .. 205
Berlin, Dresden, Praha, Vienna .. 195
Berlin, Leipsic 172
Berlin, Hamburg 169
Berlin, Hanover, Cologne 164
Berlin, Kreiensen, Soest, Elberfeld, Cologne, Aix-la-Chapelle 166
Berlin, Magdeburg 168
Berlin, Bentschen, Warsaw, Moscow 205, 226
Berlin, Stettin, Danzig 205
Berlin, Memel, Libau 208
Berlin, Riga, Reval 208
Berlin, Stralsund (Stockholm) 204, 215A
Berlin, Warnemunde, Copenhagen 204, 214
Berlin—Through Services :—
England via Flushing 130
England via Hook of Holland .. 132
England via Ostend or Calais .. 128
England—Air Service 140
Holland via Salzbergen .. 159, 163
Munich, Italy, &c. 193
Stuttgart, Italy, &c. 185
Bale, Interlaken, Lucerne, Italy, &c. 174
Bohemia, Moravia, &c. via Dresden 195
Lithuania, Latvia and Estonia .. 208
Scandinavia .. 204, 215A, 216
Poland .. 204, 205, 226, 227
Berne, Aarau, Zurich, Rorschach, &c. 282
Berne, Bienne, Chaux-de-Fonds .. 278
Berne, Lausanne, Geneva 279
Berne, Langnau, Lucerne 279
Berne, Neuchatel, Pontarlier (Paris) 267, 279
Berne, Olten, Bale 281
Berne, Thun, Interlaken, &c. .. 281
Berne, Loetschberg, Brigue .. 288
Bernhardin Pass 295
Bernina Railway 289
Beyrout, Damascus (Aleppo) .. 335
Bilbao and Irun, Saragossa, &c. .. 322
Bingen, Mainz, Frankfort, Darmstadt 176
Bingerbruck, Metz (Nancy, Paris) 179, 275
Bingerbruck, Coblence, Cologne, Bonn 177
Black Forest Lines 180, 184
Bologna, Ancona, Foggia, Brindisi 313
Bologna, Alessandria, Turin .. 303
Bologna, Florence, Rome (Naples) .. 303
Bologna, Modena (Verona), Milan .. 303
Bologna, Venice, Tarvisio (Vienna) 308
Bordeaux, Arcachon 253
Bordeaux, Biarritz, Irun (Madrid) 250
Bordeaux, Niort, Portiers, Paris .. 246
Bordeaux, Rennes, St. Malo .. 135
Bordeaux, Rochefort, La Rochelle, Nantes 246
Bordeaux, Tours, Orleans, Paris .. 248
Bordeaux, Toulouse, Narbonne (Sète, Marseilles) 252
Bordeaux, Limoges, Montlucon (Moulins), Gannat (Lyons) .. 250
Bordeaux, Narbonne, Barcelona 252, 255
Boulogne, Calais and Amiens, Paris 237
Boulogne, Folkestone and London .. 112
Bouveret, Evian, Geneva, Bellegarde 265
Breda, Bosch, Arnhem, &c. .. 155
Bregenz, Feldkirch, Lindau, &c. .. 197
Bregenz, St. Margrethen, Const'ce, &c. 285
Bremen & Berlin ; Magdeb'g, Leipsic 169
Bremen and Cologne ; Hamburg .. 161
Bremen, Hanover (Frankfort) 164, 170
Brennero, Colle Isarco, Bolzano .. 307
Brest, S. Brieuc, Rennes, Le Mans, Paris 245
Brest, Quimper, Nantes (Paris) .. 246
Briancon, Veynes, Marseilles .. 263
Brigue, Lausanne, Geneva 280
Brindisi, Ancona, Bologna (Milan) .. 313
Brindisi, Gallipoli, Otranto 313
Brindisi, Naples, Rome 311
Brunswick, Harzburg, Wernigerode 167
Brussels, Antwerp, Rotterdam, &c. .. 154
Brussels, Ghent, Ostend (Lond.) 150 (127)

Brussels, Liége, Verviers, Aachen, Cologne 151
Brussels, Lille, Calais, London .. 149 (236, 127)
Brussels, Luxemburg (Bale, &c.) 149 (178)
Brussels, Mons (Valenciennes), Paris 239
Brussels, Luttre, Charleroy 152
Bucharest, Cracow, Berlin, Dresden, Vienna 204
Bucharest, Kassa, Praha 202
Bucharest, Lemberg, Warsaw, Prague 331
Bucharest, Constanza (Stamboul) .. 330
Bucharest, Galata, Jassy 330
Bucharest, Predeal, Budapest, Vienna 203
Bucharest, Giurgiu, Sofia 330
Bucharest, Calafat, Sofia 331
Budapest, Belgrade (Istanbul) .. 200
Budapest, Kotoriba, Postumia, Nice 201
Budapest, Fiume; Budapest-Graz .. 201
Budapest, Lawoczne, Lwow .. 201
Budapest, Trieste, Rome 201
Budapest, Bratislava (Vienna), Praha 203
Budapest, Predeal, Bucharest .. 203
Budapest, Vienna (Paris) .. 200 (274)
Burgaz (Bourgas), Yambol, Plovdiv 332B
Cadiz, Seville, Madrid, &c. .. 324
Caen, Lison, Cherbourg ; Caen, Paris 243
Caen (via Lison), Avranches (S. Malo) 245
Cairo via Simplon and Taurus Express 83, 334, 335
Cairo, Alexandria, Port Said, &c. .. 338
Calais, Dover and London .. 112
Calais, Boulogne, Amiens, Paris .. 237
Calais (via Hazebrouck), Arras .. 238
Calais, Lille (Brussels), Valenciennes 236
Calais (via Lille), Tournai, Brussels 149
Calais (via Lille), St. Quentin, Laon (Reims, Chalons, Bale) 236, 268, 270
Calais (via Valenciennes), Hirson, Mezieres, Nancy, &c. 271
Cannes, Nice, &c. (Marseilles & Paris) 264
Carlsruhe-Bale, Carls.-Heidelb'g 182, 183
Carlsruhe, Stuttgart, Munich, Vienna 186
Carlsruhe, Crailsheim, Nuremberg .. 184
Cartagena, Alcazar, Madrid .. 323
Cassel, Bebra (Leipsic, Berlin) 165 (172)
Cassel, Elberfeld, Aix, Cologne .. 165
Cassel, Frankfort ; Hanover, Hambg. 170
Cassel, Giessen, Cologne 165
Cassel, Nordhausen, Berlin .. 171
Catania, Syracuse, Messina .. 314
Chalons, Paris ; Nancy, Strasbourg 272
Chalons, Chaumont (Bale) .. 270 (268)
Chalons, Reims, Laon (Calais) 270 (236)
Chambery, Grenoble, Valence .. 257
Chamonix, Fayet, Geneva 267
Chamonix, Martigny 253
Chaumont, Belfort, Bale ; Paris .. 268
Chaumont, Chalons, Reims, Laon .. 270
Cherbourg, Caen, Paris 243
Chiavenna, Colico, Lecco, Milan .. 304
Chiavenna, St. Moritz, &c. .. 295
Chiusi, Siena, Empoli, Florence .. 309
Clermont, Royat, Laqueuille .. 247
Clermont, Nimes ; St. Germain (Paris) 254
Coblence, Bonn, Cologne (Steamer) 209
Coblence, Bingerbruck, Mainz, Frankf't (Darmstadt, Aschaffenbg.) 176
Coblence, Frankfort and Wiesbaden 175
Coblence, Ems, Giessen 169
Coblence, Treves, Luxemberg, Metz 181
Coblence, Treves Steamers .. 210
Coire, Zurich (Bale) 286
Coire, Rorschach, Constance .. 285
Coire, The Engadine, Splugen, &c. .. 296
Coire, Davos & Coire, Thusis, St. Moritz 286
Col de Salvan 253
Cologne, Aachen, Verviers, Liege (Antwerp), Brussels 151
Cologne, Bremen, Hamburg .. 161
Cologne, Cleves (Rotterdam, &c.) .. 156
Cologne, Coblence, Bingen, Mainz Frankf't (Aschaffenbg., Mannheim) 176
Cologne (Ems), Rudesheim, Wiesbaden, Frankfort (Bad Nauheim) 175
Cologne, Elberfeld, Soest, Cassel .. 165
Cologne, Giessen, Cassel 165
Cologne, Hanover, Berlin 163
Cologne, Magdeburg, Berlin .. 166
Cologne, Mainz (Steamers) 209, 216
Cologne, Trèves, Saargemund (Strasbourg) 179
Cologne, Venlo, Boxtel, &c. .. 157
Cologne—Through Services :—
England via Calais or Ostend .. 128
England via Flushing .. 129, 155
England via Hook of Holl'nd 131, 132, 156
England—Air Service 140
Belgium via Verviers 152
Holland .. .. .. 155 to 157
Strasbourg, Bale, &c. 181
Bavaria, Vienna, Praha .. 188, 189
Paris 240
Como, Lecco, Bergamo, Brescia .. 304
Como, Milan ; Como, Varese .. 304
Como Lake Steamers 317
Constance, Offenburg, Carlsruhe .. 180
Constance, Romanshorn, Coire, &c. 285
Constance, Schaffhausen, Bale .. 180
Constance, Schaffhausen (Swiss Rly.) 285

Constance, Winterthur, Zurich & Bale 284
Constance Lake Steamers 294
Constance, Stuttgart 184
Copenhagen, Elsinore 214
Copenhagen, Gothenburg, Oslo .. 216
Copenhagen, Malmö, Stockholm .. 215A
Copenhagen, Nyborg, Fredericia .. 215
Copenhagen, Paddeborg, Hamb'g 162, 216
Copenhagen, Gedser, Berlin .. 214 (204)
Copenhagen, Gedser, Hamburg .. 162
Corinth, Athens, Patras, &c. .. 336
Corinth, Argos, Myli, Kalamata, &c. 336
Corsica 254
Corunna and Madrid 321
Culoz, Bellegarde, Geneva 266
Culoz, Chambery, Modane, Turin .. 265
Culoz, Lyons ; Dijon (Paris) .. 266
Cyprus 310
Damascus, Beyrout (Aleppo) .. 335
Damascus, Haifa; Damascus, Medina 335
Danish Railways and Steamers 214, &c.
Danzig, Stettin, Lubeck (Hamburg) 205
Danzig, Berlin ; Eydtkuhnen .. 205
Danube Steamers 211
Davos, Coire, 286 ; Diligences, 293, 296
Davos, Landquart, Zurich (Bale) .. 286
Dieppe, Newhaven and London .. 111
Dieppe, Le Mans, Bordeaux .. 111
Dieppe, Rouen, Nantes, Bordeaux 111
Dieppe, Pontoise, Paris 241
Dijon, Dole (Besancon, Belfort),
  Pontarlier, Berne, Lausanne .. 261
Dijon, Macon, Ly'ns, Mars'lles, Nice, &c. 259
Dijon, Paris 261
Diligences and Mail Coaches ; Switzerland and the Tyrol 212, 295, 296
Domodossola-Arona, Milan (Turin) 302
Dresden, Berlin 195
Dresden, Breslau, Bucharest .. 204
Dresden, Bodenbach, Praha, Vienna 195
Dresden, Komotau, Karlsbad .. 196
Dresden, Leipsic, Magdeburg, Hanover 168
Dresden, Hof (Munich) .. 192 (190)
Dubrovnik, Brod, Zagreb 199
Eger, Oberkotzau, Hof 192
Eger, Karlsbad, Aussig, Dresden, .. 196
Eger, Marienbad, Gmund, Vienna .. 195
Eger, Nuremberg 190
Eger, Reichenbach, Leipsic, Berlin .. 192
Eger, Weiden, Regensburg, Munich 190
Egyptian Railways 338
Einsiedeln, Wadensweil, &c. .. 287
Elsinore, Copenhagen 214
Empoli Siena, Chuisi 309
Ems, Coblence ; Ems, Giessen .. 169
Ems, Cologne 175, 177
Ephesus (Ayasoulouk), Izmir .. 333
Erfurt, Ritschenhausen, Wurzburg .. 185
Esbjerg, Copenhagen 214
Esbjerg, London (via Harwich) 136, 404
Estonia 208
Fiume, Uj-Dombovar, Budapest .. 201
Finland Railways 228
Fiume (Trieste) and Vienna 200
Fiume, Trieste, Venice, Milan .. 303
Florence, Bologna (Verona), Milan .. 303
Florence, Chiusi, Rome 303
Florence, Pisa, Leghorn 309
Florence, Perugia, Foligno (Rome) .. 309
Florence, Siena (Rome) 309
Fluelen, Lucerne (Steamers) .. 29[illegible]
Flushing, Rosendaal, Breda, Boxtel 153
France (Railways in) .. 236-275
Frankfort and Berlin :—
  Via Bebra, Eisenach, Erfurt .. 172
  Via Nordhausen 171
  Via Kreiensen 170
Frankfort, Cassel, Hanover, Hamburg 170
Frankfort, Eberbach, Stuttgart .. 185
Frankfort, Halle, Leipsic (Berlin) 171, 172
Frankfort, Neustadt, Strasbourg, Bale 181
Frankfort, Heidelberg, Carls'he, Bale 182
Frankfort, Homburg 171
Frankfort, Limburg 171
Frankfort, Mainz, Coblence, Cologne 177
Frankfort, Metz (Paris) 179, 181 (275)
Frankfort, Rudesheim, Cologne .. 17[illegible]
Frankfort, Wiesbaden (Biebrich) .. 173
Frankfort, Wurzburg, Munich .. 188
Franzensfeste, Villach, Marb'g (V'nna) 198
Fredericia, Frederikshavn .. 215A
Freiburg, Neustadt, Donuaeschingen 180
Friedrichshafen, Ulm, Stuttgart .. 186
Furka, Gletsch ; Furka Andermatt 296
Furka Railway 291
Fussen, Oberdorf, Biessenhofen .. 190
Gannat, Montlucon, Limoges, Bord'x 250
Garda Lake Steamers 318
Generoso Railway 317
Geneva, Fayet, Chamonix .. 267
Geneva, Culoz (Lyons), Macon, Paris 266
Geneva (via Culoz), Turin .. 265
Geneva Lake Steamers 293
Geneva, Lausanne, Berne, Lucerne,
  Bale 279
Geneva, Neuchatel, Bienne, Bale .. 278
Geneva, Olten, Zurich, Rorschach, &c. 282
Geneva, S. Maurice, Brigue, Simplon 280
Genoa, Milan, Novara, Luino .. 302
Genoa, Pisa, Rome (Naples) .. 301

Genoa, Turin 301
Genoa, Vintimille (Marseilles) 299 (264)
German Motor Services .. 212, 213
German Railways .. .. from 161
Ghent, Antwerp .. .. 150 or 153
Ghent, Brussels, Ostend 150
Ghent, Lille, Calais 149
Gibraltar, Bobadilla, Madrid, &c... 325
Giessen, Cologne 169
Giessen, Coblence 169
Glarus, Zurich 286
Gothenburg, Oslo, Stockholm, &c. 216
Gouda, The Hague (Utrecht) .. 159
Granada and Malaga, Cadiz, Seville Cordova, Madrid 325
Granville, Vire, Paris 245
Great Western Stations to London 98, 99
Greek Railways 336
Grenoble, Chambery 257
Grenoble, Lyons 257
Grenoble, Veynes, Marseilles .. 263
Haugesund, Odda, Oslo 438
Hague (The), Rotterd'm & Amst'dam 158
Hague, Gouda (Rotterdam) .. 159
Haifa, Kantara, Cairo .. 335, 338
Hamburg, Berlin 169
Hamburg, Bremen, Cologne .. 161
Hamburg, Hanover, Cassel, Frankf't 170
Hamb'g, Hanover, Wurzb'g, Munich 194
Hamburg, Kiel 162
Hamb'g, Lubeck, Stettin, Danzig 162, 205
Hamburg, Magdeburg, Leipsic .. 169
Hamburg, Tinglev, Copenhagen 162, 215
Hamburg, Warnemunde, Copenhagen 162
Hamburg, Sassnitz, Stockholm .. 162
Hamm, Munster, Norddeich .. 175
Hanover, Bremen 164
Hanover, Cassel, Frankfort .. 170
Hanover, Cologne 164
Hanover, Hamburg 170
Hanover, Leipsic, Dresden .. 168
Hanover, Lehrte, Stendal, Berlin .. 163
Hanover, Osnabruck, Salzbergen (Rotterdam, Amsterdam) .. 163
Harz Mountain Services 167
Havre, Amiens (via Monterollier) .. 242
Havre, Southampton, London .. 111
Havre, Rouen, Paris 242
Heidelberg, Carlsruhe, Strasbourg, Baden and Bale 182
Heidelberg, Darmstadt, Frankfort.. 183
Heidelberg, Mannheim, Mainz .. 177
Heidelberg, Wurzburg, Berlin .. 185
Heidelberg, Stuttgart (Munich) .. 184
Heiden, Rorschach 289
Hendaye, Bayonne, Bordeaux (Paris) 250
Hendaye, Bayonne 253
Herbesthal, Col'gne; Liége, Brus'ls 151, 152
Heyst, Blankenberghe, Bruges .. 153
Hirson, Soissons, Paris 238
Hof, Bamberg, Nuremberg, Munich 191
Hof, Franzensbad, Eger 192
Hof, Regensburg, Munich 190
Hof, Reichenbach, Dresden, Leipsic (Berlin) 192
Homburg, Frankfort 171
Honfleur, Lisieux (Paris) 243
Hungarian Railways .. 200 to 203
Hyères, Toulon (Marseilles) .. 263 (267)
Innsbruck, Brennero, Colle Isarco, Verona 198, 307
Innsbruck, Arlberg, Bale, Paris .. 269
Innsb'k, Buchs, Feldk'ch (Zurich) 197 (286)
Innsbruck-Kufstein, Munich .. 198
Innsbruck and Vienna 197
Interlaken-Berne-Olten Bale .. 281
Interlaken, Meiringen, Lucerne .. 281
Interlaken Steamer Services .. 294
Interlaken, Grindelw., Laut'brunn, &c. 281
Irkutsk, Omsk, Moscow ; Manchuria 232
Irun, Bordeaux (Paris) .. 250 (248)
Irun, Bordeaux, St. Malo 135
Irun, Burgos, Medina, Madrid .. 321
Irun, Saragossa, Barcelona .. 322
Ischl, Passau ; Ischl, St'nach-Irdning 196
Ischl, St. Wolfgang, Salzburg .. 198
Istanbul Through Tables, 274, 330, 332-3
Istanbul, Sofia, Belgrade 333
Istanbul, Ankara, Sivas 333
Istanbul, Adana, Aleppo, Nusaybin, Baghdad and Teheran 334
Italian Lakes Services .. 317, 318
Italian Motor Services .. 319, 320
Italy to London via M. Cenis & Paris 118
Italy to London via Simplon .. 120
Italy to London via St. Gothard .. 124
Italy to Paris via St. Gothard .. 270
It'ly to Germany, &c, 174, 178, 185, 193, 198
Izmir, Ankara, Ephesus, &c. .. 334
Jaffa, Jerusalem 335
Jerusalem, Kantara, Cairo 335, 338
Kiev, Moscow ; Odessa 230
Kiev, Warsaw ; Kiev, Shmerinka 227, 230
Knocke, Lille, Paris 239
Kroderen (Randsfjord), Oslo .. 220
La Bourboule and Le Mont Dore, Vierzon, Orleans, Paris 249
Langenschwalbach, Wiesbaden .. 171
La Rochelle, Bordeaux ; Nantes .. 246
La Rochelle, Niort, Paris 246

Laon, Reims, Chalon, Chaumont (Bale) 270
Laon, Amiens (Calais) 237
Laon, St. Quentin, Lille (Calais) .. 236
Lausanne, Berne, Lucerne and Bale 279
Laus'ne, Brigue, Simp'n & Milan 119, 280
Lausanne, Geneva, 279 ; Steamers, 293
Lausanne, Neuchatel, Bienne, Bale 278
Lausanne, Vallorbe, Dijon, Paris .. 267
Laveno, Varese (Como), Milan .. 304
Lecco (Milan), Sondrio (Chiavenna) 304
Lecco Lake Steamers 317
Leghorn, Pisa, Florence 309
Leipsic, Berlin 172
Leipsic, Cassel, Frankfort 173
Leipsic, Dresden 168
Leipsic, Hof (Weiden, Munich) 192 (190)
Leipsic, Bamberg, Munich, &c. .. 191
Leipsic (Bremen), Hamburg .. 169
Leipsic, Magdeb'g, Hanover (Col.) 168, 164
Le Mans, Rennes, St. Malo .. 244
Le Mans, Angers, Nantes 247
Le Mans, Paris 244, 247
Leningrad, Moscow and Riga .. 230
Leningrad, Tallinn 206
Liége, Antwerp, Brussels 152
Liége, Aachen, Cologne 151
Liége, Charleroy, Paris 240
Lille, Brussels, 149 ; Lille, Ghent .. 149
Lille, Arras, Amiens, Paris .. 238
Lille, Hazebrouck (Dunkirk), Calais 236
Lille, Ostend, Knocke .. 239
Lille, Val'c'nes (Mezières, Nancy) 236, 237
Lille, St. Quentin, Laon 236
Limoges, Bordeaux 250
Limoges, Orleans, Paris 249
Limoges & Agen; Mont'ban; Toul'se 249
Limoges, Moulins ; Gannat (Lyons) 250
Limburg, Frankfort 171
Lindau, Augsburg, Nuremberg .. 187
Lindau, Friedrichshafen, Schaffhaus'n 180
Lindau, Munich, &c. 187
Lisbon, Badajoz, Seville and Madrid 323
Lisbon, Medina (Bordeaux, Paris) 322 (250)
Lisbon, Oporto, Valencia, Vigo .. 327
Lisbon, Valencia Alicante, Madrid .. 325
Lisbon, Villa Real, Seville .. 327
Locarno, St. Gothard, Lucerne, &c. 287
Locarno, Domodossola 292
L.M. & S. Stations to London .. 88
London to Great Western Stations .. 99
London, Paris via Dover and Calais 112
London, Paris v. Folkestone, B'logne 112
London, Paris via Newhaven, Dieppe 111
London, Paris v. S'thampton, Havre 111
London, Dover, Ostend, &c. 127, 128, 150
London, Flushing, &c. 129, 130, 155
London, Harwich, &c. 131, 132, 136
London to Paris Air Service .. 138
London, Dover, Dunkirk, Paris, Bale 137
London to Continent—see list of
Through Routes .. .. 62 to 64
Lubeck, Hamburg .. 101, 162, 205
Lubeck, Luneburg 168
Lubeck, Warnem'de, Stettin, &c. 162, 205
Lucerne Lake Steamers 293
Lucerne, Berne, Lausanne, Geneva .. 279
Lucerne, Brienz, Interlaken (Berne) 281
Lucerne, Olten, Bale (Paris) 282, 270
Lucerne, St. Gothard, Milan, &c. .. 287
Lucerne, Zug, Zurich, Schaffhausen 284
Lugano Lake Steamers 317
Luino, Novara, Alessandria, Genoa 302
Luino, St. Gothard, Lucerne, &c. .. 287
Luxemburg, Metz, Strasbourg .. 179
Luxemburg, Brussels (London) 149, 127
Luxemburg, Spa (Liege) 152
Luxemburg, Treves, Coblence, Ems 169
Lyons (Vesoul), Belfort, Strasbourg 266
Lyons, Culoz, Geneva 266
Lyons, Mars'les ; (Nice, Mentone) 259, 264
Lyons, Macon, Dijon, Paris 261
Lyons, Roanne, St. Germain, Paris 256
Lyons, Limoges, Bordeaux 250
Lyons, St. Etienne, Roanne .. 257
Lyons, Grenoble 257
Lyons, Nimes, Sète, Barcelona .. 255
Macon, Dijon, Paris 261
Macon, Lyons, Marseilles (Nice, &c.) 259
Macon, Culoz, Geneva 266
Madrid, Burgos, Irun, Paris .. 321
Madrid, Vigo and Corunna .. 321
Madrid, Cordova, Seville, Cadiz .. 324
Madrid, Alicante (Valencia) .. 323
Madrid, Saragossa, Barcelona, &c... 326
Madrid, Badajoz, Lisbon 323
Madrid, Valencia, Lisbon 325
Magdebg., Berlin, 168, Bre'en, Hambg. 169
Magdeburg, Brunswick, Hanover .. 168
Magdeburg, Leipsic, Dresden 168 or 166
Magdeburg, Soest, Cologne, Aachen 166
Maggiore Lake Steamers 318
Mainz, Frankfurt a M., &c. .. 170
Mainz, Coblence, Cologne .. 177
Mainz, Cologne (Steamers) 209, 210
Mainz, Mannheim (Heidelberg) .. 176
Mainz, Metz (Paris) .. 179 (275)
Mainz, Carlsruhe, Bale 182
Mainz, Strasbourg, Bale 181
Malaga and Granada, Cordova,
Madrid, Seville, &c. 325

Malmö, Mjolby, Krylbo 217
Malmö, Nässjö, Stockholm ..215A
Malmö, Gothenburg, Oslo 216
Malta to London, various routes .. 343
Mannheim, Cologne, Rotterd'm St'rs. 210
Marseilles, Lyons, Paris 261
Marseilles, The Pyrenees, Bayonne .. 252
Marseilles, Cannes, Nice, Genoa .. 264
Marseilles, Briancon, Grenoble .. 263
Marseilles (via Arles and via Tarascon), Nimes, Sète, Narbonne, Barcelona 255
Mars'les (v. Sète), Toulouse, Bord'ux 252
Martigny, Chamonix 253
Messina, Catania, Syracuse .. 314
Metz-Bingerbruck (Col'gne, Frankf't) 179
Metz, Pagny, Nancy (Paris) .. 275
Metz, Saarburg, Strasbourg .. 179
Metz, Treves, Coblence, Ems .. 181
Metz, Luxemburg 179
Milan, Arona, Domodossola .. 302
Milan, Bologna, Florence, Rome .. 303
Milan, Genoa (Rome) .. 302 (301)
Milan, Turin, Modane 298
Milan, St. Gothard, Lucerne, &c. 287, 304
Milan, Simplon, Laus'ne, Geneva 280, 302
Milan, Simplon, Paris, London .. 120
Milan, Splugen, Thusis 295
Milan, Como, Chiasso, Lugano .. 304
Milan, Lecco, Colico (Chiavenna) .. 304
Milan, Varese, Laveno 304
Milan, Verona, Venice, Trieste, Fiume 305
Mont Blanc Tramway 253 ; Morocco 342
Morcenx, Tarbes, Bagnères de Bigorre 253
Moscow, Gorky 231
Moscow, Kiev, Odessa ; Sevast'p'l,&c.230
Moscow, Irkutsk, Vladivostock, &c. 232
Moscow and Leningrad ; Arkhangel 230
Moscow, Warsaw (Berlin) .. 205, 226
Moselle Steamers 210
Mosul via Simplon-Orient and Taurus Express 83, 334
Munich, Stuttgart, Carlsruhe .. 186
Munich, Innsbruck, Verona 198, 307
Munich, Lindau, Zurich 187, 283, 285
M'ich, Murnau (Ober'gau), Innsbruck 193
Munich, Oberammergau 193
Munich, Nuremb'g, Bamb'g, Hof, &c. 191
Munich, Regensburg (Eger), Hof, &c. 190
Munich, Salzburg, Vienna 187
Munich, Salzburg, Graz 199
Mun'h, Teg'see, Kochel or Schliersee 194
Munich, Wurzburg, Frankfort, &c. 189
Munich, Wurzburg, Hamburg .. 194
Munich, Bad Gastein, Villach, Triest, Zagreb and Belgrade 199
Munich—Through Services :—
England via Ostend and Calais .. 128
Berlin via Bamberg 191
Berlin via Regensburg 190
Cologne via Frankfort or Mainz.. 189
Strasbourg, Paris 274
Budapest, Istanbul, &c. 274
Murnau, Munich 193
Nancy, Chalons, Paris 272
Nancy, Contrexeville 271
Nancy, Epinal (Vesoul), Belfort .. 271
Nantes (via Angers), Le Mans (Paris) 247
Nantes, Angers, Tours (Paris), &c... 247
Nantes, Quimper, Brest 246
Nantes, La Rochelle, Rochef't, Bord'x 246
Naples, Messina (Reggio) 312
Naples, Rome (Turin, Mil'n) 310(301, 303)
Naples, Brindisi 310
Naples—Through Services :—
Genoa, Turin, Fl'nce, Milan 301, 303
London, Paris, &c. 82, 118, 270
Narbonne, Toulouse, Bordeaux .. 252
Narb'ne, Pt. Bou (Barcel'a), &c. 255 (326)
Neuchatel, Pontarlier (Paris) 279 (267)
Neuchatel, Bienne, Bale 278
Neuchatel, Berne, Interlaken .. 279
Neuchatel, Chaux-de-F., Locle .. 278
Neuchatel, Lausanne (Geneva) .. 278
Neuch'l, Olten, Zurich, Rorsch'h, &c. 282
Nile Steamers 370
Nimes, Sète, Narbonne, Barcelona 255,326
Nimes, Arles (Marseilles) ; Tarascon (Marseilles), Paris 255
Nimes, Clermont, St. Germain (Paris) 254
Norwegian Railways .. 219 to 220
Norwegian Auto-Diligences 221 to 224A
Novara, Turin ; Novara, Milan .. 298
Novara, Arona, Domodossola .. 302
Novara, Luino ; Novara, Genoa .. 302
Nuremberg, Augsb., Buchloe, Lindau 187
Nuremberg (Bayr'th), Eger, Karlsbad 190
Nuremberg, Crailsheim, Stuttgart .. 184
Nuremberg, Paris (Through Tables) 274
Nuremberg, Passau, Vienna .. 188
Nuremberg, Eger, Praha .. 188, 190
Oberammergau, Munich 193
Odessa, Cracow (Vienna, Berlin) .. 204
Offenburg (Black Forest Rly.), Schaffhausen, (Constance), Zurich .. 180
Oporto, Medina (Bordeaux, Paris)322(250)
Oporto, Lisbon 327
Oran (Algiers), Oudjda, Fez .. 342
Oslo (Dombaas), Trondheim .. 219
Oslo, Odda, Haugesund 438
Oslo, Voss, Bergen 219

Oslo, Gothenb'g, Copenh'n (Malmö) 216
Oslo, Kongsvinger, Stockholm ..215A
Oslo, Randsfjord (Kroderen), &c... 220
Ostend, Ghent (Antw'p, &c.), Brussels 150
Ostend, Dover, London 127
Ostend, Lille, Paris 239
Otranto, Brindisi (Naples), Milan .. 313
Palestine and Syrian Railways .. 335
Palermo Catania (Syracuse) .. 314
Paris, Amiens, Boulogne, Calais .. 237
Paris, Amiens, Lille, Valenciennes .. 238
Paris, Beauvais, Le Treport .. 238
Paris, Chalons, Frouard, Nancy,
Avricourt, Strasbourg 272
Via Frouard—Metz 275
Paris, Le Mans, Rennes, St. Malo .. 244
Paris, Le Mans—Angers, Nantes .. 247
Paris, Rennes—St. Brieuc, Brest .. 245
Paris, Niort, La Rochelle, Bordeaux 246
Paris, Redon, Quimper (Brest) .. 246
Paris, Chaumont, Belfort, Bale .. 268
Paris, Delle, Berne (Interlaken),
Loetschberg, Simplon, Milan .. 269
Paris, Dijon, Macon, Lyons, Mars'l's 259
Paris via Dijon—Besancon, Pontarlier
(Berne), Lausanne (Milan) .. 119, 267
Paris via St. Amour-Culoz, Geneva 121, 266
Paris via St. Amour—Modane, Turin 265
Paris via Marseilles—Toulon Cannes,
Nice, Vintimille, &c. 264
Paris, Gisors, Serq'x, Dieppe (London) 241
Paris, Lille, Ostend, Knocke .. 239
Paris, Mantes, Rouen, Havre .. 242
Paris via Rouen—Dieppe (London) 241
Paris, Mantes, Lisieux, Caen, Cherb'g 243
Paris via Lisieux—Trouville, Honfleur 243
Paris, Milan, etc., via Loetschberg .. 288
Paris, Orleans, Tours, Bordeaux .. 248
Paris, Le Mans-Nantes, Le Croisic, &c. 247
Paris, Orleans, Montlucon, Laqueuille,
Limoges (Agen, Toulouse, &c.) .. 249
Paris, Reims, Mezières, Namur .. 271
Paris, Soissons, Reims, Hirson .. 238
Paris, St. Germain, Roanne, Lyons 256
Paris via Roanne—St. Etienne .. 257
Paris via St. Germain—Clermont (F.),
Alais, Nimes (Sète, &c.) .. 254, 255
Paris, St. Quentin (or Valenciennes),
Mons, Brussels, Ostend 239
Paris, St. Quentin, Charleroy, Namur,
Liége (Cologne) 240
Paris, Vire, Granville 244
Paris, Vittel .. .. (268) 271
Paris—Through Services :—
England via Boulogne & Calais 112, 237
England via Dieppe .. 111, 241
England via Havre .. 111, 242
England via Dunkerque .. 137
England—Air Services 138
Amsterdam via Brussels 154
Brittany via Le Mans or Tours 244, 245
Barcelona via Toulouse 117, 251, 252
Barcelona via Lyons 255
Bohemia, Moravia, &c. 274
Germany via Strasbourg .. 272, 275
Germany via Metz 275
Germany via Liége 240
Germany, Hungary and Roumania 274
Istanbul 274, 232
Italy via Mont Cenis .. 118, 265
Switzerland and Yugoslavia .. 265
Italy via St. Gothard 270
Italy via Simplon 119, 280
Poland 240
Madrid and Lisbon 115, 250, 321, 322
Pyrenees via Bordeaux, 115 ; via
Agen, 252 ; via Toulouse 117, 251
Vienna via Arlberg 269
Vosges Watering Places .. 271
Parma, Spezia, Pisa, &c. 300
Passau, Attnang, Ischl 196
Patras, Corinth, Athens, Piræus, &c. 336
Perigueux, Laqueuille, (Mont Dore)
and Clermont-Ferrand 247
Piestany, Vienna (Praha) 206A
Pilatus Railway 289
Piræus, Athens, Corinth, Patras .. 336
Polish Rlys. 203 to 205, 226 to 228, 331
Porto Empedocle, St. Caterina, &c. 315
Praha, Zilina, Kassa, Jasina .. 207A
Praha, Plzen, Tuschkau-Kosolup .. 206
Praha, Dresden, Berlin 195
Praha, Linz, Villach, Rome .. 196
Praha, M'ienbad, Eger, N'remb'rg 190, 206
Praha, Paris (Through Tables) .. 274
Praha, Piestany, Zilina 206A
Praha, Bratislava, Vajnory .. 207
Praha, Vienna .. 195, 196, 206 or 206A
Praha, Zagreb, Trieste, Rome .. 196
Reggio, Bari 311
Reggio, Battipaglia, Naples .. 312
Rhine Steamers 209, 210
Riga, Wirballen, Berlin 208
Riga, Leningrad 208
Rigi Railways 294
Roccapal'mba, Agrigento, P. Empd'cle 315
Rochefort, Bordeaux, Nantes .. 246
Rochefort, Niort, Paris 246
Romanshorn, Winterthur, Zurich, &c. 285
Romanshorn, Constance, Schaffh'sen 285

Romanshorn, Rorschach, Buchs, Coire 285
Rome, Florence, Milan (Verona), &c. 303
Rome, Foligno, Ancona (Florence) 309
Rome, Naples, Brindisi 311
Rome, Pisa, Genoa (Milan), Turin.. 301
Rome, Siena, Empoli (Florence) .. 309
Rome, Trieste, Postumia, Budapest 307
Rome, Venice, Tarvisio (Vienna) 199, 308
Rome (Through Service), Germany.. 193
Rorschach, Constance, Schaffhausen 285
Rorschach, St. Gallen, Zurich .. 283
Rorschach-Heiden Railway .. 289
Rorschach, St. Margrethen, Coire .. 285
Rostov, Kozlov, Moscow 230
Rotterdam, Antwerp, Brussels (Paris) 154
Rotterdam, Breda, Boxtel, &c. .. 155
Rotterdam, Cologne, Mannheim Strs. 210
Rotterdam, Flushing, London .. 129
Rotterdam, The Hague, Amsterdam 158
Rotterdam, Hook of Holland, Harwich, London 131
Rotterdam, Nymegen, Cleves, Col'gne 156
Rotterdam, Oberhausen, Cologne .. 157
Rouen, Amiens 242
Rouen, Dieppe (London) 241
Rouen, Mantes, Paris 242
Rouen, Fecamp, Havre 242
St. Germain, Clermont, Nimes .. 254
St. Germain, Nevers, Paris .. 256
St. Germain, Roanne, Lyons .. 256
St. Germain, St. Etienne, Lyons .. 257
St Gothard Route 123 to 125, 270, 287
St. Malo, Rennes, Bordeaux, Irun .. 135
St. Malo, Rennes, Le Mans, Paris .. 244
St. Malo, St. Brieuc, Brest 245
St. Nazaire, Nantes, Tours (Paris) .. 247
Salamanca, Medina and Portugal .. 322
Salzburg, Innsbruck, Arlberg, &c. .. 197
Salzburg, Munich, &c., and Vienna.. 187
Salzburg, St. Wolfgang, Ischl .. 198
Saragossa, Bilbao and Alsasua .. 322
Saragossa, Lerida, Barcelona .. 322
Saragossa, Madrid (Barcelona) .. 326
Schaffhausen & Bale, Const'e, Lindau 180
Schaffhausen, Constance (Steamers) 294
Schaffhausen, Const'e, Rorschach, &c. 285
Schaffhausen, Offenburg 180
Schaffhausen, Stuttgart (Ulm) .. 184
Schaffhausen, Zurich, Lucerne .. 284
Scheveningen, The Hague (Amsterdam), Rotterdam 158
Schuls, Landeck 295
Selzthal, Ischl, Attnang, Passau .. 196
Sète, Nimes, Marseilles, Lyons, Paris 255
Sète, Narbonne, Cerbere, Barcelona 255
Sète (via Narbonne), Toulouse, Bordeaux 252
Sevastopol, Kursk, Moscow .. 230
Seville and Cadiz ; Cordova, Madrid 324
Seville, La Roda (Granada) .. 325
Seville, Badajoz (Lisbon) 323
Siberian Railway 232
Sihlthal Rly. (Sihlbrugg-Zurich) .. 289
Spa, Brussels ; Spa, Luxemburg .. 152
Skien, Oslo 219
Spanish, Portuguese and Balearic Isles Railways .. .. 321 to 328
Spezia, Parma (Milan) 300
Splugen Pass.. 295
Steinach, Rothenburg, Dombuhl .. 194
Stettin, Berlin; Danzig; Lubeck (Hamburg) 205
Stockholm, Gavle, Harnosand .. 217
Stockholm, Oslo 215A
Stockholm, Gothenburg, Malmö, &c. 216
Stockholm-Saltsjobaden 217
Stockholm, Trondheim and Narvik.. 218
Stockholm, Upsala, Rattvik .. 217
St'kholm, Trellborg, Berlin (H'mb'g) 215A
Strasbourg, Avricourt, Nancy, Paris 272
Strasbourg, Mainz, Cologne, &c. .. 181
Strasbourg, Heidelberg, Cologne, &c. 183
Strasbourg, Namur, Brussels, Antw'p 149
Strasbourg, Metz, Luxemburg .. 179
Strasbourg, Treves, &c., Cologne .. 179
Stuttgart, Carlsruhe 186
Stuttgart, Constance, Schaffhausen.. 184
Stuttgart, Eberbach, Frankfort .. 185
Stuttgart, Heidelberg 184
Stuttgart, Kempten, Reutte, Garm'ch 193
Stuttgart, Munich, Vienna .. 186
Stuttgart, Nuremberg 184
Stuttgart, Friedrichshafen, Zurich.. 186
Stuttgart, Wurzburg, Berlin .. 185
Sudan Government Railways .. 339
Swedish Railways .. ..215A to 218
Swiss Diligences 295, 296
Swiss Lake Steamers .. 293, 294
Switzerland to London, 120, 122, 124, 125, 127, 137
Syracuse, Catania, Messina (Palermo) 314
Syrian Railways 335
Tarbes and Agen, 252 ; Bigorre, Morcenx (Bordeaux) 253
Tarragona & Barcelona, Valencia, &c. 326
Tashkent, Bokhara, Merv. Poltoraksk 231
Teheran, via Simplon and Taurus Express 83, 334
Thessaloniki, Nisch, Belgrade .. 332
Thun, Berne, Olten, Bale 281

Thun and Brienz Lake Steamers .. 294
Thusis, Coire, Davos (Zurich) .. 286
Toulon, Hyères 263
Toulouse, Limoges (Orleans, Paris) 249
Toulouse, Narbonne, Sète (Mars'les) 252
Toulouse, Pau and Bayonne .. 251
Toulouse, Puigcerda, Barcelona .. 251
Tours, Nantes, St. Nazaire, Le Croisic 247
Tours, Orleans, Paris 248
Tours, Vendome, Paris 247
Tours, Poitiers, Bordeaux 248
Trento, Primolano, Venice .. 306
Treport, Beauvais, Paris 238
Trier, Coblence Steamers 210
Trier, Cologne; Saarbr'k, Strasbourg 179
Trier, Coblence; Luxemburg; Metz 169
Trieste, Udine (Venice, &c.) .. 308
Trieste, Semmering, Vienna .. 200
Trieste, Venice, Verona, Milan .. 305
Trondheim ; Bracke, Stockholm .. 218
Trondheim ; Hamar, Oslo.. .. 219
Trouville, Lisieux (Paris) 243
Turin, Bra, Savona (Vintimille) .. 298
Turin, Chivasso, Aosta 300
Turin, Genoa, Rome (Naples) .. 301
Turin, Milan (Venice) .. [Paris) 298
Turin, Modane, Culoz (Geneva, Ly'ns, 265
Turin, Piacenza (Bologna) .. 303
Turin, Pinerolo, Torre Pellice .. 298
Turin—Through Tables :—
London and Paris (via Modane) .. 118
Uetliberg, Zurich 289
Union of Soviet Socialist Rep'lics 230-235
Valencia, Madrid 323
Valencia and Tarragona 325
Valenciennes, Arras, Amiens, Paris 238
Valenciennes, Lille (Dunkirk), Calais 236
Valenciennes, Mezières, Nancy, &c. 271
Venice, Ancona, Naples 313
Venice, Bologna (Florence, Rome).. 303
Venice, Cervignano, Trieste, Fiume 305
Venice, Udine (Trieste) 308
Venice, Verona, Milan (Turin) .. 305
Venice, Udine, Tarvisio (Vienna) .. 308
Verona, Innsbruck, Munich .. 198
Verona, Bologna, Florence, Rome.. 303
Ver'na, Mil'n (Venice, Trieste, Fiume) 305
Vesuvius Railway 300
Vichy, Nevers, Paris 256
Vienna, Breslau, Berlin .. 203, 204
Vienna, Bodenbach (Dresden, Berlin) 195
Vienna, Zagreb, Belgrade, &c. .. 200
Vienna, Cracow, Warsaw 203
Vienna, Gmund, Prague, Marienbad,
Lobositz, Dresden, Berlin .. 195
Vienna, Fortezza, Merano, &c. .. 198
Vienna, Innsbruck (Bregenz Lindau),
Buchs (Zurich) 197 (286)
Vienna, Passau, Nuremberg, Wurs-
burg, (Frankfort, Cologne) .. 189
Vienna, Tarvisio (Venice, &c.) .. 199
Vienna, Salzburg, Munich 187
Vienna, Semmering (Fiume), Trieste 200
Vienna—Thro' Services England 124, 128
to 130, 132, Air Service, 141; Fra'ce 269
274; Bucharest, &c., 274; Istanbul, 200;
Italy, 199, 200.
Vintimille, Savona (Turin), Genoa 298, 299
Vintimille, Nice, Cannes, Marseilles 264
Visp, Zermatt, 288 ; Vittel, Paris .. 271
Vitznau, Kaltbad, Rigi-Kulm .. 289
Vladivostok, Manchuria, Irkutsk, &c. 232
Volga Steamers 233
Voss-Bergen and Voss-Oslo .. 219
Wadensweil, Einsedeln 287
Waldkirch, Freiburg 184
Warsaw, Danzig and Lemberg .. 266
Warsaw, Cracow-Vienna 203
Warsaw, Paris 240
Warsaw, Berlin, Cologne, London .. 128
Warsaw and Berlin .. 205, 226
Warsaw to Riga and Moscow .. 227
Waterloo, Brussels 151
Wengern Alp Railway 292
Wiesbaden (Coblence), Cologne .. 175
Wiesbaden, Kastel, Frankfort .. 173
Wiesbaden, Bad Schwalbach, Limb'g 171
Wiesbaden, Neustadt, Strasbourg 181
Wildbad, Pforzheim (Carlsruhe) .. 186
Wildungen, Wabern 170
Wurzburg, Bad-Kissingen 190
Wurzburg, Bamberg, Hof 191
Wurzburg, Oberhof, Erfurt, Berlin 185
Wurzburg (Heidelberg) & Stuttgart 185
Wurzburg, Nuremb., Passau, Vienna 188
Zagreb-Sarajevo-Dubrovnik .. 332B
Zermatt, Brigue Gletsch (Lucerne),
St. Moritz 291
Zilina, Cadca, Bogumin 207A
Zug Lake Steamers 294
Zurich Lake Steamers 293
Zurich, Brugg (Bale), Aarau, Olten,
Bienne, (Neuchatel, Geneva) .. 283
Zurich, Buchs (Vienna), Coire 286 (197)
Zurich, Rapperswil, Glarus, Linthal 286
Zurich, St.Gallen, Rorschach (Mun'h) 282
Zurich, Winterthur, Romanshorn,
Lindau (Munich) 285 (187)
Zurich, Wint'thur, Singen & Const'ce 284
Zurich, Schaffhausen 284
Zurich, Turgi, Waldshut 283
Zurich, Zug, Lucerne (Gothard) (284) 287

SPECIAL ACCOMMODATION.

A SUMMARY OF SLEEPING CARRIAGES, ETC., ON CONTINENTAL TRAINS.

NOTE.—Particulars of trains in which the various carriages run will be found in the notes to the time tables, particularly those of through services shown on pages 111 to 137.

SOUTHERN RAILWAY.

Pullman Cars on all boat trains from London (Victoria) to Dover, Folkestone and Newhaven and *v.v.*; supplement 3/6 to Dover and Folkestone, 2/6 to Newhaven over 1st class fare.
Corridor Lavatory Carriages on all boat trains; seats reservable in advance 1/- each, Victoria to Dover, Folkestone or Newhaven and Waterloo to Southampton.

BELGIAN NATIONAL RAILWAYS.

First and Second Class Corridor Carriages are run on the International Express Services and where indicated in the train headings. Passengers may transfer to a higher class on payment of a supplement equivalent to the following:—

2nd class to 1st class	..	One 3rd class ticket.
3rd class to 1st class	..	One 2nd class ticket.
3rd class to 2nd class	..	One 3rd class ticket.

NETHERLANDS RAILWAYS.

D.—Corridor Trains.—A supplement is charged for all journeys by trains marked **"D"** as follows: 1st, 2nd or 3rd class fl. 0.80. This supplement covers the German or Belgian as well as the Dutch portion of the journey when through place tickets are issued.
All tickets printed "Geldig in alle treinen, met inbegrip van D-treinen" are available by the D trains without supplement.

GERMAN STATE RAILWAYS.

D—Corridor Trains specially indicated in the time tables, by the letter **D** (Durchgangzug), are composed entirely of bogie corridor carriages, with lavatories, connected throughout by covered platforms.
F.D. Trains.—Special fast corridor trains, 1st and 2nd class, with extra supplements.
F.D.T.—Special trains are now in operation throughout Germany, composed of stream-lined rail cars, one class only, limited, and for which an extra supplement must be paid.
Rheingold Express.—Special Saloon and Dining Car Train (Mitropa Coy.) Hook of Holland to Bale, Lucerne and Milan, available to 1st and 2nd, class passengers.
Sleeping Cars.—In the Sleeping Cars of the Mitropa Coy. the following regulations are in force:— 2nd class passengers are entitled to one berth. A passenger holding one first-class ticket and paying one first-class supplement, gets a two-berthed compartment to himself; two passengers holding two first-class tickets and paying two first-class supplements, are entitled to a four-berthed compartment to themselves.
These Sleeping Cars run on all principal night services throughout Germany.

FRENCH NATIONAL RAILWAYS.

Couloir (Corridor) Carriages run on most of the principal services and on all International Express and Boat Trains.

Special Accommodation.—There also exists on certain trains on various sections of the National Railways, compartments of lits-salon or lits-toilette first class, as well as couchettes-toilettes first class only, and couchettes ordinaires first, second and third class. The lits-salons and lits-toilettes provide complete beds in compartments of two places side by side (West section lits-toilette provide two beds, one upper and one lower), while the couchettes-toilettes provide two couches, one upper and one lower. The couchettes ordinaires first class provide six seats by day and four couches by night; second class eight seats by day and four couches at night, while third class have six couches. Such sleeping accommodation is only available on those trains provided with the above-mentioned accommodation and passengers can only obtain berths to the extent of the number of places available, on payment of the required supplement. Passengers requiring such accommodation must be in possession of tickets of the requisite class, first class for lits-salons, or lits-toilettes compartments. Couchette compartments can only be used for sleeping purposes during night travel subject to the regulations published in the time tables from time to time; these compartments are turned into ordinary compartments during day travel. When two children between 4 and 10 years of age occupy a single berth, only one supplement is charged.

The following table shews the principal sections over which the special accommodation usually runs; and the time-tables indicate the services which are provided with the various types of accommodation.

	Lits-Salon Lits-Toilette	COUCHETTES 1st cl. Toilette	COUCHETTES 1st cl. Ordinaires	COUCHETTES 2nd. cl.	COUCHETTES 3rd cl.
Lines in the West Section	x		x	x	x
Paris-Quai d'Orsay—					
Agen			x		
Bagn.-de-Luchon..	x		x		
La Rochelle ..	x		x	x	x
Montauban ..	x		x		
Perpignan.. ..			x		
Port-Vendres ..			x		
Puigcerda	x		x	x	
Toulouse	x		x		
Paris-P.L.-M.—					
Aix-les-Bains ..	x		x		
Cannes	x	x	x	x	
Chambéry.. ..	x		x		
Clermont-Ferrand	x		x		
Dijon-Ville ..	x		x		
Genève-Cornavin..	x		x		
Lyon-Perrache ..	x	x	x		
Marseille	x	x	x	x	
Menton	x	x	x	x	
Nice	x	x	x	x	
St. Etienne ..	x		x		
Sète	x		x		
Vichy	x		x		
Paris-Est—					
Nancy-Ville ..			x	x	
Lunéville			x	x	

	Lits-Salon. Lits-Toilette	COUCHETTES 1st cl. Toilette	COUCHETTES 1st cl. Ordinaires	COUCHETTES 2nd cl.	COUCHETTES 3rd cl.
Paris-Est—					
Strasbourg ..			x	x	
Luxembourg et Metz			x		
Epinal et Gérardmer			x	x	x
St. Dié			x	x	
Bordeaux—					
Gannat	x		x		
Marseille	x		x		
Port-Vendres ..			x		
Séte	x		x		
Cerbère—					
Belfort	x				
Chambéry ..			x		
Lyon-Brotteaux ..	x		x		
Clermont-Ferrand			x		
Hendaye—					
Cannes	x				
Marseille	x				
Nice	x				
Toulon	x				
Vintimille ..	x				
Strasbourg—					
Lyon			x		
Port-Bou	x				

x Indicates that specified accommodation may run on certain trains, see time-tables.

Family Reductions.—Subject to the berths being booked in advance and that the members of the family travel together, holders of family tickets can obtain, on production of their tickets, the following reductions on the supplements for lits-salons, lits-toilettes and couchette berths:

20 per cent. for the 3rd member. 30 per cent for the 4th member.
40 per cent. each additional member.

SPECIAL REGULATIONS CONCERNING WESTERN SECTION.

(1) Exceptionally as regards toilet berths, an individual passenger may book the available berths in a compartment on payment of a supplement of Frs. 130 at the time of booking such accommodation.

(2) The Western Section issues personal cards valid for 3, 6 or 12 months, which entitle the holder to the use of first, second or third class ordinary berths without the payment of any supplement subject to the production of the requisite railway ticket.

The prices of such cards are—

		Three months.	Six months.	Twelve months.
First or second classes	Fr.	400	575	850
Third class	Fr.	325	475	650

SPECIAL REGULATIONS CONCERNING THE SOUTH-EASTERN SECTION.

(1) Subject to the same conditions as specified above, in regard to saloon or toilet sleeping berths, holders of family tickets are entitled to the following reductions on the supplements for ordinary sleeping berths:

20 per cent. for the 4th member. 30 per cent. for the 5th member.
40 per cent. for each additional member.

(2) The South-Eastern Section issues personal cards, valid for six or twelve months, which entitle the holder to a 50 per cent. reduction on the supplements (individual passengers) for lits-salons, lits-toilettes and ordinary sleeping berths.

The prices of these cards are—

Six months' validity .. Frs. 550. Twelve months' validity .. Frs. 850

ITALIAN STATE RAILWAYS.—Rapid Trains: Passengers travelling by the "Rapido" trains in Italy must hold a supplementary ticket.

NOTE.—On above railways the INTERNATIONAL SLEEPING CAR CO. run Sleeping Cars on all principal trains. **For Trains de Luxe see pp. 79 to 85.**

PRIVATE CABINS, ETC. ON CHANNEL STEAMERS.

SOUTHERN RAILWAY.

DOVER-CALAIS AND FOLKESTONE-BOULOGNE ROUTES.

Extra Charges for Private Cabins, irrespective of the number of passengers occupying them.

T.s.s. *Canterbury*.	No. available.	Charge.
Half State Cabin	2	60/-
Cabins, 15 to 18, 23 to 25	7	40/-
„ 1 to 14, 19 to 22	18	20/-
Alcoves	8	10/-

T.s.s. *Isle of Thanet* and *Maid of Kent*.	No. available.	Charge.
Half State Cabin	2	60/-
Cabins, 17 to 24	8	40/-
„ 1 to 16	16	20/-

T.s.s. *Côte d'Azur* and *Côte d'Argent*.	No. available.	Charge.
Half State Cabin	2	60/-
Cabins, 11 to 14	4	40/-
„ 1 to 10	10	20/-

s.s. *Maid of Orleans* and *Biarritz*.	No. available.	Charge.
Half State Cabin	2	60/-
Cabins, 9 to 12, 15 to 18	8	40/-
„ 1 to 8, 12a and 14	10	20/-

NEWHAVEN-DIEPPE ROUTE.

24 to 25 knot Turbine Steamers *Brighton*, *Worthing*, *Versailles*, *Paris*, *Rouen* and *Newhaven*.

Private Cabin, one passenger	20/-	Per Cabin in addition to the First Class Fares.
„ „ two or more passengers	25/-	
Grand Cabine-de-Luxe on Turbine Steamers	40/-	

Small Cabins on s.s. *Brighton*, whether occupied by one or two passengers, 15/-.

SOUTHAMPTON ROUTES.

HAVRE, ST. MALO AND CHANNEL ISLANDS SERVICES.

1. **BERTHS.**—Berths can be reserved on the Steamers from and to Southampton, on payment of 1/- per berth, 1st or 2nd class.

2. **PRIVATE CABINS** (excluding s.s. *Isle of Thanet*).—The charge for a berth in Private Cabins (1st class) on the Promenade Deck is 5/-, no reservation fee being payable when taken in advance. A 2-berth cabin may be taken for the exclusive use of one 1st class passenger or a 3 or 4-berth cabin for the exclusive use of less than three or four 1st class passengers on payment of the following charges for each unoccupied berth :—

HAVRE, ST. MALO AND CHANNEL ISLANDS STEAMERS, (excluding s.s. *Isle of Thanet*).

(*a*) **Promenade Deck.**—October to March, 31/6 ; April to September, 42/-. Inclusive of reservation fee and Promenade Deck charge for occupied berth(s).

(*b*) **Main or Lower Deck.**—October to March, 21/- April to September, 31/6. Inclusive of reservation fee for occupied berth(s).

Private Cabins (Single-berth and two-berth) on Boat Deck of the s.s. *Isle of Thanet*, 20/-. Two-berth Cabins on Awning Deck, 20/- and 30/-.

3. **CABINES-DE-LUXE.**—In the Steamers, *Hantonia*, *Normannia* and *Lorina* there are cabines-de-luxe containing a single bedstead, which can be engaged on payment of 20/- additional to 1st class fare, whether occupied by one or two passengers.

In the Steamers *Dinard*, *St. Briac*, *Isle of Guernsey*, *Isle of Jersey* and *Isle of Sark* there are cabines-de-luxe containing a single bedstead and an upholstered settee on which a second bed can be made up if required. The charge for these cabins (additional to the 1st class fare(s)) when occupied by one or two passengers is 40/-. Reservation fee of 1/- not chargeable

The charge for a Cabine-de-Luxe on the s.s. *Isle of Thanet* is 40/-.

4. **SINGLE BERTH CABINS.**—In the *Isle of Guernsey*, *Isle of Jersey* and *Isle of Sark* there are single berth cabins on the Main Deck which can be engaged at a charge of 10/- each, and on the Promenade Deck of the *Dinard*, and the *St. Briac*, at a charge of 15/- each, additional to the 1st class fare. Reservation fee of 1/- not chargeable.

DOVER-DUNKERQUE ROUTE.

Ferry Steamers, *Twickenham Ferry*, *Hampton Ferry and Shepperton Ferry.*

Private Cabins (2 berths)	Supplement	20/-
Berth in Private Cabin (Night Ferry)	„	10/-
Berths in Ladies' or Gentlemen's Saloons		1/-

(Reservation Fee includes provision of a rug and pillow.)

SOUTHERN RAILWAY—continued.

DOVER AND OSTEND.

Charges for Cabins on the Dover-Ostend Steamers are :—

MOTOR VESSEL : *PRINS ALBERT.*

FIRST CLASS.

Suite comprising Cabins Nos. 1 and 3 combined, or 2 and 4 combined, and Private Lavatory ..	300 frs.
Cabines-de-Luxe (Nos. 1 and 2) ..	200 frs.
Special Cabin (Nos. 3 and 4) ..	150 frs.
Private Cabin (two-berthed) (Nos. 5, 6, 13 and 14) ..	120 frs.
Half-Cabin (shared with another passenger) ..	60 frs.

SECOND CLASS.

Private Cabin (two-berth) (Nos. 7, 8, 9, 10, 11 and 12) ..	100 frs.
Half-Cabin (shared with another passenger) ..	50 frs.

MOTOR VESSEL : *PRINCE BAUDOUIN.*

FIRST CLASS.

Suite comprising Cabins 1 and 3 combined, or Cabins 2 and 4 combined, and Private Lavatory ..	300 frs.
Private Cabin (two-berth) Nos. 5, 6, 7, 8, 11 and 12) ..	120 frs
Half Private Cabin do. do. (shared with another passenger)	60 frs

SECOND CLASS.

Private Cabin (two-berth), Nos. 9 and 10 ..	100 frs.
Berth in Private Cabin (shared with another passenger) ..	50 frs.

OTHER DOVER-OSTEND STEAMERS

FIRST CLASS.

*Suite comprising Cabine-de-Luxe, Private Lavatory and Special Cabin ..	300 frs.
Cabine-de-Luxe (Stateroom on s.s. *P. Marie-José*) ..	200 frs.
Special Cabin ..	150 frs.
Private Cabin (two berth) ..	120 frs.
Berth in Private Cabin (shared with another passenger) ..	60 frs.

SECOND CLASS.

Private Cabin (two berth) ..	100 frs.
Berth in Private Cabin (shared with another passenger) ..	50 frs.

Nos. 25 and 26 on "Prince" class steamers. Nos. 13 and 14 on board *P. Marie-José.* Berths can be reserved in the 1st and 2nd class Ladies' and Gentlemen's Saloons on board the steamers between Dover and Ostend upon payment of 1/-.

* Not available on s.s. *Princess Marie-José.*

LONDON & NORTH EASTERN RAILWAY

(HARWICH SERVICES) STEAMERS

s.s. *AMSTERDAM, PRAGUE, VIENNA, ANTWERP, BRUGES, MALINES, ARCHANGEL, ST. DENIS.*

Charges for Cabins. (Additional to 1st Class Fare and payable at time of reservation.)

	Hook of Holland Service. s.s. *Amsterdam, Prague, Vienna.*	Antwerp Service. s.s. *Antwerp, Bruges, Malines.*	Zeebrugge Service. s.s. *Archangel, St. Denis*
Cabine-de-Luxe, 2 beds	50/-	40/-	40/-
Promenade Deck Cabin	22/6 or 17/6	—	—
Deck "A" Cabin ..	20/- or 15/-	20/-, 12/6 or 10/-	15/- or 10/-
Deck "B" Cabin ..	15/-	12/6	7/6
Deck "C" Cabin ..	10/-	10/-	—

Single Berths in certain cabins of more than one berth on Decks "B" and "C" are free.

In addition, there are, on all the Steamers, a large number of Two-Berth Cabins free of charge, when reserved for that number of passengers holding First Class Boat Tickets.

For the Reservation in advance of berths, 1st or 2nd class, Reservation fee of 1/- per berth is payable.

ZEELAND S.S. COMPANY. HARWICH-FLUSHING STEAMERS.

m.v. *KONINGIN EMMA, PRINSES BEATRIX,* and T.s.s. *PRINSES JULIANA, ORANJE NASSAU* and *MECKLENBURG.*

I CLASS.	Harwich-Flushing.	Flushing-Harwich.
Promenade Deck State Cabin ..	15/-	Fl. 7
*Special State Cabins, D1 and D2, or E1 and E2, taken together	35/-	Fl. 16
*Special State Cabins, D2 and E2 ..	20/- each	Fl. 9 each
*Special State Cabins, D1 and E1 ..	15/- ,,	Fl. 7
*Deck Cabin (1 or 2 berths) ..	10/-	Fl. 4·50
Saloon Deck Cabin (per berth) ..	5/-	Fl. 2·50

* Upper Deck.

II CLASS	Harwich-Flushing.	Flushing-Harwich.
Berth in Outside Cabin ..	4/-	Fl. 2·0
Berth in Inside Cabin ..	Free.	Free.

PULLMAN CAR TRAINS
of the International Sleeping Car Co.

GOLDEN ARROW LUXE.

From London and Paris daily.

1st and 2nd class between Calais and Paris.

London (Vic.) .	dep.	11 0	Paris (Nord) ....dep.	1030
Dover (Marine)	arr.	1235	Boulogne(Mar) arr.	1316
	dep.	1255	dep.	1345
Calais (Mar.)..	arr.	1410	Folkest'e (Mar) arr.	1515
	dep	1430	dep.	1544
Paris (Nord)	arr.	1744	London (Vic.) ..arr	1720

NORTH STAR EXPRESS.

From Paris and Amsterdam daily.

1st and 2nd class.

Paris (Nord)	dep.	1130	Amsterdam (Cen.)dp.	1259
Brussels (Midi)	arr.	1435	The Hague ....dep.	1347
	dep.	1444	Rotterdam (D.P.) dp.	1418
Antwerp (Est.)..	dep.	1526	Rosendaal (A.T.)ar.	1452
Esschen	arr.	..	(G.T.) d.	15 4
	dep.	..	Esschen ...... arr.	..
Rosendaal	(A.T.)ar.	1617	dep.	..
	(A.T.)dp.	1617	Antwerp (Est.) ..arr.	1514
Rotterdam(D.P.)	arr.	1710	Brussels (Midi) arr.	1559
The Hague	arr.	1734	dep.	1611
Amsterdam (Cen.)	ar.	1827	Paris (Nord) .... arr.	1925

COTE D'AZUR EXPRESS.

1st and 2nd class.

From Paris
From Mentone } Suspended.

(Winter only.)

Paris (Lyon)....	dep.	1015	Mentone........dep.	9 27
Lyons........	arr.	1544	Monte Carlo .... ,,	9 37
,, ...	dep.	1549	Monaco .... ,,	9 42
Avignon.......	arr.	18 8	Cap d' Ail ...... ,,	9 47
Marseilles (St. Ch.)	,,	1929	Beaulieu .... ,,	9 56
Toulon........	,,	2024	Nice .... ,,	1010
Hyeres........	,,	2129	Cannes.......... ,,	1037
St. Raphael	,,	2128	St. Raphael .... ,,	11 4
Cannes..........	,,	2155	Hyeres........ ,,	11 5
Nice	,,	2226	Toulon.......... ,,	12 9
Beaulieu	,,	2242	Marseilles (St. Ch.),,	13 8
Cap d' Ail	,,	2251	Avignon .... ,,	1425
Monaco	,,	2255	Lyons .. .. ,,	17 3
Monte Carlo	,,	23 0	,, ... dep.	1710
Mentone	,,	2310	Paris (Lyon) .... arr.	2245

BLUE BIRD EXPRESS.

From Paris and Amsterdam daily.

1st and 2nd class.

Paris (Nord)	dep.	1810	Amsterdam(Cen.)dep.	7 32
Brussels (Midi)	arr.	2110	The Hague ...... ,,	8 25
	dep.	2120	Rotterdam (D.P.) ,,	8 49
Antwerp (Est.)	arr.	22 4	Rosendaal .... arr.	9 35
	dep.	22 5	dep.	9 41
Esschen......	arr.	..	Esschen...... arr.	..
	dep.	..	dep.	..
Rosendaal	arr.	2254	Antwerp (Est.) arr.	9 52
	dep.	23 4	dep.	9 53
Rotterdam (D.P.)	arr.	2349	Brussels (Midi) arr.	1037
The Hague	,,	0 11	dep.	1047
Haarlem........	,,	0 45	Paris (Nord) .... arr.	1347
Amsterdam (Cen.)	,,	1 1		

PULLMAN CAR TRAINS—*continued.*

OSTEND-COLOGNE EXPRESS.

From Ostend and Cologne daily.
1st and 2nd class.

London (Vic.)	dep	11¶0	Cologne (Cent.)	dep.	11 8
Dover (Marine)	arr.	1235	Aachen (M.E.T.)	ar.	1158
	dep.	1255		dp	1210
Ostend (Quai)	arr.	1615	Herbesthal (G.T.)	,,	
	dep.	1651	Liege (Guill.) ..	,,	1313
Ghent........	arr.	1727	Brussels (Nord)	arr	1425
Brussels (Nrd.)	arr.	18 1		dep.	1434
	dep	1812	Ghent	arr	15 7
Liege (Guill.) ..	arr.	1927	Ostend (Quai)	arr	1546
Herbesthal ...	,,	2013		dep	1620
Aachen (G T)	,,	2033	Dover (Marine)	arr.	1940
Aachen (M.E.T.)	dep.	2043		dep.	2010
Cologne (Cent.)	arr.	2135	London (Vic.)	arr.	2150

¶ Every Saturday to Oct. 7th leave London 10.30 and Dover 12.30.

EDELWEISS EXPRESS.

1st and 2nd class.

1st & 2nd cl. Pullman Amsterdam-Bale and *v.v.* daily.

1st & 2nd cl. Pullman Amsterdam-Bale-Zurich and *v.v.* daily.

1st cl. Pullman Amsterdam-Lucerne and *v.v.* June 30 to Sept. 9. From Lucerne, July 1–Sept. 10.

Amsterdam (C) ..	dep.	8 3	Zurich ...	dp.	7 22
The Hague	dp.	8 56	Bale (Cent.) ..	ar.	8 40
Rotterdam (D.P.)	,,	9 19			
Roosendaal (A.T.)	ar.	10 6	Lucerne	dp.	7 25
Antwerp (East)	ar.	1022	Bale (Cent.)	ar.	8 55
LONDON (L'pool St.)	d.	2030	Daily.		
Antwerp (Quai.) ..	ar.	8 30	Bale (Cent.) Gr.t.	dp.	9 27
Antwerp (East.)	dp.	1028	Strasbourg	,,	1059
Brussels (Nord) ..	,,	11 7	Luxembourg .	,,	1325
Luxembourg ...	ar.	1356	Brussels (Nord) ..	ar.	16 9
Strasbourg ...	ar.	1618	Antwerp (East.)	,,	1656
Bale (Cent.) Gr.t.	ar.	1751	Antwerp (Sud.)	dp.	1945
Bale (Cent.) Sw.t.	ar.	1751	London (L'pool St.)	ar	7 53
Bale (Cent.)	dp.	1855	Antwerp (East)	dp.	1657
Lucerne	ar.	2022	Roosendaal (A.T.)	ar.	1750
			Rotterdam (D.P.)	,,	1853
Bale (Cent.)	dp.	1838	The Hague	,,	1915
Zurich	ar.	1954	Amsterdam (C) ..	arr.	20 3

THERMAL EXPRESS.
PARIS—VICHY

1st class only.

From Paris–June 1 to Sept. 30.
From Vichy–June 2 to Oct. 1.

1110	dep.	Paris (Quai D'Orsay)	arr.	1723
15 3	arr.	Moulins........	dep.	1325
15 4	dep.	,, ...	arr.	1323
1545	arr.	Vichy	dep	1240

DANUBE PULLMAN EXPRESS

Daily.

1st and 2nd class.

Bucharest ...	dep.	1925	Galatz	dep	6 0
Ploesti (Sud.) ...	,,	2021	Braïla	,,	6 42
Buzau	,,	2120	Faurei	,,	7 26
Faurei	,,	2149	Buzau	,,	8 1
Braïla	arr	2232	Ploesti (Sud.)	arr.	9 0
Galatz	,,	2315	Bucharest	,,	9 52

KING CAROL 1st EXPRESS.

To and from Constanza daily.
To and from Mangalia July 1st to Sept. 15th.
1st and 2nd class.

Bucharest (N) ..	dep.	1930	Mangalia	dep.	5 70
Ciulnita	.. arr.	2051	Carmen Sylva ..	dep.	5 42
	.. dep.	2053	Eforia	dep.	5 55
Cernavoda......	dep.		Constanza	arr.	(6?) 20
Constanza	.. arr.	2246		.. dep.	[illegible]
	.. dep.	2254	Cernavoda......	dep.	.
Eforia..........	arr.	2319	Ciulnita ...	.. arr.	8 27
Carmen Sylva ..	arr.	2329		.. dep.	8 29
Mangalia	arr.	0 7	Bucharest (N) ..	arr.	9 50

SUNSHINE EXPRESS.

From Cairo } Winter only.
From Luxor }

Cairo	dep.	8 20	Luxor	dep.	7 5
Minia	,,	12 5	Sohag	,,	1125
Assiut	arr.	1411	Assiut	,,	1312
Sohag	,,	16 0	Minia	,,	1525
Luxor	,,	2015	Cairo	,,	1910

RESTAURANT AND DINING CARS

Are run in almost all the most important day express services throughout Europe; the principal services are indicated in the notes to the various tables. 2nd & 3rd cl. passengers can usually use these cars, though on some lines they may stay in the car *during the service of meals only.*

TRAINS DE LUXE of the International Sleeping Car Co.

RIVIERA EXPRESS.

1st and 2nd class.

Berlin to Cannes and (Rome). / **(Rome) and Cannes to Berlin** — Winter only.

Berlin Anhalt) dp.	
Leipsic ...... ,,	
Frankfurt .... ,,	
Mannheim .... arr.	
Mannheim .... dep.	
Carlsruhe .... ,,	
Baden West .. ,,	
Bale (Swiss) .. arr.	
,, ... dep.	
Bellinzona .... ,,	
Lugano ...... ,,	
Chiasso ...... arr.	
,, ... dep.	
Milan .... arr.	
Milan .... dep.	
Genoa P.P..... arr.	
Milan .... dep.	
Florence ...... arr.	
Rome .... ,,	
Genoa P.P. .. dep.	
Alassio........ arr.	
San Remo .... ,,	
Ospedaletti.... ,,	
Bordighera.... ,,	
Vintimille M.E.T. a.	
,, ...G.T. dep.	
Mentone ...... arr.	
Monte Carlo .. ,,	
Cap d'Ail .... ,,	
Beaulieu ...... ,,	
Nice .... ,,	
Cannes ...... ,,	

Cannes ...... dep.	
Nice .... ,,	
Beaulieu ...... ,,	
Cap d'Ail .... ,,	
Monte Carlo .. ,,	
Mentone ...... ,,	
Vintimille G.T. arr.	
,, M.E.T. dep.	
Bordighera.... ,,	
Ospedaletti .... ,,	
San Remo .... ,,	
Alassio........ ,,	
Genoa P.P..... arr.	
Rome .... dep.	
Florence ...... ,,	
Milan.......... arr	
Genoa P.P. .. dep.	
Milan .... arr.	
Milan .... dep.	
Chiasso ...... arr.	
,, ... dep.	
Lugano ...... ,,	
Bellinzona .... ,,	
Bale (Swiss) .. arr.	
,, ... dep.	
Baden West .. ,,	
Carlsruhe .... ,,	
Darmstadt .... arr.	
Darmstadt .... dep.	
Frankfurt .... ,,	
Leipsic........ arr.	
Berlin (Anhalt) ,,	

† *Via* Aarau Rothkreuz, and *v.v.*

P. & O. EXPRESS.

Thursday.	
London (Vic.) dep.	1350
Calais .... ,,	1745
Paris (Lyon) .. arr.	2154
,, ... dep.	2230
Lyons .... ,,	5 49
Marseilles (P.& O. Quay) arr.	1045

Friday or Saturday.	
Marseilles (P.& O. Quay) dep.	1652
Lyons .... ,,	2254
Paris (Lyon) .. arr.	6 55
,, ... dep.	7 20
Calais .... arr.	1128
London (Vic.) ,,	1520

NORD EXPRESS.

1st and 2nd class.

Calais, Brussels to Warsaw daily, (to Niegoreloje, Tu.)
Warsaw, Brussels to Calais daily, (fr. Stolpce, Thur.)
Ostend, Berlin, Breslau, Cracow Lwow and Bucharest Wednesday, Friday, Sunday.
Bucharest-Ostend, Tuesday, Thursday, & Sunday.
Ostend-Warsaw, Monday, Tuesday, Thursday, Saturday.
Warsaw-Ostend, Tuesday, Thursday, Saturday, Sunday.
Paris-Warsaw daily, (to Niegoreloje Thurs).
Warsaw-Paris daily, (from Stolpce, Sats.)
Paris-Riga, and *v.v.* daily.
Paris to Hamburg and Copenhagen daily.
From Copenhagen and Hamburg to Paris daily.

London (Vic.) dep.	14 0
Calais .... ,,	1730
Brussels ...... arr.	2050
London (Vic.) dep.	15¶0
Ostend .... ,,	2038
Brussels (Nord) ,,	2210
Liege .... arr.	2325
Paris (Nord) .. dep.	1915
Liege .... arr.	2314
Liege .... dep.	2346
Cologne ...... arr.	1 46
Hanover ...... ,,	5 28
Hanover ...... dep.	5 56
Hamburg (H) .. arr.	8 4
Altona .... ,,	8 28
Copenhagen .. ,,	1927
Hanover ...... dep.	5 36
Berlin (Fried) .. arr.	8 33
,, (Schles) .. ,,	8 45
Berlin (Schles) dep.	9 12
Poznan ...... arr.	1239
Warsaw (G) .. arr.	1634
Stolpce .... arr.	2211
Niegoreloje .... arr.	1 41
Berlin (Schles) dep.	9 4
Eydtkau .. ... arr.	1822
Wirballen .... ,,	1838
Riga .... ,,	0 43
Berlin (Schles) dep.	9 30
Breslau .... arr.	1344
Breslau .... dep.	1354
Beuthen ...... ,,	1655
Katowice...... ,,	1734
Cracow........ arr.	1853
Lwow .... ,,	24 0
Oraseni ...... ,,	5 5
Oraseni ...... dp.	6 45
Cernauti ...... arr.	7 6
Pascani.... arr	9 59
Buzu ...... ,,	1415
Bucharest .... ,,	1615

¶ On Sats. until Sept. 2, leave London 14.30.
† Sats. arr. Cannon Street, 16.26.

Bucharest .... dep.	1348
Cernauti ...... ,,	0 27
Oraseni ...... ar.	0 50
Oraseni ...... dp.	0 20
Lwow .... ,,	6 15
Cracow ...... ,,	11 3
Katowice...... ,,	1244
Beuthen ...... ,,	1321
Breslau .... arr.	1547
Breslau .... dep.	16 6
Berlin (Schles) arr.	2034
Riga.......... dep.	6 25
Wirballen .... ,,	11 3
Eydtkau ...... ,,	1121
Berlin (Schles) arr.	2044
Stolpce ......dep.	6 47
Warsaw (G) .. dep.	1316
Poznan ...... ,,	1714
Berlin (Schles) arr.	2049
Berlin (Schles) dep.	2110
,, (Fried) .. ,,	2120
Hanover ...... arr.	0 11
Copenhagen .. dep.	9 15
Altona .... ,,	2117
Hamburg (H).. ,,	2140
Hanover ...... arr.	2352
Hanover ...... dep.	0 25
Cologne .... arr.	4 3
Cologne .... dep.	4 5
Herbesthal ....arr.	5 33
Liege .... arr.	6 26
Liege .... dep.	6 39
Paris (Nord) .. arr.	1055
Cologne ...... dep.	4 5
Herbesthal....dep.	6 39
Liege .... arr.	7 18
,, ... dep.	7 23
Brussels ...... arr.	8 38
Ostend........ ,,	10 8
London (Vic.) ,,	16†20
Liege ....dep.	7 0
Brussels .. ..arr.	8 12
Brussels ...... dep.	8 38
Calais .... arr.	1156
London (Vic.) ,,	1530

TRAINS DE LUXE—*continued.*

CALAIS-PARIS-MEDITERRANEAN (SAN REMO) EXPRESS.

1st and 2nd class.

From Calais and Paris.
From San Remo and Vintimille. } Daily.

London (Vic.)	dep.	11 0
Calais (Mar.)	arr.	1410
	dep.	1430
Paris (Lyon)	arr.	1825
	dep.	20 0
Marseilles	arr.	7 0
Toulon	„	8 3
St. Raphael	„	9 21
Cannes	„	9 50
Nice	„	1028
Beaulieu	„	1045
Cap d'Ail	„	1054
Monte Carlo	„	11 4
Mentone	„	1114
Vintimille (G.T.)	„	1129
„ (Etna tm.)	dp.	1250
San Remo	arr.	1314

San Remo	dep.	1552
Vintimille (Etn,tm)	a.	1617
„ (G.T.)	dep.	1655
Mentone	„	17 9
Monte Carlo	„	1719
Cap d'Ail	„	1729
Beaulieu	„	1738
Nice	„	1753
Cannes	„	1829
St. Raphael	„	1859
Toulon	„	2019
Marseilles	„	2122
Paris (Lyon)	arr.	9 0
	dep.	9 46
Boulogne (Mar.)	a.	13 5
	d.	1345
London (Vic.)	arr.	1720

ROME EXPRESS.

(1st and 2nd cl.)

From Calais and Paris to Naples, daily.
Paris-Florence and *v.v.*
From Naples to Paris and Boulogne, daily.
1 & 2 cl. Sleep. car train Rome and Naples to Syracuse and *v.v.*

London (Vic.)	dep.	11 0
Calais (Mar.)	„	1430
Paris (Nord.)	arr.	1744
„ (P.L.M.)	„	1825
„ (P.L.M.)	dep.	1930
Aix-les-Bains	„	2 43
Chambery	„	2 56
Modane (G.T.)	arr.	4 25
„ (Etna time)	dp.	4 50
Ulzio	dep.	5 36
Turin	arr.	6 50
Turin	dep.	7 3
Genoa	arr.	9 15
Genoa	dep.	9 21
Viareggio	arr.	1119
Viareggio	dep.	1135
Florence	arr.	1340
Pisa	arr.	1146
Pisa	dep.	1149
Rome	arr.	1530
Rome	dep.	1545
Naples (P. Gar)	arr.	1756
Naples (Cent.)	dep.	2148
Messina Mar.	arr.	6 45
Palermo	„	10a32
Taormina	„	8 12
Catania	„	9 10
Syracuse Mar.	„	1135

a 2 cl. Rapido.

Syracuse Mar.	dep.	19 0
Catania	„	21 7
Taormina	„	2213
Palermo	„	1810
Messina Mar.	„	2325
Naples (Cent.)	arr.	8 2
„ „	dep.	8 15
Rome	arr.	1055
	dep.	1230
Pisa	arr.	1615
Pisa	dep.	1616
Viareggio	arr.	1632
Florence	dep.	1420
Viareggio	arr.	1617
Viareggio	dep.	1634
Genoa	arr.	1847
Genoa	dep.	1854
Turin	arr.	2115
Turin	dep.	2124
Ulzio	dep.	2252
Modane (Etna tm.)	a.	2340
„ (Greenw. time)	dep.	0 0
Chambery	„	1 29
Aix-les-Bains	„	1 43
Paris (P.L.M.)	arr.	9 10
„ (P.L.M.)	dep.	9 46
„ (Nord.)	„	1040
Boulogne	arr.	13 5
London (Vic.)	„	1720

LONDON—PARIS (Ferry Service)

DAILY. 1st and 2nd class.

22 0	dep. London (Vic.)	arr.	9 10
23 36	arr. Dover (Marine)	dep	7 20
23 46	arr. „ (Ferry)	dep.	6 40
0 35	dep. „ „	arr	6 15
4 30	arr. Dunkerque (Ferry)	dep.	2 0
5 15	dep. „	arr.	1 30
5 34	dep. Dunkerque	dep.	1 12
9 0	arr. Paris (Nord)	dep.	21 50

STAR OF EGYPT EXPRESS.

From Cairo.
From Assuan. } Winter only.

Cairo	dep.	1930
Assiut	arr.	0 55
	dep.	1 2
Luxor	arr.	6 20
	dep.	6 30
Assuan	arr.	1010
Shellal	arr.	1030

Shellal	dep.	1535
Assuan	dep.	16 0
Luxor	arr.	1945
	dep.	1955
Assiut	arr.	1 53
	dep.	2 0
Cairo	arr.	7 30

VIENNA-NICE-CANNES EXP.

1st and 2nd class.

Vienna to Cannes
Vienna to Rome
Munich to Cannes
Cannes to Munich
Rome to Vienna
Cannes to Vienna } Winter only.

Vienna (East)	dep.	1930
Leoben	„	2253
Villach	arr.	2 6
	dep.	2 11
Tarvisio	arr.	2 55
	dep.	3 10
Udine	„	4 43
Venice (S.L.)	arr.	6 24
	dep.	6 37
Venice	dep.	7 7
Padua	arr.	7 46
Bologna	„	10 0
Florence	„	1130
Rome	„	1525
Munich	dep.	2350
Kufstein	„	1 30
Innsbruck	„	2 50
Brennero	arr.	3 35
	dep.	4 5
Verona	arr.	8 5
Verona P.N.	dep.	8 24
Milan	arr.	1030
	dep.	1037
Genoa	arr.	1242
	dep.	1252
San Remo	arr.	1516
Vintimille (Etna t.)	a.	1545
Vintimille (Grn.t.)	d.	1557
Mentone	arr,	16 8
Nice	„	1650
Cannes	„	1724

Cannes	dep.	[illegible]
Nice	„	1215
Mentone	„	1255
Vintimille (Grn.t.)	a.	13 5
Vintimille (Etna t.)	d.	1321
San Remo	dep.	1347
Genoa	arr.	1615
	dep.	1625
Milan	arr.	1840
	dep.	1854
Verona, P.N.	arr.	2052
Verona	dep.	22 3
Brennero	arr.	2 53
	dep.	2 55
Innsbruck	arr.	3 42
Kufstein	„	4 55
Munich	„	6 30
Rome	dep.	1425
Florence	„	1820
Bologna	„	1951
Padua	„	[illegible]
Venice	arr.	[illegible]
Venice (S.L.)	arr.	2237
	dep.	2240
Udine	arr.	0 34
Tarvisio	arr.	2 15
	dep.	2 34
Villach	arr.	3 13
	dep.	3 20
Leoben	arr.	6 32
Vienna (East)	„	9 50

SIMPLON-ORIENT-TAURUS EXP.

1st and 2nd class.

Daily, Calais and Paris to Istanbul.
Daily, Istanbul to Paris and Boulogne.
Daily, Paris to Bucharest and back.
Daily, Paris to Athens and back.
Haydarpasa to Mosul Mon., Wed. and Fri.
Mosul to Haydarpasa Tues., Thurs. and Sats.
Haydarpasa to Aleppo and Tripoli, Mon., Wed. and Fri.; returning from Tripoli, Tue., Thur. and Sat.

London (Victoria) d.	14 0
Calais.......... ,,	1735
Paris (Lyons) arr.	2117
Paris (Lyons) dep.	2220
Vallorbe .... arr.	5 25
Vallorbe .... dep.	5 45
Lausanne......arr.	6 26
Brigue .... ,,	8 38
Domodossola arr.	9 22
Domodossola dep.	9 53
Milan ....arr.	1215
Venice........arr.	16 0
Trieste........ ,,	1822
Postumia, c. ,,	1955
Postumia, c. dep.	2015
Vinkovci......arr.	4 34
Vinkovci....dep.	4 50
Jimbolia .. arr.	10 6
Jimbolia .. dep.	1128
Craiova ....arr.	1740
Bucharest .. ,,	2145
Vinkovci......dep.	4 49
Belgrade .... arr.	7 18
Belgrade .... dep.	7 55
Nisch .... ,,	1224
Skoplje ......arr.	1626
Guevgueli .. arr.	20 0
Guevgueli .. dep.	2120
Thessaloniki.. arr.	[illegible]
Athens........ ,,	1026
Belgrade ......dep.	7 45
Nisch ....arr.	1133
Tzaribrod .... ,,	1330
Sofia.......... ,,	1628
Svilengrade arr.	2257
Svilengrade dep.	2310
Istanbul ......arr.	7 20
Str. Sirkedji (Mar.) dp.	8 20
Haydarpasa .. arr.	8 40
Haydarpasa ..dep.	9 0
Ankara ......arr.	21 3
,, ...dep.	2118
Adana ....arr.	1223
Aleppo........ ,,	2042
Tripoli¶ .... ,,	6 39
Nusaybin .... ,,	7 16
Mosul .... ,,	1615
Baghdad (N) ..arr.	6 50
Baghdad (W)..dep.	19 0
Basra ....arr.	8 20
Mosul ......dep.	1330
Khanikin .. arr.	6 15
Hamadan .. ,,	20 0
Teheran .... ,,	19 0

Teheran ....dep.	6 0
Kermanshah ,,	9 0
Khanikin .. ,,	22 0
Mosul ...... arr.	1245
Basra ......dep.	1915
Baghdad (W) arr.	8 20
Baghdad (N) dep.	21 0
Mosul ....dep.	1315
Nusaybin...... arr.	2027
Nusaybin ....dep.	2033
Tripoli ¶.... ,,	2028
Aleppo........ arr.	6 56
Aleppo........dep.	7 25
Adana........ ,,	1527
Ankara ...... arr.	8 0
Haydarpasa .. ,,	20 0
Str. Haydarpasa ..dep.	20 0
Sirkedji (Mar.) arr.	2020
Istanbul ......dep.	22 0
Svilengrade arr.	6 20
Svilengrade dep.	6 50
Sofia .... ,,	1441
Tzaribrod .. arr.	1620
Tzaribrod .. dep.	1550
Nisch .... ,,	1748
Belgrade.... arr.	2149
Athens ....dep.	2045
Thessalonica ,,	8 20
Guevgueli arr.	9 59
Guevgueli dep.	9 20
Skoplje .... ,,	1322
Nisch ...... arr,	1728
Belgrade.... arr.	2149
Belgrade.... dep.	2220
Vinkovci......arr.	1 1
Bucharest ....dep.	10 5
Timisoara .... ,,	1937
Jimbolia.... arr.	2015
Jimbolia.... dep.	1937
Vinkovci......arr.	0 54
Vinkovci......dep.	1 19
Postumia .. arr.	10 0
Postumia .. dep.	1025
Trieste........ ,,	1225
Venice........ ,,	1457
Milan ....dep.	1910
Domodossola arr.	2138
Domodossola dep.	2154
Brigue........ ,,	2245
Lausanne .... ,,	0 52
Vallorbe .. arr.	1 34
Vallorbe .. dep.	2 2
Paris (Lyons)..arr.	8 40
Paris (Lyons) dep.	9 46
Boulogne .... arr.	13 5
London (Vic.) arr.	1720

¶ For connections to and from CAIRO, *see p.* 334.

ARLBERG-ORIENT EXPRESS

1st and 2nd class.

From Calais to Bucharest, Mon., Wed. and Fri.

From Paris to Bucharest and Athens, Mon., Wed. and Fri.

From Bucharest to Paris and Boulogne Tues., Thur. and Sun.

From Athens to Paris, Mon., Wed. and Sat.

London(Victoria)d.	14 0
Calais........dep.	1725
Laon ....arr.	2030
Laon ....dep.	2037
Chaumont arr.	2319
Paris (Est) ..dep.	1955
Chaumont .. arr.	23 0
Chaumont ....dep.	2331
Belfort........arr.	1 29
Belfort ...... dep.	1 35
Bale..........arr.	2 35
Bale..........dep.	2 48
Zurich (Enge) ar.	4 1
Zurich (Enge) d.	4 3
Sargans ...... arr.	5 21
Sargans .... dep.	6*†1
Coire ...... arr.	6†30
Sargans...... dep.	5 27
Buchs...... arr.	5 40
Buchs...... dep.	5 55
Innsbruck .... arr.	8 52
Innsbruck .. dep.	1028
Brennero arr.	1116
Brennero dep.	1143
Fortezza ....arr.	1230
Dobbiaco.... ,,*	1536
Cortina ,,	1710
S. Candido .. ,,*	1544
Innsbruck ....dep.	9 0
Kitzbuhel .... ,,	1023
Salzburg......arr.	1257
Vienna (W).... ,,	1715
,, (W)... dep	1728
Budapest (E) .. ,,	2355
Oradea........ ,,	6 2
Bucharest .... ,,	1955
Budapest (E).dp.	2348
Belgrade.. arr.	7 8
Nisch arr.	1215
Nisch dep	1224
Thessaloniki ar.	2255
Athens .... ,,	1026

Athens .... dep.	2045
Thessalonica ,,	8 20
Nisch .. arr	1728
Nisch .. dep.	18 9
Belgrade ar.	2240
Budapest (E). ,,	6 2
Bucharest .... dep.	13 5
Oradea......... ,,	2 7
Budapest (E).. ,,	8 15
Vienna(W).... arr.	12 5
,, (W)....dep,	1220
Salzburg...... ,,	1640
Kitzbuhel .... ,,	19 8
Innsbruck .... arr.	2033
S. Candido..dep.	14*30
Cortina ,,	8 30
Dobbiaco.... ,,	14*36
Fortezza .... ,,	1824
Brennero arr.	1920
Brennero dep.	1950
Innsbruck .. arr.	2035
Innsbruck ....dep.	2040
Buchs...... arr.	2345
Buchs...... dep.	0 0
Sargans ...... arr.	0 14
Coire ...... dep.	2239
Sargans .... arr.	2310
Sargans ......dep.	0 23
Zurich (Enge) ar.	1 36
Zurich (Enge) d.	1 38
Bale........... arr.	2 54
Bale..........dep.	3 20
Belfort........arr.	4 28
Belfort ....dep.	4 34
Chaumont .... arr.	6 40
Chaumont ..dep.	6 54
Paris (Est) .. arr.	9 45
Chaumont ....dep.	7 15
Laon ....arr.	10 5
Laon ....dep.	1013
Boulogne .... arr.	13 0
London (Victoria)a.	1720

* 2 and 3 class. † Weekdays.

ANATOLIE EXPRESS.

From Haydarpasa to Ankara and Sivas, *see page* 333.

OSTEND—VIENNA—ORIENT EXPRESS.

1st and 2nd class.

From Ostend-Budapest, From Ostend Istanbul, From Amsterdam-Bucharest } Tue., Thur. & Sat.
From Istanbul to Ostend, Tue., Thur. & Sun.
From Bucharest to Amsterdam, Mon., Wed., Fri.
From Budapest to Ostend. Tue., Thur. and Sats.

London (Vict.)	dep.	15¶0
Ostend (Quay)	,,	2038
Brussels (Nord)	arr.	2154
	dep.	2210
Aachen G.T. C.E.T.	arr.	0 26
	dep.	0 36
Cologne	arr.	1 28
Amsterdam C. d.		2041
Zevenaar	dep.	2222
Emmerich C.E.T.	arr.	2217
	dep.	2248
Cologne	arr.	0 53
Cologne	dep.	1 38
Frankfort Sud	,,	4 34
Passau	arr.	1055
	dep.	11 4
Linz	arr.	1227
Vienna (West)	arr.	1520
	dep.	1544
Nickelsdorf	arr.	1725
	dep.	1741
Budapest E	arr.	20 3
Budapest E	dep.	2348
Belgrade	arr.	7 8
	dep.	7 45
Nisch	arr.	1130
Sofia	arr.	1628
Istanbul	ar.	7 20
Budapest W	dep.	2035
Lokoshaza	arr.	0 9
	dep.	1 24
Curtici	arr.	1 35
	dep.	1 50
Ploesti (W)	,,	1140
Bucharest (N.)	arr.	1230

Istanbul	dp.	22 0
Sofia	,,	1441
Nisch	,,	1748
Belgrade	arr.	2149
	dep.	2250
Budapest W	arr	6 16
Bucharest (N.)	dep.	1945
Ploesti (W)	,,	2037
Curtici	arr.	6 26
	dep	6 41
Lokoshaza C.E.T.	arr.	6 52
	dep.	6 7
Budapest W	arr.	9 35
Budapest W	dep.	1010
Nickelsdorf	arr.	1233
	dep.	1249
Vienna (West)	arr.	1429
	dep.	1514
Linz	,,	1749
Passau	arr.	1923
	dep	1933
Frankfurt Hbf	,,	2 11
Cologne	arr.	5 14
Cologne	dep.	5 40
Zevenaar	arr.	8 38
,, Amst. T.	dp	9 15
Amsterdam C.	a.	1051
Cologne	dep.	5 26
Aachen	arr.	6 19
	dep.	6 31
Herbesthal G.T.	d.	7 14
Brussels (N.)	arr.	9 7
	dep.	9 17
Ostend (Quay)	arr.	1034
London (Vict.)	,,	1620

¶ On Sats. until Sept. 2, leaves London 14.30.

OSTEND-KARLSBAD EXP.

1st and 2nd class.

From Ostend Tues., Thurs., and Sats., June 15 to Sept. 19.
From Karlsbad Tues., Thur., and Sats., June 17 to Sept. 21.

London (Vict.)	dep.	15¶0
Ostend (Quay)	,,	2038
Brussels (N.)	arr.	2154
	dep	2210
Aachen	arr.	0 26
	dep	0 36
Cologne	arr.	1 28
	dep	1 38
Frankfort Sud	,,	4 34
Nuremberg	arr.	8 0
Eger	,,	11 9
	dep.	1121
Karlsbad	arr.	1227

Karlsbad	dep.	1832
Eger	arr.	1933
	dep.	1952
Nuremberg	,,	2235
Frankfurt	,,	2 11
Cologne	arr.	5 14
	dep.	5 26
Aachen	arr.	6 19
	dep.	6 31
Brussels (N.)	arr.	9 7
	dep	9 17
Ostend (Quay)	arr.	1034
London (Vict).	,,	1620

ORIENT EXPRESS. 1st & 2nd class.

From Calais and Paris to Vienna, Budapest and Bucharest Tues., Thurs. and Sats.
From Paris to Istanbul Tues., Thurs., and Sats.
Bucharest to Paris and Calais Mon., Wed., & Fri.
From Istanbul to Paris, Sun., Tue. and Thur.

London (Vict.)	dep.	14 0
Calais	,,	1725
Laon	,,	2037
Chalons	arr.	2148
Paris (Est.)	dep.	1955
Chalons	arr.	2146
Chalons	dep.	2210
Strasbourg	dep.	2 11
Kehl GrnT	arr.	2 22
Kehl C.E.T	dep.	2 57
Carlsruhe	arr.	3 55
Stuttgart	arr.	5 29
Munich	arr.	8 24
	dep.	8 36
Salzburg	arr.	1029
	dep	11 0
Linz	arr.	1241
Vienna (W.)	arr.	1520
	dep	1544
Nickelsdorf	arr.	1725
	dep.	1741
Budapest (E)	arr.	20 3
	dep.	2035
Arad	,,	2 7
Ploesti (W)	,,	1140
Bucharest (N)	arr.	1230
Budapest (W)	dep.	2348
Belgrade	arr.	7 10
Sofia	arr.	1625
Istanbul	arr.	7 20

Istanbul	dep.	22 0
Sofia	dep.	1441
Belgrade	dep.	2250
Budapest (W).	arr.	6 36
Bucharest	dep.	1945
Ploesti (W)	,,	2037
Arad	..	6 10
Budapest (W)	arr.	9 35
	dep.	1010
Nickelsdorf	arr.	12[illegible]3
	dep.	124[illegible]
Vienna (W.)	arr.	1429
	dep.	1514
Linz	dep.	1755
Salzburg	arr.	1943
	dep.	1953
Munich	arr.	2150
	dep.	2210
Stuttgart	dep.	1 14
Carlsruhe	dep.	2 40
Kehl C.E.T	arr.	3 44
Kehl GrnT	dep.	4 19
Strasbourg	dep.	4 36
Chalons	arr	8 20
Chalons	dep.	8 26
Paris (Est.)	arr.	1012
Chalons	dep.	8 45
Laon	,,	1013
Boulogne	arr.	13 0
London (Vic.)	,,	17[illegible]

CALAIS-PARIS-PRAHA KARLSBAD EXPRESS.

1st and 2nd class.

From Calais and Paris Tues., Thurs., and Sats., June 15 to Sept. 19.
From Karlsbad and Praha Tues., Thurs., and Sats., June 17 to Sept. 21

London (Vic.)	dep.	14 0
Calais	,,	1725
Chalons	arr.	2148
Paris (Est.)	dep.	1955
Chalons	,,	2210
Strasbourg	arr.	2 5
	dep.	2 11
Kehl C.E.T.	arr.	2 23
	dep.	2 57
Carlsruhe	arr.	3 55
Stuttgart	arr.	5 29
Eger	arr.	11 9
	dep	1137
Marienbad	arr.	1216
Tuschkau-Kosolu	,,	1336
Praha	,,	16 0
Eger	dep.	1121
Karlsbad	arr.	1227

Karlsbad	dep.	1832
Eger	arr.	1933
Praha	dep.	1520
Tuschkau-Kosolu	,,	1746
Marienbad	,,	19 7
Eger	arr.	1940
	dep.	1952
Stuttgart	dep.	1 14
Carlsruhe	dep.	2 [illegible]
Kehl C.E.T.	arr.	3 44
	dep.	4 17
Strasbourg	arr.	4 30
	dep	4 36
Chalons	arr.	8 20
Paris (Est.)	,,	1012
Chalons	dep.	8 45
Boulogne	arr.	13 0
London (Vic.)	,,	1720

TRAINS DE LUXE—*continued.*

SUD EXPRESS.

1 & 2 cl. Pullman Car Paris-Irun and *v.v.*

1 cl. Pullman Car Paris-Biarritz (Ville) and *v.v.*

1 & 2 cl. Sleeping Cars, Irun-Madrid, Irun-Lisbo n and *v.v.*

Pullman Car.	Paris(Q.d'Orsay)d	1130
Pullman Car.	Bordeaux(S.Jean)	1721
Pullman Car.	Dax ......dep.	2140
Pullman Car.	Pau ......arr.	23 4
Pullman Car.	Dax ....dep.	19 1
Pullman Car.	Bayonne .... ,,	1939
Pullman Car.	Biarritz (Ville) ar.	20 4
Pullman Car.	St.Jean de Luz,,	2016
Pullman Car.	Irun ...... arr.	2045
Pullman Car.	Irun ...... dep.	2135
	Saint Sebastian ,,	..
	Miranda ...... ,,	..
	Burgos .... ,,	..
	Venta de Banos ,,	..
	Medina .... arr.	5 44
	Medina ....dep.	5 56
	Salamanca .... ,,	7 41
	Fuentes d'Onoro	1136
	Villar Formoso dep.	1210
	Pampilhosa .... arr.	1543
	Oporto‡	..
	Coimbra Junc.	..
	Entroncamento dep.	..
	LISBON (Rocio) arr	1850
	Estoril ...... ,,	..
	Medina ....dep.	6 0
	Avila .... ,,	..
	Escorial........ ,,	..
	MADRID (N.) .. arr.	10 0

	MADRID (N.) . dep.	22 0
	Escorial ...... ,,	..
	Avila	..
	Medina .... arr.	2 20
	LISBON ....dep.	1355
	Estoril ......dep.	..
	Entroncamento ,,	..
	Coimbra Junc. dep.	..
	Oporto‡	..
	Pampilhosa .... ,,	1655
	Villar Formoso ,,	21 3
	Fuentes d'Onoro ,,	2145
	Salamanca .... ,,	0 52
	Medina ...... arr.	2 26
	Medina .. ....dep.	2 41
	Venta de Banos ,,	..
	Burgos .... ,,	..
	Miranda ...... ,,	..
	St. Sebastian.. ,,	..
Pullman Car.	Irun ...... ,,	1130
Pullman Car.	Hendaye .. arr.	1135
Pullman Car.	Hendaye .. dep.	12 0
Pullman Car.	St.Jean de Luz,,	1215
Pullman Car.	Biarritz (Ville),,	1242
Pullman Car.	Bayonne .... ,,	13 4
Pullman Car.	Pau ...... ,,	1032
Pullman Car.	Dax ...... arr.	12 8
Pullman Car.	Dax ...... dep.	1341
Pullman Car.	Bordeaux (S.J.),,	1524
	Paris(Q.d'Orsay)a	2059

ENGADINE AND OBERLAND EXPRESS.

(1st and 2nd class).

Calais and Paris to Interlaken and Coire—Mons., Weds. & Fris., June 23 to Sept. 1.

Coire and Interlaken to Paris and Boulogne—Mons., Weds. & Fris., June 26 to Sept. 4.

London (Vict.) dep	14 0
Calais .... ,,	1725
Laon .... ,,	2037
Chaumont ..arr	2319
Paris (East) ..dep.	1955
Chaumont ....arr.	23 0
Chaumont ....dep.	2331
Belfort ....arr.	1 29
Belfort ......dep.	5 10
Delle ....arr.	5 37
Berne ...... ,,	8 24
Interlaken Ct. ,,	10 2
,, Ost. ,,	10 9
Belfort ....dep.	1 35
Bale.. G.T. ar.	2 35
Bale.. M.E.T dp.	2 48
Zurich (Enge) arr.	4 1
Landquart .... ,,	7 13
Davos ...... ,,	9 12
Coire .... ,,	7 30
St. Moritz .... ,,	1012

St. Moritz ....dep.	2015
Coire .... ,,	2239
Davos ...... ,,	19 0
Sargans ...... ,,	0 23
Zurich (Enge).. ,,	1 38
Bale M.E.T. arr.	2 54
Bale G.T. dep.	3 20
Belfort .... arr.	4 28
Interlaken Os. dp.	2117
,, Cent. ,,	2125
Berne ...... ,,	2250
Delle .... ,,	1 18
Belfort ......arr.	1 46
Belfort ....dep.	4 34
Chaumont ....arr.	6 40
Chaumont ....dep.	6 54
Paris ....arr.	9 45
Chaumont ....dep.	7 15
Laon .... ,,	1013
Boulogne .... arr.	13 0
London (Vict.) ,,	1720

TIROL EXPRESS.

1st and 2nd class.

Calais to Salzburg } Winter only.
Salzburg to Calais }

London (Vic.) dep.
Calais ....dep.
Laon.......... arr
Bale (C.E.T.) arr.
Bale (C.E.T.) dep
Zurich (Enge).. arr
Buchs ...... arr.
Buchs ...... dep.
St. Anton .... arr.
Landeck ...... arr.
Innsbruck .. arr.
Innsbruck .. dep.
Kitzbuhel .... arr.
Zell-am-see.... arr.
Salzburg ...... arr.

Salzburg ......dep.
Zell-am-see ... dep.
Kitzbuhel ....dep.
Innsbruck .. arr.
Innsbruck .. dep.
Landeck ......dep.
St. Anton ....dep.
Buchs ...... arr.
Buchs ...... dep.
Zurich (Enge)..dep.
Bale (C.E.T.) arr
Bale (G.T.).. dep.
Laon..........dep.
Calais .... arr.
London (Vic.).. arr.

SIGHTSEEING ARRANGEMENTS.

Our well-known "How to See" facilities provide the best means of extracting the maximum of pleasure and interest from a visit to a strange town. They have been designed with the express object of relieving the visitor of the slightest trouble and, for the most part, they include the services of competent guide-lecturers. Descriptive programmes free on request.

COOK'S GUIDE BOOKS, Etc.

	Published.	Price s.	d.	Postage.
London (304 pages; 7 views, 11 maps and plans)	1930	3	0	3d.
London Guidebook and Atlas (320 pages) including street atlas with index of 10,000 references and 32 other maps and plans ..	1937	5	0	4d.
Belgium and Luxembourg (208 pages; 11 maps and plans)	1938	5	0	3d.
Holland (240 pages; 7 maps and plans)	1932	6	0	3d.
Rhine and Black Forest (248 pages; 18 maps and plans)	1931	7	6	4d.
Norway, Sweden, Denmark, Finland and Iceland .. .. .. (536 pages; 17 maps and plans).	1939	10	6	6d.
Paris (168 pages; 13 maps and plans)	1939	2	6	2d.
Normandy and Brittany (556 pages; 16 maps and plans)	1930	5	0	5d.
Rivieras of France and Italy (372 pages; 14 maps and plans) ..	1927	7	6	4d.
Italy : Northern and Central, including Rome .. .. (848 pages; 18 maps and plans)	1927	12	6	7d.
Southern (240 pages; 5 maps and plans)	1928	5	0	3d.
Rome (200 pages; 7 maps and plans)	1935	2	6	3d.
Venice and Venetia (272 pages; 6 maps and plans	1925	5	0	4d.
Milan and the Italian Lakes (120 pages, 2 maps and plan) ..	1926	2	6	2d.
Florence (128 pages; 5 plans)	1934	2	6	2d.
Naples (140 pages; map and 2 plans)	1928	2	6	2d.
Switzerland (478 pages; 14 maps and plans)	1929	7	6	5d
Spain and Portugal (656 pages; 36 maps and plans)	1930	18	0	6d.
North Africa : Morocco, Algeria, Tunisia, Libya .. .. .. (320 pages; 9 maps and plans)	1933	7	6	4d.
Egypt and Sudan (720 pages; 27 maps and plans)	1930	20	0	6d.
Palestine, Syria and Iraq (512 pages; 11 maps and plans) ..	1934	10	6	5d.
Loth's Conversational Guide (English, French, German and Italian)	1936	1	6	2d.

Map of Norway, 6d.; folded in cover 1/- (*postage* 1d).

MAGAZINES FOR WORLD-WIDE READING.

Postage is included in the annual subscription rates, but not in the prices for single copies.

"The Traveller's Gazette" (London), *Monthly*, 3d. (by post 4½d.). Annual sub. 3/-.
"American Traveler's Gazette" (New York), *Quarterly*, 25 cents. Annual sub. 1 dollar.
"Oriental Traveller's Gazette" (Bombay), *Quarterly*, 8 annas. Annual sub. 3/-.
"Australian and New Zealand Traveller's Gazette" (Melbourne), *Quarterly*. Annual sub. 6/-
"Far Eastern Traveller's Gazette" (Shanghai), *Quarterly*. Annual sub. 4/-.
"Malayan Traveller's Gazette" (Singapore), *Quarterly*, 30 cents. Annual sub. Str. 2 dollars.
"La Revue des Voyages" (French), *Monthly*, 8 francs. Annual sub. 60 francs.
"Het Reisblad (Dutch), *Quarterly*, 25 cents. Annual sub. 1.30 florins.
"Rivista di Viaggi (Italian), *Quarterly*, 3 lire. Annual sub. 14 lire.
"Rese-Tidningen" (Swedish), *Quarterly*, 50 ore. Annual sub. 2 kroner.
"Die Weltreise-Zeitung" (German), *Quarterly*. Annual sub. 3 marks.
"La Revista Sudamericana de Viajes" (in Spanish), *Quarterly in Buenos Aires*, 50 ctos. Annual sub. 2 pesos.

Numerous travel books are stocked. Any publication not in stock can be obtained through the Book Dept., Thos. Cook & Son, Ltd., Berkeley Street, London, W.1.

CONTINENTAL TIME TABLES

FOR INDEX OF COUNTRIES, see pages 8 and 9.

EXPLANATIONS OF THE TABLES

THE HOURS are numbered consecutively from 1 to 24, starting from midnight, as shown on the dial on the cover. A train arriving or departing at 1.10 p.m. is shown as 13.10; at 5.15 p.m. as 17.15; at 9.30 p.m. as 21.30, and so on. The figures "24.0" indicate a train arriving at midnight, but a departure at that hour is shown by "0.0" Arrivals or departures at any time between midnight and 1.0 a m. are expressed by "0.1" to "0.59."

ONE LIST OF STATIONS serves, in some of the tables, for both directions. In these cases the times on the **LEFT** of the names are to be read **DOWNWARDS**, but on the **RIGHT** must be read **UPWARDS**, from bottom to top. For instance, see page 204: *On the left* are the trains *from Berlin* to Breslau, &c.; *on the right* those returning *towards* Berlin.

STATIONS ON BRANCH OR CONTINUATION LINES are printed slightly to the right as compared with those of the primary line. When a reference, thus (*page* 200), is added the times shown must *only* be considered as *connections to or from the primary line of the table*, and the indicated page or table consulted for details of the service on the connecting line. "THROUGH TABLES" similarly show only the connections indicated by the title of the table, the pages showing further particulars being referred to.

THE CLASSES are usually printed at the head of each train, thus: 1 cl., 1 2, 1 2 3, 2 3, &c.; Trains de luxe are headed "luxe." The other descriptions, such as "Exp," "Rap," &c., correspond with the *official* classification, upon which depend certain extra charges and restrictions. *These classes and descriptions may not apply to the trains over connecting lines, regarding which reference should be made to the other tables indicated.*

b and *c* placed against the name of a Station signify Buffets and Customs respectively

GREENWICH or WEST EUROPEAN TIME is used by railways in Great Britain, France, Algeria, Belgium, Luxembourg, Portugal, Spain and Morocco.

AMSTERDAM TIME (20 minutes in advance of Greenwich time) is used in Holland.

MID-EUROPEAN TIME (one hour in advance) by railways in Germany (including Bohemia, Moravia), Slovakia, Hungary, Norway, Sweden, Denmark, Switzerland, Poland, Yugo Slavia, Lithuania and Tunis.

ETNA TIME (one hour in advance—same as Mid-European time) by railways in Italy.

EAST EUROPEAN TIME (two hours in advance) by Railways in Latvia, Esthonia, Finland, Roumania, Bulgaria, Greece and Turkey.

MOSCOW TIME.—Three hours in advance of Greenwich time and two hours in advance of Central European time, used in U.S.S.R.

EGYPTIAN TIME (two hours in advance of Greenwich time) in Egypt, Soudan and Palestine.

JULY 3rd to SEPTEMBER 24th, inclusive, 1939.

LONDON MIDLAND AND SCOTTISH RAILWAY

TO LONDON (ST. PANCRAS)

Express Train Service from SCOTLAND, YORKSHIRE, and MIDLAND COUNTIES to LONDON.

RESTAURANT CARS on Day Expresses and SLEEPING CARS on Night Trains to London (St. Pancras).

For further particulars see Company's Time Tables.

STATIONS.	WEEKDAYS.																											
dep.	B	A	B	Saturdays only. Not after Sept. 9th.	A			Saturdays excepted.	Saturdays only (Aug. 5 excepted).	Saturdays only.	Saturdays excepted.	Saturdays only.			Saturdays excepted.	Saturdays only	Saturdays only.	Saturdays excepted.	Saturdays excepted.	Saturdays only.	Saturdays only.	"The Yorkshireman"	Saturdays excepted.	Saturdays only.	Saturdays excepted.	Saturdays only.	Saturdays excepted.	Saturdays only.
EDINB'GH (Wav.)	..	..	..		..	..	9 55	..			..		..	..	..		..	..						..	..			
GLASGOW (St. E.)	..	..	..		..	9 15	..	..			..		..	..	..		..	..						..	..			
Greenock (Prin. P.)	..	..	..		..	7 30	..	..			..		..	..	..		..	..						..				
CARLISLE	..	4 24	..		..	12 5	1237	..			..		..	..	..		..	..						..				
BELFAST	..	..	..		..	..	..						..	..	9T40		9F40						9D40	..				
HEYSHAM	7c8	5 40	..		..	8c0	..						..	..	5E35		5 35						7 16	7 16				
MORECAM'E (Pm)	7c45	6 44	..		..	9 15	..						..	..	..		..		..		..		7 42	..				
Bradford (For. Sq.)	9 25	9 20	..		..	1 38	..						..	..	7 30	7§20	7 30		7 45		7 45	9§5	9 20	9 20				
Harrogate	8 53	8 55	..		..	..	..						..	..	6 50	..	6 50		7 28		7 28	..	9 0	9 0				
LEEDS (City)	1010	1015	..		..	2 41	3 10						..	..	8 0	..	8 0		8 20	..	8 20	..	9 47	9 47		..		..
Hull (Paragon)	7 55	8 40	..	..	..	..	..	..		..	..	..	..	..	..	..		..	..	..	..	5 40	..	..	..	..	..	..
York	9 32	9 32	..	..	..	..	..	2n5		2n5	..	..	..	..	..	..		..	..	..	..	7 28	..	..	..	..	..	..
BARNSLEY (C.H.)	10 3	1030	..	..	..	..	..	..		..	6 18	6 18	..	..	7 54	7 54	.	..	8 32	..	8 32	9 10	9 55	..	..	..	..	9 55
SHEFFIELD	1135	1145	1145	1 2	..	3 41	4 17	4 42		4 42	7 15	7 15	..	..	9 0	8 44	8 57	9 5	9a26	9 5	9 30	1013	1040	..	..	..	11 0	11 0
Chesterfield	12 0	1210	1210	1 26	..	1E45	..	5 13		5 13	7 36	7 36	..	..	9 20	..	9 17	9 30	9a47	9 30	9 55	1034	..	..	..	..	..	
LIVERPOOL (C.)	..	..	9 10	..	1035	..	..	..		..	..	..	..	5 5		..		..	8 5	..	8 5	..	..		8 30	8 30	..	..
MAN- (Vic.)	..	..	..	..	12 0	..	..	..		..	..	..	..	..		..		..	..	..	..	..	..		..	..	..	
CHESTER (C.)	6 40	7 25	1042	..	12 0	..	..	..		..	..	..	..	7 26		..		..	8 55	..	8 55	..	..		10 0	10 0	..	..
Buxton	3 20	8 10	..	..	..	..	..	..	..	..	..	..	..	7 52		..		..	9 43	..	9 43	..	..		..	..	..	
Matlock Bath	9 2	9 19	..	..	..	..	..	..	..	..	..	..	..	7 53		..		8 50	9 25	8 50	9 25	..	..		..	..	..	
DERBY	1055	1 10	1 10	..	2 20	3 18	4 30	6 35	5 53	6 35	7 25	7 25	8 0	8 55		..		9 35	1046	9 35	1047	..	..		1133	1131	..	
NOTTINGHAM	8 50	12 2	..	2 30	..	4 15	5 25	7 0	5 58	7 0	8 23	8 23	..	8 33	9 24	8 57	9 24	1014	..	1015	..	1118	..	..	..	..	..	..
Loughboro' (Mid.)	9 29	1 22	1 38	..	..	..	..	7 28	6 35	7 28	..	.	8 26	9 17	9 48	..	9 53	..	1045	..	1045	..	1114	1116	..	..	..	..
Burton-on-Trent	9d53	11d32	11d32	..	..	2d45	..	6L25	6L25		6d57	6d57	7d33	8d20	..	..	..	..	9d50	..	9d50	..	..	..	10d52	10d52	..	
LEICESTER	1 11	2 0	2 5	..	3 10	5 13	..	7 50	7 40	7 50	..	..	8 52	9 37	1021	10 5	1023	1028	1121	1028	1126	..	1157	12 1	12 9	1212	1218	1220
LONDON (St. P.) arr.	3 20	4 34	5 0	5 34	6 0	7 10	8 0	9 55	9 56	10 4	1035	1046	10f50	11g20	12 0	12 3	1222	1254	11 0	1 2	1 13	1H21	1 36	1 50	1 48	2 7	2 7	2 16

Train also leaves Leicester 2.5 a.m., arr. London (St. Pancras) 5.30 a.m. (Monday mornings excepted).

** For Train Services on Sundays and Bank Holidays, between "Midland" Division and St. Prancas, see Company's Time Tables.

A Sun. nights and Mon. morns. excepted. **B** Sun. nights and Mon. morns. only. **C** Commencing Sept. 10th, leaves Heysham **6.8** p.m., Morecambe **6.35** p.m. **D** Sun. nights only. **E** Mon. morns. excepted. **F** Fri. nights. **FO** Fri. only and not after Sept. 8th. **G** On Aug. 4th and 11th leaves Bradford **9.58** p.m., Leeds **11.35** p.m. **H** On Sat. arr. St. Pancras 1.37 p.m. **J** Will not apply on Sats. after Sept. 9th. On Sats. leaves Morecambe 12.40 p.m. **K** On Sats. arr. St. Pancras 3.50 p.m. **L** Via Leicester. **N** On Sept. 16th and 23rd leaves Liverpool (C.) 10.30 a.m. **P** On Sats. arr. St. Pancras **6.7** p.m. **Q** On Sats. arr. St. Pancras **7.31** p.m. **R** On Sats. arr. St. Pancras **9.4** p.m. **T** Sun. nights excepted. *a* On Mons. and Fris. leaves Sheffield 9.30 a.m., Chesterfield 9.55 a.m.

The times from 6 p.m. to 5.59 a.m. inclusive are printed in dark type, thus **12.9** meaning 9 min. aft. midn.

JULY 3rd to SEPTEMBER 24th inclusive, 1939.

LONDON MIDLAND AND SCOTTISH RAILWAY

TO LONDON (ST. PANCRAS)

Express Train Service from SCOTLAND, YORKSHIRE, and MIDLAND COUNTIES to LONDON.

RESTAURANT CARS on Day Expresses and SLEEPING CARS on Night Trains to London (St. Pancras).

For further particulars see Company's Time Tables.

STATIONS.	WEEKDAYS.																											
dep.																			Y	Z	FO	Y	Z	Y	Y	Z	Z
EDINB'GH (Wav.)	..	..	Saturdays excepted	Saturdays only	..	..	..	..	..	..	..	10 3	Saturdays excepted	Saturdays only	..	1210	1210	..	..	..	..	..	..	..	..	9 55	9 55	..
GLASGOW (St. E.)	..	..			..	..	..	..	9 35	..	9 35	..			..	1215	12 5	..	..	..	..	..	..	..	9 15	..	..	1115
Greenock (Prin. P.)	..	..			..	..	..	..	8 20	..	8 20	..			..	1015	1015	..	..	..	..	..	..	..	7 30	..	..	1012
CARLISLE	..	..			8 5	8 5	..	..	12 8	..	12 8	1240			..	2 48	2 48	..	..	4 22	6 0	..	..	..	12 5	1237	1237	2 0
BELFAST	..	..			..	..	..	..	..	..	..	..			..	..	..	..	..	..	11W0	..	..	..	..	..	..	..
HEYSHAM	..	..			8 48	8 48	..	..	..	..	..	12J8			..	1 45	1 39	..	..	5 40	8 0	..	..	..	8c 0	..	9 7	..
MORECAM'E (Pm)	..	..			9 40	9 40	..	..	..	..	12a15	12J50			..	2 37	2 37	..	..	6 44	7 40	..	..	..	9 15	..	9 25	..
Bradford (For. Sq.)	..	1038			1220	1220	..	1234	1 40	..	1 40	2 42			..	4 40	4 33	..	..	9 20	9 0	11G16	..	..	1 38	..	1 28	..
Harrogate	..	9 28			12 9	12 9	..	12 9	1 20	..	1 20	2 2			..	3 8	3V52	..	..	8 55	8 55	..	..	..	..	..	..	..
LEEDS (City)	..	11 7			1250	1250	..	1 0	2 28	..	2 31	3 13			..	5 16	5 16	5 22	..	1015	10 0	11G45	..	..	2 41	3 10	3 21	4 30
Hull (Paragon)	..	9 25	..	..	11 0	1054	..	..	..	..	..	..	..	..	2 5	..	..	..	..	8 40	8 40	..	..	..	..	..	..	..
York	..	1020	..	..	1230	1230	..	..	1 0	1 0	Saturdays only	2 25	..	..	3t10	..	..	4 17	..	9 32	9 32	..	..	..	..	..	..	..
BARNSLEY (C.H.)	..	1122	..	..	12 0	..	..	1255	1 34	1 34		2 45	..	..	4t28	Saturdays excepted	Saturdays only.	4 5'	..	1030	1030	1150	..	..	..	..	11 7	..
SHEFFIELD	..	1218	..	..	1 47	1 47	1 55	2 3	3 22	3 10		4 6	..	..	5 35			6 16	..	1145	1145	1 2	..	..	3 41	4 17	4 25	5 34
Chesterfield	..	1239	..	..	2 7	2 7	2 16	2 24	..	..		4 27	..	..	5 56			6 42	..	1210	1210	1 26	..	..	1 45	..	1 45	..
LIVERPOOL (C.)	..	..	1130	11N5	Saturdays excepted	Saturdays only	..	1230	Saturdays excepted	Saturdays only		..	3 30	3 30	..			4 55	..	6 25	6 25	..	1035	1030	..	..	..	..
MAN- (Vic.)	..	..	..	..			..	1 15				..	..	..	..			..	..	..	..	..	12 0	1145	..	..	..	..
CHESTER (C.)	..	..	1225	1225			..	2 0				..	4 25	4 25	..			5 50	..	7 25	7 35	..	12 0	12 0	..	..	..	..
Buxton	10b12	..	..	..			..	2 33				..	4 5	4 5	..	..	..	6 18	..	8 10	8 24	..	..	..	..	..	..	..
Matlock Bath	11b19	11X29	..	..			..	1h55				3X23	4 56	4 56	..	5 38	5 38	6 25	..	9 19	11v43	..	..	..	..	..	..	..
DERBY	12b5	12e10	1 54	1 54			2 7	3 36	3 41	..	..	4 8	5 48	5 48	..	6 20	6 20	7 30	7 49	1 10	1 10	1 15	2 20	2 20	3 18	4 30	4 30	..
NOTTINGHAM	1153	1 25	..	..	..	..	2 59	..	3 42	3 37	3 42	5 11	..	..	6 40	..	..	6 53	..	12 2	12 2	2 30	..	..	4 15	5 25	5 35	..
Loughboro' (Mid.)	1227	..	1 56	1 56	..	..	..	3 8	4 3	4 4	..	..	6 9	6 9	..	..	..	7 24	8 12	1 22	1 22	..	..	2 45	..	..	..	..
Burton-on-Trent	11d22	..	1d18	1d21	1L29	1L29	..	3p11	3L28	..	3L33	3d42	5d14	5d14	..	5L50	5L50	6d43	7d22	11d32	12d37		..	..	2d45	..	2d45	..
LEICESTER	1248	1 5	2 30	3 32	3 8	3 9	..	4 11	4 43	4 38	4 45	..	6 29	6 29	6 33	7 22	7 25	8 5	8 33	2 0	2 0	..	3 10	3 10	5 13	..	..	7 18
LONDON (St. P.) arr.	3 22	3K32	4 9	4 19	4 47	4 55	5 35	5P50	6 30	6 30	6 42	7Q20	8 12	8 18	8R55	9 10	9 22	9U50	1049	4 34	4 34	5 34	6 0	6 0	7 10	8 0	8 0	9 20

U On Sats. arr. St. Pancras **9.59** p.m. **V** On July 18th and Sept. 16th and 23rd leaves Harrogate 3.35 p.m. **W** Applies July 8th to Aug. 26th only. **X** Sats. only. **Y** Sat. nights and Sun. morns. excepted. **Z** Sat. nights and Sun. morns. only. *a* Applies July 15th to Aug. 12th only. *b* On Sats. leaves Derby 12.0 noon and leaves Matlock 11.18 a.m. and Buxton 10.10 a.m. *c* Commencing Sept. 4th leaves Heysham **7.50** p.m. *d* Via Derby. *e* On Sats. leaves Derby 12.18 p.m. *f* On Sats. arr. St. Pancras 11.4 a.m. *g* On Sats. arr. St. Pancras 11.30 a.m. *h* On Sats. leaves Matlock Bath 1.39 p.m. *n* Via Normanton. *p* Via Derby on Sats., leaves Burton 3.5 p.m. (2.25 p.m. on Sept. 23rd). *t* On Sats. leaves Barnsley 4.23 p.m. and on Sats. until Sept. 9th leaves York 4.0 p.m. *v* On Aug. 5th, 12th, Sept. 16th and 23rd leaves Matlock Bath **9.28** p.m. § Bradford Exchange.

The times from 6 p.m. to 5.59 a.m. inclusive are printed in dark type, thus **12.9** meaning 9 min. aft. midn.

JULY 3rd to SEPTEMBER 24th inclusive, 1939.

LONDON MIDLAND AND SCOTTISH RAILWAY

FROM LONDON (ST. PANCRAS)

Express Train Service LONDON to MIDLAND COUNTIES, YORKSHIRE, NORTH OF ENGLAND, and SCOTLAND.

RESTAURANT CARS on Day Expresses and SLEEPING CARS on Night Trains from London (St. Pancras).
For further particulars see Company's Time Tables.

WEEKDAYS.

STATIONS.			MX									
LONDON (St. Pan.) dep.	12 5	12 5	2 25	2 25	4 25	8 25	8 20	9 5	10 0	10 0	1030	1030	1047
LEICESTER ......arr.	2 43	2 43	4 26	4 26	7 13	1024	1022	..	1144	1150	12 9	1217	
Burton-on-Trent .... ,,	..	..	6d38	6d38	8d38	12d15	11d28	1d12	..	..	1d24	1d24	
Loughborough (Mid.) ,,	3 9	3 9	4 55	5 55	7 40	1043	1042	..	1212	1220	1227	1244	..
NOTTINGHAM .... ,,	3 48	3 48	7 31	7 31	8 38	..	..	11 8	1240	1252	1 34	1 34	1 25
DERBY .... ,,	3 38	3 38	5 17	5 17	8 1	11 3	11 3	12N9	Saturdays excepted	Saturdays only.	1250	1254	Runs on July 29, Aug. 5, 12, 19.
Matlock Bath ...... ,,	4f13	4f19	7 50	7 50	8 32	11f34	11f34	1254			1 54	1 54	
Buxton .... ,,	8 2	8 2	9 0	9 0	9 21	1212	1218	..			1 56	2 19	
MANCH'TER (Cen.) ,,	5 44	5 25	6 47	6 47	9 45	1240	1245	..			2 26	2 20	
MANCH'TER (Vic.) ,,	..	6 12	..	..	..	..	..				..	3 8	
LIVERPOOL (Cen.) .. ,,	7 7	7 7	8 35	8 35	1058	2 15	2 15				3 30	3 30	
Chesterfield .... ,,	..	..	7 28	6 21	9 41	..	..	1152	1245	1252		..	
SHEFFIELD ...... ,,	Monday mornings only	Monday mornings excepted.	8 17	6 52	9 6	12 2	12 2	1212	1 23	1 23	2 29	2 27	
BARNSLEY (Crt. H.) ,,			9 29	8 26	10 3	..	1246	1N 8	2 8	2 13	..	..	
York .... ,,			..	8 59	12a21	..	..	1 22	3 15	3 15	4 1	4 1	
Hull (Paragon) ...... ,,			..	1056	1145	..	..		5 8	5 8	5 40	5 40	
LEEDS (City) ...... ,,			Monday mornings only.	8 50	10 6	Saturdays excepted.	Saturdays only.	1 5	1 48	1 56	Saturdays excepted	Saturdays only	
Harrogate .... ,,				1010	1122			2 18	3 22	2G32			
Bradford (Forster Sq.) ,,				9 19	1047			2 0	2 22	2 40			
MORECAMBE (Prom.) ,,				..	1238			3h11	4 30	4 15			
HEYSHAM .... ,,				11e38	1 32			..	4 55	4 50			
BELFAST .... ,,	..	..		7e30	..	..	..	..		..			..
CARLISLE .... ,,	..	..		Mo. mrn excepted	1240	..	..	3 14	4 9	4 20			..
Greenock (Prin. Pier) ,,	..	..			4 42	..	..	6N†49	8 29	8 29			..
GLASGOW (St. E'nh) ,,	..	..			3 5	..	..	5N†45	6 38	6 54			..
EDINBURGH (Wav.) ,,	..	..	..		3 41	..	..	5 45	..	..			..

STATIONS.													
LONDON (St. Pan.) dep.	1055	1145	12 0	12 0	1215	1230	1230	1 0	1 0	2 10	2 10	2 20	2 30
LEICESTER ......arr.	1SX26	1 35	1 44	1 46	2 13	2 9	2 22	3 24	3 29	..	..	4 5	4 9
Burton-on-Trent .... ,,	..	..	..	..	3d12	3d12	3d31	..	..	..	..	5d13	5d13
Loughborough (Mid.) ,,	..	..	2 18	2 19	..	3 10	3 10	3 56	4 3	..	..	..	4 53
NOTTINGHAM .... ,,	1 44	..	2 40	2 43	..	3 41	3 41	3 45	4 0	4 13	4 26	..	5 19
DERBY .... ,,	..	Saturdays only.	Saturdays excepted.	Saturdays only	2 50	2 43	3 3	..	Saturdays only.	Saturdays excepted.	Saturdays only	4 42	4 43
Matlock Bath ...... ,,	..				..	3 29	3 42	..				..	6 7
Buxton .... ,,					..	5 25	5 25	..				..	5 54
MANCH'TER (Cen.) ,,	..				4 18	4 8	4 30	..				6 10	6 10
MANCH'TER (Vic.) ,,					..		..	..					..
LIVERPOOL (Cen.) .. ,,					5 15	5 15	6 18	..				7 15	7 15
Chesterfield .... ,,	2 31		..	3k46	Saturdays only. Aug. 5 to Aug. 26.	4D 4	3 57	..	..	4 57	5 15	..	6E6
SHEFFIELD ...... ,,	2 51	2 58	3 2	4k10		4D25	4 20	4 47	5 6	5 17	5 34	..	6E27
BARNSLEY (Crt. H.) ,,	..	4 3	4 3	..		5 20	5 25	5 56	6 10	6 10	6 50	Saturdays only.	..
York .... ,,	..	..	..	..		6 4	6 8	..	7 20	7 20	..		7 42
Hull (Paragon) ...... ,,	..	..	..	..		..	..		..		..		8 40
LEEDS (City) ...... ,,	..	3 47	3 55	3 57		5 24	5 32	..	..	6 21	6 36		Saturdays excepted.
Harrogate .... ,,	..	4 43	5 3	5 3		6 22	6 32	..	..	7 22	7 41		
Bradford (Forster Sq.) ,,	..	..	4 32	4 40		5 54	6 7	6§50	6§31	7 6	7 19		
MORECAMBE (Prom.) ,,	..	..	6 40	7 23		8 30	8 30	..		..	..	..	
HEYSHAM .... ,,		..	7 8	7 42		8 50	8 50	..		..	..	..	
BELFAST .... ,,	..	..	..	..		Saturdays excepted	Saturdays only.	Saturdays excepted.		..	..	..	
CARLISLE .... ,,	..	..	6 12	6 12					..	..		..	..
Greenock (Prin. Pier) ,,	..	..	10 4	10 3					..	..		..	..
GLASGOW (St. E'nh) ,,	..	..	8 38	8 38					..	..	..	..	..
EDINBURGH (Wav.) ,,	..	..	8 57	8 57					..	..	..	..	..

*** For Service on Sundays and Bank Holidays between London St. Pancras) and the "Midland" Division, see Company's Time Tables.

A Applies Fris., July 21st to Aug. 18th inclusive. **B** Via Derby, and Fris. only. **D** On Mons. and Fris. arr. Chesterfield 3.54 p.m., Sheffield 4.18 p.m. **E** On Mons. and Fris. arr. Chesterfield **6.0** p.m., Sheffield **6.23** p.m. **F** On July 21st, 28th, Aug. 11th, arr. Heysham 10.30 p.m. **G** Commencing Sept. 16th arr. Harrogate 3.22 p.m. **H** Via Rotherham (Masboro'). **L** Via Leicester. **MX** Mons. excepted. **N** On Sats. arr. Derby 11.59 a.m., Barnsley 1.20 p.m., Glasgow (Cent.) **6.37** p.m., Greenock (Cent.) **6.45** p.m. **S** Sats. excepted. **V** Via Derby and on Fri. nights until Sept. 1st, arr. Burton 12.5 a.m. **X** Sats. only. **Y** Sat. nights and Sun. morns. excepted. **Z** Sat. nights and Sun. morns. only. *a* On Sats. until Sept. 16th arr. York 10.42 a.m. and on Sept. 23rd arr. 11.20 a.m. *b* Fri. nights excepted. *d* Via Derby. *e* Sat. morns. only and not after Aug. 26th. *f* Matlock Station. *h* Sats. only and not after Sept. 9th. *k* Not after Sept. 16th. *n* Via Normanton. *p* Via Heysham Sat. morns. only, and not after Sept. 9th. † Central Station. § Bradford (Exchange).

The times from 6 p.m. to 5.59 a.m. inclusive are printed in dark type, thus **12.9** meaning 9 min. aft. midn.

JULY 3rd to SEPTEMBER 24th inclusive, 1939.

LONDON MIDLAND AND SCOTTISH RAILWAY

FROM LONDON (ST. PANCRAS)

Express Train Service LONDON to MIDLAND COUNTIES, YORKSHIRE, NORTH OF ENGLAND, and SCOTLAND.

RESTAURANT CARS on Day Expresses and SLEEPING CARS on Night Trains from London (St. Pancras).

For further particulars see Company's Time Tables.

WEEKDAYS.

STATIONS.													
LONDON (St. Pan.) dep.	2 30	2 40	3 15	3 25	3 25	4 0	4 20	4 30	4 30	4 55	5 0	5 0	6 20
LEICESTER ......arr.	4 15	5 8	5 11	5 49	5 49	..	6 20	6 15	6 27	6 41	7 28	7 28	..
Burton-on-Trent .... ,,	5 d28	..	6L36	7L16	..	..		7d31	7a31	..	..	..	..
Loughborough (Mid.) ,,	4 52	6 2	6 2	6 20	6 20	..	7 2	6 49	7 29	7 25	..	..	..
NOTTINGHAM .... ,,	5 19	..	5 46	5 38	5 46	6 25	7 29	..	..	..	7 21	7 21	8 23
DERBY .... ,,	4 52	Saturdays excepted.	Saturdays only.	Saturdays excepted.	Saturdays only.	Sats. only.	Sats. only.	6 52	7 5	"The Yorkshireman"	Sats. excepted.	Sats. only.	Sats. excepted.
Matlock Bath ...... ,,	6 7							7 53	7 56				
Buxton .... ,,	5 59							8 41	8 48				
MANCH'TER (Cen. ,,	6 38							8 26	8 39				
MANCH'TER (Vic) ,,	..							..	..				
LIVERPOOL (Cen.) ,,	8 52							9 38	9 48				
Chesterfield .... ,,	6 0	..	6 18	6 25	6 34	7 18		Saturdays excepted.	Saturdays only.	..	8 6	8 6	9 8
SHEFFIELD ...... ,,	6 23	..	6 39	6 45	6 54	7 38	7 48			8 0	8 26	8 26	9 28
BARNSLEY (Crt. H.) ,,	..	..	..	7 58	7 58	..				..	9 21	9 21	1039
York .... ,,	7 42	..	..	10n10	10n10	..				..	..	..	12n14
Hull (Paragon) ...... ,,	8 40	..		..	..	..	..			..	..	..	..
LEEDS (City) ...... ,,	..		7 33	7 41	7 57	8 35	..			..	9 21	9 21	1024
Harrogate .... ,,	Saturdays only.		..	9 26	..	9 26				..	..	..	1154
Bradford (Forster Sq.) ,,			8 3	8 10	8 27	9 24	9§3			9§15	10 2	9 53	11 0
MORECAMBE (Prom.) ,,		..	1034	1034	..	..	..			..	11b25	1125	..
HEYSHAM .... ,,		..	1052	10F52	..	..	..			..	1121	1121	12A32
BELFAST .... ,,		..	..	5p35	..	..	..				6 35	6 35	..
CARLISLE .... ,,	..	..	Not after Sept. 2.	..	..	..	..			Sats. excepted.	..	..	..
Greenock (Prin. Pier) ,,	..	..		..	..	..	..						..
GLASGOW (St. En'h) ,,	..			..	..	..	..				..	..	..
EDINBURGH (Wav.) ,,	..	..		..	..	..	..				..	..	..

STATIONS.									Z	Y	Z	Y	Z
LONDON (St. Pan.) dep.	6 20	6 30	7 50	8 15	8 15	9 15	9 30	9 30	1120	1150	12 0	12 5	1220
LEICESTER ......arr.	..	8 19	9 29	1049	1049	..	1135	1135	..	2 8	2 19	2 43	2 51
Burton-on-Trent .... ,,	..	9d21	11L6	12V53	12L18	..	2d55	2d55	..	..	..	..	7d 2
Loughborough (Mid.) ,,	..	8 55	1031	1116	1116	..	..	..	..	..	..	3 9	3 17
NOTTINGHAM .... ,,	8 32	9 26	1022	..	..	1141	..	1234	2 10	..	..	3 48	..
DERBY .... ,,	Sats. only.	8 57	1025	1138	1138	..	1239	1239	..	2 54	3 1	3 38	3 41
Matlock Bath ...... ,,		9 48	11x35	..	..	..	Saturday nights excepted.	Saturday nights only.	..	..	..	4f 9	7 51
Buxton .... ,,		10 0	..	..	..	..			..	..	..	8 2	9 0
MANCH'TER (Cen. ,,		1027	..	..	..	..			..	..	..	5 25	5 25
MANCH'TER (Vic) ,,		..	..	..	..	..			..	..	..	6 12	6 2
LIVERPOOL (Cen.) ,,		12 9	..	..	..	..			..	..	..	7 7	9 35
Chesterfield .... ,,	9 21	..	1038	1 6	1 6	..			3 21	3 48	3 57	..	..
SHEFFIELD ...... ,,	9 43	..	1058	1250	1250	1H16			3 50	4 23	4 37	..	..
BARNSLEY (Crt. H.) ,,	1047	..	11x42	..	..	..			..	4 56	5 40	..	..
York .... ,,	12n14	..	..	2 0	2 8	3S13			..	8n12	9n6	..	..
Hull (Paragon) ...... ,,	..	..	..	..	4 24	4S15			..	9n21	10n11	..	..
LEEDS (City) ...... ,,	1038	..	1 10	..	..	1 41	1 59	1 59	5 5	5 58	6 1	..	..
Harrogate .... ,,	1154	..	..	..	..	..	4 38	..	..	8 15	8 2	..	..
Bradford (Forster Sq.) ,,	1112	..	..	..	..	..	2 49	2 47	5 38	6 57	7 9	..	..
MORECAMBE (Prom.) ,,	..	..	..	Saturdays excepted.	Saturdays only.	..	..	..	Not after Sept. 9th.	8 52	9 35	..	..
HEYSHAM .... ,,	..	..	..			..	..	..		9 22	1055	..	..
BELFAST .... ,,	..	..	..			..	..	..		..	..	..	..
CARLISLE .... ,,	..	..	..			4 15	4 38	4 38		1042	..	..	..
Greenock (Prin. Pier) ,,	..	..	..			..	8†47	9†8		..	..	..	..
GLASGOW (St. En'h) ,,	..	..	..			..	7 31	7 28		..	..	..	..
EDINBURGH (Wav.) ,,	..	..	..	..	..	7 6	..	..		..	..	..	..

A train leaves London at 5.32 p.m., arr. Leicester **7.39** p.m., Loughborough (Mid.) **7.56** p.m. and Nottingham **8.19** p.m.

FOR NOTES SEE PAGE 90.

The times from 6 p.m. to 5.59 a.m. inclusive are printed in dark type, thus **12.9** meaning 9 min. aft. midn.

JULY 3rd to SEPTEMBER 24th inclusive, 1939.

LONDON MIDLAND AND SCOTTISH RAILWAY

Express Services from IRELAND, SCOTLAND, and THE NORTH OF ENGLAND to LONDON TO LONDON (EUSTON)

RESTAURANT CARS on Day Expresses and SLEEPING CARS on Night Trains to London (Euston).
For further particulars see Company's Time Tables.

WEEKDAYS.

STATIONS.	FO	B		B	B	A			B	B	A	A				A	A	B	A	B	A	B	A	A	B	A
			Sunday nights and Monday mornings excepted.	Third class only.			Monday mornings excepted.	Runs July 28th, Aug. 11th 18th, 25th, Sept. 1st and 8th.		"The Irish Mail."	"The Irish Mail."		Monday mornings only.	Friday nights and Saturday mornings only.	Friday nights and Saturday mornings only.	Commences July 17/18.	Not after night of July 14th.		Commencing July 18th	"Night Scot."	"Night Scot."					
STRANRAER ......dep.	..	..		..	..	3 30	..		..	..	..	..	..	..	..	..	..	..	..	..	..	..	9h37	..	..	..
INVERNESS ,,	..	..		..	..	11 5	..		..	..	..	..	..	..	..	..	..	4 10	4K20	..	..	..	..	4 40	..	..
ABERDEEN (Joint) ,,		..		..	1 20	1 0	..		..	..	..	.	..	..	..	..	..	..	..	..	..	..	..	..	7 50	7 50
DUNDEE (West) ,,	..	..		..	3 0	2 50	..		..	..	..	..	..	..	..	..	..	..	7K30	..	..	..	..	7 30	9 15	9 20
PERTH (General)...... ,,	..	..		..	3 55	3 45	..		..			..	..	..		..	..	8 45	8K40	..	..	..	..	9 10	10 0	10 5
STIRLING ,,	..	..		..	4 51	4 41			..			..	..	..		..	..	9 23	9F40	..	..	..	..	1012	1050	1054
GLASGOW (Central) ,,	..	..		..	5 30	5 40			..			..	..	..		9 25	9 25	..	..	1030	1045	..	..	..	..	..
EDINBURGH (Pr. St.) ,,		..		..	5 40	5 50			..			..	..	..		9 20	9 20	..	..	..	..	1045	11 0	..	..	..
CARLISLE (Citadel) ,,	7 12	..			8 30	8 37			..				..	..		1210	1210	1238	1223	..	..	1 7	1 15	1 25	1 33	1 37
Keswick .... ,,	6 40	..			..	6 40			..			..						..		..	..	..	..	..	..	..
Windermere .... ,,	8 35	8 5			..	8 35			..									..		..	..	..	..	..	..	..
BELFAST .... ,,	..	..			..	..			..									..				..	6Q25	..	..	..
HEYSHAM .... ,,	9 7	9 8			..	9 7			..			..						..				..	..	..	..	..
FLEETWOOD .... ,,	9 5	8 40			..	9 40			..	.	..	..						..				..	..	..	..	..
Blackpool (Central) .. ,,	9 40	9 40			..	10 0			..									..				..	..	..	..	..
PRESTON .... ,,	1035	1030			1046	1046				..								..				..	..	..	..	..
DUBLIN (W.R.) .... ,,	..	.			..	..		7 50	..	8 22	8 10				8 10			..				..	..	..	..	..
HOLYHEAD .... ,,		7 50			..	7 40		1155	..	1213	1213				1240			..				..	..	..	..	..
Llandudno .... ,,		9 5			..	9 10		..	..	1030	10J10				..			..				..	..	..	..	..
BIRK'NH'D (W'side) ,,	..	9 57			..	9 53	..	..	..	1030	1133	..	..		..		..	..				..	..	..	..	..
Chester (General).... ,,		11 0			..	11 5	..	..	.	2 0	2 0		..		..		..	..				..	..	..	..	..
LIVERPOOL (L. St.) ,,	..	1045		..	..	10 0	..	..	1155	..	..	1150	..	..	..	..	2 30	..	2 30	..	..	..	..	..	..	..
HUDDERSFIELD .. ,,	..	9 13		..	..	..	9f48	..	..	1122	1122	..	..	..	..	..	..	..	..	..	..	..	..	..	..	..
MANCHESTER (L.R.) ,,		1030		1125	1145	1030	12 0	..	..	..	..	..	12 0	..	..	..	..	..	..	..	..	..	..	..	..	..
MANCHESTER (Vic.) ,,	..	..	..	..	..	..		..	..	..	..	..		1235	..	..	..	..	..	..	..	..	..	..	..	..
CREWE .... ,,		12 5	..		1255	1250		..	1 5	2 40	2 40			..	..	3 19	3 46	3 48	3 46	3 58	4 2	4 21	4 21	4 31	4 40	4 48
WOLVERHAMPTON ,,	..	10C10	1056	*via* Stoke.	1010	..	*via* Stoke.	..	..	..	..	..	*via* Stoke.	..	..	..	..	..	..	..	..	..	..	..	..	..
BIRM'HAM (New St.) ,,	..	12C30	1220		1230	..		..	..	..	..	..		..	..	..	..	..	..	..	..	..	..	..	..	..
RUGBY .... ,,	1 38	1 38	1 25		2 44	2 45	2 57	..	3 17	..	..	3 34	3 35	3 49	..	5 0	5 16	5 18	..	5 33	..	5 52	5 52	6 2	6 11	6 24
EUSTON ....arr.	3 30	8 30	3G35	3 40	4 50	5 0	5 15	5 15	5 27	5 30	5 30	5 53	5 55	6 5	6 15	6 45	6 55	6 50	6 55	7 15	7 15	7 30	7 30	7 45	7 45	8 0

*** For Train Service on Sundays and Bank Holidays see Company's Time Table.

A Sun. nights and Mon. morns. excepted. **B** Sun. nights and Mon. morns. only. **C** Change at Rugby. **F** Will not run after Aug. 12th. **FO** Fri. nights and Sat. morns. only. **G** On Sat. morns. arr. Euston **3.18** a.m. **J** After Sept. 8th runs on Weds. and Thurs. only. **K** Commencing Aug. 14th. **Q** Via Stranraer. *f* Passengers cross Manchester from Victoria to London Road at own expense. *h* Stranraer (Harbour).

The times from 6 p.m. to 5.59 a.m. inclusive are printed in dark type, thus **12.9** meaning 9 min. aft. midn.

JULY 3rd to SEPTEMBER 24th inclusive, 1939.

LONDON MIDLAND AND SCOTTISH RAILWAY

Express Service from IRELAND, SCOTLAND, and THE NORTH OF ENGLAND to LONDON.

TO LONDON (EUSTON)

RESTAURANT CARS on Day Expresses and SLEEPING CARS on Night Trains to London (Euston).
For further particulars see Company's Time Tables.

WEEKDAYS.

STATIONS.	Saturdays excepted		Saturdays excepted	Saturdays only.		"Ulster Express."			Saturdays excepted	Saturdays only.	via Stoke.	"The Blackpool and Fylde-Coast Exp." Sats. excepted.	"The Mancunian" Saturdays excepted.
STRANRAER dep.	..	..	..	..	..	..	..	..	..	..	..	..	..
INVERNESS ,,	..	..	..	..	..	..	..	..	..	..	..	..	..
ABERDEEN (Joint) ,,	..	..	..	..	..	..	..	..	..	..	..	..	..
DUNDEE (West) ,,	..	..	..	..	..	..	..	..	..	..	..	..	..
PERTH (General) ,,	..	..	..	..	..	..	..	..	..	..	..	..	..
STIRLING ,,	..	..	..	..	..	..	..	..	..	..	..	..	..
GLASGOW (Central) ,,	..	..	..	..	..	..	..	..	..	..	..	..	..
EDINBURGH (Pr. St.) ,,	..	..	..	..	..	..	..	..	..	..	..	..	..
CARLISLE (Citadel) ,,	..	..	..	..	2M12	..	..	..	..	..	..	..	..
Keswick ,,	..	..	..	..	..	..	..	..	..	..	..	..	..
Windermere ,,	..	..	..	..	..	..	..	..	..	..	..	7 14	..
BELFAST ,,	..	..	..	..	..	9 40	..	..	..	..	..	..	..
HEYSHAM ,,	..	..	..	..	..	7 0	..	..	..	..	..	7 32	..
FLEETWOOD ,,	..	..	..	..	..	5 57	..	..	..	..	..	8 20	..
Blackpool (Central) ,,	..	..	..	..	..	6 33	..	..	..	..	..	8 25	..
PRESTON ,,	..	..	..	..	5 35	7 28	..	..	..	..	..	9 13	..
DUBLIN (W.R.) ,,	..	..	..	..	..	..	..	..	..	..	..	..	..
HOLYHEAD ,,	..	..	..	..	..	..	..	..	..	..	..	..	..
Llandudno ,,	..	..	..	..	..	6D25	6 42	..	..	..	..	..	..
BIRK'NH'D (W'side) ,,	..	..	..	..	6 0	6D50	7 35	..	..	..	..	8 0	..
Chester (General) ,,	..	..	..	..	6 42	7D45	8 20	..	..	..	..	8 50	..
LIVERPOOL (L. St.) ,,	..	..	..	..	..	..	8 15	..	..	..	..	9 10	..
HUDDERSFIELD ,,	..	..	..	..	..	..	..	..	..	..	6 54	..	8e40
MANCHESTER (L.R.) ,,	..	..	..	..	6 0	7 21	8A10	..	..	..	8 30	8 42	9 45
MANCHESTER (Vic.) ,,	..	..	..	..	..	..	..	..	..	..	..	..	9e20
CREWE ,,	..	5E10	..	..	7 46	8 50	9 8	..	..	..	..	1016	..
WOLVERHAMPTON ,,	..	6 50	8 9	8 9	..	..	..	..	9 39	9 35	..	..	..
BIRM'HAM (New St.) ,,	..	7 30	8 40	8 40	..	..	..	8 45	1015	1010	..	..	..
RUGBY ,,	7 20	8 22	..	..	9 28	..	..	9 38	..	..	1117	..	..
EUSTON arr.	9 48	9 55	1040	10 6	1050	1135	12H0	1216	1230	1237	1242	1250	1 0

STATIONS.	Saturdays excepted.	Saturdays only not after Sept. 2nd. "The Mancunian"	Saturdays only, commences Sept. 9th. "The Mancunian"	Saturdays only.	"The Merseyside Express." Saturdays excepted.	Saturdays only, and not after August 26th.		Saturdays only.	Saturdays only and not after Sept. 2nd.			Saturdays excepted.	Saturdays only.
STRANRAER dep.	..	..	..	..	..	..	..	..	..	..	..	..	..
INVERNESS ,,	..	..	..	..	..	..	..	..	..	..	..	..	..
ABERDEEN (Joint) ,,	..	..	..	..	..	..	..	..	..	..	..	..	..
DUNDEE (West) ,,	..	..	..	..	..	..	..	..	..	..	..	..	..
PERTH (General) ,,	..	..	..	..	..	..	..	..	..	..	..	..	..
STIRLING ,,	..	..	..	..	..	..	..	..	..	..	..	..	..
GLASGOW (Central) ,,	..	..	..	..	..	..	..	..	..	..	..	..	..
EDINBURGH (Pr. St.) ,,	..	..	..	..	..	..	..	..	..	..	..	..	..
CARLISLE (Citadel) ,,	..	..	..	..	..	..	..	..	..	6a25	..	..	..
Keswick ,,	..	..	..	..	..	..	..	..	..	..	..	..	..
Windermere ,,	..	..	..	..	..	..	..	..	..	7X14	..	..	..
BELFAST ,,	..	..	..	..	..	..	..	..	..	..	..	..	..
HEYSHAM ,,	..	..	..	7 32	..	..	..	..	..	..	..	..	..
FLEETWOOD ,,	..	..	..	7 45	..	..	..	..	..	8X20	..	..	..
Blackpool (Central) ,,	..	..	..	7 45	..	..	..	..	..	8 32	..	..	..
PRESTON ,,	..	..	..	8 55	..	..	..	..	..	9 29	..	..	..
DUBLIN (W.R.) ,,	..	..	..	..	..	..	..	..	..	..	..	..	..
HOLYHEAD ,,	7 30	..	..	7 10	..	..	..	..	..	..	..	..	..
Llandudno ,,	8 43	..	..	8 30	..	..	..	..	..	8X45	..	9 35	9J35
BIRK'NH'D (W'side) ,,	9 18	..	..	9 18	..	..	..	..	..	9S43	..	1050	1050
Chester (General) ,,	10 0	..	..	9 55	..	..	..	..	..	10S20	..	1127	1127
LIVERPOOL (L. St.) ,,	..	..	..	9 10	1010	10 0	..	1010	..	..	..	1115	1115
HUDDERSFIELD ,,	..	..	..	..	..	..	..	..	..	..	..	9 50	9 50
MANCHESTER (L.R.) ,,	..	9 40	9 45	..	..	..	..	..	..	1010	..	1040	1040
MANCHESTER (Vic.) ,,	..	..	..	..	..	..	..	..	..	..	..	..	..
CREWE ,,	1035	..	..	1035	..	..	..	..	..	11 8	..	1210	1210
WOLVERHAMPTON ,,	..	..	..	..	..	..	1112	..	..	..	1225	..	..
BIRM'HAM (New St.) ,,	..	..	..	..	..	..	1145	..	..	..	1 0	..	..
RUGBY ,,	..	..	..	..	..	..	..	..	1259	1252	..	..	..
EUSTON arr.	1 10	1 5	1 13	1 21	1 30	1 43	1C40	1B49	2 47	2b41	2F55	3 5	3G10

A On Sats. leaves Manchester (L. Rd.) 8.5 a.m. **B** Com. Sept. 2, arr. Euston 1.45 p.m. **C** On Sats. arr. Euston 2.5 p.m. **D** Applies July 17th, 24th, 31st, Aug. 7th, 14th, 21st only. **E** Via Birmingham and is Mons. excepted. On Sat. leaves Crewe 5.0 a.m. **F** On Sats. arr. Euston 7 mins. later. **G** On July 29th, Aug 5th, 12th and 19th, arr. Euston 3.27 p.m. **H** On Sats. arr. 12.10 p.m. **J** Comm. Sept. 9th, leaves Llandudno 9 a.m. **K** On Mons. and Fris. leaves Holyhead 10.25 a.m. **L** Not after Sept. 2nd. **M** Mon. morns. excepted. **N** On Fris. leaves Birkenhead 12. 5 p.m. **P** From Aug. 19th to Sept. 2nd arr. Euston 4.24 p.m. **S** Sats. excepted. **U** Passengers cross Manchester between Exchange and London Road Stations at own expense. **X** Sats. only. *a* On Sats. leaves Carlisle 6.15 a.m. *b* On Sats. arr. Euston 2.37 p.m. *e* On Mons. arr. Euston 1.22 p.m. *f* From Aug. 5th to 26th leaves Fleetwood 9.45 a.m. *n* Blackpool (North).

The times from 6 p.m. to 5.59 a.m. inclusive are printed in dark type, thus **12.9** meaning 9 min. aft. midn.

JULY 3rd to SEPTEMBER 24th, inclusive, 1939.

LONDON MIDLAND AND SCOTTISH RAILWAY

Express Services from IRELAND, SCOTLAND, and THE NORTH OF ENGLAND to LONDON.

TO LONDON (EUSTON)

RESTAURANT CARS on Day Expresses and SLEEPING CARS on Night Trains to London (Euston).
For further particulars see Company's Time Tables.

WEEKDAYS.

STATIONS.	"The Lancastrian" Saturdays excepted. via Stoke.	Saturdays only.	"The Lancastrian." Saturdays only.	Saturdays excepted	Saturdays only.	Saturdays only.	Saturdays excepted. "The Welshman."		Saturdays only. Lakes Express	"Lakes Express." Sats. excepted	Saturdays only. "The Welshman"	"The Royal Scot."	SX "The Royal Scot."	SO	SO "The Irish Mail"	"The Manxman"	Saturdays excepted	SO	"The Irish Mail."	SO	Saturdays excepted.	"The Manxman" Saturdays only.	SO	Saturdays only.	Saturdays excepted.	
STRANRAER ......dep.	..		..	..			..	..		..		..	7 45	..	..			..	..	7 45	..		..	..	..	..
INVERNESS ...... ,,	..		..	..			..	..		..		..	11 20	..	..			..		11 20			..	..	..	..
ABERDEEN (Joint) ,,	..		..				..	..				..	6 50		..			..		6 50			..	..	..	..
DUNDEE (West) .. ,,	..		..				..	..				..	8 15	..	..			..		8 15			..	..	..	..
PERTH (General).... ,,	..		..				..	..				..	8 55	..	..			..		8 55			..	..	..	9 SX 5
STIRLING .... ,,	..		..				..	..				..	9 41		..			..		9 41			..	..	..	9 SX 57
GLASGOW (Central) ,,	..		..				..	..				10SX0	..	..	..		..	10 0	..	..			..	..	..	..
EDINBURGH (Pr. St.),,	..		..	..			..	..		..		..	10 0	..	..		..	..	..	10 0			..	..	..	..
CARLISLE (Citadel) ,,		..		8 30	..	8 30		..	..	9 43			12 16	9 43		..	..	..		..	..		..			12 H 46
Keswick .... ,,		..		7 43	..	7 43		..	..	9 59		..	..	9 59		..	..	..	..	..	..		..			11 H 53
Windermere .... ,,		8 30		9 25	..	9 25		..	10 45	11 15		..	..	11Q5		.	..	..		..			..			11 X 53
BELFAST .... ,,		..		..	..	..		..	..	..		..	..	..			..		..		..		..			..
HEYSHAM .... ,,		8 48		9 47	..	9 47		..	10 37	10 43		..	..	..		..	..			..			..			1 10
FLEETWOOD .... ,,		9f35		9 35	..	..		..	10 30	11 20		..	..	12 0		..	..	..	.	..	..	12 30	..			1 SX 15
Blackpool (Central) .. ,,		9 55		10 10	..	10 10		..	10 55	12n10		11X15	..	12 5		..	..	..		..	..	1 N 0				1 SH 35
PRESTON .... ,,		10 50		11 15	..	11 15		..	12 6	12 48		..	..	1 9		12 57	SX	.	..		..	1 15	..			2 SH 47
DUBLIN (W.R.) .... ,,	..	..		..	..	.	..	..	..		..			..	8 25	..	..	.	8 45	..	..	..	.			..
HOLYHEAD .... ,,	..	..		..	..	8L25	9 K 0	..	..		9B40			..	12 37		..	..	12 40	SX	..	..				1 SX 0
Llandudno .... ,,	..	..		..	..	9 55	11 35	..			11E50			..	..			..	12P35	..		..	..			1 H 45
BIRK'NH'D (W'side) ,,	..	..		..	..	..	11N55	..			..			12 5	..	..			1 18	..	..	..	..			2 H 40
Chester (General) .... ,,	..	..		11 35	..	11 35	1 2	..			..			12 50	..				2 20		..	..	..			3 H 14
LIVERPOOL (L. St.) ,,	..	..	..	..	..	..		..		12 5	..			12 5	..	2SX10	..		..		..	2 15		..	..	..
HUDDERSFIELD .. ,,	10U48	..	..	..	10 52	..		..		..	..			11J14	..	11 51	..	..	..	..	1 32	1 49	1 32	..	..	..
MANCHESTER (L.R.) ,,	12 5	..	12 5	..	..	..		..	..	..	..			12 45	..	1 30	..	..	..	..	2 20	..	2 40	..	..	2 SX 30
MANCHESTER (Vic.) ,,	11 40	..	..	..	11 30	..		..	..	..	..			..	..	..	..	..	..	..	..	..	..	..	..	..
CREWE .... ,,		12 20	..	12 43	..	12 43		..	1 4	1 56	..			2 18	..	2 58	..	..	3SX2	..	..	3 12	..	..	..	3 51
WOLVERHAMPTON ,,		..	..	..	..	..		2 0	..	..	..	..	..	..	..	..	..	..	..	..	..	..	..	3 35	4 15	..
BIRM'HAM (New St.) ,,		..	..	..	..	..		2 35	..	..	..	..	..	..	..	..	..	..	..	..	..	..	..	4 50	4 50	..
RUGBY .... ,,		1 58	..	2 13	..	2 20		..	..	..	..	..	..	..	..	..	3 12	..	4 28	..	4 35	4 40	..	..	..	5 34
EUSTON ....arr.	3 40	3 41	3 50	4 2	4 0	4 10	4 20	E4 30	4P30	4 50	4 50	5 0	5 15	5 20	5 32	5 30	5 37	5 40	5G50	5 50	6 0	6 15	6 45	6 50	6 50	7 5

A Sats. excepted, and will not run on Aug. 4th and 7th. **B** From Aug. 19th to Sept. 2nd incl., leaves Holyhead 10.25 a.m. **D** On Sats. arr. Euston **8.40** p.m. **E** From Aug. 19th to Sept. 2nd incl. arr. Euston 4.30 p.m. **F** On. Sats. arr. Euston **9.15** p.m. **G** On Sats. arr. **6.0** p.m. **H** On Sats. leaves Carlisle 12.37 p.m., Keswick **11.5** p.m., Blackpool (North) 1.30 p.m., Preston 2.28 p.m., Llandudno 1.35 p.m., Birkenhead 2.30 p.m., Chester 3.10 p.m. **J** Not after Sept. 2nd. **N** Blackpool (North). **P** On Sats. until Sept. 9th incl., leaves Llandudno 12.15 p.m. **Q** Not after Sept. 9th. **SO** Sats. only. **SX** Sats. excepted. **T** Applies Sept. 16th and 23rd only. **X** Sats. only.

FOR OTHER NOTES SEE PAGE 93.

The times from 6 p.m. to 5.59 a.m. inclusive are printed in dark type, thus **12.9** meaning 9 min. aft. midn.

JULY 3rd to SEPTEMBER 24th, inclusive, 1939.

LONDON MIDLAND AND SCOTTISH RAILWAY

Express Services from IRELAND, SCOTLAND, and THE NORTH OF ENGLAND to LONDON.

TO LONDON (EUSTON)

RESTAURANT CARS on Day Expresses and SLEEPING CARS on Night Trains to London (Euston).

For further particulars see Company's Time Tables.

WEEKDAYS.

STATIONS.		Sats. only.	Sats. excepted.	Sats. excepted.	Sats. only.	A "The Coronation Scot." Reservation Fee, 2/6.	Saturdays only		Saturdays excepted.	Saturdays only.	"The Comet"	SO Not after Sept. 9th.	SX
STRANRAER ...... dep.	..					..		..	..	..		..	2 H4
INVERNESS ...... ,,	..					..		..	..	..		..	8 30
ABERDEEN (Joint) ,,	..					..		..	..	..		..	10 5
DUNDEE (West) .. ,,	..					..		..	..	..		..	1130
PERTH (General).... ,,	..	9 5				..		..					1220
STIRLING .... ,,	..	9 57				..		..					1 6
GLASGOW (Central) ,,	..	..				1 30		..	..	..			1 35
EDINBURGH (Pr. St.) ,,	..					..	..	..	..	..	..		1 40
CARLISLE (Citadel) ,,	..	1246	1 5	..	..	3 17	..	..	..	1 28	..		3 52
Keswick .... ,,	..	1153	..	..	..		..	..	..	..	..		..
Windermere .... ,,	..	..	1 53	..	..		..	..	..	2 40	..		3 55
BELFAST .... ,,	..	..	..	..	..		..	..	..	..	..		9 28
HEYSHAM .... ,,	..		1 45	..	..		..	..	..	1 39	..		3 47
FLEETWOOD ...... ,,	..	1 40	2 30	..	..		..	..	..	2 28	..		..
Blackpool (Central) .. ,,	..	1 45	2N45	..	2N45		..	..	..	3N55	..	..	..
PRESTON .... ,,	..	2 54	3 30	..	..		..	..	..	4 10	..	..	5 50
DUBLIN (W.R.) .... ,,	..	..	..	..	..		..	..	..	..	..	1145	..
HOLYHEAD ...... ,,	..	..	..	1 15	..		1 10	..	..	1T30	..	3 50	2 45
Llandudno .... ,,	..		..	2 38	..		2 0		3 25	4T0	..	4 15	4 25
BIRK'NH'D (W'side) ,,	..		..	3 35	..		3 12		4 35	4T35	..	..	5 13
Chester (General) .... ,,	..		..	4 19	..		4 5		5 18	5T25	..	..	5 54
LIVERPOOL (L. St.) ,,	..	2 55	4 5	..	4 0	..	..	..	5 25	5 25	..	..	5 30
HUDDERSFIELD .. ,,	..	..	..	3 30	2 29	..	3 30	..	..	..	..	..	4 0
MANCHESTER (L.R.) ,,	..	..	..	4 10	..	..	4 10	..	4 45	..	5 45	..	..
MANCHESTER (Vic.) ,,	..	..	..	..	..	..	..	..	..	..	..	..	5 12
CREWE .... ,,	..	4 10	4 53	5 3	..	..	4 57	..	6 12	6 12	..	..	6 55
WOLVERHAMPTON ,,	4SO15	..	..	..	..	..	..	5 43	..	..	..	..	Mid-day Scot.
BIRM'HAM (New St.) ,,	5 0	..	..	..	..	..	..	6 20	..	..	..	..	
RUGBY .... ,,	5 40	5 50	..	..	..	..	..	6 59	..	..	..	..	
EUSTON ....arr.	7 22	7 35	7 30	7 47	7 55	8 0	8 10	8D20	8 40	9 0	9F0	9 6	9 35

STATIONS.	SO	SO	July 15th to Aug. 19th.	Saturdays excepted.	Saturdays only.	SX	SO	SO	FO	Saturdays nights excepted.	Saturdays only.	SX	SO
STRANRAER ...... dep.	..	12H25		..	..	..	..	..	..	..		3 30	3 30
INVERNESS ...... ,,	..	8 30		..	..	..	..	..	..	..		11 5	11 5
ABERDEEN (Joint) ,,	..	10 5		..	..	..	..	..	..	..		1 0	1 10
DUNDEE (West) .. ,,	..	1130		..	..	..	..	..	..	..		2 50	2 50
PERTH (General).... ,,	..	1220		..	..	1230	..	1230	..	..		3 45	3 45
STIRLING .... ,,	..	1 10		..	..	1 18	..	1 20	..	..		4 41	4 41
GLASGOW (Central) ,,	1 30	..		..	..	..	..	..	..	..		5 40	5 40
EDINBURGH (Pr. St.) ,,	..	1 40		..	..	..	..	..	..	..		5 50	5 50
CARLISLE (Citadel) ,,	..	4 0	..	..	..	4 4	..	4 12	7 12	..	7 12	8 37	8 37
Keswick .... ,,	..	..	..	..	..	3 15	..	3 15	6 40	..	6 40	6 40	..
Windermere .... ,,	4 0	..	..	..	..	..	..	..	8 35	..	8 35	8 35	..
BELFAST .... ,,	..	9J28	10 0			..	..	10 0	..		..	..	..
HEYSHAM .... ,,	3 47	..	5 15			..	..	5K15	9 7		9 7	9 7	..
FLEETWOOD ...... ,,	3 45	..	..			4 50	4 50	..	9 5		9 5	9 50	9 40
Blackpool (Central) .. ,,	4 40	..	..			5N10	5N5	..	9 40		9 40	10 0	10N0
PRESTON .... ,,	..	..	..			6 3	5 53	6 16	1035		1035	1046	1046
DUBLIN (W.R.) .... ,,	..	..	..			..	..	..	..		..	..	..
HOLYHEAD ...... ,,	..	4 5	..			..	..	..	..		7 40	7 40	..
Llandudno .... ,,	..	4 30	..			..	..	..	..		9 10	9 10	..
BIRK'NH'D (W'side) ,,	..	5 13	..			5 33	..	..	..		9L53	9 53	..
Chester (General) .... ,,	..	6 10	..			6 15	..	..	..		11 5	11 5	..
LIVERPOOL (L. St.) ,,	..	..	5 3			..	5 30	..	..		10 0	10 0	..
HUDDERSFIELD .. ,,	4 0	..	..			4 41	..	..	..		9 29	9 8	..
MANCHESTER (L.R.) ,,	..	..	5 43			6 15	..	..	..		1030	1030	11G0
MANCHESTER (Vic.) ,,	5 12	..	..			..	..	..	..		..	..	..
CREWE .... ,,	6 37	6 52	7 12	..	..	7 19	7 15	..	..	..	12 5	1250	1250
WOLVERHAMPTON ,,	Mid-day Scot.	..	..	6 35	7 0	..	..	..	..	1056	1056	..	..
BIRM'HAM (New St.) ,,		..	..	7 55	7 55	..	..	..	..	1220	1215	..	..
RUGBY .... ,,		..	8 47	8 41	8 41	9 0	9 0	..	1 38	1 25	1 49	2 45	2 45
EUSTON ....arr.	9 40	9 50	1015	1025	1023	1040	1035	1052	3 30	3E35	3 35	5 0	4 50

D After Sept. 8th applies Weds. and Thurs. only. **E** On Sats. morns. arr. **3.18** a.m. **F** Commences Aug. 11th. **G** Mayfield Station. **H** Stranraer Harbour. **J** July 8th and commencing Aug. 26th. **K** July 8th, Aug. 26th, Sept. 2nd and 9th only. **L** Commencing Aug. 26th, leaves Birkenhead 10.15 p.m. **N** Blackpool (North). **P** Sun. morns. excepted. **Q** Via Stranraer. **SN** Sat. nights only. **Y** Sat. nights and Sun. morns. excepted. **Z** Sat. nights and Sun. morns. only. **FO** Fris. only. *n* Commencing August 20th.

FOR OTHER NOTES SEE PAGE 93a.

F[1] **The times from 6 p.m. to 5.59 a.m. inclusive are printed in dark type, thus 12.9 meaning 9 min. aft. midn.**

JULY 3rd to SEPTEMBER 24th inclusive, 1939.

LONDON MIDLAND AND SCOTTISH RAILWAY

Express Services from IRELAND, SCOTLAND, and THE NORTH OF ENGLAND to LONDON.

TO LONDON (EUSTON)

RESTAURANT CARS on Day Expresses and SLEEPING CARS on Night Trains from London (Euston).

For further particulars see Company's Time Tables.

STATIONS.	WEEKDAYS.													
		Y	Z	SN	Y			Y	Z					
STRANRAER ...... dep.	*Via* Stoke.	"The Irish Mail."	"The Irish Mail."			Saturday mornings only.			Commencing July 23rd.	"Night Scot."	9H37			
INVERNESS ,,								4F20	4n20			4 40	4 40	
ABERDEEN (Joint) ,,														7 50
DUNDEE (West) ,,								7F30	7n30			8 20	7 30	9 20
PERTH (General) ,,								8F40	8 40			9 10	9 0	10 5
STIRLING ,,													1012	1054
GLASGOW (Central) ,,							9 25			1045				
EDINBURGH (Pr. St.) ,,							9 20				11 0			
CARLISLE (Citadel) ,,							1210	1223	1223		1 15	1 25	1 25	1 37
Keswick ,,														
Windermere ,,														
BELFAST ,,											6Q25			
HEYSHAM ,,														
FLEETWOOD ,,														
Blackpool (Central) ,,														
PRESTON ,,														
DUBLIN (W.R.) ,,		8 10	8 10											
HOLYHEAD ,,		1213	1213											
Llandudno ,,		10D10	11 0											
BIRK'NG'D (W'side) ,,		1133	1133											
Chester (General) ,,		2 0	2 0											
LIVERPOOL (L. St.) ,,				1150	1150			2 30						
HUDDERSFIELD ,,		1122	1122											
MANCHESTER (L.R.) ,,	12 0													
MANCHESTER (Vic.) ,,						1235								
CREWE ,,		2 40	2 40				3 19	3 46	3 46	4 2	4 21	4 31	4 31	4 48
WOLVERHAMPTON ,,														
BIRM'HAM (New St.) ,,														
RUGBY ,,	2 57			3 25	3 34	3 49	5 0				5 52	6 1	6 2	6P24
EUSTON ...... arr.	5 15	5 30	5 30	5 42	5 53	6 5	6 45	6 55	6 55	7 15	7 30	7 35	7 45	8 0

FOR NOTES SEE PAGE 94.

The times from 6 p.m. to 5.59 a.m. inclusive are printed in dark type, thus 12.9 meaning ...

JULY 3rd to SEPTEMBER 24th inclusive, 1939.

LONDON MIDLAND AND SCOTTISH RAILWAY

Express Services from LONDON to IRELAND, SCOTLAND, and THE NORTH OF ENGLAND.

FROM LONDON (EUSTON)

RESTAURANT CARS on Day Expresses and SLEEPING CARS on Night Trains from London (Euston).

For further particulars see Company's Time Tables.

STATIONS.	WEEKDAYS.																							
EUSTON ....dep.	1210	12 20	1230	1245	1255	2 30	2 35	2 35	6 50	7 0	8 10	8 30	8 35	8 45	8 45	9 0	9 10	9 15	10 0	10 0	10 5	10 5	10†5	1030
RUGBY ....arr.	..	..	..	..	33	..	4 8	4 8	8 49	8 56	..	"The Irish Mail."	10 6	1018	1018	1142	1041	..	..	..	..	1132	1136	..
BIRM'HAM (N.S.) ,,	..	..	..	..	..	4 34	..	..	9 54	9 54	1010		..	..	11 1	1238	..	1110	..	..	..	1 14	1 7	..
WOLVERH'PTON ,,	..	..	..	..	..	6 9	..	..	1052	1052	1126		..	..	1151	..	..	1146	..	..	..	..	..	..
CREWE .... ,,	..	3 18	..	3 51	..	..	6 0	6 0	1046	11 2	..		1132	1144	1144	..	..	..	..	..	..	1255	1 3	1 15
MANCH'TER (Vic.),,	..	..	..	..	5 13	..	8 23	8 23	..	..	..		..	..	..	..	..	..	"The Royal Scot." Saturdays excepted.	"The Royal Scot." Saturdays only.	Saturdays only. Runs July 22 to Sept. 2 incl.	Saturdays excepted.	Saturdays only.	2 33
,, London Road) ,,	..	6SX 3	..	6 3	..	..	8 4	8 4	..	1227	..		..	..	12V58	..	..	..						2 5
HUDDERSFIELD ,,	..	7SX59	..	7 59	7 59	..	10 3	10 3	..	1 33	..		..	..	..	..	..	..						2 44
LIVERP'L (L. St.) ,,	4 3	..	4 22	5 55	..	..	6 55	6 55	..	1227	..		1235	..	..	..	..	..						2 36
Chester (General) ,,	Monday mornings only.	5SX33	..	5 33	Saturday mornings only. Commences July 22nd.	..	8 10	8 10	1132	..	..		..	1219	1219	..	..	..						2 6
BIRK'H'D (W'de) ,,		7SX15	..	7 12		..	8 45	8 45	12 7	..	..		..	1 4	1 4	..	..	..						2 51
Llandudno ...... ,,		8SX11	..	8 19		..	9 46	9 46	1 10	..	..		..	2 8	1 58	..	2 14	..						3 40
HOLYHEAD .... ,,		10SX15	..	9 58		..	11 9	1057	1 46	..	..	1 35	..	2 5	..	..	2 14	..						..
DUBLIN (W.R.) ,,		..	..	..		..	..	..	..	..	..	6 0	..	6 0	..	..	..	..						..
PRESTON ...... ,,		4 28	..	5 15		..	8 42	8 42	1214	1 22	..	Sats. only. Also runs on Fris., July 21st, 28th, Aug. 4th & 11th.	..	1 11	2 41	..	..	..					3 5	..
Blackpool (Cen.) .. ,,		6SX31	..	6 8		..	9N26	9n45	1 11	1 N 3			..	2 14	2fN5	..	..	..					3N51	..
FLEETWOOD .. ,,		7SX31	..	7 31		..	9 36	9 36	..	..			..	3 36	2f38	..	..	..					4f17	..
Heysham .... ,,		8SX40	..	8 40		..	1120	9 53	1 32	3 20	Saturdays excepted.		..	3 20	..	..	..	..	..	..		..	..	..
BELFAST ...... ,,		..	..	..		..	..	..	..	..			..	..	..	..	..	..	..	..		10 0	..	..
Windermere (Town) ,,	..	9 SX0	..	9 0	..	..	1040	1057	1 55	..			Saturdays only.	Saturdays excepted. "The Irish Mail."	Saturdays only.	Saturdays only.	Saturdays only. Runs July 15 to Sept. 2	Saturdays excepted.	..	..	..	4 18	3 50	Saturdays excepted.
Keswick .... ,,	..	8 8	..	1024	..	..	1213	1213	..	..									..	..	..	5K19	..	
CARLISLE (Citadel) ,,	..	6 35	..	9 56	..	..	1135	11 5	..	..									2 59	3F30	3 39	3 50	3 50	
EDINB'GH (P. St.) ,,	..	11 18	..	..		..	2 47	1 31	..	..									5 5	5D45	5 48	..	..	
GLASGOW (Cen.) ,,	Third class only	9E 3[illegible]	..	Saturdays only.	Third class only.	..	3 42	1 34	..	..									5 0	5 40	..	..	..	
STIRLING ...... ,,		..	..			..	4 19	2 15	..	..									..	..	..	6 33	6 40	
PERTH (General) ,,		..	..			..	Sats. excepted.	Sats. only.	Sats. excepted.	Sats. only.									..	..	..	7 25	7 30	
DUNDEE (West) ,,		..	..			..													..	..	..	8 21	8 21	
ABERDEEN .... ,,		..	..			..													..	..	..	9 52	9 52	
INVERNESS (Joint)		..	..			..													..	..	..	..	..	
STRANRAER .. ,,	..	11 5	..	..		..					..								..	7J 0	..	6H45	..	

*** For Train Service on Sundays and Bank Holidays, see Company's Time Tables.

D July 22nd to Sept. 2nd incl. excepted. **E** Glasgow (St. Enoch). **F** Applies July 8th, 15th, and commences Sept. 9th. **H** Harbour Station. **J** Harbour Station and leaves Euston 10.5 a.m. On Sept. 9th, 16th and 23rd arr. **6.45** p.m. **K** Fris. only. **N** Blackpool (North). **SX** Sats. excepted. **V** Mayfield Station. *f* Not after Sept. 2nd. *n* Blackpool (North) and commencing Sept. 9th, arrives 9.26 a.m. † From July 22nd to Sept. 2nd incl., leaves Euston 10.10 a.m.

The times from 6 p.m. to 5.59 a.m. inclusive are printed in dark type, thus **12.9** meaning 9 min. aft. midn.

JULY 3rd to SEPTEMBER 24th inclusive, 1939.

LONDON MIDLAND AND SCOTTISH RAILWAY

Express Services from LONDON to IRELAND, SCOTLAND, and THE NORTH OF ENGLAND.

FROM LONDON (EUSTON)

RESTAURANT CARS on Day Expresses and SLEEPING CARS on Night Trains from London (Euston).

For further particulars see Company's Time Tables.

WEEKDAYS.

STATIONS.								SO														H
EUSTON ....dep.	1030	1035	1040	1040	1040	1045	1050	11 0	11 5	1115	1130	1150	1135	1150	1150	12 0	12 0	12 5	12 5	1230	1 15	1 30
RUGBY ....arr.	..	1244	..	..	1223	1246	..	"The Welshman"	"The Welshman"	"The Welshman"	..	..	..	..	1 20	1 28	..	1 54	2 10	via Stoke	Not after Sept. 2nd.	..
BIRM'HAM (N.S.) ,,	..	..	..	..	..	..	..				1 25	1 39	..	..	..	Saturdays excepted.	..	3 10	3 10			..
WOLVERH'PTON ,,	..	..	..	..	..	..	..				1 58	2 16	..	..	..		..	4 9	4 2			..
CREWE .... ,,	..	2 22	..	1 56	1 37	2 28	..				Saturdays excepted.	Saturdays only.	Saturdays only.	2 35	Saturdays only.		2 57	4 12	4 9	..		"The Coronation Scot." Reservation Fee, 2/6.
MANCH'TER (V.) ,,	..	..	..	..	..	..	3 4							..			..	..	..	..		
,, London Road) ,,	..	3V53	..	..	..	..	2 40							3 20			4 5	5 25	5 30	4 28		
HUDDERSFIELD ,,	..	5 40	..	..	..	..	3 17							5e22			5 40	6 10	6 10	5 40		
LIVERP'L (L. St.) ,,	2 20	..	2 18	..	..	..	..							3 25			3 49	5 21	5 23	..		
Chester (General) ,,	2 14	3 4	Saturdays excepted.	2 47	2 47	2 57	Saturdays only.							3 9			3 34	Saturdays excepted.	Saturdays only.	"The Comet." Saturdays only.		
BIRK'H'D (W'de) ,,	2 51	3 38		..	..	..		..	..	..				3 40			4 6					
Llandudno ...... ,,	3 51	..		..	..	..		3 35	4B0	4 2				5A20			5 25					
HOLYHEAD .... ,,	Saturdays only. The "Manxman"	Saturdays only.		..	..	..		..	5D50	5E15				..			7 56					
DUBLIN (W.R.) ,,				..	..	..		..	..	..		..	..	..		..	..					
PRESTON ...... ,,				3 18	3 24	..		Runs July 15th to Aug. 26th inclusive	Saturdays only	Saturdays excepted.	..	..	3 37	"The Comet." Saturdays excepted.	4 45	4 4	Saturdays only.					
Blackpool (Cen.) .. ,,				3N55	4N22	Fridays only.					..	..	4 20		5N37	4 47						
FLEETWOOD .. ,,				4 35	4 35						..	..	..		5 50	5 19						
Heysham .... ,,				4 55	4 55						..	..	4 50		..	4 55						
BELFAST ...... ,,				..	..						..	..	..		..	..					..	..
Windermere (Town) ,,			The "Manxman"	5 14	5 14						..	..	..		5 15	5 25		..	..		..	..
Keswick .... ,,				..	..						..	..	..		6 37	6 27		..	..		7 28	..
CARLISLE (Citadel)		..		5 48	5 48						..	..	..		6 30	..		..	..	..	7 2	6 13
EDINB'GH (P. St.) ,,		..		Fridays only.	Fridays excepted.						..	..	..		"Lakes Express"	"Lakes Express"	..	..	..	..	..	..
GLASGOW (Cen.) ,,		..									..	..	..				..	..	..	..	9 12	8 0
STIRLING ...... ,,		..									..	..	..				..	..	..	..	Saturdays only.	..
PERTH (General) ,,		..									..	..	..				..	..	..	..		..
DUNDEE (West) ,,		..				..	..	..	..	..	..	..	..	..			..	..	..	..		..
ABERDEEN (Joint)		..				..	..	..	..	..	..	..	..	..			..	..	..	..		..
INVERNESS .... ,,		..				..	..	..	..	..	..	..	..	..			..	..	..	..		..
STRANRAER .. ,,		..				..	..	..	..	..	..	..	..	..			..	..	..	..		..

A Commencing Sept. 4th, arr. Llandudno 5.42 p.m. **B** Applies July 8th and commencing Sept. 2nd. On Sept. 16th and 23rd leaves Euston 11.15 a.m. **D** On Sept. 16th and 23rd arr. Holyhead 5.15 p.m. **E** Commencing Sept. 11th arr. Holyhead **6.5** p.m. **F** Until Sept. 2nd incl. leaves Euston 11.40 a.m. **H** Sats. excepted. Will not run July 28th, Aug. 1st and Aug. 7th. **N** Blackpool (North). **V** Mayfield Station. **SO** Sats. only. **SX** Sats. excepted. *e* Via Oldham (Clegg Street).

The times from 6 p.m. to 5.59 a.m. inclusive are printed in dark type, thus 12.9 meaning 9 min. aft. midn.

JULY 3rd to SEPTEMBER 24th inclusive, 1939.

LONDON MIDLAND AND SCOTTISH RAILWAY

Express Services from LONDON to IRELAND, SCOTLAND, and THE NORTH OF ENGLAND.

FROM LONDON (EUSTON)

RESTAURANT CARS on Day Expresses and SLEEPING CARS on Night Trains from London (Euston).

For further particulars see Company's Time Tables.

WEEKDAYS.

STATIONS.		SX	SO								
EUSTON ....dep.	1 30	1 35	1 35	2 0	2 0	2 0	2 25	2 30	2 35	2 40	2 40
RUGBY ....arr.	2 58	2 57	3 5	"The Mid-day Scot."	..	..	..	..	..	4 8	4 18
BIRM'HAM (N.S.) ,,	..	..	4 6		4 20	4 13	4 20	..	..	..	..
WOLVERH'PTON ,,	..	..	4 53		4 53	5C0	4 53	..	..	..	..
CREWE ,,	4 28	4 26	4 34		Runs July 8th, 15th, 22nd, 29th Sept. 9th, 16th and 23rd.	Runs Aug. 5th, 12th, 19th, 26th and Sept. 2nd.	Saturdays excepted.	..	..	5 31	5 47
MANCH'TER (Vic.) ,,	"The Mid-day Scot."	..	..					..	7 2	..	..
,, London Road) ,,		6 0	..					..	6 41	..	..
HUDDERSFIELD ,,		7 21	..					..	..	..	..
LIVERP'L (L. St.) ,,		6 17	6 25					6 18	..	6 24	6 43
Chester (General) ,,		5 1	5 22					Saturdays only.	Saturdays only, and runs July 15th to Sept. 2nd.	6 10	6 28
BIRK'H'D (W'de) ,,		6 2	..							6 42	7 8
Llandudno ,,		6 32	7 4							7 42	8 8
HOLYHEAD ,,		7 56	8 29							9 20	9 49
DUBLIN (W.R.) ,,		..	..	..						..	Saturdays only.
PRESTON ,,		5 29	6 5	6 5			..			7 19	
Blackpool (Cen.) ,,		6 30	7N9	7N3			..			8 11	
FLEETWOOD ,,	..	6 30	7 9	7 13			..			8 24	
Heysham ,,	7 8	..	8A50	7 8			..			8A50	
BELFAST ,,	..	..	..	..		..	..			..	
Windermere (Town) ,,	7 15	7 9	7 42	7 20		..	..	..		9 0	
Keswick ,,	..	..	8 50	8 50		..	..	..		Saturdays excepted.	
CARLISLE (Citadel) ,,	7 30	7 24	8 14	7 44	..	..	..	..			
EDINB'GH (P. St.) ,,	9 46	..	..	9 45	..	..	..	..	Third cl. only.		
GLASGOW (Cen.) ,,	9 42	..	..	9 55	..	..	..	..			
STIRLING ,,	Saturdays only.	9 56	1121	Saturdays excepted.	..	..	..	..			
PERTH (General) ,,		1041	1210		..	..	..	..			
DUNDEE (West) ,,		..	..		..	..	..	..			
ABERDEEN (Joint)		3 0	3 0		..	..	..	..			
INVERNESS ,,		5 25	..		..	..	..	..			
STRANRAER ,,	..	..	..		..	..	..	..	..		..

STATIONS.											
EUSTON ....dep.	2 45	2 50	3 6	3 50	4 0	4 0	4 10	4 10	4B35	5 10	5 10
RUGBY ....arr.	4 26	4 18	5 19	5 23	5 27	5 33	5 43	5 49	..	"The Blackpool & Flyde Coast Express."	6 43
BIRM'HAM (N.S.) ,,	6 12	6 12	..	..	..	..	via Stoke.	..	6 35	..	..
WOLVERH'PTON ,,	7 12	6 46	..	..	..	..		..	7 9	..	..
CREWE ,,	..	..	..	7 1	6 59	..	..	7 27	..	7 55	8 26
MANCH'TER (Vic.) ,,	7 2	7 2	..	..	..	..	..	..	..	..	..
,, London Road) ,,	6 45	6 45	..	..	..	8 5	8 5	8 48	..	8 58	..
HUDDERSFIELD ,,	8 44	8 44	..	..	..	8 51	8 51	10 8	..	..	..
LIVERP'L (L. St.) ,,	..	..	..	7 50	7 45	..	..	8 52	..	9 11	..
Chester (General) ,,	Saturdays only.	Saturdays excepted.	..	7 58	7 55	"The Mancunian." Saturdays only.	Saturdays excepted.	..	..	..	9 3
BIRK'H'D (W'de) ,,			..	8 30	8 30			..	..	..	9 39
Llandudno ,,			..	9 30	9 21			..	..	..	1051
HOLYHEAD ,,			..	11 9	..			..	..	..	1133
DUBLIN (W.R.) ,,			..	..	..		..	..	..	..	6 45
PRESTON ,,			..	Saturdays only.	8 35		..	8 55	..	9 5	9 46
Blackpool (Cen.) ,,			..		9 30		..	9NS1	..	9 57	1036
FLEETWOOD ,,			..		9 45		..	10 4	..	9 52	..
Heysham ,,			..		..		..	1030	..	10a30	..
BELFAST ,,			..		..	..	..	..	..	..	..
Windermere (Town) ,,		..	..		1030	..	"The Mancunian."	1040	..	Saturdays excepted.	Saturdays only.
Keswick ,,		..	..		..	..		..	..		
CARLISLE (Citadel) ,,		..	..		1050	..		1128	..		
EDINB'GH (P. St.) ,,	..	..	..	..	Saturdays excepted.	..		Saturdays only.	..		
GLASGOW (Cen.) ,,	..	..	..	..		..			..		
STIRLING ,,	..	..	..	..		..			..		
PERTH (General) ,,	..	..	..	..		..			..		
DUNDEE (West) ,,	..	..	..	..		..			..		
ABERDEEN (Joint)	..	..	..	..		..			..		
INVERNESS ,,	..	..	..	..		..			..		
STRANRAER ,,	..	..	..	..	..	..	..	..	..		

A Passengers cross Lancaster from Castle to Green Ayre at own expense. **B** On Sats. leaves Euston 4.30 p.m. **C** Leaves Euston 2.5 p.m. **N** Blackpool (North). **SX** Sats. excepted. **SO** Sats. only. *a* Fris., July 7th to Sept. 15th excepted.

The times from 6 p.m. to 5.59 a.m. inclusive are printed in dark type, thus **12.9** meaning 9 min. aft. midn.

JULY 3rd to SEPTEMBER 24th inclusive, 1939.

LONDON MIDLAND AND SCOTTISH RAILWAY

Express Services from LONDON to IRELAND, SCOTLAND, and THE NORTH OF ENGLAND.

FROM LONDON (EUSTON)

RESTAURANT CARS on Day Expresses and SLEEPING CARS on Night Trains from London (Euston).
For further particulars see Company's Time Tables.

STATIONS.	WEEKDAYS.										
EUSTON ....dep.	5 15	5 20	5 32	5 50	6 0	6 5	6 10	6 15	6 55	7 0	7 5
RUGBY ....arr.	..	6 52	7 45	..	..	..	..	..	..	..	8 48
BIRM'HAM (N.S.) ,,	..	..	..	7 45	..	..	..	..	8 55	..	9 48
WOLVERH'PTON ,,	..	..	..	8 15	..	..	..	..	9 26	..	1025
CREWE .... ,,	8 2	8 25	..	..	..	..	8 57	..	..	"Ulster Express."	..
MANCH'TER (V.) ,,	..	..	..	..	..	X	1022	..	..		..
,, London Road) ,,	..	..	..	..	9e15	..	10S2	..	..		..
HUDDERSFIELD ,,	..	..	..	..	..	..	10D26	..	..		..
LIVERP'L (L. St.) ,,	..	..	..	..	..	9e40	1026	10 0	..		..
Chester (General) ,,	..	9 3	..	..	"The Lancastrian."	"The Merseyside Express."	9 56	Fridays and Saturdays only.	..		..
BIRK'H'D (W'de) ,,	..	9 39	..	..			1047		..		..
Llandudno ...... ,,	..	1048	..	..			11X34		..		..
HOLYHEAD .... ,,	..	1135	..	..			..		..		..
DUBLIN (W.R.) ,,	..	6 45	..	..			..		..		..
PRESTON ...... ,,	9 13	9 43	..	..			10 3		..		..
Blackpool (Cen.) .. ,,	..	..	..	..			1057		..		..
FLEETWOOD .. ,,	..	..	..	..			1056		..		..
Heysham .... ,,	0 2	11 9	..	..			..		..	1130	..
BELFAST ...... ,,	5 35	..	..	..			..		..	6 35	..
Windermere (Town) ,,	Fridays only. Not after Sept. 15th.	Saturdays excepted	..	..			12X5		..	..	..
Keswick .... ,,			..	..			..		..	..	..
CARLISLE (Cit'del) ,,			..	..			..	..	..	..	..
EDINB'GH (P.St.) ,,			..	..	..	..	..	..	..	..	..
GLASGOW (Cen.) ,,			..	..	..	..	..	..	..	..	..
STIRLING ...... ,,			..	..	..	..	..	..	..	..	..
PERTH (General) ,,			..	..	..	..	..	..	..	..	..
DUNDEE (West) ,,			..	..	..	..	..	..	..	..	..
ABERDEEN (Joi't) ,,			..	..	..	..	..	..	..	..	..
INVERNESS .... ,,			..	..	..	..	..	..	..	..	..
STRANRAER .. ,,			..	..	..	..	..	..	..	..	..

STATIONS.	WEEKDAYS.										
EUSTON ....dep.	7 20	7 40	8 0	8 45	Y 9 15	9 25	9 25	9 25	9 35	1050	1050
RUGBY ....arr.	Saturdays excepted.	9 32	9 43	1023	..	1054	1054	1058	1114	..	Sats. only.
BIRM'HAM (N.S.) ,,		..	..	..	..	..	..	1157	1159	..	
WOLVERH'PTON ,,		..	..	..	..	..	..	..	..	..	
CREWE .... ,,	..	11 3	1120	1158	..	1237	1 5	1258	..	1 35	1 44
MANCH'TER (V.) ,,	..	..	..	..	..	Fri. and Sat. nights excepted.	Friday nights only.	Saturday nights only.	Saturdays excepted.	..	..
,, London Road) ,,	..	..	..	1 35	..					2 58	3 42
HUDDERSFIELD ,,	..	..	..	1 23	..					..	..
LIVERP'L (L. St.) ,,	..	..	..	1 5	..					..	3 45
Chester (General) ,,	"The Royal Highlander"	..	..	1234	..					2 31	2 56
BIRK'H'D (W'de) ,,		Saturdays excepted	Saturdays excepted.	..	..					4 9	7 33
Llandudno ...... ,,				..	..					4 44	..
HOLYHEAD .... ,,				2 25	..					5 31	..
DUBLIN (W.R.) ,,				6 45	..					..	..
PRESTON ...... ,,				"The Irish Mail."	..	2 4	..	..	..	2 53	3 13
Blackpool (Cen.) .. ,,		..	..		..	..	..	..	..	..	..
FLEETWOOD .. ,,		..	..		..	..	..	..	..	..	..
Heysham .... ,,		..	..		..	..	..	..	..	7 8	..
BELFAST ...... ,,		..	8 58		..	..	..	..	..	..	..
Windermere (Town) ,,		..	..		..	..	..	..	..	5 29	5 26
Keswick .... ,,		..	..		..	..	..	..	..	..	..
CARLISLE (Cit'del) ,,		2 10	..		..	3 33	4 0	4 5	..	5 10	5 21
EDINB'GH (P.St.) ,,		..	..		..	..	..	..	..	7 43	8 5
GLASGOW (Cen.) ,,		..	..		6 19	6 25	..	6A45	..	Saturdays excepted.	..
STIRLING ...... ,,	..	4 37	..	..	..	..	..	..	..		8 25
PERTH (General) ,,	4 46	..	..	..	..	..	..	..	..		9 18
DUNDEE (West) ,,	..	6 59	..	..	..	..	..	..	..		10 3
ABERDEEN (Joi't) ,,	7 10	..	..	..	..	..	..	..	..		1130
INVERNESS .... ,,	8 45	..	..	..	..	..	..	..	..		1 47
STRANRAER .. ,,	..	..	5h8	..	..	..	..	..	..		..

A Will not apply on July 29th and Aug. 5th. **D** On Sats. arrives Huddersfield **10.42** p.m. **Q** Via Stranraer. **S** Sats. excepted. **X** Sats. only
Y Friday nights only. Will also run on Saturday nights July 29th and Aug. 5th, and arr. Glasgow (Central) **5.45** a.m. *e* On Sats. arrives Manchester **9.30** p.m., Liverpool **9 47** p.m. *h* Harbour Station.

The times from 6 p.m. to 5.59 a.m. inclusive are printed in dark type, thus 12.9 meaning 9 min. aft. midn.

JULY 3rd to SEPTEMBER 24th inclusive, 1939.

LONDON MIDLAND AND SCOTTISH RAILWAY

Express Services from IRELAND, SCOTLAND, and THE NORTH OF ENGLAND to LONDON.

TO LONDON (EUSTON)

RESTAURANT CARS on Day Expresses and SLEETING CARS on Night Trains from London (Euston).
For further particulars see Company's Time Tables.

STATIONS.	WEEKDAYS.											
												FO
EUSTON ....dep.	1055	1135	1145	1145	1155	12 0	12 0	1220	1230	1230	1240	1245
RUGBY ....arr.	..	..	1 18	1 18	Saturdays excepted.	2 4	1 52	..	..	..	..	..
BIRM'HAM (N.S.) ,,	..	..	..	..		2 58	2 51	..	..	..	..	..
WOLVERH'PTON ,,	..	..	..	..		3 34	3 26	..	..	..	..	..
CREWE ,,	Saturdays excepted.	Runs nights of July 2nd and 29th and August 4th only.	2 50	2 50		Saturday nights excepted.	Saturday nights only.	3 18	..	3 41	..	3 51
MANCH'TER (V.) ,,			Saturdays excepted.	Saturdays only.				..	..	..	..	..
,, London Road) ,,					3 44			6S 3	..	..	4 45	6 3
HUDDERSFIELD ,,					5*27			7S59	..	..	..	7 59
LIVERP'L L. St.) ,,					..			..	4 22	4 49	..	..
Chester (General) ,,					..			5S33	..	9 22	..	5 33
BIRK'H'D (W'de) ,,					..			7S15	..	1051	..	7 12
Llandudno .... ,,					..			8S11	..	1120	..	8 19
HOLYHEAD .... ,,					..			10S15	..	1b39	..	9 58
DUBLIN (W.R.) ,,					..	..	..	..	..	..	..	..
PRESTON .... ,,	..		4 11	4 17	..	..	..	4 28	..	5 23	..	5 15
Blackpool (Cen.).. ,,	..		5N10	5N9	..	..	..	6S31	..	6 21	..	6 8
FLEETWOOD .. ,,	..		5 11	5 9	..	..	..	7S31	..	9 13	..	7 31
Heysham .... ,,	..		..	..	..	..	..	8S40	..	10d55	..	8 40
BELFAST ...... ,,	..		..	..	..	..	..	..	..	..	..	..
Windermere (Tn.) ,,	..	..	..	..	..	..	..	9S 0	..	..	..	9 0
Keswick .... ,,	..	..	..	..	..	..	..	8 8	..	..	..	1024
CARLISLE(Cit'del),,	5 10	6 5	6 28	6 35	..	..	..	6 35	..	..	..	9 56
EDINB'GH (P.St.) ,,	..	..	..	..	..	..	..	1115	Saturday nights excepted.	Saturday nights only.	Saturday nights only.	..
GLASGOW (Cen.) ,,	..	9a30	9 35	9 25	..	..	..	9E 8				..
STIRLING ...... ,,	8 14	..	"Night Scot."	"Night Scot."	..	..	..	Sat. nights excepted.				..
PERTH (General) ,,	9 11	..			..	..	..					..
DUNDEE (West) ,,	10 0	..			..	..	..					..
ABERDEEN(Joi't),,	1129	..			..	..	..					..
INVERNESS .... ,,	1 40	..			..	..	..					..
STRANRAER .. ,,	..	..	..	..	..	..	..	11 5				..

E Glasgow (St. Enoch). **N** Blackpool (North). **S** Sat. mornings excepted. **FO** Friday nights only. *a* On mornings of July 23rd and 30th arrives Glasgow (Central) 8.43 a.m. *b* Commencing Sept. 17th, arrives Holyhead 2.25 p.m. *d* Not after Sept. 3rd, and passengers cross Lancaster from Castle to Green Ayre at own expense. * Via Manchester, passengers cross from London Road to Exchange at own expense.

The times from 6 p.m. to 5.59 a.m. inclusive are printed in dark type, thus **12.9** meaning 9 min. aft. midn.

GREAT WESTERN RAILWAY.—PRINCIPAL TRAINS TO LONDON (Weekdays).

	a.m	a.m	a.m	a.m.	a.m	a.m	a.m	a.m	a.m	.m	no'n	a.m	a.m	a.m	a.m	a.m	a.m	a.m	a.m
		Mondays, Thursdays and Saturdays only.		Saturdays excepted.		Saturdays only.				Saturdays only.			Saturdays only.	Saturdays excepted.	Saturdays only.	Sats. only.			
PENZANCE........dep.	..		..	..	..		.	..	..	..	..	..	..	7 45	8 0		..	9 0	10j0
Falmouth ....,,	..		..	..	..	..		..	..	..	..	..	..	8 15	8 15		..	9 15	1010
PLYM'TH N. Rd. .. ,,	..		..	7 20	..	..	..	8 42	.	..	..	..	..	1035	..		..	1150	1230
Torquay ....,,	..		..	7 57	..	8 40	.	9G12	..	9 50	..	.	1150	12 0	..		..	1221	..
EXETER (S. Dd's) .. ,,	..		..	8 50	..	9 50	..	10h7	..	..	..	.	..	1240	..		..	1 25	..
Ilfracombe ....,,	..		..	..	..		..	8A15	..		..					11 0	9G50	..	..
Minehead ....,,	..		..	7 35	..		..	9 30	..		..	..				1215	11G15	..	..
Taunton ....,,	..		6 50	9 28	7S55		..	10h50	..		..	..				1 35	12G40	..	..
BRISTOL(Tp.Mds) .. ,,	7 50		9 0		9 40		..	..	1145		12 0	..				..	1 45	..	..
Bath...............,,	8 7		9 17	..	9 58		..	..	..		1220	..				..	2 5	..	..
WEYMOUTH ......,,	..	6 50	..	8 30	..		9 0	..	.		..	1145				..	..	..	..
Dorchester (G.W.).. ,,	..	7 5	..	8 45	..		9 16	..	..		..	12 0				..	.	..	..
Yeovil (Pen Mill) .... ,,	..	7 36	..	9 17	..		9 51	..	..		..	1239				..	..	..	..
LONDON (Pad'tn) ..arr.	10 0	1050	11 5	1150	1230	1250	1255	1 15	1 45	1 55	2 30	3 30	3 35	3 35	3 45	4 0	4 5	4 30	4 40

	a.m	a.m	a.m	a.m	a.m	a.m	a.m	a.m	a.m	a.m	a.m	p.m	a.m	p.m	p.m	p.m	p.m	a.m	a.m	p.m	p.m	
	Mons. only.	Mons. except.																Sats. only.			Saturdays excepted.	
Fishguard Harbour..dep.		8 55	..	..	..	4g55	5S10	..	..	..	..	..	8 25	..	.	..	..	..	1110	..	..	..
Tenby .... ,,		..	..	..	..	..	..	..	..	..	..	..	8 30	..	..		..	11 1	11G27		..	..
Carmarthen...... .. ,,		.	..	..	..	..	..	..	7 35	..	..	..	10 4	..	..	..	..	1232	1 1			..
Swansea (High Street) ,,		5 37	..	..	..	6G45	7S0	..	8 55	..	..	..	11 0	..	..	..	..	1 35	2 0			
CARDIFF (General) ,,	6 12	6 45	.	..	..	8 0	8 15	..	1015	..	..	..	1210	..	1G20	..	..	3 0	3 15	..		..
Newport ....,,	6 30	7 5	..	..	..	8 18	8 35	..	1035	..	..	..	1231	..	1G39	..	..	3 21	3 35			
Abergavenny .... ,,	4 4	3 55	..	..	..	7 10	..	..	9 39	..	..	..	11F35	..	12G25	1G0	..	2 5	1H48			..
Hereford ....,,	.		..	7 5	7D35	..	..	..	8K50	..	1020	..	..	12D55	1 15	..	2DX5			2D32		
Chel'hm Spa(St.Jms') ,,	..		6L32	8 0	..	..	..	9 20	..	10L36	1140	12L10	..	..	2 40		..		..	3L20	4 25	5E7
Gloucester ....,,	..		5L40	8 20	..	..	..	9 43	..	9L55	12 0	..	..	..	2 58	..	..		..	..	4 44	..
LONDON ....(Padd. arr)	10 0	9 45	9 52	1030	11D10	1045	1130	1230	1 5	2 10	2 30	3 0	3 10	4D20	5Z0	5 35	5D50	6 5	6 10	6 35	7 0	8 5

	a.m	a.m	a.m	a.m	a.m	a.m	a.m	a.m	a.m	a.m	a.m	a.m	a.m	a.m	p.m	p.m	p.m	p.m	p.m	p.m	p.m	p.m	p.m	p.m	p.m	p.m
LIVERP'L (Ldg Stg.)dep.	..	..			..	6 15	..	8 50	..		..	9J30	9 30	1140	..	..	..	..	2 20	..	..	4 20	..	..	..	7 0
Birkenhead (Woodside) ,,	..	..	..	..		6 30		9 5	..	..	..	9J45	9 43	1155		..	..		2 40			4 35			..	7 15
Chester ....,,			..	..	..	7 8	..	9 40	..	..		10J18	1018	1230		..	..	..	3 15	..	..	5 10	..	..	..	8 0
Shrewsbury ....,,	..		..	7 40		8 40	..	1053	..		..	11J40	1128	1 50	..	2 5	..		4 35	..	..	6 26		..	..	9 55
MANCHESTER(Lon Rd.)	..	..	..	..	..		..	8 35	..	..	..	10J10	1010	11†15		12 0	..	..	1†45			4 30				6†40
Crewe ....dep.	..			6 25	..	..	..	9 35		..	..	11J0	11 0	..		1 0	..	..				5 10			..	7 0
Wolverhampton (Low Lvl)		7 5	..	8 35		9 35	..	1137		.	..	1J35	1220	2 35		3 15	..		5 30	..		7 20			..	11t3
BIRMINGHAM (Snow H)	..	7 45	..	9 0		10 0	..	12 0	..	..	..	2J0	1245	3 0	..	3 55	..	4 5	6 0			7 50	7 55	..	..	12 0
Leamington Spa ....dep.		8 14		9 28	..	1027	..	1228	..			2J28	1 19	3 28		4 23	..	4 40	6 30		..	8 17	8 28	..		1245
Ludlow ....,,		..	4 15			7 20	..	9 20	..				11f22	1232		..	..	..	3 14		..	5 5		..		8 47
Leominster ....,,		..	4 37		7V5	.	8K2	.	8V45	..	..	..	12V20	..		..	..		2 51	3 40	4V15	4 42		7K36	..	8 23
Malvern (Great) ......,,	..	..		..	8 28			..	9 40	10R7	1149		1 31	..	2X40	..	3 45	..	..	..	5 36		6 0	..	7R50	.
Worcester (Shrub Hill) ,,	6 45	..		.	8 55	9 5	..	..	1022	..	1215		2 0	..	2X55	..	4 10	..	..		6 10	..	8 45	a.m.	a.m.	a.m.
LONDON (Paddington)ar.	9 52	10 0	1030	11 0	1110	12 5	1 5	2 5	2 10	2 30	3 0	4J0	4 20	5 5	5 50	6 0	6 35	7 28	8 5	8 45	9 30	10 5	1055	2 40	3 25	4 10

FOR FOOT-NOTES SEE PAGE 99

The times from 6 p.m. to 5.59 a.m. inclusive are printed in dark type, thus 12.9 meaning 9 min. aft. midn.

GREAT WESTERN RAILWAY—PRINCIPAL TRAINS TO LONDON (Week Days).

	p.m	n'on	p.m (Saturdays only.)	p.m	p.m (Saturdays excepted.)	p.m (Saturdays only.)	p.m (Sats. only.)	a.m (Saturdays excepted.)	p.m (Saturdays only.)	a.m (Saturdays only.)	p.m	p.m	p.m (Saturdays only.)	p.m	p.m	p.m	p.m (Saturdays only.)	p m	n'ht
PENZANCE ....dep.	..	..		..		..		1110	..	1140	..		..	..	1 30	..	2 10	2 10	9 30
Falmouth .... ,,	..	..	..	..		..		1125	..	1210			..	..	1 40	..	2 35	2 35	9 45
PLYMOUTH N. Rd. .. ,,	..	..		..		2 15		2 0		2 40	..			..	4 20	..	6 20	6 20	12 25
Torquay .... ,,	..	..		..		..	1 57	2 30	2 55	..			4 30	..	4G55	..	6 48	6 48	12 52
EXETER (St. Dd's).... ,,	..			..		..	3 5	3 28		..				..	5 50	..	7 46	7 46	2 5
Ilfracombe .... ,,	..	12 0	..	..				1 40	..	..			..	..	3k10	..	5 0	4 45	7 AA 45
Minehead............ ,,	..	1 20	2 20	..			2 30	2 30						..	5 0	..	6 52	7G25	9 T 15
Taunton .... ,,	..	2 40		1 40			3 55	4 10						..	3 35	..	8 32	8 40	2 55
BRISTOL (Tpl. Md.) .. ,,	..	..		3 15	4 30			..			5 15			6 10	..	7 35	..	1115	4 15
Bath .... ,,	2 20			3 34				..				5 20		6 29	..	7 57	..	1141	4 37
WEYMOUTH.......... ,,	..	1§50		..	..		2 40	2 40			..	4 15		..	..	..	7 15	..	..
Dorchester (G.W.)...... ,,	..	2§5		..	..	..	2 55	2 55			..	4 32		..	..	..	7 30	..	..
Yeovil (Pen Mill) ...... ,,	..	2§40		..			3 45	3 45	..			5 9		..	..	..	8 8	a.m	a.m.
LONDON (Pad'tn) ....arr.	5 20	5 30	6 0	5 35	6 15	6 30	6 50	6 50	7 0	7 10	7 15	8 10	8 30	8 45	9 0	1025	1115	2 40	7 20

	p.m. (Saturdays only.)	p.m	p.m	p.m	p.m	p.m	p.m	p.m	p.m	p.m
Fishguard Harbour ....dep.	..	12§50	..	..	1§55	..	..	..	6§40	..
Tenby .... ,,	..	..	..	..	2 40	..			7 0	..
Carmarthen .... ,,		2 47	..	..	4 10	..	..	..	8 30	..
Swansea (High Street) .. ,,		4 0	..	..	5 30	..	..	..	9 40	..
CARDIFF (General) .... ,,		5 20	..	..	6 35		..	9 50	1052	..
Newport .... ,,		5 40	..	..	6 55	..	..	10*12	1113	1154
Abergavenny .... ,,		3 45	..		5 4	..	..	9 5	..	..
Hereford .... ,,		3K27	4 10	4 45	..		..	8GK22	9§35	10K46
Cheltenham Spa (St. J's) ,,	..	..	5 26	D	..	6 39	7L5	9§20	10M55	..
Gloucester .... ,,	4 30	..	6 5		..	7 6	..	9§43	1230	a.m
LONDON (Padd.) ......arr.	8 10	8 20	8 45	9 20	9 40	1025	1055	2 40	3 25	7 20

A Via Southern Railway and Exeter. **AA** Via Southern Railway and Exeter. On Fridays and Saturdays depart **9.20** p.m. via Taunton. **B** Mondays only. **C** Malvern Road (see Note **E**). On Saturdays depart 5.47 p.m. **D** Via Worcester. **E** Malvern Road via Stratford-on-Avon and Leamington. **F** On Saturdays depart 11.30 a.m. **G** Except Saturdays. **H** On Saturday, July 29, depart 2.53 p.m. **J** Saturdays only and commences July 15. **K** Via Newport. **L** Via Kingham. **M** On Saturdays depart **11.12** p.m. **R** Via Gloucester. **S** Saturdays only. **T** On Fridays and Saturdays depart **10.50** p.m. **U** On Saturdays depart 2.40 p.m. **V** Via Bromyard. **X** One class only (limited accommodation). **Y** Via Newport. On Saturdays depart **7.50** p.m. via Newent. **Z** On Saturdays arrive Paddington 5.15 p.m. *c* Fridays and Saturdays only. *f* Via Hereford. *g* Mondays and Saturdays excepted. *h* On Saturdays depart Exeter 10.0 and Taunton 10.45 a.m. *j* On Saturdays Penzance passengers arrive Paddington 4.50 p.m. *k* On Saturdays depart 3.40 p.m. *t* On Saturdays depart **11.17** p.m. * Mondays to Fridays, one class only (limited accommodation), Newport to Bristol. On Saturdays, 1st and 3rd class. † Manchester (Exchange) via Chester. § One class only for portion of journey.

The times from 6 p.m. to 5.59 a.m. inclusive are printed in dark type, thus 12.9 meaning 9 min. aft. midn.

GREAT WESTERN RAILWAY.—PRINCIPAL TRAINS FROM LONDON (Weekdays).

Mls.		a.m.	a.m.	a.m	a.m	a.m	a.m	a.m	a.m.	a.m	a.m	a.m	a.m	a.m	a.m	a.m	a.m	a.m	a.m.	no'n	p.m	p.m	p.m	p.m	p.m	p.m	p.m
0	LONDON (Pad.) ..d.	1 35	5 30	7 30	8 30	8 50	8 55	9 0	9 15	9 30	9 35	9 40	10 0	1030	1035	1055	11 0	1110	1115	12 0	12 5	1210	1230	1 15	1 30	1 40	2 15
127	Yeovil (Pen Mill)..a.	..	1028	..	11 7	..	By Slip Carriage	..	..	..	Saturdays only.	1213	Sats. excepted	1U 5	..	.	..	..	..	..	..	..	3 20	..	..	4G20	5 3
147½	D'rch'ster(G.W.)..,,	..	11 5	..	1135	..		..	..	..		1250		1U44	..	Saturdays only.	..	Saturdays only,	..	..	..	Sats. only.	3 57		..	4G56	5A1
154½	WEYMOUTH .. ,,	..	1116	..	1146	Saturdays only.		..	..	Saturdays only.		1 10		1U55	Sat'rdays only.		..		..	..	..		4 8	.	Saturdays only.	5G9	5 55
106¾	Bath ,,	..	8 7	9 48	—				1148			—		..			..		1257	..	..	..	—	2 57		..	..
118¼	BRIST'L(T Mds) ,,	..	8 30	10 7	☞		1119	..	1257			☞	11 45	..			..		1 15	..	2F41	..	..	3 15		..	..
143	Taunton ,,	3 57	9 47	1113	Saturdays excepted.		—	1 45	—		1255	Saturdays only.	—	..			1G25		2 36	..	3k50	2 48	..	—		4G16	5 5
167¾	Minehead ,,	8 25	1148	..			..	12G55	..	..	2 45		..	..	..		2G50	..	3 50	..	4 40	..	..	..		5G40	6 2
203¾	Ilfracombe ,,	1044	1g12	..		..	..	2 28	..	..	—		..	..	..	..	4G31	..	—	..	—	..	..	..	4 40	7G0	7 45
173¾	EXETER(S.D's) ,,	4 40	1037	1156		..	..	12h25	..	..	..		..	..	..	..	2G 4	2 10	..	2G50	Fris. & Sats. only.	3 35	..	..	5 50	4G58	—
199¾	Torquay ,,	5 46	1149	1 0		1250	..	1h32	..	1 50	..		..	..	..	2 45	..	..	..	3 30		..	..	..	—	6G1	Sats. only.
225¾	PLYM'TH (N Rd.) ,,	6 10	1225	1G40		—	..	—	..	4 20	..		..	2 30	2 47	—	3k40	3 50	..	4G52		5 25	..	..	..	6 33	
291	Falmouth ......arr.	8 35	3g15	—	..	..	..	..	..	—	..	..	..	4G46	4j10	..	6k10	..	..	7G25		8 25	..	..	..	9 20	
305¼	Penzance ,,	8 52	3 35	..	..	..	..	..	..	..	..	..	..	4 55	5 10	..	6k35	6 55	..	7G30		8 40	..	..	..	9 30	

Mls.		a.m	a.m	a.m	a.m	a.m	a.m.	a.m	a.m.	a.m.	a.m.	a.m	p.m	p.m	p.m	p.m	p.m	p.m	p.m	p.m	p.m	p.m	p.m
0	LONDON (Padd) dep.	5 30	7 30	8 40	8 55	9 55	9 15	10 0	1015	1045	1155	1155	1245	1D45	1 55	3 15	3 55	4 45	5 0	5 5	5 30	5 55	6 55
114	Gloucester ...... arr.	9 2	1026	..	..	Jly. 29 only.	1211	Sats. exceptd		1 50	Not Sats.	Sats. only.	3L41	..	4 48	5 57	..	..	7 10	..	July 22 & 29 only	..	..
121	Chltnhm Sp.(St.J.),,	9 41	1051	..	..		1236		1129	2 17			3L15	..	5M5	6 15	..	..	7 30	..		..	..
144	Hereford ,,	1057	..	12D27	..		—		1D57	3 16			3D49	5D48	5J58	7 24	..	8D11	8S44	9 8		..	..
153½	Abergavenny ,,	1053	..	—	1225	1 51	..	1 51	—	—	3 11	3 11	5D4	—	5 38	—	7 27	—	—	—		9 45	11S3
133½	Newport ,,	9 53	11 0	..	1123	1226	..	1 35	..	..	2 16	2 21	—	..	4 33	..	6 16	..	..	..	8 28	8 37	9 12
145¼	CARDIFF(Gen'r'l),,	1014	1118	..	1143	1248	..	1 54	..	..	2 36	2 24	..	..	4 53	..	6 36	..	..	..	8 47	8 57	9 32
191	Swansea (H. St.) ,,	—	12S39	..	1252	2 16	..	—	..	..	3 52	3 59	..	..	6 10	..	7 52	..	..	..	10 3	1012	1040
220½	Carmarthen ,,	..	1S24	..	1 44	3 13	..	..	..	..	4 45	4 54	..	..	7 15	..	9 2	..	..	..	—	—	1135
249½	Tenby ,,	..	2S36	..	3 3	4 51	..	..	..	..	6 9	6 23	..	..	8 39	..	—	..	..	..	..	..	12S22
261¼	Fishguard Harb. ,,	..	—	..	3 2	5R46	..	..	..	..	6 26	6 38	..	..	9S51	..	..	..	..	..	..	..	1245

Mls.		a.m.	a.m.	a.m	a.m.	a.m.	a.m	a.m.	a.m	a.m.	p.m	p.m	p.m	p.m	p.m	p.m	p.m	p.m	p.m	p.m	p.m	p.m	p.m.	B	ngt.	B	ngt
	LONDON (Pad.) dep.	1 30	5 30	7 10	8 40	9 10	9 45	1015	10S20	11 5	1245	1 45	2A5	2 10	3 15	4 5	4 45	5 0	6 5	6 10	7 10	7S40	7G40	12 0	12G10	1210	12 55
120½	Worcester (S.H.) arr.	..	10 0	..	11X36	..	..	1258	..	..	2 55	4 37	..	..	..	..	7 6	..	8 50	..	..	10S30	10G58	..	..	..	..
129	Malvern (Great) ,,	..	1048	..	11X52	..	..	1 6	..	..	3 16	4 58	..	..	..	..	7 34	..	9 11	..	..	11S22	11T31	..	..	..	8 24
148	Leominster ,,	8 5	1144	K..	—	2 39	..	2 51	..	3 40	4 42	6K46	..	7 7	8 28	..	8K57	10 2	—	..	..	..	..	..	..	..	—
159	Ludlow ,,	7 41	1232	..	..	2 17	..	—	..	3 14	5 5	—	..	6 41	8 47	9 17	—	1023	..	1045	..	..	..	..	..	..	..
87½	Leamington Spa ,,	3N28	8 50	9 50	..	10G43	12G6	..	11S50	1240	—	..	..	3 40	—	5 40	..	—	..	7 40	8 40	10S10	10G10	2 14	3H15	3 2	..
110½	BIRMINGH'M(S.H.)	4N0	9 37	1026	..	1110	12G40	..	12S20	1 10	..	..	4A5	4 10	..	6 10	..	☞ Saturdays only.	..	8 10	9 10	10S40	10G40	2 50	3H50	3 42	..
123	Wolverh'pt'n(L.L.)ar.	4 32	1042	1051	..	1135	—	..	12S45	1 35	..	..	4A27	4 35	..	6 35	..		..	8 35	9 43	11S16	11G16	3 20	—	4 9	..
174½	Crewe ,,	8 49	—	1 2	..	..	..	..	—	4 0	..	..	—	6 56	..	..	..		..	10 44	..	..	—	—	..	1028	..
205½	MANC'ST'R (LR) ,,	9b8	..	2 5	..	2b38	..	..	..	4 51	..	..	..	8 10	..	10h3	..		..	1 35	..	..	..	..	..	8b32	..
152¾	Shrewsbury ,,	5 23	..	—	..	1219	..	..	..	2 15	..	..	..	5 21	..	7 21	..		..	9 24	1048	12S50	..	..	..	5 3	..
195	Chester ,,	6 49	..	..	..	1 29	..	..	..	3 26	..	..	..	6 41	..	8 34	..		..	1037	—	—	..	..	..	6 44	..
210½	Birkenh'd(Wsde) ,,	7 44	..	..	..	1 57	.	..	..	4 0	..	..	..	7 20	..	9 10	..		..	1115	..	..	..	..	..	7 33	..
211	LIVERPOOL(L.Stg.)	7 57	..	..	..	2 17	..	..	..	4 17	..	..	..	7 37	..	9 27	..		..	1137	..	..	..	..	..	7 52	..

FOR FOOT-NOTES SEE PAGE **100A.**

The times from 6 p.m. to 5.59 a.m. inclusive are printed in dark type, thus **12.9** meaning 9 min. aft. midn.

GREAT WESTERN RAILWAY.—PRINCIPAL TRAINS FROM LONDON (Weekdays).

Mls.			p.m	p.m	p.m	p.m	p.m	p.m	p.m	p.m	p.m	p.m	ngt.	p.m	nig.	a.m
				Saturdays only.							Fridays only.	By Slip Carriage		Friday nights Sun. morns only.	Not Sat. nights (Sun. morns).	Sat. nights (Sun. morns.) only.
0	LONDON (Padd..)	dep.	2 45	3 25	3 30	4 15	5 5	5 15	6 0	6 30	7 15	7 55	9 50	11 0	12 0	1230
127	Yeovil (Pen. Mill)	arr.	..	..	5 55	..	..	..	9 8		..			.		..
147½	Dorchester (G.W.)	„	..		6 27	..	..	..	9 49	.						..
154¼	WEYMOUTH	„	..		6 37	..	..	..	10 0	..						..
106¾	Bath	„	5 28			6 20	6 48	8 2	—	8 28			1233		2 47	3 24
118¼	BRISTOL (T. Mds.)	„	5 53			6 39	7 5	8 21	..	8 49		1017	1255		3 15	3 55
143	Taunton	„	—		5 56	—	8 5	—	..	10 5	..	1150	1 55		4 25	5 3
167¾	Minehead	„	..	..	7n33	..	9 35	..	..	12S8	9 40	—	..		8 25	1035
203¾	Ilfracombe	„	..	..	8 40	..	..	..	..		1050	..	..		1044	12f38
173¾	EXETER (S.D's)	„	..	7 1	6 35	..	8 47	..	..	1047	..	..	2 40		5 20	5 50
199¾	Torquay	„	..	—	7G32	..	9 49	..	..	1150	1127		4P10	..	6 42	7 2
225¾	PLYMOUTH (N. Rd.)	„	..	..	8 5		1025	..	..	1229	1229	..	4‡20	4 5	7 20	7 36
291	Falmouth	„	..	..	QQ	..	—	..	..	—	—	..	7 20	5 35	1031	10 25
305¼	Penzance	„	..	..	105		..	..	..	..	..	..	7‡25	7 0	1057	10 55

Mls.			p.m	p.m	p.m	n'gt
0	LONDON (Padd.)	dep.	6 35	7 55	9 25	1255
114	Gloucester	arr.	9 12	..	1328	4 0
121	Cheltenham Spa (S.J's)	„	9 37	..	1 6	5Y55
144	Hereford	„	1030	1J40	..	6Y35
153½	Abergavenny	„	—	..	..	7Y54
133½	Newport	„	..	1027	1Q48	5Y4
145¼	CARDIFF (General)	„	..	1047	2Q8	5Y23
191	Swansea (High St.)	„	..	1155	3Q48	7Y18
220½	Carmarthen	„	..	..	4Q44	9Y11
249½	Tenby	„	..	a.m.	6-14	11H10
261¼	Fishguard Harbour	„	..	1 40	8H 3	11H34

A Satruday, July 29 only. **B** Saturday nights (Sunday mornings)only. **C** Slip carriage. **D** Via Worcester. **E** Fridays only. **G** Saturdays excepted. **H** Sundays excepted. **J** Via Newport. **K** Via Bromyard. **L** Via Kingham. **M** Malvern Road Station (St. James') arrive 5.26 p.m. (5.41 p.m. on Saturdays). **N** Arrive 10 minutes later Mondays. **P** Torre Station. On Sunday mornings arrive Torquay 7.2 a.m. **Q** On Sundays arrive Newport **1.55** a.m., Cardiff **2.15**, Swansea **3.57**, and Carmarthen **4.54** a.m. **QQ** On Saturdays arrive **10.41** p.m. On other days arrive Falmouth (Moor) at **11.30** p.m. by Western National Bus from Truro (rail tickets available, but heavy luggage not conveyed). **R** One class only for portion of journey. **S** Saturdays only. **T** Thursdays only. **U** By slip carriage and Saturdays excepted. **X** One class only (limited accommodation). **Y** On Sundays Cheltenham Spa (St. James') arrive **4.38**, Hereford 9.13 (via Newport), Abergavenny 8.33, Newport **5.21**, Cardiff **5.40**, Swansea 7.32, and Carmarthen 11R30 a.m. *b* Manchester (Exchange) via Chester. *f* Via Exeter and Southern Railway *g* On Saturdays arrive Ilfracombe 2.8 and Falmouth 3.30 p.m. *h* 15 minutes later on Saturdays. *j* Paddington dep. 10.40 a.m. *k* On Saturdays arrive 15 minutes earlier. *n* On Fridays and Saturdays arrive **7.0** p.m. *z* Via Gloucester and Ledbury. Saturday nights (Sunday mornings) excepted. ‡ On Sunday mornings arrive Plymouth **4.30** and Penzance 7.45 a.m.

The times from 6 p.m. to 5.59 a.m. inclusive are printed in dark type, thus 12.9 meaning 9 min. aft. midn.

SERVICE TO LONDON (WATERLOO) WEEKDAYS To September 24th.

N.B.—At BANK HOLIDAY times the services shown hereon may be REVISED and certain Trains CANCELLED : reference should be made to the Special Holiday Announcements.

S. of Eng. & I. of W. to London.

					SO	SX	SO	SO		SO	SOB	K	SO	SX	SO		SX
Weymouth ...... dep.	..	..	7 42		8 35	9 25	9 25	To Sept. 9th only.	..	1020	..	1125		..	..	1225	1 35
Dorchester ...... ,,	..	..	7 57		8 57	9 42	9 42		..	1040	..	1142	..	..	..	1245	1 50
Swanage .... ,,	..		7 44		9 20	9 26	..		..	1035	..	1120	..	..	..	1 35	1 35
Bournm'th (West) ,,	7 25	7 35	8 20	8 35		1012	..		11 2	1215	11 2		..	1 0	1 11	2 20	2 20
Bournm'th (Cen.) ,,	7 35	7 45	8 40	8 45	1015	1031	1031		1112	1226	1112	1240		1 10	1 21	2 30	2 40
Totland Bay V dep.	..		Bournem'uth Limited.	7 40	..	..	..	9 50	9 50		..	..	1210	1210	..	Mons. & Fris. to Sept 1 only	1250
Yarmouth Pier ,,	..	..		8 20	..		..	1030	1030	..		..	1250	1250	..		1 30
Lymington Town ,,	7 43	8 7		9 10	9 56	9 56	..	1117	1117	..	..	..	1 37	1 34	..		2 17
Cowes Pier ...... ,,	..	7 30			9 20	9 20	..	..	11 0	..	..		1 0	1 0	..		2 0
So'h'mptn (Cent.) ,,	8 25	9 0		9 54	1058	1126	1120	1157	1220	1 6	1220	1 20	2†20	2 20	2 26		3 20
So'h'mptn (Ter.) ,,	7 52			9 40	..	..		..	..		..	..	..	..	..		..
LONDON (W'tloo) arr.	10 0	1030	1038	1136	1234	1250	1250	1R53	2 10	2 40	2 12	2 57	3†50	4 8	4 19	4 40	4 50
	R	R	R	R	R	R	R	R	R	R		R		R		R	R

Trains also leave Weymouth 1**SO**35 p.m. Dorchester 1.53, arr. London (W'tloo) 5**R**3; dep. Bournm'th (West) **SO** 10.12 a.m., Bournm'th (Cent.) 10.22, arr. London (W'tloo) 12**R**37 p.m.; dep. Swanage 11**G**20 a.m., Bournm'th (Cent.) 12.20, arr. London (W'tloo) 2**R**38.

S. of Eng. & I. of W. to London.

	SO	SO	SO	SO	SX	SO	SO	P	SO	SO		SO		SO			
Weymouth ...... dep.	1225	..	..	2 0	..	..	..	2 25	2 25	4 0	4X0	¶	5 37	¶	..	6 30	9 55
Dorchester ...... ,,	1245	..	..	2 18	..	..	..	2 45	2 45	4 16	4X16	4 43	5 53		..	6 47	1018
Swanage .... ,,	..	..	1 55	..	..	..	..	2 38	4 0	4 0	4X10	4 37	5 40	6 40		6 23	8Q41
Bournm'th (West) ,,	..	2 27	..	3†20	3 5	..	3 40	4 35		..	4H56	6 20	6 20	7 10	..	..	..
Bournm'th (Cen.) ,,	2 25	2 40	2 55	3†30	3 17	..	3 30	4 45	4 53	5 10	5 15	6 30	6 40	7 35	..	7 50	1129
Totland Bay V dep.	..	..	..	..	2 10	2 20	..		To Sep 9 only	3 5	3A55	..	..	5 45	5SX45	..	7 10
Yarmouth Pier ,,	..	..	..	..	2 50	3 0		..		3 45	4A35	..		6 25	6SX25	..	7 50
Lymington Town ,,	..	..	..	3 25	3 37	3 52	..	4SX20		4 4	5 30	6 25	..	7 14	7SX14	..	8T30
Cowes Pier ...... ,,	..	2 0	..	3 40	..	..	..	4 0	4 0	..	4SX0		6 0	7 0	..	7 0	..
So'h'mptn (Cent.) ,,	..	3 20	3 39	4 23	4 20	4 35	4 47	5 20	5 39	5 50	6 20	7 9	7 20	8 38	..	8 48	1230
So'h'mptn (Ter.) ,,	..		..	..	..			..			..		..		..	..	1 10
LONDON (W'tloo) arr.	4 36	4 50	5 12	6 3	6 26	6 37	6 39	6 45	7 22	7 41	8 15	8 44	8 50	1022	1036	1058	3 55
	R	R	R	R	R	R	R	P	R	R	R	R	R	R			a.m

Trains also dep. Southampton (Cent.) 6 47, Southampton (Ter.) 6.57, due London (Waterloo) 9.2 a.m.; dep. Southampton (Ter.) 10.7 a.m., due London (Waterloo) 12.30 p.m.; dep. Bournmouth (Cent. 2**SO**30, due London (Waterloo) 4**R**40 * To Sept. 9 only. ¶ To Sept. 2nd only.

A 10 mins. later on Sats. **B** July 8th, 15th & Sept. 9th, 16th & 23rd only. **G** Sats. only July 22nd to Sept. 9th only. **H** 9 mins. later on Sats. daily commencing September 4th. **K** Every weekday to Sept. 1st, Fris. and Sats. only thereafter. **Q** 10.0 p.m. Weds. and Sats. **P** Pullman Car Train between Bournmouth and Waterloo, 1 and 3 cl. Pullman Cars only. Supplementary fees charged. **R** Restaurant Car Train. **T** 11.14 p.m. on Weds. and Sats. **V** By coach to Yarmouth. **SO** Sats. only. **SX** Sats. excepted. **X** Mons. to Fris. and to Sept. 1st only. † To Sept. 16th only.

R ar Portsmouth to London.	MX a.m	a.m.	R a.m.	a.m	a.m	*SO a.m	a.m	SOR *a.m	SO a.m	SXR a.m	*SO a.m	SO a.m	SX a.m	*SO p.m	SO a.m	SX a.m	*SO a.m	SO p.m
Ventnor ...... dep		..	6M010	6 37	7 40	8 25	8SX40	9 3	9 3	9 42	9 55	1015	1040	1055	1115	1140	1155	1215
Shanklin ...... ,,	..		6M022	6 50	7 52	8 37	8SX52	9 17	9 42	9 54	10 7	1027	1052	11 7	1127	1152	12 7	1227
Sandown ...... ,,	..		6M027	6 55	7 58	8 43	8SX58	9 4	9 46	10 1	1013	1034	11 1	1055	1134	12 1	1155	1234
Ryde Pier ...... ,,	..	..	6 55	7 30	8 30	9 10	9SX30	9 50	1020	1035	1050	1120	1135	1150	1220	1235	1250	1 20
PortsmouthHarb. ,,	..	7 23	7 35	8 15	9 20	9 50	1020	1050	1120	1120	1150	1220	1220	1250	1 20	1 20	1 50	2 20
Prtsm'th&S'thsea ,,	12a20	7 27	7 39	8 19	9 24	9 54	1024	1054	1124	1124	1154	1224	1224	1254	1 24	1 24	1 54	2 24
LONDON (W'tloo) a.	3a55	9 10	9 26	9 49	1054	1125	1154	1226	1254	1254	1 26	1 54	1 54	2 26	2 56	2 54	3 26	3 56
		R	R	R	R	R	R	R	R	R	R	R	R	R	R	R	R	R

SO Sats. only. SX Sats. excepted.	SX p.m	*SO p.m	SO p.m	SX p.m	*SO p.m	SO p.m	SX p.m	*SO p.m	SO p.m	SX p.m	*SO p.m	SO p.m	SX p.m	*SO p.m	p.m	p.m	p.m	p.m
Ventnor ...... dep.	1240	1255	1 15	1 40	1 55	2 15	2 40	2 55	3 15	3 40	3 55	4 15	4 40	4 55	5 35	6 40	7 40	8 40
Shanklin ...... ,,	1252	1 7	1 27	1 52	2 7	2 27	2 52	3 7	3 27	3 52	4 7	4 27	4 52	5 7	5 47	6 52	7 52	8 52
Sandown ...... ,,	1 1	1255	1 34	2 1	1 55	2 34	3 1	2 55	3 34	4 1	3 55	4 34	5 1	4 55	5 54	7 18	8 19	[illegible]
Ryde Pier .... ,,	1 35	1 50	2 20	2 35	2 50	3 20	3 35	3 50	4 20	4 30	4 50	5 20	5 35	5 50	6 30	7 30	8 30	9 35
PortsmouthHarb. ,,	2 20	2 50	3 20	3 20	3 50	4 20	4 20	4 50	5 20	5 20	5 50	6 20	6 20	6 50	7 20	8 20	9 20	1020
Prtsm'th&Sthsea ,,	2 24	2 54	3 24	3 24	3 54	4 24	4 24	4 54	5 24	5 24	5 54	6 24	6 24	6 54	7 24	8 24	9 24	1024
LONDON (W'tloo) a.	3 54	4 26	4 54	4 54	5 27	5 54	5 54	6 26	6 54	6 54	7 26	7 54	7 54	8 22	8 54	9 54	1054	12 0
* To Sept. 9th only.	R	R	R	R	R	R	R	R	R	R	R	R	R	R	R	R	R	R

Also dep. Portsmouth and Southsea ....6.10 a.m. 6.37 a.m. 8.24 a.m. 8.46 a.m. **10.30** p.m. **11.0** p.m.
Arrive Waterloo ....8.16 a.m. 8.29 a.m. 10.5 a.m. 10.25 a.m. **12.38** a.m. **12.57** a.m.

a Via Eastleigh. ADDITONAL SERVICES ON SATURDAYS. **MO** Mons. only. **MX** Mons. excepted.

Portsmouth Har. dep. 9.47 a.m. 10.17 a.m. { Then at same times past each hour up to and including } Portsmouth Har. dep. 3.17 3.47 p.m.
Waterloo ......arr. 11.20 a.m. 11.50 a.m. Waterloo arr. 4.49 5.19 p.m.

The times from 6 p.m. to 5.59 a.m. inclusive are printed in dark type, thus **12.9** meaning 9 min. aft. midn.

SOUTHERN RAILWAY (Western Section).

SERVICE TO LONDON (WATERLOO) FROM THE UNDERMENTIONED STATIONS (WEEKDAYS.)

JULY 2nd to SEPTEMBER 24th, 1939.

Passengers should ascertain before commencement of journey if, and where, change of carriage is necessary.

N.B.—At BANK HOLIDAY times the services shown hereon may be REVISED and certain Trains CANCELLED, and reference should be mad·· to the Special Holiday Announcements, or enquiry made before travelling

Cornwall, North and South Devon, and West of England to London.

				SO	SO	SX	SO	SO	SO	SX	SO	SO	SX	SO	SO	SO	SX	SX	SO	SO	SO	SO			SX	SO
	a.m	a.m	a.m	a.m	a.m	a.m	a.m	a m	a.m	a m	a.m	a.m	a.m	a.m	a.m	a.m	p.m	p.m	p.m	p.m	p.m	p.m	p.m.	p.m	p m	p,m
Plymouth (Nth. Rd.) d.		..	6 5	..	8 33	8 33	..	..	..	1019	..	1041	..	..	..	..	12 9	12 9	..	..	1 10	2 19	2 SX 19	4 0	4 49	4 49
Devonport ,,	..		6 10	..	8 39	8 39	..	..		1024	..	1046	..	..	..	..	1214	1214	..	..	1 15	2 25	2 SX 25	4 5	4 55	4 55
Tavistock ,,		..	6 51	..	9 7	9 7	..	..	..	1055	..	1117	..	..	..	..	1242	1242	..		1 42	2 54	2 SX 54	4 33	5 37	5 37
Padstow ,,			Mondays only.	..	..	..	..	..	8 40	8 40	..	..	1025	1025	To Sept. 9 only.	To Sept. 9 onlo.	..	..	..	..	..	1230	12SX40	2 20	2 55	..
Bodmin ,,	..	..		..	..	..	..	..	7 27	7 27	..	..	9 0	9 0			..	..	..	..	..	1128	11SX28	2 5	..	..
Wadebridge ,,		..		..	..	..	..	..	8 51	8 51	..	..	1036	1036			..	..	..	..	..	1242	12SX52	2 30	3 18	..
Camelford ,,				..	..	..	..	..	9 26	9 26	..	..	1111	1116			..	..	..	..	..	1 18	1 SX 25	3 4	4 0	..
Launceston ,,	..	.		..	7 42	7 42	..	..	10 0	10 0	..	..	1142	1151			..	..	..	..	..	1 52	1 SX 56	3 46	4 41	..
Bude ,,	..	..			7 22	7 22	..	..	9 40	9 40	..	11 0	1625	..			..	..	..	..	..	1 30	1 SX 35	3 4	..	..
Okehampton ,,	..	..	7 32	..	9 36	9 36	..	..	11 7	1126	..	1158	1237	..	..	..	1 11	1 19	..		2 12	2 58	3 SX 24	5 8	6 17	6 17
Torrington ,,	..		7 10	7 10	8 15	8 15	..	9 0	..	1028	1022	..	..	..	..	..	..	1230	..	1240	..	1 20	2 10	2X59	4 38	4 38
Bideford ,,	..		7 19	7 19	8 24	8 24	..	9 9	..	1037	1032	..	..	..	..	..	..	1239	..	1249	..	1 29	2 19	3X25	4 47	4 47
Ilfracombe ,,	..		..	..	8 15	8 15	..	9 0	1010	1030	1030	..	..	..	1135	..	..	1230	..	1245	..	2 5	2 15	3 X 0	4 45	4 45
LYNTON ,,		..			7 15	7 15	..	..	9 0	9 20	..	..	..	..	..	..	..	..	..	..	..	1245	12SX45		3 0	3 0
for Lynmouth (¶)																										
Barnstaple Junct'n. ,,	..		7 43	7 43	8 57	8 57	..	9 42	1051	1112	1112	..	..	..	1215	..	..	1 12	..	1 30	..	2 45	2 56	3X42	5 33	5 33
Exmouth (*via* Ex'tr ,,	..	6k55	8 45	9k19	9 45	9k50	10k38	1045	..	1145	1145	1215	12k50	..	..	1k48	1 15	1 30	1k48	2 15	2 15	2 45	3 45	5 15	7 15	7 15
Exeter (Central).... ,,		7 30	9 30	9 55	1030	1030	11 5	1130	12 5	1230	1230	1245	1 30	1 22	1 30	..	2 4	2 30	..	2 50	3 0	4 15	4 30	5 53	7 50	7 50
Sidmouth ,,		7 20	8 35	9 45	..	1020	11 9	11 9	..	..	..	..	1 20	..	..	..	..	2 5	2 20		..	2A58	3 SX 24	5 30	7 45	7 40
Seaton ,,	..		9 10	1023	.	1012	..	1152	..	1148	..	..	..	..	..	..	2 20	2 27	..		..	3A40	3 SX 55	6 10	8 15	8 20
Yeovil ,,	7 15	8 24	1022	1020	1056	11 8	1130	..	..	1245	..	1 40	..	..	2 22	3 28	2 22	3 30	3 30	..	3 48	4A50	5 22	6 53	9 22	9 25
Salisbury ,,	8 44	9 31	1116	12 8	1227	1233	1 23	1 43	1 53	2 12	2 12	2 46	3 26	3 6	3 21	4 20	4 10	4 39	4 28	4 44	4 58	5 49	6 35	8 9	11 0	11 0
																									a.m.	a m
LONDON (Wat'loo) ar	1057	11 8	1245	1 40	2 2	2 2	2 58	3 19	3 34	3 40	3 43	4 33	4 58	4 43	4 53	6 0	5 43	6 15	6 6	6 21	6 29	7 35	8 37	10 8	3a55	3a55
		R	R	R	R	R	R	R	R	R	R	R	R	R	R	R	D	R	R	R	R	R	R	R		

Trains also dep. Salisbury 6.57, 8.15, 10.2, 5.20, **8.55**, arrive London (Waterloo) 9.2, 10B8, 12.30, **8.5**, **11.46**.

A To Sept. 16th only. **B** Breakfast Car provided on Mondays. **D** Restaurant Car Train between Plymouth and Salisbury. **R** Restaurant Car Train. **SO** Saturdays only. **SX** Saturdays excepted. **X** Depart Torrington 3.5 p.m., Bideford 3.15 p.m., Ilfracombe 3.10 p.m., Barnstaple 3.51 p.m. on Mondays to Fridays. ¶ Southern National Omnibus to Barnstaple Junction Station applicable July 16th to Sept. 10th only. *a* Via Eastleigh. *k* Via Budleigh Salterton.

The times from 6 p.m. to 5.59 a.m. inclusive are printed in dark type, thus **12.9** meaning 9 min. aft. midn.

SERVICE FROM LONDON (WATERLOO) WEEKDAYS. To September 24th.

Passengers should ascertain before commencement of journey if, and where, change of carriage is necessary

N.B.—At BANK HOLIDAY times the services shown hereon may be REVISED and certain Trains CANCELLED: reference should be made to the Special Holiday Announcements.

London to Isle of Wight and South of England.

				SOR	R	SOR	SOR	SOR	R	P	SO	SOR	SOR	R	SO	SOR
	a.m	a.m	a.m.	a.m	a.m	a.m	a.m	a.m	a.m	a.m	a.m	a.m	a.m	a.m	a.m	p.m
LONDON (Waterloo) d.	5 40	6 0	6 27	8 27	8 30	8 54	9 17	9 22	9 30	1030	10R47	1117	1122	1130	11R38	1222
Southampton Ter. ar.	..	8 44	9 20	..	..	..		..	..	..	..	..	..	..	..	..
Southampton Cent. ,,	7 48	8 52	9 52	10 9	10 25	1036	1049	1054	1124	1157	1218	..	1254	1 17	1 34	..
Cowes Pier ,,	9 0	1020		..	11 50		..	To Sept. 9 only.	12 40	1S030	..	..	To Sept 9 only			To Sept. 9 only.
Lymington Town .. ,,	8 44	9 49	10SX37	1048	..	..	..		12 8	1SX10	1 10	..		2SX2	2 13	
Yarmouth Slipway* ,,	9 30	..	11SX45	1145	..	..			1 0	..		..		2SX 5	3 5	
Totland Bay V ,,	1010	..	12SX25	1225	..	..			1 40	..	..	..		3SX25	3 45	
Bournemouth Cen. ,,	8 51	1013	..	11 8	11 14	1127	1134	1152	1219	1236	1 2	1 23	1 40	2 18	..	2 30
Bournemouth Wst ,,	9 23	..	..	1120	11SX33	..	..	12 6	1237	1247	To Sept. 9 only	..		2 30	..	..
Swanage ,,	10 8	1142	..	To Sep 16.	12SX33	1224	..	..c	1SX18	2SX34		2 40	2 40	..	..	3 25
Dorchester ,,	9 51	1131	..		12 8	..	1233	..c	1SX7	2 5		2 13	..		..	..
Weymouth ,,	10 5	1154	..		12 21	..	1256	..c	1SX20	2SX22		2 31	..		..	..

London to Isle of Wight and South of England.

	R	SOR	R	SX	SOR	eFO	BR	SO	R R	R	SOR	SXR	R	R	R	R
	p.m	p.m	p.m	p.m	p.m	p.m	p m	p.m	p.m	p.m	p.m	p.m	p.m	p.m	p.m.	p.m.
LONDON (Waterloo) dep.	1230	1 22	1 30	1 54	2 24	2 30	2 30	2 35	3 30	4 30	4 45	4 45	5 30	6 80	7 30	9 0
Southampton Ter. arr.	..	..	..	..	..		..	..	..		..	..		..		..
Southampton Cent. ,,	1 58	2 56	3 15	..	To Sept. 16 only.	..	3 58	4 3	5 17	Bournem'th Limited	6 16	6 16	7 19	7 58	9 28	1058
Cowes Pier ,,	3 20	..	4 40	..			5 30	5 30	..		7 45	7 45		9 45		
Lymington Town* .. ,,	3 5	..	4SO15	5 7		5 7	5 7	5 15	6 13		6 55	6 55	8 14	9 0	10SO10	1142
Yarmouth Slipway * ,,	4SX5	..	5SO15	6 0		6 0	6 0	6 0	..		7 35	7 35	..	..	..	WSO
Totland Bay V * ,,	4SX45	..	5SO55	6 40	..	6 40	6 40	6 40	..		8 15	3 15	..		..	..
Bournemouth Cent ,,	2 39	3 55	4 13	..	4 28	..	4 38	4 45	6 10	6 26	7 13	7 22	3 21	8 39	10 15	..
Bournemouth West ,,	2 55	..	4 25	..		..	4 54	..	6 22	6 43	7 25	7 34	8 33	8 55	10 28	..
Swanage ,,	3SX35	5 2	6SX1	.	5 27	6 1	5 36	6 4	..	7 21	8 36	..	..	9 40	.	..
Dorchester ,,	3 25	..	6SX2		..	6 2	5 23	5 33	..	7 12	8 25	..		9 28	11SO39	..
Weymouth ,,	3 38	..	6SX24	..	..	6 24	5 38	5 47	..	7 24	8 42	..		9 41		..

Trains also dep. London (W'tloo) 10SO38 a.m., Bournm'th (Cen.) 12.44, ar Dorchester 2.3; also 12SOR35, Southampton (Cent.) 2.12, Lymington Town* 3.12, arr. Bournmouth (Cent.) 2.50; also 2SOR30 p.m., Bournmouth (Cent.) 4.37, arr. Bournmouth (West) 4.50; also 10.30 p m. Southampton (Ter.) 12.53, Bournmouth (Cent.) 2.16, arr. Dorchester 3 14; also Thur. 12.0 midnight, arr. Southampton (Ter.) 1.45; also Wed. midnight 12.0 arr. Southampton (Cent.) 1.58; also 7.54 p.m., arr. Southampton (Ter.) 10 43.

B Mondays to Fridays to Sept. 1st. **FO** Fridays only. **P** Pullman Car Train between London and Bournemouth; 1 and 3 cl. Pullman Cars only. Supplementary fares charged. **R** Restaurant Car Train. **SO** Saturdays only. **SX** Saturdays excepted. **V** By Bus from Yarmouth. **WSO** Wednesdays and Saturdays only. *c* To Sept. 1st only. *e* Fridays only Sept. 8th, 15th, 22nd.

		SOR	R	SOR	R	SOR	R	SOR	R	SOR	R	SOR	R	SOR	R	SOR	R
	a.m	a.m	a.m	g	a.m	g	a.m	g	a.m	g	a.m	g	p.m	g	p.m	g	p.m
LONDON (Wt'loo) dep.	5 27	7 45	7 50	8 15	8 50	9 15	9 50	1015	1050	1115	1150	1215	1250	1 15	1 50	2 15	2 50
Portsmouth & Southsea	7 44	..	9 20	9 45	1020	1045	1120	1145	1220	1245	1 20	1 45	2 22	2 45	3 21	3 45	4 22
Portsmouth (Har.) arr.	7 50	9 20	9 25	9 50	1025	1050	1125	1150	1225	1250	1 25	1 50	2 27	2 50	3 25	3 50	4 26
Ryde Pier ,,	9 5	10 5	1010	1045	1115	1145	1215	1245	1 15	1 45	2 15	2 45	3 15	3 45	4 15	4 45	5 15
Sandown ,,	9 46	1040	1049	1140	11†40	1240	12†18	1 4	1†48	2 40	2†48	3 40	3†48	4 40	4†48	5 22	5*48
Shanslin ,,	9 55	1048	1055	1126	1155	[illegible]	1 6	1 26	2 6	2 26	3 6	3 26	4 6	4 26	5 6	5 29	6 1
Ventnor ,,	1012	11 7	1113	1147	1211	[illegible]	1 27	1 47	2 27	2 47	3 27	3 47	4 27	4 47	5 27	6 3	6 22

	SOR	R	SOR	SR	DR	R	DR	R	R	R	R		
	g	p.m	g	p.m	p.m	p.m	p m	p.m	p.m.	p m	p.m.	p.m	p.m
LONDON (Wt'loo) dep	3 15	3 50	4 20	4 50	5 20	5 50	6 20	6 59	7 50	8 50	9 50	1025	11 50
Portsmouth & Southsea	4 45	5 20	5 50	6 20	6 47	7 22	7 47	8 22	9 20	1020	11 20	1233	1 28
Portsmouth (Har.) arr.	4 50	5 25	5 55	6 25	6 52	7 25	7 52	8 25	9 25	1025	11 25	..	1TH.032
Ryde Pier ,,	5 45	6 15	6 45	7 5	..	8 5	..	9 25	D10SO15	..	12TH.010	..	3TH.020
Sandown ,,	6 27	6 48	7 27	7 48	..	8 48	..	10 3	D11SO5	..	..	..	4TH.028
Shanklin ,,	6 36	6 56	7 35	7 55	..	8 55	..	10 11	D11SO28	..	..	..	4TH.036
Ventnor ,,	6 52	7 13	7 52	8 12	..	9 12	..	1027	D11SO11	..	..	..	4TH.053

Also dp. W'tloo 5.57, 6.57 a.m. 4SX20, 5SX20, 6SX20. Ar. Portsm'th & S'thsea 8.14, 9.4 a.m., 6.1, 7.1, 8.1 p.m.

ADDITIONAL SERVICES ON SATURDAYS.

Waterloo ....dep.	8.20 a.m.	8.45 a.m.	Then at same minutes past each hour up to end including	Waterloo ....dep.	3.20 p.m.	3.45 p.m.
Portsmouth & Southsea arr.	9.52 a.m.	—		Portsmouth & Southsea	4.53 p.m.	—
Portsmouth Harbour arr.	9.55 a.m.	10.20 a.m.		Portsmouth Harbour arr.	4.55 p.m.	5.20 p.m.

D July 23 to Sept. 9 only. **Th.O** Thur. morns. only. **R** Restaurant Car Train. **SO** Sats. only. **SX** Sats. excepted. *g* To Sept. 9 only. † 10 mins. later on Sats. * 16 mins later on Sats.

SOUTHERN RAILWAY (Western Section).

SERVICE FROM LONDON (WATERLOO) TO THE UNDERMENTIONED STATIONS (WEEKDAYS).

JULY 2nd TO SEPTEMBER 24th, 1939.

Passengers should ascertain before commencement of journey if, and where, change of carriage is necessary.

N.B.—At BANK HOLIDAY times the services shown hereon may be REVISED and certain Trains CANCELLED, and reference should be made to the Special Holiday Announcements, or enquiry be made before travelling.

Mls.	London to of West England, North and South Devon and Cornwall.		SO R	SO R	SX R	SO R	SO R	SX R	SO R	SO R	SO R	SX R	SO R	SO AR	SO R	SO R	SX R	SO R	SO R	SO R	R	SO R	R	a
		a.m	a.m	a.m	a.m	a.m	a.m	a.m	a.m	a.m	a.m	a m	a.m	a.m	n'n	p.m	p m	p.m	p.m	p.m	p. m.	p.m	p.m	p.m
0	LONDON (Waterloo) dep.	6 0	8 35	8 45	9 0	9 0	1024	1035	1035	1040	1054	11 0	11 0	1145	12 0	12 5	1 0	1 0	1 4	2 0	3 0	3 24	6 0	10Ha30
																								a. m
83	Salisbury arr.	8 48	1028	1039	1050	1058	1152	12 1	12 1	1210	1223	1226	1232	1 19	1 31	1 41	2 39	2 30	2 50	3 30	4 27	4 55	7 45	2H36
139	Yeovil ,,	11 1	11 2	..	12 6	1213	..	..	..	..	..	2 0	2 9	..		2 45	3 54	..	4 10	..	5 SX 50	6 7	9 6	4 32
152	Seaton ,,	..	..	..	1248	1 4	..	..	..	..	..	3 2	..	..	..	3 32	4 45	..	4 50	..	6 SX 51	7 23	9 4	..
167	Sidmouth ,,	..	1239	..	1 38	1 39	..	..	..	..		2 23	..	..	3 35	4 16	5 30	..	..	5 3	6 32	8 6	1010	8Y23
171	Exeter (Central) ,,	12SX27	1229	1244	1 12	..	1 33	1 41	1 41	1 54	2 6	2 12	2 15	..	3 34	3 59	4 43	4 17	5 7	5 21	6 22	7 51	9 59	4Y39
182	Exmouth (*via* Exeter) ,,	1SX11	1 13	1k17	2k4	..		2 42	2 42		2 42	2k46	3 12	3k46	4 11	4 41	5 42	5 11	5 42	6k6	6k55d	8r25	1028	6Y24
211	Barnstaple Junction ,,	..	..	2 9	2 41	..	2 38	2 52	2 49	To Sept. 2nd only	..	5 37	3 40	..	..	..	6 30	5 25	..	6D42	7 36	9 23	11FO21	6Y22
..	Lynton for Lynmouth(¶) ,,		..	..		..	4 5	4 50	4 50		..	7 25		..	..	..	..	7 10	..	..	f	..	..	8Y35
225	Ilfracombe ,,		..	3 0	..	..	3 25	3 35	3 40		..	7 0	4 38	..	..	..	7 20	6 13	..	7D29	8 20	10 6	12FO5	7Y15
220	Bideford ,,	..	..	2 45	..	..	To Sept. 2nd only.	3 17			..	6 1	4 3	..	..	..	7 0	5 53	..	7D10	8 2	9 49	11FO48	7Y5
225	Torrington ,,		..	2 55	..	..		3 30	..		..	6 12	4 15	..	..	..	7 11	6 5	..	7D21	8 13	10 0	11FO59	7Y31
197	Okehampton ,,		1 20	2 11	2 11	..		..	..		..	3 2	3 5	..	..	..	5 37	5 14	..	6 15	7 26	9 16	1055	8Y39
226	Bude ,,	..	..	..	..	..		3 25	..		3 46	4 54	4 54	..	..	..	6 57	6 35	..	7 29	8 50	..	..	11Y17
223	Launceston ,,	..	..	..	..	..		3 9	..	3 23	3B40	4 22	4 22	..	..	..	6 42	6 25	..	7 11	8 34	..	..	10Y55
241	Camelford ,,		..	..	..	..		3 44	..	3 59	4B16	4 58	4 58	..	..	..	7 21	7 2	..	7 45	9 SO 19	..	..	11Y32
254	Wadebridge ,,	..	..	..	..	..		4 11	..	4 30	4B47	5 23	5 23	..	..	..	7 44	7 27	..	8 9	..	..	..	11Y57
271	Bodmin ,,	..	..	..	..	..		5 30	..	5 30	5 30	6 30	6 30	..	..	..	8 33	8 33	..	..	..	..	..	1Y19
259	Padstow ,,	..	..	..	..	..		4 24	..	4 43	5B0	5 36	5 36	..	..	..	7 55	7 38	..	8 22	..	..	..	12Y11
218	Tavistock ,,	..	1 48	2 59	2 39	..		..		..	..	3 31	3 34	..	..	..	6 8	5 43	..	6 45	7 58	9 52	1122	..
229	Devonport ,,		2 17	3 8	3 8	..		..	..	..		3 58	4 1	..	..	..	6 37	6 10	..	7 12	8 25	1023	1149	6Y7
230	Plymouth (North Road) ,,	..	2 23	3 15	3 13	..		..	..	..	..	4 3	4 10	..	..	..	6 42	6 15	..	7 19	8 29	1030	1154	6Y13
								Atlantic Coast Express.																

Trains also depart from London (Waterloo) at 7.24 a.m., 3.30 p.m., **6.54** p.m., 7*a***30** p.m. and **8.54** p.m., arriving at Salisbury at 10.22 a.m., 5.46 p.m., **9.23** p.m., **10***a***31** p.m. and **11.21** p.m. respectively. Train departs London (Waterloo) at 5.0 p.m., arriving Salisbury **7.0** p.m. and Yeovil **8.37** p.m.

A To Sept. 2nd only. **B** Sept. 9th, 16th and 23rd only. **C** July 29th to Sept. 9th only. **D** 25 minutes later on Sept. 16th and 23rd. **FO** Fridays only. **H** Departs Waterloo **12.0** midnight on Wednesday nights to Salisbury direct, due Salisbury **1.59** a.m. Thursdays). **R** Restaurant Car Train. **SO** Saturdays only. **SX** Saturdays excepted. **Y** Tuesday to Saturday mornings only. *a* Via Eastleigh. *f* Arrives **9.35** p.m. on Saturdays; also arrives **10.29** p.m. on Tuesdays and Fridays, July 18th to Sept. 8th. *k* Via Budleigh Salterton. *r* 10 minutes later on Sept. 9th, 16th and 23rd. ¶ By Southern National Omnibus from Barnstaple Junction Station. Applicable July 16th to Sept. 10th only. Times subject to alteration.

LONDON AND NORTH EASTERN RAILWAY.

Train Service from LONDON (King's Cross) to NORTH OF ENGLAND and SCOTLAND.

WEEKDAYS.

	FT		Q	R AA	R EE	A R	R BB	R GG	R DD	R CC	R DD	R FF	R SO	R DD
	a.m	a.m	a.m	a.m	a.m	a.m	a.m	a.m	a.m	a.m	a.m	a.m	a.m	a.m
LONDON (Kg's X) d.	1 5	1 10	4 45	7 25	9 20	10 0	10 5	10 5	1010	1010	1015	1015	1021	1028
Hull ....arr.	..	5 17	9w49	11w45	..	..		..		..	..	2X28	2t25	2 30
York .... ,,	4 45	8 27	9 18	1121	1232	..	1 22	..		1 36	1 48	2X18	2 42	2 42
Harrogate .... ,,	..	6 25	10d44	1030	1 30		..	..		..		2 45	2DD50	..
Ripon .... ,,	..	6 52	10m31	2 40	2 40	..	..			..		3 35	3DD35	..
Bridlington .... ,,	..	6 21	10g44	1N30	3 15	..	..	..		..		3X5	3ee1	3 21
Scarborough .. ,,	5 55	10 0	10 50	1p48	1 48	..	2 35	..		2s35	2cc50	3X36	4 45	—
Whitby .... ,,	6 50	1047	1155	2q42	2 32	..	3s31	..	..			4rr38	6 31	..
Northallerton.. ,,	8 24	—	1039	1 28	1 28	..	3 18	..	..	3vv34	2 34	3rr18	—	..
Darlington .... ,,	5 48	9 54	11 3	1218	1 24	..	2ab22	..	..	2 28	2 42	3rr42	..	..
Middlesbrough.. ,,	6 54	1027	1115	1256	2 5	..	2ab56	..	..	3vv27	3 27	4rr27	..	..
Stockton ...... ,,	6l48	..	1115	1256	2l5	..	2ab56	..	..	3vv25	3 25	4rr7	..	..
WestHartlepool ,,	7 40		1137	1 25	2 32	..	3ab25		..	3vv55	3 55	4rr55	..	..
Durham ...... ,,	6 26	..	1138	1 10	2 6	..	2ab55	..	..	3s7	3 28	4rr34	..	..
Sunderland.... ,,	7 36	11 7	1136	2 7	2 50	3p19	3 36		..	4bb17	3 58	5rr22	..	..
South Shields .. ,,	7 40	1127	1147	1 47	3 7	3p27	3 47		..	4 7	4 27	5rr47	..	..
Newcastle .... ,,	6 48	1047	11 5	1 10	2 17	2p36	2 55	..	..	3 22	3 35	5rr6	..	..
Berwick ...... ,,	8 21	—	1 51	2 35	3 38	..	4 16	4X16	4 40	5 44	6 2	—	..	..
Edinbro'(Wv'ly) ,,	9 36	..	1 35	3 50	4 46	5 0	5 25	5X25	5 50	—	—	..	..	..
Glasgow(Qn.St.) ,,	11 6		2 58	5 1	6 3	..	6 52	6 52	7 22	..	..	..	..	..
Stirling .... ,,	12f21			5 50	—	..	7 16	7 16	—	..	..	..	..	..
Perth .... ,,	1133		3 20	5 50	..	..	7 13	7 13	..	..	..	..	..	..
Inverness...... ,,	3 36	..	7 55	9 35	..	..	..	..	..	..	..	..	..	..
Dundee........ ,,	11k32	..	3 29	6 16	..	6 37	7 11	7 11	..		..	..	..	..
Aberdeen ...... ,,	p.m 1k21	..	p.m 5 18	— ..		8 15	9 0	9 0	..		..	..	..	..

	R EE	R HH	B PP	J	R NN	B	R KK	R KK	PR KK	R EE	R SO	R SX	R SO	R SX
	a.m	a.m	a.m	a.m	a.m	a.m	a.m	a.m	n'n	p.m	p.m	p.m	p.m	p.m
LONDON (Kg's X) d.	1050	11 0	11 0	1120	1125	1130	1140	1150	12 0	12 5	1250	1 5	1 5	1 20
Hull ....arr.	..	..	..		..	4 45	..	..	..	4 45	..	..	..	..
York .... ,,	..	2 0	2jj20	..	..		3 0	..	..	4 3	4 25	4 38	..	..
Harrogate .... ,,		3o0	3jj8	3 4	..		4 20	..	..	5 3	..	5 46	..	..
Ripon .... ,,		3o35	3jj35	3 35	..	5 48	5 9	..	..	5 30		6 32	..	..
Bridlington .... ,,	..	5 1	5dd1	..	3 25	—	4 20	..	..	5 48		..	..	
Scarborough .. ,,	3 7	2 55	3 15	..	..		4tt17	..	..	5 7	..	ee10	..	
Whitby .... ,,	—	3 55	4jj10	..	4 30		6 31	..	..	6 31	..	7 7	..	
Northallerton.. ,,	..	3 18	3jj18	..			4 49	..	..	4 49	..	5 52	..	..
Darlington .... ,,	..	3 42	3jj42	3 51	..		4 23	..	..	5 8	5 19	5 30	..	..
Middlesbrough.. ,,	..	4 27	4jj27	4 27	..		4 16	..	..	..	5 57	6 27	..	..
Stockton ...... ,,	..	4 7	4tt18	4 32	..		4 0	..	..	..	5 56	6l21	..	..
WestHartlepool ,,	..	4 55	4tt55	4 55	..		4 26	..	..	..	6 25	6 34	..	
Durham ...... ,,	..	4 34	4jj48	4ww31	..	..	4 57	..	..	5 40	..	..	..	
Sunderland.... ,,	..	4 32	5tt40	5 19	..		5 5	5 36	..	6 39	..	..	..	7 17
South Shields .. ,,	..	5 29	5tt47	5 29	..		—	5 29	..		6 47	..	..	7 7
Newcastle .... ,,	..	4 37	5tt8	4 37	..	..	..	4 45	6v0	6 0	6 10	6¶22	6v55	6 29
Berwick ...... ,,	..	7 11	—	7xx11	..	..	..	6 16	—	—	—	—	..	8 5
Edinbro'(Wv'ly) ,,	..	—	The Scarborough Flyer.	7 5	..	..	..	7 30	..	..		..	8 40	8 45
Glasgow(Qn.St.) ,,	..	The Scarboro' Flyer.		8 13	..	..	..	8‡44	..	..	..	..	9 57	9 57
Stirling .... ,,	..			9 37	..	..	..	9 37	..	..	..	..	..	..
Perth .... ,,	..			..	..	..	..	..	..	..	..	..	..	1058
Inverness...... ,,	..			..	..	..	..	..	..	..	..	..	..	a.m 5 45
Dundee........ ,,	..			8 58	..	..	..	1030	..	..	..	..	..	
Aberdeen ...... ,,	..			1045	..	..	..	..	..	..	..	..	..	..

A "The Flying Scotsman." **B** Buffet Car whole or part of journey. **C** "The Yorkshire Pullman," sup. charges. **E** "The Night Scotsman," sleeping accommodation. **F** Sleeping accommodation. **H** "The Silver Jubilee," Sats. excepted. Does not run Fri., 4th and Mon., 7th Aug. Limited accommodation, sup. charges. **J** "The Queen of Scots" Pullman, sup. charges. **K** "The Coronation," Sats. excepted. Does not run Fri., 4th and Mon. 7th Aug. Limited accommodation, sup. charges. **M** Sats. only. Runs 15th July to 2nd Sept. inclusive. **N** On Sats. arrives Bridlington 12.16 p.m. (1.23 p.m. on 16th and 23rd Sept.) **P** "The Norseman." **Q** Rest. Car York to Glasgow. **R** Rest. Car whole or part of journey. **S** or **SO** Sats. only. **SX** or **X** Sats. excepted. **T** Rest. Car Newcastle to Edinburgh. **V** "The Aberdonian, sleeping accommodation. **Y** "The Highlandman," sleeping accommodation. *b* 10.21 on Sats. *d* Via York. Passengers can arrive Harrogate 10.10 a.m. via Leeds (Cent. and City). *e* Suns. excepted. *f* On Sats. arrives Stirling 12.39 p.m. *g* Via Selby. On Sats. arrives Bridlington 11.4 a.m. via Malton. *j* Via Selby. Passengers can arrive Hull **8.15** p.m. by Pullman Car Train from Doncaster, sup. charges. *k* On Sats. arrives Dundee 11.18 a.m. and Aberdeen 1.9 p.m. *l* Thornaby Station. *m* Via Leeds (Cent. and City). *n* Sat. morns. only. *o* On Weds. arrives Harrogate 3.0 and Ripon 3.35 p.m. *p* On Sats. to 2nd Sept. incl. arrives Londesborough Road 12.37 p.m. (12.50 p.m. on 8th July). *q* Commences 11th Sept. *t* Runs 8th July, 2nd, 9th, 16th and 23rd Sept. only. *u* On Suns. arrives Perth 9.2, Dundee 9.5, Aberdeen 11.1 a.m. **AA** On Sats. leaves King's Cross 7.30 a.m. **BB** Tues., Weds. and Thurs. only; also runs on Fris., 7th, 14th July, and from 18th Aug.; Sats., 8th July, 2nd, 9th, 16th and 23rd Sept., and Mons., 11th and 18th Sept. **CC** Runs on Mons. until 4th Sept. incl. Fris., 21st July to 11th Aug. incl., and on Sats., 8th July, 2nd and 9th Sept. only.

NOTES CONTINUED ON PAGE 105A.

The times from 6 p.m. to 5.59 a.m. inclusive are printed in dark type, thus **12.9** meaning 9 min. aft. midn.

LONDON AND NORTH EASTERN RAILWAY.

Train Service from LONDON (King's Cross) to NORTH OF ENGLAND nd SCOTLAND.

WEEKDAYS.

	R SO	R SX	R SO	R SX	R SO	R M	R SO	EE	KR	R	C	HR	R	R	R FSO	R	YR SX	VR SX		E	F	F SX	F SO
	p.m	p.m	p.m	p.m	p.m	p.m	p.m	p.m	p.m	p.m	p.m	p.m.	p.m	p.m.	p.m	p.m	p.m	p.m	p.m	p.m	p.m	p.m	p.m
LONDON (King's X) dep.	1 20	1 30	1 33	1 40	1 40	2 20	2 30	2 40	4 0	4 0	4 45	5 30	5 45	5nn50	5 50	7 15	7 25	7 40	8 25	1025	1035	1045	1045
Hull arr.	..	5 23	5 29	6w21	6w21	..	..	7 34	..	8j40	8 15	..	9FSX48	10 31	9 50	11 15	..	..	1 45	..	..	4w15	4w24
York ,,	4 52			5 46	5 46	..	6 7	..	6 37	7 53		..	9 13	10x50		11s11	11 6	1 21	1 0	..	2 39	3 5	3 5
Harrogate ,,	5 48	5 53	..	6 10	6hh10	..	7 1	7 22		9 25	8 45	..	10s16	10 24	..	11 54	..	..	..	..	..	4m38	8 2
Ripon ,,	6 32	..		6 32	6hh32	..	8 29	..	8 29	9 49	9 49	..	..	11s41	..	..	..	..	..	..	..	4m59	8 30
Bridlington ,,	..	6 12	..	..	6 30	..	8h33	8 33	8 33	10b15	10b15	..	11KK25		..	12**19	..	..	..	..	..		8 11
Scarborough ,,	5 55		..	7 3	7 3	..	7 50		7 50	9ff9		..	1025	..	..		..	..		..	..	..	4 40
Whitby ,,	7 7	..	..	8gg44	8 10	..	8jj10	..	8 44	1034	ss ..	..	12mm3	..	..	..	..	..	..	..	..	..	..
Northallerton ,,	5 34	..	..	6 47		..	7jj5	..	7 43	8 52	..		1010	..	..		..	..		..	..	4 16	3 55
Darlington ,,	5 44	..	..	7 6	..	6 47	7ee24	..	8 14	9 12	..	8 48	10 4	..	..		..	..	2 3	..	..	4 7	4 18
Middlesbrough ,,	6 27	..	..	7 57	..	7 27	8ee27	..	8 56	9 46	..	9 27	11 2	..	..	..	..	..	.	..	..	5 0	
Stockton ,,	6l21	..	..	8 7	..	7 32	8ee32	..	8 50	9 26	..	9 32	1042	..	..	..	..	..		..	..	5l0	5 1
West Hartlepool ,,	7 0	..		8 35	..	7 55	8ee55	yy	9 39	9 45	..	9 55	11 4	..	..	..	..	..			..	5 26	5 32
Durham ,,	6 25	..	..	7b53	..	..	7ee56	..	..	9 46	..	9 46	1035	..	..	..	..	..			..	4 44	5 8
Sunderland ,,	7 17	..		8 33	..	8 19	8 36	..	8 36	1030	..	10 17	11r12	..	..	..	..	..		..	5e19	6 2	6 11
Newcastle ,,	6 35	..	..	9 7	..	7 36	7 49	..	7 57	10 8	..	9 30	1055	..	..	..	1253	1 8	3 3		4 38	5 10	5 33
South Shields ,,	7 27	..	..	8 15	..	8 27	8 27	..	8 47	1047	..	10 7	1136	..	..	..	..	..	4e53	..	5e30	5 52	7 27
Berwick ,,	8 5	..			..	..	9mm10	..	..		..	11 41	1s1	..	..	..		..	4 48	..	6 10		8 37
Edinbro' (Wv'ly.) ,,	9 25	..	..	..	..	..	10mm20	..	10 0	..	..			..	..	..	3 35	3 50	6 6	..	7 30	..	
Glasgow (Queen St.) ,,	1046	..	..	..	..	..	11mm57	..	1143		..	..	..	..	..	..	5 29	5 29	7*33	8 49	9†38	..	..
Stirling ,,	..	..	..	..	..	..	..	..		..		..	..	..	..	..	..	7 21	..	..	9*36	..	..
Perth ,,	1058	..	..		..	..	..	..			..		..	..	..	..	4 55	..	8x30	8u55	10e22	..	..
Inverness ,,		..			..	..	..	..	..	..			..	..	..	..	8 45	..		1 40 a.m		..	..
Dundee ,,		..			..	..	..	..	..	..		..		..	..	..	..	5 26	8x41	9u15	..	..	..
Aberdeen ,,	..	..	..	..	..	..	..	..					..	..	..	..	..	7 20	..	11u9	..	..	..

NOTES CONTINUED FROM PAGE 105.

DD Sats. only. Runs 15th July to 26th Aug. **EE** Sats. only and not after 2nd Sept. **FF** From 15th July to 26th Aug. incl. Does not run on Sats. **FSO** Fris. and Sats. only. **FSX** Fris. and Sats excepted. **GG** Mons. only, and not after 4th Sept.; also runs on Fris., 21st July to 11th Aug. incl., and Sats., 15th July to 26th Aug. **HH** Sats. excepted, and not after 8th Sept. **JJ** Runs 9th and 16th Sept. **KK** Sats. only, and not after 9th Sept. **NN** Sats. only, and not after 26th Aug. *ab* Sats. excepted; also runs on Sats., arr. Darlington 2.34, Middlesbrough 3.27, Stockton 3.25, West Hartlepool 3.55, and Durham 3.7 p.m. *bb* On Sats. arrives Sunderland 3.53 p.m. *c* Via York. On Sats. arrives Harrogate 12.46 p.m. Passengers can arrive 1.7 p.m. via Leeds (Cent. and City). *cc* Scarboro' (Londesborough Road). *dd* Runs 2nd, 9th and 16th Sept. *ee* Commencing 16th Sept., arrives Darlington **7.0**, Middlesbrough **7.57** p.m., Stockton **8.7**, West Hartlepool **8.35**, and Durham **7.46** p.m. *ff* After 16th Sept. runs on Sat. 23rd Sept. only; *gg* From 31st July to 25th Aug. incl. arrives Whitby (Westcliff) **8.23** p.m., via Scarboro'. *h* Commences 9th Sept. *hh* Until 9th Sept. leaves King's Cross 1.50 p.m. *jj* On 16th and 23rd Sept. arrives Whitby **10.10** p.m. via Scarboro' and Northallerton **6.45** p.m. *kk* Whitby (Westcliff) via Scarboro', Sats. only, and not after 10th Sept. *mm* Not after 9th Sept. *nn* On Fris. and Sats. leaves King's Cross 5.55 p.m. *pp* Sats. only, and not after 16th Sept. *qq* On Mons. and Fris., also on Sats. from 9th Sept. arrives Whitby 2.32 p.m. *r* On Sats. arrives Sunderland **11.22** p.m. *rr* Sats. excepted, commences 11th Sept. *ss* Not after 26th Aug, Whitby (Westcliff) via Scarboro'. *tt* Runs 16th Sept. only. *v* Newcastle (Tyne Commission Quay). Conveys boat passengers only. *vv* Runs 8th July and 2nd Sept. only. *w* Via Selby. *ww* On Sats. arrives Durham 4.48 p.m. *xx* On Sats. until 9th Sept. arrives Berwick **6.16** p.m. *yy* Runs 31st July to 25th Aug. incl. *z* Runs 8th July and from 2nd Sept.* On Mons. to Fris., from 24th July to 8th Sept., and on Sats. until 9th Sept. incl., arrives Scarboro' 10.35 a.m. ** Wed. and Sat. nights only. † On Suns. arrives Glasgow 10.48 a.m. †† On 9th Sept. arrives Scarboro' 4.45 p.m. ‡‡ On 2nd and 9th Sept. arrives Glasgow **9.41** p.m. ¶ Except on Fris. also arrives Tyne Commission Quay **6.55** p.m.

LONDON AND NORTH EASTERN RAILWAY.

Train Service from SCOTLAND and NORTH OF ENGLAND to LONDON (King's Cross).

WEEKDAYS.

	R	B	R SO	R SX	R SO	R	R	H R	K	R W	G R U	R XX	G R SO	C	R	N R	R	R SO	R XX	R SX	A R	R Y	R SO	R SX	R SO	R	J
	a.m	a.m	a.m	a.m	a.m	a.m	a.m	a.m	a.m	a.m	a.m	a.m	a.m	a.m	a.m	a.m	a.m	a.m	a.m	a.m	a.m	p.m	a.m	p.m	a.m	p.m	a.m
Aberdeen ....dep.	..	..	..	..	..	..	..	..	..	..	..	..	..		..	..				..	6 40	..	..	..	..	..	
Dundee .... ,,	..		..	..	..	..	..	..	..	..	..	..				..			6 15	..	8 20	..	..	..	..	.	8 40
Inverness .... ,,	..	..	..	..	..	..	..	..	..	..	..	..	..		..	..	..		11r20	..		..	..	11g20	11r20	..	
Perth .... ,,	..	..	..	..	..	..	..	..	..	..	..	..	..			..			6a25	..	..	..	..	8 35	8a35		9 17
Stirling ....,, ,,	..	..	..	..	..	..	..	..	..	..	..	..	..		..	..		..	..	..	8 10	..	..	..	8 10	..	..
Glasgow (Queen St.) ,,	..	..	..	..	..	..	..	..		..	..	..	..			..	6 30	..	7 42	..	8 35	..	8 55	8 55		..	1015
Edinburgh(Wav'ley) ,,	..		..	..	..	..	..	..	..	..	..	..	..			..	8 5	..	9 15	..	10 0	..	1010	1015	1018		1120
Berwick .... ,,	..		..	..	..	..	..	7 22	..	..		..	..	..		..	9 16	..	9 23	..	9d23	..	1117	1122	1125		11S35
South Shields .... ,,	..	..	7 34	7 34		..	..	9 17	..	8 18	8 18	8 18	8 37	8 37		..	9 59		1057	..	11d37	1137	1157	1157	1157	..	1257
Newcastle .... ,,	..	..	8 15	8 15	..	..	..	10 0	..	9 0	9 0	9 0	9 30	9 30	..	1030	10 40	..	1140		12d20	1230	1237	1242	1246		1 45
Sunderland ...... ,,	..		7 20	7 54	7 54	..	..	9 30	..	8 20	8 20	8 20	9 11	9 11		10 0	10 0	.	1058	..	11d30	1138	1138	1158	1158	..	1258
Durham .... ,,	..		8 38	8 38	.	..	..	9 54	..	8 45	8 45	8q45	9 54	9 54		..	11 4	.	1137	..		12 9	12 9	12 9	..	..	
West Hartlepool.. ,,	..	5 30	..	7 43	..	..	..	9 40		8 34	8 34	W12	9 40	9 40		..	10 11	..	1111	..	..	1211	1211	1211	..	..	1 17
Stockton .... ,,	..	5 55	..	8 20	..	..	..	10 5	..	8 57	8 57	10Wl13	10 5	10 5		..	10l52	..	11l52	..	..	1250	1250	1250	..		1 39
Middlesbrough .. ,,	..	5 44	..	8 15	8T15	..	..	10 0	..	9 5	9 5	10n7	9 45	9 45		..	10 45	..	1145	..	..	1253	1253	1253	1253	..	1 45
Darlington ...... ,,	..	6 25	..	9 8	9 8	..	..	1042	..	9 50	9 50	9 50	1028	1028		1124	11 36	..	1231	..		1 20	1 19	1 33	1 37		2 34
Northallerton .... ,,	..	7 0	..	9 5	.	..	..	..	..	9 5	..	9q5	1049	1100		..	11¶0	..	..	..	..	1 1	1 4	1 4	..	..	..
Whitby .... ,,	..		..	7j7	7j7	..	..	..	..	..	9 40	9 40	9†40	..	8†24	10 0	10 0	..	11a15	..	..		1210	1210	..	..	..
Scarborough .... ,,	..	7 15	..	8 55	8 55	..	..			1020	1040	10q5	1040	10S45	1025	11 0	11 0	..	12p10	..	..	..	1 5	1 5	..	..	..
Bridlington ...... ,,	..	6 35	..	7 56	7 56	8 15	..	..		10 0	9 49	10q0	10 0	1035	11 0	..	..	..	..	..	..	1218	..	1218	1 15	1k37	..
Ripon............. ,,	..	7 52	..	..	..	.	9 5	..	10 3	10 3	10 3	10q3	10 3	10 3	..	..	..	1121	..	1134	..	..	1246	..	..	1 30	2 43
Harrogate........ ,,	6 30	8 19	..	8 37	8 37		9 32	..	1030	1032	1032	10q32	1032	1115		1032	10 32	1155	1220	1220	..	1220	1 30	1S30	..	2 2	3 23
York .... ,,	7 49	8 20	..	9 55	9 58		..		..	1115	1135	11q25	1135	1145	.	1216	12 26	..	1 20	..		2 9	2 15	2 22	2 26		..
Hull .... ,,	7 5	7 30	..	..	..	9 30	..	..	..			..	..	1130	1145	..	..	..	..	1155	..	..	..	..		2 45	..
LONDON (King's X)ar.	11Q20	1 3	1 15	1 15	1 25	1e30	1 47	2 0	2 15	2 25	2 35	2 35	**2 45**	3 0	3 47	4 10	4 15	4 33	4 30	4 50	5 0	5 28	5 30	5 35	5 41	**6 55**	**7 5**

A "The Flying Scotsman." **B** Buffet Car whole or part of journey. **C** "The Yorkshire Pullman," sup. charges **D** "The Aberdonian," sleeping accommodation. **E** Mon. morn excepted. **F.** Sleeping accommodation to King's Cross. **G** "The Scarborough Flier." **H** "The Silver Jubilee," sup. charges (Sats. excepted). Does not run on Fri., 4th, and Mon. 7th Aug. **J** "The Queen of Scots" Pullman, sup. charges. **K** "West Riding Limited," sup. charges (Sats. excepted). Does not run on Fri., 4th, and Mon., 7th Aug. **L** "The Highlandman," sleeping accommodation. **M** On Sats. leaves South Shields **12.5**. **N** Mons., Fris. and Sats only. **P** "The Norseman." Conveys boat passengers only. **Q** Passengers from Harrogate arrive King's Cross 11.26 a.m. on Mons. and Sats. **R** Rest. Car whole or part journey. **S** or **SO** Sats. only. **SX** or **X** Sats. excepted. **T** Until 26th Aug. leaves Middlesbrough 8.28 a.m. **U** Sats. excepted, and not after 11th Sept. **V** "The Coronation," sup. charges. Does not run on Fri., 4 Aug., and Mon., 7th Aug. **W** Sats. only. Runs 15th July to 9th Sept. inclusive. **XX** Sats. only and not after 9th Sept. **Y** Fris. only; also runs on Mons., 17th July to 18th Sept. inclusive. **Z** Fris. only, and not after 15th Sept. *a* a.m. On Sats. leaves Ripon 4.15 p.m. *b* Via Thirsk and York. *c* On Sats. leaves 10.49 a.m. *d* Commences 11th Sept. *e* On Sats. arrives 1.37 p.m. *f* Tyne Commission Quay Station. *g* Fri., Sat. and Sun. nights excepted.

NOTES CONTINUED ON PAGE 106A.

The times from 6 p.m. to 5.59 **a.m. inclusive are printed in dark type**, thus **12.9** meaning 9 min. aft. midn.

LONDON AND NORTH EASTERN RAILWAY.

Train Service from SCOTLAND and NORTH OF ENGLAND to LONDON (King's Cross).

WEEKDAYS.

	RP ThO	R XX	R	R SO	R	R Z	VR SX	R		F SX	F	F	F	D	L
	p.m	a.m	a.m.	a.m	a.m	p.m	p.m	p.m.	p.m	p.m	p.m.	p.m	p.m	p.m	p.m
Aberdeen .... dep.	..	9 0	..	..	1020	..	1245	12 45	..	..	3 45	5 45	..	7 35	..
Dundee .... "	..	1038	..	..	1213	..	2 38	2 50	..	..	5 40	7 40	9 0	9 30	..
Inverness .... "	..	..	..	8 30	8 30	..	..	11 5	..	..	..	3 45	..	..	4 40
Perth .... "	..	9 17	..	1225	1225	..	2 5	3 30	..	..	5 43	8 10	..	..	9 35
Stirling .... "	..	9 52	..	12 5	12 5	..	1 41	1 41	..	..	5 52	8†25	..	..	..
Glasgow (Queen St.) .. "	..	11 0	..	1224	1SX0	1224	3 15	4 0	..	..	6 0	8‡25	..	..	10 0
Edinburgh (Wav'ley) "	..	1215	..	1 55	2 5	1 30	4 30	5 10	..	..	7 50	1030	11 0	..	..
Berwick .... "	..	1234	..	2 47	2SX51	2 51	4 4	6 26	..	..	9 11	1149	..	..	..
South Shields .... "	1257	1 57	1 57	3 37	3 37	3 37	5 57	7 17	..	1024	10 17	1117	M	..	..
Newcastle .... "	1 40	2 42	2 45	4 20	4 29	4 14	6 33	8 0	..	1045	11 10	1 13	1 31	1 43	1 55
Sunderland .... "	..	1 58	2 26	3 30	3 38	3 30	5 30	7 30	..	11 9	10s36	11s3	..	..	..
Durham .... "	..	3 32	3 8	4 2	4SX2	4 2	..	8 26	..	10 4	11 38	..	..	..	..
West Hartlepool ...... "	..	2 11	3 11	3 55	4 11	3 50	..	7 11		1139	10s50	..	..	..	..
Stockton .... "	..	2l52	4 l 2	4 20	4l53	4 20	..	8 l 22		12 1	11s14	..	..	..	..
Middlesbrough .... "	..	2 45	3 55	4 15	4 45	4 15	..	8 15	..	1140	11s15	..	..	..	..
Darlington .... "	..	3 34	3 41	5 5	5 23	5 6	..	9 1	..	..	12 18	2 7	..	..	..
Northallerton .... "	..		4 2	5 0	5SX0	5 0	..	9 24	..	1121	11s21	..	..	..	..
Whitby .... "	..	1 32	2 45	3 53	3SX53	3 53	..	7 x 0	..	7*25	7 25	..	..	..	..
Scarborough .... "	..	3 0	3 45	4 48	5SX10	4 48	..	8 x 5	..	10*0	10 s 0	..	..	..	..
Bridlington .... "		1 42	3 15	..	4 2	..	..	8 18	..	8*37	9 55	..	..	..	..
Ripon .... "		..	3a47	..	4 47	4 34	..	7 42	9 20	..			..	.	
Harrogate .... "	..		4 45	..	5 19	..	..	8 15	9 43	..	10s45				..
York .... "	..	4 27	5 13	6 3	6 13	..	..	10 20	..	1 5	1 26	3 0	3 13	3 26	3 39
Hull .... "		..	5 5	..	..	..	..	9 18	..		10 53	..	..	..	..
LONDON (King's X) arr.	7 35	7 45	9 25	9 33	9t35	9 39	1030	3 15	3u45	5 15	5 55	7 5	7 15	7 25	7 30

NOTES CONTINUED FROM PAGE 106.

j On Mons., Fris. and Sats, until 9th Sept., leaves Whitby 8.0. *k* On Sats. leaves 1.25 p.m. *l* Thornaby Station. *n* Not after 26th Aug. *p* p.m. *q* Runs 8th July only. *r* Friday nights. *s* Via York, Weds. only. *t* on Fris. arrives King's Cross **9.45** p.m. (**9.39** p.m. on 22nd Sept.), and Sats. **9.40** p.m. *u* **3.50** a.m. on Suns. *x* On Sats., until 2nd Sept., inclusive, will dep. Whitby **7.25** p.m., and Scarboro' **9.10** p.m. *z* **9.15** p.m. on Sats. commencing 11th Sept. * Not after 15th Sept. † Commencing 4th Sept. leaves Stirling **7.47** p.m. ‡ On Fris., until 25th Aug., leaves Glasgow **9.10** p.m. ¶ After 9th Sept. does not run on Sats. †† Runs 16th and 23rd Sept. only. ‡‡ Whitby (West Cliff) Sats. excepted. Commences 12th Sept.

LONDON AND NORTH EASTERN RAILWAY.

Express Train Service between LONDON (King's Cross) and NORTH OF ENGLAND and SCOTLAND.

SUNDAYS.

	F	G R M	R	R M	R	R	R	R	R	R	R	R	R	R	R A	C R		D	E	E
LONDON—	a.m	a.m	a.m	a.m	a.m	p.m	p.m	p.m	p.m	p.m	p.m	p.m	p m	p.m	p.m	p.m	p.m	p.m	p.m	p.m
(King's Cross) dp.	10 0	11 0	1110	1115	1120	1210	1220	1240	1 0	1 10	4 30	6 0	6J10	6J20	7 25	7 40	8 25	1025	1035	1045
Hull .... arr.	..		..	..	..		4 15	..	..	..	8 47	..	10 0	..	..			..	..	4s15
York .... ,,	..	..	2 36	2 55	3 48	.	..	..	..	4 47	8 55	9 35	..	..	11 6	1121	a.m 1 0	..	2 39	3 5
Harrogate .... ,,	2 0	..	..	..	4b56	5 12	..	..	..	6b17	..	..	..	1030	..		..	..	.	4H38
Ripon .... ,,	..	..		..	..	5 36	..	..	..	7b2	..	..	..	—	..			..	..	4H50
Bridlington .. ,,	..	..	..	..	5 5	..	6 27	..	..	8 46	9 46	.	..	..	..		.	..	..	..
Scarborough .. ,,	..	..	..	3 56	5 2		—	..	..	6 55	..		..	..	..			..	..	
Whitby ...... ,,	..	..	..	4 43	6d32		..	..	..	8d4	..	..	..	..	..	..		..	..	..
Northallerton ,,	..	..	..	..	—	.	..	..	..	6 42	..	..	..	..	..			..	..	4 25
Darlington .... ,,			3 29	4 27	..		..	..	..	5 41	9 53	1029	..	..	..	..	2 3	..	..	4 7
Middlesbrough ,,	..	..	4 28	5 26	..	..	..	..	..	6 28	1056	1129	..	..	..	..		..	..	5 0
Stockton...... ,,	..	..	4 33	5i20	..	..	..	..	..	6 33	10i5	11i23	..	..	..		..	..	..	5i43
West Hartlepool ,,	..	..	4 56	6 31	..	..	..	..	..	6 56	..	1213	..	..	..			..	..	6 24
Durham ...... ,,	..		5 5	5 3	..	..	..	..	..	6 17	027	11 4	..	..	..	..	3 38	..	..	4 44
Sunderland .. ,,	..	..	5 22	5 53	..	..	..	6 22	..	7 22	1128	12 3	..	..	1f39	..		..	5 19	6 44
South Shields ,,			4 57	..	..	..	..	6 27	..	7 27	..	1211	..	..	..	..	4 53	..	5 30	5 52
Newcastle .... ,,	..	..	4 20	5 25	..		..	5 38	..	6 39	1048	1125	..	..	1253	a.m 1 8	3 3	..	4 38	5 10
Berwick ...... ,,	..	..	5 45	—	..	.	..	7 35	..	8 5	—	—			..	..	4 48	..	6 10	—
Edinburgh (W.) ,,	..	6 0	7 0	..	..		..	—	8 20	9 20	..		..	..	3 35	3 50	6 6	..	7 30	
Glasgow (Queen Street) ,,		7 27	8 26	..	..		..	..	9 38	1038	..		..	..	5 29	5 29	7 33	8 49	9 38	..
Stirling ...... ,,	..	..	..	..	..	..	..	..	..	—	..		..	..	..	7 21		..	9 36	..
Perth .... ,,	..		..	..	..	..	..	..	1037	..	..	..	..	..	4 55	..	8 30	8 55	1022	..
Inverness .... ,,	..	..	..	..	..		..	..	5a30	..	..		..	..	8 45	..	..	1 40	—	..
Dundee ...... ,,	..	8 9	9 8	..	..		..	..	10p55	..	..		..	..	—	5 26	8 41	9 15		..
Aberdeen .... ,,	..	—	11 2		..		..	..	—	..	..		..	..	..	7 20	—	11 9	..	..

A "The Highlandman," sleeping accommodation. **C** "The Aberdonian," sleeping accommodation. **D** "The Night Scotsman," sleeping accommodation. **E** Sleeping accommodation from King's Cross. **F** "The Harrogate Sunday Pullman," supplementary charges. **G** "Sunday Scotsman," non-stop King's Cross to Edinburgh (Waverley). **N** Via Leeds (Cent. and City). **J** On 6th Aug. leaves King's Cross **6.0** p.m. **M** Not after 10th Sept. **R** Restaurant Cars whole or part of journey. *a* a.m. *b* Via York. *c* Whitby (West Cliff) via Scarboro'. Not after 10th Sept. On 9th July, 3rd and 10th Sept. arrives **6.55** p.m. *d* Whitby (West Cliff) via Scarboro'. *f* Not after 11th Sept. *i* Thornaby Station. *p* p.m. *s* Via Selby.

The times from 6 p.m. to 5.59 a.m. inclusive are printed in dark type, thus **12.9** meaning 9 min. aft. midn.

LONDON AND NORTH EASTERN RAILWAY.

Express Train Service between LONDON (King's Cross) and NORTH OF ENGLAND and SCOTLAND.

SUNDAYS.

	R	R	RK	R	R		GR	R	F	R	R	R	PR	R	R		E	E	E	EC
	a. m	a. m	a. m	a. m	a. m	a. m	a. m	a. m	p. m	p. m	p.m	a. m	p. m	p. m	a. m	p. m	p. m	p. m	p. m	p. m
Aberdeen ....dep.		..	..		..	..	..		..	..	..		..	..	..			3 45	..	7 35
Dundee ...... ,,		..	..	..	..	..	9 0	..	..	..	..	..	..	..				5 38	9 5	9 30
Inverness .... ,,	..	..	..	..	..	..	..		..	..	..	..	..	..				..	4 10	..
Perth .... ,,		..	..	..	..	..	..	9 25	..	..	..		..	..		..	..		9 10	..
Stirling ...... ,,		..	..	..	..	..	..	..	..	..	..		..	..					..	..
Glasgow																				
(Queen Street) ,,		..	..	..	..	..	9 45	9 55	..	..	..		..	..	10v25	..		6 10	9 25	10 0
Edinburgh (W.) ,,		..	..	..		..	11 0	1115	..	..	..	1125	..	..	11v40	..		7 50	11 0	
Berwick ...... ,,		..	..	..	..	..	..	1120	..	..	..	1242	..	..	..	4 34		9 11	1211	a. m
South Shields ,,		1015	..	..	..	..	..	12d30	..	1 55	..	1g30	..	..	4 45	6 45	1025	..	1050	..
Newcastle .... ,,	6 15	1055	..	..	11 0	..	..	1 45	..	1 15	..	2 12	1r40	..	5 20	7 20	1045	1110	1 35	1 49
Sunderland .. ,,	6 32	9 50	..	..	1030	..	..	1250	..	..	..	1 30	..	..	4 30	6 55	11 9	..	..	
Durham ...... ,,	6 0	1026	..	..	1125	..	..	..	..	..	..	..	..	..	3 10	7 51	..	1138	..	
West Hartlepool ,,	6 37	10f13	..	.	1040	..	..		..	1 10	1h45	..	..	..	4 38	7 10	1139			
Stockton...... ,,	7l27	10l51	..	..	11l26	..	..	..	..	1 39	2ul47	..	..	..	5 19	7l52	12 1	..		
Middlesbrough ,,	7 20	1045	..	..	1119	..	..	..	..	1 47	2u40	..	..	..	5 24	7 45	1135	a. m		..
Darlington.... ,,	8 16	1148	..	..	12 0	..	..	..	..	2 50	..	3 7	..	..	6 11	8 24	..	1218	2 29	..
Northallerton ,,	8 41	..	1127	..	11t27	..	..	..	..	..	..		..	..	..	8 46			..	
Whitby ...... ,,		..	10j7	..		..	..	11n46	..	..	1 55		..	..	3c24	7q35	..			
Scarborough .. ,,	8 50	..	1140	..	11t10	..	..	1 37	..	..	2 50	..	..	..	4 55	8u30		..		
Bridlington .. ,,		..	1018	1118	..	..	..	1129	..	2 0	..	..	..	..	3 30	9 12				
Ripon .... ,,	9 44	..	..		..	1157	..	..	..	..	..	..	..	..	..	9 27	..		..	
Harrogate .... ,,	1010	..	..		12b0	1231	..	1b25	3 0	2 45	..	..	..	..	6 10	9 30	9 52			
York .... ,,	11 0	..	1240		1252	..	..	3 23	..	3 44	3 55	4 6	..	..	7 2	1015	1 5	1 26	3 20	3 32
Hull.......... ,,	9 15	..	..	1225		..	..	.	..	3 4	..	..	..	5 20		8 30	..	.		
LONDON—																				
(King's Cross) arr.	3 45	4 0	4 '15	4 36	4 50	5 55	6 0	6 40	7 0	7 28	7 40	8 15	8 27	1012	1045	3 56	5 15	5 55	7 15	7 25

C "The Aberdonian," sleeping accommodation. **E** Sleeping accommodation to King's Cross. **F** "The Harrogate Sunday Pullman," sup. charges. **G** "Sunday Scotsman," non-stop Edinburgh (Waverley) to King's Cross. **K** Runs 30th July to 17th Sept. inclusive. **P** "The Norseman." Conveys boat passengers only. **R** Restaurant Car whole or part of journey. *b* Via York. *c* Whitby (West Cliff). *d* On 10th, 17th and 24th Sept. leaves South Shields 12.15 p.m. *f* On 17th and 24th Sept. leaves West Hartlepool 9.10 a.m. *g* Not after 3rd Sept. *h* Not after 10th Sept. *j* Whitby (West Cliff). Not after 27th Aug. *l* Thornaby Station. *n* Whitby (West Cliff). From 30th July to 27th Aug. leaves Whitby 12.16 p.m. *q* Until 23rd July and from 10th Sept. leaves Whitby **7.50** p.m. *r* Tyne Commission Quay. *t* Runs 9th, 16th, 23rd July, and 24th Sept. only *v* Until 27th Aug. inclusiive leaves Glasgow 10.35 and Ediburgh 11.52 a.m. *u* Not after 17th Sept.

LONDON AND NORTH EASTERN RAILWAY.

EXPRESS TRAIN SERVICE BETWEEN LONDON (KING'S CROSS and MARYLEBONE) and LEEDS (Central) and BRADFORD (Exchange).

WEEKDAYS.

			R	RM	P	RD	RSO	RSX	HR	FR	RD	R	R	P	R	R	R	GR	R	SX	SO
	a.m.	a.m.	a.m.	a.m	a.m *	p.m	p.m	p.m	p.m	p.m	p.m	p.m	p.m	p.m †	p.m	p.m	p.m	p.m	p.m	p.m	p.m
LONDON (King's X) dep.	1 10	4 45	7 25	1015	1120	12 5	1 26	1 30	1 40	1 50	2 40	..	4 0	4 45	..	5b50	..	7 10	7 15	1045	1045
(Mary'bone) ,,	..	..	..	..	..	..	..	..	..	..		3 20	..	..	4 55	..	6 20	..	..	..	
Leeds (Cent.) ar.	5 14	9 20	1115	2 3	2 31	4 3	5 13	5 14	6 32	6 27	6 38	..	7 56	8 18	..	9 43	..	9 53	11 7	3 22	5A33
Bradford (Exchange) ,,	5 49	9 47	1142	2 23	3 1	4 19	5U34	5 30	7a5	6 43	6 53	3 32	8 18	8 30	1018	10c3	1119	1015	1137	3 54	..

Trains also leave London (Marylebone) 2.32 a.m., 10R0, and 12R15, (King's X) 3D50 p.m., Leeds (Central) 7.36 p.m., arr. Bradford (Ex.) 8.8 a.m., 2.40, 6E15 & 7.48 p.m. respectively. * "The Queen of Scots." † "The Yorks. Pullman"

SUNDAYS.

		P	R	R	R	R	R	
	a.m	a.m §	no'n	p.m	p.m	p.m	p.m	p.m
LONDON (King's X) dep.	..	10 0	1210	4 30	4 55	6 20	..	1045
(Mary'bone) ,,	1240	..	..	..	..	..	5 30	..
Leeds (Cent.) ar.	..	1 25	4 2	8 29	9 22	9 53	..	3 22
Bradford (Exchange) ,,	1030	1 52	4 24	8 52	9 51	1013	1114	3 54

§ "The Harrogate Sunday Pullman."

WEEKDAYS.

	R	N	R	R	GR	R	RY	R	R	R	R	P	R	R				SO	SX
	a.m	a.m	a.m	a.m	a.m	a.m	a.m	a.m	p.m	p.m	p.m	p.m ‡	p.m	p.m	p.m	p.m	p.m	p.m	p.m
Bradford (Exchange) .. d.	7 20	8 40	7 8	9 42	1110	10 0	10e8	10e8	12T37	2 55	1 50	..	5 10	5 0	7K40	9 17	10 5	..	..
Leeds (Central) ,,	7 50	9 0	..	1010	1131	..	10e57	10e57	12T55	3 10	..	3 55	5 30	..	8K30	..	1023	10A55	10J35
LONDON (Marylebone) ar.	..	..	1 10	..	..	2 55	..	..	..	..	6 38	..	..	9 52	a.m.	a.m. 4 20	a.m.	a.m.	a.m.
(King's Cross) ,,	11L20	1 3	..	1 47	2 15	..	3 0	3 47	4T50	6 55	..	7 5	9f25	..	3 15	..	3C45	5 55	5 15

‡ "The Queen of Scots."

SUNDAYS.

	R		P	R	R	R	
	a.m	p.m	p.m ¶	p.m	p.m	p.m	p.m
Bradford (Exchange) .. d.	1035	1235	3 10	3 55	5 20	6 20	9 45
Leeds (Central) ,,	11 0	1 10	3 35		5 42	6 45	1020
LONDON (Marylebone) ar.	..	..	..	1020	..	..	a.m
(King's Cross) ,,	3 45	5 55	7 0	..	1012	1045	3 56

¶ "The Harrogate Sunday Pullman."

A Leeds (City) via York. **B** Buffet Car whole or part of journey. **C** On Sundays arrives King's Cross **3.50** a.m. **D** Saturdays only and not after 2nd Sept. **a** On Saturdays arrives Bradford **6.27** p.m. **F** Sats. only and not after 9th Sept. **G** "West Riding Limited," Saturdays excepted. Does not run on 4th to 7th Aug. Supplementary charges. Limited seating accommodation; seats bookable in advance. **H** Saturdays excepted; also runs on 16th and 23rd Sept. **J** On Wednesdays leaves **11.0** p.m. **K** On Saturdays leaves Bradford **9.5** and Leeds **9.30** p.m. **L** On Mondays and Saturdays arrives King's Cross 11.26 a.m. **M** On Saturdays from 15th July to 26th August inclusive, runs 6 minutes later. **N** Buffet Car Tuesdays, Wednesdays and Thursdays only, from Peterborough. **P** Pullman Cars only. Supplementary charges **R** Rest. Cars whole or part of journey. **SO** Saturdays only. **SX** Saturdays excepted. **T** On Saturdays leaves Bradford (Exchange) 12.18, Leeds (Central) 12.35, and arrives King's Cross 4.33 p.m. **U** Depart King's Cross 1.33 p.m. **Y** Pullman Cars from Wakefield (**SX**), Leeds (**SO**). *b* On Fridays and Saturdays depart 5.55 p.m. *c* On Fridays arrives **10.19,** and on Saturdays **10.10** p.m. *d* On 6th Aug. departs **6.0** p.m. *e* On Saturdays departs Bradford 10.40 and 11.4 a.m. *f* On Fridays arrives **9.33** p.m.

The times from 6 p.m. to 5.59 a.m. inclusive are printed in dark type, thus **12.9** meaning 9 min. aft. midn.

LONDON AND NORTH EASTERN RAILWAY.

Train Service between LONDON (King's Cross and Marylebone) and LEICESTER, NOTTINGHAM, SHEFFIELD and MANCHESTER.

WEEKDAYS.						R	R	B	R	R SX	R SO	Z R SO	U	SX	Q R	R	R SO	R SX	R SO	R	Q	SO	Q	R	G
	a.m	a.m.	a.m.	a.m	a.m	a.m	a.m	a.m	a.m	a.m.	a.m.	a.m.	p.m	p.m.	p.m	p.m	p.m	p.m.	p.m	p.m	p.m	p.m	p.m	p.m	p.m
LONDON King's X dp.	1 10	..	4 45	5 2	..	7 25	..	8 45	..	10 15	10 21	10 28	11 30	11 30	12 5	..	1 20	1 40	1r50	..	2 40	3 0	3 50	4 0	4 45
LONDON Mary'bone ,,	..	2 32	..	..	6 40	..	8 45	..	10 0	..	..	..	..	..	..	12 15	..	..	..	3 20	..	..	..	..	..
Leicester (Central) .. arr	..	4 25	..	..	10 22	..	11 0	..	12 2	..	..	..	..	..	..	2 24	..	..	..	5 9	..		..	..	..
Nottingham (Victoria) ,,	..	5 7	8 41	9 48	—	10 34	11 32	12 20	12 30	1 5	1 5	2 23	3 41	3 41	3 41	2 5k	4 50	5 7	5 14	5 36	..	6 38	..	7 23	..
Sheffield (Victoria) .. ,,	6D20	5 56	8 43	—	..	10 46	12 23	12 42	1 21	2D49	2D15	2D15	—	4 38	4 20	3 50	—	5 26	5 31	6 26	7D13	—	7D37	8 13	8D24
Manchester (Lond. Rd) ,,	9V18	9V18	10C20		..	12C17	1 34	1C55	3 17	5g3	4QD14	4h14	..	5 5b	5CD57	5 3		7Cq45	7 19	7C45	—	..	—	9C50	9h50

WEEKDAYS.	R	B	R	R	SO	SX	R	SO		SX	SO
	p.m	p.m	p.m	p.m	p.m	p.m	p.m.	p.m	p.m	p.m	p.m
LONDON King's X dp.	..	..	5k50	..	..	..	7 15	..	8 25	..	..
LONDON Mary'bone ,,	4 55	5 0	..	6 20	6 25	6 26	..	7 30	..	10 5	11 0
Leicester (Central) .. arr	6 43	7 15	..	8 19	10 4	10 [illegible]	..	11 38	..	12 8	12 53
Nottingham (Victoria) ,,	7 11	7 49	8 52	8 48	11 43	11A20	10§13	12 15	1 46	12 53	..
Sheffield (Victoria) .. ,,	8 1	—	9 44	9 38	—	—	10 35	1 3[illegible]	1D9	1 55	2 10
Manchester (Lond. Rd.) ,,	9 50	..	11 9	11 9	..	..	—	—	—	3 35	3 29

SUNDAYS.		B	B	AA B	R	R	R	R	R	R	R		B	Y
	a.m	a.m	a.m	a.m	a.m	a.m	p.m.	p.m	p.m	p.m	p.m.	p.m	p.m.	p.m
LONDON King's Cross dep.	..	..	..	10 10	..	11 20	1 10	4 30	4 55	..	6b20	..	..	
LONDON Marylebone ,,	12 40	9 50	10 5	..	11 15	..	..	..	..	5 30	..	6 40	9 0	9 45
Leicester (Central) ...... arr.	3 24	11 56	12 24	..	1 25	..	..	..	..	7 40	..	10 25	11W33	12 13
Nottingham (Victoria) .. ,,	4 3	12 29	1 0	..	2 2	2 34	3 56	..	8 56	8 14		—	12W18	—
Sheffield (Victoria) ...... ,,	5 9	1 29	—	2 35	2 56	3†15	4 50	8 26	8 48	9 5	10D¶26	..	—	
Manchester (London Road) ,,	8 36			—	4C17	4C3[illegible]	7§18	—	10 10	10 17	—	..	..	..

A On Weds. arr. Nottingham (Vic.) **11.40** p.m. **AA** 3rd Sept. excepted. **B** Buffet Car whole or part of journey. **C** Central Station. **D** Via Doncaster. **E** On Weds. and Sats. leaves Nottingham (Vic.) **11.0** p.m. **F** On Sats. leaves Leicester (Central) 1.12 p.m. **G** "The Yorkshire Pullman," between King's Cross and Doncaster, sup. charges. **H** On Sats. leaves Nottingham 3.40 p.m. **J** Via Penistone and Doncaster. **K** Via Doncaster and Gainsboro'. **L** Via Retford and Lincoln. **MX** Mons. excepted. **P** Sats. only. Runs 15th July to 9th Sept. inclusive. **R** Rest. Cars whole or part of journey. **S** or **SO** Sats. only. **SX** Sats. excepted. **T** Not after 30th July. **U** Sats. only. Commences 9th Sept. **V** On Sats. until 2nd Sept., arr. Manchester (London Road) 8.46 a.m. **W** Commencing 6th Aug. arr. Leicester **11.13** p.m., Nottingham **11.50** p.m. **Y** Commences 6th Aug. **Z** Sats. only. Runs 15th July to 26th Aug. *b* On 6th Aug. dep. King's Cross **6.0** p.m. *e* Via Bottesford. *g* On Mons. and Fris. arr. Manchester 4.10 p.m. via Doncaster. *h* Manchester (Central) via Doncaster. *k* On Fris. and Sats. dep. King's Cross 5.55 p.m. *m* Manchester (Central). On Sats. dep. 9.33 a.m. *n* On Mons., Fris. and Sats. dep. 10 minutes later. *q* Commencing 11th Sept. arr. Manchester (London Road) **6.53** p.m. *r* Commencing 16th Sept. leaves King's Cross 1.40 p.m. † On 17th and 24th Sept. arr. Sheffield 3.42 and Manchester (Central) 5.23 p.m. § Manchester (Central). On 17th and 24th Sept. arr. Manchester (London Road) **8.57** p.m. via Doncaster. ¶ On 10th and 17th Sept. arr. Sheffield **9.58** p.m. via Doncaster.

 The times from 6 p.m. to 5.59 a.m. inclusive are printed in dark type, thus 12.9 meaning 9 min. aft. midn.

LONDON AND NORTH EASTERN RAILWAY.

Train Service between LONDON (King's Cross) and Marylebone, and LEICESTER, NOTTINGHAM, SHEFFIELD and MANCHESTER.

WEEKDAYS.	MX	MX			R	R	B	R	R	PR	Q	G	R	R	R SO	RSX	R	R	R	R	R	R	R		SX	SO	
	a.m	a.m	a.m	a.m	a.m	a.m	a.m	a.m	a.m.	a.m	a.m	a.m	a.m	a.m	a.m	a.m.	p m	p.m	p.m	p.m	p.m	p.m	p m	p.m	p.m	p.m	p.m.
Manchester (Lon. Rd.) d	..	1J40	..	1L40	..	5 25	..	8 20	8D20	..	..	9Dm25	10 3	..	11C22	11C22	..	2 20	..	3 50	3Cn10	3D50	5 0	7O25	‡..	..	10 30
Sheffield (Victoria) dep	1217	..	..	4K20	7 30	8 20	8 34	9 35	9D43	10D0	11 7	10D50	1121	1137	1247	1250	..	3 30	3D16	5 2	4 30	5D15	6 21	9D0	1110	1110	12MX17
Nottingham (Vic). ...,,	1 22	..	5 30	7 44	8 21	8 30	9 38	1027	..	..	1159	..	1213	1234	1C20	..	2 26	4 21	3H19	6 9	5 0	6 14	7 13	10E41	..	..	1 MX22
Leicester (Central) ,,	2 5	..	6 21	..	8 51	..	..	1057	..	..	1233	..	1247	1F20	..	..	..	4 49	..	6 44	..	..	7 43	..	..	..	2 MX 5
LONDON { Ma'y'b'nea	4 20	..	9 45	..	1040	..	..	1 10	..	..	2 42	..	2 55	4 57	..	..	..	6 38		9 0	..	..	9 52	a.m.	a.m	a.m	4 MX 20
LONDON { King's X ,,		7 25		1028		1120	1 3		1 30	1 47		3 0			4 33	4 50	5 35		6 55		9 13	9 25		3 15	3 45	3 50	

Train leaves Nottingham (Victoria) R10.24 a.m. arrives London (King's Cross) 1.15 p.m.

SUNDAYS.				Y	BY	BT	AA	R	R	R		R		R	B	R	R	B	
	a.m	a.m	a.m	a.m	a.m	a.m	a.m.	a.m	a.m	p.m	p m	p.m	p.m	p.m	p.m	p.m	p.m	p.m	p.m
Manchester (London Rd.) dep.	..	1D30	..	..	..	.	..	1020	..	12C15	12C15	..	..	4 50	-	5C30	5C30	..	9CJ5
Sheffield (Victoria) ...... ,,	1217	3D3	..	..	..	..	8D0	1138	11D57	2 0	1 46	3D25	..	6 15	..	6 41	7 0	6 55	9D25
Nottingham (Victoria) .. ,,	1 22	..	..	..	9 55	9 55	9 18	1212		2 58	2 29	..		6 15	7 10	7 34	..	7 54	9 48
Leicester (Central) ...... ,,	2 5	..	6 11	9 30	1032	1037	..	..	..	3 38	..	..	5 15	..	7 47	8 9	..	8 30	..
LONDON { Marylebone arr.	4 24	..	10 4	11 56	1251	1 3	..	..		5 45	..	..	9 2	..	10 3	1020	..	11 6	a.m
LONDON { King's Cross ,,		7 25					1 0	3 45	4 36		5 55	7 28		1012			1045		3 56

‡ On Saturdays 15th July to 19th August, leaves Manchester (London Road) 7.58 p.m.

FOR NOTES SEE PAGE 109.

The times on the LEFT are to be read DOWNWARDS, those on the RIGHT UPWARDS.

JULY 3rd TO SEPTEMBER 23rd, 1939.

WEEKDAYS. LONDON AND NORTH EASTERN RAILWAY Via HARWICH. WEEKDAYS.

				MO	SX	SO	PV			SX	SO
	a.m	a.m	a.m	a.m	a.m	a.m	a.m	a.m.	a.m.	a.m	p.m
LIVERPOOL ST. .. dep.	5 30	..	6 55	8R15	8 45	8 45	10 0	10 20	11B30	12R33	12R33
Chelmsford .... ,,	5 50	..	8 9	9R5	9 45	9 45	"Flushing Continental"	11J9	12B17	..	12T33
Colchester .... ,,	6 50	7 48	9 0	9 45	1026	1026		11tD7	12B55	1 50	1 54
Yarmouth (South T'n) ,,	..	..	7 30	..	8R30	8R30		9SX53	10SR15	..	..
Lowestoft (Central) ,,	..	..	6B44	..	8R30	8R30		10SX0	10X3	..	..
Norwich (Thorpe) .. ,,	..	..	8R5	..	8 52	8 52		10SX28	12KR0	..	..
Ipswich .... ,,	6 24	8 7	9 9	..	1026	1038		11SX50	1 16	..	..
Manningtree .... ,,	7 6	8 27	9 31	10 0	1049	11 0		12 10	1 38	2 3	2 7
Parkeston Quay .... arr.	7a29	8 50	9 54	1021	11W00	11W21	11c30	12 34	2 1	2 18	2 22
Harwich Town ...... ,,	7a39	8 58	10 2	1028	1122	1133	11n50	12 43	2 10	2 27	2 31

							SO	SX		Q	GG		CP	F	
	p.m	p.m	p.m	p.m	p.m	p.m	p.m	p.m	p.m	p.m	p.m	p.m	p.m	p.m	p.m
LIVERPOOL ST. .. dep.	2 15	3 43	..	..	..	5 42	5 42	5 42	6B43	..	..	7R42	8 15	8 30	..
Chelmsford .... ,,	3 2	4 28	..	4 36	4 36	6E34	6 30	6 34	7B26	..	..	8R27	"Hook Continental"	"Antwerp Continental"	..
Colchester .... ,,	3 50	5 6	..	5 22	5 32	7E10	7 11	7 15	7 59	..	..	8R55			..
Yarmouth (South T'n) ,,	12b51	..	2f35	3 30	3 30	..	4Z4	..	6R35	..	..				7g30
Lowestoft (Central) ,,	12d37	..	2f33	3 33	3 33	..	3L47	..	6R38	..	..				7g33
Norwich (Thorpe) .. ,,	2 17	..	3 42	4 2	4 2	..	4 55	..	6R42	..	..				7 23
Ipswich .... ,,	3 27	..	5 15	5 57	5 57	..	7 10	6 20	8 11	8 40	8 42				9 16
Manningtree .... ,,	4 13	5 21	..	6 20	6 20	..	7 36	7 40	8 33	..	..	9 19			9h50
Parkeston Quay .... arr.	4D38	5 38	5 57	6 41	6 41	..	7 59	8 1	8 54	9 10	9 12	9 34	9 45	9 57	10h12
Harwich Town ...... ,,	4 46	5 47	6 6	6 48	6 48	7E38	8 7	8 9	9 2	9 22	9 25	9 45	—	1014	10h20

Trains also leave Liverpool St. ("The Scandinavian") at 4.10 p.m. U, arrive Parkeston Quay 5.45 p.m., Harwich Town 5.57 p.m.; Liverpool Street 4.13 p.m. CC, arrive Parkeston Quay West 5.50 p.m.; also Ipswich 4.10 p.m. FF and 8.47 p.m. Q, arrive Parkeston Quay 4.55, 9.17 p.m., and Harwich Town 5.4, 9.29 p.m.

	CP	CF			Q						SO	SX
	a.m	a.m	a.m	a.m	a.m	a.m	a.m	a.m.	a.m	a.m.	a.m.	a.m
Harwich Town ....dep.	G	..	7 6	7 6	..	7 35	8 28	8 47	9 54	10 8	10 17	1120
Parkeston Quay ...... ,,	6 20	7 0	7 13	7Rj25	7R30	7 42	8 37	8 57	10 3	10 17	10 24	1127
Manningtree .... arr	"Hook Continental"	"Antwerp* Continental"	7 36	..	..	..	9 1	9 18	1026	..	..	1150
Ipswich .... ,,			..	7 58	8 9	..	—	9 38		10 52	10 58	12 9
Norwich (Thorpe) .. ,,			..	1038	1038	..	..	11J11	..R	12SX30	12mB50	..
Lowestoft (Central) ,,			..	10847	10847	..	..	11R40	..	1SX22	1 29	2w15
Yarmouth (South T'n) ,,			..	1056	1056	..	..	11R07	..	1SX23	1 32	2w22
Colchester .... ,,			8 1	—	—	8 8	..	9 34	11 2	—	—	1219
Chelmsford .... ,,			8 38	..	..	8 52	..	10 6	1156	..	..	1R22
LIVERPOOL STREET ,,	8 2	8 41	—	..	..	9 33	..	1055	1245	..	..	2 0

	SO	SX	SO				G				
	a.m	p.m	p.m	p.m	p.m	p.m	p.m.	p.m	p.m	p.m.	p.
Harwich Town ....dep.	1130	1210	1215	3 10	4 23	5 15	"Scandinavian" leaves Parkeston Q'y during afternoon after arrival of steamer.	5 40	7 34	7 34	"Flushing Continental." 8 42
Parkeston Quay ...... ,,	1137	1219	1224	3 17	4 32	5 22		5 47	7 42	7W55	8 49
Manningtree .... arr	1159	1243	1248	3 40	4 54	5 44		6 10	8 4	8M16	9 11
Ipswich .... ,,	1223	1 17	1 11	4H25	..	6 5		7E51	8 34	..	9 29
Norwich (Thorpe) .. ,,	..	3R9	3 13	6R4	..	7R45		8YN50	..	..	2 A 5
Lowestoft (Central) ,,	2B23	3L52	4LT3	6B9	..	8R5		..	..	..	10p51
Yarmouth (South T'n) ,,	2B19	4R13	4 22	6B7	..	8R2		10YNZ6		.	10p51
Colchester .... ,,	—	1 5	1 16	4 5	5 8	—		8D36	8R43	8C43	9 5
Chelmsford .... ,,	..	2 4	2 4	5 2	5 53	..		7D9	9R20	9C20	10 45
LIVERPOOL STREET ,,	..	3 0	3 1	5x48	6 32	..		7D52	10R0	9 30	11 40

Trains also leave Harwich Town 1.45 p.m., Parkeston Quay 1.54 p.m., arr. Colchester 2.19 p.m., Liverpool St. 3.42 p.m. Also Parkeston Quay West Station 11.20 a.m. HHC, arrive Liverpool Street 1.4 p.m.

A Sun. morns. excepted. **B** Buffet Car. **C** Conveys passengers to and from the Continent only. **D** Buffet Car Sats. only. **E** On Sats. runs 4 mins. earlier. **F** Pullman Rest. Car attached to this train. **G** After 11th Sept. does not run on Mons. **GG** Tues., Weds. and Thurs. only. Commencing 15th Sept. runs every weekday. **H** On Sats. arr. Ipswich 4.3. p.m. **HH** Runs 3rd, 7th, 11th, 17th, 21st, 25th, 29th July; 4th, 8th, 12th, 16th, 21st, 25th, 29th Aug.; 4th, 11th and 18th Sept. **J** On Sats. runs 5 mins. later. **K** By "East Anglian" to Ipswich; limited accommodation. On Sats. dep. Norwich 10.35 a.m. by ordinary train without Rest. Car. **L** Via Norwich. **M** Calls when required to set down passengers from the Continent only. **MO** Mons. only. **N** Rest. Car except on Sats. **P** Rest. and Pullman Cars attached to this train. **Q** Mons., Fris. and Sats. only and not after 11th Sept. **R** Rest. Car. **S** Dep. Yarmouth (Vauxhall) by "East Anglian" from Norwich to Ipswich; limited accommodation. On Sats. dep. Yarmouth (South Town) 10.0 am. **SO** Sats. only. **SX** Sats. excepted. **T** Not after 9th Sept. **U** Pullman Car attached to this train. **V** On Sats. conveys passengers to and from the Continent only. **W** Parkeston Quay West Station. **X** Via Norwich by "East Anglian" from Norwich to Ipswich; limited accommodation. On Sats. leaves Lowestoft Central 10.0 a.m. via Beccles. **Y** Except on Sats. By "East Anglian" from Ipswich to Norwich; limited accommodation. **Z** Yarmouth (Vauxhall) via Norwich (Thorpe). *a* On Mons., Fris. and Sats. until 11th Sept. arrives Parkeston Quay 7.34 a.m. and Harwich Town 7.44 a.m. *b* Yarmouth (Vauxhall) via Norwich. On Sats. leaves at 1.0 p.m. *c* Parkeston Quay West Station. On Sats. arrives 11.35 a.m. **CC** Runs 3rd, 7th, 13th, 17th, 21st, 25th, 29th July; 4th, 8th, 12th, 17th, 21st, 25th, 29th Aug., and 5th and 12th Sept. *d* Via Norwich. On Sats. leaves 12.26 p.m. *f* On Sats. leaves Yarmouth and Lowestoft 3.10 p.m. *g* Commencing 4th Sept. leaves Yarmouth **6.55** p.m. (on Fris. **7.0** p.m.), and Lowestoft **7.3** p.m. (On Fris. **7.7** p.m.) *h* On Fris. and Sats. until 8th Sept. runs 6 mins. later. *j* On Mons., Fris. and Sats., until 11th Sept., leaves Parkeston Quay 7.20 a.m. *k* From 29th July to 9th Sept. arrives Yarmouth 11.20 a.m. *m* On 16th and 23rd Sept. arr. Norwich 12.30 p.m. *n* Sats. excepted. *p* Commencing 4th Sept. arr. Lowestoft **11.9** and Yarmouth **11.10** p.m. *s* On Sats. arrives Lowestoft 10.53 a.m. *t* On Sats. leaves Colchester 11.50 a.m. *w* On Weds. runs 5 mins. later. *x* On Sats. arrives Liverpool Street 5.42 p.m.

Via NEWHAVEN AND DIEPPE.

1 2 3 A	1 2 3 Exp	1 2 3 Exp	Mls.		1 2 3 Exp	1 2 3 Exp
9 30	10 5	2020		dep. LONDON (Victoria) ....arr.	1812	6 5
..	1024	2038	10	,, East Croydon ....arr	1753	5 43
1052	1124	2144		arr. Newhaven Harbour ....dep.	1650	4 42
1115	11†45	22† 15	56	dep. ,, ,, ...arr.	1615	4 5
1425	1455	2 5	120	arr. Dieppe Maritime ....dep.	13†5	0†15
1445	1524	2¶51		dep. ,, ,, ... arr.	1246	2325
1732	1745	5*23	224	arr. Paris–St. Lazare...... dep.	1029	20¶57
..	18‡5	5‡50		dep. ,, ,, ... arr.	10‡0	19†50
..	18‡ 20	6 ‡ 5	..	arr. Paris–Est .... dep.	9‡20	20‡0
..	18‡ 45	6‡25	..	arr. Paris–Lyon .... dep.	9‡40	19‡ 25

A Saturdays until Sept. 9, also Friday Aug. 4.

† Boat may leave up to 15 mins. earlier when possible ‡ By motor bus. * Passengers may remain in their carriages at Paris (St. Lazare) until 7.30, (except on Aug. 14, 15 & Sats. & Suns. until Oct. 1). ¶ 1, 2 & 3 cl. Couchettes between Dieppe aud Paris and *v.v.*

PULLMAN BUFFET CARS, London to Newhaven and *v.v.* Restaurant Cars Dieppe-Paris (St. Lazare) *v.v.* on DAY service.

☞ For tables of principal services beyond Paris, *see pp.* 118 to 125.

LONDON, DIEPPE, ROUEN, BORDEAUX.

1 2 3 A		Mls.		1 2 3 A	1 2 3 G
10 5	2020	0	dep. LONDON (Victoria) arr.	1812	6 5
1145	2215	56	,, Newhaven .... ,,	1615	4 5
1455	2 5	130	arr. } DIEPPE (Mar.) { dep.	13 5	0 15
1531	6a10		dep. } DIEPPE (Mar.) { arr.	1255	0 5
1631	7a10	168	arr. } Rouen (R.D.) { dep.	12 0	2321
1638	7c15		dep. } Rouen (R.D.) { arr.	1132	2319
1823	8c48	250	arr. Laigle .... p. 241 dep.	..	22 1
1922	9c34	293	,, Alencon ...... ,,	8 53	2120
2010	10c13	328	arr. } Le Mans. .. { dep.	8 13	2043
2031	1046	..	dep. } Le Mans. .. { arr.	8 6	2033
21 5	..	358	arr. Sablé (*p.* 247) ....dep.	7 28	..
2143	1133	388	,, Angers .... ,,	6 49	1926
2240	1233	442	arr. Nantes (Orleans).. dep.	5 45	1832
0 20	1242	..	dep. Nantes (Orleans) (*p* 246) a.	4 52	1741
1 41	1422	490	arr. La Roche-sur-Yon . . dep.	3 33	1638
..	15 9	512	,, Les Sables d'Olonne ,,	..	1554
3 24	..	553	,, La Rochelle .... ,,	1 44	1516
4 48	..	599	,, Saintes .... ,,	0 19	1410
7 0	..	623	,, Royan ...... ,,	2224	1315
7 18	..	678	arr. BORDEAUX (St. Jean) dp.	2210	1234

A 1, 2 & 3 cl. cars and Couchettes, Dieppe–Bordeaux and *v.v.* **B** 1, 2 & 3 cl. Auto-Rail Car Rouen-Le Mans. Supplement payable by 3 cl. passengers. **G** Auto-Rail 1. 2 & 3 cl. Le Mans–Rouen, (Le Mans–Dieppe on Suns. & Fete Days). *c* Auto-Rail; limited accommodation (3rd cl. passengers pay small supplement).

Via SOUTHAMPTON AND HAVRE.

From London—Daily except Suns., July 7–Sept. 13; Mondays, Wednesdays and Fridays from Sept. 15.
From Paris—Daily except Suns., July 8–Sept. 14; Tuesdays, Thurdays and Saturdays from Sept. 16.

Mls.	1 2 3 cl.				1 2 3 cl.
..	21* 0	dep.	London (Waterloo)	arr.	9a2
78	22*51	arr.	Southampton (Docks)	dep.	7*5
	23 15	dep.	,, ,,	arr.	6 30
198	6 20	arr.	Havre (Quay)	dep.	2330
..	6 40	dep.	,,	arr.	23 5
..	7 25	dep.	Havre (Town)	arr.	2230
252	8 23	arr.	Rouen (R.D.)	dep.	2127
339	9 49	arr.	Paris (St. Lazare)	dep.	20 0
..	10 10	dep.	Paris (St. Lazare)	arr.	1950
..	10 20	arr.	Paris (Quai d'Orsay) } Auto Bus	dep.	1940
..	10 45	arr.	Paris (Lyon) } Auto Bus	dep.	1925
..	10 25	arr.	Paris (Est) } Auto Bus	dep.	1925

Rest. Car—Havre—Paris and *v.v.* Supper Car—Waterloo—Southampton.
Breakfast Car—Southampton—Waterloo. CABINS.—For particulars as to Cabins, *see page* 77.
* 1 & 3 cl. only between London Southampton and *v.v.* Ordinary seats can be reserved in advance between London and Southampton on payment of 1/-. *a* 9.7 on Sundays.

via CALAIS, BOULOGNE or DUNKERQUE.

Daily (Sundays included), except where otherwise shown.

1 2	1 2 3		1 2		luxe	1 2	1 2 3	1 2 ‡	1 2 3	mls.				1 2 ¶	1 2 3	luxe	1 2	1 2	1 2 ¶			1 2 3	1 2	1 2 3
P	P		P		P	P	P	P	B			LONDON—		P	P	P	P	P	P			P	P	B
9 0	9 0	..	11 0		11 0	14 0	14 0	1630	22 0	0	dep.	VICTORIA b	arr.	15G30	1720	1720	1720	1720	1855	..	..	23J0	23J0	9 10
1042	1042	..	..		..	..	..	18 9	R	73	ar.	FOLKEST'N	dp	..	1544	1544	1544	1544	..	..	..	21J20	21J20	R
1055	1055	..	..		..	..	..	1825		..	dp	HARBOUR b	ar.	..	1515	1515	1515	1515	..	..	..	2050	2050	
..	..	..	1235		1235	1535	1535	..	2337	78	ar.	DOVER	dp	13G55	..	..	..	..	1720	..	..	..	..	7 20
..	..	..	1255		1255	1555	1555	..	..	..	dp	MARINE b	ar.	1320	..	..	..	..	1655	..	..	..	..	
..	..	..	..		..	..	..	..	..	..	ar.	DOVER	dp	..	..	..	..	..	..	..	..	..	..	..
..	..	1230	..		..	..	..	..	0 35	..	dp	(Ferry berth)	ar.	..	..	..	..	..	..	18 0	1830	..	..	6 15
..	..	..	1410		1410	1710	1710	..	..	103	ar.	CALAIS b	dp	12 5	..	..	..	..	1540	..	..	..	..	..
		D																		C	D			
..	..	..	1430	1450	1430	1735	18 0	..	..	..	dp	(Marit.)	ar.	1141	..	..	..	..	1523	..	..	..	..	..
..	..	1630	..	..	..	..	..	..	4 30	..	ar.	DUNKERQUE	dp	..	..	..	..	..	..	14 0	1430	..	..	2 0
..	..	..	..	..	..	..	..	..	5 15	..	dp	(Ferry berth)	ar.	..	..	..	..	..	..	..	..	..	..	1 30
..	..	..	..	..	..	..	..	..	5 33	..	ar.	DUNKERQUE	dp	..	..	..	..	..	Paris-London Midday Rapide	..	..	..	..	1 12
..	..	..	..	..	..	..	..	..	5 34	..	dp		ar.	..	..	..	..	..		..	..	..	..	1 11
..	..	..	..	..	..	..	18 5	..	..	..	ar.	CALAIS	dp	..	..	..	..	..		..	..	..	..	..
..	..	..	..	..	..	..	1813	..	..	..	dp	(Ville)	ar.	..	..	..	..	..		..	..	..	..	..
1225	1225	..	Golden Arrow.	..	..	..	..	1955	..	..	ar.	BOULOGNE	dp	..	1345	1345	1345	1345		..	..	1920	1920	..
1255	A	..		..	..	..	..	2020	..	..	dp	b (Mar.)	ar.	..	1230	13H16	13H16	13 5		..	..	1848	19 5	..
13 0	1316	..		..	..	18†10	19 5	E	S	..	ar.	BOULOGNE	dp	11†7	1225	Golden Arrow.	..	13 0		..	..	1843	19 0	..
13 1	1339	..		..	..	18†11	1915			..	dp	(Ville)	ar.	11†5	1221		..	1259		..	..	1842	1859	S
1324	14 3	..	..	..	..	..	1938	2049	..	..	ar.	ETAPLES	dp	..	1158		..	..		..	..	1818	1839	
..	1531	..	..	..	..	E	2112	..	..	207	ar.	Amiens b	dp	..	1020		..	..	E	..	..	1641	E	..
..	1536	..	..	..	..		2122	..	..		dp		ar.	..	1015		..	..		..	..	1624		..
1548	1734	..	1744	1810	1744	21 0	23 5	2311	9 0	287	ar	PARIS	dp	8 20	8 33	1030	1030	..	1215	..	..	15 0	1625	2150
..	..	..	..	1820	1753	2111	..	..	..		dp	(NORD) b	ar.	6 59	..	..	..	..	..	..	..	..	..	..
..	..	..	..	1855	1825	2133	..	..	..	290	ar.	PARIS (LYON) b	dp	6 35	..	..	..	9 46	..	..	..	..	..	..

A 13.30 from July 1 to Oct. 2. **B** 1 & 2 cl. Sleep. Cars from London to Paris and v.v.; supplements including Reservation Fee and Sleep. Car Conductor's gratuity), 1 cl. 28/-, 2 cl. 22/6. Also 1, 2 & 3 cl. Through Carriages between London and Dover, and Dunkerque and Paris. **C** Sats. only to Aug. 26. **D** Daily. **E** 1 cl. Pullman Cars Calais or Boulogne-Paris and v.v. **F** Daily (except Sats.) **G** On Sats. until Sept. 23 dep. Dover Marine 4.4, arr. London (Victoria) 15.50. **H** 13.10 from Sept. 1. **J** On Suns. until Sept. 24, dep. Folkestone Harbour 21.25, arr. London (Victoria) 23.10. **P** Pullman Cars, supplement, 3/6 over 1 cl. fare. **R** Refreshment Car. **S** Buffet Car (for Sleep. Car passengers only). † Boulogne (Tintilleries Station). ‡ 1, 2 & 3 cl. London-Boulogne. ¶ 1, 2 & 3 cl. Calais-London. *b* Buffets.

Corridor Coaches vestibuled to the Pullman Cars, with special Restaurant facilities for passengers of all classes, run in the boat trains between Victoria and Dover or Folkestone (with the exception of services **B** above). **Restaurant Cars.**—Calais, 14.50 and 17.35; Boulogne-Paris, 12.55 and 20.20; Paris-Boulogne, 10.30 and 16.25; Paris-Calais, 8.20 and 12.15. Seats of all classes can be reserved in boat trains of the Southern Railway. Charges: Ordinary seats 1/-; Pullman seats (1st class) 3/6. Seats can also be reserved in advance between Calais, Boulogne or Dunkerque and Paris in connection with the services from London on payment of 2/-. **Steamers.**—The fast turbine steamers "Canterbury," "Côte d'Argent," "Côte d'Azur," "Maid of Kent," "Isle of Thanet," "Maid of Orleans" and "Biarritz" work the services between Dover-Calais and Folkestone-Boulogne. The Ferry steamers "Twickenham Ferry," "Hampton Ferry" and "Shepperton Ferry," perform the services between Dover and Dunkerque. For Private Cabins see particulars on page 77. Luggage registerd to Paris (Nord) is examined on arrival. On the homeward journey, luggage registered to London is examined at Victoria. Sleep. Car passengers by the London-Paris Ferry Service (see Columns **B** above) have their **hand baggage** examined in the Sleep. Car just before arrival in Paris. In the reverse direction the **hand baggage** of such passengers is examined in the train on arrival at Victoria. Sleep. Car passengers' Passports will be examined in the train before arrival in Paris, and at Victoria in the return direction.

☞ **See page 484 for announcement regarding "Golden Arrow" 1 & 2 cl. Pullman Service between London and Paris.**

TO MARSEILLES AND THE RIVIERA.

NOTE.—For restrictions regarding use of these trains for short distances, *see p.* 258.

See p. 112				123			12		12 luxe	12 P		12				12
LONDON—																
Victoria *b* ..dep.	..	..		22 0		..	9 0	..	11 0	11 0		11 0			..	14 0
Dover Pier .... „	..	..		..		..	..	..	1255	1255		1255			..	1555
Calais Pier *b* .. „	..	..		¶		..	..	..	1430	1430		1450			..	1735
Boulogne Quay „	..	..		..		..	1255	..	..	..					..	..
Paris (Nord) *b* .. arr.	..	..		9 0		..	1548	..	1744	1744		1810			..	21 0
Paris (Nord) ....dep.	..	..		..		..	Drv	..	1753	1753		1823			..	2111
Paris (Lyon) .... arr.	..	..		Drive across		..	acrs	..	1825	1825		1855			..	2133
	123	123	12	12	123	123	123	12	12	123	12	123	123	123	123	123
	A	H	PP	C	I	H	J	D	L	G	F	W	E	T		K
Page 259. PARIS (Lyon) *b* dep.	8 0	8 35	1015	12 0	13 0	14 0	17 0	18 0	20 0	2040	2050	21 5	2115	2125	Fr Strasbourg	2310
Dijon *b*.......... „	12 9	1353	1346	1521	1658	1913	2055	2151	0 6	0 48	0 58	1 23	1 38	1 51		3 50
Macon *b* .... „	1344	1550	..	..	1827	2120	2230	..	..	..						5 48
Lyons arr.	1438	17 3	1544	1720	192[illegible]	2230	23 23	2358	2 29	3 11	3 21	3 55	4 12	4 28		7 0
(Perrache) *b* dep.	1452	18 6	1549	1727	1935	2335	23 40	0 20	2 35	3 17	3 27	4 11	4 25	4 40	7 15	1010
Avignon *b* ...... arr.	1737	2158	18 8	1942	2214	3 36	2 38	3 9	5 19	6 5	6 12	7 21	7 30	7 56	9 59	1259
Tarascon *b* ...... „	..	..	..	..	..	4 14	..	..	..	..		7 43		.	1019	..
Page 255. Avignon ......dep.	1749	↓	Winter only.	1952	2227	↓	3 48	↓	..	..	Limited Train.	7 26	Daily except Thurs., Marseilles-Joliette arr. 9.15.	↓	10 2	1315
Tarascon ...... „	18 9			2012	2247		4 8		..	..		7 47			1034	1345
Nimes .... arr.	1836			2040	2314		4 36		..	..		8 15			11 3	1413
Sète *b* ...... arr.	1952			..	..		5 55		..	..		9 38			1228	1531
dep	20 2			..	..		6 4		..	..		9 49			1234	1540
Narbonne...... arr.	21 9			..	..		7 6		..	..		1052			1332	1615
Cerbere *b* .. arr.	2256			..	..		9 21		..	..		1318			1527	1852
dep	..			..	..		..		..	..		..			..	..
BARCELONA *b* arr.§	..	↓		..	..	↓	..	↓	..	..		..		↓	..	..
Page 264. Tarascon ....dep.	..	..	..	..		4 19	..	..	..	..	..	..		..	1027	
MARSEILLES *b* (St. Charles) arr.	1917	0 37	1929	21 5 Z	2345	6 21	4 29	4 57	7 0	7 40	7 53	..		9 55	1150	1445
dep.	1940	0 59	1934	2115	0 59	7 15	4 44	5 12	7 5	8 9	7 59	..		1015	1235	15 0
Toulon *b* .... arr.	2044	2 7	2024	22 1	2 7	8 15	5 42	6 10	8 3	9 37	8 57	..		1124	1331	1559
Hyeres, P.L.M. arr. (*page* 263)	2121	..	2121	..	6 18	8 53	6 18	7 32	8 53	1057	..	..		1220	1423	1628
Toulon *b* ....dep.	2049	2 17	2026	22 2	2 17	8 23	5 48	6 15	8 7	..	9 1	..		1134	1336	1614
Les Arcs *b* ...... arr.	2146	3 26	..	..	3 26	9 22	6 46	..	..	..	.	..		1241	1433	1712
St. Raphael...... „	2211	3 53	2128	2259	3 53	9 46	7 12	7 32	9 21	..	1015	..		13 8	1458	1736
Cannes .... „	2238	4 37	2155	2324	4 37	1023	7 42	8 0	9 50	..	1045	..		1339	1527	18 4
Grasse (*p.* 263) „	..	6 30	..	..	6 30	1135	9 25	9 25	1135	..	1135	..		1430	1620	..
Juan les Pins.... „	2256	5 3	..	..	5 3	1042	..	8 18	..	..		..		14 1	1541	1820
NICE *b* ...... arr.	2325	5 35	2226	2350	5 35	1112	8 20	8 45	1028	..	1123	..		1430	1610	1850
dep	2340	6 0	2232	..	6 0	1140	8 28	8 59	1034	..	1131	..		1445	1620	1859
Beaulieu .... „	2355	6 15	2242	..	6 15	1155	8 39	9 13	1045	..	1145	..		1458	1634	1915
Monaco .... arr.	0 9	6 31	2255	..	6 31	1211	8 49	9 28	1059	..	1158	..		1511	1647	1933
Monte Carlo .. „	0 13	6 37	23 0	..	6 37	1216	8 53	9 33	11 4	..	12 3	..		1518	1650	1939
Mentone........ „	0 27	6 50	231[illegible]	..	6 50	1229	9 4	9 47	1114	..	1216	..		1531	17 2	1953
Vintimille *b c* G. tm. a	0 41	7 8	..	..	7 8	1246	9 19	..	1129	..	..	..		1548	1718	2014
p. 299. Etna d.	5 25	8 50	..	..	8 50	14 0	1053	..	1250	..	..	..		16 0	1828	2132
Bordighera	5 34	8 57	..	..	8 57	14 8	11 0	..	13 0	..	..	..		1610	1838	2141
Ospedaletti	5 42	9 5	..	..	9 5	1417	11 8	..	13 8	..	..	..		1619	1850	2150
San Remo ...... arr.	5 48	9 11		..	9 11	1423	1114		1314	..	..	..		1626	1857	2157

A 1, 2 and 3 cl. cars Paris-Vintimille, Rest. car Paris-St. Raphael and v.v.; 1, 2 and 3 cl. cars Paris-Grenoble via Lyons and v.v.
C Aerodynamic Train. 1 and 2 cl. cars and Rest. car Paris-Marseilles and v.v.
D 1 and 2 cl. Sleeping cars, 1 cl. Couchettes, and 1 and 2 cl. cars Paris-Mentone; Rest. car Paris-Lyons and v.v.
E 1 cl. Couchettes and 1, 2 and 3 cl. cars and Rest. car Paris-Marseilles and v.v.
F 1 and 2 cl. cars, 1 cl. Couchettes-Toilette and Lits-Salons, 2 cl. Couchettes Paris-Mentone. 1 and 2 cl. cars Calais-Mentone. Rest. car Avignon-Mentone.
G 1 and 2 cl. Sleeping cars, 1 cl. Couchettes-Toilette, 2 cl. Couchettes Paris-Marseilles; 1, 2 and 3 cl. cars Paris-Toulon. **H** 1, 2 and 3 cl. cars Paris-Vintimille. **I** 1, 2 and 3 cl. cars and Rest. car Paris-Marseilles and v.v.
J 1, 2 and 3 cl. Paris-Vintimille and v.v., and Rest. car Paris-Lyons and v.v.
K 1, 2 and 3 cl. cars Paris-Lyons and Lyons-Vintimille; return Vintimille-Lyons and Lyons-Paris. 1 and 2 cl. Sleeping car, 1 cl. Couchettes Paris-Lyons and v.v.
L Calais-Paris-Mediterranean Express Train de luxe daily.
M 1, 2 and 3 cl. cars, 1 cl. Lits-Salons and Couchettes Sète-Paris; 1, 2 and 3 cl. cars Narbonne-Paris.
¶ Via Dover and Dunkerque. ‡ 1 and 3 c*l*. only. For other notes, see page 114.

COOK'S TOURIST MAP
OF
NORTHERN FRANCE, BELGIUM,
AND THE RHINE

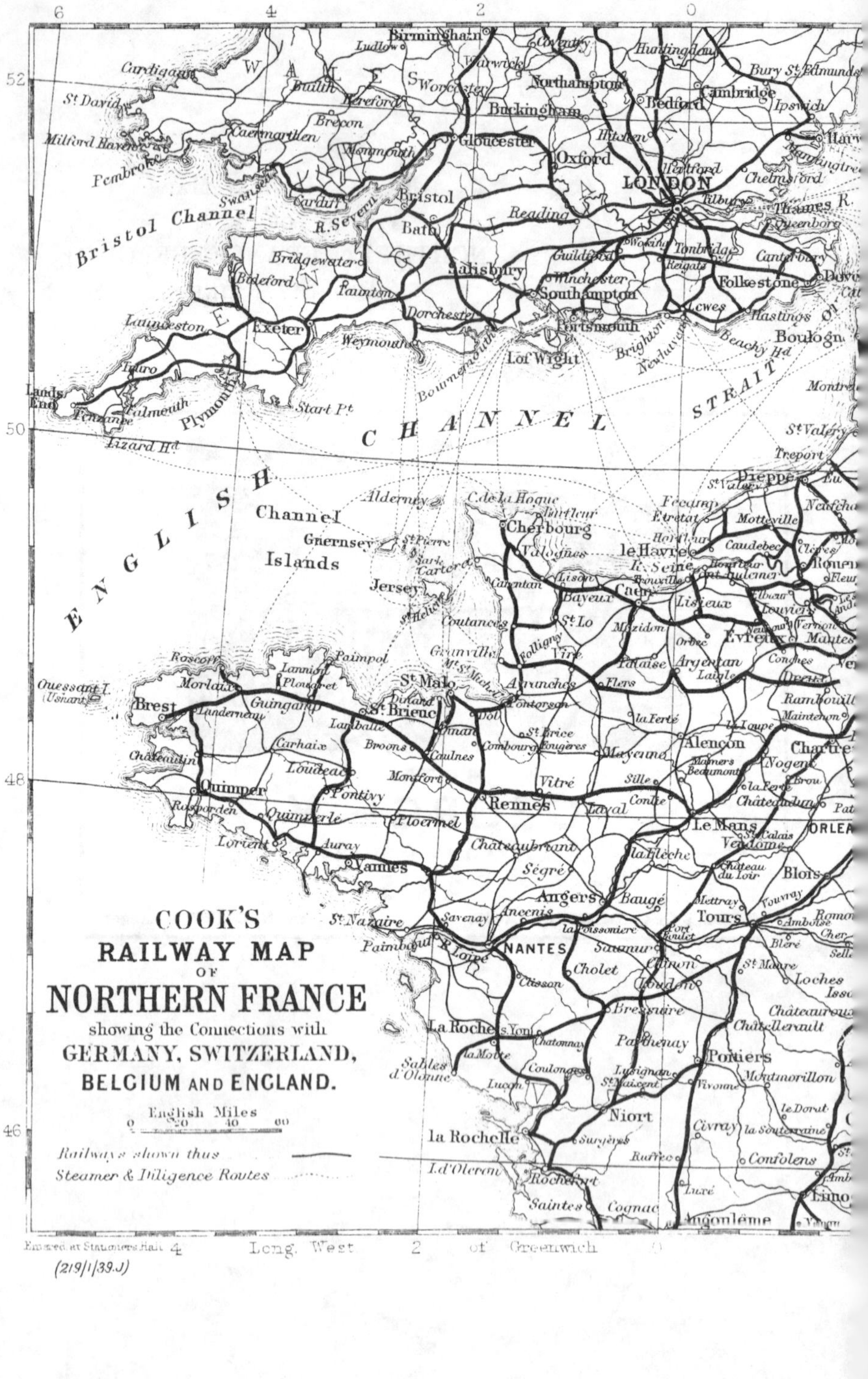

COOK'S
RAILWAY MAP
OF
NORTHERN FRANCE
showing the Connections with
GERMANY, SWITZERLAND,
BELGIUM AND ENGLAND.
English Miles
0 20 40 60
Railways shown thus
Steamer & Diligence Routes
ENGLISH CHANNEL
STRAIT
Bristol Channel
Channel Islands
WALES
ENGLAND
LONDON
Birmingham
Coventry
Huntingdon
Bury St. Edmunds
Cardigan
Warwick
Northampton
Cambridge
Ipswich
St. David's
Bedford
Buckingham
Milford Haven
Caermarthen
Brecon
Gloucester
Oxford
Hitchen
Pembroke
Hertford
Chelmsford
Swansea
Cardiff
Bristol
Reading
Tilbury
Thames R.
R. Severn
Bath
Queenborg
Bridgewater
Woking
Guildford
Tonbridge
Canterbury
Salisbury
Reigate
Bideford
Winchester
Southampton
Folkestone
Taunton
Launceston
Exeter
Dorchester
Portsmouth
Lewes
Hastings
Weymouth
Brighton
Newhaven
Boulogne
I. of Wight
Beachy Hd
Truro
Bournemouth
Lands End
Falmouth
Plymouth
Start Pt
Penzance
Lizard Hd
St. Valery
Treport
Alderney
C. de la Hogue
Dieppe
Barfleur
Fecamp
Etretat
Cherbourg
Motteville
Guernsey
St. Pierre
Valognes
le Havre
Caudebec
Honfleur
Rouen
Sark
Carteret
R. Seine
Jersey
Carentan
Lison
Trouville
Pont Audemer
Bayeux
Caen
Lisieux
St. Helier
St. Lo
Louviers
Coutances
Mezidon
Evreux
Granville
Orbec
Falaise
Argentan
Roscoff
Paimpol
Vire
Lannion
Plouaret
Morlaix
Mt. St. Michel
Avranches
Flers
Laigle
Ouessant I. (Usnant)
St. Malo
Pontorson
Brest
Guingamp
Dinard
St. Brieuc
Dol
la Ferté
Landerneau
Lamballe
Dinan
St. Brice
Carhaix
Broons
Caulnes
Combourg
Fougères
Mayenne
Alencon
Chateaulin
Loudeac
Montfort
Vitré
Sillé
Quimper
Pontivy
Rennes
Conlie
Rosporden
Quimperlé
Ploermel
Laval
Le Mans
Lorient
Auray
Chateaubriant
la Flèche
Vannes
Ségré
Angers
Baugé
St. Nazaire
Savenay
Ancenis
Tours
Paimbœuf
R. Loire
NANTES
Saumur
Cholet
Chinon
Clisson
Loudun
Bressuire
La Roche s. Yon
Chatonnay
Parthenay
Sables d'Olonne
la Motte
Poitiers
Coulonges
Lusignan
St. Maixent
Lucon
Niort
La Rochelle
Surgères
Civray
Ruffec
Confolens
Id'Oleron
Rochefort
Saintes
Cognac
Angoulême
Long. West 2 of Greenwich
Entered at Stationers Hall

(219/1/39.J)

See Map pages 162-163

ages 259-260

COOK'S TOURIST MAP
OF
NORTHERN FRANCE, BELGIUM,
AND THE RHINE

FROM THE RIVIERA AND MARSEILLES

For restrictions regarding use of these trains for short distances, *see p.* 258

NOTE. – Slp. Accom. Ex. fares *pp.* xlv.-lii.	1 2 3	1 2 3	1 2 3	1 2 3	1 2	1 2	1 2 3	1 2 3	1 2 3	1 2 3	1 2 3	1 2	1 2	1 2 3	1 2 3	1 2	1 2 3
	Auto Rail	Rap	Rap		Rap	Auto Rail	Ex;	Rap	Rap	Rap	Rap	Rap	luxe	Exp	Exp	Rap	Exp
(*p.* 299) San Remo .. dep		5 32	..	..	..		1015	..	..	..	1314	..	1552	1410	1842	..	2125
Ospedaletti ,,		5 41	..	..	..		1023	..	..	..	1321	..	16 0	1419	1849	..	2134
Bordighera ,,	..	5 52	..	..	..	..	1032	..	..	..	1329	..	16 9	1433	1857	..	2144
[Etna time] Vintimille c a	..	6 0		..		..	1040	..	..	..	1335	..	1617	1440	19 3	..	2150
	I	A	E	V	PP		K	M		X	T	N	L		J	D	S
(Complete Service, *see page* 264.) Vintimille [G. tm.] d	..	6 15		8 35	..	..	1120	..	..	..	15 6	..	1655	1715	1935	..	2245
Mentone ,,	..	6 32		8 55	9 27	..	1138	..	..	..	1522	1552	17 9	1734	1949	2045	23 3
Monte Carlo ,,	..	6 45	Dep. Marseilles-Joliette 11.40, daily except Tues.	9 11	9 37	..	1152	..	..	..	1534	16 5	1719	1747	20 1	21 0	2317
Monaco .... ,,	..	6 50		9 18	9 42	..	1157	..	..	..	1538	1610	1724	1752	20 6	21 6	2322
Beaulieu ,,	..	7 6		9 38	9 56	..	1216	..	..	..	1553	1624	1738	18 7	2019	2123	2340
Nice arr.	..	7 20		9 49	10 4	..	1231	..		..	1559	1634	1746	1818	2028	2134	2355
Nice dep.	5 45	7 35		1017	1010	1150	13 0	..	15 0	15 0	1613	1642	1753	1848	2038	2145	0 10
Juan les Pins ,,	..	8 2		..	..	..	1329	..	1522	1522	1637	..	..	1921	..	2211	0 39
Grasse *p.* 263 d.	..	7 20		9 45	9 45	..	1255	..	..	..	16 0	1630	..	..	1935	..	..
Cannes ,,	6 10	8 17		1057	1037	1215	1346	..	1533	1553	1652	1719	1829	1942	2114	2238	0 56
St. Raphael	6 34	8 46		1126	11 4	1238	1430	..	16 0	16 0	1722	1749	1859	2021	2143	2258	1 26
Les Arcs	6 47	9 11		1151		..	1458	..	1623	1623	1747	..		2050	22 9		1 57
Toulon arr	7 31	1011		1250	12 7	1336	16 0	..	1717	1717	1849	19 6	2017	2151	23 7	0 17	3 3
Hyeres, P.L.M. d *page* 263.	6 47	9 27		11 0	11 0	1258	1513	..	..	..	1759	1759	1759	..	2157	..	..
Toulon dep	7 32	1016		1255	12 9	1337	16 6	..	1732	1732	1854	1911	2019	2158	2313	0 22	3 12
Marseilles arr.	8 20	1117		1353	13 3	1425	1715	..	1836	1836	1959	2010	2117	23 5	0 15	2120	4 35
	1 2 3					1 2											
Marseilles dep	8 30	1127	1140	14 8	13 8	1440	1735	..	1850	20 0	2040	2015	2122	2345	0 30	1 35	6 40
Tarascon arr	..	..	..	..	..	..	1859			..	..	..		..	..	..	8 4
(*page* 255.) Barcelona d.	Limited Train	..	..	..	Winter only.	Limited Train	..	..	↓	↓	..	Limited Train.	↓	↓	..	† Lyons Brotteaux Station.	..
Cerbère arr.		..	..					..			..				..		..
Cerbère dep.			..	7 56			1343	..			..				1845		23 8
Narbonne ,,		7 47	..	11 6			1549	1612			..				21 2		1 53
Sète arr		9 29	..	13 0			1652	1837			..				22 9		2 57
Sète dep.		10 5	..	13 8			17 0	1855			..				2221		5 35
Nimes		1126	..	1431			1820	2022			2045				0 5		7 30
Tarascon arr.		1154	..	1458			1847	2048			2120				0 34		7 55
Avignon ,,		1219	..	1520			..	..	↓	↓	22 1		↓	↓	1 2		..
(*page* 261.) Tarascon dep.	..		..		..		19 4	2051	..	..		..		..	..	..	8 9
Avignon ... ,,	10 0	13 3	1335	16 2	1425	1556	1953	2114	2028	2142	2237	22 0	2256	2 14	2 32	3 16	8 34
Lyons (Perrache) arr.	1255	16 5	1628	19 5	17 3	1822	2315	0 40	2340	1 0	1 52	1 12	2 3	6 15	6†32	6 29	1220
Lyons (Perrache) dep.	13 7	1620	1635	2020	1710	1829	2330	0 48	0 0	1 6	2 20	1 18	2 11	8 40	7†16	7 0	1325
Macon .. arr.	1358	1711	1727	2128	..	..	0 27		0 50	..	3 17	..	..	9 47	8 9	..	1432
Dijon .. ,,	1531	1851	19 3	2338	1914	2026	1 57	3 15	2 42	3 33	5 5	3 45	4 44	1153	10 0	9 14	1639
Paris (Lyon) ,,	1925	2255	23 5	5 0	2245	2350	6 20	7 20	6 55	7 32	9 20	8 0	9 0	17 0	14 5	13 0	2145
(*See page* 112.) Paris (Lyon) dp.		..	..	6 35	..	..	drv	drv	drv	..	..	9 46		..	drive		..
Paris (Nord) arr.		..	..	6 59	..	..	acrs	acrs	acrs	..	..			..	across		..
												luxe					
	1 2 3	..	..				1 2				1 2			3	1 2		..
Paris (Nord) dep.	2150	..	..				8 20				1030	..		2150	1625		..
Boul'gne (Q.) a	..	..	..				..				1316	13 5		..	1915		..
Calais (Maritime) a	¶	..	..				1141				..			¶	..		..
Calais (Maritime) d		..	..				12 5				*	*		..	..		..
Dover Pier arr.	..	..	..				1320				..	..		..	*		..
London (Vic.)	9 10	..					1530				1720	1720		9 10	23 0		

N 1 and 2 cl. cars Mentone-Boulogne ; 1 cl. Couchettes-Toilette and Lits-Salons ; 2 cl. Couchettes, 1 and 2 cl. cars Mentone-Paris ; Rest. car Mentone-Avignon.
P Golden Arrow Pullman Car Service London-Paris.
PP Winter only. 1 and 2 cl. Pullman cars only Paris-Mentone and v.v.
S 1, 2 and 3 cl. cars Marseilles-Paris.
T 3 cl. Sleeping car, 1 cl. Couchettes and 1, 2 and 3 cl. car Paris-Vintimille and v.v. Rest. car Avignon-Nice and v.v.
V 1, 2 and 3 cl. cars Vintimille-Paris, and Rest. car Vintimille-Marseilles.
W 1, 2 and 3 cl. cars, 1 cl. Lits-Salons, Couchettes, Paris-Sète ; 1, 2 and 3 cl. cars Paris-Narbonne
X 1 and 2 cl. Sleeping car, 1 cl. Couchettes-Toilette, 2 cl. Couchettes and 1, 2 and 3 cl. car Marseilles-Paris.
Z Auto-Rail from Marseilles—Limited train—passengers for St. Raphael and beyond have priority.
b By motor. * Via Folkestone ¶ Ferry Service via Dunkerque. *For other notes see page* 113.

To THE PYRENEES, SPAIN, and PORTUGAL.

N.B.—For other restrictions regarding use of these trains for short distances see page 248.

Mls.			123		123	12	123	12	12	12	
..	p. 112 LONDON—							P	..		
..	Victoria b .... dep.	..	22 0		..	9 0	..	11 0	11 0	14 0	
..	Dover .... dep.	..			..	..	..	1255	1255	1555	
	Boulogne .... dep.	..	¶		..	1255	..	..	..	..	
108	Calais (Maritime) ,,	..	..		..	..	..	1430	1450	1735	
287	Paris (Nord) b ... arr.	..	9 0		..	1548		1744	1810	21 0	
	Paris (Nord) ....dep.	..			..	16‖0	.	18‖25	18‖25		
	Paris (d'Orsay).. arr.	..			..	1625	..	1850	18‖50	Drv acrs	
		A§	H h 123	B luxe	b G	F c	J	C† 123	E 123	123	
290	PARIS d'Orsay dep.	8 45	1010	1130	1230	1725	2030	2050	2215	0 0	
293	(Austerlitz) dep.	8 59	..	..	1242	..	2041	21 4	2227	0 15	
363	Les Aubrais b ...... arr.	1010	..	1243	1350	1838	2158	2224	2356	2 12	
365	p. 248 Orleans b......... ,,	1019	.	1251	1358	1847	22 7	2232	0 6	2 23	
433	St. Pierre b .... ,,	1126	1231	1341	15 6	1944	2310	2341	1 32	4 15	
435	Tours b .... ,,	1138	1245	1351	1518	1956	2322	2353	1 44	4 27	
496	Poitiers b ....arr.	1246	..	1439	1617	2054	0 25	0 56	2 57	6 8	
566	Angouleme b	1417	..	1540	1740	22 3	1 47	2 18	4 44	8 47	
658	BORDEAUX (S.J.) b ar.	16 7	1634	17 9	1935	2340	3 32	4 20	7 10	1220	
..	p. 247 Bordeaux......... dep.	1616	..	1733	2045	..	..	5 15	7 50	1331	
691	Arcachon......... arr.	1749	..	1820	2146		.	6 48	8 46	1434	
	p. 250					123					
..	BORDEAUX (S.J.) dp.	1648	1648	1721	1950	0 0	3 41	4 29	8 0	1345	
721	Morcenx..............arr.	18 6	18 6	..		1 33	..	..	9 29	1514	
..	p. 250 Morcenx .... dep.	18 8	18 8	..	..	1 42	..	..	9 36	1516	
746	Dax.....................arr.	1835	1835	1858	2131	2 9	..	6 12	10 9	1544	
..	p. 251 Dax.....................d.	1848	1848	..	2140	2 22	5 36	6 26	1019	1557	
766	Puyoo....................a.	1920	1920	..	22 6	2 47	6 10	7 0	1045	1632	
802	Pau b.....................,,	2016	2016	..	23 5	3 33	7 5	7 52	1140	1739	
826	Lourdes...................,,	21 1	21 1	..	2354	4 14	7 52	8 37	1232	1826	
838	p. 253 Tarbes......... arr.	2125	2125	↓	0 16	4 37	8 21	8 58	13f5	1851	
	Tarbes......... dp.	.	.	↓	6 10	4 55	8 26	9 27	..	1941	
851	p. Bag. de Bigorre a.	..	.	↓	6 50	5 25	9 15	9 59	..	2023	
..	p. Pierrefitte..............,,	..	.	..	..	5 28	8 33	1046	15 6	2012	
838	Cauterets ....,,	..	..	..	..	6 37	9‡30	1140	17‡26	21 0	
852	Luz-St.-Sauveur ..,,	..	.	..	..	6 0	9‡10	1130	17‡15	2040	
..	p. 250 Dax...................dep.	1842	1842	19 1	2134	3 27	..	6 25	1023	1549	
776	Bayonne..............arr.	1921	1921	1936	2222	4 21	..	7 11	11 7	1628	
782	Negresse............... ,,	1936	1936	1951	2235	5 12	..	7 32	1123	1642	
..	Biarritz (Ville)... ,,	1951	1951	20 4	2255	5 27	..	7 41	1134	1656	
..	Biarritz (Ville) dep.	1931	1931	..	2220	..	..	7 43	1116	1635	
..	Negresse.............. ,,	1940	1940	1959	2238	5 17	..	7 51	1126	1645	
791	St. Jean-de-Luz...... ,,	20 1	20 1	2016	2256	5 41	..	8 10	1150	17 6	
	Hendaye ....arr.	2017	2017	2031	23 8	5 56	..	8 26	12 6	1722	
800											
	p. 321 Irun b, c..............dep.	..	..	2135	..	..	..	..	..	..	
811	San Sebastian...... arr.	..	..	..	..	..	..	..	..	..	
910	Miranda b .... ,,	..	..	..	..	..	..	..	..	..	
966	Burgos b .... dep.	..	..	..	..	..	..	..	..	..	
1067	Medina b .... arr.	..	..	5 41	..	..	..	..	..	..	
1192	MADRID (Norte) b ,,	..	..	10 0	..	..	..	..	..	..	
..	p. 322 Medina b......... dep.	..	..	5 56	..	..	..	..	..	..	
1115	Salamanca ... ar.	..	..	7 29	..	..	..	..	..	..	
	Salamanca ... dp.	..	..	7 41	..	..		..	..	..	
1464	LISBON b ...... arr.	..	..	1850	..	..	..	..	..		

A 1, 2 & 3 cl. Cars Paris-Tarbes from Oct. 1; 1, 2 & 3 cl. Cars Paris-Arcachon July 1 to Sept. 30; Rest. Car Paris-Bordeaux.

B Sud Exp. Pullman Cars 1 & 2 cl. Paris-Irun and 1 cl. Paris-Biarritz Ville; Rest. Car Paris-Hendaye. Extra fares. 1 & 2 cl. Sleep. Cars Irun-Madrid and Lisbon.

C Pyrenees-Cote d'Argent Express. 1 & 2 cl. Sleep. Car Paris-Irun; 1, 2 and 3 cl. Cars Paris-Irun; 1 & 2 cl. Sleep. Cars and 1, 2 & 3 cl. Cars Paris-Tarbes from Oct. 1.

E 1 & 2 cl. Sleep. Cars Paris-Arcachon; 1 cl. Couchettes and 1, 2 & 3 cl. Cars Paris-Lourdes; 1 cl. Couchettes Paris-Irun from Oct. 1.

F 1 & 2 cl. Cars Paris-Tarbes from Oct. 1; 1 and 2 cl. Cars Paris-Pierrefitte July 1 to Sept. 30; Rest. Car Paris-Bordeaux.

G 1, 2 & 3 cl. Cars Paris-Tarbes; Rest. Car Paris-Dax, July 1 to Sept. 30 (Bordeaux from Oct. 1).

H July 1 to Sep. 30 only; 1 & 2 cl. Cars Paris-Biarritz; 1, 2 & 3 cl. and Rest. Car Paris-Tarbes.

J July 1 to Sep. 30 only; 1 & 2 cl. Sleep. Cars and 1, 2 & 3 cl. Cars Paris-Pierrefitte; 1 cl. Couchettes and 1, 2 & 3 cl. Cars Paris-Bag. de Bigorre.

P "Golden Arrow" Pullman Car Service London-Paris.

b Only takes 3rd class for 95 miles or more. *c* Only takes 2nd class for Blois and beyond. *d* Only takes 2nd class for 189 miles and 3rd class for 315 miles. *e* Saturdays and Sundays and Fete Days only. *f* Via Mont de Marsan. *d* Only takes 3rd class for Bordeaux or beyond. † Limited train, takes 3rd class for Dax and beyond. ‡ To Sept. 10. § Only takes 3rd class passengers for Tours and beyond. ‖ By Motor Bus. ¶ Via Dover and Dunkerque.

From PORTUGAL, SPAIN and THE PYRENEES.

N.B.—For other restrictions regarding use of these trains for short distances, see pages 248.

Ref	Station		1	2	3	4	5	6	7	8	9	10
			1 2 3	1 2 3	1 2	1 2	1 2 3	1 2 3	1 2 3	1 2 3	1 2 3	1 2 3
			Exp		Exp	Exp	Exp	Exp	Exp	Rap	Rap	Exp
p.322	LISBON	dep.	..	..	1355	..	..	..	..	..	..	..
	Salamanca	arr.	..	.	0 41	..	..	..	..		..	..
	Salamanca	dep.	..	..	0 52	..	..	..	..	..	..	..
	Medina	arr.	..	..	2 26	..	..		..	..	..	..
									..	..	..	..
p. 321.	MADRID (Norte)	dep.	..	..	22 0	..	..		..	..	..	..
	Medina	,,	..	..	2 41	..	..		..	..	..	..
	Burgos	,,	..	..	..	..	..	..	..	..	..	..
	Miranda	,,	..	..	..	..	..	..	..	..	..	..
	San Sebastian	,,	..	..	..	..	..		..	..	..	..
	Hendaye *c*	arr.	..	..	1135	..	..		..	..	..	..
			J	D	A	K		B	B	C *c*	H	G
	Hendaye *c*	dep.	8 37	8 45	12 0	1348	1457	..	1823	2148	21 0	2217
p. 250.	St. Jean-de-Luz	,,	8 54	9 2	1215	14 3	1516	..	1842	22 8	2122	2249
	Negresse	arr.	9 13	9 21	..	1420	1541	..	19 3	2228	2146	2310
	Biarritz (Ville)	,,	9 25	9 32	1240	1435	1552	..	1913	2238	2157	2323
	BIARRITZ (Ville)	dep.	9 5	9 5	1242	1414	1535	..	1856	2241	22 1	23 5
	Negresse	,,	9 23	9 23	..	1423	1544	..	19 5	2250	2210	2317
	Bayonne	,,	9 37	9 37	13 4	1434	1559	..	1920	23 7	2227	0 25
	Dax	arr.	1018	1018	1339	1512	1639	..	20 3	2342	23 5	1 29
p. 251.	Luz-St.-Sauveur	dep.	..	6 55	8 30	1130	1315	1535	..	1945	..	
	Cauterets	,,	..	6 37	8 20	1116	13 6	1527	..	1937	..	
	Pierrefitte	,,	..	7 28	9 10	1212	14 2	1618	..	2029	..	
	B. de Bigorre	d.	..	6 51	8 36	1023	13 8	1543	..	1920	..	
	TARBES	arr.	..	7 29	9 4	11 0	1351	1618	..	1947	..	
	TARBES	dep.	..	7 58	9 26	1233	14 1	1632	..	2122	..	
	Lourdes	,,	..	8 25	9 55	13 5	1437	1753	..	2159	..	
	PAU	,,	..	9 4	1032	1340	1516	1830	..	2236	..	
	Puyoo	,,	..	9 51	1135	1433	1612	1921	..	2324	..	
	Dax	arr.	..	1016	12 8	1458	1643	1950	..	2353	..	↓
	Dax	dep.	1034	1034	1341	1519	1651	1956	20 6	2358	23 8	2 5
	Morcenx	arr.	11 6	11 6	..	..	1724	2025	2035	..	..	2 44
	Morcenx	dep.	11 7	11 7	..	..	1726	2027	2037	..	..	2 58
	BORDEAUX (St. J.)	arr.	1220	1220	1518	1659	1843	2140	2150	1 43	0 45	4 48
p. 247	Arcachon	dep.	..	1118	13 5	16 5	18 0	20 3		..	..	7 10
	Bordeaux (St. J.)	arr.	..	1247	1359	1659	19 0	21 3		..	..	8 10
								a	*b*			
	BORDEAUX (St. J.)	dep.	1228	13 5	1524	1725	2020	2220	2220	1 52	0 55	8 30
	Angouleme		14 0	1452	1637	1850	2226	0 35	0 35	3 24	2 32	10 7
	Poitiers		1522	1614	1738	1959	0 4	2 21	2 21	4 45	3 53	1134
	Tours	dep.	1624	1723	1758	2056	1 47	3 57	3 50	5 50	4 49	1236
	St. Pierre	,,	1638	1736	1833	21 9	1 56	4 10	4 10	6 8	5 1	1250
	Orleans	,,	..	1847	19 7	2214	3 19	5 33	5 58	7 22	6 8	14 0
	Les Aubrais	,,	..	1857	1935	2221	3 30	5 48	6 5	7 29	6 15	14 9
	PARIS (Austerlitz)	arr.	1919	2018	2034	2335	5 0	7 18	7 53	8 54	7 54	1523
	PARIS (QUAI D'ORSAY)		1930	2030	2059	2345	..	..	8 5	9 5	8 5	1535
	PARIS (d'Orsay)	dep.	..	.	..			8‖20		9‖30	..	16‖30
	PARIS (Nord)	arr.	..	..	..	Drive across.		8‖40		9‖50	..	1655
				1 2 3		1 2		luxe		1 2		
	PARIS (Nord)	dep.	..	2150		8 20		1030	..	1030	..	1625
	Calais (Maritime)	arr.	..	..		1141		..	..		..	..
	Boulogne (Mar.)	,,	..	¶		..		1310	..	1310	..	19 5
	Dover Pier	,,	..	..		1320			..		..	..
	LONDON—		..	..				P	..		..	
	VICTORIA		..	9 10		1530		1720	..	1720	..	23 0

A Sud. Exp. Pullman Cars 1 & 2 cl. Hendaye-Paris via Biarritz; Rest. Car Hendaye-Paris. Extra fares. 1 & 2 cl. Sleep. Cars Lisbon and Madrid-Hendaye and *v.v.*

B 1 & 2 cl. Sleep. Cars Arcachon-Paris; 1 cl. Couchettes and 1, 2 & 3 cl. Cars Lourdes-Paris; 1 cl. Couchettes Hendaye-Paris from Oct. 2.

C Pyrenees-Cote d'Argent Exp. See also note **H.** 1 & 2 cl. Slp. Car Hendaye-Paris via Biarritz from Oct. 2; 1 & 2 cl. Sleep. Car and 1, 2 & 3 cl. Cars Tarbes-Paris from Oct. 2; 1 cl. Couchettes and 1, 2 & 3 cl. Cars Bag. de Bigorre-Paris, July 2 to Oct. 1; 1 & 2 cl. Sleep. Car and 1, 2 & 3 cl. Cars Pierrefitte-Paris, July 2 to Oct. 1; Rest. Car St. Pierre-Paris.

D 1, 2 & 3 cl. Cars Tarbes-Paris from Oct. 2; 1, 2 & 3 cl. Cars Arcachon-Paris July 2 to Oct. 1; Rest. Car Bordeaux-Paris.

G Rest. Car Bordeaux-Paris.

H July 2 to Oct. 1 only; 1 & 2 cl. Sleep. Cars Hendaye-Paris via Biarritz.

J July 2 to Oct. 1 only; 1 & 2 cl. Cars Biarritz-Paris; 1, 2 & 3 cl. Cars Tarbes-Paris; Rest. Car Dax-Paris.

K 1 & 2 cl. Cars Tarbes-Paris from Oct. 2; 1 & 2 cl. Cars Pierrefitte-Paris July 2 to Oct. 1; Rest. Car Bordeaux-Paris.

P "Golden Arrow" Pullman Car Service Paris-London.

‖ By Motor Bus. *a* July 1-October 1. *b* From October 2.

c Hendaye-Dax from October 2 only. ¶ Via Dunkerque and Dover.

N.B.—*For restrictions regarding use of these trains for short distances see page 249.*

Mls						
		1 2 3		1 2	1 2	
	LONDON:— (see p.112)					
..	VICTORIA .... dep.	22 0	..	11 0	11 0	..
..	CALAIS ...... dep.	¶	..	1450	1450	..
..	BOULOGNE .. dep.	..	..	..	..	..
	PARIS (NORD) arr.	9 0	..	1810	1810	..
287	PARIS (NORD) dep.	..	..	1825	1825	..
	Paris Quai d'Orsay	..	..	‖	‖	..
	arr	..	..	1850	1850	..
		C	J	A	B	H
			1 2 3	1 2 3	1 2 3	
290	PARIS (Quai d'Orsay) dep. (p. 249)	1015	1925	2015	2145	..
..	Austerlitz.... dep.	..	1937	2025	2159	2250
	Vierzon ...... arr.	1234	2137	..	0 3	1 34
414	Vierzon ...... dep.	1245	2139	..	0 6	1 42
	Châteauroux arr.	1332	2225	..	0 46	2 43
455	Châteauroux dep.	1337	2228	..	0 48	2 50
538	Limoges ...... dep.	1544	0 18	0 40	2 47	5 40
600	Brive .... dep.	17 9	1 40	2 1	4 18	7 33
645	Cahors .... dep.	1847	3 13	3 36	6 4	9 18
701	Montauban .... arr.	1947	4 7	4 30	7 4	1025
733	TOULOUSE .... arr.	2037	4 48	5 11	7 45	1140
..	TOULOUSE .. dep. (p. 251)	20*42	5 10	6 15	8 15	1320
798	Montréjeau .. arr.	2212	6 42	7 58	9 55	15 7
821	B.deLuchon arr.	22*57	7 29	9 0	1153	16 8
	TOULOUSE .. dep. (p. 251)	..	5 0	5 41	8 27	1350
811	Ax-les-Thermes a.	..	7 10	8 27	1043	1628
..	Ax-les-Thermes dep.	↓	7 14	8 33	1048	↓
..	La Tour de Carol ar.		8 29	9 50	12 5	
..	Odeillo-Font-Romeu ...... arr.		9 38	11 4	1314	
..	Villefranche (Vrnt.-les-Bains) arr.	↓	..	1232	1743	↓
..	TOULOUSE .. dep. (p. 252)	2132	—	5 30	8 23	1150
825	Narbonne .... arr.	2334	..	7 8	1047	1333
840	Beziers ...... arr.	0 4	..	7 43	1139	1356
808	Lamalou-les-Bains	..	..	9 0	..	..
..	Narbonne ...... dep.	2 5	..	7 40	11 7	..
850	Perpignan .... arr.	2 57	..	8 29	12 2	..
..	Perpignan .. dep. (p. 255)	5 23	..	9 20	1223	..
838	Villefranche (Vnt.-les-Bains) a.	6 38	..	1033	1330	..
..	Villefranche (Vnt.-les-Bains) d.	6 56	..	1042	1337	..
..	Odeillo-Font-Romeu .... arr.	8 36	..	1215	15 7	..
..	Perpignan .... dep. (p.)	3 7	..	8 34	12 7	..
859	Elne .... arr.	3 19	..	8†56	1219	..
879	Amelie-les-Bains a.	8 28	..	9†48	1318	..
869	Port Vendres .. arr.	3 38	..	9 2	1243	..
890	Cerbere .... arr.	3 58	..	9 21	13 6	..
892	Port Bou ...... arr.	b	..	.	..	..
.	Port-Bou ...... dep. (p. 326)	4 10	..	..	..	..
99	BARCELONA .. arr.	8 50	..	..	..	..
..	p. Sitges .... arr.	..	..	..	..	..

Sitges .... dep.	..	..	..	..	..
BARCELONA .. dep.	..	..	..	1310	..
Port Bou ...... arr.	..	..	..	2250	..
Cerbere .... arr.		..	..	b	..
	Exp	Exp	Rap	Rap	Exp
	D	E	F	G	K
	1 2 3	1 2 3	1 2 3	1 2 3	1 2 3
Cerbere .... dep.	1443	..	1931	23 2	7 56
Port Vendres .. dep	15 5	..	1952	2325	8 12
Amelie-les-Bains d.	1331	..	1824	..	..
Elne .... dep.	1528	..	..	.	..
Perpignan .... arr.	1540	..	2016	2356	8 45
Odeillo-Font-Romeu ...... dep.	11 5	..	1615	1923	5 9
Villefranche .. arr.	1232	..	1743	2048	7 36
(Vernet-les-Bains) d	1240	.	18 1	2053	7 44
Perpignan ...... arr.	1352		1911	2150	8 46
Perpignan .... dep.	1545	..	2021	0 1	8 51
Narbonne ...... arr.	1641		21 7	0 56	9 54
Lamalou-les-Bains	..	..	1935	..	..
Beziers .... dep.	1623	..	2051	0 51	9 28
Narbonne ...... dep.	1655	..	2122	1 28	9 59
TOULOUSE .... arr.	1925	..	23 2	3 47	1226
Villefranche (Vrnt.-les-Bains) d.	1042	1337	..	↓	..
Odeillo-Font-Romeu ...... dep.	15 7	1730	..		.
La Tour de Carol d.	17 9	1920	..		7 0
Ax-les-Thermes arr.	1831	2031	..	↓	8 32
Ax-les-Thermes d.	1838	2033	..	..	8 46
TOULOUSE .. arr.	2051	2236	..	..	1122
B. de Luchon dp.	1751	2028	..	..	1012
Montréjeau .. dep.	1852	2111	..		1115
TOULOUSE .. arr.	2018	2237	..	..	1235
TOULOUSE .... dep.	21 5	2250	2320	8 35	1310
Montauban .... dep.	2145	2331	0 0	9 17	1351
Cahors .... dep	2244	0 24	0 56	1013	1444
Brive .... dep.	0 29	2 0	2 30	1156	1617
Limoges ...... dep.	2 2	3 21	3 50	1335	1743
Châteauroux arr.	3 37	5 6	5 26	1526	1918
Châteauroux dep.	3 39	5 10	5 28	1528	1921
Vierzon .... arr.	4 21	6 0	6 12	1615	20 6
Vierzon .... dep.	4 24	6 3	6 23	1619	2011
Austerlitz ...... arr.	6 43	8 32	8 39	1853	2229
PARIS (Quai d'Orsay) .. arr.	6 55	8 43	8 50	19 5	2240
PARIS (Quai d'Orsay) .. dep.	7‖20	9‖30		..	..
PARIS (NORD) arr.	7 40	9 50		..	..
		1 2		1 2 3	
PARIS (NORD) dep.	8 20	1030		2150	..
CALAIS .... dep.	12 5	..		¶	..
LONDON—		a			
VICTORIA	1530	1720		9 10	

* July 2—Oct. 1. † Dep. Perpignan by Auto-rail Car 8.45, one class only.
¶ Via Dover and Dunkerque. *a* Via Boulogne. *b* Connection not guaranteed.

A Barcelona Exp., 1 & 2 cl. Sleep. Cars Paris-Cerbere; 1 cl. Lits-toilettes, Couchettes and 1, 2 & 3 cl. Cars Paris-Lamalou, July 1 to Sept. 30; 1, 2 & 3 cl. Cars Paris-Beziers from Oct. 1; 1 cl. Couchettes and 1, 2 & 3 cl. Cars Paris-Port Vendres (Quai) days prior to dep. of steamers for Algiers and Oran; and from Oct. 2—1 2 & 3 cl. Sleep. Car Paris-Toulouse and 1 cl. Lits-toilette, and 1 & 2 cl. Couchettes with 1, 2 & 3 cl. Cars Paris-La Tour de Carol. **B** 1 & 2 cl. Sleep. Car Paris-Toulouse. **C** Rest. Car Paris-Toulouse. **H** 1 cl. Couchettes Paris-Montauban; 1, 2 & 3 cl. Paris-Cahors. **J** July 2 to Oct. 1 only—1, 2 & 3 cl. Sleep. Cars Paris-Lourdes via Toulouse; 1 cl. Lits-toilettes, 1 & 2 cl. Couchettes, and 1, 2 & 3 cl. Cars Paris-La Tour de Carol and Paris-Luchon. **D** 1 & 2 cl. Sleep. Car Toulouse-Paris; 1 cl. Couchettes and 1, 2 & 3 cl. Cars Port Vendres (Quai)-Paris, days of arrival of steamers from Algiers; 1 cl. Lits-toilettes, 1 & 2 cl. Couchettes, and 1, 2 & 3 cl. Cars La Tour de Carol-Paris from Oct. 2. **E** July 2 to Oct. 1—1 cl. Lits-toilettes, 1 & 2 cl. Couchettes and 1, 2 & 3 cl. Cars La Tour de Carol-Paris and Luchon-Paris; 1, 2 & 3 cl. Sleep. Car Lourdes-Paris, via Toulouse. **F** Barcelona Exp., 1 & 2 cl. Sleep. Car Cerbere-Paris; 1, 2 & 3 cl. Cars Beziers-Paris from Oct. 3; 1 cl. Lits-toilettes, Couchettes, and 1, 2 & 3 cl. Cars Lamalou-Paris, July 2 to Oct. 1; 1 cl. Couchettes and 1, 2 & 3 cl. Cars Port Vendres (Quai)-Paris, days of arrival of steamers from Oran; Voiture Buffet Vierzon-Paris. **G** Rest. Car Limoges-Toulouse. **K** 1, 2 & 3 cl. Cars and Rest. Car Limoges-Paris.

	12	12 luxe	12	12	Mls.					12	12	12 luxe	12	12
					0		See also pp. 119 120	LONDON						
..	9 0	11 0	11 0	14 0	..	dep.		Victoria	arr.	1530	1720	1720	23 0	1521
..	..	1430	1450	1735	102	,,		Calais (Maritime) *b*	arr.	1141	..	..	..	1141
..	1255	..	..	..	..	,,		Boulogne	arr.	..	1310	13 5	19 5	..
..	1548	1744	1810	21 0	287	arr.		PARIS (Nord) *b*	dep.	8 20	1030	..	1625	8 20
..	..	1753	1823	2111		dep.			arr.	6 59	..	..	..	..
..		1825	1855	2133	290	arr.		PARIS (Lyon)	dep.	6 35	..	9 46	..	..
D	E	L	C	A						F	C	L	E	D
123	123	—	123	123						123	123		123	123
7 30	17 0	1930	2020	2310	..	dep.		PARIS (LYON) *b*	arr.	6 20	8 10	9 10	14 5	2225
1127	2049	2322	0 28	3 30	485	ar		Dijon *b*	dep.	2 12	4 3	5 8	10 7	1828
1132	2055	2331	0 37	4 9		d.			arr.	1 50	3 57	4 56	10 0	1822
1447	0 52	..	4 29	7 19	687	ar	p. 265	Culoz *b*	dep.	2145	0 20	..	5 53	15 3
1452	1 0	..	4 47	7 24		d.			arr.	2138	0 15		5 34	1447
1531	1 37	2 55	5 40	8 8	660	ar		Chambéry *b*	dep.	2051	2327	1 29	5 2	14 9
1541	1 42	2 56	6 10	8 19		d.			arr.	2037	2317	1 28	5 0	1357
1715	3 15	4 25	8 10	9 54	720	ar		[Green. T.] Modane *b c*	dep.	19 0	2145	0 0	3 30	1225
1755	4 15	4 50	9 10	1040		d.		[Etna time]	arr	18 3	2110	2340	2 35	1155
1854	5 9	5 36	10 6	1238	739	d.		Ulzio-Clavières-Sestrieres	arr.	1711	2019	2252	1 46	11 7
2020	6 30	6 50	1128	13 0	778	arr.		TURIN (P.N.) *b*	dep.	1535	1846	2124	0 15	9 36
123	123		123	12*x*						123	123	↑	123	123
21 0	7*x*0	↓	11*36	1457	..	dep.	p. 305 p. 298	Turin *b*	arr.	1450	1755		24 0	9‡15
2350	8 44		1310	1735	871	ar		Milan *b*	dep.	12 0	1620		2140	7‡36
0 16	8*x*50		1330	18*x*5		d.			arr.	1134	16 8		21*x*15	6 33
4 40	1153		1740	2110	1036	arr.		Venice *b*	dep.	6 50	12 7		18*x*15	1 25
7 0	14 5	▼	2034	23*c*10	1136	arr.		Trieste	dep.	0 5	9 30		16 5	2225
123			123	123						123	123		123	
2115	7 18	See page 82.	1218	1438	..	dep.	p. 313	Turin *b*	arr.	14 9	18*d*5	See page 82.	2353	9 22
1 0	1059		1614	1711	895	ar		Piacenza *b*	dep.	1058	1350		2120	5 17
1 10	11 9		1621	1730		d.			arr.	1040	1333		2110	5 5
3 40	1354		1820	1933	986	ar		Bologna *b*	dep.	8 40	1138		1943	2 38
3 54	1439		1835	20 5		d.	p. 313		arr.	8 28	11 5		1930	2 12
7 32	19 9		21 7	2350	1113	arr.		Ancona *b*	dep.	5 48	7 45		1626	2245
1635	3 36		3 36	5 49	1314	,,		Foggia *b*	dep.	0 25	0 40		1716	14 0
23 4	8 25		8 25	1022	1459	,,		BRINDISI *b*	dep.	2022	2022		*d*	8 57
12	123		123	1 cl.						123	123			12
2140	7 10	7 3	1210	1655		dep.	p. 301	TURIN	arr.	14 9	18‖30	2115	2345	8 20
2255	8 2	..	1320	*x*	835	dep.		Alessandria	dep.	1255	1710	..	2245	6 59
0 2	9 28	9 15	1424	1838	881	ar		Genoa *b*	dep.	1130	1555	1854	2034	5 45
0 20	9 35	9 21	1431	1840		d.			arr.	11 1	1546	1847	2018	5 35
..	..	..	*x*	..	887			Genoa (Nervi)	dep.	1040	1531	..	1958	
3 5	1213	1146	1654	2026	984	arr.		Pisa *b*	dep.	7 30	1256	1616	1655	2 48
4 10	1355	¶	17 5	0 28	..	dep.		Pisa	arr.	7 19	1243	¶	1554	2 37
5 27	1534	1340	1840	2244	1033	arr.		Florence *b*	dep.	5 10	1115	1420	1425	0 40
3 9	1217	1147	1655	2027	..	dep.		Pisa	arr.	7 21	1244	1615	1652	2 36
3 27	1236	12 4	1712	2042	994	arr.		Leghorn	dep.	7 2	1225	1558	1634	2 17
..	1521	..	1941	..	1141	arr.		Civita Vecchia	dep.	1 51	..	..	..	..
8 0	1630	1530	2045	2350	1191	arr.		ROME *b* (Termini)	dep.	0 30	8 25	1230	1135	2215
9 50	1652	1545	2115	0 40		dep.	p. 310		arr.	2350	8 0	1055	1045	2135
1247	1957	18*f*7	0 3	3 8	1353	arr.		NAPLES (Central)	dep.	2124	4 38	8 15	..	1835
1248	2010	1756	..	..	..	arr.		,, (Mergellina)	dep	2135	..	7 27	..	1819
1339	2148	2148	0 42	3 20	..	dep.	p. 314	Naples (Central)	arr.	2024	3 33	8 2	..	..
1928	5 48	5 48	8 18	1155	..	arr.		V.S. Giovanni	dep.	1132	1931	0 22	..	..
2020	6 45	6 45	9 15	1250	1648	,,		Messina	,,	1030	1830	2325	..	..
24 0	1210	1210	1435	1634	1794	,,		Palermo	,,	6 50	1445	1810	..	..
2115	1812	8 12	1031	1416	1678	,,		Taormina	,,	9‡30	1711	2213	..	..
23*a*17	1135	1135	1332	1755	1768	,,		Syracuse (Port)	,,	7 0	1340	19 0		

A 1, 2 and 3 cl. Cars Paris-Turin and v.v.; 1 cl. Couchettes Paris-Turin and v.v. Rest. Car Genoa-Turin.
C 1, 2 and 3 cl. Car Paris-Rome and v.v. 1 cl. Couchettes Paris-Turin and v.v. Rest. Cars Turin-Genoa, Florence-Pisa, Turin-Modane.
D 1, 2 and 3 cl. Cars Paris-Rome and v.v., and 1 and 2 cl. Sleeping Car Rome-Turin. Rest. Car Paris-Modane and v.v., Pisa-Rome, and Turin-Modane.

E 1 and 2 cl. Cars Paris-Rome-Naples; 3 cl. Paris-Turin and *v.v.* Rest. Car Paris-Macon and *v.v.*, Genoa-Florence.
F 1, 2 and 3 cl. Cars Turin-Paris. 1 cl. Couchettes Turin-Paris.
L Rome Express 1 and 2 cl. Sleeping Cars Calais-Paris-Rome-Naples and Naples-Rome-Paris-Boulogne; 1 and 2 cl. Sleeping Cars Paris-Florence and *v.v.*
Z Via Florence. *a* Syracuse Central. *b* Rapido supp. payable by passengers travelling Rome-Florence and v.v. only. *c* 2 cl. Rapido only. *d* 2 and 3 cl. *e* 3 cl. *f* Piaz. Gar. station.
x Supplement payable for travel by Rapido Trains, Turin-Milan, Venice-Milan and Turin-Rome.
* 2 cl. only Turin-Milan Rapido. † 1 and 2 cl. only. ‡ 2 cl. only. § Not Sundays. ¶ via Viareggio.
‖ 1 and 2 class Sleeping Cars only.

The times on the LEFT are to be read DOWNWARDS, those on the RIGHT UPWARDS.

TO LAUSANNE, MILAN (via Simplon), NEUCHATEL, BERNE, &c. Via PARIS.

NOTE.—Sleep. Accommodation, Extra fares, &c., *see* 5 to 83.

Miles via Calais.	Page	Station		1 2 luxe L	1 2 Rap A	1 2 Rap B	1 2 3 Exp C	1 2 3 Exp D	
	Page 112.	LONDON:—							
		VICTORIA	dep.	14 0	14 0	14 0	22 0	..	
72		FOLKESTONE	dep.	..	..	..	*Via Dunkerque*	..	
78		DOVER	dep.	1555	1555	1555		..	
100		BOULOGNE	arr.	..	..	..		..	
			dep.	..	..	..		..	
108		CALAIS	arr.	1710	1710	1710		..	
			dep.	1735	1735	1735		..	
287		PARIS (Nord)	arr.	21 0	21 0	21 0	9 0	..	
		Ceinture Rly.	dep.	2111	2111	2111	..	..	
290		PARIS (Lyon)	arr.	2133	2133	2133	..	..	
	Page 267.			luxe 1 2	1 2 3	1 2 3	1 2 3	1 2 3	
			dep.	2220	2255	2330	1015	1620	
485		Dijon	arr.	2 8	2 52	3 54	14 5	20 4	
			dep.	2 14	2 59	4 0	1411	2010	
562		Frasne Gr. time	arr.	..	5 14	6 12	1612	22 8	
..		Frasne Gr. time	dep.	↓	5 28	6 36	1624	2217	z
572	Page 279.	Pontarlier	arr	↓	5 45	6 49	1638	2236	z
580		Les Verrieres (M.E. time)	arr	↓	6 46	..	1710	↓	
			dep.	↓	6 50	..	1712	↓	
605		Neuchatel	arr.	↓	7 33	..	1752	↓	
			dep.	↓	7 50	..	1759	↓	
638		BERNE	arr.	↓	8 33	..	1841	↓	
674	p.231	Interlaken, Ost.	arr.	↓	10 0	..	23†12	↓	
	Page 267.	Frasne	dep.	..	5 20	6 15	1617	2213	
		Vallorbe (Gr. time)	arr.	5 25	5 49	6 40	1640	2240	
		Vallorbe (M.E. time)	dep.	5 45	6 19	7 14	1710	23 4	
578		LAUSANNE	arr.	6 26	7 0	7 55	1751	2345	
606		LAUSANNE	dep.	7 8	7 8	..	1834	2352	
		GENEVA	arr.	7 55	7 55	..	1921	0 34	
	Page 280.	LAUSANNE	dep.	6 37	7 15	8 21	18 0	2354	
..		Vevey	arr.	6 52	7 30	8 36	1815	0 9	
..		MONTREUX	arr.	6 59	7 38	8 43	1823	0 16	
618		Territet	arr.	..	r	8 48	1828	..	
..		Aigle	arr.	..	..	8 59	..	..	
..		Bex	arr.	..	..	9 0	..	..	
622		St. Maurice	arr.	..	..	9 15	1855	..	
628		Martigny	arr.	..	..	9 31	1910	..	
638		Sion	arr.	..	8 31	9 50	1931	1 12	
647		Sierre	arr.	8 4	..	10 7	1947	..	
652		Leuk	arr.	..	..	1019	1959	..	
691		Visp (Viege)	arr.	..	..	1034	2014	..	
..		Visp (*p.* 288)	dep.	¶	¶	1136	..	..	
712		Zermatt	arr.	1120	1120	13 7	..	..	
..		Visp	dep.	..	..	1035	2015	..	
697		BRIGUE	arr.	8 38	9 15	1044	2024	1 57	
			dep.	8 45	9 20	1050	2040	2 15	
722		Domodossola (Customs)	arr.	9 22	10 1	1127	2120	2 56	
			dep.	9 53	1022	1148	2140	3 30	
744		Baveno	dep.	1025	1056	1227	2213	4 4	
746		Stresa	dep.	1029	11 2	1233	2219	4 10	
757		Arona	arr.	1053	1125	13 0	2239	4 29	
798		MILAN	arr.	1215	1250	1432	24 0	5 55	
893	p.302	Milan	dep.	1334	1334	..	0 30	6 25	
		GENOA	arr.	1545	1545	..	3 39	9 10	
				1cl x	1cl x			123x	
..	p.302 p.313	MILAN	dep.	1350	1350	14 0	..	6 50	
932		Bologna	arr.	1543	1543	1718	..	9 36	
993		Florence	arr.	1638	1638	19x10	..	1140	
1189		ROME	arr.	1950	1950	23x40	..	1530	
1383	p313	BRINDISI (Marit.)	arr.	..	10[illegible]	..	..	..	
..	p. 305	MILAN	dep.	1222	1330	..	0 16	6 17	
988		Venice	arr.	16 0	1740	..	4 40	1025	
1060		TRIESTE	arr.	1822	2034	..	8 28	14 5	
..		Budapest	arr.	..	9 45	..	..	..	

N.B.—For restrictions regarding use of these trains for short distances, see page 258.

A 1 and 2 cl. Sleeping Cars Paris-Brindisi; 1 and 2 cl. Sleeping Car Paris-Budapest; 1 and 2 cl. Cars Paris-Rome; 1 cl. Couchettes Paris-Brigue; 1, 2 and 3 cl. Cars and 1 cl. Couchettes Paris-Interlaken, June 30 to Sept. 9 (Berne from Sept. 10); 1, 2 and 3 cl. Cars Paris-Istanbul; Restaurant Car Lausanne-Milan.

B June 30-Sept. 9. 1 and 2 cl. Cars and 1 cl. Couchettes Calais-Brigue; 1, 2 and 3 cl. Cars and 1 cl. Couchettes Paris-Milan; 1, 2 and 3 cl. Cars and 1 cl. Couchettes Paris-Pontarlier.

C 1, 2 and 3 cl. Cars Paris-Interlaken, July 1-Sept. 10 (Berne from Sept. 11); 1, 2 and 3 cl. Cars Paris-Milan. Restaurant Car Paris-Frasne.

D 1 and 2 cl. Sleeping Cars Paris-Venice. 1 and 2 cl. Cars Paris-Bucharest. 3 cl. Car Paris-Belgrade. Restaurant Car Paris-Vallorbe.

L Simplon-Orient Express, daily, Calais to Istanbul. Extra fares.

* 3rd cl. Auto Rail. *a* 1 cl. only Bologna-Rome. *r* Restaurant Car. *x* Rapido Train with supplement. *z* 3rd class only.

• 1 and 2 cl. only. † Interlaken (Bahnof). ¶ Via Brigue, see page 288.

FROM MILAN (via Simplon), BERNE, NEUCHATEL, LAUSANNE, &c. (Via PARIS.)

N.B.—For restrictions regarding use of these trains for short distances, *see page* 258.

Station		123 Exp B	123 Exp C	123 Exp A	luxe 1 2 L	123 Exp S	123 Exp D
p. 305 Budapest		..	..	2015	..	..	
Trieste	dep.	..	6 0	9 30	1225	1645	0 *b* 5
Venice	,,	..	1055	1215	1457	1938	5 2
MILAN	arr.	..	14 5	1641	1855	2355	9 15
*p*313 Brindisi	dep.	..	1144	2022	2022	5 58	1430
*p*303 Rome	dep.	..	0 5	7*x*10	1320	1425	0 5
Florence	,,	..	5 45	11*x*26	1611	1820	5 45
*p*303 Bologna	,,	..	7 30	13*10	17 5	1943	7*z*30
Milan	arr.	..	1035	16*17	19 0	22 0	10*z*35
p.302 Genoa	dep.	..	1140	14*x*33	15 5	2115	6 0
Milan	arr.	..	14 2	16*x*34	1745	2357	8 23
MILAN	dep.	..	1420	17 0	1910	0 15	9 35
Arona		..	1544	1821	2031	1 35	11 0
Page 280. Stresa		..	16 6	1843	2054	1 56	1126
Baveno		..	1612	1850	21 0	2 2	1134
Domodossola	arr.	..	1651	1937	2138	2 40	1214
	dep.	..	17 9	1957	2154	3 5	1233
BRIGUE (for Bel Alp)	arr.	..	1752	2040	2237	3 48	1316
	dep.	..	18 9	2050	2245	4 0	1328
Visp	arr.	..	1817	..	..	..	1336
Zermatt	dep.	..	1545	1545	1545	..	12 0
Visp (*p.* 288)	arr.	..	1732	¶	¶	..	1330
Visp	dep.	..	1818	..	..	..	1337
Leuk	dep.	..	1834	..	..	..	1353
Sierre	dep.	..	1843	2120	..	..	14 3
Sion	dep.	..	1858	2134	2327	4 45	1417
Martigny	dep.	..	1919	..	..	..	1438
St. Maurice	dep.	..	1936	..	..	..	1452
Territet	dep.	..	20 7	..	..	..	..
MONTREUX	dep.	..	2013	2225	0 18	5 42	1522
Vevey	dep.	..	2022	2234	0 27	5 50	1531
LAUSANNE	arr.	..	2038	2250	0 43	6 8	1547
GENEVA	dep.	..†	1942	21 1	..	4 45	1513
LAUSANNE	arr.	..†	2019	2228	..	5 30	1554
p. 267 LAUSANNE	dep.	..	2056	23 0	0 52	6 23	16 6
Vallorbe (M.E.T.)	arr.	..	2138	2342	1 34	7 5	1648
Vallorbe (Green. time)	dep.	..	2220	0 37	2 2	7 40	1720
Frasne	arr.	..	..	0 59	..	8 8	1742
p.281 Interlaken, Ost.	dep.	1530	..	1912	↓	↓	12 6
Page 279. BERNE	dep.	17*b*16	..	2212			1456
Neuchatel	arr.	1810	..	23 0			1543
	dep.	18*b*35	..	23 5			1557
Pontarlier (Grn. time)	dep.	2210	..	0 42		7 43	1722
Frasne	arr.	2225		0 56	↓	8 2	1736
Page 267. Frasne	dep.	2226	..	1 12	..	8 10	1755
Dijon	arr.	1 8	0 50	2 52	4 12	9 52	1940
	dep.	1 18	0 55	2 57	4 27	9 58	1946
PARIS (Lyon)	arr.	5 35	5 30	7 0	8 40	14 0	2340
				1 2		1 2	
Ceinture Rly.	dep.	6 35	..	9 35	9 35	..	Drv
	arr.	6 59	..	10 6	10 6	..	acrs
		1 2	1 2				1 2
Page 112. PARIS (Nord)	dep.	8 20	8 20	1030	1030	1625	8 20
CALAIS	arr.	1141	1141	..	..	..	1141
BOULOGNE	arr.	..	..	13 5	13 5	19 5	..
	dep.	..	..	1345	1345	1920	..
DOVER	arr.	1320	1320	..	..	..	1320
FOLKESTONE	arr.	..	..	1515	1515	2050	..
VICTORIA	arr.	1530	1530	1720	1720	23 0	1530

A 1 and 2 cl. Sleeping Car Brindisi (Mar.) (dep 14.38)-Milan-Paris; 1 and 2 cl. Sleeping Car Budapest-Paris; 1 and 2 cl. Cars Rome-Paris; 1, 2 and 3 cl. Cars Interlaken-Paris, July 1 to Sept. 10 (from Berne after Sept. 11); 1, 2 and 3 cl. Istanbul-Paris; 1 cl. Couchettes Brigue-Paris.

B 1 cl. Couchettes and 1, 2 and 3 cl. Cars Pontarlier-Paris.

C July 1 to Sept. 10, from Milan and Vallorbe with 1 and 2 cl. Cars and 1 cl. Couchettes Brigue-Calais; 1, 2 and 3 cl. Cars and 1 cl. Couchettes Milan-Paris; 1, 2 and 3 cl. Cars and 1 cl. Couchettes Pontarlier-Paris.

D 1, 2 and 3 cl. Cars Milan-Paris; 1, 2 and 3 cl. Cars Interlaken-Paris July 1-Sept. 10 (from Berne after Sept. 11). Dining Car Frasne-Paris, Milan-Lausanne.

L Orient-Simplon Express, daily, Istanbul to Paris and Boulogne. Extra fares.

S 1 and 2 cl. Sleeping Car Venice-Paris, and 1 and 2 cl. Cars Bucharest-Paris. 3 cl. Car Belgrade-Paris. Restaurant Car Venice-Verona and Vallorbe to Paris.

¶ Via Brigue. * 1 and 2 cl. only. *b* 2 and 3 cl. *x* 1 and 2 cl. Rapido with supplement. *z* 1 cl. Rapido Train with supplement.

† July 1-Sept. 10.

TO GENEVA, AIX-LES-BAINS, CHAMONIX and EVIAN, Via PARIS.

N.B.—For restrictions regarding use of these trains for short distances, *see pp.* 266 and 258.

Mls. v. Calais			E	I	D	H	F	K	J	B	A	C	G	L
						1 2 3		1 2		1 2			1 2	
..		LONDON—VICTORIA ....dep.				22 0		9 0		11 0			14 0	
72	page 112.	FOLKESTONE ....dep.				..		1055		..				
78		DOVER ....dep.				..		..		1255			1555	
100		BOULOGNE .... arr.				¶		1225					..	
		dep.						1255		..			..	
103		CALAIS .... arr.				..		..		1410			1710	
		dep.				..		..		1430			1735	
287		PARIS (Nord) .... arr.				9 0		1548		1810			21 0	
		dep.				..		..		1825			2111	
		Ceinture Rly... arr.				..		..		1855			2133	
			1 2 3	1 2 3	1 2 3	1 2	1 2 3	1 2 3	1 2	1 2 3	1 2 3	1 2 3	1 2 3	1 2 3
290	p. 266	PARIS (Lyon) .... dep.	7 30	8 0	8 20	13 0	13 5	17 0	2010	2020	2135	2135	2230	2310
435½		DIJON ....arr.	1127	12 3	1227	1652	17 0	2049	0 15	0 28	1 56	1 55	2 34	3 30
..	page 266	DIJON ....dep.	1132	12 9	1233	1658	17 6	2055	0 20	0 37	2 5	2 5	2 40	4 9
563¾		BOURG .... arr.	1328	Via Lyons, arr. 14.38	1435	19 0	1857	2316	↓	2 55	Via Lyons, arr. 4.43	4 31	4 40	5 59
		dep.	1331		1438	19 1	19 0	2318		2 56		4 32	4 42	6 2
637¾		CULOZ ....arr.	1447		1553	1958	20 7	0 52	↓	4 29		5 44	..	7 19
	page 266	CULOZ ....dep.	15 8		1558	20 5	2011	..	..	4 49		5 46	↓	7 28
658½		BELLEGARDE .... arr.	1537		1626	2026	2038	..	4 30	5 23		6 22		8 4
		dep.	1547		..	2034	2045	..	4 38	.		6 34		8 24
678		GENEVA (Swiss time)..arr.	1625		..	2110	2125	..	..	..		7 13	↓	9 8
	page 255	CULOZ ....dep.	1452		16 5	20 4	2017	1 0		4 47		..	..	7 24
		AIX-LES-BAINS ...... arr.	1512		1625	2023	2038	1 20		5 8		..	6 21	7 43
		dep.	1518		..	2024	2043	1 25		5 23		..	6 35	7 55
		CHAMBERY ....arr.	1531		..	2036	2055	1 37		5 40		..	6 43	8 8
	page 267	AIX-LES-BAINS ....dep.	1536		1630	2059	2059	..		5 38		..	6 27	7 56
		ANNECY ....arr.	1625		1719	2153	2153	..	↓	6 33		..	7 23	8 50
		LA ROCHE-SUR-FORON.. arr.	1729		1818	..	..	..	6 6	7 39		..	8 34	9 57
722		ST. GERVAIS .... arr.	1839		1925	..	..	..	7 20	9 12		..	9 45	11 3
		dep.	19 0		1937		..	..	7 35	9 29		..	10 5	1110
736		CHAMONIX-MONT BLANC arr.	20 6	↓	2043		..	..	8 42	1035	↓	..	1115	1217
	page 265	BELLEGARDE ....dep.	1555	..	1635	2111	2052	..	4 58	5 49	..	..	..	8 11
682⅜		ANNEMASSE ....arr.	1653	..	1736	22 9	2146	..	5 31	6 51	..	..	..	9 10
695		THONON-LES-BAINS ......arr.	1742	..	1816	23 6	2224	..	6 52	7 54	..	..	..	1017
700		EVIAN-LES-BAINS ....arr.	1752	..	1827	2317	2233	..	7 3	8 4		..	..	1028
..		BELLEGARDE ....dep.	..	..	1646	21 0	21 0	..	..	5 31		7 17	..	1111
..		DIVONNE-LES-BAINS ......arr.	..	..	18 0	2219	2219	..	..	6 47		8 3	..	1237
..	p257	CHAMBERY ....dep.	1634	..	..	2044	..	..	..	5 55	..	..	..	8 22
..		GRENOBLE ....arr.	1744	1653	..	22 3	..	..	..	7 18	7 9	..	..	9 32
	page 265	CHAMBERY ....dep.	1552	..	..	..	2120	..	..	7 18	..	..	6 54	1045
..		ALBERTVILLE............arr.	1643	..	..	..	2221	..	..	8 20	..	..	7 50	1158
.		MOUTIERS SALINS ......arr.	1724	..	..		23 5	..	..	9 9	..	..	8 34	
		BOURG ST. MAURICE ....arr.	1813	..	..	..	..	..	..	10 0	..	..	9 32	..

A 1 cl. Lits-Salons and Couchettes, 1, 2 & 3 cl. Cars Paris-Grenoble. **B** 1 cl. Couchettes and 1, 2 & 3 cl. Cars Paris-Chambery-Turin ; 1 cl. Couchettes and 1 & 2 cl. Cars Paris-Evian-les-Bains, from Sept. 17. **C** 1 & 2 cl. Sleep. Car, 1 cl. Couchettes, and 1, 2 & 3 cl. Cars Paris-Geneva ; 1 cl. Couchettes and 1 & 2 cl. Cars Paris-Divonne, July 8 to Sept. 16. **D** July 8 to Sept. 30, 1, 2 & 3 cl. Cars Paris-Evian-les-Bains ; 1, 2 & 3 cl. Cars and Rest. Car Paris-St. Gervais. **E** 1, 2 & 3 cl. Cars Paris-Geneva ; 1, 2 & 3 cl. Paris-Evian-les-Bains, from Oct. 2 ; 1, 2 & 3 cl. Cars Paris-Bourg St. Maurice, July 8 to Oct. 1 ; Rest. Car Paris-Chambery. **F** June 16 to Sept. 30 ; 1 & 2 cl. Cars Paris-Geneva and Paris-Chambery ; 1 & 2 cl. Cars Paris-Evian-les-Bains, July 8 to Sept. 16 ; Rest. Car Paris-Evian, July 8 to Sept. 16 (Geneva from Sept. 17). **G** June 30 to Sept. 30, 1 & 2 cl. Sleep. Cars, 1 cl. Couchettes and 1, 2 & 3 cl. Cars Paris-Bourg St. Maurice ; 1 cl. Couchettes and 1, 2 & 3 cl. Paris-St. Gervais ; 1 cl. Lits-Salons Paris-Annecy. **H** Via Macon, with change of train 18.25 ; 1 & 2 cl. Cars Macon-Geneva and Macon-Chambery. **I** 1, 2 & 3 cl. Cars Paris-Grenoble ; Rest. Car Paris-Lyons. **J** June 30 to Sept. 30, 1, 2 & 3 cl. Sleep Cars, 1 cl. Couchettes and 1 & 2 cl. Cars Paris-St. Gervais ; 1 & 2 cl. Sleep Cars and 1 cl. Couchettes Paris-Evian-les-Bains, July 7 to Sept. 16. **K** Rest. Car Paris-Dijon. **L** 1 cl. Lits Salons Paris-Chambery from Oct. 1 ; 1 & 2 cl. Sleep. Car, 1 cl. Couchettes and 1 & 2 cl. Cars Calais-St. Gervais, July 7 to Sept. 16. ¶ Via Dover-Dunkerque.

FROM EVIAN, CHAMONIX, AIX-LES-BAINS and GENEVA.

N.B.—For restrictions regarding use of these trains for short distances, *see pp.* **266 and 258**

			Rap 123	Exp 123	Rap 123	Exp 123	Rap 123	Rap 12	Rap 123	Rap 12	Exp 12	Rap 123	Rap 123	Rap 123
			C	K	J	A	F	G		L	B	H	D	E
p. 265	Bourg St. Maurice	dep.	17 0	..	1940	..	..	..	..	7 20	7 20	1140		..
	Moutiers Salins	„	1754	..	2023	..	..	..	..	8 10	8 10	1222	..	..
	Albertville	„	1845	..	21 1	..	..	..	..	9 1	9 1	13 0	..	..
	Chambery	arr.	1954	..	2153	..		..	..	1011	1011	1349	..	..
p 257	Grenoble	dep.	1822	20 0	..	2115	2042	..	..	7 54	..	1227	1355	..
	Chambery	arr.	1941	2059	..	..	22 4	..	..	9 17	..	1321		..
	Divonne-les-Bains	dep.	1850	2037		..	..	..	..	..	9 58	1210		..
	Bellegarde	arr.	20 1	2148	..	..	..	..	..	..	1110	1321		..
page 265	Evian-les-Bains	dep.	1840	1913		..	..	21 0	..	8 50		1131	↓	1315
	Thonon-les-Bains	„	1854	1930	..	..	..	2113	..	9 0	..	1147		1333
	Annemasse	„	1935	2023	..	..	..	2214	..	9 37	..	1236		1411
	Bellegarde	arr.	2031	2132	..	..		23 8	..	1024	..	1331	↓	1510
page 267.	Chamonix-Mont Blanc	dep.	1620	↓	1812	..	1720	1913		..	..	9 8	..	1052
	St. Gervais	arr.	1725		1917	..	1832	2028	..	..	..	1079	..	1159
		dep.	1735		1935	..	1849	2038		6 25	..	1043	..	1215
	La Roche-sur-Foron	„	1855		2050	..	2018	2143		7 52	..	1156	..	1327
	Annecy	„	1959		2156	..	2119	↓		8 52	1036	1318	..	1434
	Aix-les-Bains	arr.	2049	↓	2239		2212		..	9 44	1128	14 3		1518
p. 265.	Chambery	dep.	2051	21 7	2159	..	2327		5 2	1023	1142	14 9	*Via* Lyons, see p. 257. dep. 16.20.	..
	Aix-les-Bains	arr.	21 5	2122	2212		2341		5 15	1037	1153	1422		..
		dep.	2118	2129	2252		2355		5 17	1046	1154	1428		1523
	Culoz	arr.	2138	2150	..		0 15	↓	5 34	11 7	1213	1447		1541
p. 266.	GENEVA (Swiss time)	dep.	19 7	2124	↓	*Via* Lyons, dep. 0.0 see p. 257.	↓	..	..	10 0	11 5	13 6		..
	Bellegarde	arr.	2014	2159				23 8	..	1034	1139	1341		..
		dep.	2043	2220				2315	..	1049	1149	14 1		1517
	Culoz	arr.	2112	2247	↓		↓	..	..	1113	1212	1430		1543
page 266.	Culoz	dep.	2145	2248	..		0 20	..	5 53	1126	1217	15 3		16 0
	Bourg	arr.	2323	0 6	0 41		1 49	1 6	7 16	1237	1321	1623		1717
		dep.	2329	0 9	0 42		1 52	1 8	7 23	1240	1322	1626		1720
	Dijon	arr.	1 50	2 42	2 26	2 42	3 57	3 8	10 0	1428	1531	1822	1851	1920
p. 266	Dijon	dep.	2 0	2 48	2 40	2 48	4 3	3 13	10 7	1434	1537	1828	1858	1926
	Paris (Lyon)	arr.	6 20	6 55	6 50	6 55	8 10	7 15	14 5	1810	1925	2225	2255	2320
			12				12	12						
	Ceinture Rly.	dep.	6 35	..	9 46	..	9 46	9 35	..	123		..	..	..
		arr.	6 59	..	..	..	..	10 9	..			..	..	..
					..					..		..	..	..
page 112.	Paris (Nord)	dep.	8 20	..	..	..	..	1030	1625	2150		..	..	..
	Calais	arr.	1141	..	..	..	..	..	..	..		..	..	..
		dep.	12 5	..	..	..	..	..	..	..		..	..	..
	Boulogne	arr.	..	..	13 5	..	1323	1310	19 5	¶		..	..	..
		dep.		..	1345	..	1345	1345	1920	..		..	..	..
	Dover	arr.	1320	..	..	..	..	..		..		..	..	..
		dep.	1355	..	..	..	..	..		..		..	..	..
	Folkestone	arr.		..	1520	..	1520	1520	2050	..		..	..	..
		dep.		..	1544	..	1544	1544	2120	..		..	..	..
	LONDON—VICTORIA	arr.	1530	..	1720		1720	1720	23 0	9 10		..		..

A 1 cl. Lits-Salons and Couchettes, 1, 2 & 3 cl. Cars Grenoble-Paris. **B** Via Macon, change of train 13.53; 1, 2 and 3 cl. Cars Geneva and Chambery-Macon. **C** 1 cl. Couchettes and 1, 2 & 3 cl. Cars Turin-Chambery-Paris; 1 cl. Couchettes and 1 & 2 cl. Cars St. Gervais-Calais, July 2 to Oct. 1. **D** 1, 2 & 3 cl. Cars Grenoble-Paris; Rest. Car Lyons-Paris. **E** July 9 to Oct. 1, 1, 2 & 3 cl. Cars Evian-les-Bains-Paris; 1, 2 & 3 cl. Cars and Rest. Car St. Gervais-Paris. **F** 1 cl. Couchettes and 1, 2 & 3 cl. Cars Turin-Chambery-Paris; 1 cl. Couchettes and 1, 2 & 3 cl. Cars St. Gervais-Paris from Oct. 2. **G** July 1 to Oct. 1, 1 & 2 cl. Sleep. Car, 1 cl. Couchettes and 1, 2 & 3 cl. Cars St. Gervais-Paris; 1 & 2 cl. Sleep. Car, 1 cl. Couchettes and 1 & 2 cl. Cars Evian-les-Bains-Paris, July 8 to Sept. 17. **H** 1, 2 & 3 cl. Cars Geneva-Paris; 1, 2 & 3 cl. Cars Evian-les-Bains-Paris from Oct. 3; 1, 2 & 3 cl. Cars Bourg St. Maurice-Paris, July 9 to Oct. 2; Rest. Car Chambery-Paris. **J** July 1 to Oct. 1, 1 & 2 cl. Sleep. Car, 1 cl. Couchettes and 1, 2 & 3 cl. Cars Bourg St. Maurice-Paris; 1 cl. Lits-Salons Annecy-Paris; 1 & 2 cl. Sleep. Car St. Gervais-Boulogne, July 8 to Sept. 17; 1 cl. Couchettes and 1, 2 & 3 cl. Cars St. Gervais-Paris. **K** 1 & 2 cl. Sleep. Car, 1 cl. Couchettes and 1, 2 & 3 cl. Cars Geneva-Paris; 1 cl. Couchettes and 1 & 2 cl. Cars Evian-les-Bains-Paris from Sept. 18; 1 cl. Couchettes and 1 & 2 cl. Cars Divonne-Paris, July 9 to Sept. 17. **L** June 18 to Oct. 1, 1 & 2 cl. Cars Chambery and Geneva-Paris; 1 & 2 cl. Cars Evian-les-Bains-Paris; Rest. Car Evian-Paris, July 9 to Sept. 17 (from Geneva after Sept. 18). ¶ *Via* Dunkerque-Dover.

To SWITZERLAND, ITALY via the Loetschberg and the St. Gotthard, and GERMANY via the Arlberg (via Laon)

Miles fr'm Cal.	Ref.	Station		12 S	12 D	128 E
				Rap	Rap	
0		LONDON— VICTORIA	dep.	14 0	1630	..
78		Folkestone (Harbour)	,,	..	1825	..
108		Dover (Marine)		1555	..	..
		Calais	arr.	1710	..	..
..		Calais	dep.	1725	..	..
..		Boulogne	arr.	..	1955	..
..		Boulogne	dep.	..	2030	..
207		Amiens	,,	..	2159	..
271	p. 270.	Laon *b*	dep.	2037	2321	..
306	p. 270.	Reims *b*	,,	..	0 † 2	..
342	p. 270.	Chalons *b*	,,	..	0 42	..
425	p. 268.	Chaumont *b*	,,	2319	2 28	..
528	p. 268.	Belfort *b*	arr.	1 29	4 49	..
..	p. 268.	Belfort	dep.	5 10	5 10	..
551	p. 268.	Delle *b* Grn. T.	arr.	5 37	5 37	..
	p. 278.	,, M.E.T.	dep.	6 0	6 0	..
559	p. 278.	Porrentruy *b c*	arr.	6 13	6 13	..
	p. 278.		dep.	6 34	6 34	..
576	p. 278.	Delemont *b*	arr.	7 3	7 3	..
598	p. 278.	Biel (Bienne) *b*	,,	7 40	7 40	..
620		Berne *b*	arr.	8 24	8 24	..
			dep.	8 51	8 51	..
646	p. 288.	Spiez	arr.	9 29	9 29	..
688	p. 288.	Interlaken (E.) p. 281	,,	10 9	10 9	..
666	p. 288.	Kandersteg *b*	,,	..	1014	..
692	p. 288.	Brigue *b*	,,	..	11 3	..
..	p. 288.	Visp	,,	..	1259	..
..	p. 288.	Zermatt	,,	..	1435	..
794	p. 288.	Milan *b*	,,	..	1432	..
844	p. 288.	Genoa	,,	..	1752	..
..		Brindisi (Mar.) p. 313	,,	..	8 25	..
	p. 268.	Belfort	dep.	1 35	4 55	..
568	p. 268.	Mulhouse *b*	arr.	2 8	5 27	..
589	p. 268.	Bale *b* (Grn. time)	,,	2 35	5 53	..
..	p. 268.	,, (Swiss) M.E.T.	,,	2 35	5 53	..
..	p. 282	Bale (Swiss) M.E.T.	dep.	↓	6 45	..
648	p. 282	Lucerne *b*	arr.		8 1	..
			dep.		8 10	..
711	p. 287.	Goeschenen *b*	arr.		9 33	..
794	p. 287.	Lugano *b*	arr.		1114	..
810	p. 304.	Chiasso *b c*	arr.		1138	..
	p. 304.		dep.		12 0	..
813	p. 304.	Como *b*	arr.		12 8	..
842	p. 304.	Milan *b*	,,		13 7	..
1007		Venice *b* (p. 305)	,,	↓	1740	..
..		Trieste	,,	.	2034	
				S	123	
..	p. 283.	Bale (Swiss) M.E.T.	dep.	2 48	6 49	7 40
644	p. 283.	Zurich *b*	arr.	4 *f* 1	8 *f* 6	9 8
	p. 283.		dep.	4 3	8 *f* 9	9 20
701	p. 283.	Sargans *b*	arr.	5 21	9 22	1051
..	p. 197.	Sargans	dep.	5 27	9 27	1124
711	p. 197.	Buchs *b c*	arr.	5 40	9 40	1144
	p. 197.		dep.	5 55	10 0	1220
837	p. 197.	Innsbruck *b*	arr.	8 52	13 8	1555
994	p. 197.	Salzburg *b*	,,	1257	1730	2040
1189	p. 197.	Vienna (West) *b*	,,	1715	2218	.
..		Bale (Swiss) M.E.T.	dep.	2 48	7 40	7 13
..	p. 286.	Sargans	dep.	6 56	1053	*a*
708	p. 286.	Landquart	arr.	7 4	11 7	1019
740	p. 286.	Davos Platz	,,	9 12	1240	12 2
717	p. 286.	Coire *b*	,,	7 30	1122	1035
	p. 286.	St. Moritz	,,	1012	1444	1315

D 1 and 2 cl cars Boulogne-Vienna, Boulogne-Bale-Chiasso-Milan-Trieste and Boulogne-Berne-Brigue-Loetschberg-Milan-Brindisi; 1 and 2 cl. Boulogne-Interlaken to Sept. 30; 1 and 2 cl. Boulogne-Bale, from Sept. 10 to May 18, 1940; 1 and 2 cl. Sleeping Car Boulogne-Buchs, from Sept. 10 to Oct. 7; 1 and 2 cl. Sleeping Car and 1 and 2 cl. Cars Boulogne-Coire, June 30 to Sept. 9; 1 and 2 cl. Sleeping Cars Boulogne-Interlaken, June 30 to Sept. 9; 1 and 2 cl. Sleeping Car Boulogne-Berne-Brigue Thursdays and Saturdays only, July 1 to Sept. 9; Rest. Car Boulogne-Laon.

E 1, 2 and 3 cl. Cars Bale-Salzburg.

S Arlberg—Orient Express Calais to Vienna and Bucharest, Mondays, Wednesdays and Fridays. Engadine and Oberland Expresses, see pages 83 and 85.

f Zurich (Enge). † Reims-Ceres. *a* July 1 to Sept. 10.

N.B.—For conditions regarding use of these trains for short distances, see pages 237, 268 and 270.

From SWITZERLAND and ITALY via the Loetschberg and the St. Gotthard, and GERMANY via the Arlberg (via Laon)

Ref.	Station		1 2 3	1 2 3 A	1 2 B	1 2 S
p. 286.	St. MORITZ	dep	1545	..	1710	2015
	Coire b	,,	1835	..	1953	2239
	Davos Platz	,,	17 5	..	1835	19 0
	Landquart b	,,	1842	..	20 6	..
	Zurich	,,	2042	..	2149	1f38
	Bale b (Swiss) M.E.T.	ar.	22 5	..	23 1	2 54
p. 197.	Vienna b	dep.	..	..	8 5	1220
	Salzburg b	,,	..	9 30	1250	1640
	Innsbruck b	,,	..	1452	1715	2040
p. 286.	Buchs b c	arr.	..	1816	2025	2345
		dep.	..	1830	2050	0 0
	Sargans	arr.	..	1844	21 3	0 14
	Sargans	dep.	..	1859	21 9	0 23
p. 288	Zurich b	arr.	..	2029	2229	1f36
		dep.	..	2042	2236	1f38
	Bale b (Swiss) M.E.T.	ar.	..	2215	2350	2 54
	Trieste	dep.	..		9 30	Mons., Weds. and Fris. Sleep. Cars only.
	Venice b p. 305	dep.	..	..	1215	
p. 304.	Milan	dep.	..	..	1710	
	Como	,,	..	..	1812	
	Chiasso b c	arr.	..	..	1822	
		dep.	..	..	1850	
p. 287.	Lugano b	,,	..	..	1916	
	Bellinzona b	arr.	..	..	1945	
	Goeschenen b	dep.	..	..	..	
p. 282	Lucerne b	arr.	..	..	2219	
		dep.	..	..	2227	
	Bale (Swiss) M.E.T.	arr.	..	..	2341	
p. 268.	Bale (Swiss) M.E.T.	dep.	..	..	0 30	3 20
	,, (Green. time) ..	,,	..	..	0 30	3 20
	Mulhouse b	,,	..	..	1 2	3 46
	Belfort b	arr.	..	..	1 42	4 28
	Brindisi (Mar.) p. 311	d.	..	..	1951	..
page 288.	Genoa	dep.	..	..	14x33	..
	Milan	,,	..	..	1645	..
	Zermatt	,,	..	..	1555	..
	Visp	,,	..	..	1732	..
	Brigue b	,,	..	..	2030	..
	Kandersteg b	,,	..	..	2115	..
	Interlaken (East)	,,	..	..	2117	2117
	Spiez b	,,	..	..	2158	2150
page 278.	Berne b	arr.	..	..	2236	2227
		dep.	..	..	2250	2250
	Biel (Bienne) b	,,	..	..	2331	2331
	Delemont b	,,	..	..	0 12	0 12
	Porrentruy b c	arr.	..	..	0 41	0 41
		dep.	..	..	0 45	0 45
	Delle b (M.E.T.)	arr.	..	..	0 58	0 58
p. 268	,, (Gn. T.)	dep.	..	..	1 18	1 18
	Belfort	arr.	..	..	1 46	1 46
	Belfort	dep.	..	..	1 58	4 34
	Chaumont b	,,	..	..	4 13	7 15
p. 270.	Chalons b	,,	..	..	5 58	..
	Reims b	arr.	..	..	6 48	..
	Laon b	,,	..	..	7 47	10 5
p. 237.	Amiens b	arr.	..	..	9 26	..
	Boulogne	arr.	..	..	..	13 5
	Boulogne	dep.	..	..	..	..
	Calais	arr.	..	..	1136	..
	Calais	dep.	..	..	12 5	..
p. 112.	Dover (Marine)	arr.	..	..	1320	..
	Folkestone (Harbour)	arr.	..	..		1515
	LONDON (Victoria)	arr.	..	..	1530	1720

N.B.—For restrictions regarding use of these trains for short distances, see pages 237, 268 and 270.

A 1, 2 and 3 cl. Cars Salzburg-Bale

B 1 and 2 cl. Cars Trieste-Milan-Calais, Interlaken-Calais (to Oct. 2) and Vienna-Calais; 1 and 2 cl. Bale-Calais from Sept. 11; 1 and 2 cl. Sleeping Car Buchs-Calais from Sept. 11 to Oct. 6; 1 and 2 cl. Sleeping Car and 1 and 2 cl. Cars Coire-Calais, July 1 to Sept. 10; 1 and 2 cl. Sleeping Cars Interlaken-Calais, July 1 to Sept. 10; 1 and 2 cl. Sleeping Car Brigue-Berne-Calais, Fridays and Sundays only, July 2 to Sept. 10; Restaurant Car Reims-Calais.

S Arlberg—Orient Express Bucharest-Budapest-Vienna-Boulogne; Engadine and Oberland Expresses, Mondays, Wednesdays and Fridays from Vienna, St. Moritz and Interlaken, see pages 83 and 85.

x Rapido supp. payable. a July 1 to Sept. 10. f Zurich (Enge Station).

TO AND FROM SWITZERLAND via the Loetschberg and the St. Gothard, and GERMANY via the Arlberg. Via PARIS.

E	S	B	A	Miles			C	D	S	E
1 2	1 2	1 2	1 2				1 2	1 2	1 2	1 2
9 0	11 0	14 0	14 0	0	p. 112.	dep. LONDON (Victoria) b .. arr.	1530	1530	1720	23 0
..	1255	1555	1555	78		,, Dover (Marine) b ...... ,,	1320	1320	..	..
1055	..	..	..	..		,, Folkestone Harbour b .. ,,	..	.	1515	2050
..	1450	1735	1735	106		,, Calais (Mar.) b .... ,,	1141	1141	..	
1255	..	..		..		,, Boulogne (Mar.) b .... ,,	..	..	1310	19 5
1548	1810	21 0	21 0	287		arr. PARIS (Nord) b .... dep.	8 20	8 20	1030	1625
	Drive	Drive				dep. ,, ... arr.	Drive	..	..	..
	across	across				arr. PARIS (Est.) .... dep.	across	..		
1 2 3	1 2	1 2 3	1 2 3				1 2 3	1 2 3	1 2	1 2 3
1715	1955	22 0	2250	0	p. 268.	dep. PARIS (Est.) .... arr.	6 45	7 15	9 45	1415
1910	..	0 0	..	..		,, Troyes ....dep.	4 31	5 24	..	1231
2020	2331	1 24	2 7	163		,, Chaumont b............ ,,	3 17	4 21	6 54	
2243	1 29	3 48	4 37	275		arr. Belfort b .... ,,	0 27	2 10	4 34	9 23
..	5 10	..	5 10	..		dep. Belfort ....arr.	..	1 46	1 46	9 15
..	5 37	..	5 37	289		arr. Delle b Grn. T. ....dep.	..	1 18	1 18	8 48
..	6 0	..	6 0	..	p. 278.	dep. ,, M.E.T. ....arr.	..	0 58	0 58	8 33
..	6 13	..	6 13	296		arr. Porrentruy b c ....dep.	..	0 45	0 45	8 20
..	6 34	..	6 34	..		dep. ,, ...arr.	..	0 41	0 41	8 18
..	7 5	..	7 5	313		arr. Delemont b ....dep.	..	0 10	0 10	7 51
..	7 50	..	7 50	335		,, Biel b .... ,,	..	2324	2324	7 3
..	8 24	..	8 24	356	p. 288.	,, Berne b................. ,,	..	2250	2250	6 47
..	9 29	..	9 29	382		,, Spiez .... ,,	..	2158	2158	5 27
..	10¶9	..	10 9	424		,, Interlaken (E) p. 281 ,,	..	2125	21¶17	5 0
..	..	..	1016	402		,, Kandersteg b .... ,,	..	2113	.	4 45
..	..	..	11 3	428		,, Brigue b .... ,,	..	2030	..	4 2
..	..	..	1448	530		,, Milan b .... ,,	..	1645	..	0 15
..	..	..	8 25			,, Brindisi Mar. .... ,,	..	1951	..	
2250	1 35	4 15	4 45	..	p. 268.	dep. Belfort ....arr.	0 21	2 0	4 28	9 0
2329	2 8	5 6	5 20	315		arr. Mulhouse b ....dep.	2335	1 18	3 46	8 20
24 0	2 35	5 42	5 22	336		,, Bale b c Grn. T. ...... ,,	23 0	0 40	3 20	7 47
24 0	2 35	5 42	5 22	..		,, ,, (Swiss) M.E.T. .. ,,	23 0	0 40	3 20	7 4
		1 2	2 3					1 2		
..	Sleeping Cars only, Mon., Wed. & Fri.	6 45	7 18	..	p. 282	dep. Bale (Swiss) M.E.T..... arr.	22 0	2341	Sleeping Cars only, Mon., Wed. & Fri.	6 16
..		8 1	8 44	395		arr. Lucerne b ....dep.	2041	2227		4 47
..		9 35	1026	458	p. 287.	,, Goeschenen b .... ,,	1831	..		
..		1043	1156	522		,, Bellinzona b .... ,,	1717	1947		1 49
..		1120	1226	536		,, Locarno b .... ,,	1617	1743		0 30
..		1254	1254	530		,, Luino b .... ,,	1610	..		21*50
..		1045	12 0	..		dep Bellinzona b ....arr.	1712	1944		1 39
..		1115	1234	541		arr. Lugano b ....dep.	1637	1916		1 4
..		1130	13 0	557		,, Chiasso b c .... ,,	16 8	1850		0 35
..		12 0	1323	..	p. 304.	dep. ,, ...arr.	1548	1822		0 5
..		1211	1329	560		arr. Como b ....dep.	15 8	1814		2357
..		13 7	1445	754		,, Milan b................ ,,	1424	1710	‡ 1 2	2253
..	2 48	6 49	7 40	..	p. 283.	dep. Bale (Swiss) M.E.T. .... arr.	22 5	2350	2 54	6 45
..	4 a 1	8 a 15	9 8	391		arr. Zurich b ....dep.	2042	2236	1 a 38	5 35
..	5 21	9 22	1051	448		,, Sargans b............ ,,	1857	21 9	0 23	4 13
	5 27	9 27	1124	..	p. 197.	dep. Sargans................arr.	1844	21 2	0 14	4 4
..	5 40	9 40	1144	458		arr. Buchs b c ....dep.	18x30	2050	0 0	3 50
..	5 55	10 0	1220	..		dep. ,, ...arr.	1816	2025	2345	3 30
..	8 52	13 8	1555	584		arr. Innsbruck b ....dep.	1452	1715	2040	0 12
..	1257	1730	2040	741		,, Salzburg b .... ,,	9 30	1250	1640	1945
..	1715	2218	..	836		,, Vienna (West) b........ ,,	..	8 5	1220	1428
							1 2 3			
..	2¶48	7 13	7 40	..	p. 286.	dep. Bale (Swiss) M.E.T..... arr.	22 5	23 1	2 54	..
..	5 21	c	1051	..		arr. Sargans ....dep.	1859	c	0 0	..
..	7 13	1019	11 7	455		,, Landquart .... ,,	1842	20 6	..	..
..	9§12	12 2	1240	487		,, Davos Platz .... ,,	17 5	1835	19 0	..
..	7 30	1035	1122	464		,, Coire b .... ,,	1830	1953	2234	..
..	1012	1315	1444	517		,, ST. MORITZ .... ,,	1545	1710	2015	..

S Arlberg-Orient Exp. Mons., Weds. and Fris., 1 and 2 cl. Sleeping Cars Paris to Vienna and Bucharest and v.v.; also Oberland Exp. to Interlaken and Engadine Exp. to Coire, see page 85. Rest. Car Paris-Chaumont and v.v.

A 1, 2 and 3 cl. Cars Paris-Coire; 1 and 2 cl. Sleeper Paris-Coire. 1, 2 and 3 cl. Sleeper Paris-Interlaken. 1, 2 and 3 cl. Cars Paris-Milan via Loetschberg. 1, 2 and 3 cl. Cars Bale-Salzburg.
B 3 cl. Car Paris-Bale-Milan. 1 and 2 cl. Cars Paris-Budapest. 3 cl. Car Paris-Vienna. 1 and 2 cl. Sleeper Paris-Innsbruck. 3 cl. Sleeper Paris-Innsbruck June 26th to Sept. 5th. 1 and 2 cl. Sleeping Car Paris-Lucerne June 30th to Sept. 9th.
C 3 cl. Car Milan-Paris via St. Gothard. 1 and 2 cl. Sleeper Coire-Paris. 1, 2 and 3 cl. Cars Coire-Paris. 1 & 2 cl. Sleeping Car Lucerne-Paris, July 1st to Sept. 10th. 1, 2 and 3 cl. Cars Salzburg-Bale.

D 1 and 2 cl. Sleeper Innsbruck-Paris; 3 cl. Sleeper Innsbruck-Paris, June 27th to Sept. 6; 1 and 2 cl. Cars Budapest-Paris; 3 cl. Cars Vienna-Paris; 1, 2 and 3 cl. Cars Milan-Berne-Paris; 1, 2 and 3 cl. Sleeper Interlaken-Paris. E 1, 2 and 3 cl. Cars Paris-Bale and v.v.; 1 & 2 cl. Sleeping Car Vienna-Belfort; 1, 2 and 3 cl. Cars Bucharest-Paris; 3 cl. Car Milan-Paris via Berne; Rest. Car Paris-Belfort and v.v. § 2 and 3 cl. * Not Sundays. ¶ Days of running see p. 85. *a* Zurich (Enge). *c* July 1—Sept. 10.

TO AND FROM SOUTHERN GERMANY

Via Mezieres—Charleville.

A 123	123	Miles.			B 123	123
11¶0	14 0	0	p. 236. p. 112.	dep. LONDON (Victoria) .... arr.	1530	18‡55
..	..			,, Folkestone Harbour .... ,,	..	..
1255	1555	78		,, Dover (Marine) .... ,,	1320	1655
..	..			,, Boulogne (Mar.) .... ,,	..	..
1444	1758	103		,, CALAIS (Mar.) .... ,,	1026	1534
1449	18 5			,, CALAIS (Ville) .... ,,	1020	1528
2132	0 39	283		arr. Mezieres-Charleville ....dep.	5 25	8 16
23 8	2 1	336		,, Longuyon .... ,,	3 16	6 38
1831	22 0	0	p. 271.	dep. PARIS (Est.) ......arr.	9 0	11 8
2135	1 28	..		arr. Mezieres-Charleville dep.	5 37	8 10
2145	1 42	..		dep. Mezieres-Charleville .... arr.	5 5	8 1
2313	2 58	..		,, Longuyon .... ,,	3 39	6 25
0 4	3 50	366		arr. Thionville ....dep.	2 15	5 34
↓	4 5	..	p. 275.	dep. Thionville ....arr.	2 0	↑
	5 12	..		,, Hargarten-Falk .... ,,	1 4	
	6 20	..		arr. Saarbrucken ....dep.	2342	
	9 24	..		,, FRANKFORT.. .... ,,	2032	
	7 21		p. 169.	dep. Thionville..........arr.	2115	
	1023	409		arr. Treves ....dep.	1920	
	12 6	..		,, COBLENCE .... ,,	1629	
1 13	4 47	..	p. 179.	dep. Thionville ....arr.	1 50	4 17
1 38	5 30	382		arr. Metz ....dep.	1 22	3 54
3 35	8 42	483		,, Strasbourg.......... ,,	2315	2 5
5 32	1051	575		,, BALE .... ,,	2051	0 20
6 25	9 14	..		dep. Strasbourg .... arr.	2026	2224
6 36	9 26	488		arr. Kehl ....dep.	2012	2211
6 56	9 48	..		dep Kehl .... arr	1938	2155
7 9	10 4	493		arr. Appenweier ....dep.	1926	2143
7 34	1037	516		,, Baden West .... ,,	1852	2119
7 58	11 7	536		,, Carlsruhe .... ,,	1825	2055
9 38	1334	591		,, Stuttgart .... ,,	1632	1920
1252	1715	741		,, Munich .... ,,	13 6	1544
6 25	9 14	..		dep. Strasbourg .... arr.	2026	..
8 13	1046	..		,, Appenweier.......... ,,	19 7	..
8 21	1058	498		arr. Offenburg ....dep.	19 0	..
9 34	1135	519		,, Hausach .... ,,	1826	..
10 2	12 4	533		,, Triberg .... ,,	18 2	..
1134	1337	591		,, Singen .... ,,	1624	..
12 9	14 4	610		,, Constance .... ,,	1556	..
9 15	1157	537		,, Freiburg .... ,,	16 6	..
11 2	1413	557		,, Titisee .... ,,	15 6	..

¶ 3 cl. dep. 10.30. ‡ 3 cl. arr. 20.13.

A 1, 2 and 3 cl. Cars and 1 cl. Couchettes Mezieres-Bale.

B 1, 2 and 3 cl. Cars and 1 cl. Couchettes Bale-Calais.

§ Via Luxembourg.

LONDON, BRUSSELS, STRASBOURG, BALE, &c.

				Mls								
	1 2	1 2 3							1 2	1 2 3		
luxe	Exp	Exp	..		LONDON:—			..				
..	11 0	14 0	..	..	dep. VICTORIA........	p. 149	arr.	..	1530	23 0	..	
..	1255	1555	..	..	„ Dover Pier		dep.	..	1355	‖	..	
..	1444	1730	..	103	„ CALAIS PIER		dep.	..	12 5		..	
..	1619	1858	..	172	arr. Lille		d.	..	1030	1647	..	
..	1633	19 5	..		dep. Lille		a.	..	1023	1631	..	
..	1832	..	..	239	arr. BRUSSELS (MIDI)		dep.	..	..	1428	..	
..	..	2050	..	242	arr. BRUSSELS (NORD) ..		dep.		8 38	..	..	
1 2	1 2 3	1 2 3	1 2 3								luxe	B
¶	A	C	B		LONDON:—			r	1 2 r		1 2	1 2 3
11 0	1030	15 0	23 0	0	dep. VICTORIA ....dep.		dep.	1620	1620	2150	2150	7 20
1255	1255	1655	1 0	..	„ Dover Pier ....dep.		dep.	1445	1445	2010	2010	5 35
1615	1615	2015	5 0	139	arr. OSTEND (Quay) ..	p. 150	dep.	1050	1050	1620	1620	1 0
1651	1843	23 2	6 7		dep. OSTEND (Quay)		arr.	10 8	1029	1532	1546	2345
18 1	20 5	0 23	7 40	209	arr. BRUSSELS (Nord) ..		dep.	8 51	9 9	1411	1434	2224
☞	A	C						C	A		☞	
	2018	0 54	..	..	dep. BRUSSELS (Nord)	p. 149	arr.	7x48	8 53	1259		
	2113	1 46		260	arr. Namur............		dep.	7 5	8 1	1157		
	..	..		351	arr. Klein-Bettingen..		d.	..	..	..		
	..	..			dep. Klein-Bettingen		a.	..	..	..		
	2343	4 47		362	arr. LUXEMBURG		d.	3 32	5 22	9 24		
	0 10	5 1			dep. LUXEMBURG		a.	3 15	5 15	9 12		
	1 38	6 26		..	arr. METZ (p. 179)..........		dep.	1 22	3 54	7 55		
	1 41	6 28		404	dep. METZ	p179	arr.	1 18	3 52	7 53		
	3 35	8 42		503	arr. STRASBOURG		dep.	2315	2 5	6 0		
	5 43	9 14	..	..	dep. STRASBOURG	p. 182/3	arr.	2224	..	..		
	6 38	10 4	..	525	arr. Appenweier......		dep.	2143	..	..		
	7y12	1058	..	530	„ Offenburg		dep.	1955	y	..		
	9y15	1157	..	569	„ FREIBURG-I-B. ..		dep.	1741	y	..		
..	6 26	9 14	..		dep. STRASBOURG	p. 183	arr.	22 4	..	..		
..	7 42	1037	..	548	arr. BADEN BADEN ..		dep.	2039	..	..		
..	7 58	11 7	..	..	„ Carlsruhe	p.	dep.	2025	..	..		
..	9 38	1334	..	..	„ Stuttgart	p. 186	dep.	1857	..	..		
..	1252	1715	..	..	„ MUNICH		dep.	1544	..	..		
..	1510	1952	..	..	„ Salzburg		dep.	1323	..	..		
..	1950	6 44	..	..	„ VIENNA (W.)		dep.	8 50	..	..		
..	3 42	8 52	..	..	dep. STRASBOURG	p. 181	a.	2253	2 0	..		
..	5 32	1051	..	590	arr. BALE (Swiss st.) G.T.		d.	2051	0 20	..		
..	5 32	1051	..	..	„ BALE („) M.E.T.		d.	2051	0 20	..		
..	6*45	12 0	..	..	dep. BALE (Swiss) M.E.T.	p. 282	a.	20 8	23*41	..		
..	8 * 1	1330	..	..	arr. LUCERNE..........		d.	1838	2227	*..		
..	6 57	1230	..	..	dep. Bale (Swiss) M.E.T.	p. 279 281/2	a.	1855	2225	..	..	
..	8 30	14 7	..	..	arr. Berne		d.	1718	2025	..	..	
..	9 48	1540	..	..	„ Interlaken, Ost...		d	1541	19 3	..	..	
	1032	1638	..	632	„ Geneva		d.	1435	1754		..	
								C	A			
7 13	7 40	1155	..	..	dep. BALE (Swiss) M.E.T.	p. 283	arr.	1946	22 5	23 1		
8 36	9 8	1320	..	645	arr. ZURICH		dep.	1824	2042	2149		
12 2	1240	17 5	..	..	„ Davos-Platz	p. 286	dep.	1345	17 5	1835		
1035	1122	1546	..	722	„ COIRE		dep.	16 7	1830	1953		
1315	1444	1840	..	779	„ ST. MORITZ......		dep.	1236	1545	1710		
..	8 10	1344	..	..	dep. Lucerne	p. 287	arr.	1827	2219	..	..	
..	13 7	1930	..	..	arr. Milan		dep.	1220	1710	..	..	
..	19†50	6 30	..	..	„ Rome (p. 303) ..		dep.	0 5	9*15	..	..	
..	1740	2359	..	..	„ Venice (p. 305)		dep.	6*50	12 7	..	..	
..	1545	2235	..	..	„ Genoa (p. 302)		dep.	9 0	14*33	..	..	

¶ Every Sat. to Sept. 2 leave London 10.30.

1 and 2 cl. Pullman Exp. ☞ (Brussels–Strasbourg)

To Constance *via* Cologne.

1 and 2 cl. Pullman Train Brussels to Ostend. ☞

From Constance *via* Cologne.

July 1-Sept. 10 (Bale–St. Moritz trains, left column and right column).

y 2 & 3 cl. only. *r* Rest Car.

‖ *Via* Boulogne and Folkestone.

A 1 and 2 cl. Cars Ostend-Bale-Genoa-Vintimille and Ostend-Interlaken and *v.v.*: 1, 2 and 3 cl. Cars Ostend-Bale. 1 and 2 cl. Sleep. Car Ostend-Brussels-Bale-Lucerne-Milan and *v.v.*; 3 cl. Car Ostend-Milan and *v.v.* Rest. Car Ostend-Jemelle-Bale-Milan and *v.v.*

B Daily June 30-Sept. 10. 1, 2 and 3 cl. Cars Ostend-Constance *via* Cologne and *v.v.* (*See pages* 128, 180, 182/3).

C 1 & 2 cl. Sleep. Car Brussels-Bale-Rome and *v.v.*; 1, 2 & 3 cl. Cars Brussels–Bale and *v.v.*; Buffet Car Thionville-Mulhouse and Bale-Zurich-Coire. Rest Car Bale-Milan.
* 1 & 2 class only. † 1 cl. only from Milan. *a* Ostend Town Station. *x* Quartier Leopold Station.

LONDON, COLOGNE, VIENNA, BUDAPEST, BUCHAREST, BERLIN, WARSAW, MOSCOW

luxe 12	Exp 123	Exp 123						Mls.	LONDON—See p. 112.	Epx 123			Exp 123	luxe	123	luxe	
..	..	14 0					..	0	dep. VICTORIA ...... arr.	1530			1530	..	23 0	..	..
..	..	1730	Rest. Car				..	103	dep. CALAIS PIER ...... dep.	12 0	Rest. Car		12 0	..	§	..	..
..	..	2050					..	243	arr. BRUSSELS (Nord) .. dep.	8 38			8 38	..	14g28	..	..
12	123	12	123	12	123	123	123		LONDON—	12	123	123	12	12	123	12	123
11 0	1030	15 0	15 0	15 0	15 0	15 0	23 0	0	dep. VICTORIA (p. 150) .. arr.	1620	1620	1620	1620	1620	2150	2150	7 20
B	YC	O	A	N	C	D	H			E	C	A	N	O	CY	B	H
1651	17 4	2038	2120	2038	23 2	23 2	6 7	147	dep. OSTEND QUAY .... arr.	7 46	7 46	10 8	10 8	1034	1512	1546	2345
18 1	1824	2154	2238	2154	0 23	0 23	7 40	223	arr. BRUSSELS (N.) .... dep.	6 25	6 25	8 51	8 51	9 17	1411	1434	2224
1812	1832	2210	2246	2210	1 0	1 0	7 54	..	dep. BRUSSELS (N.) (p. 151) arr.	0 2	5 42	8 38	8‡38	9 7	1355	1425	2212
1927	1947	2325	0 1	2325	2 23	2 23	9 9	304	arr. Liège .... dep.	2234	4 24	7 23	7 23	7 55	1243	1313	21 0
..	2012	..	0 24	↓	2 56	6 33	9 31	317	arr. Pepinster ...... dep.	2154	3 57	7 0	7 0	..	1219	..	2037
..	2040	..	..	↓	4 38	7 27	1019	324	arr. Spa .... dep.	2124	..	..	..	..	1147	..	1956
2013	2037	0 6	0 50	↓	3 32	7 1	9 56	328	arr. Herbesthal .. d.	2130	3 36	6 39	6 39	7 14	1158	1233	2015
2015	2046	0 8	0 53	↓	4 15	7 4	9 59	..	dep. Herbesthal .. a.	21 4	2 52	6 2	5 33	6 53	1135	1232	1951
2033	21 4	0 26	1 11	0 43	4 33	7 22	1017	339	arr. AACHEN (M.E.T.) dep.	2042	2 30	5 40	5 11	6 31	1113	1210	1929
2135	2235	1 28	2 36	1 46	6 0	9 2	1146	362	arr. COLOGNE (H) dep.	1915	1 0	4 19	4 5	5 26	9 52	11 8	18 6
123	..	..	..	↓	..	1022		..	dep. COLOGNE (Deutz) (page 188) arr.	1851	..	..	↑			123	
2250	2313	1 38	2 56	↓	7 25	..	Daily to Sept. 10.	..	dep. COLOGNE (H) .. arr.	..	23 7	3 57	↑	5 14	7 10	7 57	Daily to Sept. 10.
..	..	..	5 38	↓	..	1314		478	arr. Wiesbaden .... dep.	16 5	..	1 10	↑	2 51	..	..	
1 41	2f18	4f29	6 28	↓	1036	14 8		500	arr. FRANKFORT .... dep.	1514	1935	0 14	↑	2 11	3f51	4 50	
..	..	..	7 34	↓	..	15 9		546	arr. Aschaffenburg .. dep.	1413	1847	2312	↑	..	..	..	
3 40	4 12	6 19	9 6	↓	1242	1644		609	arr. Wurzburg ...... dep.	1243	1734	2141	↑	0 7	2 0	2 54	
7 35	8 2	..	1322	↓	..	2122		770	arr. MUNICH .... dep.	8 16	..	1710	↑	..	2215	2320	
..	..	8 0	1114	↓	1424	19 8		653	arr. NUREMBURG .. dep.	1025	1558	1914	↑	2235	..	..	
..	..	11 9	1355	↓	1719	2150		748	arr. Eger .... dep.	7 16	1249	1610	↑	1952	..	..	
..	..	1227	1530	↓	1840	..		781	arr. Karlsbad .... dep.	..	11 2	1440	↑	1832		..	
..	..	8 10	1128	↓	1434	2312		..	dep. NUREMBURG .. arr.	10 7	1551	1859	↑	2225	..	..	
..	..	1055	1437	↓	1730	1 50		788	arr. Passau .... dep.	6 54	1242	1546	↑	1933	..	..	
..	..	1520	1918	↓	2210	7 45		971	arr. VIENNA (W.) .. dep.	2240	8 12	1045	↑	1514	..	..	
..	..	..	1955		..	9 15		..	arr. VIENNA (E.) .. dep.	2039	..	10 4		..	..	..	
..	..a	1544	20 0	..	..	10 0	..	..	dep. VIENNA (E.) .... arr.	1958	..	9 57	..	14a29	..	..	..
..	..	..	¶	..	..	1035	..	..	dep. Bruckneudorf .... arr.	1921	..	¶	..	..	..	..	..
..	..	20 3	2258	..	..	14 0	..	..	arr. Budapest (p. 200) d	16 0	..	7 0	..	1010	..	..	..
..	..	2034	2355	..	..	1445	..	..	dep. Budapest (p. 200) a.	1450	..	6 26	..	9 41	..	..	..
..	..	1230	1955	..	..	1015	..	..	arr. BUCHAREST (p. 203) dep.	2050	FD	13 5	..	1945		..	..
47	† The Sleeper for Calais arr. Brussels 8.12.	f Frankfort (Sud.) g Brussels (Midi). § Via Boulogne.	.. ¶ One class Limited Motor Train Vienna-Budapest and v.v., extra fares.	1 48	6 48	9 22	1153	..	dep. COLOGNE (H) .. (p. 163/4. p. 205.) arr.	19 1	2228	..	4 3	..	..	7 55	1628
2217			..	..	7 33	9 57	1223	387	arr. Dusseldorf .... dep.	1826	2154	..	..	..	..	7 19	..
3 42				5 28	1230	14 8	1628	566	arr. Hanover ...... dep.	1411	1835	–	0 25	..	..	3 7	12 8
8 0				1052	1712	1931	..	732	arr. Leipsic ...... dep.	8 32	1325	..	..	..	..	2238	7 45
10 9				1315	1922	2119	..	803	arr. DRESDEN (H) dep.	6 56	1118	..	..	..	..	2034	4 44
7 49				8 33	1613	1740	20†18	725	arr. BERLIN (Fried.) .... d.	1054	1540	..	2120	..	..	2331	8†44
..				8 36	..	1743	..	..	dep. BERLIN (Fried.) a.	1052	..	..	2118	..	..	..	..
..				9 12	..	1813	..	..	dep. BERLIN (Schles) arr.	1027	..	..	2049	..	..	..	..
..				1135	..	2213	..	837	arr. Bentschen c dep.	7 0	..	..	1816	..	..	..	..
..				1149	..	2313	..		dep. Zbaszyn .. c arr.	6 24	..	..	18 4	..	..	..	..
..				1239	..	0 22	..	883	arr. Poznan .... dep.	5 20	..	..	1714	..	..	..	..
..				1634	..	8 22	..	1072	arr. WARSAW ...... dep.	2156	..	..	1316	..	..	..	..
..				1 41	..	20 5	..	1381	arr. Niegoreloje ...... dep.	1150	..	..	5 55	..	..	..	..
..				1610	..	1120	..	1693	arr. Moscow .... dep.	23 5	..		1710	..	..	..	..
..				8 44	..	2342	..	..	dep. BERLIN (Fried) .. arr.	7 10	..	..	21 6	..	..	..	..
..				1843	..	X	..	..	dep. Wirballen .... dep.	X	..	..	11 3	..	..	..	..
..				1949	..		..	..	arr. Kaunas (Kovno) p. 206 d.		..	..	9 45	..	..	..	..
..				0 43	FDT	1735	..	..	arr. Riga (E.E.T.) .... dep.	1525	FDT		6 25	..	..	..	..
..				1 48	7 0	1113	..	..	dep. COLOGNE (p. 161) .. arr.	1824	0 23	..	4 3	..	..	..	..
..				*	1033	16 8	..	567	arr. Bremen .. .. dep.	1324	2050	..	*	..	..	..	..
..				8 4	1133	1741	..	637	arr. Hamburg .. dep.	1147	1951	..	2140	..	..	..	..

A—1 & 2 cl. Sleep. Cars, Ostend to Wurzburg & Vienna-Budapest, 1, 2 & 3 cl. Cars Ostend-Vienna-Ostend-Munich and *v.v.* Rest. Car Ostend-Herbesthal and Wurzburg-Passau and *v.v.* **B**—1 & 2 cl. Pullman Cars only Ostend-Cologne and *v.v.*, Sleeping Cars Cologne-Munich and *v.v.* **C**—1, 2 & 3 cl. cars Ostend to Cologne & *v.v.* **D**—Thro' 1, 2 & 3 cl. Cars, Calais to Brussels, Ostend-Liege and 1 & 2 cl. Liege to Berlin; 3 cl. Liege to Warsaw. Rest. Car Aachen–Bentschen. **E** 1, 2 & 3 cl. Cars Berlin-Brussels and 3 cl. Warsaw-Brussels. **FD** and **FDT** special fast train, Extra fares. **H**—1, 2 & 3 cl. Cars Ostend-Constance and *v.v.* **N**—Nord Exp. daily Ostend to Berlin, Calais and Paris to Warsaw and Paris to Hamburg and *v.v.*; also Ostend-Warsaw Mon. and Sat. and Ostend-Bucharest Wed., Fri., and Sun. and *v.v.* (*see p.* 81.) **O**—Ostend-Vienna-Budapest-Istanbul Express de luxe (also to Karlsbad, *see p.* 84). Tues., Thurs. and Sats. **X**—*via* Tilsit, *see p.* 205. **Y**—1 & 2 cl. Car Ostend-Spa and *v.v.* July 1-Sept. 1. *a* Vienna West. *See pages* 80, 81 and 84. † Berlin (Potsdam). * *via* Hanover.

LONDON & NORTH EASTERN RLY. (Gt. East. Section) via HARWICH.
TO AND FROM ROTTERDAM, THE HAGUE, AMSTERDAM, and Northern and Eastern Holland.

Mls.		1 2 3	1 2 3	1 2 3
			AP	P
0	LONDON— Liverpool St. dep.	10 0	10 0	10 0
..	Harwich (Parkeston Quay) dep.	R 1140	R 1140	R 1140
170	FLUSHING (D.S.T) a.	1735	1735	1735
	FLUSHING (D.S.T) d.	1753	1820	1842
216	Rosendaal .. arr.	19 0	1914	1938
	Rosendaal .. dep.	19 5	1925	..
242	Dordrecht .... arr.	1935	1955	..
258	ROTTERDAM B's „	..	2013	..
	ROTTERDAM DPt. „	..	2017	..
..	ROTTERDAM D.P. dep.	↓	2020	↓
..	Delft ...... arr.		2051	
267	THE HAGUE „		2041	
270	Leiden...... „		2056	
296	Haarlem .... „		2119	
307	AMSTERDAM Cen „		2137	
				1 2 3
..	Rosendaal .. dep.	19 6	1948	1942
230	Breda .... arr.	1927	..	20 4
	Breda .... dep.	1928	..	20 5
243	Tilburg .... arr.	1948	..	2024
286	Utrecht .... „	2052	..	2152
284	Nymegen.... „	21 0	..	2127
295	Arnhem .... „	2120	..	2151
..	Zutphen .... „	2145	..	2220
402	Zwolle...... „	2227	..	..
407	LEEUWARDEN „	0 10	..	..
..	GRONINGEN.. „	2357	..	..

A 1 cl. Pullman Car and 1, 2 & 3 cl. cars Flushing to Amsterdam. Rest. Car. Flushing—Amsterdam.
P 1 cl. Pullman Cars London–Harwich.
R Rest. Car. B.S.T. British Summer Time.

	1 2 3	1 2 3	1 2 3
			A
GRONINGEN ...... dep	..	7 0	..
LEEUWARDEN.... „	..	6 56	..
Zwolle .... „	..	8 25	..
Zutphen .... „	8 49	9 14	..
Arnhem .... „	9 19	9 41	..
Nymegen .... „	9 46	10 2	..
Utrecht .... „	9 40	1010	..
Tilburg.......... „	1045	1112	..
Breda .... arr.	..	1133	..
Breda .... dep.	..	1135	
Rosendaal ...... arr.	1120	1154	..
	↓	↓	1 2 3
AMSTERDAM Central dep.			1020
Haarlem .... „			1037
Leiden .... „			11 1
THE HAGUE			1117
Delft .... „			11 9
ROTTERDAM D.P. arr.			1138
ROTTERDAM D.P. dep.		..	1141
ROTTERDAM Beurs „		..	..
Dordrecht .... „		..	12 1
Rosendaal .... arr.		..	1231
Rosendaal .... dep.	1125	12 0	1239
FLUSHING (D.S.T.) ar.	1222	1328	1335
FLUSHING (D.S.T.) dp.	1350	1350	1350
Harwich (B.S.T.) (Parkeston Quay) arr.	1910	1910	1910
Harwich (B.S.T.) (Parkeston Quay) dep.	1955	1955	1955
LONDON—		P R	P R
Liverpool St.* .... arr.	2130	2130	2130

A 1 cl. Pullman Car and 1, 2 & 3 cl. Cars Amsterdam to Flushing, 1, 2 & 3 cl. cars Rotterdam—Flushing. Rest. Car from Rosendaal.
P 1 cl. Pullmans Harwich—London. † Not Sundays.
* Sundays July 9 to Sept. 24, London (Liverpool St.) arr. 21.45.

TO AND FROM COLOGNE, THE RHINE, BALE, MUNICH, &c.

Mls.		1 2 3	
0	LONDON—	PA	..
..	Liverpool St. dep.	10 0	..
170	FLUSHING (D.S.T.) d.	1820	..
..	Rosendaal...... arr.	1918	.
294	Venlo (D.S.T.) „	2112	..
	Venlo (D.S.T.) dep	2118	..
..	Kaldnk'chn C.E.T. a.	21 5	..
..	M. Gladbach .. „	2143	..
335	Neuss........ „	2158	..
338	DUSSELDORF arr.	22 9	
378	COLOGNE Hpt. arr.	2241	
..	COLOGNE Hpt. dep.	2329	
498	Mainz.......... arr.	2 38	..
578	Carlsruhe ...... „	4 55	
691	BALE (Swiss) .. „	8 30	..
..	Cologne, H..... dep.	2331	..
515	Wiesbaden .... arr.	2 4	..
..	Mannheim .... „	3 48	..
605	STUTTGART.. „	6 20	..
..	Friedrichshafen „	9 25	..
..	Lindau (p. 186) „	10 0	..
..	Innsbruck (p. 197)	1350	¶
726	MUNICH ...... „	9 54	..
..	Salzburg ...... „	14§5	
..	Cologne H. .... dep.	2313	2250
..	Mainz .... arr.	1 40	1 5
..	Frankfort (Sud.) „	2 18	1†40
..	Wurzburg...... „	4 12	3 40
..	Munich .... „	8 2	7 35
..	Salzburg .... „	1140	9 40
..	VIENNA (W).... „	1650	1442

P Pullman Cars London-Harwich and *v.v.*
A—1 & 2 cl. Sleeping Car Flushing *via* Wurzburg to Munich and *v.v.* Through 1, 2 & 3 cl. cars Flushing-Cologne-Wurzburg-Munich. Rest. Car Flushing-Cologne and *v.v.* Stuttgart-Munich and *v.v.* 1, 2 & 3 cl. Sleep. Cars Cologne-Wurzburg-Munich and *v.v.* 1, 2 & 3 cl. cars Cologne-Bale and *v.v.* Rest. Car Carlsruhe-Bale and *v.v.*

	123A	1 2 3
VIENNA (W) .... dep.	1440	..
Salzburg .... „	20 0	..
Munich ...... „	2215	2320
Wurzburg ...... „	2 0	2 54
Frankfort (Sud.) „	3 51	4†50
Mainz.......... „	4 30	5 22
Cologne .... arr.	7 10	7 57
Salzburg ...... dep.	17 5	
MUNICH........ „	1930	..
Innsbruck .... „	1452	..
Lindau ...... „	19 8	..
Friedrichshafen „	1947	..
STUTTGART.. „	2317	..
Mannheim .... „	1 49	..
Wiesbaden...... „	3 46	..
Cologne, Hpt. .. arr.	6 21	..
BALE (Swiss sta.) dp.	2239	
Carlsruhe ...... „	1 34	..
Mainz .. .. „	3 22	
Cologne Hpt. .. arr.	6 36	..
COLOGNE Hpt. dep.	8 18	
Dusseldorf.... „	8 30	
M. Gladbach .. „	9 19	..
Kaldnk'chn C.E.T. „	9 54	..
Venlo (D.S.T.) ar.	1020	..
Venlo (D.S.T.) dp.	1043	.
Rosendaal ...... „	1239	
FLUSHING (D.S.T.) a.	1335	..
	A	
FLUSHING (D.S.T.) d.	1350	
LONDON—	G	..
Liverpool St... arr.	2130	*

* Sundays July 9 to Sept. 24, London (Liverpool St.) arr. 21.45. C.E.T.—Central European Time. D.S.T.—Dutch Summer Time.
† Frankfort Cent. Station.
§ 2 & 3 cl. only.

Mls.			128	123
			A	B
	See also p. 129	LONDON— Liverpool St. ..dep.	10 0	10 0
..		Harwich (Park'nQu.) „	1140	1140
170		FLUSHING .... a.	1735	1735
		d.	1842	1842
..		Zutphen .... arr.	2220	2220
..		Hengelo .... dep.	2314	2356
..		Oldenzaal ...... arr.	2326	0 8
..		dep.	2334	0 15
..		Bentheim ...... arr.	2330	0 11
..		(C.E.T.) dep.	0 3	0 35
..		Rheine .. .. arr.	0 23	0 55
..		Osnabruck .... „	1 5	1 36
	See p. 161	Osnabruck .... dep.	2 10	3 37
508		BREMEN .... arr	3 54	5 4
578		HAMBURG (Hpt.) a.	5 44	6 36
583		Altona (Hauptb.) arr.	6 10	7 3
649		Kiel .... „	8 58	8 58
..	p. 216	HAMBURG (Hpt.) .. dep.		8 54
..		Warnemunde Stm. „		1240
..		Gedser ...... Fy. arr.		1440
..		COPENHAGEN .... „		1735
366	p. 163.	Osnabruck .... dep.	1 20	1 46
495		HANOVER .... arr.	2 58	3 28
653		BERLIN (Friedrst.) „	7 4	↓
	p. 205.	BERLIN— (Schlesischer Bahnhof) .... „	7 21	↓
..		dep.	9 4	↓
1117		Eydtkau .... arr.	1822	↓
1229		Wirballen .... „	1838	↓
1637		RIGA (E.E.T.) (p. 206) a.	0 43	↓
495	p. 168	HANOVER .... dep.	..	3 47
661		LEIPSIC .... arr.	..	8 0
		(Hauptbf.) dep.	.	8 18
735		DRESDEN .... arr.		10 9
		(Hauptbf.) dep.	..	1037
	p. 195	Praha (Mas Stn.) arr.	..	1358
..		Bratislava .... „	..	1942
1099		VIENNA (F.J.B.) „		..
..	p. 162	Hamburg ..... dep.	1040	1040
	p. 204	BERLIN (S.B.) .. „	1120	..
		Sassnitz Hafen .. „	1626	1626
		Trelleborg .... „	21 7	21 7
		STOCKHOLM .... arr.	6 30	6 30

A.T. = Amsterdam Time.

	128	123
STOCKHOLM .... dep.	2235	..
Trelleborg ...... „	8 50	..
Sassnitz Hafen .. arr.	13 0	B
BERLIN (S.B.) .... arr.	1813	..
Hamburg .... arr.	19 3	..
VIENNA (F.J.B.) dep.		9 30
Bratislava .. .. .. „	..	11 6
Praha (Mas) ..... „		1648
DRESDEN .... arr.		2018
(Hauptbf.) dep.		2034
LEIPSIC (Dred.) arr.		2218
(Haupt.) dep.	A	2238
HANOVER ...... arr.		2 34
RIGA (E.E.T.) .... dep.	6 25	↓
Wirballen .... „	11 3	↓
Eydtkau (M.E.t.) .. „	1121	↓
BERLIN (Schlesischer Bahnhof) arr.	2044	↓
dep.	2235	↓
BERLIN (Friedr.) .. „	2250	↓
HANOVER .... dep.	2 26	2 45
Osnabruck .... arr.	4 10	4 23
COPENHAGEN ...... dep.	1115	
Gedser ...... Stm. „	14 5	
Warnemunde Fy. arr.	1610	..
HAMBURG (Hpt.) .. „	1943	
Kiel (rail)	2122	
Altona (Hauptb.) .. dep.	2350	
HAMBURG (Hpt.) „	0 13	
BREMEN .... „	1 52	
Osnabruck .... arr.	3 29	..
Osnabruck .... dep.	4 44	5 15
Rheine .... „	5 23	6 5
Bentheim (C.E.T.) arr.	5 43	6 25
dep.	6 6	6 50
Oldenzaal (D.S.T.) arr.	6 41	7 25
dep.	7 15	7 50
Hengelo .... arr.	7 25	8 0
dep.	8 1	8 1
Zutphen .... dep.	8 49	8 49
Arnhem .... dep.	9 19	9 19
FLUSHING ...... arr.	1222	1222
(steamer) (D.S.T.) dep.	1350	1350
Harwich (P'kstnQu.) arr.	1910	1910
LONDON (L'poolSt.) „	2130	2130*

A Through 1 and 2 cl. Sleeping Cars Flushing-Berlin and *v.v.* Restaurant Car Flushing-Oldenzaal and *v.v.*, also through 1, 2 and 3 cl. cars Flushing, Berlin and *v.v.*

B Through 1 and 2 cl. Sleeping cars Flushing-Hamburg-Altona, and *v.v.*, also 1, 2 & 3 cl. cars Flushing-Dresden-Praha-Bratislava and *v.v.* Rest. Car Flushing-Oldenzaal and *v.v.*

* On Sundays July 9 to Sept. 24, London (Liverpool St.) arr. 21.45.

Via FLUSHING, to and from ANTWERP and BRUSSELS.

1 2	Mls.	LONDON—	123
10 0	0	dep. Liverpool St... arr.	2130*
1735	170	a FLUSHING ...... d.	1350
1820		d (D.S.T.) a.	1335
1914	216	arr. Rosendaal .. dep.	1239
20 3		dep. arr.	1145
1953	225	arr. Esschen .... dep.	1115
2015		dep. (W.E.T.) arr.	1113
2055	243	arr. ANTWERP (Cen.) dep.	1035
2131	270	„ Brussels (Nord) „	10 0
..		„ Brussels (Midi) „	..

(D.S.T.)—Dutch Summer Time.

(W.E.T.)—Western European (or Greenwich) Time.

(C.E.T.)—Central European Time.

* On Sundays July 9 to Sept. 24, London (Liverpool St.) arr. 21.45.

FLUSHING—CASSEL (Leipsic)—EGER.

2 & 3 cl. through cars Flushing to Marienbad and *v.v.*; Sleep. Car. 1 & 2 cl. Flushing-Leipsic and *v.v.*

123	23		23
..	10 0	dep. LONDON, Liverp'l St. ar.	2130*
..	1820	„ FLUSHING (A.T.) .. dep.	1350
..	2112	arr. Venlo (A.T.) .... „	1020
..	2133	„ Viersen (C.E.T.) dep.	9 28
..	22 7	dep. arr.	8 49
..	2221	arr. Crefeld .... dep.	8 36
..	2244	„ Duisburg .... „	8 12
2250	23 5	dep. Duisburg .... arr.	7 57
2313	2330	arr. Essen .... dep.	7 35
2346	0 13	„ Dortmund (Sud.) ..... „	6 55
Hbf.	0 55	„ Soest .... „	6 18
..	2 50	„ Warburg .... „	4 21
..	3 41	„ Cassel .... „	3 34
..	5 48	„ Gotha .... dep.	1 27
..	6 45	„ Weimar .... „	0 34
..	8 9	„ Leipsic .... „	2259
..	8 5	„ Gera .... „	23 0
..	9 15	arr. Plauen (L.L.) ...... „	2147
..	10 1	„ Bad Elster .... „	21 8
..	1023	„ Bad Brambach .... „	2050
..	1045	„ Franzensbad .... „	2026
..	1057	„ Eger .... „	2016
..	1139	„ Karlsbad .... „	1745
..	1153	„ Marienbad .... „	1917

To and from ANTWERP. DAILY EXCEPT SUNDAYS.

	London (Liverpool Street), train	dep.	20A30
69	Harwich (Parkeston Quay), steamer	,,	2210
210	Antwerp (Sud Quai)	arr. about	8 0
237	Brussels (Nord), train	arr.	9 6
..	Cologne	,,	1349
	Bale (Swiss)	,,	1942

Bale (Swiss)	dep.	9*27
Cologne	,,	1444
Brussels (Nord)	,,	1850
Antwerp (Sud Quai), steamer	,,	1945
Harwich (Parkeston Quay), train	,,	7 0
London (Liverpool Street)	arr.	8b41

A 1 & 2 cl. Pullman and Rest. Cars. * Connection by Edelweiss Express, 1 and 2 class Pullman train. *b* Arrive 8.30 on Sundays.

HARWICH—ZEEBRUGGE.

DAILY June 30th to Sept. 9th.

London (Liverpool Street)	dep.	20a30
Harwich (Parkeston Quay) about	dep.	2230
Zeebrugge (Quay)	arr.	7 0
	dep.	7 56
Brussels (Nord)	arr.	9 34

DAILY July 1st to Sept. 10th.

Brussels (Nord)	dep	2115
Zeebrugge (Quay) about	arr.	2250
	dep.	2310
Harwich (Parkeston Quay)	arr.	6 20
	dep.	7 [illegible]
London (Liverpool Street)	arr.	8b [illegible]

a 1 and 2 cl. Pullman and Rest. Cars. *b* Arrive 8.30 on Sundays.

Through Services to and from HOLLAND via the Hook of Holland.

LONDON (L'p'l St.)	d	2015
Harwich (P. Quay)	d.	22 0
Hk. of Hol'nd (A.T.)	d	6 51
ROTTERDAM (D.P.)	arr.	7 16
	dep	7 22
Utrecht	arr.	8 14
Arnhem	,,	9 7
Nymegen	,,	9 36

Nymegen	dep.	1949
Arnhem	,,	2032
Utrecht	,,	2122
ROTTERDAM	,,	2225
Hk. of Holl'd (D.S.T.)	a	2250
Harwich (P. Quay)	d.	6C20
LONDON (L'pl St.)	a.	8 C 2

C Sun. arr. 7.50; on Mons. from Sept. 18 Harwich (Park Q.) dp. 7.0 London (L'pool St.) arr. 8.41.

LONDON (L'po'l St)	d.	2015	2015
Harwich (Park. Qu.)	d.	22 0	22 0
Hk. of Holl'nd (A.T.)	d	6 29	7 41
THE HAGUE	arr.	7 2	8 27
Scheveningen	,,	7†24	8 58
The Hague	dep.	7 4	8 29
Leiden	arr.	7*39	8 39
Haarlem	,,	7 34	8 59
AMSTERD'M (Cn.)	a.	7 50	9 15

Hk. of Holl'd (A.T.)	dp.	7 21	9 53
Utrecht (C.) (*p.* 159)	arr.	8 44	1127
	dep.	8 53	1151
Amersfoort	arr.	9 13	12 9
Apeldoorn	,,	..	1252
Almelo	,,	..	1343
Hengelo	,,	1058	1359
LEEUWARDEN	,,	1210	..
GRONINGEN	,,	1157	..

† Not Sundays.

GRONINGEN	dep.	17 0	19 0
LEEUWARDEN		1647	1847
Hengelo	dep.	1744	↓
Almelo	,,	18 2	↓
Apeldoorn	,,	1853	↓
Amersfoort	,,	1937	2136
Utrecht (C.)	arr.	1950	2155
	dep	20 4	2212
H. of Hol'd (D.S.T.)	a.	2137	2333

AMSTERD'M (C)	d.	2137r
Haarlem	dep.	2152
Leiden	,,	2149*
The Hague	arr.	2224
Scheveningen	dp.	22 7
THE HAGUE	,,	2227
H. of Hol'd (D.S.T.)	a	23 1
Harwich (P. Quay)	d.	6C20
LONDON (L'pl St)	a.	8 C 2

r Rest. Car.

* Change at The Hague. Restaurant and Pullman Cars between London and Harwich (Parkeston Quay).

TO AND FROM COLOGNE, MAYENCE AND BALE.

1 2	1 2				1 2	1 2
2015	2015	dep.	LONDON (L'pl. St.)	arr.	8 C 2	8 C 2
22 0	22 0	,,	Harwich (Park Q.)	dep.	6 C 20	6C20
6 0	6 0	arr.	Hook of Holland (D.S.T.)	,,	23 50	2350
6 51	6 51	dep.		arr	22 50	2333
9 21	9 53	arr.	Emmerich	dep.	20 28	19 8
FDA	FD				FDA	FD
9 23	1018	dep.		arr	20 12	1853
10 6	1110	arr.	Duisburg	dep.	19 27	18 4
1022	1130	,,	Dusseldorf	,,	19 9	1745
1054	12 6	,,	COLOGNE (Cent.)	,,	18 39	1714
11 0	..	dep.	,, (Cent.)	arr.	18 32	..
13 5	..	arr.	Mainz	dep.	16 24	..
1440	..	,,	†CARLSRUHE	,,	14 46	..
15 2	..	,,	Baden-West	,,	14 21	..
16 6	..	,,	Freiburg	,,	13 21	..
17 7	..	,,	Bale (Swiss)	,,	12 18	..
1852	..	,,	Lucerne	,,	10 45	..
2247	..	,,	Chiasso	,,	7 10	..
0 5	..	,,	Milan	,,	5 50	..

FDA "Rheingold Exp.," 1 and 2 cl. special saloon dining cars. Daily Hook to Milan and *v.v.* Only takes long distance passengers. EXTRA FARES.

1, 2 and 3 cl. cars Hook-Heidelberg, Cleves-Bale, Cleves-Constance and *v.v.* Rest. Car Cleves to Bale.

1 2 3		ORDINARY EXPRESS.		1 2 3
2015	dep.	LONDON (L'pool St.)	arr.	8 C 2
22 0	,,	Harwich (Park. Quay)	dep.	6 C 20
6 0	arr.	H. of Holl'nd (D.S.T.)	dep.	23 0
7 21	dep.		arr.	22 50
1010	,,	Nymegen	,,	20 11
1032	arr.	Cleves	dep.	18 41
12 5	,,	Cologne (Cent.)	,,	17 13
1214	dep.		arr.	17 4
1454	arr.	Wiesbaden	dep.	14 34
1512	,,	Mainz	,,	14 14
1645	,,	Heidelberg	,,	12 32
1739	,,	Carlsruhe	,,	12 9
1745	dep.	Carlsruhe	arr.	12 3
1843	arr.	Offenburg	dep.	11 7
2022	,,	Triberg	,,	8 58
2239	,,	Constance	,,	6 36
18 8	arr.	Baden-West	dep.	11 38
1843	dep.	Offenburg	arr.	11 3
1934	arr.	Freiburg	dep.	10 19
2058	arr.	BALE (Swiss)	dep.	8 45

C On Suns. arr. 7.50; on Mons. from Sept. 18 Harwich (Park Q.) dep. 7.0, London (Liverpool St.) arr. 8.41.
† See note on page 213 for Motor Service to and from Freudenstadt. D.S.T.=Dutch Summer Time.
Restaurant and Pullman cars between London and Harwich (Parkeston Quay)

To and from Frankfort, Vienna, Budapest

1 2 A	1 2 3 B		FD—Special fast Corridor Exp. Extra Fares, *see p.* 75.		1 2 3 B	1 2 A
2015	2015	dep.	LONDON (L'pool Street)	arr.	8 C 2	8 C 2
22 0	22 0	,,	Harwich (Park'ton Quay)	dep.	6 20	6 20
6 0	6 0	arr.	Hook of Holland (D.S.T.)	dep.	23 50	2350
7 21	9 53	dep.	Hook of Holland (D.S.T.)	arr.	21 37	2250
9 53	1242	arr.	Emmerich (M.E. time)	dep.	17 44	19 8
F D	D				D	F D
1018	13 2	dep.	Emmerich (M.E. time)	arr.	17 29	1853
1130	1419	arr.	Dusseldorf	dep.	16 14	1745
12 6	1458	arr.	Cologne (Cent.)	dep.	15 42	1714
1211	15 4	dep.	Cologne (Cent.)	arr.	15 36	17 9
1319	1624	arr.	Coblence	dep.	14 12	1559
1459	1828	arr.	Frankfort (Cent.)	dep.	11 44	1424
15 7	1838	dep.	Frankfort	arr.	11 34	1417
1653	2049	arr.	Wurzburg	dep.	9 20	1231
17 0	..	dep.	Wurzburg	arr.	..	1224
2023	..	arr.	Munich	dep.	..	9 15
1712	2110	dep.	Wurzburg	arr.	9 0	1212
19 8	2230	arr.	Nuremburg	dep.	7 15	1025
2150	..	arr.	Eger	dep.	..	7 16
1923	2315	dep.	Nuremburg	arr.	7 0	10 7
2228	2 35	arr.	Passau	dep.	3 37	6 54
..	2 50	dep.	Passau	arr.	3 25	..
..	7 45	arr.	Vienna (W)	dep.	22 40	..
..	9 15	dep.	Vienna (W)	arr.	21 5	..
..	9 40	arr.	Vienna (E)	dep.	20 39	..
..	10 0	dep.	Vienna (E)	arr.	19 58	..
..	1352	arr.	Budapest	dep.	16 0	..

A Through 1 & 2 cl. cars Hook to Munich and Eger and *v.v.* Rest. car Hook-Munich & *v.v.* **B** 1 2 & 3 cl. cars Hook to Budapest and *v.v.*, with 1 & 2 cl. Sleeping car Wurzburg to Vienna and *v.v.* Rest. car Hook-Wurzburg and *v.v.*

London, Hagen, Cassel, Erfurt

1 2				1 2
2015	dep.	LONDON	arr.	8 C 2
2157	arr.	Harwich (Pkstn. Quay)	dp.	6 C 20
22 0	dep	Harwich (steamer)	arr.	6 0
6 0	arr.	Hook of Holland (D.S.T.)	dep.	23 50
F D				F D
7 21	dep.	Hook of Holland (D.S.T.)	arr.	22 50
9 53	arr.	Zevenaar *c*	dep.	20 15
11 0	arr.	Oberhausen	dep.	18 14
2 3				2 3
1339	dep.	Oberhausen	arr.	17 42
15 2	arr.	Hagen	dep.	16 36
D				D
1532	dep.	Hagen	arr.	16 17
1852	arr.	Cassel	dep.	12 58
2033	arr.	Eisenach	dep.	11 23
2128	arr.	Erfurt	dep.	10 28

D Corridor Express.
FD Fast Train: Special Fares: *p.* 75.
c On Suns. arr. 7.50; on Mons. from Sept. 18 Harwich (Park Q.) dep. 7.0., London Liverpool Street arr. 8.41.

To and from Northern Germany, Scandinavia, etc.

1 2	1 2 3					1 2	1 2
2015	2015	dep.	LONDON (Liverpool Street)		arr.	8 C 2	8 C 2
22 0	22 0	dep.	Harwich		arr.	6 0	6 0
6 0	6 0	arr.	Hook of Holland (D.S.T.)		dep.	2350	23 50
A							A
7 21	9 53	dep.	Hook of Holland (D.S.T.)		arr.	2137	23 33
53	1151	dep.	Utrecht		dep.	20 4	22 12
9 25	1218	dep.	Amersfoort		dep.	1937	21 36
..	1416	arr.	Oldenzaal (A.T.)		dep.	1727	..
F D							F D
..	1421	dep.	Oldenzaal (A.T.)		arr.	1651	..
11 8	1416	arr.	Bentheim (M.E. time)		dep.	1616	19 14
12 6	1540	arr.	Osnabruck		dep.	15 3	18 19
1211	1546	dep.	Osnabruck	*page* 168.	arr.	1453	18 11
1332	1738	arr.	HANOVER	*page* 168.	dep.	1249	16 51
1339	18 8	dep.	HANOVER	*page* 168.	arr.	1220	16 44
1625	22 1	arr.	BERLIN (Frd.)	*page* 168.	dep.	8 56	13 57
1637	2215	arr.	,, (Schles)		dep.	8 44	13 43
10 6	10 6	arr.	Tilsit	p. 205	dep.	2036	20 36
1735	1735	arr.	RIGA (E.E.T.) (*p.* 206)	p. 205	dep.	1525	15 25
1350		dep.	HANOVER	p. 168.	arr.		16 38
1439		arr.	Brunswick	p. 168.	dep.		15 48
1546		arr.	Magdeburg	p. 168.	dep.		14 42
1720		arr.	Leipsic	p. 168.	dep.		13 12
1922		arr.	Dresden		dep.		11 18
2 12		dep.	Dresden		arr.		3 50
5 0		arr.	Praha (*p.* 195)		dep.		23 59
2246		arr.	VIENNA (F.J.B.) *via* Gmund		d.		17 5
8		dep.	Leipsic	p. 195.	arr.	..	6 32
4 35		arr.	Passau	p. 195.	dep.	..	23 24
9 8		arr.	VIENNA (W.)	p. 195.	dep.	..	18 45
2121	..	dep.	Berlin (Sch.) *p.* 204		arr.	7 54	..
2 10	..	dep.	Sassnitz		arr.	3 4	..
1550	..	arr	Stockholm		dep.	1350	..

Thro' 1 2 & 3rd cl. car Hook to Berlin. — Thr' 1 2 & 3 cl car Berlin to Hook.

A Thro' 1 & 2 cl. cars & Rest Car Hook to Berlin and *v.v.*

1 2					1 2
2015	dep.	LONDON (Liverpool St.) ..		arr.	8 C 2
22 0	dep.	Harwich		arr.	6 0
6 0	arr.	Hook of Holland (D.S.T.)		dep	23 50
7 21	dep.	Hook of Holland (D.S.T.)		arr.	23 33
F D					F D
11 4	dep.	Hengelo		arr.	..
..	dep.	Oldenzaal (A.T.)		arr.	..
12 6	arr.	Osnabruck (M.E. time)		dep.	18 19
1229	dep.	Osnabruck		arr.	17 54
1352	arr.	Bremen		dep.	16 29
1524	arr.	HAMBURG (Hpt.)		dep.	15 1
1546	arr.	Altona		dep.	14 42
2150	dep.	Hamburg (Hpt.)	p. 162.	arr.	7 6
2246	dep.	Lubeck	p. 162.	arr.	6 12
1 25	dep.	Warnemunde	p. 162.	arr.	3 40
3 35	arr.	Gjedser	p. 162.	dep.	1 40
6 48	arr.	COPENHAGEN		dep.	22 45
1949	dep.	Hamburg (Hpt.)	p. 162	arr.	10 6
2047	dep.	Lubeck	p. 162	arr.	18 59
2 10	dep.	Sassnitz Hafen	p. 215A.	arr.	3 4
6 20	arr.	Trelleborg	p. 215A.	dep.	22 54
7 11	arr.	Malmo	p. 215A.	dep.	22 5
1550	arr.	STOCKHOLM	p. 215A.	dep.	13 50
1246	arr.	Gothenburg	p. 215A.	dep.	16 30
19 0	arr.	Oslo	p. 215A.	dep.	10 5

Through 1 and 2 cl. cars Hook to Hamburg; 1, 2 and 3 cl. cars, Hamburg–Stockholm, Copenhagen and Oslo and *v.v.*; also 1 and 2 cl. sleepers Hamburg–Oslo and *v.v.*; Hamburg-Copenhagen and *v.v.*

C On Suns. arr. 7.50; on Mons. from Sept. 18, Harwich (Park. Q.) dep. 7.0; Liverpool Street arr. 8.41.
B Rest. Car. **FD**—Special fast Corridor Express. Extra fares, see *p.* 75. D.S.T.=Dutch Summer Time.

LONDON AND ST. MALO.

Day Service.—From London: Aug. 3†, 5, 10, 12, 17†, 19, 24, 26, 31†, Sept. 2†.
From St. Malo: Aug. 4, 6, 11, 13‡, 18, 20, 25, 27, Sept. 1, 3.

Night Service.—From London: Aug. 1†, 2, 3, 4, 5, 6, 7, 8, 9, 10, 11, 12. 13, 14†, 15†, 16, 17, 18, 19, 20, 21, 22, 23, 24, 25, 26, 27, 28, 29†, 30†, 31†, Sept. 1 to 12.
From St. Malo: Aug. 1, 2, 3, 4, 5, 6, 7, 8, 9, 10, 11, 12‡, 13‡, and 14 to 31; Sept. 1 to 9.

8 15	18 40	dep.	London (Waterloo)	.. arr.	10 16	21 5
10 30	21 0	dep.	Southampton Docks	.. arr.	7 30	18 45
19 15	7 0	arr.	St. Malo Quay	.. dep.	22 0	10 0

A	7 B 30	dep.		St. Malo Quay ..	.. arr.	B	A
20 6	8 8	dep.	p. 244	St. Malo (St. Servan)	.. arr.	21 25	9 30
21 40	9 5	arr.	p. 244	Rennes	.. dep.	20 24	8 32
21 50	9 11	dep.	p. 244	,, ...	.. arr.	20 12	8 25
0 J 20	11 44	arr.		La Baule ..	.. dep.	17 36	6 J 4
0 6	11 15	arr.	p. 246	Nantes (Orleans) ..	.. dep.	18 4	6 10
0 20	11 36	dep.	p. 246	,, .	.. arr.	17 41	4 52
1 41	12 39	arr.	p. 246	La Roche-sur-Yon	.. dep.	16 38	3 33
3 24	13 58	arr.	p. 246	La Rochelle ..	.. dep.	15 16	1 44
7 18	16 42	arr.	p. 246	Bordeaux (St. Jean) p. 250	dep.	12 34	22 10
11 34	19 51	arr.	p. 250	Biarritz	.. dep.	9 5	18 37
12 6	20 17	arr.	p. 250	Hendaye	dep.	8 37	18 11
..	..	arr.	p. 250	Irun ..	dep.		

A—1, 2 & 3 cl. Cars and 1, 2 & 3 cl. Couchettes Bordeaux-St. Malo and *v.v.* B—1, 2 & 3 cl. Cars St. Malo-La Baule and *v.v.*, from July 2 to Sept. 18; then Sept. 20 and 24 to La Baule and Sept. 22 and 23 from La Baule. 1, 2 & 3 cl. Cars and Voiture-buffet St. Malo-Bordeaux and *v.v.* J—Via Savenay (change). † Passengers land by vedette; the steamer berthing at St. Malo Quay later. ‡ Passengers embark by vedette; the steamer leaving St. Malo Quay earlier.

LONDON AND THE CHANNEL ISLANDS via Southampton.

Miles	OUTWARD.		Every weekday until Sept. 23; Mons., Weds. and Fris. from Sept. 25.	Fridays until Sept. 8.	Fridays until August 25.	Saturdays until Sept. 9.	
—	London (Waterloo)	dep.	21 A 0 E	19 A 50 F	20 A 30	20 A 30	
47¾	Basingstoke	dep.	22 0	—	—	—	
79	Southampton Docks	arr.	22 51	21 40	22 10	22 10	
		dep.	23 45	22 0	23 D 0	23 30	
199	Guernsey	arr.	6 30	—	—	—	
		dep.	7 15	—	—	—	
229	Jersey	arr.	9 15	6 0	7 D 30	7 0	

Miles	HOMEWARD.		Every weekday until Sept. 23; Mons., Weds. and Fris. from Sept. 25.	Saturdays until Sept. 9.	Saturdays, July 29 to Sept. 16, inclusive.	Saturdays, July 29 to Aug. 26, inclusive.	Saturdays until July 22.
229	Jersey	dep.	8 0	7 15	11 D 0	20 0	21 0
199	Guernsey	dep.	10 15	—	—	22 30	—
79	Southampton Docks	arr.	16 30	15 0	18 D 10	6 0	6 0
		dep.	17 C 20	15 C 20	18 C 25	7 C 3	7 C 3
47¾	Basingstoke	arr.	18 14	—	—	—	—
—	London (Waterloo)	arr.	19 10	17 10	20 20	9 7	9 7

A—Restaurant Car Waterloo to Southampton. C—Restaurant Car Southampton to Waterloo. D—Second class steamer service only. E On Fris. until Sept. 22 inclusive, dep. London (Waterloo) 21.30, arr. Southampton Docks 23.10. F On Fris., July 28 and Aug. 4, a relief train will leave Waterloo at 19.15, and passengers are advised to travel by this advance portion.

For service via WEYMOUTH *see next page.*

☞ ***NOTE.—For S.R steamer servcies between Jersey and St. Malo see page 409.***

LONDON AND THE CHANNEL ISLANDS via Weymouth (G.W. Rly).

Outwards.	Every weekday to Sept. 23	Sats., Aug. 12, 19, 26	Night of Aug. 5/6
London (Pad.) d	8 G 30	—	—
Weymouth Quay.... arr.	1155	—	—
dep.	1210	1315	2 30
Guernsey arr.	1620	18 0	6 45
Guernsey dep.	1635	1810	7 0
Jersey .... arr.	1830	1945	9 30

Homewards.	Every weekday.	Sats., July 15 to Aug. 19.
Jersey .... dep.	8 30	19 J 30
Guernsey dep.	10 45	—
Weymouth Land'g Stage a.	15 15	5 30
d.	15 K 40	6 30
London (Pad.) a	19 30	10 50

G—Restaurant Car, Paddington to Weymouth.

J—Dep. 21.0 August 5. K—Restaurant Car, Weymouth to Paddington.

Services JERSEY-ST. MALO and v.v.

(*See page* 409).

FORENEDE LINE—COPENHAGEN.

HARWICH—ESBJERG SERVICE.

Departure every WEEKDAY in both directions. (Also Suns. June 18—Sept. 10)

m.s. *England*, m.s. *Parkeston*, m.s. *Jylland*, m.s. *Esbjerg*.

LONDON (Liverpool Street) dep.	1610	16 10	STOCKHOLM .. .. dep.	..	2235X
HARWICH (Parkeston Quay) dep.	18 0	18 0	OSLO .. .. dep.	..	2010
ESBJERG .. .. .. arr.	1615	16 15	GOTHENBURG .. .. dep.	8 18	2 49
ESBJERG .. .. .. dep.	1815L	17†30	MALMO .. .. dep.	13†45	..
COPENHAGEN .. .. arr.	2249	..	HELSINGBORG .. .. dep.	..	1045
ELSINORE .. .. .. arr.	0 54	..	ELSINORE .. .. dep.	..	1119
HELSINGBORG .. .. arr.	1 34	..	COPENHAGEN .. .. dep.	..	1230L
MALMO .. .. .. arr.	..	20†30	ESBJERG .. .. arr.	16†40	1655
GOTHENBURG .. .. arr.	1246	2 S 24	ESBJERG .. .. dep. about		1745
OSLO .. .. arr.	19 0	9 S 0	HARWICH (Parkeston Quay) .. arr. about	..	1645
STOCKHOLM .. .. .. arr.	1550X	6 S 30	LONDON (Liverpool St. Station) arr. about	..	§

§ The Boat Train is due London (Liverpool St.) about 2½ hours after arrival of vessel at Harwich.

X *via* Malmo.

L Limited fast train—Esbjerg-Copenhagen and *v.v.*, EXTRA FARES. Seats must be booked in advance.

† By Air Esbjerg to Malmo & *v.v.* S Sleeping Cars from Malmo to Gothenburg, Oslo, and Stockholm.

LONDON—ROTTERDAM *via* GRAVESEND. (See page 402)

(BATAVIER LINE).

Every WEEKDAY until Oct. 14th.

VICTORIA .... dep.	1830
GRAVESEND .. arr.	1923
GRAVESEND (Steamer) dep.	1930
ROTTERDAM (Jobskade) arr.	8 0

Every WEEKDAY until Oct. 12th.

ROTTERDAM (Jobskade) dep.	19 0
GRAVESEND .. arr.	8 30
GRAVESEND (Rail) .. dep.	9 7
VICTORIA .... arr.	9 54 *f*

***f* On Sundays leave Gravesend 8.50, arr. Victoria 9.35 ; on weekdays, in event of steamer arriving at Gravesend before the advertised time, passengers will be conveyed to London by an earlier train, reaching Victoria at 9.21.**

MOTOR BUS SERVICE BETWEEN STEAMER AND ROTTERDAM (D.P.) STATION

A connecting Motor Bus Service is running between the Jobskade and the Delftsche Poort (D.P.) Station *via* Schiedamschesingel (Passenger Office) in connection with the arrival and departure of Batavier Line steamers. The bus from the boat to the D.P. Station will leave the Jobskade after landing of passengers, and from D.P. Station to the boat at 18.15 *via* Schiedamschesingel (Passenger Office).

LONDON TO PARIS AND BALE and *v.v.*

	↓	↓		↑	↑	
For details of daylight Ferry service, see separate announcements.	1 2 3				1 2 3	For details of daylight Ferry service, see separate announcements.
	22 0A	..	dep. London (Victoria) ....arr.	..	9 10	
	2337	..	arr. Dover Marine..............dep.	..	7 20	
	0 35	..	dep. Dover (Ferry berth)........arr.	..	6 15	
	4 30	..	arr. Dunkerque (Ferry berth)....dep.	..	2 0	
	5 15	..	dep. Dunkerque (Ferry berth) ....arr.	..	1 30	
	..	..	arr. Dunkerque (Maritime) ......dep.	..	1 12	
	9 0	..	arr. Paris (Nord) ....dep.	..	2150	
	VF	G		G	VF	
..	6 10	6 10	dep. Dunkerque (Ferry berth)....arr.	1 8	1 8	..
..	7 37	7 37	arr. Lille ....dep.	2341	2341	..
..	..	8 18	dep. Lille ....arr.	2323	..	..
..	..	1030	arr. Brussels (Midi) ....dep.	2115	..	..
..	7 44	..	dep. Lille ....arr.	..	2331	..
..	8 49	..	arr. Aulnoye ....dep.	..	2225	..
..	1032	..	dep. Aulnoye ....arr.	..	20 4	..
..	1436	..	arr. Aachen Hbf. (G.T.)......dep.	..	1524	..
..	16 3	..	arr. Cologne ....dep.	..	14 6	..
..	20†33	..	arr. Hanover ....dep.	..	1123†	..
..	23†32	..	arr. Berlin ....dep.	..	8 20†	..
..	9 25	..	arr. Hirson ....dep.	..	2147	..
..	1019	..	arr. Mezieres-Charleville ....dep.	..	2049	..
..	1132	..	arr. Longuyon ....dep.	..	1934	..
..	1142	..	dep. Longuyon ....arr.	..	1853	..
..	1324	..	arr. Nancy ....dep.	..	17 8	..
..	1135	..	dep. Longuyon ....arr.	..	1928	..
..	1216	..	arr. Thionville ....dep.	..	1845	..
..	1244	..	arr. Metz ....dep.	..	1817	..
..	1422	..	arr. Strasbourg ....dep.	..	1633	..
..	1430	..	dep. Strasbourg ....arr.	..	1628	..
..	16 7	..	arr. Basle (Swiss)................dep.	..	1450	..

A—1 and 2 cl. Sleeping Cars from London to Dunkerque and Paris and *v.v.*; supplements (including reservation fee and Sleeping Car Conductor's gratuity), 1 cl. 28/-, 2 cl. 22/6. 1, 2 and 3 cl. carriages between London and Dover, and Dunkerque and Paris; also Refreshment Car between London and Dover, and a Supper Car (for Sleeping Car passengers only) between Paris and Dunkerque. **F**—1, 2 and 3 cl. cars Dunkerque-Bale, Dunkerque-Nancy. **G**—1, 2 and 3 cl. cars Dunkerque-Brussels and *v.v.* **V**—Rest. Car Bar Dunkerque-Strasbourg and *v.v.* For Private Cabins and Berths see page 77.
† 1 and 2 cl. F.D. train from Aachen (not via Cologne).

LONDON—BRUSSELS *via* DOVER—OSTEND.

	1 2 3	1 2 3	Ostend-Brussels Pullman Exp. 1 2	1 2 3	1 2 3	1 2 3	1 2 3
London (Victoria)dep.	8 D 0	9 A 20	11 *b* 0	10 30	14 E30	15 0	23 B 0
Dover Marine ....dep.	10 30	11 50	12 *a* 55	12 *a* 55	16 40	16 55	1 0
Ostend Quay ....arr.	13 50	15 10	16 *a* 15	16 *a* 15	20 0	20 15	5 0
Ostend Quay ....dep.	..	16 20	16 51	17 4	21 20	21 20	6 7
Bruges ....arr.	..	..	..	17 19	21 35	21 35	6 23
Brussels (Nord) ..arr.	..	17 *d* 35	18 1	18 24	22 38	22 38	7 40
	1 2 3	1 2 3	Ostend-Brussels Pullman Exp. 1 2	1 2 3			
Brussels (Nord).. dep.	9 9	14 11	14 34	22 C 24	..	..	..
Bruges ....dep.	10 13	15 16	..	23 29	..	..	..
Ostend Quay ....arr.	10 29	15 32	15 46	23 45	..	..	..
Ostend Quay ....dep.	10 50	16 20	16 20	1 0	..	..	..
Dover Marine ....arr.	14 10	19 40	19 40	5 0	..	..	..
London (Victoria) arr.	16 *e* 20	21 *c* 54	21 *c* 54	7 20	..	..	..

a Sats. until Oct. 7, Dover dep. 12.30; Ostend arr. 16.0.
b Sats., dep. 10.30 until Oct. 7.
c Suns., until Sept. 24, arr. Victoria 22.20.
d Brussels (Midi).
e Sats. until Oct. 7, arr. Cannon St. 16.25.
A Dep. Cannon St. (not Victoria); Sats. only until Sept. 2; for organised Party Traffic only.

B Nightly until Sept. 10. **C** Nightly until Sept. 10. **D** Sat. Aug. 5 only. **E** Sats. only until Sept. 2.

LONDON—(LE TOUQUET) PARIS.

	R.W.	I.W.	A.D.	A.W.X.	I.D.	A.W.	A.W.X.	I.D.	A.D.	A.W.X.
Airport (*see below*) dp.	5.25	8.45	9.0	10.0	10.45	11.0	12.0	12.45	13.0	14.0
Paris Airport .. arr.	7.5	9.55	10.15	11.15	11.55	12.15	13.15	13.55	14.15	15.15
	I.W.	A.W.	A.W.X.	I.D.	A.D.	A.W.X.	I.D.	A.D.	I.D.	I.W.
Airport (*see below*) dp.	14.45	15.0	16.0	16.45	17.0	18.0	18.45	19.0*	20.45	22.45
Paris Airport .. arr.	15.55	16.15	17.15	17.55	18.15	19.15	19.55	20.15*	21.55	23.55

PARIS-LONDON.

	I.W.	R.W.	I.W.	A.D.	A.W.X.	I.W.	A.W.	A.W.X.	I.D.	A.D.	R.W.
Paris Airport ....dp.	6.45	8.15	8.45	9.0	10.0	10.45	11.0	12.0	12.45	13.0	13.0
Airport (*see below*) arr.	7.55	9.55	9.55	10.15	11.15	11.55	12.15	13.15	13.55	14.15	14.40

	A.W.X.	I.W.	A.W.	A.W.X.	I.D.	A.D.	I.D.	A.W.X.	A.D.	I.D.
Paris Airport ....dp.	14.0	14.45	15.0	16.0	16.45	17.0	18.45	18.0	19.0*	20.45
Airport (*see below*) ....arr.	15.15	15.55	16.15	17.15	17.55	18.15	19.55	19.15	20.15*	21.55

Operating Companies.—A—Denotes Air France. Automobile connection from the Dorchester Hotel, London, to Croydon, one hour prior to departure of aeroplane. I—Imperial Airways and British Airways. Automobile connection from Airway Terminus, Victoria Station, S.W., to Croydon, 45 minutes prior to departure of aeroplane. R—Wrightways from Croydon. D—Indicates daily service. W—Weekdays only. S—Sundays only. WX Not Weds. and Thurs. * One hour earlier from Sept. 2nd. Services will be operated to Le Touquet during the summer months. Full details on application.

LONDON—BALE—ZURICH.

Imperial Airways Ltd. and Swiss Air.

Daily.

9 0	14 0	dep. London (Croydon)..arr.	1240	19 0
1145	1645	arr. Bale ....dep.	9 40	1615
1235	1725	arr. Zurich ....dep.	9 0	1525

Swiss Air and Alpar.

Weekdays.

—	—	dep. Zurich ......arr.	—	—
1210	17 5	dep. Bale ....arr.	9 10	1555
1240	1735	arr. Berne ....dep.	8 40	1525
1325	1915	arr, Lausanne ..dep.	7 50	1445
15 0	1930	arr. Geneva .....dep.	7 25	1235

Service on request, Zurich to St. Moritz, weather permitting, in 50 minutes.

LONDON—PARIS—MARSEILLES—CANNES—ALGIERS—ROME—TUNIS—GENEVA—BALE, Etc. Air France, Swiss Air, Avio Linee & Ala Littoria.

Weekdays only except otherwise shown.

9 0	9 0	11 0	13 0	15 0	15 0	—	dep. London (Croydon) ....arr.	1615	1815	1915	1215	1215	1815	2015
1015	1015	1215	1415	1615	1615	—	arr. Paris (Le Bourget)....dep.	15 0	17 0	18 0	11 0	11 0	17 0	19 0
D	†		‡			D				*			S	
1045	1045	1245	1430	1630	1635	8 0	dep. Paris (Le Bourget)....arr.	1430	1635	1730	1030	1015	1620	1835
—	—	1430	—	—	—	9 35	arr. Lyons (Bron)........dep.	1245	15 0	—	—	—	—	1 hr. earlier from Sept. 1
—	—	1535	July 1st to Sept. 3rd.	1825	—	—	arr. Geneva (Cointrin)....dep.	1145	—	—	8 30	—	—	
—	—	—		19 0	—	—	arr. Lausanne ....dep.	—	—	—	7 50	—	—	
—	—	—		—	—	—	arr. Berne ....dep.	—	—	—	—	—	—	
—	—	—		—	1825	—	arr. Basle (Birsfelden)....dep.	—	—	—	—	8 15	1420	
—	—	—		—	1840	—	dep. Basle (Birsfelden) ....arr.	—	—	—	—	8 0	1410	
1245	—	—	—	—	19 5	—	arr. Zurich (Dubendorf)...dep.	—	—	—	—	7 35	1345	1630
—	1335	1555	1725	—	—	1055	arr. Marseilles (Marignane)dep.	1120	1340	1440	—	—	—	—
—	—	1655	—	—	—	12§0	arr. Cannes ....dep.	1020	12§40	—	—	—	—	—

S Sundays only.

Daily except Mondays.	11 20	dep. Marseilles (Marignane).....arr.	13 0	Daily except Mondays.
	13 20	arr. Ajaccio (Hydrostation)....dep.	1035	
	13 50	dep. Ajaccio (Hydrostation)....arr.	10 0	
	17 0	arr. Tunis (Hydrostation) .....dep.	6 0	
	11 30	dep.Marseilles ....arr.	1310	
	12 40	arr. Alcudia (Majorca) ....dep.	9 40	
	15 30	arr. Algiers ....dep.	6 45	

9 0	9 0	9 15	9 0	*	dep. London (Croydon) ....arr.	1815	2110	1415	1215	2015
1015	1015	1015	1015	—	arr. Paris (Le Bourget) ......dep.	17 0	2015	13 0	11 0	19 0
11 0	1055	1055	1045	8 0	dep. Paris ....arr.	1635	1730	1255	1040	1835
Sats. from June 3	13 0		†	—	arr. La Baule................dep.	†	*		8 30	
	Sats. from June 3	D	1335	1055	arr. Marseilles ....dep.	1340	1440	D	Mons. from June 5	Suns. from June 4
		..	..	14 0	arr. Genoa ....dep.	1120	..	..		
		1320	..	..	arr. Turin ....dep.	..	..	10 3		
		1435	..	—	arr. Milan ....dep.	—	..	9 20		
		..	1715	16 5	arr. Rome ....dep.	8 30	11 5	..		
..	..	1550	†	*	arr. Venice ....dep.	†	*	8 0		..
1230	..	..	..	—	arr, Vichy ....dep.	—	..	..	..	17 0
Suspended					dep. Marseilles...............arr.					
					dep. Cannes..................arr.					
					arr. Ile Rousse ....dep.					

† Tues., Thurs. and Sats. * Mons., Weds. and Fris. **D** Daily. § From July 1, Fris. to Mons. ‡ Tues. and Thurs. Automobile in connection leaves Dorchester Hotel, London, and Place Lafayette, Paris. NOTE.—For Air France Services to INDIA, HANOI, SAIGON and HONG KONG, see page 147.

LONDON-BRUSSELS-ANTWERP-DUSSELDORF-ESSEN-HAMBURG-COPENHAGEN-MALMO-STOCKHOLM. British Airways, Sabena, D.L.H. and Danish.

	*	*			*		Weekdays only	*			*	*		†
8†45	8 50	9 0	1045	13†30	1450	1715	↓ dep. London (*Airport) arr. ↑	1215	1330	1555	1810	1830	20 0	2210
10 0	1020	..	..	1455	1620	1840	arr. Brussels ......dep.	1045	12 0	..	..	17 0	18†30	2045
1025	1150	..	..	1550	..	..	dep. Brussels ......arr.	9 50	1145	..	..	..	1815	..
1045	1210	..	..	1610	..	..	arr. Antwerp ......dep.	9 30	1125	..	..	..	1755	..
1030	..	..	..	..	..	..	dep. Brussels ......arr.	..	..	..	..	..	1810	..
1120	..	..	..	..	..	..	arr. Dusseldorf ....dep.	..	..	..	..	..	1720	..
1145	..	..	..	..	..	..	arr. Essen ....dep.	..	..		..	..	1655	..
..	..	12 0	1315	..	..	..	arr. Hamburg ....dep.	..	..	1320	1455	..	..	..
..	..	1340	1430	..	..	..	arr. Copenhagen ..dep.	..	..	12 5	1315	..	..	..
..	..	..	..	..	..	..	arr. Malmo ......dep.	..	..			..	..	..
1350	..	..	..	..	..	..	arr. Berlin ....dep.	..	..	..	..	..	1435	..
..	..	..	1540	..	..	..	arr. Gothenburg ..dep.	..	..	1050	..	..	..	..
..	..	..	1650	..	..	..	arr. Oslo ....dep.	..	..	9 40	..	..	..	..
..	..	16 0		..	..	..	arr. Stockholm ....dep.	..	..	§	1045		..	..

*British Airways from Heston. Other lines from Croydon.

†Daily to and from Brussels. §Leaves 8.30 until June 1st.

LONDON—BRUSSELS—COLOGNE—FRANKFORT—ROME—BUDAPEST. British Airways Ltd., Sabena, Luft Hansa, C.S.A. and Avio Linee.

	D	D	*			Weekdays only.		*		D	D	D
8 45	8 45	8 45	11 5	14 0	1715	dp. London (*Airp't) arr.	1330	1630	1830	20 0	20 0	2210
1035	1025	1015	..	1540	1840	dep. Brussels ....arr.	1135	..	1625	18 0	1810	2030
..	(Suspended)	..	..	1640	1955	arr. Cologne ....dep.	1035	..	..	(Suspended)	1710	..
↓		..	..	..	..	dep. Cologne ....arr.		..	↑		..	..
		1130	1335	..	..	arr. Frankfort ..dep.	..	14 0			..	1910
		12 0	14 5	..	..	dep. Frankfort ..arr.	..	1330			..	1840
		..	..	..	..	arr. Nuremberg ..dep.	..	..			..	..
		1310	..	..	..	arr. Munich ....dep.	..	..			..	1720
	1310	..	..	..	..	arr. Prague ....dep.	..	..		15 0	..	..
	..	1450	..	..	..	arr. Vienna ....dep.	..	..		..	..	1520
	1535	..	1720	..	..	arr. Budapest ..dep.	..	1015		1150	..	..
	19‡30	..	..	..	..	arr. Bucarest ....dep.	..	..		9†55	..	..
1320	..	..	..	..	..	arr. Milan ......dep.	..	..	13 0	..	..	..
1545	..	..	..	..	..	arr. Rome ......dep.	..	..	11 0	..	..	..

* British Airways from Heston. Other lines from Croydon. † Mons., Weds., Fris. ‡ Tues., Thurs., Sats. D Daily.

LONDON-ROTTERDAM-AMSTERDAM-BREMEN-HAMBURG-COPENHAGEN-MALMO-STOCKHOLM-GOTHENBURG-OSLO. Royal Dutch Air Line (K.L.M.), A.B. Aerotransport and D.L.H.

D.	D.	D.	W.	D.	W.	W.		W.	D.	D.	D.	W.	D.	D.
8 45	9 0	9 15	1315	1515	18 0	1945	↓ dep. Croydon .. arr. ↑	1045	1310	14 5	1635	1915	21 5	2240
1025	..	..	15 0	..	..	2130	arr. Rotterdam dep.	8 30	..	..	..	18 0	1955	..
..	1050	11 5	1530	1710	20 5	22 0	arr. Amsterdam dp.	8 0	1135	1240	1520	1730	..	2120
To Prauge, see below.	..	1125	1545	1730	2025	8 15	dep. Amsterdam arr.	..	..	1215	15 0	..	..	21 0
	..	..	..	..	2220	9 30	arr. Hamburg dep.	..	..	9 40	..	..	..	..
	..	1330	1920	1950	..	11 5	arr. Copenhagen dp.	..	..	9 9	12 0	..	..	1750
	..	..	1950	2020	..	1135	arr. Malmo ..dep.	..	..	8 30	..	..	..	1715
	..	1550	..	..	..	14 5	arr. Stockholm dep.	..	..	..	9 30	..	..	1445
	..	1855	..	..	..	1855	arr. Helsingfors dep.	..	..	..	7 30	..	..	..

D. Daily. W. Weekdays.

ROTTERDAM-VIENNA-BUDAPEST.

K.L.M. AND C.L.S.

D.		D.
1045	dep. Rotterdam ......arr.	1935
1315	arr. Prague ....dep.	1615
1445	arr. Vienna ....dep.	1435
1555	arr. Budapest ......dep.	1315

D. Daily. W. Weekdays.
Not at present calling at Prague.

PRAGUE-GENEVA-MARSEILLES.

C.L.S.

1225	↓ dep. Prague ....arr. ↑	1710
15 5	dep. Zurich ....dep.	15 5
1625	dep. Geneva ..dep.	1345
1750	arr. Marseilles dep.	12 5

Temporarily Suspended.

AMSTERDAM-BALE-ZURICH.

K.L.M. and SWISSAIR Weekdays.

9 0	dep. Amsterdam ..arr.	1830
9 30	dep. Rotterdam ..arr.	18 0
1135	arr. Bale ....dep.	1510
1220	arr. Zurich ......dep.	1430

AMSTERDAM-KRISTIANSAND-OSLO.

K.L M. and D.N.L. Weekdays.

1130	dep. Amsterdam ..arr.	15 0
14 5	arr. Kristiansand dep.	1140
1535	arr. Oslo ....dep.	1010

The times on the LEFT are to be read DOWNWARDS, those on the RIGHT UPWARDS.

LONDON—AMSTERDAM—HANOVER—BERLIN—WARSAW—DANZIG—KONIGSBERG—HELSINGFORS.

British Airways, Deutsche Luft Hansa, K.L.M. and Sabena.

via Br's'ls	Daily.	*		Daily.	Weekdays only.	Daily.		*	via Br's'ls	Daily.
8 45	9 0	12 5	1315	18 0	dep. London (Airport*) arr.	1310	1635	1725	20 0	2240
	1050	↓	1530	20 5	arr. Amsterdam ......dep.	1135	1520	↑		2120
	1110		—	2025	dep. Amsterdam ......arr.	1115	—			2045
	—		—	—	arr. Hanover ....dep.	—	—			—
1350	13 0	1550	—	2250	arr. Berlin ....dep.	8 0	—	1340	1435	18 0
—	—	1830	—	—	arr. Warsaw..........dep.	—	—	11 0	—	—
		12 0	1920	7 20	dep. Berlin ....arr.	—	10 5	1910	1650	
		14 0	2120	--	arr. Danzig ....dep.	—	7 55	17 0	—	
		1540	2220	9 45	arr. Konigsberg ......dep.	—	7 0	16 0	14 5	
				1010	dep. Konigsberg ......arr.	—	—	—	1335	
				1115	arr. Kovno ....dep.	—	—	—	1225	
				1350	arr. Riga ....dep.	—	—	—	1155	
				1535	arr. Tallin (Reval)....dep.	—	—	—	10 5	
				1555	dep. Tallin ....arr.	—	—	—	9 45	
				1630	arr. Helsingfors ......dep.	—	—	—	9 10	

* British Airways from Heston, other times from Croydon

COLOGNE—BERLIN—FRANKFURT—MUNICH—MANNHEIM—CARLSRUHE—HALLE/LEIPZIG—BRESLAU. Deutsche Luft Hansa.

Weekdays.

			Weekdays.			
7 20	1035	—	dep. Cologne....arr.	1045	1935	2220
9 45	1235	—	arr. Berlin ....dep.	8 10	1730	1930
1030	11 0	1745	dep. Cologne....arr.	1120	1310	1940
1120	1150	1835	arr. Frankfurt dep.	1030	1220	1850
12 0	1220	1845	dep. Frankfurt..arr.	1015	—	1840
—	1320	1945	arr. Nuremburg dep	9 5	—	—
1310	—	2050	arr. Munich ..dep.	8 5	—	1720
1450	—	—	arr. Vienna....dep.	—	—	1520

		Weekdays.		
7†10	1710	dep. Frankfort.... arr.	9 40	20†55
8 40	1825	arr. Halle/Leipzig dp.	8 0	19†15
1745	11 0	dep. Cologne .... arr.	1940	1120
1835	1150	arr. Frankfurt ..dep.	1850	1030
1850	1215	dep. Frankfurt....arr.	1830	7 0
—	1340	arr. Mannheim ..dep.	18 5	9 45
1930	1310	arr. Carlsruhe ..dep.	1735	6 20
—	14 0	arr. Freibnrg ....dep.	1645	—
1050	2015	dep. Cologne ....arr.	9 55	1945
1130	—	dep. Dortmund ..arr.	—	19 5
13 0	2155	arr. Leipzig ....dep.	0	1720
1345	—	arr. Dresden ....dep.	—	1630
2040	—	arr. Breslau ....dep.	—	—

DEUTSCHE LUFT HANSA, A.G.

Berlin—Stuttgart—Barcelona—Madrid.

—	dep. Berlin ....arr.	23 0
7 30	dep. Stuttgart..arr.	1950
9 20	arr. Geneva ..dep.	1810
9 35	dep. Geneva ..arr.	1755
1120	arr. Marseilles dep.	1615
1140	dep. Marseilles..arr.	1555
1330	arr. Barcelona dep.	1355
1635	arr. Madrid ..dep.	1110
1940	arr. Lisbon ..dep.	8 45

Oslo—Berlin—Dresden—Vienna.

Lufthansa.

Weekdays only.

—	9 40	dep. Oslo ....arr.	1650	—
—	1035	arr. Gothenburg dep.	1555	—
—	1050	dep. Gothenburg ..arr.	1540	
—	1140	arr. Copenhagen dep.	1450	—
9 0	1920	dep. Copenhagen arr.	2015	9 30
1045	2120	arr. Berlin ......dep.	1830	7 30
7 0	1450	dep. Berlin ......arr.	1225	1710
↓	1540	arr. Dresden ....dep.	1135	↑
	1555	dep. Dresden ....arr.	1120	
	1640	arr. Prague ....dep.	1035	
9 0	1815	arr. Vienna ....dep.	9 0	1510

Berlin—Halle/Leipzig—Nuremberg—Munich.

1125	1330	1925	dep. Berlin ....arr.	1040	1445	2155
—	1420	—	arr. Halle/Leipzig dep.	9 50	—	—
—	1540	2115	arr. Nuremberg dep.	8 30	—	20 5
1350	1640	2220	arr. Munich ..dep.	7 30	1220	19 0

Berlin—Munich—Venice—Rome.

Daily.

1125	dep. Berlin ....arr.	1445
1350	dep. Munich ....arr.	12 0
16 5	arr. Venice ....dep.	1015
1625	dep. Venice ....arr.	9 55
1820	arr. Rome ....dep.	8 0

Paris—Cologne—Berlin.

Air France and Deutsche Luft Hansa.

Daly.i

8 30	dep. Paris (Le Bourget) arr.	2150
1010	arr. Cologne ....dep.	20 0
1035	dep. Cologne .... arr.	1935
1235	arr. Berlin ....dep.	1730

Stockholm—Berlin—Zurich.

—	8 0	dep. Stockholm.. arr.	1810	—
—	11 10	arr. Berlin......dep.	15 0	—
7 0	11†30	dep. Berlin...... arr.	1320	1810
1110	14†40	arr. Zurich ....dep.	9 30	1510

DEUTSCHE LUFT HANSA, A.G.

Hamburg—Frankfurt—Stuttgart.

Weekdays only.

9 20	dep. Hamburg ..arr. ↑	2125
10 5	arr. Hanover ..dep.	2040
1015	dep. Hanover ..arr.	2025
1140	arr. Frankfurt dep.	19 0
1215	dep. Frankfurt arr.	1830
13 5 ↓	arr. Stuttgart dep.	1740

Berlin—Halle/Leipzig—Stuttgart—Zürich. Weekdays.

15 0	20 0	dep. Berlin ......arr. ↑	9 50	1320
1545	—	arr. Halle/Leipzig dep.	—	1235
1555	—	dep. Halle/Leipzig arr.	—	1220
1740	2240	arr. Stuttgart ...dep.	7 20	1035
18 0	—	dep. Stuttgart ....arr.	—	1015
1845	—	↓ arr. Zürich .....dep.	—	9 30

Stuttgart—Freiburg.

Weekdays.

18 0	dep. Stuttgart ......arr. ↑	7 10
1835 ↓	arr. Freiburg ......dep.	6 35

Hanover—Nurnburg—Vienna.

17 5	dep. Hanover......arr. ↑	1145
18 5	dep. Magdeburg ...arr.	1040
1840	dep. Leipsic ......arr.	10 5
1940	arr. Nurnberg ....dep.	9 5
2145 ↓	arr. Vienna ......dep.	7 0

C.S.A. and A.L.A. Weekdays.

7 35	8*0	16 0	dep. Prague ....arr. ↑	9 30	18*0
8 35	..	17 0	arr. Brno ......dep.	8 30	—
9 25	9 20	1755	arr. Bratislaya..dep.	7 25	1640
—	1130	—	arr. Trieste ....dep.	—	1430
—	1215	—	arr. Venice ....dep.	—	1345
—	1440	— ↓	arr. Rome......dep.	—	1120

* Suspended	7 35	16 0	dep. Prague ...... arr.	9 30	1430
	8 35	17 0	arr. Brno .... dep.	8 30	1330
	9 5	1735	arr. Zlin .... dep.	8 0	13 0
	9 40	1810	dep. Pistany ...... dep.	7 25	1225
	—	—	arr. Spisskanova ..dep.	—	—
	—	—	arr. Slatdoly ......dep.	—	—

Amsterdam—Cologne—Frankfurt—Milan—Rome.

K.L.M. AND D.L.H.

Daily.

9 30	dep. Amsterdam ..arr. ↑	1510
9 50	arr. Rotterdam....dep.	1450
10 0	dep. Rotterdam ....arr.	1440
11 0	dep. Cologne ......arr.	1310
1150	arr. Frankfurt ....dep.	1220
1210	dep. Frankfurt ....arr.	12 0
1440	arr. Milan ....dep.	9 30
18 0 ↓	arr. Rome ....dep.	7 0

Cologne-Saarbrücken.

1815	dep. Cologne........arr. ↑	7 10
1910 ↓	arr. Saarbrücken ..dep.	6 15

Berlin—Baghdad.

Every Friday.	1 0	dep. Berlin ....arr. ↑	1830 Thur.
	—	dep. Belgrade.. ....arr.	— —
	1230	dep. Athens.. ......arr.	8 30 Thur.
	—	arr. Rhodes ....dep.	— —
	18 0	arr. Damascus......dep.	3 0 Thur.
Sat.	1230	arr. Baghdad ......dep.	9 30 Wed.
Sat.	13 0	dep. Baghdad ......arr.	19 0 Wed.
Sat.	1750	arr. Teheran........dep.	5 30 Wed.
Sun.	5 30	dep. Teheran ....arr.	1330 Tues.
Sun.	1540 ↓	arr. Kabul ....dep.	5 40 Tues.

(Fortnightly beyond Teheran).

Berlin—Poznan—Warsaw.

10 0	dep. Berlin ....arr. ↑	1910
1120	arr. Poznan ....dep.	1750
13 0 ↓	arr. Warsaw ....dep.	1610

Nurnberg—Dresden—Breslau.

1655	dep. Munich ....arr. ↑	1050
1750	dep. Nurnberg .....arr.	9 55
19 0	dep. Liepsic ....dep.	8 55
1930	arr. Dresden ......dep.	7 15
2040 ↓	arr. Breslau ......dep.	6 0

PARIS—PRAGUE—VIENNA—BUDAPEST.

Air France and C.S.A.

Weekdays only.

7 45	dep. Paris (Le Bourget) arr. ↑	1230	1630
9 20	arr. Strasbourg ....dep.	1050	1450
9 30	dep. Strasbourg .... arr.	1035	1440
1040	arr. Munich ....dep.	8 30	1330
11 0	dep. Munich .... arr.	—	13 5
—	arr. Warsaw ....dep.	—	—
—	dep. Prague...........arr.	—	—
—	arr. Vienna ....dep.	—	—
—	dep. Vienna .... arr.	—	—
1315	arr. Budapest ....dep.	—	1045
—	arr. Belgrade ....dep.	—	—
—	dep. Belgrade .... arr.	12*5	—
1715 ↓	arr. Bucarest ....dep.	1110	8 45

BUCAREST—ISTANBUL (LARES).

† Tue., Thur. and Sat.	6 † 45	dep. Bucarest ...... arr.	10*30	* Mon., Wed. and Fri.
	9 0	arr. Istanbul ......dep.	8 15	

COPENHAGEN—WARSAW.

14 0	dep. Copenhagen ..arr. ↑	1130	Daily.
1525	arr. Gdynia ......dep.	10 5	
17 0 ↓	arr. Warsaw ......dep.	8 30	

Berlin—Breslau—Gleiwitz.

1035	dep. Berlin ......arr. ↑	2255
1215	dep. Breslau .....arr.	2115
13 5	arr. Gleiwitz ...dep.	2025
1440 ↓	arr. Vienna......dep.	1850

C.S.A.

†	Weekdays.	*
1330	dep. Prague ......arr.	1355
—	dep. Bratislava ..arr.	—
1445	arr. Piestany ....dep.	1240
1535	arr. Budapest ....dep.	1150
1930	arr. Bucarest ....dep.	9 55

* Mon., Wed., Fri. † Tues., Thur. Sat.

BERLIN—REICHENBERG.

1740	dep. Berlin ..arr.	9 25
1915	arr. Reichenberg dep.	7 50

COLOGNE—HAMBURG.

Weekdays only.

7 25	dep. Cologne........... arr. ↑	18 0
7 55	dep. Essen ....dep.	1740
9 30 ↓	arr. Hamburg.........dep.	1555

The times on the LEFT are to be read DOWNWARDS, those on the RIGHT UPWARDS.

TOULOUSE/MARSEILLES—CASABLANCA. Air France.

		20†15	dep. Paris .... arr.	6†55	1810
		7 50	dep. Marseilles arr.	1550	1535
		8 35	dep. Toulouse.. arr.	1515	1515
		9 0	arr. Barcelona dep.	1245	1245
		9 20	dep. Barcelona arr.	1225	Mon., Wed. and Fri.
		*	arr. Alicante .. dep.	..	
		12 0	arr. Oran .... dep.	9 45	
		..	arr. Tangier .. dep.	..	
		..	arr. Fez ...... dep.	..	
		1525	arr. Casablanca dep.	6 45	

† By train Paris to Toulouse and *v.v.*

LISBON—TANGIER.

Sun.		Wed.
10 0	dep. Lisbon .... arr.	11 5
1230	arr. Tangier ....dep.	8 45
1245	dep. Tangier .... arr.	8 30
1420	arr. Casablanca dep.	7 0

PARIS—BORDEAUX—TOULOUSE—BARCELONA.

Weekdays.

†				
1445	1645	dep. Paris ...... arr.	1040	1235
17 5	19 5	arr. Bordeaux ..dep.	8 15	1010
1715	To	dep. Bordeaux .. arr.	To	10 0
1815	July28	arr. Biarritz ..dep.	Jly. 28	9 0

† July 29 to Sept. 11.

PARIS-BRUSSELS-ANTWERP-ROTTERDAM-AMSTERDAM-HAMBURG-COPENHAGEN-MALMO. Air France ; The Royal Dutch Air Line (K.L.M.) and A.B. Aerotransport, Stockholm.

D	D		D	W	D Daily. W Weekdays.	W	D	D		
8 25	9 0	10 0	15 0	17 0	dep. Paris (Le Bourget) arr.	1115	14 5	1615	1725	1940
9 40	1010		..	1815	arr. Brussels ....dep.	10 0	..	..	1610	1825
..	..		..	..	arr. Antwerp ....dep.	..	..	..	..	..
..	..		..	1925	arr. Rotterdam ......dep.	9 50	..	..	..	..
1110	..		1715	1955	arr. Amsterdam ......dep.	9 0	1235	..	1520	..
1120	..		..	..	dep. Amsterdam ......arr.	..	1150	..	..	..
..	..		..		arr. Hamburg ....dep.		..	..	..	..
1435	..	1345	..	From May 15.	arr. Copenhagen ......dep.	From May 15.	9 0	1215	..	..
..	..	..	..		arr. Malmo ....dep.		8 30	..	..	..
17 5	..	16 0	..		arr. Stockholm ......dep.		..	9 45	..	..
..	..	1540	..		arr. Gothenburg.......dep.		..	1050	..	–
..	..	1650	..		arr. Oslo ....dep.		..	9 50	..	..

LIVERPOOL–DONCASTER–AMSTERDAM.

Weekdays.

8 0	dep. Liverpool ..arr.	1835
8 25	dep. Manchester arr.	18 5
9*0	dep. Doncaster arr.	17*25
11 5	arr. Amsterdam dep.	16 0

* Call Optional.

STOCKHOLM-ABO-HELSINGFORS. A.B. Aerotransport/Aero O.Y. (Daily).

				* Weekdays.	D	D		
8 30	9 0	1610	1830	dep. Stockholm ..arr.	13 0	9 0	19 0	2050
..	1125	..	2055	arr. Abo ....dep.	..	8 35	1835	..
Via Riga.	1140	..	2110	dep. Abo ....arr.	Via Riga.	8 20	1820	..
	1230	1855	22 0	arr. Helsingfors..dep.		7 30	1730	20 0
	13 0	From July 1.	9 10	dep. Helsingfors ..arr.		19 0	1430	From July 1.
..	1335		9 45	arr. Tallin (Reval) dep.	..	1830	1355	
1730	..		..	arr. Moscow......dep.	8 0	..	..	

OSLO—BERGEN—TROMSO. NORSKE—LUFTFARTSELSKAP.

WEEKDAYS. From June 1.

7 35	1010	dep. Oslo ....arr.	1535	1910
..	..	dep. Arendal ....dep.	..	..
..	1430	dep. Kristiansand ......dep.	1425	..
..	1545	dep. Stavanger..........dep.	1030	..
..	1620	dep. Haugesund ....dep.	10 0	..
9 10	17 0	arr. Bergen ....dep.	9 20	1730

BERGEN—TROMSO.

From June 1.

7 0	dep. Bergen .... arr.	1650
1030	dep. Trondhjem dep.	1330
1610	arr. Tromso....dep.	7 0

TUNIS—ALGIERS—ORAN.

†	*					
		1230	dep. Algiers ....arr.	9 20	arr.	arr.
6 30	1315	W.	dep. Constantine dep.	W.	8 30	15 5
7 5	14 0	1435	dep. Bone ......dep.	7 30	7 45	1420
arr.	arr.	1535	arr. Tunis ....dep.	6 10	†	*
		9†35	Algiers	1145		
		1115	Oran	10*0		

W. Weekdays. * Mo., We., Fri. † Tu., Th., Sat.

HELSINGFORS—VIIPURI—VAASA.

To Aug. 15.

	..	dep. Helsingfors ..arr.	..
	..	arr. Viipuri ......dep.	..
	9 15	dep. Helsingfors ..arr.	1855
	10 5	arr. Tampere ....dep.	18 5
	1115	arr. Vaasa ......dep.	1655
	13 0	arr. Uleaborg ....dep.	1510
	1340	arr. Kemi ......dep.	1430

BALE—BERNE—GENEVA. (Swiss Air and Alpar).

Weekdays.

1310	1455	1740	dep. Zurich ....arr.	9 5	1415	..
1350	1530	1820	arr. Berne ....dep.	8 30	1340	arr.
1430	..	19 5	arr. Lausanne ..dep.	7 50	13 0	1910
15 0	..	1930	arr. Geneva ....dep.	7 25	1235	1840

ZURICH—ST. GALLEN—MUNICH.

WEEKDAYS.

1750	9 15	dep. Zurich ....arr.	1640
1815	9 40	arr. St. Gallen ....dep.	1615
..	1050	arr. Munich ....dep.	15 0

The times on the LEFT are to be read DOWNWARDS, those on the RIGHT UPWARDS.

VIENNA—VENICE—MILAN. AND OSTERREICHISCHE LUFTVERKEHRS, A.G.

Weekdays.

8†30	—	dep. Budapest .. arr. ▲	—	17*25
9 45	15 0	dep. Vienna .... arr.	18 30	1610
—	1550	arr. Graz ......dep.	17 40	—
—	1630	arr. Klagenfurt dep.	17 0	—
12 5	—	arr. Venice ....dep.	—	1355
1230	—	dep. Venice .... arr.	—	1335
1340	—	▼ arr. Milan ....dep.	—	1225

* Mon., Wed., Fri. † Tue., Thur., Sat.

GENOA—CAGLIARI—TUNIS.

	†		*
* Mon., Wed., Fri.	10 0	dep. Genoa ...... arr.	1450
	1215	arr. Alghero ....dep.	1235
† Tues., Thur., Sat.	1430	arr. Cagliari ....dep.	1020
	1640	arr. Tunis ......dep.	8 10

ROME-BRINDISI-THESSALONIKI

*		†
9 5	dep. Rome .... arr. ▲	1250
1125	arr. Brindisi....dep.	1050
12 0	dep. Brindisi.... arr.	9 55
1255	arr. Tirana ....dep.	9 0
1610	▼ arr. Thessaloniki dp.	8 0

* Mon., Weds., Fri. † Tues., Thurs., Sats.

ROME—CAGLIARI.

Weekdays.

Tue. Thur. Sat.	Mon. Wed. Fri.			Mon. Wed. Fri.	Tue. Thur. Sat.
6 50	9 0	1215	dep. Rome .... arr. ▲	1655	1445
—	—	1445	arr. Cagliari ..dep.	—	—
1010	1220	—	arr. Palma ....dep.	1335	1125
1420	—	—	arr. Mellila ....dep.	9 30	—
1635	—	—	arr. Cadiz ....dep.	7 0	—
—	1415	—	▼ arr. Barcelona dep.	—	9 30

ROME—BELGRADE—BUCHAREST.

9*40	dep. Rome .... arr. ▲	15†40
1235	arr. Belgrade ....dep.	1245
1635	arr. Bucharest ...... dep.	1110
1750 ▼	arr. Constanza ......dep.	8 0

* Mon., Wed., Fri. † Tue., Thur., Sat.

ROME—SYRACUSE—MALTA—TRIPOLI.

*	†		*	†
7 20	7 20	dep. Rome...... arr. ▲	1555	1540
—	9 10	dep. Naples .... arr.	1345	—
—	1150	arr. Syracuse ..dep.	11 5	—
—	1350	arr. Malta ....dep.	9 35	—
9 10	—	arr. Marsala....dep.	—	1350
1220	1630	arr. Tripoli ....dep.	7 0	1030
1720	—	▼ arr. Bengasi....dep.	—	6 0

* Mon., Wed. and Fri. † Tues., Thur. and Sat.

ROME—MARSEILLES—PARIS.

Weekdays.

†	*		*	†
8 30	11 5	dep. Rome .... arr. ▲	16 5	1715
1120	—	dep. Genoa .... arr.	1330	—
1250	1355	arr. Marseilles ..dep.	12 0	1425
1355	1440	dep. Marseilles .. arr.	1055	1335
1520	—	arr. Barcelona ..dep.	9 30	—
1635	1730	▼ arr. Paris ....dep.	8 0	1045

* Mon., Wed. and Fri. † Tues., Thurs. and Sat.

MARSALA—TUNIS.

Mo., Wed., Fri.	1030	dep. Marsala .. arr.	1235	Tue., Thu., Sat.
	1150	arr. Tunis ....dep.	1115	

ROME-KHARTOUM-ASMARA MOGADISCIO.

Tu.Th Sat.	1015	dep. Rome...... ar. ▲	Aftn.	Thur. Sat., Tues.
	Aftn.	arr. Bengasi....dp.	D'wn	
Wed. Fri. Su	Dawn	dep. Bengasi.... ar.	Aftn.	Wed., Fri., Mon.
	Aftn.	dep. Cairo ......dp.	a.m.	
	Aftn.	arr. Wadi Halfa dp.	D'wn	
Thur. Sat. Mon.	Dawn	dep. Wadi Halfa ar.	Aftn.	Tues. Thu. Sun.
	a.m.	ded. Khartoum.. ar.	a.m.	
	a.m.	arr. Cassala ....dp.	a.m.	
	p.m.	arr. Asmara ....dp.	7 30	
—	p.m.	arr. AddisAbaba dp.	p.m.	—
Daily	8 0	dep. Asmara .... arr.	12 0	Daily
	—	arr. Dire Daua..dep.	—	
	12 0	arr. Addis Ababa dep.	8 0	
Tues. Fri.	6 30	dep. Addis Ababa arr.	13 0	Wed. Sat.
	1215	arr. Mogadiscio dep.	6 30	
	6 30	dp. Djibuti .... arr.	1140	
	1040	arr. Addis Ababa dp.	7 30	

▼ Weekdays only.

ROME—NAPLES—PALERMO—TUNIS—MALTA.

*	†	*		†	*	†
7 20	7 20	8 30	dep. Rome .. arr. ▲	13 0	13 0	1415
8 30	8 30	—	dep. Naples .. arr.	1150	1150	—
1015	1015	—	arr. Palermo dep.	10 5	10 5	—
—	1220	1150	arr. Tunis ..dep.	—	8 0	11 0
1135	—	—	arr. Catania..dep.	8 50	—	—
1320	—	—	arr. Malta ..dep.	7 15	—	—
—	—	1555	▼ arr. Tripoli ..dep.	—	—	7 0

* Mons., Weds. and Fris. † Tues., Thurs., and Sats.

Tirana—Valona, Tues., Thurs., Sats.
Tirana—Coriza, Mons., Weds., Fris.
Tirana—Scutari, Tues., Thurs., Sats.
Tirana—Kukas, Weds. and Sats.
Tirana—Davoli, Mons. and Sats.
Tirana—Peskopja, Fris., Mons., Weds.

ROME—TRIESTE—BRINDISI—ATHENS—RHODES—HAIFA.

Mons., Weds., Fris.	9 5	dep. Rome ....arr. ▲	14 0	Tues., Thurs., Sats.
	11 50	dep. Brindisi ....arr.	11 0	
	15 20	arr. Athens ....dep.	9 30	
	17 40	▼ arr. Rhodes ....dep.	7 0	
Tues., Thurs., Sats.	6 0	dep. Trieste .... arr. ▲	12 10	Mons., Weds., Fris.
	9 5	dep. Rome.............. arr.	10 25	
	11 50	dep. Brindisi .... arr.	8 0	
	15 20	▼ arr. Athens .... dep.	6 30	
Tues., Thurs., Sats.	15 40	dep. Athens .... arr. ▲	17 30	
	17 40	▼ arr. Rhodes.............. dep.	15 30	
Weds., Fris., Suns.	7 0	dep. Rhodes.............. arr. ▲	14 55	Suns., Tues., Thurs.
	10 10	arr. Haifa..............dep.	11 45	
	15 10	arr. Baghdad ....dep.	8 15	
	17 25	▼ arr. Basra ....dep.	6 0	

The times on the LEFT are to be read DOWNWARDS, those on the RIGHT UPWARDS.

TRIESTE-ZARA-ANCONA-ROME.

ALA LITTORIA. Weekdays.

8 20	dep. Trieste ....arr. ▲	1745
9 5	dep. Pola ....arr.	17 0
9 25	arr. Lussino ......dep.	1640
10 0	arr. Zara ....dep.	16 5
10 30	dep. Zara ....arr.	1535
11 25	arr. Ancona ....dep.	1440
13 40	▼ arr. Rome ....dep.	12 0

VENICE-FIUME.

ALA LITTORIA. Weekdays.

1030	1445	dep. Venice ....arr. ▲	9 45	1555
1115	1530	arr. Pola .....dep.	9 0	1510
..		arr. Abbazia ..dep.	..	..
12 5	1620	▼ arr. Fiume ....dep.	8 15	1425

ROME-VENICE

ALA LITTORIA.

Weekdays (except Festivals and Sundays).

7 30	1120	1630	dep. Rome ..arr. ▲	9 0	1440	1720
9 15	1315	1835	▼ arr. Venice ..dep.	7 0	1245	1535

AVIO LINEE ITALIANE.

Weekdays.

8 25	1225	1450	1820	d. Milan ar. ▲	9 0	1340	1720	19 5
9 25	1335	1550	1920	▼ a. Venice d—	8 0	1230	1620	18 5

BERLIN-VIENNA-BUDAPEST-SOFIA.

Deutsche Lufthansa and C.L.S.

Weekdays.

7 0	1450	dep. Berlin ......arr. ▲	1225	1710
..	1555	dep. Dresden ....arr.	1120	..
..	17 0	dep. Prague ....arr.	1035	..
9 0	1815	arr. Vienna ....dep.	9 0	1510
9 20	..	dep. Vienna ....arr.	..	1445
10 5	..	arr. Budapest ..dep.	..	14 0
1146	..	arr. Belgrade ..dep.	..	1215
1220	..	dep. Belgrade .. arr.	..	1150
1455	..	arr. Sofia ......dep.	..	1115
1645	..	arr. Thessaloniki dep.	..	9 25
17 5	..	dep. Thessaloniki arr.	..	9 5
1830	..	▼ arr. Athens ....dep.	..	7 40

BERLIN—BUCAREST—D.L.H.

†	*	From June 1st.	†	*
9 15	9 15	dep. Berlin ....arr.	1530	1530
1050	..	dep. Prague ....arr.	..	1355
1250	1255	arr. Budapest ....dep.	1155	1155
1930	1725	arr. Bucarest ....dep.	9 20	9 55

* Mon., Wed. and Fri. † Tues., Thurs. and Sats.

BERLIN—ISTANBUL.

Weekdays.

7 0	dep. Berlin ....arr. ▲	1710
1210	dep. Belgrade ..arr.	1140
15 5	dep. Sofia ......arr.	1045
1745	▼ arr. Istanbul ..dep.	7 55

MADRID-SEVILLE.

(Suspended). L.A.P.E.

	dep. Madrid ....arr. ▲	
	▼ arr. Seville ....dep.	

MADRID-LISBON. (Suspended).

	dep. Madrid ......arr. ▲	
	▼ arr. Lisbon ......dep.	

ISTANBUL-ANKARA-ANDANA.

Turkish State. Weekdays.

9 30	—	dep. Istanbul ...... arr.	18 0	—
1130	—	arr. Ankara ......dep.	16 0	—
1445	15 5	dep. Ankara ...... arr.	1120	12 0
—	1755	arr. Izmir ....dep.	—	9 10
1655	—	arr. Adana ....dep.	9 10	—

DUBROVNIK-BELGRADE.

1420	dep. Dubrovnik .... arr.	1135
15 0	arr. Serajevo ......dep.	1055
16 5	arr. Belgrade ......dep.	9 50

Weekdays.

ROME—VENICE—BUDAPEST—WARSAW.

Weekdays

7 30	dep. Rome .... arr.	1720
9 45	dep. Venice ...... arr.	15 5
1235	dep. Budapest .... arr.	1215
1450	arr. Warsaw ...... dep.	10 0
1655	arr. Gdynia .... dep.	8 0
1730	arr. Danzig ......dep.	7 30

AVIO LINEE ITALIANE. S.A.

Weekdays only.

7 45	11 0	16 0	16 0	d. Rome ar. ▲	8 45	9 45	1545	1550
..	13 0	..	18 0	a. Milan dp.	6 45	..	1345	..
..	1730	..	1915	d. Milan ar.	..	..	8 10	..
9 45	18 5	18 0	1950	▼ a. Turin dp.	..	7 45	7 35	1350

VIENNA-MUNICH-ZURICH

SWISSAIR AND D.L.H.

Weekdays only.

9 10	1450	1520	dep. Vienna .. arr. ▲	12 0	1450	18 5
1030	..	..	arr. Salzburg ..dep.		..	1650
1120		1650	arr. Munich ..dep.	..	1330	1555
1255	1730	..	arr. Zurich ....dep.	9 25	..	1425
1455	1820	..	arr. Bale .....dep.	8 35	..	12 5
15 0	..	..	▼ arr. Geneva ..dep.	7 25	..	..

BELGRADE-ZAGREB-VENICE, etc.

1235	dep. Belgrade ..arr.	1320
..	dep. Borovo ....dep.	..
14 5	arr. Zagreb ....dep.	1150
1430	dep. Zagreb .... arr.	1130
..	dep. Laibach ....arr.	..
1550	arr. Venice ....dep.	1010
1720	arr. Milan......dep.	8 25
18 5	arr. Turin......dep.	7 35

MELILLA—MALAGA—SEVILLE—LISBON.

Weekdays.

9 0	1550	1615	dep. Melilla ....arr.	8 40	1545	8 30
..	..	1715	arr. Tetuan ..dep.	..	..	7 30
..	..	9 0	dep. Tetuan....arr.	..	..	1830
10 0	..	9 45	arr. Malaga ..dep.	..	1445	1745
..	..	1015	dep. Malaga....arr.	..	..	1715
..	1730	11 0	arr. Seville....dep.	7 0	..	1630
..	12 0	..	dep. Seville ....arr.	1530	..	..
..	1330	..	arr. Lisbon.....dep.	14 0	..	..

The times on the LEFT are to be read DOWNWARDS, those on the RIGHT UPWARDS.

IMPERIAL AIRWAYS EMPIRE SERVICES.

TO INDIA AND AUSTRALIA.

SUBJECT TO ALTERATION.

Southampton Water	dep.	Thur.	Sat.	Sun.
Marseilles	arr.	,,	,,	,,
Marseilles	dep.	,,	,,	,,
Rome (Bracciano)	dep.	,,	,,	,,
Brindisi	dep.	,,	,,	,,
Athens	arr.	,,	,,	,,
Athens	dep.	Fri.	Sun.	Mon.
Alexandria	arr.	,,	,,	,,
Alexandria	dep.	,,	,,	,,
Tiberias	arr.	,,	,,	,,
Tiberias	dep.	,,	,,	,,
Habbaniyeh (For Baghdad)	arr.	,,	,,	,,

Basra	arr.	Fri.	Sun.	Mon.
Basra	dep.	Sat.	Mon.	Tues.
*Bahrein	dep.	,,	,,	,,
Dabai	arr.	,,	,,	,,
Jiwani	arr.	,,	,,	,,
Karachi	arr.	,,	,,	,,
Karachi	dep.	Sun.	Tues.	Wed.
Rajsamand	arr.	,,	,,	,,
Gwalior	dep.	,,	,,	,,
Allahabad	dep.	,,	,,	,,
Calcutta	arr.	,,	,,	,,
Calcutta	dep.	Mon.	Wed.	Thu.
Rangoon	dep.	,,	,,	,,
Bangkok	arr.	,,	,,	,,
Bangkok	dep.	Tues.	Thur.	Fri.

Penang	arr.	Tues.	Thur.	Fri.
Penang	dep.	,,	,,	,,
Singapore	arr.	,,	,,	,,
Singapore	dep.	Wed.	Fri.	Sat.
Batavia	dep.	,,	,,	,,
Sourabaya	arr.	,,	,,	,,
Sourabaya	dep.	Thur.	Sat.	Sun.
Koepang	dep.	,,	,,	,,
Darwin	arr.	,,	,,	,,
Darwin	dep.	Fri.	Sun.	Mon.
Townsville	arr.	,,	,,	,,
Townsville	dep.	Sat.	Mon.	Tue.
Gladstone		,,	,,	,,
Brisbane	arr.	,,	,,	,,
Sydney	arr.	,,	,,	,,

Connecting Service Bangkok to Hong Kong twice weekly.

Intermediate services to Calcutta on Wednesdays and Fridays, returning on Wednesdays and Saturdays.

Sydney	dep.	Tue.	Thur.	Sat.
Brisbane	dep.	,,	,,	,,
Gladstone	dep.	,,	,,	,,
Townsville	arr.	,,	,,	,,
Townsville	dep.	Wed.	Fri.	Sun.
Darwin	arr.	,,	,,	,,
Darwin	dep.	Thur.	Sat.	Mon.
Koepang	dep.	,,	,,	,,
Sourabaya	arr.	,,	,,	,,
Sourabaya	dep.	Fri.	Sun.	Tues.
Batavia	dep.	,,	,,	,,
Singapore	arr.	,,	,,	,,
Singapore	dep.	,,	,,	,,
Penang	arr.	,,	,,	,,

Penang	dep.	Sat.	Mon.	Wed.
Bangkok	dep.	,,	,,	,,
Rangoon	arr.	,,	,,	,,
Rangoon	dep.	,,	,,	,,
Calcutta	arr.	,,	,,	,,
Calcutta	dep.	Sun.	Tue.	Thur.
Allahabad	dep.	,,	,,	,,
Gwalior	arr.	,,	,,	,,
Gwalior	dep.	,,	,,	,,
Karachi	arr.	,,	,,	,,
Karachi	dep.	Mon.	Wed.	Fri.
Jiwani	dep.	,,	,,	,,
Dabai	arr.	,,	,,	,,
Dabai	dep.	,,	,,	,,
*Bahrein	dep.	,,	,,	,,

Basra	arr.	Mon.	Wed.	Fri.
Basra	dep.	Tue.	Thur.	Sat.
Habbaniyeh (for Baghdad)	dep.	,,	,,	,,
Tiberias	dep.	,,	,,	,,
Alexandria	arr.	,,	,,	,,
Alexandria	dep.	Wed.	Fri.	Sun.
Athens	dep.	,,	,,	,,
Brindisi	arr.	,,	,,	,,
Rome	arr.	,,	,,	,,
Rome	dep.	,,	,,	,,
Marseilles	arr.	,,	,,	,,
Marseilles	dep.	Thur.	Sat.	Mon.
Southampton Water	arr.	,,	,,	,,

* A call will be made at these places if inducement offers and circumstances permit.

AFRICAN SERVICE.

SUBJECT TO ALTERATION.

Wed.	Fri.	Sat.	dep.	Southampton Water	arr.	Fri.	Mon.	Tues.
,,	,,	,,	arr.	Marseilles	dep.	Fri.	Mon.	Tues.
,,	,,	,,	dep.	Marseilles	arr.	Thur.	Sun.	Mon.
,,	,,	,,	dep.	Bracciano (Rome)	arr.	Thur.	Sun	Mon.
,,	,,	,,	arr.	Brindisi	arr.	Thur.	Sun.	Mon.
,,	,,	,,	arr.	Athens	dep.	Thur.	Sun.	Mon.
Thur.	Sat.	Sun.	dep.	Athens	arr.	Thur.	Sun.	Mon.
,,	,,	,,	dep.	Alexandria	dep.	Thur.	Sun.	Mon.
,,	,,	,,	arr.	Cairo	arr.	Wed.	Sat.	Sun.
,,	,,	,,	arr.	Wadi Halfa	dep.	Wed.	Sat.	Sun.
Fri.	Sun.	Mon	arr.	Khartoum	dep.	Wed.	Sat.	Sun.
,,	,,	,,	dep.	Khartoum	arr.	Tues.	Fri.	Sat.
,,	,,	,,	arr.	Malakal	arr.	Tues.	Fri.	Sat.
,,	,,	,,	arr.	Port Bell	arr.	Tues.	Fri.	Sat.
,,	,,	,,	arr.	Kisumu	dep.	Tues.	Fri.	Sat.
Sat.	—	Tues.	dep.	Kisumu	arr.	Mon.	—	Fri.
,,	—	,,	arr.	Mombasa	arr.	Mon.	—	Fri.
,,	—	,,	arr.	Dar-es-Salaam	arr.	Mon.	—	Fri.
,,	—	,,	arr.	Lindi	arr.	Mon.	—	Fri.
,,	—	,,	arr.	Mozambique	dep.	Mon.	—	Fri.
Sun.	—	Wed.	dep.	Mozambique	arr.	Sun.	—	Thur.
,,	—	,,	arr.	Beira	arr.	Sun.	—	Thur.
,,	—	,,	arr.	Lourenco Marques	arr.	Sun.	—	Thur.
,,	—	,,	arr.	Durban	dep.	Sun.	—	Thur.

Connection Khartoum to Kano, Lagos and Accra on Sundays, arriving Kano on Mondays, and Lagos and Accra on Tuesdays.

South African Airways operate connecting services Durban to Germiston (Johannesburg) and Durban to Capetown, and also from Kisumu to Broken Hill and Germiston.

Wilson Airways operate from Kisumu to Nairobi, Mpika, Broken Hill and Lusaka.

Rhodesian and Nyasaland Airways operate from Beira to Salisbury, Blantyre, Bulawayo, Johannesburg and Lusaka.

Full details on application.

K.L.M. (ROYAL DUTCH AIR LINE) AND K.N.I.L.M. AMSTERDAM TO JAVA AND AUSTRALIA.

SUMMER SERVICE.

Tuesday, Thursday, Saturday	Amsterdam	Tuesday, Thursday, Saturday.	Bandoeng.
Ditto ditto	Leipzig	Ditto ditto	Batavia.
Ditto ditto	Budapest	Ditto ditto	Palembang
Ditto ditto	Athens	Ditto ditto	Singapore.
Wednesday, Friday, Sunday.	Athens	Ditto ditto	Medan
Ditto ditto	Rhodes†.	Wednesday, Friday, Sunday.	Medan
Ditto ditto	Alexandria	Ditto ditto	Penang.
Ditto ditto	Lydda*.	Ditto ditto	Bangkok.
Ditto ditto	Baghdad.	Ditto ditto	Rangoon
Ditto ditto	Basra.	Thursday, Saturday, Monday	Rangoon.
Thursday, Saturday, Monday	Basra.	Ditto ditto	Calcutta
Ditto ditto	Jask.	Ditto ditto	Allahabad.
Ditto ditto	Karachi.	Ditto ditto	Jodhpur
Ditto ditto	Jodhpur.	Friday, Sunday, Tuesday.	Jodhpur.
Friday, Sunday, Tuesday.	Jodhpur.	Ditto ditto	Karachi.
Ditto ditto	Allahabad	Ditto ditto	Jask.
Ditto ditto	Calcutta	Ditto ditto	Basra.
Ditto ditto	Rangoon.	Saturday, Monday, Wednesday	Basra.
Saturday, Monday, Wednesday	Rangoon.	Ditto ditto	Baghdad.
Ditto ditto	Bangkok	Ditto ditto	Lydda*.
Ditto ditto	Penang	Ditto ditto	Alexandria
Ditto ditto	Medan.	Ditto ditto	Rhodes†.
Ditto ditto	Singapore	Ditto ditto	Athens
Sunday, Tuesday, Thursday.	Singapore.	Sunday, Tuesday, Thursday.	Athens.
Ditto ditto	Palembang.	Ditto ditto	Budapest
Ditto ditto	Batavia§	Ditto ditto	Leipzig.
Ditto ditto	Bandoeng.	Ditto ditto	Amsterdam

† Landing at Rhodes optional.

* Lydda is the airport for Jerusalem, Tel Aviv and Jaffa.

§ On Tuesday and Thursday through connection to Sydney by K.N.I.L.M.

K.N.I.L.M. (JAVA).

Regular services Batavia-Semarang-Sourabaya, daily. Batavia-Bandoeng, thrice daily. Batavia-Palembang-Singapore, weekly. Batavia-Palembang-Pakan-Baroe-Medan, weekly. Batavia, Sourabaya, Balikpapan, Tarakan, weekly. Sourabaya-Den Pasar, twice weekly. Sourabaya-Makassar, weekly.

TIME TABLE OF THE "ZEPPELIN" AIRSHIPS.

Frankfort or Friedrichshafen.	Pernambuco Recife.	Rio de Janeiro.	Aeroplane connection of Syndicato Condor Ltda from Pernambuco.		Rio de Janeiro.	Pernambuco Recife.	Frankfort.
dep. Wednesday evening.	arr. Saturday evening.	arr. Sunday evening.	Buenos Aires arr. Tuesday	Buenos Aires dp. Tuesday.	dep. Wednesday evening.	dep. Thursday evening.	arr. Monday evening.

Suspended until further notice.

TO NORTH AMERICA (LAKEHURST).

Suspended until further notice.

MISR AIRWORK (CAIRO).

This Company operates a daily service Cairo Port Said–Lydda (for Jerusalem) and Haifa ; between Cairo and Alexandria, and Alexandria-Cairo-Assiut, and bi-weekly Cairo-Baghdad.

AUSTRALIA and NEW ZEALAND.

There are numerous services serving the whole of Australia and New Zealand, particulars of which will be furnished on application.

REGIE AIR AFRIQUE, SABENA AND REGIE MALGACHE TO THE BELGIAN CONGO AND MADAGASCAR.

Services leave Brussels via Oran and from Algiers with connection from Paris, weekly for Gao, Niamey, Zinder, Fort Lamy, Bangui, Stanleyville, Coquilhatville, Leopoldville, Brazzaville, Banningville, Elizabethville, Broken Hill and Tananarive.

The journey to Coquilhatville takes 5 days, to Leopoldville-Brazzaville 5 days, to Elizabethville 6 days, and to Tananarive 8 days.

Connection at Gao to Timbuktu, Mopti, Segou and Bamako.
Fares and full details of times on application.

LONDON—DAKAR, WEST AFRICA (Air France).

OUTWARD.

Tuesdays and Saturdays: London, Paris.
Wednesdays and Sundays: Paris, Barcelona, Casablanca, Agadir, Villa Cisneros, St. Louis, Dakar, arriving Thursday.
Sunday: Paris, Casablanca, Dakar, arriving same day.
Fridays only: Dakar, Kaolack, Tambacounda, Kayes, Bamako.

DAKAR—POINT NOIRE (Aeromaritime Co.)

Mondays: Dakar, Conakry.
Tuesdays: Conakry, Monrovia, Abidjan.
Wednesdays: Abidjan, Accra, Cotonou, Douala.
Thursdays: Douala, Libreville, Port Gentil, Pointe Noire.

HOMEWARD.

POINTE NOIRE—DAKAR (Aeromaritime Co.

Fridays: Pointe Noire, Port Gentil, Libreville, Douala.
Saturdays: Douala, Cotonou, Accra, Abidjan.
Sundays: Abidjan, Monrovia, Conakry, Dakar.

(Air France).

Saturdays: Bamako, Kayes, Tambacounda, Kaolack, Dakar.
Sundays: Dakar, St. Louis, Villa Cisneros, Agadir, Casablanca.
Mondays: Casablanca, Barcelona, Paris, London.
Tuesdays: Dakar, Paris.

LONDON—INDIA—FAR EAST—LONDON.

(LINE 260).

↓		↑
Wednesday	London, Paris, Marseilles	Friday
Thursday	Marseilles, Bastia, Tunis, Tripoli, Bengazi	Thursday
Friday	Bengazi, Amseat, Alexandria, Beyrouth, Baghdad	Wednesday
Saturday	Baghdad, Bushire, Jask, Karachi (for Bombay, Madras Colombo)	Tuesday
Sunday	Karachi, Jodhpur, Allahabad, Calcutta	Monday
Monday	Calcutta, Akyab, Rangoon, Bangkok, Saigon	Sunday
*Tuesday	Saigon, Hanoi, Hong Kong	*Saturday
Friday	Saigon, Hanoi.	Thursday
Saturday	Hanoi, Hong Kong	Wednesday

* Supplementary service to be opened shortly.

A weekly service is also operated between Marseilles and Baghdad via Corfu, Athens, Tripoli and Beyrout. Full details on application.

LONDON—OSTEND—LE ZOUTE. Sabena.

COMMENCING JULY 1st.

* Also Fris. from July 14th. † From July 14th.
‡ Also Fri. and Sat. from July 14th.
§ Also Mons. from July 14th.

Sun	† Mo., Sat.	* Sat.	Mo. to Fri.		† Mo.	Sat.	§ Tue to Fri.	Sun.
9 15	1015	14 0	1745	dep. Airway Terminus ... arr.	1054	1450	1720	2020
10 0	11 0	1445	1830	dep. London (Croydon) .. arr.	10 5	1450	1635	1935
1040	1140	1525	1910	arr. Ostend .... dep.	9 20	1320	1550	1850
11 5	12 5	1550	1935	arr. Knocke/Le Zoute .. dep.	9 0	13 0	1530	1830

LONDON—LE ZOUTE. (North Eastern Airways).

To Sept. 11th.

W	S		W	S
14 0	9 0	dep. London (Horseferry House) .... arr.	2050	2120
15 0	10 0	dep. Croydon .... arr.	1950	2020
1620	1120	arr. Le Zoute .... dep.	1830	19 0

W Weekdays. S Sundays.

LONDON—DEAUVILLE. Gt. Western & Southern Air Lines Ltd.

Services operated from Croydon to Deauville daily in 60 minutes during the Summer, from July 1st to September 4th. Special services at Whitsuntide. Full details of times, etc., on application.

LONDON (Croydon) LE TOUQUET. Gt. Western & Southern Air Lines Ltd.

Commencing May 26th to September 5th.

†	*		‡	§	Suns.
8 30	1815	dep. Croydon .... arr.	1010	1410	2010
9 10	1855	arr. Le Touquet .... dep.	9 30	1330	1930

† Mons. and Tues. * Thus., Fri., Sat. ‡ Mon., Tues., Fri., Sat. § Wed. and Fri.

LONDON—LUXEMBOURG. Gt. Western & Southern Air Lines Ltd.

Wednesdays and Fridays.

8 30	dep. Croydon .... arr.	1415
11 0	arr. Luxembourg .... dep.	1145

LONDON—DINARD.

JUNE TO SEPTEMBER.

Week-end services operated by Wrightways from Croydon in one hour 40 minutes ; also by Jersey Airways from Heston via Jersey, and by Air France via Paris, from Croydon.

NEWCASTLE—STAVANGER. (Allied Airways).

SUSPENDED.

dep. Newcastle .... arr.	
arr. Stavanger .... dep.	

BELGIUM.

[Trains run in Belgium by Greenwich (West-European) time.

THROUGH SERVICES TO BELGIUM.

From England, see also pp. 127, 128, 130, 131; *from France, pp.* 238-240; *from Holland, page* 154; *from Germany and beyond, pp.* 127, 128, 151-153.

§ (Lille) St. Andre.

(Calais) Lille, Brussels.

[French (Nord) & Belg. Nat. Rys.

123	23 Exp	123 fast	123	123	123 ‡	123	123 Exp¶	123 Exp	Mls		123 fast	123 Exp	23	123 Exp	123	123	123 fast
..		*	9 13	12 7	1444	..	1730	..	..	d. Calais (V) (*p.*236) a.	..	11‡56	18 8	18 8	2153		*
6 12	..	8 18	1117	1526	1631	1843	19 5	2038	0	d. Lille (French tm.) a.	9 27	1023	1430	1631	1954	2112	2323
6 33	..	8 42	1135	1548	1649	1916	r	21 2	7	d. Baisieux ,, a.	8 51	r	1412	1558	1918	2041	2254
6 49	..	8 59	1157	16 4	17 8	1944	..	2138	11	d. Blandain (Bl.oust) d.	8 46	..	1344	1553	1913	2035	2249
7 22	8 20	9 20	1220	1616	1720	1957	1932	2152	16	d. Tournai .... d.	8 30	9 57	..	1542	19 0	2023	2237
7 50	..	9 47	1247	1642	1747	..	..	..	35	d. Ath .... d.	7 55	9 31		1514	1815	1936	22 3
8 38	9 31	1030	1333	1720	1832	2156		..	68	a. Brussels (Midi) .. d.	7 15	..	..	1428	1722	1844	2115
..	..	..	..	..		..	2050	..	72	a. Brussels (Nord) .. d.	..	8 38	..	¶	..		

‡ Dep. and arr. at Calais (Maritime). ¶ To Boulogne (Maritime) arr. 19.15. r Rest. Car.
* From and to Dunkerque.

46 miles.

(Calais) Lille, Ghent.

[French (Nord) and Belg. Nat. Railway

Exp					Exp					Exp			Exp			Exp		
..	..	7 40	7 40	9 13	12 7	..	1449	1730	d. Calais (*p.* 236) .. arr.	1020	13 7	1529	1529	18 8	..	2153	..	..
6 33	..	9 18	11 9	13 5	1554	..	1856	1930	d. Lille .... arr.	8 1	1043	1256	1256	1638	1853	1914	2017	2236
7 29	9 2	11 5	1155	1428	1637	1740	1947	2112	d. Mouscron c .... arr.	5 14	9 57	1133	1214	1534	1758	1813	1929	2136
8 44	9 17	1119	1219	1517	1651	18 9	2018	2126	d. Courtrai ...... dep.	5 46	9 44	1118	12 1	1521	1726	18 0	1916	2123
7 14	9 55	1157	1250	1558	1721	1913	2124	22 0	a. Ghent (St. Pierre) d.	4 23	[illegible]	1036	1118	1440	1615	1727	1836	2038

Brussels, Namur, Luxemburg (Strasbourg, Bale).

[Belg. Nat. Rys.

Mls.	*Through Table, see p.* 127	123	Exp 123	Exp 123	Exp 123	luxe 12	Exp 123	Exp 123	fast 123	fast 123	Exp 123	Exp 123	Exp 123
				r	¶r	P	r	‡			S¶	A	s
..	Antwerp (Est.) (*p.* 153) dp.	..	..	..	..	1028	1155	..	..	..	..	..	2252
0	Brussels (Nord) ,,	..	7 11	7 57	10 6	11 7		1445	1647	1842	2018	2226	0 54
..	,, (Qu. Leopold) ,,	5 50	7 24	8 12	1017	..	1249	15 0	17 0	1854	2029	..	..
19	Ottignies	6 16	7 43	..	..	..	..	..	1720	..	R	..	..
39	Namur (*p.* 240) ar.	6 56	8 14	8 56	1058	1153	1333	1544	1750	1935	2113	2314	1 46
	dp.	6 59	8 25	9 0	11 3	1158	1335	1547	1753	1943	2114	2415	1 50
74	Jemelle	8 33	9 29	9 50	12 4	..	1431	1650	1853	2039	2211	0 10	2 45
124	Arlon	..	1052	1058	1323	..	1543	1822	20 3	22 2	2320	1 20	4 21
..	Sterpenich	..	..	..	..	P	Rest. Car.	..	arr.	..	..	..	..
130	Klein-Bettingen c ar.	..	..	..	..			1837	..	..	..	..	..
	dp.	..	..	..	..			1838	..	..	..	..	..
141	Luxemburg arr.	..	..	1121	1346	1356	16 8	1857	..	2226	2343	1 45	4 47
282	Strasbourg (*p.*179) ,,	..	..	1422	..	1618	19 7	2235	..	..	3 35	5 10	8 42
372	BALE (Sw's) (*p.*181) ,,	..	..	16 7	..	1751	21 0	..	..	..	5 32	7 27	1051

	Exp 123	Exp 123	Exp 123	Exp 123	Exp 123	luxe 12	Exp 123	123	Exp 123		Exp 123	fast 123
	s	S				P	r		B		r	
BALE (Swiss) .. dp.	2051	0 20		..	7 10	9 27	10 0	..	1330	..	1450	..
Strasbourg .... ,,	2315	2 5		6 0	8 58	1059	12 1	..	1550	..	1633	..
Luxemburg .. ,,	3 32	5 22	6 51	9 24	12 2	1325	1538	1627	1858	..	1946	..
Klein-Bettingen	..	R	7 9	..	Rest. Car.	..	..	1652	..	..	..	..
Sterpenich c .. ar.	..	..	..	..		P	..	1654	..		..	..
dp.	..	..	..	..		..	..	1656	..	..		..
Arlon	5 15	6 11	7 31	9 58	1236	..	1613	1741	1934	2145	2020	2032
Jemelle	6 19	7 14	8 43	11 6	1339	..	1714	1852	2037	2213	2116	2153
Namur ...... ar.	7 3	7 58	9 43	1155	1423	1519	1758	1942	2121	2232	22 2	2256
dp.	7 5	8 1	9 45	1157	1425	1525	18 4	1945	2123	2244	22 8	23 6
Ottignies	..	..	1013	1229	..	..	..	2017	..	..		2337
Brussels (Q. Leo.) ar.	7 48	8 42	1032	1245	15 6	..	1846	2035	2210	..	2247	2357
Brussels (Nord) ,,	..	8 53	1043	1259	..	16 9	1857	2045	2224	..	2257	0 8
Antwerp (Est) (*p* 153) ,,	8 39	..			16 5	1656	..	..	..	..	..	..

A Sats. only July 1—Sept. 9.

B Suns. only July 1—Sept. 10.

P Edelweiss Exp. Pullman Car train *see page* 80.

R Restaurant Car Ostend - Jemelle and *v.v.*

S 1 & 2 cl. Sleep. Car Ostend - Lucerne-Milan and *v.v.*, also 1 & 2 cl. cars Ostend-Vintimille & *v.v.* 1, 2 & 3 cl. cars Ostend-Interlaken and *v.v.*

s 1 & 2 cl. Sleeping Car The Hague-Brussels-Rome & *v.v.*; 1, 2 and 3 cl. cars The Hague-Bale & *v.v.*

‡ Only takes 2 & 3 cl. passengers from Brussels to Arlon and beyond. ¶ Only takes 2 & 3 cl. passengers from Brussels for Jemelle and beyond. r Rest. Car. * Not Suns. or Fetes.

Ostend (Bruges), Thourout, Ypres, Hazebrouck [Belgian National Railways.

123	23	23	23	23	23	123	23	123	123	123	123	Mls.		123	123	23	23	23	23	23	123	23	23	123	123
..	4 37	7 7	8 48	9 56	11 5	1213	15 5	..	1647	1745	19 1	0	dep **Ostend** .... arr.	6 41	7 54	9 16	1048	1229	1345	1527	1655	1913	1959	2136	..
..	5 13	7 27	9 3	10 7		1241	1525	..	1716	18 8	1913	..	" Bruges .... arr.		..	8 55	1033	1214	1332	..	1634	1856	1933	2139	..
..	5 52	7 53	9 27	1047	1153	1315	1558	..	1745	1832	1951	16	" Thourout .... arr.	5 54	7 4	8 27	10 6	1147	13 4	1444	1556	1815	19 5	2053	..
..	6 57	8 48	1016	1130	1246	1426	1652	..	1844	1940	2053	36	arr. Ypres .... dep.	dep	5 52	7 29	9 26	11 4	1220	14 2	15 3	1714	1815	1954	..
5 55	7 29	..	11 1	..	..	1434		17 8	..	..		0	dep. Ypres .... arr.	..	..	..	9 4	1052	..	..	1443	..	1744		2049
6 54	8 28	..	12 1	..		1532		18 7	..	..		19	arr. Hazebrouck .... dep.				8 5	9 52			1340		1638		1949

Ostend, Ghent (Antwerp, Malines), Brussels. Express Services. [Belgian National Railways.

Through Tables, see pp. 127, 128.	Exp 123	Exp 123	Exp 123	Exp 123	Exp 123	Exp 123	Exp 123	Exp 123	Exp 123	Exp 23	Exp 123	Exp 123	Exp 12	Exp 123	Exp 123	Exp 123	Exp 23	Exp 123	Exp 123	Exp 123	luxe 12	luxe 12	Exp 123	Exp 23	Exp 123	Exp 123
		Z											**E**		**A** r			**C** r			**X**	**L**			**D**	**A**
§London (p. 127) dp.	..	23 0	..	..	..	..	..	..	..	..	..		11¶0	..	1030	..	..	1030		..	15 0	15 0	15 0	..	15 0	15 0
Ostend Quay "	5 56	6 7	7 3	8 20	9 20	1020	1120	1220	1320	1420	1520	1620	1651	1657	17 4	1720	1820	1845	1920	2020	2038	2038	21 3	2113	2120	23 2
Bruges (St. A'dre) ar.		..	..	..	..	..	.	..	..	..	..	..	..	..	..	..	..	..	..	..	..	..	..		r	..
Bruges (Cent.) .. "	6 11	6 22	7 18	8 35	9 35	1035	1135	1235	1335	1435	1535	1635	..	1712	1719	1735	1835	1858	1935	2035	..	..	Sats. only.	2128	2135	2317
Ghent St. Pierre arr.	6 44	6 50	7 44	9 1	10 1	11 1	12 1	13 1	14 1	15 1	16 1	17 1	1727	1740	1746	18 1	19 1	1927	20 1	21 1	2117	2117	July 1–Sept. 9.	2154	22 1	2345
Ghent (St. P're) dp.	7 19	..	7 51	10 3		1119	12 5	..	1413	..	1610	1725	Pullman	1744	..	18 7	..	1949	2044	..	..	Nord		..	..	..
Termonde .... arr.	7 43	..	8 14	1050	..	12 7	1228		1436	..	1634	..	Cars only	1826	..	1830	..	2020	2124	..	..	Exp.		..	..	..
Antwerp (S.) "	..	..	9†0	12 8	..	1341	13†11	..	1529	†..	17†19	18†24		1937	..	..	..	2121	†.	.	..			..	..	..
Malines .. "	8 9	..	..	1211	..	..	..	..	1612	..	..			1853	..	1853	..	20 9	2242	..	..			..	..	..
Ghent (St. Pierre) d	6 46	6 52	7 48	9 3	10 3	11 3	12 3	13 3	14 3	15 3	16 3	17 3	1728	1742	1748	18 3	19 3	1929	20 3	21 3	2118	2118		2156	22 3	2347
Brussels (Midi) ar.	7 20	..	8 20	9 35	1035	1135	1235	1335	1435	1535	1635	1735	..	..	..	1835	1935	..	2035	..	..	..		2228		..
Brussels (Nord) arr.	..	7 40	..	..	..	..	..	..	..	..	.		18 1	1818	1824	..	..	20 5	..	2135	2154	2154	2217	..	2238	0 23
Cologne (p. 151) arr.	..	1146	..	..	..	..	..		..	..	..	..	2135		2235		..	..	..	..	1 28	1 46	2 58	..	2 35	6 0

	Exp 123	Exp 123	Exp 123	Exp 123	luxe 12	Exp 123	Exp 123	luxe 12	Exp 123	Exp 123	Exp 123	Exp 123	Exp 12	fast 12	Exp 12	Exp 123	Exp 123	Exp 123	Ex 123	Exp 123	Exp 23	Exp 123	Exp 123	Exp 1 3	Exp 123
Cologne (p. 152) dep.	1 0	..	..	4 19	4 5			5 26		..	..	..	..	9 52	11 8	..	..	..	..	..	..	..	w	**Z**	..
Brussels (Nord) dp.	6 25		..	8 51	8 51	..	9 9	9 17		..	..	..	..	1411	1434	..	..	..	..	..	..	..		2224	..
Brussels (Midi) "	**A**	7 0	8 0	**D** r	**L**	9 0	**C** r	**Y**	10 0	11 0	12 0	13 0	14 0	**A**	**E**	15 0	16 0	17 0	18 0	19 0	20 0	21 0	22 0	..	2234
Ghent (St. Pierre) ar.	7 1	7 32	8 32	9 27	9 27	9 32	9 45	9 53	1032	1132	1232	1332	1432	1447	15 7	1532	1632	1732	1832	1932	2032	2132	2232	23 0	Suns. only.
Malines .... dep.	4 59	..		..	Nord	..	8 32	..	9 4		1046	1136	1318		Pullman	1417	..	.	1730	..	1923	..	..	2110	July 2–Sept 10.
Antwerp (S.) "		..	6†37	..	Exp.	8†6	..	..	9†5		1018	11†48	13†24	..	Cars only	13†57		16†18	17†24	..	19†23	..	..	1954	
Termonde .... "	5 58	..	7 25	..		..	9 6	..	9 48	..	1120	1249	14 7	..		1440	..	..	18 9	..	20 8	..	..	22 9	
Ghent (St. P're) ar.	6 37	..	7 59	..		9 7	9 28	..	1010		1146	1319	1420	.		15 2	.	1721	1831	..	2031	..	..	2251	
Ghent St. Pierre dp.	7 3	7 34	8 34	9 29	9 29	9 34	9 47	9 55	1034	1134	1234	1334	1434	1449	15 9	1534	1634	1734	1834	1934	2034	2134	2234	23 2	
Bruges (Cent.) .. "	7 30	8 0	9 0	..	..	10 0	1013	..	11 0	12 0	13 0	14 0	15 0	1516	..	16 0	17 0	18 0	19 0	20 0	21 0	22 0	23 0	2329	
Bruges (St. A'dre) "	..	..	..	..	..	..	..	..	..	..	..	..	..	..	..	..	..	..	..	..	..	..	..	..	
Ostend Quay arr.	7 46	8 15	9 15	10 8	10 8	1015	1029	1034	1115	1215	1315	1415	1515	1532	1546	1615	1715	1815	1915	2015	2115	2216	2315	2345	0 7
§London (p. 127) arr.	1620			1620	1620		1620	1620		..	.			2150	2150	..		..	..			..		7 20	7 20

r Restaurant Car.

A Through 1, 2 & 3 cl. Cars Ostend-Cologne and *v.v.* **C** Sleep. Cars Ostend-Lucerne-Milan, 1 & 2 cl. Cars Ostend, Milan, Vintimille and *v.v.* **D** Sleep. Car Ostend-Cologne-Wurzburg and *v.v.* and 1, 2 & 3 cl. cars Ostend-Vienna. **E** "Cologne Pullman Exp." 1 & 2 cl. Pullman Cars only; supplement. **L** Nord Exp., *see p.* 81. **X** Ostend-Cologne-Istanbul, Tues., Thurs. and Sats. only. **Y** Suns., Weds. and Fris. only. **Z** From London daily June 30 to Sept. 10; from Brussels daily June 30 to Sept. 10. ¶ Leave London 10.30 on Sats. to Sept. 2. *w* Not Suns. or Fete days. *y* Only takes passengers to Pepinster and beyond. † Antwerp (Cen.). § Victoria. *r* Rest. Car Ostend-Jemelle and *v.v.*

The times on the LEFT are to be read DOWNWARDS, those on the RIGHT UPWARDS.

Brussels, Liege, Aachen, Cologne.

[Belg. Nat. Rlys. & Ger. State Rlys.]

EXPRESS SERVICES : for Local Services, Brussels-Liege-Verviers, see p. 152

	Exp 123	Exp 123	Exp 123	Exp 123	Exp 123	Exp 123	Exp 123	Exp 123	Exp 12	Exp 123	Exp 123	Exp 123	Exp 123	Exp 123	Exp 123	Exp 123	luxe 12	Exp 123	fast 23	fast 23	Exp 123	Exp 123	luxe 12	luxe 12	Exp 123	Exp 123	Exp 123
		a		*r*			G	*r*	G					G			P	*a*					O	N	A	B	
BRUSSELS (Nord) dep.	6 51	7 54	9 0	10 0	11 0	1152	..	1253	..	14 0	15 0	1539	16 0	*r*	17 0	18 6	1812	1832	19 7	1925	20 0	21 0	2210	2210	2246	1 0	..
LIEGE (Guillemins) ar.	8 6	9 9	1015	1115	1215	13 7	1257	14 8	1410	1515	1615	1654	1715	1817	1825	1921	1927	1947	2022	2110	2115	2215	2325	2325	0 1	2 23	—
From Paris, p. 240 d.	8 10	9 12	1018	1118	..	1318	1332	⌐	1427	..	1618	1658	..	1831	1836	1925	1932	1953	..	2133	2118	..	2329	2346	0 8	2 35	6 14
Pepinster ......arr.	8 29	9 31	1037	1137	..	1339	1351	..	..	..	1637	1717	..	1850	1857	1944	..	2012	..	22 8	2137	..	..	..	0 24	2 56	6 33
Spa ....arr.	9 13	1013	11†6	1229	..	1419	1419	..	..	..	1658	1745	..	1921	1921	2012	..	..	..	2236	22 4	..	..	..	..	..	7 27
Verviers (Central) arr.	8 37	9 38	1047	1144	..	1347	1358	..	1451	..	1645	1724	..	1859	19 6	1951	1956	2019	..	2217	2145	..	..	..	0 33	3 8	6 41
Herbesthal ......arr.	..	9 56	..	12 3	..	..	1416	..	..	..	..	1742	..	1916	..	..	2013	2037	..	2256	22 3	..	0 6	..	0 50	3 32	7 1
Herbesthal ......dep	..	9 59	..	12 6	..	..	1418	..	..	..	..	1747	..	1927	..	..	2015	2046	..	..	..	..	0 8	..	0 53	4 15	7 4
AACHEN																											
G.T. ......arr.	..	1017	..	1224	..	..	1436	..	1525	..	..	18 5	..	1945	..	..	2033	21 4	..	..	..	..	0 26	0 43	1 11	4 33	7 22
M.E.T. ....dep.	..	1050	..	1252	..	..	15 7	..	1540	..	..	1837	..	2015	..	..	2043	2134	..	..	..	..	0 36	0 53	1 41	5 3	8 3
Stolberg ....arr.	..	1059	..	13 1	..	..	..	..	..	..	..	1846	..	..	..	..	..	2144	..	..	..	..	..	..	..	..	..
Eschweiler ......arr.	..	..	..	..	..	..	1519	..	..	..	..	..	..	..	..	..	..	..	..	..	..	..	..	..	..	..	..
Duren ....arr.	..	1116	..	1319	..	..	1533	..	16 3	..	..	19 3	..	2039	..	..	..	22 2	..	..	..	..	..	..	2 5	5 26	8 28
COLOGNE (Haup.) arr.	..	1146	..	1349	..	..	16 3	..	1634	..	..	1933	..	2112	..	..	2135	2235	..	..	..	..	1 28	1 46	2 36	6 0	9 2

	Exp 123	Exp 123	luxe 12	Exp 123	123	luxe 12	Exp 123	Exp 123	Exp 123	Exp 123	Exp 123	Exp 123	Exp 123	Exp 123	luxe 12	Exp 123	Exp 123	Exp 123	Exp 123	Exp 12	Exp 123	Exp 123	Exp 123	Exp 123	Exp 123	fast 23	Exp 123
	B		N	Q	A*r*	O					G*r*		B*a*		P					G		*r*			*a*		*a*
COLOGNE (Haup.) dep.	1 0	..	4 5	..	4 19	5 26	..	..	..	8 7	8 48	..	9 52	..	11 8	..	..	..	14 6	1444	..	..	..	1643	18 6	..	1915
Duren ....dep.	1 27	..	..	..	4 49	..	..	..	..	8 35	9 19	..	1021	..	..	..	..	..	1433	1514	..	..	..	1710	1834	..	1947
Eschweiler ......dep.	1 42	..	..	..	..	..	..	..	..	..	9 34	..	..	..	..	..	..	..	..	..	..	..	..	..	*r*	..	..
Stolberg ....dep.	1 48	..	..	..	..	..	..	..	..	8 53	..	..	..	..	..	..	..	..	1450	..	..	..	..	..	1852	..	..
AACHEN																											
M.E.T. ....arr.	2 0	..	4 59	..	5 15	6 19	..	..	..	9 4	9 49	..	1048	..	1158	..	..	..	15 1	1541	..	..	..	1735	19 3	..	2016
M.E.T. ....dep.	2 30	..	5 11	..	5 40	6 31	..	..	..	9 38	1016	..	1113	..	1210	..	..	..	1524	1615	..	..	..	18 0	1929	..	2042
Herbesthal (G.T.) arr.	2 52	..	5 33	..	6 2	6 53	..	..	..	9 55	1038	..	1135	..	1232	..	..	..	1546	│	..	..	..	1822	1951	..	21 4
Herbesthal (G.T.) dep.	3 36	..	5 52	..	6 39	7 14	..	8 21	..	1016	1057	..	1158	..	1233	..	..	..	16 6	│	..	..	..	1853	2015	..	2130
Verviers (Cent.) dep.	3 51	..	..	..	6 54	..	7 30	8 36	..	1031	1112	1131	1213	..	..	1331	1432	1530	1621	│	1625	..	..	19 9	2031	..	2148
Spa ....dep.	..	..	..	..	6 2	..	7 14	8 18	9 14	1013	1058	1120	1147	..	..	1314	1412	15 8	16 2	│	16 2	..	..	1830	20 9	..	2124
Pepinster ......dep.	3 57	..	..	..	7 0	..	7 37	8 42	9 37	1037	1118	1138	1219	..	..	1338	1438	1537	1627	↓	1634	..	..	1916	2037	..	2154
LIEGE (Guillemins) ar.	4 16	..	6 26	⌐	7 18	7 50	7 56	9 1	9 56	1056	1137	1156	1238	..	13 9	1356	1456	1556	1645	1712	1652	..	..	1935	2056	..	2215
To Paris, p. 240 dep.	4 24	6 25	..	7 0	7 23	7 55	8 4	9 5	10 0	11 0	..	12 0	1243	13 0	1313	14 0	15 0	16 0	..	..	17 0	1736	18 5	1939	21 0	22 0	2234
BRUSSELS (Nord) arr.	5 42	7 37	E	8 12	8 38	9 7	9 27	1028	1112	1212	..	1312	1355	1412	1425	1512	1612	1723	E	..	1812	1851	1917	2051	2212	2312	0 2

A Sleep. Car 1 & 2 cl. Ostend-Wurzburg and *v.v.*; 1, 2 & 3 cl. Cars Ostend-Munich and Ostend-Vienna, and *v.v.*, also Nord Express Sleeper Herbesthal to Ostend. **B** 1, 2 & 3 cl. Cars Ostend-Cologne and *v.v.* **E** To or from Paris. **G** 1 & 2 cl. Cars Paris-Cologne and *v.v.* **N** Nord Express, see p. 81. **O** Ostend-Vienna-Orient Express, see p. 84. **P** 1 & 2 cl. Pullman Cars only, Ostend-Cologne and *v.v.* **Q** Carries Nord Express Sleeping Cars to Calais. *a* Limited Express. *r* Restaurant Car.

All 2 and 3 cl.]

Brussels, Louvain, Liege, Verviers.

[Belgian National Rlys.

		†				†	†			§		§	†	†			†					†				
BRUSSELS (Nord) dep.	6 54	6 57	8 25	9 25	1010	1025	..	1135	1225	13 3	1419	1514	..	16 3	1622	1630	17 4	1730	1818	1835	1925	1930	2025	2129	2213	23 6
Louvain ......dep.	7 24	7 46	8 55	9 57	1050	1055	1219	1238	1255	1333	1447	1542	..	1631	1651	1719	1732	1759	1847	19 4	1957	2038	2055	2158	2246	2357
Tirlemont ......dep.	7 42	..	9 13	1023	..	1113	1240	13 2	1311	14 1	15 3	1557	..	17 0	17 9	..	1748	1816	19 3	1922	2015	21 5	2114	2213	2324	0 26
Landen ....dep.	7 55	..	9 26	1052	..	1146	1254	1318	1323	1433	1515	16 9	..	1717	1721	..	..	1829	..	1935	2028	2121	2128	2226	2342	..
LIEGE ....arr.	8 37	..	10 9	1153	..	1258	1343	..	14 3	1541	1556	1648	..	..	18 2	..	..	1913	..	2018	2110	..	2210	2354	..	..
LIEGE ....dep.	8 45	..	1121	1156	..	..	..	..	1430	..	1612	..	1719	..	19 5	..	..	2028	..	2034	2133	..	2219	..	..	..
Chenee ....dep.	8 51	..	1129	12 3	..	..	..	..	1439	..	1628	..	1726	..	1914	..	..	..	..	2041	2140	..	2225	..	..	..
Chaudfontaine ..dep.	8 57	..	1135	..	..	..	..	..	1447	..	1634	..	1734	..	1920	..	..	..	..	2048	2146	..	2231	..	..	..
Pepinster ......arr.	9 17	..	1157	1227	..	..	..	..	1515	..	1654	..	1757	..	1940	..	..	2048	..	21 9	22 8	..	2251	..	..	..
Verviers ....arr.	9 24	..	12 5	1237	..	..	..	..	1523	..	17 1	..	1810	..	1947	..	..	2055	..	2119	2217	..	2258	..	..	..

								§				†				‡		§			†	†
Verviers ....dep.	5 21	..	..	7 55	8 57	1034	..	1217	13 2	..	1356	..	1556	1642	1738	..	..	..	1854	..	..	2049
Pepinster ......dep.	5 29	..	..	8 2	9 6	1042	..	1224	1310	..	14 6	..	16 5	17 0	1746	..	..	..	19 8	..	..	2057
Chaudfontaine ..dep.	5 50	..	..	..	9 24	11 0	..	1242	1332	..	1426	..	1627	1722	18 5	..	..	..	1937	..	..	2115
Chenee ....dep.	5 58	..	..	8 25	9 30	11 6	..	1248	1339	..	1434	..	1634	1729	1811	..	..	..	..	..	..	2122
LIEGE ....arr.	6 6	..	..	8 31	9 38	1113	..	1256	1346	..	1442	..	1641	1738	1818	..	..	..	1956	..	..	2129
LIEGE ....dep.	6 34	6 50	7 4	9 10	1010	1125	1210	1321	1410	..	1512	16 5	17 5	1810	1822	1910	..	..	2012	2035	..	22 4
Landen ....dep.	7 20	9 2	7 44	9 54	1053	1227	1253	14 4	1455	..	1627	1651	1749	1853	1947	1953	..	..	2056	2149	..	2328
Tirlemont ......dep.	7 43	9 17	7 54	10 6	11 5	—	13 5	1416	15 7	..	1639	17 3	18 0	19 6	..	20 5	..	2041	21 8	22 5	..	2343
Louvain ....dep.	8 21	9 41	8 8	1023	1121	..	1322	1432	1523	1613	17 1	1719	1832	1922	..	2021	2038	2057	2124	2229	22 7	..
BRUSSELS (Nord) arr.	8 49	..	8 35	1050	1148	..	1349	1459	1550	1647	1744	1747	19 2	1948	..	2048	2119	2123	2151	..	2247	..

† Weekdays only.
‡ Sundays only.
§ Saturdays only.

Brussels, Luttre, Charleroy.

[Belgian National Rlys.

	¶	2 3	2 3	2 3	2 3	2 3		2 3	†	2 3	2 3		2 3	†	2 3	2 3	2 3	2 3	2 3	2 3	2 3	2 3	2 3	2 3	2 3	
BRUSSELS (Midi) dep.	6 8	7 0	8 0	8 25	9 25	10 0	1025	11 0	1125	12 0	13 0	1325	14 0	1425	15 0	1525	16 0	17 0	18 0	8'28	19 0	1925	20 0	2016	21 0	22 0
Luttre	7 5	..	..	9 11	1011	..	1111	..	1211	..	..	1413	..	1511	..	1611	..	..	..	19 14	..	20 9	..	2118	..	2248
CHARLEROY (Sud) arr.	7 27	7 42	8 47	9 25	1025	1042	1125	1142	1226	1242	1342	1427	1442	1525	1542	1625	1642	1742	18 42	19 27	1947	2022	2047	2137	2142	23 8

	¶		2 3	2 3	2 3	2 3	2 3			2 3	2 3	2 3	†	2 3		2 3	2 3	2 3	2 3	2 3	2 3		2 3	2 3	2 3	2 3	2 3
CHARLEROY (Sud) arr.	5 28	5 37	7 0	7 48	8 0	8 20	9 0	9 20	10 0	1021	11 0	12 0	1220	13 0	1321	14 0	15 0	16 0	17 0	17 20	18 0	19 0	1920	20 0	21 0	22 0	2223
Luttre	5 44	6 10	..	..	..	8 38	..	9 35	..	1036	..	..	1236	..	1339	..	..	..	..	17 36	..	..	1935	..	..	..	2250
BRUSSELS (Midi) arr.	6 57	7 12	7 46	8 36	8 41	9 18	9 41	1018	1041	1117	1141	1241	1318	1341	1417	1441	1541	1641	1746	18 19	18 46	1946	2018	2046	2141	2241	2350

¶ Not Sundays and Fete Days. † Sats. only.

Pepinster, Spa (Liege), Trois-Ponts, Luxemburg.

[Belg. Nat. Rlys. & Luxemb. Rlys.

5 54	6 13	8 44	1045	1248	..	1417	1527	18 5	..	21*42	Mls.	dep. PEPINSTER ....arr.	7 17	..	8 36	9 42	..	1252	1526	16 1	..	1742	1856	2030	2144
6 22	6 36	9 13	11 6	1311	..	1440	1551	1829	..	22 6	8	dep. SPA ....dep.	6 59	..	8 18	9 22	..	1233	15 8	1541	..	1723	1830	20 9	2124
7 17	arr.	1024	arr.	14 3		..	1651	1919	..	23* 9	26	arr. Trois-Ponts ....dep.	6 6	..	..	8 24	——	1135	1418	1451	—	..	1732	..	2030
6 40	..	..	..	1232	1315	..	15 4	1839	21 0	..	..	dep. Liége (Guillemins)......arr.	..	8 9	..	8 55	1143	1314	..	..	1450	..	1916	2156	2112
7 41	..	..	..	1448	1414	..	1653	1944	2159	4 56	..	dep. Trois-Ponts ....arr.	..	7 12	..	7 34	1036	1116	..	..	1354	..	1722	20 0	2011
8 30	..	..	..	1549	..	..	18 0	2043	..	5 50	41	arr. T. Vierges (Ulfling)....dep.	..	..	..	6 6	9 48	10 3	..	..	..	..	1629	1850	1918
8 39	9 58	12 3	..	1612	A	..	1951	2044	B	6 6	..	dep. T. Vierges (Ulfling).....arr.	2140	B	8 46	..	9 39	..	..	..	A	..	16 4	1824	1917
9 2	1029	1233	..	1644		..	2024	21 9	..	6 36	..	dep. Kautenbach ....arr.	21 2	..	8 6	..	9 10	..	..	..	..	..	1529	1747	1848
9 17	11 0	13 0	1945	1712	1542	..	2046	1225	2324	7 6	65	dep. Ettelbruck ....arr.	2031	5 51	7 37	..	8 52	..	..	..	1227	..	15 1	1720	1831
9 49	1149	1349	2033	18 8	1611	..	2136	2157	2353	8 0	84	arr. LUXEMBURG ....dep.	1944	5 25	6 52	..	8 22	..	..	..	12 0	..	1416	1633	18 1

A To Oct. 10. **B** July 1—Sept. 3, 1 and 2 cl. Sleep car, Amsterdam—Bale and *v.v.* * Weekdays only. † Not Suns. or Fetes.

The times on the LEFT are to be read DOWNWARDS, those on the RIGHT UPWARDS.

Antwerp, Roermond, Gladbach. [Belgian Nat., Netherlands German State Rlys.

		1 2 3	1 2 3	1 2 3	2 3	1 2 3	1 2 3	Mls.	¶ Not Sundays.	Mls	1 2 3	1 2 3	1 2 3	1 2 3	2 3	1 2 3	2 3	1 2 3
		3 25	5 50	7 15	8 24	1553	19 0	0	dep. Antwerp (Cen) ar.	100	6¶47	8 21	1029	1125	16 4	1923	2017	2211
		5 45	7 7	..	9 21	1636	*a*	22	dep. Herenthals .. arr.	80	5 27	7 2	9 48	..	1514	18 4	1915	..
		6 28	7 35	8 3	10 8	1650	1949	33	Moll .... dep.	66	4 55	6 32	9 20	1040	1444	1734	1846	2126
		7 19	arr.	8 45	1050	1744	2038	56	dep. Hamont .... ,,	42	¶	5 40	8 17	10 4	1343	1640	18 0	2052
		arr.	..	9 9	arr.	18 8	21 1	57	arr. Budel *c* .... dep.	41	..	..	6 58	10 2	1342	1749	1749	2044
		..	..	9 58	..	1857	2150	74	a. Roermond (Holld.)	24	..	..	6 12	9 21	13 5	..	1512	20 3
		..	..	1014	..	¶	22 3	83	d. Vlodrop (Holland)	16	..	..	¶	9 8	1239	..	1444	1944
		..	..	10 2	..	..	2150	85	arr Dalheim *c* (M.E.T.)	14	..	..	..	8 31	12 3	..	1410	19 5
		..	..	1045	..	..	2234	100	arr. M.Gladbach dep.	0	..	..	..	7 59	11 9		..	1823

Antwerp, Brussels and *v.v.* [Steam Trains.

	2 3	1 2 3	2 3	2 3	1 2 3	2 3	1 2	1 2 3	1 2	1 2 3	1 2	1 2	1 2 3	1 2	1 2 3	1 2 3	1 2 3	
		¶	¶	¶		¶	luxe	Exp	luxe	Exp	Exp	luxe	¶	Exp	¶	Exp	Exp	
Antwerp (Est.) dep.	..	..	..	..	8*b*21	..	9 53	10 8	1023	1054	1228	1515	..	1915	..	2252	2340	
,, (Cent.) ,,	4 32	5 4	5 22	6 41	*	8 36	..	..	..	..	Rest. Car.	..	17 7	Rest. Car.	20 6	..	..	
Malines ...... ,,	5 0	6 5	5 57	7 21	..	9 18	..	..		..		..	..		21 5	..	..	
Brussels (Nord) arr.	5 34	6 43	6 18	7 57	9 8	9 57	..		1059	..		..	..		2144	2330	..	
,, (Midi) ,,	..		..	..	..	..	1037	1059	..	..	1314	1559	..	1958	..	..	0 26	
,, (Q.L.) ,,		..	..	..	..	..	..		..	14 8	..	..	1831	..	..	..	..	

	2 3	1 2 3	1 2 3	1 2 3	1 2 3	2 3	1 2	2 3	1 2	1 2 3	1 2	1 2	1 2 3	1 2	2 3	2 3
		¶	¶	Exp	Exp		Exp	Exp	luxe	Exp	luxe	Exp	¶	luxe		
Brussels (Q.L.) dep.	..	..	..	..	7 59	..	..	..	..	15 8	..	..	..	..	..	..
,, (Midi) ,,	..	..	..	6 40	..	..	1250	1254	1444	..	..	1751	..	2120	..	
,, (Nord) ,,	2 0	4 14	5 33	..	..	8 39	Rest. Car.	..	..	Rest. Car.	1619	..	1850	..	2219	2230
Malines .... arr.	2 19	4 53	6 7	..	..	9 8			..		..	..	..	..	2245	23 6
Antwerp (Cent.) ,,	2 42	6 0	7 4	..	..	1021		..	..		..	..	..	..	2316	2342
,, (Est.) ,,	..		..	7 25	8 39	..	1335	1340	1525	16 5	1656	1835	19*b*34	22 4	..	..

b Quai Station. * Not Mondays. ¶ Not Sundays.

Antwerp, Brussels and *v.v.* Electric Service, 2 and 3 cl. only.

					†		†		†			†		†				
Antwerp (Cent.) dep.	1 0	5 40	6 0	6 20	6 30	6 40	6 50	7 0	7 10	7 20	7 40	7 50	8 0	8 10	8 20	8 40	8 50	9 0
Malines .... ,,	1 15	5 55	6 15	6 35	6 45	6 55	7 5	7 15	7 25	7 35	7 55	8 5	8 15	8 25	8 35	8 55	9 5	9 15
Brussels (Nord) arr.	1 31	6 11	6 31	6 51	7 1	7 11	7 21	7 31	7 41	7 51	8 11	8 21	8 31	8 41	8 51	9 11	9 21	9 31

								†		†				
Antwerp (Cent.) dep.	9 30	10 0	1030	11 0	1130	Thence every 20 mins. to 20.0.	20 0	2030	21 0	2130	22 0	2245	2330	0 15
Malines .... ,,	..	1015	..	1115	..		2015	..	2115	..	2215	23 0	2345	0 30
Brussels (Nord) arr.	9 59	1031	1059	1131	1159		2031	2059	2131	2159	2231	2316	0 1	0 46

							†		†		†		†		†			
Brussels (N'd) d.	1 0	2 0	5 30	6 0	6 30	7 0	7 10	7 20	7 30	7 40	7 50	8 0	8 10	8 20	8 30	8 40	Thence every 30 mins. to 12.0.	1220
Malines .... ,,	1 15	2 19	5 45	6 15	6 45	7 15	7 25	7 35	7 45	7 55	..	8 15	8 25	8 35	..	8 55		1235
Antwerp (C't) a.	1 31	2 42	6 1	6 31	7 1	7 31	7 41	7 51	8 1	8 11	8 19	8 31	8 41	8 51	8 59	9 11		1251

Brussels (Nord) dep.	Thence every 20 mins. to 20 0.	20 0	2030	21 0	2130	22 0	2245	2330	0 15
Malines .... ,,		2015	..	2115	2145	2215	23 0	2345	0 30
Antwerp (Cent.) arr.		2031	2050	2 3[illegible]	2150	2231	2316	0 1	0 46

† Not Sundays

† June 30—Sep. 10.

(Brussels) Bruges, Blankenberghe. ¶ Not Suns.

Brussels (Midi) dep.		..	..	7 0	8 0	9 0	10 0	11 0	12 0	13 0	14 0	15 0	16 0	17 0	18 0	19 0	20 0	21 0
Brussels (Nord) ,,	..	¶	6 25	..	..	..	..	..	..	..	..	..	..	..	..	..		†
Bruges .... ,,	6 0	6 45	7 34	8 3	9 3	10 8	11 3	12 3	13 3	14 3	15 3	1615	17 2	18 4	19 3	20 3	21 5	22 3
Blankenberghe arr.	6 21	7 4	7 48	8 17	9 22	1023	1121	1224	1317	1417	1517	1635	1723	1818	1923	20 7	2119	2217

Blankenberghe dep.	6 53	7 25	8 14	9 12	1018	1114	1218	1311	1418	1518	1618	17 5	1818	1918	2014	2118	2218
Bruges .... arr.	7 7	7 44	8 28	9 32	1032	1128	1232	1332	1432	1532	1632	1726	1832	1932	2032	2132	2232
Brussels (Nord) ,,	..	¶	..	..	..	..	..	..	..		..	..	..	..	..	..	2341
Brussels (Midi) ,,	8 20	..	9 35	1035	1135	1235	1335	1435	1535	1635	1735	1835	1935	2035	2135	2228	

(Brussels), Bruges, Heyst, Knocke. ¶ Not Sundays.

Brussels (Midi) dep.	..	..	7 0	8 0	9 0	10 0	11 0	12 0	13 0	14 0	15 0	16 0	17 0	18 0	19 0	20 0
Brussels (Nord) ,,	..	..	..	..	..	..	..	..	..	..	..	..	..	..	..	..
Bruges .... ,,	5 55	7 15	8 7	9 8	10 3	11 7	12 8	13 7	14 7	15 7	16 8	17 7	18 9	1915	20 6	21 9
Zeebrugge .... arr.	6 18	7 37	8 20	9 25	..	1120	1226	1320	1420	1524	1625	..	1822	1933	2024	2122
Heyst .... ,,	6 24	7 42	8 26	9 30	1020	1126	1231	1326	1426	1529	1630	1725	1828	1938	2029	2128
Knocke .... ,,	6 33	7 50	8 34	9 38	1028	1134	1240	1335	1434	1538	1638	1732	1836	1946	2038	2136

Knocke .... dep.	6 44	8 7	9 2	9 55	11 6	1157	13 2	14 1	15 1	1558	1652	18 2	1858	1958	21 0	22 1
Heyst .... ,,	6 52	8 13	9 10	10 7	1113	12 6	13 9	14 9	15 9	16 7	17 0	1810	19 7	20 7	21 7	22 9
Zeebrugge .... ,,	6 58	8 19	..	1012	1119	1211	..	1415	1515	1612	17 7	..	1912	2012		2215
Bruges .... arr.	7 15	8 37	9 28	1028	1132	1228	1327	1428	1528	1628	1728	1828	1928	2028	2125	2228
Brussels (Nord) ,,		..	..		..		..	..	..	..		..	..			2341
Brussels (Midi) ,,	8 20	9 35	1035	1135	1235	1335	1435	1535	1635	1735	1835	1935	2035	2135	2228	..

(Paris) Brussels, Antwerp, Rosendaal, Rotterdam (Amsterdam) [Belgian Nat., Netherlands State Railways.

† Not Sundays. ‡ Quartier Leopold. ‖ Quai du Sud.
s 1 & 2 cl. Sleep. Car Paris to Amsterdam and v.v.

P "Etoile du Nord" Pullman car train Paris-Amsterdam and v.v.

PP "Oiseau Bleu" Pullman car train Paris-Antwerp-Amsterdam and v.v.

§ Thro' 1, 2 & 3 cl. carriages Paris-Amsterdam & v.v.

R Rest Car.

Mls.		123	123	123 Exp	123 Exp	23	123	123	123	Rap 12	123 Exp	luxe 12	123	Rap 123	luxe 12	123	Rap 12	123	123	Rap 12
				§ s	X					E	B	P		A	C	†	F			luxe
	Paris (Lyons) ....dep.	..	..			..	..	..	..	..		..	..	..	..	..	1232	..	..	
	Paris (Nord) (p. 239) dp.	..	..	0 15		..	..	..	..	9 10	8 0	1130	..	..	..	..	1415	..	..	1810
	Brussels (Midi) ....dep.	..	..	6 40	7‡59	..		..	..	1250	1254	1444	..	15‡ 8	..		1751	..	..	2120
0	Brussels (Nord) (153) d.	..	5 30	s	..	8†30	8 40	10 0	1130	Rest. Car.		↓	1340	Rest. car.	1619	1640	Rest. car.	19 0	1940	PP
27	Antwerp (Cent.) arr.	..	6 1	R	↓	8†59	9 11	1031	1150		..		14 9			1711		1931	20 9	..
	Antwerp (Cent.) dep.	4 57	6 19	..		9 5	9 21	1035	1225		..		1425		..	1721		1942	2025	..
..	Antwerp (Est.) .. arr.	5 2	6 22	7 25	8 39	9 8	9 24	1038	1228	1335	1340	1525	1428	16 5	1656	1725	1835	1946	2028	22 4
	Antwerp (Est.) .. dep.	5 3	6 23	7 27	8 40	9 9	9 25	1039	1229	1336	1341	1526	1429	16 7	1657	1725	1837	1947	2029	22 5
48	Esschen ....dep.	6 † 5	7†12	7 59	9 8	9 48	10 7	1115	1310	..	1412		1510	1637	1721	18 7	..	2015	2116	
53	Rosendaal e (Amst. tm.) a	6†35	7†42	8 29	9 37	..	1037	1145	1340	1426	1442	1617	1540	17 8	1750	1837	1927	2044	2146	2254
		†	†	D 123	123		23	123	123	D 12	123	P 12		123	12		↓			12
53	Rosendaal ....dep.	7 5	8 2	8 59	9 37	..	11 0	12 6	14 5	1426	15 8	1617	1628	1731	18 5	19 5	1927	21 6	22 6	23 4
77	Dordrecht .... arr.	7 37	8 36	9 29	..	..	1136	1236	1435	R	1538	↓	1711	18 1	..	1935	R	2136	2236	..
89	Rotterdam (Beurs) arr.	8 1	9 1	§	..	..	12 1	..	15 1	..	..		1731		..	20 1		..	..	..
..	,, (Delftsche Poort) ar.	8 4	9 4	9 49	1029	..	12 4	1254	15 4	1518	1559	1710	1734	1820	1853	20 4	2022	2156	2256	2349
..	p.158 The Hague ...... arr.	8 27	9 27	1013	1052	..	1227	1318	1527	1542	1620	1731	1757	1844	1915	2027	2048	2227	2327	0 11
..	p.158 Amsterdam (Cent.) arr.	9 15	1015	11 4	..	..	1315	1411	1615	1633	17 8	1827	1845	..	20 3	2115	2141	2315	0 15	1 1

A 1, 2 & 3 cl. cars The Hague *via* Brussels to Bale and v.v. Only passengers to and from Holland taken. Restrictions, see page 178.

B Thro' 1, 2 & 3 cl. cars Amsterdam to Paris and v.v.

C "Edelweiss" Pullman Car train to Amsterdam-Bale, Zurich and v.v.

E 1 and 2 cl. cars Paris-Amsterdam and v.v.

F 1 & 2 cl. thro' car Amsterdam to Paris (Lyons).

X 1 & 2 cl. Sleep car, The Hague-Rome & v.v.

Mls.		123	123	123	Exp 123	luxe 12	luxe 12	Exp 123	Exp 12	123	123	luxe 12	123	123	Exp 12	123	Exp 123	Exp 123
						PP	C	R	F R		†	P	fast		E		X	R
..	Amsterdam (Cent.) dep.	..	..	6 43	6 53	7 32	8 3	..	10 3	1043	1113	1259	1343	1550	1648	1743	..	2052
..	The Hague........dep.	..	6 20	7 32	7 52	8 25	8 55	9 54	1056	1132	1220	1347	1432	1650	1738	1832	2055	2142
..	Rotterdam (D. Pt.) ..dep.	4†54	6 49	7 55	8 20	8 49	9 19	1020	1120	1155	1249	1412	1455	1718	18 4	1855	2120	22 6
0	Rotterdam (Beurs) dep.	..	6 54	7 59	..	..	..	..	..	1159	1254	..	1459	..	..	1859		..
12	Dordrecht	5†22	7 12	8 22	8 40	..	..	1039	..	1223	1312	..	1525	1738	..	1922	2140	2225
36	Rosendaal ....arr.	6 † 2	7 56	8 52	9 16	9 35	10 6	1112	12 8	1254	1354	1458	1555	18 8	1851	1954	2210	2255
		123	123			12	12	123				Rap 12	123	123	D 12	123		Exp 123
..	Rosendaal ....dep.	6†12	8 5	9 3	9 22	9 41	1012	1119	1213	13 3	14 3	15 4	16 3	1817	19 4	20 3	2217	23 3
41	Esschen (*Belgian Customs*) (Grn. tm.) arr.	6 † 2	7 55	8 52	9 14	..	..	11 9	..	1253	1353	..	1552	18 6	R	1953	22 7	2253
	Esschen (*Belgian Customs*) (Grn. tm.) dep.	6 20	8 15	9 10	9 42	..	..	1129	..	1312	1410	..	16 6	1823		2015	2227	2314
..	Antwerp (Est.) .. arr.	6 56	8 50	9 32	10 6	9 52	1022	1153	1225	1347	1452	1514	1628	1858	1914	2050	2250	2337
	Antwerp (Est.) .. dep.	6 57	8 51	9 33	10 8	9 53	1028	1155	1228	1348	1453	1515	1629	1859	1915	2051	2252	2340
62	Antwerp (Cent.) arr.	7 1	8 55	9 37	..	..	..	..	Rest Car	1352	1457	↓	1633	19 3	..	2055	..	R
	Antwerp (Cent.) dep.	7 10	9 0	10 0	..	..	..	..		14 0	1530		1640	1920	..	21 0	..	
89	Brussels (Nord) .... arr.	7 41	9 31	1031		..	1059	..	..	1431	1559		1711	1951	..	2131	2330	
	Brussels (Midi) .... arr.	..	..	..	1059	1037	..	12‡47	1314	..	..	1559	..	..	1958	..	..	0 26
	Paris (Nord) (p. 239) arr.	..	..	..	1638	1347	..	..	1654	..	..	1925	..	..	2341	..	..	6 54
	Paris (Lyons) .... arr.	..	..	..	..		..		1725	..			..	..	..	..	..	..

Antwerp, Termonde, Ghent—31 miles.

All 2 & 3 class.] ‡ Antwerp (Cent). † Not Sundays or Fetes. [Belg. Nat. State.

6‡37	8 ‡ 6	9 ‡ 5	1018	13‡57	16‡18	1645	17‡24	19‡23	dp. Antwerp (Sud) a.	7‡45	9 ‡ 0	9‡18	1341	13‡11	15‡29	17‡19	18‡24	21‡21
7 25	..	9 48	1120	1440	..	1755	18 9	20 8	,, Termonde ..dp.	7 0	8 15	..	1236	1229	1437	1635	..	2021
7 59	9 7	1010	1146	15‡2	1721	1847	18‡31	2031	arr. Ghent (St. Pie.) d	6 36	7 51	8 19	1119	12‡5	1413	1610	1725	1949

The times on the LEFT are to be read DOWNWARDS, those on the RIGHT UPWARDS.

HOLLAND.

[Trains run in Holland by Amsterdam time, *i.e.*, 20 mins. in advance of Greenwich or European time.]

THROUGH SERVICES TO HOLLAND.

From England, see pp. 129, 131, 132 ; *from Belgium, p.* 154 ; *from Germany, pp.* 155 to 159.

Rotterdam (Flushing), Breda, Boxtel (Cologne). [Netherlands St. Rlys.

Mls		123	123	123	23	123	123	123	123	123	23	123	123	123	123	123	23	123
					†		†			†				ExD	ExD			
	Rotterdam(Del.Pt)d	6 47	7 25	8 25	1025	1125	1248	1325	1525	1625	1725	1815	..	Rest. Car.	..	1948	2125	2225
..	,, (Beurs) dep.	6 52	7 29	8 29	1029	1129	1253	1329	1529	1629	1729	..	..		..	1953	2129	2229
12	Dordrecht	7 11	7 56	8 47	1049	1153	1311	1356	1551	1647	1749	1835	..		..	2011	2149	2250
31	Breda arr.	7 40	8 18	9 12	1113	1218	1340	1416	1618	1712	1813	19 2	..		..	2040	2213	2318
..	London(L'pl St.) dp.				..	..	..	..	..	..	..	†	10 0	10 0	10 0	..	..	.
170	Flushing dep.	5†47	6 27	..	7 50	9 20	1120	..	1350	..	..	1620	1753	1820	1842	..	1920	2050
..	Middelburg ,,	5 55	6 36	..	7 58	9 29	1129	..	1358	..	..	1629	18 0	..	Rest. Car.	..	1929	2058
..	Goes ,,	6 15	6 58	..	8 15	9 51	1151	..	1415	..	..	1651	1815	Rest. Car.		..	1951	2115
..	Bergen-op-Zoom ,,	6 48	7 44	..	8 48	1037	1237	..	1448	..	..	1737	1848			..	2037	2148
216	Rosendaal arr.	7†0	7 57	..	9 0	1050	1250	..	15 0	..	..	1750	19 0		1938	..	2050	22 0
	Rosendaal dep.	7 6	..	..	10 6	11 6	13 6	..	15 6	..	..	18 6	19 6	1918	1942	..	21 6	22 6
230	Breda arr.	7 26	..	..	1026	1126	1326	..	1526	..	..	1826	1926	..	20 3	..	2126	2226
31	Breda dep.	7 42	8 20	9 14	1115	1220	1342	1420	1620	1714	1815	19 4	1927	..	20 4	2042	2215	2320
44	Tilburg	8 1	8 43	9 33	1135	1243	14 2	1443	1643	1733	1835	1927	1948	..	2024	21 2	2235	2343
54	Boxtel arr.	8 17	9 2	9 47	1150	13 2	1417	15 2	17 2	1747	1850	1944	arr.		To Hengelo	2116	2250	0 2
..	Eindhoven ,,	8 35	9 20	10 5	12 5	1320	1435	1520	1720	18 5	19 5	20 4	..	2023		2134	23 5	0 20
..	Venlo (*p.* 157) ,,	9 41	..	11 8	13 7	..	1541	..	1818	..	2016	21 2	..	2112		2238	0 9	.
..	Cologne (*p.* 157) ,,	1115	..	1456	1456	..	1855	..	2155					2241				..

	123	23	123	123	123	123	123	123	23	123	123	123	123	123	123	123	123
						ExD	fast	ExD	fast			†			†		
Cologne dep.	†	†	..	..	..	r	5 57	8 18	8 18	..	..	8 41	..	10 36	1435	1627	1821
Venlo ,,	..	5 51	..	7 18	..	..	8 55	1043	1055	..	..	13 18	..	15†55	1755	2023	2155
Eindhoven ,,	5 32	6 56	7 55	8 26	..	..	9 55	1125	1156	1256	1341	14 26	1634	16 55	1856	2126	2256
Boxtel dep.	5 49	7 11	8 12	8 44	..	..	1012	..	1211	1313	1358	14 44	1651	17 12	1913	2143	2313
Tilburg	6 19	7 28	8 29	9 1	1012	1045	1029	r	1228	1329	1419	15 1	1712	17 29	1929	22 1	2330
Breda arr.	6 40	7 45	8 45	9 19	1033	..	1045	..	1245	1345	1440	15 19	1733	17 45	1945	2219	2346
Breda dep.	7 35	8 35	..	9†35	1035	..	1135	..	1335	..	..	15 35	1735	18†35	2035	2235	..
Rosendaal arr.	7 54	8 54	..	9†54	1054	1118	1154	1231	1354	..	..	15 54	1754	18†54	2054	2254	..
Rosendaal dep.	8 0	9 0	..	..	11 0	1119	12 0	1239	14†0	..	..	16 0	1812	19 0	22 0	23 0	..
Bergen-op-Zoom ..	8 12	9 13	..	..	1113	..	1214	..	1413	..	..	16 14	1825	19 14	2214	2313	..
Goes	arr.	9 46	..	..	1146	r	1259	..	1446	..	..	16 59	19 2	19 59	2259	2346	..
Middelburg	..	10 3	..	..	12 3	..	1321	..	15 3	..	..	17 21	1919	20 21	2321	0 3	..
Flushing (*p.* 130) a.	..	10†9	..	..	12 9	1222	1328	1335	15†9	..	..	17 28	1925	20 28	2328	0 9	..
London(L'pl St.) ar.	..	..	..	..	2130	2130	..	2130	..	..	..	..	..	..	..	..	..
Breda dep.	6 42	7 47	8 47	9 21	..	..	1047	..	1247	1347	1442	15 21	..	17 47	1947	2221	2348
Dordrecht arr.	7 7	8 7	9 11	9 50	..	..	1111	..	1311	14 9	15 9	15 50	..	18 11	2011	2250	0 11
Rotterdam(Beurs) a.	7 30	8 30	9 30	1010	..	..	1130	..	1330	1430	1530	16 10	..	18 30	2030	2310	..
,, (DelftschePt.) a.	7 34	8 34	9 34	1016	..	..	1134	..	1334	1434	1534	16†16	..	18 34	2034	2316	0 31

† Not Sundays.
D—Corridor train. Extra fare, 1 fl. 20 c. See p. 75. r Restaurant car.

(Flushing), Breda, s'Bosch, Nymegen, Arnhem, Zutphen, Hengelo.

[Netherlands State Rlys.

Mls.		123	123	123	123	123	123	123	123	123	123	123	123	123	123	123
		†				†		†					ExD	ExD		
	Flushing dep.	..	5†47	6 27	7 50	..	9 20	1050	1120	1350	15†20	1753	1820	1842	1920	2050
..	Rosendaal(*above*) ,,	6 6	7 6	8 6	9 6	10 6	11 6	12 6	13 6	15 6	17 6	19 6	1918	1942	21 6	22 6
60	Breda ,,	6 27	7 27	8 27	9 27	1027	1127	1227	1327	1527	1727	1927	..	20 4	2127	2227
73	Tilburg ,,	6 50	7 50	8 50	9 50	1050	1150	1250	1350	1550	1750	1950	..	2026	2150	2250
87	s'Hertogenbosch.. arr.	7 8	8 8	9 8	10 8	11 8	12 8	13 8	14 8	16 8	18 8	20 8	..	2046	22 8	23 8
116	Utrecht ,,	7 52	8 52	9 52	1052	1152	1252	1352	1452	1652	1852	2052	..	2122	2252	2352
..	s'Hertogenbosch dep.	7 21	8 21	9 21	1021	1121	1221	..	1421	1621	1821	2021	..	2049	2221	..
..	Nymegen arr.	8 0	9 0	10 0	11 0	12 0	13 0	..	15 0	17 0	19 0	21 0		2127	23 0	..
	Nymegen dep.	8 5	9 5	10 5	11 5	12 5	13 5	..	15 5	17 5	19 5	21 5	..	2132	23 5	..
..	Arnhem arr.	8 20	9 20	1020	1120	1220	1320		1520	1720	1920	2120	..	2151	2320	..
	Arnhem dep.	8 22	9 22	1054	1122	1254	13†22	..	1522	1722	1922	2122	..	2154	2322	..
148	Zutphen (*p.* 159) arr.	8 47	9 47	1125	1147	1325	13†47	..	1547	1747	1947	2147	..	2220	2345	..
..	Hengelo (*p.* 159) arr.	9 48	1048	..	1248	..	..	..	1648	1848	2048	2248	..	2258	..	..

† Weekdays only.

Rotterdam, (Amsterdam), Nymegen, Cleves, Cologne. [Netherlands St. and Ger.St.Rys. (Koln).

	1 2 3	1 2 D	1 2 3	1 2 3	2 3	1 2 3	1 2 3	1 2 3	1 2 3	1 2 3	1 2 3	1 2 3	1 2 3	1 2 3
LONDON (L'pool St.)	†	2015		..	†	..	..	†	fast			Exp		
Hook of Holland dep.	..	7 21	8 11	1011	..	1211	..	1411		1611		1811		2011
Rotterdam (D.Pt.) „	4 54	7 52	8 55	1055	..	1255	..	1455	..	1655		1850		2055
„ (Beurs) „	..	..	8 59	1059	..	1259	..	1459	..	1659				2059
Dordrecht	5 23	R	9 22	1122	..	1322	..	1522		1722		1910		2122
Geldermalsen	6 35		1035	1235	..	1435	..	1635	..	1835		2014		2235
Amsterdam (C) dp.	5 26	8¶14	9 23	11‡33	1212	13‡33	1323	1523	1612	..	1723	18‡47	2012	
Amersfoort ... „	6 25	..	1025	..	1257	..	1425	1625	1657		1825	R	2057	
Kesteren	7 2	..	11 2	13 2	1330	15 2	15 7	17 2	1730	19 2	19 7		2130	23 2
Ressen Bemmel arr.	..	..	..	1329		..	..	1729	.		1934	..	..	2329
Nymegen „	7 25	10 4	1127	1336	1352	1527	1610	1736	1752	1925	1941	21 3	2152	2336
Amstd. time.	2 3	D	2 3			2 3		2 3				D		
Nymegen dep.	7 30	1010	1236	..	..	1532	..	18 2	..	..	..	2114	..	..
Groesbeek arr.	..	..		..	..	..	..	..	..	..			..	..
Cranenburg (C.E. time) arr.	7 26	10 9	1234	..	..	1528	..	18 0	..	.	2 3	2112	..	..
Cranenburg (C.E. time) dep.	7 33	1022	1250	..	..	1538		1815	..		..	2131	..	..
Cleves (Kleef) arr.	7 47	1032	13 0	2 3	..	1553	2 3	1825	..	2 3	..	2141	..	..
Cleves dep.	8 5	1033	13 6	1443	..	1559	1630	1826	..	1945	2148	2142	..	..
Goch	8 16		1317	15 0	..	1611	1651	1837	..	20 5	22 4	2155	..	
Kempen arr.	8 52		1351	1549	..	1648	1747	1911		21 1	2252	..	..	..
Kempen dep.	8 53		1352	1551	..	1649	1749	1912	..	21 6	2253		..	
Crefeld	9 8	1118	14 9	1612	..	17 2	1836	1926	..	2134	2331	2234	..	..
Neuss (*p.* 165) arr.	9 24	1135	1424	1633	..	1722	1858	1941		2155	2352	2250	..	..
Cologne (Haupt.) ar.	9 53	12 5	1457	1724		1810	1951	2013	..	2253	0 41	2321	..	

¶ Via Utrecht. † Weekdays only.
‡ Via Utrecht and Geldermalsen. R Rest. Car.

	1 2 3	2 3	1 2 3	1 2 3	1 2 3	2 3	1 2 3	2 3	2 3	2 3	2 3	2 3	2 3	1 2 3	1 2 3	1 2 3	2 3
				D		fast				fast				D	fast		
Cologne (Haupth.) d.	..	4 44	..	6 41	..	8 11		1015	1234	14 0	1410	1456	1555	1713	1943	.	2027
Neuss	..	5 39	..	7 8	..	8 36	.	11 5	1259	1425	15 1	1550	1653	1738	2010	..	2055
Crefeld	..	6 12	..	7 27	..	8 52	..	1145	1320	1446	1543	1645	1739	1755	2032	..	2122
Kempen ar.	..	6 23	..	R	..	9 2	..	1158	1332	1456	1556	1657	1752		2042	..	2134
to *Venlo*, *p.* 157) dp.	..	6 24	..		..	9 3	..	12 0	1334	1457	1557	17 1	1753	R	2043	..	2135
Goch	..	7 17	..	8 6	..	9 36	.	1254	1426	1531	1648	18 1	1851		2115		2226
Cleves arr.		7 34	..	8 19	..	9 47	.	1311	1441	1541	17 3	1816	19 7	1840	2126	..	2242
Cleves dep.	..	..	..	8 20	..	9 48		1319	..	1543	1715	..		1841	..	..	.
Cranenburg „	..	..	..	8 49	..	10 8	..	1340	..	16 0	1739	..	..	19 7	.		..
Groesbeek (Amst. tm.)		..	..	▼	..	..		..	..		..	..	..	..		..	..
Nymegen c arr.	†	..	..	9 28	..	1046	†	1418	.	1638	1817	..		1946	..	..	.
	1 2 3	1 2 3	1 2 3	1 2 3	1 2 3	1 2 3	1 2 3	1 2 3	1 2 3	1 2 3	1 2 3			D	1 2 3		
Nymegen dep.	6 38	8 36	9 10	9 55	1034	1210	1226	1434	1636	1710	1836	..		2011	2110	2126	..
Ressen-Bemmel „		..	..	..		..	1232	..	†	†		..	..	..	..	2132	..
Kesteren arr.	6 59	8 57	9 32	..	1057	1232	1257	1457	1656	1732	1857	..		..	2132	2157	..
Amersfoort „	7 37	9 37	10 6	..	1137	13 6	..	1537	1737	18 6	1937	..	..	..	22 8		..
Amsterdam (C) a.	8†40	1035	1055	11‡50	1235	1347		1635	1835	1847	2045	..	..	21‡51	2253	..	..
Geldermalsen .. dep.	7 35	9 35	..	1039	1135	..	1335	1535	1735	..	1935	..	..	..	..	2235	..
Dordrecht arr.	8 37	1037	..	1122	1237	..	1437	1637	1837	..	2037	..	..	..	..	2337	..
Rotterdm. (Beurs) „	9 0	11 0	..	..	13 0		15 0	17 0	19 0		21 0	..		..		24 0	..
(Delft. Prt.) „	9 4	11 4	..	1142	13 4	..	15 4	17 4	19 4	..	21 4	..	..	22‡13	..	0 4	.
Hook of Holland „	1016	1216	..	1216	1416	..	1616	1746	2015		2216	..	..	2250		..	..
LONDON (L'pool St.)	†	..	..	..	..		..	..	..	..		..	..	8 38	..		..

D—Corridor Exp., see page 75.

Zutphen, Arnhem, s'Bosch, Breda (Flushing). [Neth. St. Rlys.

	1 2 3	1 2 3	1 2 3	1 2 3	1 2 3	1 2 3	1 2 3	1 2 3	1 2 3	1 2 3	1 2 3	1 2 3	1 2 3	1 2 3	1 2 3	1 2 3
	†		†	†	ExD		Exp	†		†			†			
Hengelo dep.			6 11	7 11	8 1	8†11	D	9 11	1011	1211	1411	1611	17 11	1811	2011	2111
Zutphen „		6†14	7 14	8 14	8 49	9 14	..	1014	1114	1314	1514	1714	18 14	1914	2114	2314
Arnhem arr.		6†38	7 38	8 38	9 17	9 38	..	1038	1138	1338	1538	1738	18 38	1938	2138	2341
Arnhem dep.	5 41	6 41	7 41	8 41	9 19	9 41	..	1041	1141	1341	1541	1741	18 41	1941	2141	2350
Nymegen arr.	5 56	6 56	7 56	8 56	9 36	9 56	..	1056	1156	1356	1556	1756	18 56	1956	2156	0 8
Nymegen dep.	6 2	7 2	8 2	9 2	9 46	10 2	..	11 2	12 2	14 2	16 2	18 2	19 2	20 2	22 2	..
s'Hertogenbosch arr.	6 39	7 39	8 39	9 39	1021	1039		1139	1230	1439	1639	1839	19 39	2039	2239	
Utrecht dep.	6 10	7 10	8 10	9 10	9 40	1010	..	1110	1210	1410	1610	1810	19 10	2010	2210	..
Hertogenbosch... „	6 52	7 52	8 52	9 52	1023	1052	..	1152	1252	1452	1652	1852	19 52	2052	2252	..
Tilburg „	7 12	8 12	9 12	1012	1045	1112	..	1212	1312	1512	1712	1912	20 12	2112	2312	..
Breda „	7 35	8 35	9 35	1035	..	1135	..	1235	1335	1535	1735	1935	20 35	2135	2335	..
p. 155 Rosendaal arr.	7 54	8 54	9 54	1054	1120	1154	1231	1254	1354	1554	1754	1954	20 54	2154	2354	..
p. 155 FLUSHING „	..	10†9		12 9	1222	1328	1335		15†9	1728	1925	21 9		2328		..

R Rest. Car.
† Weekdays only.
‡ Suns. arr. 10.28

Rotterdam, Amsterdam, etc., Emmerich, Oberhausen, Cologne.

[Netherl. & Ger. State Rlys. (Essen)]

D—Corridor Exp., *see page* 75.
S Sleeping Cars Amsterdam Coire and Interlaken and *v.v.* **X** From June 30 to Sept. 9. **Z** From July 2 to Sept 11.

Mls. Miles from Amsterdam.	D Corr. Exp.; extra fares *see p.* 75.	23	12	12	23	23	123	23	23	123	23	123	23	23	23	23	23
		fast	ExD	ExD			ExD			ExD		Exp					
	Rotterdam (Maas) dp.	6 23	7*22	7*52	9 23	1023	10*26	1123	1423	..	1653	..	1723	1823	2023	2023	2123
	The Hague ...... ,,	6 15	..	7 52	9 15	1015	1027	1115	1415	..	1645	..	1715	1815	2015	2015	2115
	Gouda	6 40	..	..	9 39	1040	11 0	1139	1439	..	17 9	..	1739	1839	2039	2039	2139
	Utrecht .... arr.	7 4	8 14	8 44	10 4	11 4	1127	12 4	15 4		1734	..	18 4	19 4	21 4	21 4	22 4
							C			R		ExD				123	
0	Amsterdam (C) dep.	6 33	7 41	8 14	9 33	1033	1054	1133	1433	1452	17 3	1710	1733	1833	2033	2041	2133
..	,, Wees. Pt. d	6 43	..		9 43	1043	..	1143	1443	..	1713	S	1743	1843	2043	A	2143
22	Utrecht .... dep.	7 8	8 25	8 56	10 8	11 8	1142	12 8	15 8	1526	1738	1745	18 8	19 8	21 8	2117	22 8
57	Arnhem .... arr.	7 44	9 7	9 40	1044	1144	1225	1244	1544	16 7	1814	1827	1844	1944	2144	22 0	2244
	Arnhem .... dep.	7 49	9 9	9 41	1049	1149	1227	1249	1549	1610		1829	19 3	20 3	2149	22 4	
66	Zevenaar (Am. time) ar.	8 1	9 22	9 53	11 1	12 1	1241	13 1	16 1	1624	..	1841	1916	2021	22 1	2217	..
77	Emmerich c ... arr.	8 15	9 21	9 53	..	1212	1242	1315		1625	..	1840	1920	2015	..	2217	..
			FD	FD								X					23
..	(Mid. Eu. Tm.) dep	8 37	9 23	1018		1233	13 2	1335	..	1657	..	1910	1946	2024	..	2248	23 7
98	Wesel .... arr.	9 17		..	..	1312	..	1358	..	1721	..	1935	2013	21 5	..	2312	2348
115	Oberhausen (to Berlin p. 163 G) arr.	9 53	M	11 0	..	1337	1345	1420	..	1743	..	1957	2041	2143	..	2333	0 21
..	Oberhausen dep	10 6		11 2	..	..	1348	1422	..	1745	..	1959	2050	2150	..	2335	
134	Dusseldorf (Haupt. ar.	1055	1016	1130	..	..	1419	1451	..	1816	..	2030	2116	2220	..	0 7	..
159	Cologne Haupt. ,,	1148	1054	12 6		..	1458	1531	..	1856		2112	22 2	23 2		0 53	

	23	23	123	23	23	123	23	23	23	23	123	23	23	123	23	12	23	12	23	23
			ExD			ExD	.		†		ExD	..	fast	ExD		FD		FD		
Cologne (Haupt.) dp	..	..	5 40	..	7 9	7 55	..	..	8 40	..	12 2	.	1435	1542	..	1714	..	1832	1753	1855
Dusseldorf (Haupt.) ,,	..	..	6 25	..	7 47	8 28	..	..	9 20	..	1236	..	15 7	1614	..	1745	..	19 0	1839	1933
Oberhausen (*frm Berlin, p.* 164 *r*) ar.	..	..	6 56	..	8 14	9 0	..	..	10 9	..	13 8	..	1537	1646	..	1812	..	│	19 7	2019
Oberhausen dp	..	..	6 58	..	8 30	9 2		..	1015	..	1310	..	1539	1648	..	1814	..	│	1911	2025
Wesel .... dep.	..	..	7 20	..	8 57	9 25	..	..	1056	..	1334	..	16 0	..	..		..	↓	1956	2054
Emmerich ... arr.	..	..	7 46	..	9 24	9 51		..	1137	..	1358	..	1623	1729	..	1853	..	2012	2034	2123
			A			Z					R							M		
(Mid. Eu. Tm.) dep	..	..	8 0	..	9 35	10 6	..	..	1144	..	1413	..	1638	1744	..	19 8		2028	2045	2140
Zevenaar c ...... arr.	..		8 38	..	1013	1043	..	..	1223	..	1447	..	1712	1818		1942	..	21 2	2124	2219
,, (Ams. tm.) d	7 58	8 58	9 15	9 58	1058	1115	..	1158	1247	1358	1515	..	1740	1845	1858	2015	1958	21 2	2158	2244
Arnhem .... arr.	8 11	9 11	9 29	1011	1111	1129		1211	1311	1411	1529		1754	1858	1911	2029	2011	..	2211	2258
Arnhem dep.	8 16	9 16	9 32	1016	1116	1132	1146	1216	1316	1416	1532	1546	1816	19 0	1916	2032	2016	..	2216	2316
Utrecht .... arr.	8 52	9 52	1014	1052	1152	1214	1222	1252	1352	1452	1614	1622	1852	1941	1952	2114	2052	22 1	2252	2352
Amsterd. (Wees. P.) a.	9 18	1018	..	1118	1218	S	1248	1318	1418	1518	..	1648	1918	..	2018		2118	..	2318	0 18
Amsterdam (C) arr.	9 28	1028	1051	1128	1228	1250	1258	1328	1428	1528	1650	1658	1928	2020	2028	2151	2128	2238	2328	0 28
Utrecht .... dep.	8 58	9 58	..	1058	1158	.	1228	1258	1358	1458	..	1628	1858	20 4	1958	2122	2058	2212	2258	..
Goude .. .. arr.	9 23	1023	..	1123	1223	..	1253	1323	1423	1523	..	1653	1923	2031	2023	2153	2123	..	2323	..
The Hague ... ,,	9 43	1043	..	1143	1243	..	1313	1343	1443	1543	..	1713	1943	2057	2043	2213	2143	23 4	2343	..
Rotterdam (Maas) ,,	9 41	1041	..	1141	1241	..	1311	1341	1441	1541	..	1711	1941	21*5	2041	22*13	2141	23*3	2341	..

A Sleep. car Amsterdam-Wurzburg and *v.v.* daily; Amsterdam Bucharest, Tue. Thur. and Sat., return Mon. Wed. and Fri., *see p* 84. 1, 2 & 3cl. cars Amsterdam-Cologne-Vienna and *v.v.* **FD** Fast train special fares, *see p.* 75. **R** Restaurant Car. **C** Through 1, 2 & 3 cl. car Amsterdam Cologne-Vienna and Hook–Budapest–Dining car Hook Wurzburg and *v.v.* **M** Rheingold Express. * Rotterdam D.P. Station † Not Sundays.

(Amsterdam) Utrecht, Boxtel, Venlo. (Cologne).

23	23	23	23	23	23	23	23	(W. P. Station.)	23	23	23	23	23	23	23	23	23
fast		†											†				
7 13	1043	1313	1543	1743	1843	2013	2143	d. Amst'dm (abv) a	9 48	1118	1218	1318	1548	1718	2018	2248	0 18
7 40	1110	1340	1610	1810	1910	20 4	2210	d. Utrecht ..... a.	9 22	1052	1152	1252	1522	1652	1952	2222	2352
8 18	1148	1418	1648	1848	1948	2118	2248	d. sHertog'bosch	8 42	1014	1114	1214	1442	1614	1914	2142	2314
8 26	1156	1426	1656	1856	1956	2126	2256	a. Boxtel .... d.	8 34	10 4	11 4	12 4	1434	16 4	19 4	2134	23 4
8 27	1157	1427	1657	1857	1957	2127	2257	d. Boxtel .... a.	8 33	10 3	11 3	12 3	1433	16 3	19 3	2133	23 3
8 40	1210	1440	1710	1910	2010	2140	2310	a. Eindhovend ..	8 21	9 51	1051	1151	1421	1551	1851	2121	2251
9 41	13 7	1541	1818	20†6	2112	2238	0 9	a **Venlo** (Am. tm) d	7 18	8 55	..	1055	13†18	1455	17†55	2023	2155
23	—	23	23	—	-D-	—	23					D					
9 46	1312	1710	1843	..	2118	..	6 58	d. Venlo .. .. a.	..	8 39	..	1020	1246	1434	1729	20 3	21 2
9 32	1258	1656	1829		21 5	..	6 44	a. Kaldenkirchenc	..	8 13	..	9 54	1220	14 8	17 3	1937	2036
1023	14 3	18 4	2039	..	2152	..	7 51	a. Rheydt ...... d.	..	7 11	..	9 6	..	1148	16 1	..	1940
1115	1456	1855	20*13	..	2241	..	9 9	a. COLOGNE (155) d.	..	5 57	..	8 18	10*15	12*34	1435	17*37	18*42

† Not Sundays.
r Rest. car.

The times on the LEFT are to be read DOWNWARDS, those on the RIGHT UPWARDS.

Rotterdam, The Hague, Haarlem, Amsterdam.

[Netherlands State Railways

††2 & 3 cl., Hague Scheveningen and v.v.	123	123	Exp 12	123	123	fast 123	123	123	123	Exp 123	Exp 123	123	123	Ex D 12	123	123	Exp 12	23	Ex D 123	luxe 12	Exp 123	Exp 12	123	123	123	luxe 12
	†	†				†							†		†	*	P		A	E						P
Rotterdam (D.P.) dp.	5 53	6 36	..	7 6	7 36	7 56	8 6	8 23	9 23	9 52	1032	1136	1453	1521	1553	1653	1712	1723	1833	1854	2020	2025	2137	23 6	2336	2350
Hook of Holland ,,	..	5 43	6 29	..	7 11	..	7 41	..		..	..	1111	1411	|	..	..	Pull. Cars.	1611	..	Pull. Cars.	..	..	2111	2211	2311	..
Schiedam	6 2	6 42	6 48	7 12	7 42	..	8 12	8 28	9 28	..	..	1142	1458	|	..	..		1728	..		..	..	2143	2312	2342	..
Delft	6 12	6 51	R	7 21	7 51	..	8 21	8 37	9 37	..	..	1151	15 7	↓	16 5	17 5		1738	..		..	..	2151	2321	2351	..
The Hague ....arr.	6 18	6 57	7 2	7 27	7 57	8 13	8 27	8 43	9 43	1013	1052	1157	1513	1542	1611	1711	1734	1745	1844	1915	2041	2048	2157	2327	2357	0 11
Scheveningen†† ,,	..	7 24	7†24	7†57	8†25	..	8 58	..	..	..	..	1257	1557	..	..	1752	..		..	..	..		2257	2357	..	..
Scheveningen†† dp.	..	6†37	5†37	..	7†27	..	..	8†27	9 7	.	..	11 7	..	15 7	..	..	17 7	1657	..	..	..	20 7	21 7	23 7	..	23 7
The Hague .... dp.	6 21	6 59	7 4	7 29	7 59	8 15	8 29	8 45	9 45	1015	..	1159	1515	1544	1613	1713	1736	1746	..	1917	2043	2051	2159	2329	2359	0 12
Leiden .... arr.	6 30	7 9	..	7 39	8 9	..	8 30	8 55	9 55	..	..	12 9	1525	..	1623	1723	..	18 1	..	..	2056	..	22 9	2339	0 10	..
Haarlem ...... arr.	7 0	7 29	7 34	7 59	8 29	..	8 59	9 16	1016	..	..	1229	1547	..	1643	1744	..	..	..	..	2119	..	2229	2359	0 30	0 45
Amsterdam (C) arr.	7 16	7 45	7 50	8 15	8 45	8 58	9 15	9 32	1032	11 4	..	1245	16 3	1635	1659	18 0	1827	..	..	20 3	2137	2141	2245	0 15	0 46	1 1

P 1 and 2 cl. Pull. Cars. to and from Paris.

	123	123	123	123	Exp 123	123	luxe 12	123	123	luxe 12	123	Exp 123	123	Exp 12	fast 123	Exp 12	123	123	Ex D 12	fast 123	123	Exp 123	Exp 123	Exp 12
		†	†				P		†	E				R	P	P		†		†	*		R	R
Amsterdam (C).. dp.	..	5 43	6 13	6 43	6 53	7 13	7 32	7 43	7 58	8 3	8 58	..	9 58	10 3	1020	1259	1550	1628	1648	1658	1724	..	2052	2137
Haarlem	..	5 58	6 29	6 59	7 12	7 29		7 59	8 14	..	9 14	..	1014	..	1037	..	16 9	1644	..	1714	1740	..	..	2152
Leiden	..	6 18	6 49	7 19	7 36	7 49	..	8 19	8 35	..	9 35	..	1035	..	11 1	..	1635	17 4	..	1735	18 1	..	..	..
The Hague ....arr.	..	6 30	7 0	7 30	7 49	8 0	8 23	8 30	8 46	8 54	9 46	..	1046	1054	1114	1345	1647	1715	1736	1746	1812	..	2140	2224
Scheveningen†† ,,	..	..	7†24	7†57	..	8†25	8 58	8 58	..	..		..	..	..	1157	..	..	1752	..	..	..	..	..	2257
Scheveningen†† dp.	..	..	6†37		..	7†27	..	..	8†27	..	9 7	9 7	10 7	10 7	..	13 7	16 7	..	17 7	..		20 7	21 7	22 7
The Hague .... ,,	6 20	6 32	7 2	7 32	7 52	8 2	8 25	8 32	8 48	8 58	9 48	9 54	1048	1056	1117	1347	1650	1717	1738	1748	1813	2055	2142	2227
Delft	6 30	6 39	7 9	7 39	8 2	8 9	..	8 39	8 55	..	9 55	..	1055	..	..	..	17 0	1725	..	1755	..	..	..	..
Schiedam ......arr.	..	6 48	7 18	7 48	..	8 18	..	8 48	..	..	..	..	11 4	..	..	..	..	..	..	18 4	..	..	..	2241
Hook .... ,,	..	7 16	7 46	8 16	..	..	..	9 16	..	..	..	..	..	..	..	..	..	..	..	1916	..	..	..	23 1
Rotterdam (D.P.) ,,	6 45	6 53	7 23	7 53	8 17	8 23	8 47	8 53	9 5	9 17	10 5	1015	11 9	1117	1138	14 8	1715	1735	18 1	18 9	1829	2117	22 3	.

A 1 & 2 cl. cars from The Hague *via* Brussels to Bale and *v.v.*
D—Corridor Exp., *see page* 75.
E Edelweiss Exp., 1 and 2 cl. Pullmans to Bale and Zurich daily. Extra fares.
R Rest car. † Not Sundays.
¶ Rest. car on weekdays only
* Not Sats. or Suns.

Rotterdam—Amsterdam and *v.v.*

NOTE. Extra Trains.—The above are the principal Trains Rotterdam to Amsterdam and back. In addition there is a half-hourly service from the D.P. Station, 7.6 to 22.36, the timings being exactly similar to the 7.6 and 7.36 shown above.

From Amsterdam (C.) to Rotterdam (D.P.) half-hourly from 6.43 to 23.43, the times being exactly similar to the 6.43 and 7.13 shown above.

W Not nights of Sat./Sun., Sun./Mon or holidays.
R Rest. Car. * Via Nymegen & Amersfoort.
¶ July 1—September 3.

Amsterdam—Maastricht Liege

† Not Sundays. ‡ *via* Hilversum.

23	123	23	123	23	123				123	23	123	23	123	23	123	123
	R		ExS		W						ExS		Exp			W
7 3	9‡12	1433	1612	1733	0 22	dep.	**Amsterdam** (C.)....	arr.	9 58	1128	1418	1728	19‡49	2128	2258	2 32
7 34	9 55	15 4	*	18 4	1 0	arr.	Utrecht	dep.	9 26	1056	*	1656	19 5	2056	2226	1 52
7 40	9 58	1510	¶	1810	1 51	dep.		arr.	9 22	1052	¶	1652	19 3	2052	2222	1 17
8 16	1038	1548		1848	2 50	,,	Hertogenbosch	dep.	8 44	1014	..	1614	1823	2014	2144	0 26
8 47	11 5	1615	..	1915	3 34	,,	Eindhoven	,,	8 21	9 51	..	1551	1756	1951	2121	2335
9 28	1147	1649	..	1949	4 25	arr.	Roermond	,,	7 33	9 5	1033	1512	1710	1912	2033	2236
9 49	..	17 7	1952	20 7	4 54	,,	Sittard	,,	7 12	8 45	1012	1455	R	1855	2012	2212
1018	1228	1726	2018	2026	5 23	arr.	**Maastricht**	dep.	6 51	8 24	9 49	1437	1625	1837	1951	2144
1023	1234	1822	2022	2045	6 31	dep.	(Amst. time)	arr.	..	8 4	9 20	1225	16 0	1754	1924	2055
1017	1228	1819	2016	2040	6 29	arr.	Vise *c*	dep.	..	7 20	8 45	1152	1527	1710	1851	2011
1031	1243	1827	2016	2111	6 36	dep.	(Green. time)	arr.	..	7 10	8 39	1146	1521	1657	1845	20†3
..	..	..	2030	2144	7 12	arr.	Liege (Long.)	.....dep.	..	6 41		..	..	..		1930
1053	13 5	1850	2052	2153	7 21	arr.	**Liege** (Guil.)	......dep.	.	6 28	8 17	1124	1459	1621	1823	19†21
..	1611	2343	2353	..	1120	arr	Luxemburg	.. dep.			5 25		12 0	.	12 2	1416

Rotterdam, (The Hague), Gouda, (Amsterdam), Zwolle. [Netherlands State Rlys.

23	123	12	123	123	23	23	123	23	123	23	123	123	123	‡ *Via* Utrecht.	23	123	123	23	23	123	123	123	123	123	12	12	23	123
†		ExD	r	Exp			†	*	†		ExD		Ex †		†		ExD		†			r	ExD		ExD	ExD		Ex †
5 53	6 32	7¶52	8 32	10¶25	1053	1123	1232	1453	1632	1853	1956	2032	0¶ 3	dp Rotterdam (M) ar	9 11	1027	1058	1211	1411	1627	1827	2027	21 5	2227	23¶3	..	0 11	3¶9
5 45	6 24	7 52	8 24	1027	1045	1115	1224	1445	1624	1845	1952	2024	..	„ The Hague „	9 13	1026	1058	1213	1413	1626	1826	2026	2057	2226		23 4	0 14	..
6 9	6 53	r	8 53	11 0	11 9	1139	1253	15 9	1653	19 9	2021	2053	0 38	„ Gouda „	8 53	10 5	1032	1153	1353	16 3	18 3	20 3	2031	22 3	..	..	2353	2 38
6 34	7 19	8 44	9 19	1127	1134	12 4	1319	1534	1719	1934	2048	2119	1 10 ar	Utrecht (C) d	8 28	9 37	10 5	1128	1328	1537	1737	1937	20 4	2137	2212	2217	2328	2 7
6 38	7 25	8 53	9 25	1151	1138	12†22	1325	1538	1725	1938	2053	2125	1 40 dp	Utrecht (C) a	8 25	9 31	9 58	1125	1325	1531	1731	1931	1955	2131	2155		2325	1 32
6 51	7 43	9 13	9 43	12 9	1151	12†49	1343	1551	1743	1951	2111	2143	2 1	arr Amersfoort dep	8 12	9 14	9 37	1112	1312	1514	1714	19 4	1937	2114	2136		2312	1 11
6 17	7 0		9 1	..	1117	1144	1310	1517	1710	1917	.	21 0	0 25	dp Amsterdam C ar	9†2	9r55		1147	1347	1555	1755	1955		2155	..	¶Rotterd'm D.P Stn.	2347	2‡32
6 55	7 47	r Rest Car.	9 47	..	1155	12†54	1347	1555	1747	1955	..	2147	2 18	dep. Amersfoort arr.	8 8	9 10		11 8	13 8	1510	1710	1910	† Not Sun.	2110	.		23 8	0 58
7 33	8 32		1032	..	1233	14†12	1432	1633	1832	2033	..	2232	3 18	arr. Zwolle dep.	7 30	8 25	..	1030	1230	1425	1625	1825		2025	..		2230	2358
9 10	1010		1210	..	1410	..	1610	1810	2010	2210	.	0 10	5 18	„ Leeuwarden „	5 53	6 56	..	8 53	1053	1247	1447	1647		1847	..		2053	22†2
8 42	9 57		1157	.	1342	..	1557	1742	1957	2142	.	2357	5 18	„ Groningen „	6†20	7r0		9 20	1120	13 0	15 0	17 0		19 0	.		2120	21†49

Nymegen, Arnhem, Zutphen, Zwolle, &c. Netherlands State Rlys.

												Mls.													
†		†			†		†				ExD			†	ExD		†		†			†			
6 5	7 5	8 5	9 15	11 5	13 5	15 5	16 5	17 5	19 5	21 5	2132	0	dep. Nymegen ..arr.	8 56	9 36	9 56	1056	11 56	1356	1556	1756	1856	1956	2156	0 8
6 22	7 22	8 22	9 22	11 22	1322	1522	1622	1722	1922	2122	2154	11	„ Arnhem .. „	8 38	9 17	9 38	1038	11 38	1338	1538	1738	1838	1938	2138	2341
6 47	7 47	8 47	9 47	11 47	1347	1547	1647	1747	1947	2147	2220	29	„ Zutphen.... arr.	8 14	8 49	9 14	1014	11 14	1314	1514	1714	1814	1914	2114	2314
7 3	8 3	9 3	10 3	12 3	14 3	16 3	17 3	18 3	20 3	22 3	..	..	„ Deventer ..dep.	7 58	..	8 58	9 58	10 58	1258	1458	1658	1758	1858	2058	2258
7 27	8 27	9 27	1027	12 27	1427	1627	1727	1827	2027	2227	..	59	arr. Zwolle ..... „	7 32	..	8 32	9 32	10 32	1232	1432	1632	1732	1832	2032	2232
9 10	1010	11 3	1210	14 10	1610	1810	19 1	2010	2210	0 10	..	118	„ Leeuwarden „	5 53	..	6†56	7 47	8 53	1053	1247	1447	16 2	1647	1847	2053
8 42	9 57	1042	1157	13 42	1557	1742	1857	1957	2142	2357	..		„ Groningen.. „	6 20	.	7 0	8 0	9 20	1120	13 0	15 0	1620	17 0	19 0	2120

† Not Sunday

Amsterdam (Rotterdam), Salzbergen (Osnabruck, Hamburg, Berlin). [Netherlands State Rlys.

123	12	123	23	123	23	123	123	123	123	Mls.		123	123	123	23	123	123	123	12	23
	ExD			Exp.D R	*		ExD	fast	ExD			fast	ExD	ExD	¶		ExD		Exd	
7 0	8a38	9 1	1117	1129	1517	17 0	2036	21 0	R	0	dep. Amsterdam (C) arr.	9 55	1019	R	1347	1935	2016	2155	2217	2347
7 42	9 14	9 42	1150	1210	1550	1742	2114	2142			arr. Amersfoort Cnt. dep.	9 14	9 32	To Flushing, with Sleep. Car.	1313	1914	1932	2114	2133	2313
	7 52	..	..	1026	..	..	SZ		Fr. Flushing with Slp. Car Hamburg	..	dep. Rotterdam (D.P.) a.		ZS		..	..	21 5		23 3	..
6 32	††	8 32	1053	..	1453	1632	1956	2032		..	dep. Rotterdam (M.) ar.	1027	1038		1411	2027	R	2227	††	0 11
6 24	7 52	8 24	1045	1027	1445	1624	1952	2024		..	dep. The Hague ....arr.	1026	1058		1413	2026	2057	2226	23 4	0 13
7 25	8 53	9 25	1138	1151	1538	1725	2053	2125		..	dep. Utrecht .... arr	9 31	9 58		1325	1931	1955	2131	2155	2325
7 43	9 13	9 43	1151	12 9	1551	1743	2111	2143		..	arr. Amersfoort (C) ..dep	9 14	9 37		1312	1914	1937	2114	2136	2312
7 50	9 25	9 50	1158	1218	1558	1750	2121	2150			dep. Amersfoort (Cent.) ar.	9 7	9 28		13 5	19 7	1928	21 7	2127	23 5
8 24	..	1024	1226	1255	1626	1824	2157	2224		55	„ Apeldoorn...... „	8 33	8 51		1237	1833	1851	2033		2237
8 38	‖	1038	1238	1311	1638	1838	2213	2238			„ Deventer ...... dep	8 21	8 37	..	1226	1821	1837	2021	2039	2226
9 10	..	1110	13 5	1345	17 5	1910	R a	2310		88	„ Almelo .... „	7 48	8 0	..	1159	1748	18 2	1948	..	2159
9 26	1058	1126	1318	1359	1718	1926	2258	2326		99	arr. Hengelo........ dep.	7 31	7 44	..	1145	17 9	1744	19 4	..	21 9
9 56	11 4	1156	1320	14 4	1720	1956	2314		2356	..	dep Hengelo........ arr		7 25	8 0	1139	1656	1738	1854	..	21 4
10 9	..	12 9	1328	1416	1728	20 9	2326	..	0 8	104	arr. Oldenzaal c (Ams tm d	..	7 15	7 50	1131	1646	1727	..	a	2054
1018	11 8	1240	..	1416	..	2012	2330	..	0 11	115	„ Bentheim c (M.E.„ d.	..	6 6	6 50	1030	1547	1616	..	1014	1945
..	F‖D	13§43	..	1457	..	..	0a23	..	0 55	129	„ Rheine .... „	..	5a23	6 5	9 48	..	1543	..	F‖D	..
..	12 6	1451	..	1540	..	..	1 5	..	1 36	158	„ Osnabrück *p.* 163 dp.	..	4 44	5 15	7 48	..	15 3	..	1019	..
..	1524	..	..	1939	..	..	5 44	..	6 36		„ HAMBURG (*p.* 161) „	..	23 0	0 13	¶	..	1147	..	15 1	..
..	1625	..	..	22 1	..	..	7 4	..	7 49	..	„ BERLIN (Fr.) *p.*163 „	..	2250	2250	..	..	8 56		1357	..

†† Leaves Hook of Holland 7.21 arr. 23.33.
¶ Not Sun. * Not Sats. **R** Rest. Car.

D—Corridor Exp., *see page* 75.

a Thro' cars Amsterdam-Berlin and *v.v.*

‖ Rest. Car Hook-Hamburg and Berlin.

§ 2 and 3 class only.

S Sleep Cars Amsterdam and The Hague to Berlin and *vice versa.*

Z Slp. car Rotterdam-Hamburg and *v.v.*

The times on the LEFT are to be read DOWNWARDS, those on the RIGHT UPWARDS.

GERMANY.

Trains throughout Germany run on Mid-European time (one hour fast of Greenwich).

THROUGH SERVICES TO GERMANY.

From England, see pp. 127 *to* 130, 132, 155, 156; *from Belgium, see pp.* 127, 128, 149, 151 *to* 153; *from Holland, see pp.* 155 *to* 157, *and* 159; *from France, see pp.* 240, 269, 272, *et seq.*; *to and from Scandinavia, U.S.S.R., etc., see pp.* 203 *to* 205, 216, 217 *to* 232; *to and from Italy, pp.* 174, 178, 185, 194, 198.

Cologne, Oberhausen, Bremen, Hamburg.

[Ger. State Rlys. Essen Munster and Altona.

Mls.	*Through Tables, see pp.* 130, 132.		2 3	Rap 2 FDT	Exp 123 RD	2 3 fast	Exp 123 D	Exp 123 DY	Exp 123 DR	fast 2 3	Exp 123 DR	ExD 123 D	2 3	fast 2 3	Exp 123 SD	Exp 123 DZ	luxe 1 2
0	**Cologne** (Ht.)	dep.	4 45	7 0	7 23	8 8	9 10	10 1	1113	1133	1440	1719	1759	2021	22 7	2353	1 48
24	Düsseldorf	,,	6 2	7 26	8 8	8 47		1040		1217	1516	1753	1849	21 7	.	0 30	..
44	Oberhausen (*p.* 157)	arr.	7 7	*via* Hamm.	..	9 16	*via* Hagen.	..	*via* Hagen and Hamm	1253	1547	1820	1939	2135	*via* Hagen and Hamm.	1 3	..
		dep.	7 13		..	9 17	..	..		1255	1549	1822	1940	2137		1 5	..
59	Wanne	arr.	7 46		9 19	9 46		1153		1321	1617	1849	2010	22 1		1 39	..
		dep.	7 47		9 20	1011		1154		1325	1619	1850	2035	22 5		1 41	*via* Hanover, *page* 164.
..	Haltern	arr.	8 9		9 46	1036		..		1352	1643	..	2057	2229		..	
..	Wesel	dep.	6 15	..	8 15	..		..		1215	15 7	..	1826	212		..	
..	Haltern	arr.	7 10	..	9 6	..		..		13 2	16 0	..	1916	22 6		.	
..	Haltern	dep.	8 10	..	9 47	1037		..		1353	1644	..	2058	2230		.	
102	Münster		8 49	9 4	1024	1120	1143	1258	1356	1440	1726	1947	2156	2340	1 0	2 46	
133	Osnabrück (*p.* 16	arr.	9 26	9 31	11 0	1159	1219	1337	1433	1529	18 3	2024	23 4	0 38	1 38	3 25	
		dep.	9 35	9 32	11 6	1235	1229	1343	1439	1554	18 9	2029	..		2 10	3 37	..
207	**Bremen**	arr.	1113	1033	1234	15 4	1352	1510	16 8	1752	1938	2150	..	..	3 54	5 4	..
		dep.	1119	1034	1238	..	1357	1513	1612	1756	1943	2155	..	..	4 4	5 10	..
..	Harburg	arr.	1232	..	1353	..	15 6	1620	1725	1920	2056	23 5	..	..	5 25	6 21	..
279	**Hamburg** (Hpt.)	,,	1246	1133	14 9	..	1524	1637	1741	1939	2112	2320	..	..	5 44	6 36	8 4
284	Altona (Hpt.)	,,	1310	1150	1431	..	1546	..	18 3	20 2	2134	2341	..	..	6 10	7 3	8 28
	To Denmark, see p. 216.																

		fast 2 3	2 3	Exp 123 D	Exp 123 DR	2 3	fast 2 3	Exp 123 DY	Exp 123 DR	fast 2 3	Exp 123	Exp 123 DR	fast 2 3	Rap 2 FDT	luxe 1 2	Exp 123 DS	Exp 123 DZ
Altona (Hpt.)	dep.	..	..	5 50	7 37	..	9 22	10 5	1125	1335	1442	1625	1754	1936	2117	2238	2350
Hamburg (Hpt.)	,,	..	..	6 8	7 56	..	9 46	1023	1147	14 1	15 1	1645	1816	1951	2140	23 0	0 13
Harburg	,,	..	..	6 23	8 11	..	10 5	1038	12 3	1418	1516	17 1	1832	..		2316	0 28
Bremen	arr.	..	..	7 34	9 30	..	12 8	1147	1319	1545	1626 R	1815	1954	2049	..	0 37	1 47
	dep.	..	..	7 38	9 35	..	1235	1151	1324	1553	1629	1820	1957	2050	*via* Lehrte and Hanover, *p* 164.	0 42	1 52
Osnabrück (*p.* 163)	arr.	..	..	8 57	11 8	..	1522	1314	1457	1745	1754	1947	2133	2153		2 23	3 29
	dep.	7 28	..	9 1	1112		1534	1319	15 3	1817	1759	1954	2138	2154		2 35	3 39
Münster		8 11	11 6	9 38	1151	1325	1713	1357	1543	1910	..	2035	2230	2221		3 23	4 23
Haltern	arr.	8 43	1159	↓	*via* Hamm and Hagen.	1358	1748	..	1616	1949	*via* Hagen.		23 2	..		*via* Hamm and Hagen	4 57
Haltern	dep.	..	1224			14 8	1751			21 1							5 5
Wesel	arr.	..	1310			15 1	1823	..		2210			..				6 0
Haltern	dep.	8 44	12 5			1359	18 6	..	1617	1950			23 3	*via* Essen.			4 58
Wanne	arr.	9 11	1236	1027		1421	1837	1447	1643	2020		2128	2326	..	..		5 24
	dep.	9 13	1243	102 ,		1437	1842	1449	1645	2022		2130	2333	..	..		5 29
Oberhausen (*p.* 163)	arr.	..	1318	1054		15 0	1930	1518	1713	2053		.	0 2	..	..		5 58
	dep.		1335	1055		15 1	1935	1519	1714	2055	..		0 3	..	..		6 1
Düsseldorf	arr.	1016	1428	1123		1536	2016	1549	1744	2130	..	2238	0 40	2357	..	.	6 31
Cologne (Hb.)	,,	11 7	1540	12 0	1422	1617	2154	1629	1824	2217	21 9	2327	1 21	0 23	4 3	6 24	7 12

D—Corridor Exp., *see page* 75. **FD** and **FDT**—Special fast Exp., extra fares *see p.* 75.
R—Rest. Car. **S**—Sleep. Cars Cologne and Aix la Chapelle-Altona; also Rotterdam-Altona and *v.v.*
Y Weekdays, July 1st to Sept. 9th. **Z** - Slp. Car Cologne-Altona-Kiel and *v.v.*

Hamburg, Lubeck.

† D Express. *r* Rest. Car. ¶ Not Sundays. [Germ. Rlys. Altona.

Mls.		2 3	2 3 †	2 3	123†	123†	2 3	2 3	2 3	2 3	2 3	2 3	2 3	123†	2 3	123†	2 3	2 3
0	Hamburg (Hpt.)	5 50	6 54	6 58	8 54	1040	1220	1310	1420	1510	1550	1730	1746	1949	20 1	2150	2210	2358
39	Lübeck	7 16	7 48	8 35	9 46	1129	1343	1356	15¶1	16¶8	1651	1823	19 9	2041	2133	2240	2332	0 38
	*To Stettin, p.*162		*r*		*r*	*r*												

	2 3	123†	2 3	2 3	2 3	123†	2 3	2 3	2 3	2 3	2 3	123†	123†	2 3	2 3	2 3 †	2 3	2 3
Lübeck	5 40	6 18	6¶54	7 31	8¶5	9 9	1034	1145	1333	1542	1647	1811	1851	1933	2020	2137	2157	2250
Hamburg (Hpt.)	6 59	7 6	7 50	8 54	9 9	10 5	1114	1245	1455	17 8	1756	19 3	1943	21 4	2113	2235	2323	2330
						r						*r*	*r*					

70 miles.

Hamburg, Altona, Kiel.

[German St. R. (Hamburg).

123	23	23	23	123	23	23	23	23	Hamburg :	23	23	23	23	123	23	23	23	23
Exp	fast	fast	fast	ExD	fast	fast	fast	fast		ExD	fast	W	fast	ExD	fast	fast	fast	Exp
6 49	8 9	9 38	13 9	1531	18 6	1959	2136	0 30	dep Hauptbahn arr.	7 45	9 48	1110	1241	1455	1616	19 9	2121	0 4
7 14	8 29	10 3	1333	1553	1830	2023	2155	0 50	dep. Altona (Hptbf) arr.	7 26	9 23	1047	1218	1427	1546	1848	21 2	2316
8 22	9 37	1111	1441	17 1	1938	2131	2246	1 58	arr. Neu- dep.	6 31	8 12	9 36	11 7	1316	1435	1737	1951	22 5
8 26	9 40	1115	1445	1712	1944	2135	2251	2 2	dep. münster arr.	6 26	8 9	9 33	11 4	13 3	1432	1734	1949	22 2
8 53	10 7	1142	1512	1739	2011	22 2	2333	2 29	arr Kiel ......dep.	5 43	7 40	9 4	1035	1234	14 3	17 5	1920	2133

W Weekdays only.

Hamburg-Flensburg-Pattburg-Copenhagen.

[Ger. State Rlys. (Hamburg) and Danish Rlys.

23	23	23	23	23	123	23	23	Mls.		23	23	23	23	123	23	23	23
		Exp	‡	‡	Ex D	‡	Ex¶			Ex¶		‡		ExD	‡	ExD	
4 29	6 49	8†25	1117	13 9	1531	18 6	2136	0	dep. Hamburg (H) ....arr.	7 45	9 48	1110	14 7	1455	19 9	21†2	0 4
6 59	8 28	9 47	1317	15 5	17 8	1944	2250	50	dep. Neumunster ....arr.	6 28	7 46	9 29	1151	13 8	1721	1942	2157
8 31	9 27	1040	1416	1640	18 3	2043	2340	90	dep. Schleswig ......dep.	5 33	6 44	8 27	1023	1210	1619	1847	20 5
9 23	10 4	111[illegible]	1453	1732	1835	2120	0 10	113	arr. Flensburg ......dep.	5 4	6 14	7 57	9 31	1139	1549	18[illegible]	20[illegible]
		¶ †			23					23				23		¶ †	23
9 36	..	1151	1620	1758	1954	2249	0 30		dep. Flensburg ......arr.	4 27	..	..	8 42	1115	1440	1712	1941
9 48	..	12 3	1632	18 8	20 6	23 1	0 42	120	arr. Pattburg ......dep.	4 15	..	..	8 30	11 3	1428	17 0	1929
10 2	..	1228	1643	1817	..	2315	0 49		dep. Padborg ......arr.	3 59	..	..	8 14	..	1418	1641	1911
1927	..	1927	2257	5 58	..	7 50	7 50	245	arr. Copenhagen p. 216 dp.	2050	..	..	2340	..	7 50	9 15	1230

‡ Weekdays only. ¶ 2 & 3 cl. thro' cars Hamburg—Fredericia and Padborg—Copenhagen, see *page* 216.
† 1 and 2 cl. Sleep. Cars Paris–Hamburg–Copenhagen and *v.v.*

Hamburg, Lubeck, Stettin.

[Ger. State Rlys. (Schwerin).

23	23	123	23	23	23	23	23	Mls.		23	23	23	23	23	23	23	23
		ExD			fast	fast				fast		fast		fast	ExD		
..	..	6 54	8 9	1045	1215	1550	16 0	0	dp. Hamburg (H), p.161 ar.	1245	17 8	1636	2113	1943	2235	..	..
..	6 48	7 53	9 2	1220	..	1657	1737	39	dep. Lubeck ....arr.	1139	1515	..	2015	1846	2132	..	..
5 35	8 3	8 48	1048	1353	1421	18 1	1912	80	dep Bad Kleinen ....arr.	1037	1340	1438	1843	1757	2037	2324	..
6 40	8 51	9 19	1141	15 4	1457	1842	2015	108	dep. Butzow ....dep.	9 58	1242	14 4	1752	1726	20 5	2235	arr.
9 15	1024	1041	1352	1718	1625	2019	2313	127	arr. Neubrandenburg dep.	8 18	9 45	1223	1455	1542	1835	1915	2321
1038	1236	1112	15 5	1828	1657	2054	..	148	arr. Strasburg ......dep	7 45	8 26	1152	1333	1512	..	1829	22[illegible]
11 2	1255	1128	1533	1850	1713	2110	..	159	arr. Pasewalk ......dep	7 29	8 2	1135	1313	1457	1748	18 0	22[illegible]
1241	142[illegible]	12 4	1635	19[illegible]2	1746	215[illegible]	..	196	arr. Stettin, p. 205 dep	6 48	6 52	1037	1037	1420	1714	1642	2[illegible] 8

Hamburg, Sassnitz, Stockholm, Warnemunde and Copenhagen.

23	123	123	23	23	12	123	Mls.		123	123	23	23	123	123	23	23	23
Ex D	ExD	ExD	fast		ExD	ExD			ExD	ExD	fast		ExD	ExD		ExD	
6 54	8 54	1040	1550	16 0	1949	2150	0	dp. Hamburg (H), p.161 ar.	7 6	10 6	1245	17 8	19 3	1943	2113	2235	2330
7 53	9 52	1134	1657	1737	2047	2246	39	dep. Lubeck .... arr.	6 12	8 59	1139	1515	18 6	1846	2015	2132	2243
9 17	§	S ¶	1837	20 5	X ‡	Z §	103	arr. Butzow .... dep.	Z	X ‡	9 58	1242	S		1752	20 5	2054
9 22			1845	2017		..		dep. Butzow .... arr.	§		9 49	1230	¶	§	1743	1956	2049
9 48	1134	1310	1915	2055	2234	0 25	122	arr. Rostock ....dep.	4 36	7 0	9 22	1153	1627	17 0	17 5	1930	2020
9 55	↓	13 5	1928	..	2240	↓		dep. Rostock ...... arr.	↑	6 48	9 8	..	1622	↑	16 4	1921	1921
11 1		1413	2046	..	2343		167	arr. Stralsund, p. 204 dp		5 43	7 58	..	1518		1416	1814	1814
1234		1521	..	..	1 31		199	arr. Sassnitz dep.		3 46	6 8	..	1412		1151	1633	1633
..		1529	..	..	1 41		200	arr. Sassnitz Haven dp.		3 36	..	..	14 3		.		..
..		2036	..	..	6 20		267	arr. Trelleborg .. dep.		2254	..	..	8 50		..	..	..
..		2125	..	..	7 11		286	arr. Malmo dep.		22 5	..	..	8 0		..	..	..
..		6 30	..	..	1550		661	arr. Stockholm, p.215A d		1350	..	..	2235		..	..	..
..		2 24	..	..	1246		47[illegible]	arr. p216 Gothenburg.. dep.		1630	..	..	2 49		..	..	..
..	↓	9 0	..	..	19 0	↓	696	arr. p216 Oslo .. dep.	↑	10 5	..	..	2010	↑	..	..	..
10 0	1139	..	1930	21 5	..	0 26		dep. Rostock ......arr.	4 32	..	9 18	1149	..	1655	..	1972	2[illegible]5
1015	1152	..	1952	2126	..	0 38	130	arr. Warnemunde ..dep.	4 20	..	9 0	1130	..	1643	.	19 0	20 0
..	1240	..	..	..	..	1 25	..	dep. ,, .. arr.	3 40	..	..	..	..	16 5	..	..	..
..	1440	..	..	..	..	3 35	156	arr. Gedser ....dep.	1 40	..	..	..	..	14 5	..	..	..
..	1735	..			..	6 48	262	arr. Copenhagen, p. 216 dp.	2245	..	..	..	..	1115	..	..	..

D—Corridor Exp., *see page* 75. **S** 1, 2 and 3 cl. Sleeping Cars Trelleborg–Oslo and Trelleborg–Stockholm and *v.v.* **X** 1 & 2 cl. Sleep. Car Hamburg–Oslo & *v.v.* **Z** 1 & 2 cl. Sleep. Car Hamburg–Copenhagen & *v.v.* ¶ 1, 2 and 3 cl. Cars Hamburg–Stockholm, Hamburg–Oslo and *v.v.* § 1, 2 and 3 cl. Cars Hamburg–Copenhagen and *v.v.* ‡ 1, 2 & 3cl. Hamburg–Sassnitz.

D-Corridor Exp. *r* Rest. Car.

(Amsterdam), Salzbergen, Osnabruck, Hanover.

S Slp. Cars to and from Berlin.
SS Slp. Cars to and from Leipsic.

	2 3 fast	1 2 FD	2 3	2 3	1 2 3 ExD	2 3	2 3	1 2 3 ExD	1 2 3 ExD
p. 159 { AMSTERDAM ..dep.		8 38	..	..	1129		..	2036	21 0
p. 159 { Rotterdam (M)	..	7†52		..	10†26	dep.	..	1956	2032
Salzbergen .... ,,	8 43	¶	1146	1336	..	1618	2044	S	..
Rheine............ arr.	8 51	..	1154	1343	1457	1627	2052	0 23	3 55
Osnabruck .... ,,	9 52	12 6	1258	1451	1540	1750	22 5	1 5	1 36
(ToHambg.p.161) dep	10 5	1211	1342	15 3	1546	18 9	2236	1 20	1 46
Löhne .... arr.	1048	..	1445	16 2	1626	1911	2338		SS
See below { Hanover.... ,,	1230	1332	..	1844	1738	2159	1 24	2 58	3 28
See below { BERLIN(Frfed) ,,	1613	1625	..		22 1	4 34	5 59	7 4	7 49

	1 2 3 ExD	1 2 3 ExD	2 3	2 3	2 3	1 2 3 ExD	2 3	2 3 fast	1 2 FD
See p.164 { BERLIN(Fried.) dep.	2250	..	0 13	..	..	8 56		1327	1357
See p.164 { Hanover ,,	2 26	2 45	4 36	6 55	10 8	1249	15 7	1728	1651
Löhne.......... ,,	S	SS	6 26	8 15	1121	14 9	1747	19 3	¶
Osnabruck .... arr.	4 10	4 23	7 22	9 16	12 2	1453	1856	1944	1811
Osnabruck .... dep.	4 44	5 15	7 48	9 51	1229	15 3	1927	1959	1819
Rheine .... arr.	5 20	6 0	8 56	1050	1329	1541	2027	2049	
Salzbergen ...... ,,	..	..	9 9	1111	1351	..	21 7	21 7	
p. 159 { Rotterdam (M.) ,,	1058	..				21†5			23†3
p. 159 { AMSTERDAM ,,	1019	..		..	..	2016			2217

† Rotterdam (D.P.)
* 1 and 2 cl. only.
‡ Not Sundays.

¶ From Hook to Berlin and *v.v.* daily, with 1 cl. Saloon Cars at EXTRA FARES.

Through Service, see pp. 128, 130, 132

Cologne, Oberhausen, Hanover (Leipsic, Dresden), Berlin.

[Ger. State Rys. (Essen and Hanover).

For service via Soest, see page 166.	luxe 1 2	Exp 2 3 D	Exp 1 2 3 D r	Rap 2 FDT	Exp 1 2 3 D	Rap 1 2 FD	Exp 1 2 3 D	Exp 1 2 3 D	Exp 1 2 3 D	Rap 1 2 FD	Exp 1 2 3 D	Exp 1 2 3
Cologne(Hauptbhf.) d.	1 48	..	6 48	7 0	..	From Hook of Holland.	9 22	1038	Fr. Aachen.	1122	1153	..
Dusseldorf(Hauptbhf) a.	via Wupperthal.	..	7 33	7 25	..		9 57	11 8		1151	1223	..
*From Aix-la-C.p.*165 d.		5 44	7 37	7 26	..		10 1	1111		1153	1226	From Holland to Leipsic.
Duisburg .... d		6 2	8 0	7 45	9 42		1025	1133	1150	1213	1250	
Essen .... a		6 22	8 28	7 59	10 7		..	..	1214	1230	13 8	
Dortmund (*v.* Essen) a.		6 55	9 4	8 22	1042				1248	13 2	1343	
Oberhausen ...... a			..	..			1034	1142		..	..	
*(from Holland, p.*157) d					..		1037	1143		..	..	
Dortmund ....dep.		6 56	9 7	8 23	1044		1135	1233	1252	13 3	1345	
Hamm, *p.* 175 .. arr.	3 32	7 17	9 30	8 40	11 6		1158	1255	1315	1324	14 7	
Hamm, *p.* 175 .. dep.	3 38	7 22	9 37	8 44	1113		12 6	13 2	1325	1328	1414	
Bielefeld................	Nord Exp.	8 18	1035	..	1159		1254	1347	↓	..	15 1	
Löhne		8 40	11 1	..	..					..	..	1627
Minden		9 2	1124		1240			1426			1541	1650
Hanover .... arr.	5 28	9 55	1230	10 3	1326	1332	14 8	1516	↓	1521	1628	1738
Magdeburg *p.* 168) ,,		1222	z	1130	1546	1546	1747	1747		↓	1830	2017
LEIPSIC .. (*p.* 168) ,,		1357	1712	1239	1720	1720	1931	1931			..	2223
DRESDEN H (*p.* 168) ,,		1555	1922	†	1922	1922	2119	2119				0 15
(From Bremen, p. 164*).*	luxe							2 3				
Hanover ....dep.	5 36	1014	1242	1010	..	1339	1416	1659	To Hamburg, arr. 17.37.	1528	1636	..
Lehrte	↓	1030	1259	↓	..	↓	To Warsaw.	1725			via Magdeburg to Potsdam Bhf.	z via Vienenburg.
Oebisfelde ....arr.		via Magdeburg. to Potsdam Bhf						1856				
Oebisfelde 2nd & 3rd cl. d.			f		..			1923				
Magdeburg 2nd & 3rd cl. a.			1521		..			21 3				
Oebisfelde ....dep.					..			1921				
Stendal (*p.* 169) .... arr.			1426	↓	..	↓		2038				
Berlin { Lehrter Sta. ,,	↓				..							
Berlin { Friedrichstr. ,,	8 33		1613	1225	..	1625	1740			1814		
Berlin { Schlesisch Sta.a.	8 45	1417	1627	1233		1637	1753			1827	2018	

	Exp 1 2 3 D r	Exp 1 2 3	Exp 1 2 3 D	fast 2 3	Rap 1 2 FD	Rap 1 2 FD	fast 2 3	Exp 1 2 3 D	Exp 2 3 D X	Exp 1 2 3 D S	Exp 1 2 3 D	Exp 1 2 3	Exp 1 2 3 D S
Cologne(Hauptbhf.) d.	1241	From Aachen	1455 via Wupperthal-Elberfeld.	1645		1657 via Wupperthal Elberfeld.	1825	Fr. Aachen.	2150	2217 via Wupperthal-Elberfeld.	From Amsterdam with Sleep Car to Berlin.	.. From Flushing. Sleep Car to Leipsic.	2247
Dusseldorf(Hauptbhf) a.	1312			1718			19 4		2220			..	2317
*From Aix-la-C.p.*165 d.	1315			1721			1918		2223				2321
Duisburg .... d	1339	1521		1742	1727		20 2	2250	2246				2350
Essen .... a		1548			1743		2031	2313	.				0 17
Dortmund (*v.* Essen) a.		1624			1814		2117	2346	.				0 59
Oberhausen ...... a	1349	..		1750					2254				
*(from Holland, p.*157) d	1351	..		1753					2256				
Dortmund ....dep.	1455	1626		1850	1815		2121	2349	2356				1 1
Hamm, *p.* 175 .. arr.	1520	1648	1655	1917	1836	1838	2158	0 12	0 18	0 30			1 26
Hamm, *p.* 175 .. dep.	1524	1655	17 2	1920		1845	22 3	0 22	0 25	0 37			1 33
Bielefeld................	1619	1744	1753	2018		..	2320		1 12	1 39			2 25
Löhne	1643	..		2042		.	2351				..		..
Minden	17 6			21 4			0 19	..	1 43	2 24		2 43	..
Hanover .... arr.	1758	1852	19 5	2159	..	2033	1 24		2 30	3 16	2 58	3 28	3 42
Magdeburg *p.* 168) ,,	2017	§..	..		From Paris-Aachen.	23§30		..	4 47	6 4	6 4	6 4	6 4
LEIPSIC .. (*p.* 168) ,,	2223		..	.		1 24	..	..	8 0	8 0	8 0	8 0	8 0
DRESDEN H (*p.* 168) ,,	0 15	§..	..			7 46		..	10 9	10 9	10 9	10 9	10 9
(From Bremen, p. 164*).*										1 2 3			
Hanover ....dep.	18 8	1859	1915	2314		2040	1 35	To Hamburg, arr. 5.44	2 38	3 30	3 15	..	4 0
Lehrte	1826	..		2335		↓	1 55		ViaMagdeburg, to Potsdam Bhf				
Oebisfelde ....arr.	1912			1 7			2 51						
Oebisfelde 2nd & 3rd cl. d.	1923		f	f			5 50				..		
Magdeburg 2nd & 3rd cl. a.	21 3	..	2149	4 0			7 21				..	..	
Oebisfelde ....dep.	1914	..		1 9			2 56				..	..	
Stendal (*p.* 169) .... arr.	20 4	2043	2053	2 13	..		3 47			5 24		..	5 56
Berlin { Lehrter Sta. ,,	r			..									
Berlin { Friedrichstr. ,,	22 1	2221	2238	4 34	..	2332	5 59		..	7 12	7 4	..	7 49
Berlin { Schlesisch Sta.a.	2215	2236	2252	4 49		2344	6 15		6 55	7 27	7 21		8 3

D—Corridor Express *see p.* 75. **FD** & **FDT** Special fast Expresses, extra fares, *see p.* 75. **S** 1 & 2 cl. Slp. Car, Cologne-Berlin, *see p.* 75. **X** 1, 2 and 3 cl. Slp. Car. § 2 & 3 cl. only. † Not Sundays. *f via* Stendal. *r* Rest Car.

The times on the LEFT are to be read DOWNWARDS, those on the RIGHT UPWARDS.

Berlin, (Dresden, Leipsic), Hanover, Oberhausen, Cologne.

(Ger. State R. s Hanov., Essen and Wupp.

For services via Soest, see 166.	fast		Rap	Exp	Exp	Exp	Exp	Exp	Exp	Exp	Rap	Rap	Exp	Rap	Exp	Rap	fast	luxe	Exp	Exp	Exp	Exp	Exp	fast
	2 3	2 3	1 2	1 2 3	1 2 3	1 2 3	1 2 3	1 2 3	1 2 3	1 2 3	1 2	1 2	1 2 3	2	2 3	2	2 3	1 2	1 2 3	1 2 3	1 2 3	1 2 3	2 3	2 3
			FD	D	D	D	D r	D	D	D	FD	FD	D	FDT W	D	FDT		N	D S	D	D	D	D X	
Berlin Schlesisch Sta. d	..	..	8 7	8 29	8 44	.	9 0	1041	..	1311	1343	1527	1545		1712	19 1	1915	2110	2213	2235	Slp. Car Leipsic-Amsterdam.	2315	2315	2356
Berlin Friedrichstr. „	..		8 24	8 44	8 56	..	9 14	1054	..	1327	1357	1540	Pot-damer Bhf. via Magdeburg		Potsdamer Bhf. via Magdeburg.	1912	1931	2120	2228	2250		2331	Potsdamer Bhf. via Magdeburg.	0 13
Berlin Lehrte Stat. „	..	4 56	↓		..	..	..	↓	..		.	..		..		↓	.	.	.			S		
Stendal (p. 169)	..	7 11		1023	1031	..	1057		..	1523	..	..		..			21 8	..	0 4			1 18		2 21
Oebisfelde ..... arr.	.	8 32			..	.	1142		..	1614		..		..			2153	.		..				3 12
Magdeburg 2 & 3 cl. d.		7 10		8 36	..	..	9 27		..	1329	..	..		..			..	..	2145			2338		1 18
Oebisfelde 2 & 3 cl. a.		8 32		f	.	..	1058		.	15 4	..	..		..			..		f			f		f
Oebisfelde .. dep.		8 39		..	..	..	1144		..	1615	..	..		..			2154	.	..			..		3 16
Lehrte (pp.		1012		..	..	..	1237		..	17 3	.			..	2051		2244	..			2 17		..	4 10
Hanover 168, 170) a.		1037	1113	12 0	1220	..	1255	14 3	..	1720	1644	1828	1926	..	21 7	2117	2259	0 11	1 38	2 13	2 34	2 56	3 30	4 26
			FDT				FDT										Exp 1 2 3							
DRESDEN H. (p.168) d.	..		6 56	4 41	..	6 12	6 56	..	8 42	..	1118	1118	..	.	1413	..	Fr. Hamburg, dep. 23.0.	..	..	..	2034	2034	2118	..
LEIPSIC .. (p. 168) „	..	5 58	8 32	7 45	..	8 37	8 32	..	1025	..	1312	1325	..	1746	1624	..		..	..	..	2238	2238	2325	..
Magdeburg (p. 168) „	..	7 46	9 48	9 20	..	z	9 48	..	1212	..	1442	15*30	1731	1855	1858	..		..	..	..	0 23	0 23	1 15	..
						1 2 3	1 2 3																	
Hanover ...... dep.	6 55	10 8	1123	12 8	1235	1249	13 3	1411	1431	1728	1651	1835	1936	2032	2123	2119		0 25	1 47	2 26	2 45	3 7	3 45	4 36
Minden	7 44	1058	..	..	..	1345	1359	..	1526	1828	..		2016		2214			..	2 37	..	3 31	..	..	5 38
Löhne	8 5	1118	..	..	..	14 9	1422			1854		..			2238	.		..	.	..	To Holland.	..	..	6 6
Bielefeld	8 31	1141	..	1334	1353	..	1450	1528	1610	1923		1942	21 0	2124	23 6			..	3 17			4 29	5 3	6 37
Hamm, p.175 arr.	9 23	1231	1312	1421	1443	To Amsterdam.	1543	1619	17 0	2015	Hook of Holland	2025	2146	2154	2356	2239	3 55	2 14	4 9	To Amsterdam and Flushing.		5 19	5 58	7 47
Hamm dep.	9 30	1259	1320	1428	1451		1550	1626	17 7	2017		2029	2158	2155	0 3	2240	4 15	2 18	4 28			5 27	6 13	7 54
Dortmund ...... arr.	9 52	via Wupperthal	via Wupperthal. Elberfeld.	via Wupperthal-Elberfeld.	1514		1614	1650	1729	2041		2049	2221	Via Hagen.	0 23	2257	via Hagen.	via Wupperthal	via Hagen.			5 51	6 35	8 30
Oberhausen .. a.	1041				16 6		.	1746	..	2148		..	..		..	..						..	7 31	..
(To Holland, p.157 d.	1042				16 9		..	1751	..	2150		..			..							..	7 32	..
Dortmund (v. Es'n) d.	..				..		1616	..	1731	..		2050	2223		0 25	2258					..	5 54	..	8 34
Essen	.				.		1649	..	18 3	..		2119	2255		0 57	2321					..	6 28	..	9 15
Duisburg	1052				1622		1712	18 2	1827	22 1		2136	2314		1 17	2337				..	.	6 53	7 45	9 42
Düsseldorf (Hauptbhf) arr.	11 9				To Aachen.		1733	1823	1845	2220		2152	2333		1 36	2350				..	..	7 14	8 3	10 4
Düsseldorf (Hauptbhf) dep.	1111						1737	1826	1849	2223		2154	2335		..	2351				..	..	7 19	8 7	10 8
Cologne (Hpt.) arr.	1148	1526	1453	1628			1821	19 1	1922	23 4		2228	0 12	2328		0 17	6 20	4 3	6 50	.	..	7 55	8 45	1046

* *Via* Hildesheim. ("D" train from Magdeburg to Hildesheim).

f *Via* Stendal.

FD and **FDT** Special fast Corridor Exp., *see p.* 75.

D Corridor Exp. *see page* 75.

S Sleeping Car., Berlin-Cologne *see p.* 75.

X 1, 2 and 3 cl. Sleep. Car.

r Rest. Car.

‡ Not Sundays.

§ 2 & 3 cl. only.

z *Via* Vienenb'rg

Bremerhaven, Bremen, Hanover.

(German State Rys. (Hanover)

2 3	1 2 3	1 2 3	1 2 3	1 2 3	2 3	2 3	2	1 2 3	2 3	2 3	1 2 3		1 2 3	1 2 3	2 3	2 3	2 3	2	2 3	2 3	1 2 3	2 3	1 2 3	2 3	1 2 3
fast	ExD		ExD	ExD	fast	fast	FDT	ExD	fast		ExD		ExD	Ex D	fast		fast	FDT	fast		ExD		Ex D		Ex D
6 23	7 21	7§36	10 2	1230	1457	16 7	1743	1810	2052	23 0	.	dep. Bremerhaven .. arr.	S	8 26	1033	1345	1250	1257	1451	1846	17 3	2056	2012	2125	2310
7 11	8 1	8§9	1048	1311	1546	17 1	1825	19 6	2145	2355	..	arr. Bremen .. dep.		7 44	9 37	1225	1157	1221	14 3	1726	1613	1933	1928	2036	2227
..	5 48	7 35	9§5	1120	1346		W	1736	1955	⌣	2215	dep. Wilhelmshaven arr.	7 38	9 10	1121	..	..	W	1554	..	1810	..	2216	2216	1 1
7 19	8 10	9 15	1056	1321	16 2	1714	1832	1919	2156	..	0 2	dep. Bremen .... arr.	5 22	7 33	9 31	1126	1152	1219	1353	1650	16 7	1845	1920	2020	2212
8 54	9 39	1043	1236	1457	1745	19 0	1930	2054	2338	..	1 57	arr. Hanover .... dep.	3 36	6 1	7 54	8 37	1013	1120	1215	1345	1437	1548	1748	1850	2045
‡	‡		D	FD	D	D						(See pp. 163, 164).		2 3					Ex D	Ex D		ExD	FD	FD	‡
1417	1417	..	1613	1814	22 1	2238	2332	4 34	5 59		6‡55	arr. Berlin (Friedr.) dep.	2351	0 13	..	..		8 24	8 44	9 14	1054	1054	1357	1540	1545
1536	1536		1822	2211	2340	2340	2340	5 19	5 19	..	9 0	ar. Frankfort (p 170) dp.	21 0	0 30	..	..	..	..	8 10	8 10	8 14	8 14	12 7	1224	1457
					FDT	FDT													FDT	FDT				‖	‖

* Lehrter Station.

‖ *Via* Bebra.

§ 2 and 3 cl. only.

S Slp. car Bremen-Berlin and *vice versa.*

‡ Berlin-Potsdam

W Weekdays only.

The times on the LEFT are to be read DOWNWARDS, those on the RIGHT UPWARDS.

Aachen, Düsseldorf (Cologne), Elberfeld, Soest, Cassel, Bebra.

[Ger. St. Rys. (Wupperthal, and Cassel)

	2 3	1 2 3	1 2 3	1 2 3	2 3	1 2 3	2 3	2 3	1 2 3	2 3	1 2	1 2	2 3	1 2 3	1 2 3	1 2 3	2 3	2 3	2 3
	fast	ExD	D	Exp D	fast	D	ExD	Exp D	Exp D	fast	F D	F D	fast	Exp D	Exp D	Exp D	Exp D	Ex D	
		To Leipsic.		A; To Berlin (see page 166).		Rest. Car; To Altona.		To Leipsic	To Berlin. (see page 163).		To Berlin. (see page 163).	Paris-Berlin.		From Munich	To Altona Sleeping Car.	B; To Berlin.	C		
Aachen Hpt.d.	4 27		6 25		7 42		1039			1452	..	16 3	1640					2131	2154
Aachen West.	4 32		6 30	..	7 47		7 15		..	1457	..	..	1645		..	..	..		2159
p.153 Antwerp	..		..	..	..		..		..	.	..	..	8 24		..	..	..	19 0	
M. Gladbach dep.	5 57		7 26	..	9 5		1142		..	1552	..	1648	1745		..	..	..	2235	2331
Neuss	6 25		7 42	..	9 20		1156		..	16 5	..		1759		..		..	2255	2355
Dusseldorf (Haupt.) ar.	6 37		7 53		9 32		12 7		..	1617	..		1811		..			23 6	0 8
Dusseldorf (Haupt.) dp.	7 3	..	8 2		9 46		1210		..	1620	..		1820		..	..	..	2314	0 24
Vohwinkel .. arr.	7 27		R		1010		..		..	1645	..		1846		..	..	..	2339	0 46
Cologne(H) d.	6 45	7 33	..	8 32	9 34	1113	1210	1412	1455	1611	1657	..	1825	18‡55	22 7	2217	2248	..	0 8
Vohwinkel arr.	7 37	..	..		1017	..		..	..	1653	..		19 5	..	..	..	..	..	..
Vohwinkel .. dep.	7 38	..	.	..	1018	.	..	..	.	1654	..		19 6		..	..	..	2340	0 48
Wupperthal-Elberfeld .. a.	7 45	8 17	8 37	9 15	1025	1156	1251	1454	1537	17 0	1735		1913	1950	2251	23 0	2332	2346	0 55
Wupperthal-Elberfeld .. d.	7 56	8 25	8 39	9 17	1034	1158	1257	1457	1540	17 4	1741		1917	1952	2255	23 6	2336	2348	0 57
Wup't'l-Barmen	8 2	8 31	8 46	9 24	1040	12 5	..	15 5	1548	17 9	..		1923	1959	23 4	2315	2343	2353	1 2
Oberbarmen	8 8				1046	..		..	..	1714	..		1929	..	..	..	..	2356	..
Hagen .... arr.	8 30	8 54	9 10	9 48	11 6	1230	1321	1528	1610	1736	18 2		1951	2023	2328	2337	0 7	0 36	..
Hagen .... dep.	8 36		9 17	9 51	1117	1233			1614	1742	18 3		2027		2333	2343	0 12	..	..
Schwerte	8 50			..	1130				..	1754			2038			2358	..	..	..
Hamm .... arr.	9 25			..	12 1	1315			1655	1828	1838	1836	21 9		0 16	0 30	..		..
Soest (p.16) a.		↓	10 3	1036	13 6	..	↓	↓	..	19 4			..	2 3	..	..	1 0	2 3	..
Hagen .... dep.	..	8 57	..	..	1128	..	1324	1532		1810		..	2010	21 3				4 45	
Schwerte	..	9 10	..		1148	..	..	1546		1829		..	2024	2115				5 6	..
Bestwig .... arr.	..	1014	..		1336		..	1658		20 6		..	22 2	2216			↓	6 53	..
Soest .... dep.	..	..	10 5		1415		..	16 9		2132		..	..	2132			1 13	5 56	..
Altenbeken ,,	..	..	1112		1541		..	1724		2242		..	..	2242			2 18	8 12	..
Warburg .... arr.	..	1115	1146		1559		..	18 0		2321		..	..	2321			2 50	9 7	..
Cassel .... ,,	..	12 7	1237		1736		1613	1852		0 13		..	..	0 13			3 41	1025	..
Cassel .. dep.	..	1215	1250		19 0	..	1623	19 0		0 20		..	..	0 20			3 48	1039	..
Bebra .... arr.	..	13 8	1343	..	1951	..	17 9	1951		1 43		..	..	1 43			4 39	1135	..

(From Leipsic, see p. 173.)	1 2 3	1 2 3	2 3	1 2 3	2 3	2 3	1 2	2 3	1 2 3	2 3	2 3	2 3	2 3	2 3	1 2 3	1 2 3	1 2 3
	Exp D	Exp D	ExD	Exp D	fast	Exp D		fast	Exp D	fast	D	fast		Ex D	ExD	Exp D	ExD
	From Hamburg with Sleep Car.	From Berlin Sleep. Car.				From Altona.	From Berlin (see page 164).		From Berlin (see page 164.)						From Hamburg	A	
Bebra .... dep.			2 38		5 29			..		8 19	12 4	..	10 3	16 6			1655
Cassel .. arr.		..	3 27	..	6 58	..		..		9 16	1251	..	1056	1655		..	1745
Cassel .... dep.			3 34	..	7 41			..		9 25	1258	..	1130	17 2		..	1752
Warburg .. ,,			4 21	..	8 31			..		1051	1346	..	13 2	1749		..	1840
Altenbeken arr.			4 57	..	9 3			..		1048	1456	..	1339	..			1917
Soest .... ,,			6 5	..	10 7			..		1153	1625	..	1528	..		..	2023
Bestwig .... dep.			↓	..	9 42			1042		1240	1458	..	1517	1854		↓	↓
Schwerte .. arr.				..	1043			1220		1417	16 4	..	1713	1951			
Hagen .... ,,		..		..	1056	..		1239		1439	1617	..	1744	20 5			
Soest .... dep.	..	..	6 21	..	9 49	..	F D	1218	..	↓	↓	..	1629	↓	..	20 9	2025
Hamm .... ,,	4 15	4 28	..	8 0	1022	1223	1320	1259	1428			..	1721		19 9	..	..
Schwerte	..	5 1	7 1	8 27	1052	..	.	1332	..			1721	18 1		1938	..	21 1
Hagen .... arr.	4 53	5 14	7 15	8 40	11 5	13 2	1354	1346	15 7	↓	↓	1734	1815	↓	1951	2056	2114
Hagen .... dep.	4 57	5 21	7 21	8 46	11 8	13 5	1355	14 1	1512	1525	1623	1744	1823	20 7	1954	21 0	2118
Oberbarmen ..	..	..	..	..	1128	..	..	1425	..	1544	..	1811	1844		2018	.	2145
Wup't'l-Barmen	5 26	5 50	7 47	9 12	1132	1333	..	1430	1538	1548	1649	1817	1848	2032	..	2128	..
Wupperthal-Elberfeld .. a.	5 31	5 56	7 52	9 17	1136	1339	1415	1434	1543	1552	1654	1822	1852	2037	2024	2134	2151
Wupperthal-Elberfeld .. d.	5 34	6 1	7 56	9 19	1139	1341	1419	1438	1546	1555	1658	1828	1854	2040	2027	2137	2154
Vohwinkel .. arr.	..	..	..	..	1146	..	..	1444	..	16 1	..	1836	19 0	..	..	..	..
Vohwinkel dep.			..	..	1147	..	..	1445	..	..	.	19 7	19 7		..	..	..
Cologne(H) a.	6 20	6 50	8 40	10‡18	1229	1422	1453	1526	1628	..	1741	1947	1947	2123	21 9	2220	..
Vohwinkel .. dep.	(see page 164)	6†51	..	To Munich.	..	..	..	1454	..	16 2	..	1837	19 1	..	..		..
Dusseldorf (Haupt.) a.		7 9	..		..	..	..	1512	..	1619	..	1857	1920	..	2110		2222
Dusseldorf (Haupt.) d.		7 22	BC		..	..	..	1516	..	1621	..	1911	20 8	..	2112		2228
Neuss .... arr.		7 33			..	..	..	1528	..	1632	..	1924	2021	..	2123	From Berlin.	2239
M.Gladbach arr.		7 47	..		..	..	15 2	1542	..	1645	..	1949	2042	..	2137		2253
p.153 Antwerp a.		1125	..		..	..	..	..	..	2211	..	..	..	..	..		R
Aachen West.		9 4	..		..	..	.	1646	..	1759		2115	2216	..	2239		2347
Aachen Hpt. a.		9†10	..		..	..	1550	1653	.	18 5		2121	2221	..	2245		2354

R Rest. Car Berlin Dusseldorf and v.v. † 2 and 3 cl. only.

A Rest. Car Cologne-Berlin and v.v. B Sleep Car Cologne-Berlin, Cologne-Dresden and v.v. (see page 163). C Sleep Car Cologne-Eger-Marienbad and v.v. ‡ Cologne, Deutz Station.

Cologne Giessen Gr.St.Ry. Frankf't

Cologne (H) dp.	7 45	8 24	9 28	12 1	1435	18 0	2145
Troisdorf dp.	8 2	8 42	10 3	1219	1515	1820	22 3
Betzdorf dep.	8 58	9 54	1146	1323	1656	1925	23 7
Giessen .. arr.	1024	12 7	1522	1522	1934	2132	.
Cassel .. arr.	1318	1456	1729	1729	23 5	0 3	

Cassel dep.		5 55	7 41	1010	1259	1549	..
Giessen dep.		8 43	1033	1247	1517	1822	
Betzdorf dep	6 40	1036	13 9	1419	1716	2028	2140
Troisdorf ar.	7 44	1141	1447	1512	1816	2131	2310
Cologne(H) ar.	8 1	1158	1522	1529	1833	2149	2343

Aachen, Cologne, &c., Kreiensen, Brunswick, Magdeburg (Berlin) [German St. Rlys.]

2 3	1 2 3	1 2 3	2 3	2 3	2 3	1 2 3	1 2 3	2 3	R Rest. Car.	1 2 3	2 3	2 3	2 3	1 2 3	1 2 3	1 2 3	2 3	1 2 3
ExD	ExD	ExD		fast	ExD	ExD	ExD	r xD		ExD		ExD	fast	ExD	ExD	Exp	ExD	ExD
	..	6 25	..	9 36	1244		1252	2134	d. Aachen ... (H) ar (p. 165)	19 3	2022		2121	19 2	2354	2354	9 49	
	..	8 2		1139	1210	r	14 0	2238	,, Dusseldorf .. arr.	1729	1834	..	1857	17 6	2222	2222	..	
From Frankfort.	8 32	..	11 1	1113	1356	From Frankfort	1412	2248	,, Cologne ,,	1741	1853	r	1947	155	..	2220	8 40	To Frankfort.
	1038	Z	1450	1415	16 9		Z	1 13	,, Soest ...... ,,	Z	1528	1359	1625	1535	Z	20 7	6 5	
	1148		1659	1540	1717			2 18	Altenbeken ..		1345	1256	15 5	1432		19 3	5 0	
		1228	1759	1635	..			C	arr. Holzminden dp.		1225	1158	1355		18 5		C	
		1231	18 2	1640	.				dep. Holzminden ar.		1218	1157	1352		18 1			
3 0	via Hildesheim arr. 13.25.	13 9	1855	1735		1915	via Cassel, arr 18.52 and Bebra.	via Cassel, arr. 3.41 and Bebra.	ar. Kreiensen dp.	via Bebra and Cassel, dep. 12.58.	1125	1117	1257	via Hildesheim dep. 12.53	1721			3 48
3 6		1318	1938	1743	via Hildesheim arr. 18 54	1917			dp. Kreiensen (Frnk, p.170) ar.		1053	11 8	1249		1712	via Hildesheim. dep. 17.16.	via Bebra and Cassel, dep 3.34.	3 40
		1339	20 4	18 6		1937			arr. Seesen .... dep.		1027	1050	1227		1655			
		1340	20 9	18 7		↓			dep. Seesen .... arr.		1020	↑	1225		1654			
3 52		14 5	2040	1833					ar. Goslar (see below) dp.		9 53		1159		1632			3 5
3 54		14 7	2045	1837					dp Goslar ar.		9 23		1154		1630			3 2
4 35		1456	2148	1926					arr. Halberstadt dp.		8 5		1042		1534			2 12
7 25		1638	..	2144					,, Halle .. dep.		6 21		7 57	↑	1358	↑		
7 59		1712	..	2226		↓	2314	8 9	,, Leipsic ,,	8 36	5 20		7 2		1325		2258	
4 40	..	15 3		1933				..	dep. Halberstadt arr.		7 55		1032		1527			2 7
4 55	..	1519		1952		..			arr. Oschersleben d.	..	7 34	..	1011		1510	..		1 51
↓	..	↓	2014	↓	↓	1938		..	dep. Seesen .... arr.		1025	1049	↑		↑	..		↑
	..		21 4			20 9	..	..	arr. Börssum .... dep.		9 31	1018				..		
	1410		2136		1927	2045	..	..	,, Brunswick d.	..	9 1	9 46		1220		1635	..	
	..		2133		..			..	,, Jerxheim .. dep.	..	7 40	..				..	..	
4 57	..	1520	e	1954	..	..			dep. Oschersleben arr.		7 33		1010		15 8	..	..	1 50
5 27	1518	1553	2330	2030	2031	2112		..	ar. Magdeburg dp.		6 51	9 17	9 31	1118	1441	1530	..	1 22
7 17	17 2	1751	..	2234	22 9	2251		..	ar. Berlin (p.168) dp.	..		7 43	7 10	9 42	1250	1350	..	2342

C Sleep. Car Cologne-Eger-Marienbad, and *v.v.* — *e via* Eilsleben. — *r* Rest. Car. — **Z** *via* Hagen and Schwerte. — *v via* Vienenburg.

Cologne, &c., Hildesheim, Brunswick (Berlin), Halle, &c. [Ger. State Rys., Elber Cassel, Han]

	2 3	2 3	2 3	1 2 3	2 3	1 2 3	2 3	2 3		2 3	2 3	1 2 3	1 2 3	2 3	2 3	2 3	2 3
				D		D		Ex		fast		ExD	D			Ex	fast
Dining car Cologne Berlin	..	..	..	8 2	..	14 0	1519	From Hanover 2.38.	dp. Düsseldorf (p. 165) ar	1410	1857	1746	2222	1 47	..	To Hanover arr. 3.30.	D Corridor Exp. (see page 75).
	..	..		8 32		1356	1455		,, Cologne ,,	1422	1947	1755	2220	..	..		
		..	7 56	1038	1154	16 9	1759		,, Soest ...... ,,	1153	1625	1535	20 7	2258			
		7 3	9 17	1148	1346	1717	1928		,, Altenbeken .. ,,	1028	15 0	1431	19 0	2042	arr.		
		7 58	10 7	1222	1442	1753	20 8		Pyrmont	9 15	14 7	1350	1817	1938	2334		
	..	8 25	1030	1239	15 9	18 9	2024		arr. Hameln ... dep.	8 42	1341	1333	1758	1911	2258		
	..	9 33	1035	1240	1520	1810	21 7		dep. Hameln .... arr.	8 26	1312	1332	1756	1854	2136		
	..	1019	12 0	1325	1641	1854	2227		arr. Hildesheim dp.	7 0	1225	1253	1716	1738	2052		
		1020		1336	1726	1856	2240	3 9	dep. Hildesheim arr	6 35	1159	1252	17 5	..	2048	2 58	
		1051	..	1410	1835	1927	2341	3 41	arr. Brunswick d.	5 35	11 1	1220	1635	..	2015	2 26	
		1222		1518	2017	2031	..	4 47	,, Magdeburg ,,	..	9 20	1118	1530		1858	1 15	
		1417	..	17 2	2234	22 9	..	6 55	,, Berlin .. ,,	..	7 10	9 42	1350		1712	2315	
						1 2 3 D		2 3									
† Not Sundays.	6 28	9 44	1140	1248	1623	18 8	22 5		dep. Hanover .... arr	7 42	1153	1237	1740	1822	2054		2339
	7 3	1023	1222	1337	1720	1859	23 0		,, Hildesheim ,,	6 40	1047	12 3	17 4	1650	20 8		23 6
	7 49	1111	1334	1424	1831	1945	0 11	—	a. Goslar (p.167) d.	5 30	9 30	1121	1623	1532	19 3		2225
	7 52	1114	1437	1427	1843	1949	0 19	5 38	d. Goslar a.		9 23	1113	1619	1522	1857		2222
	8 41	1158	1611	1511	2024	2035	1 33	6 56	arr. Halberstadt .. ,,		8 5	1022	1529	14 9	1723		2128
	1014	1322	1922	1638	..	2151		9 36	,, Halle ...... ,,		6 21	8 56	1358	1121	1333		20 0
	1052	1357	2011	1712	..	2226		1038	,, Leipsic .... ,,		5 20	8 22	1325	1025	1230		1923
	1312	1555	2211	1922		15		1312	,, Dresden (p168) d.			6 12	1118	8 42	1013		1744

Magdeburg, Zerbst (Leipsic), Dresden. [Ger. St. Rys. and Halle.

s Sleeping Car Altona-Leipsic & *v.v.*

2 3	2 3	2 3	2 3	2 3	2 3	1 2 3	2 3	2 3		2 3	2 3	2 3	2 3	2 3	2 3	2 3	2 3	2 3
4 10	6 16	7 45	8 32	1056	13 9	1758	2046	2343	dep. Magdeburg .. arr.	8 11	1020	1427	1510	17 7	2013	2115	2311	1 9
s	7 9	..	9 4		1338	..		.	Gutergluck	7 25	9 52	1343		..	1912		2240	s
4 45	7 20	8 20	9 12	1125	1346		2121	0 20	Zerbst	7 14	9 44	1332	1436	1630	19 0	2042	2231	0 34
4 59	7 37	8 36	9 26	1137	1358	..	2133	0 30	Rosslau (p. 171)	6 57	9 33	1314	1425	1619	1843	2130	2220	0 22
5 27	8 29	9 4	10 5	12 4	1426	19 1	2154	1 3	arr. Bitterfeld dep.	5 56	9 5	12 4	1357	1551	1723	20 1	2126	2353
5 59	9 24	9 35	1046	1236	1457	1931	2247	1 32	,, Leipsic (Ht.) ,,	5 23	8 37	1120	1330	1514	1631	1932	2057	2325
5 54	8 42	8 42	9 39	1140	14 8	..	..		dep. Rosslau .. arr.	6 52	9 18	1234		1550	1819	2024	22 0	† Not Sundays
5 58	9 10	9 10	1020	1258	1514		.	..	Wittenberg	5 58	8 47	1150		15 1	1737	1940	2132	
7 56	9 54	9 54	1113	1352	1612	..	..	..	arr. Falkenberg dep.	4 49	6 39	9 53		14 3	1626	1826	2047	
10 9	1225	1225	1225	17 0			..		,, Dresden (p.195) ,,	..		7 8		1118		1558	1912	

Goslar (Brunswick)—Halberstadt—Frose. [Ger. St. Rlys. Hanover

Ex D	2 3	2 3	2 3	2 3	Ex D	Ex D	2 3	Ex D		2 3	Ex D	2 3	2 3	Ex D	2 3	2 3	2 3	2 3
3 54	7 52	8 37	1114	1234	14 7	1427	1837	1949	dep. Goslar (p. 166) a.	9 23	1113	1227	1522	1619	1857	1958	2021	2222
↓	7 18	8 0	1049	1149	..	1338	1757	19 0	dp. Brunswick p.168 a	9 46	1136	..	1558	1724	19 1	2041	2045	2256
	8 7	9 0	1135	1254	..	1443	1847	20 6	dep. Vienenburg arr.	8 56	1051	..	1457	1629	..	..	1938	22 0
	8 21	9 14	1147	13 8	..	1457	1858	2018	arr. Harzburg dep.	8 48	1043	12 6	1449	1620	1838	..	1930	2152
	8 5	9 1	1126	1253	1419	1440	1852	20 3	dep Vienenburg arr	8 54	1053	..	1458	1559	..	1941	1954	22 3
	8 26	9 28	..	1326	1441	..	1912	..	arr. Heudeber ..dep.	8 25	..	11 8	1429	..	1741	1920	19 9	2143
4 35	8 41	9 45	1158	1340	1456	1511	1926	2035	arr. Halberstadt dep	8 5	1022	1052	14 9	1529	1723	19 6	1849	2128
5†15	9 32	1115	1228	1423		16 6	20 9	2133	„ Quedlinburg „	7†8	9 34	1024	1331	1428	1629	..	18 0	2052
5†35	9 46	1134	1244	1440	..	1630	2024	2148	„ Thale.... „	6†54	9 18	1010	1314	1414	1614	..	1742	2033
5 8	8 56	9 57	..	14 0	..	..	1942	..	arr. Wegeleben .dep.	7 47	..	1029	1352	..	1616	1851	1825	2115
5 34	..	1023	1219	1426	..	..	20 7	..	arr. Frose ...dep.	7 32	..	10 3	1326	..	1550	..	1759	..
5 43	9 17	1031	1227	1435	..	1545	2016	21 4	„ Aschersleben „	7 21	9 49	9 55	1318	1452	1542	1832	1750	2053
7 25	1014	12 0	1322	1618	..	1638	2144	2151	„ Halle .... „	6 21	8 56	7 56	1121	1358	1333	1742	1613	20 0

Goslar—Harzburg—Halberstadt.

2nd and 3rd cl. only.

5 55	9 4	1015	13 3	1524	1655	1843	1955	2054	de. Goslar arr.	9 43	11 5	1227	1453	1558	1741	1857	2121	2328
14	9 23	1033	1523	1540	1715	19 3	2011	2116	arr. Ha..burg dep.	9 27	1046	12 6	1436	1541	1719	1837	21 2	23 5
6 57	10 5	1114	14 5	1618	1759	1949	2058	2155	arr. Wernigerode dep	8 48	10 6	1124	1357	15 0	1625	1757	2020	2219
7 31	1039	1150	1439	1655	1832	2024	2136	2231	ar. Halberstadt (ab.) d	8 13	9 34	1052	1322	1426	1550	1723	1948	2135

Wernigerode—Brocken—Nordhausen.

All 2nd & 3rd cl. | Hanover Rly.

7 32	7 55	9 15	1150	1222	1418	1633	1816	2025	a. Wernigerode (abv) a	6 52	9 48	1112	1344	1550	1750	1844	1940
7 47	8 10	9 33	12 5	1237	1433	1647	1833	2041	d. Hasserode Bhf. d	6 37	9 34	1059	1330	1536	1736	1831	1927
8 11	8 35	9 57	1230	13 2	1458	1711	1858	21 0	a. Dreiannen Hohne d	6 16	9 11	1036	13 6	1512	1712	18 5	19 2
8c34	8 58	1021	..	1326	15d8	..	b	2125	a Schierke ...... d	5 55		1020	1246	14d52	1654	1750	
9c12	9 34	1058	..	14 4	16d0	..		..	a. Brocken d	..		9 42	12 7	14d14	1615	1710	
8 17		10 2	1236	..	15 7	1718	19 1	..	d. Dreiannen Hohne a	..	9 10		1258	15 4	..		19 0
8 45	a	1030	13 6	..	1535	1752	1928	..	a. Sorge (below) .. d	..	8 46	a	1227	1437	..	d	1830
9 31		11 0	1352	..	1615	1846	20 3	..	a. Elsfeldr-Talmühl d	..	8 6		1146	1358	..		1750
1013	..	115	1438	..	1653	1930	2050	..	a Nordhausen (p.171) d	..	7 28	..	11 0	1315	..		17 5

a Suns. May 28 to Sept. 10. *b* Suns. to Sept. 10. *c* July 1 to Aug. 31. *d* May 27 to Aug. 31.

Halberstadt—Blankenburg—Tanne.

† Not sundays. § Only 3 cl. | Hanover Rly.

3 cl.	2 3	2 3	2 3	2 3	2 3	2 3	2 3	2 3		2 3	2 3	2 3	2 3	2 3	2 3	2 3	2 3
	8 8	1051	1325	14 5	1535	1725	1948	2155	d. Halberstadt (abv) a.	6 50	8 41	1015	1315	1453	1650	1920	2120
	8 38	1120	14 5	1435	16 6	1756	2016	2225	a. Blankenburg d.	6 20	8 4	9 45	1245	1421	1620	1850	2050
	7 35	10†38	..	1329	..	1754	1955		d. Quedlinburg a.	7 25	..	1036	1320	†	1746	1944	..
	8 2	11 2	..	1359	†	1822	2024		d. Thale (above) a.	6 55	..	1010	1251	15 4	1712	1916	..
	8 22	1123	..	1420	..	1843	2045	..	a. Blankenburg d.	6 35	..	9†50	1232	1440	1650	1855	..
6 45	8 42	1125	..	1440	1611	..	2047	..	d. Blankenburg a.	6†15	..	9 40	1227	1416	1610	1847	2046
7 30	9 22	12 6	1426	1519	1652	..	2125	..	a Rübeland d.	5†34	..	9 0	1144	1335	1531	1758	20 4
7 40	9 32	1225	1437	..	1716	..	2131		a. Elbingerode W. d.	..	..	8 48	1117	1324	1521	1744	1954
	9 47	..	1450	..	1713	..	..	..	a. Dreiannen Hohne d.	..	..	..	11 5	13 8	1511	1732	1934
7 41	..	1226	..	..	1722	..			d. Elbingerode W... a.	..	..	8 46	..	1323	..	..	1952
8 7		1249	..	..	1749	..	..	..	a. Tanne d	..	..	8 21		1255	..	..	1925

Tanne—Braunlage.

† Only Sun., Tue. Fri. [Sud Harz Rly. All 2 and 3 cl.

			8†14	..	..	13 0	..	1817	d. Tanne a.	8†10	..	..	1234	..	18 8
			8 23	8 49	1034	1313	1538	1829	d. Sorge (abv.) d.	8 2	8 44	1028	1225	1433	1755
			..	9 10	1055	1334	1559	1850	a. Braunlage d.	7†40	8 23	10 7	12 1	1412	1735

Frose—Quedlinburg—Nordhausen.

[Ger. State Rlys.

2 3	2 3	2 3	2 3	2 3	2 3	2 3	2 3	2 3	¶ Weekdays only.	2 3	2 3	2 3	2 3	2 3	2 3	2 3	2 3	2 3
6 24	7 32	1027	1152	1322	1514	17 1	19 4	2138	dep Frose .... arr.	7 30	9 46	12 7	1422	1524	1725	1854	20 3	2235
6 50	8 0	1048	1219	1348	1538	1723	1929	2210	dep. Ballenstedt E. ar.	7 4	9 22	1144	14 1	1459	1659	1832	1941	2216
7 8	8 14	11 0	1233	14 4	1551	1735	1944	2229	arr. Gernrode .dep.	6 44	9 4	1132	1345	1444	1644	1816	1928	2153
7 25	8 30	1115	1247	1419	16 8	1749	20 3	2243	arr. Quedlinburg dep.	6¶25	8 47	1120	1330	1431	1631	1758	1916	2140
8 40	9 9	1140	1311	1410	1559	1830	1949	..	dep. Gernrode .. arr.	..	8 52	1050	1339	..	1549	18 3	1915	2027
8 50	9 50	1228	1341	1452	1642	1914	2021	..	arr. Alexisbad ..dep.	..	8 5	1018	1256	..	1 17	1717	1842	1943
8 51	9 58	1231	1342	1455	1648	1925	2022	..	dep. Alexisbad arr.	..	7 59	1017	1254	..	1516	1714	1841	..
9 2	10 7	1240	1353	15 4	1657	1937	2033	..	arr. Harzgerode dp	..	7 50	10 5	1245	..	15 5	17 5	1830	..
..	9 54	..	..	..	17 0	1926	..	..	dep. Alexisbad arr.	arr.	7 51	..	..	..	1515	1644	..	1026
..	1043	..	..	..	1758	202	..	..	arr. Stiege dep.	8 36	6 44	..	..	..	1418	1546	..	1837
..	1115	..	..	..	1819	2046	..	..	arr Hasselfelde dep.	¶	6 24	..	..	..	..	1511	..	1822
..	11 9	..	..	..	1833	..	..	..	a. Elsfeldr-Talmül. d	8 10	..	..	..	..	1356	..	..	1746
..	1150	..	..	..	1930	..	..	..	a. Nordhausen (p.171) d	..	..	..	..	..	1315	..	..	17 5

Nordhausen—Herzberg.

† Weekdays only. Cassel & Sud. Harz. Rlys.

23	23	23	23	23	23	23	23	23		23	23	23	23	23	23	23	23	23
6 30	7 20	8 34	9 26	1316	1555	1740	1934	2237	d Nordhausen p.171a	6 39	1026	1327	1421	1552	1650	1716	1945	21 4
6 56	7 40	9 9	9 57	1338	1615	18 5	1958	23 4	arr. Walkenried dep.	6 11	9 58	1258	14 0	1524	1629	1649	1919	2037
7 1	..	10 6	10 6	14 6	17 6	..	2040	..	dep. Walkenried arr.	6 5	9 28	1245	1345	..	16 9	16 9	..	1951
8 1	..	11 9	11 9	15 6	18 9		2140	..	arr. Brauniage dep.	5 5	8 23	1145	1245	..	1515	1515		1852
6 57	7 41	9 10	9 58	1339	1617	18 6	1959	23 5	dep. Walkenried arr.	6 9	9 55	1257	1359	1523	1628	1648	1918	2036
7 31	8 5	9 46	1031	14 2	1641	1834	2024	2334	arr. Herzberg p. 170d	5 36	9 23	1217	1336	1445	16 3	1616	1851	20 2

Hanover. Brunswick, Magdeburg, Leipsic, Dresden.

For service via Oebisfelde p. 1?3. *From Cologne, &c., see p. 163.*

[Ger. Stat. Rlys. Hanover and Dresden.

§ 2 & 3 cl. only. † via Hildesheim,	23 D	123 D a Exp	23 fast	23 —	2cl. FDT Rap	123 — Exp	23 D Exp	23 fast	123 D Exp	123 D Exp	123 D Exp	123 D Exp	123 D	123 D Exp	23 — fast	2 FDT Rap	123 D Exp	23 —
Hanover ....dep.	2 38	3 47	6 16	7 39	10 6	From Hamb'rg p. 169.	1014	..	1248	1248	1350	1535	1636	1718	18 3	1933	1915	2123
Lehrte		4 4	6 32	8 14	W		1030	..	†	†	14 7	1554	..		1820	..	via Stendal	2139
Brunswick arr.	3 41	4 44	7 10	9 10	1044		11 7	..	..	1410	1439	1634	1722	18 3	1856	2016		2215
Brunswick dep.	3 46	4 51	7 15	9 21	1046		1112	..	Z	1417	1444	1639	1729	18 8	19 3	2019		222[illegible]
Helmstedt	..	5 23	7 49	10 8	..		1143	..		..	..	1710	..		1937	W		225[illegible]
Jerxheim (p.166)d.	..		7 8	..	..		..	..	..	..	..	..	..	Y	1814	..		2146
Eilsleben	..	..	8 4	1031	..		..	..		..	..	..	..		1953	..		23 6
Magdeburg (Hauptbhf.) ar.	4 47	6 4	8 28	11 0	1130	1220	1222	..	..	1518	1546	1747	1830	1916	2017	21 6	2149	2330
	23			123		D	—			23		D						
Magdeburg (Hauptbhf.) dp.	5 53	6 24	8 40	1054	1132	1228	..	1359		1528	1552	1758	..	1922	..	..	2158	2348
Halle (pp. 166, 171, 172, &c.) ar.	7 41	7 24	9 44	1150	1214	1326	..	1456	1638	1630	1645	19 1	..	2018	..	..	2256	1 34
Halle dp.	7 54	7 30	1020	1157	1215	1330	..	1458	1649	1634	1649	19 7	..	2023	..		23 3	1 44
Leipsic (Haupt.) ar.	8 44	8 0	1052	1229	1239	1357	..	1530	1720	17 3	1720	1931	..	2051		..	2331	2 34
Leipsic (Haupt.) dep.	9 10	8 18	1128	1247	..	14 5	..	1618	1733	—	1733	1944	..	21 2	..	..	2358	4 41
Dresden (Neust.) arr.	1136	10 0	13 5	1415	..	1545	..	1743	1913		1913	2110	..	2222	..	..	1 33	7 35
Dresden (Hptbf.) arr.	1144	10 9	1312	1423	..	1555		1754	1922		1922	2119	..	2230	..	..	1 43	7 46

Z *Via* Hildesheim.

mls	D Corridor Express, r Rest. Car	123 Ex D	23 fast	2 cl. FDT	123 Ex D	23	123 Ex D	23	23	1 3 Exp	123 Ex D	123 Ex D	23 Ex	2cl. FDT	23 Ex D	23 fast	123 Ex D	23 fast
0	Dresden (Hptbf). d.	4 41		6 56	..	2 10	8 42	7 56	9 41	1118	1118	1413	1413		1554	1744	2034	2118
2	Dresden (Neust.) dep.	4 53	..	7 3	..	2 29	8 50	8 4	9 54	1126	1126	1427	1427		16 2	1753	2044	2126
78	Leipsic (Haupt.) arr.	6 28	..	8 11	..	5 15	1019	9 42	1228	13 4	13 4	1613	1613	..	1733	1916	2218	23 5
..	Leipsic (Haupt.) dep.	6 51	7 45	8 32	9 5	6 7	1025	9 57	1230	1	1325	1631	1631	1746	1752	1938	2238	2325
88	Halle (pp. 166, 171 to 173) .. arr.	7 18	8 15	..	9 31	6 51	1052	1046	1319		1351	17 6	17 6	18 9	1820	2025	23 6	c
	Halle dep	7 26	8 17	..	9 38	6 58	1057	11 3	1354		1358	1712	1712	1810	1826	2030	2312	..
146	Magdeburg (Hf) a	8 27	9 14	9 46	1038	8 55	1155	1255	1535		..	18 9	18 9	1852	1923	2136	0 12	1 [illegible]
				W			D			L	Z				23		D	
	Magdeburg (Hf) d	8 36	9 20	9 48	1040	9 25	1212	1313	1630	1442	..	1812	1858	1855	1947	2154	0 23	1 15
165	Eilsleben	via Stendal.	9 42	.		1019	..	1359	1715	..	..	To Hamburg. p. 169	..		2034	2216	..	
	Jerxheim (p. 166) a.		1124		Y	1124	..	1459	1815	..	..		..	W	2138		..	
192	Helmstedt		9 57			1045	1249	1423	1738	..	..		1935		2059	2231		1 52
216	Brunswick (p. 166) .... arr.		1029	1034	1145	1139	1320	1512	1828	1543	..		20 3	1947	2156	23 2	1 31	2 20
	Brunswick dep.		1057	1037	1150	1153	1326	1645	1854	1548	..		20 9	1950	2210	23 8	1 37	2 26
244	Lehrte		1137			13 4	14 7	1748	1957	..	..		2051		2314	2349	2 17	
254	Hanover ...... arr.	12 2	1154	1118	1238	1329	1423	1810	2022	1638	1740		21 7	2020	2332	0 5	2 34	3 30

Y June 24 to Sept. 3. **W** Weekdays only. *c via* Dessau. **Z** *via* Hildesheim

Berlin, Magdeburg. 88 miles.

[Ger. St. Rlys. Hanover.

D Corridor Exp. see page 75. Potsdamer Sta.	23	23	Ex D 123	23	Ex D 123	Ex D 23	23	Ex D 123	Exp 123	Ex D 23	Ex D 123	Ex D 23	23	fast 23	Ex D 123	Ex D 23	Ex D 123	23
Berlin ....dep.	5 30	7 10	7 43	8 15	8 45	9 42	1020	1250	1350	1446	1545	1712	1815	1950	2120	2315	2342	0 24
Potsdam	5 55	7 33	8 4	8 41	9 7	10 3	1040	1313	1411	15 8	16 6	1733	1835	2014	2142	2337	0 3	0 55
Magdeburg (p. 166) a	8 29	9 9	9 14	1134	1026	1115	12 6	1437	1526	1618	1724	1852	20 9	2145	23 2	1 4	1 15	3 7

	23	Exp 123	Ex D 123	Ex D 123	23	fast 23	fast 23	23	Ex D 23	23	Ex D 123	Ex D 123	Ex D 123	fast 23	Ex D 123	Ex D 123	Ex D 23	Ex D 123
Magdeburg (Hbf.) d.	4 22	5 3	5 32	6 46	6 58	7 25	8 37	1034	1228	13 0	14 3	1523	1557	18 3	1836	1950	2035	2110
Potsdam .... arr.	7 23	6 28	6 50	7 59	9 32	8 52	9 59	1254	1354	1521	1529	1639	1726	1931	1954	21 3	2144	2228
Berlin (Potsd.) ,,	8 0	6 55	7 17	8 29	10 1	9 15	1021	1322	1417	1546	1550	17 2	1751	1955	2018	2129	22 9	2251

¶ Not Sundays

Lubeck, Luneberg.

[Ger. St. Rlys., Hamburg.

	23	23	23	23	23	23
Lubeck .. dep.	5 25	8 20	1249	1330	1740	2154
Büchen ,,	6 32	9 28	1338	1435	1953	2333
Lüneburg ,,	7 23	10 4	14 3	1515	2017	0 10

	23	23	23	23	23	23
Lüneburg ,,	5¶38	9 51	1353	1615	1826	2248
Büchen .. ar.	6 17	1030	1430	1644	19 6	2321
Lubeck .. ,,	7¶49	1140	1554	1733	2028	0 30

The times on the LEFT are to be read DOWNWARDS, those on the RIGHT UPWARDS.

From Denmark, *pp.* 216/7 **Berlin (Dresden-Leipsic)—Hamburg** (Germ. Rys. Hamburg).

Mls.		2 FDT	123 D	123 D	123 D	23	123 D	123 D	23	2 FDT	123 D	23	12 FD	123 D	123 D	123 D	2 FDT	23
0	Berlin (Lehrte) dp.	7 37	7 56	..	8 56	9 20	10 6	1156	1226	1411	1536	1630	1811	1826	1835	2038	2157	2342
90	Wittenberge arr.	W	9 30	..	1023	1153	1137	1330	1517	W	17 6	19 5	W	1958	20 5	22 1	..	2 28
..	Dresden dep.	↓	r	4 41	r	..	r	8 42	..	↓	r	1118	↓	1413	1413	1554	↓	..
..	Leipsic (*p.* 169) dep.	↓		6 51	..	..	..	1025	..	↓	..	1330	↓	1631	1631	1752	↓	..
..	Wittenberge dep.	↓	9 35	1016	1026	12 6	1142	1335	1612	↓	1711	1918	↓	20 0	2010	22 5	↓	2 29
105	Ludwigslust .. dep.	↓	..	1052	11 0	1254	..	14 7	1713	↓	1744	2021	↓	2037	2044	2239	↓	3 32
120	Hagenow ......dep.	↓	..	11 8	1117	1319	..	1424	1810	↓	18 3	2110	↓	2053	21 1		↓	3 55
150	Buchen dep.	↓	..	..	to Kiel	1411	..	r	1914	↓	1839	2212	↓	to Kiel	..	2325	↓	4 49
178	Hamburg Haupt. arr.	9 56	1125	1213		1514	1325	1531	20 8	1628	1916	23 5	2040		22 5	0 5	0 17	5 46
183	Altona .....arr.	0 1	1145	1238		..	1348	1554	2042	651	1937	2333	2059		2233	0 28	0 35	6 18

	23	12 FD	123 D	123 ExD	23 D	23	2 FDT	123 D	23	2 FDT	123 D	2 FDT	123 D	123 D	123 D	123 D	2 FDT	23
Altona . dep.	5 5	6 40	6 51	From Kiel	8 25	9 13	1036	1234	1312	1438	1550	1723	1735	18 5	From Kiel	1920	2125	2327
Hamburg Haupt. dep.	5 30	7 3	7 10		8 59	9 39	1050	1252	1337	15 0	1620	1740	18 0	1830		1950	2140	0 0
Buchen . . dep.	6 28	W	r		9 27	1039	W	r	1437	↓	1659	W	r	r		2027	W	0 59
Hagenow .....dep.	7 25	↓		8 25	1013	1141	↓	1359	1551	↓	1733	..	.	.	1917	r	↓	1 52
Ludwigslust .. dep.	7 55	↓	8 31	8 46	1022	1213	↓	1417	1620	↓	1751	..	..	1953	1940	2114	↓	2 21
Wittenberge .. arr.	8 47	↓	9 2	..	1053	13 3	↓	1448	17 9	↓	1822	..	1945	2023	2314	2146	↓	3 6
Leipsic *p.* 169 arr.	..	↓	1229	..	17 3	..	↓	..	..	↓	r	2120	..	2331	r	5 59	↓	8 0
Dresden ...arr.	..	↓	1423	..	1922	..	↓		..	↓	.	2235	.	1 43	..	8 4	↓	10 9
Wittenberge .. dep.	8 51	↓	9 7	..	1058	1313	↓	1453	1714	↓	1827	..	1951	..	2017	2151	↓	3 11
Berlin (Lehrte) arr.	1110	9 30	1040	1044	1230	1542	13 9	1625	1951	1720	20 0	..	2120	..	2156	2316	2358	5 22

D Corridor Exp., *see page* 75. **FD** and **FDT** Special fast trains, extra fares.
W Weekdays only. *r* Restaurant Car.

Bremen, Hamburg, (Stendal) (Berlin), Magdeburg. [German State Rys. (Hanover).

23 fast s	23	Exp	ExD	23		ExD	23	ExD		23 fast s	23	ExD	23	23	ExD	Exp	23	ExD
	4 58	7 44	.	1026	..	1555	1643	1912	dp. Bremen .... ar.		13 3	1341	1720	2345	1747	..		2314
	7 46	9 17		1339		1734	1938	2050	ar. Uelzen ......dp.		1026	1154	1432	2031	16 4			2137
0 3	6 17	8 8	8 59	1155		1622	1830	1830	dp. HAMB'G (*p.* 170) a.	5 27	1034	13 4	1632	2229	..	2243		2243
1 41	7 58	9 25	1018	1431	..	1742	2021	2056	dp. Uelzen ......arr.	3 51	9 17	1140	1335	1958	1558	2132	.	2124
3 5	1018	1046	1134	1649		19 5	2250	2218	arr. Stendal ....dep.	2 22	7 59	1015	1046	1736	1442	2015	.	20 7
5d30	1340	1212		1940	..	2 37	1 6	2340	ar. Berlin (*Lehrt*) dp.	0d13	4 56	8 48	6 35	1450	1310			1850
		23			ExD							ExD	23	23				
↓	5 30	8 50	↓	1252	1830	0 0	1950	..	dp. Hmb'g (*above*) a.	↑	..	1213	1514	22 5	22 5	↑	5 46	..
↓	8 55	12 7	↓	1611	2025	3 15	22 6	..	dp. Wittenberge a.	↑	..	1011	1137	1847	1949	↑	2 2	
↓	9 56	13 7	↓	1715	21 4	4 15	23 8	..	ar. Stendal ..dp.	↑		9 28	1040	1738	19 9	↑	1 0	..
3 10	1035	1313	1137	1728	21 7	4 22	2316	..	dp. Stendal ...... ar.	2 11	7 57	9 18	1026	1721	19 4	2013	0 52	..
4 0	1150	1427	1220	1851	2149	5 35	0 31	..	ar. Magdeburg dp.	1 18	7 5	8 36	9 6	16 4	1812	1931	2338	..
5 59	1615	17 3	1357	2226	2331	8 44	5 59	..	ar. Leipsic...... dp.	2325	..	6 51	6 7	1330	1624	1752	2018	..

d Fried. Station. *s* 1, 2 & 3 cl. Sleeping Car Hamburg-Leipsic and *v.v.*

† Not Sundays. **Coblence, Ems, Limburg, Giessen** (Berlin). [German State Rys. (Frankfort)

23	23	123 ExD	23	23 fast	23	23	23	23 fast	§ Berlin (Schl.)	23	123 ExD	23 fast	23	23	23 fast	23	123 ExD	23
48	7 7	11 8	1237	1348	15 0	1635	1811	2136	dp. Coblence .. ar.	8 53	7 54	1015	1355	1531	1652	1737	19 9	2131
19	7 36	1129	13 9	14 8	1529	1710	1840	2159	,, Ems ...... ,,	8 21	7 33	9 55	1326	1459	1631	17 5	1844	21 3
5	8 18	1159	1352	1437	1612	1752	1924	2229	,, Diez (*p.* 171) dp.	7 39	7 4	9 25	1243	1418	16 1	1624	1815	2021
10	8 23	12 4	1357	1442	1616	1756	1929	2234	ar. Limburg .. ar.	7 26	6 57	9 16	1228	14 5	1555	1548	18 6	20 7
40	1043	1253	1522	1529	1746	1922	2056	2324	Wetzlar .. ,,	5 53	6 13	8 16	1110	1247	15 8	1429	1717	1835
56	1058	13 4	1537	1540	18 2	1938	2112	2336	ar. Giessen.... dp.	5 39	6 1	8 0	1054	1232	1457	1410	17 6	1815
751	..	2129	2251	2251	..	.	7 17	7 17	ar. Berlin (Pots) dp.	20§35	..	2342	..	..	7 43	..	8 45	..

Coblence, Bad Ems. [Ger. State Rys. (Frankfort)

	23	23	23	23	23	123	23	23	23	23	23	23	23	23	23	23	23	23
Coblence .. dep.	5 45	7 7	8 31	9 45	1045	11 8	1149	1237	1348	15 0	1547	1635	1811	1842	2040	2136	2218	0 16
Bad Ems .. arr.	6 17	7 35	8 59	1017	1114	1128	1221	13 8	14 7	1528	1619	17 9	1839	1914	21 6	2158	2244	0 47

	23	23	23	23	23	23	23	23	23	23	23	23	23	123	23	23	23	23
Bad Ems .. dep.	6 0	6 22	7 17	7 34	8 22	9 56	11 6	1256	1328	15 0	1632	17 7	1743	1845	19 1	20 4	21 4	2326
Coblence .. arr.	6 32	6 55	7 46	7 54	8 53	1015	1132	1330	1355	1531	1652	1737	1817	19 9	1931	2039	2131	2358

Hamburg, Hanover, (Berlin) Kreiensen, Cassel, Frankfort.

[Ger. St. Rys. Hanover, Cassel, & Frankfort)

R—Rest. Car.	Exp 123 D	23 fast	Exp 123 D a	Exp 123 D	Exp 123 D	23	Exp 123 D	23 fast	Exp 123 D e	Exp 123 D	23 fast	Rap 2 cl. FDT	23 fast	23 fast	Exp 123 DS	Exp 123 D	123 D	Exp 123 DS
Hamburg (Hpt.) d.	8 59	6 17	7 15		..	8 16	1038		1333	..	1622	18	0 3	20 1	2140	2226		2345
Harburg ......dep.	9 17	6 34	7 30		..	8 33	1052		1348	..	1637	W	0 24	2026	..	2241		0 0
Lüneburg	9 46	7 1	7 58	From Bremen.	..	9 28	1119	..	1419		17 9	|	0 59	21 1	..	23 8	Sleep. Car Berlin-Frankfort.	0 30
Uelzen (*see p.* 169)	1016	7 29	8 29			1025	1150	..	1452		1740	|	1 34	2137		2338		1 3
Lehrte	..		..		..	12 7	1259			..	1854	↓	..	2250	..	A		..
Hanover..... a.	—	8 42	9 39		..	1232	1316	..	16 6	..	1910	1930	..	23 5	2346	0 47		2 20
	23	D	d	—									—		d			
(*Fr. Bremen, p.*164 d.	7 7	123	10 1	9 53		1425	1325	1331	1613		1939	1935	D	0 26	0 2	0 55		2 47
Kreiensen ......arr	8 8	..	1056	..		1544		1432	1714		2039	..	123	2 8		..		3 48
BERLIN (Potsdr) d.	fast	8 45	..	..	7 43	..		..	1250	1446	..	|	2120	..		..	2342	..
Magdeburg (*p.* 168)		1033	..		9 17			..	1441	1626	..	|	23 9	..	Sleeper to Bale.	..	1 22	
Kreiensen ....dep.	8 10	|	1057	..	11 9	1549	..	1434	1717	1851	2041	|		4 11		..	3 46	3 53
Northeim ...... arr.	8 34	|	1114	1057	..	16 9	..	1453	1734	..	21 3	|		4 35		..	..	4 10
Herzberg (*p.*168) a.	9 20	|	1216	1216		1722	..	1614	1918		2134	↓		5 34		..		5 3[illegible]
Göttingen ......arr.	8 52	|	1132	1116	1138	1629	1443	1512	1753	1921	2121	2038	1 36	5 22	1 23	2 14	4 14	4 29
Göttingen....dep.	..	↓	1135	|	|	|	|	1516	1756	|	2129	..	..	..	..	2 17	..	..
Eichenberg .. arr.	..	1357	1155	|	|	|	|	1533	1817	|	2145	..		..		2 36	..	
Bebra (*p.* 171) ,,	..	..	1259	|	|	|	|	..	1932	|	..		..	..		3 42		..
Frankfort ,,	..	..	1531	↓	↓	↓	↓	..	2223	↓			..	..		6 8		
Göttingen..... dep.	8 57			1128	1143	1636	1444	1516	1756	1924	2129	2039	1 41	5 48	1 26	..	4 17	4 31
Cassel ...... arr.	10 3	1445		1233	1249	1747	1541	1625	19 9	2026	2233	2129	2 42	7 13	2 30	..	5 17	5 44
Cassel ...... dep	1010	1458		1241	1259	2039	1549	1632	1916	2034	2312	2131	2 49	7 41	2 37	..	5 26	5 55
Wabern (*below*)	1041	1529		..		2138		17 4	1946	21 4	0 2	|		8 11		..	..	6 25
Marburg	1140	1627	To Bale.	14 7	1420	2347	17 5	18 5	2042	22 1	1 26	|		9 8		..	6 45	7 25
Giessen (*Cobl., p.*169)	1212	17 1		1433	1446	0 24	1727	1830	21 8	2226	..	|	4 32	9 36	4 24	..	7 13	7 55
Bad Nauheim	1239	1728		15 0	1513		1751	19 0	2136	2254	..	↓	4 59	10 3		..	7 41	8 23
Frankfort (Hauptbf)	1315	18 5		1536	1544		1822	1944	2211	2329		2340	5 31	1028	5 10	..	8 1[illegible]	[illegible]

D Limited Corridor Exp.	Exp 123 D	Rap 2 FDT	Exp 123 D e	23 fast	Exp 123 D	Exp 123 D	Exp 123 C	Exp 123 D	Exp 123 D a	Exp 123 D	23 fast	Exp 123 DS	Exp 123 D	Exp 123 D	Exp 123 D	Exp 123 DS	23 fast
Frankfort (Hauptbhf) dp	7 17	8 10	8 14	10 5	12 7	1215	..	1438	..	1450	16 8	21 0	2240	..	0 20	0 30	..
Bad Nauheim	7 51	|	8 51	1047	1239	1256	..	1515		1524	1648	2140	2315	B	..	1 3	..
Giessen	8 20	|	9 20	1119	13 8	1333	..	1545		1553	1723	2212	2343	..	1 20	1 33	..
Marburg	8 45	|	9 45	1144	1332	1358	..	16 9	From Bale.	1617	1748	2239	0 8	..	..	..	..
Wabern (*below*)	9 38	↓	1039	1242	..	1453	..	..		..	1847	..	..	..	..	..	..
Cassel .... arr.	1010	1017	1115	1318	1456	1525	..	1729		1737	1921	0 3	1 28	..	3 4	3 17	..
Cassel .... dep.	1025	1019	1122	1344	15 7	1533	..	1738		1748	1933	0 18	1 35	..	3 11	3 24	7 11
Göttingen.......... arr.	1124	11 7	1232	1457	1559	..	..	1838		1851	2039	1 26	2 30	..	4 8	4 22	8 14
Frankfort (*p.* 172) dep.	5 50	|	7 2	..	|	..	1224	..	1457	..	1425	|	.	0 1	..	|	..
Bebra....(*p.* 171) ,,	9 20	|	1022	1331	|	..	15 9		1728	.	1852	|	.	2 21	..	|	6 27
Eichenberg...... ,,	1028	|	1214	1438	|	1619	16 5	..	1828	..	2023	|	..	3 18	..	↓	7 57
Göttingen ....arr.	1046	|	1232	1457	|		1623	..	1845		2039	↓		3 33	..	..	8 14
Göttingen ....dep.	1127	11 8	1234	15 2	16 2	|	1626	1842	1848	19 6	2044	1 30	2 32	3 36	4 14	4 26	8 20
Herzberg (*p.* 168) ,,	..	|	1040	1441	|	|	..	..	1820	..	2025	2339	..	..	|		8 6
Northeim.......... ,,	..	|	1252	1523	|	|	1643	..	19 7		21 3	1 48		..	|	Sleeper Bale-Altona.	8 37
Kreiensen .... arr.	1157	|	1310	1541	|	↓	17 0	1915	1925		2124	2 5	3 0	4 6	↓		8 56
Magdeburg (*p.* 168) arr.	1358	..	1553	..	..	1943	..	2112	..	..		..	5 27	..	6 38		..
BERLIN (Potsdamer) arr.	1550		1751	..	..	2129	..	2251	..	..			7 17	..	8 29		..
Kreiensen .... dep.	..	..	1315	1547	..		17 1	..	1926	..	2129	2 7		4 7	fast		8 57
Hanover .... arr.	..	1210	1418	1647	1718	..	1758	..	2022	2030	2235	3 2		5 0	..	5 43	10 2
			R				..		a	123					23		
Hanover .... dep.	..	1212	1426	..	1725	..	18 6	..	2045	ExD	2240	3 22	Sleep. Car Frankfort-Berlin.	5 10	7 54	5 56	1018
Lehrte	..	|	..	..	..	..	..	..	21 7		..	..		..	8 14	..	..
Uelzen	..	|	1542	..	1836		..	..	2214	2134	2347	4 44		..	9 22	..	1146
Lüneburg	..	|	1610	..	19 1	..	..	..	2242	22 0	0 16	5 15		..	9 50	..	1213
Harburg	..	↓	1644	..	1929	..	1957	..	2311	2229	0 47	5 55		7 34	1021	..	1250
Hamburg (Hpt.)....arr.	..	1347	1659		1944	..	2011	..	2326	2243	1 0	6 14		7 50	1034	8 4	13 4

A July 1 to Sept. 7. **B** July 4 to Sept. 10. **C** June 30 to Sept. 15. **D** Corridor Exp., *see page* 75. **S** Sleep. Car **W** Weekdays only. *a* Dining Car Hamburg-Frankfort-Stuttgart and *v.v.* *d* Hamburg-Bale and *v.v.* *e* Rest. Car Hamburg-Frankfort and *v.v.* *h via* Hildesheim.

Wabern, Wildungen.

Ger. St. Rys. (Cassel)

6 29	8 16	10 6	1156	1350	1648	1859	1951	2140	dep. Wabern ..arr.	5 59	8 6	1028	1131	1344	1521	1642	18 3	2049
7 0	8 46	1039	1225	1415	1713	1932	2028	2214	arr. Wildungen dep.	5 30	7 38	9 59	11 0	1320	1450	1616	1734	2017

The times on the LEFT are to be read DOWNWARDS, those on the RIGHT UPWARDS.

(Frankfort), Cassel, Halle, Berlin, via Nordhausen. [Gr.St.Rys.(Cassel) Halle

D—Corridor Exp.	23	23 fast	23	23 fast	23	23 ExD	123 ExD	23 fast	123 ExD	23 ExC	123 D
p. 170 { Frankfort (Haupt.) d	..	..			..	8 14	1215	16 8	2240	2248	0 20
p. 170 { Giessen .... dep.	..	..				9 20	1333	1723	2343	0 2	1 20
Cassel .... dep.	3 31	6 16	7 18	10 0	1132	1250	1533	1933	1 35	1 55	3 11
Eichenberg .... arr.	4 33	7 0	8 21	1045	1235	1336	1617	2020	.	2 37	S
							R			¶	
Frankfort (Hpt.) dp.	..	↓	..	..	7 a 2	↓	↓	14a57	↓	..	↓
Bebra .... dep.	..		6 27	..	1022			1728		..	
Eichenberg .... arr.	..		7 52	..	1153			1826		..	
Eichenberg .... dep.	4 57	7 1	8 30	1048	1251	1337	1619	2028	*via* Kreiensen, *p.* 170 With Sleeping Car.	2 39	*via* Kreiensen *see p.* 170.
Nordhausen ...... ,,	7 3	8 8	1039	12 3	15 0	1451	1739	2134		3 41	
Sangerhausen ...... arr.	7 50	8 40	1128	1233	1551	1522	18 7	22 6		4 8	
Sangerhausen .... dep.	7 57	8 49	1144	1234	16 5	1525	18 2	22 8		..	
Halle .... arr.	9 29	9 43	1310	1324	1736	1626	1858	2256		..	
BERLIN (Anb.) (*p.* 172)	1244	1244	1520	1520	1955	1830	2259	4 58		..	
						23				¶	
Sangerhausen ...... dep.	8 44	8 44	1138	..	1618	1538	18 9	2237		4 9	
Güsten .... arr.	9 40	9 40	1246	..	1743	1631	19 1	2355		5 5	..
Güsten .... dep.	9 42	9 42	1346	..	18 7	1632	19 2	0 7		5†24	..
Magdeburg .... arr.	1029	1029	1455	..	1916	1713	1943	1 9	5 27	6†39	6 38
Güsten .... dep.	1022	⁀	1321	..	1822	1942	..	..	..	5 11	..
Dessau .... { arr.	..	..	1426	..	..	2030	↓	..	↓	6 4	↓
Dessau .... { dep.		..	1433	..		2032		..		6 8	
Rosslau .... dep.		..	1441	..		2039		..		6 15	
Güterglück dep.	1110	..	1437	..	1916	..	..	..	..	¶	..
Berlin { Friedrichstre, ar.	14 0		1731	..	2215	2245	..	..	..	8 13	..
Berlin { Schlesisch sta. ar.	1413		1745	..	2229	2258	21†29		7†17	8 28	8†29

	23	23 fast	23	123 ExD	23 D	23 fast	23	23 fast	23	23 fast	23 ExD	123 D	123 ExD
Berlin { Schlesisch sta. d.	..		4 18	8‡45	..	1115	8 23	..	1350	1610	2035	21‡20	2342
Berlin { Friedrichstre. dp.			4 33	R	..	1129	8 38	..	14 5	1622	2049	..	‡
Güterglück	..	..	7 27	..	..	..	11 7	..	17 2	1914	¶	S	..
Rosslau .... dep.	..	..	..	↓	..	1323	..	..	1640	..	2253	↓	↓
Dessau .... { arr.	..	..	..		..	1329	..	..	1646	..	23 0		
Dessau .... { dep.	..	..	..		..	1332	.	..	1657		23 8		
Güsten .... arr.	..	..	8 6	.	..	1422	1143	..	1752	1950	0 2	..	
Magdeburg .... dep.	..	6 52	7 57	1033	..	1310	..	..	1650	19 6	2255	23 9	1 22
Güsten, ar. fr. Magdbg.	..	7 38	8 57	1115	..	1419	..	..	1754	2011	2358		
Güsten .... dep.	..	7 39	9 11	1116	..	1423	1423	..	1813	2016	0 9	*via* Kreiensen *see p.* 170	*via* Kreiensen *p.* 170 With Sleep Car
Sangerhausen ...... arr.	..	8 34	1032	12 7		1552	1552		1933	2136	1 2		
					Exp				fast				
BERLIN (Anh.) (*p.* 173) d.	0 9	0 15	..	.	1150	↓	1150	1436	1645	1729	..		
Halle .... dep.	5 6	7 40	8 59	..	1357		14 6	1659	1850	20 1	¶		
Sangerhausen .... arr.	6 39	8 39	1038	.	15 0		1546	1750	1946	2131	..		
Sangerhausen ...... dep.	6 50	8 43	1051	1211	15 2	1557	16 5	1753	1948	2140	1 4		
Nordhausen ...... ,,	8 7	9 19	12 0	1244	1540	1634	1749	1825	2022	23 0	1 39		
Eichenberg .... arr.	9 53	1023	1350	1357	1651	1824	20 3	1932	2134	1 4	2 39		
Eichenberg ...... dep.	↓	1043	1444	↓	↓	1830	2036	..	..	↓	..	↓	↓
Bebra .... arr.		1136	1626			1932	2138	..	..		..		
Frankfort (Hpt.) ,,		1512	1931			2223	..	..	..				
						123D							
Eichenberg .... dep.	9 57	1024	1416	14 0	1652	1821	2037	1949	2147	1 15	2 41	..	..
Cassel .... arr.	11 0	11 9	1523	1445	1738	19 9	2151	2035	2233	2 15	3 26	2 42	5 17
p. 170 { Giessen ...... arr.	1430	1430	1826	1651		21 5	..	..	..	..	5 34	4 30	7 11
p. 170 { Frankfort (Hpt) ,,	1536	1536	1944	18 5		2211	..	..	..		6 47	5 31	8 17

‡ Potsdamer Stn.

¶ 1 & 2 cl. Sleep. Car. Berlin to Wiesbaden and *v.v.*

S Sleeping Cars Bale-Berlin and *v.v.*

a "D" Train. **R** Restaurant Car. † Not Sundays.

Wiesbaden Langen-Schwalbach Diez [Gr.St.R. (Frank.)

2 & 3 cl. only.

a Weekdays only.

Wiesbaden .. dep.	*a* 6 40	8a40	1143	1346	1610	1919	
Bad Schwalbach ..	6 2	7 42	9 35	1243	1446	18 0	2019
Diez .... arr.	7 0	8 42	1033	1341	1545	19 3	2117
Limburg (*p.* 169) ,,	7 8	8 52	1045	1352	1555	1914	2128
Limburg .... dep.	4a47	7 57	11 5	1332	1624	1829	19a24
Diez (*p.* 169) ,,	4 57	8 7	1116	1342	1635	1840	1930
Bad Schwalbach ..	6 13	9 14	1216	1444	1744	1956	2052
Wiesbaden .. arr.	7 8	10 3	13 3	1533	1846	2046	2142

Frankfort and Bad Homburg.

dep. Frf.	arr. Hm.	dep. Hm.	arr. Frf.
6†12	6†44	5 27	5 59
7 0	7 27	6 3	6 34
7 41	8 14	7† 3	7†35
8 25	8 57	7 16	7 42
9 30	9 59	8 26	8 54
1010	1038	9 41	10 9
1140	12 8	10†46	11†17
13 1	1334	1132	12 2
1346	1418	1242	13 9
1430	15 3	1341	14 8
1537	16 4	15 3	1531
16†50	1725	1552	1618
1735	18 9	1623	1653
1822	1849	1710	1738
1917	1943	1832	19 3
1950	2020	1920	1950
2038	21 6	1954	2026
2154	2221	2038	21 6
2236	23 9	21 6	2144
2335	0 1	2235	23 4
0 45	1 12	2335	0 2

† Not Sundays

Limburg, Frankfort. [Gr. St. Rys. (Frankft.)

23	23	23	23	23	23	23	23	*Coblence p.* 58)	23	23	23	23	23	23	23
7 35	9 54	1052	1228	1410	1620	1932	2055	d. Limburg ar.	8 41	9 4	1158	1327	1654	1959	2212
[illegible] 19	1051	1157	1328	1453	1724	2041	2138	Niedernhausn	7 45	8 25	11 5	1248	1557	19 4	2130
[illegible] 55	..	1232	1446	1519	1754	21 8	22 6	a. Wiesbaden d.	7 14	7 14		1217	1520	1834	2040
8 56	1137	1246	1414	1531	1810	2129	2216	a. Frnkfrt. (H) d.	6 44	7 41	[illegible]	12 3	15 1	1758	2046

☞ *Frankfort to Berlin via Nordhausen see p. 171*

Frankfort, (Cassel), Bebra, Erfurt, (Leipsic), Halle, Berlin.

[Ger. State Rlys. (Frankfort and Halle).

z Sleep. Cars, Frankfort to Leipsic and Dresden. e *via* Eichenberg. § 2 & 3 cl. only. ‖ *via* Halle. ‡ Berlin (Fried).

† Not Sundays.	Exp 23	23	Exp 123	Exp 123	Rap 2	Exp 123	Exp 23	Exp 123	Exp 123	Exp 23	fast 23	Exp 123	Exp 123
	D		D	Db	FDT	D	D r	D r	D	D		D	D R
Frankfort (Haup.) d	From Cologne	..	5 50	7 2	8 12	9 43	..	..	..	.	1052	1224	From Stuttgart.
Hanau (Haupbanh'f)		..		7 29	W	10 7	.	..	..	..	1122	1250	
Fulda		5 2	7 17	8 53	..	1120	.		..	.	1249	14 8	
Bebra (*pp.* 170, 171) a.		6 11		9 43	..	..	.	..	..	⌒	1342	r	
Cassel (*p.* 165) dep.	3 48	5 0	..	8§56	..	..	1113	1122	From Munich (*p.* 80)	1250	1250	..	
Bebra dep.	4 43	6 15		9 55	..	..	12 9	e		1352	1420	..	
Eisenach	5 23	6 57		1039	..	1242	1249	.		1438	1515	1534	
Gotha	5 51	7 22	..	1111	..		1320	1353		15 6	1551	16 4	
Neudietend'f (*p.* 185)		7 35	..	..	..	..	..	14 8		..	..	..	
Erfurt	6 16	7 48	9 22	1138	1042	1335	1352	1435		1532	1650	1631	1652
Weimar	6 44	8 7	9 44	12 1	1057	1357	1414	1456		1554	..	1654	1714
Naumburg	7 20	8 46		1234	.	..	1452	1533	1547	1627	..	..	1751
Weissenfels (*p.* 191) a.	7 34	8 59	1024	1252	..	1438	15 9		..	1643		1735	18 7
Weissenfels dep.	7 35	9 1		1259	..	1439	1526	..	‖	1644	To Berlin *via* Sangerh'nsen	⌒	18 8
Leipsic (Haupt.) a.	8 9	9 53	.	1339	1155	1512	16 0	..	1712	1719		..	1840
Dresden (*p.* 168) a.	10 9	12 9		1555	..	1754	1754	..		1923		..	2032
Weissenfels dep.	Sl'p Car	9 1	1026	1252	..		1518			..		1736	..
Halle arr.		9 31	1051	1323	*via* L'psic	*via* L'psic	1546	1613	1630	..		18 3	*via* L'psic
Halle dep		9 35	1059	1330			1553	1620	1638	..		18 9	
Bitterfeld (*below*) arr.		9 57	..	1351			1615	1643	..			..	
Berlin (Anhalt) arr.		12‡12	1250	1520	1317	1718	1758	1824	1830	..	22‡45	1955	21‡27

† Not Sundays.	Exp 123	Rap 2	fast 23	Rap 12	Exp 23	Rap 2	Exp 123	fast 23	Exp 123	fast 23	Exp 123	Exp 123	Exp 123
	D	FDT		F D	D b	FDT	D		D S		D z	DS	D
Frankfort (Haup.) d	13 5	..	14 0	1440	1444	16 0	1645	17 0	2251	2158	0 22	0 28	From Stuttgart, with Sleep Car.
Hanau (Haupbanh'f)	1331	..	1424	↓	1510	↓	17 4	1725	2320	2237	0 43	0 58	
Fulda	1441	From Stuttgart	1543		1630		1810	1844	0 43	0 33	1 56	2 16	
Bebra (*pp.* 170, 171) a.	..		1630		.		..	1931	..	1 30	..	..	
Cassel (*p.* 165) dep.	..		1623 (1 2 3)	.	..		..	19 0 (1 2 3)	..	0 20	..	..	
Bebra dep.	..		1710	..	..		..	1955	..	1 48	..	..	
Eisenach	16 2		1746		18 5		1925	2037	2 16	3 52	..	3 46	..
Gotha	1631		..	..	1834		1954	21 6	2 46	4 36	..	4 17	..
Neudietend'f (*p.* 185)	..		..	..	..		..	..	..	4 51	..	..	..
Erfurt	17 5	1732	1841	1747	19 1	1836	2023	2131	3 16	5 26	4 1	4 47	4 34
Weimar	1728	.	19 1	.	1926	..	2043	2151	3 40	5 50	4 24	5 10	4 56
Naumburg	..	..	..	..	1955	..	2118	2224	4 16	6 42	4 58	5 48	..
Weissenfels (*p.* 191) a.	1814	..	1939	.	2011	..		2239	..	6 56	..	6 2	5 38
Weissenfels dep.	1815		1940	..	2013	..	..	2240	..	7 47	..	..	..
Leipsic (Haupt.) a.	1849	1855	2013	19 8	2046	..	22 8	2314	..	8 46	5 49	..	..
Dresden (*p.* 168) a.	2032	2119	2211	2119	2235	..	0 15	1 43	..		8 4		..
Weissenfels dep.	..		..		..		..	..	..	7 23		6 15	5 40
Halle arr.	..	*via* L'psic	..	*via* L'psic	*via* L'psic	1939	*via* L'psic	..	4 59	8 1	..	6 47	6 6
Halle dep	..		..			1941			5 6	8 34	..	6 54	6 13
Bitterfeld (*below*) arr.	..		..			..		..	5 30	8 59	..	7 18	6 35
Berlin (Anhalt) arr.	..	2040	..	2055	2259	21 0	0 22	..	7 16	1111	..	8 59	8 7

D Corr. Exp. **FD** and FDT Special fast Corridor Exp. EXTRA FARES, *see p.* 75. **R** Rest. Car. **S** Sleeping cars Frankfort-Berlin.
W Weekdays only. *r* Rest Car.

Berlin, Leipsic.

s Sleeping car, Berlin-Munich. [German State Rlys. (Halle).

Mls.	Anhalter Sta.	123 ExD	23 fast	23 ExD	123 ExD	123 ExD	12 FD	123 FD	123 ExD	123 ExD	123 ExD	12 luxe	23 fast	123 ExD	2 FDT	23 Exp	23	2 FDT	123 ExD	123 ExD	123 ExD	123 ExD	123 ExD	23	23
0	Berlin dep.	5 38	6 19	7 36	7 58	8 4	9 20	9 28	1031	1239	1340	1420	1436	1532	1640	1715	1719	1840	19 0	2020	2129	2137	2250	0 9	0 15
59	Wittenberg	6 43	7 33	8 48	..	..	..	.	..	..	..		1554	1635	..	.	19 2		..	..	..	..	.	1 44	2 35
82	Bitterfeld *above* arr.	7 8	8 4	9 14	..	..	..	..	..	..	..	X	1626	17 1	W	1849	1933	W	..	..	s	..	0 28	2 20	3 25
	Bitterfeld *above* dep.	7 10	8 6	9 16	..	..	..	..	..	..	..	..	1627	17 2		1850	1943	..	..	..	..	..	0 30	2 31	3 33
101	Leipsic (Haupt.) arr.	7 36	8 47	9 43	9 49	10 0	1058	11 8	1224	1430	1530	16 3	17 1	1732	18 6	1914	2016	1958	2056	2213	2335	2347	1 0	3 12	4 12

Mls.		23	123 ExD	123 ExD	123 ExD	123 ExD	23 ExD	23 ExD	23	23 fast	2 FDT	2 FDT	123 ExD	23 fast	12 luxe	123 ExD	123 ExD	123 ExD	12 FD	12 FD	123 ExD	123 ExD	23 D	123 ExD	23
0	Leipsic (Haupt.) dp.	1 8	5 9	6 2	6 40	7 6	7 19	8 18	8 37	1010	1157	12 6	12 9	1342	14 2	1519	1555	1735	19 2	1915	2010	2042	2057	2227	2236
19	Bitterfeld arr.	1 49	..		..	..	..	8 42	9 3	1040	..	..	..	1410	..	1546	..	..	..	..		..	2121	2250	23 5
	Bitterfeld dep	2 4	..	s	..	..	..	8 44	9 8	1045	W	W	..	1412	X	1547	..	..	..	..	..	..	2123	2251	23 9
42	Wittenberg	2 56	..	.	..	..	..	9 12	9 44	1115	..	..		1442	..	..	..	..	..	..	..	..	2149	2317	2342
101	Berlin (Anhalt) arr.	4 58	7 23	8 2	8 44	9 7	9 14	1024	1111	1244	1317	1324	1358	16 3	16 2	1718	1746	1927	2040	2055	22 0	2234	2259	0 22	1 8

FD Special fast Corridor Exp. EXTRA FARES. *See p.* 75.
D Corridor Express. *See p.* 75.
X Riviera Express. *See p.* 81.
W Weekdays only.

☞ *Berlin to Frankfort via Nordhausen, see p.* 171.

Berlin, Halle, (Leipsic), Corbetha, Erfurt, Bebra, Frankfort.

[German State Rlys. (Halle, Erfurt, & Frankfort).

	fast	fast	Exp	Exp	Exp	Rap	Exp	Rap	Rap	Exp	Exp	Rap	Exp	Exp
D Corridor Exp. see p. 75	2 3	2 3	1 2 3	2 3	2 3	2 cl.	1 2 3	1 2	1 2	1 2 3	1 2 3	1 2	1 2 3	1 2 3
			D	D S	D r	FDT	D r A	F D	F D r	D	D	FD	D	D
Berlin (Anhalt) dep.	0 9	..	5 38	..	7 36	7 54	8 24	9 20	9 28	8‡31	..	1013	1023	..
Bitterfeld (p. 172) ..	2 26	..	7 10		9 16	..	..	Via L'psic	Via L'psic	1049		..	1150	..
Halle arr.	2 51	..	Via L'psic		Via L'psic	9 19	1016			Via L'psic	..	1151	1213	..
Halle dep.	3 13					9 21	1023				..	1159	1220	..
Weissenfels ....arr.	3 51	..		..			..				..	..	1252	..
Dresden (p.168) dp.	..	..	..	6 12	7 56	↓	..	9 18	9 18	..	1013	↓	..	1013
Leipsic (Haupt.) „	..	6 10	7 45	8 36	9 54	↓	..	11 6	1119	1124	12 [illegible]	↓		1253
Weissenfels .. „	..	6 56	..	..	1026	↓			..	1156	12[illegible]	↓		
Weissenfels (p. 191)	4 1	6 58	..	..	1027	↓	..	..	..	1157	1237	To Munich.	1253	
Naumburg	4 20	7 10	8 28	9 20	1040	↓	11 4	..	..	1210	1250		13 6	..
Weimar	5 21	7 54	9 2	9 58	1119	↓	To Munich	1211	..	1248	1330		1347	14 7
Erfurt	6 40	8 22	9 27	1028	1144	1024		1235	1249	1313	1356		1411	1431
Neudietendorf (p.185)	6 52	8 35	..	..	..	..		↓	To Stuttgart.	To Stuttgart.	..		.	
Gotha	7 6	8 50	..	1056	1214	↓		↓			1426		1439	1459
Eisenach	7 35	9 19	1012	1123	1239	↓		↓			1452		15 4	1522
Bebra (pp.170, 171) a.	8 16	10 0	..	12 1	R	↓		↓			..			16 3
Cassel (p. 165) arr.	9 16	1056	..	1251 (2 3)	..	↓	..	..			..	..	..	1655
Bebra ....dep.	8 30	1022	..	1225	..	↓	..	..			..	..	..	..
Fulda	9 20	1139	1132	1317	14 6	↓	..	..			1615	..	1631	..
Hanau (Hauptbhf.)	1031	1326	1228	1441	1511	..	..	..	..	..	1715	..	1732	..
Frankfort (Haupt.) a.	1055	1402	1250	1512	1539	1255	..	1546	..	..	1739	..	18 1	..

	Exp	Exp	Exp	Exp	Exp	Exp	Exp	Exp	Rap	Exp	Exp	Exp	Exp	Exp
D Corridor Exp. see p. 75	1 2 3	1 2 3	1 2 3	1 2 3	1 2 3	1 2 3	1 2 3	2 3	2 cl.	1 2 3	2 3	1 2 3	1 2 3	2 3
	D r	D	D r	D	D	D	D	D r	FDT W	s	D	D S	D	D S
Berlin (Anhalt) dep.	..	1125	1150	1239	..	1546	1645	1729	1840	20 5	..	2212	Sleep Car fr. Leipsic	23 5
Bitterfeld (p. 172) ..	..	13 7	..	Via L p i	..	1713		1912	Via L'psic	2141	..	..		0 48
Halle arr.	..	1332	1342		..	1736	1833	1936		22 6	..	0 3		1 13
Halle dep.	..	1338	1351		..	1742	1840	1944		2213	..	0 10		1 29
Weissenfels ....arr.	..	..				1810		2014		2239	..	..		2 2
Dresden (p.168) dp.	1118	..	..	12 4	1330	1413		1744	1845	1912	2034	..	23 1	..
Leipsic (Haupt.) „	1322	..	..	1437	1523	1719	..	1931	20 0	2158	2258	..	0 50	..
Weissenfels .. „	1355	..	..	1511	1555	18 3		20 5	2032	2233	2331	..	1 26	..
Weissenfels (p. 191)	1356	..	..	1512	1556	1816		2015	2033	2241	2332	..	1 28	2 5
Naumburg	1410	1420	1429	..	..	1829		2037	..	2254	2345	..	1 42	2 20
Weimar	1449	15 6	To Munich.	1555	1643	19 4	1950	2124	..	2337	0 34	..	2 24	3 3
Erfurt	1513	1557		1620	17 8	1929	2015	2156	2114	0 6	1 0	1 40	2 49	3 29
Neudietendorf (p.185)	..	1613		..	..	..	↓	..	↓	To Stuttgart.	..	..	..	..
Gotha	1540	1636		..	..	1958	↓	2223	↓		1 27	..	3 20	3 59
Eisenach	1610	..		17 6	1755	2024	↓	2253	↓		1 54	..	3 46	4 26
Bebra (pp.170, 171) a.	1652	e		..	1835	..	↓	2238	↓		2 34	..	..	..
Cassel (p. 165) arr.	1745 (2 3)	19 9	..	..	1928	..		0 29	↓		3 27	..	..	..
Bebra ....dep.	17 3	..	..	..	..	..		..	↓		To Cologne	..	..	..
Fulda	1751	..	..	1824	..	2142	2219	..	↓			3 49	5 13	6 5
Hanau (Hauptbhf.)	19 7	..	..	1919	..	2238		..		..		4 50	6 11	7 9
Frankfort (Haupt.) a.	1931	..	..	1945	..	23 7	2333	..	2340	..		5 20	6 39	7 41

A June 15–Sept. 15. **S** Sleep. Car Berlin-Frankfort. **FD** and FDT Special fast Corridor Exp., *see page* 75, Extra Fares. *r* Rest. Car.
e Via Eichenberg. *s* Sleep. Cars Berlin-Stuttgart and Zurich. ‡ Fried. Stn. § 2 & 3 cl. only.

¶ Weekdays only.

Wiesbaden, (Biebrich-Rh.), Kastel, Frankfort.

[Ger. State Rly. (Cologne)

Hauptbhf.	2 3	123D	2 3	2 3	2 3	2 3	2 3	2 3	2 3	2 3	123D	2 3	2 3	123D	2 3	2 3	2 3	2 3	2 3	123D	2 3	2 3	2 3	2 3	123D	2 3	123D	2 3
Wiesbaden ....dep.	5 21	5 44	6 42	6 51	7 14	7 52	8 15	8 39	1015	11 0	1130	12 1	1240	1320	1411	15 0	15¶45	1632	1721	1752	1827	1928	20 5	2011	2152	22 3	2211	2343
Wiesbaden-Ost	5 26	..	6 47	6 56	7 19	7 57	8 20	8 44	..	11 5	..	..	..	..	1416	..	1550	1637	1726	..	..	1933	..	2016	..	22 8	..	..
Kastel (Mainz) ..	5 33	5 54	6 53	7 3	7 26	8 3	8 27	8 51	1024	1111	1139	1210	1250	1331	1422	15 9	1556	1644	1732	..	1836	1940	2014	2022	22 1	2214	2221	2352
Höchst	6 10	6 16	7 11	7 40	7 47	8 23	9 2	9 9	1043	1147	1158	1230	1310	1355	1456	1527	1631	1720	18 6	..	1855	2016	2033	2059	2219	2257	2245	0 17
Frankfort (H.)‡ arr.	6 21	6 28	7 23	7 51	7 59	8 33	9 17	9 19	1053	12 2	..	1242	1321	14 8	15 6	1540	1642	1736	1822	1828	19 6	2031	2044	2115	2230	23 7	2258	0 28

Mls.	Hauptbhf.	123D	2 3	2 3¶	2 3	123D	123D	2 3	2 3	2 3	2 3	2 3	123D	2 3	2 3	2 3	2 3	123D	2 3D	2 3	2 3	2 3	2 3	2 3	2 3	2 3	2 3	2 3
0	**Frankfort** ....dep.	0 14	0 28	5 28	6 25	7 23	7 57	8 50	9 26	9 59	11 2	1110	1144	1238	1322	1349	1446	1514	1555	16 3	1657	1740	1754	1848	2027	2116	2122	2241
6	Höchst	0 27	0 43	5 43	6 46	7 35	8 9	9 8	9 36	10 9	1111	1125	1155	1249	1334	14 1	15 3	1527	16 6	1615	17 8	1751	18 5	1859	2038	2126	2138	2259
21	Kastel (Mainz) arr.	0 49	1 16	6 16	7 21	7 57	8 32	9 44	9 55	1029	1130	1157	1217	1322	14 6	1420	1537	1549	1626	1634	1741	1811	1838	1919	2111	2144	2210	2332
23	**Wiesbaden-Ost**	..	1 22	6 23	7 29	..	..	9 50	..	..	..	12 4	..	1328	1413	..	1544	..	..	1641	1748	1818	1845	1925	2118	..	2217	2339
26	**Wiesbaden** ....arr.	1 1	1 28	6 28	7 35	8 7	8 42	9 56	10 3	1038	1138	1210	1226	1334	1419	1429	1549	1559	1637	1647	1753	1824	1851	1931	2124	2154	2223	2345

For other routes between Berlin and the South, see pp. 185 (via Stuttgart) *and* 192 (via Munich).
RIVIERA EXPRESS. *See p.* 81.

	A	B	C	E	O	F	G		H	J	K		P	M	L	N
..	7 15	..	1333	2140	..	..	2345	dep. HAMBURG (p. 170) arr.	1944	2326	6 14	..	..	..	8 4	1659
..	8 11	..	1321	2156	..	..	0 2	,, Bremen (p. 164) ,,	1920	2212	5 21	..	..	..	7 33	16 7
..	1531	..	2210	5 19	—	2 8	9 0	arr. FRANKFORT......dep.	12 7	1457	21 0		..	—	0 30	8 14
FDT	FD	..	1246	2120	..	20¶49	2342	dep. BERLIN Potsd. (p.170) a.	..	FD	..	FDT	8¶13	..	8 29	1517
			2211	5 31	..	6 49	8 17	arr. FRANKFORT........dep.	..		..		2248	..	0 20	6 50
7 54	9 20	1023	1645	..	2212			dep. BERLIN Anh. (p.178) ar.	1955	2055	0 22	21 0	7 15	8 59	..	1250
1255	1546	18 1	2333	..	5 20		..	arr. FRANKFORT........dep.	1224	1440	1645	16 0	2251	0 28	.	5 50
	1 2 3					1 2 3		(*via Carlsruhe*)		1 2 3						
13 0	16 3	1829	2353	5 55	5 43	7 10	9 34	dep. FRANKFORT .. (p. 182-3) arr.	12 6	1419	1632	1555	2231	0 3	0 3	5 32
1318	1633	1857	0 21	..	6 10	7 38	10 1	,, Darmstadt .... ,,	113[illegible]	1351	16 6	1535	22 2	2336	..	
			..	7 4	..		1115	,, Mannheim .... ,,	..			15 0	..	..	2255	4 20
14 0	1729	20 0	1 31	.	7 15	8 55	..	,, Heidelberg .... dep.	1053	13 4	1516	..	21 9	2251	..	
1434	1816	2050	2 27	7 56	8 4	9 52	1214	,, Carlsruhe .... ,,	10 4	1217	1427	1424	2021	22 4	2212	3 34
1630	2052	2330	5 25	1038	1052	13 0	1520	arr. BALE (D.R.B.) ,,	7 25	9 38	1141	1230	1735	1917	1928	0 30
1652	2120	24 0	6 8	1118	1125	1338	1549	,, BALE (Swiss) c ,,	6 39	9 5	1030	1210	17 7	1835	1842	0 0
..	2138	↓	7 13	..	1155	1454	1714	dep. Bale (Swiss) p. 283 arr.	6 45	8 40	..	..	1644	1811	..	23 1
..	2256		8 36	..	1320	1614	1831	arr. ZURICH.... dep.	5 35	7 22	..		1529	1655	..	2149
..			1035	..	1546	1841	2034	,, Coire (p. 286).... ,,	..	..	..		1310	1310	..	1953
..	0 23	0 23	6 57	..	1230	16 8	16 8	dep. Bale (Swiss)......arr.	..	8 55	∞	..	1531	1855	..	2225
..	2 23	2 23	8 30	..	14 7	1748	1748	arr. Berne ....dep.	..	7 0		.	1345	1718		2050
..	7 44	7 44	1948	..	1540	1929	1929	,, Interlaken (East) dep.	..	5 0	..	..	1215	1541	..	19 3
						w	w	w (West). (p. 381)		w						
..	..	0 23	7 25	FDT—2 cl. only. Special fares Berlin-Bale and v.v.	1230	..	16 8	dep. Bale (Swiss) p278/9 .. arr.	6 16	..		..	1531	1855	..	2225
..	..	2 23	9 26		14 6		1748	arr. Berne .... ..dep.	4 19	..		..	1345	1718	..	2050
..	..	5 36	1223		163[illegible]	..	2023	,, GENEVA... .. ,,	1 15	..			1115	1435		1754
..	..	9 35	1625		2020	..	a	,, Lyons (p. 266).... ,,	1955	..	..	..	6 40	1155		a
..	..	1445	21 5		.	..	5 24	,, MARSEILLES (p.259) ,,	14 8	..	..		0 30	..		7 30
..	..	1650	2350		..	..	9 18	,, Nice .... ,,	1017	..			2038	..	..	0 10
1 2 3	..	2014				..	1030	,, Vintimille (p. 264) ,,	8 35	..		1 2 3	1935	..	..	2245
1730	2142		6 45		12 0	1450	1730	dep. BALE (Swiss) ......arr.	6 16	8 55	..	12 0	1648	1648	..	2341
1852	2320		8 1		1330	1615	1852	arr. LUCERNE (p. 282) ..dep.	4 47	7 25	..	1045	1524	1524	..	2227
2221	3 45	..	1115		1725	2022	2231	,, Lugano .... ,,	1 8	2 34	..	7 36	1144	1144	..	1917
2247	4 15		1138		1750	2050	2247	,, Chiasso c (p. 287) .. ,,	0 35	2 7		7 10	1116	1116		1850
0 5	5 58		13 7		1924	2224	0 5	,, MILAN (p. 304) .... ,,	2252	0 20		5 58	9 42	9 42	..	1715
..	6 25	..	1334		20 0	0 30	0 30	dep. MILAN (p. 302) .... arr.	2231	24 0			9 33	9 33		1636
..	9 10		1545		2235	3 39	3 39	arr. Genoa ....dep.	1946	2115	..	..	7 1	7 1	..	14x33
.	1440		19 3		2 40	8 39	8 39	,, Vintimille (p.299).. ,,	1545	1715		..	0 50	0 50		1053
	1559		2028		..	1118	1118	,, Nice .... ,,	14 5	1445			22 0	22 0		8 8
.	9 35		1655		23 9		7 0	dep. Genoa (p. 301)...... arr.	1847	2018		..	6 36	6 36	..	11 1
	163[illegible]		2350		6 55		1310	arr. ROME (p. 301) ....dep.	1230	1135			23 0	23 0	.	0 30
	6x50	..‖	1350		1940	2250	..	dep. Milan ....arr.	22 0	2325	..	..	9 15	9 15	.	1628
..	9 36	‖	1543		2140	1 57	..	arr. Bologna ...... (p. 303) dep.	1943	2130	..	..	7‖15	7‖15	..	1451
.	[illegible]	‖	1638		..	3 25	..	,, FLORENCE .... ,,	18‖20	2036	..		5 45	5 45	..	1311
	[illegible]40	‖	1930		..	8 0		,, ROME .... ,,	1425	1725‖	..		0 5	0 5	..	9x15

A—1, 2 & 3 cl. Cars Hamburg, Berlin and Bremen-Bale ; 1 & 2 cl. Berlin (Anh.)-Bale-Milan-Rome ; Rest. Cars Hamburg-Bale, Berlin (Anh.)-Frankfort. **B**—1, 2 & 3 cl. Cars and Rest. Car Berlin (Anh.)-Bale. **C**—1, 2 & 3 cl. Cars Hamburg-Frankfort, Berlin (Anh.)-Bale-Geneva ; 1 & 2 cl. Cars Berlin (Anh.)-Vintimille ; Sleep Cars Berlin-Lugano, Berlin (Anh.)-Bale, Berlin-Coire (June 30 to Sept. 9) and Berlin-Interlaken (June 30 to Aug. 31); Rest. Cars Hamburg and Berlin (Anh.)-Frankfort and Bale-Milan. **E**—1, 2 & 3 cl. Cars Hamburg and Berlin (Pots.)-Bale ; 1 & 2 cl. Cars Hamburg-Rome ; 3 cl. Cars Hamburg-Genoa ; Sleep. Cars Hamburg-Bremen Berlin (Pots.)-Bale; Rest. Car Mannheim-Bale. **F**—2 & 3 cl. Cars Berlin-Frankfort ; Sleep. Cars Berlin-Frankfort. Rest. Car Frankfort-Bale. **G**—1, 2 & 3 cl. Hamburg-Bale-Milan and Berlin (Pots.)-Frankfort ; Sleep. Cars Hamburg and Berlin (Pots.)-Frankfort ; Rest. Car Frankfort-Bale. **H**—1, 2 & 3 cl. Cars Bale-Berlin (Anh.) ; 1, 2 & 3 cl. Vintimille-Berlin (Anh.) ; 1 & 2 cl. Rome-Berlin ; Rest. Car Bale-Berlin. **J**—1, 2 & 3 cl. Cars Bale-Hamburg and Bremen ; 1 & 2 cl. Bale-Berlin (Anh.) ; Rest. Cars Bale-Hamburg and Frankfort-Berlin. **K**—1, 2 & 3 cl. Cars Milan-Bale-Hamburg and Bale-Berlin (Pots.) ; Sleep. Car Frankfort-Hamburg ; Rest. Car Bale-Frankfort. **L**—1, 2 & 3 cl. Cars Bale-Hamburg and Berlin (Pots.) ; 1 & 2 cl. Rome-Bale-Hamburg ; 3 cl. Genoa-Bale-Hamburg ; Sleep. Cars Bale-Hamburg-Bremen and Berlin (Pots.) ; Rest Cars Bale-Mannheim. **M**—1, 2 & 3 cl. and 1 & 2 cl. Sleep. Car Frankfort-Berlin (Anh.) ; Rest. Car Bale-Frankfort. **N**—1, 2 & 3 cl. Cars Geneva-Bale-Berlin (Anh.), Frankfort-Hamburg ; 1 & 2 cl. Vintimille-Berlin (Anh.) ; Sleep Cars Lugano-Berlin, Bale-Berlin, Coire-Berlin (July 1 to Sept. 11) and Interlaken-Berlin (July 1 to Sept. 1) ; Rest. Cars Frankfort-Hamburg and Berlin. **O**—1, 2 & 3 cl. Cars Berlin-Bale-Coire and Rome; Sleep. Cars Berlin-Bale-Nice; Rest. Car Frankfort-Bale. **P**—1, 2 & 3 cl. Cars Rome and Coire-Bale-Berlin. Sleep. Cars Nice-Bale-Berlin ; Rest. Car Bale-Frankfort. **FD**—Special Fast 1 & 2 cl. Corridor Exp. Extra Fares. ‡ Via Bienne. § Via Sarzana. ‖ 1st cl. only. ¶ Berlin (Fried.), via Sangerhausen, see page 171. † Lyons Brotteaux. *a* Via Grenoble. *x* Rapide Train, extra supplement.

The times on the LEFT are to be read DOWNWARDS, those on the RIGHT UPWARDS.

[German St. Rys. (Cologne).

D—Corridor Exp., see page 75. (Cologne—Frankfort 137 Miles).

Through Services, see also pp. 128, 129, 132, 188. Greenwich Time.	1 2 luxe O	Exp 1 2 3	Exp 1 2 3 D	fast 2 3	fast 2 3	Exp 1 2 3	Exp 1 2 3 Y	Exp 1 2 3 D	2 3	Exp 1 2 3 D	Exp 1 2 3	fast 2 3	fast 2 3	2 3	Exp 1 2 3 D	Exp 1 2 3 D	Exp 1 2 3 D
Cologne (Hauptbahnh) dp	1 38	2 56	7 0	8 15	9 19	..	1153	1214	1323	15 4	15 6	1510	1647	1825	19 3	2313	2331
Cologne (Deutz) .... ,,	Sun., Wed. and Fri. only	↓	..	8 18	9 22	1022	..	↓	1327	↓	..	1513	..	1829	..	↓	↓
Troisdorf			..	8 37	9 38	..	..		14 1		..	1529	17 5	19 3	..		
Beuel (Bonn)			..	8 47	9 47	1049	..		1417		..	1537	1715	1916	..		
Obercassel			..	..	..	..	..		1422		..	..	..	..	..		
Königswinter			7 28	8 57	9 56	..	1222		1442		1537	1546	1725	1939	1934		
Linz			..	9 16	1012	..	..		15 9		..	16 2	1742	20 2	..		
Neuwied		↓	7 58	9 45	1031	1126		↓	1546		1610	1621	18 3	2032	20 6		↓
Ehrenbreitstein				10 5	1047				1610		..	1637	1820	2053	..	↓	
Niederlahnstein .... arr.		L	L	1013	1055	1148	L	1333	1621	↓	L	1647	1828	21 1	L		0 45
Ems ,,				1114	1128	1221	..	14 7	17 9	L	..	17 9	1914	2158	..	L	..
Cologne (*see p.* 176) dep.	..	..	6 33	..	9 17	..	..	..	..	..	..	14 5	1643	19 6	..	..	2255
Coblence .... dep.	..	4 15	8 18	9 45	1045	1116	1310	1315	1635	1626	1634	1635	1819	2052	2027	0 32	0 16
Niederlahnstein .... arr.	..	..	8 24	9 52	1051	1124	To Constance	1323	1641	..	..	1641	1827	21 0	2033	..	0 24
Niederlahnstein .. dep.			8 25	1017	1059	1150		1335	1655	..	To Heidelberg.	1650	1831	21 4	2034		0 46
St. Goarshausen			..	1051	1130	..		..	1736	..		1721	1859	2144	21 1		..
Rudesheim			9 13	1125	1159	1241		1426	1814	..		1757	1927	2220	2128		1 36
Eltville		5 23	..	1140	1214	1258			1842	..		18 6	1943	2245	2144		..
Wiesbaden-Biebrich dep.	↓	..		..	1224	..	↓	↓	19 0	..			1953	23 1	..	↓	..
Wiesbaden (Haupt.) arr.	..	5 38	9 39	1154	1231	1314	1425	1454	19 6	1746		1821	1959	23 7	2159		2 4
Mainz (Haupt.) .... arr.	3 52	5 57	9 56	1223	1248	1337	1441	1512	1931		1753	1848	2016	2321	2214	1 40	2 32
Wiesbaden (Haupt.) .. dep.	..	5 44		12 1	1240	1320	..	To B'le	1928	1752	..	1827	20 5	2316	2211	..	To B'le
Frankfort (Haupt.) arr.	‡1 20	6 28	1036	1242	1321	14 8			2031	1828	.	19 6	2044	0 16	2258	2‡18	

Frankfort, Kastel, Biebrich and Wiesbaden, see p. 173.	Exp 1 2 3 D	Exp 1 2 3 D	luxe 1 2 O	Exp 1 2 3 D	Exp 2 3 D	Exp 1 2 3 D	Exp 1 2 3	fast 2 3	Exp 1 2 3 D	Exp 1 2 3 D	Exp 1 2 3 Z	Exp 1 2 3 D	fast 2 3	fast 2 3	fast 2 3	Exp 1 2 3 D	fast 2 3
Frankfort (Haupt.) dep.	0 14	0 20	2 11	*	7 23	7 57	* *	9 59	1144	‖	..	1514	16 3	1740	1848	1935	2116
Wiesbaden (Haupt.) arr.	1 1	1 7	2 45	..	8 7	8 42	.	1038	1226	..	..	1559	1647	1824	1931	.	2154
Mainz (Hpt.) .... dep.	0 39	..	..	3 8	7 58	8 33	9 41	1025	1224	1414	1506	1538	1636	18 2	19 0	2011	2145
Wiesbaden (Haupt.) .. dep.	1 10	1 20	2 51	3 46	8 13	8 49	..	1044	1247	1434	1524	16 5	1655	1831	1937	2029	22 0
Wiesbaden-Biebrich ,,	..	↓	↓	..	..	..	↓	..	..	↓	↓		..	1837	..		..
Eltville	1 25			..		9 4		1057	..			1619	17 9	1847	1951	..	2213
Rudesheim	1 41			4 12	L	9 21		1112	1315			1636	1724	19 7	20 6	2055	2229
St. Goarshausen	..			..	..	9 47		1141	..	↓		..	1754	1940	2034	..	2257
Niederlahnstein .. arr.	..	↓	↓	5 1	..	1015	↓	1212	..	1548		1727	1827	2011	21 2	2143	2327
Niederlahnstein .. dep.			..	..	.	1018	L	1241	..	1552	↓	1731	1831	2013	2114	..	2328
Coblence .... arr.	2 37	2 45	..	..	9 38	1025	11 2	1250	1410	16 1	1642	1737	1840	2019	2120	..	2334
Cologne (*see p.* 177) arr.	..	..	..	..	..	..		..	..	..		1927	2125	..	2252		2 14
Ems .... dep.				..	..	..		11 6		15 0	L	17 7	1743	..	2036	L	2326
Niederlahnstein .. dep.			Sun., Wed and Fri. only.	5 2	..	..		1217		1550	..	1729	1833	L	21 8	2144	0 4
Ehrenbreitstein				..	..		↓	1224			..	..	1841	.	2115	2152	0 12
Neuwied				..	9 59	L	1124	1240			..	1748	1858	2039	2131	22 6	0 32
Linz				..	..	..	..	1259				..	1919	21 4	2149	..	0 59
Königswinter				..	1030	..	1154	1316			1727	..	1936	2122	22 4	2235	..
Obercassel .... arr.				..	..	..	..	..			..	..	..	..	..	..	..
Beuel (Bonn) .... ,,				5 52	..	..	..	1325		↓	..	1824	1946	2131	2213		..
Troisdorf .... dep.				..	..	..	..	1334	↓		..	..	1956	2145	2222	..	..
Cologne (Deutz) .. arr.	↓	↓		..	..	..	..	1349		..	..	1851	2013	22 1	..		..
Cologne (Hauptbahnh) ,,	3 57	4 5	5 14	6 21	11 2	1158	1227	1353	1536	17 4	1759	..	2018	22 6	2239	23 7	..

L *via* Coblence. O Ostend (Karlsbad)-Vienna Exp. Sleeping Cars only, *see page* 84. Extra Fares.
Y July 1–Sept. 11. Z June 30–Sept. 10. * From Munich. * * From Heidelberg.
‡ Frankfort (Sud.) + Not Suns. § 3 & 3 class only. „ Mainz (Kastel). ‖ Fr. Bale.

† Emden (South)

HAMM—MUNSTER—NORDDEICH

a 2 and 3 cl. only

2 3	fast 2 3	2 3	fast 2 3	Exp 1 2 3	2 3	fast 2 3	2 3	2 3	155 Miles	fast 2 3	2 3	2 3	Exp 1 2 3	2 3	fast 2 3	2 3	2 3
6 4	9 35	1028	12 5	1325	1441	19 7	2033	1 21	dep. Hamm p. 163/4 arr.	1020	1355	1518	16*a*21	1832	2111	2311	..
6 46	10 4	1110	1234	1354	1524	1936	2113	2 1	arr. Munster.. dep.	9 53	1310	1436	15*a*52	1750	2040	2229	..
6 57	1026	1115	1258	1435	1550	2025	2156	4 32	dep. Munster..... arr.	9 32	1247	1432	1516	1720	2028	2156	0 24
7 42	11 1	1157	1332	15 6	1635	2055	2242	5 18	arr. Rheine..... dep.	9 1	12 2	1348	1444	1636	1953	21 8	2340
7 50	11 3	1214	1338	15 8	1641	21 4	2250	5 33	dep Rheine........ arr.	8 55	1154	1335	1442	1627	1951	2059	2332
9 59	1258	1413	1530	1633	1851	2253	0 53	7 45	arr. Leer......... dep.	7 15	9 42	1120	1312	1350	18 2	1846	2126
1111	1328	1446	1558	17 1	1949	2319	1†50	8 40	arr. Emden, West dep.	6 45	9 5	1035	1243	13†16	1730	18†10	2036
1228	1421		1650	1753	2047	..	..	9 46	arr. Norddeich dep	..	8 4	9 25	1157	..	1627	1510	1925

F D—Special fast corridor Express, EXTRA FARES, *see page* 75. J—Rheingold Exp., See Note, *p.* 75.

Cologne, Coblence, Bingen, Mainz, Frankfort, Aschaffenburg, Mannheim.

[German State Railways. (Cologne).

☞ *Cologne-Frankfort via Rudesheim, see page* 175.

Mls.	Station	2 3	Exp 1 2 3 D	Exp 2 3 D	Exp 1 2 3 D	2 3	Rap 2 cl. FDT	Exp 2 3 D	Exp 1 2 3 D	Exp 1 2 3 D	fast 2 3	Rap 1 2 FD J	Rap 1 2 FD	fast 2 3
..	Cologne (Deutz.) dep.	5 19	..	..	..	7 31	..	8 16	..	..	..	J	..	1159
0	Cologne (Hptbhf.) ,,	5 30	6 33	..	7 25	7 51	8 16	8 31	9 17	9 24	1032	11 0	1211	1218
21	Bonn	6 20	7 2	..	7 53	8 42	8 38	8 59	9 47	9 55	1059	↓	1238	1245
25	Gödesberg	6 28	..		..	8 51	W	R	R		11 7			1252
29	Rolandseck	6 39	..	..	..	9 1								..
33	Remagen arr.	6 49	7 21	..		9 11		9 18	10 7	1013	1120			13 4
..	Neuenahr (Bad.) ,,	7 17	8 6	..	..	9 41		9 41	1036	1036	1143		↓	14 2
46	Andernach	7 21	7 38	..	..	9 48		9 36		1033	1138			1322
48	Weissenthurm	7 27		..	..	9 53	↓					↓	..	1327
57	Coblence arr.	7 46	7 57		8 38	1011	9 18	9 54	1041	1054	1256	12 3	1319	1342
..	Bad Ems (p.169) ar.	8 59	8 59	..	1017	1114	1017	1114	1114	1128	13 8		14 7	14 7
..	Coblence dep.	8 27	7 59	.	8 42	1019	9 19	9 58	1045	1058	1211	12 4	1320	1346
61	Capellen-Stolzenfels ,,	8 34				1025	..	.	.					..
69	Boppard	9 0	8 16			1045		1014		1116	1229			14 2
78	St. Goar	9 19	..			11 4		1027	..		1243			1415
87	Bacharach	9 36	..			1128			..	.	13 0			1431
95	Bingerbruck (p. 179) arr.	9 55	8 49			1146		1049	1132	1151	1313			1443
	dep.	1015	9 2	8 59	↓	1250	↓	1051	1134	1153	1317		↓	1446
96	Bingen	1020	..	9 3	..	1254	..	1055		1157	1321	↓		1450
114	Mainz (Hauptbf.) arr.	11 7	..	9 28	9 52	1327	1017	1117	1159	1223	1350	13 5	1425	1516
									2 3					
	dep.	1154		9 31	10 4	1332	1018	1120	1232	..	1355		1427	1519
137	Frankfort (Hpt.) arr	1256		10 6	1036	1412	1043	1153	13 8		1435	To Milan.	1459	1555
		2 3	To Bad Munster and Munich.	2 3					2 3					
114	Mainz (Hpt.) dep.	12 9		9 35		14 5	To Bale.	12 9	12 9		14 5		.	1535
136	Darmstadt arr.	13 0		10 6		1437		13 0	13 0		1437		..	16 6
	dep.	1331		1015	..	1448		1331	1331		1448		..	1656
162	Aschaffenburg ar.	1433		1052	..	1550		1433	1433	↓	1550		..	18 0
		2 3			2 3				1230	2 3	2 3			
114	Mainz (Hpt.) dep.	1115		9 42	9 51	..		..	12 3	1227	1436	13 7	1514	1542
150	Worms	1231		1015	11 6			..	1239	b	1556	b	1550	1653
164	Mannheim arr.	14 8		1048	12 8	..	..	..	1320	1326	1648	1358	1623	1812
..	Heidelberg	1426		1122	1245		..	..	1349	..	1717		1645	1852

Mls.	Station	fast 2 3	Exp 1 2 3 D	Exp 1 2 3 D	Exp 1 2 3 D	Exp 1 2 3 D	2 3	Exp 2 3 D	Exp 1 2 3 D	fast 2 3	Exp 1 2 3 D M	Exp 1 2 3 D	Exp 1 2 3 D	Exp 1 2 3 D
..	Cologne (Deutz.) dep.		.		..		1517	..	R	..	..	..	..	..
0	Cologne (Hptbhf.) ,,	14 5	1452	15 4	15 6	1538	1545	1643	19 6	2021	2120	2250	2255	2329
21	Bonn	1437	1519	1533	↓	16 6	1631	1710	1936	2049	2149	2317	2323	2357
25	Gödesberg	1446	..			1615	1638	..	..	2057	..	↓	↓	..
29	Rolandseck	..				..	1648	R	..	..	↓			..
33	Remagen arr.	1458	1537	1551		1628	1658	1728	1954	21 9				..
..	Neuenahr (Bad.) ,,	1537		..		1646	1726	1750	2056	2152				..
46	Andernach	1517	..	..	↓	1646	1730	1747	2014	2134				..
48	Weissenthurm		.			..	1736	.	..					..
57	Coblence arr.	1536	1611	1624	1630	17 6	1755	18 7	2035	2150	2236		0 10	0 44
..	Bad Ems (p.169) ar.	1619	17 9	17 9	17 9	1748	1839	1839	21 6	2244	.	..	0 47	..
..	Coblence dep.	1543	1613	1626	1634	1711	1822	18 9	2038	2156	2250		0 16	0 46
61	Capellen-Stolzenfels ,,					..	1828	..						..
69	Boppard	1559			1651	1727	1848	..	2055	2211				..
78	St. Goar	1616			..	1741	19 7	..	2110	2226	↓			..
87	Bacharach	1632			..	..	1924	..	.	2242				..
95	Bingerbruck (p. 179) arr.	1644	1659		1724	18 3	1942	1856	2132	2252	2337			1 32
	dep.	1646	17 1		1726	18 5	20 8	1858	2134	2257	2339	↓	↓	1 33
96	Bingen	1650			1730	..	2012	19 3	2138	23 1		..	..	
114	Mainz (Hauptbf.) arr.	1716	1726		1753	1829	2059	1927	22 2	2326	0 4	1 5	1 24	2 38
	dep.	1719	1732	↓			2114	1931	22 7	2331		1 8	1 26	..
137	Frankfort (Hpt.) arr	1757	18‡1	1828	To Heidelberg.	To Bale,	2214	20 5	2245	0 10	To Bale.	1 40	1 58	..
								2 3						
114	Mainz (Hpt.) dep.	1759	To Munich.	..			2216	1939	2216	2339		To Munich.	To Munich.	2 41
136	Darmstadt arr.	1830		..			2247	2010	2247	0 24				3 11
	dep.	1835		..			2317	2022	2317	..				3 14
162	Aschaffenburg ar.	1912		..			0 13	2136	0 13	..				
114	Mainz (Hpt.) dep.	..		..	18 4	1831	2224	..	..	2335	0 7	..		To Bale.
150	Worms	..		..	1843	b	23 1	..	..	0 22	0 44	..		
164	Mannheim arr.	..	..	..	1926	1930	2338	..	..	0 56	1 16		..	
..	Heidelberg	..	..	..	20 0	..	24 0	..	..	1 17		..	..	4 5

D Corridor Exp. **M** June 30–Sept. 9. **R** Rest. car. **W** Weekdays only. *b via* Biblis. † Not Suns. ‡ Frank'ort Sud.

D—See *p.* 75.

Mainz, Worms, Ludwigshafen.

[German State Rlys., Mainz.

Mls.	Station	1 2 3 D	2 3	2 3	2 3	2 3	2 3 D	2 3	2 3	1 2 3 D	2 3	2 3	1 2 3 D	2 3	2 3	2 3	1 2 3 D	2 3	2 3	2 3	2 3	1 2 3 D	2 3
	Wiesbaden dep.	2 20		5 44	6 46	8 58	9 28	9 33	1056	1135	1238	1325	15 0	1527	1614	1720	1746	1816	1935	2014	2121	2210	2311
0	Mainz (Hauptb.) ,,	2 35	4 22	6 10	6 58	9 11	9 42	9 51	1115	12 3	1250	1345	1514	1542	1647	1740	18 4	1847	1950	2032	2145	2224	2335
8	Worms arr.	3 10	5 36	7 26	7 44	9 59	1015	11 6	1231	1239	1333	1438	1550	1653	1758	19 4	1843	1959	2037	2141	23 8	23 1	0 22
	dep.	3 11	5 42	7 30	7 45	10 1	1016	1118	13 2	1240	1335	1440	1551	17 0	18 2	1921	1845	20 6	2038	2146	2316	23 2	0 24
	Ludwigshafen arr.	3 34	6 11	7 58	8 5	1023	1036	1147	1331	13 4	1357	15 2	1610	1730	1829	1948	19 9	2034	2058	2212	24 0	2322	0 45
	Mannheim ,,	3 48	6 24	8 16	8 16	1036	1048	12 8	14 8	1320	14 8	1515	1623	1812	1849	2025	1926	2045	2111	2248	0 48	2338	0 56

¶ Not Sundays

Mannheim, Aschaffenburg, Frankfort, Mainz, Coblence, Cologne.

[German State Rys. (Cologne).

Thro' Tables, pp. 128, 129, 132, 178, 189	123	123	123	23	23	123	123	23	23	123	123	23	123	12
	ExD	Exp	D	fast		Exp	ExD		Exp	ExD	Exp		Exp	Rap
Heidelberg .. dep.	..	D			6 58	D	8 4	8 55	D	..	D	..	1232	FD
Mannheim .... dep.	2 23	4 0			7 17		8 23	9 17	R	..	..	..	1258	..
Worms	↓	4 33			7 48		8 57	9 54		..	..	..	1335	
Mainz .... arr.	↓	5 7			8 31	..	9 37	1038		1155	..	..	1411	
	From Bale.	B			23		23	23					23	From Munich.
Aschaffenburg d.			..	.	6 16	.	7 54	9 12	..	..	..	1121	12 9	
Darmstadt .. arr.	..				7 27	..	8 56	9 49		..	..	1221	1321	
Darmstadt .. dep.	..	↓	..	5 8	7 48	..	9 0	1016	1016	..	..	1232	1331	
Mainz (Gr. tm.) a.	3 20		..	5 57	8 27	..	9 31	1045	1045		.. ‡	1324	14 1	
							123						23D	
Frankfort (Hpt.) dp.	↓		4 50	5 49	7 43	7 57	↓	9 58	1015		1152	1227	1334	1424
Mainz (Hauptbhf.) arr.	↓	↓	5 20	6 22	8 46	..	↓	11 4	1050		x	1330	14 6	1454
Mainz (Hauptbhf.) dep.	3 22	5 9	5 22	6 32	9 10	..	9 41	1114	1053	1157	..	1355	1417	1456
Bingen	..			6 58	9 58	Via Niederlahnstein, see p. 175.	10 3	1159	1116		Via Niederlahnstein, see p. 175.	1448	..	↓
Bingerbruck arr.	↓		5 45	7 1	10 1		10 7	12 2	1119	1220		1451	1440	
Bingerbruck dep.			5 47	7 4	1017		10 9	1229	1121	1221		1459	1442	
Bacharach			↓	7 17	1036		..	1247	.	↓		1517		
St. Goar				7 33	1053		1032	13 4	..			1541	..	
Boppard	↓	↓		7 47	1113		1045	1323	1155			16 1	1517	
Capellen-Stolzenfels	..		↓	..	1132			1342	..	↓		1620	..	↓
Coblence ...... arr.	5 14	6 17	6 36	8 4	1138	1025	11 2	1348	1213	13 7	14 1	1626	1534	1558
Ems (p. 169) .. dep.		..	6 0	7 34	11 6	9 56	..	1328	11 6		1328	1632	15 0	15 0
Coblence ...... dep.	5 18	6 31	6 41	8 9	1152	1029	11 6	1424	1219	1312	14 3	1712	1538	1559
Weissenthurm	..		..	8 24	1213	..	..	1443		..	..	1730	..	..
Andernach	..			8 31	1219	1047	..	1449	1236	..	..	1744		..
Neuenahr .... dep.	..		6 27	8 32	1221	1019	..	1424	1221	13 8	1424	1748	1519	..
Remagen	..		7 11	8 53	1259	11 5	..	1518	1254	1343	1434	1812	1610	..
Rolandseck	..			..	13 8	..	..	1528	..	..	..	1821	..	..
Godesberg	..	↓		9 6	1319	1118	..	1538	..	..	..	1830	..	..
Bonn	6 4	7 19	7 29	9 14	1328	1127	..	1548	1314	14 1	1452	1839	1628	1642
Cologne (H.) .. arr.	6 36	7 50	7 57	9 45	1412	1158	1227	1633	1344	1431	1523	1922	1659	17 9
Cologne (Deutz.) ,,					1430		..	1651	1354	..	..	1936	..	..

Thro' Tables, pp. 128, 129, 132, 178, 189	23	23	12	123	123	23	23	23	123	3 cl.	23	123	23
			Rap	ExD	ExD	fast		fast	ExD	Rap	fast	Exp	
Heidelberg .. dep.	1347	..	FD	1450	1450	..	..		..	FDT	19 0	D	1846
Mannheim .... dep.	14 5	..	1531	1516	1526	..	..		..	W	1924	..	19 8
Worms	1436		b	1553	16 5	..	..	..	..	..	2016	.	1946
Mainz .... arr.	1520	..	1622	1628	1640	..	..	..	..	..	2126		2021
	fast		From Milan	↓	↓	23				From Bale		From Munich via Bad Munster.	
Aschaffenburg d.	1326	12 9				1527	..	1655			..		1820
Darmstadt .. arr.	1421	1321				1630	..	1759	..		..		1928
Darmstadt .. dep.	1444	1411				1651	..	1812	..		..		2020
Mainz (Gr. tm.) a.	1515	15 4				1739	..	1843	..		..		2047
Frankfort (Hpt.) dp.	1448	1344	J			17 4	1719	1815	.	2051	2058		20 0
Mainz (Hauptbhf.) arr.	1525	1449		..	↓	1744	1815	1852	.	2115	2135		2059
Mainz (Hauptbhf.) dep.	1529	15 8	1624	1632	1644	1747	1830	1856	2020	2116	2138		2122
Bingen	1555	1551	↓		17 8	1819	1915	1924	..	↓	22 4		2212
Bingerbruck arr.	1558	1554		1658	1712	1822	1918	1927	2044		22 7	2048	2215
Bingerbruck dep.	16 0	1611		17 0	1714	1825	20 2	1930	2046		22 9	2054	2225
Bacharach	1612	1630			..	1838	2020	1943	..		2221	..	2244
St. Goar	1628	1647		1724	..	1855	2037	20 0	..		2237		23 1
Boppard	1645	17 0		1738		1912	2058	2014	..		2250	2126	2322
Capellen-Stolzenfels	..	1734	↓		..	..	2117				..		2341
Coblence ...... arr.	17 1	1740	1726	1755	18 2	1929	2123	2031	2133	2213	23 6	2142	2347
Ems (p. 169) .. dep.	1632	1743	..	17 7	17 7	19 1	21 4	19 1	21 4	..	21 4	21 4	2326
Coblence ...... dep.	17 7	1835	1727	18 0	18 9	1936	2149	2037	2137	2214	2310	2144	0 3
Weissenthurm	1722	1855	↓			1951	22 6		..	↓	2325		0 22
Andernach	1728	19 0		1818	1828	1957	2212	2055	..		2330	22 0	0 29
Neuenahr .... dep.	17 9	1825		1748	1825	1948	2155	2051	..		..	2155	..
Remagen	1745	1930		1837	1847	2022	2242	2120	..		2347	2217	0 57
Rolandseck	..	1940		..	..		2251		.		..	..	1 7
Godesberg	18 4	1950			.	2035	23 1	2134		↓	2359		1 18
Bonn	1813	20 0	↓	1857	19 8	2045	2310	2145	2221	2253	0 7	2234	1 29
Cologne (H.) .. arr.	1843	2045	1832	1927	1940	2125	2353	2219	2252	2316	0 36	23 3	2 14
Cologne (Deutz.) ,,		21 3	..				0 6		..		0 51		2 38

B Rest Car. b Via Biblis. x From Frankfort via Wiesbaden. z Via Worms. ‡ Frankfort-Sud

B July 2–Sept. 11. D Corridor Exp., *see p.* 75. J Rheingold Exp., see note *p.* 75. FD Special fast Corridor Exp. EXTRA FARES, *see p.* 75.

Ludwigshafen, Worms, Mainz.

[German State Rys. (Mainz).

D—See page 75.

	23	23	23	123D	23	23	123D	23	123D	23	23	123D	123D	23	23	23	123D	23	23	23	23	23	123D
Mannheim .... dep.	4 40	6 15	7 17	8 23	9 17	1012	11 4	1140	1258	14 5	1435	1516	1526	..	1738	..	19 8	1924	2040	2136	2225	23 4	1 49
Ludwigshafen .... ,,	5 8	6 46	7 28	8 36	9 32	1030	1118	1220	1315	1416	1448	1529	1541	1631	1750	1841	1921	1940	2052	2148	2235	2326	2 4
Worms .... arr.	5 29	7 14	7 47	8 56	9 52	1056	1138	1250	1333	1435	1510	1552	16 4	1655	1820	19 9	1945	20 8	2118	22 8	23 2	2345	2 27
Worms .... dep.	5 31	7 38	7 48	8 57	9 54	1117	1139	1310	1335	1436	1512	1553	16 5	17 1	1830	1924	1946	2016	2130	22 9	2310	2346	2 28
Mainz (Hauptbhf.) ...... arr.	6 17	8 55	8 31	9 37	1038	1237	1215	1431	1411	1520	16 5	1628	1640	1810	1940	2045	2021	2126	2238	2252	0 18	0 27	3 5
Wiesbaden (p. 175) .... ,,	6 34	9 27	8 44	9 55	1052	13 0	1230	15 1	1427	1534	1620	1649	1711	1830	20 0	21 5	2035	2156	23 0	23 6	0 36	0 45	3 20

THROUGH SERVICES between HOLLAND, BRUSSELS, BALE, etc.

and Heidelberg, Bale, Zurich, Coire, St. Moritz, Interlaken, Lucerne and Italy, via the St. Gothard.

P	FD	A	C	X	E	H	G			G	E	X	C	A	P	FD
1 2	1 2	1 2 3	1 2 3	1 2 3	1 2 3	1 2 3	1 2		1 2 3	1 2 3	1 2 3	1 2 3	1 2 3	1 2 3	1 2	1 2
Pull. Car Train Amsterdam to Zurich	7 41	8 14	1452	1710	1947	..	1041	dep. AMSTERDAM (C.) p 157 a	..	1051	1150	1250	1650	2151	Pull. Car Train Zurich to Amsterdam	2238
	7 15	7 52	1415	1645	1813	..	2015	,, The Hague.... ,, ,,	..	1113	1213	1313	1713	2226		23 4
	1054	12 6	1856	2112	2321	..	0 53	arr. Cologne (Cent.)....dep.	..	5 40	6 41	7 55	12 2	1714		1839
	11 0	1214	19 6	2120	2329	..	2 56	dep. COLOGNE (C.) (p.175) a.		3 57	6 36	7 50	1158	17 4		1832
	..	15 0	..	..	2 26	..	5 44	,, Wiesbaden.... (pp. 182-3) ..dep.	..	1 10	3 54	..	8 49	1434		..
	..	..	2245	..	..	..	6 28	ar. Frankfort .... ,,	..	0 14		..	7 57	..		..
	..	..	2353	..	..	..	7 10	d. Frankfort .... arr.	..	0 3		..	5 32			
	14 3	1626	*	1 22	*	..	*	dep. Mannheim.... .. ,,	..	2355	2 17	3 45	4 20	1254		1525
	1440	1739	2 11	2 5	4 55	..	9 40	arr. Carlsruhe .... ..dep.	..	2212	1 34	3 0	3 34	12 9		1449
	1650	2025	5 25	4 55	5 2	..	13 0	,, BALE (Badisch) .. ,,	..	1928	23 5	0 17	0 30	9 22		1238
	17 7	2058	6 8	5 40	8 30	..	1338	,, BALE (Swiss) c .. ,,		19 2	21 0	2327	0 0	8 45		1218
8 3	↓	..	1543	June 1 – Sept. 9	..	1943	↓	dep. Amsterdam ...... arr.	9‡15	↑	1145	..	1416	1945	20 3	↑
8 56		9 54	1632		..	2055		,, The Hague ...... ,,	8‡27		1052	..	1327	1844	1914	
..		..	1842		..	2220		,, Ostend (p.127) .. ,,	..		10 7		1032	..		
11 7		1249	2020			0 54		,, Brussels (p. 149) .. ,,	2255		7 48	July 1 – Sept 10	8 53	15 5	16 9	
1356		16 8	2343		..	4 47		arr. Luxemberg (p. 179) dp.	1946		3 32		5 22	12 2	1325	
↓		1254	1612	From July 1	..	↓		dep. Amsterdam (p. 158) ar.	↑		..		1418 (From July 1)	1949	↑	
		14 2	2022		..			,, Maastricht ...... ,,			..		9 20	16 0		
↓		..	2333		..	↓		arr. Luxemburg (p. 158) dp.					5 25	12 0		
14 2		1625	0 10	..	..	5 1		dep. Luxemburg . arr.	1930		3 15	..	5 15	1150	1319	
1618		19 7	3 35	..	..	8 42		arr. Strasbourg ....dep.	1633		2315		2 5	8 58	1059	
1751	↓	21 0	5 32	..		1051	↓	arr. BALE (Swiss Sta.) dep.	1450		2051	..	0 20	7 10	9 27	
1838	1838	2138	6 49	7 13	8 5	1155	1454	dep. Bale (Swiss) .. p. 283 ar.	1425	1813	1946	2350	22 5	6 45	8 40	1123
1954	1954	2256	8 17	8 36	10 4	1320	1614	arr. ZURICH (Cent.) dp.	1312	1655	1824	2236	2049	5 35	7 22	1018
2327	2327		1122	1035	12 3	1546	1841	,, Coire .... p. 286 ,,	1052	1310	16 7	1953	1830		.	7 11
			1444	1315	1759	1840	22 0	,, St. Moritz ,,	8 0	1025	1236	1710	1545		..	..
↓	1855	2142	6 57	6 57	..	1230	16 8	dep. Bale (Swiss) p. 281 arr.	1531	1855	1555	2225	2225	6 16	..	..
	2042	2328	8 30	8 30	..	14 7	1741	arr. Berne.... dep.	1345	718	1718	2050	2050	4 19	..	..
↓	..	.	9 48	9 48		1540	1929	,, Interlaken (Ost.) .. ,,	12 5	1541	1541	19 3	19 3	..		
			1 2	1 2								1 2	1 2			
1855	1730	2142	5 42	6 45	9 0	12 0	1450	dep. BALE (Swiss)...... arr.	1425	1648	20 8	2341	2341	6 16	8 55	12 0
2022	1852	2320	7 58	8 1	1028	1330	1615	arr. LUCERNE (p. 282) dep.	1253	1524	1838	2227	2227	4 47	7 25	1045
..	2247	4 15	1138	1158	1457	1755	2050	,, Chiasso c (p. 287).. ,,	8 32	1116	1410	1850	1850	0 37	2 5	7 10
..	0 5	5 55	13 7	13 7	1640	1924	2224	,, MILAN (p. 304).... ,,	6 55	9 42	1225	1715	1715	2252	0 20	5 58
												1 2	1 2	1 2		
..	6 25	..	1334	│	1712	20 0	0 30	dep. Milan .... arr.	5 34	9 40	1145	1636	634	2230	..	..
..	9 10	..	1545	│	1947	2235	3 39	arr. Genoa (p. 302) ....dep.	1 4	7 1	9 0	1433	1433	1946	..	..
..	1630	..	6 40	↓	6 40	6 51	1310	,, ROME (p. 301) .... ,,	18 0	23 0	2350	0 30	0 30	1220	..	..
..	6 50		13x50	14x20	18 0	1940	2250	dep. Milan .... arr.	5 10	1035	1035		1345	22 0		..
..	9 36	..	1543	1543	1953	2 40	1 57	arr. Bologna .... p. 303 ..dep.	2 38	7‖20	8 50	..	1410	1948	..	..
..	1140	.	1638	1638	2018	2253	3 35	,, FLORENCE.. .. ,,	2328	5 48	5 48	..	11 35	1820	..	..
..	1530		1950	1950	24 0	..	8 0	,, ROME .... .. ,,	1910	0 5	0 5	..	7 5	1425	..	..

A—1, 2 & 3 cl. Amsterdam-Cologne-Genoa-Vintimille, and 1, 2 & 3 cl. Hague-Bale and v.v. Rest. Car Rotterdam-Cologne-Bale-The Hague-Bale and v.v. B—1, 2 & 3 cl. Cars Amsterdam-Coire and Interlaken and v.v. Rest. Car Amsterdam-Coblence and v.v. 1 & 2 cl. Sleep. Cars Amsterdam-Coire and Amsterdam-Interlaken and v.v. C—1, 2 & 3 cl. Amsterdam and Hague-Frankfort. 1 & 2 cl. Car Frankfort-Milan-Vintimille and v.v. Rest. Car Amsterdam-Frankfort and v.v. 1 & 2 cl. Sleep. Car Ostend-Bale-Lucerne and v.v., and Amsterdam-Bale. E—1, 2 & 3 cl. Amsterdam-Cologne-Milan-Genoa and v.v. Rest. Cars Rotterdam-Cologne and v.v. 1 & 2 cl. Sleep. Car Amsterdam-Bale and v.v. 1 & 2 cl. Sleep. Car Rome-Bale-Brussels-The Hague. G—1, 2 & 3 cl. Amsterdam-Cologne-Frankfort and v.v. 1, 2 & 3 cl. Frankfort-Milan and v.v. Rest. Car Amsterdam-Cologne, Frankfort-Bale and v.v. Sleep. Car Amsterdam-Frankfort and v.v. H—1 & 2 cl. Sleep. Car The Hague-Bale-Rome and 1, 2 & 3 cl. Cars The Hague-Bale. P—"Edelweiss" Pullman Express daily. S—Rest Car Amsterdam-Frankfort and v.v. 1 & 2 cl. Sleep. Cars Amsterdam-Bale and Frankfort-Lugano and v.v. X—1, 2 & 3 l. Amsterdam-Interlaken and Coire. Rest. Car Amsterdam-Coblence and Bale-Olten. 1, 2 & 3 cl. Sleep. Car Amsterdam-Interlaken and Coire. FD—Rheingold Express, 1 & 2 cl. Saloon Car Train, Hook-Milan and v.v. **Extra Fares.**
* Via Heidelberg. Zurich, Enge Station. ‡ Weekdays only. § Interlaken (Bahnhof). ‖ 1 cl. only.
x Rapido train, supplement payable. *o* 1st class Rapido only.

☞ For Through Services from Flushing and Hook of Holland to Bale, etc., see pages 129 and 131.

D Corridor Exp. see p. 75.

(Frankfort) Bingerbruck, Metz.

[Ger. St. Rlys. Mayence & Trier Saabrg & French Rlys. (Est),

	2 3	2 3	2 3	1 2 3	1 2 3	2 3	2 3	2 3	2 3	2 3	2 3	2 3	1 2 3	2 3	1 2 3	
Frankfort p.177 dp.	4 50	4 50	5 49	7 23	8 30	1015	1110	13 8	1448	16 7	..	17 4	2032	..		
Mainz ....dep.	5 22	5 22	6 32		9 3	1053	1218	1342	1529	1651		1747	21 6	2020		
						Exp							D		Exp	
Cologne (p.176) dep.	1 25	..	1 25	6 33	6 33	9 24	1032	1032	1218	15 6	15 6	1643	..	19 6	..	
			fast	ExD	ExD			s x D					s			
Bingerbruck ..dep.	5 45	6 58	7 18	9 2	..	1156	1324	1414	1632	1731	1743	19 4	..	2137	.	
Kreuznach-Bad dep.	6 12	7 20	7 36	9 18	9 35	1217	1352	1430	17 1	1749	18 9	1920	2142	2153	..	
Munster a. S. arr.	6 18	7 34	7 41	9 24	9 40	1222	1358	1435	17 6	1755	1814	1925	2148	2158	..	
Munster a. S. dep.	—	7 47	7 42	To Munich.	9 41	1224	14 0	1436	17 8	1756	1817	1926	22 1	22 1	..	
Saarbrucken ¶arr.	..	1116	9 42		1138	1555	1728	1633	21 0	20 9	22 4	a	0 9	0 9		
Saarbrucken dep.	8 15	..	1045		1136	1543	18 9	17 0		2016	.		..		6 0	
Forbach ....arr.	8 24	..	1054		1156	1557	1825	1710		2030	..		..	..	6 10	
Metz	9 39	..	12 2		1338	1747	2011	1833	..	2219	..		..	..	7 27	

a To Carlsruhe. s Slp.-cars Frankfort-Paris & v.v.

† Weekdays only. § 2 and 3 cl. only. ¶ German (Mid-European) Time.

Mls	From Paris, p. 275.	2 3	2 3	2 3	1 2 3	2 3	2 3	2 3	2 3	2 3	1 2 3	1 2 3	2 3	1 2 3	2 3	2 3	1 2 3	
		fast	Exp		ExD						Exp	D		Exp	A		Exp	
0	**Metz** ....dep.	..	.	5 8	7 32	7 32	9 0	1143	1325	..	From Munich.	1630	1630	1812	1855	2132	2312	
48	Forbach............	..	..	7 13	8 40	8 40	1046	1252	1434	..		1811	1811	1925	2115	2343	0 18	
49	Saarbrucken arr.	..	..	7 27	8 50	8 50	1054	13 2	1444	..		1825	1825	1936	2135	2356	0 28	
	Saarbrucken ¶ dep.	..	6 5	7 49	8 50	9 25	1134	1310	1452	1630		1910	1848					
															2 3	2 3		
125	Munster a. S. arr.	..	8 10	1125	1046	1317	1455	1515	1817	1830		21 7	2213					
	Munster a. S. dep.	8 15	8 11	1126	1047	1332	1456	1516	1819	1831	2026	21 8	2221		9 39	1054		
128	Kreuznach-Bad	8 21	8 17	1133	1053	1339	15 3	1522	1828	1836	2033	2114	2229		9 46	1059		
137	**Bingerbruck** .. arr.	8 36	..	12 0	..	14 0	1528	1536	19 1	1852	2048	↓	2247	.	10 3	1116	..	
			s															
..	Cologne (p. 177) a.	11 2	..	1431	..	1659	1843	1843	2219	2219	23 3	↓	5 30	.	1227	1344	..	
156	p176 Mainz ....arr.	9 28	8 50	1327	1125	1457	1611	1611	20 2	20 2	22 2	2146	2326		111	1159	..	
180	p176 **Frankfort** .... arr.	10 6	9 24	1112	12 0	1616	1653	1653	2050	2050	2245	2221	0 10	..	1153	..		

A Not Sundays or Fete days.

Luxemburg, Metz, Strasbourg.

[French Rlys. (Est.)

Mls	From Belgium, see pp. 127 & 149.	1 2 3	1 2 3	1 2 3	1 2 3	1 2 3	1 2 3	1 2	1 2 3	1 2 3	1 2 3	1 2 3	2 3
		Ex s	Exp	Exp	Exp	Exp	Exp	P	Exr	Exp		Exp	Exp
0	**Luxemburg** ....dep.	0 10	1 53	5 1	6 5	8 8	1132	14 2	1625	1634	..	1912	2240
20	Thionville..........	1 13	2 40	6 0	6 53	9 8	1222	1428	1653	1723	1816	2012	2326
41	**Metz** .... arr.	1 38	3 3	6 26	7 22	9 37	1244	1448	1717	1752	19 2	2039	2353
	Metz .... dep.	1 41	3 10	6 28	7 36	9 39	1246	1449	1720	1755	1925	2043	
95	Saarbourg .... arr.	..	B	¶	8 44	1048	..	..	..	19 1	2131	¶	
	Saarbourg .... dep.	..			8 53	1056		..	..	19 7	..		
149	**Strasbourg** .... arr.	3 35	5 10	8 42	9 55	1156	1422	1618	19 7	20 1	..	2235	.
	BALE p. 181 arr.	5 32	7 27	1051	1211	1413	16 7	1751	21 0	2228	..	..	

s Sleeping car. ¶ Via Reding. v Buffet Car. † Not Sundays and Fetes.

	1 2 3	1 2 3	1 2 3	1 2 3	1 2	1 2 3	1 2 3	1 2 3	1 2 3	2 3	1 2 3	1 2 3	1 2 3
	Exp	Exp		Exp	P		Exp	Exp	Exp		Exp	Ex s	Exp
BALE (p. 181) dep.	..	..	..	7r10	9 27	..	10r0	1330	1450	..	17v8	2051	0 20
Strasbourg ....dep.	..	6 0	6 30	8 58	1059	1010	12 1	1550	1633	1442	19 0	2315	2 5
Saarbourg .... arr.	..	¶	7 30	¶		12 5	1255	B	..	1628	20 2	¶	s
Saarbourg .... dep.	..		7 37			1235	13 0			1652	20 7		
Metz .... arr.	..	7 53	9 26	1054	1227	1444	14 4	1733	1814	1916	2115	1 18	3 52
Metz .... dep.	6 50	7 55	..	1056	1229	..	14 7	1745	1817	2016	2118	1 22	3 54
Thionville..........	7 25	8 30	..	1120	1250	..	1441	18 6	1847	2122	2155	2 8	4 25
Luxemburg .... arr.	8 5	9 12	..	1150	1319	..	1529	1852	1930	2220	2235	3 15	5 15

* Express. r Rest. car. § 2 & 3 cl. only. P Pullman Train. 1st and 2nd class. B Suns. only, July 2–Oct. 10.

Cologne, Trier, Saarbrucken, Strasbourg.

[Saarbrg. and French Rlys. (Est.)

2 3	2 3	D2 3	2 3	2 3	2 3	2 3	2 3	D2 3		2 3	2 3	2 3	D2 3	2 3	2 3	2 3	D2 3	2 3
	6†54	8 25	10†32	1228	1336	1622	1830	2026	de. **Cologne (Hpt.)** arr	9 52	11 4	13‡44	1638	1946	2155	0 1	2224	..
	9 52	1130	14 0	17 8	1648	1932	2113	2325	arr. Trier (Hptb.) dep.	6 50	8 22	1027	1340	1635	1728	946	1928	
7 35	10 0	1140	14 5	1749	1653	1940	2117	2330	dep. **Trier** ...... arr	6 45	8 18	1023	1335	1615	1721	1922	924	2215
[illegible] 3	1127	13 0	1530	2019	1816	2110	2232	0 53	arr. Saarbrücken dep	4 33	7 9	9 0	1215	1455	15 2	171[illegible]	18 2	2053
9 7	1135	1320	1627	..	..	..	..	6 35	dep ¶Saarbrücken¶ arr	2224	..	..	12 5	..	1450		1657	2035
10 6	1212	15 3	1652	..	..	..	..	7 7	a. Saargemund d	2127	..	..	1121		1412	..	614	1952
12 4	1512	1512	1843	..	.	..	..	6 25	d. (Grn. time) a	2117	..	..	1010	..	1345	.	1529	1835
1344	1649	1649	..	..	..	..	..	7 18	arr. Ober- dep	2020	..	..	8 40	..	1215	..	1358	1657
1355	1657	1657		..	.	..	..	7 19	dep. modern arr	2018	..	..	8 32	..	12 6		1346	1649
1445	1741	1741	20 9	..	..	..	..	7 46	arr. **Strasbourg** dep	1948	..	..	7 44	..	1115	..	1258	6 0
1727	2051	2051	2228	..	..	..	..	1051	arr. BALE (p. 181) d	17 8	..	..	..	..	7 10	..	..	1313

† Via Coblence. ‡ Weekdays only. ¶ Cent. European time.

(Black Forest Line.) Offenburg, Constance, Schaffhausen. [Ger. State Rlys., Carlsruhe.

23	123	23	23	23	23	123	12	3	123		123	123	123	23	23	23	123	123
fast	Ex D	fast		Ex D		Ex D	F x D		Ex D		Ex D	Ex D	Ex D	Ex D	fast	fast	Ex D	fast
2329	..	3 6	3 6	7 25	..	9 24	1153	9 19	1214	dp. Cologne .. (p183/3) ar.	17 4	1759	1940	2252	..	..	3 57	6 21
4 14	7 15	8 55	8 55	11 6	11 6	1345	16 0	1521	1729	„ Heidelberg „	1159	1343	1453	1850	2055	21 2	2244	1 1
5 1	8 4	9 52	9 52	1221	1230	1455	1641	1618	1816	„ Carlsruhe „	11 7	1257	1346	1745	1920	20 6	2158	0 5
6 18	9 8	11 8	1135	1347	1442	1622	1742	1750	1922	„ **Offenburg** .. „	9 51	1152	1230	1646	1735	1852	2043	2236
6 34	..	..	1154	..	1512		A	1820	..	▼ Biberach .... ▲		B		..	1711		2027	..
6 49	9 33	1133	1210	1413	1533	1648	18 8	1842	1948	arr. Hausach .... dp.	9 24	1126	12 4	1620	1653	1826	2012	2210
7 35	9 39	1220	1220	1425	..	1710	..	19 6	2046	dp. Hausach .. ar.	8 42	1117	1117	A	1640	..	1941	22 4
8 52	11 5	14 4	14 4	1540	..	1833	..	2029	2224	arr. Freudenstadt d.	7 43	9 54	9 54		1545	..	1836	21 3
6 50	9 34	1135	1213	1415	1535	1650	18 9	1848	1949	dp. Hausach .... ar.	9 23	1125	12 3	1619	1651	1825	2011	22 9
7 2	9 46	1147	1231	1430	1558	17 6	..	1910	20 2	Hornberg .... ▲	9 13	..	1153	1610	1640	1816	20 2	2159
7 20	10 3	12 5	1255	1453	1629	1734	1844	1944	2023	Triberg	8 58	11 2	1139	1556	1623	18 2	1948	2145
7 57	1038	1241	1344	1537	1737	1823	1920	2051	21 5	Villingen	8 22	1032	11 5	1524	1546	1729	1915	2113
8 10	1051	1254	14 5	1550	1811	1837	1933	2123	2118	▼ Donaueschng.	8 5	1017	1049	15 7	1518	1713	19 0	2057
8 25	11 6	13 8	1426	16 5	1840	1853	..	2149	2135	ar. Immendingn.	7 48	..	1033	1452	1456	1657	1844	2041
8 55	1134	1337	1459	1635	1941	1925	2012	2239	22 2	„ Singen ...... dp.	7 9	9 28	9 59	1420	1359	1624	18 7	2011
9 38	12 9	14 4	1538	1712	2049	1956	2040	2349	2239	„ **Constance**.... „	6 36	9 0	9 28	1351	1325	1558	1739	1940
9 55	12 9	1448	1552	17 9	20 6	20 6	..	..	2242	„ **Schaffhausen** „	..	..	9 14	..	1250	1515	17 0	1943
1125	13 5	1727	1727	1757	2144	2144	.	..	2332	„ Zurich (p. 284) „	..	..	8 16	..	1039	1427	16 7	1757

A July 1st to Sept. 11th. **B** June 30–Sept. 10. **D** Corridor Exp., *see page* 75.

Hollenthal Line.) Freiburg-in-Breisgau, Neustadt, Donaueschingen. [Ger. St. Rys. Carlsruhe.

For trains on Suns. and Fete days see local bills.

A July 2nd to Sept. 9th. *w* Weekdays.

	A	fast				fast			2 and 3 cl.						A		fast	
7 15	8 37	9 10	10 1	1130	1310	1510	1557	1843	dep. **Freiburg** .. arr.	9 50	13 4	1518	1548	1724	1815	1917	1953	2325
8 21	9 10	9 46	11 3	1215	1417	1542	1649	20 2	Titisee ..	9 10	1217	1429	15 6	1635	1739	1829	1914	2239
8 28	9 16	9 52	1110	1223	1427	1549	17 0	2011	arr. } **Neustadt** { dp.	9 3	12 7	1419	1459	1628	1731	1818	19 6	
8 45	9 22	9 58	1118	1235	1440	1554	1726	2017	dep. } **Neustadt** { ar.	8 57	12 1	1412	1453	1622	1725	1811	1859	6 3
9 53	10 6	1042	1214	1334	1555	1638	1828	2113	ar. Donaueschingen d.	8 13	11 0	1310	14 2	1527	1639	17 5	18 8	2120

Bale, Schaffhausen, Constance, Friedrichshafen, Lindau. [Ger State Rlys., Carlsruhe.

23	2	23	23	23	23	23	23	23		23	23	23	23	23	23	23	23	23
w		fast			fast		fast				fast			fast			fast	
..	5 6	7 0	9 4	1131	1323	1423	18 9	1944	dp. **Bale** (D.R.B.) arr.	1047	1033	14 2	1714	1622	19 5	2119	2135	2328
..	5 54	7 30	9 49	1220	1353	1522	1839	2030	Säckingen ..	9 50	10 3	1310	1626	1552	1817	2034	21 8	2243
..	6 20	..	1015	1246	..	1555	..	2055	Albbruck ..	9 22	..	1237	1554	..	1745	20 6	..	2221
..	6 30	7 51	1026	1256	1414	16 7	1859	21 3	arr. } Waldshut { dp.	9 11	9 41	1222	1540	1532	1733	1955	2047	22 9
5 14	6 40	7 58	1038	13 7	1420	1618	19 8	21 8	dep. } (p. 213) { ar.	9 3	9 33	12 0	15 8	1525	1718	1932	2042	22 2
5 48	7 21	..	1117	1348	..	1659	..	2145	Erzingen c ..	8 38	..	1135	1442	..	1649	19 1	..	2136
6 12	7 43	..	1137	1413	..	1728		22 8	Neuhausn. (Fls)	8 4	..	11 2	14 8	..	1617	1829	..	21 5
6 15	7 47	8 30	1147	1417	1453	1732	1941	2212	arr. } **Schaff-** { dep.	7 58	8 58	1056	14 0	1450	1610	1823	20 8	2058
6 44	8 4	8 32	1215	1422	1455	1743	1943	2216	dep. } **hausen** { arr.	7 50	8 56	1042	1351	1448	1552	1819	20 6	2055
7 29	8 42	8 51	1253	15 3	1514	1821	20 3	2252	arr. } Singen c { dep.	7 18	8 37	10 3	13 7	1428	1516	1740	1946	2018
8 1	10 8	9 0	13 8	15 8	1524	1831	2033	23 0	dep. } Singen c { arr.	7 7	8 27	9 34	1256	14 9	1418	1729	1935	20 8
8 13	1020	9 10	1320	1517	1534	1843	2043	2312	arr. Radolfzell ..	6 56	8 17	9 21	1243	1358	14 9	1718	1923	1959
8 56	11 3	9 38	14 4	1538	1616	1922	21 3	2349	„ **Constance** .. dep.	6 36	8 0	8 35	1156	1325	1351	1657	19 0	1940
9 23	12 8	9 11	1422	1748	1536	1942	2050	6 34	dep. Radolfzell .. arr.	5 49	8 10	..	1015	1356	1343	1650	1911	
10 0	1246	9 39	1458	1827	16 1	2016	2121	7 12	Ueberlingen	5 18	7 32	..	9 39	1333	13 7	1619	1843	..
1026	1334	9 54	1523	1858	1616	2040	2142	7 40	a. {¶Mimmemb's-sen-Neufrach} d.	..	7 0	..	9 3	1319	1238	1547	1826	..
1059	1418	1014	16 1	1938	1637	2113	2210	8 16	arr. **Friedrshfn.** * dep.	..	6 20	..	8 24	1257	1144	1513	18 3	..
1110	15 0	1026	..	..	1643	..	..	8 22	„ „ (Hafen) „	..		..	8 12	1135	1135	14 0	1650	..
1251	1526	1017	..	1957	1647	2120	2215	8 24	dep. Fried'hafen* arr.	..	6 2	..	8 5	1250	1127	1453	1750	..
1335	16 6	1043	..	2040	1712	22 4	23 4	9 4	arr. **Lindau** .... dep.	..	5 22	..	7 24	1227	1046	1411	1725	..
2114	..	15 3	..	..	2130	..	..	13 1	„ Munich (p. 187) „	..	.	..	..	8 0	6 25	..	1312	..

* Stadtbahnhof. ¶ Junction for Salem; or by Road 3 miles. *w* Weekdays only.

Rastatt—Freudenstadt.

All 2 & 3 class. 36 miles

5 41	8 45	1013	1128	1320	1547	1720	1850	19 9	dp. Rastatt ... ar.	8 59	1117	1225	1452	1628	1732	1830	1938	21 5
6 58	9 50	..	1239	1427	17 4	1831	A	2016	dp. Raumanzach dp.	8 0	1023	1117	1324	1526	A	1724	1832	1957
8 7	1059	12 2	1355	1532	1817	1943	2030	2123	ar. Freudenstadt dp.	7 0	9 28	10 6	1210	1426	1555	1610	1728	1852

A June 26th to Sept. 17th.

WALDSHUT and IMMENDINGEN 2, 3cl. [G. St., Carlsrh.					Mls						
	6 40	8 47	1428	1727	0	dep. Waldshut .. arr.	6 56	13 6	1518	1948	2143
	8 38	1057	1629	1931	47	arr. Immendingen dep	4 52	1119	1341	1750	1945

The times on the LEFT are to be read DOWNWARDS, those on the RIGHT UPWARDS.

(Cologne), Wiesbaden, Mainz, Neustadt, Strasbourg, Bale.

German Railways, Mainz, Ludwigshafen: French, Est.

Mls.		23	23	23	23	Exp 23	Exp 123	Exp 123	23	23	Exp 123	Exp 123	Exp 123	fast 23	23	Exp 123	fast 23	Exp 123
							D	D			D	D	D					B
0	COLOGNE (p.176) dep.	..	..	3 6			6 33	9 27	1022	..	1214	15 6	..	1643	..	19 3	2033	2120
122	**Wiesbaden** .. ,,	..	..	6 46	8 58	9 28	*Via* Bingerbruck.	↓	1325	..	15 0	..	..	1935	2014	2210	2311	2340
127	MAINZ .. .. arr.	..	..	6 56	9 8	9 39		12 0	1337	..	1512	1757	..	1946	2027	2220	2321	2353
..	FRANKFORT p.177 d.	..	..	5 49	8 30	8 59		11 4	1227	..	1424	..	1819	1911	1929	2144		23 0
..	MAINZ .... ,,	..	4 22	6 58	9 11	9 42		12 3	1345	..	1513	18 4	*a*	1950	2032	2224	2335	0 7
170	LUDWIGSHAFEN ar.	..	6 11	8 5	1023	1036		13 4	15 2	—	1610	19 9	1931	2058	2212	2322	0 45	1 2
	LUDWIGSHAFEN dp	..	6w42	8 21	1040	⌐		1318	15 6	1514	16†12	¬	1937	2155	23 0	0†10	0 53	..
177	Schifferstadt .... ,,	..	7 2	8 34	..			1330	1530	|	|	..	..	2217	2325	0 32	..	..
187	Neustadt-Wein arr.	..	7 22	8 49	..		1031	1344	1555	|	|	..	20 1	2240	2351	0†51	1 14	..
	Neustadt-Wein dep.	5 50	7 29	8 58	..	..	1034	1410	1637	*b*	*b*	..	20†6	2257	0 19	..	..	..
198	Landau ...... ,,	6 33	8 9	9 39	*b*	..	11 2	1445	1717	|	|	..	2035	2324	0 46	..	..	..
216	Weissenb'g M.E.T. a.	7 22	8 56	1120	|	..		1539	18 6	|	|	..	2115	..	..	..	..	..
	Weissenb'g Gr.T. d.	8 0	9 5	1155	↓	..		1630	1812	↓	↓	..	2131	..	..	..	..	..
260	**Strasbourg** .... arr.	8 5	9w55	1342	1343	..	to Munich arr. 17.15.	18†11	1954	19 5	21 9	..	2226	..	..	..	..	..
		123	A	123	⌐—	123			123	123		P		123	123		123	..
0	**Strasbourg** ....dep.	8 52	1028	1430	..	1635		1816	2015	1914	..	1623	23 5	6 10	7 35	..	12 6	..
27	Selestat .. .. ,,	9 22	1057			1711		1856	2048	..		..	2342	6 43	8 15	..	1239	..
43	Colmar .... arr.	9 43	1112	1512	.	1733		1918	2112	1958	..	17 1	0 3	7 2	8 37	..	1258	..
68	Mulhouse .. . arr.	1018	1143	1542	.	1816		1957	2157	2033	..	1728	0 43	7 26	9 18	..	1337	..
89	**Bale** (Swiss Stn.) arr.	1051	1211	16 7		1850		..	2228	21 0	..	1751	..	[illegible]	[illegible]		1413	..

Mls.		Exp 123	Exp 123	23	23	Exp 123	Exp 123	Exp 123	Exp 123	P	Exp 123	Rap 123	Exp 123	Exp 123	Exp 123	Exp 123	Exp 123	123
0	**Bale** *c* (Swiss Sta.) dp.	2318	..	..	..	..	.	7 10	..	9 27	10 0		1450	1313	17 8	1753	2051	2145
21	Mulhouse	2353	..	..	..		..	7 42	7 58	9 50	1033		1516	1342	1734	1828	2125	2242
46	Colmar	0 27	..	..	..	..		8 12	8 39	1016	11 6		1546	1418	18 6	19 7	22 3	2312
62	Selestat .. .... arr.	0 46	..	..	..	..	..	..	9 0	..	1123			1435	1823	1928	2222	2328
89	**Strasbourg** .... arr.	1 19	..	..	..	..	..	8 53	9 40	1054	1153	From Munich. 13.6.	1626	15 6	1854	20 6	2253	2358
		23						23	23	23			23	23	23			
0	**Strasbourg** ....dep.	..	..	..	..	From Paris.	..	9 3	1036	11 4	12†28		..	1547	1912	..	.	..
44	Weissenb'g Gr. T. a.	..	..	..	..		..	1038	|	1221	14 9		..	|	2014		.	..
	Weissenb'g M.E.T. d.	..	..	..	7 48		..	1148	|	1432	1640		..	|	2120	..	.	..
62	Landau .... ,,	6 10	..	8 5	9 58		..	1258	*b*	1529	1759	19 0	20w5	*b*	2222	..		..
78	Neustadt-Wein arr.	6 36	..	8 23	1025	..	..	1325	|	1556	18†28	1916	2037	|	2248	..	Exp	..
	Neustadt-Wein dep.	6 43	..	8 41	1030	1231	..	1344	|	1658	1840	1918	2048	|	2254	..	123	..
83	Schifferstadt .... ,,	7 7	..	8 56	1051	1246	..	14 7	↓	1719	..		2110	↓	23 8	..		..
90	LUDWIGSHAFEN ar.	7 23	..	9 9	1110	1259	..	1423	16 9	1740	19 4	*Via* Bingerbruck.	2128	2158	2321	..	B	..
	LUDWIGSHAFEN dp	7 28	8 36	9 32	1118	13 5	1315	1448	1631	1750	1921		2148	2235	2326	..	4 14	..
133	MAINZ .... arr.	8 31	9 37	1038	1215	*a*	1411	16 5	1810	1941	2022		2252	0 18	0 27	..	5 7	..
..	FRANKFORT (p 176) a.	..	1036	1153	13 8	1419	..	1653	..	2050	2122		0 10	1 20	..	..	6 38	..
..	MAINZ ....dep.	8 33	..	1041	1218	..	1414	16 8	1817	1944	2024		2255	0 25	0 34	..	5 26	..
138	**Wiesbaden** .... arr.	8 44	..	1052	1230		1427	1620	1830	1954	2035		23 6	0 36	0 45	..	5 39	..
260	COLOGNE (p.177) arr.	1158	1227	1344	1523	..	17 4	1927	..	2254	..	23 7	..	..	3 57	..	7 50	.

A Auto Rail. **B** June 30–Sept. 9. **P** 1 & 2 cl. Pullman Train. *a Via* Biblis. *b Via* Speyer and Lauterburg. *w* Weekdays only. † 2 & 3 cl. only.

† Auto Rail.

Coblence, Trier (Luxemburg), Metz.

[Ger. State and French Rlys.

23 fast	23 fast	23	23 fast	23 fast	23	23 Ex D	23 fast	¶ Not Saturdays.	23 fast	23 Ex D	23 fast	23	23 fast	23	23	23 fast	23 ¶	23 ..
8 12	9 50	1046	1220	1629	1711	1911	2138	dep. Coblence .. arr.	7 54	1053	12 6	1446	1523	1731	18 3	2021	2243	..
8 51	1038	1156	1259	1710	1826	1950	2217	Cochem.....	7 15	1012	1124	1329	1443	1619	1719	1940	2133	..
9 52	1135	1334	14 0	1812	20 1	2051	2319	arr. Trier (Hptb.) d.	6 20	9 13	1022	1156	1345	1447	1620	1842	1940	..
9 58	1212		1422	1825	2018	2118	2230	dep. Trier .. arr.		9 1	..	1131	..	1353	1615	1810	..	2115
1046	1248	..	15 7	1918	21 4	2118	2310	,, Wasserbillig dp.	..	8 20	..	1051	..	1314	1538	1727	..	2034
1145	1354	..	16 6	2016	22 7	2235	2348	arr. Luxemb'g ,,		7 37	..	10 0	..	1214	1440	1630	..	1935
10 3		1340		1915			..	dep. Trier (Hptb.) a.			9 33	..	13 6	..	1556	18 2	..	2115
1213	..	1511	..	2115		..	..	arr. Diedenhofen dep.		..	7 21	..	9 55	..	1352	1510	..	2015
1222		1622		2120	†..	..	..	dep. (Thionville) .. arr.		..	7 16	..	9†41	..	1346	15 3	..	1918
1244		17 3	..	22 0	†..		..	arr. Metz ......dep.			6 50	..	9†1	..	13 7	1418		1846

All 2 & 3 cl.

Oppenau Branch.

[Ger. State Rlys., Carlsruhe.

7 1	9 32	1139	1337	16 8	1826	2016	2213	dep. Appenweier arr.	6 30	7 32	10 0	1250	14 5	1642	1854	2044
7 36	10 5	1211	1411	1642	19 0	2050	2244	arr. Oppenau ....dep.	6 6	7 0	9 26	1216	1331	16 8	1820	2010
8 11	1037	1244	1448	1714	1933	2122	2316	arr. Bad Gr'isbach dp.	5 46	6 30	9 5	1154	13 9	1544	1758	1948

The times on the LEFT are to be read DOWNWARDS, those on the RIGHT UPWARDS.

Frankfort (Cologne, Mannheim), Heidelberg (Stuttgart), Carlsruhe, Baden (Strasbourg), Bale [German State Rlys. Mainz and Carlsruhe.]

Mls		1 2	1 2 3	1 2 3	2 3	1 2 3	1 2 3	1 2 3	1 2 3	1 2 3	1 2 3	1 2 3	2 cl.	2 cl.	1 2 3	1 2 3	1 2	1 2 3	2 3	1 2 3	1 2 3	1 2 3	1 2 3	1 2 3	1 2 3	2 3	2 3
		luxe	ExZ	ExD	fast	ExD	ExD	ExD	ExD	ExD	Ex	ExD	FDT	FDT	ExD	Ex	FD	ExD	fast	ExD	ExD	ExD	ExD	ExD	Exp	fast	ExD
0	**Frankfort** (Hpt) d.			2353	2 45	S	5 36	5 55	5 43	7 10	9 44	9 34	1050	13 0		12 8	J	13 5	1346	X	..	1556	16 3	1836	1829	1955	2232
17	Darmstadt .. arr.	Orient Express—from Carlsruhe Wed., Fri. and Sun. only.	..	0 18	3 8		6 0	..	6 8	7 35	10 9	9 59	11 7	1317		1233		1329	14 9			..	1629	..	1854	2018	2254
..	p. 176 { COLOGNE dep.			S		2329	S	↓	..	2 56	..	..	W	..	..	8 31		..	..	1153	..	..		1538	..	1643	
..	p. 176 { Mainz „				..	2 41	..			z	..	..			..	z			..	1442	..		..	1831	1759	1939	2216
..	Darmstadt .. dep.		..	0 21		3 15	6 2		6 10	7 38	1013	10 1	11 8	1318	..	1236	..	1331	1412	1510		..	1633	..	1857	2021	2257
48	Friedrichsfeld arr.		..	1 9	..	g	..	↓	..	8 24		1047	..		..	1322			15 0	..	..	..		..	..	21 5	2339
54	Mannheim „		..	..		..	6 48	6 54		..	..	1058	1144		..	..	..	..	..	..	..	1659		1930		..	..
55	**Heidelberg** .. „			1 24	..	4 5	↓		7 8	8 40	11 7		..	1354		1338	..	1422	1515	1554	..		1722		1952	2122	2355
Miles from Heidelberg	(See p.) 176		K																								
	COLOGNE dep.		2120			..				..	To Munich.		..	↓	9 24		11 0	9 19	..	↓	1214	..	..		..	..	19 3
	Mainz (p. 65) dp.		0 7	..	..	..			..	..			..		1227	..	13 7	1250			1514				..	..	2224
	Ludwigshafen „		1 8	..			↓	↓	..	..		↓	..		..	..		14 2			1616		..	↓	..		2331
	Mannheim .. „		1 22	..	6 0	..	6 55	7 4		..	1040	1115	1148		1337	..	14 3	1411	1453		1626	17 7	..	1947	..	2050	2343
	Heidelberg arr.			..	6 15			..		..	1059			↓	..			1426	1510	↓	1645		..	..	..	21 7	24 0
0	**Heidelberg** .. dep.		↓	1 31	6 22	4 14	↓	..	7 15	8 55	1114	..	..	14 0	..	1345		1431	1521	16 0	1657	..	1729		20 0	2128	0 15
20	Bruchsal .... arr.				6 49	..	↓		..	9 19	1139		..	..	..	1411		..	1550			..				2154	0 40
	STUTTGART	dep.	↓	n t	b	y k	u	d	f r	a r	dep	e r			r k	r v	r	d r	a	g	h r	l r	d	r o	d r	p	arr.
..	(page 184 arr.	1 14		..	..		..	..	..	1140	1024	..			..	..			..				r m	..			2 21
31	Durlach (p. 186)				7 3			..			..		..	..	..		..	..	16 6							2211	1 2 3
33	**Carlsruhe** { arr.	2 34	2 5	2 11	7 9	4 55	7 39	7 46	7 55	9 40	1145	12 1	1221	1430	1430	1440	1440	1511	1613	1638	1739	1754	1810	2030	2042	2217	ExD
	Carlsruhe { dep.	2 40	2 12	2 27	7 15	5 1	..	7 56	8 4	9 52	1152	1214	1224	1434	1449	1455	1441	1515	1618	1641	1745	18 0	1816	2035	2050	2224	2055
..	Rastatt ... „		..	..	7 33	5 21	..		..		..	..				1514	..	..	1636	..		1820		..	..	2244	
54	Baden-West .. arr.	..		2 52	7 41	5 30	..	8 20	8 28	1016	1213	1237	1242	1453	1513	1523	15 2	1537	1645	17 3	18 8		1839	2059	2112	2253	2117
56	**Baden-Baden** ar	..		3 31	7 54	5 42	..	8 31	8 44	1029	1224	1256		15 3	1525	1535	1516	1549	1656	1714	1824	1836	1850	21 9	2122	23 4	2137
	Baden-Baden dp	..		1 56	7 25	5 16		8 12	8 12	10 8	12 4	1233		1444	15 4	1512	1455	1529	1633	1654	18 0		1831	2051	21 3	2245	21 3
..	Baden-West			2 54	7 42	5 32		8 22	8 30	1019	1214	1247	1243	1454	1516	1525	15 3	1539	1647	17 5	1811		1841	21 1	2114	2255	2119
73	Appenweier .. arr.		..	↓	8 12		..	..	1, 2 & 3 cl. sleep. car.	1043	1241	1311		↓	..	..	..	16 3	1719	↓		..	..		..	2329	2142
	Kehl ...... arr.	3 44			8 41		..	..		11 4	1256	..	..		..			1631	1753				..			2359	2155
86	**Strasbourg** { ar.	4 31			9 31	..	..	..		1155	1340				..	..	..	17 2	..			..	..			..	2224
	Strasbourg { dp.	4 36	K		6*37		..			9 14	14 2	..			..	..	..	..	..		j		..			2014	23 7
	Kehl ...... dep.	..			7 40		..			9 48		1222	..				..	..	1653				..		..	2225	
..	Appenweier .. dep.				8 13					1046		1315	..					16 6	1721			..	..			2330	To Paris.
78	Offenburg .. arr.	To Paris.	3 4	3 26	8 21	6 4	..	8 54	9 2	1058	To Paris.	1327	..		1548	16 7		1616	1730	1735	1843	..	1913	2133	2145	2340	
117	Freiburg-in- { arr.		4 0	4 26	9 15	7 6	.	9 46	9 55	1157		1422	1337	1549	1644	To Constance	16 6	17 4	1835	To Constance	1934	..	20 2	2224	2234	0 43	
	Breisgau { dp.		4 5	4 32	9 18	7 10	..	9 49	9 58	12 3		1426	1338	1550	1647		16 7	17 7	1843		1937	..	20 5	2227	2238	..	
156	**Bale** (D.R.B.) ar.		4 55	5 25	1013	8 2	..	1038	1052	13 0		1520	1417	1630	1740		1650	1758	1936		2025		2052	2315	2330	.	
159	Bale (Swiss) c ar.		5 40	6 8	..	8 30		1118	1125	1338		1549	1439	1652	1818		17 7	..	..		2058		2120		24 0	..	

Through Carriages in Trains marked { *a* Frankfort-Bale. *b* Mannheim-Bale. *d* Berlin-Bale. *e* Hamburg-Bale-Milan. *f* Berlin-Coire and Rome. *g* Ostend-Cologne-Constance. *h* Amsterdam-Vintimille. *k* Dortmund-Bale. *l* Berlin-Baden Baden. *m* Berlin-Rome. *n* Berlin-Geneva. *o* Hamburg-Bale. *p* Frankfort-Freiburg. *r* Restaurant Car. *t* Praha-Bale. *u* Hamburg-Rome. *v* Frankfort—Constance. *y* Amsterdam-Rome. *z* Via Frankfort, page 175. **D** Corridor Exp., see p. 75. **K** June 30 to Sept. 9. **S** Sleeping Cars. **W** Weekdays only. **X** July 1 to Sept. 11. **Z** Sleeping Cars and 1, 2 & 3 cl. Cars Amsterdam-Bale, Interlaken and Coire. **FDJ** Rheingold Express and **FDT** Extra Fares, see p. 75.

Bale (Strasbourg), Baden, Carlsruhe (Stuttgart), Heidelberg, (Mannheim, Cologne), Frankfort.

[German State Railways, Carlsruhe and Mayence.

A Sleep. Cars Lugano-Berlin. B Sleep. Cars and 1, 2 & 3 cl. Cars Interlaken and Coire-Amsterdam. G July 1 to Sept. 10. S Sleep. Cars. X June 30 to Sept. 10. FDJ Rheingold Express. FDT—*see page* 75.

D Corridor Exp. *see page* 75. ‡ 1 & 2 cl. only.	Exp 123	Exp 123	luxe 12	fast 23	Exp 123	Exp 123	Exp 123	Exp 123	Exp 123	Exp 123	Exp 123	Exp 123	Exp 123
		D			D	D		D	D		D	D	D
Bale (Swiss) dep.	From Paris.	From Paris.	From Paris.	..	..	6 54	From Paris.	8 45	9 5	From Constance	From C'stance	1030	..
Bale (D.R.B.) „				..	7 11	7 25		9 22	9 38			1058	1141
Freiburg-in- arr.				..	8 2	8 14		1015	1028			1151	1237
Breisgau dp.				6 30	8 5	8 17		1019	1032			1155	1241
Offenburg				7 27	8 54	9 5		11 7		12 3	1238	1249	
Appenweier .. arr.				7 35	..	..		..		X	1247	1259	
Kehl .... arr.				8 0		..		..			1350	..	
Strasbourg ar.	0 11	0 11	2 5	..		..	7 30	..			14*24		
Strasbourg d.	0 30	1 5	2 10	6 25		..	9 14	..				..	
Kehl .... dep.	1 15	2 0	2 57	6 56		..	9 48	..	..		1222	1222	
Appenweier .. dep.	..	..	..	7 37		..	1012	..	..		1249	13 0	
Baden-West .. arr.	1 52	2 41	..	8 9	9 22	9 33	1037	1135	1144	1232	1315	1324	1351
Baden-Baden arr.	3 15	3 15	..	8 18	9 42	9 42	1048	1144	12 2	1241	1324	1336	14 9
Baden-Baden dep.	0 20	1 56	..	8 0	9 14	9 14	1030	1127	1137	1224	13 7	1318	1345
Baden-West .. „	1 54	2 42	..	8 10	9 24	9 35	1040	1138	1146	1234	1318	1327	1354
Rastatt ...... „		2 52	..	8 20	..		1049	..	..			1336	..
Carlsruhe arr.	2 20	3 14	3 55	8 38	9 49	9 59	11 7	12 3	1212	1257	1346	1355	1420
				p	*g r*	*e*		*b r*	*g e*	*d r*	*v r*	*f r*	*e*
Carlsruhe dep.	2 26	4 40	4 1	8 43	9 54	10 4	1142	12 9	1217	13 1	14 2	14 8	1428
Durlach	..	..	..	8 49	..	*a r*	..	..	*r*	..	..	..	..
St'tg'rt (p184, d	3 58	6 28	5 29	..		..	1334	..	..		1248	..	..
Bruchsal	arr.	arr	arr	9 5	..	..	arr.	..	..	..	1425	..	..
Heidelberg .. arr.	To Vienna	To Prague	Orient Express— Wed., Fri. and Suns. only.	9 33	..	1045	To Munich, arr. 17.15.	..	1258	1343	1453	..	15 0
Heidelberg dep.				9 36	..	..		..	1325		..	..	..
Mannheim arr.				9 52	1038	..		1254	1353		..	15 6	..
Ludwigshafen, a.				1018	..	..		13 6	..		..	1534	..
Mainz (p. 177) a.				1237	..	..		1411	..		..	1640	
COLOGNE arr.	..	..		..	..	..		17 4	..		..	1940	..
Heidelberg .. dep.		..		9 43	..	1053		..	13 4	1351	15 0	..	1516
Mannheim „	..	..		..	11 0	..		..	..	..	..	..	..
Friedrichsfeld ..	..	..		9 58	..			..	..		..	..	..
Darmstadt .. arr.	..	..		1045	*x*	1138	..	..	1351	1434	1557	..	16 6
p177 Mainz .... arr.	..	..		1222	1155	1222	..	..	..		..	..	..
p177 COLOGNE .. „	..	..		1523	1431	1536	..	..		1759	..	..	..
Darmstadt .. dep.	..	..		1048	..	1141	..	..	1354	..	16 0	..	16 8
Frankfort .. arr.				1112		12 6	..		1419	..	1625		1632

D Corridor Exp. *see page* 75. ‡ 1 & 2 cl. only.	Rap 2 cl.	Rap 12	fast 23	Exp 123	Exp 123	fast 23	Rap 2 cl.	Exp 123	Exp 123	Exp 123	fast 23	Exp 123	Exp 12	Exp 123
	FDT	FDJ		D	D		FDT W	D S	D	D S		D S	B G	D A
Bale (Swiss) dep.	1210	1218	..	From Paris.	1443	..		17 7	1835	19 2	2020	2239	2327	0 0
Bale (D.R.B.) „	1230	1238	1244		1510	1525	1724	1735	1917	1928	2045	23 5	0 17	0 30
Freiburg-in- arr.	13 8	1320	1333		16 3	1621	18 2	1825	20 6	2018	2142	2352	1 6	1 24
Breisgau dp.	1310	1321	1340		16 6	1625	18 3	1829	20 9	2021	2148	2355	1 10	1 28
Offenburg		..	1440		1659	1752		1917	21 0	2110	2252		1 58	2 21
Appenweier .. arr.		..	1448		..	18 1		..	..		23 0			
Kehl .... arr.		..	1631		..	1938		..	..	..	2359			
Strasbourg ar.		..	17 2	14 1	..	2026			..	..	..			
Strasbourg d.		..	13*40	1428	..	17*17		..	..	..	2014			
Kehl .... dep.		..	1412	1514	..	1741			..	..	2225			
Appenweier .. dep.		..	1449	..	..	18 4			..	..	23 2			
Baden-West .. arr.	14 1	1420	1520	1553	1728	1842	1854	1945	2128	2138	2334	1 5	2 28	2 50
Baden-Baden arr.	14 9	1430	1535	16 4	1740	1850	19 2	1954	2137	2148	2344	1 26	3 15	3 15
Baden-Baden dep.	1345	1410	1512	1545	1720	1831	1842	1932	2114	2130	2327	0 20	1 56	1 56
Baden-West .. „	14 2	1421	1522	1555	1730	1845	1855	1948	2130	2141	2336	1 6	2 29	2 52
Rastatt ...... „	..	..	1532		..	1856	..		2139	..	2345		..	..
Carlsruhe arr.	1422	1443	1551	1620	1755	1921	1914	2015	2158	22 7	0 5	1 30	2 54	3 18
			h		*g k*	*h v*		*e r*	*l r*	*e m*	*n v*	*o f*		*e t*
Carlsruhe dep.	1424	1446	1559	1683	18 9	1930	1915	2020	22 4	2212	0 12	1 34	3 0	3 34
Durlach	..	..	16 6	..	..	1937	..	*a*	..	*r*	0 19	..	..	*u y*
St'tg'rt (p184, d	..	..	..	18 7	..	..		..	..	..	..	..	..	..
Bruchsal	..	..	1623	arr.	..	20 5	..	..		..	0 35	..	..	..
Heidelberg .. arr.	..	..	1652	To Vienna.	*r*	..	..	21 2	2244	..	1 1	..	..	..
Heidelberg dep.	..	..	17 5		..	..	..	2115	..	..	1 6	..	..	..
Mannheim arr.	1457	1526	1722		1855	2058	1946	2139	..	2255	1 23	2 17	3 45	4 20
Ludwigshafen, a.	..	..	..		1915	..		2142	..	..	..		4 8	4 47
Mainz (p. 177) a.	..		..		2012	..	..	2252	..	..	..		5 7	6 17
COLOGNE arr.	..	..	..	2 8	2252	..		..	..	..	..		7 50	9 45
Heidelberg .. dep.		..	17 0	1810	..	..	..	21 9	2251	.	1 29		* Not Suns. & Fetes.	..
Mannheim „	15 0	1531	..	..	19 6	2119	1950	..	..	23 5	..	2 23		4 28
Friedrichsfeld ..	..	..	1717	1826	..	2145	..	..	..	..	..	..		..
Darmstadt .. arr.	1535		18 5	1911	1958	2254	20 6	22 2	2336	..	2 18	..		..
p177 Mainz .... arr.	..	1622	1843	1954	..	0 31		*z*	*z*	..	..	3 20		..
p177 COLOGNE .. „	..	1832	2219	2252	..	3 57	..	3 57	3 57	*x*	..	6 36		*x*
Darmstadt .. dep.	1536	..	18 8	1914	20 2	23 0	2027	22 5	2339	..	2 29	..		..
Frankfort .. arr.	1555		1834	1939	2027	2334	2016	2231	0 3	0 3	2 53			5 32

Through Carriages in Trains marked — *a* Rome-Berlin. *b* Bale-Amsterdam. *d* Constance-Cologne-Ostend. *e* Bale-Berlin. *f* Bale-Dortmund. *g* Bale-Hamburg *h* Bale-Frankfort. *k* Milan-Hamburg. *l* Bale-Dresden. *m* Rome-Hamburg. *n* Bale-Mannheim. *o* Rome-Amsterdam. *p* Freiburg-Frankfort. *r* Restaurant Car. *t* Vintimille-Berlin. *u* Geneva-Berlin. *v* Constance-Frankfort. *x Via* Biblis. *y* Bale-Praha. *z Via* Frankfort.

Heidelberg, Muhlacker, Stuttgart.

[German State Railways Carlsruhe and Stuttgart

D Corridor Exp., see page 75.

	1 2 3	2 3	2 3	2 3	1 2 3	1 2 3	2 3	1 2 3	2 3	2 3	1 2 3	2 3	1 2 3
	Exp D		fast		Exp D	ExD		Exp D d	A		Exp D		Exp D
Heidelberg .... dep.	4 20	6 44	8 45	8 55	1114	From Landau	13 8	14 5	1544	1625	2011	1830	0 15
Bruchsal ...... „	4 46	8 15	9 12	9 31	1140		14 8	1431	via Heilbronn	1730	2038	2010	0 43
Bretten ...... arr.	a	8 38	9 27	9 49	..		1435	1448		1755	2052	2033	0 59
Bretten ...... dep.		8 45	9 28	9 51		a	1457	1449		1757	2055	2035	1 0
Muhlacker .... arr.	5 28	9 16	9 48	1020	1217	1238	1527	..		1828	2118	21 3	1 22
Stuttgart (p. 186) „	6 20	1030	1035	1140	13 4	1334	1640	16 3	1817	2037	2213	22 3	2 21
Friedrichshaf (p.186)	9 25	..	15 9	1634	1634	..	..	..	21 2	..	..	..	7 1
Munich (p. 186) arr.	9 54	..	1527	1637	..	1715	..	1843	2143	..	..	..	6 33

R Rest Car.

	2 3	2 3	1 2 3	2 3	2 3	1 2 3	2 3	1 2 3	1 2 3	1 2 3	2 3	2 3	1 2 3	1 2 3
		fast	Exp			ExD		Exp	ExD	ExD	fast		Exp	ExD
Munich (p. 186) dep.	..	..	..	7 22	..	8 56	..	13 6	13 6	14 2	1544	.	1930	2235
Friedrhshaf. (p.186) d	..	..	5 20	5 1	..	9§38	..	1323	1323	1323	..		1947	..
			D		A			D						
Stuttgart (p. 186) dp.	6 0	7 43	8 33	1055	1114	1248	1442	1632	1645	17 5	1913	2033	2317	2 12
Muhlacker .... „	6 44	8 29	9 22	1150	via Heilbronn	1342	16 4	1726	1734	..	1957	2128	0 13	2 59
Bretten ...... arr.	6 59	8 45	d	1210		a	1631	a	d	..	2010	2154	0 33	d
Bretten ...... dep.	7 0	8 46		1211			1639	to Landau			2013	2156	0 34	
Bruchsal ...... arr.	7 14	9 0	9 55	1226		1413	17 0		18 4	.	2027	2219	0 49	3 32
Heidelberg .... „	7 50	9 33	1021	14 7	14 6	1442	1814		1832	1840	2055	0 14	1 18	4 2

A See page 185.

Thro' Carriages in trains marked:

a Cologne-Munich and *v.v.*

d Frankfort-Munich and *v.v.*

¶ Not Sundays.

§ 2 & 3 cl. only.

† FDT 2 cl.

Carlsruhe, Stuttgart, Crailsheim, Nuremberg.

[German State Railways, Stuttgart and Munich.

a Via Aalen. *d*—*Via* Muhlacker. *e* Via Eppingen. **K** Calais-Paris-Prague Express (see page LIII) † Via Backnang. ¶ Via Stuttgart.

1 2	1 2 3	2 3	1 2 3 D	2 3	2 3	1 2 3	2 3	1 2 3				2 3	2 3	2 3	2 3	2 3	1 2 3	1 2 3	1 2 3	1 2
4 1	4 40	7 12	9 55	..	10 0	1418	16 9	..	dep.	Carlsruhe..	arr.	12 8	..	1356	1356	1928	..	2039	1 58	2 34
..	..	8 35		..	1146	..	1722	..	arr.	Heilbronn *c*	dep.	1013	..	12 5	12 5	1814	..	..		K
¶	¶	*e*	¶	..	*e*	¶	*e*	..	dep.	Bietigheim	arr.	*e*	..	*e*	*e*	*e*	..	¶	¶	¶
K	..	8 43	..	..	1217		1825	..	„	Heilbronn	„	10 3		12 0	12 0	18 9	..	..	..	..
..	..	1035	..	..	1457	..	2047	..	arr.	**Crailsheim**	dep.	8 3	..	1044	1044	1625	..	..	..	..
luxe	ExD			ExD		ExD		D					D		D		D		D	lux
5 48	6 50	7 49	1130	1135	1343	1646	1729	1946	dep.	**Stuttgart**	arr.	1012	9 39	1331	1226	1832	1842	19 2	23 7	0 5
↓	*a*	8 42	.	*a*	*a*	1718	*a*	..	„	Backnang ..	„	*a*		1224	*a*	*a*	*a*	..	*a*	↑
	9 1	1036	13 4	1318	1537	1822	2121	2128	arr.	**Crailsheim**	dp	7 43	8 3	1044	1040	1629	17 5	1739	2056	
	D																		D	
	9 3	1045	13 5	1319	1542	1824	2129	2143	dep.	**Crailsheim**	ar	7 34	7 54	8 42	1038	1621	17 4	1737	2051	
	9 55	1134	1343	1359	1631	19 6	2210	2227	arr.	Ansbach	dep.	6 51	7 7	7 42	9 58	1529	1628	1657	1958	
↓	9 57	1138	1344	14 0	1632	19 7	2212	2229	dep.	Ansbach	arr.	6 49	7 5	7 35	9 56	1526	1627	1656	1951	
[illegible] 47	1036	1222	1420	1438	1715	1944	2251	23 8	arr.	**Nuremberg**	dep.	6 10	6 21	6 30	9 22	1430	1551	1620	1910	2 21

Stuttgart, Constance, Schaffhausen (Zurich).

[German State Rlys., Stuttgart and Carlsruhe.

C *via* Tuttlingen.

† Dining Car Stuttgart-Arth-Goldau and *v.v.* ¶ Not Sundays.

‡ Thro' car Stuttgart-Cannes & *v.v.* D—Corridor train Berlin-Milan.

2 3	1 2 3	2 3	1 2 3	2 3	1 2 3	2 3				2 3	1 2 3	1 2 3	2 3	2 3	1 2 3	1 2 3	2 3	2 3
	ExD		ExD	fast	ExD	ExD				fast	ExD	ExD	fast		ExD	Ex(		
6 35	7 52	1113	1338	1434	1740	1917	dep.	**Stuttgart**	arr.	8 40	11 9	1259	14 7	1826	1841	2058	2255	..
8 17	9 7	1311	1444	1551	1842	2018	arr.	Horb	dep.	7 30	1014	1159	1251	1628	1740	1948	2111	..
8 24	9 9	1325	1445	1555	1845	2020	dep.	Horb	arr.	7 22	1013	1151	1250	1619	1739	1946	21 4	..
1216	C	1612	C A	1816	C	C	arr.	Immendingn.	dep.	5 6	C	C	1117	1352	C	C	1714	..
1114	..	1122	↓	1514	..	..	dep.	**Ulm**	arr.	1013	↑ A	..	1350	1814	↑ A	..	2133	..
1229	†	1335		1632	.	..	„	Mengen ..	„	8 23		..	1226	1542		..	1932	..
1240	..	14 6		1645	..	..	„	Sigmaringen	„	8 4		..	1214	1515		†	19 5	2127
1335	..	1612		1744		..	arr.	Immendingen	dep.	6 42			1117	1352		..	1714	195[illegible]
1548	..	1917	↓	1953	..	..	„	Freiburg ..	„	..	..	..	9 10	10 1			1510	1557
1338	..	17 9	..	1854		..	dep.	Immendingen	arr.	..	..	..	1032	1327	..	..	1656	[illegible]
1416	1118	1753	1627	1925	2031	2155	arr.	Singen .... p. 180	dp.	..	8 40	10 7	9 59	1228	1558	1747	1624	[illegible]
1517	1155	1922	..	1956	21 3	2239	„	Constance ..	„	..	8 0	9 28	9 28	1129	..	1657	1559	1739
1443	12 9	1853	17 9	20 6	..	2242	„	Schaffh'sen	„	..	7 56	9 14	9 14	10 8	1515	17 0	1515	17 0
1727	13 5	20 5	1757	2144	..	2332	„	Zurich (p.284)	„	..	7 7	8 16	8 16	8 16	1427	16 7	1427	16 7

Freiburg, Waldkirch, Elzach.

¶ Not Sundays. All 2 & 3 cl.] [Ger. State Rlys., Carlsruhe.

5 57	8 45	1114	1327	1438	1655	1733	1922	22 9	dep.	Freiburg	arr.	6 58	8 33	1115	1351	1533	..	1855	1949	2137
6 12	8 59	1123	1342	1453	1710	1749	1936	2223	„	Denzlingen ..	„	6 41	8 16	1056	1333	1516	1614	1844	1931	2122
6 28	9 15	1136	1358	15 0	1724	18 6	1952	2238	„	Waldkirch ..	„	6 26	7 57	1041	1312	15 2	16 2	1829	1915	21 7
6 56	9 42	12 [illegible]	1425	1530	1750	1833	2018	23 4	arr.	Elzach	dep.	6 1[illegible]	7 32	1016	1249	1438	1540	18 4	1840	204[illegible]

23	23	123	23	23	23	23	23	23	A July 2—Sept. 8	23	23	23	23	23	23	23	23	123
		A						fast		fast							fast	A
..	5 5	6 2:	6 30	10 2	1224	1346	16 4	1945	dep. **Frankfort** ..arr.	10 25	1339	1443	1725	1625	2223	2222	..	2345
..	5 43	*Via* Heidelbg dep. 7.48.	7 3	1032	1248	*Via* Heidelberg 15.44.	1633	2010	arr. Hanau ......dep.	10 0	13 3	14 2	1644	*Via* Heidelberg arr. 14.6.	2158	*Via* Heidelb'g 20.11	..	*Via* Heidelberg arr. 22.24.
..	6 5		7 25	1112	1311		1647	2011	dep. **Hanau** ......arr.	9 59	1257	1344	1639		2145		..	
..	6 3		7 46	1056	1327		1647	2015	,, Darmstadt ,,	10 2	1138	14 8	1640		2122		..	
5 18	7 11		8 44	1223	1426		1758	2055	Wiebelsbach ,,	9 19	1046	1238	1540		2023		..	
6 34	8 33		10 3	1341	1543		1915	2155	arr. } Eberbach { dep.	8 17	9 34	1124	1420		1856		..	
7 32	9 33		1016	1434	1758		1919	2158	dep. } (*below*) { arr.	8 16	..	1011	1345		1727	1928	2227	
8 0	10 9	8 38	1048	1457	1856		1947	2224	,, Neckarelz.... ,,	7 58	..	9 44	1316		17 1	1854	2138	
8 20	1038	..	1112	1529	1927	1654	..	2245	arr. Jagstfeld	7 35	..	9 6	1228	1245	1619	1832	21 9	
8 34	1055	9 7	1128	1551	1948	17 7	..	2258	arr. } Heilbronn { dp.	7 20	..	8 47	12 7	1219	16 0	1816	2047	21 4
8 40	1150	9 9	⌣	..	2046	1713	..	23 1	dep. } { arr.	7 18	..	8 38	1158	1212	1514	1756	2033	21 1
9 8	1219	..	.	..	2136	1746	..	2328	arr. Bietigheim ..	6 52	..	7 54	1115	1141	1433	1726	20 4	..
9 34	1246	10 0		..	2230	1817	..	2355	,, **Stuttgart** ....dep.	6 25	..	7 4	1025	1114	1350	1655	1933	2012

Stuttgart, (Heidelberg), Osterburken, Wurzburg

[Ger. State Rlys., Stuttgart & Carlsruhe.

D Corr. Exp. *s* Thro' & Sleeping cars to & from Berlin. ‡ Thro' car. and Rest. car. to & from Berlin.

23	23	123	123	12	23	23	23	123	*a Via* Hof, *p* 191.	123	23	23	23	12	23	123	123	23
fast		ExD	ExD	F D		ExD	fast	ExD		ExD			fast	F D	fast	ExD	ExD	
6 25	..	7 25	9 43	1148	1250	..	655	1825	dep. **Stuttgart**.... arr.	7 25	12 0	1246	1817	1848	..	2030	2236	2349
6 52	..	..	1012	..	1336	..	1726	2151	,, Bietigheim .. ,,		11 2	1219	1746	..	..	1958	..	2314
7 20	..	8 14	1038	1234	1420	..	18 0	2220	,, Heilbronn .. ,,	6 32	9 59	1146	1626	18 0		1930	2139	2224
7 34	..		..	↓	1430	..	1814	..	arr. Jagstfeld ....dep.	..	9 42	1132	16 7	↑	..	..		22 5
8 45	..	8 56	1123		1557	⌣	1851	..	arr. Osterburken dep.	5 48	8 46	1056	1515		..	1848	2059	2111
6 55	8 45	..	9 45		14 2	1729	1830	2113	dep. **Heidelberg** arr.	7 9	1019	1225	1644		2011	2033	..	2313
7 32	9 33	..	1016		1434	1758	1919	2147	,, Eberbach.. ,,	6 38	9 45	1152	1610		1928	1959	..	2227
8 9	10 6	..	1037		1454	1819	1951	2211	,, Neckarelz ,,	6 14	9 24	1130	1548		1851	1938	..	2155
9 11	1139	8 57	1130	↓	1620	1912	21 2		dep. Osterburken arr.	5 47	8 14	1048	1510		18 8	1842	2056	2048
10 5	1246	9 36	12 5		1736	1948	2219	2341	Lauda	5 7	7 12	10 9	1432		1725	18 3	2020	1950
1110	1353	1018	1245	s1420	1840	2030	2320	0 24	arr. **Wurzburg** ..dep.	4 13	5 46	9 22	1347	16 4	1612	1715	1930	1838
1 8	..‡	1819	..	2040	..	8 a 2	..	8 7	arr. Berlin(*below*) dep.	20 5	.	2137	a..	9 28	7 30	9 38	1125	..

Stuttgart, Wurzburg, Erfurt, Berlin.

[Ger. State Rlys. Nuremburg.

Rest. Car Stuttgart—Berlin and *v.v.*	23	123	123	123	123	23	123	123	*a* Berlin (Fried)	123	123	23	123	123	123	123	23	*s* Sleeping Cars Berlin—Zurich and *v.v.*
		D	D	F D	D		D	D A	A July 2—Sept. 17.	D	D A		D	D	F D	D		
	..		9 45	..	..	14 2	2113	..	dep. Heidelberg arr.	7 9	..	1644	..	2033	..	..	..	
	..	7 25	9s43	1148	13 9		2125	23 5	,, Stuttgart .. ,,	7 31	1020	1817	1728	2030	1848	2236	..	
	7 10	1030	1255	1426	1558	1740	0 34	2 7	,, **Wurzburg** .. ,,	3 57	6 58	1132	1429	17 3	1559	1924	24 0	
	7 59	1121	1348	15 9	1648	1831	1 27	3 1	,, Schweinfurt ,,	3 11	6 10	1040	1343	1615	1515	1838	2315	
	8 4	1128	1348	↓	..	1810	..	..	,, Kissingen.. ,,	..	..	1118	..	1621	↑	1841	2340	
	8 16	1149	14 5		..	1848	..	..	,, Ebenhausen ,,	..	..	1034	..	16 0		1819	23 0	
	9 43	1249	15 9		1810	2026	2 46	4 18	arr. { Grim- } dep.	1 58	4 55	9 14	1231	15 1		1733	2139	
	9 45	1250	1510		1811	2028	2 48	4 22	dep. { menthal } arr.	1 56	4 51	9 13	1230	15 0		1722	2136	
	9 26	..	..		..	20 2	s	..	arr. Meiningen ..dep.	..	..	9 28	..	..		..	2154	
	1027	1340	1557		..	2112	3 39	..	,, Oberhof .... ,,	1 23	..	8 42	12 2	1427		1650	21 5	
	11 9	..	..	↓	..	2158	..		,, Neudietendorf ,,	..	..	7 45	..	..		..	20 2	
	1121	1428	1645	1726	1937	22 9	4 27	5 55	,, **Erfurt** (*p*.172),,	0 6	3 2	7 33	1053	1314	1249	1534	1945	
	1520	1819	21a27	2040	23 4	4 58	8 7	9 34	,, BERLIN (Anh) ,,	20 5	23 0	0 9	7 30	8a28	9 28	1125	1546	

Through Services between Berlin and Nuremberg, Stuttgart, &c

D	FD	FD	D	FDT	D	D	D		D	D	D	D	FDT	D	FD	D
8 24	9 28	1013	1125	1640	20 5	2137	2240	dep. BERLIN (Anh.) a	7 8	7 23	8 7	9 24	1324	1830	2040	2234
c	1119	*c*	*b*	18 9	*b*	2358	*c* B	,, Leipsic (*p*.182),,	B	4 59	..	8 9	12 4	*c*	1855	2032
1023	*b*	1159	1338	*c*	2213	*c* *	0 38	,, Halle ...... ,,	4 48	* *c*	6 s6	..	.	1630	*b*	.
1419			..	W	*s*	4 38	4 55	,, Bamberg .... ,,	0 34	0 23		A	W	1220	..	1457
15 1	..	1610	..	2142		5 43	5 52	arr. } NUREM- { dep.	2345	2332	†	..	8 37	1128	..	1438
1551	..	1618	..	2146		6 21	6 21	dep. } BERG { arr.	23 6	23 6			8 21	..	..	1420
1842	1848	19 2	2236	2353	7 28	9 39	9 39	arr. } STUTTG'RT { dp	1946	1946	2125	23 5	6 15	6 50	1148	1120
..	1917	1917	..	..	7 52		1338	dep. } { ar		1841	2058	..	..		11 9	11 9
C	2242	2242	..	..	12 9	..	17 9	arr. Schaffhausen dep.	..	1515	17 0	..	..	..	7 56	7 56
..	2332	2332	.	..	13 5	..	1757	,, ZURICH *p*. 384 ,,	.	1427	16 7	..	..	..	7 7	7 7
..	5 58	5 58	..	..	1930	..		,, MILAN (*p*. 287),,	..	..	9 42	..	..	..	0 25	0 25
..‡	1045	1045	..	..	2253		..	,, Florence .. ,,	..	..	5 45	.	..	..	2036	2036
..‡	1415	1415	..	..	6 30			,, ROME .... ,,	..	..	0 5	..	..	..	1725	1725

b Via Erfurt. *c Via* Probstzella. *s* Sleeping cars. Berlin-Stuttgart and Zurich and *v.v.* * Thro' car. and sleep. car. Berlin-Stuttgart and *v.v.* † Thro' car. and Rest. car. Berlin-Stuttgart and *v.v.* Thro' car. Berlin and Leipsic to Rome. Dining car. Stuttgart-Arth-Goldau. ‡ Rapido. **A** July 1—Sept. 16. **B** June 14—Sept. 9. **C** June 15—Sept. 15. **D** Corridor Express. **FDT and FD,** *see page* 75. **W** Weekdays only.

The times on the LEFT are to be read DOWNWARDS, those on the RIGHT UPWARDS.

Carlsruhe, Wildbad, Stuttgart, Ulm, Augsburg, Munich. [Ger. St. Rys., Carlsruhe Stuttgart and Augsburg

Through Table see p. 274.	Exp	luxe	Exp	Exp	fast	Rap	Exp	fast	Exp	Exp	Rap	Exp	fast	Exp	Exp		Exp	fast	Exp
	123	12	123	123	23	2cl	123	23	123	123	2cl	123	23	123	123	23	23	23	123
	D†	O	D	D S		FDT	D		D	D	FDT	D		D	D		D		D
Carlsruhe ..dep	2 26	4 1	↓	4 40	7 4	..	8 9	9 16	9 55	1152	..	1418	1615	1636	1816	1939	2021	2220	0 15
Durlach	..	..		4 47	7 10	..	..	9 23	..	.	..	..	1622	..	..	1947	..	2226	0 22
Pforzheim ..arr.	2 59	..		5 19	7 39	..	8 43	10 0	1026	1228	..	1451	1651	17 8	1847	2040	2053	2257	0 55
Pforzheim dep.	..	..		..	7 44	..	8 54	..	1215	1410	..	1543	..	..	1851	21 3	21 4	23 3	
Wildbad ..arr.	..	..		..	8 28	..	9 41	..	13 0	1458	..	1629	..	..	1941	2152	2152	2347	
Pforzheim ..dep.	3 1	..		5 21	7 40	..	8 45	10 7	1027	1231	..	1453	1652	1711	1849	21 1	2055	23 0	0 57
Muhlacker ar.	..	..	↓	5 36	7 53	..	.. r	1025	..		..	15 4	17 3	.. r	19 0	2123	21 8	2314	1 10
Muhlacker dp.		..	..	5 37	7 54	..	.	1033	..		..	15 5	17 4	..	19 1	2133	21 9	2315	1 28
Bietigheim		..	..	5 58	8 16	..	..	11 7	..	13 4	..	1526	1724	..	..	2211	2130	2336	..
Stuttgart arr.	3 58	5 29		6 28	8 43	..	9 38	1140	1120	1334 r	..	1556	1751	18 7	1942 A	2253	22 3	24 0	2 21
Stuttgart dep.	4 10	5 34	6 36	6 50	..	8 52	9 48	1150	1130	1346	1610	16 2	..	1822	20 2	..	2225	..	2 36
Ulm (*to Frdrichshafen., below*) a.	5 25		7 58	..	..	9 54	11 2	1343	To Nuremberg.	15 9	1712	1730	..	1934	2111	..	2355	..	4 0 D
Ulm d.	5 29	..	8 8	To Prague.	..	9 55	11 7	1359		1517	1713	1749	Exp	1950	2114			..	4 14
Augsburg arr.	6 29	..	9 6		..	1047	12 4	1520		1622	18 2	1856	123	2054	2213	.	..	..	5 33
Augsburg dep.	6 31	..	9 8		..	1049	12 6	1534		1626	18 3	1859	6 16	2058	2215	..	..		5 37
Munich (Hpt.) a.	7 20	8 24	9 54		..	1131	1252	1627		1715	1843	1946	7 5	2143	23 4	..	..		6 33
(p. 187) Salzburg ar	9 40	1029	..		..	1510	1510	1952	..	1952	.	2310	9 40	0 5	..	..	..		9 40
(p. 187) VIENNA ar	1442	1520	..		..	1950	1950	5 24	..	6 44	..	6 44	1442	6 44		..	.		1442

† 1 & 2 cl. only.	fast		fast	fast	Exp	Exp		Exp	Exp				Exp	Exp	Exp	Rap	luxe	Exp
	23	23	23	23	123	123	23	2cl	123	23	23	23	123	123	123	2cl	12	123
					D			FDT			fast		D	D	D S	FDT	B	D
p187 VIENNA (W) d		..	..	..	2315	2315	..	..	2315	2315	..	..	8 50	1120	..	..	1514	1440
p187 Salzburg dp.		..	..	..	5 0	6 23	..	..	9 41	5 45	..	..	1323	1635	..	.	1953	20 0
Munich (Hpt.) d.		..	..	6 8	7 22	8 56	5 36	12 0	13 6	1033	..	..	1544	1930	From Prague	2035	2210	2235
Augsburg .. a.		..	..	7 12	8 8	9 43	6 53	1236	1354	1148	..	..	1630	2015		2 18		2323
Augsburg .. d.		..	..	7 17	8 10	9 47	8 24	1237	1357	1243	..	..	1632	2018		2119	..	2325
Ulm (*below*) a.	..	..	..	8 41	9 7	1055	1038	1326	15 2	1447	..	..	1731	2120		22 8	..	0 26 t
Ulm d.	.	6 8	7 2	8 54	9 9	11 8	1225	1327	15 8	1610	1741	..	1734	2138	..	2210		0 30
Stuttgart a.	..	8 9	8 22	1034	1019	1231	1425	1430	1622	18 1	19 8	..	1846 r	23 0	23 7	2312	0 56	1 51
Stuttgart d.	7 43	8 20	9 5	1055	1024	1240	1435	¶ Not Sundays FDT See page 75.	1632	1815	1933	2033	1857	2322	0 27		1 14	2 1
Bietigheim	8 8	8 50	9 29	1124	..	13 9	15 0		..	1849	2011	21 0	..	..	0 55	..	..	..
Muhlacker a.	8 27	9 33	9 51	1146	.. r	1331	1519		.. r	1914	2032	2121	..	0 12	..		..	2 47
Muhlacker d.	8 36	9 40	9 53	1243	..	1332	1520		..	1917	2033	2123	..	0 15	..	..	..	2 48
Pforzheim ..arr.	8 48	9 59	10 5	13 3	1116	1345	1532		1731	..	2046	2135	1949		1 27	..	..	3 0
Wildbad ..dep.	8 17	..	9 10		10 8	1320			1643	*	20 6	..	18 7	..	..		..	..
Pforzheim arr.	8 49	..	9 47	..	1045	1356	..		1722		2050	..	1842	*	..		..	..
Pforzheim dep.	8 54	1014	10 7	1310	1118	1348	1534		1734	..	2055	2137	1951	..	1 30	..	..	3 3
Durlach ....arr.	9 16	1055	1029	1354	..		1557		..	2038	2137	2159		..	..		..	..
Carlsruhe .. ,,	9 22	11 2	1036	14 1	1145	1417	16 4		18 3	2045	2144	22 6	2020	1 6	1 55		2 34	3 29

O Orient Exp. Train de luxe, Wed., Fri. & Suns. * Via Bruchsal. § 2 & 3 cl. only.

r Rest car. *t* Sleep. car Nancy-Munich & *v.v.* **S** Sleep. car Paris-Prague & *v.v.* **A** July 1–Sept. 17 from Stuttgart. **B** Orient Express. Train de luxe, Tues., Thurs. & Sats. *see p.* 84. **D** Corridor Exp., *see p.* 75.

(Nuremberg), Crailsheim, (Stuttgart), Ulm, Friedrichshafen. [Ger. State Rys., Stuttgart.

	23		23			23		23	*a* July 2–Sept. 8. ‡ Not Sundays.	23		23	23		23		23
			Exp							Ex D							Ex D
..	1910	..	6 10	..	..	9 22	..	1439	dep. Nuremberg arr.	1036	..	1420	1715	..	1944		2251
..	1930	..	*	..	..	9 44	..	1554	,, Nordlingen ,,	9 10	..	1458	1828	..	1828		*
..	2056	..	7 43	..	..	1040	.	1629	,, Crailsheim ,,	9 1	.	1238	1537	..	1818	..	2121
..	2212	..	8 21	..	..	1117	..	1715	,, Aalen ...... ,,	8 17	..	12 6	15 4	..	17 3	..	2041
	2354	..	9 25	..	..	1323	..	1913	arr. **Ulm** ......dep.	7 13	..	11 5	1153	..	1518		1938

123		123	123	23		Exp		23	* *via* Crailsheim.	123	23	23		23	123	123	23	123
		D	D			D		fast		D					D	D	D	
6 36	6 36	7 53	1010	1050	1346	1326	1822	1938	dep. **Stuttgart** (*abv.*) a.	8 22	1019	1231	1231	1521	1617	1955	2116	23 0
8 8	8 36	9 23	1124	1223	1532	1515	1939	2125	,, Ulm ....arr.	6 46	7 55	1027	11 2	1344	1454	1828	1929	2110
9 54	1150	..	*a*	1350	1841	1841	22 3	2348	arr. Kempten ..dep.	4 30	4 30	8 15	9 20	1114	..	*a*	1720	1933
9 25	1115	1047	1243	15 9	1759	1634	21 2	23 0	,, **Friedrichshafn** d.	5 20	5 1	8 34	9 38	1043	1323	17 3	1754	1947
9 30	1120	1057	1251	1515	18 9	1643	21 7	..	,, ,, (Hafen) d.	..		8 27	9 34	1035	13 9	1650	1742	1942
10 0	13†25	1139	1332	16 6	1855	1712	22 4	2357	arr. Lindau (rail) dep.	4 23	..	7 24	8 31	8 31	1227	1614	1725	19 8
1155	1335	1335		17 0	1925	1735	..	..	,, Romanshorn (Str.)	..	..	7 20	8 40	8 40	12 5	..	1530	1730
1311	1520	1520		1931	2246	2014	..	..	,, Zurich (*p.* 285) dp.	..	..	4 54	..	6 56	1015		1338	.

† Steamer.

For other services Munich-Salzburg, *see page* 199.

	Exp 123	23	23	Exp 123	luxe 12	Exp 23	Exp 123	Exp 12	Exp 123	fast 23	23	Exp 123	Exp 23	23	Exp 23	23	Ex 23	Exp 123	Exp 123
	D		fast	D r	O	D	D	Z	D			D	D		D		D	D A	D
Munich (Hpt.) d.	S	..	6 55	7 40	8 36	8 55	9 35	From Innsbruck	From Passau	1048	1232	1312	1610	1650	1740	1925	2055	22 5	From Innsbruck
Rosenheim	From Berlin	..	7 47		..	9 45	1022			1212	14 9	..	1658	1810	1827	2048	2146	↓	
Freilassing .. a.		..	9 8	9 29	..	1055	1130			1355	16 9	1458	1813	20 8	1940	2229	2259		
B.Reichenh'll a			9 29	1018	..	1116	12 0			1419	1640	1521	1836	2047	20 2	2325	2325		
Berchtesg'den a		..	1013	1055	..	12 2	1247		..	15 1	1725	16 1	1940	2131	2043	0 6	0 6		
Salzburg c .. a.		..	9 20	9 40	1029	..	1140		..	14 5	1622	1510	Y	2020	1952	2242	2310	0 5	
	r		ExD		luxe				r								23	D	
Salzburg c .. d.	..	7 35	9 25	10 0	11 0	..	12 5	13 7	..	1535	1643	1525	..	23 0	2115	23 0	5 35	1 25	3 20
Attnang (*p.* 196)	..	9 42	1029	11 8		..	1317		..	17 2	19 1	1628	..	0 7	2235	0 57	7 16	2 36	4 27
Wels (*p.* 188) a.	5 49	1027	1054	..	..	..	1341	.	1617	1735	1947	..	..	1 38	23 4	1 38	7 55	3 0	..
Wels (*p.* 188) d.	5 51	1036	1056	..	..	..	1342	..	1619	1738	1952	..		1 43	23 5	1 43	8 2	3 2	..
Linz ...... a.	6 12	1112	1117	1153	1241	..	14 0	1447	1638	1758	2028	1712	..	2 10	2325	2 10	8 23	3 25	5 10
Linz ...... d.	6 20	1215	1125	12 4	1255	..	14 8	1455	1645	1815	..	1718	..	2 25	..	2 25	8 34	3 38	5 20
St. Valentin	6 43	1322		..	..	..	..		..	1844	..	..	..	3 0	..	3 0	9 0	..	5 44
Amstetten	7 18	1434	1218	..	..	..	15 1		..	1931	..	..	..	3 59	..	3 59	9 41	4 42	..
Vienna (West) a.	9 8	1752	14 5	1442	1520		1650	1715	1918	2133	..	1950	..	7 31	..	7 31	1140	6 44	8 0

From Budapest & the East, see p. 200, &c.	fast 3 cl.	fast 23	Exp 123	Exp 123	Exp 123	Exp 12	Exp 23	Exp 123	Exp 123	luxe 12	Exp 123	Exp 123	Exp 123	Exp 23	Exp 123	Exp 12	23
			D	D r	D	Z	D		D r	O	D S	D	D A	D	D	D	
Vienna (West) dep.	2 42	7 25	8 50	1045	1120	1210	.	1015	1440	1514	1845	2135	2315	..	..	..	2050
Amstetten..........	4 52	9 26	..	..	1315		..	1217	..		2033	2320	1 15	..	..	..	0 17
St. Valentin........	5 29	10 0	..	1259	..		..	..	..		..		1 51	..		..	1 15
Linz .... arr	5 56	1025	1120	1320	1413	1438	..	1312	1727	1741	2127	0 10	2 15	..		..	1 48
Linz .... dep.	6 30	1045	1125	1328	1422	1445	..	1340	1738	1755	2137	0 18	2 25	..	6 22		2 8
Wels .... arr.	7 7	11 5	1143	1350	1443		..	14 1	..		2157		2 47	..	6 44	..	2 40
Wels .... dep.	7 15	1117	1145	1352	1445	.	..	14 3	..		2159	..	2 50	..	6 46	..	2 56
Attnang	8 12	1145	1216	.	1520	..	..	1449	1835	..	..	1 10	3 39	..	7 30		4 14
Salzburg c .. arr.	10 7	13 2	1313	..	1620	1630	..	1550	1935	1943	..	2 10	4 35	..	8 38	..	6 20
	23							23		O	r				DX		23
Salzburg c .. dep.	1135	15 0	1323	To Passau.	1635	To Innsbruck.	..	1835	20 0	1953	To Berlin.	To Innsbruck	5 0	6 23	8 43		9 5
Berchtesgaden dp.	1035	1355	1226		..		17 5	1730	..				..	5 25		8 45	8 0
B. Reichenhall dp.	1120	1441	1310		..		1749	1815	..				..	6 10	8 32	9 30	8 42
Freilassing	1151	1510	1334		1644		1810	1851	..	↓			..	6 36	8 58	9 54	9 16
Rosenheim	1347	17 2	..		1756		1923	2131	2111				..	7 50	1019	11 7	1127
Munich (Hptb) arr.	15 8	1816	1525		1845		2015	2252	22 2	2150			7 3	8 42	1110	1155	1247

A Sleep. Car Vienna to Munich and *v.v.*
S Sleep. Car Vienna-Berlin and *v.v.*

O—Orient Express, Sun., Wed. and Fri. from Munich; Tue., Thur. and Sat. from Vienna, *see page* 84.

Y June 17—Sept. 17. **X** June 18 - Sept. 18.

Z Arlberg Express Mon., Wed. & Fri. from Vienna. Tue., Thur. and Sat. from Salzburg. *r* Rest. Car.

Munich, Buchloe, Lindau (Zurich). [Ger. State Rlys., Augsburg.

123	123	123	23	123	123	123	23	183 miles to Lindau.	23	23	123	23	12	123	12.	12..	23
fast	ExD	ExD		ExD	ExD	ExD	fast		fast		ExD		ExD	ExD	ExD	ExD	fast
6 25	8 0	8 51	1028	1312	1345	1728	1940	dep. **Munich** (Hpb.) ar	1012	1230	13 1	1448	1643	..	2016	2130	2234
7 44	9 10	r	1154	1412	..	1832	2058	dep. Buchloe ....dep	9 9	1046	12 7	1317	1545	2016	.	2031	2130
8 5	9 32	A	1216	1433	..	r	2122	Kaufbeuren......	8 43	1016	..	1249	1522	20 0	A	20 8	2111
8 53	1017	1041	13‡14	1517	1534	1933	22‡9	arr. Kempten- d.	7‡50	9‡21	11 7	11‡55	1434	1912	1827	1922	2023
8 55	1019	..	1322	1528	..	1935	2218	dep Hegge a.	7 51	9‡ 4	11 7	1145	1433	19 8	..	1919	2021
9 15	1038	1058	1354	1537	1551	1952	2238	arr. Immenstadt dep	7 20	8 33	1050	11 0	1416	1851	1811	19 3	20 4
1027	1134	12 8	1527	1659	1659	21 3	2348	arr. Oberstdorf ..dep.	5 8	7 40	9 30	9 28	1257	1752	17 0	1752	1849
1028	1152	12 0	1548	1646	1655	2057	2352	arr. **Lindau**......dep	6 7	6 57	9 35	9 12	1247	1720	1655	1732	1827
1121	1244	1244	1642	1735	1735	2132	0 20	,, Bregenz (*p*197) ,,	5 42	6 30	8 59	..	1141	1618	⌒	1618	18 5
..	1310	1310	1814	1814		..	.	,, Rorschach 282 ,,	..	..	..	..	1130	1617		1617	..
..	..†	1520	20†9	20†9	..	23†40	..	,, Zurich (283) ,,	..	..	6†55	..	9†26	1338	..	1338	..
..	1340	1340	1815	1815	..	..	..	,, Romanshorn (st) ,,	..	..	8 18	..	..	1515		1515	..
..	1520	1520	20 9	20 9	..	..	..	,, Zurich (*p.* 285) ,,	..	..	6 56	..	..	1338	..	1338	..

D Corridor Exp. *see page* 75.

A June 11—Sept. 17. ‡ Kempten Hbf.

† *Via* Bregenz, St. Margrethen (railway). *r* Restaurant Car Munich-Lindau and *vice versa.*

(Lindau), Buchloe, Augsburg, Nuremberg. Ger. State Rlys., Augsburg.

23	23	123	123	123	12	23		23	123	123	123	23	123	23	23
	fast	ExD	ExD	ExD	ExD				ExD	ExD	ExD	fast	ExD		
6 7	6 57	9 35	1247	1720	S	1750	dep. Lindau (*abv.*) arr	1116	..	1130	1646	2137	2137	..	..
9 7	1050	1212	1552	2020		2227	dep. Buchloe......arr	7 39	S	8 48	1412	1823	1838	22 9	0 24
9 42	1145	1240	1626	2053	..	2321	arr. **Augsburg** dp.	7 0	..	8 14	1325	1754	1815	2120	2332
9 50	1217	1250	1637	2121	2310	0 0	dep. **Augsburg** arr.	6 9	7 8	8 4	1228	1620	1743	2059	2223
‡	1311	..	B	..	..	‡	arr. Treuchtlingen....	‡	..	S	1139	1529	FD	‡	2121
1118	1357	1420	1811	23 0	1 0	1 34	arr. **Nuremberg** ..dep.	4 28	4 55	6 28	10 3	1444	1618	1913	2015

B To Sept. 30
S Sleep. Cars only
r Rest Car.
‡ 1, 2 and 3 cl.

THROUGH SERVICES BETWEEN COLOGNE AND MUNICH, VIENNA, BOHEMIA, MORAVIA, etc.

[German State Railways.

Mls.	D—Corridor Express, *see page* 75.	1 2 luxe	1 2 3 D s	1 2 3 D	2 3 fast	1 2 3 D Z	1 2 3 D	Exp D	1 2 F D	2 3 fast	1 2 3 DA	1 2 3 DJ	1 2 3 D	1 2 3 DS	1 2 3 DY	1 2 3 DC
0	**Cologne** (Haupt.) *p.* 175 d.	1 38	2 56	3 6		6 33	7 25		1211	1218	1452	15 4	19 3	2250	2255	2313
..	Cologne (Deutz) .... ,,	O		..			..	1022		*a*		..	S	*a*		.
..	Frankfort (Hptbhnhf.) .... arr.	4*m*29	6 28	6 36			1036	14 8	1459	1555	18*m*1	1828	2258	1 40	1 58	2*m*18
..	Frankfort (Hptbhnhf.) .... dep.	4 34	6 46	6 53	10 2		1046	1420	15 7	16 4	18 2	1838	2321	1 47	2 5	2 19
..	Aschaffenburg ...... arr.		7 34	7 41	1058		..	15 9	..	1659	1839	1917	0 13	..	.	
0	**Coelogne** (*p.* 176) .... dep.		..	—	6 33			9 17		1032	..	15 6	19 6			
114	Mainz .... arr.		..	..	9 25			1159		1350	..	1753	22 2			
	Mainz .... dep.		5*14	..	9 35			1317		14 5	..	1759	2216			
135	Darmstadt .... ,,		6*19	..	1015			1420		1448	..	1835	2317			
164	Aschaffenburg ...... arr.	↓	7*22	..	1052		↓	15 0	↓	1550	..	1912	0 13	↓	↓	↓
..	Aschaffenburg ...... dep.	..	7 35	7 43	11 0		..	1510	..	17 5	1840	1918	0 17			..
196	Gemunden .... arr.	..	8 51	8 39	1159		..	1610	..	1757	..	2014	1 14		..	
..	Gemunden .... dep.	..	8 43	8 43	12 9			1624		1857		2017				
216	Hammelburg ...... arr.	..	9 24	9 24	1254			1655		1938		2059				
229	Bad Kissingen .... ,,	..	9 43	9 53	1323		↓	1715	↓	20 6	↓	2129	↓		↓	↓
..	Gemunden .... dep.	..	8 32	8 40	12 1		..	1611	..	1759	..	2015	1 16	..		..
227	Wurzburg .... arr.	6 19	9 6	9 13	1236		1242	1644	1653	1834	1955	2049	1 50	3 40	4 2	4 12
..	Wurzburg .... dep.	..	9 9	—	1235	↓		1911		1911		2120	..			
..	Schweinfurt ...... arr.	..	10 5	..	1342			2012		2012	..	22 0	..			
..	**Kissingen** ...... ,,	..	1033	..	1421			2053		2053	..	23 1	..			
..	Bamberg .... ,,	..	1130	..	1448			2149		2149		23 2	..			
..	Bayreuth .... ,,	..	1423	..	1653			1 24		1 24	..	1 24	..			
..	Eger .... ,,	..	1811		21 2		↓	6 4	↓	6 4	..	6 4	..	↓		↓
227	Wurzburg .... dep.		9 35	9 30	13 2		..	17 7	17 0	1845	20 3		2 0	3 45		4 20
248	Steinach .... arr.		1014	1029	1351		..	1812		1951	..		S			
..	Rothenburg ...... ,,		1048	1053	1415		..	1839		2011	..		*Via* Nuremberg.			
263	Ansbach .... arr.		1048	11 3	1419		..	1848		2022	..					
	Ansbach .... dep.		1049	11 5	1421		..	1849		2027	..			↓		
318	Treuchtlingen .... arr.		1136	1151	15 5		..	1936		2113	..			..		
	Treuchtlingen .... dep.		1143	1159	1515	↓	..	1945	↓	2121				..		
350	Augsburg .... arr.	↓	1257	1248	1612	1622	..	2034	*z*	2223	Z					↓
389	**Munich** .... ,,		1322	1340	17 7	1715	..	2122	2023	2325	2336		6 55	7 35	↓	8 2
								D			1 2 3 D *y*					
..	Wurzburg .... dep.	6 24	9 24	..	1310	..	1249	1712		..		2110	2 0	..	4 10	
285	Furth .... ,,		11 5	..	1443	..	..	1857		..	From Berlin		3 37	..	5 48	
291	Nuremberg .... arr.	8 0	1114	..	1454	..	1424	19 8		..		2230	5 50	..	6 0	
	Nuremberg .... dep.	8 10	1132	..	1515	..	1434	1922		..		2315	8*15	..	6 14	
353	Regensburg ...... arr.	9 29	1313	..	1647	..	1555	2047		..		0 52	1046	..	7 52	
	Regensburg ...... dep.	9 30	1318	..	17 5	..	16 5	2051		..	3 1	0 59	1224	..	8 11	
..	Plattling .... ,,		1412	..	18 6	..	..	2142		..			1422	..	9 9	
426	Passau .... arr.	1055	15 0	..	1855	..	1740	2228		..	4*r*35	2 35	1536	..	9 58	
	Passau .... dep.	11 4	1510	..	19 12	..	1753	..		..	4 45	2 50	15 43	..	1010	
..	Scharding .... ,,	..	..	..	1933	..	18 8	..			4 59	3 5	16 8	..		
..	Wels .... arr.	..	1617	..	21 2	..	19 5	..			5 49	4 7	1736	..	1111	
..	Linz .... ,,	1227	1638	..	2131	..	1925	..		..	6 12	4 32	1812	..	1132	
610	**Vienna** (W.) (*p.* 187) ,,	1520	1918	..		..	221	..			9*r*8	7 45	‡	..	1420	
													2 3			
..	Nuremberg ...... dep.	9 0	1123	..	..	..	1438	1925		..	..	2326	7 29	..	6 30	
..	Bayreuth ...... arr.	*g*			..	..	1551	..			..	0 36	9 55	..		
..	*p.* 190 Eger .... ,,	11 9	1355	..	..	..	1719	2150		..	..	2 32	1143	..	8 52	
399	*p.* 190 Karlsbad ...... ,,	1227	1530	..	..	..	1840	23 2		..	..	..	1318	..	1012	
396	*p.* 190 Marienbad ...... ,,	1216	1444	..	..	..	18 8	..		..	..	..	1542	..	9 57	
..	*p.* 190 Tuschkau-Kosulup *c*	1336	1614	..	..	..	1940	..			..	..	1733	..	1257	
..	*p.* 190 Plzen .... ,,	1412	17 0	..	..	..	2028	..			..	..	1929	..	1344	
..	*p.* 190 Praha .... ,,	16 0	1855	..	..	..	2225	..		..	..	..		..	1550	
								2 3			2 3					
0	Nuremberg .... dep.	8 54	..	..	..	..	15 0	2045			4 22		..	..	..	
..	Munich (*p.* 190) .. ,,	8 0	..		..	..	1336	1944					..	..	..	
101	Furth i. W. *c* ...... arr.	1144	..	..	..	..	1743	0 49		..	9 4		..	..		
..	Taus (Domazlice) *c* .. dep.	1253	..	..	..	..	1918	..			1046		..	..	..	
151	Plzen .... arr.	1350	..	..	..	..	2124	..		..	1222		..	..	..	
224	**Praha** .... ,,	1550	..		..	..	..	..			1724		..	..	..	

Y 1 & 2 cl. Sleep. Cars Essen–Cologne–Vienna and Karlsbad.

s Through Sleeping Cars Ostend to Wurzburg daily. y Sleep. Cars only.

A June 20-Sept. 16. C 1 & 2 cl. Sleep. Car Flushing-Munich. J Sleep. Car Wurzburg-Vienna. z via Ingolstadt.

a via Mainz to Frankfort. r Restaurant Car Passau to Vienna.

g June 16-Sept. 20. * 2 and 3 cl. only.

m Frankfort (Sud). ‡ 3rd class only.

O Ostend-Vienna-Orient Exp. Tues. Thurs. and Sats. only. *See page* 84. S 1, 2 & 3 cl. Sleep. Car Cologne-Munich. Z *Via* Bingerbruck, Landau, Carlsruhe. *See pages* 176, 179 and 186. FD *See p.* 75.

THROUGH SERVICES BETWEEN COLOGNE AND MUNICH, VIENNA, BOHEMIA, MORAVIA, etc.

[German State Rlys.

			1 2 3	1 2	1 2 3		1 2 3	2 3	1 2	2 3	1 2 3		1 2 3		1 2 3	2 3
Praha dep.	..		Exp	..	D	..	D		luxe		D		1535			9 45
Plzen	..	..	DJ		..	..	7 50	5 20	O	5 20	..	..	1737	..	..	1410
Taus (Domazlice) c dep.	..	..			..	..	1024	7 50	..	7 50			1855	..	..	1649
Furth i. W. c dep.	..	..			..	..	1218	1239	..	1218	..		1946	..	..	1817
Munich (p. 190) arr.	..	..	..	..	..		1730	1730	..	1730			2335	..	..	2335
Nuremberg arr.	..	..		..	..		15 6	1740	..	15 6			2234	..	..	2310
								1 2 3							..	
p. 190 Praha dep.	..	..	.	..	..	.	7 35	11 0	1520	..	..		P	..	..	..
Plzen "	..		..	..	..	..	9 37	13 0	17 8	..	..		..	..		..
Tuschkau-Kosolup c	..	..	..	..	..	..	1024	1348	1746	7 10	.		..		..	..
Marienbad "	..	..	..	..	..		1158	1522	19 7	9 7			..		..	..
Karlsbad "	..	..		..	..	..	1234	1440	1832	..	..		19 3	..		..
Eger "	..	..	..		..	..	1249	1610	1952	1111	..		2026	..		1845
Bayreuth "	..	..			..		1434	..	g	1241			..	..		21 7
Nuremberg arr.	..	..	..		..		1553	1847	2156	1422	..		2250	..		2340
	2 3				Exp	D										1 2 3
Vienna (W.) p. 187 dep.	fast	..	2240	..	1845	..	8 12	1045	1514	..		P 1 & 2 cl. Sleep. Cars Karlsbad and Vienna–Cologne–Essen.	1428	..	..	..
Linz			1 42	..	2137	..	11 0	1328	1749	..	..		1726	..	..	..
Wels	..		2 7	..	2159	..	1122	1352	1813	..			1750	..	..	..
Schärding			3 10	..	2258	..	1217			..	.			..		..
Passau arr.	..	..	3 25		2312	..	1230	15 8	1923	..	..		1857		..	D
						1 2 3				2 3						
Passau dep.	..	..	3 37	..	2324	6 54	1242	1523	1933	1120	..		19 7	..	..	..
Plattling	..		..			7 38	..	16 7		1211			1952	..	..	..
Regensburg arr.	..	..	5 17	..	0 56	8 30	1420	1711	2057	13 9	..		2053	..	..	..
Regensburg dep.	..	..	5 24	..	To Berlin.	8 34	1430	1721	2058	1317			2110	..		..
Nuremberg arr.	..	..	7 0	..		10 7	1551	1859	2225	1456	..		2248	..	..	2 40
Nuremberg dep.	5 8		7 15	..		1025	1558	1914	2235	1514	..		2322	..	..	2 50
Fürth "	5 17	..	7 26	..		1036		1927	..	1525	..		2333	..		3 2
Wurzburg arr.	6 53	..	9 0	..	—	1212	1724	21 6	0 6	1655	..	..	1 8	..	..	4 33
		1 2 3 D Y		FD 1 2	2 3	1 2 3 D	Exp X		..	fast 2 3		Exp 1 2 3		Exp 1 2 3	Exp 1 2 3	1 2 3
Munich dep.	..	6 45	..	9 15	7 5	8 16	1350			13 0	13 6	1710		2215	2320	0 [illegible]
Augsburg	..	a	..	a	7 59	9 4	a			1349	1355	..		C	T	a
Treuchtlingen arr.	..		..		8 58	9 53				1445	..	1915				S
Treuchtlingen dep.	..		..		9 7	10 1				1457	..	1917				
Ansbach arr.	..		..		9 54	1051				1538	..	20 2				Via Nuremberg.
Ansbach dep.	4 32	↓	..		10 0	1053			↓	1539	Z	20 4				
Rothenburg "	..		..	↓	9 45	1058			..	1536		..				
Steinach "	5 10	..	..		1028	1122	↓		..	16 6		2032		↓	↓	
Wurzburg arr.	5 28	10 4	..	1224	1133	1214	1720	↓	..	1658		2125	↓	1 45	2 49	4 33
Eger dep.	..	..	2322							11 2		11 2				..
Bayreuth "	..	..	4 14		4 14					1325		1450				..
Bamberg "	..	..	6 52		6 52	..				1515		1830				..
Kissingen "	..	..	7 9		9 26	..				1534		1935				2340
Schweinfurt "	..	..	8 1		1055	..				1621		2015				3 17
Wurzburg arr.	..	..	8 41	↓	1132	..	↓	↓	↓	17 3		2113	↓	↓	↓	3 58
Wurzburg dep.	7 37	1012	9 20	1231	1145	1243	1734	2141	0 7	1712		2152	1 30	2 0	2 54	4 42
Gemunden arr.	8 10	..	9 48		1219	1311		2212		1752		2222	..		..	5 12
Bad Kissingen dep.		..	8 36		1010	1212				1625		..	..			
Hammelburg "			9 3		1038	1234		..		1655		..	..			
Gemunden arr.	↓	..	9 42	↓	1119	13 5				1735		..	..		↓	↓
Gemunden dep.	8 12	..	9 49	..	1221	1312	↓	2213		1754		2223	..		..	5 13
Aschaffenburg arr.	9 7	1117	1048	..	1322	1411	1846	2310		1857		2319	..		..	6 9
Aschaffenburg dep.	9 12		11 0	z	1326	1420		..		1919						6§16
Darmstadt	1016		1150	..	1444	1556		.		2020		..				7§30
Mainz (p. 177) arr.	1045		1223	1454	1515	1633		..		2052		..				8§18
Mainz (p. 177) dep.	..	↓	13 5	1456	1529	1647		..	↓	..	↓	..				9 41
Cologne arr.	..	..	1535	17 9	1843	1940	↓	..		..	23 3	..	↓	↓	↓	1227
Aschaffenburg dep.	9 8	1118	1049	..	1326	1413	1847	2312		1858	..	2320	..	..		6 12
Frankfort (Hptbahnhof) arr.	9 54	11†50	1134	1417	1443	1503	1924	24 0	2 0	1952	..	0 6	3 29	3†49	4 42	6 58
Frankfort (Hptbahnhof) dep.	1015	1152	1144	1424	1448	1514	1935	0 14	2 11	..	..	0 20	3 35	3 51	4 50	7 23
Cologne (Deutz) p. 175 arr.	..	..	..			1851	..	..		..	..	.				
Cologne (Haupt.) arr.	1344	1523	1536	17 9	1843		23 7	3 57	5 14	..	..	4 5	6 44	7 10	7 57	11 2

C 1 & 2 cl. Sleep. Car Munich–Flushing. **D** and **FD** *See p.* 75. **J** Sleep. Car Vienna-Wurzburg. **O** Orient-Vienna-Ostend Exp. from Budapest Tues., Thurs and Sat. **S** Sleep. Car Munich *via* Nuremberg to Frankfort and Cologne. **T** 1, 2 and 3 cl. Sleep Car Munich Cologne.

X Munich—Wurzburg, July 1–Sept. 15 only. **Y** July 1–Sept. 17. **Z** *Via* Carlsruhe—Landau, *see pages* 179, 177, 186. *a* via Ingolstadt. *g* June 17–Sept. 21. *z* via Frankfort to Mayence. † Frankfort (Sud.) § 2 and 3 cl. only.

Nuremberg, Bayreuth, Eger, Praha.
(German State Railways)

Mls.		123 ExD	23 fast	23	12 luxe	123 ExD	23 fast	123 ExD	123 ExD	23	123 ExD	123 ExD
	Nuremberg ....dep.	6 30	6 55	7 29	9 0	1123	1245	1428	1438	1746	1925	2320
47	Schnabelwaid .. arr.	..	8 8	9 21	..	..	14 6	..	..	1934	2025	..
59	Bayreuth .... arr.	..	8 25	9 55	P	..	1430	1540	1551	1958	..	0 36
..	Schnabelwaid ..dep.	..	8 12	9 27	..	..	1410	..	..	1940	2030	..
78	Marktredwitz ..dep.	8 26	9 16	11 5	..	1323	1514	..	1654	2137	2122	1 59
95	Eger .... arr.	8 52	9 49	1143	11 9	1355	1546	..	1719	2212	2150	2 32
	Eger dep.	..	1018	1451	1137	14 9	..	..	1733	..	..	..
114	Marienbad .... arr.	..	11 8	1542	1216	1444	..	..	18 8	..	..	..
	Marienbad dep.	..	1116	1544	1221	1448	..	..	1814	..	..	..
154	Tuschkau- arr.	..	1257	1733	1336	1614	..	..	1940	..	..	..
	Kosolup c dep.	..	1318	..	1349	1632		..	20 0	..	..	..
234	Praha (Wils.) p.206 a.	..	1550	..	16 0	1855		..	2225	..	..	..

Mls		123 Exp	123 ExD	123 ExD	23 fast	123 ExD	123 ExD	23	123 ExD	12 luxe	23	123 ExD
..	Praha (Wils.) p.206 d.	..	..	..	..	7 35	..	..	11 0	1520	..	..
80	Tuschkau- arr.	..	..	..	..	10 7		..	1330	1730	..	..
	Kosolup c dep.	..	..	..	7 10	1024	..	1058	1348	1746	..	..
120	Marienbad .... arr		..	..	9 3	1150	..	1253	1517	19 2	..	..
	Marienbad dep.	..	..	..	9 7	1158	..	13 0	1522	19 7	1747	1917
139	Eger .... arr.	..	..	..	9 54	1238	..	1346	1555	1940	1838	1953
	Eger dep	..	..	7 16	1111	1249	..	14 0	1610	1952	1845	2026
156	Marktredwitz ..dep.	..	5 7	7 55	1155	1327	..	1452	1643	..	2028	2058
..	Schnabelwaid .. arr.	..	..	8 45	13 3		..	1551	..	P	2136	2149
175	Bayreuth ....dep.	4 28	6 7	..	1241	1434	1449	..	..	..	21 7	..
187	Schnabelwaid ..dep.	..	..	8 50	13 9		..	1558	..		2155	2150
234	**Nuremberg** .... arr.	5 50	7 45	9 53	1422	1553	16 5	1753	1847	2156	2340	2250

P Calais (Ostend)-Paris-Praha Express de Luxe, *see page* 84. Rest. Car Nuremberg-Prague and *v.v.* Summer only. Extra Fares.
c Customs examination.

Wurzburg, Kissingen.
[Ger. St. Rys.

Mls		23	23	23	23	23	123	23	23	23	23
	Wurzburg ......dep.	4 39	6 41	9 9	1030	1143	1255	1620	1740	1911	2120
..	Bamberg (p. 191) ,,	4 20	6 52	9 10	..	10 0	1224	1515	1723	1835	..
27	Schweinfurt .... ,,	6 22	8 9	1037	1121	1317	1348	1720	1831	2025	2225
42	**Bad Kissingen** .. arr.	7 2	8 40	1118	12 0	1342	1421	1753	1927	2053	23 1

	23	23	23	23	23	23	123	23	23	23	23
Bad Kissingen ..dep.	4 56	7 9	9 25	1053	12 3	1423	1534	1631	1810	1935	2217
Schweinfurt .... arr.	5 39	7 32	1049	1119	1236	1450	1615	17 0	1838	20 3	2315
Bamberg (p. 191) ,,	7 32	8 50	1214	1214	1345	1859	1859	1859	21 0	2149	2 49
Wurzburg ...... ,,	7 22	8 41	1132	1256	1420	1559	17 3	1824	1924	2113	2 40

Biessenhofen Fussen.
[German State Rlys.]
2 & 3 class.

Kaufbeuren d.	8 17	9 41	1141	1443	1731	1913	2015	2131	
Biessenhfn. d.	8 25	9 49	1149	1452	1739	1921	2023	2139	
M.Oberdorf a.	8 36	9 59	12 0	15 6	1750	1932	2035	2150	
Fussen ..arr.	9 44	1056	13 6	16 [illegible]	1857	2034	2140	2255	
Fussen ..dep.	6 23	7 15	10 0	1122	1340	1512	18 1	1940	
M.Oberdorf ..	7 24	8 10	11 3	1224	1440	1611	19 4	2040	
Biessenhofn.	7 38	..	1115	1248	1454	1624	1916	2052	
Kaufbeuren a.	7 45	8 27	1123	1255	15 1	1632	1924	21 0	

Munich, Regensburg, Hof (Berlin, etc.)
[Ger. St. Rlys., Regensburg.

	23	123 ExD	23	123 ExD	123 ExD	23	23 fast	123 ExD	123 ExD	123 ExD	123 ExD	23 ExD	123 ExD
+ *Via* Marktredwitz.	..												
Munich (Hptb.) dep.	6 12	8 r 0	1022	12 7	1242	1336	1525	1613	2145	2280		2349	0 5
Landshut	7 16	8 54	1140	..	1342	1444	1626	17 9	2244	2257	2347	0 46	1 11
Regensburg .. arr.	8 12	9 44	13 0	1343	1432	1538	1717	1758	2336	2348	0 37	1 36	2 1
Regensburg dep.	8 37	9 52	1310	1350	1440	1549	1730	18 5	2344	2357	0 47	1 44	2 8
Schwandorf	9 16	1029	1431	1425	..	1625	18 7	..	0 24	0 36	..	..	..
Weiden	9 54	11 5	1531	..	1548	17 5	1846	1912	1 1	1 15	..	..	3 17
Wiesau .... arr.	1024	1139	1611	1527	..	1744	1920	..	s	..	..	..	
Eger .... ,,	1155	1339	1853	16 4	..	1853	1957	A	2‡32		..	..	B
Praha (*above*) ,,	1855	1855	..	2025	..	..	..		..			..	..
Marktredwitz ..dep.	1041	12 4	1630	..	1637	18 5	1938	..	1 55	2 11	..	..	4 7
Hof............ arr.	1126	1247	arr.	1620	1724	1851	2021	2042	2 37	2 55	3 30	4 14	4 50
p. 192 Dresden (Hptb.),,	1955	1726	..	2025	2148	2359	..	0 34	7 31	7 31	9 13	9 13	9 13
p. 192 Leipsic...... ,,	1836	1546		20 1	20 1	2224	..	.	5 51	6 43	6 43	7 4	8 5
p. 192 BERLIN (Anh.) ,,	2234	1746	..	22 0	22 0	1 8	..	..	8 2	9 7	9 7	9 14	102[illegible]

‡ 1 & 2 cl. "D" train	23 fast	23 fast	123 ExD	23	123 ExD	123 ExD	123 ExD	123 ExD	123 ExD	123 ExD	123 ExD	123 ExD	23 ExD
p. 192 BERLIN (Anh.) dp.	..	0 15	5 38	6 19	7 58	1340	19 0	19 0	2020	..	2129	2137	2250
p. 192 Leipsic ...... ,,	..	4 27	8 8	9 6	9 59	1538	21 8	21 8	2232	..	2348	0 7	1 12
p. 192 Dresden...... ,,		..	7 11	9 35	8 16	1430	1842	2045	2045	2216	2226	2226	
Hof............dep.	7 38	1015	1115	1346	13 2	1848	0 10	1 36	1 52	2 47	3 4	3 26	4 10
Marktredwitz	8 37	1056	1158	1445	1341	1930	..		..	3 26	3 44	..	4 47
Praha (*above*) dep.	..	..		7 35		11 0	..	..	..	..	s	..	
Eger .... ,,	8 10	1026	A	1355	..	18‡45	..	B	..	..	..	..	4 2[illegible]
Wiesau	8 54	1113	..	15 2	..	..	..	..	..	3 43		..	5 4
Weiden	9 27	1143	..	1542	1424	2015		..		4 13	4 28	..	5 34
Schwandorf	10 5	1219	1324	1621		2054	..	..	..	4 49	..	..	6 10
Regensburg .. arr.	1041	1254	14 4	1658	1537	2133	2 53	4 10	4 23	5 28	5 40	6 12	6 48
Regensburg dep.	1051	13 5	1411	1711	1545	2141	..	4 17	4 30	5 36	5 47	6 55	6 55
Landshut .... . arr.	1148	1355	1458	18 8	1631	2231	..	5 8	5 22	6 25	6 37	7 42	7 42
Munich (Hptb. arr.	1255	15 0	1558	1922	1730	2335	..	6 10	7 32	7 32	7 40	8 43	8 43

A July 1–Sept. 15. **B** June 15–Sept. 15. **D** Corridor Exp., see p. 75. *r* Rest. Car. *s* Sleeping Cars.
+ Not Suns. ‡ *Via* Marktredwitz.

[German State Rlys., Munich & Erfurt.

Fr. Stuttgt. p. 185,186	1 2 3 ExD	2 cl. FDT	2 3 ExD	1 2 3 ExD	1 2 3 ExD	2 3 fast	2 3 fast	1 2 F D	1 2 3 ExD	1 2 3 ExD	2 3 fast	2 3 fast	1 2 3 ExD	1 2 3 ExD	1 2 ExD	1 2 3 ExD	1 2 3 ExD
Munich (Hpt.) dep.	..	6 40	8 35	9 8	9 17	9 25	..	12 5	..	1220	13 0	1750	From Stu'gart	From Lindau.	2220	2312	2350
Ingolstadt .... ,,	..		9 34	*a*	A	1035	..	*a*	..	*a*	*a*	1849			..	..	..
Treuchtlingen (188)	..	W	A		*a*	1141	..	.	..	C	1450	1950			*a* Z	..	*a*
Pleinfeld (*p.* 187) ..	..	..	..	..		1158	..	..			15 8	..			..	*a* S	..
Nuremberg .. arr.	..	8 31	11 3	1118	1140	1239		14 4	..	1456	1552	2038	23 6	23 0	1 0	1 34	2 16
Nuremberg .. dep.	7 10	8 37	1112	1128	1149	1249		1413		15 4	1614	2054	2332	2345	1 12	1 43	2 27
Bamberg ...... arr.	7 52	..	..	1217	1238	1358	..	..	..	1547	1712	22 2 Exp	0 20	0 32 B S		..	3 13
(*p.*185) Heidelberg dp.	..	|	|	6 56	|	..	6 56	|	9 46	..		1729	S	|	|	..	Slp. Car. fr. Rome
Wurzburg .. dep.	.			1030		..	1143		1255	..		2120				..	
Schweinfurt	..			1121		..	1241		1355	..		22 9				..	
Bamberg .. arr.	..			1214	▼		1345	▼	1448	..		23 2				..	
												1 2 3					
Bamberg .... dep.	7 53			1220	1241	14 4	1355	.	1457	1549	1718	2315	0 23	0 34		..	3 16
Lichtenfels .... arr.	8 15			1243	13 3	1434	1424	.	1521	1611	1742	2340	0 45			2 50	
Probstzella arr.	..		▼	▼	.	1633				..	19 8		..	..	..		
Saalfeld .... arr.	9 40		1336	1416	1434	17 2		1629		1740	1932		2 17	2 33	3 52	4 24	5 15
Jena	..	▼	..	151[illegible]	1528	*z*		..		1837	*z*		*z*	3 28		5 23	6 16
Leipsic (*p.* 172)	1148	12 4	17‖3	1719	.	2019		..		2013	22‖8		4 59	5‖51	7‖1		8 9
▼ Halle ...... arr.	¶	¶	1539	1630	1610	22 4		1816		1954	23 6		¶	4 48	5 47	6 40	7 46
BERLIN (*p.*172) ,,	13[illegible]8	1324	1734	1830	1839	2234	▼	20 2	▼	2152	0 22	▼	7 23	7 8	7 55	8 53	9 49
Lichtenfels .... dep.	..	..	..	..	..		1440	..	1523	..	..	2345	..			..	..
Neuenmarkt-Wirs. a	..	..	..	..	..	..	1525	..	16 3		..	0 30	..		..		..
Bayreuth .. arr.	..	..	..	..	..	..	1653	..	1653		..	1 24	..	..		..	..
Bayreuth .. dep.	..	..	..	..		..	1450	..	1557	..		2232	..	..	..	..	..
Neuenmarkt-W. ,,	..	..	..	..	..	..	1535	..	1624			0 39	..	..	..	..	..
Oberkotzau (*p.*192) a.	..	..	..	..	..	..	1637	..	..			..		..	..	..	..
Hof .... ,,	..	..	..	..	..	..	1646	..	1731	..	..	1 53	..	..	..		
p. 193 Dresden (H) ar.	..	..	..	..		..	21 0	..	2148	..	..	7 51	..	..	..	..	..
p. 193 Leipsic (Hpt.) ,,	..	..	..	..	..		2046	..	2032	..		5 51	..				..
p. 193 BERLIN (Anh) ,,	..	..	..	..	..	..	22 0	..	2234			8 2	..				..

For service via Weiden, see p. 190.	2 3 fast	2 3 ExD A	1 2 3 ExD C	1 2 3 ExD	1 2 F D	1 2 3 ExD A	2 3 fast	1 2 3 ExD	1 2 3 ExD	2 cl FDT W	2 3 fast	1 2 3 ExD	1 2 3 ExD S	1 2 FxD Z	1 2 3 ExD S	1 2 3 ExD B	2 3 ExD
p. 192 BERLIN (Anh) dp.				7 58	.		0 15	..			..	..					2250
p. 192 Leipsic (Hpt.) ,,	..	..	..	9 59			6 49	..	1415	..	..	..	..				1 12
p. 192 Dresden (Hpt) ,,	..	..	..	8 16	..	.	6 0	..	1254		..	..		..	..	..	2226
Hof .... dep.	..		..	1257	..	..	1039	..	1814	..	..	..			..		4 15
Oberkotzau	..	..	..	..		..	..	..	1822		..	..	..	..	..	S	4 25
Neuenmarkt-Wirsb.	..		..	1356	.		1149	..	1922		..	..		.	..		5 28
Bayreuth .. arr.			..	1423		..	1237	..	2020	..		..		..	..		7 36
Bayreuth .. dep.	..	..	..	1325	..		11 3	..	1842			..		..	..	..	4 14
Neuenmarkt-Wirs. d	..		..	14 3	..	..	1155	..	1926		..	..			.		5 30
Lichtenfels .... arr.	..	..	..	1440	..	..	1240	..	2022			..		..	.	.	6 13
BERLIN ‡ (173) dp.	0 15	8 24	8 31	|	1013	103		1150	1532	1640	1719	21 3	2112	2118	2137	2240	|
Halle ...... dep.	¶	1023	1037		1159	1241		1351	¶	¶	¶	2258	2314	2325	¶	0 58	
Leipsic (*p.* 173)	7 10	9 54	..		11‖23	12 0		1322	1749	18 9	2030	22‖1	2258	22‖58	2358	..	
Jena ...... dep.	*z*	1137	..		..	1356		15 2	*z*		*z*	..	0 33	.	*z*	1 49	
Saalfeld .... ,,	9 52	1228	1245		1343	1456		16 0	20 3		0 2	1 0	1 30	1 47	2 35	2 53	
Probstzella dep.	1022	1258	1315	▼	..	..	▼	1630	2032		0 36	1 30	1 58		3 3	3 22	▼
Lichtenfels	1149	..	1417	1442		1648	1252	1737	2133	|	2 16	2 31	..			..	6 16
Bamberg ...... arr.	1217	1417	1440	15 8	..	1712	1321	18 1	2155	|	2 44	..	3 20		4 36	4 52	6 42
Bamberg .. dep.	|	..	|	1515	|	|	14 6	|	2212	|	4 20	|	..	|	|	|	6 52
Schweinfurt arr.		..		16 7			15 0		23 3		5 53						7 51
Wurzburg .. ,,		..		17 3			1550		0 20		7 22						8 41
(*p.*185) Heidelberg ,,	▼	.	▼	2033	▼	▼	2011	▼		▼	1438	▼		▼	▼	▼	1225
Bamberg .... dep.	1226	1419	1443		..	1714	..	18 3	2158	..	2 58	..	3 22		4 38	4 55	6 52
Nuremberg .. arr.	1329	15 1	1529	..	1610	1817	..	19 0	2251	2142	4 8	3 38	4 17	4 39	5 43	5 52	8 14
Nuremberg .. dep.	1349	1513	1537	..	1618	1827	..	1913	..	2146	4 35	3 50	4 28	4 55	6 21	6 28	8 38
Pleinfeld (*p.* 187) ..	1436		..	..		..	..	..			..	..	..	..	To Stu'gart	To Lindau	9 8
Treuchtlingen .. arr.	1458		1620		*a*	*a*	..	..		..	5 37	..	..				9 21
Ingolstadt .... ,,	*a*	1641	*a*			..	..	*a*	..	..	*a*	*a*	*a*	*a*			..
Munich (Hptb.) arr.	17 7	1757	1820		1828	21 5		2152	..	2344	7 54	6 20	7 5	8 2			1123

A June 15–Sept. 15. **B** June 15–Sept, 10. **C** June 30 Sept. 15. **D** Corridor Exp., *see p.* 75. **FD** and **FDT** see *page* 75. **S** Sleep. Cars. **Z** Sleep. Cars only Munich to Berlin and *v.v.* *a Via* Augsburg. *z Via* Zeitz. ¶ To and from Berlin *via* Leipsic. ‖ Connection at Halle.

Berlin, Leipsic, Dresden, Reichenbach, Hof. [Ger. Rlys., Dresden

1 & 2 cl. D—Exp., see p. 75.	2 3	fast 2 3	Exp 2 3 D	fast 2 3	1 2 3 D	1 2 3 D	Exp 1 2 3 D	Exp 1 2 3	Exp 1 2 3 D	2 3	Exp 1 2 3 D r	fast 2 3	fast 2 3	Exp 1 2 3	Exp 1 2 3 D	Exp 1 2 3 D	Exp 1 2 3 D s	Exp 2 3 D
BERLIN (p. 172) dep.	0 15		5 38	6 19	7 58	8 4		..	1031	8 40	1340	1532	1715	19 0	2020	..	2129	2250
Leipsic (Haupt) dep.	4 27	6 49	8 3	9 6	9 59	10 8			1235	1415	1538	1738	1939	21 8	2232	..	2348	1 12
Reichenbach .. arr.	7 18	8 53	9 35	11 4	..	..		..	14 8	1551	17 5	1911	2125		0 8	..	1 31	..
Dresden (Haupt) d.	..	6 0	7 11	..	8 16	↓	9 35	9 47	1110	1254	1430	1622	1842	↓	2045	2216	2226	..
Chemnitz Haupt dp.	..	7 39	8 40	..	10 0		11 2	1123	1248	1425	16 3	1750	2016		2226	2355	0 5	..
Reichenbach .. arr.	..	8 58	9 48	..	..	↓		1239	1359	1537	1716	19 6	2134	↓	2354	1 12	1 20	..
Reichenbach dep.	7 24	9 3	9 58	1146	..	..		1241	1416	1552	1722	1915	2136	..	0 20	1 13	1 33	..
Plauen (Upper St.) ar.	8 5	9 36	1022	1221	1153	12 7	1231	13 6	1446	1617	1746	1943	22 2	23 1	0 46	1 38	1 58	3 6
Hof ,,	9 23	1030	1113	1331	1247	13 3	1319	1354	..	18 2	1836	2030	..	24 0	1 44	2 32	2 54	3 59
Munich (p. 190) arr.	15 0	..	..	1922	1730			1835		..	2335	..	..	..	..	7 32	7 40	8 43

r Rest. Car. *s* Sleep. cars Berlin-Munich and *v.v.* Berlin-Rome.

§ 2 and 3 cl. only.	1 2 3 D	1 2 3 D	1 2 3 D	1 2 3 D	2 3 D	2 3 fast	2 3 fast	2 3	2 3 fast	1 2 3 D	1 2 3 D	1 2 3 D	2 3 fast	1 2 3 D	2 3	1 2 D	1 2 3 D	1 2 D
Munich (p. 190) dep.	2145	22 0	..	..	2349		1945			8 0	8 0	..	..	12 7	8 30	..	1242	1242
Hof .... dep.	2 50	3 10	3 40	3 51	4 22	..	5 15	8 4	1015	13 6	1319	..	..	1627	1656	1721	1726	1748
Plauen (Upper Stn.)	3 41	3 59	4 30	4 40	5 9	6 14	7 48	9 24	11 1	1354	14 6	1523	1639	1712	1752	18 4	1813	1834
Reichenbach .. arr.	4 9	4 26	4 56		5 35	6 39	8 12	10 3	1129	1419	1433	1552	17 4	1737	1821	..	..	19 0
Reichenbach dep.	↓	4 32	..	↓	6 16	7 1	8 24	10 7	1136	..	1439	16 7	1712	1739	1914		..	19 1
Chemnitz Haupt. ar.		5 54	..		7 39	8 15	1033	1149	1248	..	1555	1720	1829	1853	2142	1934	..	2017
Dresden (Haupt) ar.	↓	7 31	..	↓	9 13	9 44	1254	1615	1416	..	1726	1844	1955	2025	2359	21 0	..	2148
Reichenbach ...dep.	4 15	..	5 14	..	5 38	6 40	8 14	1014	1142	1422	..	1559	1720		1843	..	..	..
Leipsic (Haupt) arr.	5 51	..	6 43	6 32	7 4	8 5	9 47	1217	1312	1546	..	1727	1850	..	2046	..	20 1	..
BERLIN (p. 172) arr.	8 2	..	9 7	8 44	9 11	1024	1244	1613	1612	1746	..	1927	..	..	2234	.	22 0	..

(Berlin) Leipsic, Dresden, Eger. [Ger. Rlys., Dresden.

1 2 3 D	2 3 D	2 3	2 3	2 3	1 2 3 D	2 3 fast	1 2 3 D	1 2 3	¶ 2 & 3 cl. only.	2 3	1 2 3 D	1 2 3 D	1 2 3 D	2 3	2 3	2 3 D s	1 2 3 D
2250	From Gera	5 38	7 58	..	1031	8 40	1340	1532	dep. **Berlin** .. (above) .. arr.	1530	..	1746	1927	2234	1 8	To Weimar	8 2
1 12		8 8	9 59	1128	1235	1415	1538	1745	dep. Leipsic (above) .. arr	1217	1255	1546	1727	2046	2224		5 51
2226		6 0	8 16	9 35	1110	1254	1430	1622	dep. Dresden (above) .. arr.	1615	1416	1726	1844	2025	2359		7 31
1 52	*s*	9 39	1119	13 8	1416	1559	1722	1926	dep. Reichenbach .. arr.	10 3	1118	14 9	1552	1737	2027		4 9
2 18	..	10 6	1143	1351	1446	1641	1746	1953	arr. Plauen .. dep.	9 24	1050	1325	1523	1712	1959		3 41
¶							¶					¶					
5 55	9 22	1012	12 0	1356	1448	1649	1758	1955	dep. Plauen .. arr.	9 18	1048	1310	1521	17 7	1935	2146	2239
6 54	10 1	1119	1238	1446	1535	1741	1852	2039	arr. Bad Elster ....dep.	8 23	10 8	1215	1440	1614	1845	21 8	2139
7 17	1022	1140	1257	15 6	1559	18 2	1914	2059	arr. Bad Brambach dep.	8 1	9 48	1155	1418	1554	1826	2050	2120
7 37	..	1158	..	1524	..	1820	..	..	arr. Voitsersreuth dep.	7 42	..	1136	.	1535	18 5	..	21 0
7 46	1045	12 8	1320	1533	1623	1830	..	2123	arr. Franzensbad ..dep.	7 31	9 19	1124	1343	1524	1754	2026	2049
7 58	1057	1219	1331	1544	1635	1841	..	2134	arr. **Eger** ....dep.	7 20	9 8	1114	1332	1514	1744	2016	2039

s Sleep. car, Cologne-Eger-Marienbad and *v.v.*

Leipsic, Chemnitz. *Via* Gethain. [Ger. Rlys., Halle.

80 Klms. All trains 2 and 3 cl.

8 20	9 57	13 5	14 5	1541	1740	1952	2354	dep. **Leipsic** . arr.	7 50	9 26	1056	1314	1448	1729	1952	2128	0 32
9 53	1118	1126	1534	1710	1913	2126	1 23	arr. **Chemnitz** *abn.* dep.	6 30	8 1	9 34	1155	1328	16 5	1827	21 7	2315

Hof, Oberkotzau, Eger. [Ger. State Rys., Regensburg.

All 2 and 3 cl.

4 45	5 28	7 26	1111	1356	1635	1934	2332	dep. **Hof** .... arr.	6 52	9 41	1229	1515	18 3	2056	2330	0 45
..	..	..	7 40	9 14	1355	..	1646	dep. Bamberg (p. 191) arr.	11 1	1323	1454	2055	2055	2 44	..	6 42
4 53	5 38	7 35	1120	14 7	1644	1943	2339	dep. Oberkotzau ...... arr.	6 43	9 31	1218	15 5	1752	2046	2321	0 34
5 30	6 28	8 13	12 6	1452	1735	2027	0 22	dep. Asch .... dep.	5 57	8 50	1141	1426	1711	20 6	2248	2359
5 53	6 54	8 36	1233	1517	18 0	2051	0 46	arr. Franzensbad .. dp.	5 22	8 8	1112	1355	1638	1931	2220	2332
6 4	7 7	8 47	1243	1528	1811	21 2	0 56	arr. **Eger** .. ..dep.	5 12	7 58	11 2	1344	1626	1921	2210	232

Garmisch-Partenkirchen—Zugspitzgipfel. May 15—Oct. 7.

2 and 3 cl. only.

a			c	b									a	
7 45	9 25	11 0	1355	1640	18 0	1910	dp. Garmisch-P. (p. 193) ar.	7 38	8 26	10 8	1343	1512	1720	1841
8 9	9 48	1123	1417	17 3	1819	1929	,, Grainru-Bad .. ,,	7 20	8 8	9 50	1325	1454	17 2	1823
8 28	10 8	1141	1435	1723	..	..	,, Eibsee .... ,,	..	..	..	..	1435	1642	18 4
9 27	11 7	1240	1534	1822	..	..	a. Hot'l Schne'fernerha's d	..	..	..	..	1333	1549	17 4

Aerial Railway from Hotel Schneefernerhaus to Zugspitzgipfel from 9.0 to 17.0 every 30 mins. Cars leave valley and mountain top every hour and half-hour. Length of journey 4 minutes. Cable Railway from Obermoos at 8.30, 9.30, 10.30, 11.30, 12.30, 13.30, 14.30, 15.30, 17.0, 18.0.

a June 4—Oct. 1, in every case weather permitting. *b* Sats. only. *c* July and Aug.

Munich (Oberammergau), Partenkirchen, Innsbruck. [German Rys.

Mls		2 3	2 3	1 2 3 ExD	2 3	1 2 3 ExD	2 3 ExD	1 2 3 ExD	2 3	2 3 ExD	2 3	2 3	1 2 3 ExD	2 3	2 3 fast
0	**Munich** (Starnberg) .. dep.	5 5	6 38	7 38	7 50	8 55	B	9 8	1128	1358	1533	1723	19 3	2040	2230
18	Starnberg .... ,,	5 42	7 8	C	8 22	E	..	9 32	1158	..	16 3	1755	..	21 6	..
24	Tutzing .... arr.	5 57	7 22	↓	8 37	↓	..	9 43	1213	..	1618	18 9	1936	2116	2255
33	Weilheim .... ,,	6 16	7 39		8 53		9 44	9 56	1231	.	1638	1825	1948	2135	23 7
46	Murnau .... ,,	6 46	8 8		9 22		10 5	1015	13 1	15 0	17 7	1852	20 8	22 2	2320
0	**A** Murnau .... dep.	7 3	8 18		..		..	1025	1340	1516	1715	1911	2015	2210	.
15	**A** Oberammergau .... arr.	7 58	9 11		..		..	1118	1435	1559	1810	20 6	2110	23 5	..
..	Murnau .... dep.	6 50	8 10	↓	9 26	↓	10 6	1018	13 5	15 1	1711	1854	20 9	22 5	2321
63	Garmisch- arr.	7 25	8 42	9 7	9 59	1020	1034	1046	1339	1526	1744	1935	2034	2235	2339
	Partenkirchen dep.	7 40	8 50	9 22	10 8	1035	⌐	1055	1355	1540	1815	1955	2039		2340
73	Mittenwald .... arr.	8 15	9 26	9 54	1041	11 5	..	1125	1431	1610	1850	2030	2110		0 8
	Mittenwald .... dep.	8 21	..	10 0	1043	1112	..	1130	1437	1617	1856	2038	2113	..	0 10
77	Scharnitz .... arr.	8 33	..	1010	1052	1122	..	1140	1449	1628	19 7	2049	2123	..	0 41
97	Seefeld .... ,,	8 59	..	1030	1113	1142	..	12 2	1514	1650	1932	2113	2142	..	..
99	**Innsbruck** (Central) .. ,,	9 45	..	1110	1157	1230	..	1248	16 1	1735	2020	22 4	2223		..

	2 3	2 3	2 3	1 2 3 ExD	2 3	2 3	1 2 3 ExD	2 3	1 2 3 ExD	2 3	1 2 3 ExD	2 3 ExD	2 3	2 3 fast	2 3
Innsbruck (Cent.) p. 197 dp.	..	..	5 18	7 26	8 0	1010	1158	1310	1430	1520	1645	..	18 2	1922	2116
Seefeld .... ,,	..	..	6 15	8 11	8 58	1112	1242	14 4	1515	1620	1736	B	19 3	2011	2222
Scharnitz .... ,,	..	..	6 39	8 31	9 18	1139	..	1423	C	1644	1754	..	1925	2029	2242
Mittenwald .... arr.	..	..	6 48	8 40	9 27	1149	13 9	1433	1542	1653	18 3	..	1934	2038	2252
Mittenwald .... dep.	..	6 28	6 52	8 45	9 32	1154	1315	1440	1547	17 3	18 9		1947	2045	..
Garmisch- arr.	..	6 59	7 26	9 16	10 6	1227	1346	1514	1620	1737	1840	⌐	2022	2118	..
Partenkirchen dep.	5 20	7 6	7 48	9 26	1034	13 0	14 0	1527	1630	1750	1855	19 3	2035	2123	..
Murnau .... arr.	5 51	7 31	8 21	9 51	11 8	1334	1423	1559	↓	1822	1919	1929	21 8	2152	..
A Oberammergau .... dep.	..	6 38	7 16	8 57	10 2	1242	..	15 5		..	1823	..	2014	E	..
A Murnau .... arr.	..	7 25	8 5	9 44	1050	1331	..	1554		..	1910	..	21 4		..
Murnau .... dep.	5 53	7 33	8 25	9 53	1111	1338	1424	16 2		1823	1920	1930	2111	2153	..
Weilheim .... ,,	6 22	7 53	8 53	1013	1138	14 3	1443	1628	↓	1848	1938	1948	2140	2211	..
Tutzing .... ,,	6 39	..	9 12	..	1156	1421	..	1647		19 5	1954	..	2157	2224	..
Starnberg .... ,,	6 51	..	9 28	..	12 7	1436	..	17 3	C	1917	20 5	..	2213	2238	..
Munich (Starnberg) .. arr.	7 20	8 41	10 0	11 1	1236	15 9	1530	1737	1757	1946	2032	..	2245	23 5	..

E July 1–Sept. 17. † Not Sats. ‡ 1, 2 & 3 cl.

A 2 and 3 cl. only Murnau-Oberammergau and *v.v.* **B** From Berlin. **C** July 1–Aug. 31. **D** Exp.

(Stuttgart) Kempten, Reutte, Garmisch-Partenkirchen.

2 3	2 3	2 3	2 3	2 3	2 3	2 3	2 3	**A** July 1—Aug. 31.	2 3	2 3	2 3	2 3	2 3		2 3	2 3
..	..	..	6 36	7†53	1050	1346	1613	dep. **Stuttgart** (*p.* 186) arr.	1658	..	1846	2116	23†0	..	9 57	1231
..	..	..	7 58	9 15	1218	15 9	1737	arr. Ulm .... dep.	1548	..	1734	1949	2138	..	8 49	11 8
..	..	..	8 19	9 30	1225	16 5	1755	dep. Ulm .... arr.	1540	..	1726	1927	21 2	..	8 26	1048
..	..	..	9 54	1150	14 2	1841	1942	arr. Kempten .... dep.	1326	..	16 6	1719	1933	..	6 55	9 20
..	5 27	7 11	1054	1324	1551	19 4	2055	dep. Kempten (*p.* 187) .. arr.	1143	..	1510	17 6	1842	22 9	6 41	8 54
..	6 51	8 41	1217	1457	1715	2029	2219	arr. Pfronten-Ried ...... dep.	1022	..	1351	1542	1717	2045	5 18	7 34
..	7 38	9 30	13 2	1547	18 1	2114	..	arr. Reutte .... dep.	9 35	A	13 5	1456	1628	20 0	..	——
5 50	8 18	1033	1340	1610	18 7	..	..	dep. Reutte .... arr.	9 15	1110	1230	..	1528	1948	..	2215
6 33	9 4	1131	1424	1653	1850	..	..	arr. Lermoos .... dep.	8 33	1024	1146	..	1444	1915	..	2132
6 40	9 10	1139	1434	17 0	1857	..	..	arr. Ehrwald-Zugspitzbahn dep.	8 26	1015	1138	..	1437	1858	..	2125
6 42	9 12	1140	1435	17 1	1859	..	..	dep. Ehrwald-Zugspitzbahn arr.	8 24	1012	1135	..	1436	1855	..	2120
6 59	9 28	1156	1451	1717	1916	..	..	dep. Griesen .... dep.	8 7	9 52	1116	..	1416	1836	..	21 6
7 25	9 55	1222	1518	1743	1942	..	..	arr. Gar. Partenkirchen dep.	7 40	9 23	1050	..	1350	1810	..	2040

THROUGH SERVICE, Berlin, Munich and Italy.

1 2	1 2 3	2 cl.	1 2 3	1 2 3	1 2 3	*a* Via Probstzella.	2 cl.	1 2 3	1 2	1 2 3	1 2 3
10 13	1150	1640	2112	2118	21 29	dep. BERLIN (*p.* 191) arr.	1324	1830	20 2	7 55	9 49
FzD	*a*	FDT	S	¶	C *a*		FDT	*a*	FzD	¶	S *a*
18 28	2150	2344	7 5	8 2	7 40	arr. MUNICH (*p.* 190) dep.	6 40	9 8	12 5	2220	2350
18 50	2355	⌐	7 55	8 15	10 20	dep. MUNICH (*p.* 198) arr.	⌐	6 30	1144	..	2310
21 31	2 40	..	1028	11 3	14 10	,, Innsbruck ...... ,,	..	3 48	8 57	..	2035
22 52	4 5	..	1145	..	15 50	,, Brennero *c* .... ,,	..	2 29	7 23	..	1920
..	6 47	..	1447	..	19 31	arr. Merano ...... dep.	..	2122	..	..	9 45
3 15	8 5	..	1532	..	20 35	,, Verona .... ,,	..	22 3	2 55	..	1511
6 33	1024	..	1815	..	23 45	,, MILAN .... ,,	..	20 8	0 16	..	1228
5 25	1025	..	1740	..	22 55	,, Venice ...... ,,	..	1938	0 1	..	1215
9 36	14 6	..	2130	..	0 32	,, Bologna .... ,,	..	1950	1 5	..	1310
11 40	1549	..	0 45	..	2 15	,, FLORENCE ...... ,,	..	1820	2328	..	1135
15 30	2020	..	6 30	..	6 50	,, ROME .... ,,	..	1425	1910	..	7 10

S 1 & 2 Sleep. Car Berlin-Munich-Rome and *v.v.*

¶ Sleeping Cars only, Berlin-Munich and *v.v.*

a 1 & 2 cl. Cars Berlin-Rome and *v.v.*

C 1, 2 & 3 cl. Sleep cars Berlin-Munich.

FD and **FDT** see page 75.

Hamburg—Hanover—Wurzburg—Munich.

[Germ. Rlys.

Exp 123 A¶	FD 12	Exp 123 ¶	Exp 123 A§	Ex 123 A§	Exp 123 S¶	Exp 123 T§		(515 miles).		Exp 123 A§	Exp 123 A§	Exp 123 ¶	F D 12	xp 123 A¶	Ex 123 T§	Exp 123 S¶
6 31	..	7 49	8 57	1150	1810	2357	dep.	HAMBURG-ALTONA	arr.	1813	2030	2150		2357	6 53	9 41
6 50	..	8 8	9 17	12 8	1830	2359	,,	HAMBURG HBF.	,,	1754	2011	2125	..	2338	6 31	9 17
..	..	9 23	r	..	1944	1 24	,,	Uelzen (p. 170)	,,	..	r	2012	..	..	4 53	8 7
8 51	..	1045	1123	1426	2054	2 40	arr.	HANOVER	dep.	1528	18 6	1850	..	2126	3 41	6 57
8 59	..	1058	1131	1440	21 5	3 3	dep.	HANOVER	arr.	1540	1758	1833	..	2118	3 20	6 50
r		r	1227	1536	2215	4 1	,,	Kriensen	dep.	1445	17 1	1740		..	2 21	5 55
1136		1345	1415	1724	0 16	5 56	arr.	Bebra	,,	1253	15 9	1543	..	1840	0 27	4 6
1142	..	1355	1418	1729	0 23	6 5	dep.	Bebra	arr.	1246	15 4	1534	..	1834	0 17	3 58
1227	..	1449	15 4	1814	1 13	7 1	,,	Fulda	,,	12 1	1417	1448	..	1748	2327	3 7
1332	.	1556	16 5	1917	..	8 9	arr.	Gemunden	dep.	1055	13 7	1325		1640	22 5	
1333	..	1558	16 6	1918	..	8 10	dep.	Gemunden	arr.	1054	13 6	1324	..	1639	22 3	
14 5	—	1629	1537	1949	2 50	8 48	arr.	Wurzburg (p. 188/9)	dep.	1023	1237	1250	—	16 8	2132	1 23
1412	17 0	1642	—	20 3	2 59	9 10	dep.	Wurzburg	arr.	10 4	—	1237	1224	16 0	2115	1 13
..		18 2	..	..		1043	arr.	Ansbach	dep.	↑	..	1126	↑	..	1955	↑
1624		..	..	..		1131	,,	Treuchtlingen	,,		..			1413	19 3	
1723		..	..	..		1228	,,	Augsburg	,,		..			1314	1756	
..	↓	1940	..	2232	↓	..	,,	Ingolstadt	,,	7 36	..	9 50		..	..	
1820	2023	2045	..	2336	7 3	1322	,,	MUNICH	,,	6 45	..	8 55	9 15	1220	17 0	2140

A June 30 to Sept. 15. **S** Sleep. Cars 1, 2 and 3 cl. Hamburg-Munich and *v.v.* **T** Sleep. Car 1, 2 and 3 cl. Hamburg-Wurzburg and *v.v.* *r* Rest. Car. ¶ 1, 2 and 3 cl. Cars Hamburg-Munich and *v.v.* § 1, 2 and 3 cl. Cars Hamburg-Wurzburg and *v.v.*

(Wurzburg)—Steinach—Rothenburg—Dombuhl—(Augsburg).

All trains 3 cl. unless otherwise stated.

	7 0		10 0	13 2	1430	1845	dep.	Wurzburg	arr.	9 41	12†14	15 0	1650	19 6	0 33	0 33
5 12	8 22	9 48	1135	1356	1612	1955	,,	STEINACH	,,	8 13	1116	1334	1554	1740	2039	2254
5 30	8 39	10 5	1153	1415	1631	2011	arr.	Rothenburg-	dp	7 55	1058	1315	1536	1722	2021	2236
5 35	8 42	1010	1220	15 0	1822	2017	,,	o/Tauber	ar.	7 37	1050	12 1	14 5	1718	20 9	..
6 27	9 32	11 5	1314	1548	1920	21 1	arr.	Dombuhl	dep.	6 45	9 48	1115	1319	1630	1925	
7†33	10†19			1557	20†25	21 3	dep.	Dombuhl	arr		9 34	1110	12 3	1626	8 46	..
9 3	1226			1832	23 7	0 42	arr.	STUTTGART	dep.		6†50	7 49	9 10	[illegible]	6†46	
6 37	9†35	1111		16 7	1924	2113	dep.	Dombuhl	arr.	..		1018	1316	[illegible]	1921	21 1
8 17	1036	1222		1715	2040	2240	arr.	NUREMBURG	dep.		..	9†22	1122	1430	1734	1932
6 40	1023	..	1327	1645	1932	2119	dep.	Dombuhl	arr.	6 27	9 26	1057	..	1541	1840	2056
7 15	11 2		14 2	1723	2010	2154	arr.	Dinkelsbuhl	,,	5 50	8 49	1018	..	15 1	18 2	2019
8 6	1156		1454	19 9	21 3	..	,,	Nordlingen	dep.	4 55	7 21	9 18	..	1338	17 4	1923
9 15	1255		15 4	1936	21 7	..	,,	Nordlingen	,,	..	6 50	9 8	..	12 7	1655	1913
9 42	1332		1533	2016	2142		,,	Donauworth	,,		6 14	8 40	..	1130	16 8	1832
1014	1430		1612	2059	2223	..	dep.	AUGSBURG	arr.	..	5 3	7 59	..	1019	1530	1756

† 1, 2 and 3 cl. "D" Train.

Munich—Schaftlach—(Tegernsee)—Bad Tolz.

All 2 and 3 cl. — 41 miles.

5 45	8 30	1140	1348	15 3	1718	20 0	dep.	MUNICH (Holz Bhf)	arr.	7 28	9 31	1144	1322	1525	1837	1924	2051
7 7	9 23	13 6	1441	16 5	1814	21 5	arr.	Schaftlach	dep.	6 28	8 43	11 5	1218	1442	1737	1845	20 0
7 10	9 25	13 9	1443	16 8	1816	21 6	dep.	Schaftlach	arr.	6 23	8 38	11 0	1213	1437	1732	1840	1955
7 36	9 44	1331	15 2	1631	1835	2131	arr.	Tegernsee	dep.	6 0	8 15	1040	1147	1417	17 0	1820	1930
7 10	9 25	13 9	1444	16 8	1817	21 8	dep.	Schaftlach	arr.	6 23	8 38	11 0	1213	1437	1732	1840	1954
7 22	9 35	1320	1453	1619	1826	2119	arr.	Bad Tolz	dep.	6 7	8 22	1049	1157	1426	1716	1827	1936
7 42	9 46	1338	15 6	1637	1840	2137	,,	Lenggries	dep.	5 51	8 5	1035	1140	1413	1659	1812	1917

Munich—Tutzing—Kochel.

All 2 and 3 cl. — 46 miles.

5 13	8 23	1036	1329	1633	1954	dep.	MUNICH (Starnberg Bhf)	arr.	7 33	9 1	1251	1552	19 0	21 4
5 56	9 15	1117	1422	1723	2046	arr.	Tutzing	dep.	6 45	8 13	12 2	15 6	18 9	2013
5 57	9 16	1119	1424	1725	2048	dep.	Tutzing	arr.	6 43	8 11	12 0	15 5	18 7	20 9
7 52	10 4	1211	1520	1820	2142	arr.	Kochel	dep.	5 45	7 20	11 0	1415	1717	19 5

Munich—Schliersee—Bayrischzell.

All 2 and 3 cl. — 48 miles.

6 15	8 38	12 6	1442	1938	dep.	MUNICH (Holz Bhf)	arr	7 17	9 46	13 0	16 0	21 0
6 58	9 36	1252	1541	2024	,,	Holzkirchen	,,	6 29	8 57	1224	1516	2023
7 48	1022	1341	1628	2112	arr.	Schliersee	dep.	5 52	8 20	1148	1438	1943
7 56	1029	1349	1634	2118	dep.	Schliersee	arr.	5 46	8 14	1142	1429	1934
8 33	11 3	1423	17 7	2152	arr	Bayrischzell	dep.	5 15	7 40	1110	1355	19 1

D—Corridor Exp. (*p.* 75).

Berlin, Dresden, Praha, Gmund, Vienna.

[German State Rlys.

123 ExD	23	123 Exp	123 ExD	23	123 ExD	23 ExD	123 ExD	¶ Sleep. Car Berlin-Vienna & *v.v.*	23	123 ExD	23 ExD	123 ExD	23 fast	23	123 ExD	123 ExD	23	123 ExD
7 25	8 47	..	1334	14 7	17 7	..	2326	dep. **Berlin** (Anhalt) ar.	8 22	6 58		1219	1339	17 0	..	2020	0 5	2321
9 19	1141	..	1510	1647	..	..	1 4	arr. } Elster- { dep.	5 36	5 12	..	▲	1133	1432	..	1837	2050	r
9 21	1147	..	1511	1653	..	..	1 5	dep. } werda { arr.	5 4	5 11	..	|	1131	1429	..	1835	2044	
1023	13 2		16 6	1813	1928	..	1 56	arr. **Dresden** (Hpt.) dp.	3 45	4 21	..	9 49	1033	1314	..	1738	1926	2044
..	↓	10 0	↓	..	..	1921	..	dep. **Berlin** (Anhalt) ar.	▲	.	9 35		..	..	*5 3		..	2327
..		1120		..	..	2046	¶	Falkenberg	|	¶	8 13	..	..	..	..	..	..	22 8
..		..			..	21 8		dep. Röderau .. dep.	|		7 51	..	..	..	..		..	2146
..	▼	1225	▼	..	..	2153		arr. Dresden (Hpt.) dp.	—	..	7 8	..	..	..	1254	..	..	2034
1037	1324	1236	1632	1830	1942	2252	2 12	dep. Dresden (Hpt.) ar.	2348	3 50	6 42	9 33	9 13	11 1	1236	1723	1921	2018
..	1415	13 6	17 3	1925	..	2340	..	arr. Bad Schandau ,,	2257	..	5 50		8 22	1010	12 0	1647	1831	..
1128	1455	1331	1729	20 4	2035	1 24	3 4	,, Bodenbach dep.	2220	2 56	5 16	8 43	7 42	9 32	1141	1625	1757	1926
1137	15 5	1341	1743	2022	2043	..	3 14	dep. Bodenbach arr.	2156	2 46		8 35	7 17	9 22	1131	1615	1746	1911
1158	1547	14 2	1812	2118	21 2	..	3 36	arr. Aussig ...... dep.	2116	2 25		8 15	6 31	8 41	11 8	1554	17 0	1850
..	1952	1627	2052	..	2330	..	..	,, Karlsbad .... ,,	..	..	..	5 50	.	..	7 32	1330	..	1336
1220	1635	..	1841	22 1	2135	..	3 57	,, { Lobositz *c* } ,,	..	2 4	..	8 1	5 51	8 1	1046	..	1618	1830
1245	1734	..	1911	..	22 0	..	4 27	dep. { Lobositz } a.	..	1 34		7 36	..	..	1016	..	..	18 0
1358	2130		21 0	..	2313		6 0	arr. Praha (Mas.) dp.	.	2359		6 24	..		8 30	.	..	1648
1440		..	..		..		6 32	dep. Praha (W.) .. arr.	.	2320		..	..		..			1010
18 0	..	..	..	..	..	..	1010	,, Gmund .. dp.	..	2011	..		..	..	..		..	1255
21 4	..	..	..	..	..	..	1246	arr. VIENNA (F.J.B.) ,, (*p.* 196).	..	17 5	..	..	..				..	9 30

Berlin. Leipsic, Passau. Vienna.

A Sleep. Car and 1, 2, 3 cl. Leipsic–Vienna.

B Sleep. Cars and 1, 2 & 3 cl. Cars, Berlin-Vienna and *v.v.*

123 Exp *r*	123 Exp	123 ExD B	123 Exp A	German State Railways.	123 Exp *r*	123 Exp	123 ExD A	23 ExD B
7 58	1340	19 0	2137	d. BERLIN (Anh.) *p.* 192	1746	8 2	..	8 44
9 49	1530	2056	2347	arr. } Leipsic .. { dep.	1555	6 2	..	6 40
9 59	1538	21 8	0 7	dep. } Leipsic .. { arr	1546	5 51	6 26	6 32
..	17 5	..	1 50	arr. Reichenbach dep.	1422	4 15	..	
8 16	1254	..	..	dep. Dresden .... arr.	1726	7 31	..	
..	17 7		1 52	dep. Reichenbach arr.	1419	4 9	..	
1247	1824	2 40	3 16	arr. Hof .... dep.	13 6	3 10	3 30	3 51
1537	2133	2 53	6 12	arr. } Regens- { dep.	9 52	2357	0 33	1 4
16 5	0 59	3 1	6 22	dep. } burg { arr.	8 30	2110	0 20	0 56
1740	2 35	4 35	8 2	arr. } Passau .. { dep.	6 54	19 7	2245	2324
1753	2 50	4†45	8 12	dep. } Passau .. { arr.	3 25	1857	2235	23†12
2210	7 45	9†8	1245	arr. **Vienna** (W.) dep.	2240	1428	1815	18†45

r Rest. Car Berlin-Regensburg. † Rest. Car Passau to Vienna and *v.v.*

Berlin—Troppau.

[German Rlys.

ExD 23		ExD 23
7 5	dep. BERLIN (Gor Bhf.) arr.	2051
1252	arr. Glatz .... dep.	15 5
1312	dep. Glatz .... arr.	1444
1336	,, Kamenz ...... ,,	1422
14 4	arr. Neisse .... dep.	1353
1411	dep. Neisse .... arr.	1343
1448	,, Ziegenhals .... dep.	1323
1539	,, Jagerndorf .... ,,	1239
1614	arr. TROPPAU ...... dep.	1154

All 2 and 3 cl.

Dresden, Zittau, Liebenau, Praha (170 miles).

[German Railways.

									† Denis Stn. *a* Via Loban								
..	6 16	7 51	9 58	1210	1338	1549	1627	2122	dep. DRESDEN ..... arr.	8 51	1232	1420	1617	19 3	2047	2339	..
..	7 8	8 36	1051	13 0	1429	1634	1730	2210	,, Bischofswerda ,,	8 10	1146	1340	1523	1819	20 9	2258	..
5 17	8 21	9 21	1155	1343	1538	*a*	1846	23 0	,, Ebersbach .... ,,	7 25	1039	1253	1418	17 3	1922	2147	..
6 20	9 3	9 51	1234	1414	1617	1755	1928	2332	arr. ZITTAU .... dep.	6 50	9 53	1220	1330	1619	1846	2055	..
6 30	9 10	9 57	1329	1422	1722	18 0	1938	2337	dep. ZITTAU .... arr.	6 42	8 50	12 9	1259	1419	1839	20 2	2320
7 32	9 55	1128	1415	1454	18 8	1840	2026	0 12	arr. Reichenberg ... dep.	5 42	8 6	1140	1220	1337	1812	1919	2239
8 30	1150	1150	⌣	1730	1953	..	..	..	dep. Reichenberg ... arr.	..	6 37	1037	..	1320	..	1910	2227
9 10	1230	1230	..	1812	2033	..	..	..	arr. Liebenau *c* ..... dep.	..	6 0	10 0	..	1243	..	1835	2150
..	..	..	..	1858	..	..	..	..	dep. Liebenau *c* ..... arr.	..	5 10	..	..	1154	..	1825	2132
..	..	..	..	21*52	..	..	..	..	arr. PRAHA (Wils.) .. dep.		2330		..	8†3	..	1437	19 1

(Electric Line).

Berlin, Gorlitz. Breslau.

[German Railways.

	Exp	fast	Exp		fast			fast		(255 miles.)				Exp		fast	Exp		
..	7 5	8 45	1125	1245	1415	1425	15 5	1925	2145	dp. BERLIN (Gor. Bhf.) ... ar.	9 31	1051	1451	1511	2159	1931	2051	2331	..
5 58	8 43	1042	1310	1550	1545	1640	1810	2126	0 21	,, Cottbus ,,	7 31	9 8	1248	1329	1720	1735	19 7	2125	1 7
7 47	10 2	1220	1433	1744	17 5	1820	20 4	2257	2 3	ar. GORLITZ dp.	6 12	7 56	1058	1217	1536	1614	18 0	20 0	2320
7 54	1016	1230	1443	18 0	1715	1845	22 7	23 5	3 39	dp. GORLITZ ar.	6 4	7 47	1050	12 8	1530	16 4	1753	1951	23 6
8 24	..	1251	15 3	1630		1913	2235	2323	4 19	,, Lauban dp.	5 45		1022	1150	15 1	1546	..	1932	2234
9 17	1112	1333	1544	..	1816	20 1	..	0 7	5 30	ar. Hirschb'g d.	4 55	6 49	9 21	11 8	1356	15 4	1658	1843	2132
⌐	1123	1348	1558	.	1834	2011	..	..	5 54	dp. Hirschb'g ar	..	6 1	9 16	1059	1327	1453	1546	1822	20 7
..	1216	1439	1646	..	1922	2110	..	..	7 2	,, Wal'nb'g ,,	..	4 59	8 28	1021	1223	14 7	15 7	1730	1911
..	1258	1516	1724	..	20 0	2147	..	..	7 42	ar. K'nsz'lt ,,	..	..	7 45	9 34	1130	..	1427	1650	1822
..	1358	1551	1757	..	2034	2232	..	..	8 38	ar. BRESLAU Freib. Bhf. dp.	..	..	7 16	9 5	1032	..	1352	1611	1715

The times on the LEFT are to be read DOWNWARDS, those on the RIGHT UPWARDS.

Eger, Karlsbad, Aussig, Dresden. [German Rlys.

2 3 Exp	2 3	1 2 3 Exp	2 3	2 3 fast	2 3 Exp	2 3	2 3		2 3	1 2 3 Exp	2 3	2 3 fast	2 3	1 2 3 Exp	2 3	1 2 3 Exp	2 3	1 2 3 Exp
6 15	8 38	12 6	14 5	16 6	1733	18 6	2010	dep. **Eger** ...... arr.	1055	12 5	16 2	1410	19 8	18 0	2124	22 2	2318	..
7 23	10 2	1318	1530	1711	1840	1932	2137	arr. } **Karlsbad** { dp.	9 31	11 2	1440	13 0	1745	1647	20 0	2059	2158	..
7 32	1015	1330	1546	1716	1848	1940	2144	dep. } **Karlsbad** { arr.	9 22	1054	1433	1250	1737	1627	1952	2052	2150	2330
8 37	1143	1430	1722	1818	1951	2120	2316	arr. } Komotau { dep.	7 47	9 49	1310	1145	1606	1525	1824	1946	2017	2226
8 45	12 4	1440	1740	1826	1959	2134	..	dep. } Komotau { arr	7 35	9 40	1118	1136	1414	1516	18 8	1936	1956	2217
9 36	1341	1531	1925	1915	2046	2252	..	dep. Teplitz...... arr	5 59	8 50	9 55	1042	1230	1424	1630	1844	18 3	2124
9 57	1417	1551	20 0	1957	21 5	2324	..	arr. **Aussig**...... dep.	5 22	8 32	9 18	1023	1147	14 5	1553	1826	1721	21 6
1026	1523	1615	..	..	2131	0 9	..	arr. Bodenbach.. dep.	4 30	8 8	..	10 0	1055	1341	15 5	1755	1632	2043
1236	1713	1723	..	..	2348	..	..	arr. **Dresden** .. dep	2 12	6 10	..	8 9	9 10	1236	1324	1632	1437	1042

Eger—Franzensbad.

7 20	9 8	1041	1332	1514	1744	20 0	2210	dep. Eger .. ... arr.	7 58	9 42	1057	1219	1528	1841	20 4	2134	..	..
7 29	9 18	1050	1342	1523	1753	20 8	2219	arr. Franzensbad dep.	7 48	9 32	1046	12 9	1518	1831	1954	2124	..	..

Praha, Linz, Tarvisio, Rome.
(Ger. & It. Rlys.)

A 2 3		A 2 3
2216	dep. **Praha** (Wils.) arr.	6 20
1 18	,, Budweis ...... ,,	3 20
3 42	,, Kaplitz *c* ...... ,,	1 54
5 45	arr. } Linz ...... { dep.	2340
6 26	dep. } Linz ...... { arr.	2315
8 57	,, Selzthal .... ,,	2056
1223	,, Leoben ...... ,,	1838
1527	,, Klagenfurt.. . ,,	1526
1613	arr. } Villach.... { dep.	1442
1636	dep. } Villach.... { arr.	1418
1750	arr. Tarvisio *c* .... arr.	1330
2138	,, Trieste (*p*.199) dp.	9 47
2227	,, Venice........ ,,	8 47
1 48	,, Bologna ...... ,,	5 10
3 10	,, Florence...... ,,	3 40
7 50	,, Rome .... dep.	2325

A 1 & 2 cl. Sleep. Car Praha-Rome and *v.v.*, Tues., Thurs., Sats.; 2 & 3 cl. Cars Praha-Linz and *v.v.* Rest. Car Bruck-Venice & *v.v.*

Praha, Linz, Graz, Trieste (Rome).
(Ger., Yugoslav. & It. Rlys.)

B 2 3		B 2 3
2216	dep. **Praha** (Wils.) arr.	6 20
1 18	,, Budweis ...... ,,	3 29
3 45	,, Kaplitz *c* .... ,,	1 54
5 45	arr. } Linz ...... { dep.	2340
6 26	dep. } Linz ...... { arr	2315
8 38	arr. Salzburg .... dep.	2115
11 0	arr. } Bruck .... { dep.	852
11 1	dep. } Bruck .... { arr.	1846
1151	arr. } Graz *p.* 200 { dep.	1758
1215	dep. } Graz *p.* 200 { arr.	1733
1316	arr. Maribor *c* .... dep.	1632
1710	,, Zagreb ... ,,	1240
7 10	,, Split (*p.* 199) ,,	2330
2010	,, Trieste (*p.* 200) ,,	9 37
8 25	,, Rome .... dep.	2140

B 1 & 2 cl. Sleep. Car Praha-Salzburg, Suns., Mons. Weds. and Fris.; from Salzburg Mons., Tues., Thurs. and Sats. 2 & 3 cl. Cars Praha-Trieste and Praha-Split and *v.v.*

Vienna, Gmünd, Suchdol (Praha.) [Ger. State Rlys.

2 3	1 2 3 Exp	1 2 3 Exp	2 3	2 3 Exp	1 2 3 Exp	2 3	2 3	* 3 cl. only.	2 3	2 3	2 3	1 2 3 Exp	2 3	1 2 3 Exp	1 2 3 Exp	2 3
6 30	7 50	9 30	13 6	1425	17 5	1820	21 0	dep. **Vienna** F.J.Bf.(*p*.206) arr.	8 50	10 7	1311	1246	1838	21 4	2137	2255
7 12	..	..	1351	1456	..	19 6	2129	,, Tulln .... arr.	8 10	9 34	1226	..	1756	..	..	..
9 21	9 13	11 2	1530	1557	1831	2051	2223	dep. Sigmundsherberg .. dep.	5 48	8 46	1043	1123	1625	1857	2019	2129
1130	1029	1223	1743	1718	1951	23 8	2341	arr. Gmünd .... dep.	4 44	7 35	8 48	1010	1420	1822	19 8	2010
12 0	1049	1255	1810	..	2011	..	..	dep. Gmünd *c* .... arr.	..	6 16	8 14	9 50	13 8	18 0	1843	1950
1228	..	..	..	..	..	..	..	arr. Gratzen *c* .... dep.	..	5 58	7 10	..	1250	..	..	..
18 5	14 8	..	..	..	..	..	..	,, Plzen .... ,,	..	..	..	..	7*50	..	1526	
1234	..	1313	1842	..	2029	..	..	arr. Suchdol *c* .... dep.	..	..	7 25	9 32	..	1741	..	..
..	..	1610	..	..	2320	..	..	arr. Praha W. .... dep.	..	..		6 32	..	1440	..	..

(Passau), Scharding, Attnang, Ischl, Stainach-Irdning. [German State Rlys.

2 3	2 3	2 3	2 3 A	1 2 3	2 3 A	2 3	2 3	2 3	+ Weekdays only.	2 3	2 3	1 2	2 3	2 3 B	2 3 B	2 3	2 3
..	5 4	1017	..	1130	..	..	1555	..	dep. Passau (*p*.188) a	10 2	1151	1151	1517	..	1851	21 1	2210
..	5 23	1034	..	1149	..	1410	1612	1630	,, Schärding .. arr.	9 43	1133	1133	1448	16 6	1832	2042	2151
.	7 5	12 5	..	1352	—	1611	1742	1845	arr. Attnang .. dep.	8 5	1010	1010	1326	1412	1558	1911	2032
2315	2 42	8 50	8 50	8 50	1015	1120	1420	1420	dep. Vienna (*p* 187) a	1140	14 5	14 5	1650	1824	2133	2218	..
5 22	7 37	1217	1336	1411	15 0	17 0	1813	1910	dep. **Attnang** .. arr.	7 10	9 20	9 51	1311	1350	1641	1826	2019
5 47	8 3	1237	1352	1430	1515	1716	1826	1934	Gmunden......	6 50	9 1	9 38	1253	1337	1625	18 8	20 6
6 3	8 16	1255	14 4	1442	1530	1729	1839	1957	Traunkirchen ..	6 36	8 45	9 25	1240	1325	1610	1755	1952
6 23	8 33	1316	1414	1455	1539	1743	1849	20 9	Ebensee	6 22	8 31	9 18	1225	1318	1559	1743	1943
6 47	8 54	1337	1432	1519	1559	18 6	19 7	2034	arr. **Ischl** .... dep.	6 0	8 2	9 0	12 1	13 0	1538	1718	1925
7 57	9 57	1438	1517	1625	1657	19 8	1958	2147	arr. } Bad { dep.	5 6	6 55	8 8	11 4	12 6	1450	1626	1840
8 58	..	1445	..	1640	1733	1914	2044	..	dep. } Aussee { arr.	..	6 45	..	1056	..	1427	1614	1821
9 44	..	1526	..	1721	1820	1958	2126	..	arr. Stainach-Ird. dp.	..	6 4	..	10 8	..	1337	1535	1740
1035	..	16 0	..	1755	1846	2030	..	..	,, Selzthal .. dep.	..	5 40	..	9 24	..	1255	1455	1713

A June 17—Sept. 17. **B** June 18—Sept. 18.

The times on the LEFT are to be read DOWNWARDS, those on the RIGHT UPWARDS.

N

2 3	1 2 3	2 3	1 2 3 ExD	2 3	2 3 fast	1 2 3 ExD	2 3	1 2	1 2 3 ExD	2 3	1 2 3 ExD	1 2 3 ExD	2 3 fast		1 2 3 ExD	1 2 3 ExD	1 2 S	2 3 fast	2 3	1 2 3 ExD	2 3	1 2 3 ExD	2 3	1 2 3	2 3	2 3 fast
..	..	2315	..	..	7 25	..	8 12	Sleeping Cars only.	..	1420	..	..	1845	dep. **Vienna** (West) ar.	..	..	Sleeping Cars only.	..	..	..	..	..	..	..	14 5	9 8
..	..	3 15	..	7 22	9 42	..	1010		..	1633	..	..	22 0	Amstetten .. arr.	..	..		21 0	..	..	..	..	..	..	1136	7 13
..	..	4 42	..	8 39	1054	..	1150		..	18 9	..	..	2316	Klein Reifling	..	..		1947	..		..	..	..	..	10 0	5 58
..	..	6 45	..	1023	1236	..	1343		..	20 0	..	..	0 50	arr. Selzthal ....dep.	..	..		1810	..	.	..	..	..	..	8 8	4 27
..	..	8 5	..	1053	1255	..	1455		..	2120	..	..	1 10	dep. Selzthal .... arr.	..	1232		1755	..	.	..	..	..	..	7 50	4 15
..	..	8 35	..	1124	1325	r	1530		..	2148	..	..	1 31	Stainach-Irdng	..	..		1733	..	..	..	..	..	..	7 27	3 54
..	..	1049	..	1330	1457	..	1755		..	2340	..	..	2 55	arr. Bischofshofen dp.	..	1050		1520	..	.	..	..	..	..	4 53	2622
	Exp Tr		A K	1 2 3 fast	↓			S	E r			Z	↓		E r			fast		A K		T r				Z
2050		..	8 5	7 25		1120	7 25	1220	1428	1712	1712	2135		dep. **Vienna** (p. 187) arr.	14 5	1650	1715	2133	2133	2218	7 31	..	7 31	6 44	14 5	8 0
7 15	9 30	9 45	1250	1330		1655	17 0	1640	1945	0 0	1 10	2 30		dep. **Salzburg** .... arr.	9 10	1145	1257	15 0	1452	1730	1928	2040	2230	0 50	6 12	2 50
8 27	102	11 0	1334	1425	↓	1750	1810		2030	1 22	2 3	..	↓	arr. Bischofshofen dp.	8 25	1055	..	14 2	1339	1645	1815	1948	2115	2350	4 48	..
8 28	1023	1115	1336	1432	1515	18 5	1816	..	2032	1 38	2 8	..	3 5	dep. Bischofshofen ar.	8 22	1045	..	1358	1319	1644	18 8	1947	21 6	2348	4 30	..
8 47	1042	1135	1350	1450	1531	1822	1835	1738	2047	1 57	2 25	3 28	3 19	arr. Schwarzach dep.	8 5	1030	1156	1340	13 2	1630	1750	1932	2048	2332	4 10	1 48
..	12 8	..	1435	..	..	1936	1936	1826	2146	..	3 12	..		arr. Badgastein dep.	..	9 41	..	..		1446	..	..	1944	2242	2 30	..
..	10 5	..	..	1359	1446	1740	1740		1944	..		2 30	..	dep. ,, .. arr.	9 30		..	1435	1353	1718	1826	..	2146	..	4 38	3 12
8 50	1045	1138	1352	1455	1543	1828	1840	1740	2050	2 27	..	3 45	.	dep. Schwarzach .. arr.	8 3	1028	1155	1335	1250	1627	1744	1930	2035	2324	3 48	1 39
9 35	1123	1223	1427	1540	1622	19 7	1925	1815	2125	3 22	..	4 20	..	Zell-am-see ..	7 28	9 52	1121	1258	1210	1552	17 2	1855	1953	2245	3 3	1 6
9 58	1140	1247	1444	1558	1640	1924	1945	..	2145	3 55	..	4 37	..	Saalfelden ..	7 12	9 38	..	1242	1152	1535	1642	1840	1933	2228	2 41	0 53
104	121	1328	..	1635	1715	1957	2028	..	2218	4 42	..	..	..	St. Johann	6 33	9 2	..	12 2	11 3	..	1550	18 3	1844	2143	2 5	..
1053	1225	1340	1528	1648	1728	2010	2040	19 8	2230	4 58	..	5 20	.	Kitzbühel ..	6 23	8 52	1023	1152	1053	1450	1540	1753	1834	2133	1 42	0 9
1141	13 3	1431	16 6	1727	18 8	2049	2147	..	23 7	6 2	..	6 0	..	Wörgl	5 48	8 17	..	1115	1010	1413	1450	1718	1746	2052	0 57	2335
12 8	1324	15 2	.	1754	1830	2110	2216	..	2328	6 36	..	6 21	1 2 3	Jenbach	5 22	7 55	..	1047	9 16	.	1416	1656	1712	2015	0 20	2311
1249	1355	1548	1655	1835	19 5	2145	2258	2033	24 0	7 24	..	6 50	ExD	arr. *Munich* (198) d.	4 50	7 20	9 0	1010	8 36	1320	1328	1620	1628	1930	2330	2240
			r	X		2 3		S			2 3		Y	**Innsbruck**	D	2 3	S	X		r						Z
1512	1452	1720	1715	1915	1926	2157	0 25	2040	0 12	8 10	6 0	7 20	10 0	dep. **Innsbruck** ar	4 40	7 12	8 52	9 55	6 24	13 8	1212	1555	1510	1752	2125	2218
1647	1535	1841	1753	1953	2031	23 2	1 31	..	..	9 34	7 7	7 57	1038	Oetzthal	..	6 12	..	9 18	4 49	1230	11 0	1519	1356	1642	2032	2138
1654	1546	1856	..	20 3	2043	2313	1 44	..	..	9 48	7 18	8 10	1049	Imst (p. 213)	..	6 1	..	9 7	4 31	..	1049	15 7	1343	1632	2021	2128
1720	16 5	1932	1824	2022	22 8	2335	2 16	2145	1 22	1020	7 48	8 33	1110	Landeck	3 32	5 40	7 49	8 50	4 0	12 3	1022	1450	1320	1611	1958	21 9
18 1	1635	2038	1854	2058	..	..	3 0	2215	1 52	11 1	8 30	9 4	1146	St. Anton	2 58	4 52	7 17	8 14	3 10	1131	9 30	1417	1218	15 1	1915	2030
1812	1647	2050	19 6	21 9	..	..	3 12	2227	2 4	1112	8 41	9 15	1157	arr. Langen .. dep.	2 38	..	7 4	8 1	2 56	1117	9 18	14 3	1149	1448	19 1	2016
1920	1726	22 8	1945	2147	..	..	4 2	23 8	2 52	1215	10 1	9 55	1235	Bludenz	2 5		6 33	7 29	2 10	1044	8 30	1331	11 8	14 2	1820	1944
1954	1743	2237	20 3	22 5	..	..	4 30	2326	3 11	1244	1031	1012	1252	arr. Feldkirch .... dep	1 29	..	6 11	7 6	1 12	1020	7 46	1310	1032	1316	1748	1915
20 8	1751	2242	↓	22 7	..	..	4 38	↓	..	13 6	1034	1018	1254	dep. Feldkirch .. arr.	..	..	↑	7 4	1 5	↑	7 45	13 5	10 9	1254	1746	1846
21 8	1835	2340		2240	..	..	5 27		..	1357	1133	1052	1330	arr. Bregenz .. dep.	..	..		6 30	0 24		6 50	1225	9 16	12 2	1652	1810
2119	..	0 26		..	..	..	5 31		..		1147	..	..	,, ,, (Hafen ,,	..	..			0 20		6 14	..	9 11	..	1641	
2141	1858	0 46		23 5	..	..	5 51		..	1424	12 7	1110	1348	,, Lindau *c* ,,	..	..		6 12	0 2		5 55	12 0	8 48	..	1620	1747
..	1750	..	20 7	..	..	..	..	2328	3 12	1310	11 7	1026	1310	dep. Feldkirch .... arr.	1 28	..	6 10	..	..	1017	7 42	1250	8 54		1648	19 0
..	1816	..	2025	..	..	..	..	2345	3 30	1342	1132	1045	1342	arr. **Buchs** *c* .... dep.	1 10	..	5 55		..	10 0	7 9	1220	8 26	..	1618	1840
..	2029	..	2229	..	..	..	..	1‖38	5 28	18 2	..	1250	..	,, Zurich p. 286 ,,	2312	..	4‖3			8‖9	..	9 20	..	..	1021	1624
..	22 5	..	2350	..	..	..	..	2 54	6 45	1946	..	1425	..	,, Bale (Swiss) ,,	2138	..	2 48		..	6 49	..	7 40	..	..	8 50	1454
													..	(p. 283)										..		
..	6 45	..	7 15	..	..	..	..	9 45	1415	..	..	2125	..	Paris (p. 268) ,,	1430	..	1955	..	..	22 0	..	2250	..	..	..	8 5

e Connection at Schwarzach. *r* Rest. Car.

A 1 & 2 cl. cars Budapest-Paris and Vienna-Calais, 3 cl. Vienna-Paris and *v.v.* **E** 1 & 2 cl. Sleep. Car Vienna-Belfort, and 1, 2 and 3 cl. Cars Budapest-Vienna-Paris and *v.v.* **K** 1 & 2 cl. Sleep. Car Innsbruck-Paris and *v.v.* (also 3 cl. June 27-Sept. 6). **S** Arlberg—Orient Express from Paris, Mon., Wed. and Fri., from Vienna Mon., Wed., Fri. **T** 1, 2 & 3 cl. Salzburg-Bale and *v.v.* **X** Innsbruck-Lindau and *v.v.*, June 15–Sept 10 only. **Y** July 3–Sept. 9. **Z** 1 & 2 cl. Sleep. Car Vienna-Zurich, 1 & 2 cl. Cars Bucharest-Budapest–Vienna–Paris, 1, 2 & 3 cl. Cars Vienna-Paris; Rest. Car Innsbruck-Buchs & *v.v.*

Munich (Vienna), Innsbruck, Verona.

German & Italian State Rlys.

Mls.		3 cl.	1 2 3 DY	2 3	1 2 3 ExD	1 2 3 ExD	1 2 3 ExD	2 3	2 3	1 2 3 DZ	1 2 3 ExD	2 3	1 2 3 ExD
0	**Munich** (Hpt.) dep.		6 45	6 55	7 55	8 15	1020	1232	1350	14 0	1850	2055	2355
40	Rosenheim........	5 45	7 37	8 8		..	1117	14 5	15 0	1452	..	2154	0 47
62	Kufstein *c* .. arr.	6 28	8 5	8 53	9 13	9 29	1149	1449	1538	1523	20 8	2233	1 15
	dep.	7 4	8 8	8 56	9 16	9 32	1157	15 2	1541	1526	2011	2244	1 18
	Vienna .... ,,	2135	..	2135	..	..	..	..	8 5	..	8 5	1428	..
71	Wörgl (*p.* 197)	7 30	8 25	9 40	..	9 52	1219	1523	1613	1545	2027	23 7	1 34
107	**Innsbruck**.. arr.	8 48	9 20	11 8	1019	1053	1330	1638	1730	1647	2119	24 0	2 30
	dep.	9 10	9 36	1130	1028	11 3	1410	1840	1740	17 5	2131	..	2 40
132	Brennero *c* .. arr.	10 5	1025	1223	1116	1150	15 6	1938	1836	1753	2222	..	3 27
	dep.	..	1055	1245	1143	1220	1550	..	1910	1823	2252	..	4 5
158	Fortezza ...... arr.	..	1141	1333	1230	13 6	1643	..	2016	1916	2345	..	4 54
188	Bolzano ...... ,,	..	1252	1437	1329	14 6	1749	..	2141	2023	0 50	..	5 55
285	**Verona** (P.N.) arr. (*p.* 307).		..	18 7	15*x*32	1655	2035	..	..	..	3 15		8 5

x 1 & 2 cl. Rapido train with supplementary charge.

Mls.		1 2 3 ExD	2 3	1 2 3 ExD	2 3	3 cl.	1 2 3 DZ	1 2 3 ExD	1 2 3 ExD	2 3	1 2 3 DY	1 2 3 ExD	2 3
0	**Verona** (P.N.) (*p.* 307) dep.	22 3	..	2 55	17 2		5 16	..	9 0	..	1250	15*x*11	1250
97	Bolzano .. ,,	0 38	..	5 22	2034	7 30	9 12	1135	1213	..	1640	1721	1755
122	Fortezza .. ,,	1 39	..	6 30	22 8	9 4	1023	1253	1325		1754	1824	19 3
152	Brennero *c* a.	2 29		7 23	2311	1021	1120	1350	1422	..	1850	1920	2031
	d.	3 2	..	8 3	6 22	1048	1145	1432	15 0	16 6	1915	1959	2050
178	**Innsbruck** a.	3 48		8 57	7 15	1145	1236	1526	1551	17 0	20 1	2035	2146
	d.	3 58	5 10	9 12	7 40	1218	1246	1540	16 7	1720	2016	2045	2210
214	Wörgl .... arr.	..	6 17	10 6	9 2	1327	1345	1643	17 9	1838	21 7	2132	2322
..	**Vienna** ,,	..	14 5	2133	2133	2218	..	..	..	..	..	..	8 0
223	Kufstein *c* a.	5 0	6 38	1022	9 27	1346	14 5	17 4	1729	19 0	2122	2147	2353
	d.	5 3	6 51	1024	9 45	16 0	14 8	1710	1733	1957	2125	2149	..
245	Rosenheim ar	5 29	7 35		1027	1644	1439	1740	18 2	2038	..	..	..
85	**Munich** .. ,,	6 30	8 42	1144	124[illegible]	1816	1535	1839	19 2	22 2	2245	2310	..

Y From June 15.
Z Innsbruck-Brennero and *v.v.* June 25-Sept. 29 only.

Innsbruck—Igls.

a July 8–Sept. 2.

All 3 cl. Weekdays only.

				a			*a*				*a*
Innsbruck d.	8 15	9 45	1115	1215	1315	1415	1448	1545	1715	1845	2015
Igls ......ar.	8 51	1021	1151	1251	1351	1451	1524	1621	1751	1921	2051

					a						
Igls......dp.	7 15	9 0	1030	12 4	13 4	15 0	1630	18 0	1925	..	..
Innsbuck a.	7 54	9 39	11 9	1243	1343	1539	17 9	1839	20 4	..	..

2nd and 3rd cl. only.]

Salzburg, St. Wolfgang, Ischl (40 miles).

[Salzkammergut Rly.

	a			*a*		*a*						*a*		*a*		*a*	
..	6 20	8 0	1015	1210	1420	1630	1750	20 5	dep. **Salzburg** .. arr.	7 22	9 35	1149	1430	1640	19 0	1957	21 6
..	7 34	9 18	1132	1325	1537	1747	19 6	2118	St. Lorenz* ..	6 18	8 35	1050	1329	1539	1750	1857	20 4
6 50	8 1	9 46	12 0	1352	16 4	1815	1934	2143	St. Gilgen ..	5 50	8 3	1020	1258	15 6	1719	1817	1933
7 7	8 19	10 5	1218	1410	1622	1833	1952	..	St. Wolfgang†	..	7 45	10 2	1240	1448	17 1	1758	1914
7 45	8 57	1046	1256	1448	17 0	1912	2030	..	arr. Ischl ...... dep.	..	7 4	9 20	12 0	14 7	1620	1720	1830

a June 26–Sept. 17. * St. Lorenz to Mondsee, local trains 10 minutes journey. † St. Wolfgang to Schafbergspitze—connecting services. ‡ Weekdays only.

Fortezza, Lienz, Villach, Vienna.

[Ital. & Ger. Rlys.

ExD 2 3	2 3	2 3	fast 2 3	2 3	ExD 1 2 3 C	2 3	2 3	ExD 1 2 3 DS	C June 25- Sept. 18.	Exp 1 2 3 DS	2 3	2 3	2 3	Exp 1 2 3 C	2 3	2 3	2 3	Exp 1 2 3
..	..	..	..		5 45	5 45	1125	1544	dep. Merano .. arr.	14 3	1939	..	..	2359	..	10 9	..	..
..	..	..	..	2 50	2 50	..	1130	1410	,, Innsbruck ,,	1550	2030	..	..	3 42	..	1145	..	..
..	..	..	..	6 53	8 18	9 38	1338	1830	,, **Fortezza** .. arr.	1128	16 3	..	..	2138	..	7 29	..	..
..	..	..	..	8 49	10 7	1115	1556	2029	a. Dobbiaco d.	9 48	1436	..	..	2012	..	5 51	..	..
..	..	..	..	8 50	10 9	1116	1538	2031	d. (Toblach) a.	9 46	1435	..	..	2011	..	5 50	..	..
..	..	..	..	8 56	1015	1122	1644	2037	a. S. Candido d.	9 40	1430	..	..	20 5	..	5 45	..	..
..	..	6 18	..	9 20	1045	1345	1730	21 3	d. Innichen *c* a.	9 10	1314	..	17 4	1947	2144		..	..
..	..	7 39		1045	1145	1510	1859	2217	a. Lienz.... d.	7 50	1148	..	1540	1828	2010	fast	..	..
..	5 4	7 48	10 0	1054	12 2	16 2	1912	2230	d. Lienz.... a.	7r42	9 58	1245	1532	1820	1945	21 0	2257	..
..	6 29	9 14	11 9	1219	1310	1734	2049	2337	a. Spittal (*p.* 199) .. d.	6 30	8 27	1110	14 2	1711	1816	1950	2126	..
dep.	7 30	10 6	1151	1312	1347	1830	2152	0 11	a. Villach .... d.	5r54	7 27	1020	1310	1635	1718	1912	2032	..
6 23	7 45	1016	12 0	1723	1442	2035	22 4	0 35	d. Villach .... a.	5 24	7 8	9 56	1157	1613	1645	1857	2017	225[illegible]
6 39	8 13	1041	1217	1739	15 1	2058	2232	0 51	arr. Velden .... dep.	5 6	6 40	9 29	1411	1555	1619	1839	1953	22[illegible]
7 3	8 45	1115	1244	18 6	1526	2130	23 5	1 16	,, Klagenfurt ,,	4 40	6 0	8 50	1116	1527	1536	1811	1915	22[illegible]
7 12	9 26	..	1253	1810	1530	2140	..	1 22	dp. Klagenfurt .. a.	4 31		8 36	1110	1522	1510	18 3	..	22
1023	1333	..	1610	2059	1833	1 15	..	4 29	arr. Leoben .... dep.	1 33	..	4 20	8 34	1223	11 5	1457	..	18[illegible]
14 2	1728	..	1945	5 54	21*53	5 54	..	8 0	a. VIENNA (S.) *p.* 199 ,,	22 0	..	2250		8*55	6 5	1112	..	151[illegible]
..	8 54	1312	1312	2015	1536	..	..	S	dep. Klagenfurt .. arr.	S	..	..	9 19	15 2	15 2	1714	1714	..
..	9 46	14 1	14 1	21 4	1624	..	..	..	arr. Bleiburg *c* dep.		..	..	8 29	1414	1414	1626	1626	..

D 1, 2 & 3 cl. car Vienna-Merano and *v.v.* **S** 1 & 2 cl. Sleeping cars Vienna to Merano and *v.v.* From Vienna Tue., Thur. and Sat., and Merano Wed., Fri. and Sun. * Vienna (East)

Vienna, Klagenfurt Villach, Tarvis (Venice).

German State and Italian State Rlys.

123 ExD	23 fast	23 fast	123 ExD	12 luxe	123 ExD	23	Mls.	r Rest. Car.	12 luxe	123 ExD	23 fast	123 ExD	23	23	123 ExD
8 55	..		A	1950	S	..	0	dep. Vienna (E) arr.	9 50	A	..	2152	1945	..	S
r	1112	1340	1510	V	22 0	2250	0	dep. **Vienna**(S)(p200)a.	V	14 2	1728	..	..	5 54	8 0
11 6	1330	1552	1726	2140	0 9	1 53	70	dep. Semmering arr.	7 58	12 9	1532	20 4	1740	3 25	6 3
12 1	1423	1656	825		1 2	3 23	107	arr } Bruck .. { dep.	6 54	1055	1420	1857	1634	1 48	4 54
12 4	1435	1730	1840	2236	1 12	3 55		dep. } Bruck .. { arr.	6 50	1042	14 3	1854	1628	1 35	4 49
1221	1452	1751	1856	2252	1 29	4 15	117	arr. Leoben dep.	6 34	1026	1342	1838	1613	1 18	4 33
1223	1457	1756	1859	2253	1 33	4 20	125	dep. Leoben .. ...arr.	6 32	1023	1333	1833	1610	1 15	4 29
15 1	1734	2211	2138	V	4 8	7 51	204	a. } St. Veit a.d. { d.	V	7 33	10 1	1552	1320	2215	1 45
15 4	1745	2218	2142		4 13	8 2		d. } Glandorf { a.		7 30	9 58	1549	1312	22 5	1 41
1522	18 3	2248	22 1	1 26	4 31	8 36	216	arr Klagenfurt dep	3 58	7 12	9 26	1530	1253	2140	1 22
1527	1811	2317	22 6	1 31	4 40	8 50		dep Klagenfurt .. arr.	3 52	7 3	8 45	1526	1244	2130	1 16
1555	1839	2348	2232	..	5 6	9 29	230	arr. Velden .... dep.	..	6 39	8 13	15 1	1217	2058	0 51
1613	1857	0 10	2250	2 6	5 24	9 56	236	arr. Villach ..dep.	3 20	6 23	7 45	1442	12 0	2035	0 35
1728	1954	..	0 18	2 34	6 28	11 4	279	dep. Arnoldstein arr.	2 53	5 12	6 27	1342	9 4	1930	2337
1750	2015	..	0 40	2 55	6 50	1125	286	arr. { Tarvisio } dep.	2 34	5 0	6 13	1330	8 50	1915	2325
1815	5 50	..	1 10	3 10	7 10	1225		dep. { Tarvisio } arr.	2 15	4 35	..	13 9	8 1	9 55	2250
20 0	8 2	..	2 44	4 37	8 56	1455	344	arr. Udine .. ...dep.	0 39	2 45	..	1117	4 40	7 23	2059
2138	1058	..	..	7 49	1058	1755	396	arr. Trieste ... dep.	21 0	1950	..	9 47	..	..	19 0
2227	12 0	..	5 12	6 24	11 1	1733	430	arr. Venice (p.308)dp.	2240	0 8		8r47	..	..	18r40

A Sleep. Car 1 & 2 cl Vienna-Rimini and *v.v.*

S Sleeping cars Vienna-Venice-Rome, daily, Vienna-Merano, Tues., Thur., Sats. only and *v.v.*

V Vienna-Cannes Express for days of running, see p. 82. Winter only.

† Not Sundays.

Munich (Vienna), Badgastein, Trieste, Zagreb.

Ger. State, Italian & Yugo.-Slav. Rlys.

123D	123D	123D	123D	123D	123D	123D	123D	23	R—Rest Car.	123D	23	123D	23	123D	123D	123D	123D	23
A		A													A			
..	7 48	7 48	9 45	..	1350	..	2220	..	dep. MUNICH ..arr.	6 55	..	1456	1920	1920	..	2211	..	..
..	..	2325	R	8 5	1015	1440	1712	2050	dep. VIENNA(W) arr.	1140	1442	1824	..	2218	2218	..	..	7 31
8 30	1020	1138	1215	1250	1625	1945	1 10	7 0	dep. Salzburg .. arr.	4 38	9 50	1155	1638	1648	1715	1938	21 0	2230
9 28	1120	1230	1322	1336	1715	2032	2 8	8 3	dep. Bischofshofen a	3 34	8 48	11 1	1514	1548	1619	1844	20 2	21 6
9 45	1125	1245	1339	1350	1730	2047	2 25	8 22	arr. SchwarzSt.Veitd	3 20	8 30	1045	1451	1532	16 5	1830	1945	2048
1033	12 8	1333	1435		1816	2146	3 12	9 30	arr. Badgastein dep.	2 30	7 46	10 5	1359	1446	1521	1740	19 5	1944
1048	1220	1346	1450	..	1839	22 4	3 25	9 46	arr. Bockstein.. dep.	2 19	7 32	9 49	1344	1436	1512	1723	1854	1926
1144	1317	1453	1544	..	1935	23 3	4 20	1047	arr. Spittal ....dep.	1 23	6 34	8 45	1236	1338	1417	1622	1753	1815
1228	14 2	1540	1627	..	2018	0 11	5 5	1143	arr. Villach ....dep.	0 40	5 54	7 55	1142	1255	1333	1538	1710	1718
..	3cl		R X				S	3 cl		S		3 cl	3 cl	R X		23		
..	..	..	8 55	..	..	..	22 0		dep. Vienna(*abv.*)ar.	8 0	..	..	1945	2152	..	..	..	..
..	1326	..	1527	..	..	..	4 40	1326	dep. Klagenfurt arr.	1 16	..	..	1244	1526	..	..	..	..
..	1448	..	1642	..	..	..	5 38	1215	dep. Villach ....arr.	0 23	..	7 22	1130	1240	..	1515	..	..
..	1529	..	1713	..	..	..	6 9	1259	arr. Rosenbach dep.	2357	..	6 42	1050	1210	..	1433	..	..
..	1540	..	1739	..	..	..	6 29	1315	dep. Rosenbach arr.	2336	..	..	1036	1152	..	1421	..	..
..	1556	..	1755	..	..	..	6 45	1331	arr. Assling ....dep.	2320	..	..	1020	1136	..	14 5	..	..
..	..	..	2214	..	..	..	10 8	..	ar. TRIESTE ....dep.	19 0	..	..	..	7 10	..	..	..	..
..	..	..	1825	..	..	..	7 45	..	dep. Jesenice p332A a	2215	..	..	..	1110	..	..	..	..
..	..	..	1842	..	..	..	8 2	..	arr. Lesce Bled dep.	2155	..	..	..	1051	..	..	..	..
..	..	..	2240	..	..	..	12 0	..	arr. Zagreb ....dep.	1740	..	..	..	6 50	..	..	..	..
..	..	..	6 20	..	..	..	2015	..	arr. Belgrade dep.	9 2	..	..	..	2312	..	..	..	..

A June 15—Sept. 15. **S** 1 and 2 cl. Sleep Car Munich to Trieste, Sun., Tue., Thur. and Fri.; Mon., Wed. and Sat. to Zagreb; from Trieste Mon, Wed., Fri., and Sat.; from Zagreb Tue., Thur. and Sun.

X 1 and 2 cl. Sleep. Car Assling to Belgrade and *v.v.*

Munich, Salzburg, Bruck, Graz.

German Rlys.

23	23	123	23	123	3cl.	23	23		23	3cl.	23	23	123	23	23	23	23
		E		B	C		B			C	B		E			B	
..	..	6 55	..	9 45	..	1048	2220	dep. Munich .....arr.	1816	..	1920	..	22 2	..	..	6 55	..
..	..	9 20	..	1156	..	14 5	0 20	arr. Salzburg ...dep.	15 0	..	17 5		20 0	..	..	4 52	..
	7 0	9 40	..	1215	1615	1530	1 10	dep. Salzburg .. arr	1452	1225	1648	1928	1950	0 50	..	4 38	1242
..	8 0	1035	..	1315	1658	1650	2 3	arr. Bischofshofen dep.	1339	1137	1555	1815	19 5	2350		3 44	1122
4 53	8 5	1050	..	1353	17 0	1720	2 22	dep. Bischofshofen arr.	1330	1134	1457	1755	1857	2340	2340	2 55	1049
7 50	1035	1232		16 0	1846	2030	4 15	arr. Seltzthal ....dep.	1053	9 42	1255	1455	1713	2120	2120	1 10	8 5
8 16	1113	1242	1418	1617	1858	2116	4 28	dep. Seltzthal .. arr.	1030	9 37	122	1448	17 2	2045	2056	0 55	7 54
10 2	1253	1352	1552	1737	20 1	23 3	5 45	arr. St. Michael ..dep.	8 51	8 28	1 9	1310	1553	1850	1941	2337	6 20
1020	1315	14 2	16 9	1742	20 8	2318	5 50	dep. St. Michael ..arr.	8 39	8 26	11 6	1250	1549	1837	1932	2332	6 15
1033	1333	1417	1627	1756	2021	2341	6 3	arr. Leoben ....arr.	8 0	8 12	1049	1210	1532	18 6	1910	2312	5 48
1051	14 3	1438	1655	1818	2037	0 4	6 22	arr. Bruck a/M. dep.	7 38	7 57	1032	1148	1515	1744	1853	2255	5 27
1151	1531	1538	1758	1925	2132	1 11	7 35	arr. Graz .....dep.	6 20	7 3	9 30	1025	1415	1540	1758	2150	4 8

B 2 & 3 cl. Munich—Graz, and *v.v.*

C 3 cl. Salzburg-Graz and *v.v.* **E** 1, 2 & 3 cl. Munich-Graz and *v.v.*

The times on the LEFT are to be read DOWNWARDS, those on the RIGHT UPWARDS.

Vienna, Maribor (Belgrade), Fiume, Trieste.

German, Yugoslav. and Italian State Rlys.

1 2 3	2 3	2 3	2 3	1 2 3	1 2 3	2 3	Mls.	Vienna-Bruck, see also p. 199.	2 3	1 2 3	2 3	2 3	1 2 3	2 3	2 3	1 2 3
Ex O	fast			fast	DS					fast			ExD		fast	DS
8 0	1112	9 30	1340	1510	2120	2250	0	dep. **Vienna** (Süd) ar.	15 0	1728	1816	2210	2135	5 54	14 2	8 50
1010	1330	1228	1552	1726	2326	1 53	80	Semmering	1216	1532	1542	1914	1948	3 25	12 9	7 4
1113	1448	1420	17 3	1832	0 25	4 0	123	dep. Bruck ...... arr.	10 6	1410	1320	1646	1838	0 56	1025	5 52
1215	1538	16 5	20 0	1925	1 20	6 40	155	dep. **Graz** ......dep.	8 58	1310	12 5	1532	1748	2340	9 30	5 3
1254	..	17 5	21 2	..	1 59	7 47	186	arr. Spielfeld *c* ..	7 32	1145	1033	1339	1653	2138	..	4 7
1255	..	1714	2110	2 3	2 0	7 56		dep. Spielfeld *c* ..arr.	7 26		1027	1329	1652	2126	..	4 6
1316	..	1740	2137	..	2 21	8 22	195	arr. Maribor .. dep.	7 0	..	10 0	13 0	1632	21 0	..	3 46
1343		1758	2340	2055	2 48	9 16		dep. (Marburg) arr.	..	..	..	1144	16 8	1720	..	3 20
1412	..	1831	..	2129	3 20	9 47	206	dep. Pragersko ..dep.	..	..	..	1116	1551	1652	..	3 3
1531	..	2012	..	23 5	4 37	1131	265	arr. Zidani Most dep.	..		..	9 33	1426	15 6	..	1 37
1549	..	2025	..	2319	6 2	1154		dep. Zidani Most arr.	..	1 2 3	..	8 12	14 3	1440	..	2358
1710	..	22 5	..	0 40	7 30	1340	311	arr. Zagreb dep.	..	Exp	..	6 50	1240	1250	..	2225
1835	1 2	2310		1 10	8 0	1835		dep. Zagreb arr.	..	.	..	6 25	1150	..	1 2	2150
6 8	luxe	6 20		8 40	1517	6 8	583	arr. Belgrade....dep.	..		..	2312	2333	..	luxe	1423
1538	7 13	1 2 3	2 3	0 10	4 44	1153		dep. Zidani Most arr.	..	21 4	..	9 15	1414	1455	2255	1 24
1642	8 17			1 15	5 48	1322	279	arr. Ljubljana dep.	..	20 0	..	7 52	1311	1340	2152	0 21
1652	8 27	10 0		1 33	5 54	1345	..	dep. (Laibach) arr.	..	19 5	..	..	13 3	1326	2142	0 15
1756	9 31	1120		2 38	6 58	15 4	302	arr. Rakek *c* dep.	..	1756	..	..	12 8	1217	2047	2320
1842	1025	1155	1410	3 45	7 40	1715		dep. Postumia *c* arr.	..	17 0	..	..	1113	9 26	1955	222[illegible]
1856	1036	1211	1425	3 59	7 54	1732	32[illegible]	arr. St. Pietro ..dep.	..	1643	..	..	1059	9 10	..	2215
2026	12 2	1524	1759	7 14	9 31	2026	36[illegible]	ar. **Fiume** (*p.* 305) dp.	..	1355	..	.	7 50	7 50	..	18 2
1858	1039	1212	1510	4 0	7 56	1738		dep. St. Pietro .. arr.	..	1638	..	..	1057	9 3	..	2714
R	..	13 8	1611	4 57	..	1842	359	arr. Aurisina ..dep.	..	1538	..	..	9 58	..	..	2121
2010	1145	1329	1635	5 20	9 4	1853	368	arr. **Trieste** (*p.* 305) d.	..	1520	..	..	9 37	8 0	1840	21 3

R Rest. car Vienna-Trieste & *v.v.* ¶ 1 & 2 cl. Sleeping Car, Vienna-Zagreb-Susak & *v.v.*

S Sleeping car 1 & 2 cl. Vienna-Trieste & Vienna-Zagreb and *v.v.* daily. § 2 & 3 cl. only.

Vienna, Hegyeshalom, Budapest (Belgrade).

German, and Hung Rlys.

Mls			2 3	2 3	1 2 3	1 2 3	2 3	1 2 3	2 3	1 2	1 2	1 2 3	2cl.	2 3	1 2 3
					Exp	Exp		Exp		luxe	luxe	Exp	Rap		Exp
	Vienna (West)	dep.	..	..	7 20	9 15	..	15 0	..	1544	1728	..	1935	..	2245
0	**Vienna** (East)	,,	6 25	7 38	8 15	10 0	1232	1552	16 0	..	..	1820	20 0	2035	2250
25	Bruckneudorf ..	,,	7 45	8 56	8 50	1035	1345	1627	1710	O	X	1855	Z	2145	0 57
30	Parndorf	,,	8 6	9 8	r	r	14 6	..	1720	..	.	..		2154	1 6
45	Strass-Somerein *c*	a	8 35	9 46	9 18	11 3	1435	1655	1749	1725	1847	1925	↓	2223	1 35
	Nickelsdorf......	d	8 57	10 5	9 43	1128	16 0	1719	1836	1741	19 0	1948		6 11	2 7
73	Györ (Raab)	dep.	9 59	11 8	1025	12 5	17 4	1751	1950	1814	1932	2028		7 45	3 30
97	Komarom	,,	1058	..	1053	1233	1750	1819	..	..	..	2056	▼	8 30	4 16
167	**Budapest** .... K.p.u. (East)	arr.	1327	..	1220	14 0	2035	1945	..	20†3	2120	2235	2258	1045	6 20
					2 3							¶ S			2cl.
		dep.		..	1445	1434	..	..	..	20†35		2348	..	..	7 50
234	Kis-Körös	,,	..	..	1818	1624	..	..	..	To Bucharest.	To Bucharest.	2 1	..	..	9 2
269	Kelebia *c*	arr.	..	..	1921	1716	..	..	..			2 56	..	..	9 44
380	**Belgrade** (*p.*332)	arr.	..	..	..	2142	..	..	..			7 8	..	..	1753

		2 3	2 3	2cl.	1 2 3	1 2	Exp	1 2	2 3	1 2 3	1 2 3	2 3	1 2 3	2 3
				Rap	Exp	luxe	1 2 3	luxe		Exp	Exp		Exp	
						From Bucharest.		From Bucharest.						
Belgrade (*p.*332)	dep.	..	..	Z	2250	..	2250	..			8 0	..		1134
Kelebia *c*	,,	..	..	..	3 4	..	3 4	..	..	..	1216	7 5	..	1717
Kiskörös	,,	..	..	..	4 2	..	4 2	..	5 53	..	1313	8 36	..	1850
Budapest ...... K.p.u. (East)	arr.	..	..	..	6 2	6 26	6 2	9†35	8 50	..	1456	11 8	..	2115
							¶ S							
	dep.	..	..	7 0	7 5	8 15	9 25	10†10	1016	13 0	16 0	1320	2335	
Komarom	,,	..	..		8 43	X	1051	O	1242	1431	1727	1547	1 24	
Gyor	,,	3 1	5 19		9 15	10 3	1119		1348	15 3	1759	1650	2 23	
Nickelsdorf *c*	ar.	4 19	6 50		9 49	1035	1150	1233	1443	1537	1834	1745	3 17	
Strass-Somerein..	dp	5 26	7 26		1020	1046	1211	1249	1533	1550	1854	1931	4 2	
Parndorf	..dep	6 6	8 14		1044	..	..	..	16 2	..	..	20 9	4 31	
Bruckneudorf	,,	6 22	8 33	▼	1053	..	1239	..	1629	1624	1922	2027	4 50	
Vienna (East)	arr	7 25	9 35	9 57	1129	..	1315	..	1733	17 0	1958	2134	5 55	
Vienna (West)	arr.	..		1027	..	12 5	14 0	1429	..	1748	21 0		7 12	

O Orient Exp. from Vienna Wed., Fri. and Sun.; returning from Budapest Tues., Thur. and Sat.
R—Rest. Car. X Arlberg Exp. Tues., Thur. and Sat. from Vienna, Mon., Wed. and Fri. from Budapest.
S Sleep. Car Budapest-Istanbul & *v.v.* daily Z One class limited Motor Train, Buffet Car. *Special* tickets required. ¶ Thro' 1 & 2 cl. cars Vienna, Praha & Warsaw to Belgrade & *v.v.* † West Station.

Budapest—Maribor—Trieste—Rome (Vintimille)—Cannes.

[Hung. Yugoslav and Italian Rlys.

1 2 3	1 2 3	2 3	1 2 3	2 3		1 2 3	2 3	2 3	1 2 3	2 3
Exp	Ex A		S			¶ S			Ex B	
7 20	8 10	1455	2015	2225	dep. Budapest (Sud) ...... arr.	9 45	16 0	2046	2145	6 15
9 20	..	1737	2219	1 52	dep. Siofok (Balaton) ... dep.	7 41	1243	1732		2 42
1115	1125	2020	0 4	4 42	arr Nagy-Kanizsa ... dep.	5 44	9 44	1430	1830	2345
2254	1956	..	..	1225	arr Vienna (Sud) dep.	..	..	7 14	..	1640
1354	1133	2023	0 24	4 57	dep. Nagy-Kanizsa ..... arr.	5 30	9 35	..	1820	2235
14 7	1144	2036	0 36	5 10	arr. } c Murakeresztur .. { dep	5 17	9 24	..	18 8	2217
1433	1149		0 48	5 20	dep. } c Murakeresztur .. { arr	5 12	..	..	18 3	..
1440	1156	..	0 55	5 27	arr. } Kotoriba c .... { dep	5 5	..	..	1756	..
..	1213	..	1 17	..	dep. } Kotoriba c .... { arr	4 47		..	1744	..
..	1756	..	6 58	..	arr } Rakek } p. 332A { dep	2320	..	..	12 8	..
..	18 6	..	7 8	..	dep. } Rakek } p. 332A { arr.	23 0	..	..	1148	..
	1842	..	7 40	..	dep. Postumia } p. 332A .. arr.	2228		..	1113	..
..	2026	..	9 31	..	arr. Fiume .... dep.	2055		..	9 33	..
..	2010	..	9 4	..	arr. Trieste p. 307 .... dep.	21 3	..	..	9 37	..
..	4 2	..	1549	..	arr. Florence .... dep.	1355	..	..	3 40	..
..	8 25	..	2020	..	arr Rome p. 307 ...... dep.	9 30	..	..	2325	..
..	0 12	..	1147	..	arr. Venice (S. L.) p. 305 dep.	18 2		..	7 27	
..	6 33	..	16 8	.	arr. Milan p. 305 .... dep.	1330	.	..	0 16	..
..	9 45	..	1947	..	arr. Genoa p. 302 .. .... dep.	9 0	..	..	1946	..
..	1335	..	2 40	..	arr. Vintimille p. 299 .... dep.	5 25	..	..	1545	..
..	1559	..	7 20	..	arr. Nice .... dep.	2340	..	..	14 5	..
..	1647	..	8 12		arr. Cannes .... dep.	2243	..	..	1240	..

A 1, 2 & 3 cl. carriages Budapest to Rome and to Vintimille; 1 & 2 cl. Sleep. Car Budapest-Nice Mon Wed. & Fri. Winter only. Rest. Car Budapest-Pragersko.

B 1, 2 & 3 cl. carriages Vintimille and Rome to Budapest; 1 & 2 cl. Sle-p. Car Nice-Bupadest Mo., We. & Fri. Winter only. Rest. Car Pragersko-Budapest. ¶ Rest. Car Nagy-Kanizsa to Budapest † 1 and 2 class.

S 1st & 2nd cl. Sleep Car, Budapest-Venice-Milan and v.v. daily; also 1st & 2nd cl. cars Budapest, Trieste, Venice, Florence, Rome and v.v.

Budapest, Fiume (Susak).

Hun. & Yugo Slv. Rly.

1 2 3	1 2 3	2 3	1 2 3	1 2 3	2 3		2 3	1 2 3	1 2 3	2 3	1 2 3	2 3	1 2 3
	r		Exp	Exp	s	K.p.u. (East Sta.)	s	Exp	Exp		Exp		r
	9 0	1340	1455	19 0	23 0	dep. **Budapest**..arr.	6 50	9 49	9 49	14 8	1450	2021	2040
..	1155	1728	1740	2149	3 7	arr. Ujdombovár	2 24	6 58	6 58	9 55	12 7	1535	1741
..	1313	1912	1912	23 0	5 27	arr. Pécs....dep.	0 7	5 43	5 42	7 58	1026	1335	1618
..	1551	23 0	23 0	..	9 59	arr. Osijek ..dep.	2010	..	..	4 10	..	..	13 8
..	1210	1755	1750	2158	3 50	dep. Ujdombovár ..	1 35	..	6 47	9 28	1153	1520	1718
..	14 5	2034	1928	2347	7 10	arr. Gyékényes dep.	2227	..	5 0	5 54	1020	1250	1522
8 10	↓	..	↓	..	2225	dep. Budapest (s) arr.	↑		↑	..	..	..	2115
1354	↓	..	↓	.	4 57	dp. Nagykanizsa ar.	↑	..	↑	..	..	..	1542
1434	▼	..	▼	..	5 42	arr. Gyékényes dep.	↑		↑	..	..		15 6
1453	1453	..	1955	0†19	7 24	dep. Gyékényes arr.	2213	..	1†32	..	9 54	..	1452
17 0	17 0	..	2210	2†20	1050	arr. Zágreb dp.	19 0	..	2†30		7 46	..	1245
2255	2255	..	7 37	8 5	1952	arr. **Fiume** ..dep.	8 22	..	1957	..	2047		5 21
2250	2250	..	7 30	8 0	1945	arr. **Susak**	8 32	..	20†6	..	2057		6 30

s 2 & 3 cl. Sleep. Car Budapest-Pécs-Osijek-Vinkovci and v.v.
r Rest. Car, Budapest–Susak.
† To Sept. 15th.

Budapest-Graz.

[Hung. and German Rlys.

2 3	1 2 3	2 3	2 3	2 3		2 3	2 3	2 3	2 3	1 2 3
	Exp									Exp
..	7 5	13 0	16 0	2335	dep. Budapest (East) arr.	6 20	1220	1718	1945	2235
6 12	9 25	1513	18 6	2 20	dep. Győr .... dep.	3 20	1025	1355	1751	2028
8 1	1038	17 0	1946	4 10	arr. } Celldomolk { dep.	0 41	8 30	1152	1612	19 3
8 31	1043	17 5	1952	4 30	dep. } Celldomolk { arr.	0 21	8 25	1148	16 7	1859
9 29	1131	1846	2052	5 34	arr. Szombathely ..dep.	2316	7 16	1050	1516	1815
1054	1232	1948		7 22	arr. Szentgotthard..dep.	2040	6 0	9 26	..	17 7
1336	1438	2256		1018	arr Graz ...... dep	1746	..	6 15	..	15 0

S 2 & 3 cl. Sleeping Car Budapest-Szentgotthard, returning from Graz.

Budapest-Lwow.

[Hung. & Polish Rlys.

1 2 3	1 2 3 ¶	1 2 3	2 3		2 3	2 3	1 2 3 ¶	1 2 3
7 30	1045	1410	0 45	dep. Budapest (East) .... arr.	5 0	1556	1930	23 0
1029	1326	1742	7 36	„ Miskolt .... „	2259	1310	1649	1953
1149	1435	19 2	9 34	arr. } Satoraljaujhely { dep.	2023	1120	1536	1836
1159	1438	..	9 56	dep. } Satoraljaujhely { arr.	1953	11 6	1535	1823
1240	1531	..	11 2	„ Csap .... dep.	1856	1010	1456	1745
1331	1614	..	12 9	arr. Munkacs .... „	1733	8 49	14 0	1646
..	19 0	..	..	„ Lawoczne c ...... dep.	..	..	1135	..
..	1920	..	..	dep. } Stryj .... { arr.	..	..	1113	..
..	2040	..	..	arr. } Stryj .... { dep.	..	..	9 45	..
..	2217 ¶		..	arr. Lwow (p. 226)..... dep.	..	..	8¶20	..

¶ Through 1, 2 and 3 class Cars and Rest. Car Budapest to Lwow and v.v.

Budapest—Galanta—Praha—Berlin.
Hung. and German Rlys.

123 Exp	123 Exp		123 Exp	123 Exp
7 5	20 0	dep. Budapest (West) ...... arr.	2331	10 0
9 31	2234	,, Galanta .... dep.	2112	7 27
9 51	2254	arr. } Szenc c .... { dep.	2047	7 5
1011	2318	dep. } Szenc c { arr.	2028	6 44
1019	2326	arr. } Ceklis c .... { dep.	2020	6 36
1039	2351	dep. } Ceklis c { arr.	20 5	6 15
1057	0 9	arr. Bratislava .... dep.	1950	6 0
13 2	2 32	,, Brno .... ,,	1752	3 33
1636	6 45	,, Praha (Mas.) .... ,,	1410	2311
A	S		A	S
1648	8 30	dep. Praha (Mas.) .. .... arr.	1358	21 0
2018	1236	arr. Dresden .... dep.	1037	1632
2321	15 3	arr. Berlin (Anh.) (p.195) dep.	7 25	1334

S 1 and 2 cl. Sleeping Car Budapest-Praha and *v.v.*

A 1 and 2 cl. Sleeping Car Berlin–Athens and *v.v.*, from Berlin, Weds., Fris. and Suns.; from Athens, Tues., Thurs. and Suns.

Praha-Kassa-Bucharest.
German, Hung. & Roumanian Rlys.

		dep. Praha(W) (p. 207A) arr.		
		,, Prerov .... ,,		
		,, Zilina .... dep.		
		arr. Poprad-velka .... arr.		
		arr. } Kassa .... { dep.		
		dep. } Kassa { arr.		
		arr. } Csap.......... { dep.		
		dep. } Csap { arr.		
		arr. } Halmeu H.E.C { dp		
		dep. } Halmeu H.E.O { ar.		
		arr. } Orade .... { dep.		
		dep. } Orade { arr.		
		arr. } Teius .... { dep.		
		dep. } Teius { arr.		
		dep. Brasso .... dep.		
		arr. Bucharest (p. 231) dep.		
		arr. Constanza .... dep.		

S 1, 2 & 3 cl Sleep. Car, Praha–Bucharest and *v v.*

Budapest—Galanta—Ceklis (Praha)
(Hung. Rlys.)

123 Exp	23	23	123 Exp		23	123 Exp	23	123 Exp	23
7 5	1250	1520	20 0	dep. Budapest (West) ...... arr.	1057	10 0	2122	2331	5 37
..	1419	1639	..	,, Sob .... ,,	8 46	..	1954	..	3 46
..	1450	17 5	21 9	,, Parkanynana .... ,,	8 19	8 49	1929	..	3 16
8 52	16 2	18 4	2155	,, Ersekuyvar .... ,,	7 17	8 11	1840	2147	2 4
9 27	17 0	19 2	2231	arr. } Galanta .... { dep.	6 10	7 27	1730	2112	1 4
9 31	..	19 7	2234	dep. } Galanta { arr.	6 0	7 24	1723	21 6	0 59
9 51	..	1939	2254	arr. Szenc .... dep	5 29	7 5	1650	2047	0 28
1011	..	20 4	2318	dep. Szenc c .... arr.	5 0	6 44	1615	2028	0 8
1019	..	2018	2326	arr. Ceklis c (p. 207) .... dep.	4 48	6 36	16 3	2020	2356
1636	..	..	6 45	arr. Praha (p. 207) .... dep.	..	2311	..	1410	..

Budapest—Salgotarjan—Losonc.
Hung. and German Rlys.

23 fast	123 Exp	23	123 Exp		23	123 Exp	23	123
6 55	6 55	1225	1525	dep. Budapest (East) .... arr.	1042	1410	1653	22 4
8 16	8 11	1435	1628	dep. Hatvan .... arr.	9 25	13 3	15 6	21 5
1019	9 16	1614	1751	arr. } Salgotarjan .... { dep	7 51	12 0	1337	20 4
1023	9 17	1619	1732	dep. } Salgotarjan { arr.	7 48	1159	1334	20 3
1150	10 5	1725	1825	arr. } Losonc c .... { dep.	6 42	1113	1226	1912
..	..	..	1850	dep. } Losonc c { arr.	..	1051	..	..
..	..	..	1927	dep. Lovinebana ...... dep.	..	1039	..	..
..	..	..	2219	arr. Vrutky .... arr.	..	7 34	..	..
..	..	..	2250	arr. Zilina .... dep.	..	7 12	..	..
..	..	..	1 23	arr. Bogumin .... dep.	..	4 44	..	..
..			8 26	arr. Warsaw (p 227). dep.	..	22 4	..	

Budapest-Kassa-Poprad-velka (Tatra).
Hung. & German Railways.

123 Ex†	23	123 Ex:	23	123 Exp	23		123 Exp	123 Exp	123 Ex†	23	23
7 30	8 12	1410	1410	1919	0 10	dp. Budapest (East).. ar.	1042	1556	23 0	5 0	5 45
1015	1244	1725	1725	2147	4 20	ar. } Miskolc ...... { dp.	7 40	1330	2013	2347	1 54
1022	1343	1735	1757	2157	4 38	dp. } Miskolc { ar.	7 23	1320	20 3	21 6	1 24
1120	1511	..	1932	..	6 25	ar. } Hidasnemeti { dp.	6 32	..	19 0	1939	2355
1120	1513	..	1938	..	6 35	dp. } Hidasnemeti { ar.	5 32	..	1859	1937	2354
1147	1559	19 3	2027	23 2	7 23	ar. } Kassa c ...... { dp.	6 10	1217	1836	1845	2311
12 6	..	1920		..	7 50	dp. } (Kosice) { ar.		9 57	1822	..	2217
1447		2213		..	1050	ar. Poprad-velka ....dp.		7 27	1552	..	1946

† 1, 2, 3 cl Cars and Rest. Car Budapest-Kassa & v v **S** 2 & 3 cl Sleep. Car.

Budapest, Szeged.
Hung. Rlys.

S 2 & 3 cl. Sleep Car.	23	123 Exp	23	123 Ex r	123 Exp	23 S		23	123 Ex r	123 Exp	23	123 Exp	23 S	r Rest. Car.
	4 40	7 30	8 25	1415	1850	2320	dp **Budapest** (West) ..ar	7 59	9 31	1712	1927	2219	5 0	
	6 41	8 44	1018	1529	20 4	0 42	dp Czegled ....dp	5 51	8 22	16 9	18 8	2112	3 20	
	..	1028	1326	1713	2145	3 35	ar Szeged ....dp	..	6 28	1416	1422	1920	2320	

(Vienna), Budapest, Predeal Bucharest.

[Hungarian and Roumania Ry.

123	12	23	123	23	123	23	c Customs Ex.	12	12	123	123	23	123	23
Exp	luxe		Exp		Exp			Exp	luxe		Exp		Exp	
10 0	15†44	..	17†28	..	2350	2350	dp. Vienna (E) ...... ar.	12†5	14†29	..	1958	..	5 55	1346
1445	O	2140	2355	6 0	7 0	7 48	dp. Budapest (East) ..ar.	6 26	O	1750	1450	1913	22 5	4 50
..	2035	..	..	..	S	8 28	dp. Budapest (West)	Z	9 35	1739	S	..	S	..
1629	2210	0 53	¶	9 15	8 35	¶	dp. Szolnok ....dp.	..	8 12	¶	13 9	1626	2037	2 41
1731	..	2 31	..	1040	9 36	..	dp. Gyoma ....dp.	¶	..	..	12 1	1430	1932	2334
1810	2332	3 20	Z	1125	1011	..	ar. Bekescsaba ......dp.	..	6 42	..	1126	1326	19 2	2222
1854	0 9	5 4	..	1439	1050	..	ar. Lokoshaza ......dp.	..	6 7	..	1051	1111	1829	1948
	luxe				123				luxe				123	
2013	1 24	7 41	..	1630	1214	..	d. Lokoshaza (E.E.T.) a.	..	6 52	..	1110	1130	19 6	1950
2025	1 35	7 59	..	1648	1255	..	ar. Curtici ....dp.	..	6 41	..	1059	1115	1855	1932
21 7	2 5	8 55	..	1741	1310	..	ar. Arad ....dp.	..	6 10	..	10 8	1020	18 9	1820
1015	1230	..	1955	..	0 27	8 10	ar. Bucharest p. 331 dp.	13 5	1945	1955	2050	..	6 55	..

† Vienna (West). ¶ Via Oradea—Mare. **O** Orient Ex See p. 84.

S 1, 2 & 3 cl. Sleep Car Budapest-Bucharest and v.v. **Z** 1 & 2 cl. Sleep. Car Paris-Budapest-Bucharest & v.v.

Berlin—Breslau—Vienna.

[German State Rlys.

123	123	123		123	123	123
	A	B	**Berlin—**		A	B
7 44	19 1	20 3	dep. Friedrichstr.......... arr.	2037	7 52	8 12
8 3	1922	2025	dep. Schles .... arr	2014	7 30	7 55
9 7	2027	..	arr. Frankfort /Oder ...... dep	19 9	6 27	..
9 12	2031	..	dep. Frankfort /Oder ...... arr.	19 4	6 23	..
1210	2340	0 30	arr. Breslau.......... dep.	1613	3 25	4 0
1218	2351	0 40	dep Breslau.......... arr.	16 3	3 15	3 50
1357	1 29	2 18	arr. Heydebreck...... dep	1425	1 40	2 15
14 3	1 35	2 24	dep. Heydebreck...... arr.	1359	1 34	2 9
1542	3 12	3 44	arr. Zauchtel c .... dep	1220	2357	0 39
1554	3 24	3 56	dep. (Suchdol) ...... arr	12 5	2342	0 24
18 3	5 33	6 21	arr. Lundenburg c ...... dep.	1026	2141	2217
1925	6 56	7 44	arr. Vienna (East) ...... dep	9 8	2020	2050

A Sleep Cars and 1, 2 and 3 cl Cars Berlin-Vienna and v.v. Rest. Car Berlin-Breslau.

B Sleeping Cars only Berlin-Vienna and v.v. Rest Car Berlin-Sommerfeld and v.v.

Vienna (Praha), Bogumin, Cracow, Warsaw.

[German and Polish Railways.

123	23	123	123	123	123	¶	123		123	123	123	123	¶	123	123	123	123	23
		ExR	Exp	Exp	Exp		S r		ExR		S r	Exp		Exp		Exp		
..	..	9 50	15†0	..	..	..	2320	dp. Vienna (East.) ..	2033	..	6 31	..	..	11†10	To Sept. 30th.	Suspended.	¶ Rail Car Limited, one class only EXTRA FARES.	..
..	..	11 5	1614	..	..	..	0 40	ar. Lundenburg dp	1915	..	5 10	..	..	9 57				..
..	..	1118	1638	..	..	..	1 0	dp. Lundenburg ar	19 0	..	4 55	..	..	9 35				..
..	..	1322	1845	..	..	..	3 5	a Prerov ...... d.	1659	..	2 56	..	..	7 35				..
..	..	1332	19 0	..	..	..	3 18	d Prerov ...... a.	1644	..	2 51	..	..	7 25				..
..	..	9 15	1442	..	..	..	23 3	d. Praha (W) 207 a.	2119	..	6 53	..	..	1130				..
..	..	16 9	21 0		..	..	5 9	ar. Bogumin c ....dp.	1510	..	0 30	..	..	5 30				..
..	11 7	1620	2120	Suspended.	1 50	..	5 47	dp. Bogumin...... ar.	1357	..	2355	..	..	4 27				11 0
..	1140	1644	2142		2 14	..	6 10	ar. Zebrzydowice.. dp.	1333	..	2333	..	..	4 5				1026
..	1144	1645	↓		2 15	..	6 11	dp. ,, ar.	1332	..	2332	..	..	↑	☞	..		1024
..	1224	1712			2 44	..	6 39	a Dziedzice .... d	13 5	..	23 6	..	..			..		9 45
..	1240	1719				..	6 46	d Dziedzice .... a	1245	..	23 0	..	..			..		9 35
..	1349	18 4				..	7 32	ar. Trzebinia......dp.	1156	..	2213	..	..			..		8 28
..	1458	1839	↓		↓	..	8 8	ar. **Cracow** (p.204) d.	1118	..	2135	..	..		..	..		7 30
..		1725	2143	☞	2 15	..	6 24	dp. Zebrzydowice .. ar.	1332	..	2318	..	arr.	4 5	Sleep. car.	..	8 25	1024
1037	.	1751	2244		2 53	5 2	7 21	dp. Dziedzice ......d.	13 5	..	2250	..	0 7	3 39		..	7 42	9 45
1256	..	1840	0 9		3 42	6 46	7 49	dp. Katowice ......ar.	1210	1631	2151	..	2256	2 42		..	5 52	7 55
1347	..	19 8	1 9		..	7 16	8 17	ar. Zabkowice ......d.	1142	1554	2123	..	2226	2 12		..	4 56	6 57
5 37	1120	1120	1, 2 & 3cl. Sleep. Car	2117	↓	↓	2230	dp. Krynica ...... ar	2058	0 12	7 22	7 21	↑	↑	1224	9 0	15 3	..
1128	1734	1734		..			5 11	ar. Cracow ...... dp.	1415	1815	0 35	0 35			..	Sleep. car.	8 35	Sleep. Car.
6 35	1253	1253		Sleep. car.			2310	dp. Zakopane...... ar.	1743	2350	6 23	6 25			8 27		1421	
7 12	1323	1323					0 4	dp. Nowy Targ .... ar.	17 3	2316	5 23	5 23			7 49		1338	
1040	1710	1710					5 3	ar. Cracow ....dp.	1325	1925	0 45	0 45			..		9 10	
12 2	1743	1748	↓	..			7 0	dp. **Cracow** ...... ,,	13 0	1740	2257	2328			..		6 43	
1258	Via Radom	1827					7 38	,, Trzebinia .... ar.	1225	1647	2219				4 10		5 55	..
1342		19 2	↓	Via Radom	↓	↓	8 12	ar. Zabkowice .... dp	1151	1559	2140	Via Radom			3 19	Via Radom	5 9	..
1353		1914	1 16		4 14	7 16	8 23	dp. Zabkowice .... ar.	1137	1539	2118		2225	2 11	3 18		4 48	6 55
1834		2156	5 9		6 52	9 16	11 1	Koluszki ......dp	8 52	1114	1827		2022	2328	0 18		1 17	2 22
1918	..	R	5 57		..	..	..	Skierniewice .. ,,	..	1021	r		..	..	2337		0 24	1 29
2034	2230	2322	7 6	8 10	8 26	1026	1222	ar. **Warsaw** (Gl.).. ,,	7 28	9 8	1652	1824	1912	22 4	2228	2212	23 8	0 8
	R						S				S	R						

A 1, 2 & 3 cl. Sleep Car, Warsaw-Zakopane & v.v. daily. **S** 1 & 2 cl. Sleep. Car Vienna-Warsaw, and Karlovy-Vary-Praha-Warsaw and v.v. daily. *s* 1 & 2 cl. Sleep. Car Warsaw-Cracow. **R** Rest. Car. *r* Rest. Car Warsaw-Zebrzdowice and v.v. † Nord Station. ‡ Mas. Station.

The times on the LEFT are to be read DOWNWARDS, those on the RIGHT UPWARDS.

(Ger. St. Rys. (Osten Halle, Breslau Oppeln & Pres.) & Polish Rys.)

☞ See also services Berlin—Vienna, page 203.

123	123	123	23	123	123	23	123	123		123	123	23	123	123	23	123	123
ExD	ExD	D H	fast	ExD	D X	FDT	ExD	Ex D	**Berlin—**	Ex D	ExD	FDT	D X	Exp	fast	D H	Ex D
6 52	..	9 6	1056	1417	1727	2010	2016	2328	dep. Friedrichstrasse .. arr.	7 18	9 18	9 51	1251	1511	1712	2055	2254
7 16	..	9 30	1116	1438	1747	2020	2036	2350	,, Schlesisch station ,,	6 59	9 9	9 42	1232	1450	1654	2034	2233
8 18	..	1037	1227	1545	1850	↓	2139	0 55	,, Frankfort-on-Oder ,,	5 32	7 57	↑	1127	1345	1539	1926	2132
9 20	..	1135	1336	1651	1951		2242	2 3	,, Sommerfeld ...... ,,	3 53	7 1		1028	*Via* Glogau.	1433	1828	2035
6 20	..	..	1025	1216	1447		1712	..	,, **Leipsic** (H.) .... ,,		..		..		1725	2150	0 36
6 0	..	..	1021	1143	1416		1657	..	,, Halle .... ,,	..	..		..		1736	2214	1 11
7 27	..	..	1138	14 1	1623		1822	S	,, Falkenberg (p166) ,,		..		..		1620	2041	2256
8 44	..	..	1256	1557	1814		1942	..	,, Cottbus .... ,,		..		..		1510	1925	2121
10 3	..	12 3	14 7	1734	2021		2323	Z	,, Sagan .... ,,	Z S	6 35		9 59		14 5	1748	20 5
1055	..	1254	15 5	1829	2114	↓	0 14	4 36	arr. Liegnitz ...... dep.	1 14	5 31		9 5		13 5	1652	1914
1147	..	1344	16 9	1925	22 6	2254	1 7	5 35	,, **Breslau** (Hptbf.) .. ,,	0 20	4 45	7 1	8 16	1010	12 3	16 6	1826
8w17	8 17	..	1021	1423	1754		2111	1 41	dep. **Dresden** (Hptbf.) arr	4 21	9 25	↑	..	1414	1751	2028	..
9 32	1011		1214	1611	1941		2246	3 35	,, Görlitz .... ,,	2 32	7 52		..	1222	1610	1839	..
FDT	1034	H	1243	1635	20 2		..	4 0	,, Kohlfurt ...... ,,	2 0	7 28		..	1154	1541	18 9	..
	1135		1343	1730	21 0		2357	4 57	arr. Liegnitz ...... dep.	0 59	6 38		..	1055	1444	17 9	..
11w3	1226	..	1445	1817	2149	↓	0 45	5 47	,, **Breslau** (Hptbf.) ,,	0 11	5 57		..	10 5	1356	1620	..
1156	1242	1354	1619	1935	2218	2257	1 17	5 57	dep. **Breslau** (Hptbf.) .. arr.	24 0	4 35	6 58	8 3	10 0	1148	1547	1817
1336	1421	1527	1810	2113	2355	2358	3 0	7 47	arr. Heydebreck ...... dep.	2218	2 50	5 55	6 32	8 33	9 56	1414	1647
1443	..		20 8	↓	1 0	.	4 10	9 4	arr. Bogumin ...... dep.	2110	1 38	..	5 27	↑	..	..	1540
2033	†..		..	↓	6 35	†..	1110		,, VIENNA (N.) (p. 203) ,,	15 0	..	..	23†20		..	..	9†50
1348	1427	1531	1814	2116	0 6	0 0	3 5	7 52	dep. Heydebreck ...... arr.	22 5	2 44	5 54	6 23	8 30	9 52	1411	1634
1418	1455	1559	1843	2147	0 35	0 20	3 32	8 24	arr. Gleiwitz .... dep.	2135	2 17	5 34	5 56	8 5	9 25	1344	16 8
1442	1518	1623	19 7	2211	0 58	0 37	3 55	8 49	,, Beuthen c .... ,,	2112	1 56	5 18	5 34	7 40	9 4	1321	1548
..	1617	1716	2042	23 7	1 52	1 52	4 59	9 46	,, Katowice (p. 228) .. ,,	1955	0 15	..	4 43	6 52	8 16	1230	1430
..	..	1853	2241	0 24	..	..	7 45	1127	,, **Cracow** .... ,,	18 3	22 0	..		..	6 30	11 3	1258
		123	x			Exp	..				123	..			123	123	
		9 50	..	..	..	2320	..	2320	dep. VIENNA (E.) (p. 203) a.	..	6 35	..		..	x	2033	
		9 5	0 15	..	..	8 35	..	1142	,, **Cracow** (p. 228) .. ,,	1734	2110	..		..	6 0	1055	
		24 0	6 20	..	..	1355	..	1645	arr. Lemberg (Lwow) dp.	1247	1552	..		.	2345	6 15	
		0 30	7 20	..	..	..	..	17 2	dep. Lemberg (Lwow) ar.	1227	..	..		..	2252	5 40	
		7 16	1835	z..	..	..	..	2316	,, Cernauti .... arr.	7 40	..	..		..	183	0 7	
		9 7	2055		..	..	..	1 18	arr. Burdujeni .... dep.	5 36	..	..		..	1650	22 2	
		9 59	22 7		..	..	..	2 19	,, Pascani (p. 331) .. ,,	4 30	..	..		..	1554	2055	
		1415	3 46		..	..	..	6 57	,, Buzau (p. 330) .... ,,	2338	..	..		..	1135	1554	
		1950	14 5		..	..	..	14 5	,, CONSTANZA (p. 331) ,,	1530	..	..			..	..	
		1615	6z0		..	..	.	9 5	,, BUCHAREST (p. 331) ,,	2124	..	..			9 40	1343	
		0 15	7 20		..	1435	..	1820	dep. Lemberg (Lwow) .. arr.	1120	1237				20 5	5 50	
		1 34	9 0			1549	..	1859	Krasne	9 55	1129			..	1831	4 7	
		3 32	11 7			..	..	2013	arr. Tarnopol .... dep.	7 56	..				1615	1 30	
		7 23	15 4			..	..	..	,, Podwoloczyska c .. ,,	6 13	..				1345	..	
		8 10	..			..	..	..	dep. ,, (Moscow tm.) arr.	..	..			..	1150	..	
		8 36	..			..	..	..	,, Volochisk c		..			..	1130	..	
		..	..			..	..	..	arr. Shmerinka (p. 230) dep.		..				..	.	
		1246	..			..	..	..	,, ODESSA (p. 230) .. ,,		..				1826	..	
		..	..			..	..	..	dep. Shmerinka .. arr.		..				..	..	
					..	..	..	..	arr. KIEV .... dep.		..	..					

e *Via* Shmerinka.

w Weekdays only.

H 1 & 2 cl. Sleep Car Ostend-Berlin-Bucharest and *v.v.* for days of running, *see p.* 81.

x 1 & 2 cl. Sleep. car Cracow-Lemberg and *v.v.*

Z *Via* Sorau Kohlfort.

§ 2 & 3 cl. only.

† East Stn.

X Sleeping Car, 1 and 2 cl. Berlin-Vienna and *v.v.*

S—1 & 2 cl. Sl. Car Berlin-Bucharest & *v.v.* also 1, 2 & 3 cl. Sleepers to Beuthen & *v.v.*

z 1 and 2 cl. Sleeping Cars Cernauti-Bucharest and *v.v.*

Berlin, Stralsund, Sassnitz, Warnemunde. [Ger. State Rlys.

S 1 & 2 cl. Sleep. car Berlin-Stockholm and *v.v.* **Z** 1 & 2 cl. Sleep. car Berlin-Copenhagen and *v.v.*
¶ 1 & 2 cl. Slp. Malmo-Stockholm 1, 2 & 3 cl. Malmo-Oslo and *v.v.*

D23	D	D ¶	23	23	23	fast	Ex D	D		D	Ex D	fast	23	23	¶ D	D †	23
8 20	8 42	1120	1021	1345	1527	19 4	2121	2132	dep. **Berlin** (Stet) .... arr.	7 21	7 54	1011	1157	1630	1813	1955	215
9 46	10 2	..	1250	1525	1746	2039	S	2252	arr. Neustrelitz .... dep.	6 6	S	8 47	1016	15 7	..	1839	1938
A	↓	1430	1629	..	2121	↓	0 31	Z	arr. **Stralsund** .. dep.	Z	4 48	↑	8 15	1150	15 0	↑	1529
..		1441			..		0 41		dep. **Stralsund** .. arr.	↑	4 38		..	8 40	1449		..
..		1537			..		1 31		arr. Sassnitz .... dep.		3 46		..	7 20	1352		..
..		2036			..		6 20		,, Trelleborg ...... ,,		2254		.	..	8 50		..
..	↓	6 30	↓	↓	..	↓	1550	↓	arr. Stockholm (p. 215A) ,,		1350		..	..	2235		..
9 48	10 4	..	1315	1527	1752	2042	..	2257	dep. Neustrelitz ...... arr.	6 4	..	8 42	9 43	15 2	↑	1837	175
1137	1149	..	16 0	1712	2033	2224	..	0 32	arr. Rostock .... dep.	4 26	..	6 55	6 23	1320		1646	142
..	12 6	..	17 1	1730	2126	2250	..	0 48	,, **Warnemunde** .. ,,	4 10	..	6 40	5 55	13 0		1633	14
..	1440	..		..	..	..	..	3 35	arr. Gedser .... dep.	1 40	..	..	..	.		14 5	..
..	17†35	..	..	..	..	..	..	6 48	,, Copenhagen (p. 214) ,,	2245	..	..	..	.	†	1115	..
..	6 30	¶	..		..	..	S	2235	arr. Stockholm (p. 216) dp.	8 0	S	..	..	..	¶	2235	..
..	9 0	9 0	..		..	..	1910	1910	,, Oslo ..... (p. 216) ,,	10 5	10 5	..	..	..	2010	2010	..

A June 17–Aug. 14. † 1, 2 & 3 cl. cars Berlin–Copenhagen and *v.v.*

The times on the LEFT are to be read DOWNWARDS, those on the RIGHT UPWARDS.

Berlin (Danzig) (Memel), Eydtkau, (Riga).

Ger. State, Pol., Lithuanian & Latvian Rlys.

1 2 3	1 2 3	1 2 3	1 2 3	1 2 3	1 2 3	1 2 3	1 2 3		1 2 3	1 2 3	1 2 3	1 2 3	1 2 3	1 2 3	1 2 3	1 2 3	1 2 3
DN	ExD	ExD	ExD	ExD	FD	DS	ExD	**Berlin—**	ExD	ExD	ExD	ExD	DN	FD	ExD	D X	ExD
8 44	9 14	11 3	10†35	1332	1637	2255	2342	dep. Friedrichstrasse ar.	15 4	1844	18 9	19 2	21 6	23 1	6 38	7 10	7 43
9 4	9 34	1122	r	1352	1650	2316	0 5	,, Schlesicher .. ,,	1444	r†	1748	1843	2044	2244	6 23	6 50	7 22
..	..	r	*Via* Stettin.	r	r		..		r	*Via* Stettin.	r	..	..	..	r	..	..
1157	1245	1424		1657	1923	2 16	3 23	dep. Schneidemuhl .. arr.	12 2		1449	1532	1750	2015	3 7	3 21	4 5
14 8	..	..		..	..	4 42	5 41	arr. Dirschau ......dep.	..		A		1530	..	A	0 54	1 30
x	↓	↓	..	x	x	..	..	dep. Tczew c ...... arr.	x	..	x	x	14 3	↑	..	x	x
1656			1812	2147	2355	7 4	7 4	arr. } Danzig (p.227) { dep.	7 32	1119	10 2	10 2	1316		..	2318	2318
1316			1819	..	19 7	..	X	dep. } Danzig (p.227) { arr.	..	1113	↑	..	1656		..	..	S
14 3	↓	↓	1850	..		..		arr. Tczew ....dep.	..	1042		..	1623		..	..	
1413	r	..	1855	..	..	4 47	5 46	dep. Dirschau........ arr.	..	1038		r	1523	..		0 49	1 25
1439	1536	17 8	1924	1946	2159	5 14	6 13	,, Marienburg ....dep.	9 22	1022	12 9	1240	15 7	1743	0 16	0 32	1 8
15 1	16 0	1730	1946	20 9	2218	5 40	6 38	,, Elbing.......... ,,	8 51	9 49	1139	12 5	1436	1716	2342	0 0	0 36
1620	1724	1847	21 8	2132	2328	7 15	8 5	arr. Konigsberg......dep.	7 37	8 30	1016	1037	1316	16 6	2213	2233	2316
1730		1956	..	2239	1 2	8 27	9 15	,, Insterburg...... ,,	5 39	7 17	8 29	9 30	12 9	..	..	2123	22 4
1738	..	20 3	See below.	2245	..	..	9 21	dep. Insterburg .... arr.	..	7 11	8 24	9 24	12 0	..		2117	..
1836	..	2048		2323		..	10 6	arr. Tilsit ....dep.	..	6 33	7 26	8 43	1051	..	..	2036	..
..	..	2229		..	..	..	1148	,, Memel (p.208) ,,	..	..	..	7 0	7 55	..	..	1837	..
1733	..	..		..	..	8 30	..	dep. Insterburg ...... arr.	..	See below.	8§25	..	12 6	..	..	..	22 0
1822	..	‡		..	..	9 21	..	arr. Eydtkau ....dep.	..		7§4	..	1121	..	..	‡	21 0
1838	..	..		..	..	9 55	‡	,, Wirballen ...... ,,	..		..	..	11 3	..	..		2021
0 43	..	..		..	..	1736	1736	,, Riga............ ,,	..		..	..	6 25	..	..	1525	1525

D Corridor Exp. **N** Nord Express, 1 & 2 cl. Sleep. Cars; EXTRA FARES, also 1, 2 & 3 cl. Car Berlin-Riga and *v.v.* **S** 1, 2 & 3 cl. Sleep. Car Berlin-Eydtkau, 1 & 2 cl. Sleep. Car and 1, 2 & 3 cl. Cars Berlin-Riga, & *v.v.* **X** 1, 2 & 3 cl. Sleep. Car Berlin-Memel, 1 & 2 cl. Sleep Car Berlin-Dunaberg and *v.v.* † Stettin Stn. ‡ *Via* Tilsit. § 2 & 3 cl. only. *r* Rest Car. *x Via* Marienburg. **A** June 27—Sept 10.

Berlin, Poznan, Warsaw.

[Ger. State and Polish Rlys.

2 3	1 2 N	1 2 3	2 3	1 2 3	1 2 3	Mls.	*c* Customs Exam.	1 2 3	1 2 N	2 3	1 2 3	1 2 3	2 3
	luxe	Exp		ExD	Ex S			Exp	luxe	2 3	Ex S	Exp	
0 48	8 36	9 49	12 0	1743	2349	0	dp. **Berlin** (Fried). ar.	1917	2118	1 22	8 0	1052	1652
1 10	9 12	10 8	1222	1813	0 10		,, Berlin (Schles.) ,,	1856	2049	1 2	7 43	1027	1635
4 40	10 4	11 6	14 2	1934	1 5	50	,, Frankfort-Oder ,,	1749	1950	2253	6 28	9 7	1449
6 48	1114	1225	16 5	21 6	2 25	..	ar. } Neu Bentschen *c* { dp.	1627	1842	2026	5 8	7 41	1239
9 0	1129	1255	1730	22 5	2 48	..	dp. } Neu Bentschen *c* { ar.	1557	1824	1855	4 34	7 8	1050
9 9	1135	13 3	1739	2213	2 56	112	ar. Bentschen *c* ..dp.	1549	1816	1844	4 25	7 0	1039
1230	1149	1343	2030	2313	3 38	..	dp. Bentschen ....ar.	1519	18 4	1715	3 40	6 24	9 41
14 5	1239	1437	2211	0 22	4 32	158	ar. Poznan (*p.* 226) dp.	1427	1714	1535	2 44	5 20	8 0
..	1634	1938	6 6	8 22	9 2	347	,, **Warsaw** (G.) *p.*226 ,,	9 24	1316	..	22 8	2156	0 16

N Nord. Exp., Daily, *see page* 81.
S 1 & 2 cl. Sleep. Car Berlin-Warsaw and Berlin-Niegoreloje and *v.v.*

Berlin (Hamburg), Stettin, Belgard, Danzig.

[Ger. State & Polish Rlys.

2 3	123D	123D	2 3	123D	2 3	2 3	2 3	2 3	**Berlin—**	2 3	2 3	2 3	123D	123D	2 3	123D	2 3	2 3
7 0	8 28	1035	1238	16 0	1620	1815	2245	2343	dep. Stettin Sta. ..arr.	1152	1321	19 8	1553	1844	2340	2046	1 30	7 12
7 58	9 27		1342	1658	1759	1917	0 22	0 51	,, Angermunde .. ,,	1047	1145	1729	1446		2237	1942	2359	6 10
8 45	1014	1210	1432	1746	1922	20 5	1 38	1 43	arr. Stettin ....dep	10 0	1024	16 9	14 1	17 7	2151	1858	2253	5 25
..	..	6 54	..	1215	..	1045	1550	..	d. Hamburg { p. 162 ar.	2113	1636	2235	1943	2235	..	..	..	1245
		7 53	6 48	..	..	1220	1657	⌣	d. **Lubeck** .. { p. 162 ar.	2015	..	2132	1846	2132	..	..	..	1139
9 50	1020	1216	1437	1752	1935	2010	1 55	7 45	dep. Stettin ...... arr.	9 54	1014	1558	1355	17 1	2011	1852	2240	4 0
1038	1049	1244	1512	1820	2024	2038	2 38	8 13	arr. Stargard ....dep.	9 24	9 29	15 0	1325	1631	1920	1821	22 7	3 13
1347	1226	14 2	1733	20 3	23 8	2217	4 55	9 46	arr. } Belgard.. { dep	7 40	6 8	12 7	1138	1513	1648	1641	2035	1 6
1412	1228	14 4	1747	20 6	2316	2220	5 3	9 48	dep. } Belgard.. { arr.	7 35	5 57	1149	1132	1511	1614	1636	2029	0 58
1444	1245	1423	1814	2024	2346	2237	5 30	10 5	arr. } Köslin .. { dep.	7 15	5 32	1120	1112	1451	1544	1616	20 5	0 27
1453	1247	1425	1818	2026	..	2239	5 37	10 7	dep. } Köslin .. { arr.	7 13	..	1046	1110	1449	1537	1613	20 3	0 18
1621	1338	1522	1950	2120	..	2334	7 22	1059	arr. Stolp........dep.	6 25	..	9 11	1019	14 1	1419	1527	1915	2245
1857	..	1627	..	..	..	..	9 22	..	arr. } Gross Boschpol } dep.	..	..	..	8 45	1258	..	..	1424	2010
1927	..	1637	..	..	..	..	..	..	dep. } Gross Boschpol } arr.	..	..	..	8 26	1248	..	..	..	..
21 9	..	1737	..	..	..	..	..	..	arr Gdynia......dep.	..	..	..	7 14	1153	..	..	..	..
2156	..	1759	..	..	..	..	..	..	arr. Zoppot ......dep.	..	..	..	6 45	1133	..	..	..	..
2212	..	1812	..	..	..	..	..	..	arr. **Danzig** ....dep.	..	..	..	6 30	1119	..	..	..	..
..	..	21 8	..	..	..	..	..	..	arr. Konigsberg ..dep.	..	..	..	..	8 30	..	..	..	..

The times on the LEFT are to be read DOWNWARDS, those on the RIGHT UPWARDS.

BOHEMIA, MORAVIA AND SLOVAKIA.

Trains throughout Greater Germany run on Mid-European time (one hour fast of Greenwich).

Praha—Vranany—Lobositz (Dresden).

123 Exp	23	123 Exp	23	23	123 Exp	3 cl	23	123 Exp	Mls.		123 Exp	3 cl	23	123 Exp	23	23	123 Exp	123 Exp
..	..	..	..	..	..	..	..	2342		d. Praha (Wil.) arr.	6 15	..	..	..	..	..	..	..
5 24	6 28	8 30	1030	1326	1648	1840	1930	2359	0	d. ,, (Mas.) arr.	6 0	8 20	1048	1358	1511	2130	21 0	2313
R	7 44	..	1140	1444	R	1921	2046	..	25	d. Vranany ....dep.	..	7 41	9 39	..	14 5	20 4	..	..
..	8 16	9 28	1215	1527		1946	2120	0 56	42	d Roudnice n Lab. d.	5 4	7 18	9 7	R	1325	1920	20 3	R
..	8 32	9 40	1235	1544	..	1958	2139	1 8	49	a. Terezin- dp.	4 53	7 7	8 46	..	13 4	1858	1952	..
..	9 3	1010	..	1635		..	2217	1 28		d. Bohusovice *c* a.	4 33	..	7 38	..	1128	1742	1917	..
7 36	9 10	1016		1643	18 0	..	2225	1 34	54	a. Lobositz *c*.... dp.	4 27		7 30	1245	1120	1734	1911	22 0
9 33	1318	1236	..	20 9	2018	..	..	3 50	..	a. Dresden (*p.* 195) d.	2 12	..	..	1037	..	1324	1632	1942

R Rest Car.

Praha—Plzen—Domazlice (Furth-i-W).

23	123 Exp	23	123 Exp	23	23	23	23	Mls.		23	23	23 fast	123 Exp	23	123 Exp	123
..	7 35	9 45	11 0	1212	1535	1842	20 0	0	dep. Praha (Wil.) .. arr.	9 44	1724	1550	1855	..	2225	..
..	9 27	1310	1250	1520	1726	2045	2311	72	arr. } Plzen .... { dep.	7 48	1335	1358	1710	..	2040	..
7 50	..	1410	⌒	..	1737	2146	2328		dep. } Plzen .... { arr.	7 24	1222	1350	..	1727	..	2124
9 33	..	1557	..	..	1819	2327	0 53	96	dep. Stankov *c*...... dep.	5 38	1131	1311		1553	..	1950
9 59	..	1625	..	..	1838	2354	1 20	108	arr. } Domazlice .. { dep.	5 7	1046	1253	..	1521	..	1918
1024	..	1649	..	..	1855	..	..		dep. } (Taus) { arr.	4 51	1021	1233	..	15 0	..	1851
1110	..	1736	..	..	1936	..	..	122	ar. Furth-i-W. (*p.* 188) dp.	4 10	9 34	1154	..	1415	..	18 6

Praha, Plzen—Krimice (Nuremberg.)

123 Exp	23 Exp	123 Exp	23	123 Exp	23	12 luxe	Mls		23	23	23	23	12 luxe	123 Exp	123 Exp	123 Exp
7 35	..	..	9 45	11 0	1425	1520	0	dep. Praha (Wil.) ...... arr.	1025	9 44	12 6	1550	16 0		1855	2225
A				S		*a*							*b*		S	A
9 27	..		1310	1250	1717	1658	72	arr. } Plzen .... { dep.	6 47	7 48	1014	1358	1425	..	1710	2040
9 37	13 0	1418	1451	13 0	1812	17 5		dep. } Plzen .... { arr.	6 20	7 37	..	1344	1412	1518	17 0	2028
9 45	13 8	1426	15 3	13 8	1823	1713	76	arr. } Krimice *c* .... { dep.	6 9	7 26		1333	14 5	1511	1653	2021
10 0	1323	1441	.	1323	1833	1723		dep } Krimice *c* .... { arr.	..	7 16	..	1322	1335	1456	1638	20 6
10 7	1330	1448	.	1330	1842	1730	79	arr. Tuschkau-Kosolup *c* dep.	..	7 7	..	1318	1349	1450	1632	20
1150	..	..	..	1517	2048	19 2	..	arr. Marienbad .... dep.	..	5 9	..	1111	1221	..	1448	1814
1553	..	..		1847		2156	..	arr. Nuremberg (*p.* 190) dep.		2320	..	..	9 0	..	1123	1438

A 1, 2 & 3 cl. Cars Paris—Praha and *v.v.* **S** Sleep. Car 1, 2 cl. and 1, 2 & 3 cl. Cars Praha-Paris and *v.v.*
a Tues., Thurs., Sats., June 17—Sept. 21. *b* Weds., Fris., Suns., June 16—Sept. 20.

Praha—Suchdol—Vienna (Linz).

123 Exp	23 fast	123 Exp	23 fast	23 Exp		23 fast	123 Exp	23	23	123 Exp	123 Exp	23 Exp
6 32	7 12	14 10	1725	2216	dep. Praha (Wil.) ...... arr	8 45	1610	1827	2215	2110	2320	6 20
8 12	9 7	1620	1927	0 8	dep. Tabor .... dep.	6 54	1438	1558	1935	1929	2150	4 40
8 32	9 31	1640	1952	0 30	arr. Mezimosti- dep.	6 28	1416	1515	1838	19 4	2128	4 17
8 57	↓	1645	↓	↓	dep. Veseli n. Luz arr.	↑	1411	.	1815	↑	2124	↑
9 12		1717			arr } Suchdol *c* .... { dep.		1340		1720		2050	
9 32		1932			dep. } Suchdol *c* .... { arr.		11 0				2020	
9 50		18 0			arr. Gmund *c* (*p.* 196) .. dep.		1255	..			2011	
1746	↓	21 4	↓	↓	arr. Vienna F.J.B. .... dep.		9 30				17 5	
	9 35	..	1956	0 34	dp. Mezimosti V. n. Luz arr.	6 23		15 7	1828	19 0	..	4 12
	1011	..	2030	1 10	ar. } Ceske Budejovice { dep	5 50	.	1410	1733	1823	..	3 35
	1040	..	21 4	1 18	dp. } Ceske Budejovice { arr.	.		1333	..	17 7	..	3 29
..	1128	..	2152	1 55	arr. Velesin *c* .... dep.	..	.	1253	..	1624	..	3 4
..	1152	..	..	2 25	arr. Kaplitz .... dep.	..	..	1216	..	..	..	2 36
..	15 8		..	5 45	arr. Linz (*p.* 196)...... dep.		..	7 38	..	..	..	2340

Praha (Vienna)—Piestany—Zilina.

2 3	1 2 3	2 3	1 2 3	1 2 3	2 3	2 3	2 3	1 2 3		1 2 3	1 2 3	2 3	2 3	1 2 3 Exp	2 3	1 2 3 Exp	2 3
..	2311	..	..	..	..	..	6 47	1410	dep. Praha (Mas) arr.	..	1636	20a40	..	..	6 45	..	..
..	3 33	..	5†10	..	..	..	1440	1752	,, Brno...... ,,	..	13 2	1635	..	..	2 32	..	..
..	5 40	..	8†30	..	..	..	18 5	1942	arr. Bratislava dep	..	11 6	1413	..	..	0 25	..	..
..	..	..	6 28	1135	..	1350	..	21 5	dep. Vienna (E) arr.	9 43	14 8	7‡13	..	19 7	..	..	..
..	..	..	8 15	1240	..	1522	..	22 4	,, Marchegg.. ,,	8 32	1237	1443	..	1755	..	..	..
..	..	..	9 6	1322	..	16 9	3 cl.	2244	arr. Bratislava dep.	7 48	1152	14 2	..	1712	..	..	..
4 28	6 5	8 0	9 42	1338	1427	1655	1836	2257	dep. Bratislava arr.	7 30	1043	1325	1641	1656	2127	2044	1 7
6 5	7 3	9 37	1038	1434	1556	1833	1932	2357	arr. Leopoldov dep.	6 23	9 45	1140	15 5	1558	1952	1946	2327
6 42	7 24	1012	11 8	1458	1639	1913	1950	0 12	arr. } Piestany { dep.	6 5	9 29	11 6	1433	1534	19 2	1923	2245
6 44	7 26	1015	*1110	15 0	1643	1916	1951	0 13	dep. } Piestany { arr.	6 3	9 27	11 4	1431	1532	1858	1921	2242
7 48	8 3	1125	1147	1537	1754	2017	2027	0 51	arr. Trencin .. dep.	5 27	8 52	10 1	1333	1455	1750	1844	2123
8 3	8 12	1140	1156	1546	1811	2030	2036	1 0	,, Trencianska- ,,	5 18	8 43	9 48	1321	1446	1735	1835	21 4
8 35	8 17	12 7	1159	1550	1823	2047	2040	1 7	dep. Tepla arr.	5 11	8 40	9 35	1312	1443	1723	1833	2049
1024	9 26	1353	13 0	1655	2010	2236	2149	2 20	arr. Zilina .... dep.	4 0	7 31	7 50	1131	1345	1537	1738	1857
..	..	..	1529	..	..	..	1 23	..	arr. Bogumin dep.	..	4 44	..	..	..	..	15 1	..
..	..	..	2254	..	..	..	9 18	..	,, Berlin (Fried) ,, (p. 204)	..	2016	..	..	..	..	6 52	..

a Praha (Wils.) ‡ Vienna Nord Station. † 2 and 3cl. class only.

Brno—Trencianska—Tepla—Piestany.

2 3	2 3	2 3	2 3	1 2 3 Exp	2 3	2 3		2 3	2 3	2 3	2 3 Exp	2 3	2 3	2 3	2 3
3 10	5 50	7 41	1157	1315	1448	1918	dep. Brno...... arr.	8 20	11 5	1522	1614	1813	21 4	2332	4 39
8 2	1022	1234	1653	1637	20 2	0 12	arr. } Byinica } dep	3 38	5 44	1033	1256	1240	1536	1920	2242
8 3	1035	1238	1655	1638	20 3	0 13	dep. } Byinica } arr	3 35	5 41	1030	1254	1237	1533	1917	2235
8 30	1121	1318	1732	1713	2032	0 56	arr. Trencianska- dp	3 0	5 14	9 53	1220	12 2	1450	1845	2138
8 43	..	1321	1735	1735	21 4	..	dep. Tepla arr.	1 0	..	8 12	1156	1140	1428	1811	2036
9 27	..	1431	1858	1858	2242	..	arr. Piestany .. dep.	0 13	..	7 26	1110	1015	1313	1643	1951

Praha—Prerov—Lundenburg (Vienna).

1 2 3 Exp	2 3	2 3	1 2 3 Exp	1 2 3 Exp	M'ls.		2 3	1 2 3 Exp	2 3	2 3	1 2 3 Exp
..	..	9 15	..	2138	0	dep. Praha .... arr	1636		2119	6 38	7 56
7 35	8 38	1552	1659	2 56	171	,, Prerov .... ,,	1211	1322	1654	2316	3 5
8 47	1044	1753	1812	4 6	221	,, Hodonin .. dep.	10 3	12 7	1449	2110	1 54
9 1	11 8	1850	1829	4 22	231	arr. } Hrusky { dep.	9 36	1149	1422	2046	1 36
9 27	1148	1912	1852	4 47		dep. } (*c*) { arr.	9 10	1124	14 2	2026	1 6
9 36	1150	1917	19 0	4 55	238	ar. Lundenburg(*c*) dp	8 57	1118	1355	2020	1 0
11†10	14†57	..	2033	6 31	285	,, Vienna (East) ,,	6†18	9 50	..	18†0	2320

† Vienna, Nord Stn.

Praha—Otrokovice—Zlin.

1 2 3	1 2 3	2 3	2 3	1 2 3	1 2 3 S	196 miles.	1 2 3	1 2 3	2 3	2 3	1 2 3 S
..	9 15	12†0	1442	1837	23 3	dep. Praha (Wils) arr.	1130	16†36	2119	6†38	6 53
7 35	1334	2123	19 0	23*2	3 46	dep. Prerov ..arr.	7*31	1211	1654	2316	2316
8 5	1424	2215	1950	2332	4 28	arr. Otrokovice dep.	6*43	1117	16 7	2223	2223
3 cl.	3cl.	2 3	3 cl.	2 3	2 3		3 cl.	3 cl.	3 cl.	2 3	2 3
8 8	1430	2230	1959	2332	5 35	dep. Otrokovice arr.	6 32	11 2	1550	22 3	22 3
8 28	1453	2253	2023	2352	5 59	arr. Zlin .... dep.	6 7	1040	1530	2140	2140

S 2 & 3 cl. Sleep Car Praha-Zlin and *v.v.* † Praha (Mas.) * 3rd class.

Praha—Brno—Bratislava—Vajnory

Mls.		2 cl. M	1 2 3 Exp	2 3	1 2 3 Exp	1 2 3 Exp	1 2 3 Exp	2 cl. M	2 3 SS	1 2 3 Exp	1 2 3 Exp	2 3	1 2 3 Exp	1 2 3 Exp
0	Praha (Wilson) ......dep.	..	8 40	..	9 15	R	1442	1834	..	1837	2138	..	23 3	S
..	„ (Mas.) .... „	6 12	R	6 47	..	1410	..	..		..	..	2220	..	2311
65	Pardubice .... „	..	10 7	1012	1048	..	1611	..	..	20 6	23 6	1 10	0 30	0 40
102	Ceska Trebova ...... „	8 0	1113	1225	1148	..	1715	..	..	2117	0 7	2 49	1 30	1 44
..	Blansko ....arr.	..	..	..	To Bogumin.	..	To Bogumin.	..	..	To Bogumin.	To Bogumin.	..	To Bogumin.	
145	Blansko (Caves) ...... „		1211	1346		..		..	..			4 5		..
159	Brno .... arr.	9 3	1235	1421		1748		2121	..			4 40		3 3
	dep.	9 6	1247	1440		1752		2124	..			5 10		3 33
197	Lundenburg ...... arr.	..	..	..		..		..	..			SS		..
	dep.	..		..		..		..	..			..		..
208	Kuty ....dep.	9 58	1352	1635		1854		..	..			7 2		4 45
248	Bratislava ....arr.	1037	1444	18 5		1942		2253				8 30		5 40
			2 3	2 3		1 2 3						2 3		1 2 3
..	Bratislava ....dep.	..	1516	1840	..	1950	..	..	23 4	..	..	1028	..	6 0
259	Ceklis c .... arr.	..	1543	1912	..	20 5	..	..	2336	..	..	1056	..	6 15
	dep.	..	16 3	..	..	2020	..		2356	..	..	1116	..	6 36
262	Szeno c (p. 202) ....arr.	..	1615	..	..	2028	..	..	0 8	..	..	1129	..	6 44
372	Budapest (W) ......arr.	..	2122	..	..	2331	..	..	5 37	..	..	1649	..	10 0
..	Bucharest (p. 203)....arr.	..	..	..	..	1955	..	..	..	..	..	..	..	..

R Rest. Car. S 1, 2 & 3 cl. Sleep. Car Praha—Budapest.

	1 2 3 Exp	1 2 3 Exp	1 2 3 Exp	2 cl. M	1 2 3 Exp	2 3	1 2 3 Exp	2 3	1 2 3 Exp	3 cl. M	2 3	2 3	1 2 3 Exp S	2 3 SS
Bucharest (p. 203) ......dep	..	..	..	..	..	..	13 5	..	..	..	..			..
Budapest (p. 202) ..... „	..	..	..	..	..	..	7 5	7 33	..	..		1520	20 0	0 5
Szene c (p. 202) ....dep.	..	..	..	..	..	..	1011	1210	..	..	..	20 4	2318	5 40
Ceklis c ....arr.	..	..	..	..	..		1019	1224	..	..		2018	2326	5 52
Ceklis ....dep.		..	..	..	..	..	1039	1244	..	..	..	2038	2351	6 12
Bratislava................arr.		..	..	..	..	..	1057	1312	..	..	..	2113	0 9	6 36
							1 2 3	1 2 3					1 2 3	
Bratislava.................dep.	From Bogumin.	From Bogumin.	..	6 0	From Bogumin.	6 15	11 6	1413	From Bogumin.	1851	1915	2132	0 25	..
Kuty .... „			..	..		7 55	1157	1526		..	21 1	2257	1 23	..
Lundenburg .... arr.				..		..	..	..		..	..	arr.	..	..
dep.			..	..			..	..		..	..	..	..	..
Brno .... arr.			..	7 26		9 41	13 2	1635		..	2240	..	2 32	
dep.			6 5	7 29		1041	13 6	1645		2022	2310	..	2 52	..
Blansko (Caves) .... „			6 29	..		1122	..	1711		..	2359	..	..	..
Blansko .... „	..	..	..	..	..	..	..	..	..	..	0 2	..	..	..
Ceska Trebova .... „	4 34	5 28	7 41	..	9 8	1316	1427	1820	1851	..	3 9	..	4 19	..
Pardubice ....arr.	5 21	6 21	8 32	..	9 59	1444	..	10 8	1944		4 17	..	5 13	..
Praha (Mas.) .... „	..	..	..	..	..	1726	1636	R	..	2313	6 38	..	6 45	..
Praha (Wilson) .... „	6 53	7 56	10 3	1018	1130		R	2040	2119		..	..		

M Motor-Rail Service, 2nd cl. only. SS 2 & 3 cl. Sleeping Car Bratislava to Budapest & v.v.

Praha—Zilina—Bogumin—Cracow (Warsaw)—Berlin

[German and Polish Railways.

1 2 3 Exp	1 2 3 Exp	1 2 3 Exp	1 2 3 Exp	1 2 3 Exp	1 2 3 Exp	1 2 3 Exp	1 2 Exp	Mls		1 2 3 Exp	1 2 3 Exp	1 2 3 Exp	1 2 3 Exp	1 2 3 Exp	1 2 3 Exp	1 2 3 Exp	2 3
9 15	From Vienna.	1442	From Vienna.	1837	2138	..	23 3	0	dep. Praha (Wil).. arr.	6 53	..	7 56	1130	.	..	2119	..
..		..			..	From Vienna.	S	..	dep. Praha (Mas) arr.	S	To Vienna.		..	To Vienna.	To Vienna.	..	6 38
1143		1710		21 6	0 2		1 25	102	a. Ceska Trebova (abv)	4 34		5 28	9 8			1851	3 9
1259		1821		2236	1 17		2 42	156	arr. } Olomouc { dep.	3 1		4 11	7 54			1732	0 54
13 1		1823		2237	1 19		2 44		dep. } Olomouc { arr.	2 59		4 9	7 52			1730	0 37
1319	1322	1841	1845	2256	1 37	3 5	3 4	171	arr. } Prerov dep.	2 36	2 56	3 50	7 34	7 35	1659	1711	0 10
1329	1335	19 0	19 0	2328	1 45	3 10	3 18		dep. } (p. 203) arr.	2 22	2 51	3 42	7 25	7 25	1654	1654	2350
1357	14 1	1929	929	0 5	2 13	3 38	3 46	189	arr. Hranice ....dep.	1 59	2 27	3 19	7 2	7 2	1632	1632	2316
14 5	↓	..		..	2 14	..	3 5	..	dep. Hranice ... arr.	1 40		3 18	..	..	..	1625	..
1557			..	..	3 54	..	5 40	247	arr. Puchov n/V dep.	2354	..	1 38	..	..	..	1438	..
1645	▼	..	..		4 42	..	6 33	274	arr. Zilina ...... dep.	2312		0 52		..	..	1354	..
14 2	14 2	1930	1930	..	..	3 39	3 47	..	dep. Hranice ....arr.	1 58	2 26		7 1	7 1	1631	1631	..
1522	1522	21 0	21 0	..	..	5 9	5 [illegible]	229	ar. Bogumin (p.203) dp.	0 30	1 10	..	5 30	5 30	1510	1510	..
1620	1620		2120	..	..		5 47		dp. Bogumin (p.203) ar.	2355		..	4 27			1357	..
1839	1839		..	..	..	..	8 8	327	arr. Cracow (p 203) dep	2135	..	..	..	..	..	1118	..
2322	2322	..	7 6	..	..		1222	477	arr. Warsaw (p 203) dp.	1652	..		22 4	..		7 28	..
1540	..	2110	..	..	..	..	5 27	..	dep. Bogumin.... arr.	..	1 0	..	4 10		..	1443	..
1817	..	24 0	..	..	..	..	8 3	..	arr. Breslau.....dep.	..	2218	..	1 17	..	..	1156	..
2254	..	7 18	..	..	..	..	1251	..	arr. Berlin (Fried) dep.	..	1727	..	2016	..	..	6 52	..

S 1, 2 & 3 cl. Sleeper Praha-Warsaw and v.v.

The times on the LEFT are to be read DOWNWARDS, those on the RIGHT UPWARDS.

Praha—Zilina—Kassa—Jasina.

1 2 3	1 2 3	1 2 3	1 2 3	2 3	1 2 3	2 3	Mls.		2 3	1 2 3	2 3	1 2 3	1 2 3	1 2 3
Exp	Exp	Exp	Exp		Exp					Exp		Exp	Exp	Exp
..	2138	23 3	..	..	9 15		..	dep. Praha (W) *p.*207 arr.	..	2119	..	6 53	7 56	..
..	4 42	6 33	..	..	1645		274	arr. Zilina ....dep.	..	1354	..	2312	0 52	..
2 39	4 52	9 35	1310	1530	1710	0 12	0	dep. Zilina .... arr.	1357	1330	1733	1720	0 42	3 44
3 11	5 13	9 56	1332	1610	1730	0 57	12	,, Vrutky .... ,,	1235	13 7	1636	1658	0 20	3 10
5 8	7 7	1154	1528	19 5	1920	3 43	62	,, Strba ....dep.	9 36	1127	1356	1524	2248	1 28
5 25	7 23	1210	1544	1930	1936	4 5	74	ar. } Poprad-Velka { ,,	9 0	11 0	1320	1454	2216	0 58
5 28	7 27	..	1552	1952	1946	4 20		dp. } Poprad-Velka { arr.	8 47	1050	13 9	1447	2213	0 55
7 10	9 7	..	1734	2217	2134	6 49		arr. } Kysak...... { dep.	5 55	8 44	1025	13 0	2015	23 8
7 20	9 15	..	1750	2227	2142	7 2	133	dep. } Kysak...... { arr.	5 43	8 34	1013	1247	1957	2255
7 42	9 37	..	1812	2250	22 4	7 30	144	arr. Presov ......dep.	5 10	8 12	9 42	1225	1935	2233
7 16	9 17	..	1743	..	2144	7 3	..	dep. Kysak .... arr.	5 40	8 30	1020	1244	20 5	2253
7 24	9 25	..	1751	..	2152	7 13	137	arr. Kostolany *c* ....dep.	5 30	8 22	10 9	1236	1957	2245
..	9 57	..	1822	..	2217	..	142	,, } Kassa *c* .. { ,,	..	7 50	..	12 6	1920	..
..	..	..	..	..	..	..		dep. } Kassa *c* { arr.	..	..	..	..	..	..
..	..	..	..	..	..		209	arr. Csap (*p.* 202) . dep.	..	..	..	..	..	..
..	..	..	..	..	..		247	,, } Tiszaujlak *c* { ,,	..	..	..	..	..	..
..	..	..	..	..	..	..	..	dep. } Tiszaujlak *c* { arr.	..	..	..	..	..	..
..	..	..	..	..	..		255	arr. Sevlus ....dep.	..	..	..	..	..	..
..	..	..	..	..	..	..	261	,, Kralovo *c* .... ,,	..	..	..	..	..	..
..	..	..	..	..	..	..	272	,, Chust .... ,,	..	..	..	..	..	..
..	..	..	..	..			320	,, } Valea Visului *c* { ,,	..	..	..	..	..	..
..	..	..	..	..	..	..		dep. } Valea Visului *c* { arr.	..	..	..	..	..	..
..	..	..	..	..		..	350	arr. Jasina ...... dep.	..	..	..	..	..	..

Zilina—Cadca—Bogumin.

3 cl.	3 cl.	1 2 3	2 3	2 3	3 cl.	1 2 3	Mls.		2 3	1 2 3	2 3	3 cl.	3 cl.	3 cl.	1 2 3	2 3
		Exp				Exp				Exp					Exp	
..	6 5	9 42	..	1338	..	1836	0	dep. Bratislava .... arr.	..	1048	1325	..	1656	..	2044	..
..	..	7 † 5	..	..	..	1525	..	,, Budapest (*p.*202) ,,	..	1410	..	..	..	..	23†31	..
7 32	1030	1318	1415	1823	2316	23 9	127	,, Zilina .... ,,	6 28	6 57	7 34	9 8	1216	1434	17 8	18 5
8 16	1116	1344	1457	19 8	2359	2336	145	arr. } Cadca *c*.... { dep.	5 45	6 30	6 48	8 26	1135	1352	1643	1720
..	..	1411	..	..	..	0 5		dep. } Cadca *c* { arr.	..	6 3	..	..	..	..	1621	..
..	..	1529	..	..	..	1 2	189	arr. Bogumin *c*.... dep.	..	4 44	..	..	..	..	15 2	..
..	..	2254	..	..	..	9 18	..	,, Berlin *p.* 204 ,,	..	2016	..	..	..	..	6 52	..

† *via* Leopoldov, *see below.*

(Budapest) Galanta—Leopoldov—Zilina.

3 cl.	1 2 3	3 cl.	3 cl.	3 cl.		3 cl.	3 cl.	3 cl.	3 cl.	3 cl.	1 2 3
	Exp										Exp
..	7 5	..	8 50	..	dep. Budapest (W).. arr.	..	1431	..	..	..	2331
..	9 27	..	1448	..	arr. } Galanta *c*.. { dep.	..	10 0	..	..	..	2112
8 24	9 51	..	15 8	2126	dep. } Galanta *c* { arr.	..	9 14	1348	..	1843	2042
8 31	9 58	..	1516	2133	arr. } Gan *c* .... { dep.	..	9 7	1341	..	1836	2034
8 51	1018	1356	1536	2153	dep. } Gan *c* { arr.	6 55	8 50	1321	1657	1816	2014
8 59	1025	14 4	1545	22 2	arr. Sered .... arr.	6 46	8 41	1312	1648	18 7	20 6
9 22	1043	1427	16 8	2226	,, Leopoldov (*p.*207) dp.	6 25	8 17	1250	1626	1745	1950
1012	11 8	1458	1639	2258	,, Piestany ...... ,,	6 5	7 50	11 6	1534	17 6	1923
1353	13 0	1655	2010	..	,, Zilina .... ,,	4 0	4 32	7 50	1345	14 1	1735
..	1529	..	..		arr. Bogumin (*abv.*) dep.	..	..	..	..	..	15 1
..	2254	..	..	..	,, Berlin (F) *p.* 204 ,,	..	..	..	..	..	6 52

LITHUANIA, LATVIA and ESTONIA.

Cent. European time in Lithuania. East European time (2 hours in advance of Greenwich time), in Latvia and Estonia.

(Berlin) Tilsit—Memel Liepaja.

2 3		2 3
0 5	dep. Berlin (S) (p. 205) .... arr.	6 50
9 26	dep. Insterburg .... arr.	2117
10 6	arr. } Tilsit c .... { dep.	2036
1016	dep. } Tilsit c { arr.	2012
1148	arr. } Memel ....(C.E.T.) { dep.	1837
12 5	dep. } Memel { arr.	1812
1239	arr. Bajohren c .... dep.	1734
1710	arr. Priekule c ....(E.E.T.) dep.	1438
1725	dep. Priekule c .... arr.	1424
1818	arr. Liepaja (Libau)........ dep.	1330

Through 2 & 3 cl. Cars Berlin to Liepaja and *v.v.*, *via* Schneidemühl.
1, 2 & 3 cl. Sleeping Cars Berlin-Memel and *v.v.*

(Berlin) Riga—Valka—Tallinn.

2 3	2 3	2 3		2 3	2 3
9 4	..	0 5	dep. Berlin (S) p. 205 arr.	7 22	2044
R		S		R	S
8 20	1520	0 58	dep. Riga ..... arr.	1458	6 0
12 4	1851	4 0	arr. } Valka (L.) c { dep.	1215	2 22
1240	1935	4 15	dep. } Valka (L.) c { arr.	1157	2 8
1250	1948	4 23	arr. } Valka (E.) c { dep.	1151	2 2
1315	2045	4 32	dep. } Valka (E.) c { arr.	1145	2 0
15 0	2335	6 0	dep. Tartu ...... dep.	1020	0 41
1722	..	8 0	dep. Tapa .... dep.	8 9	2244
1825	6 30	9 10	arr. Tallinn (Reval) dep.	6 40	21 0

S 1, 2 and 3 cl. Sleep. Cars Riga-Tallinn and Zemgale-Riga-Tallinn and *v.v.*
R Rest. Car Riga-Tallinn and *v.v.*

Berlin—Tilsit—Moscow.

2 3		2 3
ExS		ExS
0 5	dep. Berlin (S) p. 205 .... arr.	6 50
10 6	arr. } Tilsit .... { dep.	2036
1029	dep. } Tilsit { arr.	2026
11 2	arr. Langszargen ...... dep.	1952
1343	dep. Radviliskis .... dep.	1712
1620	arr. } Obeliai c .... { dep.	1417
1630	dep. } ,, (C.E.T.) { arr.	14 0
18 0	arr. } Daugavpils { dep.	1335
1927	dep. } (E.E.T.) { arr.	13 5
21 0	arr. } Indra c .... { dep.	1142
2135	dep. } Indra c { arr.	1120
2315	arr. } Bigosovo .... { dep.	1038
0 35	dep. } Bigosovo { arr.	1040
1440	arr. Moscow (p. 230) ... dep.	2030

S 1 & 2 cl sleeping car Berlin-Daugavpils and *v.v.*
Rest. Car Laugszargen-Daugavpils and *v.v.*

Liepaja—Skrunda—Riga.

2 3	2 3	2 3		2 3	2 3	2 3
		S				S
6 0	1647	2125	dep. Liepaja........ arr.	1147	21 5	8 25
7 28	1820	1 33	dep. Skrunda ......dep.	1022	1936	4 54
8 7	19 2	3 14	dep. Saldus ....dep.	9 47	19 0	3 30
9 13	20 6	4 58	dep. Dobele .... dep.	8 37	1750	1 29
9 46	2040	5 45	arr. Jelgava........dep.	8 0	1713	0 36
1021	2118	6 50	arr. Riga ..... dep.	7 20	1635	2320

S Sleeping Cars.

Wirballen—Riga.

1 2 3	1 2 3	2 3		1 2 3	2 3	1 2 3
9 4	0 5	2316	dp. Berlin S (p. 205) ar.	2044	7 22	6 50
S	R	SR		S	SR	R
1843	¶	10 7	dp. Wirballen c .... ar.	1058	2020	¶
1949		112	ar. } Kaunas ....dp.	9 45	1918	
1954	..	1130	dp. } Kovno .... ar.	9 39	19 5	
2133	1344	1344	dp. Radviliskis .... ar.	7 52	1658	1658
2221	1454	1454	ar. Joniskis c .. dp.	6 50	16 0	16 0
2226	1459	1459	dp. ,, (C.E.T.) ar.	6 45	1555	1555
2340	1614	1614	ar. Meitene c dp.	7 27	1637	1637
2348	1634	1634	dp. Meitene c (E.E.T.) a.	7 20	1627	1627
0 9	17 0	17 0	ar. Jelgava ....dp.	6 59	16 0	16 0
0 43	1736	1736	ar. Riga .... dp.	6 25	1525	1525

R Rest. Car Wirballen Riga and *v.v.* ¶ *via* Tilsit.
S 1 & 2 cl. Sleep. Car Berlin-Riga and *v.v.*

Riga—Indra—Bigosovo Moscow.

2 3	3cl.		2 3	3cl.
1550	7 13	dep. Riga (p. 230) .... arr.	1759	2332
1927	1540	dep. Daugavpils .... dep.	1330	1952
21 0	1716	arr. Indra c .... dep.	1142	1755
2335	..	arr. Bigosovo c (p. 230) ..dep.	1050	..
1440	..	arr. Moscow . .. dep.	2030	

(Tallin) Riga—Zemgale

	S			S		
..	21 0	6 40	dep. Tallin (side) arr.	9 10	1825	..
0 20	7 13	1550	,, Riga .... arr.	2332	6 37	1759
4 40	12 2	1854	ar. } Daugavpils { dp.	1952	3 37	1330
4 59	1243	1915	ap. } Daugavpils { ar	1940	3 20	1311
5 29	1328	1951	dr. } Zemgale .. } dp	19 8	2 44	1237
6 2	14 0	2035	dp. } Zemgale } ar.	1840	2 17	1212
1342	2130	6 30	ar. Warsaw p. 227 dp.	9 24	17 8	0 16

S 1, 2 & 3 cl. Sleep. Car Tallin-Zemgale.

Riga—Ritupe.

2 3	2 3		2 3	2 3
	¶			¶
7 0	16 7	dep. Riga ....arr.	2118	7 25
11 8	2019	arr. } Gulbene .... { dep.	1717	3 24
1118	2029	dep. } Gulbene { arr.	17 7	3 10
1148	21 0	dep. Sita .... dep.	1639	2 46
1349	23 0	arr. Ritupe .... dep.	1420	2346
..	10 0	arr. Leningrad (p. 230) ..dep		1434

¶ 2 & 3 cl. thro' car Riga-Ritupe-Leningrad & *v.v.*

Kaunas—Warsaw.

1 2 3		1 2 3
S		S
2055	dep. Kaunas.. ....arr.	9 20
23 3	arr. } Landwarow c { dep.	7 31
2343	dep. } (p. 227) { arr.	7 9
6 30	arr. Warsaw (Gl.) ...... dep.	0 16

S 1, 2 and 3 cl. Sleeping Cars.

Tallinn—Leningrad.

1 2 3		1 2 3
2330	dep. Tallinn (Reval) ......arr.	6 30
3 25	arr. } Tapa .... { dep.	2 52
3 50	dep. } Tapa { arr.	2 10
4 58	dep. Rakvere ....dep.	1 8
8 45	dep. Narva c ....arr.	2145
11 0	dep. Kingisepp c...........arr.	21 0
1420	arr. Leningrad ....dep.	1740

GERMAN AND HUNGARIAN RIVER STEAMERS.

THE RHINE.

(See also *page* 210.)

COLOGNE-DUSSELDORF STEAMBOAT COMPANY.

	To Sept. 10th.											Sept. 11—Sept. 24.					
				F		E									F		
Cologne dep.	..	..	..	..	5 45	8 0	..	8 30	10 0	1415	1750	..	..	..	8 0	8 30	1415
Bonn ,,	..	..	5 0	6 30	8 10	1015	..	11 0	1230	1645	2020	..	..	8 10	1015	11 0	1645
Godesberg ,,	..	..	5 30	7 0	8 40	1045	..	1130	13 0	1715	2050	..	..	8 40	1045	1130	1715
Königswinter ,,	..	..	5 45	7 10	8 55	1055	..	1145	1315	1730	21 5	..	..	8 55	1055	1145	1730
Honnef ,,	..	..	6 5	7 30	9 15	↓	..	12 5	1335	1750	2125	..	B	9 15	..	12 5	1750
Rolandseck ,,	..	..	6 12	..	9 22	↓	..	1212	1342	1757	2132	..		9 22	..	1212	1757
Remagen ,,	..	..	6 45	8 3	9 50	↓	..	1240	1410	1825	2158	..	..	9 50	1140	1240	1825
Linz ,,	..	..	7 7	8 20	10 7	↓	..	1257	1427	1842	..	..	..	10 7	..	1257	1842
Andernach ,,	..	..	8 25	9 25	1125	↓	..	1415	1545	20 0	..	..	..	1125	..	1415	20 0
Neuwied ,,	..	..	8 46	9 45	1146	↓	..	1436	16 6	2021	..	..	..	1146	..	1436	2021
Coblence arr.	..	..	10 3	11 0	13 3	1430	..	1553	1720	2138	..	..	..	13 3	1430	1553	2138
Coblence dep.	..	7 30	1015	1110	1315	1435	1445	16 0	1730	..	..	1015	1215	1315	1435	16 0	..
Niederlahnstein ,,	..	7 54	1039	1130	1339	..	15 9	1624	1754	..	..	1039	1239	1339	..	1624	..
Boppard ,,	..	9 5	1150	1230	1450	1555	1620	1735	19 5	..	..	1150	1348	1450	1555	1735	..
St. Goar ,,	6 30	1011	1256	1325	1556	1650	1726	1841	2010	..	..	1256	1456	1556	165	1841	..
Bacharach ,,	7 23	1110	1354	1420	16 4	..	1824	1939	..	..	..	1354	1554	1654	1745	1939	..
Assmannshausen ,,	8 13	12 3	1445	15 5	1745	1830	1915	2030	..	..	..	1445	1645	1745	1830	2030	..
Bingen ,,	8 35	1230	1510	1530	1810	1855	1940	2055	..	..	..	1510	1710	1810	1855	2055	..
Rüdesheim ,,	8 45	1245	1525	1540	1825	19 5	1955	21 5	..	..	..	1525	1725	1825	19 5	21 5	..
Eltville ,,	9 55	14 2	1650	..	1942	..	2112	..	..	..	..	1642	1842	1942	20 5	..	..
Wiesb'n-Biebrich ,,	1035	1445	1735	1720	2025	2045	2155	..	..	..	..	1725	1925	2025	2045	..	..
Mainz arr.	1055	15 5	1755	1740	2045	21 5	2215	..	..	..	..	1745	1945	2045	21 5	..	..

	To Sept. 10th.											Sept. 11—Sept. 24.						
						E	G	F		F					F			
Mainz dep.	..	..	..	7 45	8 45	9 15	9 45	1030	11 0	13 0	1530	..	6 30	7 45	9 15	..	11 0	1430
Wiesb'n-Biebrich ,,	..	..	..	8 7	9 7	9 35	10 7	1050	1122	1320	1552	..	6 50	8 7	9 35	..	1122	1452
Eltville ,,	..	..	..	8 35	9 35	..	1035	1110	1150	1340	1620	..	..	8 35	9 55	..	1150	1520
Rüdesheim ,,	..	..	8 0	9 33	1033	1045	1133	12 0	1248	1430	1718	..	8 0	9 33	1045	..	1248	1618
Bingen ,,	..	..	8 15	9 45	1045	11 0	1145	1215	13 0	1440	1730	..	8 15	9 45	11 0	..	13 0	1630
Assmannshausen ,,	..	..	8 30	10 0	11 0	1115	12 0	1230	1315	1455	1745	..	8 30	10 0	1115	..	1315	1645
Bacharach ,,	..	..	8 58	1032	1132	..	1232	1255	1347	1520	1817	..	8 58	1032	1140	..	1347	1717
St. Goar ,,	..	..	..	1110	..	..	1310	1325	1430	1550	..	..	..	1110	1210	..	1430	..
Boppard ,,	..	..	1020	1155	1255	1235	1355	14 0	1515	1625	1945	..	1020	1155	1245	..	1515	1845
Niederlahnstein ,,	..	..	11 8	1238	1343	..	1443	1440	16 3	17 5	2033	..	11 8	1238	1325	..	16 3	1933
Coblence arr.	..	..	1125	1255	14 0	1325	15 0	1455	1620	1720	2050	..	1125	1255	1340	..	1620	1950
Coblence dep.	..	8 30	1130	13 0	..	1330	1515	15 5	1630	1730	..	8 30	..	13 0	1350	..	1630	..
Neuwied ,,	..	9 15	1215	1345	..	↓	16 0	1545	1715	1810	..	9 15	..	1345	..	..	1715	..
Andernach ,,	..	9 30	1230	14 0	..	↓	1615	16 0	1730	1825	..	9 30	..	14 0	..	..	1730	..
Linz ,,	8 15	1015	1315	1445	..	↓	1715	..	1815	19 5	..	1015	..	1445	..	1715	1815	..
Remagen ,,	8 30	1030	1330	15 0	..	↓	1730	1650	1830	1920	..	1030	..	15 0	1535	1730	1830	..
Rolandseck ,,	8 50	1050	1350	1520	..	↓	1750	..	1850	..	..	1050	..	1520	..	1750	1850	..
Honnef ,,	8 55	1055	1355	1525	..	↓	1755	..	1855	1945	..	1055	..	1525	..	1755	1855	..
Konigswinter ,,	9 10	1110	1410	1540	..	↓	1810	1720	1910	20 0	..	1110	..	1540	16 5	1810	1910	..
Godesberg ,,	9 20	1120	1420	1550	..	↓	1820	1730	1920	2010	..	1120		1550	1615	1820	1920	..
Bonn arr.	9 45	1145	1445	1615	..	1555	1845	1750	1945	2030	..	1145		1615	1635	1845	1945	..
Cologne ,,	1115	1315	1610	1745	..	1715	2015	1915	2115	2155	..	1315	..	1745	18 0	2015	2115	..

B Weekdays only Coblence-Boppard.

F Fast Service. **E** Express Service. **G** Suns. only.

a To Sept. 10.

Steamers on the Upper Elbe.

b May 27—Aug. 27-

a	*a*		*a*		*a*		*b*		↓		↑	*a*		*b*	*a*	*b*	*b*	[illegible]		*b*
..	6 30	8 0	10 0	11 0	1215	14 0	15 0	17 0		d. Dresden		8 15	11 5	1250	1415	17 0	8 0	19 0	20 0	2230
..	8 55	1025	1225	1320	1440	1625	1725	1920		Pirna		6 30	9 20	11 5	1230	1515	615	1715	1815	2045
7 50	1115	1240	1445	1535	7 0	1840	1940	..		Schandau		..	7 30	9 15	1035	1320	420	1520	1620	1850
10 0	1340	..	1710	..	1917	..	..	..		Tetschen		..	..	7 35	9 5	1140	..	1330	..	1725
10 5	1345	..	1715	..	1920	..	..	..		Bodenbach		..	..	7 30	8 58	1135	..	1323	..	1718
1245	1625	..	1955	..		..	..	..		a. Aussig		..	..	..	7 0	..	..	1115	..	1530
1625	1955	..	..	..	..	..	..	..		a. Leitmeritz		..	..	..	..	..	..	8 30	..	13 0

To October 22nd. **NETHERLANDS—RHINE S.S. COY.** SUMMER SERVICE.

Rotterdam	dep.	Mo. 8 0	Tue 8 0	We. 8 0	Thr 8 0	Fri. 8 0	Sat. 8 0	Sun 6 0
Nymegen	,,	..	..	,, 1515	..	,, 1515		,, 12 5
Arnhem	,,	,, 1545	,, 1545	..	,, 1545	..	,, 1545	..
Emmerich (M.E.T.)	arr	,, 1735	,, 1735	,, 17 5	,, 1735	,, 17 5	,, 1735	,, 14 0
	dep	,, 1915	,, 1915	,, 1915	,, 1915	,, 1915	,, 1915	,, 1615
Wesel	arr.	,, 22 0	,, 22 0	,, 22 0	,, 22 0	,, 22 0	,, 22 0	,, 1853
Wesel	dep	Tu. 3 0	We. 3 † 0	Thr 3 0	Fri. 3 0	Sat. 3 † 0	Sun 8 15	Mo. 3 0
Duisburg	,,	,, 6 15	,, 6 15	,, 6 15	,, 6 15	,, 6 15	,, 1135	,, 6 15
Dusseldorf	,,	,, 11 0	,, 11 0	,, 11 0	,, 11 0	,, 11 0	,, 1445	,, 11 0
Cologne	arr.	,, 1630	,, 1630	,, 1630	,, 1630	,, 1630	,, 2015	,, 1630
	dep.	,, 19 0	,, 19 0	,, 19 0	,, 19 0	,, 19 0	,, 2130	,, 19 0
Bonn	arr.	,, 2130	,, 21†30	,, 2130	,, 2130	,, 21†30	,, 24 0	,, 2130
Bonn	dep.	We. 5 0	Thr 5 0	Fri. 5 0	Sat 5 0	Sun 5 0	Mo. 5 0	Tue 5 0
Godesberg	,,	,, 5 30	,, 5 30	,, 5 30	,, 5 30	,, 5 30	,, 5 30	,, 5 30
Remagen	,,	,, 6 50	,, 6 50	,, 6 50	,, 6 50	,, 6 50	,, 6 50	,, 6 50
Andernach	,,	,, 8 35	,, 8 35	,, 8 35	,, 8 35	,, 8 25	,, 8 35	,, 8 35
Neuwied	,,	,, 9 0	,, 9 0	,, 9 0	,, 9 0	,, 8 46	,, 9 0	,, 9 0
Coblence	arr.	,, 1030	,, 1030	,, 1030	,, 1030	,, 10 3	,, 1030	,, 1030
	dep.	,, 11 0	,, 11 0	,, 11 0	,, 11 0	,, 1015	,, 11 0	,, 11 0
Boppard	dep.	,, 1250	,, 1250	,, 1250	,, 1250	,, 1150	,, 1250	,, 1250
St Goarhausen	,,	,, 14 0	,, 14 0	,, 14 0	,, 14 0	,, 1252	,, 14 0	,, 14 0
Bingen	,,	,, 1640	,, 1640	,, 1640	,, 1640	,, 1510	,, 1640	,, 1640
Rudesheim	,,	,, 1655	,, 1655	,, 1655	,, 1655	,, 1525	,, 1655	,, 1655
Eltville	,,	,, 18 8	,, 18 8	,, 18 8	,, 18 8	,, 1642	,, 18 8	,, 18 8
Wiesbaden-Biebrich	,,	,, 19 0	,, 19 0	,, 19 0	,, 19 0	,, 1725	,, 19 0	,, 19 0
Mainz	arr	,, 1930	,, 1930	,, 1930	,, 1930	,, 1745	,, 1930	,, 1930
	dep	Thr 6 0	Fri. 6 0	Sat. 6 0	Sun 18 0	Sun 18 0	Tue 6 0	We. 6 0
Mannheim	arr	,, 12 0	,, 12 0	,, 12 0	,, 23 0	,, 23 0	,, 12 0	,, 12 0

Mannheim	dep.	Mo. 5 0	Tue 5 0	We 5 0	Thu 5 0	Fri. 5 0	Sat. 5 § 0	Sat. 7 ¶ 0	Sun 7 0
Mainz	arr.	,, 9 20	,, 9 20	,, 9 20	,, 9 20	,, 9 20	,, 9 20	,, 1045	,, 1045
	dep	,, 10 0	,, 10 0	,, 10 0	,, 10 0	,, 10 0	,, 10 0	,, 11 0	,, 11 0
Wiesbaden-Biebrich	,,	,, 1150	,, 1150	,, 1150	,, 1150	,, 1150	,, 1150	,, 1122	,, 1122
Eltville	,,	,, 1215	,, 1215	,, 1215	,, 1215	,, 1215	,, 1215	,, 1150	,, 1150
Rudesheim	,,	,, 1315	,, 1315	,, 1315	,, 1315	,, 1315	,, 1315	,, 1248	,, 1248
Bingen	,,	,, 1330	,, 1330	,, 1330	,, 1330	,, 1330	,, 1330	,, 13 0	,, 13 0
St. Goarhausen	,,	,, 15 0	,, 15 0	,, 15 0	,, 15 0	,, 15 0	,, 15 0	..	..
Boppard	,,	,, 1545	,, 1545	,, 1545	,, 1545	,, 1545	,, 1545	,, 1515	,, 1515
Coblence	arr.	,, 17 0	,, 17 0	,, 17 0	,, 17 0	,, 17 0	,, 17 0	,, 1620	,, 1620
	dep.	,, 1730	,, 1730	,, 1730	,, 1730	,, 1730	,, 1730	,, 1630	,, 1630
Neuwied	,,	,, 1820	,, 1820	,, 1820	,, 1820	,, 1820	,, 1820	,, 1715	,, 1715
Andernach	,,	,, 1840	,, 1840	,, 1840	,, 1840	,, 1840	,, 1840	,, 1730	,, 1730
Remagen	,,	,, 1940	,, 1940	,, 1940	,, 1940	,, 1940	,, 1940	,, 1830	,, 1830
Godesberg	,,	,, 2040	,, 2040	,, 2040	,, 2040	,, 2040	,, 2040	,, 1920	,, 1920
Bonn	,,	,, 21 5	,, 21 5	,, 21 5	,, 21 5	,, 21 5	,, 21 5	,, 1945	,, 1945
Cologne	arr.	,, 2230	,, 2230	,, 2230	,, 2230	,, 2230	,, 2230	,, 2115	,, 2115
Cologne	dep.	Tue 7 0	We. 7 0	Thr 7 0	Fri. 7 0	Sat. 7 0	Sun 9 45		Mo. 7 0
Dusseldorf	,,	,, 1130	,, 1130	,, 1130	,, 1130	,, 1130	,, 1230		,, 1130
Duisburg	,,	,, 1340	,, 1340	,, 1340	,, 1340	,, 1340	,, 1415		,, 1340
Wessel	,,	,, 1620	,, 1620	,, 1620	,, 1620	,, 1620	,, 1655		,, 1620
Emmerich (M.E.T.)	arr.	,, 18 5	,, 18 5	,, 18 5	,, 18 5	,, 18 5	,, 1845		,, 18 5
	dep.	,, 19 0	,, 19 0	,, 19 0	,, 19 0	,, 19 0	,, 1930		,, 19 0
Arnhem	arr.	,, 2140	..	,, 2140		,, 21‡40	..		,, 2140
Nymegen	,,	..	,, ‡2140	..	,, 2140	..	,, 22 0		..
Arnhem or Nymegen	dep.	We. 8 0	Thu 8 0	Fri. 8 0	Sat. 8 0	Sun 8 0	Mo. 8 0		Tue 8 0
Rotterdam	arr.	,, 14 0	,, 13 0	,, 14 0	,, 13 0	,, 14 0	,, 13 0		,, 14 0

† Wesel dep. 5.0 from June 28—Sept. 9, arr. Bonn 24.0. ‡ arr. 22.0 from May 27—Sept. 9.
§ From Sept. 16. ¶ To S pt 9.

THE MOSELLE.

				Sats. only
Coblence	dep.	8 30	1430	
Cochem		1355	1945	
Alf (Bullay)		17 0	—	
Reil	dep.	1830	..	
Trarbach	arr.	1930	..	
Trarbach	dep.	..	8 0	
Berncastel	arr.	..	1010	9 15
Trier §	arr.	..	..	1445

			Suns only	
Trier §		8 0	..	..
Berncastel		1110	..	1115
Trarbach			..	13 0
Reil	dp.		..	1335
Alf (Bullay)			..	1455
Cochem	dp.		9 30	1655
Coblence	arr.		1235	20 0

THE MEUSE.

a	*b*				*b*	*a*
9 20	1420	dep.	Namur	arr.	1215	1715
1010	1510	,,	Tailfer	dep.	1130	1630
1115	1615	,,	Hun	,,	1025	1525
1145	645	,,	Houx	,,	9 50	1450
1230	1730	arr.	Dinant	,,	9 20	1420

a To Sept. 24. *b* To Sept. 3.

Mls.		a	b	f	e
..	**Passau** ....dep.	7 0	1510		
..	Engelhartszell	8 5	1615		
57	**Linz** ....arr.	1050	19 0		
		a		f	e
..	**Linz** ....dep.	1235		..	..
91	Grein	1440		..	..
..	Ybbs ....dep.	1535		1335	..
118	Melk	1630		1440	1515
139	Krems	1755		1650	1725
185	**Vienna** (Reichsbr.),arr.	2035		1950	2025
		k			
..	**Vienna** (Reichsbr.) dp.	8 30			
222	Bratislava (Pressburg)	1115			
..	Gönyü ....arr.	1425			
..	Györ (Raab) .. arr.	1830			
	Györ (Raab) .. dep.	1250			
..	Gönyü ....dep.	1435			
..	Esztergom (Gran)..arr.	1735			
310	**Budapest** ....arr.	21 0			

	m	b	h	c
Budapest........dep.	8 0			
Esztergom (Gran)....	1235			
Gönyü ....arr.	1645			
Györ (Raab).... arr.	1830			
Györ (Raab).... dep.	1250			
Gönyü ....dep.	1650			
Bratislava (P'sb'g) a.	2310			
Bratislava (P'sb'g) d.	1 0			
Vienna (Reichsbr)ar.	6 30			
	d		h	c
Vienna (Reichbr.)dep.	7 15		22 0	9 0
Krems	1315		4 45	1630
Melk............	1615		8 10	2010
Ybbs ....arr.	1810		1035	..
Grein	1945		..	..
Linz ....arr.	0 25		..	..
		b		
Linz ....dep.	8 0	6 0	..	..
Engelhartszell ..arr.	14 0	12 0	..	..
Passau ....arr.	1610	1410	..	..

a Daily to Sept. 3. *b* Suns. and Holidays, May 28–Sept. 3. *c* Fris. to Sept. 15. *d* Daily to Sept. 1. *e* Suns. to Sept. 17. *f* Daily to Sept. 17. *h* Daily to Sept. 16. *k* Suns. and Thurs. (also Tues. July 4–Aug. 29). *m* Suns. and Thur. (also Tues. July 11–Sept. 5).

Vienna, Budapest, Belgrade, Orsova, Turn-Severin, Giurgiu.

		Time. arr.	Time. dep.	Days.
Vienna (Reichsbr.) ..	Mid-Europ. time.	..	8 30	Tues. *k*
Bratislava		1045	1115	Thurs.
Budapest........		21 0	2315	Suns.
Mohacs		7 40	8 20	Wed. *k*
Bezdan		9 20	9 35	Fris.
Vukovar........		1330	1340	Mons.
Novi Sad		17 0	1720	
Belgrade		2045	2215	
Moldova........		5 0	5 20	
Orsova	E. Europ. time.	9 25	9 35	Thurs. *k*
Turn-Severin		1035	1045	Sats.
Widdin		16 5	1620	Tues.
Lom		1810	1840	
Orehovo........		2110	2120	
Giurgiu		5 5	5 35	Fris. *k*
Bucharest (*rail, p.* 330)		9 5	..	Suns.
Rousse		5 55	..	Weds.

k To Aug. 29.

		Time. arr.	Time. dep.	Days.
Bucharest (*rail, p.* 330)	E. Europn. time.	..	1810	Weds.
Giurgiu		..	22 0	Fris. *n*
Rousse........		2220	..	Suns.
Rousse........		..	0 10	Thurs.
Somovit		6 50	7 20	Sats. *n*
Lom		1515	1730	Mons.
Widdin........		2010	2115	
Turn Severin		5 5	5 25	Fris.
Orsova		9 15	9 25	Suns. *n*
Moldova	M. Europon. time.	1535	1545	Tues.
Belgrade		2230	..	
Belgrade		..	0 35	Sats.
Novi Sad		5 0	5 10	Mons. *n*
Vukovar		9 30	9 35	Weds.
Bezdan........		1425	1435	
Mohacs........		1545	17 0	
Budapest		5 0	8 0	Sun., Tue. *n*
Bratislava		2310	..	Thurs.
Bratislava		..	1 0	Mon., Wed. *n*
Vienna		6 30	..	Fris.

n To Sept. 1.

ROYAL HUNGARIAN CO.

Mon., Wed., Sat.				
8 30	dep. Vienna (Reichbr.) arr.	16 5	TuThSa	
1410	,, Gönyü .... dep.	3 50	,, ,, ,,	
21 0	arr. Budapest........ ,,	18 0	MoWeFr	
Daily				
22 0	dep. Budapest........ arr.	4 0	Daily	
8 30	arr. Mohacs.........dep.	1130	Daily	

ROYAL YUGOSLAV CO.

↓ Daily				↑ Daily
	Sat. 8 0	dep. Vienna (Reichbr.) arr.	Thu 1515	
	,, 2015	arr. Budapest ..... dep.	We. 18 0	
	,, 2115	dep. Budapest ...... arr.	,, 1445	
	Sun 5 30	arr. Mohacs ...... dep.	,, 2 25	
	,, 5 35	dep. Mohacs .... arr.	,, 2 5	
	,, 6 50	,, Bezdan .... dep.	,, 0 45	
	,, 1110	,, Vukovar........ ,,	Tue 1855	
	,, 15 0	,, Novi Sad........ ,,	,, 1355	
	,, 1850	,, Zemun. .... ,,	,, 9 0	
	,, 1910	arr. Belgrade ...... dep.	,, 8 30	
1430	,, 2130	dep. Belgrade ...... arr.	,, 4 30	4 30
1735	Mo. 0 5	,, Smederevo......dep.	,, 0 45	0 45
22 0	,, 3 40	arr. Golubac........dep.	Mo. 19 0	19 0
..	,, 4 0	dep. Golubac........ arr.	,, 1855	1855
..	Mo. 8 25	dep. Orsova .... dep	Tue 1220	1220
..	,, 9 30	arr. Turn Severin .. dep.	,, 9 40	3 35
..	,, 1425	arr. Radujevac......dep.	..	18 0

Black Forest Area.

Freiburg—Todtmoos.

7 40	1325	1715	1850	dp. Freiburg arr.	9 35	1425	1955
9 45	1530	..	2055	arr. Schonau arr.	..	1225	1755
..	..	1935	..	arr. Todtmoos dep.	7 0		..

Baden—Baden—Freudenstadt.

To Sept. 14.

7 0	8 55	1055	1345	16 0	d. Baden-Baden a.	1215	1441	1522	1745	1920
9 0	1135	13 0	1610	1820	a. Freudenstadt d.	9 10	1231	1314	1545	1710

Waldshut—St. Blasien.

9 45	1330	1830	2110	dp. Waldshut arr.	7 40	13 0	1520	2010
1055	1446	1955	2220	ar. St. Blasien dp	6 30	1155	1410	19 0

Heidelberg—Lucerne.

b	*a*	*a*		*c*	*c*	*b*
..	..	7 45	dep. Heidelberg ....arr.	2020	..	..
..	..	8 50	,, Carlsruhe ......arr.	1925	..	..
..	..	1040	arr. } Baden-Baden { dep.	18 0	..	..
..	..	11 0	dep. } Baden-Baden { arr.	1755	..	..
..	..	1410	dep. Freudenstadt ....arr.	1455	..	..
..	..	1550	arr. } Triberg .... { dep.	1315	..	..
..	..	1640	dep. } Triberg .... { arr.	1125		..
..	8 10	18 5	,, Titisee .... ,,	9 55	1915	
9 35	9 5		,, St. Blasien ...... ,,	..	1820	1750
1020		..	,, Waldshut ...... ,,	..	..	17 5
1120	..	..	,, Baden (Swiss).... ,,	..	..	16 5
12 5	..	..	,, Zurich .... ,,	..	..	1525
1310	..	..	arr. Lucerne ....dep.	..	..	1415

a July 1-Sept. 14. *b* Tu., Th. & Sa. July 4-Sept. 14. *c* July 2-Sept. 16.

Daily Motor Coach Service in connection with Rheingold Express.

			dep. Karlsruhe, (Hbf.) ......arr.			
			arr. Freudenstadt (Market P.) dep.			
			arr. ,, (Hbf.) ..dep.			

Schonau—St. Blasien.

a Wed., Sats. & Suns. only.

	a		*a*
11 0	2050	dep. Schonau arr.	7 15
1215	22 5	arr. St. Blasien dp	6 10

Frankfort—Baden-Baden.

a Via Mannheim.

7 0	12 0	dp. Frankfort arr.	1256	1859
7 28	1228	dp. Darmstadt dp.	1227	1831
8 8	*a*	dp. Heidelberg dp.	1150	*a*
8 54	1358	dp. Carlsruhe dep.	11 0	17 0
9 53	1453	ar. Baden Baden d	10 0	16 3

Also a departure from Baden-Baden at 20.15 due Frankfort 23.6.

Baden-Baden—Lindau.

July 1-Sept. 15.

..	7 0	dp. Baden-Baden a.	20 0	..
..	9 10	,, Freudenstadt a.	1755	..
.	12 0	a. { Freiburg { dp.	1515	
7 30		d. { Freiburg { ar.	..	20 0
9 30	..	a. } St. Blasien { d.	..	18 0
10 0	..	d. } St. Blasien { a.	..	1730
1330	..	arr. Constance dep.	..	14 0
17 0	..	arr. Lindau ..dep.	..	1030

Lindau—Oberstdorf.

7 30	17 0	dep. Lindau .. arr.	10 0	19 0
10 0	1930	arr. Oberstdorf dp.	7 30	1630

Harz District. Bad Harzburg—Braunlage.

† Suns. only.

8 25	9 30	11†10	12 0	1330	1510	1550	1910	dep. Bad Harzburg ......arr.	8 30	1020	1350	1525	1820	1920	20†30
9 31	1036	12†15	13 6	1436	1616	1656	2016	arr. Braunlage.........dep.	7 30	9 15	1235	1420	1718	1815	19†30

Braunlage—Schierke.

8 40	9 35	1035	1225	1430	1450	1710	1820	dep. Braunlage ....arr.	9 12	1030	1224	1310	1420	17 0	1755	1858
9 30	1030	1128	1320	1535	1540	1750	1910	arr. Schierke ....dep.	8 30	9 50	1145	1225	1350	1625	17 5	1810

Bavaria. Berchtesgaden—Hintersee.

6 0	8 25	9 20	11 5	1325	1515	18 5	2030	dep. Berchtesgaden ....arr.	7 30	9 55	11 6	1340	1540	1823	1941	2156
6 40	9 5	10 4	1149	14 9	1555	1850	2112	arr. Hintersee ....dep.	6 50	9 15	1025	13 0	15 0	1740	19 0	2115

Salzburg—Berchtesgaden—Lindau.

To Sept. 15.

..	7 0	dep. Salzburg ......arr.	..	19 5
..	7 50	,, Berchtesgaden .. ,,	..	1815
..	8 42	,, Bad Reichenhall ,,		1721
..	14 0	,, Tegernsee........ ,,	2115	1240
..	1535	,, Kochel .... ,,	1920	..
..	1645	,, Mittenwald ...... ,,	1810	..
..	1720	arr. } Garmisch .... { dep	1733	..
8 0		dep. } Garmisch .... { arr.	17 0	..
8 40	..	,, Oberammergau .. ,,	16 0	..
1056	..	,, Hohenschwangau ,,	13 4	..
1110	..	,, Fussen.......... ,,	1255	..
14 0	..	,, Oberstdorf ...... ,,	11 0	..
1440	..	,, Immenstadt .... ,,	9 55	..
1615	..	arr. Lindau ....dep.	8 15	..

Munich—Bad Tolz.

‡ Weekdays only.

7 35	1220	1810	dep. Munich ....arr.	8 40	13 0	19‡10
9 46	1431	2021	arr. Bad Tolz ..dep.	6 35	1050	17‡ 0

Munich—Tegernsee.

7 40	1310	1825	2335	dep. Munich ....arr.	7 50	1038	1653	2143
8 53	1423	1938	1 25	arr. Tegernsee ..dep.	6 0	9 25	1540	2030

Tegernsee—Scholastika.

7 45	1035	1340	1635	dep. Tegernsee.. arr.	1010	12 5	1755	1930
8 40	1130	1435	1720	dep. Glashutte.. arr	9 17	1110	1640	1840
9 15	1215	1510	1755	arr. Scholastika dep	8 40	1030	16 0	18 0

Munich—Vienna.

Daily Service.

7 0	dep. Munich ....arr.	1815
9 55	dep. Salzburg ..arr.	1530
1815	arr. Vienna ....dep.	7 0

MOTOR COACH SERVICES IN GERMANY—*continued*

Bavaria (*continued*) and Tyrol.

Oberammergau—Garmisch—Partenkirchen.

a Sundays only. *b* Weekdays only. *c* To Aug. 31.

										a	*b*	*c*
Oberammergau........dep	7 15	8 22	1030	1220	1245	1450	1658	1756	1815	19 0	1930	2055
Oberau..............arr.	7 51	8 44	11 0	1256	1321	1526	1734	1818	1851	1936	20 6	2125
Garmisch-Partenkirchen ar.	8 13	9 0	1120	..	1343	1548	1756	1834	1913	1958	2028	2147
												c
Garmisch-Partenkirchen dp	7 5	7 40	9 25	1014	..	1350	1510	17 0	1710	19 0	2030	2337
Oberau .... dp	7 25	8 0	9 50	1037	1327	1413	1537	1717	1733	1924	2049	2359
Oberammergau.... ..arr.	8 0	8 21	1025	1111	14 2	1448	1610	1739	18 8	20 0	2118	0 23

Oberammergau—Linderhof.

To Sept. 15.

8 15	9 50	1440	1730	d. Oberammergau a	7 44	1239	1459	1819
8 32	1010	1458	1751	dep. Ettal ....arr.	7 27	1222	1442	18 2
8 54	1032	1520	1813	arr. Linderhof dep.	7 5	12 0	1420	1740

Garmisch-Part.—Fussen.

7 40	17 0	d. Garmisch-Prt. a	9 0	1834
8 2	1742	a. Oberammergau a	8 22	1756
9 57	1913	ar. Fussen.. dep.	6 45	1620

Tegernsee—Garmisch-Partenkirchen.

To Sept. 15.

6 40	1340	14 0	1640	dep. Tegernsee arr.	11 5	1140	16 0	2115
7 40	1440	15 0	1732	,, Bad Tolz ,,	1022	1045	15 0	2015
8 31	1530	1535	1815	,, Kochel .. ,,	9 39	1011	14 5	1921
9 10	1615	..	..	,, Walchensee ,,	8 58	..	1318	1847
9 50	17 0	1645	1931	,, Mittenwald ,,	8 21	8 46	1235	1810
1028	..	1720	20 5	arr. Garmisch-Pt. d	7 50	8 15	..	1733

Tegernsee—Kufstein.

To Sept. 20.

8 0	1635	dep. Tegernsee arr	1025
1015	19 0	arr. Kufstein dep.	8 0

Munich—Berchtesgaden.

8 40	dp Munich....arr.	1950
1138	a. Berchtesgaden d	1655

Munich—St. Moritz.

To Sept. 15.

8 0	dep. Munich ......arr.	19 0
11 0	,, Garmisch-Part. ,,	1540
1340	,, Imst.......... ,,	1355
1420	,, Landeck ...... ,,	1215
17 0	,, Schuls ...... ,,	1010
1755	,, Zernez ...... ,,	9 10
1915	arr. St. Moritz ....dep.	7 30

Fussen—Reutte.

6 30	8 20	1220	1617	1930	dep. Fussen arr.	7 40	9 55	1335	1745	2115
7 0	9 0	1255	1655	2010	arr. Reutte dep.	7 10	9 15	13 0	17 5	2030

Kochel—Murnau.

a To Aug. 31.

	a		*a*					*a*		*a*
8 0	1010	1215	1530	1825	dep. Kochel ..arr	6 50	1056	14 0	1755	2058
8 45	1052	1259	1610	19 8	arr. Murnau dep	6 5	1012	1320	1710	2012

Langen—Zurs—Lech.

9 25	1410	1655	1910	dep. Langen ....arr.	7 50	1235	1345	18 0
10 5	1445	1735	1945	arr. Zurs ......dep.	7 9	1154	1313	1728
1025	15 3	1755	20 3	arr. Lech ......dep.	6 45	1130	1255	1710

Oetzthal—Obergurgl.

a To Sept. 20.

a		*a*	*a*		*a*		*a*				*a*		*a*		*a*		*a*	
6 15	8 0	1125	13 0	1435	1540	1650	18 0	1850	dep. Oetzthal....arr.	7 35	9 5	1045	1215	1345	15 5	1625	1745	2015
8 20	10 5	1330	1455	1640	1745	1855	20 5	2055	arr. Zweiselstein dp.	5 30	7 0	8 40	1010	1140	13 0	1420	1540	1810
9 0	1055	1420	..	1725	..	1950	..	..	arr. Obergurgl..dep.	..	6 10	..	9 10	..	12 0	..	1450	..

Lienz—Heiligenblut—Zell-am-See. Grossglockner Road (101 Klms.)

a	*b*	*b*	*c*	*a*	*c*	*c*	*c*	*c*		*c*	*a*	*a*		*c*	*b*	*b*	*a*
7 25	7 55	8 0	..	8 50	..	1010	13 0	1610	dep. Lienz ....arr.	1324	1530	..	1735	18 5	19 0	1855	2045
8 15	8 45	8 50	9 27	9 35	1018	1057	1345	17 5	,, Winklern...... ,,	1243	1445	..	1650	1720	1814	1813	20 5
9 40	9 40	9 45	1045	1055	12 0	1220	1445	18 5	,, Heiligenblut .. ,,	1155	1355	—	16 5	1630	1730	1730	1915
..	1040	11 0	1220	1355	1430	1445	16 0	19 5	,, Franz-J. Hohe ,,	1045	12 0	1145	1445	15 0	16 0	1620	18 0
1015	1145	1130	1255	1425	15 1	1520	1630	..	,, Guttal Post.... ,,	9 5	1036	1115	1220	1230	1430	1510	1646
1110	13 5	1235	1415	1540	1650	1640	1725	..	,, Fuschertorl.... ,,	8 10	9 45	1025	1130	1135	1340	1420	1555
..	1450	1436	1545	17 6	..	18 6	1855	..	,, Bruck .... ,,	6 30	7 40	..	..	9 35	..	1145	1355
..	15 0	1450	16 0	1720	1810	1820	1910	..	arr. Zell-am-See..dep.	6 10	7 20	8 5	9 35	9 10	11 0	1120	1330
..	1855	..	..	..	..	..	..	..	,, Munich .... ,,	..	..	..	..	..	7 0	..	..
..	..	1730	1950	..	2050	..	..	..	,, Salzburg ..... ,,	..	..	..	6 50	..	..	8 20	..

a To Oct. 7. *b* To Sept. 15. *c* To Sept. 18.

Trains run in Denmark, Norway and Sweden by Mid-European time, 1 hr. fast of Greenwich.

CLASSES : Only two classes on Danish trains, First class and General class. International trains have 1, 2 & 3 class cars.

There are numerous trains designated "Lyntog" (Lightning Trains) marked **L** in the following tables which have limited accommodation. Seats must be reserved in advance, supplementary charges.

Copenhagen—Fredericia—Esbjerg—Struer.

Mls		*w*			L		L						S	
0	Copenhagen (*p.* 215)..dep.	1 30	..	..	7 50	9 15	1230	..	..	17†52	2050	..	2340	2340
112	Odense ....dep.	6 9	8 15	..	1058	1313	..	1548	17 20	20†56	0 57	..	4 3	4 3
..	Aarhus ....dep.	5 0	8†30	8 40	..	1215	..	..	17†40	19 15	0 4	..	..	
152	Fredericia (*p.* 215) ..dep.	8 14	9 45	1111	1136	1439	1554	1728	19 40	22 0	2 11	3 22	5 13	5 34
165	Kolding ....arr.	8 41	10 6	1141	1150	15 3	16 9	1754	20 4	22 18	2 28	..	5 40	5 54
173	Lunderskov ....arr.	8 59	1022	1232	..	1523	..	1817	20 21	22 33	..	4 0	6 5	6 15
198	Bramminge ....arr.	9 58	11 6	1355	1227	1616	..	1921	21 6	23 16	..	5 32	7 12	7 12
208	Esbjerg ....arr.	1023	1124	1426	1240	1638	1655	1947	21 26	23 34	3 20	6 17	7 37	7 37
..	Esbjerg ....dep.	..	1136	1431	1243	17 0		20 8	..	23 44	3 27	6 42		7 55
246	Skern ....dep.	..	1241	1557	1332	1822	..	2128	..	0 45	4 24	8 4	..	9 31
261	Ringkobing ....arr.	..	13 6	1625	1350	1854	..	2156	..	1 10	4 46	8 34	..	1022
290	Holstebro ....arr.	..	1357	1731	1439	1956	..	2258	..	..	5 34	9 26	..	1143
300	Struer ....arr.	..	1411	1752	1457	2016	..	2317	..	..	5 52	9 45	..	1210

w Weekdays only. **L** See note above. **S** 1, 2 and 3 cl. Sleeping Car Copenhagen to Esbjerg.
† Connection by "Lyntog" Express.

Struer—Esbjerg—Fredericia—Copenhagen.

				¶			L	L		*w*	S
Struer ....dep.	..	6 30	8 21	9 *w* 0	1211	14 25	..	16 8	..	18 4	2030
Holstebro ....dep.	..	6 48	8 46	9 *w* 46	1232	14 42	..	1625	..	1835	2055
Ringkobing ....dep.	5 47	7 42	9 48	11 *w* 25	1351	15 30	..	1728	..	1954	22 1
Skern ....dep.	6 15	8 12	1028	12 21	1422	15 57	..	1747	..	2036	2236
Esbjerg ....arr.	7 25	9 18	1153	14 15	1537	16 59	..	1838	..	2210	0 3
Esbjerg ....dep.	7 36	9 28	12 7	14 23	1548	17 10	1815	1843	19 0	2225	0 15
Bramminge ....dep.	7 55	9 43	1223	14 45	16 3	17 28	..	1855	19 22	2259	0 35
Lunderskov ....dep.	8 43	1024	1325	15 38	1654	18 10	..	..	20 17	2358	1 14
Kolding ....arr.	8 54	1036	1339	15 54	17 4	18 22	..	1934	20 31	0 13	1 30
Fredericia (*p.* 215)....arr.	9 17	1059	14 5	16 23	1723	18 45	1915	1950	20 59	0 40	1 52
Aarhus ....arr.	1110	12†20	1624	20 3	20 3	21 *w* 56	..	..	22†37	..	4 12
Odense ....arr.	10†9	1240	1537	17 39	19 7	19†46	1956	2034	22 44	..	3 36
Copenhagen (*p.* 215)..arr.	13†20	..	1927	21 40	..	22†57	2249	2346	5 58	..	7 50

¶ 2 and 3 cl. Cars Esbjerg—Copenhagen. *w* Weekdays only. **S** 1, 2 and 3 cl. Sleeping Car Esbjerg—Copenhagen. † Connection by "Lyntog" Express.

† Weekdays only.

Tommerup—Assens—Aarosund.

5†11	7 10	8 56	11 2	1313	14 0	1611	1840	22†0	dep. Odense *abv.* ....arr.	7 48	1118	1353	1448	16 7	1739	2020
5 38	7 41	9 27	1131	1335	1437	1641	1910	22†28	dep. Tommerup *p.* 216 ar.	7 25	1054	1319	1418	1540	1719	1955
6 26	8 33	1022	1218	1428	1530	1733	2011	23†20	arr. Assens........dep.	6 34	9 53	1225	1318	1438	1626	19 0
6 45	..	1025	1230	1450	1655	..	2015	..	dep. Assens } *ferry* arr.	..	8 40	1220	..	1425	..	1850
7 40		1120	1325	1545	1750	..	2110	..	arr. Aarosund } *ferry* dep.	..	7 45	1125	..	1330	..	1755

(Berlin) Warnemunde—Gedser—Copenhagen.

				128			123				123						123
	Exp			Exp		Exp	Exp				Exp					Exp	Exp
w			*w*	† *r*	*w*		¶		*w*		† *r*		*w*				¶
..	..	..	..	8 42	..	..	2132	dp. Berlin (*see p.* 204) a	..	..	1955	..	..	..	..	..	7 21
..	..	..	..	8 54	..	..	2150	dp. Hamburg (*p.* 162) a	..	..	1943	..	..	..	..	..	7 6
..	..	..	..	1240	..	..	1 25	dep. Warnemünde ar.	..	..	16 5	..	..	..	..	..	3 40
..	..	..	..	1440	..	..	3 35	arr. Gedser (*ferry*) dp	..	..	14 5	..	..	..	..	..	1 40
..	6 25	..	9 42	15 2	1520	19 5	4 4	dep. Gedser (*rail*) ar.	arr.	1112	1341	1743	2220	2220	arr.	0 15	1 11
5 25	7 15	6 36	11 7	1529	1623	2012	4 33	dep. Nykobing ..dep.	9 53	1040	1320	1710	2140	2140	2240	2345	0 50
5 48	7 43	7 17	1134	1559	1711	2044	..	dep. Vordingborg dep.	9 1	9 59	1253	1520	1940	1931	2155	23 2	0 24
8 1	9 20	9 31	..	..	2029	2217	..	dep. Roskilde ..dep.	6 49	8 36	..	1311	1655	..	19 8	2135	..
8 37	9 50	10 3	13 3	1735	21 4	2244	6 48	arr. Copenhagen dp	6 4	8 3	1115	1238	1611	1756	1820	21 0	2245

† 1, 2 & 3 cl. thro' cars Berlin and Hamburg to Copenhagen and *v.v.* ¶ 1 & 2 cl. Sleeping Cars Berlin and Hamburg to Copenhagen and *v.v.*, also 1, 2 & 3 cl. thro' cars Hamburg-Copenhagen and *v.v.* *r* Rest. Car Copenhagen–Gjedser & *v.v.* *w* Weekdays only.

COPENHAGEN—ELSINORE. A frequent service of trains to and from Elsinore both *via* Rungsted and Hillerod in 65 to 70 minutes. Express trains (in 46 minutes) shewn on page 217.

Copenhagen, Nyborg, Fredericia.

Mls		†		L	L	L		S		L				L	L			Z
0	Copenhagen d.	1 30	..	7 35	7 50	8 0	8 20	9 15	1032	1230	..	1440	16 0	1740	1752	1840	2050	2340
20	Roskilde.. arr.	..	..	7 56	..		8 52	..	11 5		..	15 8	1638	1811		1919	2123	0 13
40	Ringsted arr.	..	..	..	..		9 30	..	1148		..	1535	1726	..		20 3	2152	0 42
69	Korsor.. arr.	2 47	..	8 45	8 58		1019	1049	13 0		..	1621	1841	19 0		21 8	2242	1 34
	Korsor dep. (ferry)	2 56	..	8 49	9 10		1028	11 0	..		14 47	1630	..	19 9		2117	2253	1 53
94	Nyborg arr.	4 11	..	9 59	1020		1141	1215	..		16 0	1743	..	2022		2235	0 6	3 8
94	Nyborg.. dep.	4 31	7 5	10 4	1030		..	1237	..		16 20	18 2	..	2032		2255	0 26	3 32
112	Odense.. dep.	4 59	8 15	1025	1053		..	1313	..		17 20	1835	..	2056		2335	0 57	4 3
122	Tommerup arr. (p. 214)	..	8 33	..	..		..	1331	..	↓	17 43	arr.	..	..	↓	0 3	..	..
152	Fredericia arr.	5 51	9 15	11 2	1133		..	1415	..	1551	18 54	..	..	2137	2122	1 8	1 53	4 59
..	Hamburg arr.	..	..	19† 9	19† 9		..	21 2	..	0 4	..	..	..	..	..	..	7 45	14 7
..	Esbjerg.. arr. (p. 214)	..	1124	..	1240	↓	..	1638	..	1655	21 26	..	..	2334	2334	..	3 20	7 37
	Aarhus.. arr.	8 51	1110	1220	14 8	1230	..	1624	..	..	21†56	..	..	23 0	2237	..	4 12	7 28

Fredericia, Nyborg, Copenhagen.

	Z					L	L		S		X	L	L	L	L		
Aarhus dp.	0 4	..	..	..	5 0	8 5	8 30	..	1215	..	1310	17 40	..	19 0	..	19 6	1915
Esbjerg dp.	0 15	..	..	..	..	7 36	7 36	..	12 7	..	1423	17 10	1815		1843	19 0	19 0
Hamburg d	2136	..	..	..	..	..	..	..	8 25	..	..	11†17	..		..	13†9	13†9
Fredericia d.	2 28	..	..	6 15	8 0	9 29	9 44	9 50	1439	1531	1637	19 5	1920		1954	2120	2214
Tommerup d (p. 214)	..	..	..	7 29	9 7	..		11 0	..	1641	1724	..	..		..	2226	2329
Odense dep.	3 40	..	5 10	7 55	9 32	1011		1135	1542	1659	1744	19 48	1958		2036	2250	2358
Nyborg arr.	4 10	..	5 48	8 33	1010	1032		1215	16 8	1747	18 9	20 8	..		2056	2328	0 26
Nyborg arr. (Ferry Stn)	4 14	..	5 51	8 42	1014	..		1222	1613	..	1813	..	..		..	..	0 34
Nyborg dep. (ferry)	4 32	..	6 0	8 49	..	1042		1233	1627	..	1823	20 20	..	↓	21 9	..	0 55
Korsor arr.	5 47	..	7 10	10 2	..	1155		1351	1740		1938	21 33	2133	2222	2222	..	2 8
												a	*a*	*a*	*a*		
Korsor dep.	6 16	6 29	7 22	1014	..	12 7		14 3	1746	1756	1951	21 44	..	..	2234	..	3 12
Ringsted ar.	..	7 38	8 33	11 5	..	..		1453	..	..	2042	..	..	..	..	..	4 19
Roskilde ar.	..	8 19	9 4	1131	..	1257	↓	1523	1854	..	21 9	22 34	..	..	2324	..	5 5
Cop'h'g'n a.	7 50	9 3	9 45	12 0	..	1320	13 7	1556	1927	1937	2140	22 57	2249	2335	2346	..	5 58

L Lyntog Exp.—See Note, p. 214. † Weekdays only. **S** 1 & 2 cl. Sleeping Cars Copenhagen to Paris and *v.v.* ‡ Connection by "L" Train. ¶ 1, 2 & 3 cl. Sleep. Car Copenhagen-Hamburg and *v.v.*, and 2 & 3 cl. cars Copenhagen-Frederikshavn. **Z** 1, 2 & 3 cl. Sleep. Cars Copenhagen to Aalborg and Esbjerg, and 2 & 3 cl. cars Copenhagen-Frederikshavn and *v.v.* **X** 2 & 3 cl. cars Esbjerg to Copenhagen. *a* The times of these services Korsor to Copenhagen are altered on Sundays and Fete Days, and made a few minutes later.

(Copenhagen) Fredericia, Padborg (Hamburg).

Exp				Exp	Exp N				Mls.				Exp N	Exp					Exp
2050	2340	1†30	7‡50	9 15	From Aarhus	12‡30	..	17‡52	0	d. Copenh'en a.	..	1927	To Aarhus	1927	2140	2257	5 58	..	7 50
2 20	5 13	8 1	1142	1431		1624	1925	2144	152	d. Fredericia a.	1048	13 3		1419	1623	1858	2113	2312	2 17
..	6 10	8 51	1215	15 8		17 9	2018	2226	173	d. Lunderskovd	1010	1215		..	1538	1822	2025	2226	
3 38	7 49	1023	1357	1619		1842	2131	2343	212	a. Tinglev d.	8 47	1035		1245	1344	17 7	1844	2047	..
3 59	8 14	1053	14 8	1641	1717	1911	2157		221	a. Padborg *c* d.	..	10 2	1155	1228	1313	1644	1817	2016	0 49
7 45	14 7	1455	19†9	21 2	..	0 4	..	..	..	a. Hamburg d.		4 29	..	8 25	..	11†17	13†9	1531	2136

‡ Connection by "L" Train—see above. † Weekdays only. **N** North Arrow Motor Express to Frederikshavn and *v.v.*

The times on the LEFT are to be read DOWNWARDS, those on the RIGHT UPWARDS.

(Hamburg) Fredericia, Frederikshavn. [Danish State Rlys.

¶	S	L	L	LN	r		L	L		L	L	r		LN	L	L		
2130	..	..	..	8 25	8 25	..	13 9	..	dep. Hamburg ar.	..	..	21 2	0 4	21 2	..			7 45
2050	2340	7 3[illegible]	3 0	↓	9 15	12‡30	1752	1740	dep. Copenhagen ar.	1320	13 7	1927	2140	↑	2257	2335		7 50
2 24	5 21	11 5	↓		1434	1730	2125	2140	dep. Fredericia ar.	9 25	9 40	1417	1610		19 1	↑	0 18	2 2
3 48	7 0	12 4			16 0	1930	..	2242	arr. Skanderborg dp.	8 22	..	1246	1347		1758		22 4	0 34
6 41	8 19	1251	▼	▼	1648	2027	..	2330	arr. Silkeborg..dp.	7 19	..	1155	1253		17 0		20 7	2332
4 12	7 28	1220	1230	1440	1624	20 3	2237	23 0	arr. Aarhus ....dp.	8 5	8 30	1215	1310	1428	1740	19 0	2118	0 4
5 15	8 48	..	1318	1532	1732	22 0	2325	2356	arr. Randers ....dp.	7 2	7 43	1110	1122	1339	1638	1814	1934	23 0
6 33	1020	..	1423	1632	19 0	0 10	0 30	..	arr. Aalborg ....dp.	..	6 40	9 45	..	1237	1425	1710	1717	2135
8 45	1245	..	1855	†..	2115	..	.	..	arr. Hirtshals dp	..	..	7 10	..	1050	9 30	13†5		19†10
..	..	..	2315		.	..		..	arr. Christianssand (p.416) (str.) d.	..	..	..	..	5 30	..	5 30		..
6 45	1033	..	1426	1634	1912	..	..		dp Aalborg ....arr.	..	..	9 35	..	1235	14 5	17 7	..	2121
8 22	1219	..	1530	1740	2053	..	..	..	ar. Fredrikshavn d		..	8 2		1124	1155	1353	..	1956
..	..	..	2130	2130		..		.	ar. Goth'burg (str.) d	..	..	..	..	7 20	7 20	..		..
..		..	..		5a15	..			ar. Larvik (p.420) dp.	..	..	..			..	..		11a40

L See note *page* 215. N North Arrow Motor Exp. Padborg-Fredrikshavn and *v.v.* Supplement 2 kr. 1st cl., 1 kr. general class. S Sleep. Car 1, 2 & 3 cl. Copenhagen-Aalborg and *v.v.* *a* To Sept 10. *r* Rest Car Aalborg-Nyborg and *v.v.* † Not Suns. ¶ Thro' Cars Copenhagen-Fredrikshavn.

(Berlin, Copenhagen,) Trelleborg, Malmö, Stockholm [Swedisn States Rly.

2 3	1 2 3 ExA	1 2 3 Exp	2 3	1 2 3 Exp	2 3 Z	1 2 3 ExS	2 3 ‖ Exp		1 2 3 Exp	2 3	2 3 Exp	1 2 3 ExA	2 3	2 3 ‖ Exp	1 2 3 ExS	2 3 Exp
..	2121	..	..	..	..	1120	¶	dep. BERLIN (*p.* 204)..arr.	..	..	..	7 54	..	¶	1813	Z
..	1949	..	..	R	..	1040	..	dep. Hamburg (*p.* 162) arr.	..	..	..	10 6	..	..	19 3	..
..	2 10	..	..		..	1626	..	dep. Sassnitz (*ferry*) ..arr.	..	..	..	3 4	..	..	13 0	..
..	6 45	..	8 55	1330	..	21 7	..	dep. Trelleborg ....arr.	1648	..	..	2231	..	..	8 13	1256
..	7 11	..	9 33	14 8	..	2138	..	arr. Malmö ....dep.	1610	..	..	22 5	..	..	7 45	1218
..	R	..	..	2132	..	8 42	8 42	dep. BERLIN † ....arr.	7 21	..	..	R	..	1955	1955	..
..		..	..	2150	..	8 54	8 54	dep. Hamburg† (*p.* 164)arr.	7 6	..	..	..	..	1943	1943	..
..	5 25	..	..	9 56	14 0	1917	1917	dep. Copenhag. (Cent.) arr.	1833	..	..	24 0	..	10 2	10 2	1411
.	5 47	..	..	1017	1420	1945	1945	dep. Copenhag. Free Har. a	18 6	..	..	2335	..	9 30	9 30	1350
.	7 17	..	..	1147	1548	2115	2115	arr. Malmö ....dep.	1636	..	..	22 5	..	8 0	8 0	1220
6 40	7 35	7 42	9 50	1422	17 8	2155	22 5	dep. Malmö ....arr.	16 5	2032	2135	2148	..	7 28	7 36	12 5
8 8	8 38	8 51	1115	1550	1830	23 6	2325	arr. Hassleholm ....dep	1456	19 5	2026	2040	..	6 10	6 25	1052
..	7 0	7 5	9 10	1356	1622	2113	2113	dep. Hälsingborg ...arr.	1628	2218	2218	2218	..	8 15	8 15	1320
8 14	8 46	8 55	1136	1534	1843	2312	2330	dep. Hässleholm......arr.	1451	1858	2021	2035	arr.	5 59	6 17	1044
1027	10 2	1012	1350	1650	2044	0 30	1 0	dep. Alvesta .. ...dep.	1340	17 6	19 7	1921	2253	4 36	4 58	8 52
1245	1114	1124	1650	18 3	2255	1 43	2 10	Nassjo *p.* 217 ......dep.	1235	1521	18 0	1816	2225	3 27	3 48	7 2
1452	1221	1234	1829	1911	1 38	2 57	..	Mjölby .... „	1122	1345	1643	..	2045	..	2 20	4 34
1530	..	13 1	19 6	1940	2 19	3 25	X	Linköping ...... „	1052	1256	1612	..	20 3	X	1 46	3 34
1556	..		1934	..	2 39	3 44		Norsholm........ „	R B	1224	1547	..	1931		..	2 48
1629	1324	1340	2026	2020	3 19	4 10	..	Norrköping...... „	1013	115[illegible]	1524	16 1	19 3	..	1 2	2 20
1722	..	1427	2126	21 6	4 7	4 58	..	arr. Nyköping........ „	9 24	1015	1430	..	1757	..	0 7	0 41
1928	1550	16 5	2333	2235	5 45	6 30	8 45	arr. Stockholm .... „	8 0	8 23	13 0	1350	1610	21 1	2235	2310

A 1 & 2 cl. Sleep. cars Berlin Stockholm and Hamburg to Malmo & *v.v.* R Rest. Car. Malmo-Stockholm and *v.v.* S 1, 2 & 3 cl. Sleep. cars from Trelleborg to Stockholm and *v.v.* X *Via* Falkoping and Katrineholm, *p* 216. Z 1, 2, 3 Sleep. cars Stockholm to Alvesta & *v.v.* ¶ Sleep. cars, 1 & 2 cl. Copenhagen-Stockholm and 1 2 3 cl. Malmo-Stockholm and *v.v.* ‖ No ordinary 1 cl. cars. B 2 & 3 cl. cars Stockholm—Copenhagen. † *Via* Warnemunde.

Stockholm, Laxa, Karlstad, Oslo. [Swed. & Norw. St. Rys.

2 3 Exp R	2 3	1 2 3 Exp ¶	2 3 r	2 3 ‡ Exp ‡		2 3 r	2 3	2 3 Exp R	2 3	2 3	2 3 ‡ Exp ‡
8 49	8 49	1240	1640	22 5	dep. **Stockholm** ....arr.	1455	2056	2056	..	2253	6 25
1047	1047	r	1825	0 12	dep Katrineholm ....arr.	13 0	1843	1843	..	21 2	4 16
12 5	1255	16 9	1957	1 42	dep. Laxå .. .... arr.	1130	1547	1713	1923	1937	2 19
1333	1455	1759	2125	3 9	arr. Karlstad (Cent.).. .. dep.	9 33	14 0	1549	17 5	18 7	0 58
1340	1528	18 4	2130	3 15	dep. Karlstad (Cent.) ......arr.	9 16	1355	1545	1635	18 1	0 54
1357	1553	1824	2150	3 31	arr. Kil (*p.* 216)............dep.	8 56	1333	1530	1616	1741	0 39
14 1	1610	1827	22 0	3 40	dep. Kil ....arr.	8 40	1319	1527	16 1	⁓	0 35
1442	1659	1919	2250	4 18	arr. Arvika .. .. dep.	7 45	1226	1448	1510	..	2356
1514	1732	1951	2322	4 49	arr. } Charlottenberg .. { dep.	7 10	1153	1417	1430	..	2323
1529	1750	20 5	..	5 4	dep. } Charlottenberg .. { arr.	..	1133	1359	..	..	23 2
1618	1858	2055	..	5 48	dep. Kongsvinger ....dep.	..	1032	13 8	..	..	2214
1825	2130	2310	..	7 55	arr. **Oslo** (East) ....dep.	..	8 0	11 5	..	..	2010

‡ 1, 2 & 3 cl. sleep. cars, Stockholm Oslo & *v.v.* R Rest. car Stockholm-Oslo and *v.v.*

r Rest. Car.

¶ Weekdays from June 20 to Sept. 3.

The times on the LEFT are to be read DOWNWARDS, those on the RIGHT UPWARDS.

(Berlin), Malmö, (Copenhagen), Gothenburg, Oslo

Swed. & Norg. St. Rlys & Berg. & Dals. Rlys.

23	123	23	23	23	23	23	23*		123	123	23	23	2	23	23*
..	Exp	..	Exp			Exp	Exp	R Restaurant Car.	Exp	Exp		Exp			Exp
..	21‖21	..	..	..	..	..*	1120	dep. BERLIN (p. 204)......arr.	7‖54	..	..	..	..	..	1813
	19‖49	..	..	..	..	..	1040	dep. Hamburg (p. 162)....arr.	10 6	..	..	..	..	..	19 3
..	2 10	..	..	..	..	..	1626	dep. Sassnitz ....arr.	3‖4	..	..	..	arr.	..	13 0
..	6 45	8 55	11 0	11 0	1330	..	2059	dep. Trelleborg ....dep.	2254	..	..		1638	2253	8 50
..	8 ‡ 4	9 53	1158	12 6	1523	1730	2148	dep. Malmö ....arr.	2121	0 2	9 58	13 0	1555	21 9	7 42
..	9 18	1128	1311	1359	1659	1843	23 2	arr. Engelholm ....dep.	20 5	2246	8 21	1144	14 0	1917	6 22
..	2132	..	X	..	..	..	8 42	dep. Berlin v Warnemunde.arr.	7 21	▲	..	..	..	..	1955
..	7 5	8 49	1049	..	1434	1610	2043	dep. Copenhagen (H) arr	2212	│	1017	1417	1617	2117	9 [illegible]
..	8 7	10 5	12 2	..	1542	1727	2148	dep. Elsinore *ferry* ...... arr.	2110	│	9 9	13 4	15 6	1952	8 4
..	8 29	1027	1224	..	16 4	1749	2210	arr. Hälsingborg *ferry*....dep.	2048	│	8 47	1242	1444	1930	7 6
	‡						*		‡						*
..	8 49	1116	1241	1322	1620	18 9	2227	dep. Hälsingborg. (Fy)..arr.	2029	2322	8 40	1215	1433	1917	6 46
..	9 17	1147	13 6	1355	1656	1836	2254	arr. Engelholm ....dep.	20 2	2255	8 6	1149	14 3	1843	6 18
..	9 28	1152	1317	1411	1711	1849	2313	dep. Engelholm ....arr.	1951	2240	8 1	1140	1346	1840	6 7
..	1038	1326	1422	1555	1850	1957	0 19	dep. Halmstad ....dep.	1840	2134	6 40	1034	1222	1711	5 0
..	1143	1542	1526	1732	2035	21 9	1 24	dep. Varberg ....dep.	1733	2028	——	9 26	1035	1529	3 53
..	1246	1716	1629	19 0	2230	2215	2 24	arr. } Gothenburg ... { dep.	1630	1920	23	8 18	8 55	14 0	2 49
9 25	13 5	..	1725	20 5	..	2230	2 40	dep. } Gothenburg ... { arr	16 8	1818	20 4	..	8 30	1355	2 31
1024	14 0	..	1851	2131	..	2345	3 35	dep. Trollhättan .... dep.	1515	1633	1911	..	6 50	1231	1 38
1125	1447	..	1951	arr.	..	0 48	4 25	dep. Mellerud.......... dep.	1425	1522	1818	..	..	1130	0 56
1520	16 0	..	arr.	..	..	arr.	5 40	dep. Kornsjö ....dep.	1316	..	1512	..	..	..	2345
1843	1725	..	..	..	..	..	7 15	arr. Fredrikstadt ¶ ......dep.	1140	..	1037	..	..	..	2156
1952	18 0	..	..	..	..	..	7 53	dep. Moss ....dep.	11 6	..	9 47	..	..	..	2118
2135	19‡0	..	..	..	..	..	9*0	arr. Oslo (East) ....dep.	10‡5		8 15	..	..	..	20*10

* Sleeping cars 1 & 2 cl. Copenhagen to Oslo, 1, 2 and 3 cl. Berlin-Oslo & Hamburg Oslo & *v.v.* 1, 2 & 3 cl. Trelleborg to Gothenburg and Oslo and *v.v.*; also from Gothenburg (passengers can join same 21.0) to Oslo and *v.v.* Passengers may remain in car at Gothenburg until 7.55. ‖ Thro' 1 and 2 cl. Sleep. car, Hamburg to Oslo and *v.v.* ‡ Rest. Car. Oslo–Malmo and *v.v.*

X Thro' 2 and 3 cl. cars Copenhagen-Gothenburg-Stockholm, arr. Stockholm 22.53 (*see below*).

¶ Ferry to Larvik, Mon., Weds., Sats. and Suns., May 27–Sept. 10, *see p.* 420.

Gothenburg, Laxå, Stockholm.

[Swedish State Rlys.

23	123	123	23	23	23	23	23		23	23	123	123	123	23	23	23	23
..	Ex¶	Ex¶	Ex ¶		Exp	Ex*	Exp				Ex¶	Ex*	Ex¶	r	Exp	Exp	Exp
3 25	8 42	1415	1650	18 0	..	2245	..	dep. Gothenburg arr.	..	12 0	1454	19 2	2245	..	..	..	6 35
4 35	9 44	1519	1749	1923	..	0 9	..	dep. Herrljunga ..arr.	..	1042	1350	18 1	2142	..	..	..	4 57
5 6	1010	1546	1815	1957	..	0 36	..	arr. Falköping ..dep.	..	1011	1326	1731	2117	..	..	..	4 32
2 10	6 54	1238	1523	1825	..	2235	2 10	dep. Nässjö ....arr.	11 6	1219	1743	..	..	..	3 23	..	6 42
2 46	8 10	1325	1616	19 5	..	2319	2 46	dep. Jönköping arr.	1028	1132	1558	..	2242	..	2 45	..	5 51
3 43	9 21	1430	1723	20 2	..	0 27	3 43	arr. Falköping dep.	9 33	1023	1449	..	2121	..	1 53	..	4 45
5 25	1013	1551	1817	2015	dep.	0 48	3 48	dep. Falköping ..arr.	9 25	10 5	1321	1729	2115	0 12	1 49	arr.	4 16
7 17	1138	1728	1942	2222	2 56	2 31	5 20	ar. Laxa (p. 215A) dp.	7 20	8 29	1154	1555	1947	2221	0 19	1 34	2 36
1051	1333	1935	2125	0 13	..	..	7 51	arr. Karlstad dep.	5 30	..	9 33	14 0	18 7	..	2135	..	0 58
7 51	12 6	18 3	2010	2259	3 21	3 10	5 47	arr Hallsberg....dep.	6 43	8 0	1125	1527	1919	2143	2351	1 10	2 [illegible]
8 37	1245	1855	21 3	2333	5 0	5 0	6 43	arr. Orebro ....dep.	6 0	7 17	1030	1440	1838	21 3	23 8	2356	2356
7 17	1135	1730	1935	..	2356	2356	5 25	dep. Orebro ......arr.	..	8 37	1153	1555	1949	22 3	0 20	..	5 [illegible]
8 r 0	1212	1814	2014	..	3 28	3 48	5 53	dep. Hallsberg ..arr.	..	7 53	1119	1521	1914	2129	2349	0 59	1 53
9 5	13 3	1914	21 4	..	4 23	4 43	6 48	d. Katrineholm.. dep.	..	6 51	1032	1432	1825	2019	23 2	0 12	1 3
1134	1455	21 2	2253	..	6 25	7 15	8 45	arr. Stockholm dep.	..	5 0	8 44	1240	1640	18 8	21 1	22 5	23 0

¶ Restaurant car Gothenburg-Stockholm and *v.v.* *r* Rest. car Stockholm–Hallsberg and *v.v.*

* 1, 2, & 3 cl. Sleeping cars, (but not first cl. Ordinary cars) Gothenburg-Stockholm and *v.v.*

All 2 & 3 class]

Gothenburg (Stockholm), Gävle.

[Bergslagernes & Gävle Rly. Cos.

2 40	..	7 50	9r25	1415	..	1725	2230	dep **Gothenburg**..arr	1044	1245	17 ρ	20r4	2 31	2 31	6 42
3 35	..	8 45	1024	1513	..	1851	2345	dep Trollhattan dep	9 8	1148	16 7	1911	1 38	1 38	5 30
4 19	..	9 26	1115	1555	..	1951	0 48	arr Mellerud ....dep	7 55	1057	1515	1818	0 56	0 56	4 27
7 20	⌐	11 7	1325	1735	⌐	2155	2 55	arr Kil ... dep	5 31	8 55	1332	16 8	22 2	22 2	2 33
7 47	..	1140	1355	18 1	..	2222	..	arr Karlstad dep.	3 9	8 24	1249	1528	2130	2130	..
8 56	7 57	1114	1336	1741	1744	0 43	3 2	dep Kil ...... arr	3 31	▲	1316	1556	2055	2150	2 25
¶	1148	1419	1711	¶	2127	¶	6 32	arr Ludvika dep	¶	│	1020	1221	1727	¶	23 4
1455	1624	..	2142	2253	..	6 25	1123	arr Stockholm dep	22 5	│	..	8 0	13 0	1640	1815
1317	..	1511	1825	..	..	..	7 48	arr Borlange......dep	..	│	9 24	1059	1612	..	2158
1350	..	1537	1852	..	..	..	8 23	arr Falun ....dep	..	│	9 0	1031	1538	..	2128
..	..	1742	21 2	..	..	..	1043	arr Gävle .. ....dep	..	│	7 15	8 17	12 7	..	1915

¶ via Laxa, p. 215A.

Stockholm—Gavle—Harnosand.

[Swedish State Rlys.

2 3	2 3	2 3	2 3¶	2 3	2 3	2 3		2 3	2 3	2 3¶	2 3	2 3	2 3	2 3	2 3
			Exp		R					ExR					
2055		4 45	8 40	9 0	1513	..	dep. Stockholm ....arr.	1352	1543	1651	..	2042	..	..	7 37
A	..	5 45	9 33	10 2	16 7	..	dep. Uppsala ....dep.	1258	1451	1559	..	1950	..	..	A
↓	..	8 10	11 5	12 8	1750	1825	dep. Gavle ....dep.	1058	1250	1434	..	1818	21 5	..	A
↓	..	10 6	1220	14 3	1916	2023	dep. Soderhamn ....dep.	8 36	1050	1315	..	1638	1919	..	↑
↓	7 10	1134	1321	1524	2022	2137	dep. Hudiksvall ....dep.	7 17	9 35	1211	..	1525	18 2	2017	↑
↓	7 42	1210	1348	1559	2046	..	dep. Harmanger ....dep.	..	9 0	1140	..	1448	1722	1945	↑
7 14	8 57	1326	1448	1719	2153	..	arr. Sundsvall ....dep.	..	7 40	1045	arr.	1346	16 1	1825	22 0
7 37	1115	1340	1451	1732	22 5	..	dep. Sundsvall ....arr.	..	7 33	1042	12 5	1338	1534	..	2142
9 16	1310	1519	16 4	1915	2334	..	arr. Harnosand ....dep.	..	5 52	9 30	1028	1210	1330	..	20 0

A Sleep. Car Stockholm-Harnosand and *v.v.* via Ange, page 218.
R Rest Car. ¶ June 15th to Sept. 3rd only.

Malmo—Mjolby—Kryl o—(Rättvik)

[Swedish State and Dalarnes Rlys.

2 3	2 3	2 3	†	2 3	2 3	1 2 3			2 3	1 2 3	2 3	2 3	2 3	2 3	2 3
				ExR		Exp				Exp		Exp			
2155	..	..	..	7 35	..	1422	..	dep. Malmö ....arr.	..	16 5	2032	2135	..	..	7 36
1 43	6 50	..	8 47	1114	1245	18 3	..	dep. Njasso ....arr.	11 9	1230	15 9	1753	2210	..	3 40
2 50	8 18	..	1016	1218	1421	19 8	—	arr. Mjolby ....dep.	9 44	1122	1345	1643	2045	..	2 20
5 10	8 37	..	1125	1242	1457	1915	1924	dep. Mjolby ....arr.	8 30	11 0	1333	1624	2020	23†34	1 33
5 44	9 8	..	12 0	13 5	1529	1941	20 5	dep. Motala ....dep.	8 3	A	13 5	16 2	1953	23 1	1 7
7 2	1021	dep	1329	1357	1646	2033	2116	arr. Hallsberg ....dep.	6 41	9 43	1137	15 8	1820	21†34	2353
1134	1455	8 44	1737	1737	..	A	6 25	arr. Stockholm ......dep.	23 0	5 0	8 44	..	1240	18 8	21 1
7 20	1030	1126	1333	14 2	1825	2041	2136	dep. Hallsberg ....arr.	6 32	9 35	11 2	15 2	18 4	2131	2340
7 57	11 2	1153	14 6	1428	1915	21 8	2218	dep. Orebro ....dep.	6 0	9 10	1034	1440	1730	21 3	23 8
8 17	1122	arr.	..	1443	1938	2124	2244	dep. Ervalla ....dep.		8 39	9 49	1419	1651	2026	2236
9 42	1320	..	..	1548	2117	2232	..	dep. Vastanfors ....dep.		7 29	8 14	1312	..	..	2047
9 54	1334	..	..	..	2132	..	..	dep. Snyten ....dep.		..	7 59	R	..	..	2027
1017	14 2	..	..	1617	2154	23 0	..	arr. Krylbo ....dep.	—	7 0	7 34	1242	..	..	20 0
1044	1428	..	..	1852	2217	..	7 30	dep. Krylbo ....arr.	22 0	..	..	1025	16 7	..	1922
1110	1459	..	..	1922	2248	..	8 2	arr. Hedemora ....dep.	2130	..	..	9 59	1540	..	1858
1210	16 0	..	..	2018	..	..	9 8	arr. Borlange ....dep.	2033	..	..	9 10	1448	..	1811
13 1	1712	..	..	2128	..	..	1026	arr. Leksand ....dep.	19 9	..	..	8 5	1331	..	1712
1328	1741	..	..	2157	..	..	1057	arr. Rättvik ....dep.	1837	..	..	7 35	13 0	..	1645

† Rail Car 3 cl. only. **A** Sleep. Cars 1, 2 & 3 cl. Mjolby-Storlien. Rest Car to Krylbo and *v.v.*
¶ June 3rd to Sept. 2nd. **R** Rest. Car.

† Not Sundays.

Stockholm—Rättvik.

[Swedish State and Dalarnes Rlys.

2 3	2 3	2 3	2 3	2 3	2 3	2 3		2 3	2 3	2 3	2 3	2 3	2 3
..	6 55	8 20	1125	1355	1635	1955	dep. Stockholm ....arr.	10 5	1243	1445	19 5	2147	..
..	8 6	9 10	1227	1457	1724	2049	arr. Uppsala ....dep.	9 11	1153	1350	1810	2057	..
..	8 18	9 14	1232	1535	1727	2054	dep. Uppsala ....arr.	9 3	1146	1347	18 5	2053	..
..	1010	1031	1414	1727	1839	22 9	arr. Krylbo ....dep.	7 30	1034	1231	1623	1940	..
7 30	..	1044	1428	..	1852	2217	dep. Krylbo ....arr.	7 18	1025	..	16 7	1922	22 0
8 2	..	1110	1459	..	1922	2248	arr. Hedemora ....dep.	6 50	9 59	..	1540	1858	2130
9 8	..	12 0	16 0	..	2018	..	arr. Borlänge ....dep.	6 0	9 10	..	1448	1811	2033
9 25	..	12 9	1613	..	2028	..	dep. Borlänge ....arr.	..	9 5	..	1435	18 0	2015
1057	..	1328	1741	..	2157	..	arr. Rättvik ....arr.	..	7 35	..	13 0	1645	1837

Electric Rly. all 3rd class.

Stockholm—Saltsjobanen.

Weekdays.

Stockholm . . d.	6 55	7 32	8 20	8 56	9 35	10 0	1035	11 0	1135	12 0	1235	13 0	1335	14 0	1435	15 0	1535	16 0	1635
Saltsjobanen a.	7 24	7 59	8 52	9 27	9 53	1027	1053	1127	1153	1227	1253	1327	1353	1427	1453	1527	1555	1622	1657

Stockholm . . dep.	17 5	1720	1740	18 5	1840	19 5	1935	20 0	2035	21 0	2135	22 0	2235	23 0	2335	0 0	0 35	1 0
Saltsjobanen arr.	1732	1738	18 0	1832	1910	1928	1955	2025	2053	2127	2155	2227	2253	2327	2355	0 27	1 0	1 20

Saltsjobanen dep.	6 55	7 32	8 3	8 20	8 45	9 0	9 32	10 0	11 0	1132	12 0	1232	13 0	1332	14 0	1432	15 0	1532
Stockholm . . arr.	7 22	7 59	8 27	8 47	9 5	9 27	9 52	1027	1127	1152	1227	1252	1327	1352	1427	1452	1527	1554

Saltsjobanen dep.	16 0	1630	17 5	1739	18 5	1837	19 5	1932	20 0	2032	21 0	2133	22 0	2232	23 0	2333	0 0	0 40
Stockholm . . arr.	1627	17 0	1732	18 0	1832	1859	1930	1952	2027	2052	2127	2153	2227	2252	2327	2353	0 27	0 56

On Sundays and Holidays a reduced service is operated.

Stockholm—Trondheim (Lulea)—Narvik. [Swed. & Norw. State Rlys.

2 3	2 3	2 3	1 2 3	2 3	2 3	2 3		2 3	1 2 3	2 3	2 3	2 3	2 3	2 3
	R		X		¶	S			X		R		S	¶
6 55	8 20	1125	1415	1635	1955	2055	dep. **Stockholm** .. arr.	1243	1445	19 5	2147	2319	7 37	8 58
8 18	9 14	1232	15 9	1727	2054	2150	dep. Uppsala .. arr.	1146	1347	18 5	2053	2151	6 38	8 3
1049	1040	1420	1636	1850	2219	2347	dep. Krylbo .... dep.	1034	1231	1623	1940	1953	5 22	6 50
13 0	1130	155	1723	2013	23 7	0 41	dep. Storvik ... dep	9 10	1132	1417	1845	1726	4 26	5 58
15 4	1253	1755	1846	22 0	0 24	2 11	dep. Bollnas ... dep.	7 19	1010	12 8	1715	15 8	3 5	4 40
1816	15 0	arr.	2056	arr.	2 29	4 42	arr. Ange ... dep.	..	8 0	8 16	15 4	1152	0 38	2 30
2029	1716	..	2310	..	..	7 14	arr. Sundsvall dep.	..	5 32	5 32	1240	9 18	22 0	..
..	1240	..	1817	..	22 0		dep. Sundsvall arr.	..	10 3	..	1116	..		7 14
..	1510	..	21 6	..	2 39	4 56	dep. Ange .... arr.	..	7 51	..	1451	..	0 12	2 18
..	1534	..	2130	..	3 5	5 20	arr. Bracke .... dep.	..	7 28	..	1427	..	2348	1 50
..	1535	..	2131	..	↓	5 21	dep. Bräcke .... arr.	..	7 27	..	1425	..	2347	↑
..	1642	..	2238	..	↓	6 30	arr. Ostersund .. dep.	..	6 15	..	1318	..	2240	↑
..	1919	..	..	..	↓	9 29	arr. Are .... dep.	..	..	..	1032	..	1950	↑
..	2035	..	..	..	↓	1050	arr. } Storlien { dep.	..	..	..	9 25	..	1840	↑
..	21a0	..	..	..	↓	1115	dep. } Storlien { arr.	..	..	..	..	..	18 5	↑
..	23a50	..	..	..		1330	arr. **Trondheim** dep.	..	..	..	..	..	1537	
..	1523	..	2119	..	2 39	5 16	dep. Ange .... arr.	..	7 37	..	1436	..	2225	2 18
..	1548	..	2146	..	3 5	6 5	dep. Bräcke .... arr.	..	7 4	..	1411	..	2126	1 50
..	1750	..	2333	..	4 44	8 31	arr. Langsele .. dep.	..	5 14	..	12 8	..	1917	2359
..	..	..	8 55	..	1419	2014	arr. Boden .. dep.	..	1049	..	..	..	7 45	1423
..	..	..	9 56	..	1513	21 5	arr. Lulea .. dep.	..	1854	..	..	..	6 53	1330
..	..	..	1244	..	1735	..	arr. Karungi .. dep.	..	16 0	..	..	..	..	1058
..	..	..	1326	..	1810	..	arr. Haparanda dep.	..	1518	..	..	..	..	1025
..	..	..	1510	..	1016	..	arr. Tornio (p. 228) d.	..	1520	..	..	..	..	1055
..	..	..	9 22	..	1439	..	dep. Boden .... arr.	..	1924	..	..	..	..	1359
..	..	..	1354	..	1826	..	arr. Kiruna .... dep.	..	15 4	..	..	..	..	1016
..	..	..	1552	..	1955	..	arr. Abisko .... dep.	..	1318	..	..	..	..	8 46
..	..	..	1625	..	2026	..	a. } Vassijaure .. { d	..	1244	..	..	..	..	8 14
..	..	..	1628	..	2029	..	d } Vassijaure .. { a.	..	1241	..	..	..	..	8 11
..	..	..	1725	..	2125	..	arr. **Narvik** .... dep.	..	1145	..	..	..	..	7 15

R Rest. car Stockholm-Storlien and *v.v.*; 2 & 3 cl. cars Stockholm-Bracke (Umea) and *v.v.*

S—1, 2 and 3 cl. Sleep. cars Stockholm to Storlien and *v.v.*; Stockholm-Harnosand and *v.v.* via Sundsvall, (see p. 217); also 2 and 3 cl. cars Stockholm-Trondheim and *v.v.*

X—1, 2 & 3 cl. Sleep. cars, also 2 & 3 cl. thro' cars Stockholm to Narvik and *v.v.* Rest. car Stockholm-Ostersund, Boden-Kiruna and *v.v.*

¶ 1, 2 and 3 cl. Sleep. cars Stockholm-Narvik and *v.v.*; also 2 and 3 cl. thro'cars Stockholm-Lulea and *v.v.*

a Suns. and Holidays June 20–Sept. 3 between Storlien–Trondhiem.

Rättvik—Gothenburg (Oslo).

7 36	8 30	11 3	1429	1753	dep. **Rättvik** ..... arr.	1524	17 5	2025	21 4	..	1142
8 36	9 55	12 8	1529	1851	arr. } Falun ..... { dep.	1420	1548	19 0	20 5	..	1039
9 0	10 0	..	1538	2128	dep. } Falun ..... { arr.	1350	1537	1852	..	2310	8 23
1010	1157	..	17 5	2250	arr. } **Ludvika** .... { dep.	1220	1422	1727	..	2139	6 49
1020	1221	..	1727	23 4	dep. } **Ludvika** .... { arr.	1148	1419	1711	..	2127	6 32
1316	1556	..	2055	2 25	arr. Kil ..... dep.	7 57	1114	1336	..	1744	3 2
17 0	20 4		2 31	6 42	arr. **Gothenburg** dep	2 40	7 50	9 25	..	1415	2230
14 1	1610		..	3 40	dep Kil .. arr.	..	..	1319	..	1527	0 35
1825	2130	..	..	7 55	arr. Oslo (p. 215A) dep.	..	..	8 0	..	11 5	2010

Oslo—Gjovik. [Norw. State Rlys.

2 3	2 3 ¶	2 3	w	2 3		w	2 3	2 3	2 3 ¶	2 3
8 0	9 55	1420	1620	1910	dep Oslo .. ..arr.	8 25	11 3	1720	19 0	2220
9 33	11 8	1553	18 8	205.	dep. Roa ...... dep.	6 50	9 35	16 0	1750	2056
9 51	..	1611	1835	211.	arr. Jaren ...... dep.	6 10	9 3	1532	1731	2030
1034	12 0	1654	..	215.	arr Eina, p. 220 dep	..	8 23	1455	1658	1945
1040	12 .	1656	..	2156	dep. Eina .. arr	..	8 20	1453	1650	1938
1047	1212	17 3	..	22 3	arr. Reinsvold .. dep.	..	8 12	1445	1640	1930
1115	1240	1730	..	2230	arr. Gjovik...... dep.	..	7 40	1415	16 5	19 0

¶ June 18th to Aug. 27th. *w* Weekdays only.

The times on the LEFT are to be read DOWNWARDS, those on the RIGHT UPWARDS.

Oslo. Dombaas (Aandalsnaes) Trondheim.—346 miles. {Norw. State Rlys

3 cl	2 3	2 3	2 3	2 3	2 3	2 3	Mls		2 3	2 3	2 3	2 3	2 3	2 3
		Exp	Exp	r		Exp			Exp	Exp			r	Exp
☞ Not Sundays.	8 10	9 40	1035	1440	1745	21 0	0	dep. **Oslo (East)** arr.	1925	1946	1120	1725	2215	7 0
	9 33	11 1	¶	16 8	1931	2228	42	,, Eidsvold dep.	18 2	1824	9 37	1546	2050	5 40
	1053	12 0	1255	1715	2050	2327	79	arr. Hamar ,,	1642	1717	8 15	1410	1930	4 34
	11 5	12†30	X	1730	21 0	S	..	dep. Hamar .. arr.	¶R	X	..	1340	1912	..
	1236	14†32	..	1933	2315	..	119	arr. Rena dep.	..	..	..	1135	1732	..
	1635		..	..	..	..	217	arr. Tynset .. dep.	..	..	..	..	1338	S
	1756	R	..	..	..	..	249	arr. Röros dep.	..	..	..	..	1217	..
..	..	1210	13 2	1735	21 5	2334	..	dep. Hamar arr.	1632	17 7	8 5	1345	1910	4 24
..	..	1320	14 9	19 5	2225	0 40	115	arr. Lillehammer dp	1523	16 5	6 40	12 3	1715	3 22
..	..	1325	1413	1923	—	0 44	.	dep. Lillehammer ar.	1520	16 0	—	1151	—	3 18
..	..	14 4	1446	2012	..	1 15	135	arr. Tretten ....dep.	1448	1523	w	1057	..	2 46
dep.	..	1436	1515	2052	..	1 43	152	arr. Ringebu... dep.	1414	1449	arr.	10 7	..	2 17
5 55	..	16 0	1627	2233	..	2 47	185	arr. Otta dep.	1257	1333	2210	8 10	..	1 15
8 10	..	1714	1737	..	..	3 41	214	arr. Dombaas dep.	1155	1230	2025	..	..	0 24
9 20	..	1730	..	w	3 cl.	4 0	..	dep. Dombaas arr.	1140	..	1930	..	3 cl.	2348
1221	..	1917	..	..	w	5 31	261	dep. Verma .. dep.	9 44	..	1646	..	..	2158
1246	..	1935	¶	..	..	5 47	269	dep. Flatmark dep.	9 22	..	1617	..	..	2137
1335	..	2010		w	..	6 20	280	arr. Aandalsnaes dep.	8 45	..	1520	..	w	21 0
9 0	..	17‡22	1748	..	..	3 50		dep. Dombaas .. arr.	..	1220	1938	..	arr.	0 15
1240	..	1912	1938	..	7 0	5 17	268	arr. Opdal .... dep.	¶	1028	1513	..	2143	2244
1512	..	20 0	2027	..	7 47	5 56	292	dep. Berkak (p.221) dp.		9 37	1247	..	2055	2155
1643	..	2042	21 9	..	8 44	6 29	313	arr. Stören......dep.	..	8 47	1042	..	1956	2117
1915	..	21‡48	2215	..	1025	7 25	346	arr **Trondheim** dep.	..	7 45	8 5	..	1815	2020

R Rest. Car Oslo-Favang. **S** Sleeping Cars 1, 2 and 3 class Oslo–Trondheim and Aandalsnaes and v.v.; no ordinary 1 cl. cars

r Rest. Car. w Weekdays only + Sundays only.
‡ From Aug. 28th.
¶ Daily to Aug. 27th.
X Rest. Car Oslo to Trondheim and v.v.

Bergen, Voss, Oslo. {Norw. State Rlys.

3 cl.	2 3	2 3	2 3	3 cl.	2 3	2 3	Mls		2 3	2 3	3 cl.	3 cl.	2 3
†	Exp	Exp	†		S¶	S			Exp	Exp	†		S¶
..	8 0	9 30	1432	1745	20 5	2230	0	dep. **Bergen** .... arr.	1917	21 0	1634	2214	9 0
..	8 17	A	1455	18 2	2021	2246	5	dep. Nestun .. dep.	19 3	2047	1615	22 0	8 45
..	R	..	..	..	X	Z	22	dep. Garnes .. dep.	A	R		..	
	9 0	..	1554	1912	21 0	2325	25	dep. Trengereid.. dep.	..		1512	21 2	..
..	1026	1139	1742	2115	2223	0 48	67	arr. Voss, p. 220 dep	17 0	1830	1310	1855	6 40
3 20	1036	1147	—	—	2235	0 56		dep. Voss arr.	1650	1819	—	—	6 30
7 11	12 9	1317	..	..	0 7	2 4	98	dep. Myrdal dep.	1558	1717	2 3	..	5 36
8 56	13 9	1416	..	..	1 3	2 50	119	dep. Finse dep.	1519	1637	†	..	4 58
9 49	1336	1444	..	..	..	..	136	a. Haugastol, p.221 d.	1443	1559	..	..	4 26
11 2	14 9	1517	..	..	1 58	3 47	149	dep. Gjeilo dep.	14 5	1520	..	..	3 50
1330	1447	1551	..	..	2 32	4 21	164	dep. Aal arr.	1318	1428	2035	..	3 4
1846	1636	R	..	..	.	..	180	dep. Gulsvik dep.	..	1235	1833	..	..
2145	1745	1822	2 3	2 3	5 12	6 53	251	arr. Honefoss dep.	1040	1135	1710	2 3	0 23
..	1755	1835	1440	1948	5 22	7 2		dep. ,, .. arr.	1030	1125	1650	2155	0 13
	1838	..	16 0	2056	..		271	dep. Roa . dep.	9 50	1044	16 0	21 0	..
..	1950	2030	1720	2220	7 5	8 50	307	arr **Oslo** (East) dep.	8 35	9 30	1420	1910	2230

R Rest. Car Oslo-Bergen and v.v.

A June 18th to Aug. 27th only.
S 1, 2 and 3 class Sleeping cars and 2 and 3 class ordinary coach.
X From Bergen Mons., Tues., Thurs., Fris. and Sats. only.
Z Suns. and Weds. only from Bergen.
* No 2 cl. on Sundays. † Not Sundays.
¶ Rest. Car Bergen-Voss and v.v.

Oslo, Kongsberg (Arendal), Kristiansand.

2 3	2 3	2 3	2 3	2 3	2 3	2 3	2 3	Mls		2 3	2 3	2 3	2 3	2 3	2 3	2 3	2 3
R	Exp		R		Exp		S			S			Exp	R		Exp	R
8 0	8 33	9 35	13 0	1435	1633	18 0	23 0	0	dep Oslo (West) arr	6 55	12 0	1522	1630	17 0	2025	2130	22 0
9 0	9 29	1050	1358	1550	1729	1858	2354	33	arr. Drammen dep	5 55	11 0	14 5	1532	16 0	19 5	2032	21 0
9 3	9 31	11 0	14 3	16 0	1730	19 3	2358		dep Drammen arr	5 50	1055	1355	1529	1555	1855	2029	2055
9 21	¶R	1125	1421	1625	Z	1921	0 15	44	arr Hokksund ..dep.	5 32	1035	1330	R¶	1535	1830	¶	2035
9 22	..	1130	1422	1630	..	1922	0 16		dep. Hokksund arr	5 30	1034	1323	..	1534	1823	..	2034
10 1	..	1215	15 1	1715	1818	20 1	0 50	62	dep. Kongsberg dep.	4 58	10 0	1245	1440	15 0	1745	1943	20 0
1046	..	..	1546	..	1858	2046	1 30	85	arr. Hjuksebo (p.220) d.	4 15	9 5	..	..	14 5	..	1859	1913
11 2	11 8	..	16 2	..	1920	21 2	1 43	91	arr. Nordagutu dep	4 2	8 47	..	1340	1347	..	1846	1853
1146	⌣	..	1646	..	20 1	..	2 24	110	arr. Lunde...... dep.	3 26	7 40	..	⌣	1252	..	..	1821
1231	..	..	1734	..	2042	..	3 13	138	arr. Neslandsvatn dep.	2 43	.	..	..	1157	..	..	1734
1320	..	..	1830	..		..	4 0	154	arr. Kragero dep.	1 30	..	..	..	11 0	..	..	1635
1236	..	..	1741	..	2048	..	3 17	..	dep. Neslandsvatn arr.	2 37	..	..	..	1150	..	..	1726
1344	..	..	1854	..	2155	..	4 22	176	arr Nelaug (p.220) dp.	1 28	..	..	..	1040	..	..	1619
1455	..	..	20 0	..	..	..	5 25	198	arr. Arendal ....dep.	0 40	..	..	..	9 25	.	..	1510
15 0	..	..	2021	..	23 8	..	5 33	215	arr. Grovane ..dep	0 12	..	..	..	9 19	..	..	15 0
17 0	..	..	..	..	..	..	10 10	252	arr. Byglandsfjord d.	1915	..	..	..	7 15	..	..	1140
15 2	..	..	2023	..	2311	..	5 35	..	dep. Grovane ... arr.	0 10	..	..	..	9 17	..	..	1457
1525	.	..	2045	..	2335	..	5 55	228	arr. Kristiansand dep.	2350	..	..	..	8 55	..	..	1435

R Restaurant Car. **S** 1, 2 and 3 cl. sleep. cars, Oslo-Kristiansand and Arendal & v.v.

† Not Sundays. ¶ June 18th to Aug. 27th. **Z** Saturdays only June 17th to Aug. 26th.

2 3	2 3	2 3	2 3	2 3	2 3	2 3	Mls.		2 3	2 3	2 3	2 3	2 3	2 3	2 3
8 0	9 35	13 0	1435	18 0	1935	23 0	0	dp. **Oslo** (West) ..ar.	10†22	12 0	1522	17 0	2022	22 0	1 10
9 5	11 5	14 5	16 5	19 5	21 5	0 5	33	dp. Drammen ....ar.	8 40	1055	1350	1555	1850	2055	2350
10 5	1216	15 5	1720	20 5	2220	1 20	62	ar. Skoppum ....dp.	7 15	9 51	1227	1451	1735	1951	2227
1020	1240	1520	1750	2020	2240	1 40	67	ar. Horten ......dp	6 45	9 30	12 5	1430	17 5	1930	22 5
9 30	12 5	1430	17 5	1930	22 5	1 5		dp. Horten ......ar.	7 20	1020	1240	1520	1750	2020	2240
10 6	1220	15 6	1732	20 6	2227	1 27		dp. Skoppum ....ar.	7 5	9 50	1219	1450	1731	1950	2221
1026	1245	1526	1758	2026	2258	1 58	78	ar. Tonsberg ....dp.	6 40	9 30	1153	1430	17 8	1930	2153
11 2	1327	16 2	1855	21 2	2355	2 50	88	dp. Sandifjord ..dp.	5 50	8 55	11 1	1355	1630	1855	21 1
1126	1355	1626	1930	2126	0 30	3 20	99	ar. Larvik (*p.* 216) dp.	5†20	8 27	1020	1327	1555	1827	2020
1217	1445	1717	..	2217	..	..	120	ar. Eidanger ....dp.	..	7†30	9 25	1235	15 0	1735	..
1245	..	1745	..	2245	..	..	126	ar. Brevik ......dp	..	7 0	9 5	12 5	..	17 5	..
1250	1515	1750	..	2251	..	..	127	ar. Skien (*p.* 221) dp.	..	6 50	9 0	1157	1430	1657	..

† Weekdays only.

Oslo—Honefoss.

3 cl.	2 3	2 3	2 3	2 3	2 3	2 3	Mls.		2 3	2 3	2 3	2 3	2 3	2 3
w		*w*					0		*w*		*w*			
..	8 0	9 35	13 0	1435	18 0	1935	33	dep. **Oslo** (W) *p.* 219 ar.	1022	12 0	1522	17 0	2022	2245
6 30	9 45	1128	1445	1630	1945	2150	43	dep. Hokksund .. arr.	8 5	1015	1320	1515	1915	2140
7 15	1025	1226	1525	17 6	2025	2230	60	arr. Vikesund ..dep.	7 15	9 33	1230	1437	1827	21 0
..	1155	..	..	..	22 0	..	73	arr. Kröderen..dep.	..	8*w*0	..	1320	*w*..	..
7 20	1028	1235	1528	17 8	2028	2235	..	dep. Vikesund.... arr.	7 5	9 30	1225	1435	1835	2055
8 15	11 5	1350	16 5	1745	21 5	2310	78	arr. Honefoss....dep.	6 15	8 50	1130	14 0	18 0	2015

w Weekdays only

Voss-Granvin (Eide).

3 cl.	3 cl.	3 cl.	3 cl.	3 cl.	Mls.		3 cl.	3 cl.	3 cl.	3 cl.	3 cl.
6 55	1040	1430	1855	2230	0	dep. Voss (*p.* 219) ..arr.	6 34	9 55	1250	1810	22 0
7 40	1137	1515	1930	2310	17	arr. Granvin (Eide). dep.	5 50	9 0	1210	1710	2115

Valders Railway.

2 3	2 3 Exp ¶	3 cl.	3 cl.		3 cl.	2 3 Exp ¶	2 3
8 0	9 55	1420	1910	dep. **Oslo** (East) arr.	1720	19 0	2220
1048	12 3	17 5	2220	dep. Eina ...... arr.	1448	1651	1930
1158	13 7	1813	2330	dep. Odnes ....dep.	1342	1538	1815
1211	1318	1824	2342	arr. } Dokka { dep.	1330	1525	18 0
1217	1324	1829	..	dep. } Dokka { arr	1321	1519	1753
1322	1426	1921	..	dep. Tonsasen ..dep.	1236	1431	17 2
1415	1515	2010	..	arr. **Fagernaes** dep.	1145	1330	16 5

¶ June 18th to Aug. 27th.

Arendal—Nelaug. (3rd class).

				†			§
Arendal....dep.	6†0	9 25	1235	1410	1510	1740	0 0
Rise........arr	6 20	9 44	1255	1432	1529	18 0	..
Nelaug (*p.* 219) a.	7†0	1030	1335	1545	1610	1845	1 0
	§						
Nelaug (*p.* 219) d.	4 30	8 30	1045	1355	1625	17†0	19 5
Rise........arr	..	9 7	1122	1435	..	1830	1942
Arendal ....arr.	5 25	9 25	1140	1455	1720	19†5	20 0

† Weekdays only. § 1, 2 & 3 cl. Sleep. Car to and from Oslo (*see page* 219).

(Rjukan) Tinnoset—Brevik. All 3rd class.

..	..	9 15	..	1415		..	dep. Rjukan ..arr	..	1540	..	2040	..		..
6*w*50	..	1235	..	1735	1820	2310	dep. Tinnoset .... arr.	1120	1215	..	1715	..	2220	6*w* 0
8 0	1025	1330	1525	1830	2025	2 40	dep. Notodden.. .... arr.	9 30	1110	1430	1610	1935	2110	2 0
8 20	1043	1350	1543	1850	2043	3 0	arr. Hjukesbo ....dep.	9 10	1055	1410	1555	1915	2055	1 45
12 0	..	17 0	..	22 0	..	6 55	arr. Oslo (W) *p.* 219 ..dep.	..	8 0	..	13 0	..	18 0	23 0
..	8 0	..	13 0	..	18 0	23 0	dep. Oslo (W)..........arr.	12 0	..	17 0	..	22 0	..	6 55
8 21	1050	1410	1550	1920	2030	3 35	dep. Hjukesbo ....arr.	9 0	1040	14 0	1530	1910	2030	1 25
8 36	11 2	1425	16 2	1935	21 2	3 50	arr. Nordagutu (*p.* 219) dep.	8 47	1025	1347	1515	1857	2015	1 10
9 50	1150	1555	1650	2055	2150	5 0	arr. Skien (N.)...........dep	8 0	8 55	13 0	1345	18 0	1840	0 0
..	1221	..	1721	..	2221	6 11	arr Eidanger ....dep.	7 22	..	1227	..	1727	..	2327
..	1245	..	1745	..	2245	6 30	arr. Brevik ....dep.	7 0	..	12 5	..	17 5	..	23 5

w Weekdays only.

Trondheim—Hell (Namsos)—Storlien.

2 3 *r*	3 cl.	3 cl.	3 cl. W	3 cl. W	2 3	3 cl.	3 cl. W	Mls.		3 cl. W	3 cl.	3 cl. W	3 cl.	2 3	2 3 *r*	3 cl. W
7 50	8 20	1415	..	1430	1537	1750	1915	0	dep. **Trondheim** arr.	8 40	9 55	1135	1310	1330	20 2	22 2
8 28	9 6	1515	..	1632	1614	1835	2014	20	arr. Hell .. dep.	7 36	9 7	10 2	1221	1253	1927	2050
8 30	↓	1517	—	..	↓	1837	↓	.	dep. Hell .. arr.	↑	9 2	↑	1229	↑	1925	↑
1038	↓	1752	18 0	..	↓	2050	↓	77	arr. Stenkjaer dep.	↑	6 50	↑	10 3	↑	1721	↑
1225	↓	..	2137	..	↓	2255	↓	137	arr. Grong ....dep.	↑	..	↑	8 0	↑	1535	↑
1345	↓	..	..	..	↓	..	↓	174	arr. Namsos ..dep.	↑	..	↑	5W30	↑	1410	↑
..	9 8	..	..	1648	1616	..	2016	..	dep. Hell ... arr.	7 35	..	9 48	..	1251		2048
..	1051	..	..	21 0	18 5	..	2212	66	arr. Storlien ....dep.	5 55	..	6 45	..	1115	..	1835

W Not Sundays.
r Rest Car Trondheim-Grong and *v.v.*

The times on the LEFT are to be read DOWNWARDS, those on the RIGHT UPWARDS.

BANDAK CANAL.—Lakes Bandak, Kvideseid, Flaa, and Nordsjo.

Weekdays fr. June 15, also Suns. July 3 to Aug. 14.

Skien ....dep.	7 0	* At Lunde 11.54 an Auto meets train from Oslo 8.0 (p. 219) and conveys passengers to Strengen, where steamer awaits arrival.
*Lunde, p. 219 ar.	11 0	
Strengen	1230	
Bandaksli........	17 0	
Laardal ......arr.	1715	
Dalen ....arr.	18 0	

Weekdays fr. June 15, also Suns. July 3 to Aug. 14.

Dalen ......dep.		7 0	¶ Connects at Strengen with motor to Lunde, corresponding with 12.52 train due Oslo 17.0 (p. 219).
Laardal ....dep.	about	7 30	
Bandaksli	,,	7 45	
Strengen ....dep.	,,	1130¶	
Lunde ......dep.	,,	1245	
Ulefos	,,	1415	
Skien ....arr.	,,	1630	

DAILY from July 3rd.

Skien ....dep.	6*0	7†30
Ulefos .... dep.	8 0	9 30
Notodden .... arr.	12*0	13†0

Notodden ....dep.	13 0	17†0
Ulefos ....dep.	1545	1945
Skien........ .... arr.	17*40	21†45

* Weekdays only. † Sundays only.

GOTA CANAL STEAMERS. Stockholm, Gothenburg.

From May 16th to Sept. 15th.

Stockholm dp.	Su., Tu., We., Th.‡, Fri., Sa.†	10 0
Norsholm ,,	Mo., We., Th., Fri., Sat, Su.	4 0
Motala ... ,,	,, ,, ,, ,, ,, ,,	13 0
Töreboda ar.	,, ,, ,, ,, ,, ,,	2230
Trollhättan ,,	Tu., Th., Fri., Sa., Su., Mo.	14 0
Gothenb'g ar.	,, ,, ,, ,, ,, ,,	18 0

Gothenb'g dp.	Su., M.§, Tu., Wd., Fri., Sa.†	10 0
Trollhättan ,,	,, ,, ,, ,, ,, ,,	17 0
Töreboda.. ,,	Mo., Tu., We., Th., Sa., Su.	7 0
Motala ... ,,	,, ,, ,, ,, ,, ,,	1630
Norsholm ,,	Tu., We., Th., Fri., Su., Mo.	1 0
Stockholm ar.	,, ,, ,, ,, ,, ,,	1830

† July 1st to Aug. 19th. ‡ July 6th to Aug. 24th. § July 3rd to Aug 21st.

JÖNKÖPING to LINKÖPING and vice versa.

Daily from June 1st to Aug. 31st.

10 0	(by bus) .. dep.	Jönköping..arr.	1745
1245	,, .. arr.	Vadstena..dep.	15 0
15 0	,, .. dep.	Vadstena..arr.	14 0
1525	,, .. arr.	Motala ....dep	1335
1530	(by steamer) dep.	Motala ....arr.	1330
2030	,, .. arr.	Malfors....dep.	8 30
2035	(by bus) .. dep.	Malfors....arr.	8 25
[illegible]	,, .. arr.	Linköping dep	8 0

AUTOMOBILES IN NORWAY. (Summer.)

The following are the Time Tables of the Principal Tourist Automobile Services, but there are a number of other services of which Thos. Cook and Son *can supply details on application.*

Aandalsnes—Valldal.

June 24th to Aug. 20th.

8 45	15 0	21†0	dep. Aandalsnes.... arr.	8*30	1430	20†30
1110	1715	23†0	arr. Valldal ......dep.	6*30	1150	18 0

† Sun., Tue., Thur., Sats. * Sun., Mon., Wed., Fri.

Arendal—Bygland.

10 0	dep. Arendal............arr.	1510
14 0	arr. Byglandsfjord......dep.	1140
1450	,, Bygland .... ,,	1030

Bergen—Norheimsund—Oystese & *v.v.*

9 30	1615	dep. Bergen .... arr.	1135	1735
1240	1925	arr. Norheimsund...... dep.	8 30	1430
..	2030	,, Alvik .... ,,	6 0	..
1255	1940	,, Oystese .... ,,	8 15	1410

Note: On Mon., Wed., Thur. and Sat. special bus from Oystese 7.30 and Norheimsund 7.45 due Bergen 10.15 if ordered the night before.

Berkak—Trondheim. 44

6 15	1025	dep. Berkak (p 219) ar.	1710	2115
8 0	1225	arr. Løkken dep	1510	1920
9 0	14 0	dp. Løkken arr.	1350	1820
1030	1540	arr Trondheim dep.	1220	17 0

Bjorgo—Sorum and *v.v.*

From July 1st. 47

1550	dep........ Bjorgo .... arr.	1415
1850	arr........ Sorum .... .. dep.	11 0

Byglandsfjord—Hovden.

Daily, June 1st to October 31st.

¶			¶	
1135	12 0	dep. Byglandsfjord ......arr.	1320	1320
1235	1245	dep. Bygland ....dep.	1215	1215
1335	1315	dep. Ose ....dep.	1130	1145
18 0	16 0	dep. Bykle ....dep.	7 30	9 10
1930	17 0	arr. Hovden ....dep.	6 30	8 20

¶ Weekdays only.

Dokka—Gjovik and *v.v.*

On Weekdays 42

Dokka Hotel, dep.	8 20	Gjovik, dep.	18 0
Odnes. dep.	9 38	Odnes, dep. ..	1936
Gjovik. arr ..	1010	Dokka, arr.	1954

Eidfjord (Vik)-Fossli (Vøringfoss)-Haugastol

June 1 to Sept. 20.

	¶	‡		‡	¶	
..	1050	1810	dep Kinsarvik ....arr.	1040	18 0	..
9 30	12 0	1945	dep Eidfjord...... arr	9 0	17 0	1915
9 45	1215	1955	arr. Saebo ....dep.	8 45	1650	19 0
1030	1235	2030	arr Fossli ......dep	8 15	1615	1830
11 0	13 0	2130	dep ,, ... arr	7 45	16 0	18 0
1115	1315	2145	arr Maurset ...... arr	7 30	1550	1745
1135	1335	2220	arr Dyranut ...... arr.	7 0	1530	1715
12 0	14 0	2250	arr Kroekja Bro .. arr	6 30	15 5	1630
1230	1430	2320	arr Haugastol .... dep	6 0	1445	1615

¶ June 10—Aug. 27. ‡ July 1—Sept. 20

AUTOMOBILES IN NORWAY—continued.

Distance in Kilometres.

Fagernes, Bygdin, Bygdisheim. 55

a	*b*	*c*		*a*	*a*
9 0	1430	1530	d Fagernes (p 220 a	12 0	1855
1015	1545	1645	a. Bygdin ... d.	1045	1735
1020	1550	1650	▼ a. Bygdisheim d	1040	1730

a June 15–Sept. 15. *b* June 15–17 & Sept. 4–15.
c June 18–Sept 3.

Fagernes—Gol.

June 15th to Sept. 15th. 55

1130	1315	15 0	dep. Fagernes.. arr.	13 0	arr.	1830
123[illegible]	141[illegible]	16 0	,, Sandestolen..dep	12 0	15 0	1730
133[illegible]	151[illegible]	17 0	arr. Gol .. ..dep.	1045	14 0	1630

Fagernes, Tyin, Laerdal and *v.v.* 160

a	*b*	*c*		*a*	*a*
8 30	1430	1530	d.Fagernes ..a. (p 220)	1250	2010
1050	1650	1750	a. Tyin } p d.	1030	1750
1120	1720	1820	d.Tyin } 222 a.	9 50	1715
1135	1735	1835	a.Nystuen ..d.	9 35	17 0
12 0	18 0	19 0	a.Maristuen d.	9 10	1637
1342	1923	2025	a.Laerdal ..d.	8 0	1515

a June 15–Sept. 15 *b* June 15–17 & Sept. 4–15.
c June 18–Sept. 3.

Haugesund—Olen. 50

	¶			¶	
Haugesund ......dep.	5 0	8 0	1515	1715	1915
Skjoldevik ...... ,,	6 0	8 55	1615	..	2015
Olen (*p.* 223) .. arr	6 45	9 40	1655	2020	21 0
	¶	¶			
Olen (*p.* 223)......dep.	7 15	8 10	9 45	17 0	2115
Skjoldevik ...... ,,	8 0	8 45	1030	1745	2150
Haugesund ...... arr	8 55	9 45	1125	1845	2250

¶ Weekdays only.

Hellesylt-Oie. (June 24 to Aug. 20.) 30

Leave Hellesylt 6.15, 9.10, 11.30, 16.5, 19.10, 20.0.
(1 hr.).
Leave Oie 8.0, 8.30, 12 15, 15.0, 18.0, 20.15.

Kristiansand—Flekkefjord.

Oslo (rail) (*p.* 220) ..dep.	23 0	..	..	8 0
Kristiansand .... arr.	6 10	..	..	16 5
Kristiansand .... dep.	6 30	1030	1430	1630
Mandal ....dep.	7 45	1145	1550	21 0
Flekkefjord........arr.	1055	1455	1915	..
Flekkefjord dep.	8 30	14 0	1825	
Mandal ....dep.	12 0	1720	2130	
Kristiansand .... arr.	1315	1835	2250	
Kristiansand .... dep.	1345	..	2310	
Oslo (rail) ....arr.	22 0	..	6 45	

Kristiansand—Stathelle. 202

8 45	15 0	17 0	19 0	dp.Kristiansand ar.	1455	2015	17 5
1020	1630	1830	2030	dp.Lillesand....dp.	1325	1845	1535
11 0	17 5	19 5	21 5	dp.Grimstad ..ar.	1250	1810	1450
1145	1745	1945	2145	ar. } Arendal { dp.	1210	1730	14 5
1215	1830	..	..	dp. } Arendal { ar.	12 0	17 1	22 5
1255	1935	..	..	dp. Tvedestrand dp	11 5	16 5	21 0
..	213.	..	..	ar. Kragero ....dp.	9 5	..	19 0
16 0	..	..	..	ar. Stathelle....dp.	..	13 5	..

Distance in Kilometres.

Laerdal to Gol, and *v.v.* 124

a	*b*		*a*	*b*
1415	1630	Gol .. ▲	1320	1510
1815	2030	Laerdal ..	9 30	1130

a May 20–Sept 10. *b* July 1–Aug. 31.

Maristuen to Gol, and *v.v.*

From May 20th to Sept. 10th. 90

1045	dep. Maristuen.... arr. ▲	17 0	1915†
1315	▼ arr. Gol .... dep.	1415	1630†

† Must be ordered in advance.

Maristuen to Tyin, and *v.v.* 27

17†0	1920	d Maristuen a.	10†45
1750	20 0	a. Tyin d.	10†0

† Must be ordered in advance.

Merok-Grotli (Otta) Visnaes, Loen.

June 20th to Sept. 20th.

6 35	9 0	1430	dp.Merok....ar	1425	1850	7 55	..
8 0	12 0	16 0	ar. Grotli....dp	13†0	1615	6 30	..
	¶	8 0	dp.Otta *p.* 224 ar.	2013	¶	..	
8 15	1230	615	d. Grotli....arr.	1225	1540	..	8 0
9 5	1320	1715	d. Videseter arr.	1110	13 0	2015	7 15
9 40	1450	18 0	d. Hjelle ..dep.	1030	1215	1945	dep.
1010	1525	1840	d.Mindresunde d	9 45	1125	18 0	
1050	1545	19 0	ar.Visnaes....d.	9 20	1040	1825	..
1110	1550	1910	d. ,, arr.	9 10	1030	1815	2140
1130	16 5	1930	ar.Loen ....dep.	8 55	1015	1755	2120
1140	1610	1940	d. ,, ...arr.	8 45	1010	1745	2115
12 0	1625	20 0	ar.Olden ..dep.	8 30	10 0	1730	21 0

† To Aug. 25th. ¶ July 1 to Sept. 1.

Molde to Gjemnes, and *v.v.* 40

1045	1730	2330	dep. Molde . arr. ▲	1030	1615	23 0
12 0	19 0	1 0	▼ arr. Gjemnes dep.	9 0	1445	2130

Molde—Flemma. To Aug. 31st.

1115	1630	1645	dep.Molde .. arr. ▲	1535	16 5	2050
1255	1810		arr. Angvik ..dep.	1355	..	1910
1330	..	1845	▼ ,, Flemma ..dep.	..	1415	..

Molde—Eikesdalsvatn.

Services will be run from June 15 to Sept. 15.

	Sun.	Mon., Wed., Fri.	Sat.
Molde ..... dep.	8 0	1715	18 0
Eidsora.... arr.	9 30	1845	1930
Eikesdalsvatn arr.	11 0	20 0	21 0
	Sun.	Tue., Fri.	Sat.
Eikesdalsvatn dep.	1920	10 0	10 0
Eidsora ......arr.	2020	11 0	11 0
Molde.... arr.	22 0	13 0	13 0

Mundal—Böyum and Suphelle.

From Mundal Hotel every hour from 8.0 to 18.0.
30 minutes to *each* Glacier.

The times on the LEFT are to be read DOWNWARDS, those on the RIGHT UPWARDS.

Distance in Kilometres.

Nesflaten—Breifon and v,v.

(Bratlandsdal Coy.)

June 15th to Aug. 31st, daily.

9 30	1730	dep. ....Breifon ... arr.	1130	21†15	23‡10
1030	1830	arr. ... Nesflaten .. dep.	1030	20‡30	22‡5

† Not Sats. ‡ Sats. only

Notodden—Kviteseid and v.v. 85

14 0	dep. ....Notodden (p. 220) .. arr.	11 0
1630	arr. ....Kviteseid .... dep.	8 30

Notodden—Seljord.

Weekdays, June 20th to September 20th.

1115	1430	dep. Notodden (p. 220) .. arr.	9 30	1510
12 0	1520	dep. Sauland ....dep.	8 45	1425
1230	16 5	dep. Hjartdal ....dep.	8 10	1355
1310	1650	arr. Seljord ....dep.	7 30	1315

Notodden—Tinnoset—Bolkesjo.

Weekdays, June 20th to September 20th.

1430	dep. Notodden (p. 220) arr.	1015
1530	dep. Tinnoset ....dep.	9 0
1650	arr. Bolkesjo Hotel ....dep.	8 15

Notodden–Tuddal.

From June 15th. 55

15 0	dep. Notodden, (p 220) ...... arr.	1030
1730	arr. Tuddal .... dep.	8 30

Odda, Breifonn, Dalen, Bo and v.v.

June 20–Sept. 10. 174

7 45	9 0	1230	dep. Odda .. .. arr	12 0	1745	2145
9 0	1045	14 0	,, Breifonn dep	1030	1615	2025
1030	12 0	arr.	arr. Haukelister dep	..	1430	1925
1045	..	..	dep Haukelister ar	..	..	1920
1445	..	..	arr. Dalen .... dep.	..	..	16 0
1750		.	arr. Bo............dep.	..	..	12 0

Odda, Breifonn, Nesflaten and v,v. 64

June 15 to Aug. 31.

Odda ....dep.	..	1230
Breifonn ..dep.	8 0	2030
Nesflaten .. arr	8 45	2115
Nesflaten .. dep.	9 0	2130
Breifonn... arr.	10 0	2215
Odda ......arr.	12 0	..

Odda—Fjaera.

June 1st to Sept. 20th. 35

1230	dep. Odda .... arr.	1515
1345	arr. Fjaera ......dep.	14 0

Odda—Ringøy—Eidfjord.

June 1st to Sept. 20th, daily 70

8 0	13 0	1630	dep. Odda arr.	1215	1530	20 0
9 10	1415	1745	dep. Loftus .. dep.	11 5	1415	1845
1015	15 0	1830	arr. Ringøy . dep.	1015	..	1815
1045	1530	19 0	arr. Eidfjord	9 45	13 0	1730

Distance in Kilometres.

Øie–Hellesylt–Visnaes–Olden and v.v.

June 24th to Aug. 20th. 64

Øie .... dep.	8 0	15 0
Hellesylt .... dep	9 5	1610
Visnaes .... dep	1110	1910
Loen .... dep	1140	1940
Olden .. .. arr.	12 0	20 0
Olden .. .. dep.	8 30	1630
Loen .... dep	8 55	17 0
Visnaes .... dep.	9 20	1740
Hellesylt .. .. arr	1130	1945
Øie .... arr.	1145	21 0

Olden–Visnaes–Nordfjordeid, and v,v.

Weekdays, June 10th to Sep. 20th. 121

10 0	17¶ 0	dep. Olden .... arr.	12¶0	20†0	20‡0
1025	17 30	dep. Loen .... arr.	1130	1930	1930
1040	17 50	arr. Visnaes .. dep.	1110	1910	1910
1045	19 10	dep. Visnaes .. arr.	1035	18 0	1855
1230	21 ¶0	arr. Nordfjordeid dp.	8¶40	16†0	1715

† Daily except Tues. ‡ Tues. only.

¶ July 1st to Aug. 20th only.

Olen—Skanevik—Kyrping.

	¶	¶		¶		
9 45	17 0	2115	dep. Olen .... arr.	9 40	17 0	21 0
1015	1730	2045	,, Etne ....dep	9 10	1630	2040
..	1830	2245	arr. Skanevik .... ,,	8 0	..	1930
11 0	..	..	arr. Kyrping......dep.	..	1545	..

¶ Weekdays only.

Olen—Sauda and v.v.

7 0	9 45	2115	dep. Olen .... arr.	9 40	1515	21 0
1010	1230	24 0	arr. Sauda ......dep.	7 15	1215	18 0

Opdal-Kvisvik (Kristiansund).

June 1st to Sept. 15th.

	¶	S			Z	X
21 0	..		dep. Oslo (rail) arr.	..	7 0	7 0
..	7 45	7 45	dep. Trondhjem a.	2215		..
5 50	1110	1110	dep. Opdal arr.	1715	2210	2210
8 10	1330	1330	arr. Sunndalsora dep.	15 0	20 5	20 5
8 35	14 5	14 5	dep. Sunndalsora arr.	1445	1955	1955
1020	1545	1545	arr. Tingvoll dp	1315	1830	1830
1030	16 0	18 0	dep. Tingvoll ar.	13 0	1820	17 0
1045	1620	1820	arr. Sandvika dep.	1240	..	..
1135	17 5	19 5	arr. Kvisvik dep.	1145	1715	1545
1145	1715	1930	d. Kvisvik Ferry) a.	1145	1715	1545
1245	1815	2030	a. Khristi'nsund ,, d.	1030	16 0	1430

¶ Weekdays. S Suns. only.

X Sats. only. Z Daily except Sats.

Oslo—Telemark—Kristiansand.

403

7 30	dep. Oslo .. .. arr.	2045
1015	,, Kongsberg .... dep.	1830
1645	,, Tveitsund ...... ,,	12 0
2045	arr. Kristiansand .. .. dep.	7 45

AUTOMOBILES IN NORWAY—continued.

Distance in Kilometres

Otta, Grotli, Merok (Geiranger) & *v.v.*

June 20th to Sept. 10th.

Otta, dep. ..	—	—	8 0	1630 ..	—
Grotli arr. ..	—	¶	1215	2120 ..	125
Grotli, dep ..	6 30	13 0	1615	— ..	—
Merok Union ..	7 45	1415	1840	— ..	177
Geiranger. arr.	7 50	1420	1845	— ..	—
Merok, arr. ..	7 55	1425	1850	— ..	—
				¶	
Merok, dep. ..	6 35	—	9 0	1430 ..	—
Geiranger ..	6 40	—	9 5	1435 ..	0
Merok Union	6 45	—	9 20	1445 ..	
Grotli, arr. ..	8 0	—	12 0	16 0 ..	52
Grotli, dep. ..	8 15	—	—	1615 ..	—
Otta, arr. .	1230	—	—	2013 ..	177

¶ June 25th–August 25th.

Otta—Elveseter—Krossbu.

June 20th to September 10th. 100

1715	dep. Otta	arr.	1245
1925	arr. Fossheim (Lom)	dep.	1020
2020	,, Roisheim	,,	9 40
2050	,, Elveseter	,,	9 10
22 0	,, Krossbu....	,,	8 0

Odda—Kristiansand. 357

7 45	dep. Odda..................	arr.	2145
12 0	arr. Hovden	dep.	1730
13 0	dep. Hovden	arr.	1630
15 0	,, Valle	dep.	1430
1540	,, Granheim	,,	1330
1550	,, Ose	,,	1320
1630	,, Bygland	,,	13 0
17 0	arr. Byglandsfjord	dep.	1130
1730	dep. Byglandsfjord	arr.	1130
20 0	arr. Kristiansand	dep.	9 0
6 45	arr. Oslo (rail) *p.* 219	dep.	23 0

Oslo—Kristiansand. 395

7 30	dep. Oslo	arr.	2045
8 40	,, Drammen	dep.	1935
9 10	,, Hokksund	,,	19 0
1015	,, Kongsberg	,,	1830
14 0	,, Seljord	,,	15 0
1645	,, Tveitsund	,,	12 0
1825	,, Svenes	,,	9 55
1925	,, Birkeland	,,	8 50
2045	arr. Kristiansand	dep.	7 45

Sogndal-Jostedal (Kroken), and *v.v.* 70

June 1 to Sep. 10.

1515	dp. Sogndal.. ... ar.	11 0
17 0	dp. Marifjoeren ..dp.	9 45
1915	ar. Kroken (Jostedal) d	7 50

Sogndal-Fortun, and *v.v.* 70

From June 18 to Sept. 4.

1 0	1515	dep. Sogndal......	arr.	11 0	18 0
1045	17 0	dep. Marifjoeren ..	dep.	9 45	1620
12 0	1830	arr. Fortun	dep.	8 15	15 0

Distance in Kilometre

Stenkjaer—Namsos. 85

Trondheim, rail (*p.* 220) .... dep	7 50	1415
Stenkjaer, rail .. .. arr	1038	1752
Stenkjaer, motor .... dep.	1045	18 0
Namsos .... arr.	1245	20 0
Namsos ....dep	7 15	1430
Stenkjaer . ... arr	9 30	1645
Stenkjaer. rail ....dep.	10 3	1721
Trondheim. rail .... arr.	1310	20 2

Suldalsosen-Sand, and *v.v.* 19

From Suldalsosen, Sun. 11.0 and 18.0; Mon., Tue., Wed., Thur. and Fri. 11.0 and 21.0; Sats. 11.0. From Sand, Sun. 12.45 and 20.0; Mon., Tues., Wed., Thur. and Fri. 16.45 and 23.15; Saturday 18.15. Journey about 45 minutes.

Trengereid—Oystese. 57

June 3rd to Sept. 20th.

9 5	1740	2030	dep. Trengereid ..arr.	8 40	1725	2030
11 0	1930	2210	,, Norheimsund dp.	7 0	1520	1830
1120	1940	2225	arr. Oystese ..... dep.	6 45	15 0	18 5
1210	2030	2310	,, Alvik ...... ,,	6 0	1410	1710

Trondhjem—Kvisvik.

June 1st to Oct. 1st. 217

¶	S			
1130	1130	dep. Trondhjem	arr.	1930
1310	1310	,, Svorkmo	dep.	1750
1510	1510	arr. Surnadal Hotel	,,	1550
1810	1755	,, Tingvoll	,,	1250
1930	19 0	,, Kvisvik (*p.* 223)	,,	1130
2045	20 0	arr. Christiansund	dep.	1030

¶ Not Sats. and Suns. S Sats. and Suns. only.

Ulvik—Granvin.

Daily. 25

8 0	16 0	dep. Ulvik .... arr.	1230	2025
8 50	1650	arr. Granvin (*p.* 220) dep.	1140	1935

Ulvik—Gudvangen.

June 18th–August 20th. 92

9 30	15 0	dep. Ulvik .... arr.	1330	1845
1145	17 0	,, Voss .... dep.	1145	17 0
13 0	1815	,, Stalheim...... ,,	10 5	1530
1340	1855	arr. Gudvangen.... dep.	9 25	1235

Vadheim—Sandane—Stryn and *v.v.*

Summer service June 20 to September.

Distance in Kilometres. 167

	Sunday		Monday		Tuesday		Wed.		Thurs.		Friday		Saturd'y	
Vadheim....dep.	8 30	1645	6 30	1645	8 30	1645	8 30	1645	8 30	1645	8 30	1645	8 30	1645
Förde......arr.	9 45	18 0	7 45	18 0	9 45	18 0	9 45	18 0	9 45	18 0	9 45	18 0	9 45	18 0
Förde......dep.	10 0	1810	8 30	1810	1010	1810	1010	1810	1010	1810	10 0	1810	1010	1810
Vassenden ..dep.	1040	1845	9 10	1845	1050	1845	1050	1845	1050	1845	1040	1845	1050	1845
Egge ......dep.	1150	2040	1020	2040	1225	2040	1225	2040	1225	2040	1150	2040	1225	2040
Björkelo... arr.	12 5	2050	1030	2050	1235	2055	1235	2050	1235	2050	12 0	2050	1235	2050
Sandane.. arr.	1240	2130	1110	2130	1315	2130	1315	2130	1315	2130	1240	2130	1315	2130
Sandane dep.	1130	2020	10 0	2020	12 5	2020	12 5	2020	12 5	2020	1130	2020	12 5	2020
Björkelo.. ➤d.	12 5	2055	1035	2055	1240	2055	1240	2055	1240	2055	12 5	2055	1240	2055
Olden ......dep.	1340	2220	12 0	2220	1415	2220	1415	2220	1415	2220	1340	2220	1415	2220
Loen ......dep.	1355	2235	1215	2235	1430	2235	1430	2235	1430	2235	1355	2235	1430	2235
Stryn { Visnes ar.	1415	2250	1230	2250	1450	2250	1450	2250	1450	2250	1415	2250	1450	2250
Stryn { Tonning a	1420	2255	1235	2255	1455	2255	1455	2255	1455	2255	1420	2255	1455	2255

	Sunday		Monday		Tuesday		Wed.		Thurs.		Friday		Saturd'y	
Stryn { Tonning d	6 40	1550	6 40	1225	6 40	1550	6 40	1550	6 40	1550	6 40	1550	6 40	1550
Stryn { Visnes dp.	6 45	1555	6 45	1230	6 45	1555	6 45	1555	6 45	1555	6 45	1555	6 45	1555
Loen ......dep.	7 0	1615	7 0	1245	7 0	1615	7 0	1615	7 0	1615	7 0	1615	7 0	1615
Olden ......dep.	7 15	1630	7 15	13 0	7 15	1630	7 15	1630	7 15	1630	7 15	1630	7 15	1630
Björkelo... arr.	8 40	1750	8 40	1420	8 40	1750	8 40	1750	8 40	1750	8 40	1750	8 40	1750
Sandane.. arr.	9 15	1835	9 15	15 0	9 15	1835	9 15	1835	9 15	1835	9 15	1835	9 15	1835
Sandane dep.	8 5	1725	8 5	1350	8 5	1725	8 5	1725	8 5	1725	8 5	1725	8 5	1725
Björkelo.. ➤d.	8 40	18 0	8 40	1425	8 40	18 0	8 40	18 0	8 40	18 0	8 40	18 0	8 40	18 0
Egge ......dep.	8 50	1810	8 50	1435	8 50	1810	8 50	1810	8 50	1810	8 50	1810	8 50	1825
Vassenden ..dep.	1120	1920	1120	1655	1120	1920	1120	1920	1120	1920	1120	1920	1120	1920
Förde ......arr.	1155	20 0	1155	1730	1155	20 0	1155	20 0	1155	20 0	1155	20 0	1155	20 0
Förde ......dep.	12 0	2045	12 0	1745	12 0	2030	12 0	2030	12 0	2045	12 0	2030	12 0	2045
Vadheim ....arr.	1315	22 0	1315	19 0	1315	2145	1315	2145	1315	22 0	1315	2145	1315	22 0

Vestnaes-Sjoholt-Aalesund, and *v.v.*

(June 10 to Sept. 10). 70

Vestnaes dep. ..	8 25	1330	1815	2015
Sjoholt dep ..	9 15	1445	19 0	21 0
Aalesund arr. ..	1015	1545	20 0	22 0
Aalesund dep. ..	6 45	1330	1615	1830
Sjoholt dep. ..	7 45	1430	1715	1930
Vestnaes arr. ...	8 25	—	18 0	2010

Vadheim-Vetlefjord and *v.v.*

88

	a	*b*	*c*	*d*		
Vadheim ......dep.	6 30	8 30	15 0	1645	..	
Sande..........dep.	7 0	9 0	1530	1715	..	
Viken ....arr.	8 0	10 0	1630	1815	..	
	e	*f*			*g*	
Viken ....dep.	1140	1210	..	..	1845	
Vetlefjord ......arr.	1320	1350	..	..	2025	
			g			*g*
Vetlefjord ......dep.	..	..	14 0	..		2030
Viken ....arr.	..	..	1540	..		2210
	h	*k*	*a*	*d*	*l*	..
Viken ....dep.	1140	1250	1730	1820	2015	..
Sande..........dep.	1240	14 0	1830	1930	2115	..
Vadheim........arr.	1310	1430	19 0	20 0	2145	..

a Mons. only. *b* Daily except Mons. *c* Tues., Thurs., Sats. *d* Suns. only. *e* Suns., Tues., Thurs., Sats. *f* Mons., Weds., Fris. *g* Daily. *h* Tues., Sats. *k* Suns., Weds., Fri. *l* Daily except Suns. and Mons.

Voss-Stalheim-Gudvangen and *v.v.*

From June 18th to Sept 3rd.

Distance in Kilometres. 48

Voss .. .. ..dep.	7 30	1030	1145	1430	17 0	1825
Stalheim .. arr	8 45	1145	13 0	1545	1815	1940
Gudvangen ....ar.	9 25	1225	1340	1625	1855	2020
Gudvangen ....dp.	8 0	9 25	1235	—	16 0	20 5
Stalheim ......dp.	9 0	10 5	1315	1530	1640	2045
Voss .. ..arr	1015	1120	1430	1645	1755	22 0

Voss to Ulvik, and *v.v.*

June 4–Sept. 20.

44

Voss dep.	1145	17 0
Ulvik arr....	1330	1845
Ulvik dep. ..	9 30	15 0
Voss arr (*p.* 219)	1115	1645

Vetlefjord-Stryn and *v.v.*

89

	c	*b*	*c*
Stryn ....dep.	6 40	..	
Loen ....dep.	7 0	..	..
Olden ....dep.	7 15	..	..
Sandane ......dep.	8 5	..	..
Vassenden ......dep.	1010	1010	1720
Forde ....dep.	1010	1010	1720
Holsen ....dep.	1050	1050	1755
Viken ....dep.	1140	1210	1845
Vetlefjord ...... arr.	1320	1350	2025
	c	*c*	*c*
Vetlefjord ......dep.	14 0	1530	2030
Viken ....dep.	1540	1710	8†30
Holsen ....dep.	1630	..	9 20
Forde ....dep.	1710	..	10 0
Vassenden ......arr.	1710	1840	10 0
Sandane ....dep.	..	2130	
Olden ....dep.		2220	..
Loen ....dep.	..	2235	..
Stryn .... arr		2255	..

a Suns., Tues., Thurs. and Sats.
b Mons., Weds. and Fris.
c Daily. † arr. 22.10.

The majority of the Services given below apply from June until the end of August only.

Aardal.—s.s. *Aardal*, Ovre Aardal to Aardalstangen (Aardal) (1¼ hrs.), June to Sept. 8, Sun., 4.0, 9.30 and 22.0, Mon. 15.0, Tues., 20.0., Wed. 22.0, Thur., 6.0 and 19.30, Fri. 22.0, and Sat, 8.0; returning from Nedre Aardal Sun., 6.0 and 12.45, Mon. 0.30 and 18.0, Tues., 22.0., Thur., 0.30, 9.0 and 22.0, Sat., 0.30 and 12.0.

Bandak.—See under CANALS, page 221. † To Aug. 14th only. ‡ From Aug. 15th.

Bygdin.—Motor Boat *Bitihorn* July 1st-Sept. 1st.

11 0	18 0	dep.	Bygdin Hotel ...... arr.	10 30	17 0
13 0	20 0	arr.	Eidsbugaren ...... dep.	8 30	15 0

Byglandsfjord.—s.s. *Bjoren* and *Dolen* (to August 31st).

Weekdays	13 45	dep	Byglandsfjord Stn. arr.	12 30	Weekdays
(except Sats.)	18 30	arr.	Ose .... dep.	7 30	(except Mons.)

Eikesdal.—s.s. *Eikisdal*, June 30 to Aug. 24. From Overaas via Osen to Eikiesdal (about 1¾ hour), Sun. 10.0, Mon. 16.0, Wed. 10.30, Thur. 10.0, and Fri. 10.30; return Sun. 14.0, Tues. 7.15, Wed. 16.30, Thur. 16.0 and Sat. 12.0.

Ekern.—s.s. *Stadshauptmand Schwartz* from Eidsfoss to Vestfossen, Mons. and Sats. only.

Femunn.—s.s. *Fæmund II.*, Nordendon, dep. 10.0 Mon., Wed. † and Fri., return from Sydenden Tues. Thur. † and Sat. 10.0. †To August 31st only.

Flaa.—See under CANALS, page 221. (Bandak Canal).

Fredrikshalds Canal.—SUSPENDED.

Hornindal. s.s. *Dolen*, Nor to Sanden (2½-4 hrs.), calling at intermediate stations: *Sun.*, 8.15, Mon. 14.0, Wed. 14.0, and Fri. 13.0. Returning from Sanden *Sun.* 14.0, Wed. 9.0, Fri. 8.0, and Sat. 9.0.

Hjelle to Mindresunde.—*See below*, Opstryn.

Jolster.—s.s. *Skjold*, Skei to Nedre Vasenden.

Kroderen.—s.s. *Norefjeld*, Kroderen to Gulsvik (3-3½ hrs.) daily, in July and August, 13.30; returning from Gulsvik 9.15.

Kvideseid.—See under CANALS, page 221. (Bandak Canal).

Mjosa. Exp. Stmr. *Skibladner.* Daily	June 24–Aug. 20.	To Aug. 21. Exp Stmr. *Skibladner*, Daily.
9 35	Eidsvold	20 20
12 10	Hamar	..
13 15	Gjovik	17 20
..	Modalen	16 35
..	Eriksrud	..
15 15	Lillehammer	15 20

Also steamer (Weekdays) leaving Modalen 6.15, due Hamar, 10.30; returning from Hamar, 14.30, reach Modalen 18.55 and Sundays, from Modalen 7.20, returning from Hamar 14.30.

Nisser and Vraa.—s.s. *Dolen*, Vraaliosen to Treungen, weekdays, 6.50; return 14.0.

Nordsjo.—See under CANALS, page 221.

Olden.—s.s. *Brixdal*, and m.b. *Alda*, Eide to Rustoen (1 hr.). From Eide 11.0 returning from Rustoen 16.30 every day.

Opstryn, or Stryn.—s.s. *Fridtjof Nansen.* Leave Hjelle Mo., We. & Sa. 8.0. Leave Mindresunde, 10.40.

Randsfjorden.—s.s. *Randsfjord* between Engelien and Onsaker as follows:—

	Mon., & Sat.	Wed., & Sat.
Engelien	—	4 50
Roykenvik Stn..............	11 0	9 0
Onsaker	12 0	10 0

	Wed.	Tues. & Fri.	Mon., & Sat.
Onsaker ....dep.	1420	—	13 5
Roykenvik Stn. ...arr.	1520	—	1425
Roykenvik ....dep.	—	11 0	
Engelien ....arr.	—	1415	2115

Saetersdalen.—s.s. *Bjoren*, see Byglandsfjord above.

Selbusjoen.—s.s. *Kong Sverre*, Havernes to Brottem (about 3 hours), Mon., Wed., 8.0, Fri., 16.0, Sats. 14.30, Sun. 6.0 & 19.0; returning from Brottem, Mon., Wed., 10.30, Fri. 18.30, Sats. 17.0, Sun. 8.30, 21.30

Siljord.—s.s. *Fjollgutten*, Ulvenæs to Næs.

Sirdal.—s.s. *Fram I.* Tonsad to Osen (Bakke), Mo., Tue., Thu., & Sat. 8.0, We. 7.30, ret. fr. Osen We., 16.30

Snaasen.—s.s. *Bonden*, and Motorboat *St. Olaf*, Sunnan to Seem (4½ hrs.) Mon., Tue., Wed., Thur., Fri. and Sat., 15.30; returniug from Seem, Mon., Tues., Wed., Thur., Fri. and Sat. 6.30.

Sperillen.—s.s. *Baegna*, from May 27 to June 22 and from August 25 until service ceases.

dep.	Sorum daily except Mondays	8.10	dep.	Sperillen daily except Sundays	13.50
arr.	Sperillen „ „ „	10.40	arr.	Sorum „ „ „	16.20

From June 23 to Aug. 24.	Sun., Wed., Fri.	Tue., Thu., Sat.	Daily except Sundays.	
dep. Sorum ..	8.10 ..	11.0	dep. Sperillen ..	13.50
arr. Sperillen ..	10.40 ..	13.20	arr. Sorum ..	16.20

Telemarken Lakes.—See Bandak CANAL, page 221. **Suldal.**—Full particulars page 431.

Tinnsjo.—s.s. *Tinn* and *Gausta*—Moel to Tinnoset daily 7‡55 and 14†50; arr. Tinnoset 10‡20 and 16†50 Returning from Tinnoset, daily 14‡20 and 22‡10; arr. Moel 15‡30 and 0†45.

Tyin.—Motor boat *Tyin* from Tyin hotel 7.45, 13.30, 18.20, return from Tyinholmen 9.0, 16.0, 19.30 (1 hour).

Tyrifjord.—s.s. *Ringerike*, Svangstrand to Sundvolden and *v.v.* (1¾ hours), from Svangstrand 10.30, return 5.10 daily. † 1st July to August 15th. ‡ From September 1st to 15th.

Trains throughout Poland run on Mid-European time; *i.e.*—One hour fast of Greenwich time.

Warsaw—Danzig (Gdansk)—Hel

123	123	123	123	123	123	123	Mls.	R Rest. Car.	123	123	123	123	123
	Exp		Exp	Exp	Exp	Exp			R	Exp	Exp	Exp	Exp
0 16	9 12	1128	1528	16†2	2114	2352	0	dep. WARSAW (Gl.) arr.	1454	21†42	2210	5 50	8 2
X	X‡	X	X	..	¶	S	87	,, Ilowo dep.	..		X	S	¶
	..		R	..	1 42	3 48	144	,, Jablonowo ,,	X‡	R		2 53	4 3
8 25	1358	1847	20 9	20 4	2 49	4 47	176	arr. Laskowice ,,	..	1740	1733	1 51	3 (
9 32	15 0	2042	2121	2121	4 0	5 57	223	,, Tczew c dep	9 5	1630	1630	0 42	1 42
1015	..	2147	2211	2211	6 22	7 4	244	,, Danzig ... p. 205 ,,	7 32	1515	1515	2318	.
..	..	..	..	..	..	..	..	dep. Gdansk .. arr.	..	..	..	..	..
..	..	..	..			..	264	arr. Zoppot dep.	..	..	..	..	..
1029	16 2	2156	2220	2220	5 0	7 8	256	,, Gdynia ,,	8 3	1525	1525	2335	0 31
1124	18 1	..	..	..	5¶53	9 36	277	,, Puck ,,	7 0	1430	..	2237	2338
1252	..	..	..		7†29	11 9	305	,, Hel ,,	5 50	13 0	..	21 1	2212

S 1, 2 & 3 Slp. Car Warsaw-Gdynia and Hel and *v.v.*

‡ Sep. 3 to Oct. 7. X *via* Torun *see below.* ¶ June 17 to Sept. 2. † Gdanska Stn.

(Berlin) Poznan—Warsaw (Moscow)

12	123	123	23	123	12	Mls.		123	12	123	123	123	123
luxe	Exp			ExA	ExS			Exp	luxe		ExD	ExA	
8 36	9 49	..	12 0	1743	2349	0	dep. Berlin (Fr.) p. 205 arr.	1917	2118	..	8 0	1052	1652
1149	1343	..	2030	2313	3 38		dep. Zbaszyn arr.	1519	18 4	..	3 40	6 24	9 41
1239	1437	..	2211	0 22	4 32	158	arr. Poznan dep.	1427	1714	..	2 44	5 20	8 0
124	15 5	1610	2255	0 56	4 4		dep. Posen arr.	14 5	1713	2253	2 34	5 8	7 40
	1643	1848	1 36	*via* Lodz.		220	dep. Konin dep.	1230	..	2046	..	*Via* Lodz.	4 58
1459	1755	2045	3 30		7 r 9	269	dep. Kutno dep.	1119	1456	19 6	0 37		3 20
N		1126	4 24		S	297	arr. Lowicz	r	N	1820	S r		2 4
1634	1938	2218	6 6	8 22	9 2	347	,, **Warsaw** (G.) dep.	9 24	1316	17 8	22 8	2156	0 16
1647	20 3	2255	6 35	8 55	9 19	..	,, ,, (W.) ,,	9 2	1258	1650	2134	2126	2354
2257	..	..	.	17 0	17 0	..	arr. Stolpce (p. 230) ,,	..	6 47	.	1320	1320	..
2322	..	..	..	20 5	20 5	..	arr. Negoreloje ,,	..	5 55	..	1150	1150	..
1610	..	..	..	1120	1120	..	,, Moscow (p. 230) ,,	..	1710	..	23 5	23 5	..

S Sleep. Car, 1 & 2 cl. Berlin-Warsaw-Stolpce and *v.v.*

A 1, 2 and 3 cl. cars Paris-Stolpce, and *v.v.* N Nord Exp., daily to Warsaw; 3 times weekly Warsaw-Moscow and *v.v.*, *see p.* 230. r Rest Car.

Warsaw—Lodz—Poznan.

123	123	¶	123	¶	123	¶	123	Mls.	R Rest. Car.	123	¶	123	¶	123	¶	123
		Exp		Exp		Exp				ExS	Exp		Exp		Exp	
5 50	8 40	1014	1312	1444	1625	21 8	2156	0	dep. Warsaw (G) arr.	8 22	8 58	1446	1751	19 8	2054	23 8
7 35	1015	X	1427	X	1813	X	2314	50	,, Zielkowice dep.	7 1	X	13 4	X	1733	X	2146
8 44	1127	12†12	1532	15†12	192	22†36	0 28	87	arr. Lodz-Kal ,,	6 2	7†30	1158	16†26	1627	19†26	2040
8 54	1138	..	1540	..	1935	..	0 40		dep. Lodz-Kal arr.	5 54	..	1145	..	1617	..	2030
11 6	1348		1736	..	2152	..	2 39	157	dep. Kalisz dep	4 5	..	9 39	..	1410	..	1830
1143	1429	..	18 6	..	2235	..	3 2	72	arr. Ostrow dep	3 35	..	8 57	..	1330		1745
1437	1711		2330		..		5 [illegible]	244	arr. Poznan dep.	0 56		6 15		9 25	..	1331

X *via* Skierniewice. ¶ Special Rail car Limited Train, one class only: EXTRA FARES. † Lodz Fabr. Stn.

Warsaw—Danzig—Gdynia.

			123	ExR	123	ExR	123	123	Mls.		R Rest Car.	123	ExR	123	ExR	123	123
			7 0	9†12	1128	1528	23 8	0 16	0	dep.	Warsaw (G) .. arr.	1558	1454	2350	2210	6 6	9 34
			9 52	11 1	1358	1712	0 20	3 1	79	,,	Kutno dep.	1345	1310	2132	2031	3 30	6 28
			1053	1143	15 2	1754	1 26	4 3	113	,,	Wloclavek .. ,,	1239	1222	2019	1944	2 12	4 48
			1142	1215	1552	1823	2 11	5 3	136	,,	Alexandrovo ,,	1125	1153	19 9	1916	1 21	4 4
			12 5	1230	1622	1839	2 36	6 2	147	arr.	Torun ...... dep.	1052	1137	1840	19 2	0 45	3 45
			..	..	2147	2211	3 11	1015	278	,,	Danzig (p. 205) dp.	5 57	7 32	1316	1515	1928	2218
			1745	16 2	2156	2220	3 20	1029	291	,,	Gdynia ...... ,,	6 12	8†3	13 14	1525	1935	2240

† Sep. 3 to Oct. 7.

Warsaw—Lwow (Lemberg).

R Rest. Car. S Sleeping Car.

123	123	123	123	123	123	123	123	Mls.		123	123	123	123	123	123	123	123
	Exp	Exp		R	Exp	S	S			Exp	Exp	R	R	Exp		S	
..	..		1512	1544	..	2012	2252	0	dep. Warsaw (Glo.) arr.	..	R	2254	2326		6‡38	7 42	8 50
..	..		1520	..		2025		..	,, Warsaw (... sc.) ,,	..	..		2316		..	..	8 34
..	..		17 0	Z	..	222	Z	65	,, Deblin dep.	..	..	Z	2150	..	5 6	Z	6 49
..	..	..	1853		..	0 55		109	,, Lublin ,,	..	..		2035		3 47		5 30
..	..	.	2033	2028		2 35	3 58	174	arr. Rozwadow dep.	..	..	1830	1825	..	1 15	2 42	3 8
6 34	..	..	—	2038	..	2 45	3 48		dep. Rozwadow arr.			1822	—	..	1 7	2 30	—
8 9	1143	1428	..	2131	2155	3 50	4 51	220	,, Preswork arr.	8 14	1448	1719	..	18 3	2346	1 27	..
8 26	1158	1454		2158	2211	4 5	5 [illegible]	235	,, Jaroslaw dep.	8 1	1435	17 7		1751	2333	1 15	..
9 11	1232	1529	..	2227	2245	4 4	5 43	251	,, Przemysl ,,	7 32	14 5	1636	..	1719	23 0	0 43	..
1027	1355	1645	..	2343	24 0	6 5	7 0	282	arr. Lwow (p. 204) ,,	6 15	1247	1520	..	16 0	2135	2325	..

Z *Via* Radom. ‡ Warsaw Gdanska Stn.

The times on the LEFT are to be read DOWNWARDS, those on the RIGHT UPWARDS.

(Berlin) Chojnice—Marienburg.

2 3	1 2 3 ExD	1 2 3 Exp	1 2 3 Exp	2 3	1 2 3 ExD	1 2 3 ExD	Mls.		2 3	1 2 3 ExD	1 2 3 ExD	1 2 3 ExD	1 2 3 ExD
..	8 44	From Danzig	From Danzig.	..	2255	2342	..	dep. Berlin (Fr.) (p. 205) arr.	To Danzig.	To Danzig.	21 0	7 10	7 43
..	1253			..	3 24	4 23	..	arr. Konitz.......... dep.			1659	2 26	3 2
5 15	13 1			2040	3 32	4 31	0	dep. Chojnice c...... arr.			1651	2 18	2 54
6 46	..			22 3	..	..	45	,, Starogard ....dep			..	..	..
7 11	1418	1658	1847	2229	4 42	5 41	61	arr. Tczew (p.205) c dep.	6 28	1046	1530	0 56	1 32
7 38	1423	..	..	23 9	5 20	6 28	..	dep. Dirschau arr.	..	..	14 4	2352	..
8 14	15 0	..	..	2355	6 22	7 4	..	arr. Danzig ....dep	..	..	1316	2318	..
8 21	1413	17 3	1855	2356	4 47	5 46	81	dep Tczew .... arr	6 20	1038	1523	0 49	1 25
8 46	..	1712	..	0 5	..	..	66	dep. Simonsdorf........ dep.	..	..	..	..	..
9 0	1429	1721	1911	0 15	5 4	6 3	74	arr Marienburg ....dep.	6 0	1022	15 7	0 32	1 8
1155	1620	..	21 8		7 15	8 5		arr Konigsberg (p 205)..dep	..	8 30	1316	2233	2316

(Warsaw) -Bogumin—Cadca- (Budapest)

2 3	1 2 3 Exp	1 2 3 Exp	2 3	2 3	Mls.		1 2 3 Exp	2 3	2 6	1 2 3 Exp	2 3	3 3
..	22 4	7 2	..	..		dep. Warsaw (p. 208). .. arr.	5 26	..	..	2 22		
3 57	4 46	15 3	1815	2015	0	dep. Bogumin ....arr	1 23	8 8	1051	1549	1945	2340
4 58	5 24	1538	1919	2120	..	arr Cieszyn Zachodni dep.	0 47	7 5	9 53	1453	1845	2247
5 8	5 25	1539	1925	2126	20	dep Cieszyn Zachodni arr	0 46	6 40	9 38	1452	1840	2236
7 8	S	..	2030	23 5	37	arr. Mosty Slaskie .....dep	S	5 0	8 44	..	1728	2051
	6 8	1622	..	..	44	arr Cadca c ....dep.	0 5	..	6 26	1411	1710	
..	6 57		..	..	63	arr. Zilina............ dep	23 9	..	..		..	..
..	1410				310	arr. Budapest (p. 202) dep	525	..	..		..	

S 1, 2 & 3 cl. Slee car Warsaw—Zilina & v.v.

Warsaw—Moscow.

1 2 3 Exp	1 2 3 Ex	r Rest. Car.	1 2 3 Exp	1 2 3 Exr
9 12	1644	dep. Warsaw (G) .. arr.	1254	2142
9 58	..	,, Warsaw (W) .. ,,	‡	2044
1227	1912	,, Bialystok	11 2	18 6
1558	22 0	,, Baranowicze ..dep	7 44	1424
17 0	2251	ar Stolpce ...... ,,	6 47	1320
1730	2318	dep. Stolpce ...... arr.	5 54	1225
18 5	2348	a. Negoreloje M.E. tm d.	5 22	1145
1837	2 8	d. Negoreloje E.E. tm a	6 42	1236
1120	1610	arr Moscow (p. 230) dep	17‡10	23 5

Warsaw—Wilno—Turmont (Riga).

Exp	Exp	S	S 1, 2 & 3 cl. Sleep. Car.	Exp	r	S
9 24	1644	0 16	dep. Warsaw (Gl.) .... arr.	1342	2130	6 30
9 37	1659	0 29	,, ,, (Wsc.) .... ,,	1328	2116	6 8
1150	1938	3 29	,, Bialystok............ ,,	1111	19 0	3 5
13 0	2039	4 58	,, Grodno .... ,,	10 6	1756	1 37
..	..	7 9	arr. Landwarow .. dep.			2343
1450	2231	7 45	arr. Wilno .... ,,	8 15	16 5	2310
15 5	2246	8 5	dep. (Vilna) .... arr.	8 0	1548	2250
1735	0 47	1044	arr. Turmont ....dep.	5 32	13 5	9 40
1840	2 17	1212	,, Zemgale .... ,,	6 2	14 0	2035
2332	6 37	1759	,, Riga (p. 208) .... ,,	0 20	7 13	1550

r Rest. Car, Warsaw-Wilno and v.v.

§ Mon., Wed. and Fri. from Warsaw. ‡ Sun., Wed. and Fri. from Moscow. † Weekdays only.

Warsaw—Kowel—Mobilany (Kiev).

1 2 3	1 2 3	1 2 3 Exp	1 2 3 Exp	1 2 2 ExS	Mls		1 2 3 ExS	1 2 3 Exp	1 2 3	1 2 3 Exp	1 2 3
1 20	..	1512	2012	23 4	0	dep. Warsaw (Gl.).... arr.	8 6	8 50	..	2326	5 26
1 33	8†35	1520	2025	2317	10	,, ,, (Wsch.) ,,	7 50	8 34	19†23	2311	5 8
5 2	1051	17 0	2223	0 43	70	,, Deblin .... ,,	5 56	6 44	1655	2145	2 30
7 5	1213	18 9	2349	1 44	115	ar. Lublin.......... dp	4 59	5 30	1526	2035	0 10
7 30	1221	1819	..	1 55		dp. Lublin.......... ar	4 50	..	1511	2026	2344
11 2	1620	21 0	..	4 52	215	,, Kowel .... dep	1 31	..	1121	1752	1920
1227	1747	2218	..	6 18	259	,, Kiwerce.......... ,,	0 12	..	9 49	1633	1718
1347	19 9	2335	..	7 40	299	arr Rowne .... ,,	2237	..	8 16	15 5	1541
1416	1940	2355	..	8 2	307	,, Zdolbunow...... dep	22 6	..	7 55	1210	15 5
1558		2 4	..		324	,, Mobilany (p. 327) ,,	..	..	6 35	1019	
..	..	..	..	1119	355	arr. Shepetovka .... dep.	1945		..	..	..
..	..	..	..	2033	547	,, Kiev (p. 231 .... ,,	1140		..	..	..

S 1 & 2 cl. Sleep. Car from Warsaw to Zdolbunow and v v daily

† Gdanska Station.

r Rest. Car.

(Warsaw) Lwow—Oraseni.

1 2 3	1 2 3	1 2 3	1 2 3 Exp	1 2 3 Exp	Mls.		1 2 3 Exp	1 2 3 Exp	1 2 3	1 2 3	1 2 3 Exp
2252		..	..	1544	..	dep. Warsaw (p. 216) .... arr.	.	2254	2254	6 38	7 42
0 15	2310	8 35	1142	19 5	..	,, Cracow (p. 228)...... ,,	1055	1734	2110	5 25	6 0
7 2	1038	1515	17 2	0 30	0	,, Lwow.................. ,,	5 40	1227	15 5	21 0	2252
1020	1340	1753	1859	2 43	87	arr. Stanislawow...... dep.	2 53	1022	12 8	1736	2049
1033	14 0	18 8	19 2	2 5	..	dep. Stanislawow...... arr.	2 36	1015	1134	1716	2043
1232	16 7	2010	2025	4 20	140	arr. Sniatyn Zaluaze c dep.	0 56	8 53	9 37	15 0	1913
1255	1621	..	2058	4 53	..	dep. Sniatyn Zaluaze c arr.	0 32	8 17	9 5	1420	1852
13 7	1639	..	21 5	5 5	152	arr. Oraseni (p. 331) .. dep.	0 25	8 5	8 45	14 0	1840
6 0		..	9 5	1615	504	,, Bucharest (p. 331) .... ,,	13 0	2124	..	2340	9 40

The times on the LEFT are to be read DOWNWARDS, those on the RIGHT UPWARDS.

Bogumin—Cracow—Lwow.

123	123	123	123	123	123	23	123	Mls.		123	123	123	123	123	123	123	123	23
Exp	Exp		Exp	Exp	Exp		Exp			Exp	Exp		Exp	Exp	Exp		Exp	
		..	Fr Berlin, p 204	From Berlin.			From Berlin.				To Berlin		To Berlin, p.204		To Berlin		s To Berlin	
..	5 47	..			1620	1820		..	d. Bogumin (p.203) a.	1339		2122		2355				9 8
..	6 11	..			1645	1853		0	,, Zebrzydowice ,,	1315		2048		2332		..		8 25
..	7 3	..			1735	2033		32	arr. Oswiecim ..dep.	1225		1914		2240		..		7 9
6 17	..	..	10 6	1734	..	..	22 5	..	dep. Katowice arr.	..	1218	..	1926	..	2332		8 7	..
..	7 6	..	S	..	1736	2038	s	..	,, Oswiecim .. ,,	1224	..	1911	S	2239	..		..	7 5
7 5	7 32	..	1050	1818	18 4	2121	2254	47	,, Trzebinia.. ,,	1155	1138	1813	1845	2212	2242	..	7 16	6 35
7 45	8 8	..	1127	1853	1839	2210	2334	72	arr. Cracow dep.	1118	11 3	1728	18 3	2135	22 0	..	6 30	5 49
⌣	8 35	7 56	1142	⌣	19 5	2310	0 15	..	dep. Cracow arr.	1055	⌣	17 3	1734	2110	⌣	5 25	6 0	⌣
..	9 53	1028	1253	..	2018	1 2	1 57	121	,, Tarnow.... ,,	9 52	..	1510	1626	1950	..	3 34	4 26	..
..	1143	13 5	1438	..	2155	3 36	4 2	194	,, Przeworsk dep.	8 15	..	1220	1449	18 5	..	1 10	2 19	..
..	1158	1328	1454	..	2211	4 25	4 20	204	,, Jaroslaw ,,	8 1	..	1152	1435	1751	..	0 46	2 2	..
..	1232	1421	1529	..	2245	5 17	4 56	225	,, Przemysl .. ,,	7 32	..	1055	14 5	1719	..	2349	1 23	..
..	1355	1630	1645	..	24 0	7 35	6 20	287	arr. Lwow ....dep.	6 15	..	8 40	1247	16 0	..	2142	2345	..
	R		R		R		s			R			R	R			s	

S 1 and 2 cl. Sleep. Car Berlin-Bucharest and v.v.

R Rest. Car Cracow-Lwow & *v.v.* *s* 1, 2 & 3 cl. Sleep. Car Katowice-Lwow & *v.v.*

☞ NOTE.—For Services (Vienna) Cracow-Warsaw, *see page* 203.

FINLAND.

Trains in Finland run on East European time, two hours fast of Greenwich time, and one hour fast of Mid-European time.

Helsinki—Rajajoki (Leningrad).

123	23	23	123	23	123	23	S 23	Mls		23	S 23	23	23	123	23	123	23
7 25	7 40	9 30	1245	1515	1710	2135	2320	0	Helsingfors dep. (Helsinki) .... arr.	7 0	7 50	8 35	1120	1140	1741	1832	23 6
A	8 55	1048	R	1633	R	23 2	0 37	37	,, Hyvinkaa...... ,,	5 26	6 35	7 13	1023	R	1626	1734	A
8 23	9 23	1115	1348	1710	1822	2350	1 6	44	,, Riihimaki ....dep.	5 10	6 20	6 57	1010	1045	1610	1746	22 2
10 0	12 0	1355	1527	1949	1959	2 31	3 35	120	arr. Kouvola.... dep.	2 30	3 1	3 45	7 22	8 54	13 5	1546	2015
1010	1236	16 8	1542		2011	3 20	4 0		dep. Kouvola.... arr.	..	2 41	2 25	..	8 44	1231	1536	20 1
1158	1516	19 4	1724	..	2214	6 33	7 0	195	arr. Viipuri dep.	..	2350	2320	..	7 5	9 50	1348	1818
..	1622	..	1735	†	..	7 15	7 15		dep. (Wiborg) arr.	..	2252	2252	..	..	9 34	13†23	18 6
..	1852	..	1946	†	..	1017	1017	255	arr. Rajajoki ......dep.	..	2025	2025	..	..	6 55	10†55	1550
..	..	..	..	..	..	14 5	14 5	..	,, Leningrad .... ,,	..	1836	1836	..	..	..	R	..

A To Sept. 14.

R Rest. Car Helsinki-Viipuri & *v.v.* **S** 1 & 2 cl. Sleeping Car Helsinki-Leningrad & *v.v.* † 2 & 3 cl. only.

Hanko (Turku) Helsinki.

23	23	12	123	23	23	123	Mls.	R Rest. Car.	123	23	23	123	23	123	23	123
		Exp	Exp			Exp			Exp			Exp		Exp		
5 12	9 35	R	R	1512	1910	R	0	dep. Hanko (Hango) .... arr.	..	1235	1740	R	1740	R	22 0	..
6 16	1050			1621	2022		36	arr. Karjaa (Karis)......dep.	..	1120	1635		1635		2055	..
↓	8 10	9 12	1420	..	1724	2024	0	dep. Turku (Abo)...... arr.	1132	1340	↑	1835	⌣	2036	..	2337
	9 25	10 3	1519	..	1855	2119	35	,, Salo .... ,,	1037	1226		1739	..	1940	..	2222
	1046	1057	1628	..	2025	2215	71	arr. Karjaa ....dep.	9 32	1110		1630	..	1841	..	21 5
6 30	1114	11 6	1634	1644	2050	2224	71	dep. Karjaa .... arr.	9 29	1052	1612	1624	..	1834	2040	2050
8 55	13 6	1225	18 0	1845	2255	2345	125	arr. Helsinki ....dep.	8 5	8 40	1348	15 0	..	17 5	1825	192[illegible]

Helsinki—Seinajoki—(Rovaniemi)—Tornio

23	23	¶ 23	23	23		23	Mls			23	23	¶ 23	23	23	23
Exp		Exp R	Exp		S	Exp			S			Exp R	Exp		Exp
8 25	9 30	14 0	1725	1820	2050	2220	0	dep. Helsinki ...... arr.	8 0	9 55	1241	1445	18 8	2340	2350
9 20	11 5	15 2	1826	20 7	22 5	2327	44	arr. Riihimaki......dep.	6 37	8 25	1056	1347	17 7	2212	2250
9 22	1125	15 4	1831	2024	2212	0 56		dep. Riihimaki ......arr.	6 27	8 15	1041	1342	17 2	2143	2242
11 4	1426	1651	2020	23 9	0 4	4 46	117	arr. Tampere .. dep.	4 20	5 30	7 40	1158	15 5	1830	2050
1250	1515	17 8	..	0 31	0 20	8 2		dep. ,, .. arr.	4 6	5 11	..	1148	1414	1746	2030
1948	1835	1938	..	3 46	2 55	1118	188	dep. Haapamaki .... arr.	1 8	1 43	..	9 35	1045	1345	1720
2327	2130	2154	..	6 47	5 20	1426	262	arr. Seinajoki ......dep.	2220	2241	..	7 30	7 44	1045	1427
..	..	2215	..	7 36	5 35		.	dep ,, ...arr.	22 2	2135	..	7 9	..	..	..
..	..	1 13	..	1049	7 56	..	332	arr. Kokkola ....dep.	1947	1820	..	4 13	..	..	..
..	..	4 59	..	1428	1040	..	437	arr. Lappi .... dep.	17 8	1438	..	0 38	..	..	..
..	..	6 20	..	1545	1134	..	471	arr Oulu .... dep.	1615	1318	..	2315	..	..	..
	..	9 10	..	1919	1342	..	537	arr Kemi .. .. dep.	14 4	1023	..	2017	..	..	..
	..	1215	..	2350	1650	..	558	arr. Rovaniemi .. dep.	1116	5 6	..	1655	..	..	..
..	..	1019		2024	1452		608	arr. Tornio (p 218) ..dep.	13 5	9 10		1025			..

R Rest. Car Helsinki Tampere and *v.v.* **S** 1. 2 and 3 cl. Sleeping Car train Helsinki-Seinajoki and *v v.*, with Sleepers to Oulu. ¶ 1, 2 and 3 cl. Sleeping Car Haapamaki to Tornio and *v.v.*

The times on the LEFT are to be read DOWNWARDS, those on the RIGHT UPWARDS.

UNION OF SOCIALIST SOVIET REPUBLICS.

These tables (except the Central Asia Rlys.) are according to Moscow time. This (differing sometimes considerably from local time) is 3 hrs. 1 min. fast of Green., or 2 hrs. 1 min. fast of Mid-European time.

Leningrad, Ritupe (Riga).

2 3	Mls.		2 3
		(Varshavsk Sta.)	
1435	0	dep. **Leningrad** .. arr.	10 0
21 0	122	Pskov	3 35
2210	139	arr. Ostrow	1 59
2335	171	arr. Ritupe ...... dep	0 20
7 26	358	,, Riga, *p.* 208 ,,	16 7

Moscow Arkhangelsk. 2, 3 cl.

9 40	0 10	dep. **Moscow** (Sev.) arr.	1930	6 15
1221	2 31	Alexandrov .. ,,	1645	3 44
1936	9 23	arr. Danilov ...... dep.	8 45	2049
1950	9 33	dep. Danilov ...... arr.	8 30	2039
2337	13 0	arr. Vologda ...... dep.	4 45	1710
0 12	1332	dep. Vologda ...... arr.	4 7	1637
1915	6 30	arr. **Arkhangelsk** dep.	9 0	2340

Leningrad, Moscow.

1 2 3	1 2 3	2 3	2 3	Mls		1 2 3	1 2 3	2 3	2 3
Exp	fast	fast	fast		(October Station).	Exp	fast	fast	fast
0 30	0 40	2125	2150	0	dep. Leningrad .. arr.	1025	13 5	9 5	1010
5 47	7 13	3 50	4 18	196	Bologoe (*below*)	5 40	7 7	3 0	4 4
..	9 19	5 51	6 19	271	Likhoslavl ..	..	4 54	0 52	1 56
8 13	1014	6 46	7 14	297	Kalinin (Tver)....	3 18	4 2	0 0	1 5
1045	1330	10 0	1025	405	arr. Moscow (Oct.) dep.	0 30	0 40	2025	2140

S Sleeping Car. r Rest Car. + Kursk Station.

Stolpce, Minsk (Leningrad), Moscow.

Exp	Ex ¶	Mls.		Ex X	Exp
1733	2252	0	dep. Stolpce *c. p.* 226 arr.	6 27	1225
18 8	2322	7	arr. } Negoreloje { M.E.t. dep.	5 55	1150
2137	2 38	..	dep. } Negoreloje { E.E.t. arr.	6 42	1236
2229	3 30	38	arr. } Minsk .... { dep.	5 54	1148
2246	3 42		dep. } Minsk .... { arr.	5 39	1133
2 14	7 10	170	arr. Orsha .... dep.	2 11	8 5
3 10	..		dep. Orsha .... arr.	..	4 41
1845	..	540	arr. Leningrad ...... dep.	..	1245
2 31	7 25	..	dep. Orsha .... arr.	1 56	7 50
4 12	9 6	245	arr. Smolensk .... dep.	0 17	6 11
7 16	1211	417	,, Vyazma ,,	2112	3 7
1120	1610	506	,, Moscow (Smolenskii) ,,	1710	23 5

¶ Mon., Wed. and Fri.
X Sun., Wed. and Fri.

(Riga) Bigosovo—Moscow.

1550	dep. Riga (*p.* 208) .... arr.	1759
0 15	arr. } Bigosovo .... { dp	1050
0 35	dep. } Bigosovo .... { ar	1040
1440	arr. Moscow (Smolenskii) dp	2030

Moscow, Kiev, Odessa.

1 2 3	1 2 3	Mls.	* Bryansk station.	1 2 3	1 2 3
fast	fast			fast	fast
20 0	2215	0	dep. **Moscow*** .. arr.	8 10	9 25
4 19	8 1	238	,, Bryansk .. ,,	2234	0 59
S	..	..	dep. Moscow .. arr.	..	
	..	..	,, **Kursk** ...... ,,	..	
9 40	1356		dep. Konotop .. arr.	1630	1938
1013	1430	399	Bakhmatch	1559	1912
1348	1817	415	arr. **Kiev** (*below*) dp.	12 7	1540
..	1840	0	dep. **Kiev** ...... arr.	1142	..
..	22 7	99	,, Kazatin (*below*) a	8 33	..
..	..		,, Volochisk arr.	..	..
..	0 25	165	,, Shmerinka ,,	6 16	..
..	6 18	361	arr. Razdelnaya	0 7	..
..	7 45	406	,, **Odessa** .... dep.	2235	..

S Sleeping Car.

(Volochisk) Shmerinka—Kiev.

Mls.	
	d. Volochisk (*p.* 204) a.
	a. Shmerinka (*p.* 204) a.
0	dp. Shmerinka .. ar.
26	ar. Kalinovka .. dp.
67	ar. Kazatin .. dp.
127	ar. Fastov ...... dp.
166	ar. Kiev dp.

Moscow, Kursk, Sevastopol.

1 2 3	Mls.	S Sleep. car.	1 2 3
fast		(Kursk Station).	fast
2353	0	dep. **Moscow** arr.	1139
3 58	121	Tula	7 34
8 22	237	Orel	3 37
1122	333	arr. } **Kursk** { dp.	0 28
1137	..	dep. } **Kursk** { ar.	0 16
1620	485	arr. Charkov ..	1937
1936	577	,, Lozovaya	1633
22 2	638	dep. Sinelnikovo	1417
2 5	755	,, Melitopol ..	9 28
5 27	849	arr. Djankoi ..	5 54
9 52	921	arr. Feodosia dep.	2248
10 7	954	,, **Sevastopol** ,,	0 59

Bucharest, (Odessa), Moscow

2 3		1 2 3
2245	dep. Bucharest (*p.* 330) .... arr.	7 25
1357	arr. } Tighina *c* .... { dep.	1737
1555	dep. } Benderi .... { arr.	1330
1625	arr. } Tiraspol .... { dep.	13 0
20 0	dep. } Tiraspol .... { arr.	1214
2141	arr. Razdelnaya .... dep.	1055
22 0	dep. Razdelnaya .... arr.	1035
2341	arr. Odessa .... dep.	8 49
0 7	dep. Razdelnaya .... arr.	6 18
1142	arr. } Kiev .... { dep.	1840
12 7	dep. } Kiev .... { arr.	1817
8 10	arr. Moscow .... dep	2215

The times on the LEFT are to be read DOWNWARDS, those on the RIGHT UPWARDS.

Tbilisi, Ordzhonikidze (Automobile Service).

7 5	7 55	8 10	9 30	dep. Tbilisi	arr.	1720	18 0	1820	2320
17 0	1830	18 5	20 5	arr. Ordzhonikidze	dep.	7 0	7 10	7 20	13 0

Moscow, Gorky.

1 2 3 S	272 Miles.	1 2 3 S
2310	dp. Moscow (Kursk) a	9 55
3 20	Vladimir	5 47
9 0	arr. Gorky	2340

S Sleeping Car.

Shepetovka, Kiev, Kharkov, Baku.

Exp	Mls			Exp
1125	0	dep. Mobilany (p. 227)	a	2251
1314	29	a. Shepetovka p. 227	d	1953
1440	..	d. Shepetovka p. 227	a.	1753
1731	121	arr. Kazatin ...	dep.	1450
1756		dep. Kazatin ...	arr.	1414
1919	180	arr. Fastov	dep.	1240
2032	220	arr. Kiev	dep.	1120
2057	0	dep. Kiev	arr.	10 9
5 52	442	,, Poltava	dep.	0 38
9 3	530	arr. Kharkov	dep.	21 6
9 28		dep. Kharkov ..	arr	2037
22 4	857	arr. Rostov	dep.	7 53
2236		dep. ..	arr.	7 23
13 6	1279	arr. Beslan ..	dep.	1749
4 20	1649	arr. Baku (*below*) ..	dep.	1 35

Moscow, Kharkov, Rostov.

fast 1 2 3	fast 1 2 3	Mls.			fast 1 2 3	fast 1 2 3
1155	1725	0	dep. **Moscow** (Kursk) (*page* 230)	arr.	5 47	2018
1611	2146	121	,, Tula	dep	1 44	1612
2021	1 55	237	,, Orel	,,	2135	12 3
2324	5 3	333	,, Kursk	,,	1815	8 54
3 54	9 36	485	arr. Kharkov	dep	13 8	4 3
4 14	10 3		dep. Kharkov (p. 230)	arr	1243	3 43
7 5	1254	579	arr. Lozovaya	dep.	9 59	0 59
10 3	16 2	673	,, Konstantinovka	,,	6 44	2140
1055	1655	691	,, Nikitovka	,,	6 12	21 7
12 3	18 6	719	,, Khartsisk	,,	5 0	2010
1656	2229	845	arr. **Rostov**	dep.	0 17	15 5

r Restaurant Car.

Rostov, Baku.

2 3 fast	1 2 3 fast			2 3 fast	1 2 3 fast
1716	2233	dep. **Rostov**	arr.	7 29	1445
3 14	8 22	arr. Mineralnye Vodi	dep	2210	5 28
3 38	8 42	dep. Mineralnye Vodi	arr	2148	5 10
7 24	1237	arr. Beslan	dep.	18 5	1 42
9 35	1355	arr. Ordzhonikidze	dp	1645	2341
7 39	1251	dep. Beslan	arr	1744	1 26
1257	1826	arr Machatch-Kala	dep.	1059	1845
2140	4 40	arr. **Baku**	dep.	0 55	10 0

Baku, Tbilisi, Batumi.

2 3	2 3	Mls.			2 3 fast	2 3
14 45	2226	0	dep. **Baku** ..	arr.	16 50	9 17
4 12	9 24	232	dep. Akstafa	dep.	3 56	2228
7 41	12 3	340	arr Tbilisi ..	dep	0 45	20 0
8 30	..		dep. Tbilisi ..	arr	23 55	..
20 45	..	558	arr. **Batumi** .	dep	12 0	..

Tbilisi, Yerevan, Dzhulfa.

2 3	2 3	1 2 3			2 3	1 2 3	2 3
6 40	1432	2242	dep Tbilisi (*abv.*)	arr	6 7	1141	1959
1323	2112	5 7	,, Kirovakan ..		0 14	5 1	13 5
1612	0 2	7 56	arr Leninakan ..	dep	2120	2 17	1013
2123	5 37	1311	arr Yerevan	dep	1418	1926	3 40
5 33	..	..	arr. Dzhulfa	dep.	..	..	19 5

Moscow. Tashkent, Ashkhabad.

1st day	..	dep.	Moscow (Kazan) arr.	..	7th day
3rd ,,	..	,,	Kuibishev .... dep.	..	6th ,,
3rd ,,	..	,,	Orenburg ...... ,,	..	6th ,,
4th ,,	..	,,	Kazalinsk ...... ,,	..	4th ,,
5th ,,	..	arr.	Tashkent ...... ,,	..	3rd ,,
6th day	..	dep.	Tashkent .... arr.	..	3rd day
7th ,,	..	arr.	Samarkand ...... dep.	..	2nd ,,
7th ,,	..	,,	Kagan .... ,,	..	2nd ,,
7th ,,	..	,,	Bokhara .... ,,	..	2nd ,,
8th ,,	..	,,	Mary (Merv) ...... ,,	..	1st ,,
8th ,,	..	,,	Ashkhabad .... ,,	..	1st ,,

SIBERIA, MANCHURIA, CHINA & JAPAN.

Sun.	Tue.	Wed.	Fri.	2349	dep Berlin (Fried)	arr.	8 0	Tue.	Thu.	Fri.	Mon.
Mon.	Wed.	Thu.	Sat.	0 10	dep. Berlin (Schles.) p. 205 ..	arr.	7 43	,,	,,	,,	,,
,,	,,	,,	,,	9 12	dep. Warsaw (G) p. 227 ...	arr.	2142	Mon.	Wed.	Thu.	Sat.
,,	,,	,,	,,	1733	dep. Stolpce c	dep.	1320	,,	,,	,,	,,
,,	,,	,,	,,	2137	dep. Negoreloje	arr.	1236	,,	,,	,,	,,
Tue.	Thu.	Fri.	Sun.	112[illegible]	arr Moscow (Smolenski) ...	dep	23 5	Sun.	Tue.	Wed.	Fri.
,,	,,	,,	,,	..	dep. Moscow (Smolenski)	arr.	..	,,	,,	,,	,,
,,	,,	,,	,,		arr. Moscow (Severnii)	dep.	..	,,	,,	,,	,,
Tue.	Thu.	Fri	Sun.	17 0	dep. **Moscow** (Severnii) ..	arr.	1330	Sun.	Tue.	Wed.	Fri.
Wed.	Fri.	Sat.	Mon.	1121	dep Kirov (Viatka) ..	arr.	1841	Sat.	Mon.	Tue.	Thu.
Thu.	Sat.	Sun.	Tue.	5 17	dep. Sverdlovsk	dep.	0 47	,,	,,	,,	,,
,,	,,	,,	,,	2311	arr. Omsk	dep.	6 23	Fri.	Sun.	Mon.	Wed.
Thu.	Sat.	Sun.	Tue	2331	dep. Omsk	arr.	6 3	Fri.	Sun.	Mon.	Wed.
Fri.	Sun.	Mon.	Wed.	1110	dep. Novosibirsk	dep.	1849	Thu.	Sat.	Sun.	Tue.
Sat.	Mon.	Tue.	Thu.	3 39	dep. Krasnoyarsk	dep.	2 51	,,	,,	,,	,,
,,	,,	,,	,,	9 15	dep. Kansk (Eniseiski) ...	dep	21 7	,,	,,	,,	,,
Sun.	Tue.	Wed.	Fri.	4 50	arr. **Irkutsk**	dep.	1 18	Wed.	Fri.	Sat.	Mon.
,,	,,	,,	,,	5 2[illegible]	dep. Irkutsk	arr.	0 43	,,	,,	,,	,,
Mon.	Wed.	Thu.	Sat.	8 6	arr. Karymskaya	dep.	23 3	Mon.	Wed.	Thu.	Sat.
Mon.	↓	Thur.	↓	8 16	dep. Karymskaya	arr.	2255	↑	Wed.	↑	Sat.
Wed.		Sat.		1630	arr. } Chabarovsk	dep.	14 0		Mon.		Thr.
,,		,,		17 0	dep. } Chabarovsk	arr.	1330		,,		,,
Thur.		Sun.		1818	arr. Vladivostock‡	dep.	2350		Sun.		Wed.
—	Wed.	—	Sat.	8 16	dep. Karymskaya	arr.	2255	Mon.	—	Th.	—
—	,,	—	,,	23 0	arr. Manchouli ¶	dep.	8 34	,,	—	,,	—
Daily			1st day	13 0	dep. Manchouli *	arr	1050	2nd day	Daily		
			2nd day	1410	arr. Harbin	dep.	1030	1st day			

HARBIN—MUKDEN—DAIREN.

Daily.	1st day	17 0	dep. Harbin	arr.	8 0	2nd day	Daily.
	2nd day	2 42	arr. Mukden	dep.	23 5	1st day	
	,,	9 40	arr. Dairen	dep.	17 0	,,	

HARBIN—MUKDEN—TIENTSIN—PEKING.

Daily.	1st day	22 0	dep. Harbin	arr.	8 0	2nd day	Daily.
	2nd day	7 5	arr. } Mukden	dep.	23 5	1st day	
	,,	8 0	dep. } Mukden	arr.	2250	,,	
	,,	2125	arr. Tientsin	dep.	8 55	,,	
	,,	2355	arr. Peking	dep.	6 25	,,	

HARBIN—MUKDEN—KEIZYO—HUSAN—JAPAN.

Daily.	1st day	2330	dep. Harbin	arr.	7 10	4th day	Daily.
	2nd day	1230	arr. Mukden	dep.	1710	3rd day	
	3rd. day	3 15	arr. Keizyo	dep.	2 35	2nd day	
	,,	11 5	arr. Husan	dep.	1855	,,	
	4th day	1525	arr. Tokyo	dep.	15 0	1st day	

TIENTSIN—PUKOW—NANKING—SHANGHAI.

SUSPENDED.

Steamer services from Dairen to Shanghai, *p.* 471, and from Vladivostock to Tsuruga, *p.* 477.

TIME.—Moscow time is three hours later than that of Greenwich. When it is 12.0 noon at Moscow, it is 16.56 at Irkutsk, 18.0 at Harbin. Times at intermediate stations on the Trans-Siberian Railway are given in Moscow time. ¶ Moscow time. ‡ Vladivostock time 8 hours fast of Moscow time. * Manchukuo time: 6 hours fast of Moscow time. From Niegoreloje to Moscow, and from Moscow to Manchuria and Vladivostock (*via* Chabarovsk), Sleeping Cars of direct communication, soft and hard class cars.

VOLGA STEAMERS. (Summer only.)

Volga.			
Rybinsk	dep.	1730	Daily.
Yaroslavl	,,	0 0	,,
Kostroma	,,	7 30	,,
Kineshma	,,	1750	,,
Gorky (Nishni-Novgorod)	arr.	6 10	,,
	dep	14 0	Daily.
Kazan	,,	1430	,,
Ulianovsk	,,	2 5	,,
Kuibishev	arr.	12 0	,,
	dep.	16 0	,,
Saratov	arr.	12 0	,,
	dep.	16 0	,,
Stalingrad	arr.	9 15	,,
	dep	1415	,,
Astrakhan	arr.	12 0	,,
Astrakhan	dep.	14 0	Daily.
Stalingrad	arr.	20 0	,,
	dep.	1 0	,,
Saratov	arr.	5 0	,,
	dep.	8 0	,,
Kuibishev	arr.	1310	,,
	dep.	1640	,,
Ulianovsk	,,	7 55	,,
Kazan	arr.	2240	,,
	dep.	2 40	,,
Gorky (Nishni-Novgorod)	arr.	9 0	,,
	dep.	18 0	Daily.
Kineshma	,,	1215	,,
Kostroma	,,	2140	,,
Yaroslavl	arr.	6 0	,,
Rybinsk	arr.	1330	,,

U.S.S.R. CASPIAN SEA STATE S/S LINES

Astrakhan, Baku, Krasnovodsk.

Astrakhan dep.		Krasnovodsk dp.	
Petrovsk ..dep.		Baku next day, a.	
Baku......arr.			
		Baku ......dep.	
Baku ....dep.		Petrovsk ..dep.	
Krasnovodsk a.		Astrakhan ..arr.	

Meshedesser Line.—Weekly

Astrakhan dep.	
Alexandrovskd.	
Krasnovodsk arr.	
Krasnovodsk dep.	
Astrabad ..dep.	
Meshedesser, a.	
Meshedesser, d.	
Astrabad ..dep.	
Krasnovodsk arr.	
Krasnovodsk dep.	
Alexandrovskd.	
Astrakhan ..ar.	

Astara Line.

Astrakhan dep.	
Petrovsk ..dep.	
Baku .... arr.	
Baku .... dep.	
Astara .... arr.	
Astara ....dep.	
Baku .... arr.	
Baku .... dep.	
Petrovsk ..dep.	
Astrakhan..arr.	
Baku ......dep.	
Lenkoran arr.	
Lenkoran dep.	
Baku ...... arr.	

Baku—Pechlevi.

EXPRESS SERVICE.

s.s. *Chaumian*

Baku ....dep.	14 0 We.	16 0 Sat.
Pechlevi..arr.	7 0 Th.	9 0 Sun.
Pechlevi..dep.	16 0 Mo.	19 0 Th.
Baku .... arr.	9 0 Tue.	12 0 Fri.

Routes to Teheran, Iran (Persia).

I.—Via Simplon-Orient-Taurus Exp., *see page* 83 and 334 **(8½ days).**

II.—Via U.S.S.R. { **Moscow and Baku** (9¾ days). **Shepetovka and Baku** (7½ days).

III.—Via Istanbul, Batumi, Baku (15 days).

FRANCE. (Greenwich Time).

THROUGH SERVICES TO AND FROM FRANCE.

With England, see pp. 111, 112, *et seq.*, 135, 237, 241, 242.
,, *Belgium pp.* 239, 240.
,, *Holland p.* 154.
,, *Germany: via Cologne p.* 240; *via Metz, p.* 275.
via Strasbourg, pp. 272 to 274
With Switzerland, pp. 119, 120, 266, 267, 268, 269
,, *Italy pp.* 118 124 264, 265, 270.
,, *Spain & Portugal, pp.* 115-117, 250, 255, 321
,, *Germany and the Orient, pp.* 269, 274.
,, *U.S.S.R., p.* 226, 240.

Calais, Hazebrouck, Lille, (Brussels, Valenciennes). [French Rlys. (Nord).

Mls.	*Thro' Tables pp.* 127, 128	123	123	123	123	123	123		123	123	123	123	123	123	123		123	
		Exp			Exp			A	Exp			Ex§§		Exp		A		A
	LONDON (*p.* 112) d.	To Bale.	..	..	..	..	..	..	..	..	..	11 0	..	14 0	..	..	..	..
..	Calais (Maritime) d.		..	..	..	..	..	..	..	..	..	1444	..	1730	..	..	..	..
0	Calais (Ville) dep.		5 37	6 43	7 40	9 13	..	..	..	12 7	..	1449	1641	R	..	..	1940	2313
26	St. Omer		6 33	7 29	8 9	10 8	..	..	..	1258	..	1519	1737		..	..	2035	2345
38	Hazebrouck .... arr.		6 51	7 53	8 26	1032	..	..	..	1322	..	1536	18 1	1820	..		2059	0 2
..	LONDON *p.* 137) d.	22 0	..	..	..		..	..	..	..	..	..		..	..	..		..
..	Dunkerque .. dep.	6 31	6 31	..	..	9 48	..	..	1255	.	1549	1444	1737	..	1825	1936	2015	..
..	Hazebrouck .... dep.	7 2	7 5	8 0	8 34	1037	1113	1154	1329	1335	1637	1539	1817	1822	1916	2012	2110	0 3
..	Armentieres .. arr.	..	7 38	8 33	8 53	11 2	1151	1215	1349	14 8	1711	1558		..	1949	2034	2143	0 23
63	La Madeleine	..	7 59	..	..	..	1212	..	..	1436	1737	..	..	..	..	2049	22 6	
65	Lille .... arr.	7 37	8 7	8 54	9 13	1122	1220	1235	14 9	1447	1745	1619	..	1858	20 9	2056	2214	0 41
							¶	¶										
84	*p.* 149 Tournai .... arr.	..	9 12	..	..	..	1415	1415	..	1616	..	1718	..	1931	2140	..	..	..
136	BRUSSELS (Midi) a.	..	1030	..	..	..	1530	1530	..	1720	..	1832		20*50	..	..	..	..
						A							A			123		
..	Lille .... dep.	7 44	8 28	..	..	1127	..	..	1415	..	..	1757	1955	..	2015	2117	..	..
107	Valenciennes .. arr.	8 20	9 40	..	..	1210		..	1452	..	..	1845	2042	..	2130	22 0	..	..

From Nancy, &c., page 271.	123	123	123	123		123		123	123	123		123	123	123	123	123	123	123
		Exp		Exp	A	Exp	A			Exp	A	Exp					Rap	
Valenciennes . dep.	..	..	6 10	7 44	..	..	9 26	1110	1150	13 9	14 7	..	1623	..	18 7	..	2254	..
Lille .... arr.	..	..	7 28	8 30	..	..	1010	1153	1312	1346	1459	..	17 9	..	1852		2331	..
								A										
BRUSSELS (Midi) d.	..	..	..	..	7 15	8*38	..		..	..	..	1428	..	..	16¶15	1722	2115	..
Tournai (*p.* 149) dp.	..	5 25	6 37	..	8 33	9 57		1030	..	..		1542	..	..	17¶43	19 0	2237	..
			A			R	123				123					A		
Lille .... dep.	5 13	7 3	8 12	8 37	9 39	1030	1048	1241	1314	1353	16 3	1647	1745	1818	19 0	2011	2341	0 0
La Madeleine .. dep.	..	7 12	8 17	..	9 44			1246	..	..	1612	..	..	1827	..	..	..	0 9
Armentieres .. dep.	5 35	7 29	8 31	8 57	9 59	..	11 7	1249	1336	1413	1639	..	18 5	1848	1919	2030	..	0 28
Hazebrouck .... arr.	6 8	7 54	8 58	9 17	1025	11 5	1130	1320	1410	1434	1712	1720	1829	1922	1943	2052	0 16	..
Dunkerque .. arr.	7 5	8 47	9 34	1024	..	1213	..	..	..	1522	..	..	1918	..	2034	2135	1 8	..
LONDON (*p.* 137) a.	..		..	..	..		..	..	..		..	..			..	..	9 10	..
Hazebrouck .... dep.	6 35	8 5	..	9 18	..	1116	1150	..	1442	1612	..	1722	1835	1949	..	21 0	..	..
St. Omer	7 3	8 22	..	9 36	..	.	1216	..	15 0	1647	..	1739	19 1	2013	..	2116	From Bale.	..
Calais (Ville) .. arr.	7 58	8 51	..	1020	..	1150	13 7	..	1529	1740	..	18 8	1953	21 5	..	2153		..
,, (Gare Mari) a.	..	§	..	1026	..	..	..	..	1535	..	..	‡‡	..	..	..			..
LONDON (*p.* 112) ar.	..	..	..	1530	..	1530		..	1855	..	..	23 0	..	..	..	..	..	..

A Auto-Rail Car, Supplement. § arr. Boulogne V. 9.41. ‡‡ *Via* Boulogne.
§§ 3 cl. dep. London 10.30. ¶ Not Sundays or Fetes. * To and from Brussels (Nord).
R 1, 2 and 3 cl. Cars and Rest. Car, Calais–Brussels and *v.v.*

(Calais), Lille, St. Quentin, (Laon). [French Rlys. (Nord).

123	123	123	123	123	123	123	123	Mls.	*Thro' Table, see p.* 123.	123	123	123	123	123	123	123	123
	Exp				Exp							Exp					Exp
..	A	6 43	9 13	1449	1449	..	1730	0	dep. Calais .... arr.	1020	1528	13 7	1528	1740	2134	..	A
6 50	8 14	9 22	1134	1644	1734	..	1923	69	dep. **Lille** .... arr.	7 33	1258	1040	1258	14†0	1848	2020	2256
7 35	8 43	1049	1243	1718	18 3	..	2020	87	dep. Douai ...... arr	5 55	1217	1010	1217	1330	1755	1922	2228
8 1	..	1112	13 6	1743	A		2044	90	dep. Aubigny ...... arr.	5 33	1149	A	1149	1312	1731	19 0	..
8 50	9 12	1137	16 5	1844	1831	1948	2144	122	dep. Cambrai .... arr.	5 10	8 24	9 45	1044	1248	1659	18 8	22 3
9 27	9 42	12 5	1640	1923	19 1	2023	2222	137	arr Busigny (*p.* 239 dp	4 32	7 52	9 21	1011	1221	1624	1736	2138
..	10 8	1413	17 7	21 8	1929	21 8	..	..	arr. **St. Quentin** dep.	..	7 6	8 51	9 43	1147	..	1646	21 9
..	1028	1438	1728	2129	1949	2129	..	..	arr. Tergnier dep.	..	6 35	8 31	9 6	1127	..	1613	2049
..	11 6	1518	18 3	22 7	2017	22 7	..	..	arr **Laon** *p* 237 d.	..	5 30	8 7	..	9 52	..	..	2023

A 1, 2, & 3 cl. cars Lille-Dijon and *v.v.*

P

The times on the LEFT are to be read DOWNWARDS, those on the RIGHT UPWARDS.

Calais, Boulogne, Amiens, Paris. [French Rlys. (Nord).

Thro' Tbles, pp. 118 to 122 & 125, 126.	123	Exp 123	A	123	123	Rap 12	Exp 123	12	Rap 12	Exp 123	123	luxe 12	Rap 12	Exp 123	Rap 12	Rap 12	123
p. 112 { LONDON— (Victoria) dep.	..	..	..	..	..	9 0	9 0	11 0	11 0	..	..	14 0	14 0	14 0	1630	1630	..
									Rc				Rc		c	a	
Calais (Maritime) d.	..	..	..	..	..	R	..	1430	1450	..	..	1725	1735	18 0	..	..	..
Calais (Ville) dep.	..	6 0	8 19	8 56	1024	c	1244	..	..	..	1533	..	..	1813	P	..	21 5
Boulogne-Tintelleries	..	6 52	8 54	..	1121	..	1340	..	|	..	..	..	1811	..	..	..	2158
Boulogne (Ville) .. ar.	..	..	..	9 41	1126	..	..		|	..	1627	..	P	19 5	..	..	22 4
Folkestone (str.) dp.	..	..	..	123	.	1055	1055	"Golden Arrow" Pullman Car Train	|	..	..	..	--	..	1825	1825	..
Boulogne Quai dep	..	..	..			1255	1330		|	..	..	..	..	..	2020	2030	..
Boulogne (Ville) dep.	5 11	..	..	..	1130	13 1	1345		|	1559	1653	..	..	1915	2026	..	2212
Etaples .... arr.	5 48	7 15	9 16	..	1213	..	14 3		|	1623	1730	1818	..	1938	2049	2057	2250
Abbeville ...... dep.	7 8	8 16	10 0	1130	1316	..	1459		|	1731	1919	To Laon.	..	2035	|	..	2352
Longpre	7 33	..	..	1155	1340	|	..		|	1747	1943		..	2051	|	..	..
Amiens (b) .... ar.	8 12	8 48	1031	1231	1418	|	1531		|	18 8	2020		..	2112	|	2158	..
			123		..												
(to Rouen, p. 242) dp.	9 8	8 58	1034	13 3	1454	|	1536		|	1812	..		..	2122	|	2159	..
Clermont	1033	..		1435	..	↓	1631		↓	1913	..		..	..	↓	To Laon	..
Creil	1056	9 59	..	1457	..	..	1647	..		1932	..		..	2224			..
Paris (Nord) b .. arr.	1141	1010	1215	1554	1625	1548	1734	1744	1810	2019	..		21 0	23 5	2311		..

For other trains, Paris and Amiens, see p. 238.	123	Exp 123	Rap 12	Rap 12	Exp 123	luxe 12	Exp 123	Rap 12	123	Rap 12	123	Exp 123	Exp 12	Exp 1/23	123	Exp 123	Exp 123
				Rc	C			**		cR			c				
Paris (Nord) b .. dep.	..	7 10	From Laon	8 20	8 30	From Laon.	8 33	1030	1043	1215	1345	15 0	1625	1720	1828	1940	2315
Creil	..	7 49		..	..		9 17	..	1133	..	1431	..	..	..	1913	2019	0 2
Clermont	..	..	e	..	..		..	..	1154	..	1450	..	..	..	1931		0 19
Amiens b .. arr.	..	8 52	9 26	..	9 57		1015	..	1328	P	1624	1636	P	1856	2033	2119	1 9
Amiens b .. dep.	7 5	8 55	9 30	..	10 0		1020	..	..	..	18 2	1641	..	1858	..	2123	1 49
Longpre	7 46	..	..	..	..		1042	..	..	|	1842	..	..	..	..	..	..
Abbeville	8 18	9 29	..	..	1034		11 0	..	..	|	1938	1717	..	1931	..	2157	2 26
Etaples	9 28	1024	1035	..	1134		1158	1248	..	|	2049	1818	1839	2013	..	2253	3 17
Boulogne (Ville) arr.	10 4	1048	..	..	1155	1254	1221	1311	..	|	2125	1842	1859	..	..	2321	3 48
Boulogne (Quai) ar.	..	..	..	..	..	13 0	1230	1316		|	..	1848	19 5	..	..	..	..
Folkestone (str.) ar.	..	..	..	..	..	1515	1515	1515	123	|	..	..	2050	..	..	..	..
Boulogne (Ville) dep.	..	1119	..	..	..	..	..	..	1651	|	..	1848	|	..	..	2327	..
Boulogne Tintelleries	..	..	11 0	11 7		..	..	..	1656	|	..	1854	|	2036	..	2333	3 59
Calais (Ville) arr.	..	1211	..	..	..	..	..	..	1757	↓	..	1946	|	2110	..	0 18	4 51
,, Gare Maritime) a.	..	..	1136	1141	..	..	..	..	..	1523	..	..	|	..	..	..	..
p. 112. { Dover Pier .. dep.	..	..	1355	1355	..	..	..	..	..	1720	..	..	↓	..	..	..	..
LONDON— Victoria .. arr.	..	..	1530	1530		1720	1720	1720	..	1855	..	..	23 0	..	..	..	..

A Auto rail. **C** July 1-Oct. 2. **P** Pullman Cars between Calais or Boulogne and Paris. **R** Rest. car. *a* Only takes 2 cl. for Laon and beyond. *c* Takes 1 and 2 cl. local passengers between Boulogne or Calais and Paris, if without baggage. *d* Only takes for beyond Amiens. *e* Only takes 2 cl. for Amiens and beyond. ** "Golden Arrow" Pullman Car Train.

Amiens, Laon (Reims). [French Rlys. (Nord).

Mls.		123	123	123	1/23	123	1/23	123	123	12	12	123
			Exp	Exp			D	Exp		luxe	Rap	
..	Calais ...... dep.	..	6 5	Fr. Lille.	..	..	1234	From Lille	..	1725	†	18 3
.	Boulogne .... ,,	..	6‡57		..	..	1339		..	..	20†30	1918
0	**Amiens** ...... dep.	5 49	9 6		9 46	1258	16 2		1745	..	2159	22 6
50	Tergnier .. arr	7 29	1019	1028	1119	1436	1724	1949	1933	B	SR	2340
	Tergnier .. dep	7 38	1021	1040	1126	1444	1733	1950	2133			2358
67	**Laon** ...... arr.	8 13	1047	11 6	1156	1518	18 3	2017	22 7	2030	2314	0 30
.	Reims (p. 270) ar.	..	1155	1155	..	1855		21 7	..	..	‖	
..	Bale (p. 268) ,,	..	2051	2051	..	..		5 42	..	2 35	5 33	

B Arlberg-Orient Express. *See page* 83 for days of running.
D Auto-rail
R Rest. Car.
S Sleeping Cars.

Mls.		123	123	123	12R	123	12	123	1/23	123	123	1/23
					Rap	Exp	luxe				Exp	
..	Bâle (p. 268 dep.	..	..	..	0 30	23 0	3 20	..		..	1126	
.	Reims (p. 270 ,,	..	5 27	..	6 57	7 7	B	9 45	D	1234	1937	D
0	**Laon** .... ,,	5 30	7 4	7 40	7 58	8 7	1013	1155	1345	1746	2023	
7	Tergnier .. arr	6 1	7 29	8 15	8 22	8 30	..	1231	1417	1820	2048	
	Tergnier .. dep.	6 10	7 39	9 1	8 24	8 32	..	1245	1419	1828	2049	2132
67	**Amiens** ...... arr.	7 47	8 50	1034	9 26	To Lille.	..	1428	1527	2010	To Lille.	23 6
..	Boulogne ... arr.	..	1048	1552	S		13 0	..	1839	2323		..
.	Calais ...... ,,	..	1211		11†36		..	..	1944	0 20		..

† Maritime Station.
‡ Tintelleries Station
‖ See note ¶ page 270.

(Valenciennes), Lille, Arras, Amiens Paris. [French Rlys. (Nord

Miles from Lille.		123	123	123	123	123	123	12	123	123	123	123	12	123	123
		Rap From Dunk'rque	Rap		Exp From Dunkerque	Rap		Auto Rail				Rap	Rap		
	Valenciennes dep.		..	6 21		8 47	..	1114	1125	1241	1514	1632	..	1833	..
	Somain...... ,,		..	6 49		9 10	..	1139	1151	13 6	1541	1650	..	19 0	..
	Douai ...... arr.		..	7 4		9 25	..	1154	12 6	1321	1556	17 5	..	1915	..
	Lille ...... ,,			7 52		1040	..	1258	..	15 3	1636	1848		2028	.
				123								1 2		Exp	
0	**Lille** ....dep.	↓	6 45	6 50		9 5	9 22	1134	1212	1310	1531	1644	19 0	1910	1923
21	Douai .... ,,		7 9	7 18	..	9 32	1019	1158	1315	1338	1643	1711	1927	1943	2037
37	Arras (*below*)		7 28	7 41	8 1	9 58	1058	1216	14 7	14 2	1736	1732	1952	20 6	2216
78	Longueau......arr.		..	8 36	..	1044		..	..		..	1814	R	..	.
81	**Amiens**...... ,,		..	8 37	8 47	1055	1227	1253	1531	1448	1913			2111	2343
			¶					B							
..	**Amiens** ....dep.		..	..	8 58	1034	13 3	1256	1536	1454	..	..		2122	..
78	Longueau...... ,,		..	8 38	..	1046	1310	..	..		..	1815		..	..
124	Creil .... ,,		..	..	9 59	..	1457	..	1647		..		↓	2224	..
156	**Paris** (Nord) .. arr.	9 0	9 15	10 4	1040	1215	1554	14 9	1734	1625		1936	2156	23 5	..

A Limited train. B Buffet Car. a Does not take 2 cl. at Lille for Douai.

Mls.	Other trains, Paris & Amiens, see p. 237.	123	12	123	123	123	12	123	123	123	12	123	12	123	123	123
		Exp	Rap	Exp	Rap		¶ B	Exp	Exp		Auto Rail	Rap	Rap	Exp	Rap	fast
0	**Paris** (Nord) ..dep.	7 10	8 15	8 33	10 0	1043	1125	13 0	15 0	..	17 0	1720	1925	1940	2150	2315
32	Creil ....arr.	7 48	↓	9 16	R	1131	..	1337	..	..			R	2018	..	2358
78	Longueau ...... ,,	8 44		..	1122	1321	..	..	..		¶	1846	2043		..	..
81	**Amiens**...... ,,	8 52		1015	1133	1328	1238	1436	1636	..	..	19 2	2054	2119	..	1 9
	Amiens ....dep.	9 2		1022	1112	14 0	1241	1443	1645	17 0	..	1837	2029	2126		1 26
78	Longueau...... ,,	..		..	1124	..	..	..	..		..	1848	2044	..		..
119	Arras..........arr.	9 56	1014	1154	12 9	1528	1318	1545	1749	1833	1848	1935	2127	2219	To Dunkerque.	2 39
135	Douai.......... ,,	1019	1035	13 2	1230	1625	1335	16 5	1814	1928	19 5	1958	2147	2244		3 21
156	**Lille** .... ,,	1050	11 2	15 3	1258	18 9	14 0	1636	1848	2117	1930	2028	2215	2323		4 0
								Auto Rail					123			
..	Lille ......dep.		9 22	..	1134	1531	..	..	1816	..	1816	19 1	..	2219		..
..	Douai ...... ,,		1043	..	1238	17 2	..	16‖10	1913	..	1913	20 5	2152	2316		..
..	Somain ......arr.	..	1058	..	1253	1717		1623	1927	..	1927	2020	22 7	2331		..
..	Valenciennes ,,	..	1125	..	1322	1743	..	16‖42	1952	..	1952	2045	2225	2356		..

b Does not take 3 cl. at Paris for Amiens. c 3 d cl. carried for Paris only.
¶ Not Sundays and Fetes. † 1 & 2 cl. only. ‖ Supplement. R Rest. car Paris-Lille and *v.v.*

‖ Supplement.

Dunkerque, (Calais), Hazebrouck, Arras. [French Rlys. (Nord).

123	123	123	‖	123	123	‖	123	123	B Buffet Car.	123	123	123	123	‖	123	‖	123	123
	ExB	Exp	Auto Rail			Auto Rail	Exp						Exp	Auto Rail		Auto Rail	Exp	ExB
	22 0	..		.	..		..		dp. London (*p.*137) a.	..	..	..			..		..	9 10
..	6 24	7 51	1033	1255	1444	1549	1737	1936	dp. Dunkerque ..arr.	8 47	1016	1330	1216	14 2	1918	1933	2135	0 24
.	5 37	7 40	9 13	12 7	..	1449	1641	18 0	,, Calais .... ,,	8 51	1020	1150	13 7	1528	1953	21 5	2153	..
6 15	6 57	8 31	11 9	1343	1634	1625	1818	2016	,, Hazebrouck ,,	5 57	8 23	10 0	1136	1324	1816	1857	2056	2336
7 2	7 21	9 5	1136	1429	1721	1652	1854	21 1	arr. Bethune ....dep.	6 10	7 33	9 15	11 2	1256	1725	1829	2022	23 2
9 35	7 59	9 45	1211	1648	1844	1727	1933	2211	,, Arras ...... ,,		6 13	7 56	1029	1221	1614	1754	1945	2222

Paris, Soissons, Laon, Hirson, Aulnoye. [French Rlys. (Nord).

123	123	123	123	123	123	123	123		123	123	123	123	123	123	123
		Exp					Exp			Exp				Exp	
..		8 0	10 0	1240	1430	1726	1810	dep. **Paris** (Nord) arr.	8 55	9 58	1438	1648	1940	2043	2325
..	..	9 25	12 5	1435	1629	1953	1935	arr. Soissons ....dep.	6 58	8 34	1239	1435	1741	1919	2125
5 52	9 2	9 26	12 7	1439	1631	1955	1937	dep. Soissons .... arr.	6 56	8 32	1236	1433	1739	1917	2123
6 59	9 48	9 59	1251	1524	1717	2040	2010	arr. Laon ......dep.	6 12	8 2	1151	1349	1655	1845	2039
9 15	1223	11 0	1411	..	1833	..	2122	,, Hirson...... ,,	..	7 3	9 32	1231	..	1745	1857
1020	..	1233	1531	..	..		2211	,, Aulnoye .... ,,	..	6 14	8 55	1123	..		

A June 4-Sept. 4.

Paris, Beauvais, Treport. [French Rlys. (Nord).

123	123	123	123	123	123	123	Mls.		123	123	123	123	123	123	123	123	123
A		Exp		Exp		Exp				Exp	Exp						Exp
7 10	7 30	8 33	1130	15 0	1745	1847	0	dep. **Paris** (Nord) arr.	1425	1040	11 8	14 9	1647	1734	19 7	2225	23 5
..	9 13		1313		1924	2011	49	arr. Beauvais ..dep.	1245		9 54		15 8	..	1728	2052	
↕	9 56	↕	1339	↕	1942	2013	..	dep. Beauvais....arr.	8 3	↕	9 51	↕	15 0	↕	1720	2040	↕
	11 6	..	1456		2116	21 8	78	,, Abancourt .. ,,	6 49		9 6		1338	..	1610	1922	
1018	1214	1151	16 0	1823	2226	2154	112	arr. Eu ....dep.	5 22	7 20	8 5	1040	1216	1357	1454	18 0	1945
1023	1219	1156	16 5	1828	2231	22 0	114	ar. **Le Treport** Mersd.	5 17	7 16	7 59	1035	1211	1352	1449	1755	1940

↕ via Abbeville.

The times on the LEFT are to be read DOWNWARDS, those on the RIGHT UPWARDS.

Paris, St. Quentin, Mons, Brussels (Ostend).

[French Rlys. (Nord) and Belg. Nat. Rlys

Thro' Services to and from Holland, see p. 154	1 2 3	1 2 3	1 2	1 2 3	1 2	1 2 3	1 2	1 2 3	1 2 3	1 2	1 2	1 2 3	1 2	1 2 3
	Exp	Exp	Rap		Rap		Rap		Exp	Rap	Exp	Exp	Rap	Exp
Paris (Nord)....dep.	6 40	8 0	9 10	9 23	1130	1245	1415	1528	1630	1810	1820	1824	20 3	0 6
Creil	7 24	A	R	10 6	Pullman Car Train, Paris-Amsterdam.	1331		1612	1713	Pullman Car Train Paris-Amsterdam	..	19 2	..	..
Compiègne	7 55	8 56		1037		1428	..	1754	1740		1917	1933	..	1 10
Tergnier........arr.	9 4	..	‡	1118		15 8	‡	19 7	1823		..	2014	..	..
		†		†			R						R	S
Tergnier ......dep.	9 6	..	..	1127		1613		1950	1825		..	2016		..
St. Quentin (p. 236) arr.	9 35	9 42	1045	1145		1643	1548	2016	1844		20 2	2039	2133	2 2
St. Quentin (p. 236) dep.	9 52	9 43	1046	1147		1646	1549	..	1846		20 4	2049	2134	2 6
Busigny .... arr.	1020	10 6	..	1216		1729	..	..	1915		2027	2127	..	2 32
Busigny .... dep	..	10 7	..	1218		1732	..	..	1916		2028	2128	.	2 36
Aulnoye...... (p. 271) arr.	..	1031	1130	1255		1822	..	..	1953		2052	22 7	2215	3 4
Aulnoye...... (p. 271) dep.	..	1042	1137	1257		1850	..	..	1954		2054	2248	2222	3 50
Maubeuge ......dep.	..	..	..	1318		1911	..	..	2012		2113	23 1	..	..
Feignies............	..	1057	..	1329		arr.	..	..			2127	..	..	4 23
Quévy *c* ...... arr.	..	11 3	..	1335		..	..	..	..		2133	..	..	4 29
Quévy *c* ...... dep.	..	1118	..	1350		..	..	..	.		2149	..	.	5 9
Mons ....arr.	..	1136	..	14 6		..	1655	..	..		2210	..	2247	5 32
Mons ....dep.	..	1138	..	14 8		..	1656	..	..	..	2212	..	2248	5 38
Braine le-Comte	..	..	..	..		..	..	..	..	..	2240	..	..	6 5
Brussels (Midi) arr.	..	1216	1240	1454	1435	..	1740	..	..	2110	23 1	..	2325	6 27
Ostend .... „	..	1415	1415	1615	1615	..	1915	.	..	2315	..	..		8 15

Mls.		1 2 3	1 2 3	1 2 3	1 2 3	1 2	1 2 3	1 2	1 2 3	1 2	1 2	1 2 3	1 2 3	1 2	1 2 3
		Exp		Exp		Rap		Rap	Exp	Rap	Rap			Rap	Exp
..	Ostend ....dep.	..	..	..	..	7 3	..	9 20	9 20	1120	1420	..	1520	1820	..
0	**Brussels** (Midi).. „	..	..	7 27	..	9 15	..	1047	11 9	1326	1611	..	1741	20 8	0 55
19	Braine-le-Comte......	..	..	..	..	R	..	..	..	R	Pullman Car Train Amsterdam-Paris	..	..	R	1 26
38	**Mons**............arr.	..	..	8 5	..	9 53	..	Pullman Car Train, Antwerp-Paris.	12 1	14 7		..	1826		1 53
									†	B			†	‡	S
38	**Mons** ....dep.	..	..	8 6	..	9 54	..		12 2	14 8		1427	1828	..	2 1
47	Quévy	..	..	8 28	..	..	..		1224	..		1452	1851	..	2 26
50	Feignies *c* .... arr.	..	..	8 34	..	..	..		1230	..		1457	1857	..	2 32
	Feignies *c* .... dep.		..	8 54	..	..	..		1251	..		15 2	1922	..	3 21
51	Maubeuge	5 43	..	9 10	..	..	12 6		..	..		1558	1945	..	..
59	Aulnoye ...... arr.	6 1	..	9 26	..	1022	1224		13 9	..		1615	20 4	2115	3 35
	Aulnoye ...... dep.	6 3	..	9 28		1032	1225		1312	..		1617	20 7	2124	3 46
81	Busigny ...... arr.	6 44	..	9 53	..	..	13 6		1348	..		1643	2040	..	4 13
	Busigny ...... dep.	6 51	7 12	9 55	9 44	..	13 8		1350	..		1646	2043	..	4 15
98	**St. Quentin**......arr.	7 15	7 47	1015	10 8	1112	1343		1417	1515		17 7	21 8	22 5	4 36
112	Tergnier ...... arr.	7 36	8 19	1035	1028	..	1413		1439	..		1728	2129	..	4 57
	Tergnier ...... dep.	7 37	8 34	1036	1236	..	1557		1441	..		1729	2131	..	4 58
141	Compiègne ......dep.	8 23	9 40	11 9	1354	..	1722		1528	..		1814	2218	..	5 46
161	Creil ....arr.	..	10 5	..	1423	..	18 8	..	1553	..	.	1839	2247	..	6 12
194	**Paris** Nord)......arr.	9 25	1051	12 5	1510	1250	19 3	1347	1640	1655	1925	1920	2330	2345	6 55

R—Rest. Car. **V**—Voiture Buffet.
S—1 & 2 cl. Sleep. Car and 1, 2 and 3 cl. cars Paris-Brussels-Amsterdam and *v.v.* See page 154.
‡ 1st & 2nd cl. Cars Paris Brussels-Amsterdam
† 1, 2 & 3 cl, Cars Paris Brussels and *v.v.* ‖ and *v.v.*

A—Only takes 3 cl. for Busigny and beyond.
B—Only takes 2 cl. passengers for St. Quentin and beyond. ‖ Stops to set down only.

Paris, Lille, Ghent, (Knocke, Ostend).

[French Rlys (Nord) and Belg. Nat. Rlys.

1 2 3	1 2 A	1 2 3	1 2 3	1 2 3	A 1 2	Mls.		1 2 3 A	1 2	1 2 3	1 2	1 2 A	1 2 3
	Rap	Rap			Exp			Rap	B	Exp	Rap	Rap	
..	8 15	10 0	13 0	15 0	1720	0	dep. **Paris** (Nord) ...... arr.	1215	14 9	1625	1936	2159	..
..	11 2	1258	1636	1848	2028	156	arr. Lille .... dep.	9 5	1134	1310	1644	19 0	..
4 41	11 9	13 5	1758	1856	2035	..	dep. Lille .... arr.	8 58	1043	1256	1638	1853	2236
5 28	1139	14 5	1628	1937	21 8	167	arr. Mouscron..........dep.	8 10	9 59	1215	1550	1819	2154
5 58	12 8	1450	1912	20 7	2124	175	arr. Courtrai ...... dep.	7 40	9 44	12 1	1521	18 0	2123
6 18	1212	1517	1917	2018	2126		dep. Courtrai ...... arr.	7 38	9 43	1152	1518	1758	2119
6 56	1250	1558	1959	2124	22 0	201	arr. Ghent (St. Pierre) dep.	6 19	9 12	1118	1440	1727	2038
5 41	1155	1428	19 0	1947	2112	..	dep. Mouscron ....arr.	8 4	9 57	1214	1534	1813	2136
5 58	12 8	1450	1912	20 7	2124	.	arr. Courtrai ....dep.	7 40	9 44	12 1	1521	18 0	2123
6 57	13 7	16 6	2010	21 8	..	197	arr. Thourout..........dep.	5 49	8 30	1034	14 4	17 5	1945
7 26	1332	1634	2034	2132	..	208	arr. Bruges ....dep.	5 13	8 5	10 7	1339	1641	1913
7 48	1415	1723	2119	2237	..	218	arr. Blankenberghe ....dep.	..	7†25	9 12	1314	1618	1818
8 34	1434	1732	2136	..	..	221	arr. Knocke ....dep.	..	6 44	9 2	13 2	1558	18 2
7 4	1311	1610	2055	..	..		dep. Thourout.......... arr.	..	7 40	1029	1356	1546	1941
7 54	1345	1655	2136	..	..	212	arr. Ostend ....dep.	..	7 7	9 56	1323	15 5	19 1

A 1 and 2 cl. cars Paris-Ghent and *v.v.* **B** Buffet-Bar Tourcoing-Paris. *r* Rest. Car Paris-Tourcoing.
a *Via* Bruges. † Weekdays only

Paris, St. Quentin, Charleroy, Namur, Liege (Cologne) [French Rlys. (Nord)

Mls.		1 2 3	1 2 3	1 2 3	1 2 3	1 2	1 2	1 2 3	1 2 3	1 2 3	1 2	1 2 3
				Exp	Exp	Rap	Rap			Exp	luxe	
0	p. 239 Paris (Nord) dep.	..	..	8 0	9 23	10 6	1335	..	1245	1820	1915	0 6
81	Tergnier ......dep.	6 23	8 31	D	1127	..	F	..	1613	B	L	S
96	St.Quentin dep.	7 6	8 51	9 43	1147	E	15 4	..	1646	20 4		2 6
134	Aulnoye ...... arr.	8 30	1013	1031	1255		1545	.	1822	2052		3 4
134	Aulnoye (p. 271) dep.	9 24	1046	1032	1257		1546	1552	1850	2054		3 7
142	Maubeuge	10 6	1128	1045	1324		1558	1710	1924	2114		..
148	Jeumont	1023	1152	1056	1341		16 9	1726	1941	2125		3 29
149	Erquelines c arr.	1027	1156	11 0	1345		1613	1730	1946	..		3 33
	Erquelines c dep.	1044	1246	1114	1355		1629	1741	20 1	..		3 57
168	Charleroy ...... arr.	1131	1336	1136	1435	1251	1653	1828	2051	2149		4 21
	[Belgian Nat. Ry.]	2 3	2 3	B			B					
168	Charleroy ......dep.	1214	1418	1137	1456	1254	1656	19 9	..	2150		4 24
190	Namur ....arr.	1342	1533	12 7	1537	1324	1726	1936	..	2217		4 52
	[Nord-Belgian]											
..	Namur ....dep.	..	..	12 9	1547	1325	1727	1938	..	2218	..	4 54
210	Huy	..	..	1233	1616	..	1753	20 2	..	2239		5 19
228	Liege (Guillemins) ar.	..	..	1257	1644	14 7	1817	2023	..	23 0	2314	5 45
	p. 151 Liege	..	..	1332	1658	1427	1831	..	..	0 5	2346	6 14
248	Spa .... arr.	..	..	1419	1745	..	1921	..	..	..	..	7 27
262	Aachen ...... arr.	..	..	1436	18 5	1525	1945	..	.	1 11	0 43	7 22
305	COLOGNE...... arr.	..	..	16 3	1933	1634	2112			2 36	1 46	9 2

A 1 and 2 cl. Sleeping car Cologne-Paris, and 1, 2 and 3 cl. cars, Stolpce—Paris.
B 1 and 2 cl Cars Paris Liege and v.v.
D 1, 2 and 3 cl. Cars Paris-Cologne and v.v.
E 1 & 2 cl cars Paris-Cologne-Berlin and Hamburg, and v.v., Rest. Car Paris Liege and v.v.
L Nord Express.

	1 2 3	1 2 3	1 2	1 2	1 2 3	1 2 3	1 2 3	2 3	1 2	1 2 3	1 2	1 2 3
	Exp		luxe	Exp		Rap			Rap	Exp	Exp	Exp
p. 151 COLOGNE ......dep.	..	..	4 5	4 19	..	8 48	..	..	1444	14 6	..	1915
Aachen ......dep.	..	..	5 11	5 40	..	1016	..	..	1615	1524	..	2042
Spa ....dep.	..	..	..	6 2	..	1013	..	..	..	1541	..	2124
Liege ....arr.	..	..	6 26	7 18	..	1137	..	..	1712	1645		2215
[Nord-Belgian.]			L			F r		1 2 3	E	D		A
Liege (Guillemins) d.	..	..	6 39	8 18	..	1149	..	1355	1733	1658	..	2344
Huy	..	..		8 39	..	1214	..	1425	..	1725	..	0 13
Namur ....arr	..	..		9 0	..	1239	..	15 4	1815	1752	..	0 42
[Belgian-Nat.]												
Namur ....dep.	‡	..		9 1	..	1240	..	1512	1816	1753	..	0 46
Charleroy ......arr.		..		9 28		1310	..	1550	1844	1832	..	1 27
[Nord.]				1 2 Rap		1 2 B			1 2		1 2	
Charleroy ......dep.	..	8 10		9 29	1054	1311	1356	1557	1846	1835	..	1 31
Erquelines	..	8 41		..	1139	1337	1443	1638	..	1910	..	2 10
Jeumont c ...... arr.		8 44		9 53	1142	1340	1446	1641	..	1913	..	2 13
Jeumont c ...... dep.	5 28	8 54		9 56	1152	1359	1546	1658	..	1925	2038	3 3
Maubeuge	5 43	9 10		10 6	12 6	1410	1558	1713	1916	1945	2048	3 15
Aulnoye ....arr.	6 1	9 26		1017	1224	1423	1615	1731	..	20 4	21 5	3 29
Aulnoye ....dep	6 3	9 28		1032	1225	1424	1617	1735	..	20 7	2124	3 46
p. 239 St. Quentin...dep.	7 17	1017		1113	1345	15 6	17 9	1912	20 4	2111	22 6	4 38
Tergnier ....arr	7 36	1035		..	1413	..	1728	1940	..	2129	..	4 57
Paris (Nord) ...arr.	9 25	12 5	1055	1250	1640	1645	1920		2137	2330	2345	6 55

S 1 and 2 cl. Sleeping Car Paris-Cologne, and 1, 2 and 3 cl. Cars Paris to Niegoreloje.
F 1, 2 cl. Cars and Rest. Car Paris-Cologne & v.v.

Through Services to and from Hamburg, Berlin, Riga, Warsaw.

(1 and 2 class except otherwise indicated).

	ED	luxe		Rap		Rap	luxe			ED
8 0	10 6	1915	1820	0 6	dep. PARIS (Nord) arr.	6 55	1055	1250	1645	2137
16 3		1 46	2 36	9 2	arr. Cologne ....dep.	1915	4 5	4 19	8 48	
2321		8†11	14 9	1516	arr. HAMB'G (p. 161) „	1147	21†31	1645	0 13	
2150		1 48	6 48	9 22	dep. Cologne .. p. 168 ar	19 1	4 3	2228	7 55	
10 9		N	1923	A	arr. Dresden p. 168 dp	A	N	1118	2034	
6¶55	2344	8 45	1627	1753	arr. BERLIN (S.) p. 168 dp	1041	21 8	1527	2316	8 7
..		9 4	..	0 5	dep. BERLIN (S.) arr.	6 50	2044	..		..
..	..	1822	..		arr. Eydtkau .. dep.	..	1121	..	..	..
..	..	0 43	..	1736	arr. Riga (E.E.T.) dep.	1525	6 25	..	..	..
..	..	9 12	1813	0 10	dep. BERLIN (S.) arr.	1027	2049	..	..	..
..	..	1135	2213	2 56	a. Bentschen (c) (205) d.	7 0	1816	..	..	..
..	..	1239	0 22	4 32	arr. Poznan (205) dep.	5 20	1714	..	..	..
..	..	1634	8 22	9 2	arr. WARSAW (226) dep.	2156	1316	..	..	..

¶ Potsdam Station.

A—1 & 2 cl Sleeping Car Paris-Cologne, 1, 2 & 3 cl. Cars Paris-Niegoreloje, & v.v.
N—Nord Exp. Train de luxe, see p. 81.
† Via Hanover, p. 170.

E 1 & 2 cl. cars Paris to Berlin *via* Aachen, Krefeld and Hamm, and *v.v.*

Dieppe, Rouen (Paris). [French Rlys. (Ouest).

Mls.		123	1/23	1/23	1/23	1/23	1/23	123	123	1/23	1/23	123	1/23
	LONDON—	Exp						Exp	Rap			Exp	
	Victoria ......dep.	2020	..	..	..	..	.	10 5	10 5	..	..	..	..
	Newhaven ...dep.	2215	..	..	..	..	.	1145	1145	..	..	..	..
	Dieppe M { arr	2 5	..	..	..	..	..	1455	1455	..	..	..	..
	Dieppe M { dep.	2 51	..	..	.	..		1524	1531	..	..	..	..
0	Dieppe Ville dep.	C	6 10	7 13	8 14	11 3	1248	R	1543	1648	1810	19 2	20 8
25	Clères	via Pontoise	6 50	7 53	9 2	1143	1336	via Pontoise	D V	1728	1914	Via Pontoise.	2052
32	Malaunay		7 0	..	9 15		1350			1738	1932		..
38	Rouen (R.D.) b a		7 10	8 10	9 26	12 0	14 0		1631	1748	1945		2111
				123	123	123	123			123			123
..	p. 242 Rouen (R.D)dp	..	..	8 26	1036	1245	1411	..	1645	1812	..		2132
125	Paris (S.L) arr	5 23	..	9 49	1159	1447	1546	1745	1836	1935	..	2141	2255

C 1, 2 & 3 cl. Couchettes Dieppe-Paris and v.v.

R Restaurant Car.

r Rest. Car.	1/23	1/23	1/23	1/23	123	123	123	123	1/23	123	123	123	123	123
					R	V							C	
			Exp		Exp	Rap	Exp	Exp		Rap	Exp	Rap	Rap	Exp
Paris (p.242)d.	..	..	8 5	..	1029	..	1130	1320	..	1715	1720	20 0	2057	2120
Rouen(R.D.)ar.	..	..	9 28	..	..	..	1332	1510	..	1838	1910	2123	..	2310
						D V	1/23				1/23	1/23		A
Rouen (R.D.)dp.	6 28	7 51	9 38	1116	Via Pontoise.	12 0	1337	1520	1725	19 0	1945	2134	Via Pontoise	2321
Malaunay	6 42	8 1	..	1124		..	..	1530	1737	1911	1958	2142		.
Clères	7 1	8 14	9 58	1137		..	1357	1543	1752	1924	2014	2156		..
Dieppe Ville arr.	7 53	8 52	1036	1215		1245	1435	1621	1837	20 3	21 1	2234	2313	2357
Dieppe M ..arr.	..	..	..	..	1246	1255	..	..		..	..	..	2323	0 5
London—														
Victoria arr.	..	..	..	..	1812	1812	..	..	..	..	..	..	6 5	6 5

A Auto-Rail, extra fare. Suns. only.

D 1, 2 & 3 cl. Couchettes 1, 2 & 3 cl. cars Dieppe-Bordeaux and v.v. (July 1–Sept. 30 to Lourdes.)

V Buffet Car.

Rouen, Serquigny (Caen)., Le Mans. [French Rlys. (Ouest).

Mls.		1/23		1/23	1/23	1/23	1/23	1/23	123	1/23	1/23	1/23
		A	A	A	A	A		A	Rap	A	A	
0	Rouen { R. Droite ..dep.	5 46	7 15	7 35	9 47	1219	13 8	1532	1638	17 0	2023	2138
	Rouen { R. Gauche..dep.			..		..	..	..	¶	..	..	
12	Elbeuf-St.-Aubin	6 7	7 33	7 57	10 6	1240	1334	1552	1659	1723	2046	2156
32	Glos-Montfort	6 37	↓	8 27	1030	1311	1415	1623	↓	1750	2120	..
44	Serquigny .... arr.	6 56		8 48	1049	1329	1438	1641		18 6	2142	..
100	Caen (p. 243) .... arr.	8 19	↓	1015	1235	1450	16 6	18 3	↓	1945	2327	..
89	Laigle ....arr.	..	8 48	..	..	..	..	..	1823	..	..	..
82	Alencon .... ,,	..	9 34	..	..	..	..	..	1922	..	..	..
117	Le Mans .... ,,	..	1013			..	..	..	2010	..	..	..

Thro' 1, 2 & 3 cl car Dieppe-Bordeaux.

¶ 13 minutes later on Suns.

Mls.		1/23	1/23	1/23	1/23	12/3	123	1/23	1/23	1/23	1/23	1/23	123
						A	Rap	A		A	A	A	Rap
0	Le Mans (p. 244) ..dep.	..	..	..	..	..	8 13		..		..	..	2030
35	Alencon .... ,,	..	..	..		..	8 53	..	..	..	..	..	2120
78	Laigle .. ,,	..		..	..	..	..		..	..	..	..	22 1
0	Caen (p 243) ....dep.	..	..	5 48	7 32	8 17	↓	1052	1242	1625	1821	2022	↓
56	Serquigny	..	..	7 10	9 1	9 53		1254	1515	1823	1948	22 4	
68	Glos-Montfort	4 25	..	7 31	..	1012	↓	1314	1537	1843	20 4	2222	↓
88	Elbeuf-St.-Aubin	4 58	6 58	8 1	9 46	1039	1115	13 4	1613	1910	2032	2243	23 4
	Rouen { R. Gauche..arr.	5 38	7 34	..	..	..	¶	..	..	..	..	..	..
100	Rouen { R. Droite ..arr.	..	..	8 21	10 5	1059	1132	14 3	1636	1929	2054	23 2	2310

A Auto-Rail.

Dieppe, Serqueux, Pontoise, Paris. [French Rlys. (Ouest).

123	1/23	123	123	123	1/23	123	Mls.		1/23	123	123	123	123
Rap		¶										w	Rap
cc	A	Exp	Exp	Rap		Exp				Exp	Rap	Exp	cc
2*51	6 14	7 42	1449	15*24	17 5	19 2	0	dep. Dieppe ..ar.	1015	1131	12*45	1958	23*23
↓	6 57	8 12	1521	R	1759	1936	21	Neufchâtel	9 24	11 1	..	1926	↑
	7 13	8 27	1538	..	1819	1952	31	ar. Serqueux dp.	9 5	1047	..	1911	
	7 26	8 29	1540	..	1828	1954	..	dp Serqueux ar.	9 2	1045	R	19 9	
	8 21	9 10	1626	..	2045	2035	62	Gisors ....dp.	7 50	9 53	..	1815	
↓	9 17	9 47	17 5	..	22 1	2111	87	Pontoise ..dp.	6 43	9 10	..	1730	
5 23	1014	1017	1738	1745	2239	2141	105	ar. Paris (S.Laz.) d.	6 7	8 40	10r29	1657	2057

* Maritime Stn. ¶ 13 minutes later on Suns. cc 1, 2 & 3 cl. Couchettes Dieppe-Paris and v.v.

A Auto-Rail Car—one class only. R Restaurant Car. w Weekdays only.

The times on the LEFT are to be read DOWNWARDS, those on the RIGHT UPWARDS.

Paris, Mantes—Gassicourt, Rouen (Fécamp), Havre. [French Rlys. (Ouest).

Mls.	English Services, see p. 111.	Exp 123	Rap 123 B	Rap 123	Exp 123	Rap 123	123	Exp 123 E	Exp 123	Exp 123 E	Rap 123	Exp 123	Auto Rail	Rap 123	Exp 123	Auto Rail	123
0	**Paris** (St. Lazare d.	7 20	7 52	8 5	9 20	1015	1130	1315	1320	1515	1715	1720	..	20 0	2120	*from Bordeaux.	2245
36	Mantes(Gassicourt)d.	7 58	..		9 58	..	1222	..	1358	1553		1758	..	R	2158		2327
50	Vernon	8 17	..	*h*	1017	..	1240	..	1417	1611	*h*	1817	..	*h*	2217		2346
78	Oissel	8 58	..	..	1058	..	1320	..	1458	1650		1858			2258		0 38
87	**Rouen** (Rive Dr.) *b* a.	9 10	9 21	9 28	1110	1138	1332	1438	1510	17 2	1838	1910		2123	2310	2319	0 50
		Auto Rail					¶		C	1/23		1/23					
	Rouen (R. Droite) d.	1032	9 24	9 32	..	1140	1343	1442	1514	1734	1842	1915	21 4	2127	..	2342	..
98	Malaunay	1041	↓		..		..	..	..	1744	..	1926	2114	..	..		..
106	Motteville	11 2	↓	9 57	..		1414	15 7	1539	18 9	.	1952	2136	..	..		..
111	Yvetot	11 9	↓	10 3		12 8	1421	1513	1545	1817	1913	1959	2142	2157	..	0 13	..
126	Bréauté-Beuzeville a.	1132	↓	1020	..	1225	1444	1530	16 2	1843	1930		..	..	..	0 30	..
	Bréauté Beuzevil. d	..	↓	1028	..	1246	..	1540	1612	..	1945		..	..	..		..
	Fécamp .... arr.	..	↓	1056	..	1314	..	16 6	1637		2013	..		..	..		..
138	Harfleur ..... dep.	..	↓		..		..	..	..	19 9		..	..	..	..		..
141	**Le Havre** . arr.	1153	1025	1041	..	1245	15 5	1551	1623	1919	1951	..	..	2230	..	0 48	..
..	p. 111 Southampton arr.	..	..	..	..	..	..	..	..	..	..	..	..	6 30	Ev'ry wk'dy		
..	p. 111 LONDON (Waterl.) a.	..	..	..	..	..	..	..	..	..	..	..	..	9 2	Jly. 8-Sep. 14		

	Auto Rail 1/23	Exp 123	Rap 123	Rail 1/23	Rap 123	Auto Rail 1/23	Exp 123	1/23	Rap 123	Auto Rail 1/23	Auto Rail 1/23	Rap 123	123
p. 111 LONDON (Waterl.) d.	..	..	21 0	Every weekday, July 7–Sept. 13				..	*g*		..	*g*	
p. 111 Southampton dep.	..	..	2315					..	..	..	..	..	
			g R										
Le Havre .... dep.	5 50	..	7 25	7 48	9 18	1114	1256	1456	1654	1755	1844	2018	2237
Harfleur	..	..	..	7 56	..	..	..	..					2248
Fécamp .. dep.		..	..	..	9 3	¶	1231	.	1643		1835	1835	
Bréauté-Beuzev. ar.	..	..	..	..	9 36	..	13 5	..	1714		19 4	19 4	..
Bréauté Beuzeville d.	6 12	..	..	8 19	9 43	1133	1323	1521	1719	1814	19 9	2043	2319
Yvetot	6 31	..	..	8 44	10 2	1158	1342	1549	1738	1839	1937	21 3	2352
Motteville	..	..	..	8 51	1011	12 5	..	1556	1747	1846	1945		0 2
Malaunay		..	..	9 8	..	..	..	.		19 3	20 7	..	..
Rouen (Rive Dr.) arr.	6 58	..	8 23	9 20	1032	1231	14 7	1625	18 8	1913	2018	2128	0 30
						123		123			123		
Rouen (Rive Droite) *b* .. dep.	..	7 3	8 26	8 45	1036	1245	1411	1645	1812	..	2045	..	1 45
Oissel	..	7 17	↓	8 59	↓	1258		1659	..	..	2059	..	2 7
Vernon	..	7 57	↓	9 39	↓	1337	1455	1739	..	..	2139	..	3 2
Mantes (Gassicourt)	..	8 14	V	9 57	V	1354		1757	..	..	2159	..	3 32
Paris (St Lazare) a.	..	8 52	9 49	1035	1159	1447	1546	1836	1935	..	2235	2255	4 34

B Suns. only to Oct. 1. **C** Daily except Sats. Rouen—Havre. **E** Sats. only.

R Restaurant Car Paris to Havre and *v.v.* **V** Buffet Car. *g* Does not take 3 cl. between Rouen and Paris unless travelling 103 miles or more. *h* 3 cl. passengers only accepted at Paris if travelling 103 miles or more. *k* Only takes 3 cl. for beyond Vernon. ¶ Not Suns. and Fetes.

Amiens, Rouen (Havre). [French Rlys. (Nord and Ouest).

1/23 *	1/23	1/23	123	1/23 *	1/23 *	1/23 *	Mls.		1/23 *	1/23 *	1/23 *	1/23 *	123	1/23 *	1/23 *
5 40	8 0	8 58	1258	1645	1826	2133	0	dep. Amiens (*p.* 237) arr.	7 40	..	1015	1236	1552	1626	2212
6 57	1113	9 33	14 6	1727	1928	2223	32	dep. Abancourt arr.	6 40	9 3	9 36	1155	1447	1545	21 3
7 18	1134		1429	1746	1959	2245	44	arr } Serqueux { dp.	6 17	8 40	9 16	1136	1423	1523	2040
7 19	1135		1430	1747	20 2	22 6		dp } Serqueux { arr	6 16	8 21	9 15	1135	1419	1522	2038
7 40	1156	..	1450	18 3	2023	23•6	56	Montéroller-Buchy d.	5 57	8 2	9 0	1118	1358	15 5	2019
8 16	1232	1026	1525	1830	2059	2334	78	a. Rouen (Rive-Droite) d	5 15	7 21	30	1046	1313	1431	1937
1041	14*1	1153	16†57	1951	2230	0*48	119	,, **Havre** (abv.) dep.	..	5 50	7 25	9 18	11†14	1256	1654

* Auto-Rail Supplement for 3rd class. † Weekdays.

The times on the LEFT are to be read DOWNWARDS, those on the RIGHT UPWARDS.

Paris, Mantes, (Gassicourt), Lisieux, Caen, Cherbourg. [French Rlys. (Ouest).

Mls.		1/23	1/23	123	123	A	123	1/23	1/23	123	123	1/23	123	123	123
	To Trouville, see below		*	B	Rap	..	Rap	*	*	Rap	D		Exp	Exp	Exp
0	**Paris** (St.Lazare) dep.	..	..	6 50	7 5	..	9 5	..	..	13 5	1424	..	1624	20 5	2213
36	Mantes (Gassicourt)	..	..	..	..	..	V	..	..	..	..	..	V	..	23 1
67	Evreux-Embranch...	..	..	..	8 24	..	1029	..	..	1424	..	..	1745	2130	0 0
93	Serquigny (*p.* 241) ..	..	6 57	..	8 54	..	1059	1049	1329	1454	.	..	1816	22 2	0 35
119	Lisieux (*p.* 243)	..	7 33	9 17	9 33	..	1140	1157	1405	1530	1645	..	19 0	2244	1 30
150	**Caen** .... arr.	..	8 19	9 55	1015	..	1219	1235	1450	16 6	1725	..	1945	2327	2 8
							Exp								C
	dep.	6 13	..	..	1021	11 5	1225	..	..	1615	1731	1825	1951	..	2 24
168	Bayeux	6 52	..	..	1047	1131	1251	..	..	1640	18 1	1854	2026	..	2 57
185	Lison (*p.* 245) arr.	7 21	..	..	11 7	1152	1315	..	..	1659	1824	1917	2051	..	3 20
	dep.	7*29	..	..	1110	1213	1319	..	..	17 9	1827	1920	2054	..	3 40
214	Valognes	8 9	..	..	1147	1254	1357	..	..	18 1	19 9	20 9	2143	..	4 36
232	**Cherbourg** ....arr.	8*35	..	..	12 8	1318	1418	..	..	1830	1933	2039	22 6	..	5 10

	A	A	123	A	1/23	123	123	123	123	123	123	123
			Exp			Exp	E	Exp	Exp	Exp	B	Exp
Cherbourg ....dep.	..	..	6 20	8 45	10 0	1115	..	1455	*	1822	..	2016
Valognes	..	..	6 42	9 11	1042	1140	..	1517	..	1844	..	2058
Lison	..	..	7 19	9 54	13 4	1217	..	1552	..	1921	..	2155
Bayeux	..	5 49	7 45	1020	1338	1240	..	1618	..	1944	..	2223
Caen .... arr.	..	6 15	8 7	1045	1421	13 1	..	1639	..	20 6	..	2251
		123	V								V	C
dep.	..	6 22	8 17	1052	..	13 9	1322	1649	1821	2014	2022	2335
						V	V			V		
Lisieux	.	7 5	9 6	1219	..	..	14 7	1733	1911	..	21 8	0 56
Serquigny	6 2	7 45	9 48	1253	..	..	1448	1811	1948	..	2148	1 55
Evreux-Embranch...	6 45	8 22	1024	..	..	..	1524	1847	To Rouen	..	2224	2 47
Mantes (Gassicourt)	8 14	..	..	..	..	..	..	..		..	..	3 52
Paris (St.Lazare) arr.	8 52	9 45	1145	..	..	16 3	1645	20 5		2318	2345	4 50

* Auto Rail.

a From Cherbourg to Caen takes 3 cl. for Paris only.

A Auto-Rail Car, one class. **B** From Sept. 4. **C** 1, 2 & 3 cl. Couchettes Paris-Cherbourg and *v.v.* **D** Daily except Suns., June 30-Sept. 4. **E** From Oct. 2. **V** Buffet-Bar.

To Oct. 1. **(Paris), Lisieux, Trouville—Deauville, Honfleur.** [French Rlys. (Ouest).

Mls.			123	123		123	123			12	123	12	123	123		123
			Exp	Rap		Exp	Rap			A	Rap	A		Exp		Exp
0	**Paris** (S.L.) *above* dep	..	6 50	7 5	..	9 2	9 5	..	..	1025	13 5	1410	1424	1624	..	20 5
119	Lisieux .... arr.	..	9 13	9 31	..	1128	1135	..	..	D	1527	E	1640	1855	..	2241
		1/23	B	A	A	C	A	A	A		A		F	A	A	A
119	Lisieux ......dep.	7 47	9 25	10 0	11 0	1130	1143	1230	1411	↓	1555	↓	1653	1916	2111	2247
129	Pont l'Eveque arr.	8 12	9 42	1015	1111	1143	12 2	1245	1426		16 9		17 9	1934	2126	23 2
145	**Honfleur** ,,	..	1014	1028	..	..	1234	..	1457		..		1741	21 4	..	..
136	**Trouville-Deau** ,,	8 35	9 55	1028	1120	1154	1218	1258	1439	1227	1621	1610	1720	1948	2132	2315
0	Trouville-Deau dp.	..	10 0	..	..	12 2	1236	..	..	1230	1613	1627	1727			
12	Houlgate .... arr.	..	1039	..	..	1242	1314	..	..	1252	1635	1712	1813			
15	Dives-Caborg arr.	..	1044	..	..	1248	1318	..	..	1256	1639	1716	1818			

		1/23	12	12			1/23	123	1/23	12	1/23	12	1/23
			G	H				J		D		K	
Dives-Caborg ..dep.	..	7 37	8 28	9 20	..	..	1210	1323	1556	1750	1920	2021	2048
Houlgate	..	7 43	8 35	9 24	..	..	1217	1331	16 2	1754	1928	2029	2055
Trouville-Deau arr.		8 22	9 13	9 46		..	1310	1415	1642	1816	20 7	2113	2133
	A			A	A	A				A			A
Trouville-Deau dep.	6 25	8 35	9 23	9 50	1033	13 6	1329	1429	1648	1820	2017	2123	22 2
Honfleur .... ,,	6 6	..		..	1047	13 3		..	1627				..
Pont l'Eveque	6 38	8 45		..	1042	1316	1342	..	17 0		2033		2215
Lisieux .... arr.	6 53	9 0		..	1053	1331	1359	1455	1714		2056		2230
	123	123							123		123		123
Lisieux .... *abv.* dep	7 6	9 6	↓	..	..	..	14 7	1457	1733	↓	21 8	↓	0 54
Paris (S.L.) arr.	9 45	1145	1156	1150	..	..	1645	1737	20 5	2020	2345	0 7	4 50

A Auto-Rail Car, one class. **B** July 13–Sept. 3. **C** To Sept. 3. **D** July 22–Sept. 5. **E** Daily, except Suns., July 21–Sept. 4. **F** Daily, except Suns., to Sept. 4. **G** Sats. and Mons. July 17–Sept. 11. **H** Tue., Wed., Thu. and Fri., July 18–Sept. 8. **J** July 29–Oct. 1. **K** Suns. to Sept. 24.

Paris, Chartres, Le Mans, Rennes, St. Malo. [French Rlys. (Ouest).

Mls.		123	123	123	123	123	123	123	123	123	123	123	123	123	123
		Rap	Rap	Rap	Exp	Rap	Exp	Rap	Exp	Exp	Exp	Exp	Exp	Exp	Exp
	Paris ....dep.	**X**	**R**	..	..	**R**	*e*	**R**			**Z**		**FZ**	**C**	..
0	,, (Mpn.).. ,,	8 35	1010	13 0	1310	16 5	17 0	1810	1923	2040	21 5	22 0	23 0	0 15	..
9	Versailles .. ,,	..	1027	..	1329	..	1719	..	1941	21 5	2126	2219	2322	0 34	From Bordeaux.
55	Chartres arr.	..	1111	**V**	1427	..	1817	..	2037	2154	2226	23 8	0 26	1 36	
	Chartres dep.	..	1112	..	1429	..	1819	..	2039	2158	2228	23 9	0 28	1 31	
132	**Le Mans** .. arr.	1040	1225	1515	16 3	1810	20 1	2020	2235	2332	0 10	0 30	2 15	2 52	
	(*To Angers, b'low*)		*m*	**Y**	**A**							*m*			
	Le Mans ..dep.	1046	1231	1528	1620	1816	..	2038	..	..	0 16	0 37	2 22	3 55	
188	Laval...... arr.	1150	..	1635	1758	1919	..	2153	..	..	..	1 43	3 30	5 16	
234	**Rennes** .. ,,	1243	1435	1729	1914	2011	..	2250	..	..	2 20	2 51	4 28	6 25	..
	(*To Brest*, 245.)		‡	*m*										‡	**L**
	Rennes....dep.	1255	1634	1734	..	2024	..	..	..	..	..	3 4	4 33	6 45	8 32
270	Dol........ arr.	1343	1736	1820	..	21 5	..	..	..	..	..	¶	5 28	7 55	9 12
281	Dinan .. ,,	1422	1812	1858	..	2147	..	..	..	..	..	7‡46	6 6	8 34	..
294	Dinard .. ,,	1455	1924	1929	..	2217	..	..	..	..	..	8 27	6 46	9 5	..
288	**St. Malo** .. ,,	14 5	18 6	1842	..	2125	..	..	..	..	..		6 0	8 23	9 30

	123		123	123	123	123		123	123	123	123	123	123
	Exp	**A**	Rap	Exp	Exp	Exp	**A**	Exp	Rap	Exp	Exp	Exp	Exp
St. Malo ..dep.	..	6 24	8 8	1039	..	1357	1524	1711	1711	20 6	..	..	2258
Dinard .. ,,	..	..	7‡19	9 45	..	1310	..	1622	1622	..	..	2121	2219
Dinan .. ,,	..	..	7‡47	1020	..	1341	..	1657	1657	19‡28	..	2153	2254
Dol........ ,,	..	6 49	8 26	11 2	..	1425	1547	1735	1735	2032	..	..	2335
Rennes arr.	..	7 49	9 5	1146	..	15 8	1642	1821	1821	2140	..	1¶11	0 24
		123		**X**	**B**	**B**		**L**			**D**		**YF**
Rennes dep.	..	8 0	..	12 0	13 5	1520	1720	..	1833	2227	1 6	1 29	0 29
Laval......	..	8 56	..	1258	..	..	1835	..	1930	2349	2 20	2 43	1 38
Le Mans arr.	..	10 1	..	14 1	15 3	1710	20 3	To Bordeaux.	2036	1 8	3 33	3 53	2 51
				R						**F**			
Le Mans dep.	7 0	10 7	..	14 7	1510	1720	2052		2045	3 0	3 39	4 0	3 0
Chartres arr.	8 31	1118	..	1522	..	..	2222		..	4 50	5 28	5 42	4 50
Chartres dep.	8 32	1120	..	1523	**R**	..	..		**R**	4 53	5 30	5 44	4 53
Versailles.. arr.	9 26	12 2	..	16 7	..	..	..		2241	6 0	6 32	6 42	6 0
Paris (Mpm.) ,,	9 43	1220	..	1625	1720	1935	..		23 0	6 20	6 50	7 0	6 20

A Auto Car—one class only. **B** July 2-Oct. 1. **C** 1, 2 and 3 cl. Couchettes and cars Paris-St. Malo and *v.v.* **D** July 1-Oct. 1. **F** 1, 2 and 3 cl. cars and 1, 2 and 3 cl. Couchettes Paris-St. Malo and Dinard and *v.v.* **L** 1, 2 & 3 cl. Couchettes and 1, 2 & 3 cl. cars Bordeaux-St. Malo and *v.v.* **R** Rest. Car. **V** Buffet Car. **X** 1, 2 and 3 cl. cars to St. Malo and *v.v.* **Y** From Le Mans to St. Malo and *v.v.* July 1-Sept. 30. **Z** June 30-Sept. 30. *a* 3 cl. from Lavel and beyond. *b* 3 cl. for Lavel and beyond. *c* Until Rennes 3 cl. 63 mls. and beyond. *e* Only 3 cl. for Le Mans and beyond. *h* 1, 2 & 3 cl. cars, 1 cl. Lits-Toilettes and 1, 2 & 3 Couchettes Paris-Dinard; Couchettes 1, 2 & 3 Paris-St. Malo. *k* Only 3 cl. 155 mls. or more from Rennes. *m* Only takes 3 cl. for beyond Le Mans. *n* At Rennes 1 cl. without baggage, and at Dol all classes. ¶ *via* Lamballe. ‖ Not Suns. or Fetes. ‡ 3 cl. Auto-Rail.

Paris, Laigle, Granville. [French Rlys. (Ouest).

	123		123	123		123	123	Ms		123	**A**	123	**A**	**A**	123	123	**A**
A	Exp	**A**	Exp	Ex †	**A**	Ex**V**	Ex *c*		Montparnasse Statn.	Exp		Exp		..	Ex**V**	Ex *c*	
..	8 20	..	1123	1351		18†2	2238	0	dep. **Paris** ......arr.	12 0	1539	1820	22 2	..	232	5 28	9 57
..	9 30	..	**B**	15 0	1512	1916	0 2	51	,, Dreux ......dep.	1046	1412	17 5	2010	..	22 6	3 52	8 38
..	1018	9 41	1316	1550	1612	2010	1 12	88	,, Laigle ...... ,,	9 59	13 7	1612	19 5	..	2116	2 48	7 34
..	1052	1041	*r*	1624	1656	2052	1 59		,, Surdon ...... ,,	9 18	1220	1534	1818	arr.	2038	2 0	6 52
7 12	11 8	12 8	1357	1640	1810	21 9	2 32	124	,, Argentan .... ,,	9 4	12 6	1521	18 3	1941	2024	1 44	6 38
7 56	12 0	1310	1436	1724	19 0	2153	3 25	152	,, Flers .... ,,	8 19	1119	1425	..	1859	1931	0 39	..
8 22	1225	1340	15 2	1747	1926	2218	4 5	169	,, Vire .... ,,	7 53	..	1348	..	1830	19 4	2359	..
9 0	1259	1433	1538	1823	20 4	2252	5 21	195	,, Folligny .... ,,	7 18	..	13 8	..	1751	1823	23 5	..
9 14	1313	1447	1549	1834	2017	23 4	5 38	205	arr. **Granville** ..dep.	7 0	..	1250	..	1735	18 5	2230	..

A Auto-Rail: one class. **B** Sats. July 1–Sept. 2. **V** Buffet Car. *c* 1, 2 and 3 cl. Couchettes Paris-Granville and *v.v.* *r* Rest. Car. † Takes 3 cl. for 63 miles or more.

(Paris), Rennes (St. Malo), St. Brieuc, (Lannion), Brest. [French Rlys. (Ouest).

123 Rap Y	123 Rap Z	123 Rap X	123 Rap	123 Rap T	123 Exp	123 Exp	Ms	(Montparnasse Stn.)	123 Rap Y	123 Exp U	123	123 Rap	123 xp U	123 Rap
8 35	1010	13 0	16 5	21 5	22 0	0 15	0	dep. **Paris** (p.244) arr.	1625	1720	..	23 0	6 50	7 0
1243	1435	1729	2011	2 20	2 51	6 25	234	arr. Rennes .... dep.	12 0	13 5		1833	1 6	1 29
r	r	V	r	a	b	g			r			r	a g	b
1250	1450	1740	2018	2 27	3 4	9 15	.	dep. **Rennes** ....arr.	1152	1257	1853	1826	0 56	1 11
1350	1555	1834		3 34	4 4	101	282	arr. Lamballe....dep.	1044	1149	1745	1732	2346	0 6
1411	1617	1851	2125	3 58	4 25	1031	295	,, **St. Brieuc** .. ,,	1026	1129	1726	1716	2317	2346
10‡39	12‡59	..	1856	‡ ↓	↓	5 24	..	dep. **St. Malo** .. arr.	10‡12	14 3	1952	1952	↑	↑
1110	1351	..	1935		‡	8 0	..	,, Dol ...... ,,	9 43	13‡25	1920	1920		
1116	1231	..	19‡31			7 19	.	,, Dinard.. ,,	..	1457	19‡21	19‡21		
12 1	1425	..	20 1			8 35	..	,, Dinan.... ,,	9 18	12‡57	1855	1855		
13 3	1523	..	2111	↓	↓‡	9 36	.	arr. **St. Brieuc** dep.	8 19	11‡56	1757	1757		
1419	1625	1854	2129	5 13	4 35	1035	295	dep. **St. Brieuc** ..arr.	1017	1119	1651	1711	23 2	2331
15 8	1715	1941	2218	6 12	..	1125	323	arr. Plouaret .... dep.	9 26	1027	1545	..	22 5	2238
	1734	1958	23 0	6 40	.	115	332	,, Lannion .. ,,	6 20	10 3	1455	..	2123	21‡54
1535		..	2246	6 49	5 51	115	350	,, Morlaix	8 59		15 1	1559	2136	2210
1614	..	..	2319	..	6 31	1226	375	,, Landerneau dep.	8 24	..	1410	..	..	2119
1632	..	..	2335	..	6 49	1244	387	,, **Brest** ...... ,,	8 7	..	1353	1516	..	21 0

A Auto Rail—one class. **S** Saturdays only. **T** July 30–Sept. 30. **U** July 2–Oct. 1. **V** Buffet-bar. **X** July 1–Sept. 30 (Sats only beyond Rennes) **Y** 1, 2 & 3 cl. Car Paris-Rennes (St Brieuc, July 1–Sept. 30). **Z** July 1–Sept. 30. *a* 1 cl. Lits-Toilette & 1, 2 & 3 cl. Couchettes Paris-Lannion & *v.v.* *b* 1 cl. Lits-Toilette, 1, 2 & 3 cl Couchettes Paris-Brest *g* 1, 2 & 3 cl. Couchettes Paris-Rennes and *v.v.* *h* Only takes 3 cl. at St. Brieuc and Lamballe for Laval and beyond. *r* Rest. Car. ‡ 3 cl. Auto Rail.

(Caen), Lison, Coutances, Avranches, Dol, (St. Malo). [French Rlys. (Ouest).

A	1/23	123	1/23	1/23	1/23	A	Ms		1/23	A	1/23	A	1/23	123	‡ Auto-Rail.	A Auto-Rail Car—one class.
..	6 13	1032	1225	1615	..	1825		dep. Caen (p. 243) arr.	8 7	1045	1253	1639	20 6	2251		
..	7 25	1124	1325	17 3	..	1924	0	,, Lison........ ,,	7 10	9 45	1155	1543	1912	2148		
..	7 59	1142	1357	1721	..	1950	12	St. Lo	6 45	9 24	1125	1525	183	2131		
..	8 47	1210	15 2	1751	..	2056	30	Coutances ..	5 56	8 45	1044	1457	1729	21 1		
5 29	9 34	1239	1559	1828	..	2258	47	d. Foligny (*below*) a.	5 16	8 18	9 58	1428	1636	2033		
6 11	10 1	1256	1619	1846	..	2315		dep. Avranches ..	..	..	9 32	14 8	16 4	2013		
6 57	1029	1316	1650	19 6	dep.	arr.	59	,, Pontorson ..	..	..	9 2	1348	1533	1954		
7 9	1053	1335	1716	1924	2111	..	73	arr. Dol (*above*) ..dep.	..	..	8 32	1328	15 7	1933		
8 23	11‡27	14 5	18 6	1958	..	..	86	,, St. Malo .. ,,	..	..	8 8	1259	..	1856		
8 34	11‡43	1422	18‡12	1959	2147	..	100	,, Dinan ...... ,,	..	..	7 47	13 0	1341	1859		
9 15	12‡43	15 4	..	2048	..	..	104	,, Lamballe.... ,,	..	..	7 6	1211	..	18 6		
9 36	15‡3	1523		2111			129	,, St. Brieuc.... ,,			6 46	1152		1745		

(Paris), Poitiers—Niort—(Royan)—Bordeaux.

123 Exp	123 Exp	A	1/23	A	123 Rap	123 Rap	123 Rap	Ms		123 Exp	12 Exp	1/23	123 Exp	123 Rap	123 Rap	1/23	123 Exp	12 Exp
From Rennes.	2255	..	..	..	From St. Malo	8 45	1230	0	dep. Paris (Orsay) (page 248) arr.	1235	To Rennes.	..	1750	23‡45	To St. Malo.	..	6 15	To St. Malo.
	2 15	..	..	6 40		1117	1456	149	,, Tours .. ,,	9 58		..	1439	21‡14		..	2 51	
	3 32	..	..	9 10		13 0	1631	210	,, Poitiers.. ,,	8 26		..	13 5	19 4		..	1 23	
	4 46	..	..	11 1		14 6	1737	259	arr. Niort.... dep.	7 19		..	1155	1632		..	0 6	
						A	1/23						A					
..	5 37	..	7 50	1110	..	1425	1751	..	dep. Niort........arr.	7 11	..	..	1140	1529	..	..	2235	..
4 48	6 49	..	9 42	12 4	15 2	1519	1849	305	arr. Saintes..... dep	5 58	8 12	..	1042	1414	1410	..	2130	0 19
..	8 19	..	1113	..	1552	1552	2132	329	arr. **Royan** ......dep.	..	..	..	9 51	..	1315	..	20 5	..
.	7 6	9 51	9 51	..	1315	..	1847	..	dep. ,, ...arr.	..	9 2	..	1113	..	1552	2132	..	..
				123		123							123					
4 57	7 54	1035	1052	1212	15 5	17 1	1948	..	dep Saintes ......arr.	..	7 55	8 57	1028	1323	14 7	20 4	2113	0 8
5 20	8 14	1052	1122	1231	B	1731	2014	320	arr. Pons ....dep.	..	..	8 30	10 8	1245	B	1932	2052	2345
7 18	9 56	1211	13†49	14 6	1642	1928	2148	385	,, **Bordeaux**.... ,,	..	6 20	6a30	8 40	9†39	1234	16†39	1920	2210

A Auto-Rail Car—one class. **B** Buffet Car. † Deschamps Station. ‡ 1 & 2 cl. only.

(Paris) Poitiers—Niort—La Rochelle. [French Rlys. (Ouest).

123	123	1/23	123	123	1/23	12			123	123	123	1/23	1/23	12	123
Exp			Rap	Rap		Rap	Mls	p. 248.	Exp	Rap	Rap			Rap	Exp
2255	2215	..	8 45	1230	..	1725	0	dp. **Paris** (Qu. d'Orsay) ar	1535	1235	1750	..	..	2345	6 15
3 26	2 57	..	1246	1617		2054	210	arr. Poitiers ..... dep.	1134	8 34	1327	..	..	1959	1 30
¶	1/23					A			1/23					A	¶
3 32	5 27	9 10	13 0	1631	18 4	21 4		dep. Poitiers ...... arr.	10 3	8 26	13 5	19 8	2234	1945	1 23
4 46	7 7	1059	14 6	1737	20 1	22 4	259	arr. Niort .... dep.	8 5	7 19	1155	1632	2057	1833	0 6
..	..	..	7 0	1025	..	..	..	dp. Paris (M'tparnass) a	..	..		..			..
4 58	7 41	1149	1416	1740	2058	22 6	..	dep. Niort .... arr.	7 1	7 16	1151	1459	1940	1830	2354
6 2	9 20	1331	15 7	1831	2210	2255	301	arr. **La Rochelle** . dep.	5 40	6 26	11 1	1311	1711	1742	2249
6 45	10 3	1427	1553	1914	..	2323	320	arr. Rochefort .... dep.	..	5 51	1019	1225	16 1	1714	22 7
9 56	14 6	1642	1928	..	..		426	arr. Bordeaux (*below*) dp	..	..	6 2[illegible]	..	1234	..	1920

A Auto-Rail, one cl. only.
¶ Through 1, 2 & 3 cl. cars Paris-La Rochelle-Bordeaux and *vice versa*.

(Paris) Tours, Thouars, La Roche-sur-Yon.

123	123	1/23	123	123	123	123	Mls.	**B** July 1–Sept. 30.	1/23	123	123	123	1/23	1/23	123
Exp	fast	..	fast	Rap	Rap	B				fast	fast	B		..	Exp
2255	..	..	0 0	8 45	1230	..	0	dep. **Paris** (Q. d'Orsay) a.	..	1750	..	..	2345	..	6a15
2 2	..	..	4 27	1138	1520	..	..	arr. } Tours.... { dep.	..	1451	..	..	‡	..	1 47
2 21	..	..	6 30	1154	1618	..	149	dep. } Tours.... { arr.	1336	1445	..	..	..	..	1 16
3 57	..	..	9 7	1357	1910	..	210	arr. Thouars ...... dep.	11 2	1214	..	..	1858	..	2325
..	..	..		7 0	..	13 0	0	dp Paris M'tparnasse ar	..	1929	1652	1935	23 0	6 20	..
..		..	..	1254	..	..	204	arr. Thouars ...... dep.	..	1318			¶		..
4 5	4 52	5 7	9 23	14 9	2011	*via* Nantes	..	dep. Thouars .. ..arr.	8 54	1228	*via* Nantes	*via* Nantes	1850	*via* Nantes	23 5
4 37	5 19	5 52	1013	1456	2127		228	ar. Bressuire ....dep.	4 20	12 2			1818		2238
..	7 55	..	..	..	..		298	arr. La Rochelle dep.	..	..			..		19 7
4 45	..	5 57	1037	1512	..		..	dep. Bressuire ....arr	8 16	11 5	..	..	1759	..	2235
6 3	..	7 56	1226	1717	..	1915	..	ar } La R'che-s'r-Yn { d	6 18	10 3	1049	1326	1542	1959	2054
6 14	..	8 21	1250	1727	..	1916	282	de } La R'che-s'r-Yn { a	5 57	9 26	1042	1324	1531	1947	2049
6 45	..	8 58	1327	18 0	..	1950	304	ar. Les Sables d'Olone d	5 15	8 40	10 3	1242	1452	19 0	2010

A auto-Rail Car, one cl. only. *a* arr. Paris (Austerlitz) 5.0 by changing at Tours.
‡ *via* St. Pierre des Corps to Paris.
¶ *via* Nantes to Paris.

Nantes, La Rochelle, Bordeaux. [French Rlys. (Ouest).

▼ Voiture-Buffet.

123	A	123	123	123	1/23	A	1/23	1/23		123	A	123	1/23	A	123	123
Exp		Exp	Rap			* ‡		Exp		‡		Rap			Exp	Exp
From Paris.	6 53	8 25	1136	‡	1242	1550	..	0‡20	dep. **Nantes** (Etat) arr.	1151	1347	17‡41	2137	..	To Paris.	4‡52
	8 16	9 29	1239		1422	1648	..	1 41	a. La Roche-sur-Yon d.	1049	1231	1638	1959	..		3 33
	1013	1055	1358		1721	18 2	..	3 24	a. } **La Rochelle** { dp.	9 27	1037	1516	17 0	..		1 44
6 16	..	11 2	14 5	1515	1818	18 9	..	3 35	d } **La Rochelle** { ar.	9 20	..	15 9	1638	..	2237	1 34
6 45	..	1124	1427	1553	19 0	1835	..	4 1	arr. Rochefort ....dep.	8 53	..	1446	16 1	..	22 7	1 7
7 37	..	12 4	15 2	1654	2038	1915	..	4 48	arr. } Saintes .. { dep	8 12	..	1410	15 1	1730	2120	0 19
7 54	..	1212	15 5	17 1	..		1948	4 57	dep } Saintes .. { arr.	7 55	..	14 7	..	1711	2113	0 8
9 56	..	14 6	1642	1928	..	..	2148	7 18	arr. **Bordeaux**† ..dep.	6 20	..	1234	..	1538	1920	2210

* Auto-Rail Nantes-La Rochelle & *v.v.*

A Auto Rail one class. † St. Jean Stn. ‡ Arrive or depart Nantes (Orleans). *r* Rest. Car.

(Paris), Nantes, Redon, Quimper, Brest. [French Rlys. (Ouest).

1/23	123	123	‡	123	123	123	123		123	123	123	123	123	123	123
	Rap	Exp		Exp	Exp	Rap	Exp		Rap	Exp	Exp	Exp	Rap	Exp	Exp
..	8 15	1010	..	..	16 5	22 0	0 15	dep. Paris (*p.* 245) ..arr.	..	..	1720	23 0	23 0	6 20	7 0
		B *r*			*r*	C		Montparnasse			B		*r*		C
10‡5	1230	1442	1610	17‡55	2032	¶	6 50	,, Rennes ....arr.	9‡37	1140	1243		1810	22 7	1 11
11‡7	1342	1537	17 3	1918	2124		8 14	arr. Redon .....dep.	8‡40	1021	1148	¶	1710	2035	0 6
9‡40	1250	1410	1535	1815	1010	3 10	7 2	dep. **Nantes** (or)..arr.	10 4	1130	..	18 6	1826	22 7	..
1032	1331	1455	1516	1913	2114	..	7 52	,, Savenay .... ,,	8 30	1016	..	16 8	1715	2037	..
1125	14 4	1545	17 5	1959	2126	4 29	8 35	dep. Redon ...... ,,	8‡25	1011	1145	1549	17 8	2026	0 1
1220	1446	1631	1759	2056	22 8	5 18	9 24	arr. Vannes ....dep.	7‡33	9 27	11 1	1445	1627	1939	2310
1320	1536	1727	1854	22 4	2258	6 19	1022	,, Lorient .... ,,	6‡42	8 29	10 6	1328	1539	1837	22 6
1342	1557	1750	1916	..	2318	5 46	1050	,, Quimperlé .. ,,	6‡21	8 9	9 46	1250	1520	1812	2141
1430	1639	1834	20 4	..	0 3	7 36	1135	,, Quimper .... ,,	5‡41	7 2[illegible]	9 0	1145	1437	1722	2045
..	1814	2058	..	..	..	9 22	1336	,, Landerneau dep.		5‡51	..	9 43	12‡55	1515	1816
	1830	2116	..	..	..	9 44	14 5	,, **Brest** (*above*) dp.	..	5‡35	..	9 18	12‡35	1446	1755

B July 1–Sept. 30. **C** 1 cl. Lit, Toilette, 1, 2 and 3 cl. Couchettes and Cars Paris-Quimper and *v.v.*
* 1 and 2 cl. only. *r* Rest. Car. ‡ Auto rail, one class. ¶ *uia* Le Mans & Nantes page 247.

(Paris), Le Mans, Angers, Nantes, St. Nazaire, Le Croisic.

French Rlys. (Ouest).

Mls.		123	123	123	123	123	123	123	123	123	123	123	123	123	123	123
			fast	Exp	Rap	fast	Exp	Rap		Exp		Rap	Exp	Rap	Exp	Exp
0	p.244 Paris (M'parnasse) d	0 15	..	..	8 15	1010	..	13 0	13 0	..	16 5	1810	22 0	..	23 0	
132	Le Mans ...... arr.	2 52	..	..	1020	1225	..	1515	1515	..	1810	202..	0 30	..	2 15	
		A							A			R			T	
..	Le Mans ...... dep.	4 40	..	..	1026	13 0	..	1521	1535	..	1835	2031	0 42	..	2 29	..
162	Sable .... dep.	5 45	..	..	..	1344	..	..	1619	..	1939	21 7		..	3 10	..
190	Angers (St. Laud) ar	6 54	..	..	1133	1436	..	1631	1712	..	2050	2143	1 58	..	3 57	..
0	Paris (Orsay) dep.	..	0 0	..	..	..	8 5	..	..	1432	..		↓	21a41	Y	2255
149	Tours .... de .	..	5 23	8 1	10 0	..	1049	1456	.	1758	..	1935	↓	0 21	..	3 18
152	Angers .... arr.	..	7 2	9 22	1123	..	1238	1623	..	1921	..	21 6	↓	1 48	..	4 45
0	Angers ...... dep.	..	7 19	9 25	1136	15‡5	1246	1641	18 0	1926	..	2146	2 5	——	4 0	4 55
55	Nantes (Orl) arr.	..	8 46	1028	1233	1648	14 2	1748	1943	2045	..	224..	3 3	..	5 15	6 1
	Nantes (Orl) dep	..	8‡54	1033	1240	..	1424	1754	..	..	..	2250	3 10	..	5 20	6 20
97	St. Nazaire .... arr.	..	10‡1	1135	1336	..	1539	1859	..	..	..	2351	To Brest	..	6 35	7 29
107	Pornichet .... arr.	..	1031	12‡1	14 1	..	15‡54	1919	..	..	..	0 15		..	7 12	8 0
110	La Baule-Es'blac ar	..	1041	1210	1410	..	16‡1	1929	..	..	..	0 24		..	7 21	8 10
115	Le Croisic .... arr.	..	11 1	12‡29	1431	..	16‡17	1953	..	..	..	0 43		..	7 43	8 35

	123	123	123	123	1/23	123	A	123	A	123	123	123	123	123
	Rap	..	Rap	Z		Exp		Rap		Rap	fast	Exp	X	Exp
Le Croisic .... dep.	..	..	5 40	6 21	..	9 36	..	1240	..	1624	..	1927	..	2143
La Baule Es'blac ,,	..	..	5 59	6 40	..	9 59	..	13 0	..	1645	..	1955	..	22 7
Pornichet ...... ,,	..	..	6 9	6 52	..	1011	..	13 6	..	1656	..	20 8	..	2220
St. Nazaire .... ,,	..	..	6 32	7 20	8 41	1041	..	1335	..	1721	..	2032	..	2245
Nantes ...... arr.	..	..	7 31	8 20	10 4	1146	..	1433	..	1816	..	2140	..	2355
Nantes ...... dep	5 45	..	7 37	8 29	1010	12 0	..	1440	..	1832	1915	2210	2342	0 13
Angers (St. Laud) ar.	6 47	..	8 31	9 32	1213	13 7	..	1546	..	1926	2121	2313	0 55	1 24
Angers .... dep.	↓	5 36	8 33	9 35	..	1325	1410	1555	..	1935	..	2318	↓	1 35
Tours .... arr.	↓	7 51	9 55	1053	..	1438	16 7	1713	..	2114	..	0 39	↓	3 21
Paris (Orsay) .. arr.	↓	1235	1235	1535	..	1750	2030	2030	——	2345	..	5a0	↓	7 7
				A	A			Rap		r		..		T
Angers (St. Laud) dp.	6 49	..	..	10 8	1220	1310	..	1549	1632	1928	2132	..	1 2	1 29
Sables .... arr.	7 27	..	..	11 0	1313	1350	..	..	1725	..	2211	..	..	2 8
Le Mans ...... arr.	8 6	..	..	1145	1358	1429	..	1710	1810	2033	23 0	..	2 30	2 47
Le Mans (p. 244 dp.	10 7	..	..	1219	14 7	1435	..	1720	1835	2045	3 0	..	2 36	3 0
Paris (M'parn) arr.	1220	..	..	1523	1625	1652	..	1935	2110	23 0	6 20	..	5 50	6 20

‡ Auto-Rail, one class.
a Paris Austerlitz Station.

r Rest Car Nantes—Le Mans.

A Auto-Rail Car, one class only. **R** Rest Car, Paris—Nantes.
T 1 & 2 cl. Sleep. Car, Paris—Le Croisic and *v.v.* **X** July 1–Oct. 1.
Y June 30–Sept. 30. **Z** July 2–Oct. 1.

Paris, Vendome, Tours.

[French Rlys. (Sud-Ouest).

A	1/23	123	1/23	1/23	123	123	Mls.		Mls.	A	A	1/23	A	123	123	A
..	6 35	8 0	1221	17 6	18 6	21†10	0	dep. **Paris** (Orsay) arr.	149	9 12	1332	1515	1847	1951	2147	..
6 30	8 55	1014	1551	1938	2037	2328	85	Chateaudun dep.	64	6 36	1043	1215	16 3	1744	1857	arr.
7 12	arr.	1058	1651	2019	arr.	0 10	125	Vendome .... dep.	24	5 48	..	1126		1659	1814	21 6
8 22	..	1225	1814	2125	..	1 18	149	arr. **Tours** ...... dep.	0	4 40	..	10 4	..	1530	..	1917

† Austerlitz Stn.

Perigueux—Brive—Royat—Clermont Ferrand.

[French Rlys. (Sud-Ouest).

1/23	1/23	A	3 cl.	1/23	1/23	3 cl.	Mls.		A	1/23	123	1/23	A	1/23
..	..	8 58	..	..	..	..	0	dep. Perigueux ...... arr.	1221	..	16 1	..	2130	..
..	5 25	10 5	..	1359	1630	..	45	dep. Brive .... arr.	9 42	1349	1435	16 6	2025	..
5 46	9 0	1156	1212	1635	1930	1943	104	dep Ussel .... arr.	6 51	9 40	1140	1320	1835	22 4
7 0	1019	1242	1350	1742	⌐—	21 3	128	arr. Laqueuille ...... dep.	dep.	8 24	1045	1224	1751	21 6
8 59	1123	1325	1658	1823	..	2153	138	arr. Mont Dore .. dep.	..	6 38	9 57	1146	17 2	2017
8 47	12 1	1351	1555	1914	..	2251	159	arr. Royat .... dep.	..	6 23	8 56	1043	1640	1922
8 56	1210	1359	16 7	1923	..	23 3	162	ar. Clermont Ferrand dp.	..	6 10	8 42	1031	1630	1910

A Auto-Rail Car, one class only.

Bordeaux, Arcachon.

[French Rlys. (Sud Ouest).

1/23	1/23	1/23	1/23	123	1/23	1/23	123	1/23		1/23	1/23	123	1/23	1/23	1/23	123	123	123	1/23
6 31	7 50	9 30	1120	1331	1616	1733	1832	2045	d. Bord'x, *p*.248 a	7 28	8 10	8 52	1244	1359	16 1	1659	1750	19 0	21 3
7 27	8 25		1159	1410	1724	18 4	1911	2128	dp. Lamothe dp.	6 37	7 33	8 19	1155	1327	15 2	1629	17 8	1823	2026
7 51	8 46	1019	1223	1430	1749	1823	1934	2146	ar. Arcachon dp.	6 15	7 10	8 1	1118	1351	1411	16 5	1650	18 0	20 3

Paris, Orleans, Tours, Bordeaux.

[French Rlys. (Sud-Ouest).

Ml	Thro' services, see also pp. 115, 116, 250.	Exp 123	Rap 123	Rap 123	luxe 12	Rap 123	Exp 123	Exp 123	Rap 12	Exp 123	Rap 123	Rap 123	Rap 123	Exp 123	Exp 123	Exp 123	1/23	Exp 123
			R*a*	**Y**	**B**	**R**	**Y**		**R**		**Y**	*g***S**		**E**	**Z**			
0	**Paris**(Qu.d'Orsay)dp.	8 5	8 45	1010	1130	1230	1240	1432	1725	1728	2030	2050	..	2215	2220	2255		0 0
	,, (Austerlitz) dep	8 17	8 59	..		1242	1251	1443	*p*	1738	2041	21 4	2141	2227	2231	2311	..	0 15
77	Les Aubrais .... arr.	9 25	1010	*t*	1243	1350	14 0	16 3	1838	1859	2158	2224	23 2	2356	0 4	0 36	..	2 12
78	**Orleans**.... arr.	9 35	1019	|	1251	1358	14 9	1610	1847	19 6	22 7	2232	2315	0 6	..	0 45	..	2 23
	Orleans.... dep.	9 13	10 4	|	1237	1344	1354	1615	1831	1911	2152	2218	2250	2350	2358	0 28	..	2 8
..	Les Aubrais ....dep	9 21	1013	|	1243	1353	14 3	..	1839	..	22 0	2226	23 5	2359	0 7	0 38	..	2 22
114	Blois	1017	1053	|	..	1433	1445	17 0	1913	2019	..	23 6	2351	0 46	0 58	1 20	..	3 21
147	St. Pierre-des-Corp a.	1058	1126	1231	1341	15 6	1518	1743	1944	2117	2310	2341	0 29	1 32	1 45	1 55	..	4 15
149	**Tours**...... arr.	11 7	1138	1245	1351	1518	1531	1751	1956	2126	2322	2353	0 41	1 44	2 8	2 3	..	4 27
	Tours...... dep.	1049	1117	1221	1329	1456	1510	19 1	1936	..	23 2	2333	0 7	1 23	1 37	2 15	..	4 17
..	St.Pierre-des-Corps d.	11 6	1133	1236	1342	1510	1522	..	1948	..	2314	2348	0 36	1 38	1 50	..	..	4 32
210	**Poitiers**...... arr	To La Croisic.	1246	|	1439	1617	1630	2113	2054	..	0 25	0 56	..	2 57	3 12	3 26	..	6 8
	Poitiers...... dep.		1252	|	1440	1623	..	..	2056	..	0 29	1 0	To Brest.	3 2	3 16	To La Rochelle	5 40	6 20
281	Angoulême .. arr.		1417	|	1540	1740	..	..	22 3	..	1 47	2 18		4 44	5 0		7 3	8 47
	Angoulême .. dep.		1421	|	1541	1744	..	..	22 5	..	1 51	2 21		4 50	To Royan.		7 4	9 5
332	Coutras		1515	|	..	..	..	..	..	..	..	..		6 8			8 11	1058
342	Libourne		1531	|	..	19 0	..	..	23 9	..	..	..		6 27			8 24	1119
364	Bordeaux (Bast.) a.		..	↓	..	..	..	..	..	..	..	..		..			..	1150
368	**Bordeaux**(St.Jean)a		16 7	1634	17 9	1935	..	..	2340	..	3 32	4 20	..	7 10			8 55	1220
...	p. 250. Bordeaux(S.J) dp	..	1648	‿	1721	1950	..	..	0 0	..	3 41	4 29	..	8 0	..	..	..	1345
...	Pau (*p*. 251) arr.	..	2016	..	23 4	23 4	..	..	3 33	..	7 5	7 52	..	1140	..	..	..	1739
...	Hendaye ....arr.	..	2017	..	2031	23 8	..	..	5 56	..	..	8 26	..	12 6	..	..	..	1722
...	MADRID (*p*. 321) a	..	..		10 0	..		..	2130	..	..		..	..		..	..	..

	123	123 Exp	123	123 Rap	123 Exp	123 Exp	123 Rap	luxe B	1/23 fast	12 Rap	1/23	123 Exp	123 Exp	123 Exp	123 Rap	123 Exp	123 Rap
MADRID (*p*.321) dp	..	..	..	..	..	..	..	22 0	..	..	..	..	..	..	..	..	..
p. 250 Hendaye...... ,,	..	..	..	..	..	8 37	8 45	12 0	..	1348	..	15 1	..	**X**	1823	21 0	2148
Pau (*p*. 251) ,,	..	..	..	..	..	9 4	9 4	1032	..	1340	..	1516	..	..	1830	..	2236
Bordeaux (S.J) ar	..	..	..	..	..	1220	1220	1518	..	1659	..	1843	..	From Royan.	2150	0 45	1 43
Bordeaux (St.Jn.) d.	..	..	..	8 30	From La Rochelle	1228	13 5	1524	..	1725	1748	2020	From La Rochelle		2220	0 55	1 52
Bordeaux (Bast) dp.	..	From La Rochelle	..	**R**		**X**	**R**	..	1523	**R**	..				**E**	**X**	..
Libourne	..		..	8 59		..	1336	..	1551		1819	2058			2256	1 23	*g***S**
Coutras	..		..	..		..	1351	..	16 7	*q*	1832	2115			2316	..	..
Angoulême .. arr.	..		..	10 3		1356	1448	1636	1725	1848	1937	2219		..	0 30	2 29	3 21
Angoulême .. dep.	..		..	10 7		14 0	1452	1637	..	1850	1946	2226		0 20	0 35	2 32	3 24
Poitiers ...... arr.	..		..	1130		1519	1610	1737	..	1957	2159	2357		2 2	2 17	3 49	4 42
Poitiers ...... dep.	..	8 34	8 40	1134	1327	1522	1614	1738	..	1959	..	0 4	1 30	2 6	2 21	3 53	4 45
St. Pierre-des-Corp a.	..	9 41	..	1244	..	1632	1731	1832	..	21 4	..	..	2 43	3 51	4 5	4 57	5 53
Tours...... arr.	..	9 58 *r*	1034	1256	1439 *r*	1644	1744	1845	..	2114	..	1 32	2 51	4 6	4 16	5 9	6 10
Tours...... dep.	6 15	9 35	11 9	1236	1451	1624	1723	1758	..	2056	..	1 47	2 58	3 40	3 57	4 49	5 50
St. Pierre-des-Corp ,,	6 23	9 55	1116	1250	1458	1638	1736	1833	..	21 9	..	1 56	..	4 1	4 10	5 1	6 8
Blois	7 20	1030	1228	1326	1538	|	1813	..	..	2143	..	2 42	3 39	4 42	4 52	..	6 46
Les Aubrais .... arr.	..	11 6	..	14 6	1618	|	1854	1930	..	2219	..	3 25	4 22	5 25	5 38	6 12	7 27
Orleans...... arr.	8 24	1114	1345	1416	1627	|	19 4	1939	..	2232	..	3 36	4 33	5 33	5 47	6 21	7 36
Orleans...... dep.	8 34	1059	14 0	14 0	1612	|	1847	19 7	..	2214	..	3 19	4 17	5 20	5 33	6 8	7*r*22
Les Aubrais ...... ,,	8 40	11 8	14 9	14 9	1620	↓	1857	1930	..	2221	..	3 30	4 25	5 28	5 42	6 15	7 29
Paris (Austerlitz) arr.	1015	1225	1523	1523	1739	1919	2018	2034	..	2335	..	5 0	6 0	6 55	7 18	7 54	8 54
,, (Qu. d'Orsy) arr.	1025	1235	1535	1535	1750	1930	2030	2059	..	2345	..	..	6 15	7 7	..	8 5	9 5

For full details of Through Coaches and Sleeping Cars see pages **115 & 116.**

B Sud Express, Pullman Cars to Irun, daily train de luxe with Sleeping Cars Irun-Madrid and Lisbon, *see page* 85. Extra Fares. **E** 1st and 2nd cl. Sleeping Car Paris-Arcachon and *v.v.* **R** Restaurant Car Paris-Bordeaux and *v.v.* **S** 1st and 2nd cl. Sleeping Car Paris-Irun and Tarbes and *v.v.* **X** July 2—Oct. 1. **Y** July 1—Sept. 30. **Z** June 30—Sept. 30. *a* Only takes 3 cl. for beyond Orleans and Les Aubrais. *b* Takes 3rd cl. 94 miles or more. *g* Limited train takes 2nd cl. for St. Pierre-des-Corps and beyond; 3rd cl. passengers for Dax or beyond, and before Dax for Paris in reverse direction. *k* Does not take 3rd cl. for Les Aubrais and Orleans. *p* Only takes 2nd cl. for Blois and beyond. Limited train. *q* Limited train. *r* Rest. Car. *s* Takes 2 cl. for 190 miles, and 3 cl. for 315 miles or more. *t* Only carries 3 cl. for Bordeaux and beyond. † 1 and 2 cl. only. *** For other trains, Paris-Orleans, *see p.* 249.

(Paris), Orleans, Vierzon, Mont Dore, Limoges. [French Rlys. (Sud-Ouest).

See also p. 248.

Mls.		1 2 3	1 2 3 r	1 2 3	1 2	1 2 3	1 2 3	1 2 3	1/2 3	1 2 3	1 2 3	1 2 3	1 2 3	1 2 3	1 2 3	1 2	1 2 3	1 2 3
		Exp	Exp	Exp	Rap		Exp	Exp		Exp	Rap	Rap	Exp	Rap	Exp	Y	Exp	fast
0	Quai d'Orsay, Paris........dep.	..	..	10r15	1110	..	1310	1432	15 6	1728	1925	2015	d	..	2145	22 40	..	0 0
0	Paris (Austerlitz) ,,	7 5	9 27	1028	B	..	1319	1445	1515	1738	1937	2025	2112	2130	2159	..	2250	0 19
74	Les Aubrais ..arr	8 22	1039	1139	1223	..	1427	16 3	1716	1859	2045	i	2232	2250	23 9	via Nevers and Clermont.	0 21	2 12
75	Orleans .... ar.	8 31	1050	1149	..	..	1436	1610	1723	19 6	2056	↓	2249	23 0	2319		0 31	2 23
..	Orleans .... dp.	8 16	1033	1133	1217	..	1420	1615	1735	1919	2038		2225	2245	23 3		0 15	5 33
..	Les Aubrais....dep	8 24	1041	1142	1224	..	1429	..	..	V	2046		2235	2253	2312		0 24	
126	Vierzon ....arr.	9 15	1151	1234	1315	..	1520	1718	1856	2041	2137		2332	2350	0 3		1 34	6 55
..	Vierzon......dep.	9 23	1157	..	⌣	1329	1530	..	..	..	..		..	..	..		1 41	..
..	Bourges .... arr.	..	1222	..	..	A	1748	..	..	..	..		..	..	..		2 15	..
207	Montlucon ..arr.	1110	1410	..	..	1511	2012	..	..	..	..		..	A	..	..	6 2	..
278	Laqueuille.. arr.	1323	1742	..	..	18 8	..	..	..	..	..		..	..	..	8 13	1019	..
284	La Bourboule ,,	1338	1813	..	..	1836	A	..	..	..	..		..	..	..	8 41	11 9	..
287	Le Mt. Dore ,,	1347	1823	..	..	1849	..	..	..	..	..		..		..	8 59	1123	..
124	Vierzon........dep	9 19	12 8	1245	..	..	1522	1720	..	..	2139		2335	2353	0 6	..	1 42	7 20
165	Chateauroux	10 8	1517	1337	..	..	1610	1826	..	..	2228		0 17	0 37	0 48	..	2 50	1040
230	St. Sulpice Laurière	1136	17 5	15 0	..	..	1734	2015	..	..	2353	↓	..	..	..	..	4 43	1238
248	Limoges ...... arr.	12 1	1741	1529	..	..	18 0	2045	..	..	0 15	0 36	1 57	2 22	2 32	..	5 10	1318

Toulouse, Agen, &c. see Table below.	1 2 3	1 2 3	1 2 3	1 2 3	1 2 3	1 2 3	1 2 3	1 2 3	1 2	1/2 3	1 2 3	1 2 3	1 2 3	1 2 3	1 2 3	1 2 3
	Exp	Exp	Exp	Rap		Exp	fast	Rap	Rap	Exp	Exp	Exp	Rap	Exp	Exp	Y
Limoges......dep.	2 2	2 12	3 21	3 50	..	7 21	8 55	..	..	..	1335	1540	1743	2350	..	2042
St. Sulpice Laurière		..	3 51	..	..	7 49	9 39	D	B	..	14 5	1610		0 23	..	21 0
Chateauroux	3 39	3 49	5 10	5 28	6 0	9 7	1128	..	..	..	1528	1731	1921	1 51	..	2125
Vierzon ...... arr.	4 21	4 31	6 0	6 12	6 55	9 53	1230	..	..	..	1615	1816	20 6	2 37		..
		C	V	i r									r			
Le Mt. Dore dep.	..	↓	e	..	..	..	..	9 40	..	6 38	r	D	1518	..	2017	..
La Bourboule ,,	..			..	..	..	..	9 53	..	6 48	..	..	1525	..	2027	..
Laqueuille..dep.	l			..	..	..	..	1018	..	8 24		..	1542	..	21 6	
Montlucon	..			..	..	6 45	9 42	1310	..	1320	..	1435	1812	..	0 39	via Clermont and Nevers.
Bourges ....dep.	..			..	..	9 16	12 4	..	..	15 9	..	17 8	..	..	2 23	
Vierzon......arr.	..	↓	↓	..	..	9 45	1238	1453	⌣	1538	..	1731	20 0		2 55	
Vierzon ......dep.	4 24	4 34	6 3	6 23	7 0	10 0	1243	..	1510	1544	1619	1821	2011	2 44	3 1	
Les Aubrais .. arr.	5 20	5 32	7 4	..	..	1115	14 4	..	16 1	1656	1719	1935	21 7	3 45	4 10	
Orleans.... ar.	5 28	5 40	7 13	..	8 19	1125	1416	..	1640	17 6	1730	1945	2118	3 55	4 21	
Orleans.... dp.	5 15	5 27	6 58	..	8 27	11 9	14 0	..	1555	1650	1715	1930	21 1	3 40	4 5	
Les Aubrais ..dp.	5 21	5 35	7 6	..	8 40	1117	14 9	..	16 2	1659	1724	1938	2110	3 48	4 14	..
Paris (Auster.) arr.	6 43	7 4	8 32	8 39	1015	1234	1523	..	1714	1828	1853	2058	2229	5 17	5 51	..
,, (Quai d'Orsay) ,,	6 55	7 17	8 43	8 50	1025	1244	1535	..	1723	1840	19 5	2110	2240	5 30	6 4	6¶10

See p. 248

A July 1—Sept. 30. **B** Thermal Exp., see pp. 80 and 254. **C** July 3—Oct 2. **D** July 2—Oct. 1. **V** Voiture Buffet.

a Only takes 2 and 3 cl. for Chateauroux and beyond. *b* At Paris, does not take 3 cl. for Les Aubrais and Orleans. *d* Only takes 1, 2 and 3 cl. for 125 miles or more. *e* Does not take 3 cl. at Les Aubrais and Orleans for Paris. *i* Does not carry local passengers. *j* Only takes 2 cl. for Limoges and beyond, and 3 cl. for beyond Limoges. *k* Only takes 2 cl. for 250 miles or more. *l* Takes 3 cl for 63 miles. *r* Rest. Car. ¶ Paris (Lyon). **Y** 1 & 2 cl. Sleep. Car, Paris–Mont Dore and *v.v.* to Sept. 2.

(Paris), Limoges, Agen, Montauban, Toulouse. [French Rlys. (Sud-Ouest).

1 2 3	1 2 3	1 2 3	1 2 3	1 2 3	1 2 3	1 2 3		1 2 3	1 2 3	1 2 3	Exp	1 2 3	1 2
Rap	Exp	Rap	Exp	Exp	Exp	Rap		Exp	Rap	Exp	1 2 3	Exp	Rap
7 5	1015	1925	2015	2112	2145	2250	dep. Paris (*above*) arr.	19 5	2240	5 30	6 55	8 43	8 50
12 1	1529	0 15	0 36	1 57	2 32	5 10	arr. Limoges ....dep.	1335	1743	2350	2 2	3 21	3 50
	r	r			A				r		A		c
1212	1551	Z	..	..	2 41	5 35	dep. Limoges .... arr.	1325	1736	2312	1 39	..	
1355	1720	..	..	..	4 21	7 36	arr. Perigueux dp.	1152	1538	2137	2359	Z	V
1430	18 3	..	..	..	4 36	9‡ 2	dep. Perigueux ar.	1146	..	2051	2346	..	
1818	2140	..	..	..	7 25	12‡48	arr. Agen ......dep.	7 35	..	1645	21 4		..
											a		
12 6	1544	0 18	0 40	2 8	2 47	5 40	dep Limoges ....arr.	1320	1734	2318	1 49	3 14	3 47
1328	17 3	1 34	1 56	3 31	4 3	7 20	arr. Brive .. dep.	1156	1617	22 0	0 29	2 0	2 30
1354	17 9	1 40	2 1	3 47	4 18	7 33	dep Brive .. arr.	1149	1611	2152	0 23	1 54	2 24
B	1947	4 7	4 30	B	7 4	1023	arr Montauban (see p 252) dp	9 17	1351	B	2145	2331	0 0
	1953	4 13	4 36		7 10	11 5	dep Montauban (see p 252) ar	9 11	1345		2139	2325	2354
1913	2037	4 48	5 11	9 56	7 45	1140	ar Toulouse (p.252) d	8 35	1310	1545	21 5	2250	2320
..	0 20	5 10	6 15	1035	8 15	1320	dep Toulouse .. arr.		1041	..	2018	2237	22 4
..	2 4	6 42	7 58	1240	9 55	15 7	ar. Montréjeau (see p. 251) dp	..	9 3	..	1852	2111	2029
..	5 28	6 50	8 14	1249	10 6	1525	dp Montréjeau (see p. 251) ar		8 55		1840	2056	2023
..	8 4	7 29	9 0	1339	1053	16 8	arr. Luchon ....dep.		8 5	..	1751	2018	1942

A 1 cl. Couchettes & 1, 2 & 3 cl. cars Paris-Agen & 1 & 2 cl. Sleep. Car Toulouse & *v.v.*
C 3 cl. Sleep. Car Couchettes Paris-Toulouse & *v.v.*

a Only takes 3 cl. for beyond Limoges. *b* Only takes 2 cl. for 250 miles or more. Special accommodation, etc., *see page* 117. **B** *Via* Capdenac. *c* Takes 2 cl. 250 miles or more, except from branches. *r* Rest. Car. **V** Voiture Buffet. **Z** Limoges-Toulouse-Luchon and *v.v.*, July 2 - Oct. 1. ‡ Tue., Wed. and Sat. only. Daily from July 1.

The times on the LEFT are to be read DOWNWARDS, those on the RIGHT UPWARDS.

Thro' Service, see pp. 115, 116, 251.	123	123	1/23	123	123	123	1/23	123	1/23	123	12	123	123	12
		Rap		Rap		Exp	..	Exp		Exp	luxe	Exp	Rap	Rap
PARIS (Quaid'O'sy)	..	2050	..	2215		From Toulouse.	..	0 0	.	8r45	1130	..	1230	1725
BORDEAUX ....arr.	..	4 20	..	7 10	..		..	1220	..	16 7	17 9	..	1935	2340
		L r									G			123
Bordeaux S. Jean) d.	..	4 29	5 15	8 0	From Toulouse		1130	1345	1411	1648	1721	1814	1950	0 0
Lamothe	..	..	6 11	8 34			1234	1421	1512	1722	1750	19 2	2022	0 42
Morcenx ....dep.	..	..	7 39	9 36			14 3	1516	1628	18 8	..	2013		1 42
Dax .... arr	..	6 12	8 32	10 9		..	1457	1544	1712	1835	1858	2055	2131	2 9
To Pau, p.251 dep.	dep.	6 25		1023		..	16 0	1549	1718	1842	19 1		2134	3 27
Bayonne ...... arr.	6 47	7 11	..	11 7	1216	14 1	1741	1628	1820	1921	1936	..	2222	4 21
Negresse .... arr.	6 58	7 29	..	1123	1239	1424	1754	1642	..	1936	1951	..	2235	5 11
Biarritz (Ville) arr.	7 12	7 39	..	1134	1251	1435	1810	1656	..	1952	20 4	..	2255	5 27
Biarritz ......dep.	6 51	7 42	..	1116	1233	1414	1743	1635		1931	..	..	2220	
Negresse........dep	7 12	7 50	..	1126	1243	1427	18 1	1645	..	1940	1959	.	2238	5 17
Guethary ...... arr	7 11	7 59	..	1138	1253	1438	1813	1657	..	1952	20 6	.	2247	..
St Jean de Luz	7 21	8 9	..	1150	13 2	1447	1834	17 6	..	20 1	2016	..	2256	5 41
Hendaye ...... arr	7 36	8 25	..	12 6	1316	15 3	1852	1722	..	2017	2031	..	23 8	5 56
Irunc .... arr.	..	..	..	..	..	..	..	..	..	..	2045	..	..	..
pp 321 & 322 Irun ......dep	..	..	..	..	..	..	..	.	..	..	2135	..	.	8 0
LISBON.... arr.	..	..	..	..	..	..	..	..	.	.	1850	..	..	..
MADRID .... ,,	..	..	..		..	..	..	..	..	..	10 0	..		2130

G Sud Ex. daily. *See p.* 85. Ex. Fares. **L** 1 and 2 cl. Sleeping Cars, Paris-Biarritz-Irun and *v.v.*, also 1, 2 & 3 cl. thro' Cars. *r* Rest. Car.

	123	123	123	12	123	123	12	123	123	123	123	123	123	1/23
				luxe								Y L	H	
pp 321 & 322 MADRID ..dep.	..	..	..	22 0		..	..	..	..	..	..	..	..	
LISBON.. ,,	..	..	..	1355	..	..	..	..	..	..	..	.	..	..
Hendaye *c* arr.	..	..	..	1135	..			..	..	..	..	.	..	..
	Exp	Rap		G		Exp	Rap	Exp		Exp	Rap	Exp	Rap	
Hendaye ......dep.	6 23	8r37	9 31	12 0	1240	1321	1348	1457	..	1823	20 9	21 0	2148	2217
St Jean de Luz ..	6 41	8 54	9 48	1215	1256	1345	14 3	1516	.	1842	2030	2122	22 8	2249
Guethary......dep.	6 50	9 2	9 57		13 6	1353	1412	1527	.	1852	2038	2123	2218	23 0
Negresse ...... arr.	7 1	9 13	10 8	..	1318	14 1	1420	1541	..	19 3	2046	2146	2228	2310
Biarritz (Ville) ar	7 12	9 25	1019	1240	1330	1412	1435	1552		1913	2057	2157	2238	2323
Biarritz (Ville)dp.	6 51	9 6	10 1	1242	1312	1354	1414	1535		1856	2038	22 1	2241	23 5
Negresse	7 3	9 23	1011	..	1322	14 4	1423	1544	..	19 5	2049	2210	2250	2317
Bayonne ......dep.	7 19	9 37	1030	13 4	1350	1424	1434	1559	..	1920	21 9	2227	23 7	0 25
Dax .... arr.	8 0	1018	1138	1329	1455		1512	1639	.	20 3		23 5	2342	1 29
Dax dep	8 3	1034	..	1341	1524		1519	1651	18 0	20 6		23 8	2358	2 5
Morcenx ......dep.	8 40	11 7	..	..	1625	To Toulouse.		1726	19 2	2037	To Toulouse.			2 58
Lamothe	9 29	1150	..		1735		1629	1811	2015	2120		..	..	4 0
Bordeaux (S.Jean) a	9 59	1220	..	1518	1821		1659	1843	2055	2150		0 45	1 43	4 48
		Exp		luxe										
BORDEAUX ..dep.		13r5	..	1524			1725	2020	..	2220		0 55	1 52	..
PARIS(Quai d'Osy)		2030		2059		..	2345	5 *a*0	..	7 18		8 5	9 5	

H Hendaye–Bordeaux from Oct. 2.

Y July 2—Oct. 1. *a* Austerlitz Stn.

Bordeaux, Limoges, Montlucon, Gannat (Lyons, Moulins). [French Rlys. (Sud-Ouest)

A	123	A	A	123	Mls.		123	A	A	A	123	A
	D			C			C				D	
7 20	1030	13 5	17 4	1950	0	d. **Bordeaux** (St Jean) a	7 36	10 3	1440	1728	1920	2310
8 0	1117	14 4	1743	2031	32	dep Coutras...... arr	6 46	9 21	1342	1644	1826	2229
8 56	1222	1514	1839	2126	79	arr Perigueux....dep.	5 44	8 23	1223	1528	1728	2132
.	14 7	1726	20 5	2312	141	arr. **Limoges** dep.	4 17	7 0	1010	1212	1551	
..	1417	1834		2327		dep. *also p* 249 arr	4 2	..	9 47	.	1539	
	15 6	1943	..	0 7	161	dp S. Sulpice Lau. d.	3 34	..	9 16	..	1510	*Via* Ussel & Brive
Via Brive & Ussel	1553	2113		0 58	189	arr. Gueret .... d.	2 41	..	8 13	..	1417	
	1720	..	..	2 48	237	arr. **Montlucon** d.	1 7	..	6 23	..	1246	
	1734	.	.	2 55		dep. **Montlucon** a.	1 0	..	..	..	1232	
	V											
	19 0	..	..	4 40	279	arr **Gannat** (*p* 254) d.	2331	..	..	.	11 7	
	1927	..		5 4	294	arr. S. Germain d F d	23 5	..	..	.	1042	
..	2240		..	8 41	388	,, LYONS (*p* 256) d	1925	..	..	..	7 40	..
2134				12 0		,, Geneva (*p* 266) d.	16 8	..			V	9 3
	1745	..		6 48	237	dep. Montlucon..arr	21 9	..		..	1148	..
..	1921			8 31	288	arr Moulins ....dep	1925	..	..	..	10 7	..
..	5 54	..	..	2358	610	arr. **Strasbourg** d p.	6 10	..	..	..	2311	..

A Auto Rail.
C 1, 2 & 3 cl. cars and Coucnettes Bordeaux-Geneva and *v.v.*
D 1, 2 & 3 cl. cars Bordeaux-Strasbourg and *v.v.*
V Buffet Car, Bordeaux–Lyons and *v.v.*

The times on the LEFT are to be read DOWNWARDS, those on the RIGHT UPWARDS.

Bayonne (Dax), Pau, Tarbes, Toulouse (Paris). [French Rlys. (Sud.-Ouest)

	123 Exp	1/23	1/23	123 Exp	123 Rap	123 Rap	123	123 Exp	123 Rap	123 Exp	1/23	123 Exp	123 Exp	123 Exp	123 Exp	123 Rap	123 Exp
Hendaye dep.	..	..	..	..	..		..	..	6 23	9 31	..	1321	..	..	1620	..	20 9
Bayonne					A	B			A						A		
p 250 dep.	..	..	..	..	..	..	5 45	..	7 25	1030	..	1424	..	..	1714	..	21 9
Puyoo arr	..	..	..	..	..	..	7 7	..	8 18	1125	..	1520	..	..	1814	..	22 3
Bordeaux d	0 0	..	..	..	3 41	4 29	..	7 43	..	8 0	..	..	1345	..	..	1648	1950
Dax p.250 d	2 22	..	..	..	5 36	6 26	..	9 39	..	1031	..	1146	1557	..		1843	2146
Puyoo ... dep.	2 49	..	..	..	6 13	7 3	7 20	1010	8 19	1128	..	1522	1636	..	1816	1924	2213
Pau .... arr.	3 33	..	..	..	7 5	7 52	8 32	11 4	9 5	1220	..	1611	1739	..	1852	2016	23 5
Pau .... dep.	3 39	..	5 52	6 40	7 10	7 56	9 14	11 9	9 7	1254	..	1621	1744	..	1853	2020	2312
Lourdes arr.	4 14		6 41	7 23	7 52	8 36	10 9	1156	9 44	1333	..	17 3	1826	..	1930	21 1	2354
Lourdes dep.	4 19	5 30	6 46	7 28	8 2	8 39	1016	..	9 50	1345	..	17 8	1831	1852	1939	21 5	2356
Tarbes arr	4 37	5 54	7 11	7 49	8 21	8 58	1042	..	10 9	14 6	..	1729	1851	1912	1958	2125	0 16
Tarbes dep.	..	6 1	..	7 54	..	..	11 5	..	1011	1411	1525	1734	..	1915	20 1	..	0 21
Montréjeau ..d.	..	7 30	..	9 5	..	..	1248	..	1115	1522	1711	1852	..	2029	2111	..	1 27
Boussens ..	..	8 2	..	9 39	..	..	1332	..	..	1556	1753	1926	..	21 3		..	..
Toulouse arr.	..	9 1	..	1041	..	..	1456	..	1235	1653	1915	2018	..	22 4	2227	..	2 50
PARIS (p. 249) a.	..	..	..	..	..	..	..	..	2240	..	6 55	6 55	..	8‡50	..	..	..

	123 Exp	123 Exp	1/23	123 Rap	123 Exp	123 Exp	123 Rap	123 Exp	123 Exp	123 Exp	12 Rap	123	123 Exp
PARIS p.249 d.	1015	..	..	1925	2145	..	2250	..	..	..	..	..	1015
Toulouse ..dp.	0 20	..	5 33	6 15	8 15	..	13 0	1320	..	1550	..	1832	2042
Boussens .	1 20	..	6 54	7 14	9 16	..	A	1424	..	1654	..	1953	A
Montréjeau.. ar	2 10	..	7 40	7 58	9 55	..	1428	15 7	..	1733	..	2039	2212
Tarbes .. ar	3 26	..	9 48	9 21	1111	..	1538	1627	..	19 0	..	..	2320
Tarbes .. dp	3 32	7 58	..	9 26	1114	1233	1541	1632	..	19 4	2122	..	2324
Lourdes .. ar	3 56	8 22	..	9 50	1140	1257	16 3	17 2	.	1928	2146	..	2345
Lourdes .. dp	4 0	8 26	..	9 55	1143	13 5	16 6	17 8	1753	1930	2159	..	2347
Pau ...... ar	4 38	9 0	..	1027	1217	1337	1638	1755	1825	20 7	2231	..	0 19
Pau ...... dp	4 48	9 4	..	1032	1222	1340	1641	18 4	1830	2012	2236	..	..
Puyoo ... ar	5 36	9 49	..	1121	1313	1414	1726	19 5	1918	2059	2324	..	..
Dax (p.250) ar	7 56	1016	..	12 8	1458	1458	..	..	1950	2128	2333	..	..
Bordeaux arr	9 59	1220	..	16 2	1821	1659	..	..	2140	..	1 43	..	..
Puyoo ..dp	5 40	9 51	..	1126	1314	..	1727	1912	1921	21 1	..	..	..
Bayonne ar	6 32	11 7	..	1216	14 1	..	1824	2019	2222	2222	..	..	..
Hendaye .. arr. (p. 250)	7 36	12 6	..	1316	15 3	..	1922	23 8	23 8	23 8	..	..	..

‡ 1 and 2 cl. only. * 1st cl only.

A July 2-Oct. 1. B From Oct. 2.

Montrejeau, Bagneres de Luchon. [French Rlys. (Sud-Ouest).

5 28	6 50	8 14	9 11	10 6	1249	1525	1740	2112	dep. Montrejeau arr.	7 25	8 55	9 49	11 2	1420	15 3	17 6	1840	2056
8 4	7 29	9 0	10 6	1053	1339	16 8	1837	2152	arr. Luchon ..dep.	6 26	8 5	9 11	1012	1342	1421	1617	1751	2018

Lourdes, Pierrefitte, Cauterets (Luz). [French Rlys. (Sud-Ouest).

5 0	8 3	8 27	1015	12 6	1435	1610	1715	1940	dp. Lourdes......ar.	6 38	7 57	9 40	1131	1250	1427	1653	1826	2055
5 28	8 33	9 0	1046	1234	15 6	1639	1748	2012	ar. Pierrefitte ...., ,,	6 8	7 28	9 10	11 4	1212	14 2	1618	1757	2029
6 37	9‡30	10‡0	1140	1330	1554	1726	1840	21 0	,, Cauterets .... ,,		6 37	8 20	1020	1116	13 6	1527	17 2	1937
6 0	9‡10	9 45	1130	1320	1545	1715	1830	2040	,, Luz St. Sauveur dp	..	6 55	8 30	1010	1136	1315	1535	1715	1945

Toulouse, Ax-les-Thermes, Puigcerda. [French Rlys. (Sud-Ouest).

123	123	123	123	1/23	123	1/23		1/23	123	123	1/23	1/23	123	123
1925	20†15	2145	2145	2250	..	..	dep. Paris .. } p. ar.	19 5	..	2335	..	6 55	6 55	8 43
4 48	5†11	7 45	7 45	1140	..	..	arr. Toulouse } 249 dp.	8 35	..	1325	..	21 5	21 5	2250
5 0	5 41	8 27	11 0	1350	18 3	1824	de Toulouse . arr	8 7	8 45	1122	14 8	1933	2055	2236
6 13	7 16	9 48	1234	1524	1921	2020	arr. Foix dep.	6 24	7 33	9 49	1235	1743	1937	2126
7 10	8 27	1043	1339	1628	2026	..	arr. Ax-les-Thermes d.	..	6 28	8 46	1133	1638	1838	2033
7 14	8 33	1048	..	1635	..	..	dp Ax-les-Thermes ar.	..	..	8 32	1128	1612	1831	2031
8 29	9 50	12 5	..	1758	..	..	arr. Tour-de-Carol dp.	..	..	7 0	10 2	1420	17 9	1920
8 35	10 4	1211	..	1816	..	..	dep. Tour-de-Carol¶a.	..	..	..	9 43	1320	1619	1834
9 38	11 4	1314	..	1922	..	..	a. Odeillo Font Romeu d	..	..	..	8 39	1215	15 7	1730
A	1232		..	2048	..	..	arr Villefranche-Vernet-les-Bains ¶dp.	..	..	..	6 56	1042	1337	B ..
..	..	..	..	..	..	..	dep. Tour-de-Carol arr.	..	..	..	..	..	..	..
..	..	..	..	..	..	..	arr. Puigcerda dep.	..	..	..	..	..	..	..
..	..	..	..	..	..	..	dep. Puigcerda .. arr.	..	..	..	..	..	..	..
..	..	..	..	..	..	..	a. Barcelona (Nor.) d.	..	..	..	..	..	..	..

† 1 and 2cl only.

¶ Tour-de-Carol to Vernet-les-Bains 1 & 2 cl. only.

A July 1-Sept. 30. B July 2-Oct. 1.

The times on the LEFT are to be read DOWNWARDS, those on the RIGHT UPWARDS.

Mls		1/23 fast	123 Exp	23 Rap A	123 Rap B	123 Exp B	1/23	1/23	123 Exp	3 cl.	123 Exp	123 Rap L	123 Rap C	123 Exp D
	(S. Jean Sta.)													
0	**Bordeaux** ....dep.	0 30	..	7 55	8 0	8 7	.	8 20	1326	1332	From Paris.	1733	20 0	2220
85	Agen ...... arr	3 37	From Paris	9 48	9 42	1026	.	1224	1539	1713		1923	2143	0 42
	dep	3 59		9 52	9 47	1031	..	—	1544	1725		1927	2148	0 52
128	Montauban arr	5 16		1059	1042	1138	..	..	1653	1838		2022	2250	2 3
	dep	5 45	7 10	11 5	1050	1146		..	17 0	1844	1953	2028	2256	2 11
160	**Toulouse** ....arr	6 53	7 45 r	1140	1125	12 0	..		1744	1930	2037	2112	2333 ‖	2 58
..	p. 251 Bayonne..dep	..	..	r	..	..	..	..	1030	..	..	1424		
..	p. 251 Pau ...... "	..	..	6 40	..	9 7	..	..	1254	..	..	1621		
..	p. 251 Lourdes .. "	..		7 28	..	9 50	..	..	1345	..	..	17 8	1852	..
..	**Toulouse** ....dep	7 20	8 23	1150	1139	13 0	1355	1751	1817		..	2132	2347	3 21
193	Castelnaudary	8 32	9 13	1229	1222	1355	1517	1853	19 7	..	—	..	0 26	4 24
216	Carcassonne arr	9 18	9 45	1253	1247	1429	16 2	1929	1940	..	..	2243	0 50	4 58
	dp	1035	9 50	1254	1249	1434	1720	..	1944	..	..	2246	0 54	5 20
252	**Narbonne**(p.255) a.	1143	1047	1333	1328	1532	1828	..	2042	..	..	2334	1 33	6 36
..	p. 255 Barcelona arr	..			..	..	.		..	..	..	..	..	..
295	p. 255 Sète .... arr.	13 0	1234	1434	1434	1652	2050	.	2210	..	..	0 47	2 56	8 28
..	p. 255 Tarascon "		14 9	1635	1635	1845	..		0 25	..	..	3 44	4 58	1016
..	p. 255 MARSEILLES a.	..	1550	18 5	18 5	2025	..		..	..		5 11	6 35	1150

‖ Takes 2 cl for 63 miles, and 3 cl. for 125 miles.
z 1 cl only in Spain.
r Rest Car

‖ Between Toulouse and Sète, only takes 2 cl. for 32 miles and 3 cl. for 63 miles, but without conditions for beyond Sète.

	123	123 Exp	123 Exp	123 Rap	123 Exp	1/23	123 Exp	123 B	123	123 Rap	123 Exp D	123 Rap C	1/32	123 L	123 Exp
p. 255 MARSEILLES dep.	..	5 22	..	9 0	..	..	1140	..	1230	..	1413	2025	..	0 20	..
p. 255 Tarascon .... "	4 8	6 51	..	1030	..	..	1318	..	14 2	..	18 9	2157	.	1 59	..
p. 255 Sète .. .... "	6 4	8 44	..	12r36	..	..	1540	..	1627	1833	20 2	0 7	..	4 27	..
p. 255 Barcelona .. dep.	..		..	..	..	..	..	..	..	..	.	..	..		..
Narbonne........dep.	7 20	9 59	..	1340	..	..	1655	1830	1910	2122	2132	1 28	..	5 35	..
Carcassonne .... arr.	8 34	1058	..	1424	..	..	1756	1917	2030	22 3	2231	2 22		6 44	..
dep.	8 41	11 3	..	1427	..	..	18 2	1918	2050	22 4	2235	2 25	..	6 46	..
Castelnaudary	9 26	1140	..	1458	..	..	1840	..	2147	..	2310	3 1	..	7 20	..
Toulouse ......arr.	1030	1226		15r38	..		1925	2024	2232	23 1	2359	3 47		8 3	..
p. 251 Lourdes ......arr.	..	17 2	..	1928	..	..	..	..	..	..	3 56	..	..	1143	..
p. 251 Pau .... "	..	1755	..	20 7	..	..	..	..	..	..	4 38		..	1218	..
p. 251 Bayonne...... "	..	2020	..	2222	..	..	..	..	..		6 32		..	14 1	
‖**Toulouse** ....dep	11 0	1252	1310	1552	1720	19 4	21 5	2034	..	2320	0 23	3 58	5 40	8 18	8 35
Montauban .... arr.	1142	1329	1345	1626	18 3	1946	2130	21 8	.	2354	1 6	4 38	6 29	8 55	9 11
dep.	1148	1335	To Paris.	1632	18 9	1953	To Paris.	2114	..	To Paris.	1 12	4 45	6 37	9 1	To Paris.
Agen .... arr.	13 5	1442		1721	1917	2125		22 9	..		2 19	5 34	8 10	10 5	
dep.	1321	1447		1726	1922	..		2214	..		2 28	5 40	8 21	10 8	
Bordeaux (S. Jean) arr	1638	1659		1911	2141	..		2356			4 47	7 31	1137	115·	

* 1 & 2 class only.
a 1 & 3 class only.

A From Oct. 1. **B** July 1-Sept. 30. **C** 1 cl. Lits-toilette, Couchettes, 1, 2 & 3 cl Bordeaux-Marseilles and *v v*. **D** 1 cl Couchettés, 1, 2 & 3 cl. Bordeaux-Port Vendres. **L** 1 cl. Couchettes, 1, 2 & 3 cl. Cars Bordeaux-Marseilles-Vintimille.

(Paris). Agen. Tarbes, &c. [French Rlys. (Sud-Ouest).

..	..	..	7 5	1015	2145	dep PARIS } p.249 ar	..	19 5	5 30	6 55
..	..	..	1212	1551	2 41	dep Limoges } .... arr	..	1325	2312	1 39
..	..	..	1818	2140	7 25	arr **Agen**........dep.	..	7 35	1645	21 4
5 50	1040	16 1	..	..	7 45	dep **Agen**........arr	9 42	..	1430	1848
10 0	1612	2017	..	..	1059	arr. Tarbes ......dep.	5 46	..	1016	1435
1130	1821	..	..		13 4	arr. B deBigorre (120A	..	..	9 18	13 5
1140	17 2	2143			1140	arr. LOURDES. (251) d	4 19	..	9 50	14 0

A July 2-Oct. 1.

Pau-Canfranc *via* Somport Tunnel.

[French Rlys (Sud-Ouest and N. of Spain Rly).

1/23	1/23	1/23	1/23	Mls.		1/23	1/23	1/23	1/23
3 41	4 29	7 43	1345		dep. Bordeaux arr.	1220	1821	1843	2156
7 31	8 22	1145	1815	0	dep. Pau .... arr.	8 45	1130	13 2	1738
8 54	9 47	1323	1945	37	dep. Bedous ....dep.	7 9	9 59	1227	16 7
9 35	1026	1431	2024	55	ar. Forges d'Abel ..dep.	6 13	A	..	1510
A		..		..	dep. Canfranc ..... arr.		..	..	..
..	..	..	..	70	arr. Jaca .... dep.	..	.	..	..
..	..	..		147	arr. Zuera .. .. dep.	..			..
..	..	..	..	163	ar. Saragossa (p. 326) dep.	..	..	..	..
..		..	.	382	ar. Valencia (p. 326) dep		..	..	..

Q The times on the LEFT are to be read DOWNWARDS, those on the RIGHT UPWARDS.

A Auto Rail. [French Rlys (Sud-Est.)]

Besancon—Vesoul.

1/23	A	1/23	1/23	1/23		1/23	1/23	1/23	A	1/23
6 14	1115	1410	1740	1950	dep. Besancon (p. 267) ...... arr.	7 24	9 33	12 2	1638	2058
7 38	1241	1537	19 0	2115	arr. Vesoul (p. 268) ....dep.	5 52	8 16	1035	1514	1928

Morcenx, Tarbes, Bagneres de Bigorre. French Rlys. (Sud-Ouest).

..			..	..	8 0	..	1411	1648	1814	d. Bord'x, p.250 a	9 59		16 1	..	..	2055	2146		..
..	..	..	..	..	9 42	..	1640	1810	2030	dp. Morcenx arr.	8 22	..	1321	..	..	1855	20 0		..
..	..		7 25	..	1040		1740	1851	2110	Mont-de-Marsan	7 32		1240	..	..	1759	1920		..
..	..		9 21	..	13 5		1956	—	..	ar. Tarbes ..dep.	4 54	..	9 34	..	..	1515	..		..
6 10	8 26	9 27	1120	1230	1431	1740	1828	1941	..	dp. Tarbes .. arr.	6 46	7 29	9 4	11 0	1351	15 6	1618	1816	1947
6 50	9 14	9 59	12 8	13 3	15 4	1821	1915	2023		ar. B.deBigor dp.	6 3	6 51	8 36	1023	13 8	1422	1543	1731	1920

2 and 3 class Martigny-Vallorcine.

COL DE SALVAN ROUTE.

a Suns., June 4–Sept. 10
c June 15–Sept. 15
d June 1–Sept. 30.
f To Sept. 20.

	a		*d*	*c*	*b*	*c*		
Martigny dp.	6 55	8 10	9 40	1120	13 0	1440	1540	1752
Vernayaz ,,	7 7	8 22	9 51		..	1452	1552	18 5
Finhaut ,,	7 57	9 12	1036		..	1540	1645	1858
Chatelard Ville a	8 12	9 27	1050		..	1555	1659	1913
Vallorcine (Swiss) a.	8 25	9 41	11 3	1320	1430	16 8	1712	1926
Greenwich time d.	8 38	9 55	1116	1327	1437	1624	1718	1939
Montroc dp.	8 57	1013	1134	1343	1456	1641	1735	1957
Argentiere ,,	9 12	1024	1147	1355	15 8	1652	1746	20 9
Les Tines ,,	9 28	1040	12 1	1414	1523	17 8	18 2	2024
Chamonix Mt. Blanc a.	9 39	1052	1213	1420	1534	1720	1812	2035

	f							
Chamonix-Mont Blanc d.	6 50	8 11	1037	1117	14 6	1557	1653	1750
Les Tines .. ,,	7 1	8 24	1049	1128	1421	1610	17 7	18 4
Argentiere .. ,,	7 19	8 43	11 5	1146	1439	1627	1723	1821
Montroc ....ar.	7 30	8 55	1116	1157	1454	1642	1736	1834
Vallorcine(Gn) a	7 47	9 12	1134	1213	1511	1659	1753	1851
					d		*a*	
Swiss time dep.	7 57	9 20	1222	..	1530	1712	18 0	19 2
Chatelard Vill.,,	..	9 34	1235		1545	1726	1815	..
Finhaut .... ,,	..	9 56	1251	..	16 0	1743	1833	..
Vernayaz.... ,,	..	1043	1343	..	1648	1838	1933	..
Martigny....ar.	9 26	1055	1355	..	1658	1850	1945	2040

COL DE VOZA.

A			B	C						B			B		
6 46	9 13	1053	1428	1540	1623	1723	dep. Chamonix-Mt.-B.......... arr.	8 7	1035	1217	1354	1622	1855	20 6	23 1
7 6	9 34	1115	1448	16 2	1643	1746	dep. Les Houches .... arr.	7 43	1011	1153	1330	16 0	1832	1943	2239
7 53	1019	1159	1534	1649	1725	1832	arr. } St. Gervais le Fayet { dep.	7 1	9 29	1110	1247	1518	1741	19 0	2158
E	F	G											F	G	
8 0	1025	1335	..	..	..	..	dep. } St. Gervais le Fayet { arr.	..	..	..	..	..	1656	1840	..
8 19	1044	1354	..	..	..	..	arr. } St. Gervais les Bains { dep.	..	..	..	..	..	1641	1825	..
8 20	1045	1355	..	..	..	..	dep. } St. Gervais les Bains { arr.	..	..	..	..	..	1640	1824	..
9 23	1138	15 0	..	..	..	..	arr. Col de Voza ....dep.	..	..	..	..	..	1552	1734	..

A July 1—Sept. 17. **B** July 8—Sept. 7. **C** July 1—Oct. 1.
E To Sept. 10. **F** To Sept. 20. **G** To Sept. 15.

CHAMONIX—MONT BLANC—MONTENVERS. [Electric Rly.

a		*a*				*a*	*a*		*a*	*a*		*a*				*a*
7 0	8 20	10 0	1130	1210	1425	1543	1620	dep. Chamonix, Mont Blanc ar.	8 55	1034	12 4	14 0	1420	1618	1737	1845
7 53	9 13	1053	1223	13 3	1518	1636	1723	arr. Montenvers ....dep.	8 5	9 44	1114	1310	1330	1528	1647	1755

a To Sept. 10.

The times on the LEFT are to be read DOWNWARDS, those on the RIGHT UPWARDS.

(Paris), St. Germain-des-Fosses, Clermont Ferrand, Nimes. [French Rlys (Sud-Est).

123 Exp D	12 Rap Z	123 Exp Ar	123 Rap Br	123 Exp C	123 Exp E	123 Exp F	1/23	Ml.		123 Exp Av	12 Rap Z	123 Exp Br	123 Exp D	123 Exp B	123 Exp C	123 Exp E	123 Exp F
7 40	11 10	1230	1720	2110	2240	2255			dep. **Paris** (Lyons) p.256 a	1430	17 23	19 0	2315	2327	5 20	6 10	6 35
1327	..	1753	22 4	2 44	4 38	4 51		221	arr. St. Germain d.	9 25	..	1325	1742	1859	2354	0 45	0 57
1332	..	1759	22 9	2 59	4 43	5 20	9 27		d. **St. Germain d. F.** a.	9 12		1313	1730	1847	2339	0 39	0 34
1343	1545	18 9	2218	X	..	5 30	9 36	235	arr. Vichy .. dep	9 2	1240	13 4	1720	1838	2 30	X	0 25
1347	1550	1813	2223		X	..	9 38		dep. Vichy .. arr	8 58	1225	13 1	1717	1835	2324		..
1426	1621	1851	2243	3 54	5 42		1013	253	arr. Riom........dep.	8 21	1156	1228	1644	18 3	2249	2351	..
1441	1638	19 5	2312	4 10	6 0	..	1026	261	,, **Clermont Ferr** d.	8 5	1135	1215	1631	1750	2233	2336	..
..	17 0	..	..	5 10	6 18	..		264	,, Royat (p. 247) ,,	..	1113	12 1	1542	17 3	2118	2251	..
1457	..	1937	..	4 27	6 22	..	1055		dp. **Clermont Ferr** a	7 52	..	..	1624	..	2213	2324	..
1540	..	2013	..	5 3	7 12	..	1140	283	arr. Issoire ......dep	7 19	..	..	1552	..	2140	2245	..
1611		2043	..	5 39	7 51	..	1215	298	arr Arvant.......dep	6 52	..	..	1526	..	2113	2212	..
1631	..	2056	..	6 8	8 10	..	1234	304	arr. Brioude ....dep	6 41	..	..	1515	..	21 1	2147	..
1720	..	2143	..	6 55	9 3	..	..	323	arr Langeac ....dep	5 56	..	..	1431	..	2015	21 0	..
1913	..	2326	..	8 39	..	..	..	365	arr. Langogne dp	4 18	..	..	1250	..	1836	..	..
1935	..	2331	..	8 45	..	..	..		dep Langogne ar	4 15	..	..	1243	..	1828	..	..
2158	..	1 47	..	11 6	..	..	..	419	arr Alès ....dep	1 33	..	..	9 34	..	1542		..
23 8	..	2 45	..	1157	..	..	..	450	arr **Nimes** (p. 255) dep.	0 30	..	..	8 30	..	1445		..
5 11	..	5 11	..	1430	.	..	..		arr. **Marseilles** ..dep	2130	..	..	5 25	..	1210	..	..

A 1, 2 and 3 cl. cars Paris-Vichy-Clermont-Marseilles and *v.v.*
B 1, 2 and 3 cl. cars Paris-Clermont-Ferrand and *v.v.* also Rest. Car Bar Paris Clermont and *v.v.*
C 1st cl. Couchettes and 1, 2 and 3 cl. cars Paris-Nimes and *v.v.*
D 1, 2 and 3 cl. Paris-Nimes and *v.v.* **E** 1st cl. Couchettes and 1, 2 and 3 cl. Paris-Langeac and *v.v.* 1 & 2 cl. Sleep. car Paris-Mont Dore *via* Clermont and *v.v.* (*see page* 249) to Sept. 2.
F 1 cl. Couchettes and 1, 2 and 3 cl. cars Paris-Vichy, June 24 – Sept. 30.
X *Via* Gannat, see below. **Z** Lits Salons and 1 and 2 cl. cars Paris-Quai D'Orsay-Clermont and *v.v.*; 1 cl. Pullman (to Sept. 30), 1 and 2 cl. cars and Rest. Car Paris-Vichy and *v.v.*
r Rest. car. *v* Voiture-bar. ¶ Paris Quai D'Orsay.

☞ For Paris-Vichy Services, *see page* 256.

St. Germain-des-Fosses, Gannat, Clermont Ferrand. French Rlys. (Sud-Est)

123	123	1/23	1/23	123	123	123	1/23	123		1/23	123	1/23	123	123	123	123	1/23	123
2 59	4 43	6 9	8 5	1042	1332	1759	1828	23 5	d. St.Germain-d-F. a	6 54	9 12	13 5	1313	1716	1847	2119	2339	0 39
3 25	5 11	6 38	8 36	11 2	..	..	1856	2326	a. Gannat .... d.	6 24	..	1236	..	1649		2051		0 17
3 27	5 13	6 43	8 40	1110	..	..	19 8	2335	d. ,, ... a.	6 14	..	1233	..	1648	..	2046		0 15
3 54	5 42	7 14	9 14	1142	1426	1851	1939	0 0	a. Riom.......... d.	5 42	8 21	12 0	1228	1617	18 3	2016	2249	2351
3 56	5 45	7 15	9 17	1143	1428	1853	1940	0 1	d. ,, ... a.	5 39	8 19	1158	1227	1616	18 2	2015	2246	2350
4 10	6 0	7 31	9 33	1159	1441	19 5	1956	0 15	a. Clermont Ferrand d.	5 23	8 5	1143	1215	16 0	1750	20 0	2233	2336

Nevers, Chagny. [French Rlys. (Sud-Est).

4 55	7 0	..	1157	..	1630	..	1845	2045	d. Nevers p.256 a.	9 27	1030	1424	..	1755	2010	2127	..	..
6 2	7 50	..	13 2	..	1722	..	20 4	2134	Cercy-la-T. ▲	8 22	9 35	1315	..	1647	1914	2032	..	..
7 11	8 44	..	14 8	..	1817	1855	2115	2220	Etang	7 17	8 48	12 6	13 5	1541	1815	1938		2055
7 50	9 7	1233	1443	17 0	1843	1957	2141	2239	▼ Le Creusot	6 44	8 16	1132	1235	1512	1745	1917	1931	2025
8 1	9 17	1243	1453	1712	1853	20 9	2151	2247	ar. Montchanin d	6 27	8 2	1114	1219	1455	1712	19 4	1920	2010
9 1	9 44	1331	1539	18 3	1924	2120	2229	2317	,, Chagny..dep. (*Dijon, &c.*, 259.)	5 30	7 1	1022	1132	14 2	1630	1830	1838	1922

Corsica.

12			12		Mls.			12	12			
7 45	8 15	1315	1620	1740	0	dep. Bastia .... arr.	8 49	10 0	1120	1511	1840	..
9 0	10 0	1438	1719	1924	29	arr. Pte. Leccia ....dep.	7 42	9 0	1022	1328	1722	..
¶	1153	1729	1853	..	62	arr. Ile Rousse ....dep.	..	7 20	7 59	..	1545	..
	1226	1820	1925	..	75	arr. Calvi ....dep.	..	6 45	7 0	..	1510	arr.
9 40	1124	1535	..	1941	46	arr. Corte..........dep.	7 2	..	9 42	1214	1630	1950
1145	1521	1830	..	..	99	arr. Ajaccio ....dep.	.	..	7 35 ¶	7 45	1320	1635

¶ Limited train carries for 25 miles or more.

			Mls.				
7 45	14 7	1740	0	dep. Bastia .... arr.	8 49	1156	1710
8 20	1451	1810	54	dep. Casamozza .... arr	8 20	1115	1643
9 53	17 3	1943	.	dep. Ghisonaccia .... arr.	6 47	9 11	1510
1030	1755	..	69	arr. Solenzara ....dep.	..	8 20	1430
1125	1910	..	95	arr. Porto Vecchio ......dep	..	7 0	1335

(Paris), Marseilles, Nimes, Cette, Narbonne, B'celona. [French Rlys Sud-Est & Sud-Ouest]

Mls		1 2 3	1 2	1 2 3	1 2 3	1 2 3	1 2 3	1 2 3	1 2 3	1/2 3	1 2 3	1 2 3	1 2 3
		Rap	Rap	Exp	Rap	Exp	E	Exp	Exp	Exp	Exp	Exp	Exp
..	p. 259 Paris (Lyon) dep	17 0	18 0	..	21 5	2310	..	..	8 0		12†0	13 0	
..	p. 259 Lyons ......dep	2340	0 20	..	4 11	7 15	1010	13 0	1452		17†27	1935	
..	p. 259 Avignon ....dep	3 48	3 9		7 26	10 2	1315	1638	1749	1952	2127	2227	..
..	p. 259 Tarascon .... arr	4 6	arr.		7 43	1019	1333	1655	18 7	2011	2144	2244	..
		A	—	B	C	D			JF		G		H
..	(p. 261 **Marseilles** d		..	5 25	..	9 5	1210	14 8	14 8		2030	..	0 8
0	**Tarascon** ......dep	4 8	..	6 51	7 47	1034	1345	17 7	18 9	2012	22 5	2247	1 47
17	**Nimes**..........arr	4 36	..	7 19	8 15	11 3	1413	1737	18 36	2040	2234	2314	2 26
	p. 254 *(via Clermont)*												
..	p. 254 **Paris** (Lyon) dep	..			..		2110	..			*a*		1230
..	p. 254 **Nimes** ...... arr				..	*r*	1157	.				..	2 45
..	**Nsmes**..........dep	4 45	..	7 26	8 27	1119	1423	1812	1845	2042	2244		3 3
34	Lunel .... arr	5 5	..	7 45	8 48	1140	1443	1851	19 4	21 2	23 5		3 24
..	Lunel ....dep	5 7	..	7 46	8 50	1141	1445	1914	19 6	21 3	23 7	..	3 28
48	Montpelier .. arr	5 26	..	8 5	9 10	12 2	15 4	1947	1924	2121	2328	..	3 47
	Montpelier .. dep	5 31	..	8 9	9 16	12 5	15 7		1928	..	2333	..	3 55
65	**Sète** (Midi) .. arr	5 55	..	8 33	9 38	1228	1531	..	1952	..	2359	..	4 18
	Sète (Midi) .. dep	6 4	..	8 44	9 50	1236	1540	..	20 2	..	0 7	..	4 27
93	Beziers ....dep	6 50	..	9 28	1035	1314	1623		2051		0 51	..	5 9
108	**Narbonne** (*to* arr	7 11	..	9 49	1056	1334	1644		21 2		1 12	..	5 29
	Bordeaux, p252 dep	7 40	..	10 5	11 7	1345	1656		2114		2 5		5 50
148	Perpignan ...... arr	8 29	..	1056	12 2	1430	18 2		2214	..	2 57	..	7 10
177	V. Vernet les B arr	1033	..	..	1330	17 0	1919	..		..		..	8 48
167	Port Vendres....dep	9 2	..	1148	1243	1511	19 5	..	2241		3 35	..	8 6
178	Cerbère .... arr	9 21	..	12 5	13 6	1528	1925		2256		3 58		8 26
174	Port Bou *c* .... arr		..	..	..		..	..		..			
279	(p. ,, (Green. t.) d	..	..	..	..		..	..		..	4 10	..	..
..	326) **Barcelona** arr.	..	..	..	..	..	..	..	..	..	8 50	..	..

J 1, 2 and 3 cl. Avignon-Irun. **K** 1, 2 and 3 cl. Narbonne-Avignon.
a Only takes 2 and 3 cl. for Nimes and beyond. *b* Only takes 2 and 3 cl. for Tarascon and beyond. *c* 1 and 3 cl. *d* Takes between Sete and Tarascon for not less than 94 miles, after Tarascon not less than 187 miles: also from Port Bou line without conditions. * 1 and 2 cl. only. * For restrictions for these trains between Paris and Tarascon and v.v., see page 259/261 (and notes, page 258).

Mls		—	1 2 3	1 2 3	1 2 3	1 2 3	1 2 3	1 2 3	1 2 3	3 cl.	1 2 3	1/2 3
0			Exp	Exp		Exp	Exp		Exp		Rap	..
	p. 326 **Barcelona** dep			..	..	..	..	..		..	1810	
	p. 326 Port Bou *c* arr.					..	..	..		..	2250	
		Z	F	K	B	D	C		FA	H	G	D
112	Cerbère (Frnch. t.) d.c	..		7 58	1051	..	..	..	1845		23 2	
..	Port Vendres			8 12	1116	..	..	..	19 2		2325	
..	V. Vernet les B dp	..		7 44	1040	.		..	18 1	2052	2052	
131	Perpignan	5 12	6 2	8 51	1210	..	1445	..	1935	2155	0 1	
171	**Narbonne** (*to* a	6 3	7 7	9 54	1323	..	1539		2027	23 5	0 56	
										1 2 3		
	Toulouse, &c., p252) d.	6 5	7 47	11 8	1336	1544	17 0	.	21 0	2342	1 55	
186	Beziers .... p	6 32	8 33	1145	1357	1612	1736	—	2125	0 6	2 18	
214	**Sète** (Midi) .. arr	7 17	9 29	1234	1434	1649	1838	1 2 3	22 9	0 47	2 56	
											b	
	Sète (Midi) .. dep	7 18	10 5	13 8	1445	17 0	1855	..	2221	1 0	3 8	5 35
231	Montpellier .. arr	7 40	1030	1333	15 9	1726	1919	..	2250	1 28	3 31	6 0
	Montpellier .. dep	7 43	1036	1338	1512	1730	1925	1837	2256	1 35	3 36	6 3
245	Lunel .... arr.	8 0	1053	1357	1532	1749	1945	1910	2317	1 58	3 55	6 36
							d					
..	Lunel ....dep	8 1	1055	1359	1533	1751	1948	1913	2319	2 2	3 57	6 38
282	**Nimes** .... arr	8 21	1116	1421	1557	1813	2012	1952	2344	2 30	4 20	7 17
via Cl'mont	Nimes ..dep		..	1445					0 16	..		8 25
711	*p.* 252 **Paris** (Lyon) a	1 2 3	..	5 20	.				1430	..		2315
..	**Nimes**..........dep	9 0	1126	1431	16 6	1820	2022	2045	0 5	3 10	4 30	7 30
279	**Tarascon** ...... arr	9 25	1154	1458	1635	1847	2048	2120	0 34	3 39	4 58	7 55
341	(p. 259) **Marseilles** arr	1150	1415	..	18 5	2025		23 6		5 11	6 35	9 18
		*					*	*	1 2		..	1 2
	p. 26 Tarascon ....dep	9 27	12 0	15 0	17 3	19 4	2051	2135	0 39	..	..	8 9
	p. 26 Avignon .... arr.	9 46	1219	1520	1729	1934	2111	22 1	1 2	..	..	8 28
	p. 26 Lyons ...... arr	1255	16 5	1822	†.	2315	0 40	1 52	6 29	..		1220
	p. 26 **Paris** (Lyon) arr	1925	2255	2350	†..	5 20	7 20	9 20	13 0		..	2145

Through Carriages, etc.—A 1 cl. Couchettes and 1 and 2 cl. Cars Geneva-Port Bou and v v. 1, 2 and 3 cl. Cars Avignon-Narbonne. **B** 1, 2 and 3 cl. Cars Milan-Bordeaux and v.v. **C** 1 cl. Lits-Salons, Couchettes and 1, 2 and 3 cl. Cars Paris-Sete, 1, 2 and 3 cl. Cars Paris-Narbonne and v.v. **D** 1, 2 and 3 cl. Cars Marseilles-Bordeaux and v.v. **E** 1, 2 and 3 cl. Cars Avignon-Cerbere. **F** 1, 2 and 3 cl. Cars Avignon-Bordeaux and v.v. **G** 1 cl. Couchettes and 1, 2 and 3 cl. Cars Marseilles-Port Bou, 1 cl. Lits-Salons, Couchettes, and 1, 2 and 3 cl. Cars Marseilles-Bordeaux and v.v. **H** 1 cl. Lits-Salons, Couchettes and 1, 2 and 3 cl. Cars San Remo-Irun and *v v.*; 1 cl. Couchettes and 1 and 2 cl. Cars Vichy-Port Bou, June 25-Oct. 1 1 cl. Couchettes and 1, 2 and 3 cl. Cars Vintimille-Bordeaux and *v.v.*

Mls.		123 Exp	123 Exp	123 Rap	123 Exp	..	123 Rap	123	123 Exp	123 Exp	123 Exp	123 Exp	123 Exp
0	**Paris** (Lyons) ..dep.	..	7 40	.	1230	..	1720	1830	21 0	2110	2240	2255	..
37	Fontainebleau-Avon	..	V *d*	..	AC	..	AC		J	D	H	E	..
42	Moret	..	A	..	*d r*	..	*r*			*e*		*e*	..
74	Montargis .... arr.	..	9 36	..	14 3		1841	2023	2247	23 1	0 42	0 53	..
	dep.	..	9 39	..	14 6		1850	2028	2250	23 4	0 45	0 57	..
97	Gien	..	1013	..	1441		1920	21 0	2324	2338	1 20	1 33	..
150	Pougues-les-Eaux....	..	1135	..	16 0	..	..	2219	.		..	..	..
158	**Nevers** *p.* 254) arr.	.	1147	..	1612	..	2038	2234	0 48	1 5	2 53	3 5	
	dep.	8 0	1154	..	1620	..	2041		0 55	1 12	3 0	3 12	3 40
195	Moulins-sur-All..arr.	8 45	1245	..	1714	..	2128	..	1 45	2 2	3 53	4 4	5 0
	(*see page* 250)												..
..	Paray-le-Monial ar.		1531	..	1848	..	2250	..	..	..	..	6 5	..
	Moulins-sur-All..dep.	8 47	1248	..	1717	..	2130	..	1 50	2 7	3 56	4 10	5 3
220	**St. Germain-F.** arr.	9 21	1327	..	1753	..	22 4	..	2 29	2 44	4 43	4 51	5 37
..	Vichy .. .. arr.	9 36	1343	..	18 9		2218			.	..	5 30	6 0

Mls.		123 Exp	123 Exp	123 Rap	123 Exp	V*k*	123 Rap	123	123 Exp J	123 Exp D	123 Exp H	123 Exp E	123 Exp
	Vichy ....dep.	9 16	13 4	..	1720	1923	2114	..	To Nimes.	..	To Langeac and Mont Dore.	4 25	.
220	**St. Germain-F.** dep.	9 30	1340	1511	18 8	1943	2215	..		3 5		5 15	5 44
243	St. Martin Sail-les-ba.	10 1	1411	..	..	..		..		..		..	..
261	Roanne ... .. arr.	1026	1437	16 6	19 7	2045	23 5	..		3 57		6 14	6 40
310	St. Etienne ....arr.	..	1550	..	2028	2221	0 15	..		5 25		7 31	8 44
290	Tarare ....arr.	1124		1657	..	2147	..	..				..	7 44
314	Lyons (Vaise) ..arr.	1212	..	..	..	..	..	..		..			8 32
317	**Lyons** (Perrache) arr.	1220	..	1746	..	2240	..	..		7 6		8 41	8 40

	1/23	123 Exp	123 Rap	123 Exp	123 Exp	123 Exp	123 Exp	123 Exp	123 Exp	123 Exp	123 Exp
Lyons (Perrache) dep	..		7 40	*r*	1437		1655	1930	1925	H	D E
Lyons (Vaise) ..dep.	.	..	*k*	AC	..	AC	17 3	1937	E	From Langeac & Mont Dore.	..
Tarare ....dep.	..	..	8 45		..	..	1759	2039			.
St. Etienne ..dep.	..	7 0	8 17	11 5	1539	1645	17 3	..	2046		..
Roanne .. ....dep.	6 30	8 13	9 36	1218	1645	1757	1856	2138	22 0		2225
St. Martin Sail les-ba.	7 2			..	..		1923	..			2349
St. Germain-F...arr.	7 37	9 9	1030	1310	1734	1845	1954	2229	2255		0 43
Vichy ....arr.	7 50	9 36	11 1	1343	1747	1911	20 8	2320	2320		

	123 fast	A *nr*		*n*	C			*h* A	*l*		
Vichy ....dep.	..	9 2	..	13 4	1720	1838	1923	2214	2330	..	
St. Germain-F. dep.	..	9 25	..	1325	1742	1859	20 4	2236	2354	0 45	0 57
Moulins-s-Allier .arr.	..	9 59	..	14 4	1818	1932	2037	2310	0 32	1 22	1 34
(*see page* 250)											
Paray-le-Monial d.		8 18	..	1045	1550	1812	1812	2141	..	..	..
Moulins-sur-All. dep.	5 45	10 1	.	14 7	1821	1935	2039	2313	0 39	1 24	1 36
Nevers ...... arr.	6 45	1048		1456	1913	2015	2126	0 17	1 29	2 13	2 28
dep.	6 55	1055	..	15 3	1920	2018	..		1 36	2 19	2 35
Pougues-les-Eaux....	7 8	11 9		1517	1934		..	..	1 50		..
Gien...........dep.	8 15	1219	..	1636	2055		..	..	..	3 44	4 4
Montargis .... arr.	8 40	1248	..	17 7	2125	2152	..	..	3 30	4 16	4 36
dep.	8 47	1251	..	1710	2128	2155	..	..	3 33	4 19	4 39
Moret	..		..	*l*	V	..	.	..	..	..	
Fontainebleau-Avon		.	..			.		..	..	.	..
Paris (Lyon) ..arr.	1030	1430	..	19 0	2315	2327	..		5 20	6 10	6 35

A 1, 2 and 3 cl Cars Paris St. Etienne and *v.v.*

B 1st cl. Lits-Salon with sheets, and 1 & 2 Car and Rest Car Paris-Vichy and *v.v.*

C 1, 2 and 3 cl. Cars Paris-Vichy and *v.v.*

D 1st cl. Couchettes, and 1, and 2 cl. Cars, Paris-St. Etienne-Le Puy and *v.v.* 1, 2 and 3 cl. cars Paris-St. Etienne and *v.v.*

E 1 cl. Lits Salons, Couchettes and 1, 2 & 3 cl. Cars Paris-St. Etienne and *v.v.*, and Paris-Vichy (June 24-Sept. 30) and *v.v.*

H June 24–Sept. 30 only, 1 cl. Couchettes and 1, 2 & 3 cl. cars Paris-St. Germain-Langeac, also 1 and 2 cl. Sleep. car Paris-Mont Dore *via* Clermont and *v.v.* (*see page* 249) to Sept. 2.

J June 24–Sept. 30 only, 1 cl. Couchettes and 1, 2 and 3 cl. Cars Paris–St. Germain.

V Voiture-bar.

a—At Paris only takes for 150 miles and until Moulins for 63 miles or more. *c*—Only takes passengers for 94 miles or more from Vichy outwards. *d*—Does not take 2 and 3 cl. north of Nevers unless travelling 63 miles. *e*—Takes between Paris and Nevers 2 and 3 cl. for 94 miles or more except from branches. *h*—After St. Germain only takes 2 and 3 cl. for 94 miles or more. *k*—Takes 3 cl. from St. Germain for 63 miles and upwards. *l*—Takes 2 and 3 c. for 63 miles or more after St. Germain. *n*—After Nevers only takes 2 cl. for 63, and 3 cl. for 94 miles or more. *o*—2nd and 3rd for Moulin or beyond. *p*—At Paris only takes passengers for 150 miles from Fontainebleau-Avon to Moulin for 63 miles or more. *r*—Rest. car. ¶ Limited train.

(Paris), Roanne, St. Etienne, Givors, Lyons (Chasse). [French Rlys. (Sud-Est).

Mls.		1 2 3	1 2 3	1 2 3	1 2 3	1 2 3	1 2 3	1 2 3	1 2 3	1 2 3	1 2 3	1 2 3
		Exp	Exp	Exp	Exp	Exp	Exp	Exp	Rap	Exp	Rap	Rap
..	p. 256 Paris (Lyon) dep.	2110	2255	..		..	..	7 40	..	1230	..	1720
	St. Germain-	C	A							B r		B r
220	des-F. ... dep.	3 5	5 15	5 44	..	9 30	..	1340	1511	18 8	1943	2215
261	Roanne .... dep.	4 7	6 17	6 47	..	1029	..	1440	16 8	1910	2049	23 8
..	St. Just .... dep.	..	..	..	..	..	..		..	..	..	..
310	**St. Etienne** .. arr.	5 25	7 31	¶	..	¶	..	1550	¶	2028	¶	0 15
	dep.	5 45	7 36	..	1017	..	1313	16 0	..	2058	..	..
332	Givors .... arr.	6 37	8 15	..	1053	..	1349	1636	..	2136	..	..
346	**Lyons** (Perrache) arr.	7 6	8 41	8 40	1120	1220	1416	17 3	1746	22 4	2240	..

C—1 cl. Couchettes, 1, 2 & 3 cl. Paris-St. Etienne and *v.v.*

¶ *Via* Tarare, *see p.* 256.

M.s	To & from Marseilles, *pp.* 259, 261.	1/23	1 2 3	1 2 3	1 2 3	1 2 3	1 2 3	1 2 3	1/23	1 2 3	1/23	1 2 3	1 2 3	1 2 3	1 2 3
			Exp Br	Rap	Exp Br		Rap	r	Exp	Rap		Exp		Exp C	A Exp
0	**Lyons** (Perrache) dp.	4 9	..	6 39	..	9 45	1235	1311	1437	..	1510	1655	1833	1925	2028
14	Givors.......... dep.	4 41	..	7 15	..	1011	..	1340	15 0	B	1538	..	19 0	1950	2059
36	**St. Etienne** .. arr.	5 38	..	8 11	..	1051	¶	1420	1536	..	1630	¶	1948	2034	22 5
	dep.	5 56	7 0	8 17	11 5	⁀	..		1539	1645	1657		1956	2046	2225
44	St. Just	6 15	..	..		..	..	..	.	..	1717	..	2014	..	..
85	Roanne .... arr.	7 36	8 10	9 25	1215	..	1421	..	1644	1754	1842	1853	2125	2157	2344
126	p. 256 St. Germ.-des-F. a.	..	9 9	1030	1310	..	1515	..	1734	1845	..	1954	..	2255	0 43
346	**Paris** (Lyon) arr.	..	1430	..	19 0	..	..	..	2315	2327	..	..	..	5 20	6 35

A 1 cl. Couchettes, Lits-Salons and 1, 2 & 3 cl. cars, Paris–St. Etienne and *v.v.*
B 1, 2 and 3 cl. cars Paris-St. Etienne and *v.v.* **r** Rest. Car.

Lyons, (St. Rambert), Voiron, Grenoble. [French Rlys. (Sud-Est).

A 1 cl. Lits-Salons, and Couchettes, 1, 2 & 3 cl. car, Paris-Grenoble and *v.v.*
B 1, 2 & 3 cl. cars Paris-Grenoble and *v.v.*

1 2 3	1 2 3	1 2 3	1/23	1 2 3	1 2 3	1 2	1 2 3	1 2 3	Mls.		1 2 3	1 2 3	1 2 3	1 2 3	1 2 3	1 2	1 2 3	1/23
18 0	2135	2310	..		8 0	12 0	13 0	14 0	0	dep. **Paris** (*p.* 259) arr.	6 55	13 0	1810	1925	2255	2350	5 0	..
	A 1 2 3				B	1 2 3					A		1/23		B	1 2 3		
0 23	4 55	7 25	1040	1315	1453	18 5	20 2	2248	317	dep **Lyons** (Perrache) a	2346	6 23	1129	1250	1555	18 6	20 5	2214
1 52	6 1	8 25	1132	1425	1554	19 5	21 5	2340	357	arr. St. André le Gaz. d.	2240	5 23	1036	1152	1457	17 2	19 8	2044
2 0	6 5	8 27	1133	1428	1555	19 6	21 7	2341	..	dep. St. André le Gaz. a.	2237	5 22	1031	1151	1456	17 4	19 6	2041
..	..	7 19		1117		..	1940	..	..	dp. ‡St. Rambert (259) a	.	8 40	..	1534	..	19 3	..	..
3 0	6 37	8 55	12 0	1456	1622	1935	2140	0 8	376	↓ Rives...... ↑ a.	22 4	4 54	10 5	1123	1427	1632	1836	20 5
3 21	6 47	9 4	1210	15 6	1631	1944	2149	0 17	383	Voiron .... d.	2145	4 43	9 54	1111	1416	1620	1824	1951
3 31	6 53	9 11	..	1513	1638	1951	2156	0 22	387	Moirans .. d	2132	4 36	9 47		..	1611	1816	1938
3 50	7 9	9 26	1230	1528	1653	20 6	2211	0 37	399	arr. **Grenoble** .... dep	2115	4 23	9 33	1050	1355	1556	18 0	1916
6 13	7 55	1022	1328	1630	1745	21 5			..	arr. Uriage ..... dep.	2020	..	8 10	9 12	1317	1515	17 2	1825

Valence, Grenoble, Montmelian, Chambery. [French Rlys. (Sud-Est).

1 2 3	1/23	1/23	1 2 3	1/23	1 2 3	1/23	Ml		1/23	1/23	1/23	1 2 3	1/23	1/23	1/23	1 2 3
2358	..	0 30	7 30	1210	14 8	..	151	(*p.* 261) Marseilles a.	1150	1445	..	1844	1917	23 6	..	5 24
3 39	..	5 10	1045	1629	1750	1818	0	dep. Valence .. arr.	7 20	9 52	..	1421	1546	1950	..	1 43
A	..	6 2	1120	17 1	1828	19 4	23	St. Hilaire St. N.	6 44	9 11	..	1349	1512	1919	..	A
4 58	..	7 4	12 3	1743	1912	20 2	49	Moirans	6 0	8 18	..	13 7	1424	1841	..	
5 17	..	7 24	1221	1759	1930	2025	..	arr. Grenoble dep.	5 40	7 55	.	1250	14 5	1824	..	0 17
5 29	5 42	7 54	1227	1822	20 0	2042	61	dep. Grenoble arr.	..	7 18	9 32	1223	1339	1816	22 3	0 7
6 16	6 34	9 2	1310	1926	2046	2148	92	Montmelian.. dep.	..	6 12	8 36	1142	1236	1735	21 1	2326
6 29	6 48	9 17	1321	1941	2059	22 4	10	arr. Chambery.... dep.	..	5 55	8 22	1128	1220	1722	2044	2311

A 1 & 2 cl. Sleeping car, 1 cl. Couchettes and 1, 2 & 3 cl. cars Vintimille-Geneva and *v.v.* 1 & 2 cl. cars and 1 cl. Couchettes Cerbere-Geneva add *v.v.* Classes to and from Marseilles *see pp.* 259, 261.

French Rlys. (Sud-Est.).

Notes to Main Line Trains.

a—At Lyons takes 2 and 3 cl. for Valence and beyond; also to Vienne if places available.

aa—Only takes 1 cl. for 125 miles; 2 cl. from Paris to Lyons or from Lyons for 150 miles.

b—At Paris takes for 378 miles or more, and from Laroche 312 miles or more, at Lyons for Pas-des-Lanciers, Marseilles and beyond.

bb—Only takes from Switzerland for Nord Rly. and England, and if places available for Paris.

c—Only takes at Paris and Laroche 2 and 3 cl. if travelling 188 miles or more.

cc—Only takes 1 and 2 cl. for Aix-les-Bains and beyond, but 2 cl. only if travelling 125 miles or more, and 3 cl. only at Paris and only for beyond Aix-les-Bains; also at Aix-les-Bains 2 cl. for St. Pierre d'Albigny and beyond. At Chambery all classes for St. Pierre d'Albigny if places available.

d—Only takes 2 and 3 cl. for Dijon and beyond.

e—Only takes for Avignon and beyond, and at Dijon from Est Rly. via Is-sur-Tille for Lyons and beyond. At Avignon 3 cl. for Marseilles and beyond.

ee—Only takes passengers for Chalons-s-Saone and beyond; also at Paris and Laroche (if places available) 1 and 2 cl. to Dijon.

f—Only takes 2 and 3 cl. for beyond Dijon.

ff—Only takes 2 and 3 cl. for Sens and beyond, except on Sundays and fetes when takes 2 cl. for Fontainebleau.

g—Only takes 2 and 3 cl. for Dijon and beyond.

gg—At Paris and Laroche for 140 miles or more. From Dijon 2 cl. for 65 miles and 3 cl. for 95 miles.

h—From Dole only takes 2 and 3 cl. for 125 miles or more except at Laroche takes for Paris.

hh—Only takes 1 cl. for Toulon and beyond (Marseilles if places available); 2 cl. for St. Raphael and beyond, but takes without restriction passengers holding through tickets and arriving from the Nord by train leaving Calais Maritime at 14.50.

i—Only takes for Montelimar and beyond. From Avignon to Toulon 3 cl. for 63 miles or more.

j—Only takes 3 cl. for Laroche and beyond.

k—Only takes 2 and 3 cl. for Nimes and beyond, but if seats available at Marseilles for Aries and Tarascon.

kk—From Dole and beyond only takes 2 and 3 cl. for 94 miles or more, but at Dijon takes for Tonnere and at Tonnere for beyond Laroche towards Auxerre and Paris.

l—Only takes 1 cl. for 125 miles; 2 cl. for 155 miles or more.

ll—Only takes for Bourg and beyond.

m—Takes between Paris to Dijon for beyond Bourg. From Bourg to Culoz 2 and 3 cl. for 63 miles or more; also at Paris 1 and 2 cl. for Dijon.

mm—Takes all classes for 188 miles or more.

nn—From Lyons (incl.) 2 cl. for 63 miles or more; 3 cl. for 95 miles or more; also at Macon and Chalons for Dijon and beyond.

o—From Laroche only takes 3 cl. for 63 miles or more.

oo—Until Marseilles 3 cl not less than 32 miles.

p—Only takes 2 and 3 cl. for Nimes and beyond.

q—After leaving Chambery only takes 2 and 3 cl. 63 miles or more.

qq—Onlyt akes from Marseilles to Valence for 125 miles 2 cl., and 220 miles 3 cl. From Lyons for 190 miles 2 cl. or 310 3 cl. Exceptions: At Avignon from Nimes and beyond for Valence and beyond. At Valence 2 cl. for Lyons and beyond. At Lyons 2 and 3 cl. for Dijon and beyond.

ss—Only takes for 187 miles or more, but takes at Laroche for Paris, if places available.

t—Only takes 2 and 3 cl. between Toulon and Vienne for 60 miles or more.

tt—At Lyons only takes 2 and 3 cl. for Valence and beyond.

u—From Marseilles to Valence only takes 2 and 3 cl. for 94 miles or more and from Lyons 3 cl. 32 miles or more if places available; from Marseilles 2 and 3 cl. for Avignon. At Avignon 2 cl. for Valence.

uu—Only takes from St. Gervais to Annemasse incl., and for not less than 118 miles.

v—Only takes up 313 miles or more.

vv—From Nice until Marseilles only takes for 187 miles or more. Exceptions: From Nice to Toulon (but not from Mar. 15 to Apl. 30) takes for Toulon and beyond. Takes for Aries and beyond. Takes at Nice from Breil for Marseilles and beyond.

w—Only takes for Valence and beyond; also at Dijon for beyond Lyons towards St. Etienne.

ww—Only takes between Vintimille and St. Raphael for Avignon and beyond. At Toulon 1 cl. only for 315 miles or more. At Marseilles and Lyons 1 cl. only for Paris. At Vintimille passengers from the direction of Genoa.

x—From Paris to Villefranche-sur-Saone only takes 2 and 3 cl. for 220 miles or more, but takes at Macon 2 and 3 cl. for Avignon and beyond. Between Lyons and Avignon 2 cl. for 125 miles and 3 cl. for 190 miles.

xx—From Toulon until Valence only takes 2 and 3 cl. fo 163 miles or more.

y—Only takes passengers for 188 miles or more.

yy—From Vintimille to Marseilles takes for 187 miles or more, and from Marseilles for 375 miles or more; and from Vintimille to Toulon 1 and 2 cl. for Avignon and beyond (except Mar. 15 to Apl. 30). At Vintimille passengers from the direction of Genoa.

z—Between Marseilles and Valence only takes passengers for 315 miles or more.

zz—Only takes up passengers from Culoz to Dijon and for not less than 125 miles.

French Rlys. (Sud-Est.). *Through tables pp.* 14, 15.

					1 2 3					1 2				luxe 1 2		
LONDON (p. 112) ..dep	..	..	..		22 0			..		9 0				11 0		
Boulogne Mar. .... ,,	..	..	..		¶					1255				P		
Calais (Mar.) ...... ,,	..	..	..		..									1430		
Paris (Nord) ......arr.	..	..	..		9 0			..		1548				1744		
,, (Lyon) ......arr.	..				..					..				1825		
	Rap 1 2 3	Rap 1 2 3	Rap 1 2 3	Rap 1 2 3	Rap 1 2	Rap 1 2 3	Exp 1 2 3	Rap 1 2 3	Rap 1 2 3		Rap 1 2	Exp 1 2 3	luxe 1 2		Exp 1 2 3	Rap 1 2 3
		Z	**B**		**I**	**N**	**B**		**J**		**C**		**L**			**F**
Paris (Gare de Lyon) d.	7 30	8 0	8 35	1015	12 0	13 0	14 0	1620	17 0	..	18 0	18 5	20 0	..	2020	2040
Fontainebleau-Avon ..	*d*	..	9 25	*d*	*a a*	*g g*	*j*	*c*		..	*b*	1856	..	..	..	..
Moret (p. 256)	*r*	*x*	*ff*	*r*	*r*	*r*		*r*	*r*	..	*r*	*r*	*r*		..	*e*
Sens		*r*	10 4		..	..	1531	..	..	..	..	1942		..	..	
Laroche *b* ...... arr.	9 23	9 53	1038	12 6	1335	1449	16 2	18 9	1847	..	1947	2021	2154	..	2218	2234
dep	9 28	9 59	1044	12 9	1337	1455	16 7	1815	1852	..	1952	2031	22 0	..	2224	2240
Tonnere	..	..	1123			..	1643	..	..	..		21 9		..	..	
Dijon *b*(p. 267) arr.	1127	12 3	13 0	14 5	1515	1652	1821	20 4	2049	..	2146	23 5	24 0	..	0 28	0 42
dep	1132	12 9	1353	1411	1521	1658	1913	2010	2055	..	2151	..	0 6	..	0 37	0 48
Chagny (p. 254)	To Modane.		1444	To Vallorbe.			20 4	To Vallorbe.	2133	..		..	..	..	To Modane.	..
Chalons-s-Saone arr.		1258	1457		..	1744	2018		2145	..	..	..		..		..
dep		13 0	15 1		..	1746	2030		2147	..		..	..	..		..
Macon *b* (to Geneva, p. 266) .. arr.		1342	1546		..	1825	2116		2226	..	..	..	..	..		..
dep		1344	1550		..	1827	2120		2230	..	..	..		..		..
Villefranche s/Saone d.		1412	1627		..	1856	2154		2255	..	..	.	..	..		..
Lyons (Vaise)......arr.		..	1654			..	2219	..	..	Rap		..		.		..
Lyons (Perrache) *b* arr.		1438	17 3	1 2 3	1720	1921	2230	..	23†23	1 2 3	2358	..	2 29	..		3 11
p. 266 GENEVA (Corna.) d.	..	..	13 6	15 7	13 6	16 8	1937	..	..	2035		..	..		..	..
p. 266 Lyons (Perrache) a.		..	1625	..	1625	1911	2320	..	..	..		..	..		..	..
Grenoble, &c., p. 257	Exp			**V**						**Y**				Rap		
Lyons (Perrache)..dep	1 2 3	1452	18 6	From Geneva	1727	1935	2335		*a*	From Geneva	0 20	.	2 35	1 2 3	..	3 17
Lyons Brotteaux ..dep.	From Bordeaux.	..			..	..	..	..	2340		..		..	From Bordeaux.	..	..
Chasse (p. 257).......		..	1824		..	..	..	..			..	..			..	..
Vienne		..	1835		..	..	0 22	..	0 15		..				..	..
St. Rambert d'A.(p.257)		..	19 5	..		..	0 48	..			..	..			..	..
Valence .... arr.		16 6	1944	1950	1833	2048	1 26	..	1 7	1 43	1 37		3 49		..	4 33
dep		16 9	20 5	1958	1834	2051	2 0	..	1 10	1 50	1 40	..	3 52		..	4 36
Orange ....arr.		..	2130	..	..	..	3 11	..			..	..			..	..
Avignon *b* ...... arr.		1737	2158	2124	1942	2214	3 36	..	2 38	3 22	3 9	..	5 19		..	6 5
dep		1743	2234	2127	1945	2218	3 56	..	2 52	3 36	3 19	..	5 22	..	..	6 8
Tarascon *b* (*to Sete, p.* 255) arr.	1847	..	..	2144	..	..	4 14	..	..	..	..	..	..	4 58	..	..
dep	1853	..	.	2148	..	..	4 19	..		..	..	..	..	5 3	..	..
Arles ....arr.	19 5	18 8	2258	2159	..	..	4 31	..				..	..	5 16	..	..
Marseilles (St. Ch.) ar.	2025	1917	0 37	23 6	21 5	2345	6 21	..	4 29	5 24	4 57		7 0	6 35	..	7 40
page 264: Marseilles ....dep.	2115	1940	0 59	..	2115	0 59	7 15	..	4 44	5 40	5 12	..	7 5	7 15	..	8 9
Toulon ....arr.	22 1	2044	2 7	..	22 1	2 7	8 15	..	5 42	6 38	6 10	..	8 3	8 15	..	9 37
Hyères P.L.M. ,, (p 263)	..	2121	.	..			8 53	..	6 18	7 32	7 32	..	8 53	8 53	..	1057
Cannes ......arr.	2324	2238	4 37	..	2324	4 37	1023	..	7 42	8 35	8 0	..	9 50	1023	..	..
Nice .... ,,	2350	2325	5 35		2350	5 35	1112	..	8 20	9 18	8 45	..	1028	1112	..	..
Mentone ...... ,,	..	0 27	6 50		..	6 50	1229	..	9 4	1014	9 47	..	1114	1229	..	..
Vintimille .... ,,	..	0 44	7 8	..	..	7 8	1246	..	9 19	1030	..		1129	1246	..	..

† Lyons-Brotteaux. ¶ Ferry Service via Dunkerque. *r* Rest. Car.

A 1 & 2 cl. Sleeping Car and 1, 2 & 3 cl. Cars Paris-Lyons.

B 1, 2 & 3 cl. Paris-Vintimille.

C 1 & 2 cl. Sleeping Car; 1st cl. Couchettes; 1 & 2 cl. Cars Paris-Mentone. Rest. Car Paris-Lyons.

D 1 cl. Lits-Salons and Couchettes and 1, 2 & 3 cl. Cars Strasbourg-Nice.

E Daily, except Thurs.; 1 cl. Couchettes, 1, 2 & 3 cl. Cars Paris-Marseilles-Joliette. Limited Train. Only takes passengers for Algiers.

F 1 & 2 cl. Sleeping Car, 1 cl. Couchette-Toilette, 2 cl. Couchettes, Paris-Marseilles and 1, 2 & 3 cl. Cars Paris-Toulon.

I Aerodynamic Train with 1 & 2 cl. Cars and Rest. Car Paris-Marseilles, Limited Train.

J 1, 2 & 3 cl. Cars Paris-Vintimille; Rest. Car Paris-Lyons.

French Rlys. (Sud-Est.)

1 2		1 2						1 2					
11 0		11 0						14 0				..	dep. LONDON (p 112)
..		..						..				..	,, Boulogne (Mar.)
1450		1450						1735				..	,, Calais (Mar.)
1810		1810						21 0				..	arr. **Paris** (Nord)
1855		1855						2133				..	,, ,, (Lyon)
Rap 1 2	..	Rap 1 2 3	Rap 1 2 3	Rap 1 2 3	Rap 1 2 3	luxe 1 2	Rap 1 2 3	Exp 1 2 3	Rap 1 2 3	Exp 1 2 3	Exp 1 2 3	Exp 1 2 3	
2050	..	21 5	2115	2125	2135	2220	2255	2310	2310	2340	..		d. **Paris** (Gare de Lyon)
M	..	*w*	**E**	*i*	*ee*	..		*f*	*g*			**U**	,, Fontainebleau-Avon
hh	..	**O**	*r*	**Q**	**S**	..	..	**A**	..	..	..		,, Moret (p. 256)
..	..		..		..	..		..	..		..	..	,, Sens
2244	..	23 4	2316	2328	2340	0 9	0 47	1 15	1 15	1 47	..	..	arr. } Laroche *b*
2250	..	2310	2322	2334	2346	0 15	0 53	1 21	1 21	1 53	..	..	dep. }
	..			.						2 29	.	..	,, Tonnere
0 52	..	1 17	1 31	1 44	1 56	2 8	2 52	3 30	3 30	4 10			arr. } **Dijon** *b* (p. 267)
0 58	..	1 23	1 38	1 51	2 5	2 14	2 59	3 50	3 56	4 20	5 10	9 20	dep. }
..	..	..		..				4 40		..	6 8	10 7	,, Chagny (p. 254)
		..	..	..	3 0			4 53			6 27	1020	arr. } Chalons-s-Saone
Limited Train.	..	..	..	..	3 2	Simplon-Orient Express To Vallorbe.		4 57			6 31	1023	dep. }
		..	..	..	3 45		To Vallorbe	5 44	To Modane.	To Pontarlier.	7 28	11 8	arr. } **Macon** *b* (to Geneva. p. 266)
	..	..		..	3 52			5 48			7 30	1110	dep. }
	..	..	..	..				6 24			8 14	1140	d. Vilefranche s/Saone
..	..	..	..					6 51			8 46	12 2	arr. Lyons (Vaise
3 21	..	3 55	4 12	4 28	4 43			7 0			8 55	1211	arr. **Lyons** (Perrache) *b*
..	..	..		..	..		..	Rap		..	6 15	9 3	d. GENEVA (Corna.) } p. 266
..	..	.		..	..		..	1 2 3	Exp	..	9 35	12 9	a. Lyons (Perrache) }
	Exp					..		*tt*	1 2 3				*Grenoble &c* p 257.
3 27	1 2 3	4 11	4 25	4 40	4 55	..	..	7 15	8 10	.	1010	13 0	dep. **Lyons** (Perrache).
..	..		..	..		..		..				..	dep. Lyons (Brotteaux)
..		..	..	..	..	..	..		8 30	..			,, Chasse (p. 257)
..		4 39	..		..	..	..	7 40	8 41	..	1036	1328	,, Vienne
.		..		..	..	..	..	**D**	9 13	..		1354	St. Rambert d'A. (p. 257)
4 42	From Bordeaux.	5 37	5 58	6 13	..	..	..	8 30	10 1	..	1128	1433	arr. } Valence
4 45		5 47	6 1	6 16	..	..	..	8 33	10 7		1131	1440	dep. }
		6 56		*r*		..	..	..	1136	..	*r*	16 4	arr. Orange
6 12		7 21	7 30	7 56		..	..	9 59	12 4	..	1259	1632	arr. } Avignon *b*
6 24	.	7 26	7 35	8 10	To Grenoble.	..	..	10 2	1225	..	13 5	1638	dep. }
	7 55	7 43		..		..	..	1019	1250		..	1655	arr. } **Tarascon** *b* (*to Cette, p.* 255)
r	7 58	7 47				..	..	1027	1312	..		17 2	dep. }
..	8 9	*r*		8 38		..	..	1039	1313		1329	1714	arr. Arles *b*
7 53	9 18		..	9 55		..		1150	1430		1445	1844	ar. **Marseilles** (St. Ch.)
7 59	9 25			1015	..	..		1235	..	..	15 0	1940	dep. Marseilles } page 262.
8 57	1027			1124	..	..	..	1331	..	..	1559	2044	arr Toulon
1057	1057	To Narbonne	a r. Marseille Quai Joliette 9.15	1220	..	..	..	1423	..	..	1628	2121	,, Hyères, P.L.M. p. 263.
1045	..			1339	..	..	..	1527	..	..	18 4	2238	arr. Cannes
1123	..			1430	..	..		1610	..	..	1850	2325	arr. Nice
1216	..			1531	..	..		17 2			1953	0 27	,, Mentone
..	..			1548	..	..		1718			2014	0 44	,, Vintimille

L Calais-Paris-Mediterranean Luxe daily.
M 1st cl. Lits-Salons, Couchettes-Toilette, 2 cl. Couchettes and 1 & 2 cl. Cars Paris-Mentone; 1 & 2 cl. Cars Calais-Mentone. Rest. Car Avignon-Mentone.
N 1, 2 & 3 cl. Cars and Rest. Car Paris-Marseilles.
O 1 cl. Lits-Salons and Couchettes, and 1, 2 & 3 cl. Cars Paris-Sete; 1, 2 & 3 cl. Cars Paris-Narbonne.
P Golden Arrow Pullman Car Service, London-Paris.
Q 1st cl. Couchettes and 1, 2 & 3 cl. Cars and 3 cl. Sleeping Car Paris-Vintimille; Rest. Car Avignon-Vintimille.
S 1, 2 & 3 cl. Cars, 1 cl. Couchettes and Lits-Salons Paris-Grenoble.
U 1, 2 & 3 cl. Cars Dijon-Marseilles.
V 1, 2 & 3 cl. Cars Geneva-Marseilles.
Y 1 & 2 cl. Sleeping Car, 1 cl. Couchettes and 1, 2 and 3 cl. Cars Geneva-Vintimille.
Z 1, 2 & 3 cl. Cars Paris Vintimille Rest. Car Paris-St. Raphael.

For other Notes and References, see page 258.

(Vintimille), Marseilles, Tarascon, Lyons, Macon, Paris.

French Rlys. (Sud-Est.)

Miles from Marseilles.																	
		1 2 3	1 2 3	1 2 3	1 2 3	1 2 3	1 2 3	1 2 3	1 2 3	1 2	1 2 3	1 2 3	1 2 3	1 2 3	1 2 3	1 2 3	1 2 3
		Exp	Exp	Rap	Rap	Exp	Rap	Rap	Exp	Rap	Exp	Exp			Exp	Rap	Rap
	page 264. Vintimille ....dep.	2245	..	..	..		Dep Marseilles-Joliette 11.40.	6 15	–	..	8 35	..	..	..	1120	..	From Narbonne
	page 264. Mentone ...... ,,	23 3	..		..	..		6 32		..	8 55	..	..	..	1138		
	page 264. Nice .... ,,	0 10	..	5 45	Auto Rail	..		7 35	..	1150	1017	..	..	..	13 0	15 0	
	page 264. Cannes........ ,,	0 56	..	6 10		..		8 17	..	1215	1057	..	..	..	1346	1533	
	page 264. Hyeres, PLM (263)		.	6 47		..		9 27	..	1258	11 0	..	..	..	1513	..	
	page 264. Toulon........dep.	3 12	..	7 32		7 37		1016	11 0	1337	1255	..	..	.	16 6	1732	
	page 264. Marseilles .... arr.	4 35	..	8 20		8 54		1117	12 0	1425	1353		..	..	1715	1836	
		Y r		I				J q q	1 2 3	H	N u	p			E D	z	y O
0	**Marseilles** (St. Ch.) d.	6 40	7 30	8 30	5 25	9 5		1127	1210	1440	14 8	2030	..	..	1735	1850	..
53	Arles (p. 255) .... ,,	7 52	8 35	l r	6 36	1015			1323	..	1515	2144	..	..	1846	.	r
61	**Tarascon** p. 255 arr.	8 4	..	..	6 48	1028	M	r	1335	..	..	2158	..	..	1859	..	2048
	Tarascon p. 255 dep	8 9	..		6 51	1034			1350		..	22 5	..	..	19 4	..	2051
75	Avignon ...... arr.	8 28	9 1	9 57		..	1329	1258	1410	1553	1542		..	.	1931	2023	2111
	Avignon ...... dep.	8 34	9 4	10 0	..		1335	13 3	1420	1556	16 2	..	..	..	1953	2028	2114
..	Orange ....dep.	9 2	..	..	..	To Bordeaux.			1449	..	..			..	2018	..	2140
152	Valence (p. 257) arr.	1027	1037	1133	.		15 6	1439	1621	17 9	1736	To Bordeaux.		..	2140	22 8	23 0
	Valence (p. 257) dep.	1049	1045	1136	To Bordeaux.		15 9	1442	1625	1710	1740				2143	2211	2314
180	St. Rambert (p. 257) ,,	..	To Geneva	..			..		17 9				..	..	2223	..	↓
198	Vienne .... ,,	..		..			..		1741	..	1839			..	2248	2312	
204	Chasse (p. 257) ,,	..		..			..		1752			..	..	..		.	
..	Lyons (Brotteaux) arr.			..			..			..	..	..	..	..		..	
218	**Lyons** (Perrache) b ,,	1220		1255			1628	16 5	1812	1822	19 5	—		.	2315	2340	0 40
..	p. 266 Lyons ......dep.	1310		..		..		1810	..		1955			..			
316	p. 266 GENEVA .... arr.	1625	1533	..			..	2131	..		2330		..	..	..		..
		n n			1 2 3 Rap	1 2 3 Rap						1 2 3 Exp	1 2 3 Rap	1 2 3 Rap			
218	**Lyons** (Perrache) dep.	1325		13 7	From Modane.	From Vallorbe.	1635	1620	..	1829	2020	..	q	From Vallorbe	2330	0 0	0 48
221	Lyons (Vaise) ,,	1333		..					..	..	2029	From Belfort.	From Modane.		2338	..	
237	Villefranche s/Saone d.	14 0	..	..					..	..	2055				0 2	..	..
262	**Macon** b (p. 266) arr.	1432	..	1358			1727	1711	..	..	2128				0 27	0 50	
	Macon b (p. 266) dep.	1437	..	14 0			1728	1713	..	..	2132				0 29	1 5	..
297	Chalons-s-Saone arr.	1524	..	1439			18 9	1754	..		2224				1 7	..	
	Chalons-s-Saone dep.	1527	..	1440	r	h	1810	1756	.		2228				1 9	..	..
307	Chagny .... ,,	1548	..	..	z z	r	1825	1811	..		2248						..
340	**Dijon** b (p. 267) arr.	1639	..	1531	1822	1940	19 3	1851		2026	2338	1 8	1 50	2 52	1 57	2 42	3 15
	Dijon b (p. 267) dep.	17 0	..	1537	1828	1946	19 9	1858	..	2032	0 8	1 18	2 12	2 57	2 12	2 48	3 20
412	Tonnere.......... ,,	1842	..	..					..	..	1 50			..			
439	Laroche b ...... arr.	1917	..	1728	2021	2136	2111	2050		22 8	2 21	3 16	4 10	4 54	4 10	4 45	5 17
	Laroche b ...... dep.	1923	..	1734	2027	2142	2116	2056		2210	2 32	3 22	4 16	5 0	4 16	4 51	5 23
465	Sens .... ,,	20 5	..	..	..	..	..	..		..	3 14	..	..	..	..	..	
498	Fontainebleau-Avon ,,	2051	..	..	..	..	..	..			..	..	..	..	..	..	..
535	**Paris** (Lyon) .. arr.	2145	..	1925	2225	2340	23 5	2255	..	2350	5 0	5 35	6 20	7 0	6 20	6 55	7 20
	See Thro' Tables, p. 112.	..	..	1 2 3							1 2				1 2		
	Paris (Lyon) ....dep	..	..	..	..	..	..	..	..	..	6 35						
	Paris (Nord.) ....dep.	.	..	2150	..	..	..	..	..	..	8 20				8 20		
	Boulogne (Mar.) ...... arr.	..	..	¶	..	..	..	..	..								
	Calais (Mar.) .... arr.	..	..		..	..	..	..	..	..	1141				1141		
	LONDON (p. 112) .. .. ,,	..	..	9 10	..	..	..	..	..	..	1530				1530		

* 3rd cl. Auto-Rail. † Brotteaux Station. *r* Rest. Car. ¶ Via Dunkerque and Dover.

A 1 & 2 cl. Sleeping Car, 1 cl. Couchettes-Toilette, 2 cl. Couchettes, and 1, 2 & 3 cl. Cars Marseilles-Paris.

B 1 & 2 cl. Car Mentone-Boulogne ; 1 cl. Couchettes-Toilette and Lits-Salons ; 2 cl. Couchettes and 1 & 2 cl. Cars Mentone-Paris ; Rest. Car Mentone-Avignon.

C 1 & 2 cl. Sleeping Car, 1 cl. Couchettes, and 1 & 2 cl. Cars Mentone-Paris ; Rest. Car Lyons-Paris.

D 1, 2 & 3 cl. Cars, 1 & 2 cl. Sleepers and 1 cl. Couchettes, Lyons-Paris.

E 1, 2 & 3 cl. Cars Vintimille-Lyons.

G 3 cl. Sleeping Car, 1 cl. Couchettes and 1, 2 & 3 cl. cars Vintimille-Paris ; Rest. Car Nice-Avignon.

H 1 & 2 cl. Cars and Rest. Car Marseilles-Paris. Limited Train.

I 1, 2 and 3 cl. Cars and Rest. Cars Marseilles-Paris.

J 1, 2 & 3 cl. Cars Vintimille-Paris ; Rest. Car St. Raphael-Paris.

(Vintimille), Marseilles, Tarascon, Lyons, Macon, Paris.

French Rlys. (Sud-Est).

123	123	12	123	1/23	123	12	123	123	123	123	123	12	
Rap	Rap	Rap	Exp	Exp	Rap	luxe	Exp	Exp	Rap	Exp	Rap	Rap	
..	..	..		..	15 6	1655	1715	1845	..	.	1935		d. Vintimille .. (page 264.)
..	..	1552	..	..	1522	17 9	1734	19 0	..	..	1949	2045	,, Mentone ....
..	..	1642	..	..	1613	1753	1848	1955	..	..	2038	2145	,, Nice........
	..	1719	..	..	1652	1829	1942	2042	..	..	2114	2228	d. Cannes .
	1716	1759	..	1759	1759	1759	..	2157	..	..	2157		Hyères PLM 263
	18 0	1911	..	1923	1854	2019	2158	2240	..	..	2313	0 22	d. Toulon ....
	1910	2010	..	2048	1959	2117	23 5	2340	..	.	0 15	1 20	a. Marseilles
From Briancon.	A	B			G	L	U	S	T		X	C	
		ww			*yy*			*xx*			*t*	*ss*	
	20 0	2015	2030	2130	2040	2122	2345	2358	0 8	..	0 30	1 35	d. **Marseilles** (S.Ch.)
	21 8	..	2144	23 7		..	1 34	..	1 25	..	..	..	,, Arles (*p.* 255)....
		r	2158	..	r	..	..	..	1 38	..		..	a. **Tarascon**, *p*255
			22 5				..	.	1 47	..	..	.	d.
	2137	2145		2349	2223	2253	2 4	1 32	..	..	2 17	..	a. Avignon.......
	2142	22 0	..	—	2237	2256	2 14	1 47	To Bordeaux.	..	2 32	3 11	d.
			To Bordeaux				2 43	..		..	..	3 16	d. Orange ....
2252	2331	2345			0 20	0 31	4 17	3 30		..	4 31	..	a. Valence (*p.* 257)
2314	2334	2346		..	0 23	0 34	4 43	3 39		..	4 39	4 58	d.
↓	..	..		..	..	↓	5 14	To Geneva.		..		5 1	,, St Rambert(*p*257)
	..	..		.	..		5 41			..	5 52	..	,, Vienne ....
		..		..			5 53			..	..	..	,, Chasse (*p.* 257)
	..			..	..		..			..	6 32	..	a. Lyons (Brotteaux
0 40	1 0	1 12			1 52	2 3	6 15			..		6 29	a **Lyons** (Perr che *b*
..	..	..	12	12		..	..	S		..	6†53		d. Lyons (*p* 266)
..	.		luxe	luxe	..	..	..	9 8			1030		a. Geneva..
										kk 123		r	
0 48	1 6	1 18	Simplon-Orient Exp. fr. Vallorbe.	Rome luxe.	2 20	2 11	8 40	..	..	Rap	7†16	7 0	d. **Lyons** (Perrache
..	..	..			..		8 47	..	..		*y*	..	,, Lyons (Vaise)....
..	..	Limited Train.			..		9 15	..	..		7 45	..	d. Villefr'che s/Saone
..	..				3 17		9 47	..	..	From Vallorbe.	8 9	..	a. **Macon** *b* (*p.* 26·)
..	..				3 19		9 52	..	..		8 22	..	d.
..	..				4 3		1039	..	..		9 1	..	a. Chalons-s-Saone
..	..				4 6	↓	1045	..	..		9 3		d.
..	..	..			..		11 5	..	..		9 19		,, Chagny.......
3 15	3 33	3 45	4 12	4 56	5 5	4 44	1153	..	..	9 52	10 0	9 14	a. **Dijon** *b* (*p.* 267
3 20	3 39	3 52	4 27	5 8	5 15	4 50	1225	..	..	9 58	10 7	9 20	d.
..			..	..			14 9	..	..		1133	..	,, Tonnere .....
5 17	5 32	5 45	6 27	6 57	7 7	6 47	1443	..		1151	12 3	11 6	a. Laroche *b* ....
5 23	5 37	5 51	6 32	7 3	7 17	6 53	1449	..		1157	12 9	1112	d.
..			..		7 51		1528	..		..		..	,, Sens ....
..	..	.	..	..		..	1610	..	..	..	r	..	,, Fontainebl'u-Av'n
7 20	7 32	8 0	8 40	9 10	9 20	9 0	17 0	..	..	14 0	14 5	13 0	a. **Paris** (Lyon)
12						..	..	..	..	12			*See Thro' Tables,* *p* 112.
..						9 46	..	..	..	..			d. **Paris** (Lyon) ..
1030							..	..	..	1625			d. Paris (Nord) ..
1310						13 5	..		..	19 5			a. Boulogne (Mar.)
..						..	..	..	..	..			a Calais (Mar.)
1720						1720	..	..	..	23 0			a. London (*p.* 112)

L Calais-Mediterranean Luxe, daily.
M Daily, except Tues .; 1 cl. Lits-Salons, 1, 2 & 3 cl. Cars Marseilles-Joliette-Paris. For travellers from Algiers, but if seats available, from Marseilles or Avignon, 1 & 2 cl. for 63 miles and 3 cl. for 95 miles.
N 1, 2 & 3 cl. Cars Vintimille-Paris ; Rest. Car Vintimille-Marseilles.
O 1, 2 & 3 cl. Narbonne-Paris ; 1 cl. Lits-Salons and Couchettes, 1 ,2 & 3 cl. Cars Sete-Paris.
S 1 & 2 cl. Sleeping Car, 1 cl. Couchettes and 1, 2 & 3 cl. Cars Vintimille-Geneva ; 1 cl. Couchettes ; 1 & 2 cl. Cars Cerbere-Geneva. See also *pp.* 257 & 260.
T 1 cl. Lits-Salons and Couchettes ; 1 & 2 cl. Car San Remo-Irun ; 1 cl. Couchettes ; 1, 2 & 3 cl. Cars Vintimille-Bordeaux.
U 1 cl. Couchettes ; 1, 2 & 3 cl. Cars Vintimille-Paris.
X 1, 2 & 3 cl. Cars Vintimille-Paris ; 1, 2 & 3 cl. Cars and 1 cl. Couchettes Vintimille-Strasbourg.
Y 1, 2 & 3 cl. Cars Marseilles-Paris.

For other Notes see page 25

Toulon, Hyeres. [French Rlys. (Sud-Est),

Mls.		1/23	1/23	1/23	1/23	1/23	1/23	1/23	1 2 3	1/23
0	Toulon ....dep.	5 55	7 5	8 30	1035	12 0	14 0	16 5	1810	2058
13	Hyeres P.L.M. .. arr.	6 18	7 32	8 53	1057	1220	1423	1628	1834	2121
18	Les Salins d'Hyeres arr.	6 32	7 52	9 7	..	1237	1437	1642	1850	2135
		1/23	1/23	1/23	1/23	1/23	1/23	1/2 3	1/23	1/23
..	Les Salins d'Hyeres dep.	5 10	6 34	9 15	..	1245	15 0	1653	1745	2145
..	Hyeres P.L.M. .... dep.	5 23	6 47	9 27	11 0	1258	1513	1716	1759	2157
..	Toulon ....arr.	5 47	7 11	9 51	1124	1322	1537	1744	1823	2221

Cannes—Grasse (Auto Bus Service).

5 55	8 50	11 0	1355	1545	17 0	18 0	2125	dep. Cannes arr.	5 35	7 55	1020	1245	1330	1635	17 5	2010
6 30	9 25	1135	1430	1620	1735	1835	22 0	arr. Grasse dep.	5 0	7 20	9 45	1210	1255	16 0	1630	1935

Marseilles, Veynes, Grenoble, Briancon. [French Rlys. (Sud-Est),

A Extra Fares 3 cl.

1/23	1/23	1 2 3	1/23	1/23	1/23	1/23	Mls.		1 2 3	1/23	1/23	1/23	1 2 3	1/23	1/23	1/23
5 7	5 20	8 4	1020	1610	1725	1856	0	dep. **Marseilles** ..arr.	8 43	10 0	1155	1420	1724	2234	2354	..
5 52	6 22	9 6	1115	17 0	1818	1951	18	Aix-en-Pr...	7 53	9 10	1113	1331	1630	2140	2313	..
6 27	7 10	9 49	12 2	1735	19 6	2037	38	arr. Pertuis ....dep.	6 50	8 20	1034	1235	1541	2040	2237	..
..	..	..	..	8 40	..	..		dep. Avignon.. arr.	..	..	1412	..	2132	..	..	..
6 30	..	9 55	..	1737	..	..		dep. Pertuis .... arr.	..	..	1029	..	1535	..	2236	..
7 35	..	1115	..	1842	..	..	80	St. Auban ..dep.	..	..	9 17	..	1422	..	2131	..
8 41		1240	..	1950	..	..	122	arr. Veynes ....dep.	..	..	8 7	..	1258	..	2025	..
8 49	..	1310	1615	2018	..	5 8		dep. Veynes....arr.	8 25	..	..	8 18	1228	1612	1937	..
1111	..	1543	1858	2220	..	7 45	190	arr. **Grenoble** dep.	5 25	..	..	5 10	9 40	1350	1730	..
1 2 3		1/23													1 2 3	
9 0	..	1321	1625	2018	2010	..	..	dep. Veynes....arr.	..	..	8 4	..	1011	1529	20 2	2134
9 32	..	14 0	17 6	2250	2037	..	138	Gap	..	..	7 35	..	9 39	1446	1930	2040
1029	..	15 2	18 7	..	2120	..	178	Embrun ..	..	..	6 43	..	8 36	1339	1834	1935
1135	..	1616	1921	..	2210	..	246	arr. **Briancon** dep.	..	..	5 47	..	7 35	1234	1740	1830

Toulon—St. Raphael.

1 & 2 class.] [Chemin de Provence.

								Mls.								
5 42	7 47	8 56	1110	1215	1324	1538	1752	0	dep. Toulon (Prov.) p. 264 arr.	6 15	8 20	1034	1248	15 2	1716	1930
7 8	8 19	9 22	1138	1247	1350	16 4	1818	10	arr. San Salvadour......dep.	5 43	7 53	10 7	1221	1435	1649	19 3
7 19	8 29	9 33	1147	1257	14 1	1615	1829	14	arr. Hyeres (Ville) ...... dep.	5 33	7 44	9 58	1212	1426	1640	1854
7 43	..	9 57	1211	..	1425	1639	1853	26	arr. Bormes les Mimosas dep.	5 4	7 17	9 31	1145	1359	1613	1827
7 47	..	10 1	1215	..	1429	1648	1857	27	arr. Le Lavandou ...... dep.	5 0	7 13	9 27	1141	1355	16 9	1823
7 58	..	1012	1226	..	1440	1654	19 5	31	arr. Cavaliere .... dep.	..	7 3	9.17	1131	1345	1559	1813
8 4	..	1018	1232	..	1446	17 0	1914	33	arr. Le Canadel ....dep.	..	6 57	9 11	1125	1339	1553	18 7
8 17	..	1031	1245	..	1458	1713	1927	38	arr. Cavalaire ....dep.	..	6 44	8 58	1112	1326	1540	1754
8 20	..	1034	1248	..	15 2	1716	1930	39	arr. Pardigon ....dep.	..	6 41	8 55	11 9	1323	1537	1751
8 27	..	1041	1255	..	15 9	1723	1937	42	arr. La Croix de Cavalaire dp.	..	6 35	8 49	11 3	1317	1531	1745
8 45	..	1059	1313	..	1527	1741	..	44	ar. Guerrevieille-Beauvallond	..	..	8 28	1042	1256	1510	1724
8 50	..	11 4	1318	..	1532	1746	20 0	52	arr. Ste. Maxime ...... dep.	..	6 9	8 23	1037	1251	15 5	1719
9 25	..	1139	1353	..	16 7	1820	..	65	arr. St. Raphael (p. 264) dep.	..	..	7 51	10 5	1219	1433	1647

RAILCAR*

GRENOBLE—DIGNE.

Suspended.

8 55	dep. Grenoble .... arr.	1748
1058	arr. Veynes ...... dep.	15 9
1059	dep. ,, ... arr.	15 8
1212	arr. St. Auban.... dep	1357
1215	dep. ,, ... arr.	1354
1229	dep. Mallemoisson dep.	1343
1238	arr. } Digne .... { dep.	1333
1345	dep. } Digne .... { arr.	1150
1711	arr. Nice ....dep.	8 20

*3rd class passengers pay supplement.

P.L.M. MOTOR SERVICES.

Marseilles—Nice. Daily.

8 15	0	dep. Marseilles P.L.M. St. arr.	18 0
9 52	27	,, Les Leques .... ,,	1615
1053	50	,, Toulon P.L.M. St. .. ,,	1510
1132	61	,, Hyeres .... ,,	1425
..	76	,, Bormes .... dp.	..
1330	80	,, Le Lavandou........ ,,	1350
1343	84	,, Cavaliere .... ,,	1220
1350	87	,, Le Canadel.......... ,,	1212
1355	90	,, Le Rayol .... ,,	12 7
14 5	92	,, Cavalaire .... ,,	1157
1415	97	,, La Croix de Cavalaire ,,	1147
1427	102	,, La Foux .... ,,	1135
1432	104	,, Beauvallon........... ,,	1130
1450	106	,, St. Maxime .... ,,	1115
1535	125	,, St. Raphael P.L.M. St. ,,	1035
1555	131	,, Agay .... ,,	1010
1710	153	,, Cannes .... ,,	9 13
1820	176	arr. Nice.. .... ,,	8 0

Paris, Marseilles, Toulon, Nice, Mentone, Vintimille. [French Rlys. (Sud-Est).

Mls.	Through Tables, see pp. 113 & 259.	Exp 123	Rap 123	Rap 12	Rap 123	1cl.	luxe 12	Exp 123	Rap 12	Exp 123	1cl.	Rap 123	Exp 123	Exp 123	Rap 123	Rap 123	Rap 12	123
												i						
0	Paris (Lyon) d.	8 35	17 0	18 0	..	..	20 0	14 0	2050	2040	D	2125	2310	..	..	8 0	12 0	..
317	Lyons........d.	18 6	23†40	0 20	G	..	2 35	2335	3 27	3 17	..	4 40	7 15	1010	..	1452	1727	18 6
535	Marseilles....a.	0 37	4 29	4 57	5 24	..	7 0	6 21	7 53	7 40	..	9 55	1150	1445	..	1917	21 5	23 6
	Marseilles dp.	0 59	4 44	5 12	5 40	6 47	7 5	7 15	7 59	8 9	10 0	1015	1235	15 0	1815	1940	2115	2315
567	Bandol	..	..	..	..	D	C	..	r	9 15	..	11 7	..	..	..	..	D	0 8
571	La Seyne-Tamar	..	..	..	..	..		..	hh	9 30	..	r	..	..	r	r		..
577	**Toulon** b arr.	2 7	5 42	6 10	6 38	7 40	8 3	8 15	8 57	9 37	1046	1124	1331	1559	1911	2044	22 1	0 24
	(p. 263) dep.	2 17	5 48	6 15	6 43	7 42	8 7	8 23	9 1	..	1047	1134	1336	1614	1916	2049	22 2	..
620	Les Arcs b ..arr.	3 26	6 46	..	7 43	..	..	9 22	..	..	..	1241	1433	1712	2010	2148	..	..
634	Fréjus......arr.	3 49	7 8	7 28	8 4	..	..	9 42	..	..	1141	13 4	1454	1732	2029	22 8	.	..
636	St. Raphael ,,	3 53	7 12	7 32	8 8	8 41	9 21	9 46	1015	..	1144	13 8	1458	1736	2033	2211	2259	..
641	Agay	4 9	..	..	..	..	..	9 59	.	..	..	H	..	..	..	..	.	..
647	Le Trayas......	4 20	..	..	..	..	..	1010		..	..	..	..	..	..	..		..
656	**Cannes**....arr.	4 37	7 42	8 0	8 35	9 6	9 50	1023	1045	..	12 9	1339	1527	18 4	21 4	2238	2324	..
662	Juan-les-Pins ..	5 3	..	8 16	8 51	..		1042		..	..	14 1	1541	1820	2119	2256		..
663	Antibes ....arr.	5 9	7 59	8 24	8 57	9 18	10 7	1048	11 3	..	1220	14 7	1547	1826	2125	23 2	2335	..
675	**Nice** b .... ar.	5 35	8 20	8 45	9 18	9 33	1028	1112	1123	..	1235	1430	1610	1850	2145	2325	2350	..
	d.	6 0	8 28	8 59	9 28	..	1034	1140	1131	..	13 0	1445	1620	1859	22 0	2340	..	..
678	Villefranche arr.	6 10	..	9 7	9 38	..		1150	1138	..	..	1453	1629	1910	22 8	2350		..
679	Beaulieu.... ,,	6 15	8 39	9 13	9 43	..	1045	1155	1144	..	13 8	1458	1634	1915	2213	2355	Auto Rail from Marseilles	..
683	Cap d'Ail .. ,,	6 27	..	9 23	9 53	..	1054	12 7	1153	..		15 7	1644	1928	2222	0 5		..
686	Monaco .... ,,	6 31	8 49	9 28	9 57	..	1059	1211	1158	..	1316	1511	1647	1933	2227	0 9		..
691	Monte Carlo ,,	6 37	8 53	9 33	10 1	..	11 4	1216	12 3	..	1319	1518	1650	1939	2232	0 13		..
692	**Mentone**	6 50	9 4	9 47	1014	..	1114	1229	1216	..	1327	1531	17 2	1953	2245	0 27		..
..	Mentone-Gar. ..	6 58	..	..	1021	..	..	1236	..	..	..	1538	17 9	20 3	..	0 34		..
697	**Vintimille** c ar.	7 8	9 19	..	1030	..	1129	1246	..	..	..	1548	1718	2014	23 0	0 44		..
p. 299	SanRemo a	9 11	1114	..	1114	..	1314	1423	..	..	..	1857	1857	2157	1 11	5 48	..	..
	Genoa arr.	1210	1415		1415	..		1734	..	..	..	..	2343	..	5 25	8 50	..	..

(Etna time).	1/23	123 Rap	123 Exp	1/23 Exp	123 Exp	123 Rap	123 Rap	12 Rap	123	luxe 12	1cl. Rap	123 Exp	123 Rap	123 Rap	1/23	12 Rap	123 Exp
p. 299 Genoa ......dep.	D	0 50	4 0	6 57	6 57	..	1120	..	1120	..	..	1120	G	16 0	16 0	..	1810
San Remo .. ,,	..	5 32	8 15	1015	1015	..	1410	..	1410	1657	..	1410	..	1842	1842		2125
(Green. time).				E			yy	ww	1/23	C			xx	t		ss	Exp
Vintimille ....dep.	..	6 15	8 35	1025	1120	..	15 6	..	1610	1655	Auto Rail to Marseilles.	1715	1845	1935	2015	..	2245
Mentone-Garavan ..	..	6 26	8 47	1034	1131	..	1516	..	1619			1726	..		2024	..	2256
Mentone	..	6 32	8 55	1039	1138	..	1522	1552	1624	17 9		1734	19 0	1949	2029	2045	23 3
Monte Carlo	..	6 45	9 11	1050	1152		1534	16 5	1635	1719		1747	1913	20 1	2041	21 0	2317
Monaco	..	6 50	9 18	1053	1157	..	1538	1610	1639	1724		1752	1917	20 6	2045	21 6	2322
Cap d'Ail	..	6 55	9 24	1056	12 3	..	..	1615	1642	1729		..	1922	2011	2049	2112	2328
Beaulieu...........	..	7 6	9 38	11 6	1216	..	1549	1624	1652	1738	..	18 7	1931	2019	2059	2123	2340
Villefranche	..	7 10	9 42	11 9	1220	..	1553	1628	1656		D	1811	1935		21 3	2127	2344
Nice b .... ar.		7 20	9 49	1118	1231	..	1559	1634	17 5	1746	..	1818	1942	2028	2112	2134	2355
d.	5 45	7 35	1017	1150	13 0	15 0	1613	1642	1710	1753	1840	1848	1955	2038	..	2145	0 10
Antibes	6 0	7 57	1038	12 4	1324	1518	1633	17 3	1735	1814	1856	1915	2019	2059	..	22 5	0 33
Juan-les-Pins		8 2	..	..	1329	1522	1637	.	1738		..	1921	2024	..	..	2211	0 39
Cannes (p. 126) dep.	6 10	8 17	1057	1245	1346	1533	1652	1719	1748	1829	19 7	1942	2042	2114	..	2228	0 56
Le Trayas ...... ,,	.			..	14 8	..		..	arr.	..	..	1956	..	..	..		
Agay .... ,,	.	r		..	1419	..	¶	¶	—	..	..	20 7		..	..	..	
St. Raphael	6 34	8 46	1126	1238	1430	16 0	1722	1749	..	1859	..	2021	2110	2143	..	2258	1 26
Fréjus..............	..	8 50		..	1435	16 4	H	..	..	..	1930	2027	2115	2147	..	..	1 33
Les Arcs b ......dep.	6 47	9 11	1151	..	1458	1623	1747	..	..	..	..	2050	2137	22 9	..		1 57
Toulon b p. 263 arr.	7 31	1011	1250	1336	16 0	1717	1849	19 6	..	2015	..	2151	2234	23 7	..	0 17	3 3
dp.	7 32	1016	1255	1337	16 6	1732	1854	1911	..	2019	2029	2158	2240	2313	..	0 22	3 12
La Seyne-Tamaris ..	..		r	..	..	..	r	r	..	..	2030		..	..	..	r	..
Bandol ....dep.	..	..		..	..	..	1911		..	..	..	2215	..	..	..		..
Marseilles ....arr.	8 20	1117	1353	1425	1715	1836	1959	2010	..	2117	2125	23 5	2340	0 15	..	1 20	4 35
p. 201 Marseilles .. dep.	8 30	1127	14 8	..	1735	1850	2040	2015	..	2122	2345	2345	2358	0 30	..	1 35	6 40
Lyons ...... arr.	255	16 5	19 5	..	2315	234	1 52	1 12	..	2 3	6 15	6 15	G	6†32	..	6 29	1220
Paris (Lyon) arr.	1925	2255	5 0	..	6 20	6 55	9 20	8 0	..	9 0	14 5	17 0		14 5	..	13 0	2145

C Calais-Paris-Mediterranean luxe, daily. **D** Auto-Rail Exp., supplement according to destination. **E** Auto-Rai Nice-Marseilles. **G** To and from Geneva. **H** 3 cl. W.L. Paris-Vintimille and *v.v.* † Lyons (Brotteaux). *r* Rest. Car. Other Notes see *p.* 258. ¶ See *pp.* 259/262 for notes *re* limited places. For 1 and 2 cl. Sleeping Car Nice-Postumia-Budapest see *p.* 201 : Riviera Express see *p.* 81, and Vienna-Cannes Express see *p.* 82.

Thro' Services, p.p. 118,121,122

(Paris) Culoz, Aix-les-Bains, Modane, Turin. [French Rlys. (Sud-Est).

Mi fr. Paris		123	12	12	123	12	12	123	123	123	123	3cl.	123	123	12	123
	see p. 266: LONDON dep.	C	11 0	11 0	..	..	14 0	..	..	..	..	..	..	22 0	..	..
	Calais (Mar.) d	B	1430	1450	..	..	1735	..	..	..	..	..	..	..	..	..
		Rap	L	123	X		123	..	Exp		Rap				Y	
0	**Paris** (Lyon) d	17 0	1930	2020	2230	..	2310	..	..	..	7 30	..	..	13 0	13 5	..
195	**Dijon** ..dep.	2055	2331	0 37	2 40	..	4 9	..	..	..	1132	..	..	1658	17 6	..
	Lyons ,,	2258	..	..	..	..	5 30	6 40	8 55	9 40	1155	..	..	1810		1955
	Geneva ,,	2124	..	..	..		5 17	6 15	9 3	11 5	13 6	..	15 6	18 8		2035
				m		1/23	A	1/23			R		1/23	123		
347	**Culoz** ......dep.	1 0	..	4 47	..	6 15	7 24	8 42	1045	1244	1452	16 7	1720	2026	2011	2221
361	**Aix-les-Bains** a	1 20	2 42	5 8	6 21	6 40	7 43	9 4	11 5	1311	1512	1629	1746	2052	2038	2244
	d	1 25	2 43	5 23	6 35	6 44	7 55	9 55	1110	1323	1518	1650	1751	2056	2043	2251
369	Chambery ..arr.	1 37	2 55	5 40	6 43	7 0	8 8	1012	1123	1339	1531	17 5	18 7	2112	2056	23 5
372	Montmelian	..	..	6 24	7 8	7 34	..	1059	1142	1413	..	1751	1837	2150	2135	2326
384	St.Pierre d'Albig.	..	..	6 35	7 20	7 46	..	1113		1425	1614	18 6	1850	2159	2148	..
	St. P.d'Albig.d.	..	..	..	7 21	7 47	r	1124		1435	1615	..	1852	..	2149	..
	Albertville arr.	..	..	..	7 50	8 20	..	1158		15 8	1643	..	1930	..	2221	..
..	Moutiers-Sal.a.	..	..	..	8 34	9 9	..	..		1556	1724	..	2147	..	23 5	Z
418	Brg St. Maur a.	..	..	..	9 32	10 0	..	..		1645	1813	..	..	..	..	..
421	St.Jean-de-Maur.	2 36	3 45	7 22	..	..	9 12	1212	To Valence.	1524	1634	19 3	..	2251	.	..
430	**Modane** e ..arr.	3 15	4 25	8 10	.	..	9 54	13 0		1612	1715	20 0	..	2337	..	..
								2 3				2 3				
	M'd'ne (Etnat.) d.	4 15	4 50	8 10		..	1040	1530		..	1755	2040	..	..	..	..
495	**Turin** ....arr.	6 30	6 50	1128		..	13 0	1818	..	..	2020	2345	..	..	..	..

	1/23	1/23	1/23	1/23	1/23	1/23	123	123	123	1/23	1/23	123	123	123	123	12	12
Turin ......dep.	..	..	..		..	..	..	..	9 36	..	13 2	..	1535	..	1846	2124	0 15
Modane e .. arr.	..	..	..	..	..	..	..	..	1155	..	16 0	..	18 3	..	2110	2340	2 35
													123				
							Rap	U	Rap				Exp	T	Exp	L	B
Modane (Gn.t.) d	From Grenoble.	..	5 35	8 0	..	1130	From St. Gervais.	..	1225	..	1618	..	19 0		2145	0 0	3 30
St. Jean de Maur.		..	6 28	8 52	..	1219		..	13 9	..	1711	..	1946		2227	..	4 12
Bourg St. Maur d.		..	..	7 20	..	..		1140	..	..	..	17 0	r A	1940	..	..	..
Moutiers-Sal. d.		..	..	8 10	..	..		1222	..		..	1754		2023	..	..	..
Albertville		..	5 55	9 1	..	1223		13 0	..	..	..	1845	↓	21 1	..	..	..
St. Pierre d'A.a		.	6 26	9 33	..	1257		1327	..	..	..	1919		2130	..	..	..
St. Pierre d'Albig.	..	..	7 18	9 43	..	13 9		1328	R	..	18 5	1922	↓	2131	..	..	..
Montmelian, p. 257	6 16	..	7 30	9 56	..	1322		..	..	..	1819	1938	2027		23 7	..	..
Chambery ..dep.	6 40	7 0	8 46	1046	1118	1344	..	14 9	14 9	1630	1915	20 5	2051	2159	2327	1 29	5 2
Aix-les-Bains a	6 55	7 16	9 0	11 3	1132	14 0	14 2	1422	1422	1646	1931	2022	21 5	2212	2341	1 42	5 15
d	7 2	7 18	9 54	1136	1136	..	14 9	1428	1428	1655	1937	2049	2118	2252	2355	1 43	5 17
Culoz ...... arr.	7 23	7 47	1019	12 1	12 :	..	1430	1447	1447	1721	2003	2111	2138	..	0 15	..	5 34
see p. 266: Geneva arr.	9 8	1012	12 0	..	1423	..	1625	..	1625	..	2125	..	2330	..	..	..	7 13
Lyons.. ,,	9 35	9 35	12 9	..	1415	..	1625	..	..	2034	..	2320	..	..	..	..	7 15
Dijon .... ,,		.	..	1331	..	..	..	1822	1822	..	..	..	1 50	2 36	3 57	4 56	10 0
	Z								zz				q				
Paris (Lyon) a		.	..	1925	..	..		2225	2225	..	..	..	6 20	6 50	8 10	9 10	14 5
p. 112: Calais (Mar.) a	..		..	..	..	..	.	..	..	..	..	..	1141		1523		..
LONDON ..arr.	..			9 10	..	..	..	..	..	..	..	..	1530		1855	1855	23 0

A 1 cl. Couchettes, and 1, 2 & 3 cl. Paris-Turin and *v.v.* **B** *Via* Lyons. **C** 1 & 2 cl. Paris-Naples and 3rd Paris-Turin. **L** Rome Luxe daily. **R** Rest. Car Paris-Modane and *v.v.* **T** July 1—Oct. 1 **U** July 2 Oct. 2. **X** June 30—Sept. 30. **Y** June 17—Sept. 30. **Z** Through accommodation Geneva *via* Grenoble to Vintimille and *v.v.*, *see pp.* 257, 259 262. (*m*, *q*, *zz*, *see* notes on *p.* 258). *r* Rest Car.

Bellegarde, Geneva (Eaux Vives), Evian-les-Bains, Bouveret.

¶ To and from Paris, see *p.* 266 and notes 258.

12	1/23	1/23	1/23	1/23	1/23	123	1/23	123	Ms	[P.-L.-M. Co.]	1/23	12	1/23	1/23	1/23	123	1/23
4 38	5 49	8 11	9 20	1134	1555	1635	2052	2111	0	dp. **Bellegarde** .. arr.	9 23	1024	1331	1510	16 9	2031	2132
5 31	6 51	9 10	1023	1234	1553	1736	2146	22 9	23	ar. Annemasse .. dp.	8 21	9 37	1236	1411	15 7	1935	2023
A	6 30	8 46	9 58	12 9	1625	B	2124	2124	..	dp. **Geneva** (E.V.) ‡ar.	8 39	9 52	13 0	1452	1527	1955	2034
6 1	7 6	9 32	1030	1245	1659	1739	2151	2218	..	,, Annemasse .. ,,	8 8	9 31	1231	14 6	15 1	1930	2014
6 52	7 54	1011	1113	1331	1742	1816	2224	23 6	43	,, Thonon-les-Bains	7 19	9 0	1147	1333	1418	1854	1930
7 3	8 4	1028	1123	1342	1752	1827	2233	2317	49	ar. **Evian-les-Bains**	7 5	8 50	1131	1315	14 2	1840	1913
..	1020	..	1212	1445	1849		C	¶	59	,, St. Gingolph	6 18	C	1038	B	1233	1712	..
..	1028	..	1220	1453	19 0	..	..	..	63	,, Bouv'et (p. 288) d.	6 10	..	1030	..	1225	17 6	..

By Auto Evian to Le Bouveret.

A June 30—Sept. 30. **B** July 8—Sept 30. **C** July 8 - Sept. 16. ‡ Central European time.

(Paris), Dijon, (Lyons), Culoz, Geneva

[French Rlys. (Sud-Est).

Mls	Special Accomod'tn. see p. 121, 122.	123 Rap	1/23	12 Rap	12 Rap	123 Rap	123	123 Rap	12 luxe	123 Rap	123 Rap	123 Rap	123 Rap	123 Z	123 Exp	123 Exp
0	**Paris** (Lyon) ....dep.	7 30	..	13 0	13 5	..	..	17 0	1930	2020	2135	..	2310	..	..	2340
197	Dijon .... ,,	1132	..	1658	17 6	..	..	2055	2331	0 37	2 5		4 9	..	..	5 5
417	St. Amour ...... ,,	..	..	**	..	r	..	r	..	m	ll		f	..	..	7 33
285	Bourg ....arr.	1328	..	B	..	B	..	2316	1 10	2 45	4 31 **		5 59	..	..	8 5
..	Macon ......dep.	R	1247	1833	F	..	..	**	L	..	Y		..	6 7	..	..
	Bourg........ arr.	..	1325	19 0	..	..	..	..	..	..	..		..	6 45	..	
	Bourg ....dep.	1331	1357	19 1	19 0	..	..	2318	1 13	2 56	4 32		6 2	7 0		1026
305	Ambérieu ...... arr.	..	1435	..	↓	..	..	2348	..	3 26	..		6 27	7 32	..	11 [illegible]
0	**Lyons** (Perrache) d	..	..	↓	↓	1810	1955	2258	..	..	↓		5 30	..	8 55	1155
	,, (Brotteaux d.	..	1336	↓	↓	1825	2010	2310	..	..	↓		5 40	7 54	9 8	12 6
37	Ambérieu .... arr.	..	1442	▼	↓	19 4	2052	2345	..	..	▼		6 15	8 24	9 42	1241
..	Ambérieu ......dep.	..	1526	..	↓	19 9	2057	0 0	..	3 33	..		6 32	8 25	9 44	124[illegible]
330	Virieu-le-Grand	..	1610	..	▼	..	2140	..	..	4 17	..		..	..	..	..
337	**Culoz** (to Modane p. 265) arr.	1447	1624	1958	20 7	1953	2151	0 52	..	4 29	5 44	7 23	7 19	9 2	1030	1317
	dep.	15 8	163[illegible]	20 5	2011	1956	22 1	To Modane.	To Modane.	4 49	5 46	7 28	7 28	9 3	1033	131[illegible]
357	Bellegarde(265) arr.	1537	1712	2026	2038	2024	2233			5 23	6 22	8 4	8 4	9 25	11 2	1340
	dep.	1547	1733	2034	2045	2033	2248			..	6 34	8 22	8 22	9 31	1120	1347
377	**Geneva** (Cornav.) ar.	1625	1831	2110	2125	2112	2330			..	7 13	9 8	9 8	10 5	12 0	1423

123 Rap column (11th train column): From Vintimille & Grenobl. Special accom. see p. 292.

† Rest. Car.

** Via Chalon- to Macon & ...

L Rome luxe daily.

Z Not Suns. or Fêtes.

B From Oct. 1. **E** June 18—Oct. 1. **F** June 17—Sept. 30.

Y 1 & 2 cl. Sleep. Car, Couchettes and 1, 2 & 3 cl. Car Paris-Geneva and *v.v.*

Swiss Railways pp. 278-280, &c.	123 Rap	123 Rap	123 Exp	123 Rap	12 Rap	1/23	123 Rap	1/23 Exp	123 Exp	12/3 Exp	123 Rap	123 Rap	123 Rap	123 Exp	12 luxe
Geneva (Cornav.) dp.	From Md'ne	..	6 15	9 3	10 0	10 9	13 6	..	16 8	18 0	From Modane.	2035	2124	..	..
Bellegarde *e* .. arr.		From Modane.	6 54	9 38	1034	1059	1341	..	1643	1833		2117	2159	..	
dep.			7 18	9 58	1049	1121	14 1	..	17 3	1844		2147	2220	..	From Modane.
Culoz (*Modane Line see p.* 265) arr	5 34		7 47	1025	1113	1158	1430	..	1729	19 7		2215	2247	0 15	
dep.	5 44		7 50	1028	1126	1211	15 3	..	1731	19 8	2144	2221	2248	0 20	
Virieu-le-Grand	..	..	8 2	..	E	..	1517	..	..		..	..	↓	0 35	..
Ambérieu ...... arr.	6 26	..	8 4	1115	↓	1314	..		1822	1946	2246	..	↓	1 17	..
Ambérieu ....dep.	6 28	..	8 43	1117	↓	1322	..	..	1824	1947	..		↓	..	..
Lyons(Brotteaux)a.	7 1		9 21	1155	↓	14 0	..		1857	2020	..		↓	..	..
Lyons (Perrache)a	7 15		9 35	12 9	▼	1415	..		1911	..	..		↓	..	..
							zz								
Ambérieu ......dep.	To Bordeaux.	6 45	..	..	..	..	..	1658		..	2253		▼	1 22	..
Bourg .... arr.		7 16	..	..	1237	..	1623	1733	.	..	2323		0 6	1 49	3 11
Bourg ....dep.		7 23	..	..	1335	..	..	1823	..	..	..			..	..
											q		Y **		L
Macon........ arr.		8 0	..	..	1414	..	..	19 1	..	..	..			..	..
Bourg ....dep.		**	..	..	1240	..	1626	1753	..	..	2329		0 9	0 58	3 14
St. Amour .... ,,		..	..	..	..	..	..	1832	..	..	..		..	..	
Dijon .... arr.		10 0	..	..	1428	..	1822	2134	..	..	1 50		2 42	3 57	4 56
Paris (Lyon).... ,,		14 5	..	..	1810	..	2225	5 0	..	..	6 20		6 55	8 10	9 10

123 Rap column (12th train column): To Grenoble and Vintimille. Special accom. see p. 259.

See notes on p. 258 as to use of these trains, *f, g, ll, m, q, zz.*

Marseilles, Lyons, Besancon, Belfort (Bale), Strasbourg.

[French Rlys. (Sud-Est)

123 Exp	123 Exp	123 Rap	12 Exp	123 Rap	123	123 Exp		123 Exp	123 Rap	1/23 Rap	123 Rap	123 Exp	123 Exp	123 Rap	1/23 Exp
..	..	0 30	8 30	1127	1210	1850	dp. **Mars'lles**(*p* 261)a.	..	1917	21 5	4 29	..	..	1150	..
..	..	A	1320	1620	1850	2356	,, Lyons (Perr.) ,,	..	1415	1710	..	..	..	6 50	..
..	..	6 59	1331	1639	19 3	0 10	,, Lyons (Brot.), ,,	..	14 0	1659	23 0	..	..	6 36	..
..	..	7 58	1415	1737	20 9	1 16	a. Bourg (*above*) ..d.	..	1249	1610	22 0	..	..	5 43	..
..	..	8 1	1417	1741	2030	1 19	d. ,, a.	..	1246	16 9	2155	..	..	5 39	..
..	..	1012	..	1936	2516	3 11	,, Mouchard.. ..d.	..	1054	1453	1943	..	..	3 54	..
..	..	1059	1610	2019	2356	3 50	a. Besancon .... ,,	..	10 8	1420	1849	..	..	3 10	..
				C		B			C		A			B	
4 20	6 25	↓	↓	1831	1 45	↓	d. Dijon ..a.	9 40	1147	▲	▲	2346	1 8	▲	5 35
5 10	7 8	↓	↓	1916	2 42	↓	,, Dole (*p*.267) a	8 55	11 0	↑	↑	23 1	0 11	↑	4 42
5 47	7 42	▼	▼	1957	3 30	▼	a. Besancon . d.	8 21	1025	↑	↑	2220	2332	↑	4 5
5 58	7 48	11 9	1613	2026		4 4	d. Besancon ..ar.	8 15	9 58	1418	1839	2210	2316	3 2	
7 18	8 59	1221	1713	2137		5 14	,, Montbeliard ....d.	6 59	8 52	1321	1731	2034	2158	1 55	
7 39	9 18	1242	1727	2157	..	5 32	a. Belfort .... ,,	6 40	8 36	13 7	1714	2010	2135	1 40	
8 55	1011	1330	18 2	2236		6 10	,, Mulhouse ......,,	..	7 46	1230	1625	1827	2043	0 50	
9 41	1020	1343	1829	2332	..	7 38	d. Mulhouse .. a.	..	7 40	1157	1543	1822	2020	0 44	
1011	1051	1413	1921	24 0		8 7	a. Bale (*p*. 268) d.	..	7 10	1126	1514	1753	1936	0 20	
1153	1153	15 6	1015	2358		7 38	a. **Strasb'rg** (182/3) d.	..	6 10	1123	1453	1635	1816	23 5	

A 1st class Couchettes and 1, 2 & 3 cl. cars Vintimille, Marseilles, Strasbourg and *v.v.*

B 1 cl. Couchettes and 1, 2 and 3 cl. cars Nice—Strasbourg and *v.v.*

C 1, 2 & 3 cl. cars Vintimille—Strasbourg and *v.v.*

The times on the LEFT are to be read DOWNWARDS, those on the RIGHT UPWARDS.

	1/23	123	123 Rap	123	123 Exp	1/23	123 Rap	123 Exp	12 luxe	123 Exp	123 Rap	123 Rap
Paris (Lyon)....dep.	..	7 30	1015	13 0	14 0	..	1620	18 5	2220	2255	2330	2340
Dijon ....arr.	..	1127	14 5	1652	1821		20 4	23 5	2 8	2 52	3 54	4 10
			r				r		L			
Dijon ....dep.	7 45	12 0	1411	1713	1831	1930	2010	1 45	2 14	2 59	4 0	4 20
Dôle ....arr.	8 47	1257	1446	18 9	1913	2022	2045	2 37	..	3 34	4 41	5 0
p. 266 Dôle ....dep.	9 5	13 3	..	1814	1916	2053	..	2 42	↓	..		5 10
p. 266 Besancon (p.253) ar	9 55	14 0	..	1910	1957	2139	..	3 30		..	A	5 47
p. 266 Belfort (p. 268) ,,	1242	16 7	..	2134	2157		..	5 32		..	..	7 39
p. 266 Besancon ....dep.	..	1419	..	20 6	..	..	..	..		..	..	6 3
Morteau ....arr	..	1633	..	2222	..	..	..	..		..		8 22
Le Locle Ville¶ ,,	..	18 9	..	..	..		..	..	↓	..	..	9 58
Dôle ....dep.	8 55	..	1449	1838	..	..	2048		..	3 38	4 47	5 4
Andelot ....arr.	1018	..	1548	21 6	..	..	..		..	4 45	..	6 8
Morez (p. 279) ,,	..	..	1750	..	..	..	..		..	6 48	..	8 48
Frasne.......... ,,	1052	..	1612	2140	..		22 8	To Strasbourg.	.	5 14	6 12	6 33
Frasne ......dep.	11 1	..	1623	2145	..	..	2217		↓	5 28	..	6 36
p. 279 Pontarlier .. ,,	1120	..	1655	22 5	..	..	2236			6 30	..	6 49
p. 279 Neuchatel ¶..arr.	1350	..	1752	arr.	..	..	..			7 33	..	
p. 279 BERNE ¶ .... ,,	1522	..	1845	..	..	..	..		↓	8 33	..	..
Frasne ....dep.	1058	..	1617	..	..	..	2213			5 20	6 15	
Vallorbe c......arr.	1127	..	1640	..	..	..	2240		5 25	5 49	6 40	..
,, ¶......dep.	13*15	..	1710	..	..	..	23 4		5 45	6 19	7 14	..
Lausanne ¶ ....arr.	13*56	..	1751	..			2345		6 26	7 0	7 55	..

Thro' Services between London and Paris and Berne, Interlaken, Lausanne, Zermatt, Brigue &c., see pp. 119.

Luncheon Car Paris to Dôle.
Couchettes, Lits Salons, &c. *see pp.* 76, 119, 120.

L Simplon Exp. Daily train de luxe Paris Trieste and *v.v.* EXTRA FARES

r Rest Car.

* 3rd cl. only.

(Simplon Line, p. 280).	123 Exp	123	3 cl.	123 Rap	123 Exp	123	123	123 Rap	123 Exp	123	123 Exp	123 Exp	123 Rap	12 luxe
Lausanne ¶ ....dep.	..	..	..	6 23	..	..	..	..	16 6	..	2056	..	23 0	0 52
Cossonay ...... ,,	From Strasbourg.	..	..	..	..	..	..	..	..	..	..	..	..	..
Vallorbe ¶ ......arr.		..	..	7 5	..	..	..	..	1648	..	2138	..	2342	1 34
,, (Green.tm.) dep.		..	5 10	7 40	..	9 5	..	..	1720	..	2220	..	0 37	2 2
Frasne e ....arr.		..	5 41	8 8	..	9 36	..	..	1742	..			0 59	..
p. 279 BERNE (M.E.t.) d.		..	..	..	..	5 18	..	..	1455	..	..	17*16	2212	L
p. 279 Neuchatel ..dep.		..	..	..	..	6*52	..	..	1557	..	..	18*35	23 5	..
p. 279 Pontarlier (Gr.t.) d		..	5 31	7 43	..	9 27	..	..	1722	..	..	2210	0 42	..
Frasne ......arr.		..	5 51	8 2	..	9 46	..	..	1736	..	..	2225	0 56	..
Frasne ....dep.		..	5 56	8 10	..	9 50	..	..	1755	..	..	2226	1 12	..
Morez (p. 279) ,,		..	4 48	..	..	8 24	..	..	..	..	..	21 0	..	..
Andelot .... ,,		..	6 27	..	..	1019	..	..	1815	..	..	2249	..	..
Dôle ....arr.	..	..	7 52	9 14	..	1140	..	..	19 2	..	2359	2348	2 15	..
Le Locle Ville ¶ d.	..	..	..	Rest. Car.	7 4	9a24	..	1254	..	1812	..	..	↓	↓
Morteau .... ,,	..	..	5 42		7 42	10 2	..	1332	..	20 9	..	..		
Besançon (p 253) ar.	..	..	7 37		9 39	1154	..	1526	..	2157	..	..		
Belfort (p. 268) dep.	1 40	..	6 40		8 36	..	1045	1437	..	2010	..	2135		
Besançon .... ,,	4 5	..	8 21		1025	1228	1327	1650	h	2220	..	2332		
Dôle ....arr.	4 42	..	8 55		11 0	13 0	1424	1729	..	23 1	..	0 11		
Dôle ....dep.	4 47	6 4	8 57	9 16	11 3	13 2	1429	1733	19 3	23 4	0 12	0 25	2 16	..
Dijon..........arr.	5 35	7 5	9 40	9 52	1147	1338	1528	1815	1940	2346	0 50	1 8	2 52	4 12
		12	12	kk		r		r	r	Exp				
Dijon ....dep.	..	9 20	10 7	9 58	1225	1537	1537	1828	1946	0 8	0 55	1 18	2 57	4 27
Paris (Lyon) ..arr.	..	13 0	14 5	14 0	17 0	1925	1925	2225	2340	5 0	5 30	5 35	7 0	8 40

* 2nd and 3rd class.
For notes on h, ll, kk, see p. 258.
¶ M.E. Time.
A From Paris, June 30–Sept. 9.
B July 1–Sept. 10.
a Le Locle-Besançon July 1-Oct. 1 only.

(Geneva), Aix les Bains Annecy, Chamonix-Mont Blanc.

12 *A	1/23 †	1/23	1/23 A	1/23	1/23	1/23	1/23		123	1/23 ‡	1/23	1/23	1/23	1/23	12 *A
..	5 34	6 48	..	9 58	1247	1628	19 8	dp.**Geneva** (E.V.) arr.	8 39	1050	13 0	1452	..	2115	..
4 38	..	5 49	‡	9 20	1134	1555	..	,, Bellegarde .. ,,	9 23	1123	1331	16 9	‡		23 8
5 42	5 59	7 14	..	1043	1317	17 1	1940	dep.Annemasse ..arr.	8 15	1025	1220	1426	..	2051	22 3
6 6	6 27	7 41	..	11 7	1344	1725	20 7	arr.La Roche-sur-F. d.	7 50	10 3	1158	14 1	..	2026	2145
↓	..	5 38	7 56	9 9	1113	1536	1758	dep.Aix-les-Bains arr.	9 44	1128	14 3	1552	2043	2212	..
	..	6 33	8 50	10 6	1220	1628	1858	arr.Annecy ......dep.	8 52	1036	1318	1452	1959	2119	..
	..	6 42	8 57	1015	1252	1635	1913	dep.Annecy ......arr.	8 43	1032	1250	1445	1950	2110	..
	..	7 39	9 57	1112	1352	1729	2016	arr.La Roche-sur-F. d.	7 52	9 38	1156	1354	1855	2018	..
6 9	6 30	7 58	10 2	1118	14 4	1735	2024	dp.La Roche-sur-F.ar.	7 44	9 32	1150	1342	1847	20 9	2142
7 20	7 44	9 12	11 3	1214	1512	1839	2143	arr. Fayet (St. Gervais) d.	6 25	8 16	1043	1228	1735	1849	2038
7 35	7 58	9 29	1110	1247	1518	19 0	2158	dep. Fayet (St. Gervais) a.	..	7 53	1019	1159	1725	1832	2028
8 44	9 7	1037	1217	1354	1622	20 6	23 1	ar.Chamonix-Mt. B. d.	..	6 46	9 8	1052	1620	1720	1913
..	..	7 50	10 3	1121	14 1	1740	2026	dp.La Roche-sur-F.ar.	7 41	..	1144	1344	1847	20 7	..
..	..	8 15	1025	1148	1426	18 2	2051	arr.Annemasse ..dep.	7 14	..	1115	1317	1821	1940	..

A From and to Paris.
* July 1–Sept 1.
‡ July 8–Sept 17.
† Suns. and Fete days only.

RAILWAY MAP

OF

NORTHERN AND CENTRAL GERMANY,
CZECHO-SLOVAKIA AND POLAND

See

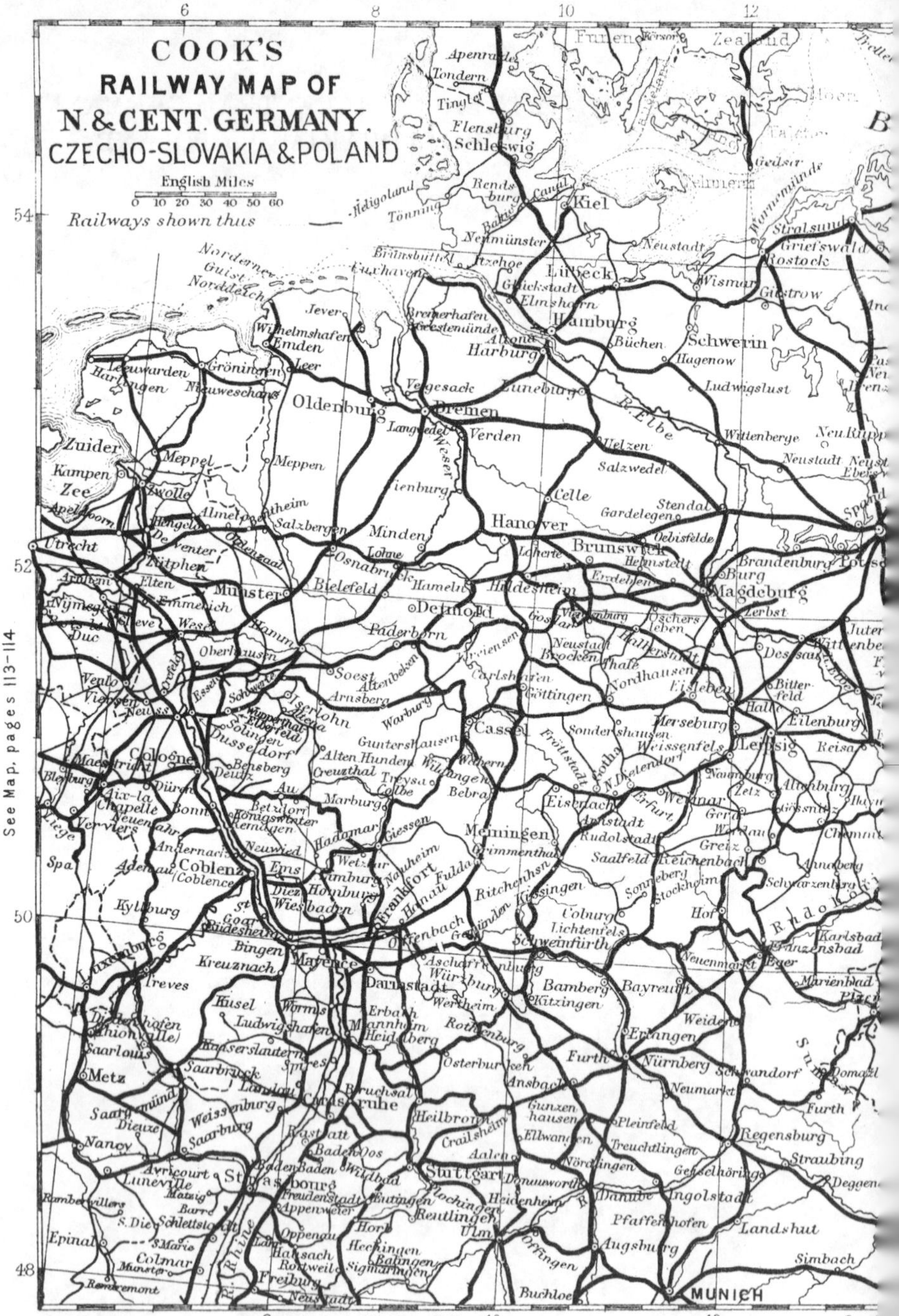

See Map. pages 113–114

(219/1/39.J) Entered at Stationers Hall.

See Map. pag

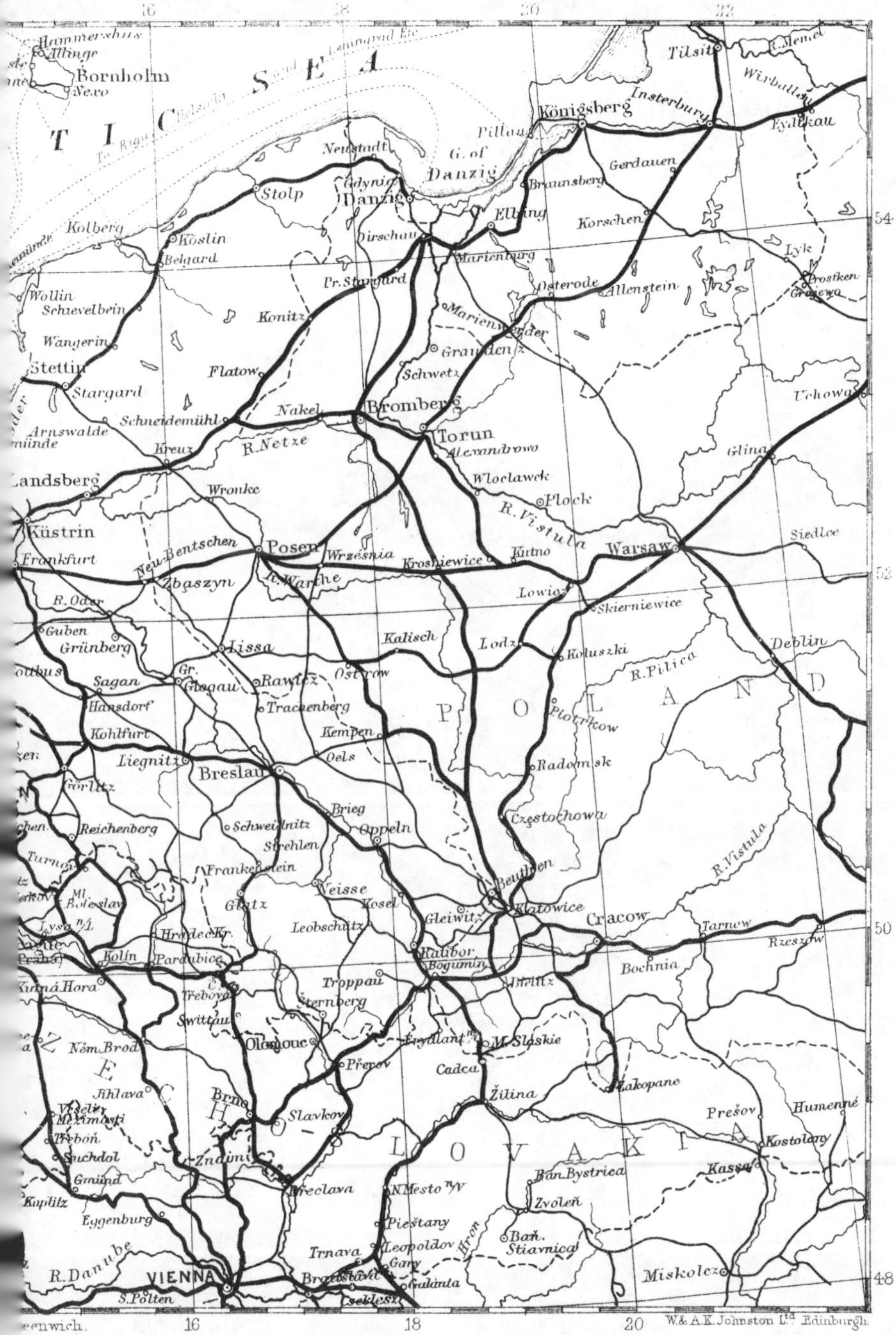

Bornholm
Allinge
Nexo
Hammershus
S E A
T I C
Königsberg
Insterburg
Tilsit
R. Memel
Wirballen
Eydtkau
Pillau
G. of
Danzig
Neustadt
Gdynia
Danzig
Stolp
Kolberg
Köslin
Belgard
Braunsberg
Gerdauen
Korschen
Elbing
Dirschau
Marienburg
Lyk
Prostken
Grajewo
Osterode
Allenstein
Pr. Stargard
Konitz
Marienwerder
Graudenz
Schwetz
Wollin
Schievelbein
Wangerin
Stettin
Stargard
Flatow
Uchowa
Nakel
Bromberg
Schneidemühl
Torun
Alexandrowo
Arnswalde
Kreuz
R. Netze
Glina
Wloclawek
Plock
Landsberg
Wronke
R. Vistula
Küstrin
Posen
Września
Warsaw
Siedlce
Frankfurt
Neu-Bentschen
Zbąszyn
R. Warthe
Kroshiewice
Kutno
Lowicz
Skierniewice
R. Oder
Guben
Grünberg
Lissa
Kalisch
Lodz
Koluszki
R. Pilica
Deblin
Sagan
Gr. Glogau
Rawicz
Ostrow
Hansdorf
Trachenberg
P O L A N D
Piotrkow
Kohlfurt
Kempen
Liegnitz
Breslau
Oels
Radomsk
Görlitz
Brieg
Reichenberg
Schweidnitz
Oppeln
Częstochowa
Strehlen
Frankenstein
Beuthen
R. Vistula
Ml. Boleslav
Glatz
Neisse
Kosel
Gleiwitz
Katowice
Cracow
Tarnow
Rzeszow
Leobschütz
Hradec Kr.
Ratibor
Bogumin
Kolin
Pardubice
Bochnia
Troppau
Bielitz
Kutná Hora
C. Trebová
Šternberg
Swittau
Olomouc
Frydlant
M. Slaskie
Něm. Brod
Cadca
Přerov
Jihlava
Brno
Žilina
Zakopane
Prešov
Humenné
Veselí
Slavkov
Třeboň
Kostolany
Suchdol
Znojmo
L O V A K I A
Kassa
Ban. Bystrica
Gmünd
Breclava
N. Mesto n/V
Zvoleň
Eggenburg
Pieštany
Ban. Stiavnica
Hron
Trnava
Leopoldov
Gary
Miskolcz
R. Danube
VIENNA
Bratislava
Galánta
S. Pölten
16
18
20
22
54
52
50
48
W. & A. K. Johnston Ltd Edinburgh.

RAILWAY MAP

OF

NORTHERN AND CENTRAL GERMANY,

CZECHO-SLOVAKIA AND POLAND

Paris, Chaumont, Belfort, Bale (Delle, Berne). [French Rlys. (Est).

Mls.	Thro' Tables, see pp. 269-271, 123, 124.	123	123	123	123	123	12	123	12	123	123	12
		g r Rap	r C Exp	V b Rap	D e Rap	b r Rap	L luxe		Rap	S g Rap	Z j Exp	h Rap
	Paris ....dep.	8 5	9 0	1155	1430	1715	1955	2015		22 0	2250	..
104	Troyes...... arr.	9 48	1047	1338	1613	19 5		2250	..	2356	..	B
	Troyes...... dep.	9 53	1052	1340	1618	1910		23 5	..	0 0	..	..
163	Chaumont ..arr.	A	1211	1448	1723	2015	23 0	0 50	..	1 18	2 1	
	Reims (p. 270) dep.			12 7	r				..	2125	..	0 2
	Chalons (p. 270) ,,			1259		..	..	.	2231	2236	..	0 42
	Chaumont ..dep.		1214	15 2	1727	2020	2331	4 5	0 20	1 24	2 7	2 28
184	Langres (p. 271) ..		1243	1535		2049		5 20		..	2 39	
208	Vitrey-Vernois			1612	..			6 26		S	..	
	Bourbonne-l-Bs. a		13p0	1641	..	..		..	SUSPENDED	..	7a10	
224	Port d'Atelier p. 271			1640	..	2133		7 4		..		
237	Veso'l (p. 253) arr.		1339	1657	1844	2149		7 31		..	3 38	
	Veso'l (p. 253) dep.		1341	17 0	1846	2152		7 46		..	3 41	
	p. 271 Nancy-Ville dep.	8 55		1134	16 3	1940		5 56		..	..	
	p. 271 Aillevillers .. ,,	1025		13 5	1736	2119		7 30		..	..	
	p. 271 Lure........arr.	1053	k..	1332	18 3	2149		7 59		..	..	
255	Lure ....dep.		14 5	1727	r	2217		8 25		.		
275	**Belfort** (p. 266) arr.	1255	1429	18 0	1935	2243	1 29	arr.	2 43	3 48	4 37	4 49
	Belfort ......dep.	13 2	1435		1945	2250	1 35		3 5	4 15	4 45	4 55
305	Mulhouse ....arr.	1335	1510		2020	2329	2 8	..	3 48	5 6	5 20	5 27
326	**Bale** (Sw.)(G.T.) arr.	14 3	1537		2051	24 0	2 35		4 16	5 42	6 22	5 53
	Belfort ......dep.		1440		1955	..	5 10	..	2 51	..	5 10	5 10
289	Delle (G.T.) arr.	..	15 7		2022	..	5 37	..	3 20	..	5 37	5 37
	,, Mid-E. tm.) dep.		1523	..	2032	..	6 0	..	4 35	..	6 0	6 0
296	Porrentruy....arr.	..	1539	..	2045	..	6 13	..	4 48	..	6 13	6 13
313	Délémont .... ,,	.	1622		2133	..	7 3	.	5 37	..	7 3	7 3
363	Berne (p. 278) ,,	..	1740	..	2253	..	8 24	..	7 0	..	8 24	8 24

a Takes 3 cl. 156 mls. or more. *b* 3 cl. not less than 125 mls. *c* 2 cl. for 94 mls. and 3 cl. 156 mls. or upwards. *d* 2 cl. for 125 mls. and 3 cl. 220 mls. or more. *e* Takes 3 cl. for 187 mls. or upwards. *f* Takes 2 cl. at Langres for Paris only and 3 cl. 250 mls. or more. *g* Only takes 3 cl. 220 mls. or more. *h* Only takes local passengers 187 mls. or more. *i* 3 cl. not less than 217 mls. *j* 3 cl. not less than 156 mls. *l* From Troyes only takes 3 cl. for 125 miles or more. *m* 3 cl. not less than 94 miles. † 2 and 3 cl. only.

	123	123	123	123	123	123	12	12	123	12
	fast	Rap	Rap	Rap	Exp	Exp	Rap	Rap	Rap	luxe
Berne (p. 278) dep.	..	6 30	..	1337	..	..	2338	2250	2250	22¶50
Délémont .... ,,		7 53	..	1456	..	..		0 12	0 12	0 12
Delle c (M.E.T.) ar	..	8 33		1540	..	..	0 35	0 58	0 58	0 58
,, (G.T.) dep.	..	8 48		1558	..	..	2355	1 18	1 18	1 18
Belfort ......arr.	..	9 15	r	1625		..	0 24	1 46	1 46	1 46
		123 r m	f	A i r	l V	Z		B h	S c	L
Bale (Sw.)(G.T.) dp.	..	7 47	1126	1514	17 8	23 0		0 30	0 40	3 20
Mulhouse ...... ,,	6 19	8 20	12 0	1547	1744	2335		1 2	1 18	3 46
Petit-Croix....dep.	7 29	D		..	..			..		
Belfort........arr.	7 44	9 0	1252	1621	1821	0 21		1 42	2 0	4 28
Belfort ......dep.	7 49	9 23	13 6	1633	1825	0 27	1 0	1 58	2 10	4 34
Lure ....arr.	8 14		1335			0 51	..			
Lure ....dep.		9b30	13‡21	17†5	19*33		SUSPENDED			
Aillevillers ..arr.		10 3	1354	1732	20 1	..				
Nancy-Ville ,,		1150	1523	19 9	2147					
Veso'l (p. 253) arr.	8 38	10 4	14 0	1714	19 6	1 14				
Veso'l (p. 253) dep.	8 41	10 6	14 3	1716	1911	1 17				
Port d'Atelier	8 59	..	1423							
Bourbonne-le-B. d	8 46		1418		17t24	19a9				
Vitrey...........	9 25		1450							
Langres..........	10 9	11 6	1540		2021	2 43	..			
Chaumont ..arr.	1034		16 6		2047	3 11	3 14	4 7	4 15	6 40
Chalons .... ,,	1415	..	18 6			5 27	5 5	5 53	..	..
Reims ...... ,,	..		1932		..	6 51	..	6 48	..	
Chaumont ..dep.	1040		1612		2052	3 17	..	..	4 21	6 54
Troyes .... arr.	1151	1226	1722	1934	2156	4 26	..	..	5 21	
Troyes .... dep.	1156	1231	1725	1939	2159	4 31	..	..	5 24	..
Paris (Est) ..arr.	1411	1415	1930	2125	2345	6 45	..	..	7 15	9 45

A 1 and 2 cl. Cars Paris-Bucharest; 2 and 3 cl. Cars Paris-Belgrade; 3 cl. Car Paris Budapest and *v.v.*
B Anglo-Swiss Express, *see pages* 123/5.
C 1, 2 and 3 cl. Cars Paris-Berne-Milan. Paris-Interlaken, from July 1 to Sept. 29. 1, 2 and 3 cl. Paris-Bale.
D 1 and 2 cl. Cars Paris-Berne-Milan-Venice and *v.v.*, 3 cl. Paris-Berne-Milan, 1, 2 and 3 cl. Cars Bucharest and *v.v.*
L Arlberg Exp. Mon., Wed., Fri., from Paris-Vienna, Sleep. Cars only, 1 and 2 cl. For Engadine Exp. to Coire and Oberland Exp. to Interlaken, see *p.* 85.
S 1 and 2 cl. Sleep. Car Paris-Bale-Innsbruck & *v.v.*, 3 cl. Sleep. Car Paris-Innsbruck & *v.v.* June 26-Sept. 5. 1 and 2 cl. Cars Paris-Budapest and *v.v.*, 3 cl. car Paris-Vienna and *v.v.*, 1, 2 & 3 cl. sleeper Paris-Lucerne June 30-Sept. 9 out, July 1-Sept. 10 home.
Z 1, 2 and 3 cl. cars Paris-Coire, 1 and 2 cl. Sleeping Cars Paris-Coire and *v.v.*, 1, 2 and 3 cl. Sleeping Car Paris-Interlaken and *v.v.*

a Change at Chalindrey. *b* dep. Belfort 9.5. *k* arr. Belfort 11.21. *t* arr. Langres 19.32. † dep. Belfort 16.42. *p* dep. Langres 12.11. * dep. Belfort 19.10. ‡ dep. Belfort 12.58. *r* Rest. Car. **V** Rest. Car Bar.

Paris & Zurich to Coire, & Germany (Arlberg Route), Yugo Slavia
(Tauern Route)

123	123	123	12	123	123				123	123	123	12	123	123
Fr		D r	C	A	E				Fr	E	A	C	D	r
8 5	9 0	1430	1955	22 0	2250	dep. PARIS (Est) ..	p.268	arr.	2125	6 45	7 15	9 45	1415	1930
1335	1510	2020	2 8	5 6	5 20	arr. Mulhouse ..		d.	1547	2335	1 18	3 46	8 20	12 0
1338	1512	2023	2 9	5 9	5 56	dep. Mulhouse ..		a.	1543	2329	1 9	3 45	8 15	1157
14 3	1537	2051	2 35	5 42	6 22	arr. *BALE (Swiss)		dep.	1514	23 0	0 40 r	3 20	7 47	1126
1454	1714	2138	2 48	6 49	7 40	dep. §BALE (Sw.)	p. 283	arr.	1425	22 5	2350	2 54	6 45	8 40
1614	1831	2256	4 † 1	8 † 7	9 8	a. ZURICH ..		d.	1312	2042	2236	1†39	5 35	7 22
1624	18‖38	2312	4 † 3	8 † 9	9 20	d. ZURICH ..		a.	1250	2029	2229	1†38	5 28	..
1746	20 8	0 29	5 21	9 22	1051	arr. Sargans		dep.	1130	1859	21 9	0 23	4 13	..
1819	2021	↓	7 13	↓	11 7	arr. Landquart ..	p.286	dp.	11 7	1842	..	..	↑	..
20 5	22 5		9‖12	‖	1240	arr. Davos		dp.	9 30	17 5		19 0		..
1841	20‖34		7 30		1122	arr. COIRE		dp.	1052	1830	..	2239		..
22 0		↓	1012	↓	1444	arr. St. Moritz ..		dp.	8 0	1545	..	2015		..
1810	2050	0 52	5 40	9 40	1144	arr. Buchs c ..	p.197	dp.	11 8	1830	2050	0 0	3 50	..
1840		1 10	5 55	10 0	1220	dep. Buchs c ..		arr	1045	1816	2025	2345	3 30	..
19 0		1 28	6 10	1017	1250	arr. Feldkirch ..		dep.	1026	1750	20 7	2328	3 12	..
21 8	..	..	7 40	1052	1357	arr. Bregenz ..		dep.	9 16	1652	1815	2241	..	..
2218		4 40	8 52	13 8	1555	arr. INNSBRUCK ..		dep.	7 20	1452	1715	2040	0 12	..
2240		4 50	..	1320		dep. Innsbruck ..	p.197	arr.	6 50	1355		..	24 0	..
3 12	..	9 30	..	1718	..	arr. Bad Gastein	p.197	dep	2 30	10 5	..	..	1944	..
5 5		1143		2018	..	arr. Villach		dep.	0 40	7 58	.	..	1718	
6 45		1556	..	..	..	arr. Assling c	p.199	dep.	2320	..	..	..	1136	..
7 45		1825	..		..	dep. c Jesenic		arr.	2215	..		.	1110	..
2015		6 20	..		..	arr. BELGRADE		dep	9 21	..	..	..	2312	..
2240	..	4 50	9 0	1320	1620	dep. Innsbruck	p. 197	ar.	6 50	1355	1655	2033	24 0	..
2 50	..	9 10	1257	1730	2040	arr. Salzburg		dp.	2 30	9 30	1250	1640	1945	..
8 0		14 5	1715	2218	..	arr. VIENNA (W)		dp.	2135	..	8 5	1220	1428	..
14 0		1945	2120	6 20	..	arr. Budapest........		dep.	16 0	..	2335	8 15	9 25	..

* Greenwich time. § Mid-European time. ‖ 2nd and 3rd cl. only.

E 1 and 2 cl. Sleep. Car Paris-Coire, 1, 2 and 3 cl. Cars Paris-Bale-Coire and v.v.; 1, 2 and 3 cl. Cars Bale-Salzburg and v.v.; Rest. Car. Bale-Coire and v.v.

r Rest. Car. † Zurich Enge.

A 1 & 2 cl. Sleep. Car Paris-Bale-Innsbruck, 3 cl. Sleeper Paris-Innsbruck & *v.v.*, from June 26-Sept. 5 with 1 and 2 cl. Cars Paris-Budapest; 3 cl. Car Paris-Vienna and *v.v.*, Rest. Car Bale-Vienna and *v.v.*
C Arlberg–Orient Express, 1 & 2 cl. Sleep. Cars only—Mons., Weds. & Fris. Paris to Vienna, Bucharest, Belgrade and Athens and *v.v.*; also Paris-Coire, days of running, *see page* 85. Rest. Car Paris-Chaumont and *v.v.*
D 1, 2 & 3 cl. Car Paris–Bucharest and *v.v.* 1 & 2 cl. Sleeping Car Bale-Vienna and Vienna to Belfort.
F 3 cl. Cars Paris-Budapest and *v.v.*, 1 and 2 cl. Sleeping Car Zurich-Vienna and *v.v.*, 1 and 2 cl. car Paris-Bucharest and *v.v.*, 2 & 3 cl. cars Paris-Belgrade and *v.v.*, Rest. Car Paris-Bale.

THROUGH SERVICES via Delle—BERNE.
To Interlaken, Loetschberg, Milan.

123	123	12	123	Mls.				123	123	123	12
E	A	C	B D					A	E	B D	C
9 0	1430	1955	2250	0	dep. PARIS (Est)	p268	.. arr.	1415	2125	7 15	9 45
15 7	2022	5 37	5 37	..	arr. Delle		.. dep.	8 48	1558	1 18	1 18
1523	2032	6 0	6 0	289	dep. Delle		.. arr.	8 33	1540	0 58	0 58
1740	2256	8 24	8 24	330	arr. Berne		.. dep.	6 30	1337	2250	2250
18 9	2338	8 51	8 46	..	dep. Berne ..	p.281	.. arr.	6 11	1321	2236	2227
1848	0 33	9 29	9 22	355	arr. Spiez		dep.	5 27	1245	2158	2150
1858		9 40	9 24		dep. Spiez		arr.	5 22	1243	2147	2147
1929	..	10 9	9 48	391	arr. Interlaken (East)		dp.	5†a0	1215	2112	2117
18 6	2117	..	9 2	..	dep. Interlaken (East)		ar.	7 54	1320	2218	†..
1853	0 36	..	9 38	..	dep. Spiez	p.288	arr.	5 25	1231	2149	..
1930	1 12	..	1014	375	arr. Kandersteg....		dep.	4 46	1156	2115	..
2017	1 58	..	11 3	402	arr. Brigue		dep.	4 2	1110	2030	..
2120	2 56	..	1157	427	arr. Domodossola		dep.	3 5	10 5	1930	..
2140	3 30	..	1217		dep. Domodossola		arr.	2 40	9 30	1912	..
2219	4 4	..	13 1	452	arr. Stresa		dep.	1 57	8 45	1826	..
24 0	5 50	..	1435	504	arr. MILAN		dep.	0 15	6 50	1645	..
3 39	9 9	..	1752	554	arr. Genoa		dep	2120	1 * 9	1235	..

† Interlaken (West). * 2 and 3 cl. only. a 3rd class.

A 3 cl. Cars Paris-Milan and *v.v.*, 1 & 2 cl. Paris-Venice and *v.v.* **B** 1, 2 & 3 cl. Sleeper Paris-Interlaken and *v.v.* **C** Oberland Express from Calais and Paris. Rest. Car Bienne-Berne and Spiez-Berne Days of running, *see p.* 85. **D** 1, 2 & 3 cl. Cars Paris-Milan and *v.v.* Rest. Car Milan-Berne and *v.v.* **E** 1, 2 & 3 cl. Car Paris-Milan and *v.v.* 1 & 2 cl. cars Paris-Interlaken, from July 1-Sept. 29, from Interlaken July 2-Sept. 30. Rest. Car Paris-Belfort

Paris, Lucerne, and Italy via the St. Gothard.

123	123	123	123	123	Mls.		123	123	123	123	123
8 5	9 0	1430	22 0	2250	0	dep. PARIS (Est) } p. 268 a.	6 45	7 15	1415	1930	2125
1335	1510	2020	5 6	5 20		arr. Mulhouse .. } p. 268 d.	2335	1 18	8 20	12 0	1547
14 3	1537	2051	5 42	6 22	326	arr. BALE (Swiss) } p. 268 d.	23 0	0 40	7 47	1126	1514
C r		s	r A	r D			D r E	12 r	s		r C
1450	1730	2142	6 42	6 54	..	d. BALE (Sw.) (p. 282) a.	22 0	2341	6 16	8 55	1415
1617	1853	2320	7 55	8 28	385	arr. Lucerne d	2041	2230	4 47	7 23	1253
1627	1858	0 5	8 7	8 40		dep. Lucerne a	2028	2219	4 39	6 44	1242
1940	2150	3 3	1045	1141	494	arr. Bellinzona (p. 287) d.	1717	1945	1 49	3 7	9 41
2010	2239	5 51	1120	1226	..	,, Locarno ,,	1617	1743	2259	..	8 52
..	.	5 5	1254	1254	529	,, Luino .... ,,	1610	..	22 0	..	8 42
..	..	..	..	1450	..	dep. Novara .. ,,	1414	..	..	..	
	..	..	..	2145	..	arr. Genoa .... ,,	9 20		..	..	
2050	2247	4 15	1140	1248	520	,, } Chiasso c dp.	16 8	1850	0 35	2 7	8 32
2114	23 7	4 50	12 0	1323		d. } Chiasso c ar.	1548	1822	0 5	1 43	8 10
2122	2324	4 58	12 8	1331	523	arr. Como .. p. 304 dp.	1538	1812	2355	1 33	8 0
2230	0 5	5 58	13 7	1445	553	,, MILAN .. p. 304 ,,	1424	1710	2253	0 25	6 50
4 40	5 25	1025	1740	2012	697	arr. Venice } p. 305 dep.	8 40	1215	1815	1938	1 25
7 0	8 28	14 3	2034	2310	..	,, Trieste } p. 305 ,,	6 0	9 30	1343	1645	2225
			12	123			12				
0 30	..	6 25	1334	15 5	..	dep. MILAN.... } p. 301 ar.	14 2	1634	2230	2357	5 34
3 39	..	9 10	1545	1752	646	ar. Genoa .... } p. 301 dp.	1140	1433	1946	2113	! 4
1310	..	1530	2350	6 55	954	,, ROME .... ,,	2350	2350	1220	1220	18 0
..	..	1756	9 52	9 52	..	,, Naples (C) ,,	2018	2018	9a52	9a52	13a0
..	..	..	1016	1016	..	,, NAPLES (Merg.) ..	2135	2135	10C2	10C2	1312
		12 x	1cl c	12 x				12	12	1cl. x	
2250	..	6 50	1350	1520	..	dep. MILAN .... } p. 303 arr.	9 0	1617	22 0	19 0	5 10
1 57	...	9 36	1543	1733	..	arr. Bologna .. dep.	5 38	1310	1943	17 5	1 25
3 25	..	1140	1638	1855	770	,, FLORENCE ,,	4 5	1126	1820	1611	23 1
8 0	..	1530	1950	2255	966	,, ROME .... ,,	2350	7 10	1425	13 0	18 5
..	..	1838	2310	3 8	..	,, Naples (C) ,,	2035	3 53	1140	..	
1038	..	1836	..	..		,, NAPLES (Merg.) ..	20 0	3 49	..	..	1316
		12	12	12						12 x	
0 25	x	7 55	1530	1530		dep. MILAN........arr.	6 22	1140	..	22 0	6 22
1635	..	23 0	3 36	3 36	1015	arr. Foggia .. } p. 313 dep.	1843	0 38	..	7 16	1357
2045	..	6 10	8 13	8 13	1188	,, Naples .. ,,	1455	2037	..	0 13	9 28
23 4		6 21	7 59	7 59	1159	,, Brindisi ,,	15 5	2022	..	..	8 57

† Venice Mestre Stn. ‡ 1 & 2 class.

a Naples (Piazza Garibaldi) * Sunds.

A 1 & 2 cl. Sleeping Car Paris-Lucerne June 20-Sept. 9; 3 cl. Car Paris-Milan, dep. Bale 6.54, dep. Milan 14.20, see p. 287.
C 1 & 2 cl. cars Paris-Milan and v.v.
D 1 and 2 cl. Sleeping Car and 1, 2 and 3 cl. Cars Paris-Bale and v.v.
E 3 cl. car Milan-Paris. 1 and 2 cl. Sleeping Car Lucerne-Paris July 1-Sept. 10.
c 1st class Rapido only. r Rest. car.
s 1 & 2 cl. Sleeping Car Bale-Genoa on odd dates; Genoa-Bale, even dates.
x Rapide, with supplement (1 & 2 class).

(Boulogne) (Calais) Laon, Reims, Chalons, Chaumont (Bale).

Through Tables see pp. 123, 124. [French Rlys. (Nord & Est).

Mls.		1/23	1/23	1/23	1/23	123	1/23	123	1/23	123	12	12
	Boulogne......dep.	..	..	..	..	Exp	..	..	..	Exp	..	2030
..	Calais .... (p. 236 or 237)	..	..	..	..	6 5	..	..	..	1234	1725 L	A ¶
0	Laon .... ,,	..	..	..	7 22	1110	1120	1442	1750	2024	2037	2321
33	**Reims** ...... arr.	..	..	..	8 25	1155	1222	1543	1855	21 7		0 1
	Reims ...... dep.	..	5 22	7 14	9 31	12 7	1256	1615	..	2125	..	0 2
68	**Chalons-sur-Marne** b arr.	..	6 40	8 25	1030	1254	1357	1716	..	2217	..	0 40 ¶
	(p. 272) dep.	5 5	..	8 46	..	1259	16 0	1724	..	2236	..	0 42
	Vitry-le-francois ..	7 14	..	10 7	..	1324	1643	18 3	..	23 3	..	
153	**Chaumont** ....arr.	9 45	..	1153	..	1452	1931	arr.	..	0 39	2319	2 22
	Bale (p. 268) ,,	1537			..	2051	24 0	..	..	5 42	2 35	5 53

¶ These trains do not enter Reims but call at Reims-Bethany where local trains carry passengers and baggage to and from Reims.

Mls.		123	123	12	1/23	123	12	1/23	1/23	1/23	123
..	Bale (p. 268) ..dep.	..	23 0	0 30	..	..	3 20	..	..	..	1126
..	**Chaumont** .... ,,	..	3 27	4 13	..	4 57	7 15	..	12 0	1318	1626
..	Vitry-le-françois	..	4 58	B	5 54	7 37	..	1048	1353	16 8	..
..	**Chalons-sur-Marne** .... arr.	..	5 27	5 53	6 30	8 0	.. L	1111	1415	1635	18 6
	Chalons-sur-Marne .... dep.	..	5 47	5 58	6 45	..	..	1116	15 0	..	1814
..	**Reims** ...... arr.	..	6 51	6 48	7 44	..	..	1226	1559	..	1932
	Reims ...... dep.	5 27	7 7	6 57	9 45	..	..	1234	1718	..	1937
..	Laon ....arr.	6 40	7 55	7 47	1048	...	10 5	1335	1822	..	2020
..	Bo'logn (236, 237) a.	..	..		..	..	13 0	..	..	..	..
..	Calais ....arr.	1211	..	1136	..	..	..	1944	..	..	..

A. B. Only take local passengers on Est Rly, for 187 miles or more.

L Arlberg-Orient Express.

Paris, Reims, Mezieres, Givet, Namur. [French Rlys. (Est & Nord-Belge).

1/23	1/23	1/23	1/23	123	123	123	123	Mls.		123	123	1/23	123	1/23	1/23	123	1/23	123
				Exp	Rap	Exp	Exp			Exp	Exp		Rap			Exp		Rap
..	8 0	..	..	1422	1831	22 0	2240	0	dep. **Paris** (Est) .. arr.	9 0	11 8	..	1356	..	..	19 0	..	2250
..	9 57	..	..	16 4	2016	0 11	1 27	98	arr. Reims ......dep.	7 0	9 24	..	12 5	..	..	1712	..	2057
	V	..	B		V								V B			B		V
..	10 2	..	..	16 9	2021	0 16	1 40	98	dep. **Reims** ...... arr.	6 52	9 18	..	1159	..	..	17 7		2051
..	1124	..	..	1727	2135	1 28	3 27	153	arr. Mezières .. Charlevll. d.	5 37	8 10	..	1052		..	1553		1942
8 6	1130	13 7	1551	1842	2150	..	4 33		dep. Mezières Charlevll. a	..	7 29	9 27	..	1142	14 8	1532	17 7	1910
9 38	1254	1437	1653	2016	2320	..	6 37	198	arr. Givet.... dep.	..	5 52	7 56	..	1011	1236	1427	1530	1737
1030	..	1524	18 5	2041	..	..	6 56		dep. Givet.... arr.	..		7 30	..	10 6	1211	1415	1415	1637
11 8	..	16 0	1843	2118	..	..	7 33	237	arr. Dinant ......dep.	..	..	6 57	..	9 37	1137	1342	1342	16 6
1152	..	1643	1928	22 0	..		8 13	252	,, Namur ...... ,,	..	..	6 10	..	9 3	1052	1255	1255	1510

B Auto-Rail Mezieres-Givet and *v.v.* **V** Buffet Car.

† Maritime Stn.]

(Calais), Valenciennes, Mezieres, Sedan, Nancy. [French Rlys. (Nord & Est).

..	..	..	5 24	..	..	12 7	1444	1758	dep. Calais (p. 236) arr.	15†34	15†34	21 3	..	..	..	10†24
..	..	..	8 21	..	..	1454	1847	22 7	,, Valenciennes ,,	11 7	13 7	18 5	..	..	2252	7 55
..	..	..	8 55	..	..	1532	1932	2246	,, Aulnoye	1020	1233	1728	..	..	2217	7 20
..	..	..	9 25	..	..	1617	2027	2333	arr. Hirson .. dep.	9 34	1152	1642	..	..	2147	6 33
..	..	..	9 26	..	..	1623	2034	2342	dep. Hirson .. arr.	9 23	1151	1639	..	..	2145	6 10
..	..	..	1019	..	..	1724	2132	0 39	arr. Mezières Char. dp.	8 16	1054	1544		..	2049	5 13
2240	..	..	..	8 0	..	1422	1831	22 0	dep. **Paris** .... arr.	11 8	1356	..	19 0	2250	..	9 0
4 13	5 48	9 37	1023	1131	1338	1736	2145	1 42	,, Mezières Char. ,,	8 1	1043	1439	1539	1933	2044	5 5
4 32	6 31	9 56	..	1150	14 9	1755	22 4	2 1	arr. Sedan ......dep.	7 41	1023	1349	1519	1913	2023	4 44
6 5	8 54	1122	1132	1258	1614	19 4	23 8	2 52	arr. Longuyon ..dep.	6 38	9 24	1155	1426	1816	1934	3 47
..	..	1314	1314	1429	2030	2030	0 20	8 17	,, Luxemburg ,,	4 23	7 53	..	13 0	1653	1653	2243
8 33	..	1325	1244	..	20 6	2039	0 37	5 30	,, Metz ...... ,,	3 54	7 55	..	1250	14 7	1817	1 22
7 47	1117	..	1248	..	20 4	2037	..		,, Pagny-s-Mosel ,,	..		1017	1256	..	..	..
8 23	1154	..	1324	..	2058	2111	..	8 23	,, Nancy-Ville.. ,,	..	7 9	9 23	1219	..	17 8	..

Thro' accommodation see p. 126. * 1 & 2 cl. only.

Vesoul, Port d'Atelier, Plombieres (Epinal). [French Rlys. (Est).

123	123	1/23	123	1/23	1/23	1/23	1/23		1/23	1/23	123	1/23	1/23	123	1/23	123	123
..	22 0	..	..	..	..	1155	..	dep. **Paris** (*p.* 268.) arr.		1411	..	1930	..	..	..	..	6 45
Paris dep. 22.40 *via* Nancy	..	..	7 56	1248	..	1620	1815	,, Vesoul ...... ,,	8 14	9 26	..	1444	19 5	2149	..	arr. Paris 6.55 *via* Nancy.	..
	3 0	..	8 38	1313	..	1653	1856	,, Port d'Atelier ,,	7 56	8 51	..	1418	1830	2122	..		1 11
	3 26	..	9 17	1343	..	1731	1932	arr. Aillevillers ..dep.	7 35	8 11		1348	1755	21 0	..		0 44
	6 20	..	1028	14 2	.	18 5		dep. Aillevillers arr.	.	8 5	..	1320	1722	1952	..		↑
	6 44		1055	1429	.	1829	..	arr. Plombières dep.	..	7 42		1251	1659	1929	..		
	..	5 55	9 5	1258	1356	1642	1910	dep. Belfort (*p.* 268) ar.	8 22	..	1121	1355	1826	..	2219		
	..	6 18	9 30	1321	1430	17 5	1933	,, Lure .... ,,	7 59	..	1053	1332	18 3		2149		
	3 30	6 48	10 3	1356	15 8	1738	20 3	,, Aillevillers .. ,,	7 29	8 8	1023	13 4	1735	2057	2117	.	0 43
4 52	4 20	7 21	1043	1427	1550	1812	2040	arr. Epinal ......dep.	6 57	7 14	9 50	1233	17 4	2018	2034	2248	0 1
6 45	6 45	9*23	12*31	..	1834	..*	2229	,, Gerardmer ,,	4*54	4*54	7*18	10*12		1848	1848	2110	..
..	5 45	8 22	1150	1523	1655	19 9	2147	,, Nancy-Ville.. ,,	5 56	..	8 55	1134	16 3	19 9	1940		2243

† Auto-Rail. * By Autobus.

(Paris), Langres, Vittel, Contrexeville, Nancy (Paris) [French Rlys. (Est)

1/23	1/23	1/23	1/23	1/23	1/23	1/23	1/23	1/23		1/23	1/23	1/23	1/23	123	1/23
..	..	0 10	..	7 25	..	1159	1159	1740	dep. **Paris** .... arr.	1230	1654		2341	6 55	..
..	..	6 3	7 32	12 9	1555	1757	1915	2231	,, Nancy-Ville ,,	8 43	1030	1646	1850	2120	..
4 58	..	8 2	8 53	1323	17 4	19 9	20 2	2349	,, Mirecourt.... ,,	7 35	9 9	15 5	1742	1926	2236
5 25	..	8 40	9 14	1355	1747	arr.	2022	arr.	,, Vittel ......dep.	7 1	8 43	1431		1833	22 9
5 31	..	8 47	9 20	14 3	1755	..	2028	..	,, Contrexeville ,,	6 51	8 37	1422	..	1822	22 3
5 41	dep.	8 59	9 28	1416	18 8	..	2038	..	,, Martigny- -B ,,	6 37	8 28	14 8	..	18 8	2154
6 4	9 38	9 32	9 48	1438	1842	..	2058	..	arr. Merrey ...... ,,	6 4	8 5	1335	.	1731	2130
6 43	10 3	1112	..	1530	1939	..	2137	..	,, Langres .... ,,	5 10	7 19	1249	..	1628	2055
1411	1411	..	..	1930	2345	..	A	..	,, **Paris**........ ,,	2250	..	9 0	..	1155	1715

A July 1—Sept. 15.

Cook's Tourist Map

of

SOUTHERN and CENTRAL FRANCE

See Map, pa

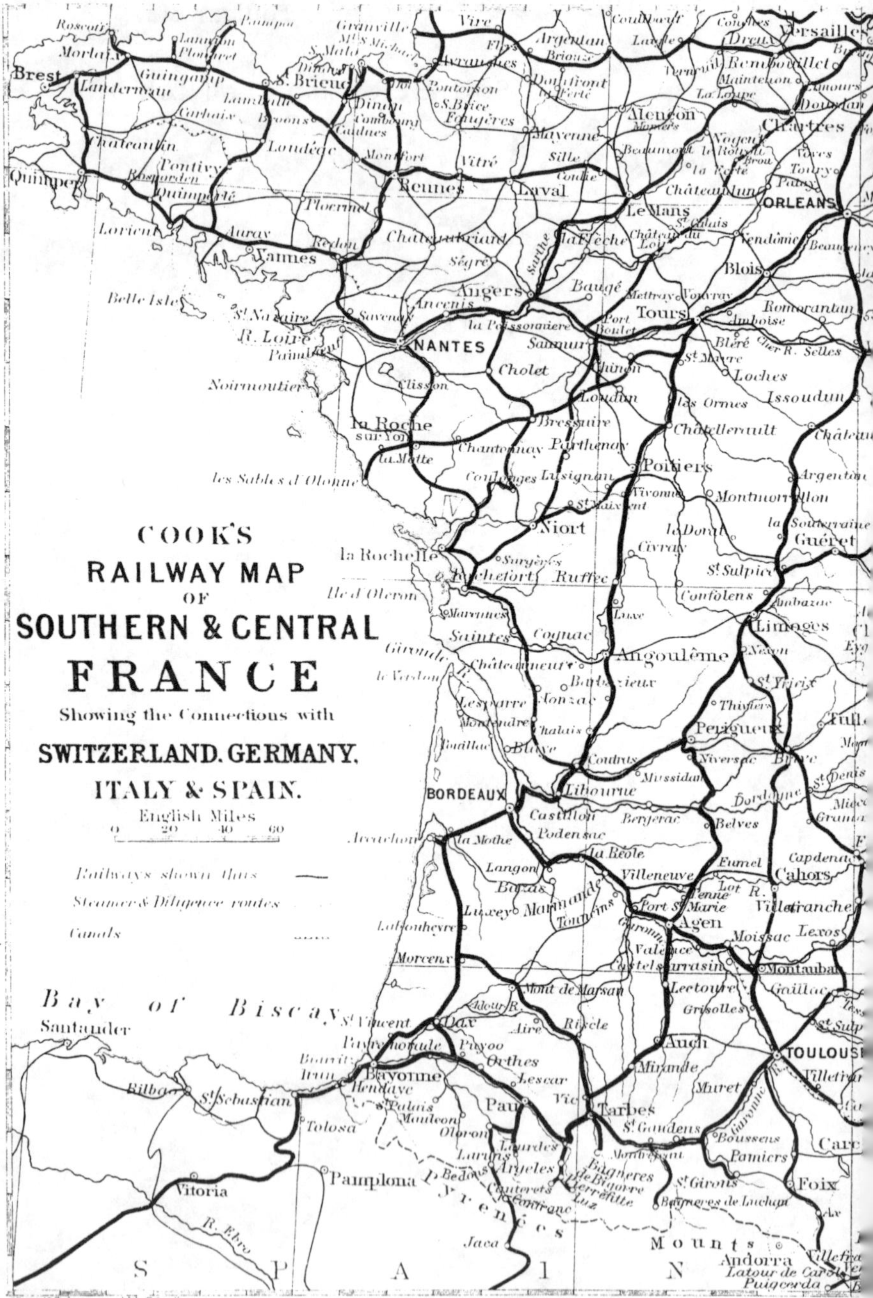

(219/1/39 J.)

See Map, pages 321-322

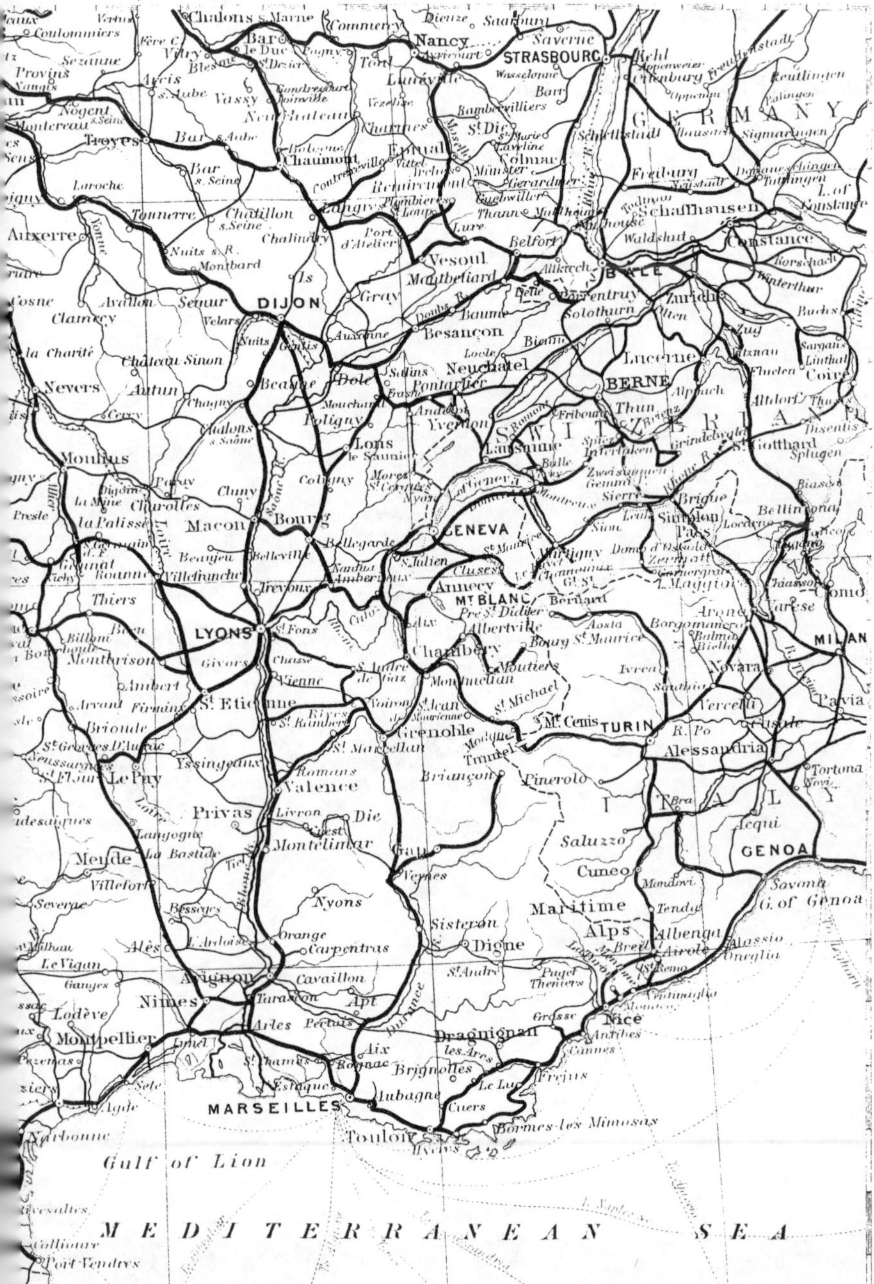

See Map.pages 279-280

See Map.pages 298-299

See Map.pages 338-339

Cook's Tourist Map
of
SOUTHERN and CENTRAL FRANCE

COOK'S TOURIST MAP
OF
GERMANY, HUNGARY,
YUGO-SLAVIA, ETC.

See Map, pages 162-163

See Map, pages 279-280

W.&A.K.Johnston Ltd Edinburgh

(219/1/39 J.)

See Ma

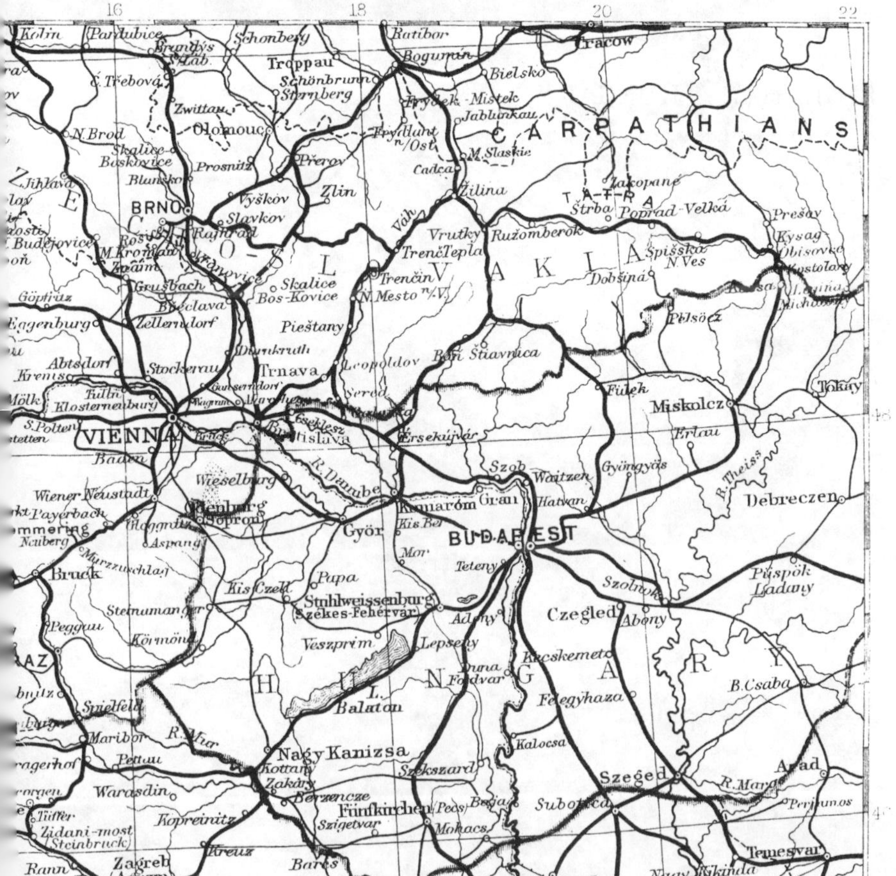
COOK'S RAILWAY MAP OF
S.GERMANY, HUNGARY,
CZECHO-SLOVAKIA,
N. ITALY, YUGOSLAVIA &c.
English Miles
0 10 20 30 40 50 60
Railways shown thus
Steamer Routes
Auto
CARPATHIANS
TATRA
VAKIA
HUNGARY
YUGOSLAVIA
VIENNA
BRNO
BUDAPEST
Kolin
Pardubice
Brandys
Schonberg
Ratibor
Cracow
Troppau
Bogumin
Bielsko
Schönbrunn
Sternberg
Frydek-Mistek
Jablunkau
Č. Třebová
Zwittau
Olomouc
N.Brod
Skalice-Baskovice
Prosnitz
Prerov
Cadca
M.Slaskie
Zilina
Zakopane
Jihlava
Blansko
Vyškov
Zlin
Slavkov
Štrba
Poprad-Velká
Prešov
Rajhrad
Vrutky
Ružomberok
Trenč.Tepla
Spišska N.Ves
Kysag-Obisovce
Trenčin
N.Mesto n/V.
Skalice
Bos-Kovice
Dobšiná
Grusbach
Břeclava
Göpfritz
Zellerndorf
Eggenburg
Piešťany
Pelsöcz
Dürnkruth
Ban. Štiavnica
Abtsdorf
Stockerau
Trnava
Leopoldov
Krems
Tulln
Klosterneuburg
Sered
Fülek
Miskolcz
Tokay
S.Polten
Bratislava
Érsekújvár
Erlau
Baden
Szob
Waitzen
Gyöngyös
R. Danube
R. Theiss
Wieselburg
Gran
Hatvan
Debreczen
Wiener Neustadt
Komaróm
Payerbach
Sopron
Györ
Kis Ber
Aspang
Mor
Teteny
Mürzzuschlag
Bruck
Papa
Szolnok
Püspök Ladany
Kis Czell
Stuhlweissenburg
(Szekes-Fehervar)
Steinamanger
Adony
Czegled
Abony
Peggau
Veszprim
Lepseny
Körmönd
Duna Foldvar
Kecskemet
B.Csaba
Spielfeld
L. Balaton
Felegyhaza
Maribor
R. Mur
Kalocsa
Nagy Kanizsa
Pettau
Kottany
Szekszard
Szeged
Arad
Warasdin
Zakány
Berzencze
Fünfkirchen (Pecs)
Baja
Subotica
R. Maros
Perjamos
Tüffer
Koprcinitz
Szigetvar
Mohacs
Zidani-most
(Steinbruck)
Kreuz
Temesvar
Rann
Zagreb
(Agram)
Barcs
Sombor
Nagy Kikinda
Karlova
R. Drave
Slatina
Szebely
Sissek
Osijek
Novi Sad
Peterwardein
Karlstadt
Petrinia
Lipik
Jasenovatz
Vinkovci
Versecz
R. Danube
India
Ogulin
Brod
Novi
R. Save
Jassenova
Pancsova
Semlin
(Zimony)
Belgrade
Basiasch
(Bazias)
Banjaluka
Gracac
Jajce
Travnik
Lasva
Zara
Knin
Bugojno
Sarajevo
Sibenik
Split
16
18
20
22
44
46
48
Entered at Stationers Hall.

8-299

Cook's Tourist Map
of
S. GERMANY, HUNGARY,
YUGO-SLAVIA, Etc.

COOK'S TOURIST MAP
OF
NORWAY, SWEDEN AND DENMARK

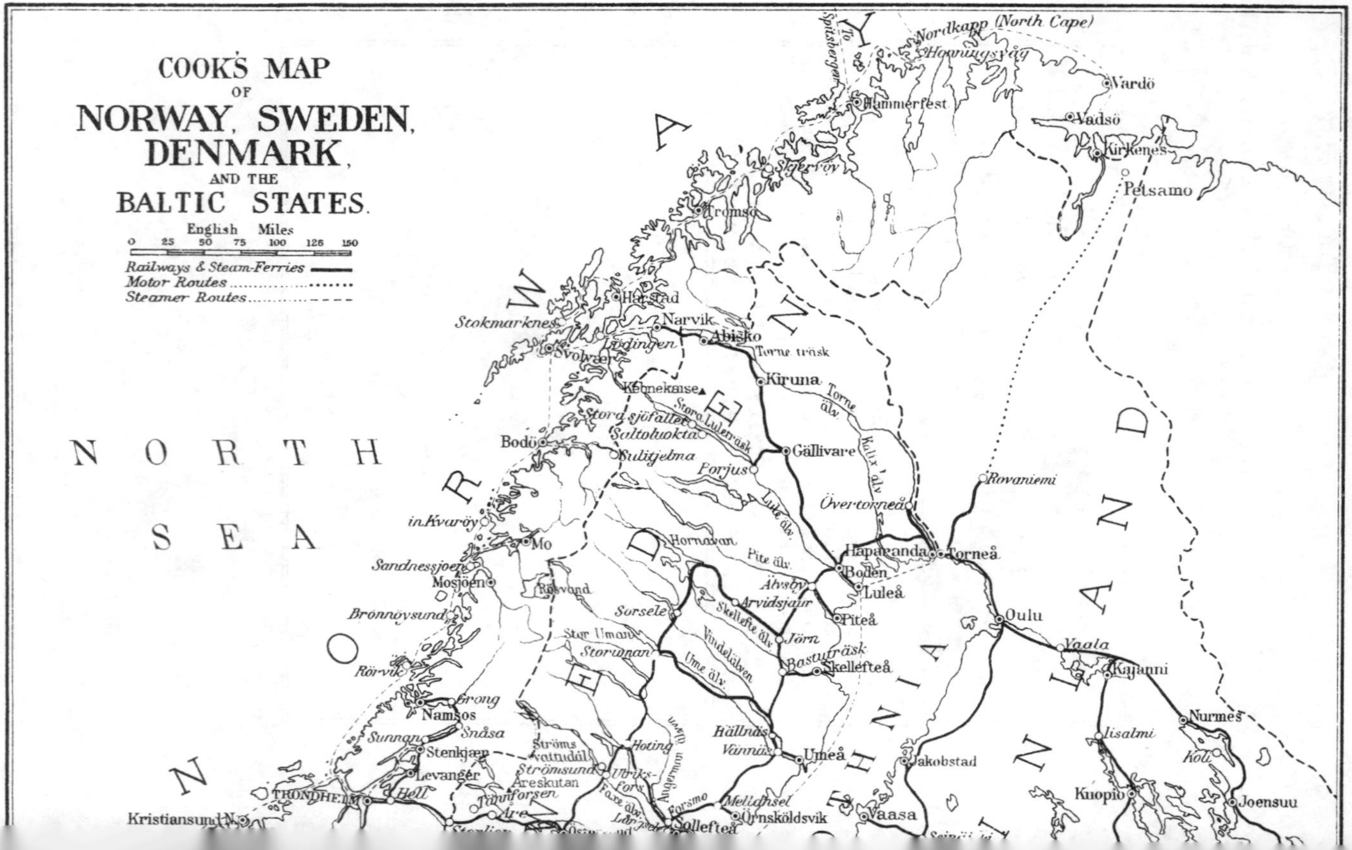
COOK'S MAP
OF
NORWAY, SWEDEN, DENMARK, AND THE BALTIC STATES.
English Miles
0 25 50 75 100 125 150
Railways & Steam-Ferries
Motor Routes
Steamer Routes
NORTH SEA
NORWAY
SWEDEN
FINLAND
GULF OF BOTHNIA
To Spitsbergen
Nordkapp (North Cape)
Honningsvåg
Hammerfest
Vardö
Vadsö
Kirkenes
Petsamo
Skjervöy
Tromsö
Harstad
Narvik
Abisko
Torne träsk
Stokmarknes
Lödingen
Svolvaer
Kiruna
Torne älv
Kebnekaise
Stora sjöfallet
Stora Luleträsk
Saltoluokta
Bodö
Sulitjelma
Gällivare
Kalix älv
Forjus
Lule älv
Övertorneå
Rovaniemi
in Kvaröy
Mo
Hornavan
Pite älv
Haparanda
Torneå
Boden
Luleå
Sandnessjoen
Mosjöen
Rösvand
Älvsby
Arvidsjaur
Brönnöysund
Sorsele
Skellefte älv
Piteå
Oulu
Stor Uman
Storuman
Vindelälven
Jörn
Bastuträsk
Vaala
Kajaani
Rörvik
Ume älv
Skellefteå
Grong
Namsos
Snåsa
Nurmes
Hällnäs
Vännäs
Umeå
Sunnan
Stenkjaer
Ströms vattudal
Hoting
Ångermanälven
Iisalmi
Levanger
Strömsund
Ulriksfors
Jakobstad
Koli
TRONDHEIM
Hell
Åreskutan
Tännforsen
Åre
Faxe älv
Forsmo
Mellansel
Kuopio
Joensuu
Kristiansund N.
Sollefteå
Örnsköldsvik
Vaasa

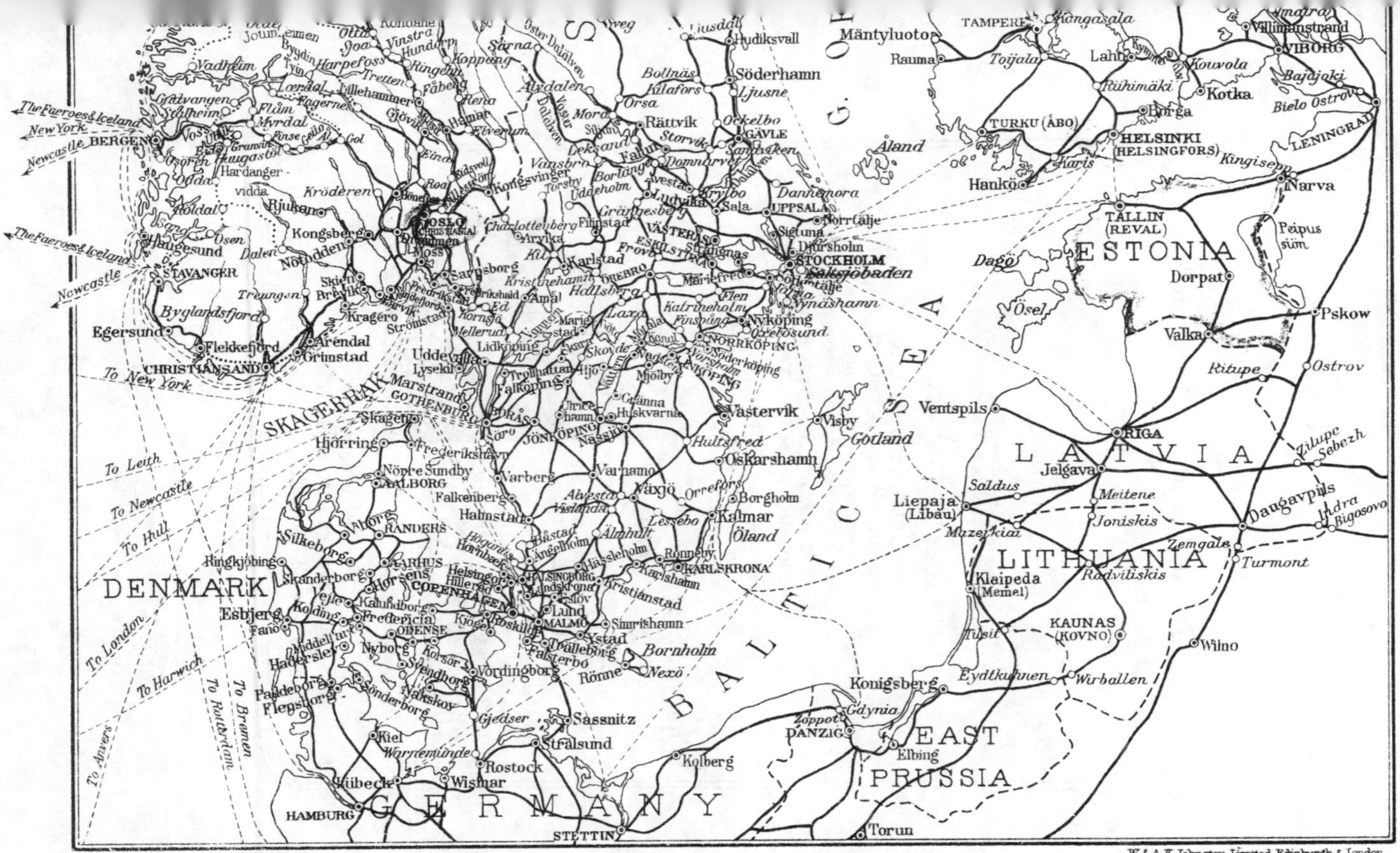

(219/1/39.J.)

W. & A. K. Johnston, Limited, Edinburgh & London.

See Map, pages 162-163

Cook's Tourist Map

of

NORWAY, SWEDEN and DENMARK

Mls.	Through Services *see pp.* 273 to 275.	fast 1 2 3	Exp 1 2 3	Exp 1 2 3	Rap 1 2 3	Rap 1 2	Exp 1 2 3	Rap 1 2	luxe 1 2	Rap 1 2 3	Rap 1 2 3
			V	V *c*	*f*	V	D *c*	V	L	S *b*	*b*
0	**Paris** (Est) ....dep.	6 25	7 25	1159	1335	1730	1740	1950	1955	2240	0 10
58	Chateau Thierry ..	7 42	..	13 7	│	A	*r*	..		2355	B
87	Epernay........arr.	8 14	..	1344	│		1921	..	..	0 35	1 51
..	Reims .... „	8 53		1430	│		20 8	..	..	E	..
	Epernay ......dep.	8 16	.	1346	│	Auto-Rail Car, Limited train	1922	..	..	0 39	1 52
107	**Chalons-s-Marne** a.	8 38	9 27	14 9	│		1946	..	2146	1 4	2 17
	Reims (*p*. 270) dep.	7 14	..	1256	│		1840	..		2342	
	Chalons-s-Marne d.	8 46	9 30	1414	│		1950	..	2210	1 9	2 22
135	Vitry-le-Francois ..	9 11		1441	↓		2017	..	..	..	2 49
159	Bar-le-Duc .. { arr.	9 53	1037	1519	1624		2057	22 4	..	2 17	3 31
	Bar-le-Duc .. { dep.	9 58	1043	1526	1630		21 4	22 6	..	2 23	3 36
200	Toul .... { arr.	1058	..	1620			..	..	..	│	4 32
	Toul .... { dep.	11 0	..	1621			..	..		↓	4 34
220	**Nancy-Ville** ....arr.	1126	12 0	1645	1737	2032	2216	23 2	0 20	3 41	5 2
(*p*.	271) Contrexeville arr.		1357	..			..	..	..		8 47
266	*p*. Epinal....arr.	..	1458	..	1934		2349	..	..	4 52	6 42
293	271 Aillevillers „	..	1725	..	2057		0 43	..	..	..	7 29
	Nancy-Ville....dep.	..	12 6	1651	1744	2036	2225	..	0 26	4 1	5 12
240	Luneville	..	1230	1728	1811	│	2249	..	│	│	5 45
256	Igney Avricourt	..	..	1749		│		..	│	│	6 10
268	Sarrebourg .. { arr.	..	13 2	18 6		│	2321	..	│	│	6 28
	Sarrebourg .. { dep.	..	13 3	18 7		│	2322	..	│	│	6 33
	Saverne ....arr.	..	1327	1830	↓	↓	2341	..	↓	↓	6 59
318	**Strasbourg** .... „	..	1358	19 1	1928	2155	0 11	..	2 5	6 0	7 30
..	Kehl.......... „	..	1442	2025	2025	0 44	0 44	..	2 23	6 36	8 14

E 1, 2 and 3 cl. Couchettes & through cars Paris-Strasbourg and *v.v.*
S 1 and 2 cl. Sleep. Car Paris-Stuttgart and *v.v.* **V** Buffet Car.
L Orient Express, *see page* 84.
† Weekdays only.

	fast 1/2 3	Exp 1 2 3	luxe 1 2	Rap 1 2	Exp 1 2 3	Rap 1 2	Exp 1 2 3	Exp 1 2 3	Exp 1 2 3	Rap 1 2 3	Rap 1 2 3
			L		D *d*		*d r*		*i*	*h r*	*g*
Kehl ....dep.		–	4 17	..	5 14	6 28	..	..	1326	1648	2150
Strasbourg .... „			4 36		6 30	8 8	9 54	..	14 3	1740	23 7
Saverne .... „		..	│	..	7 3	..	1026	..	│	│	2343
Sarrebourg .. { arr.		..	│	..	7 30	A	1052	..	│	│	0 9
Sarrebourg .. { dep.	..		│	A	7 31		1053	..	│	│	0 10
Igney Avricourt „	..		│	..	..	..			│	│	0 32
Luneville		5 21	↓	..	8 6	..	1130		↓	↓	0 53
Nancy-Ville.... arr.		5 53	6 19	..	8 30	9 26	1156		1539	1914	1 23
Aillevillers ..dep.		..		..	6 48	6 48	10 3	..	1356	1738	20 3
Epinal ...... „	..	..	..	5 20	7 29	7 29	1051		1430	1818	2248
Contrexeville dep.	..	..	..	..	..	6 51	8 37	..	..	..	1822
			L	V	V	V					S B
Nancy-Ville....dep.	3 50	6 5	6 25	7 32	8 41	9 30	12 1	..	1545	1920	1 31
Toul ....dep.	4 40	6 31		..	9 7	..	1227				2 0
Bar-le-Duc .... „	6 37	7 30		8 30	1014	..	1332	1518	17 4	2034	3 8
Vitry-le-Francois ..	7 37	8 8	..	..	1048			16 8	1738		3 53
Chalons-s-Marne a.	8 0	8 30	8 20	..	1111	Limited train.	1428	1635	18 1	2133	4 19
Reims (*p*. 270) arr.	..	..		..	1226		1559	1932	1932		6 51
Chalons-s-Marne d.	..	8 35	8 26	..	1114		1431	1645	1812	2137	4 24
Epernay ...... arr.	..		..	..	1137		1456	17 9	1835	..	4 49
Reims ......dep.	..	..	..	..	1045		13 0	1618	..	..	..
Epernay ...... „	..	.		..	1138		1457	1711	..	..	4 50
Chateau Thierry arr.	..	9 31		..	1211		1538	1750	..	..	
Paris.......... „	..	1037	1012	1040	1320	1230	1654	19 6	2015	2341	6 55

A Auto-Rail Car, Limited train, supplement.
B 1, 2 & 3 cl. Cars to Prague; 1, 2, 3 cl. Couchettes, and 1 cl. Lits-Toilettes Paris-Strasbourg and *v.v.*
D 1 and 2 cl. Sleep. Cars and 1, 2 and 3 cl. Cars Paris-Prague and *v.v.*
r Rest. Car Paris-Nancy and *v.v.*

a Paris dep. 3 cl. 125 miles, and from Chalons 2 cl. 50 miles and 3 cl. 80 miles or more. *b* Paris dep. 2 cl. 94 miles, 3 cl. 125 miles or more. *c* 3rd class not more than 63 miles. *d* Takes 3 cl. for Paris only. *e* Between Nancy and Paris, 3 cl. 94 miles or more. *f* From Paris, 2 cl. 187 miles and 3 cl. 235 miles or more, and from Bar-le-Duc, 2 and 3 cl. 125 miles or more. *g* Between Nancy and Paris 3 cl. 187 miles or more. *h* From Strasbourg to Nancy, from Nancy, 3 cl. 155 miles or more. *i* 1 and 2 cl. only at Strasbourg for Nancy, at Nancy and Bar-de-Duc, 2 cl. for 218 miles, and 3 cl. 250 miles or more. *j* Limited Train. *k* Paris dep. 2 cl. not less than 94 miles, and 3 cl. 187 miles, and from Chalons, 3 cl., 65 miles or more. *l* Only takes at Paris 2 and 3 cl. for 187 miles or more. *m* At Paris 3 cl. not less than 125 miles. *p* At Paris takes 3 cl. 187 miles or more. *x* 2 and 3 cl. only.

Paris and Black Forest, Baden, Carlsruhe, Heidelberg, Stuttgart, &c.

Mls.		Exp 123	Rap 123	Rap 12	Rap 123	luxe 12	Rap 123	Rap 123
		E		C		L	S	A
0	p. 272 PARIS (Est) ..dep	7 25	1335	1740	..	1955	2240	0 10
257	Nancy-Ville .. ,,	12 6	1744	2225	..	0 26	4 1	5 12
..	Sarrebourg....arr.	13 2	..	2321	..	..	..	6 28
313	STRASBOURG .. ,,	1358	1928	0 11		2 5	6 0	7 30
..	p. 177 Strasbourg .. dep.	1547	..	..	5 16	↓	..	9 3
..	Ludwigshafen a.	2158	..	..	1019		..	1423
..	Ludwigshafen d.	2235	..	..	1118		..	1448
..	Worms ......arr.	23 2	..	..	1138		..	1510
..	Mayence...... ,,	0 18	..	..	1215		..	16 5
..	WIESBADEN .. ,,	0 36	..	...	1230	V	..	1620
			2 3					
	p. 183 STRASBOURG..dep.	1428	2014	0 30	1 5	2 10	6 25	8 3
353	Baden-West ..arr.	1553	2120	1 52	2 41		7 34	9 13
355	Baden-Baden ,,	16 4	2137	3 15	3 15	.	7 42	9 23
373	CARLSRUHE .. ,,	1620	2149	2 20	3 14	3 55	7 58	9 40
..	Carlsruhe ..dep.	1652	22 4	..	..	.	8 43	10 4
..	HEIDELBERG ar.	1814	2244	.	..	.	9 43	1045
	p. 186 CARLSRUHE ..dep.	1633	2220	2 26	4 40	4 1	8 9	9 55
393	Pforzheim .... arr	17 8	2257	2 59	5 19	..	8 43	1026
407	Wildbad.... ,,	1842	2347	..	6‡40	..	9 41	13 0
..	Muhlacker.. arr.	..	2314	..	5 36	..	..	..
..	Muhlacker.. dep.		2315	..	5 37	..	..	..
42[illegible]	STUTTGART arr.	18 7	24 0	3 58	6 28	5 29	9 38	1120
..	p. 186 Ulm...... ,,	1934	4 0	5 25	7 58	.	11 2	1344
..	Friedrichshf a	21 2	7 1	9 5	9 25	..	15 9	1634
..	Lindau .. arr.	22 4	8 3	10 0	10 0	..	16 6	1712
..	Bregenz.. ,,	..	8 30		1154	..	..	1728

L—Orient Exp. Paris-Vienna Tues., Thurs. and Sats.

‡ Not Sundays.

	123	123	luxe	123	23	123	23	23
	Exp	Rap	12	Rap		Rap	Exp	..
Bregenz ....dep.	12 0	12 0		18 6	..	..		..
Lindau...... ,,	1240	1240	L	1837	..	4 10	8 31	..
Friedrichshfn ,,	1323	1323		2033	..	5 20	9 38	..
Ulm .... ,,	15 8	1734		0 30	..	9 9	11 8	..
STUTTGART ,,	1632	1857	1 14	2 1	4 31	1024	1240	..
Muhlacker .. arr.	..	..	↓	2 47	5 45	..	1331	..
Muhlacker .. dep.		..		2 48	5 52	..	1332	..
Wildbad .... ,,	1646	19 5		..	..	10 4		..
Pforzheim .... ,,	1734	1951	V	3 3	6 19	1118	1348	..
CARLSRUHE .. arr.	18 3	2020	2 34	3 29	7 11	1145	1417	..
		B		C			E	
HEIDELBERG dep.	1729	1830	.	1 31	6 22	11 6	1431	..
Carlsruhe.... arr.	1810	1950	..	2 11	7 9	1147	1511	..
CARLSRUHE ..dep.	1825	2025	2 40	3 44	7 15	1152	1515	..
Baden-Baden ,,	1842	2039	..	..	7 25	12 4	1429	..
Baden West.... ,,	1852	2049		4 10	7 42	1214	1539	..
STRASBOURG .. arr.	2026	2248	4 31	5 28	9 31	1340	17 2	..
p. 176 WIESBADEN dep.	1325	1746	↓	↓	2 20	6 46	↓	8 58
Mayence .... ,,	1345	18 4			2 35	6 58		9 11
Worms...... ,,	1440	1845			3 11	7 45		10 1
LUDWIGSHAF'N a	15 2	19 9			3 34	8 5		1023
LUDWIGSHAF'N d	1514	1937			5 0	8 40		1040
STRASBOURG arr.	19 5	2226	V	V	8 5	1155	V	1343
STRASBOURG ..dep.	..	23 7	4 36	6 30	9 54	14 3	1740	..
Sarrebourg .... arr.	..	0 9	..	7 30	1052	..		..
Nancy-Ville.... ,,	..	1 23	6 19	8 30	1156	1539	1914	..
PARIS (Est) .. ,,	..	6 55	1012	1320	1654	2015	2341	..

L Orient Express Mons. Weds. and Fris., from Strasbourg.

¶ Not Sundays.

V Buffet Bar.

A 1, 2 and 3 class cars and Couchettes Paris-Strasbourg and 1, 2 and 3 class cars, Paris-Stuttgart.
B 1 & 2 class Sleep. car Stuttgart-Paris. 1, 2 & 3 class Couchettes and 1, 2 & 3 class cars, Strasbourg-Paris.
C 1, 2 and 3 class cars Paris-Stuttgart and *v.v.*
E 1, 2 & 3 class cars and Rest. car, Paris-Strasbourg.
S 1 and 2 class Sleep. car Paris–Stuttgart, 1, 2 and 3 class Couchettes Paris–Strasbourg, and 1, 2, 3 class cars Paris–Stuttgart.

Paris and Munich Vienna, Budapest, Bucharest, and Istanbul.

123	123	123	12	12	123	123			123		12	123	123	123
Rap	Rap	Rap	Rap	luxe	Rap	Rap			Rap		luxe	Exp	Rap	Rap
7 25	1335	1740	1740	1955	2240	0 10	dep. PARIS (Est) ...... arr.		1320		1012	2015	6 55	6 55
1358	1928	0 11	0 11	2 5	6 0	7 30	arr. Strasbourg .. dep.	see p. 273	6 30		4 36	14 3	23 7	23 7
C		Z	123	L	B					Z	M	C	..	B
1428	2014	0 30	1 5	2 10	6 25	8 3	dep. Strasbourg .. arr.	see p. 273	4 57	5 28	4 31	1340	2026	2224
1514	2038	1 15	2 0	2 57	6 56	8 34	dep. Kehl ....arr.	see p. 273	4 25	4 52	3 44	1256	1938	2155
1620	2149	2 20	3 14	3 55	7 58	9 40	arr. Carlsruhe .. .. dep.	see p. 273	3 0	3 44	2 40	1152	1825	2055
1633	0 15	2 26	4 40	4 1	8 9	9 55	dep. Carlsruhe .. .. arr.		1 58	3 29	2 34	1145	18 3	2019
18 7	2 21	3 58	6 28	5 29	9 38	1120	arr. STUTTGART ...... dep.		0 27	2 1	1 14	1024	1632	1857
1822	2 36	4 10	6 50	5 34	9 48	1346	dep STUTTGART ...... arr.		23 7	1 51	0 56	1019	1622	1846
1950	4 14	5 29	To Nuremberg and Prague.	..	11 7	1517	dep. Ulm .... dep.	p.186	From Prague and Nuremberg.	0 30	..	9 9	15 8	1734
2143	6 33	7 20		8 24	1252	1715	arr. MUNICH .... .. dep.	p.187		2235	2210	7 22	13 6	1544
22 5	7 40	7 40		8 36	1312	1740	dep. MUNICH .... .. arr	p.187		22 2	2150	7 3	1155	1525
0 5	9 40	9 40		1029	1510	1952	arr. Salzburg .... .. dep.	p.187		20 0	1953	5 0	9 41	1323
1 10	..	1215		..	..		dep. Salzburg .. ....arr.	p199		1648	..	4 38		..
10 8	..	2214		..	..		arr. Trieste .. ....dep.	p199		7 10	..	19 0		..
1 25	10 0	10 0		11 0	1525	..	dep. Salzburg .. ....arr.	p187		1935	1943	4 35	6 20	1313
6 44	1442	1442		1520	1950	..	arr. VIENNA (W.) ....dep.	p187		1440	1514	2315	2050	8 50
7 49	..	1525		..		..	arr. VIENNA (E.) ....dep.			1335	..	2039		6 42
												123 Exp		Exp
8 15	..	1552	L Orient Exp. Tus., Thrs. and Sats. from Boulogne & Paris to Vienna & Bucharest.	1544*	2350	..	dep. VIENNA (E.) ....arr.	p.200	..	1129	1429*	1958		5 55
8 49	..	1626		..	0 56	..	arr. Bruckneudorf ....dep.	p.200	..	1052	..	1922	..	4 50
1220	..	1945		20 3	6 20	..	arr. BUDAPEST .. dep.	p.200	..	7 5	1010	16 0	..	2335
1445		2355		2034	..	..	dep. K.p.u.(East) .... arr.		..	6 26	9 45	1450		22 5
2123	..	¶		2 7	..	..	dep. Arad (p.203)........ arr.		..	¶	6 10	10 8	..	18 9
1015	..	1955		1230	..	..	arr. BUCHAREST (p 203) ..dep		..	13 5	1945	2050	..	6 55
1920	..	..		17 5	..	..	arr. Constanza (p.330) ..dep.		..	6 0	14 3	14 3	..	2353
8 ‡ 0	..	..		8 ‡ 0	..	..	arr. ISTANBUL (p.393) str.)dp.		..	..	22a0	22a0	..	22a0
10 0	..	1820		..	2350	..	dep. VIENNA (E.) .. ....arr.	p. 200	..	1129	..	1958	..	5 55
8 35	..	1855		..	0 56	..	dep. Bruckneudorf ....arr.	p. 200	..	1053	..	1920	..	4 49
14 0	..	2235		..	6 20	..	arr. BUDAPEST .. dep.	p. 200	..	7 5	..	16 0	..	2335
1435	..	2348		..	8 2	..	dep. K.p.u (East) arr.	p. 200	..	6 32	..	1456	..	2115
2142	..	7 8		..	1753	..	arr. Belgrade ....dep.	p. 200	..	2250	..	8 0	..	1134
4 22		1130		..	..	..	arr. Nisch ....dep.	p.332	..	1748	..	0 53	..	..
1353	..	2255		..	..	..	arr. Thessaloniki ....dep	p.332	..	8 20	..	1253	..	..
..	..	1026		..	..	..	arr. Athens ....dep.	p.332	..	2045	..	..	..	..
1040	..	1628		..	..	..	arr Sofia ....dep.	p.332	..	1441	..	2025	..	
6 40	..	7 20		..	..	..	arr. ISTANBUL ....dep		..	22 0	..	2235	..	..

M Orient Exp. from Bucharest Mon., Wed. and Fri., from Vienna Tues., Thurs. & Sats. to Paris & Calais.

* West Station. ¶ Via Oradea-Mare

a Sats. only. ‡ Fridays. † 2 & 3 class only.

B 1 & 2 cl. Sleeping CarParis–Strasbourg-Stuttgart and *v.v.*, 1, 2 & 3 cl. cars Paris-Salzburg-Vienna and *v v.*

C 1, 2 & 3 cl. cars Paris-Vienna and *v.v.*, 1 & 2 cl. Sleeping Car Carlsruhe-Vienna and *v.v.* 1, 2 & 3 cl. cars Paris-Salzburg-Jesenice and *v.v.*

Z 1 & 2 cl. Sleeping Car Nancy-Strasbourg-Munich & *v.v.* and 1, 2 & 3 cl. cars Paris-Vienna & *v.v.*

Paris. Nuremberg (Karlsbad), Praha and Warsaw.

123	luxe	123	12	Mls.			12	123	luxe	123
7 25	1955	1740	0 10	0	dep. PARIS (Est.).. arr		6 55	1320	1012	2015
	K	A	B				B	A	K	..
1428	2 10	1 5	8 3	313	dep. Strasbourg .. arr.	see p. 273	2224	4 57	4 31	1340
1514	2 57	2 0	8 34	..	dep. Kehl .. .. arr.	see p. 273	2155	4 25	3 44	1256
1633	4 1	4 40	9 55	373	dep CARLSRUHE .. arr.	see p. 273	2040	1 58	2 34	1145
..	..	5 58		..	arr. Bietigheim .. dep.	see p. 273	..	0 55	..	..
18 7	5 29	6 28	1120	429	arr. STUTTGART dep.	see p. 273	1920	0 27	1 14	1024
1946	5 48	6 50	1130	0	dep. STUTTGART .. arr.	p. 184	19 2	23 7	0 51	9 39
		9 1	13 4	63	arr. Crailsheim .. dep.	p. 184	1738	2056	..	8 3
23 8	8 47	1036	1420	119	arr. NUREMBERG .. dep	p. 184	1620	1910	2210	6 21
2320	9 0	1123	1438	0	dep. Nuremberg .. arr.	p. 190	1553	1847	2156	..
2 32	11 9	1355	1719	95	arr. Eger .... dep	p. 190	1249	1610	1952	..
6 56	1227	1530	1840	128	ar. KARLSBAD .. dep.	p. 190	11 2	1440	1832	
2320	9 0	1123	1438	0	dep. Nuremberg arr.	p. 190	1553	1847	2156	..
2 32	11 9	1355	1719	95	arr. Eger ...... dep.	p. 190	1249	1610	1952	..
4 56	1216	1444	18 8	114	arr Marienbad .. dep.	p. 190	1158	1522	19 7	..
6 49	1336	1614	1940	154	ar. Tuschkau dep	p. 190	1024	1348	1746	
7 7	1349	1632	20 0		d. Kosolup c arr.	p. 190	10 7	1330	1730	..
9 44	16 0	1855	2225	233	arr. PRAHA W... dep.	p. 190	7 35	11 0	1520	..
..	..	13 3	..	..	arr. WARSAW p. 203..dep		1640	..	..	..

A—1 & 2 cl. Sleeper and 1, 2 & 3 cl. cars Paris-Praha and *v.v.* daily.

B 1.2 & 3 class Cars Paris-Praha & *v.v.*

K Calais-Paris-Karlsbad and Prague Exp. de luxe. Tues., Thurs., Sats. from Paris, June 15–Sept 19. Tues., Thurs., Sats. from Prague, June 17–Sept. 21.

Paris, Nancy, Pagny-sur-Moselle, Metz. [French Rlys. (Est).

1 2 3	1 2 3	1 2 3	1 2 3	1 2 3	1 2 3	1 2 3	1 2 3		1 2	1 2 3	1 2 3	1 2 3	1 2 3	1 2 3	1 2 3	1 2 3	1 2 3
Exp	Exp	Exp	Exp	Exp	Exp	Rap	Exp		Rap	Rap	Rap	Exp	Rap	Exp	Rap	Rap	Exp
6 25	7 25	1159	1335	1740	2240	0 10	0 10	dep Paris (*p.* 272) ar.	1035	1230	1654	19 7	2015	2341	2349	6 55	7 55
1126	12 0	1645	1737	..	..	..	5 2	arr. Nancy-Ville dep.	..	9 30	12 1	..	1545	1920		1 31	..
				z	A	z			z		r	A				z	X
1133	1219	1715	1749	..	*via* Verdun.	↓	6 15	dep. **Nancy-Ville** a.	..	9 19	1154	*via* Verdun.	1539	1856	*via* Verdun.	1 0	
.	..	..	..	..			..	dep. Frouard .... arr	..	9 6			..	..			..
12 6	1253	1749	1823	..		..	6 50	arr. Pagny-s Mos. dep.	..	8 26	1118			..		0 21	..
12 7	1259	1750	1824	..		..	6 51	dep. ,, arr.	..	8 21	1113			..		0 20	..
	13 4	..	..	..		..	.	dep Noveant arr.	..	8 15	11 6		..	..		0 13	..
1223	1320	18 6	1841	2230	6 11	5 15	7 13	arr. **Metz** (*p* 179) dep.	7 15	7 56	1052	1218	1453	18 5	1714	2358	..
1316	1429	1429	1839	0 56	7 16	7 16	8 21	arr. Thionville dep.	5 35	6 58	1135	1135	..	1723	1544	2325	1 15
1453	1529	1529	1930	2 16	8 5	8 5	9 12	,, Luxemburg ,,	4 31	6 10	10 0	10 0	..	1634	1517	2239	2356
..	..	18 3	2219		1023	1023	13 6	,, Treves .... ,,	..	..	7 34	7 34	..	1340		1920	..
..	.	2021	..	..	12 6	12 6	1523	,, Coblentz .... ,,	..	..		..	..	1046	..	1629	..

A 1, 2 & 3 cl. cars Paris-Thionville. *z Via* Bar le Duc and Thiaucourt. *r* Rest. Car.
X *Via* Mezieres Charleville.

THROUGH SERVICES via Metz. Paris & Mayence, Frankfort, Wiesbaden

b via Worms. ‖ *via* Gau-Algesheim.

2 3	1 2 3	1 2 3	1 2 3	1 2 3	1 2 3	1 2 3		1 2 3	1 2 3	1 2 3	1 2 3	1 2 3	1 2 3
Exp	A		A	A	Exp	S		S	A	A		A	Exp
.	7 25		1335	1740	22 0	0 10	dep. PARIS (Est) .... arr.	6 55	1320	1654	2015	2341	7 55
..	12 5		1758	2230	..	5 15	arr. METZ .... dep.	0 30	8 50	12 9	1453	1848	
		r						Z				r	
..	1228	1325	1812	2312	z	5 35	dep. METZ .... arr.	2342	7 22	12 2	1422	1833	z
—	1351	1444	1936	0 28	6 20	6 52	arr. SARREBRUCK G.T. dep.	2216	7 57	1045	1256	1658	2342
					r			r					
11 0	1432	17 1	21 0	.	7 10	↓	dep. SARREBRUCK .... arr.	2143	..	1026	..	1521	↑
1129	15 3	1730	2132	..	7 40		arr. Homburg (Saar) dep.	2112	..	9 58	..	1450	
1259	1636	19 4	..	..	9 9		,, Ludwigshafen .. ,,	1937	..	8 21	..	1318	
1325	..	1932	23 1	..	9 52	Z	,, Worms .... ,,	19 9	..	7 53	..	1240	
1411	h	2020	0 27	..	1038		,, Mainz .... ,,	18 4	..	6 58	..	12 3	
		2034	0 36	..	1051		,, Wiesbaden ...... ,,	1746	..	6 46	..	1135	
1419	1834	2024	23*b*53	..	11*h*12	↓	,, FRANKFORT M.E.T. d.	1819	*b*	6*b*58		11*h*4	
								2 3		2 3			
1310	..	1910	..	..	6 5	8 50	dep. SARREBRUCK .... arr.	20 9		9 42	1138	1633	0 9
1516	..	21 8	..	..	8 11	1046	,, Munster A/S .... dep.	1756	..	7 42	9 41	1436	22 1
1541	..	‖	..	..	‖	‖	,, Bingerbruck .... ,,	1731	..	7 18	‖	1414	‖
1611	..	2146	—	..	8 50	1125	arr. Mainz .... ,,	1651			9 3	1342	21 6
1633	..	2223	..	..	9 12	1142	,, Wiesbaden .... ,,	1614	..		8 50	1318	2049
1653	..	2221	..	.	9 24	12 0	,, FRANKFORT M.E.T. d.	16 7	.		8 30	13 8	2032

A 1, 2 & 3 cl. cars Paris-Sarrebruck and *v.v.*

S Sleeping Car, 1 & 2 cl. Paris-Frankfort; 1, 2 & 3 cl. cars, Paris-Frankfort-Berlin and *v.v.*

Z 1st class Couchettes Paris-Metz-Forbach and *v.v.*

z Via Thionville and Hargarten-Falk.

§ 2 & 3 cl. only. *h Via* Mannheim. ‡ *Via* Mainz. *r* Rest. Car.

SAVOY—STEAMERS ON THE LAKE OF ANNECY

(*Steamer*)
dep. Annecy .. ar.
↓ Veyrier .. ↑
Menthon ..
Talloires ..
Duingt ....
Angon ..
Bredannaz
Lathuille ..

The times on the LEFT are to be read DOWNWARDS, those on the RIGHT UPWARDS.

Cook's Tourist Map of
SWITZERLAND and the ITALIAN LAKES

See Map, pages

See Map, pages 113-114

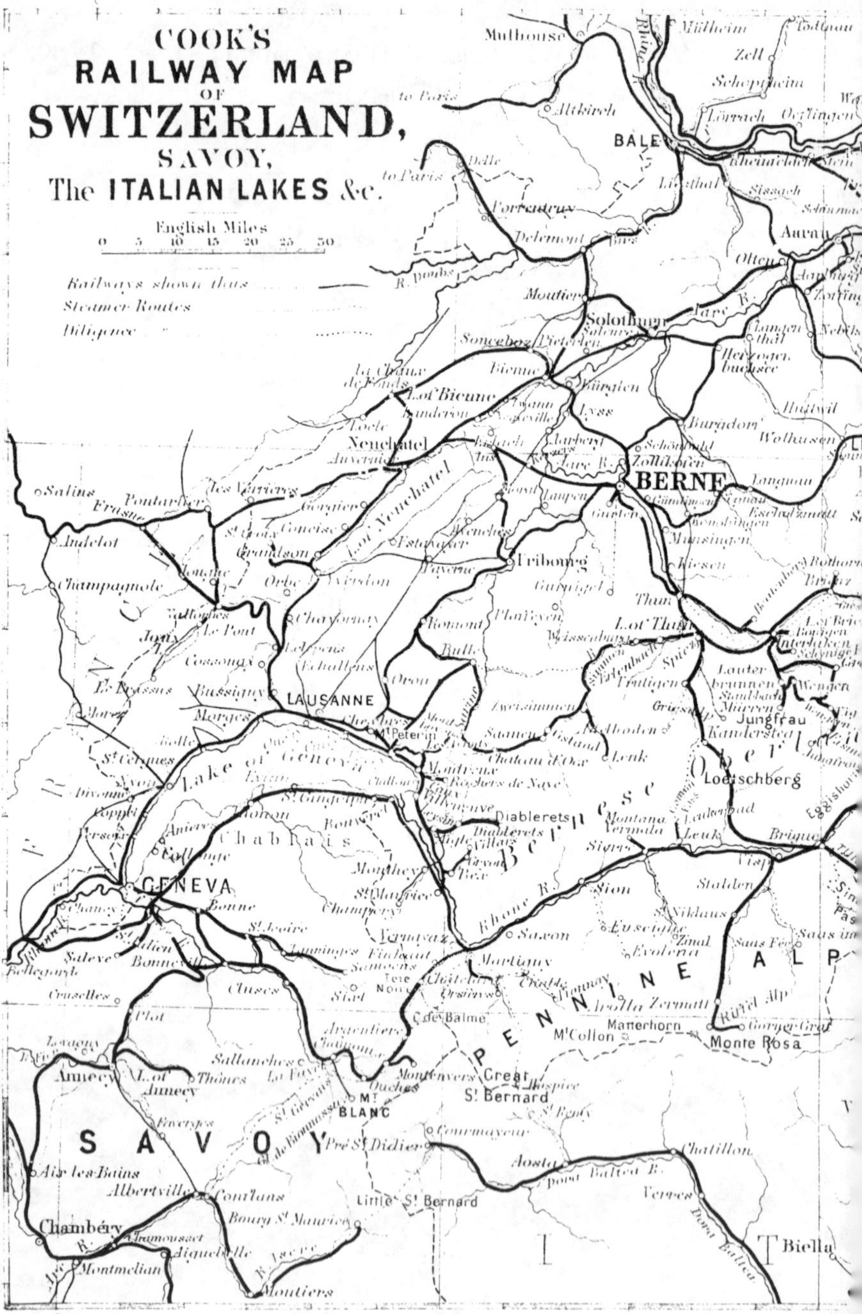

(219/1/39.J)

See Map

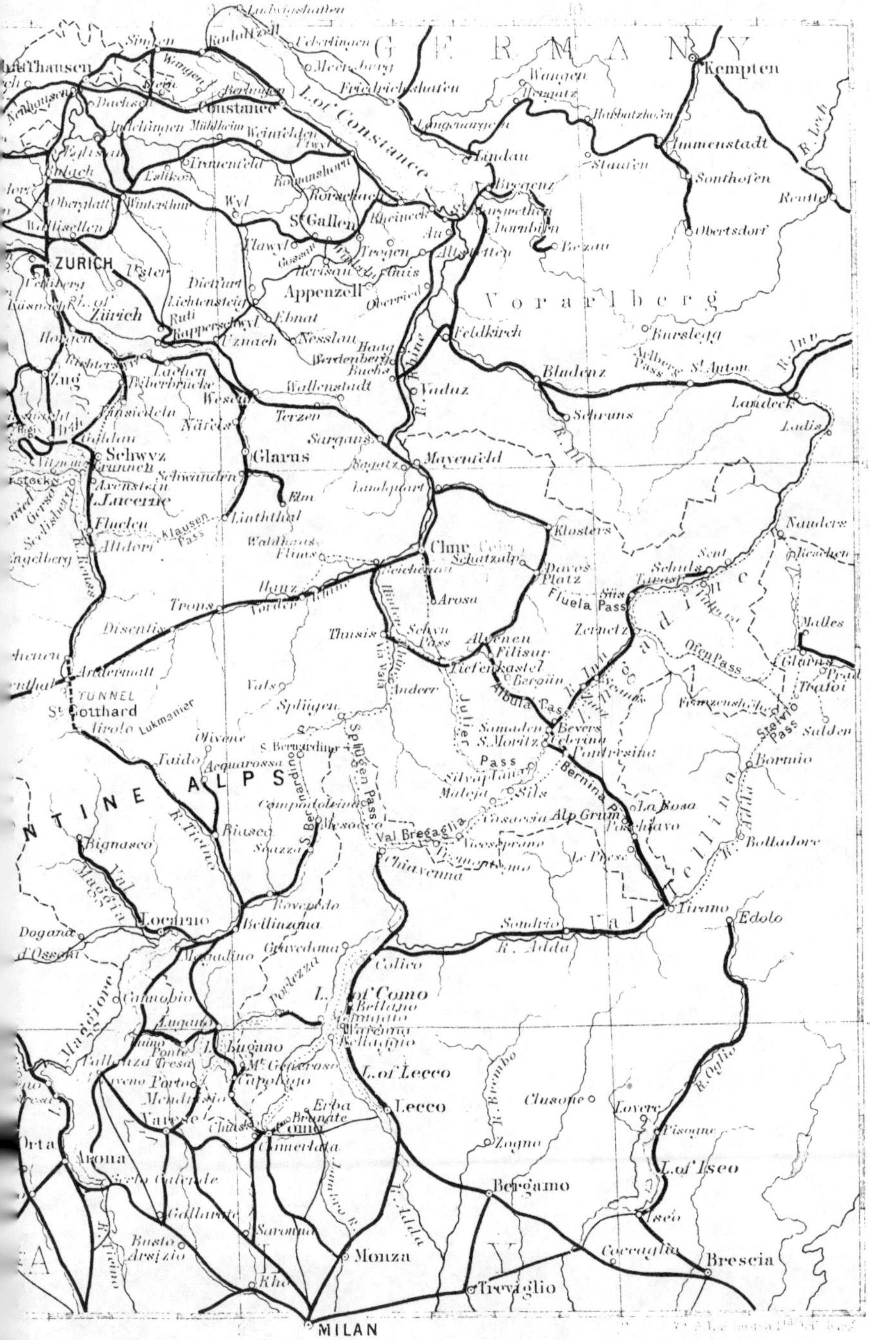

See Map, pages 190-191

Cook's Tourist Map
of
SWITZERLAND
and the
Italian Lakes

Trains throughout Switzerland run by Mid-European time, which is one hour fast of Greenwich (West-European) time. 1 2 3 means 1st 2nd and 3rd class.

THROUGH SERVICES TO AND FROM SWITZERLAND.

From England, see pp. 83, 85, 119 *to* 127, 131; *from France, pp.* 119 *to* 125, 267 *to* 270; *from Belgium, pp.* 80, 7, 178; *from Germany, pp.* 174, 178, 180, 184 *to* 187, 197, 286; *from Italy, pp.* 284, 287, *&c.*

Bale, Delemont, Bienne, Neuchatel, Lausanne. [Swiss Federal Rly.

Mls.	(Electric)	123 Exp	23	123 Exp	123 Exp	23	23 Exp	23	23	123 Exp	123 Exp		123 Exp	123 Exp
0	**Bale** (Swiss Sta) dep.	..	5 24	..	7 55	1013	1135	1214	1452	..	16 8	1726	1945	20†36
24	Delémont arr.	..	6 18	..	8 34	11 8	1210	1322	1550	..		1824	2021	21†26
..	Delle (*p.* 268) dep.	..	..	6 0	7*19	9 30	B	11*31		1523	*Via* Olten	..	1855	2032
	Delémont dep.	5 58	6 30	7 5	8 39	1118	1215	1334	1559	1624		1835	2025	2135
31	Moutier .... arr.	6 13	6 48	..	8 52	1136	..	1353	1616	1636		1853	2037	2147
54	Sonceboz arr.	6 3	8 4	..	9†35	13*41	..	15*19	1 20	1815	..	..	2129	..
53	Bienne (Biel) arr.	..	7 27	7 40	9 19	1210	1245	1427	1649	17 2	1743	1925	21 3	2214
	Bienne ......dep.	6 22	7 50	7 50	9 24	1237	1319	1437	↓	1710	↓	1934	21†24	2224
74	Berne.... ..arr	7 0	8 24	8 24	9 52	1330	1344	1525	↓	1740	↓	2029	22†6	2253
	Fr. Zurich, &c., p. 283.	2 3	Exp	*a* Also 1st class.				Exp						
53	Bienne (Biel) dep.	5 48	7 35		9 30	..	1247	1528	1718	..	1751	1935	2117	23*4
62	Neuveville ..	6 10	*a*		..	..	..	*a*	1743	..	*r*	1959	2130	2319
71	Neuchatel *Pontarlier, &c., p.* 279 a	6 34	7 58		9 56	..	13 9	1551	18 3	..	1815	2019	2143	23*36
	d	6‡39	8 0		10 0	..	..	1553	1823	..	1818	2042	2146	..
94	Yverdon (*p.* 287) d.	7 15	8 32		1032	..	..	1623	1915	..	1850	2137	2217	..
108	Cossonay . dep.	7 36			..	..	..	..	1953	..	..	22 3	..	..
118	Lausanne arr.	7‡50	9 0		11 6	..	14 4	1651	2011	..	1924	2222	2248	..
155	GENEVA (*p.* 279)..arr.	9 6	9 49	..	1146	..	15 1	1741	2136	..	20 4	..	2340	..

Mls.		123 Exp	123 Exp	123 Exp	123 Exp	23	23 Exp	123 Exp	123 Exp	123 Exp	23
..	GENEVA ... dep	4 45	7 55	1120	..	..	13 8	1513	1818	..	1942
0	Lausanne *p.* 279 dp.	5 34	8 42	1157	..	12 5	1412	16 0	1852	..	2059
9	Cossonay	..	..	*r*	..	1227	B	*r*	*r*	..	2117
24	Yverdon (*p.* 287 dep.	6 3	9 14	1234	..	13 6		1633	1930	..	2142
47	Neuchatel .. arr.	6 30	9 44	13 6	..	14 5	15 5	17 3	20 2	..	2232
	dep	6 32	9 49	1310	..	1412	15 6	17 6	20 6	..	2235
56	Neuveville		10 2		..	1435	..	..	..	..	2255
65	Bienne (Biel) arr.	6 55	1015	1336	⌣	1456	1528	1730	2032	..	2313
	Berne (*below*) dep.	6 30	9†35	..	1335	1412	..	16 2	1950	2250	..
	Bienne arr.	7 3	10†17	..	14 8	1456	..	1652	2038	2324	..
65	Bienne (Biel) dep.	7 14	1029	1343	1416	15 4	1529	1739	2050	2331	..
	Sonceboz dep.	6 28	10 0	*Via* Olten	13*20	1440	..	*Via* Olten	20†2	21†57	..
87	Moutier ... dep.	7 39	1053		1442	1536	..		2117	2357	..
94	Delémont .... arr.	7 51	11 5		1454	1554	1559		2129	0 10	..
119	Delle (*p* 268) arr,	8 33	1232		1540	1724	1724		..	0 58	..
94	Delémont dep	8 1	1110		..	1610	16 3		2136	..	..
118	**Bale** (Swiss Sta) arr.	8 41	1148	1530	..	17 2	1638	1946	2213	..	..

* Weekdays. *r* Rest. Car † 2 & 3 class B Buffet Car. ‡ 3rd class only.

Neuchatel, Chaux-de-F. Locle (24 miles)

Swiss Federal Ry. (Electric) † Sundays. * Weekdays.

	23	23	23	2*3	23	23	23	23	23*	23	23	23
Neuchatel ..dep.	dep.	6 42	8 9	1017	1217	1313	1414	1710	dep.	1830	2037	22 8
Chaux-de-Fonds a	6 7	7 36	8 57	1110	1315	1358	15 4	1758	19 0	1923	2120	2256
Locle (Ville) arr.	6 20	7 54	9 11	1123	1342	1415	1524	1819	1925	1942	2135	2315

	23	23	23	23	23	23	23	23	23	23	23	23	23
Locle (Ville) dep.	5 10	6 31	7 5	8 36	1040	1152	1244	1431	1658	1833	2032	2214	2322
Chaux-de-Fonds d	5 37	6 53	7 37	8 57	11 0	1212	13 5	1451	1719	19 0	2054	2227	2333
Neuchatel arr.	6 26	7 47	8 26	9 47	1148	13 2	1354	1545	1813	1950	2141	..	..

(Electric) Berne, Bienne, Chaux-de-Fonds. [Swiss Federal Rly.

Mls.		23	23	23	3	23 *	23 *	23	23	23	23	23	23	23	123 Exp	23
0	**Berne**............dep.	..	6 30	..	8 4	9 35	12 8	1211	1412	16 5	1727	..	1825	2033	2250	2332
21	Bienne (Biel) .. arr.	..	7 3	..	8 54	1017	1234	13 1	1456	1651	1758	..	1913	21 2	2324	0 12
	dep.	6 3	7 15	7 48	9 27	1058	1238	1344	15*a*32	17 9	18 4	1811	1931	2125	..	..
39	Sonceboz (*above*) ,,	6 25	7 30	8 7	9 48	1121	13 2	1410	15*a*45	1733	1821	1831	1957	2151	..	..
40	Chaux-de-Fonds arr.	7 18	8 10	8 50	1035	1219	1345	1459	16*a*17	1825	1857	1912	2048	2237	..	..

* Weekdays. *a* 3 cl.

		23	23	23	23	23	23	3	23	23	23	23	23	3
0	Chaux-de-Fonds dep.	..	5 27	6 12	8 21	9 5	1123	1224	13 0	1512	18 3	1912	2058	2237
19	Soncboz (*above*) ..arr.	..	6 7	6 56	8 54	9 51	1257	1256	1346	16 0	1846	1957	2143	23 5
28	Bienne .... arr.	..	6 28	7 25	9 11	1017	1228	1312	1411	1620	19 8	2020	22 7	2323
	dep.	5 30	6 37	7 50	9 24	1036	1237	1319	1437	1710	1914	2124	2224	..
49	**Berne** ....arr.	6 16	7 29	8 24	9 52	1126	1330	1344	1525	1740	1940	22 6	2253	..

(Bale), Lucerne, Berne, Lausanne, Geneva. Swiss Federal Railway.

ELECTRIC.	123 Exp	123	123	23	123 Exp	23		123 Exp	123	123	123	123 Exp	123 Exp	123	23
Bale } p. 281 ..dep.	0 23	..	..		7 25	9 45	..	1230	* Weekdays.	1230	..	16 8	..	..	
Berne ..arr.	2 23	..	..		9 26	1120	..	14 6		14 7	..	1748	..	..	
		2 3			123			Exp		2 3		2 3		2 3	
Lucerne ....dep.	..	5*33	..	Weekdays only.	8 15	..	..	1249		1111	..	1411	1842	1659	Weekdays only.
Langnau ....dep.	..	7 14	..		9 8	..	..	1342		1238	..	1542	2017	1824	
Berne ......arr.		8 15	..		9 40	..	..	1416		1340	..	1640	2113	1927	
			Exp		Exp					2 3		123			
Berne ....dep	2 50	..	..	8 42	9 57	1124	..	1421	r Rest. Car.	1440	..	18 0	..	..	21 4
Fribourg .... arr.	3 20	..	..	..	1023	12 8	..	1447		1530	..	1826	..	..	..
Fribourg .... dep.	3 25	..	..	..	1025	1217	..	1449		1536	..	1828	..	..	..
Romont ....arr.	..	..	..	..	1046	1258	..	..		1614	..	1849	..	..	..
Bulle } 2 & 3 cl. arr.	..	..	..	..	1128	15*9	..	..		..	..	r	..	..	..
Bulle } 2 & 3 cl. dep.	..	..	..	..	9*50	..	..	..		13 2	..		..	..	..
Romont ...... dep.	..	..	..	..	1047	13 0	..	..		1616	..	1850	..	..	..
Lausanne (to Simplon p. 280) arr.	4 25	123	..	9 53	1128	1352	..	1547	Exp	17 9	Exp	1932		..	2214
		Exp	r		r	123	2 3		123		123		Exp	Exp	
Lausanne dep.	4 49	7 8	9 5	9 55	1136	1415	1430	1556	1657	1715	1912	1939	2050	2256	2216
Morges .... dep.	5 1	7 18	9 15		1147	1426	1446	..	..	1732		r	21 1	23 6	↓
Rolle .... dep.	..	7 30	..	..	..	..	1511	r	..	1758	r		..	..	↓
Nyon (side) ....dep.	5 20	7 40	9 34	..	1217	1445	1522	..	1725	1812	..	20 7	2120	2325	↓
Geneva .... arr.	5 36	7 55	9 49	1032	1223	15 1	1550	1638	1741	1851	20 4	2023	2136	2340	2253

French Lines, p. 266, &c.	123 Exp	123 Exp	123 Exp	23	23	123	123 Exp	123 Exp	123 Exp	123 Exp	123 Exp	123 Exp	123 Exp	123 Exp	23	123 Exp
Geneva ..dep.	1 15	4 45	7 17	6 30	8 5	1026	1115	1120	13 8	1435	1513	1652	1754	1818	1942	2253
Nyon (side) dep.	1 32	5 1	7 35	..	8 33	1043	..	1137	1325	..	..	17 8	1811	r	..	23 9
Rolle	1 42	..	..	..	8 48	11 0	..	r	1336	..	..	..	..	..	..	..
Morges	1 54	5 20	7 55	..	9 8	11 9	r	1155	1349	..	..	1728	1831	..	..	2328
Lausanne arr.	2 7	5 30	8 7	7 7	9 23	1121	12 0	1210	14 1	1519	1554	1742	1843	19 4	2019	2338
		2 3						2 3			2 3		r			
Lausanne dep.	2 20	6 2	8 18	7 8	9 41	..	12 6	1245	..	1524	1646	..	1848	..	2021	..
Romont .... arr.	..	6 54	9 1	Weekdays only.	1032	..	..	1338	..	..	1736	..	1931	..	Weekdays only.	..
Bulle } 2&3 cl. a.	..	8 21	r		1128	..	..	15*9	..	..	2018	..	2017	..		..
Bulle } 2&3 cl. d.	..	6*0			9*50	..	..	13 2	..	..	..	..	1843	..		..
Romont ....dep.	..	6 56	9 2		1034	..	..	1342	..	..	1738	..	1932	..		..
Fribourg arr.	3 23	7 33	9 27		11 9	..	13 2	1418	..	1626	1814	..	1953	..		..
Fribourg dep.	3 28	8 0	9 29		1114	..	13 3	1424	..	1628	1821	..	1955	..		..
Berne .... arr.	3 55	8 44	9 55	8 18	1155	..	1330	15 6	..	1655	19 8	..	2022	..	2131	..
	Exp	2 3	2 3				Exp			Exp	2 3			2 3		
Berne ..dep.	6 40	9 10	11 8	..	..	..	1340	..	..	1714	1922	..	..	2054	..	..
Langnau arr.	7 14	1011	1213	..	..	..	1412	..		1746	2030	..	..	2143	..	..
Lucerne arr.	8 5	1128	1336	..	..	..	15 1	..	..	1837	2156	..	..	2250	..	..
Berne } p. 281 dep.	4 19	..	1010	..	1230	..	1345	..	..	1718	..	..	2050	..	..	..
Bale .. } arr.	6 16	..	1155	..	1524	..	1531	..	..	1855	..	..	2225	..	..	..

Nyon—St. Cergue—Morez. (Electric)

2 & 3 class. * Weekdays.

Nyon (side) d. p.	7 42	11 7	1330	1818	2025
St. Cergue arr.	8 30	1154	1421	19 5	21 7
St. Cergue dep.	8 32	12 1	1425	1911	..
Morez (P.L.M.) arr.	9 40	13 7	15*57	20*18	..

Morez (P.L.M.) dep.	..	10*54	18 0
St. Cergue ....arr.	..	1159	1910
St. Cergue ....dep.	6 30	12 4	1913
Nyon (side) ....arr.	7 20	1249	20 3

Special Sun. and Hol. Services, see bills.

Interlaken, Berne, Neuchatel, Pontarlier (Paris).

Mls.	ELECTRIC.	23 a	23	23	3 cl.	123 Exp	23	23	123 Exp
0	Interlaken (East) p. 281 dep.	..*	6‖18	8 15	1033	1215	1541	18 6	19 3
36	Berne ....dep.	5 18	8 43	1024	1248	1455	1716	1943	2212
	(Via Direct Line) arr.	6 20	9 43	1127	1350	1543	1810	2031	23 0
69	Neuchatel .... dep.	6 52	1026	..	14 4	1567	1835	2034	23 5
94	Verrières (Mid. Eu. time) arr.	8 9	1145	..	1536	1640	1958	2145	0 1
102	Pontarlier .... ,,	8 39	1214	..	*	1655	2022	..	0 17
						Exp	*		
384	Paris (p. 267) .... ,,	1925	..	..	..	2340	5 35	..	7 0

Mls.		23	123 Exp	23	23	23	23	123 Exp	23	
0	Paris (p. 267).......... dep.	..	2255	..	..	..	..	1015	..	‖ Bhf.
282	Pontarlier .... ,,	..	6 30	..	..	1020	1221	1655	17*55	..
90	Verrières e (Md.Eu. time) arr.	..	6 46	..	..	1040	1241	1710	18*27	
	Verrières dep.	5 21	6 50	7 5	..	1050	1249	1712	1851	2036
315	Neuchatel .... arr.	6 18	7 33	8 6	..	1155	1350	1752	1954	2136
	Neuchatel dep.	6 48	7 50	8 37	1020	1213	1419	1759	20 7	2225
348	Berne ....arr.	7 46	8 33	9 46	1128	1313	1522	1845	21 5	2324
384	Interlaken (East) p. 281 arr.	..	9 48	1132	1320	1550	18 6			..

* Weekdays.

a 3 cl. Berne–Neuchatel.

Vallorbe, Le Pont, Brassus.

	23	23	23	23
Vallorbe (p.267) dp.	7 47	1115	1511	21 8
Le Pont .... dep.	8 8	1135	1531	2132
Brassus ......arr.	8 35	12 9	16 0	2159

	23	23	23	23
Brassus ....dep.	5 57	9 48	1325	1752
Le Pont ....dep.	6 25	1017	14 0	1823
Vallorbe ....arr.	6 45	1037	1420	1843

ELECTRIC.] (See Note *re* Domo d'Ossola-Milan, *page* 120.) [Swiss Federal Rly.

Mls.	*Thro' Services from London (p. 119) from*	1 2 luxe	2 3	2 3	1 2 3 Exp	1 2 3 Exp	2 3	1 2 3	2 3	1 2 3 Exp	2 3	1 2 3 Exp	2 3	2 3	1 2 3 Exp
0	PARIS (267) dep.	2220	—	..	2255	2330	A..	..	..	..	..	1015	..	*	1620
316	Lausanne .. ar.	6 26	..	..	7 0	7 55	A..	..	..	..	..	1751	..	..	2345
..	Geneva (279) d.	4 45 G	1 15	5*5	6 30 r	7 17 r	8 5	1026 r	1120	13 8 r	1435	1654 r	1826	21 1	2253
0	**Lausanne** a.	5 30	2 7	6*40	7 7	8 7	9 23	1121	1210	14 1	1519	1742	1949	2228	2338
	Lausanne d.	6 37	5*0	6 52	7 15	8 21	9 30	1135	1215	1410	1530	18 0	1952	2232	2354
12	Vevey .... arr.	6 52	5 21	7 15	7 30	8 36	9 53	1150	1242	1425	1554	1815	20 9	2257	0 9
15	Clarens .. dep.	.	5 30	7 28	..	..	10 4	.	1255	..	16 8	.	2010	23 7	.
15½	Montreux arr.	6 59	5 32	7 30	7 38	8 43	10 6	1158	1257	1433	1610	1823	2019	23 9	0 16
17	Territet .. dep.	EXTRA FARES.	5 38	7 35	..	8 48	1012	12 4	1259	1438	1616	1828	2024	2313	↓
17¼	Veytaux .. dep.		5 41	7 38	..	..	1014	..	13 4	.	1618	.	..	2315	
19	Villeneuve ,,		5 45	7 41	..	..	1019	12 9	13 7	1448	1622	..	2029	2318	
25	Aigle (p. 290) ar.		5 58	8 1	..	8 59	1031	1217	1319	1451	1636	1839	2038	2330	
30	Bex (p. 290) ,,		6 10	8 12	..	9 8	1043	1226	1331	15 0	1648	1848	2047	2340	
32	St. Maurice a		6*17	8 18	..	9 15	1049	1233	1337	15 7	1656	1855	2054	2346	
	St. Maurice d		6 25	8 23	..	9 17	1055	1234	1349	15 9	17 1	1857	2058	*	
38	Vernayaz .. ,,		6 37	8 38	..	..	11 6	..	14 1		1713	.	21 8		
41	Martigny .. arr.	..	6 42	8 41	..	9 31	1111	1247	14 6	1522	1718	1910	2113		
58	Sion ...... ,,	..	7 23	9 15	8 31	9 32	1146	13 8	1440	1544	1753	1931	2143		1 12
68	Sierre .. dep.	8 6	7 46	9 20	..	10 8	1211	1326	15 5	16 0	1831	1947	22 4		↓
73	Loëche (Leuk) d	..	7 57	9 50		1019	1223	1337	1518	1612	1846	1959	2219		
85	Viège (Visp) ar.	..	8 17	1011	‡	1034	1245	1355	1541	1627	19 9	2014	2239		
106	*p.* Zermatt .. a.	..	1040	*	1120	13b7	..	1616	..	1855	..	..	..		
112	288 Gornergrat ,,	..	..	..	13c0	14c53	..	17c40	..	20d20	..	.			
91	**Brigue** (Brig) arr.	8 38	8 28	1021	9 15	1044	1255	14 5	1550	1638	1920	2024	2245		1 57
	Brigue (Brig) dep.	8 45	..	..	9 20	1050		1416	..	1652		2040	..		2 15
116	Domo d'Ossola arr.	9 22	..	..	10 1	1127	..	15 0	..	1733	..	2120	..		2 56
	Domo d'Ossola dep.	9 53	..	..	1022	1148	..	1530	..	1752	—	2140	..		3 30
..	Turin .... arr.	..	..	..	1516	1610	..	1950	..	2210	..	..	..		8 45
138	Baveno	1024	..	..	1055	1235	..	1614	..	1835	..	2214	..		4 4
140	Stresa	1029	..	..	11 0	1240	..	1619	..	1841	..	2219	..		4 9
192	MILAN (p. 302)	12 4	..	..	1240	1428	..	1744	..	2022	..	24 0	..		5 50

Miles from Brigue.		1 2 3 Exp	2 3	2 3	2 3	2 3	1 2 3 Exp	1 2 3 fast	1 2 3 Exp	2 3	1 2 3	2 3	1 2 3 Exp	1 2 3 Exp	1 2 luxe
	MILAN (*see p.* 302) d.	0 15	..	..	..	..	..	7 0	9 45	..	1025	..	1420	17 0	1910
	Stresa	1 57	..	..	..	..	..	8 45	1131	..	..	..	16 7	1845	2055
	Baveno	2 3	..	..	..	..	..	8 51	1138	..	..	..	1613	1852	21 1
	Turin ..... dep.	..	..	..	..	..	..	..	7 22	..	..	..	1319	..	..
	Domo d'Ossola ...... arr.	2 40	..	..	..	..	..	9 30	1214	..		..	1652	1937	2139
	Domo d'Ossola .... dep.	3 5	..	..	..	..	..	10 5	1233	..	1347	..	17 9	1957	2154
..	**Brigue** .... arr	3 48	..	..	..	..	..	1053	1316	..	1432	..	1752	2040	2237
0	(Brig) .. dep.	4 0	..	..	4 56	6 21	9 8	1116	1328	1419	1540	..	18 9	2050	2245
..	*p* Gornergrat dep.	..	..	..	..		..	7d10	10c30	..	11d40	..	13c30	15c45	..
..	288 Zermatt . dep.	..	..	..	..		7 10	9b10	12 0	..	14 5	..	15d50	18‡15	..
6	Viège (Visp) .. dep	..	..	..	5 4	6 32	9 16	1125	1337	1428	1549	..	1818	r	..
18	Loëche (Leuk) *p.* 153	..	..	..	5 20	6 50	9 30	1146	1353	1449	1611	..	1834	—	..
23	Sierre (Siders)	..	..	..	5 48	7 10	9 40	1156	14 2	15 1	1623	..	1843	2119	..
38	Sion (Sitten) dep.	4 45	..	..	6 5	7 32	9 54	1215	1417	1521	1642	1711	1858	2134	2327
49	Martigny .... dep	..	..	..	6 34	8 5	1013	1238	1438	1557	17 4	1745	1919	21c53	G
52	Vernayaz	—	..	..	6 40	8 11	..	..	r	16 3		1751	r	..	EXTRA FARES
58	St. Maurice .. arr.	..	..	..	6 51	8 21	1024	1251	1451	1613	1717	18 2	1932	..	
	St. Maurice .. dep.	..	5 22	6 11	6 56	8 25	1028	1255	1452	1620	1721	18 9	1936	..	
60	Bex (p. 290)	..	5 28	6 18	7 2	8 31	1034	13 1	1458	1626	1728	1813	1941	..	
66	Aigle (p. 290) .. dep.	..	5 39	6 30	7 12	8 41	1041	1310	15 6	1636	1737	1828	1952	..	
72	Villeneuve .	—	5 51	6 44	7 26	8 55	..	1320	..	1651	1747	1843	20 2	..	
73	Veytaux-Chillon ..	..	5 54	6 47	7 29	8 58	..	..	..	1654		1846	..	..	
74	Territet-Glion .. dep.	..	5 57	6 50	7 32	9 1	1056	1325	.	1657	1752	1849	20 7	..	
75	Montreux (Vernex) d.	5 42	6 1	6 55	7 35	9 6	11 2	1330	1522	17 2	1758	1855	2013	2225	0 19
76	Clarens	..	6 4	6 59	7 40	9 9	..	..		17 5	..	1859		..	..
79	Vevey	5 50	6 14	7 12	7 49	9 18	1111	1339	1531	1717	18 7	19 7	2022	2234	0 26
91	**Lausanne** .. arr.	6 8	6 44	7 45	8 7	9 44	1127	1355	1547	1745	1823	1934	2038	2250	0 43
	Lausanne .. dep.	7 8	7 8	..	8 20	9 55	1136	1415	1556	..	1834	1939	2050	2256	4 49
128	Geneva (p. 279) ar.	7 55	7 55	..	9 6	1032	1223	15 1	1638	..	1921	2023	2136	2340	5 36
0	p267 Lausanne dep.	6 23	..	..	..	..	..	..	16 6	..	..	..B	2056	23 0	0 52
316	p267 PARIS (Lyon) arr.	14 0	..	..	..	..	..	..	2340	..	..	..B	5 30	7 0	8 40

G Simplon Orient Train de luxe—*see page* 83.
* Weekdays. ‡ Via Brigue to and from Zermatt, *see page* 288. *r* Rest. Car.

A From Paris June 30–Sept. 9 only.
B From Lausanne July 1–Sept. 10 only.
a Suns. and Hols., July 1—Aug. 31. *b* June 15—Sept. 10.
c June 1—Sept. 30. *d* July 1—Aug. 31.

VEVEY—MONT PELERIN, (14 Minutes). 2,700 ft.—From Vevey and Mont Pelerin dep. 6.35, 7.10, 7.30, 8.30, 9.0, 9.30, 10.30, 11.30, 12.18, 13.10, 13.35, 14.0, 14.20, 14.40, 15.0, 15.40, 16.20, 17.0, 17.40, 18.0, 18.20, 18.40, 19.0, 20.0, 20.30, 22.0, 23.35

(ELECTRIC). (Bale) Olten, Berne, Interlaken. [Swiss Fed. and Berne-Loetschberg-Simplon Coy's.

Mls.		123	123	123	12	123	123	123	123	23	123	23	123	123	123	123
		Exp	Exp	Exp	luxe	Exp	Exp	Exp	Exp		Exp		Exp	Exp	Ex r	Exp
0	(p. 282) **Bale** (Swiss) dep.	0 23	..	6 57	¶	7 25		9 45	1230	1330	16 8	..	1725	1725	1855	2142
25	Olten ....dep.	1 14	..	7 34	..	8 20	8 50	1019	13 9	15 5	1646	..	1759	1759	1938	2229
42	**Berne** *(from Geneva, &c., pp, 278, 279)* arr.	2 23	..	8 30	..	9 26	9 45	1120	14 7	1649	1748	..	1848	1848	2042	2328
		23					23	123		23			b	23		
	dep.	5 45	6 51	8 46	8 51	1014	1115	12 0	1432	1449	18 9	1835	1856	1947	2110	2336
47	Gümligen	5 56	..		..		1127	r	r	15 0		1846	b	1957	..	2347
61½	**Thun** (Bahnf.) arr.	6 26	7 14	9 9	9 16	1040	1156	1223	1456	1530	1834	1916	1922	2028	2135	0 15
	dep.	6a35	7 16	9 18	9 18	1042	12a8	1228	1458	1540	1837	1930	1924	20a35	2141	0 22
68	Spiez ....arr.	6 55	7 27	9 22	9 29	1053	1227	1239	15 9	16 0	1848	1950	1935	20a55	2152	0 33
78¼	**Interlaken** (West) arr.	7 30	7 48	9 42	10 2	1124	..	1312	1534	1640	1921	20a18	20 5		2218	..
79½	Interlaken(East)(*below*)a	7a44	7 54	9 48	10 9	1132	..	1320	1540	1648	1929	..	..	..	..	

From Lucerne, &c., see below.	123	23	123	123	23	123	123	23	123	23	123	23	123	123	123
	Exp		Exp	Exp		Exp	Exp		Exp		Exp		Exp		Exp
Interlaken (East) ....dep.	..	..	8 15	1015	1033	1215	1335	13c42	1541	..	1740	18 6	19 3	19b58	2117
Interlaken (West) ....dep.	5a0	6 18	8 22	1021	1037	1221	1340	1351	1548	1650	1745	1816	1910	20b5	2125
Spiez ....dep.	5 27	6 49	8 51	1048	11 4	1245	14 5	1425	1619	1720	18 8	1849	1947	2032	2158
Thun (Bahnf.) .... arr.	5 39	7 9	9 2	1059	1121	1256	1415	1443	1630	1738	1819	19 0	1958	2050	22 9
dep.	5 44	7 13	9 5	11 1	1126	1258	1417	1454	1633	1752	1821	19 6	20 0	21 6	2211
Gümligen ....arr.		..	r	..	x	r	b	1526	r	1824	r	..	r	2135	r
Berne *(To Geneva, &c., pp. 278, 279)* arr.	6 11	7 49	9 31	1124	1225	1321	1443	1537	1658	1835	1844	1931	2025	2146	2236
	Exp			Exp			b								
dep.	7 0	..	1010	1135	..	1345	1510	1621	1718	..	19 0	1943	2050	To Paris.	..
Olten ....arr.	8 1	..	1113	1226	..	1446	1556	1757	1816	..	1952	2120	2148		..
(p. 282) **Bale** (Swiss) ....arr.	8 55	..	1155	13 7	..	1531	1629	.	1855	..	2025	22 0	2225		

* Weekdays. *a* 3 class only. *b* July 1-Sept. 10. *r* Rest. car. † Sundays. *x* Via Belp.

¶ Tue., Thur. and Sat. to Sept. 2nd.

(Berne), Interlaken, Brienz, Meiringen, Lucerne. [Swiss Federal Rly.

123	23	23	23	123	23	23	23	123		23	123	123	23	123	23	123	23	23
..	6 51	6 51	8 46	1014	12 0	a	1449	1618	dep.Berne(*above*)arr.	..	1225	1321	..	1653	1844	1844	2236	2236
7 22	8 6	9 14	1030	1227	1410	1528	1719	1815	,, **Int'laken**(East) ,,	9 25	1030	12 9	13 5	1431	1718	1731	1938	2044
..	8 19	..	1041	1241	1423	b	1732	..	,, Niederried ..dep.	9 13	..	a	1254	1421	17 6			2034
7 41	8 36	9 36	1058	1259	1440	1549	1749	1834	arr.Brienz ...... ,,	8 55	1010	1147	1231	14 3	1645	17 9	1918	2016
..	..	8 25	9 46	1151	13 0	1436	1557	1730	dp. Interlaken Str. arr.	10 6	1120	1255	1415	1512	1753	1827	..	..
..	..	9 23	1046	1246	1349	1533	1655	1819	,, Giessbach ,,	9 6	1022	1159	1310	1415	1656	1723	..	..
..	..	9 35	1057	1258	14 0	1547	17 6	1831	arr. Brienz(*p.*294) dp.	8 56	1012	1149	13 0	14 5	1646	1710	..	.
7 43	8 38	9 39	11 1	13 3	1444	1551	1751	1835	dep.Brienz ....arr.	8 52	10 9	1146	1229	14 2	1643	17 7	1917	2014
8 4	9 10	10 3	1126	1332	1515	1616	1816	1858	,, Meiringen dep.	8 31	9 56	1132	12 8	1345	1623	1652	19 4	1955
8 30	9 42	1040	1212	14 4	1550	1657	1848	1924	,, Brunig .... ,,	8 4	9 37	11 9	1137	1315	16 0	1629	1843	1932
..	9 55	1053	1227	1418	16 5	1712	19 3	..	,, Lungern .... ,,	7 33	..	1035	1112	1247	1532	16 3	..	19 5
9 3	1019	1115	1251	1441	1630	1734	1926	1956	,, Giswil ..... ,,	7 6	8 57	1012	1045	1223	15 8	1538	18 7	1839
..	1051	1139	1317	1518	17 2	18 5	1956		dep.Alpnachstad ,,	6 27	..	9 40	10 9	1155	1429	15 6		18 3
9 42	1115	1158	1339	1542	1725	1827	2019	2032	arr. **Lucerne** ..dep.	6 4	8 15	9 17	9 44	1133	14 2	1445	1725	1735

* Weekdays. † Sundays. *a* To Sept. 10. *b* Also 1 cl. June 15-Sept. 10.

(ELECTRIC.) Bernese Oberland Railway. (2nd & 3rd class.)

For Wengeralp and Murren Railways, see page 292. For Jungfrau Railway, see page 289.

	a		b	b		a		b					
Interlaken (Ost)........dep.	7 20	8 10	9 15	10 0	1035	1150	1340	15 8	1558	1818	1943		
Wilderswil ....dep.	7 27	8 18	9 23	10 7	1043	1158	1349	1516	16 6	1825	1950		
Zweilutschinen .... arr.	7 38	8 30	9 35	1018	1054	12 8	1359	1527	1617	1836	20 1		
Zweilutschinen ......dep.	7 39	8 31	9 37	1019	1055	12 9	14 0	1528	1618	18c37	20 2		
Lauterbrunnen ...... arr.	7 55	8 46	9 52	1035	1110	1223	1415	1544	1634	1852	2017		
Zweilutschinen ....dep.	7 41	8 33	..	1021	1057	1212	14 2	1530	1620	18c39	20 4		
Grindelwald .... arr.	8 21	9 14		11 1	1137	1252	1442	1610	17 0	1918	2043		

				c				d					
Grindelwald ....dep.	6 55	8a50	1112	1230	1418	1625	1753	1843					
Zweilutschinen .... arr.	7 36	9a31	1141	1310	1459	17 5	1833	1922					
Lauterbrunnen ......dep.	7 20	9 23	1125	1255	1443	1650	1818	19 6					
Zweilutschinen ...... arr.	7 35	9 37	1140	13 9	1458	17 4	1832	1921					
Zweilutschinen ....dep.	7 39	9 41	1144	1313	15 3	17 8	1836	1925					
Wilderswil .... arr.	7 49	9 52	1155	1323	1513	1718	1848	1936					
Interlaken (Ost)........ arr.	7 56	10 0	12 2	1330	1520	1725	1855	1943					

a June 15–Sept. 10.
b June 15–Sept. 17.
c June 1–Sept. 17.
d July 1–Sept. 10.

Thro' Tables, see pp. 123 to 127, 270.

Bale, Olten, (Berne) Lucerne:

[Electric.] Swiss Federal Ry.

	123	23	12	123	123	123	23	23	123	23	23	123	123	123	123	23	123	123
	Exp	*	Exp		Exp	Exp			Exp	b		Exp		Exp	Exp		Exp	Exp
Bale (Sw. st.) d.	0 23	5 11	6 45	7 18	7 25	9 0	..	1021	12 0	13 7	1330	1450	16 8	1725	1730	1820	1855	2142
Liestal ....dep.	0 36	5 32	r	r	7 42	9 13	..	1043	r	1319	1352	..	1621	..		1843	19 8	2155
Olten(*below*)arr.	0 58	6 7	7 16	7 52	8 9	9 34	..	1120	1237	1343	1425	1522	1642	1756	18 2	1919	1929	2220
Berne (*p.*281) a.	2 23	8 20	..	..	9 26	..	..	1334	1357	..	1649	..	1748	1848	..	..	2042	2328
	23	*			23	r							23					
Olten ....dep.	5 41	6 12	7 17	7 56	8 54	9 37	1053	1156	1240	1345	1451	1527	1651	..	18 5	2018	1934	2225
Zofingen dep.	5 54	6 22	..	8 5	9 4	9 47	11 2	1210	..	1353	15 1	1535	17 1	..	..	2028	1943	2235
Sursee ..dep.	6 30	arr.	..	..	9 35	10 5	1127	1244	..	..	1532	..	1736	..	..	21 1	..	
Lucerne arr	7 10		8 1	8 44	1010	1028	1156	1323	1330	1433	16 6	1615	1819	..	1852	2135	2022	2320

	123	123	23	23	123	23	123	23	123	23	123	123	23	123	12
	Exp	Exp			Exp		Exp		Exp		Exp	Exp		Exp	Exp
Lucerne dep.	4 47	7 25	8 5	9 40	1045	12 6	1253	1415	1524	17 4	1838	..	1950	2041	2227
Sursee ..dep.	..	..	8 35	1021	..	1248	r	1454	..	1744	r	..	2031	r	r
Zofingen dep.	..	8 3	9 1	1056		1320	..	1525	16 2	1817	1920	..	21 2	..	..
Olten ....arr.	5 32	8 12	9 10	11 8	1128	1331	1339	1536	1611	1829	1929	..	2114	2125	2310
Berne ..dep.	..	7 0	7 25	..	..	1230		..	1510	1718	..	19 0	..	1943	..
Olten ....dep.	5 40	8 19	9 18	1137	1130	1430	1343	1625	1614	1847	1934	1954	2229	2128	2311
Liestal ..dep.	..	8 42	9 45	12 8	..	15 4		1656	1635	1923		..	23 1	..	..
Bale(Sw. s.) a.	6 16	8 55	10 1	1228	12 0	1524	1415	1719	1648	1946	20 8	2025	2321	22 0	2341

b Sats. June 24–Sept. 9. *r* Rest. Car. * Weekdays.

(Geneva), etc., Bienne, Olten, Aarau, Brugg, Zurich, Winterthur, St. Gallen (Munich)

Electric] [Swiss Federal Ry.

	123	23	23		23	123	123	23	123	123	23	123	123	23		123	
	Exp					Exp	Exp			Exp			Exp			Exp	
Geneva (*p.* 278) dp.	..		..	..	.	4 45	7 55	.	..	1120	Limited Train.	..	1513	..	Limited Train.	1818	..
Lausanne .... dep			..	..	..	5 34	8 42	..	..	1157		..	16 0	..		1852	..
Neuchatel ....dep.	.	..	..	..	..	6 32	9 49	1113	..	1310		..	17 6	..		20 6	..
Bienne (Biel) ..dep.	.	..	5 40	..	..	7 0	1024	1248	..	1343		..	1739	1744		2044	..
Selzach .... dep.		..	6 9	..	..	..	..	1318	..	..		..		1815			..
Solothurn .... arr.			6 20	..	..	7 21	1045	1329	..	14 6		..	18 1	1825		21 5	..
Solothurn .... dep.			6 30	..	..	7 23	1047	1338	..	14 8		..	18 4	1833		21 7	..
Olten.......... arr.	..		7 25	..	..	7 52	1116	1435	..	1443	..	..	1833	1929		2135	..
				23		Exp	Exp		Exp	Exp		Exp	Exp		23	Exp	23
Geneva (*p.* 279) dp.	1 15	*	..	6 30	..	..	7 17	8 5	..	1115	..	1435	..	..	1518	1754	1942
Lausanne .... dep.	2 20		..	7 8	..	..	8 18	9 41	..	12 6	..	1524	..	..	1646	1848	2021
Berne .. dep.	4 19		5 49	8 20		7 0	1010	1230	1135	1345	1510	1710	1718	1813	1913	2038	2133
Olten ....dep.	5 37	6 20	7 48	* Limited Train. ↓	9 41	8 3	1125	1446	1229	1455	16 0 ↓	18 4	1839	2025	20 1	2148 r	Limited Train. ↓
Aarau .... arr.	5 50	6 40	8 7		9 57	8 14	1140	15 2	1241	15 9		1816	1851	2046	2011	22 1	
Aarau .... dep	5 53	6 42	8 15		9 59	8 15	1142	1520	1243	1511		1818	1853	2054	2012 ↓	22 3	
Brugg .... arr.	6 10	7 10	8 41		1021	8 30	1158	1543	..			..	19 9	2120		2219	
Brugg ....dep	6 11	7 14	8 51		1025	8 31	12 0	1550	r	r		r	1910	2129		2220	
Turgi		7 19	8 57		1029	..	..	1554					..	2136			
Baden	6 22	7 25	9 4		1038	8 40	1210	16 0	.	1537	17 1	1841	1919	2144		2229	
Zurich ....arr.	6 42	7 48	9 38	9 50	11 4	8 59	1230	1626	1324	1558	1650	1859	1939	2216	2049	2249	23 3
Schaffhausen, Lucerne, &c., (*p.* 284.)									23	123			23				
						Exp	Exp			Exp		Exp					
Zurich........ dep.	6 56	4 54	1019	..	1131	9 15	1342	..	1347	1621	18 5	19 9	2134	..	21 5	2315	..
Wallisellen .... dep.	r	5 12	1028	..	1143		..	..	..		..	..	2149	..	..	..	..
Winterthur .... arr.	7 17	5 30	1059	..	12 0	9 37	14 4		1427	1642	1829	1930	2214		2124	2336	..
Bale (*via* Bulach) d.		..	..	..	7 40	7 2	1034		..	1352		..	1934				
Winterthur .... dep	7 19	5 40	..	..	12 7	9 40	14 8	..	1430	1645	1837	19 2	2222	..	2125	2338	..
Wil ....arr.	7 39	6 30	.	..	1246	10 1	1428	..	1513	17 7	1913	1954	2254	..	..	2357	..
Gossau ....arr	7 55	7 6	..	..	1320	1023	1450	..	..	1725	1938	2016	2319	..	2157	0 16	..
St. Gallen ......arr.	8 6	7 22	.	..	1337	1034	15 1	..	..	1735	1948	2027	2333	..	22 5	0 27	..
,, ...dep.	8 10	7 43	.	..	14 0	1036	15 6	..	..	1737		2033	2338	..	22 6		..
Rorschach (Bhf) arr.	8 26	8 5	..	..	1424	1052	1522	..	..	1753	..	2054	2358	..	2222	..	..
St. Margrethen..arr	8 36	8 21	..	..	1444	1110	1533	..	..	18 9	..	2110	..	..		..	..
(*p.* 285) ..dep	8 43	..	..	..	..	1118	16 0	..	..	1820	..	2150	..	..	..	..	..
Lindau ....arr.	9 12	..	..	..	..	1155	1632	..	..	1931	..	2229	..	..	..	..	..
Munich (*p.* 187) arr.	13 1	..	..	..	..	16 2	2130	..	..	..	..	..	..	..	..	..	..

* Weekdays. *r* Restaurant Car.

Electric **Bale, Brugg, (Zurich).** Swiss Federal Rly.

Mls.		1 2	2 3	1 2 3	1 2	1 2 3	1 2 3	2 3	2 3	1 2 3	1 2 3	2 3	1 2 3	1 2 3	2 3	1 2 3	2 3	1 2 3
		D	*	Exp	Exp	Exp	Exp			Exp			Exp	Exp		Exp		Exp
	Bale (Swiss Stn.) dep.	2 48	5 3	6 49	7 13	7r40	8 50	9 8	1034	1155	1320	1352	1454	1714	1719	1838	1947	2138
10½	Rheinfelden	|	5 24	..	..	7 57	9 6	9 30	1059	1212	..	1419	1510	1728	1744	1853	20 9	2154
18¾	Stein-Sackingen dp.	|	5 41	r	r	8 10	..	9 51	1118	r	..	1442	..	1739	18 8	..	2028	..
36¼	Brugg ....arr.	|	6 17	..		8 35	9 39	1026	1156	1248	..	1520	1545	18 3	1850	1936	21 6	2229
41¼	Baden.... dep.	▼	6 32		8 13	8 48	9 49	1040	1222	13 0	..	..	1555	1813		1936	2122	2239
55½	**Zurich** (p.282) arr.	4 a 1	7 2	8 17	8 33	9 8	10 7	11 4	1254	1320	1432	..	1614	1831		1954	2148	2256

(see below).	1 2	1 2 3	2 3	1 2 3	1 2 3	2 3	2 3	1 2 3	2 3	1 2 3	1 2 3	1 2 3	1 2 3	2 3	1 2 3	1 2	1 2 3
	D	Exp		Exp				Exp		Exp	Exp	Exp	Exp		Ex r	Exp	Exp
Zurich ......dep.	1a38	5 35	6 49	7 22	8 49	9 36	1018	1140	1217	1312	1529	1655	1824	1918	2042	2149	2236
Baden........dep.	|		7 26	7 42	9 9	1011	r	1158	1257	..	1548	1714	1843	1959	21 2		..
Brugg ....arr.	|	..	7 37	7 50	9 17	1023	..	12 6	13 9	..	1556	1722	1853	2022	2111	F	r
Stein (Sackingen) dep.	|	..	7 57	..	9 44	1111	..	..	1437	r	r	1743	1913	21 6	2136	..	..
Rheinfelden	▼		9 3	8 25	9 54	1126	..	1239	1452	..	1628	1756	1925	2127	2148	..	..
Bale (Swiss) ....arr.	2 54	6 45	9 26	8 40	10 8	1144	1123	1255	1512	1425	1644	1811	1940	2151	22 5	23 1	2350

D Ariberg Orient and Engadine and Tirol Express special running. (*see pp.* 83 and 85.) * Weekdays.
F July 1 to Sept. 10. *a* Zurich (Enge) Station. *r* Rest. Car.

(Munich), St. Gallen, Winterthur, Zurich, Brugg, Aarau, Bienne (Geneva, &c.) Electric Swiss Federal Rly.

	1 2 3	1 2 3	2 3	1 2 3	1 2 3		2 3	2 3	1 2 3	1 2 3			1 2 3	1 2 3
		Exp							Exp	Exp	..		Exp	Exp
Munich (p.187) dep.	.	..	..			..	..	.	8¶50	..	..	..	1345	1728
Lindau ...... „	.		..	5 55	8 8	..	..	9 58	1230	1345	..	..	1722	2120
St. Margrethen arr.	.	..	..	7 16	9 2	..	..	1044	13 2	1434	..	..	1757	2150
(p. 285) dep.	.	..	~	7 34	9 8	..	..	1057	1328	1524	..	..	1822	22 4
Rorschach (Bhf) dep.	..	..	..	7 57	9 17	..	..	1117	1340	16 0	..	..	1835	2216
St. Gallen ......arr.		..	..	8 13	9 49	..		1134	1356	1624	..	..	1852	2232
„ ....dep.	5 20	..	..	8 14	9 54	..	1058	1139	14 1	1654		..	1858	2233
Gossau ....arr.	5 28	..	dep.	..	10 2	..	1111	1147	14 9	17 8	..	..	19 6	..
Wil ....arr.	5 50	..	5*56	..	1023	..	1130	12 7	1427	1721	..	..	1923	..
Winterthur......arr.	6 15	..	6 35	8 53	1046	..	12 3	1230	1450	1742	..	..	1946	2317
Bale (via Bulach) a.	..				..	..	1512	1512	1924	2031	..	..	..	
Winterthur ....dep.	6 24		6 59	8 54	1050		1210	1232	1456	1745	..	..	1948	2318
Wallisellen	6 50	..	7 3			..	1238				..	..	..	..
Zurich ....arr.	6 47	..	7*15	9 13	1112	..	1255	13 0	1520	18 6	..	..	20 9	2339
Schaffhausen, Lucerne, &c. (p. 284)	2 3	1 2 3	1 2 3	2 3	1 2 3	2 3	1 2 3	2 3	1 2 3	1 2 3	1 2 3	2 3	1 2 3	1 2 3
		Exp	Exp		Exp		Exp		Exp	Exp	Exp			Exp
Zurich ....dep.	7 7	7 16	7 51	9 20	1154	1217	1324	1443	1557	1830	19 9	1932	2120	2355
Baden..........dep.	..	7 35	8 10	..	1214	1257	1343	1516	1556	1850	1928	..	2139	0 15
Turgi ....dep.	Limited Train.	.		..	r	13 5		1522				Limited Train.		
Brugg ....arr.		7 43		..	..	13 9	..	1526		1859			2147	0 24
Brugg...........dep.		7 44		..		1314		1529		19 0	.		2148	0 25
Aarau .... arr.		8 0	8 33	9 55	1233 r	1345	14 6	1554	1619	1915 r	1952 r		22 3	0 41
Aarau dep.		8 2	8 35	9 56	1240	1355	14 8	1558	1620	1917	1954		22 5	0 45
Olten ....arr.	..	8 15	8 47		1254	1415	1421	1617	1635	1930	20 6	..	2217	0 59
Berne (p. 281) ..arr.	8 40	9 26	9 45	1054	1357	1649	16§49	1840	1750	2042	23§16	21 2	2328	2 23
Lausanne ....arr.	9 53		1127	1352	1547	1924	19§21	..	1932	..		2214	..	4 25
Geneva (p. 280) „	1022		1223	15 1	1638		..	..	2023	..		2253		5 36
	2 3		2 3	2 3	2 3						r			2 3
Olten ....dep.	5 22	8 21	8 51	1139	1313		1429	..	1651	17 0	2011	..	..	2024
Solothurn .... arr.	6 19	8 50	9 44	1224	1418	.	1459	.	1719	175[illegible]	2040	..	..	2121
Solothurn .... dep.	6 28	8 52	9 50	1226	1420	..	15 1	..	1721	1812	2043		..	2143
Selzach ....dep.	6 39		10 3	1236	1453	..	..	..	..	1824		..	..	2155
Bienne (Biel) .. arr.	7 7	9 14	1030	1259	15 2	..	1523	..	1743	1852	21 8	..	..	2221
278 Neuchatel .. „	7 58	9 56	11*49	14 0	..	..	1551	..	1815	2018	2143	..	..	23*36
278 Lausanne ... „	9 0	11 6	13*51	1549	..	..	1651	..	1924	2222	2248	..	..	
278 Geneva..... „	9 49	1146	15*1	1638	..	..	1741	..	20 4	..	2340	..	..	..

a Suns. and Holidays. * Weekdays. † Sundays. § 2nd and 3rd class only. *r* Rest. Car.
¶ dep. 8.51 June 11-Sept. 17.

Waldshut, Turgi (Zurich) Swiss Federal Rl

2 3	2 3	2 3	2 3	2 3	2 3	2 3	3 cl.	2 3	p. 69	2 3	2 3	2 3	2 3	2 3	2 3	2 3	2 3
*					†		*					b	b		*		
..	..	8 3	9 40	12 7	15 1	1729	1816	2030	d. Waldshut a.	7†29	9 30	1143	1219	1424	1716	arr.	2021
6 5	6 24	8 12	9 49	1238	1532	1735	19 9	2045	d. Koblenz d.	7†24	9 25	1138	1214	1419	1710	1847	2016
6 25	6 44	8 31	10 9	1258	1551	1754	20 0	21 5	a. Turgi dep.	6 58	8 58	1118	1147	1330	1458	1828	1949
7 6	7 39	9 8	11 4	1349	1626	1855	2113	2148	„ Zurich „	6 2	8 6	1037	1037	1217	1347	1720	19 6

a Daily except Saturdays. *b* Sats. only.
* Weekdays. † Sundays.

Lucerne, (St. Gothard), Zug, Zurich, (Winterthur) Schaffhausen. [Swiss Fed. Ry.

ELECTRIC.	2 3	2 3	1 2 3 Exp	2 3	1 2 3 Exp	2 3	2 3	1 2 3 Exp	2 3	1 2 3 Exp	2 3	2 3	2 3	1 2 3 Exp	2 3	1 2 3 Exp	1 2 3	2 3
Lucerne ......dep.	..	5 18		6 50	8 36	9 9	1049	..	13 4	B	1359	1555	1710	..	1845	C	2047	2140
Rothkreuz ....dep.	..	5 42	S	7 10	..	9 36	1112	..	r	..	1422	1617	1735	r	D	..	..	22 4
Zug ....arr.	..	6 0	..	7 22	9 1	9 49	1126	..	1330	..	1440	1630	1751	..	1910	..	2114	2217
														g			Exp	
p287 { MILAN (Cen.) dep.	2252	..	0 20	..	..	..	..	6 55	..	9 42	..	..	..	1225	..	1421	1715	..
p287 { Bellinzona .. ,,	1 49	..	3 7	..	4†56	..	6 45	9 41	..	1218	..	..	1325	1520	..	1717	1945	..
Zug ....dep.	4 53	6 19	6 6	7 24	9 8	9 58	1137	1238	1334	1511	1448	1635	1757	1822	1912	2020	2116	2221
Sihlbrugg (p.289) dep.	5 5	6 32	..	..	..	1015	1152	..	..	..	..	..	1811	..	..	..	..	2232
Thalwil ....dep.	5 24	6 46	6 24	7 45	9 26	1029	12 9	1256	1359	1531	1517	1657	1823	1840	1952	2039	2135	2246
Zurich { arr.	5 48	7 8	6 39	8 0	9 41	1052	1231	1312	1414	1543	1539	1715	1849	1854	1947	2054	2152	23 9
					2 3							2 3						
Zurich { dep.	6 28	..	7 7	8 16	1039	..	..	1330	..	..	16 7	1759	..	..	2059	23*9	..	..
Bulach ....arr.	7 3	..	..	8 40	1111	..	..	..	..	..	..	1821	..	..	2123	2339	..	..
Eglisau (below) dep	7 12	..	r	8 48	1121	..	..	..	..	..	r	1826	..	..	2130	2347	..	..
Neuhausen (Falls) arr.	7 36	..	..	9 6	1149	..	..	..	..	..	..	1849	..	..	2148	0 13	..	..
Schaffhausen arr.	7 42	..	7 49	9 10	1154	..	..	1428	..	..	1650	1853	..	..	[illegible]	0*19	..	..
p184 { Immendingen arr.	9 37	..	V	V	1444	..	..	V	..		V	2147	..	..	..	..	..	..
p184 { Stuttgart .. ,,		..	11 9	1259	1939	..	..	1841	..	..	2056	..	..	..	..	..	..	..

	2 3	2 3	2 3 Exp	1 2 3 Exp	2 3	1 2 3 Exp	2 3	1 2 3 Exp	2 3	1 2 3 Exp	2 3	1 2 3	2 3	2 3	1 2 3 Exp
p.184 { Stuttgart ....dep	..	..	..	..	D	..	..	7 52	..	..	1042	1338	1113	1434	917
p.184 { Immendingen ,,	..	..	..	..	..	..	8 27	V	..	1118	1338	V	17 9	1854	V
Schaffhausen dep.	..	5*12	5 54	..	8 9	..	10 0	1222	1234	1423	16 6	1715	1917	2022	2250
Neuhausen (Falls) ..	..	5 16	5 59	..	8 13	..	10 5	..	1239	1427	1612	..	..	2027	..
Eglisau ....arr.	..	5 35	6 23	..	8 31	..	1053	r	13 7	1447	1642	r	1935	2053	r
Bulach ....dep.	..	5 51	6 32	..	8 40	..	1050	..	1323	1457	1654		1943	21 6	..
Zurich { arr.	..	6*30	6 55	..	9 3	..	1125	13 5	1353	1525	1727	1757	20 5	2144	2332
		1 2 3	1 2 3					B		2 3	1 2 3				
Zurich { dep.	5 19	6 53	7 1	8 27	9 30	1015	1214	1322	1416	16 9	1831	..	2033	2235	2347
Thalwil ......dep.	5 45	7 10	7 16	8 42	9 44	1030	1241	1338	1436	1624	1846	..	2047	2256	0 0
Sihlbrugg (p.289) dep	5 59			..	..	r	1257	..	1446		..	..	2059	23 7	S
Zug ....arr.	6 11	7 27	7 33	9 0	10 1	1047	13 8	1356	1456	1640	19 3	..	2111	2317	0 17
p287 { Bellinzona ...arr.	1033	..	..	1141	..	1350	..	1647	1922	1940	2156	..	..	..	3 3
p287 { MILAN ...... ,,	..	..	..	1440	..	1640	..	1924	..	2224	0 18	..	..	..	3 55
Zug.......... dep.	6 25	7 29	..	..	10 4	11†15	1314	14 5	15 1	1642	1913	..	2115	2318	..
Rothkreuz .... dep.	6 46	7 40	..	..	1015	1127	1335	..	1516	..	1925	..		2330	..
Lucerne ......arr.	7 9	7 58	..	..	1033	11†48	1357	1430	1535	17 7	1942	..	2140	2349	..

B Rome-Stuttgart-Berlin. Rest. Car Arth-Goldau-Stuttgart and *v.v.* **C** Milan-Zurich *via* Arth-Goldau. **D** Thro' Car Constance Schaffhausen-Lucerne and *v.v.* **S** Sleeper Zurich-Genoa, on even dates and *v.v.* on odd dates. **V** *Via* Tuttlingen. *g* Genoa-Milan-Zurich *via* Arth-Goldau. *r* Rest Car. * Weekdays only. † 2 & 3 cl. only.

(Bale) Stein & Schaffhausen, Winterthur, Constance & Singen. [Swiss Fed. Ry.

2 3	2 3	2 3	2 3	2 3	2 3	2 3	Mls.		2 3	2 3	2 3	2 3	2 3	2 3	2 3	2 3
..	7 2	7 40	1034	1352	1719	1934	0	d. Bale (Sws. (p283) a.	7*35	8 40	1020	1512	15*24	1924	2151	
5 4	7 42	8 39	1130	1450	1811	..	19	,, Stein(Sacking)arr.	6 55	8 4	9 49	1430	1643	1850	2058	..
5 41	8 10	9 16	12 9	1526	1851	2034	36	arr. Koblenz ....dep	5*15	7 21	9 21	1330	1741	1822	2015	.
6 21	8 42	10 2	1250	16 1	1925	21 5	53	arr. Eglisau ....dep.	5 30	6 45	8 54	13*9	1644	1756	1938	
7 12	8 48	10 9	12*53	1614	1930	2131	..	dep. Eglisau .. arr.	5 35	6 23	8 31	13 7	1642	1750	1935	
7 42	9 10	1033	13*26	1644	20 3	2153	..	arr. Schaffhausen d	5 12	5 54	8 9	1234	16 6	1728	1917	
..	9 18	13 3	1526	17 5	..	22 1	..	dep. Schaffhausen a.	..	..	7 26	1210	1546	1712	..	.
..	9 46	1330	1550	1732	..	2227	..	arr. Etzwilen ‡ dep	..	..	6 56	1145	1518	1645	..	..
..	1035	1426	1637	1825		2313	..	arr Constance dep	..	..	5 50	1051	1421	1545	..	..
6 29	8 43	10 3	1252	16 2	1926	21 6	..	dep Eglisau (above)arr	5 38	6 43	8 53	1257	1625	..	1937	..
6 39	8 52	1013	13 2	1611	1935	2114	57	arr. Bulach ......dep	5 29	6 33	8 46	1248	1610	.	1930	
7 ‖ 8	9 18	1045	1344	1638	20 9	2133	67	arr. Winterthur ..dep.	*	6 5	8 14	12*13	15*27	..	1841	*..
7 22	..	1131	15 0	1640	21 5	..	..	dep. Zurich (p 282) a	..	..	8 29	1147	14 9	1749	1931	2127
8 14	..*	1214	16 0	17*47	2141	..	..	dep. Winterthur ..arr	..	..	7 45	11 7	1339	1715	1823	2032
8 55	..	1324	1643	1829	2222	..	..	arr. Etzwilen ..dep.	..	..	6 53	9*56	12*48	15*27	1739	1945
1017	..*	14 2	17 9	18*55	2250	..	..	arr. Singen ....dep.	..	..	6 20	8*20	1210	14*22	17*11	19 9

‖ **3rd Class.** ‡ *Via* **Singen,** *see page* 180. * **Weekdays.**

Zurich, Winterthur, Romanshorn (Friedrichshafen) (Munich). (Electric)

[Swiss Federal Rly.

Mls.		2 3	1 2 3	2 3	1 2 3	2 3	2 3	1 2 3	2 3	2 3	2 3	2 3	2 3
					Exp			Exp				Exp	
0	Bale v. Eglisau (p. 284) dep.	..	..	..	7 40	8 50	..	1155	..	1454	..	1838	..
56	Zurich (p. 282) ,,	4 54	6 56	7 22	9 15	1015	1219	1342	15 0	1640	18 5	20 9	2134
73	Winterthur .. arr.	5 30	7 17	7 49	9 37	1036	1258	14 4	1539	1725	1829	2032	2214
..	Winterthur .. dep.	5 40	7 26	7 56	9 45	1038	1313	1412	1551	1738	1837	2036	2222
83	Frauenfeld .... arr.	6 3	7 38	8 16	10 3	1049	1332	1424	1613	18 1	1850	2057	2240
94	Weinfelden .... arr.	6 29	7 52	8 38	1023	11 2	1352	1437	1639	1830	19 4	2123	23 0
98	Sulgen .. .... arr.	6 41	7 58	8 47	1031		14 0	1443	1650	1844	1911	2134	23 8
108	Romanshorn arr.	7 7	8 13	9 6	1050	1121	1424	1459	1713	19 9	1928	2155	2325
108	Romanshorn (Str.) dep.	..	8 35	1030	..	12 5	..	1510	1645	..	1938	..	..
115	Friedrichshafen arr.	..	9 13	1110	..	1245	..	1548	1725	..	2016	..	..
..	Stuttgart (p. 186) a.	..	1231	..	..	1617	..	2116	..	..	..	..	..
122	Lindau (stmr.) .. arr.	..	9 25	..	1212	..	..	17 7	..	..	2135	..	..
..	Munich (p. 187) ,,	..	13 1	..	1643	..	..	2130¶		..	..	..	..

	2 3	2 3	2 3	2 3	1 2 3	2 3	1 2 3	2 3	2 3	2 3	1 2 3	2 3
Munich (p. 187) dep.	..	..	..	..	..	..	8¶0	..	..	..	1345	..
Lindau (stmr) .. ,,	..	..	..	6 20	..	9 40	1222	..	1434	..	1723	..
Stuttgart (p. 186) dep.	..	..	..	..	..	7 53	7 53	..	1050	..	1326	..
Friedrichshafen (Str.) dp.	..	..	6 27	..	..	1117	13 4	..	1553		1815	1815
Romanshorn arr.	..	..	7 5	..	..	1155	1342	..	1631		1853	1853
Romanshorn (rail) dep.	5 2	5 46	7 16	8 41	1016	12 5	1354	1532	1640	1720	19 0	2043
Sulgen .. .. arr	5 21	6 6	7 31	9 3	1034	1218	14 9	1553	1654	1738		21 3
Weinfelden .... arr.	5 28	6 16	7 38	9 15	1042	1224	1416	16 5	17 0	1747	1920	2113
Frauenfeld .... arr.	5 48	6 46	7 54	9 42	11 2	1237	1431	1629	1713	18 8	1935	2137
Winterthur .... arr.	6 10	7 22	8 9	10 8	1122	1249	1446	1655	1726	1829	1950	22 2
Winterthur .... dep.	6 24	7*30	8 12	1019	1126	1250	1456	17 5	1727	1845	1953	2210
Zurich (p. 283) ... arr	6 47	7 55	8 39	1058	1147	1311	1520	1742	1749	1931	2014	2246
Bale via Eglisau (p.284) ,,	8 40	..	10 8	1255	1425	..	1644	..	1940	..	22 5	..

* Weekdays. † Sundays. ¶ arr. 20.16 } dep. 8.51 } June 11-Sept. 17.

Schaffhausen (Constance), Rorschach, Buchs (Coire).

Swiss Federal Rly.

2 3	2 3	2 3	1 2 3	2 3	2 3	2 3	2 3	2 3		2 3	2 3	2 3	2 3	2 3	1 2 3	2 3	2 3	2 3
..	6 20	9 18	..	13 3	1526	17 5	1910	22 1	dp Schaffhausen ar	7 26	9 28	1210	1546	1712	..	2010	..	2232
..	6 57	9 48	..	1336	1551	1737	1939	2228	dp Etzwilen (p. 284)	6 56	8 58	1145	1518	1645	b	1942		22 6
..	7 46	1035	..	1426	1637	1823	2024	2313	ar. } Constance { d.	5 55	7 53	1051	1421	1545	..	1840	..	2118
6 12	7 50	1037	1229	1428	1638	1825	2028	..	dp } Constance { ar	5 48	7 50	1049	1419	1543	1642	1838	20 8	2116
6 44	8 30	1119	1259	15 6	1713	19 6	21 4	..	a } Romanshrn .. { d	5 16	7 17	1015	1347	1512	1622	1757	1938	2045
7 37	8 38	12 6	13 5	1522	1718	1913	21*11	..	d } (fr. Zur above) { a	4 54	7 9	9 56	1340	1454	1617	1750	1910	2039
7 57	9 1	1225	1317	1543	1736	1926	2135	..	a. Rorschach (Hfn) dp	4 31	6 50	9 37	1317	1435	16 3	1725	1847	2019
8 2	9 5	1230	1325	1548	1740	1930	21*39	..	a } Rorschach .. { d	4 27	6 46	9 32	1312	14*32	1556	1721	1842	2014
									Bahnhf (from									
8 10	9 29	1234	1327	1612	1839	2056	2236	..	d } Zurich p.282/3) { a	..	6 43	9‡23	13 4	1339	1554	1543	1810	20 8
8 21	9 41	1249	1336	1626	1852	2110	2249	..	arr. St. Margrethen dp	..	6 28	9 8	1247	1328	1543	1524	1754	1956
		3 cl.		3 cl.	3 cl.	3 cl.			[German Rlys]	..	3 cl.	3 cl.	3 cl		3 cl.		3 cl.	
8 42	9 48	1328	a	1632	1922	2150	23 6	..	dep. St. Margrethen ar	..	6 16	9 0	1228	13 2	1434	1434	1620	1845
8 57	10 4	1350	..	1651	1938	22 5	2322	..	arr. Bregenz (p.197) dp	..	5 55	8 38	12 8	1246	1412	1412	1555	1821
9 12	1051	1424	..	1757	2011	2229	0 46	..	,, Lindau (p.197) ,,	..	..	8 8	1058	1230	1345	1345	1510	1747
8 22	9 42	..	1343	1629	1853	2112	..	..	dep St. Margrethen ar.	..	6 27	9 7	1244	..	1540	1522	1753	1955
8 59	1023	..	1413	1717	1941	22 2	..	..	a. Buchs ...... dep.	..	5 36	8 21	1151	..	15 8	1431	17 4	1924
9 13	1048	..	..	1743	20 3	2230	..	..	arr. Sargans } p.286 dep.	..	5 12	8 2	1124	..	..	14 4	1639	1910
9 43	1132	..	1456	1841	2034	2327	..	..	,, Coire .. } p.286 ,,	..	4 8	7 13	10‡52	..	1426	1323	1547	1842
1255	1444	..	1750	22 0	..	..	..	..	,, St. Moritz } p.286 ,,	..	..	..	8 0	..	1150	1025	1236	1545

* Weekdays. ‡ 1st, 2nd & 3rd class. *a* June 15—Sept. 9. *b* June 16–Sept. 10.

(Electric) 2 & 3 class. * Weekdays Gossau. Appenzell. † Suns. [Appenzell Rly.

										Mls									†	*
6 25	7 59	8 50	1027	1325	1454	16 4	1827	1951	22 0	0	d. Gossau a.	7 20	7 52	9 57	1139	14 6	1659	19 2	2035	2050
6 54	8 12	9 3	1045	1337	15 6	17 0	1840	20 2	2210	2	d. Herisau d.	7 14	7 45	9 50	1132	1359	1652	1835	2028	2043
7 34	8 50	9 45	1128	1417	1553	1742	1919	2042	2250	14	a. Ap'enzell d	6 11	6 55	9 6	1045	1250	16 8	18 6	1940	20 1

Electric] Zurich, Sargans, (Buchs, Vienna) Ragaz (Davos), Coire, St. Moritz. [Swiss Federal Rhætian Rlys.

12	123	123	123	12	123	123	123	23	123	23	23	123		123	23	23	123	123	23	123	23	123	123	123	12
luxe			Exp	Exp	Exp		Exp	c	Exp			S		Exp			Exp	Exp		Exp	..	Exp	Exp	Exp	luxe
2 48	b		6 49	7 13	7 40	8 50	1155	1320	1454	1714	1838	2138	d. Bale (p. 283) a.	6 45	1123		1425	1644	..	1946	.	22 5	23 1	2350	2 54
4 ‡ 3	5 55	7 8	8 ‡ 9	8 47	9r20	1021	1345	1455	1624	1838	2055	2312	d. Zurich ...... a.	5 28	10 2	1350	1250	1510	1841	18 2	20 1	2029	2141	2229	1 38
..	6 17	7 24	..	..	9 33	..	1358	15 8	S	1853	21 8		a. Thalwil ... d.	..	9 42	1328	.	1458	1819	1747	1941	2016		2216	
A B	6 58	8 16	r	a	1017		1442	1555	1713	1935	22 8		d. Ziegelbrucke a.	S	8 39	1154	12 1	1413	1657	17 8	1836	1931	a	..	A B
..	7 3	8 21		r	1022	a	1447	16 0	r	..	2212		d. Weesen d.	..	8 35	1150	r	r	1653	a	1832	1927	..	r	
5 21	7 35	8 58	9 22	..	1051		1517	1631	1746	20 8	2250	0 29	a. Sargans d.	4 13	7 56	11 7	1130	1340	1615	1636	1752	1859		21 9	0 23
5 27	8 2	9 32	9 27	..	1124	..	r	1639	1757	2028	2311	0 39	d. Sargans a.	4 4	7 48	1048	1122	13 9	1557	1557	1743	1844	A ↑	21 3	0 14
5 40	8 19	9 54	9 40	..	1144	..	↓	1658	1810	2050	2330	0 52	a. **Buchs** .. d.	3 50	7 27	1030	11 8	1246	1539	1539	1722	1830	↑	2050	0 0
8 52	..		13 8		1555	..	↓	..	2218			4 40	,, Innsbruck p197 ,,	0 12	..	..	7 20	..	..		..	1452	↑	1715	2040
1715	..		2218		..	..	↓		8 0			14 5	,, VIENNA(W) ,,	1428	..	..	2135		..			r	r	8 15	1220
6 56	7 36	8 59	..	..	1053	..	1518	1634	18 1	20 9	2257	..	d. Sargans a.		7 46	1053	1119	1338	1614	1634	1750	1855	..	..	2310
7 4	7 43	9 6	..	1013	11 0	1145	1525	1642	1810	2016	23 4		d. Ragaz (Pfafers) d.		7 40	1046	1113	1332	16 8	1628	1744	1850	2015	..	23 3
7 13	7 49	9 12	..	1019	11 7	1150	1532	1651	1819	2021	2312	..	a. Landquart .. d.	..	7 29	1036	11 7	1324	16 0	1620	1734	1842	20 6		A
9g12	9g25	1132	..	12 2	12g40	13g45	17 5	19 0	20 5	22 5	..		a. Davos Platz ,,		5 20	8 42	9 30	1150	1345	1345	..	17 5	1835		19 0
7 30	8 3	9 25	..	1035	1122	12 3	1546	17 7	1841	2034	2327		a. **Coire 291** d.		7 13	1017	1052	1310	1547	16 7	1722	1830	1953		2239
			23					23		..				23e					123		123			23	
7 48	6 48	9 57	1140	1055	12r8	15f10	16 3	1720	19 5	..	..		d. **Coire** a	1157	6 44	8 32	1030	1250	14h14	1530	1837	1813	1937	2215	2230
..	7 4	1015	12 9	..	1221	1525	1617	1738	1920		.		a. Reichenau d	1140	6 25	8 15	1015	1236	14 1	1512	1820	18 0	..	2159	
..	7 41	1050	1318	..	1248	1555	1641	1812	1954	..			a. **Thusis** d.	11 0	5 55	7 40	9 50	1212	1335	1438	1740	1736		2126	..
..	8 15	1114	1423	a	1312	1617	17 2	1836	2018		..		d. Tiefencastel .. d.	1026	..	7 12	9 29	1151	1313	1413	17 0	1715	a	21 3	r
r	8 35	1135	1451	r	1330	1634	1718	1854	2037	..			a. Filisur d.	9 58	..	6 51	9 12	1135	1258	1353	1638	1656	r	2044	..
..	8 57	1222	1553		1347	1651	1739	1913	21 3				d. Bergun d.	9 26		6 33	8 55	1118	1242	1336	1619	1640	..	2027	..
..	9 40	1237	1638		1426	1729	1820	1952	2143	..	..		a. Bevers p. 291 d.	8 38		5 56	8 19	1044	12 7	1258	1541	16 5	..	1950	..
10 2	9 46	1242	1646	13 2	1431	1738	1825	1957	2148	..			a. Samaden d.	8 30		5 52	8 14	1038	12 2	1250	1535	1559	1726	1942	2028
10 4	9i52	1244	e	13 9	1435	1740	1832	1959	2251		..		d. Samaden a.	8 6		5 48	8 6	1029	1155	1229	1517	1550	1718	1934	2022
1014	10i2	1253		1319	1444	1750	1842	20 8	22 0				a. Pontresina d.	7 57	..	5 39	7 57	1020	1145	1220	15 7	1540	17 9	1925	2013
10 3	9 55	1250	1658	1310	1439	1745	1835	20 3	2150				a. Celerina d.	8 18		5 45	8 5	1030	1155	1241	1525	1550	1715	1932	2020
1012	10 0	1255	17 3	1315	1444	17f50	1840	20 8	22 0				a. S. Moritz 289, 291 d	8e12		5 40	8 0	1025	11h50	1236	1520	1545	1710	1927	2015

r Rest. Car. * Weekdays. † Zurich (Enge. Stn.)

A Engadine Express, Sleep. cars only, special running (*see pp.* 85, 123, 124).
B Arlborg Orient Exp., Sleep. cars only, special running (*see pp.* 83, 123, 124). **S** Sleeper. *a* July 1–Sept. 10.
b Suns. nly to Sept. 10. *c* Sats. July 1-Sept. 9. *e* Weekdays only.
f June 15–Sept. 9. *g* 2 & 3 cl.
h June 16–Sept. 9. *i* From Sept. 3.
Suns., Mons., Weds. Fris. June 25-Sept. 1.

‖ 2 and 3 class.

Landquart, Davos, Filisur. (Electric)

23	23	123	12	123	23	3 *	123	123	23	123	23				23	23	123	23	123	123	23	3	Exp		123
5 35	6 53	8 50	‡	1046	‡	1215	14 6	1510	1630	1753	20 0	Mls.	dep.	Coire .... arr.	7 18	1054	1137	1316	1346	16 0	1727	*	19 0	‡	2010
6 5	7 30	9 36	1033	1116	12 0	13 0	1445	1542	17 7	1827	2028	0	dep.	Landquart (*above*) .. arr.	6 52	1025	1058	1246	1315	1532	17‡1	18 8	1827	1957	1936
7 15	8 36	1051	1130	12 5	13 8	1447	1554	1634	1821	1927	2130	32	arr.	Klosters .... dep	5 51	9 21	10 4	1130	1223	1425	1553	17 5	1737	19 7	1839
7 51	9 12	1132	12 2	1240	1345	1545	1635	17 5	19 0	20 5	22 5	51	,,	Davos Platz .... ,,	5 20	8 42	9 30	1050	1150	1345	15‡15	1537	17 5	1835	18 4
7 58	10r55	..		12‖54	1440	‡	1640	..	..	20 9	..	..	dep.	Davos Platz .... arr.		7 34		9 52	..‖	1213	1429	‡	1615	‖..	1756
8 31	1128	..		13‖27	1518		1715	..	..	2040	..	73	arr.	Filisur (*above*) ..... dep.		6 53		9 13	..‖	1138	1354		1530	‖..	1723

* Weekdays † Sundays. ‡ July 1–Sept. 10.

(Electric) (2 & 3 cl.) Zurich, Rapperswil, Glarus Linthal. † Sun. * Weekdays. [Swiss S. Ry.

..	4 46	6 5	8 17	1044	1441	1625	1737	1812	1917	2021	2130	2347	dep. Zurich .... arr.	7 0	7*19	9 13	9 54	1115	1224	1354	1553	1843	2034	2251
..	5 21	6 43	9 1	1121	1519	17 2	1814	1855	20 4	2057	22 3	0 22	,, Meilen .... dep.	6 26	6*48	8 41	9 29	1044	1142	1323	1525		20 4	2223
dep.	5 44	7 10	9 22	1149	1542	1731	1840	1918	2028	2120	2229	0 41	arr. Rapperswil (*p.* 287) ,,	5 58	6*16	8 9	9 5	10*14	1026	1252	1450	1748	1930	2156
5 52	6 43	8 5	10 7	1242	1649	..	1924	..	..	22 0	..	..	arr. Ziegelbrucke (*abv.*) arr.	5 20	5 20	6 50	7 45	8 35	1013	1158	1410	1652	1828	21 6
6 9	7 20	8 37	1040	13 4	1737	..	1959	..	..	2229		..	arr. Glarus .... dep.	5 4	5 4	6 34	7 20	8 32	9 54	1142	1352	1633	18 8	2048
6 41	8 2	9 0	1118	1337	1812	.	2034		..				,, Linthal .... ,,		..	6 4	6 49	7 47	9 19	11 6	1317	16 2	1731	1926

Goeschenen—Andermatt. Time 22 mins. [Electric Rly.
2nd and 3rd class.

From Goeschenen—7.0, 9.39, 11.10, 12.35, 14.32, 15.38, 17.25, 18.58, etc.
From Andermatt—7.38, 10.15, 11.58, 13.48, 15.0, 16.18, 17.56, 10.42.

A All trains Bellinzona-Locarno and Bellinzona-Luino 2 and 3 cl. only.
r Restaurant Car. * Weekdays. § 2 & 3 class.
G Sleeping Car Bale-Genoa on odd dates; *v.v.* even dates.
H Sleeping Car Zurich-Genoa on even dates; *v.v.* odd dates.

Electric] (Bale), Lucerne (Zurich), Zug, St. Gothard (Luino), Lugano, Como, Milan. [St. Gothard Rly.

23	23	12	123	23	123	23	123	123	123	123		123	23	23	123	123	123	123	23	123	123	12	123
		Exp	Exp		Exp		Exp	Exp	Exp	Exp		Exp			Exp		Exp	Exp		Exp	Exp	Exp	Exp
..	..	6 45	7 18	..	9 0	..	12 0	1450	1730	2142	dep. Bale (p. 282) arr.	8 55	10 1	1155	12 0	..	1415	1648	2040	20 8	22 0	2341	6 16
														23		23							
5 4	6 28	8 10	8 54	8 21	1040	12 3	1344	1627	1858	0 5	dep. Lucerne ..arr.	6 44	7 33	9 9	1038	10 6	1242	1514	1749	1827	2028	2219	4 39
5 22	6 49	..	.	8 43	r	1226	..	..		G H	dep. Küssnacht ..dep.	6 19	7 14	8 45	..	9 47	..	..	1730	..	..	r	G
5 26	6 54	..	..	8 47		1231	..	..	..		dep. Immensee ..dep.	6 14	7 10	8 39		9 43	..	..	1724	..	..		
5 35	7 3	..	9 21	8 56	11 7	1240	1411	1654	1925	0 32	arr. Arth-Goldau dep.	6 4	7 1	8 27	1011	9 34	1214	1446	1714	1759	20 0	2152	4 10
..	..		.		8 14		1222	1423	1715	2250	dp. Schaffhausn (284) a.	7 49	9 10	1155		1337	1427	1650	..	..	2153	0 40	7§42
..	7 1	..	8 27	7 26	1015	1123	1322	16 4	1831	2347	dep. Zurich (p. 284) ar.	6 39	8 0	9 41	1115	1052	1312	1543	1849	1854	2054	2240	5 48
..	7 35	..	9 2	8 28	1049	1211	1358	1637	19 5	0 18	dep. Zug ....arr.	6 6	7 18	8 51	1036	9 52	1236	15 9	1738	1820	2019	2212	4 50
..	7 50	..	9 18	8 48	11 5	1234	1414	1652	1924	0 33	arr. Arth-Goldau dep.	5 49	6 58	8 31	1019	9 36	1220	1453	1720	18 4	20 3	2158	4§33
5 42	7 52		9 31	9 3	1118	1252	1425	17 4	1935	0 47	dep. Arth-Goldau arr.	5 41	6 52	8 16	10 9	9 32	1210	1442	17 3	1755	1955	2149	4 7
5 52		r	r	9 15	1127	13 6		1713	..	.	dep. Schwyz ....dep.	5 32	6 42	8 4	..	9 23			1652		..	↑	↑
5 57	8 3	..	9 44	9 20	1133	1312	1436	1718	1946	.	dep. Brunnen ....dep.	5 27	6 37	7 58	..	9 18	1158	1430	1646	1743	1942		
6 10	8 15	..	10 0	9 34	1147	1328	1448	1731	1958		dep Flüelen ....dep.	5 14	6 24	7 42		9 3	1145	1417	1631	1730	1929		
6 28	..	..		9 55	..	1356		r	r	.	dp Amsteg-Silenen ..	H	6 5	7 18	..	8 43	r	r	16 2	..	..		
6 54	8 54	9 33	1041	1025	1229	1427	1530	1818	2037	1 47	ar. } Gœschenen { d.	4 33	5 39	6 47	..	8 17	11 6	1330	1528	1650	1851	..	
6 59	8 56	9 35	1046	1053	1234	1432	1535	1823	2039	1 50	dp. } (see side) { a.	4 32	..	6 44		8 13	11 1	1334	1522	1645	1846	..	
7 16	9 9			11 9	1248	1450		1837	2052	..	dep Airolo ......dep.	4 20	..	6 30	..	7 59	1048	1321	15 7	1633	1832	..	2 56
8 14	..			12 0	1334	1554		1923	..	..	dep. Biasca (p. 295) dp.	3 24	..	5 22		7 7	9 58	1235	1351	1538	1737	..	..
8 36	10 7	1043	1156	1223	1350	1618	1647	1940	2150	3 3	arr Bellinzona dep	3 7	..	4 56	8 5	6 45	9 41	1218	1325	1520	1717	1947	1 49
9 39	1052	1052	1211	1328	1410	1622	1717	1949	2214	3 15	dep. Bellinzona arr.		..	.	7 49	6 37	9 22	1152	1318	15 0	1649	1817	23*24
9 49	11 4	11 4	1222	1341	1422	1635	1728	1957	2224		dep. Cadenazzo dep.	..	..	..	7 36	6 27	9 11	1142	13 6	1448	1637	18 6	23*14
10 6	1118	1118	1239	1358	1441	1654	1743	2010	2239	4 0	arr. A Locarno dep.	..	..	..	7 20	6 12	8 53	1128	1248	1427	1618	1748	22*59
	..	..	12 4	..	1433	18 7	18 7		..	3 35	dep. Bellinzona arr.		..	..	..	6 31	9 38	..	..	1433	17 4	..	23*4
	..	..	1254	..	1531	19 8	19 8	..	..	5 5	arr. Luino .. A dep		..		..	5 30	8 42		..	1332	1610	..	21*50
..	..	..	1446		1858					7 8	arr. Novara (p. 302) d.	..	..	..	..	..	6 55	..	..	1135	1416		1915
..	..	..	2148	..	0 2		..	..	..	1150	arr. Genoa (p. 302) d.	..	..	..	..	..	3 28	..	..		9 4		15 0
9 17	1010	1045	12 0	1312	1355	1628	1652	1944	2153	3 10	dep. Bellinzona arr.	3 4	..	..	8 4	6 42	9 33	1213	1158	1510	1712	1944	1 39
9 59	1014	1115	1236	14 5	1430	1754	1730	2023	2223	3 49	dep. Lugano ....dep.	2 34	..	..	7 36	6 5	9 4	1144	1113	1441	1641	1917	1 8
1015		..	..	1419		1812	..	r	..		Capolago (M Generoso)	..	..	..		5 47		r	1049	r	r	r	..
1029	11 6	1138	13 0	1436	1457	1829	1756	2050	2247	4 15	ar. } Chiasso { dep.	2 7	..	.	7 10	5 33	8 32	1116	1032	1410	16 8	1850	0 35
.	1126	12 0	1323	..	1528	1853	1824	2114	23 5	4 50	dp } { arr.	1 43	..		7 0	..	8 10	1053	9 55	1345	1548	1822	0 5
..	1134	12 8	1331	..	1536	19 2	1832	2122	2313	4 58	arr. Como ......dep.	1 35	..	..	6 50	..	8 0	1043	9 45	1335	1538	1812	2355
	1238	13 7	1445	..	1645	2050	1930	2230	0 5	5 58	arr. Milan (p. 304) dep.	0 25	..		5 50	..	6 50	9 42	8 38	1220	1424	1710	2253

Rapperswil, Wadenswil, Biberbrucke (Einsiedeln) Arth-Goldau.

						Mls.								
6 41	9 28	8 26	1315	1538	1855		dep.	Rapperswil arr.	8 26	10 3	1313	1553	1822	212[illegible]
6 48	9 36	8 32	1321	1547	19 1	2	dep.	Pfäffikon ..dep	8 21	9 57	13 8	1548	1816	2114
7 13	10 6	8 55	1346	1615	1922	12	arr.	Biberbrücke dep.	7 54	9 30	1244	1521	1745	2045
5 46	9 44	..	1238		1824		dep.	Zurich .. arr.	9 24	1049	1324	1612	1925	2217
6 41	9 50		13 0		1833		dep.	Wädenswil ..arr.	9 20	1039	1316	16 8	1921	2215
7 7	1012	..	1326	..	1854		arr.	Biberbrücke dep.	8 55	1012	1249	1541	1854	2045
7 23	1022	1022	1356	1625	1932	15	arr.	Einsiedeln ..dep.	7 43	9 19	1234	15 8	1734	2034
7 14	1013	8 56	1348	1616	1923	..	dep.	Biberbrucke arr.	7 53	9 29	1243	1520	1744	2043
7 47	1046	9 26	1420	1655	1951	24	arr.	Arth-Goldau dep.	7 15	9 0	1214	1447	17 8	20 4

Sierre—Montana. (About 35 mins.)

From Sierre, 6.35, 7.10, 8.20, 8.56, 9.46, 10.22, 12.18, 12 56, 13.36, 15.30, 16.30, 18.4, 18.51, 20.10.
From Montana, 6.53, 7.26, 8.39, 9.30, 10.5, 11.9, 12.36, 13.20, 15.12, 15.49, 17.48, 18.28, 20.29.

Yverdon—Ste. Croix. (50 mins.)

Dep. Yverdon, 9.16, 13.0 16.33, 19.34.
Dep. St. Croix, 7 7, 11.30, 14.15, 17.55.

Lötschberg Route.—Berne—Kandersteg—Brigue.

Mls.	ELECTRIC.	3	123	123 Exp	123 Exp	123	123 Exp	123 Exp	123 Exp
0	Paris (Est.) p. 268 d.	..	..	2250	..	..	..	9 0	1430
363	Berne arr.	..	..	8 24	..	r	r	1740	2253
326	Bale (Swiss) dep.	..	..	6 57	7 25	9 45	1230	16 8	2142
	Berne .. arr.	..	r	8 30	9 26	1120	14 7	1743	2328
	Berne .. dep.	..	6 35	8 51	1014	12 0	1425	18 9	2336
0	Thun .... dep.	..	7 6	9 18	1042	1228	1453	1837	0 22
19¼	Spiez .. dep.	5 30	7 23	9 38	11 1	1246	15 8	1853	0 36
26	Mulenen for Niesen Rly. (p 292) arr.	5 39	..	r ..	1110	..	..	r ..	..
33½	Frutigen (p. 296) dep.	5 52	7 46	9 55	1122	13 2	1525	1911	0 51
45¾	Kandersteg dep.	6 15	8 13	1016	1150	1324	1546	1930	1 12
72¼	**Brigue** p 280 arr.	7 0	9 0	11 3	1236	14 5	1630	2017	1 58
	dep.	..	9 20	1117	..	1416	1652	2040	2 15
85½	Domodossola arr.	..	10 1	1157	..	15 0	1733	2120	2 56
102¼	Milan p. 302 arr.	..	1240	1435	..	1744	2022	24 0	5 50
172½	Genoa (p 302) arr.	..‡	1545	1752	‡..	20 0	0‡2	3‡39	9‡9
188	Turin (p 302) arr.	..a	1516	16a10	..a	1950	2210	a	8 35 a

	123	3	123 Exp	3	123 Exp	123 Exp	23	123 Exp	123 Exp
Turin .... dep.	..	..	..	..	..	7a28	a	1319	..
Genoa .... dep.	21‡20	..	..	..	1‡10	7‡5	..	11‡45	14‡33
Milan (p 302) . dep.	0 15	..	..	..	7 0	1025	..	1420	1645
Domodossola dep.	3 5	..	..	..	10 5	1347	..	17 9	1930
Brigue p. 280 arr.	3 48	..	..	..	1053	1432	..	1752	2015
dep.	4 2	..	7§10	9§5	1110	1445	17 5	18 7	2030
Kandersteg ... dep.	4 46	5 50	7 57	9 52	1156	1534	1757	1859	2115
Frutigen ...... dep.	5 10	6 18	8 22	1017	1216	1557	1821	1922	2135
Mulenen .... dep.		6 31	8§34	1027	r	r	1832	r	r
Spiez .... dep.	5 27	6§49	8 54	11 4	1235	1619	1849	1947	2158
Thun .... dep.	5 45	7 22	9 5	11§26	1248	1633	19 6	20 0	2211
Berne .... arr.	6 11	7 49	9 31	12§25	1313	1658	1931	2025	2236
Berne .... dep.	7 0	..	1010	..	1345	1710	1943	2050	..
Bale (Swiss) .. arr.	8 55	..	1230	..	1531	1859	22 0	2225	..
Berne .. dep.	6 30	..	..	..	1337	..	..	..	2250
Paris (Est.) p. 268 a.	1415	..	..	..	2125	..	..	..	7 15

† Via Milan, see page 302. * Weekdays. § 2 & 3 class.

a Via Arona.

Oberland Express, to Sept. 4. Special running, p. 85.

r Rest. Car.

(Landquart)—Coire—Ilanz—Disentis. (Rhætian Rly (Electric)

Mls.		23	23	23	123	123	23	23	23	23
0	Landquart (p. 286) .. dep	*	†	7 15	b	1152	..	..	1518	1822
8	Coire .... dep.	5 25	6 10	8 8	1010	1228	..	..	1552	1915
15	Reichenau ..... dep.	5 51	6 28	8 27	1029	1246	..	..	16 9	1934
26	Ilanz .... arr.	6 33	7 3	9 2	1058	1322	..		1650	2015
45	Disentis (p. 291) .... arr.	8 0	8 0	10 5	1142	1415	a	..	1753	2110
Mls.	Disentis .... dep.	5 0	..	8 35	1415	..	11 5	16 6	..	19a0
19	Ilanz .... dep.	5 51	..	9 38	1456	..	12 0	1655	..	1951
30	Reichenau ..... dep.	6 52	..	1025	1525	..	1246	1728	..	2030
37	Coire .... arr.	7 10	..	1042	1540	..	13 2	1745		2052
45	Landquart ...... arr.	7 27	..	11 4	b	..	1322	1832	..	2253

‡ 2 & 3 cl. † Sundays. * Weekdays.

a To June 14.
b June 15 Sept. 30.

(Electric) Brigue, Visp, Zermatt, Gornergrat.

* Weekdays
† Sundays.

123 *a	123 †a b	123 c	123	123 d	123	123	Mls.	From Lausanne (p. 280.)	123	123 d	123	123	123 b	123
5 10	6 30	..	9 30	1120	1425	17 5	0	dep. Brigue arr.	8 58	1057	1350	1555	1740	20 0
6 25	6 45	..	9 45	1134	1440	1720	5	arr. Visp dep.	8 43	1042	1334	1540	1725	1945
6 35	6 48	9 10	9 47	1136	1442	1723		dep. (Viege) .. arr.	8 41	1040	1330	1536	1721	1943
7 0	7 5	9 27	10 5	1153	15 0	1740	10	Stalden	8 26	1026	1315	1521	17 6	1929
7 30	7 32	9 55	1032	1220	1528	18 8	15	St. Nicolas	7 58	9 58	1248	1454	1638	19 2
8 25	8 20	1011	1120	13 7	1616	1855	27	arr Zermatt dep.	7 10	9 10	12 0	14 5	1550	1815

June 1—Sept. 30.

	b						b	Mls.	One class only.	b			b			
7 20	8 50	10 0	1150	1340	1415	1630	1910	..	dep. Zermatt arr.	8 26	9 52	1140	1252	1440	1656	19 0
7 53	9 21	1033	1221	1411	1445	17 1	1941		dep. Riffelalp dep.	7 55	9 22	1110	1222	1410	1626	1830
8 12	9 40	1055	1240	1433	1455	1720	20 0	29½	dep. Riffelberg dep	7 31	9 3	1051	12 3	1351	16 6	1811
8 22	9 50	11 5	1250	1443	..	1730	2010	31	dp. Rotenboden dp.	7 20	8 47	1040	1150	1340	1555	18 0
8 32	10 0	1115	13 0	1453	..	1740	2020	32¾	arr. Gornergrat dp.	7 10	8 37	1030	1140	1330	1545	1750

a From Sept. 1-Oct. 7.
b Daily, July 1-Aug. 31.
c Suns. July 1-Aug. 31.
d June 15-Sept. 10.

☞ For through Service Zermatt—Brigue—Furka—St. Moritz, see page 291.

* Weekdays. † Suns. and Fete Days. (Geneva), Bouveret, St. Maurice. [Swiss Fed. Rys

			† 123	123	123
p. 265 Geneva (Eaux Vives) dep.	..	..	6 30	12 9	1628
Bouveret arr.	..	..	1028	1453	19 0
[Mid-Europn time.	23	23	23*	23*	23
Bouveret .... dep.	5 29	7 30	1025	1610	20 5
Monthey .... arr.	5 53	7 54	1117	1630	2031
Champery arr.	8 10	1046	..	1844	..
St. Maurice .. arr.	6 5	8 13	1143	1652	2044

	23	23		* 23	† 23		23	23
St. Maurice .. dep.	6 22	8 38	..	1207	1214	..	1724	21 0
Champery dep.	..	..	..	8 58	8 58	..	1638	19 6
Monthey .... dep.	6 37	8 53	..	1230	1228	..	1737	2113
Bouveret .... arr.	7 1	9 18		1322	1253		18 0	2138
[Gr'nwich time]			123			123		
p. 265 Bouveret dep.	.	1030	1225	..	..	17 6	..	..
Geneva (E.V.) a.	.	13 0	1527	..	..	1955	..	..

Vitznau-Rigi Railway (Electric) (Weather permitting).

One Class only.

	a					Mls						
6 20	8 8	9 15	1144	1512	1815	0	d. Vitznau (p. 293) ar.	8 50	1120	1327	1638	1932
6 40	8 29	9 34	12 5	1533	1834	3	ar. Kaltbad .. dp.	8 23	1055	13 0	1611	19 7
6 44	8 32	9 40	1211	1538	1839	..	ar. Staffelhobe dp.	8 18	1025	1255	16 5	19 2
6 55	8 42	9 50	1221	1549	1849	4½	ar. Rigi-Kulm dp	8 8	1015	1245	1555	1854

a July 2–Aug. 27.

Arth-Rigi Railway. (Electric) (Weather permiting). 12 miles.

a		a						a	a					
8 6	8 44	9 50	1033	14 6	15 9	1648	dep. Arth (p. 294) arr.	9 37	1027	1156	1447	1722	1835	20 7
8 12	8 50	9 56	1039	1412	1515	1654	dep. Oberarth dep	9 31	1021	1150	1441	1716	1829	20 1
8 18	8 56	10 2	1045	1419	1522	17 0	arr. Arth-Goldau dp.	9 25	1015	1144	1435	17 9	1823	1955
8 21	9 40	1040	1121	1430	1540	17 8	dep. ,, (p.287) arr	9 5	10 2	1143	1430	1624	17 6	1937
8 50	10 9	11 9	1150	1459	16 9	1737	d. Rigi-Klosterli dp.	8 31	9 28	11 9	1356	1550	1718	19 3
8 56	1015	1115	1156	15 5	1615	1743	d. Wolfertschen-Fst d.	8 24	9 21	11 2	1349	1543	1711	1856
9 2	1021	1121	12 2	1511	1621	1749	arr. Rigi-Staffel dep.	8 18	9 15	1056	1343	1537	17 5	1850
9 7	1026	1126	12 7	1516	1626	1754	arr. Rigi-Kulm dep.	8 12	9 9	1050	1337	1532	1659	1844

a June 1–Aug. 31 daily.

Brienz—Rothorn.

9 46	1113	13 5	15 3	1720	18 0	dp. Brienz (p. 281, 294) ar.	8 17	1355	1459	1659	1755
1041	12 8	1359	1557	1750	1855	ar. Rothorn-Kulm....dp.	7 18	1256	14 0	16 0	1657

Pilatus Railway. (Electric).

9 39	1015	1155	1426	1550	0	d. Alpnachstad (p. 281, 293) a.	1130	1420	1547	17 0	18 0	19 0
10 9	1045	1225	1456	1616	4	a. Pilatus-Kulm ....d.	1048	1335	15 0	1617	1715	1815

Jungfrau Railway. (Electric).

(Weather permitting). (6 miles). *d* July 1–Sept. 10.

a	b		c	b		b			b	b	a	b			d
7 35	9 30	1025	1125	1157	1235	1345	16 0	d. Scheidegg (p. 292) a.	9 15	10 0	13 5	1420	1517	1635	1733
7 50	9 45	1040	1140	1212	1250	1442	1615	a. Gletscher ....d.	9 0	9 45	1250	14 5	15 2	1620	1718
8 10	10 5	11 0	12 0	1230	1310	1419	1635	a. Eigerwand ....d.	..	..	..	..	..	..	..
8 25	1020	1115	1215	1245	1325	1432	1650	a. Eismeer ....d.	8 30	9 10	1220	1335	1432	1550	1650
8 45	1040	1135	1235	13 5	1345	1452	1710	a. Jungfraujoch ....d.	8 10	8 50	12 0	1315	1412	1530	1630

a June 1–Oct. 7. *b* June 15–Sept. 10. *c* June 15–Sept. 17.

St. Beatenberg Railway. (Cable).

1 mile. Journey 14 mins.

Steamers to and from Beatenbucht p. 292.

From Beatenbucht, 8.24, 9.18, 10.26, 11.26, 13.16, 14.22, etc.
From Beatenberg, 8.24, 9.50, 10.50, 11.26, 13.16, 14.22. etc.

Uetliberg Railway. (Electric).

5½ miles. 26 minutes.

From Zurich-Selnau, 6.48, 9.0, 11.0, 12*12, 14.0, 15.0, 16.15, 17.15, 18.20, 19.27, 21.10.
From Uetliberg, 7.18, 9.33, 11 33, 13*18, 14.33, 15.33, 16.43, 17.45, 18.53, 20.2. 21.38.

* Weekdays

Rorschach Heiden Railway. (Steam).

4 miles. 2 and 3 class.

From Rorschach (Bhf.) (p. 282), 8.22, 9.28, 11.22, 14.29, etc.
From Heiden, 8.55, 10.43, 12.43, 15.24, 17.52, etc.
Time, Rorschach (Bahnhof) and Heiden, 28 mins.

Sihlthal Railway.

11¼ miles. Electric.

3	3	3	2 3	3	3	3	2 3	2 3		3	3	3	2 3	3	3	3	3
7 11	8 16	1022	1215	13 8	14 7	1510	1724	1830	dp. Zurich (Sel.) arr.	8 48	1010	1149	1347	1454	1546	1923	2050
7 43	8 45	1052	1244	1344	1436	1541	1756	19 3	ar. Sihlwald ...	8 19	9 42	1121	1316	1424	1517	1854	2020
7 50	8 52	1059	1251	1351	1443	1548	18 3	1913	ar. Sihlbrugg (p. 284) d.	8 12	9 35	1114	13 9	1417	1510	1847	2014

Burgenstock Railway. (Cable).

Time occupied 7 mins.

From Kehrsiten (p. 293) and Burgenstock. 9.45, 10.0, 11.15, 11.30, 12.0, 12.13. 14.18, 14.30, etc.

Martigny Orsieres Rly. (Electric).

Time, 50 minutes. 12 miles. 2 & 3 class.

From Martigny (p. 285), 9.40, 12.55, 15.35, 17.55, 19.30.
From Orsieres (p. 296), 8.27, 11.35, 14.25, 15.55, 18.15.

Bernina Railway (2 & 3 cl.) (Electric).

				a									a			a	
..	..	8 5	1058	1320	1435	1650	1836	0	d. St. Moritz (p. 286) a.	8 0	1139	1414	1514	1718	1854	2118	..
.	..	8 22	1114	1335	1451	17 6	1853	3½	dep. Pontresina dep.	7 45	1124	14 0	15 0	17 4	1840	21 4	
..	..	9 0	1153	..	1531	1743	1930	14	ar. Bernina Hospiz d.	7 7	1049	1325		1627	18 5	2029	..
dep.	dep.	9 11	12 4	..	1542	1754	1941	—	ar. Alp Grum dep.	6 54	1038	1313	.	1616	1754	2018	arr.
7 25	9 0	9 55	1248	..	1626	1838	2025	27¼	arr. Poschiavo dep.	6 7	9 55	1220	1336	1533	17 4	1932	2217
8 15	9 49	1044	1549	1541	1716	1928	2115	38	arr. Tirano (p. 304) dp.	5 10	8 55	1120	1240	1430	16 5	1835	2125

a July 1—Sept. 10.

Montreux-Oberland-Bernois (Electric.)

1 2 3	1 2 3	1 2 3	1 2 3	2 3	1 2 3	1 2 3	1 2 3	2 3		2 3	1 2 3	1 2 3	1 2 3	1 2 3	1 2 3	1 2 3	1 2 3	1 2 3
b †	§ *	—	—	—	—	—	—			—	—	—	—	§	—	a	* b	† e
7 32	7 42	9 7	10 9	1215	1411	1455	1614	2027	d { Montreux (p. 285) } a	8 41	1054	1256	1428	16 8	1818	1846	2115	2220
7 58	8 12	9 36	1043	1248	1441	1527	1648	21 2	a. Les Avants d	8 11	102[illegible]	1228	1355	1539	1751	1748	2041	2151
8 23	8 36	10 2	1112	1317	15 9	1556	1716	2133	a. Montbovon d.	7 35	9 54	1159	1321	15 9	1723	1718	20 6	2123
..	..	..	1117	1320	1532	..	1720	..	d Montbovon a	..	7 32	1044	1250	..	§	..	1910	..
..	..	..	1155	14 3	..	..	18 4	..	arr. Bulle ..dep.	..	6 49	10 0	1255	..		..	1814	..
8 24	8 37	10 3	1113	1319	1510	1558	1717	2134	d. Montbovon a.	7 33	9 53	1158	1319	15 8	1722	1717	20 4	2122
8 44	8 58	1024	1136	1344	1531	1620	1739	2157	a. Chat. d'Oex d.	7 14	9 35	1139	13 0	1448	17 4	1659	1943	21 4
..	9 16	1044	12 0	14 7	..	1640	1752	2213	dep Saanen dep.	6 50	9 15	1120	1240	1429	..	..	1923	2044
9 7	9 22	1049	12 6	1412	1554	1644	1757	2218	arr. Gstaad dep	6 45	9 9	1116	1236	1425	1644	1637	1918	2040
9 43	10 3	1128	1249	1455	1632	1723	1838	2253	a. Zweisimmen d.	6 7	8 32	1038	1158	1350	1610	1610	1841	20 2
‖ 2 3	2 3		2 3	2 3		‖ 2 3	2 3				‖ 2 3		2 3			2 3	2 3	
9 47	10 6	1134	13 2	15 9	1637	1738	18‖44		d. Zweisimmen a.	..	8 25	1032	1154	1346	16 6	16 6	1835	1958
1012	1014	12 1	1341	1535	17 0	18 3	19 9	..	d. Weissenburg d.	..	7 56	10 2	1129	1317	1540	1557	18 9	1930
1040	1057	1228	1359	16 8	1726	1837	1939		arr. Spiez ..dep.	..	7 27	9 36	11 3	1247	1515	1512	1737	19 2
1124	1124	1312	1426	1640	1756	1921	20‖18		a Interlaken B. d	..	6§53	9 10	1037	1221	1444	1444	1650	1816
..	1132	1318	1431	1638	..	1930	..	..	a. Interlaken (E) d	..	..	8 20	1028	1159	..	1444	17 8	..

† Suns. * Weekdays. ‖ Also 1 cl. July 1–Sept 10. § July 1–Sept. 10. *a* From Sept. 11. *b* Daily, July 1—Sept. 10. *c* Suns., June 4—Oct. 1.

Zweisimmen Lenk. (Electric).

2 & 3 class. † Suns. 8 mls. Time about 30 mins.

From Zweisimmen (above), 7†*a*45, 8.34, 10.34, 11.59, 13.49, 14.58, 16.11, 17.37, 18.43, 20.0.
From Lenk, 9*b*13, 11.8, 12.34, 14.30, 15.38, 17.10, 18.13, 19.30. *a* To Oct. 7. *b* July 1—Sept. 10.

Leuk (Loeche)—Leukerbad (Loeche-les-Bains) (Electric).

7 miles. 2 & 3 class.

	a							a		
8 0	1040	1356	1615	19 5	dep. Leuk (p. 280) arr.	7 50	1010	1330	16 3	1825
9 0	1145	1456	1718	20 8	arr. Leukerbad..dep.	6 50	9 10	1230	15 3	1725

a June 10—Sept. 17.

Bex—Villars—Chesieres. (Electric).

6 35	9 16	10‖55	1250	1515	17§32	1854	0	dep. Bex (p. 280) arr.	8 23	1021	12‖40	1439	18 0	19§21	2040
7 53	1028	12 8	14 5	1629	1844	20 6	8	dep. Villars S/Bex dp.	7 14	9 11	1130	1328	1650	18 9	1929
7 59	1034	1214	1411	1635	1850	2012	8¾	arr. Chesieres ..dep.	7 6	9 3	1122	1320	1641	18 0	1920

§ Sats., Suns. July 15—Sept. 17. ‖ July 15—Sept. 17.

Aigle-Monthey-Champery. (Electric).

15½ miles.

2 3	3 cl.	2 3	2 3	2 3	3 cl.	3 cl.		3 cl.	2 3	3 cl.	3 cl.	2 3	3 cl.	3 cl.	3 cl.	2 3
9 10	1050	1225	15 1	1650	1845	2048	dp. Aigle (p 280) a.	6 52	8 30	1028	1210	13 1	1455	1720	1810	2035
9 20	11 4	1234	1511	17 0	1855	2058	ar. Ollon.... d.	6 43	8 21	1021	12 0	1252	1446	1710	18 6	2026
9 40	1120	1255	1531	1720	1915	2120	ar. Monthey V d.	6 20	8 0	10 0	1137	1230	1425	1646	1745	20 3
1046	..	1419	16a28	1844	2015	..	ar. Champery d.	..	..	8 58	..	1130	..	15a33	1638	19 6

a July 1—Sept. 10.

(Lucerne), Stansstad, Stans, Engelberg. (Electric). 2 and 3 cl.

			a				a		b		
Lucerne (Str.) dep.	5 45	..	8 25	9 2	..	1043	13 0	..	1548	1718	1859
Stansstad .. arr.	6 19	..	8 59	9 40	..	1116	1358	..	1646	1752	1933
Stansstad ..dep.	6 25	7 5	9 9	9 50	1036	1124	14 5	1516	1655	18 0	1946
Stans (*below*) arr.	6 32	7 12	9 16	9 57	1043	1134	1412	152[illegible]	17 5	1810	1953
,, ...dep.	6 33	..	9 19	9 58	..	1135	1413	1525	17 6	1816	1954
Engelberg....arr.	7 31	..	1015	1055	..	1245	1510	1624	1817	1921	2046
Engelberg dep.	5 39	..	8 27	9 21	..	1055	1231	..	1456	1628	1827
Stans .....arr.	6 31	..	9 27	1027	..	1152	1329	..	1555	1725	1925
,, ...dep.	6 32	7 43	9 36	1029	1110	1153	1330	1438	1557	1726	1926
Stansstad ..arr.	6 39	7 50	9 43	1036	1117	12 0	1337	1445	16 4	1783	1933
Stansstad (Str.) dp.	6 45	..	9a54	1047	..	1210	13b55	14a50	1616	1748	1942
Lucerne arr.	7 45	..	10a32	1130	..	1240	14b41	15a35	712	1826	2024

a June 25—Sept. 10. *b* To Sept. 24.

STANS, STANSERHORN. (Cable).

40 Minutes. (6233 ft. above s.l.)

From Stans ...... 8.15, 9.24, 10.2, 11.40, 13.47, 15.30, 17.10, etc.
From Stanserhorn 7.59, 8.58, 9.46, 11.14, 13.54, 14.16, 16.44, 17.18, etc.

Lugano-Ponte-Tresa. (Electric).

2 and 3 cl. Time 28 mins.

Leave Lugano) p. 287), 6.16. 7.56, 9.7, 11.0, 12.7, 14.1, 15.5, 16.56, 18.35, 19.43.
Leave Ponte-Tresa (p. 317) 5.34, 7.0, 8.27, 10.15, 11.37, 13.17, 14.33, 17.46, 19.13.

Monte-San-Salvatore (Funicular).

Time 18 minutes.

From Lugano (Paradiso) and from S. Salvatore, 7.20, 8.20, 9.0, 10.20, 11.35, 15.0, etc.

Montreux, (Territet), Glion, Rochers de Naye. (Electric, Cable and Steam.)

Weather permitting Caux to Rochers-de-Naye.

Mls.													
0	Montreux (p.280) dep.	7 44	8 54	10 8	1129	1347	1438	1532	1613	1725	18 9	1831	2022
..	Glion ....arr.	7 57	9 7	1020	1142	14 0	1451	1545	1626	1738	1821	1844	2035
0	‡Territet ....dep.	7 49	9 2	1013	1134	1351	1443	1539	1619	1729	1812	1836	2028
	Glion ......arr.	7 57	9 10	1021	1142	1359	1451	1547	1627	1737	1820	1844	2036
	Glion ....dep	7a59	9 11	1027	1144	14 2	1453	1550	1628	1740	1823	1847	2037
1¼	Caux ....arr.	8 11	9 21	103	1157	1414	15 7	16 2	1639	1752	1833	1859	2049
5	Rochers-de-Naye ar.	8a41	9 49	11 3	1226	1445	1536	..	17b9	..	..	..	.

Rochers-de-Naye d.		8a50	9 53	11 6		..	15 0	16b0	1631	17b38	..	..	..
Caux..........dep.	8 13	9 23	1021	1133	13 0	1440	1526	1630	17 0	1810	1836	1956	2055
Glion ....arr.	8 25	9 35	1033	1144	1311	1452	1538	1642	1710	1822	1847	1948	21 7
Glion ......dep.	8 26	9 36	1034	1146	1313	1454	15 9	1641	1712	1823	1851	1949	21 9
‡Territet ....arr.	8 34	9 44	1042	1154	1321	1452	1547	1649	1720	1831	1859	1957	2117
Glion ....dep.	8 27	9 37	1035	1145	1313	1454	1545	16b44	1712	1824	1850	1949	21 8
Montreux ....arr.	8 39	9 49	1047	1157	1325	15 6	1558	16b56	1723	1836	19 2	20 1	2120

a Suns. June 4–Sept. 10. † Suns. ‡ Change at Glion. b July 1–Sept. 10.

* W ekdays

Aigle, Sepey, Diablerets. (Electric)

Mls.	b daily to Aug. 31.	2 3 a *	2 3 b	2 3	2 3	2 3 c
0	Aigle (p. 280) ..dep	7 15	9 10	1045	15 0	2058
8¼	Sepey dep.	8 6	9 59	1134	1557	2144
13¼	Diablerets (p.296) ar.	8 34	1027	12 3	1618	2214

	2 3	2 3	2 3	2 3 c	2 3 c
Diablerets dep.	7 22	1142	1511	17 6	1947
Sepey ,,	7 54	1214	1541	1738	2017
Aigle arr.	8 34	1254	1621	1818	2057

a To Sept. 9. c To Sept. 24.

2 and 3 cl. * Weekdays. † Sundays.

Aigle, Leysin.

a 3 cl. only. (Electric)

a	*	†	†						Mls		a	†				a	
6 30	9 5	9 20	1045	1228	15 8	1655	1842	2055	0	dep. Aigle (p 280) arr.	8 32	1024	1258	1444	1725	1940	204
7 26	9 49	1012	1132	1325	1556	1745	1928	2149	3¾	ar. Leysin Village dp.	7 37	9 38	12 3	1349	1638	1846	195
..	10 3	1026	1146	1332	1610	1759	1942	2155	4	ar. Leysin Gd. Htl. dp.	..	9 20	1156	1342	1621	1839	194

(Zermatt), Brigue, Gletsch, Disentis (Furka Railway).

	123	3 a	123	2 3	3 a	2 3	Weather permitting. page 288	3 a	2 3	2 3	2 3	3	123	3 a	123
..	7 10	7 10	9 10	12 0	14 5	14 5	dep. Zermatt arr.	1120	1120	13 7	1616		1855	..	..
..	8 58	8 58	1057	1350	1555	1555	arr. } Brigue { dep.	9 30	9 30	1120	1425		17 5	..	..
			c							c					
6 31	9 27	9 20	1116	1431	1650	1720	dep } Brigue { arr.	8 30	8 50	1049	1317		1649	1745	1955
7 20	10 9	1016	1158	151	1740	1816	dep. Fiesch .... dep.	7 45	8 2	10 6	1235	..	1610	17 0	1913
7 59	1048	11 7	1235	1556	1823	19 0	dep. Munster dep.	7 4	7 14	9 25	1156	..	1536	1619	1836
8 15	1056	1120	1246	1612	1840	1915	arr. Oberwald dep.	6 45	6 56	9 10	1141	..	..	16 0	1821
8 4	125		13 9	1655	..	1958	arr. Gletsch dep	..	6 36	8 50	1121		15 4	..	18 2
9 55	1251		1420	1748	..		arr. Andermatt dep.	..	..	7 30	10 5	..	1345	..	1640
1015	13 7		15 0	1756		..	dep. Andermatt ar.		..	7 22	10 0	..	1257		16 0
1037	1320		1522	1818			ar. Goeschenen dp			7 0	9 39	..	1235		1538
9 39	12d4		13d40	1725		..	dp. Goeschenen ar.			..	1037		1410		1640
10 0	12d26		14d2	1747			ar. Andermatt dep.				1015	c	1348		16 8
10 0	1236		1425	1754			dep. Andermatt arr.		..		9 51	1152	1338		16 7
1026	..		1445	1814			arr. Natschen dep.		..	..	9 32	1133			..
1039	13 8		1455	1827		..	dep. Oberalpsee dep.		..	.	9 19	1121	13 7		1536
112	1347		1539	19 9		..	dep. Sedrun dep.			..	8 35	103	1224		1454
1145	1410		16 2	1933			arr. Disentis dep.				8 10	1012	12 0		1430
1155	1415		16 6	1938		..	dep. Disentis arr.		..	..	8 0	10 5	1142		1415
1350	1540	..	1745	2150	..	..	arr Coire dep.	..	..		5 25	8 8	1010	..	1228
18b40	18b40		20 8	..		..	ar. St Moritz p286 dp.	..	..		..	5 40	8 0	..	1025

a To June 14 and Oct. 1–7. b June 15–Sept. 9 arrive 17.50 c July 1–Aug. 31. d June 15–Sept. 30.

1, 2 & 3 cl.

St. Moritz, Schuls-Tarasp.

(Rh'n Rlys.

a		a				b a		a		b	a †	a *		b	a	a c
6 55	9 25	1215	1412	1717	18 5	1935	d. St. Moritz (p.286) a.	7 40	8 23	1055	1150	1224	1619	1720	20 0	2056
7 7	9 37	1230	1423	1730	1817	1949	dp. Samaden .. arr.	7 30	8 10	1046	1141	1210	16 9	1711	1950	2046
7 12	9 45	1237	1430	1737	1826	1954	dp. Bevers (p.286) dp.	7 25	8 6	1041	1137	1157	16 3	17 4	1945	2041
7 27	10 3	1251	1447	1755	1843	2010	dp. Zuoz ......dep.	7 10	7 50	1028	1123	1137	1547	1648	1926	2025
7 54	1032	arr.	1517	..	1912	204	ar. Zernez ....dep.	..	7 21	10 1	1057	11 0	1520	1618	1854	1956
8 32	1119	..	16 5	..	20 0	2125	ar. Schuls-Tarasp d.		6 35	9 25	1010	10 0	1435	1530	18 5	1915

c June 15–Sept. 9. b July 1–Sept. 10

a 2nd and 3rd Class. Motor Dil. to Landeck, see p. 295 † Sundays. * Weekdays.

2nd & 3rd class. (Electric)

Coire (Chur), Arosa.

a June 16–Sept. 10.

	*		a		a									a				
7 0	8 55	9 50	1045	1237	1518	16 5	19 8	2045	Coire (p. 286)	6 43	8 30	1025	1251	14 2	1531	1810	1920	2024
7 56	9 51	1036	1129	1333	1610	17 1	20 3	2131	Langwies....	5 51	7 35	9 30	1159		1422	1718	1828	1933
8 20	1015	1056	1149	1357	1634	1 25	2027	2151	▼ Arosa	5 28	11	0 6	1136	1252	1416	1655	18 5	1910

* Week-days.

2 & 3 class. **Wengernalp Railway** (Electric). § Jungfrau Railway—*page* 289.

a		a	a		a							‖					c	
8 5	8 58	10 0	1043	1120	1228	1425	1648	2022	d.	Lauterbrunnen	a.	7 15	9 19	11 7	12a50	1425	1645 1813	1852	19‖15
8 32	9 26	1027	11 8	1145	1253	1451	1715	2047	a.	Wengen....	d.	6 50	8 59	1040	1224	14 0	1620 1746	1825	1855
8 34	9 27	1029	1110	1147	1256	1452	17b20	..	d.		a.	..	8 58	10a27	1213	1358	1619 1745	1822	1854
9 10	10 1	1112	1153	1230	1340	1536	18b5	..	a.	Scheidegg §	d.	..	8 15	9 43	11a27	1314	1536 17 0	1738	18‖10
9‖50	11a23	..	..	13 8	1522	17c38	18c20	..	d.		a.	..	7 30	9 25	1020	1215	3a38 1515	..	18c8
1050	12a23	..	..	14 8	1622	18c38	19c20	..	a.	Grindelwald	d.	..	6‖30	8a25	9 20	1115	12a38 1415	..	17c3

a June 15–Sept. 10. *b* Sats, from June 1. *c* July 1–Sept. 10. ‖ June 1 Oct. 7.

Lauterbrunnen Murren Railway (Electric).

a		b	c		a		b								b	a			
8 7	9 0	10 8	1050	1117	1230	1420	1550	1648	d	Lauterbrunnen	a	7 15	8 55	1110	1250	1415	1438	1640	1810
8 47	9 39	1046	1130	1157	13 9	1457	1634	1727	a.	Murren	d.	6 35	8 15	1031	1210	1335	14 0	16 0	1730

a June 15–Sept. 10. *b* June 15–Sept. 17. *c* June 1–Sept. 10.

One class only. **Schynige Platte Railway (Electric)**

a		b		a		b	a				a		b	c	d		b
7 20	8 10	9 15	1035	1150	1340	15 8	1818	d.	Interlaken (Ost)	a	9 36	12 2	1330	1520	1553	18 2	1855
7 26	8 16	9 21	1041	1156	1346	1514	1824	a.	Wilderswil	d	9 30	1156	1324	1514	1547	1756	1849
7 30	8 20	9 30	1045	12 0	135	1520	1855	d.		a.	9 27	1153	1310	15 2	1515	1755	1847
8 20	9 10	1020	1135	1250	1445	1610	1945	a.	Schynige Platte	d.	8 31	1058	1212	14 6	1450	17 0	1753

a June 15–Sept. 10. *b* June 15–Sept. 17. *c* From Sept. 11. *d* July 1–Sept. 10.

THUN, BEATENBUCHT, INTERLAKEN. Electric Tramway.

Thun Bhf. ..dep.	7 19	1052	13 3	14 5	15 2	1740	
Merligen ......arr	8 2	1123	1346	1445	1548	1826	
Beatenbucht ..arr	8 9	1126	1352	1450	1556	1832	
Beatushohlen arr	8 29	1138	14 5		..	1847	
Interlaken Bhf arr	8 51	12 0	1427	..	..	19 9	
Interlaken Bhf dp	7 42	1036	1318	14 47		17 23	1825
Beatushohlen dep.	8 4	1057	1340	15 8		1745	1847
Beatenbucht ..dep.	8 16	11 9	1351	1520	1711	1757	1858
Merligen ....dep.	8 24	1117	14 4	1526	1718	18 4	1859
Thun .. .. arr	9 10	1150	1445	16 8	18 0	1852	1948

Distance 2¼ miles
35 minutes.

NIESEN RAILWAY.

Altitude 8,760 ft.
(Electric).

Mulenen (*p* 288) dep. 7.7, 7.45, 10.0, 11.20, 13.10, 13.47, 14.37 15.35, 16.40, 18.2.
Niesen-Kulm ... dep 7.27, 9.43, 10.20 13.30, 14.20, 14.57, 16.23, 17.0, 17.45.

Treib—Seelisberg.

Distance about ¾ miles. Duration of journey 8 mins. Altitude: Treib, 441 metres; Seelisberg, 761 metres.
Treib (*p.* 293) and Seelisberg dep 7 30, 8.30, 10.10, 10.35, 13.35, 15.19, 16 22, 18.25, 19.22, etc.

LOCARNO—DOMODOSSOLA. (CENTOVALLI RAILWAY)—(Electric).

	2 3	1 2 3	1 2 3	1 2 3	1 2 3
Page 143.			Exp	Exp	Exp
Lausanne dp.	..	7 15	..	1135	1410
Berne *p* 151 dp.		6 35	8 51	12 0	1425
Domodossola a	..	10 1	1157	15 0	1753
		2 3	2 3	2 3	2 3
Domodossola dp.	7 16	1017	1221	1516	18 0
S.M. Maggiore d	8 15	1111	1314	1611	1848
Dogana Ital'na d	8 52	1144	1345	1639	1922
Camedo ....dep.	8 56	1150	1351	1645	1928
Cavigliano..dep	9 27	1212	1423	1715	1959
Locarno .. . arr	9 50	1243	1445	1736	2021

Mls.		2 3	2 3	2 3	2 3	2 3
0	Locarno ...dep.	7 22	1015	1426	17 4	1920
5	Cavigliano..dep.	7 47	1042	1458	1729	1952
12	Camedo . dep	8 22	11 6	1524	18 2	2016
20	Dogana Ital'na d	8 28	1110	1530	18 8	arr.
	S. M. Maggiore d	9 1	1144	16 7	1838	..
31¼	Domodossola ar.	9 49	1228	1655	1925	..
		1 2 3	1 2 3	1 2 3	1 2 3	
		Exp	Exp	Exp	Exp	..
	Domodossola d	10 5	1235	17 9	1930	..
	Berne ... arr.	1313		2025	2236	..
	Lausanne arr.	1355	1547	2038	2250	..

(Electric). **LUGANO—MONTE BRÉ.** Altitude 933 metres.

7 40	8 40	9 20	1020	1110	1350	1440	1540	1720	d.	L'gano (Pi'za Giardino)	a.	8 40	9 40	1020	1120	1210	1450	1540	1640	182
7 55	8 55	9 35	1035	1125	14 5	1455	1555	1735		Cassarate ..		8 30	9 30	1010	1110	12 0	1440	1530	1630	181
8 0	9 0	9 40	1040	1130	1410	15 0	16 0	1740		Suvigliana		8 20	9 20	10 0	11 0	1150	1430	1520	1620	18
8 10	9 10	9 50	1050	1140	1420	1510	1610	1750		Aldesago		8 10	9 10	9 50	1050	1140	1420	1510	1610	175
8 20	9 20	10 0	11 0	1150	1430	1520	1620	18 0	a.	Monte Bré	d.	8 0	9 0	9 40	1040	1130	1410	15 0	16 0	174

June 17–Sept. 10.
* Weekdays.

LAKE OF GENEVA. (Lac Leman.)

Sunday Services, see bills.

							Mls						
..	9 5	..	1345	..	1730	..		d. Geneva (Mt. Blanc)	..	..	..	..	..
6 45	..	11 0	..	..	..	..	0	d. Geneva (Jard Angl) a	1117	1310	..	1840	2155
7 33		1148	1424	..	18 9	..	8¾	Coppet......	1027		..	1736	2115
8 1	10 5	1216	1448		1833	..	14½	Nyon (p. 279)	9 59	12 4		1721	2047
..	..	..	..	1430	..	..		d. Geneva (Jar. An.) a	..	..	1910	..	..
..	..	..		1557	..	..		Nyon	..		1741	..	..
	..	..	15 6	1620	..	..	..	Yvoire	..	1145	1717	..	..
..		..	1540	1710	..	..	..	Thonon-les-B.		1111	1631		
..	..		1612	1745	..	..	..	Evian-les-B.	..	1040	1555	..	
..	..		1644	1820		..	..	arr. Ouchy .... dep.			..		..
8 32	..	1247	..		..	..	22	Rolle	9 28	..	..	1650	2017
9 15		1330	..		..	..	31¼	Morges	8 46		..	16 8	1936
9 47	12 3	14 1	..	..	2038	..	38	a. } Ouchy d.	8 14	10 5	1520	1535	19 4
9 50	12 7	14 5	1647	1830	20*45	14 0		d. } (Lausanne) a.	8 10	10 0	1515	1530	1859
1048	1252	15 3	1732	1930	2130	1455	50	**Vevey** (Marché)	7 15	9 15	1415	..	1815
1053	1257	15 8	1737	1935	2135	..		Vevey (La Tour)	7 10	9 10	1410	..	1810
11 8	1312	1522	1751	1950	2150	..	53¾	Clarens	6 55	8 55	1355	..	1756
1113	1317	1527	1756	1955	2155	1515	54¼	Montreux (Vernex)	6 50	8 50	1350	..	1751
..		..	..		22 2	..	55	Territet	6 42	8 42	1342		1743
1133	1334	1547	1813	2013	22*12	..	57½	Villeneuve	6 30	8 31	1327		1730
1153	1354	16 7	1853	2055	..	1537	64¼	**Bouveret**	..	7 50	13 5	1355	17 9
12 5	14 6	1620	..			1550	62	arr. St. Gingolph dep.		..	1250		1655

							Mls						
10 5	1115	1212	14 6	1520	1720	19 5	0	dep. Ouchy (Laus.) arr.	7 18	12 3	1355	1820	2045
1040	1150	1247	1440	1555	1755	1940	8	arr. Evian-les.B. dep.	6 45	1130	1320	1745	2010
1111	1230	1320	1511	1631	1826	2015	8¾	arr Thonon-les-B dep.	6 10	1058	1245	1710	1937

* Weekdays. † Suns.
a June 4–Sept. 17, daily.

LAKE OF LUCERNE.

b To Sept. 24, daily.
c Change in Lucerne.

*	†		*a*	*b*		†		Lucerne				*a*		*b*		†
9 1	9 15	1041	1141	13 3	1415	1510	1712	dep. station arr.	1033	1237	1456	1650	18 0	1943	2028	21 0
9 32	9 41	1111	12 7	1331	1443	1548	1748	Hertenstein	10 8	1159	1414	1613	1731	1914	20 3	2034
9 46	9 51	1122	1219	1342	1454	1558	1759	Weggis ...... ▲	9 59	1149	14 4	16 4	1721	19 5	1954	2025
9 56	10 4	1135	1232	1356	15 7	1612	1811	**Vitznau** (p. 289)	9 42	1132	1348	1547	17 4	1849	1937	20 9
1017	1024	1156	1314	1444	1547	1632	1848	Beckenried....	9 5	1045	1312	..	..	18 6	1859	1951
1034	104	1213	1331	15 1	16 4	1650	19 3	Gersau	8 48	1027	1255	1524	1640	1749	1842	1935
1051	1056	1229	1348	1518	1621	17 8	1918	Treib (p. 292)	8 32	10 9	1239	15 8	1623	1733	1825	1919
1057	11 1	1235	1354	1524	1627	1715	1923	Brunnen	8 23	10 0	1231	15 0	1615	1725	1817	1912
1125	1128	13 8	1427	1557	1656	1749	..	Tellsplatte		9 24	12 3	1433	1540	1648	1746	1844
1138	1140	1322	1440	1610	1710	1817	1054	arr. **Fluelen** ....dep.	7 43	9 10	1148	1418	1525	1633	1731	1829

d June 25–Sept. 10.

	d			*d*				Mls	Lucerne	*d*			*b*	*a*			*d*
	8 25	9 2	1043	13 0	1548	1718	1859	0	dep station arr.	1032	1130	1240	1441	1535	1712	1826	1935
	..	..	..	1339	1628	..	..	7½	dep Kehrsiten- ▲ Burgenstock	..		..	1414	15 9	1636	..	19 9
	9 2	9 43	1121	14 1	1649	17a56	1933	11½	▼ Stansstad	9 54	1047	1210	1355	1450	1616	1748	1849
	9 22	10 2	1140	1421	17 8	18a16	..	15⅝	a. **Alpnachstadt** d	9 30	10 6	1146	1420	1425	1550	1711	1820

							Mls							
	b	9 30	10 6	1146	14a25	1550		dep. **Alpnachstadt** ..arr.	11 42	14a21	1545	1 a8	18a16	*b*
	8 0	9 54	1047	1210	1450	1616	3¼	,, Stansstad (p. 290) dp.	1116	14 1	1514	1649	1757	1950
	8 36	*c*	*a c*	*c*	15†37	1737	6½	,, Kehrsiten .... ,,	1044	13a39	1448	1628	1740	1930
	8 54	1120	1217	1339	1556	1756	9½	arr. Weggis........ ,,	10b23	1149	14 4	16 4	1723	..
	9 10	1135	1232	1356	161	1811	12½	,, **Vitznau** (p. 289) ,,	9 42	1132	1345	154	17b6	19 4
	..	1322	1440	1610	1817	1954		,, **Fluelen** ......dep	7 43	9 1	1148	14 18	1525	16b33

					e	*b*		Mls.		*e*	*b*	*f**
					8 18	1049	1425	0	dep. Lucerne ....arr.	1035	1316	1825
					9 12	1154	1528	9¼	arr. Küssnacht ..dep.	9 45	1214	1735

e July 2–Aug. 27 *f* May 15–July 1.

LAKE OF ZURICH.

* Weekdays.

							a	Mls		*a*			*b*	*c*
			1110	1335	1415	15 0	1910	0	d. Zurich ....a.	9 0	14 0	1845	1945	2045
			1148	1420	..	..	..	5	Thalwil ..d.	..		..	1914	1941
			12 6	1448	..	..	1958	8	a. Horgen ..d.	..	1316	..	1856	1924
			1216	15 4	15 3	1550	20 9	8¾	a. Meilen a.	8 6	13 5	1754	1845	1914
			1243	1546	1521	1615	2035	11¾	Wadenswil d.	7 40	1238	1724	1827	1855
			1244	1532	1535	..	2038	13	Stäfa ..d.	7 25	1221	1710	..	..
			...	..	16 0	1655	2115	17½	a. Rapperswil (p. 286) d.	7 0	12 0	1645	1745	1815

a June, July and August. *b* Sept. 1–Oct. 7. *c* To Aug. 31.

For Steamers on Sundays and Holidays see special bills.

LAKE OF CONSTANCE (Boden See).

..	7 30	..	10 3	1225	..	1425	1555	..	d. Ueberlingen a	7 3	9 37	..	1355	..	1550	1730	1910	23 0
..	8 20	..	11 0	1330	..	1525	1650		a. Meersburg ..d	6 24	8 47	..	13 0	..	1455	1635	1820	22 5
..	9 5	..	1145	14 0	..	1555	1730		a. Constance d.	5 45	8 20	..	1230	..	1415	16 5	1750	2140
		A			A			Mls.						A				
5 30	8 0	9 48	1220	1340	1445	1558	1740	0	d. Constance a	6 28	9 10	1120	1312	1435	1515	1650	1825	2220
6 0	8 27	..	1250	1410	..	1627	1810	5	d. Meersburg . . a.	6 0	8 40	1051	1242	..	1446	1620	1755	2150
7 8	9 27	1058	1350	1510	1555	1727	1910	17	a. Friedrich- d	5 0	7 40	9 50	1140	1325	1346	1520	1655	2050
7 15	9 40	11 7	14 0	1520	16 0	1735	1915		d. shafen a	..	7 35	9 45	1125	1320	1335	1515	1640	2040
8 40	11 5	1211	1525	1645	17 5	19 0	2040		a. Lindau d.	..	6 10	8 20	10 0	1217	1210	1350	1515	1915
8 45	1115	1225	1535	1655	1710	1912	2050	33	d. Lindau a.	..	6 0	8 10	9 50	1211	1155	1345	15 5	19 5
9 5	1135	1245	1555	1720	1730	1937	2115	37½	a. Bregenz ....d.	..	5 40	7 50	9 25	1151	1130	1325	1440	1845

A June 25-Sept. 10.

Lindau—Rorschach.
13 miles.

6 20	9 40	1222	1434	1723	d Lindau ar.	9 25	1047	1426	17 7	2135
7 40	1055	1312	1549	1813	a. Rorschach d	8 35	9 40	1336	1617	2025

Friedrichshafen—Rorschach.

		Ms			
7 40	12 0	0	dp. Friedrichshaf ar	1055	1715
9 1	1257	16½	ar. Rorschach dp	9 37	1618

Friedrichshafen—Romanshorn.

9 45	1117	13 4	1815	2024	d. Friedrichshaf a.	9 13	1110	1245	1548	1725	2016
1025	1155	1342	1853	21 2	ar. Romanshorn d.	8 35	1030	12 5	1510	1645	1938

Lindau—Romanshorn.
14¼ mls.

1225	1820	dep. Lindau arr.	1213	1630
1335	1925	a R'm'nshorn d	11 5	1520

Constance—Schaffhausen

	c	a	a	c		a			a	d	c		c	a	
750	9 20	9 30	1320	1330	1410	17 5	.	dep. Constance ....arr	1155	1320	1520	17 5	17 5	1920	2018
8 44	1010	1014	1414	1420	1454	18 1	..	arr Reichenau ....dep	11 8	1220	1430	1614	1615	1833	193[illegible]
..	1011	..	1425	1425	1620	18 3	.	dep. Reichenau ......arr.	1013	..	1428	..	1610	1758	..
..	1040	..	15 5	15 5	17 0	1843	..	arr. Radolfzell ....dep.	9 43	..	1350	..	1530	718	.
8 45	..	1015	1415	..	1455	18 2	..	dep Reichenau ....arr.	11 7	1219	..	1613	..	1832	1930
9 57	..	11 5	1530	..	16 5	1915	..	dep. Stein .... .. dep.	9 55	1115	..	15 0	..	1720	1825
11 0	..	12 0	1630	..	..	2015	..	arr Schaffhausen ......dep.	8 10	9 35	..	1315	..	1535	1645

a To Sept. 9. Daily July 1-Aug. 31. *c* To Sept. 10. *d* Sun. only.

LAKE OF ZUG.

a July 1–August 20.

		a	Ms.			*a*	
8 35	1330	..	0	Zug (Stadt.)	1152	..	1842
8 45	..	16 8	0	Zug (Bhf.) (*p.* 284) ..	..	16 5	..
9 35	1428	1648	6	Immensee	1045	1525	1740
10 5	1458	17 8	7¾	Arth (*p* 289)	1015	15 5	1710

LAKE OF THUN.

§ Beatenberg Rly., see p. 289. * Weekdays.

				*		
	Thun (Bahnhof)........dep.	9 19	1045	13 0	1459	1717
..	Hilterfingen.............. ,,	9 33	1059	1324	1512	1740
2½	Oberhofen .... ,,	9 37	11 3	1328	1516	1744
4½	Gunten .... ,,	9 51	1117	1344	1531	1758
6¼	Spiez .... arr.	10 1	1127	1353	1541	18 8
9¼	Beatenbucht § .... ,,	1020	1147	1414	16 0	1827
18¾	Interlaken ....,,	11 3	1229	1454	1640	19 7

Interlaken .... dep.	..	8 58	..	1111	..	13 7	1535	1912
Beatenbucht § .... ,,	8 6	9 36	..	1146	1336	1344	1613	1953
Spiez .... ,,	8 24	9 57	1113	12 6	14 3	14 3	1633	2013
Gunten .... ,,	8 36	10 8	1123	1216	1413	1413	1643	2023
Oberhofen.............. ,,	8 51	1022	1138	1231	1426	1426	1656	2037
Hilterfingen .... ,,	8 55	1026	1142	1235	1430	1430	17 0	2041
Thun (Bahnhof)........ arr.	9 10	1040	1156	1251	1448	1448	1715	2056

LAKE OF BRIENZ

					Mls.							
8 25	1151	1338	1557	1810		dep. Interlaken (str.).. arr.	8 5	1120	1512	1753	1827
8 41	12 6	..	1612	1825	2	,, Bonigen (str.).... ,,	7 48	11 3	1456	1736	1811
9 4	1228	1410	1636	1847	6½	,, Iseltwald ....dep.	7 27	1041	1434	1714	1745
9 23	1246	1429	1655	1913	10½	arr. Giessbach Falls † ,,	7 9	1022	1415	1656	1723
9 35	1258	1440	17 6	1928	13	,, Brienz (*p* 281) .. ,,	6 56	1012	14 5	1646	1710

† Funicular Railway to and from Grand Hotels.

ALPINE DILIGENCES.

The following are the principal Motor Diligences, but there are many others for which consult the Swiss "Indicateur Officiel."

Coire—Tiefencastel—St. Moritz.

	d	*d*	*a*	50 Miles. (Motor).	*b*	*d*		*d*
6 50	11 0	9 35	1530	dp. Coire (Stat) arr.	1036	1251	18 5	1811
7 21	1132	0 2	..	a. } Churwalden { d	..	1221	1735	..
7 22	1133	10 3	..	d. } 4036 ft. { a.	..	1220	1734	..
7 41	1152	1022	1612	a. } Lenzerheide { d.	9 54	12 0	1714	1729
7 45	1245	1025	1615	d } 4848 ft { a.	9 52	1142	17 7	1727
8 9	13 8	1047	1637	a. Tiefencastel d.	9 30	1113	1643	17 5
8 20	1318	1049	1639	dep. Station arr.	9 20	11 5	1640	1656
8 23	1322	..	..	d. Tiefencastel Pst.)	..	11 4	1639	..
8 51	1345	1114	..	,, Savognin	..	1030	1610	..
9 17	1412	1132	..	a. } Mühlen ...... { d	..	10 8	1543	..
9 18	1415	1134	..	d. } ,, 4793 ft. { a.	..	10 7	1542	..
9 42	1433	1152	1737	▼ Bivio 5827 ft ▲	8 22	9 49	1519	1558
10 4	1455	1213	1757	a. Julier-Hospiz ...d.	8 2	9 27	1457	1538
1024	15 5	1233	1817	ar. Silvaplana ... d	7 42	9 5	1433	1518
1031	1522	1237	..	d Campfer .... ,,	..	8 59	1429	1514
1036	1527	1241	1828	a. St. Moritz-Bad ,,	7 20	8 54	1424	1510
1041	1532	1245	1833	a. St Moritz-Bahn ,,	7 25	8 42	1413	15 0
1047	1538	1250	1840	a ,, ,, Dorf ,,	7 30	8 49	1419	15 5

a Tues., Thurs., Sat-. to Sept. 2. *b* Mon., Wed., Fri. o Sept. 4. *d* To Sept. 10.

Buchs—Unterwasser—Nesslau

(2972 ft.)

1247	1730	d. Buchs (*p* 286) ar	1054	1410	1717	1930
1346	1910	a Unterwasser dp.	9 37	12 7	1630	1850
1416	1940	a. Nesslau(Stat.) dp.	9 7	1137	1540	..

Umbrail.

33 Miles. (8220 ft.)

8 3	dep. St. Moritz (Stat) .. arr.	1859
9 35	dep. Zernez .... arr.	1746
1129	arr. S Maria 1/M......dep	1540
1240	arr. Stilfserjoch (Stelvio) dp.	1425

Splügen and St. Bernhardin.

43 miles. (Motor.) (6770 ft.)

8 0	1740	d Thusis (Sta.) a.	9 36	1726
8 42	1822	,, Andeer ......dp.	9 1	1651
9 17	1857	a. Splügen 4429 ft	8 23	1613
1045	..	dp Spl gen ... ar	..	1530
1135	..	a Mt Splügen dp.	..	14 0
1150	..	da Mt Splügen a	..	1230
1340	..	a Chiavenna d	..	1030
1550	..	dp ,, (rail) a	..	10 8
1751	..	arr. Milan (,,) d.	..	7 0
9 22	19 2	dp Splügen ... ar	8 18	1550
9 47	1925	,, Hinterrhein d	7 55	1528
1037	arr. a	} St. Bern- { d.	..	1438
1 30	..	d } hardin Pst { a.	..	14 4
1314	..	a Mesocco ...... d.	..	1345
1317	..	d Mesocco rly. ar	..	1155
1442	..	a. Bellinzona d.	..	1032

Ofen.

Ofenberg Pass. 7070 ft.

25 Miles.

..	8 10	11 0	dp **Zernez** (Sta.) ar.	9 33	1510	..
..	8 56	146	arr. Il Fuorn dep.	8 47	1424	..
..	9 0	1150	dep. Il Fuorn¶ arr	8 45	1243	..
..	9 24	1212	,, Ofenberg dep.	8 24	1222	..
..	9 46	1234	,, Cierfs .. ,,	8 3	12 1	..
..	1011	1259	arr. St Maria ,,	7 39	1137	..
..	102	1427	,, Münster dep.	7 30	1125	..
..	..	1440	dep. Münster arr.	..	1120	..
..	..	17 0	arr. Merano dep.	..	8 40	..
..	..	18 0	arr. Bolzano. .dep.	..	7 45	..
7 30	1415	..	dep. Münster arr.	..	10 0	1835
8 40	1525	..	arr. Mals ...... dep.	..	9 15	1720
1123	1631	..	ar. Merano (rail) d.	..	6 14	1515

19 Miles. (Motor) 3550 ft.

		c Dec 15 to Mar. 15.		
8 42	1615	d. Schuls-Tar (*p* 291) a.	1210	1759
8 45	1618	a. } Schuls Post { d.	12 7	1756
8 50	1620	d } Schuls Post { a.	12 3	1752
9 38	17 1	ar Martinsbruck dp	1115	1712
1025	1749	a } Pfunds { dp.	1028	16 2
1030	1752	d } Pfunds { ar	1021	1631
1130	1852	a Landeck (*p* 213) (Stadt) d.	9 10	1537
1140	19 6	ar. Landeck (Bhf.) d.	8 55	1530

Klausen.

6404 ft.

34 Miles (Motor.)

8 40	14 0	dep. Fluelen .... arr	1319	1718
8 53	1413	dep Altdorf Post...dep.	13 9	17 6
9 34	1453	dep. Unterschachen ...	1229	1626
9 48	15 7	arr Urigen ....dep	1 15	1612
1119	1713	arr. Urnerboden .. arr	9 54	1427
1156	1715	arr Linthal Post .. dp	9 18	1351
1159	1722	arr. Linthal Stat ...dp.	8 50	1344

Lukmanier.

30 Miles. 6,296 ft.

a			*a*	
8 35	1425	dep. **Disentis** (Sta.) ar.	1115	1750
9 4	1454	arr. Platta ......dep.	1118	1723
9 49	1631	Lukmanier....	9 35	1639
1215	1743	dep. Olivone ...... arr.	8 23	15 0
1248	1816	arr. Acquarossa ..dep.	7 50	1427
1253	1810	dep ,, (rail) arr.	7 38	1422
1320	1[?]47	arr **Biasca** (Stat) dep.	7 8	1352

a July 10—Aug. 31.

Flims.

3618 ft. 8¾ Miles. (Motor).

Chur (Bhf) dep.	7 0	1048	1215	16 5	1725
Flims-Dorf ......dep.	8 3	1144	1318	17 1	1825
Flims-Waldhaus arr.	8 7	1148	1322	17 5	1829

Flims-Waldhaus dp.	9 25	1155	1712	1835
Flims Dorf ....dep.	9 31	12 1	1718	1841
Chur (Bhf) ....arr.	1032	1255	1814	1940

Lugano—Menaggio—Maloja—St. Moritz.

	Excursion							Excursion	
1420	7 0	..	7 42	..	dep. Lugano (Post) a.	..	1846	2020	1153
1435	..	..	7 57	..	,, Gandria .. arr.	..	1838	..	1127
1539	..	..	9 1	..	,, Menaggio .. arr.	..	1820	..	1028
1658		..	1020	..	arr. Chiavenna. .dep.	..	1721		9 9
17 0		7 15	1025	1525	dep. Chiavenna arr.	1145	16 2		9 7
1726		7 45	1051	1551	dep. Castasegna. . arr.	1010	1529		8 36
1747		8 15	1112	1623	arr. Vicosoprano dep.	1013	15 8		8 15
1819		8 49	1144	1657	,, Maloja ....dep.	9 37	1436		7 43
1838	..	9 13	12 2	1722	,, Sils Maria ..dep.	9 15	1418	..	7 25
1848	..	9 24	1212	1733	,, Silvaplana. .dep.	9 3	14 8	..	7 15
19 0	1125	9 38	1224	1747	,, St. Moritz Bad dp.	8 50	1358	1540	7 4
19 5	1130	9 46	[illegible]	1752	,, St. Moritz Stn. dp.	8 40	1345	1530	7 0

The times on the LEFT are to be read DOWNWARDS, those on the RIGHT UPWARDS.

COOK'S TOURIST MAP
OF
NORTHERN ITALY

See M

See Map, pages 259-260

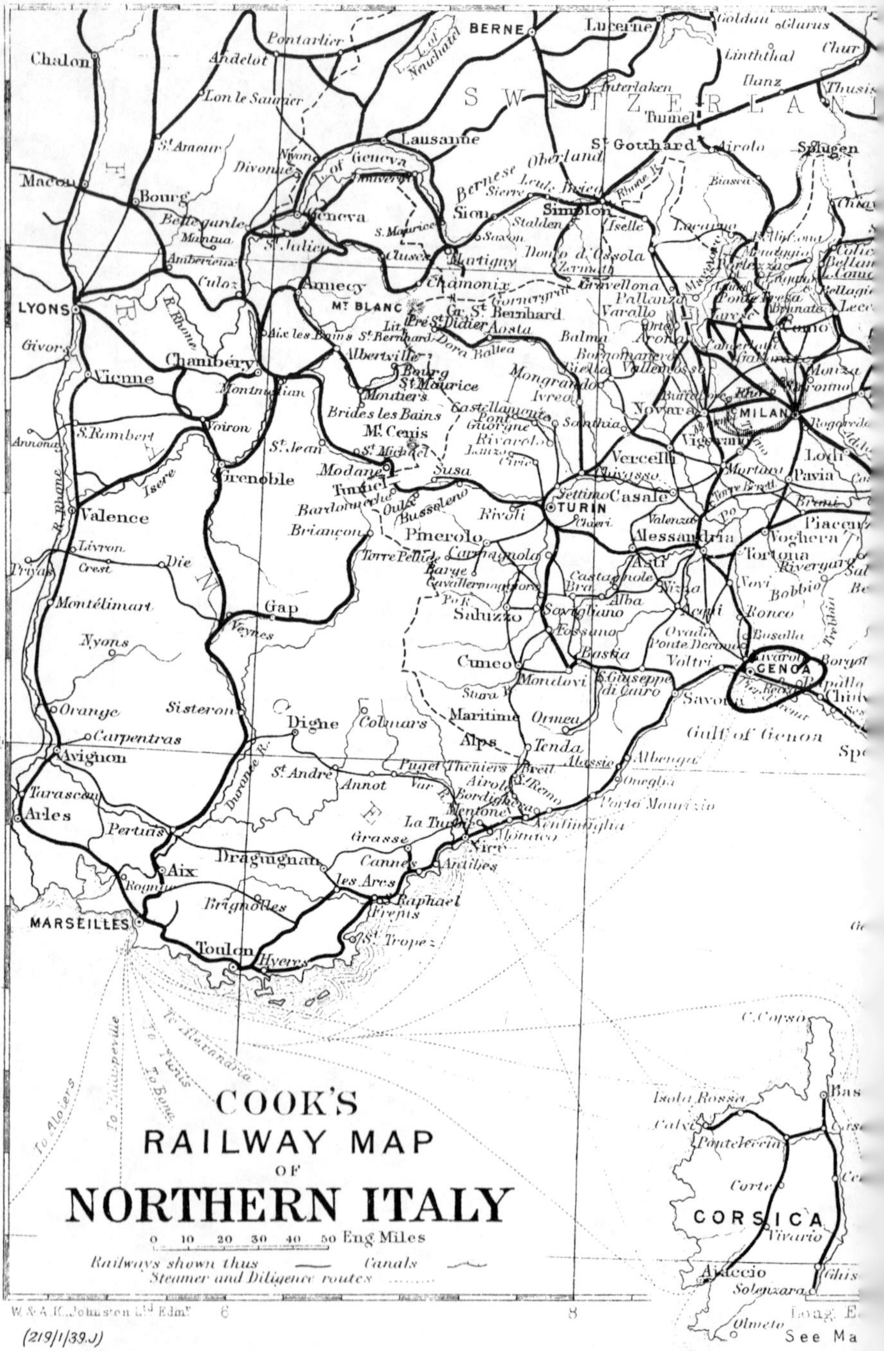

(219/1/39.J)

See Ma

s 279-280

See Map, pages 338-339

2-313

Cook's Tourist Map

of

NORTHERN ITALY

Grimsel. 7,159 ft. (Motor).

a To Aug. 31. *b* To Oct. 1.

			a		*a*		*b*		
7 15	1010	12 8	1620	dep. **Meiringen, sta.** arr.	9 40	13 4	1545	1645	1847
7 17		1210	1622	dep. Meiringen (Post) arr.	9 39	13 3	1544	..	..
7 32	1025	1225	1636	dep Innertkirchen dep	9 24	1249	1529	..	1833
7 56	1050	1249	17 0	dep. Guttannen dep	9 0	1225	15 5		18 9
8 15	11 8	13 7	1718	arr. Handeck Falle dep.	8 45	12 5	1446	1555	1750
8 49	1138	1340	1751	arr. Grimsel Hospiz dep.	8 14	1052	1415	..	1720
9 56	1243	1441	18 0	arr. Gletsch (5776 ft.) d.	7 30	10 8	1320	15 0	1640

Furka. 7,990 ft.

19 Miles (Motor)

			a					*b*
7 30	1020	1345	1611	d Andermatt a	1220	1330	1545	1741
7 40	1030	1350	1615	d *p* 150 (Post) a	1218	1328	1543	1739
7 48	1037	1357	1623	a. Hospenthal d	1212	1322	1537	1733
8 4	1052	1412	1638	a Realp d	1156	13 7	1522	1717
8 48	1135	1455	1721	d. Furka d.	1112	1224	1439	1632
9 54	1314	1555	1758	a. **Gletsch** d. *p.* 291 (Rhone Glc.)	10 6	1128	1330	1525

a To Aug 31 *b* To Oct. 1.

St. Gotthard. 6,929 ft.

10 Mls. (Motor)

a To Sept. 17.

	a				*a*	
8 0	1345	1615	d Andermatt (St.) a	9 50	1539	18 9
8 5	1350	1620	d ,, (Post) ... a	9 48	1537	18 7
8 13	1358	1628	d. Hospenthal ... d	9 42	1531	18 1
8 42	1427	1657	a } St Gott- { d.	9 11	15 0	1730
9 30	1456	1735	d } hard Hsp. { a.	8 57	1417	1723
1014	1540	1821	a. Airolo (St.) ..... d	8 10	1330	1636

Simplon (6,582 ft.) 39 Miles.

a Summer auto service. *b* Horse post Dec. 16—May 14.

b	*a*		*a*	*b*
7 15	9 25	d. **Brigue** (Sta.) a.	1715	1545
1220	1058	a. Simplon Hospiz d.	1551	13 0
13 5	1130	a. } Simplon Dorf d.	1521	11 0
1450	1230	d. } (4930 ft.) a.	1516	1025
1545	13 5	a. Gondo d	1445	8 5
1635	1333	a. Iselle di Trasqra d.	1415	6 40

Sierre—Ayer [Zinal]. 5500 ft

Private carriage Ayer to Zinal (5 Km.)

*	*a*		(*p.* 285)		*a*	
8 10	1220	1615	Sierre (Pst)	1121	1542	19 7
9 22	1332	1727	Ayer (Post)	1010	1430	1755

* Weekdays. *a* To Aug. 31.

Adelboden. 4450 ft. (Motor).

10¼ Mls.

	a	*a*	*c*	*a*					*a*				*b*
8 5	1016	1130	1150	1316	1545	1922	d. **Frutigen** (Sta.) ar	7 43	9 50	1140	1520	1850	2050
8 55	11 6	1220	1240	14 5	1635	2010	arr Adelboden .. dep	6 55	9 0	1050	1430	18 0	20 0

a To Sept. 10. *b* Suns. to Aug. 31. *c* Sept. 11—Oct. 7.

Pillon. 5,085 ft.

4 Miles (Motor)

9 15	1437	1750	d. Diablerets (p. 291) a	1050	1455	1810
9 40	1435	1748	d Col. du Pillon .. arr	1030	1435	1750
10 5	1427	1740	a. } Gsteig { dep.	10 5	1410	1727
1010	1418	1731	d. } Gsteig { arr.	10 0	14 5	1725
1018	1410	1723	Feutersœy	9 52	1357	1717
1027	14 5	1720	Grund	9 43	1348	17 8
1035	1345	17 0	Gstaad Post	9 35	1340	17 0
1037	1320	1635	a Stat. dp.	9 26	1330	1650

Grand St. Bernard. 16 Miles.

(Motor).

*		
9 50	d. **Martigny** For Rail a	1632
1033	a Orsieres see p 289 d	1552
1038	dp. ,, Post .. a	1549
1116	ar Bourg St. Pierre dp	1511
12 1	ar. **Gd. St. Bernard** dp. 8114 ft.	1430
1450	dp. Gd St. Bernard ar.	1130
1650	ar Aosta .... .. dp.	9 30

* Weekdays.

Bagnes. (Motor).

16½ Miles

7 0	1255	dep. **Martigny** (rail) arr	1224	19 4
7 42	1340	dp. Sembrancher (sta.) ar	1140	1815
7 47	1345	dp Sembrancher (Post) ar	1135	1810
8 6	14 2	dep. Le Chable dep.	1121	1756
8 16	1412	dep Versegères dep	1110	1745
8 31	1427	arr. Lourtier dep.	1054	1729
8 58	1454	arr. Fionnay dep	1030	17 5

Les Mosses. (Motor) 15 Miles.

4750 ft.

8 20	1630	d. **Chat. d'Oex** (St.) a.	9 26	1711
9 9	1719	a La Lécherette d.	8 43	1629
9 18	1725	Les Mosses	8 34	1620
9 26	1737	La Comballaz	8 26	1612
9 43	1754	ar. **Le Sepey** (Stn.) d.	8 6	1552
1018	913	,, Leysin-Tour d'Aïd	7 34	1515

Martigny—Champex.

June 1 to Sept. 30.

† Suns. * Weekdays.

†	*						†	*			
8 10	9 45	1255	1535	1745	dep. Martigny (Sta.) arr.	7 47	9 15	1225	1514	1837
9 15	1050	1355	1640	1850	arr. Champiex (Post) dep.	6 50	8 10	1120	1417	1732

Clavadel to Davos, 9.13, 14.0, 18 0.
Davos Platz (Station) to Clavadel, 7.55, 13.0, 17.15.
Films to Ilanz, 8.3, 15.56.
Hauderes to Sion, 7.25, 13010, 15.50.
Ilanz to Vals, 9.45, 17.5.
Ilanz to Films, 9.7. 17.5.
Melchthal to Sarnen, 10.30, 18.45
Saas-Grand to Stalden 7.12, 12.7, 1600.
Sarnen to Melchthal, 9.36, 15.0

Orsieres-Champex.

8 5	dep. Orsieres (St.) a.	1125
8 45	arr. Champex dep.	1045

Stalden to Saas-Grund (for Saas Fee) 10.30, 1526, 17.50.
Sion to Hauderes, 9.45, 1300, 18010.
Vals to Ilanz, 7.40, 15.20
e To Aug. 31.

ITALY.

Trains run in Italy by "Etna" time, which is one hour fast of Greenwich (West-European) time, and the same time as Mid-European time, which applies in Switzerland and Germany.

Supplement payable for Supplementary Ticket to travel by "Rapid" trains.

THROUGH SERVICES TO AND FROM ITALY.

From England, see pp. 113, 114, 118-120, 123.
From France, see pp. 113, 114, 118-120, 265, 269, 270.
From Switzerland, see pp 269, 270, 280, 287; *also Diligence routes, pp.* 295, 296.
From Germany, see pp. 174, 178, 185, 193, 198-200.
From Hungary, see p. 87A.

Modane, Turin, Milan. [State Rly.

Mls	* 1 & 2cl. r Rest. Car.	2 3	1 2 3	Rap 1 2 3	Exp 1 2 3	luxe 1 2	2 3	Rap 1 2	Exp 1 2 3	Exp 1 2 3	auto 2 cl.	2 3	auto 2 cl	2 3	Exp 1 2 3	auto 2 cl.
	Modane........dep.	2040		..	4 15	4 50	5 30	9 10	..	1040	..	..	..	1530	1755	..
0	Ulzio-Clavières-			x						r	x		x	r	b r	x
22	Sestrieres	2143		..	5 9	5 36	6 27	10 6	..	1130	..	..	..	1622	1854	..
66	Turin (P N.) arr.	2345		..	6 30	6 50	8 15	1128	..	13 0	..			1818	2020	..
	Turin (P N.) dep.	3 40	5 20	7 0	7 15	—	9 10	1136	12 0	1457	1624	1632	18 5	1838	21 0	2230
84	Chivasso (p. 300) ..	4 29	5 54	..	7 45	..	9 46	..	1230	1531	|	1727	|	1910	2140	..
103	Santhia	5 23	6 34	..	8 11	..	1015	..	1256	16 2	|	19 7	|	1938	2212	..
115	Vercelli	5 46	6 53	..	8 28	..	1032	r	1313	1621	|	1936	|	1957	2233	2324
128	Novara	6 40	7 16	..	8 50	..	1059	x	1336	1645		2124		2020	2257	2339
142	Magenta	7 8	7 40		..	..		a		17 5		2151		e		..
150	Rho	7 32	7 54		..	..	e	..	r		↓	2215	↓	2052	2332	..
159	Milan (Centrale) ar.	7 56	8 12	8 44	9 35	..	1148	1310	1424	1735	1757	2239	1940	2111	2350	0 0
		1 2 3		1 2 3			1 2 3	1 2 3		1 2 3						
		x		x	r		r			x r						
0	p. 305 Milan ..... dep.	8 50	..	8 50	9 52	..	1228	1330	1545	18 5	..	..	..	..	0 16	..
166	p. 305 Venice ..... arr	1153	..	1153	1432	..	1636	1740	2012	2110	..	..	..	..	4†20	..

a 2 cl Turin—Milan. *b* Ex Turin June 15—Sept. 30

	Exp 1 2 3	Exp 1 2 3	1 2 3	auto 2 cl.	Rap 1 2 3	Rap 1 2 3	1 2 3	auto 2	1 2 3	Exp 1 2 3	auto 2 cl.	luxe 1 2	Exp 1 2 3	auto 1 2 3	Exp 1 2 3	auto 2
Venice..........dep.	0 1	1 25	..	..	8 40	..	8 40	..	12 7	12 7	..	..	1510	1815	..	..
Milan ....arr.	5 40	6 33	..	..	1310	..	1310	..	16 8	16 8	..	..	1913	2115	..	..
				x		x		x			x		r	x		x
Milan (Cent.) ......dep.	6 22	7 40	8 55	1038	12 0	1412	15 2	1620	17 9	17 7	1850		1932	2123	2140	7 36
Rho..	..	..	9 12	..	..	r	..	|		Via Mortara.	..		..	2nd cl.		|
Magenta	..	..	9 25	..	r		..	|					..		..	|
Novara	7 13	8 28	9 51	..	1253	..	1552	|	18 0		..		2024		2226	|
Vercelli	7 38	8 48	1012	..	1317	..	1614	|	1824				2046		2245	|
Santhia	8 0	9 7	1034	..	1342	..	1634	|	1845		..		21 9		..	|
Chivasso..........	8 31	9 34	1118	..	1412	..	17 2	↓	1918	2036	..	..	..		..	↓
Turin (P.N ...... arr.	9 7	1010	12 0	1212	1450	16 0	1736	1755	1953	2114	2028		2212	2256	24 0	9 15
Turin (P.N ...... dep.	9 36	..	13 2	13 2	1535	..	1846	1846	..			2124	..	..	0 15	..
Ulzio-Clavières-Sestrieres	11 7	..	15 2	15 2	1711	..	2019	2019		..	..	2252	..	..	1 46	..
Modane ....arr.	1155	..	16 0	16 0	18 3	..	2110	110		..	..	2340	..	..	2 35	..

e Also 1 cl. from Turin. *x* Supplement payable for travel by Rap. trains. † Mestre.

Turin, Fossano, Savona. [State Rly.

a 2 & 3 cl. Savona-Fossano.

1 2 3	1 2 3	1 2 3	2 3	2 3	1 2 3	2 3	Mls.		1 2 3	1 2 3	2 3	1 2 3	2 3	1 2 3	1 2 3
5 28	6 45	7 24	13 7	14 8	1932	2128	0	dep. Turin (P.N.) ....arr	7 45	8 58	1148	1450	1645	1950	2335
6 40	7 33	8 43	1430	†	2022	2248	31	dep. Fossano ......dep.	†	7 53	1037	1341	1540	19 0	2224
9 5	9 17	11 4	1647	1812	2213	arr.	91	arr. Savona (p. 299) dep.	3 55	6 0	8 25	1114	1328	17 3	20 2
								† Via Bra.				a			a

Turin—Torre Pellice. [State Rly. Electric

a Not Suns.

2 3	2 3	2 3	2 3	2 3	a 2 3	2 3	2 3	Mls.		2 3	2 3	2 3	2 3	2 3	2 3
6 37	8 8	1151	1321	1718	1818	19 0	2034	0	dep. Turin (P.N.) ....arr.	7 0	8 3	8 28	1432	1821	20 7
7 41	8 55	1241	1427	1816	1915	1945	2129	24	arr. Pinerolo ... dep.	6 2	6 58	7 43	1327	1723	1916
7 46	8 57	1245	1430	1822	..	1948	..	..	dep. Pinerolo ... arr.	5 56	..	7 41	1322	1719	19 7
8 18	9 23	1317	15 2	1858	..	2022	..	35	arr. Torre Pellice ..dep.	5 25	..	7 13	1247	1650	1829

The times on the LEFT are to be read DOWNWARDS, those on the RIGHT UPWARDS.

Turin—Cuneo—Breil—Vintimille.

123	123	123	123	123	123	123	2 3		Station		123	123	123	123	123	123	123
		T			Exp								B			T	
..	1230		2142	..	6 57	6 57	9 45	dep.	Bale.. (page 288)	arr.	1855	..	2225	8 55		1531	..
..	1425	..	2336	..	8 51	8 51	12 0	dep.	Berne (page 288)	arr.	1658	..	2025	6 11	..	1313	..
..	4 48	7 24	1116	1512	1624	1828	2128	dep.	Turin (P.N.)	arr.	8 58	8 10	1252	1450	2040	2335	..
..	6 55	9 6	1313	1716	1734	2010	2321	arr.	Cuneo......	dp	7 11	6 21	1145	1314	1822	2149	..
..	7 22	9 14	1411	1848	1741	..	..	dep.	Cuneo......	ar.	6 58	—	1138	1258	18 6	2139	..
..	8 49	1034	1536	2014	19 0	..	..	arr.	S. Dalmazzo	dp	5 36		1022	1135	1640	2016	..
5 5	9 1	1044	1546	..	19 9	..	..	dep.	di Tenda	ar.		9 0	1014	1122	1626	20 7	2146
					B				(Etna time)								
5 31	9 27	1111	1620	..	1936	..	..	arr.	Breil (G.T.) ..	dp.	..	8 32	9 46	1044	1558	1938	2118
6 0	..	1150	1655	..	2015	..	..	dep.	Breil (G.T.)	arr.		7 48	8 14	..	1520	19 5	2047
7 7	..	1250	1830	..	2114	..	..	arr.	Nice	dep.	..	6 28	7 0	..	14 0	1755	1920
5 45	9 32	1122	1633	..	1950	..	..	dep.	Breil (Etna tm.)	ar.	..	8 12	9 30	..	1544	1918	21 6
6 22	1010	1157	17 9	..	2023	..	..	arr.	Vintimille ..	dep.		7 33	8 53	..	15 6	1840	2024
6 51	11 3	1314	1857		2055		..	arr.	S. Remo ..	dep.		5 32	8 15		1314	1743	1842

B 1 and 2 cl. cars Geneva-Lausanne-Simplon-Turin-S. Remo, also 1, 2 and 3 cl. cars Bale-Berne-Brigue-Simplon-Arona-Turin-Nice and *v.v.* **T** Through cars Turin-Cuneo-Nice and *v.v.*

Vintimille, Savona, Genoa.

[State Rly.

Mls.	**R** Rest. Car.	2 3	1 2 3	1 cl.	1 2 3	1 2 3	1 2 3	1 2 3	1 2	1 2 3	1 2	1 2 3		1 2	1 2 3	1 2 3	1 2 3
				Auto		Exp			luxe		Rap			luxe		R	Exp
	p. 264. Marseilles dep.	..	..	x	1940	0 59	4 44	5 40	7 5	7 15	7 59	..	..	..	1015	1235	1815
	p. 264. Cannes .. ,,	..	..		2243	4 47	7 47	8 40	9 54	1027	1050	..	..	1515	1346	1532	21 9
	p. 264. Nice .... ,,	..	..		2340	6 0	8 8	9 28	1034	1140	1131	14 5		1558	1445	1620	22 0
	p. 264. Mentone ,,	..	..		0 30	6 53	9 7	1017	1117	1231	1219	1452		1640	1534	17 5	2248
	p. 264. Vintimille arr.	..	..		0 44	7 8	9 19	1030	1129	1246	1230	15 5			1548	1718	23 0
	(Etna time).						R				1 2 3	1 2 3	2 3	C	2 3	B	S
0	**Vintimille** ..dep.	..	..	5 10	5 25	8 50	1053	1250	1250	13 5	14 0	1545	16 0	1710	1828	2010	0 50
3	Bordighera......	..	..	5 16	5 34	8 57	11 0	13 0	13 0	1313	14 8	1553	1610	1717	1838	2017	0 57
7	Ospedaletti......	..	..	5 23	5 42	9 5	11 8	13 8	13 8	1322	1417	16 1	1619	1725	1850	2025	1 5
10	**San Remo** .. arr.	..	..	5 28	5 48	9 11	1114	1314	1314	1330	1423	16 7	1626	1730	1857	2031	1 11
25	Oneglia ....dep.	..	5 19	..	6 30	9 45	1153	14 3	..	..	15 4	1650	1717		1943	2110	1 51
27	Diano Marina ..	..	5 26	..	..	9 52	12 0	1410	..	..	1512	1657	1726	R	1951	2117	1 59
33	Alassio.........	4 30	5 54	6 6	6 53	10 8	1218	1437	..	..	1530	1713	1753	1820	2020	2136	2 26
42	Albenga ....dep.	4 40	6 21	..	7 3	1018	1227	1447	..	..	1540	1723	18 4	..	2030	2146	2 36
47	**Loano**.........	4 54	6 37	..	..	..	1237	15 3	..	..	1552	1733	1821		2014	2156	2 50
67	**Savona** (*p.*298) ar.	5 46	7 35	6 46	7 46	11 3	1310	16 4	..	..	1627	1815	1927	19 7	2150	2229	3 42
88	Genoa Pegli ..dp.	6 44	9 4	..	8 33	12 2	1359	1749		..	1718	19 7	2058	1950	..	2322	4 58
91	Genoa Sampier ,,	6 59	9 18	..	8 45	1214	1410	1810	.	..	1729	1919	2124	..	..	2335	5 20
93	**Genoa** (P.P.) arr.	7 4	9 23	7 28	8 50	1219	1415	815	..	..	1734	1924	2129	20 5	..	2340	5 25

	1 2 3	1 2 3	1 2 3	1 2 3	1 2 3	1 2	1 2 3	1 2 3	1 2	1 2	1 2	2 3	1 2 3	1 2 3	1 cl.	1 2 3
		G	ExS	B		luxe	R	R	luxe	..	luxe			R	Auto	Exp
Genoa (P.P.) dep.	0 50	4 0	4 20	6 57	8 5	9 12	10 5	1120	...		1252	1250	16 0	1810	2030	225[illegible]
Genoa Sampier ..	0 57	4 6	4 30	7 12	8 11	..	1012	1127	..	..	..	13 0	16 6	1817	..	2258
Genoa Pegli	1 11	4 16	4 45	7 21	8 23	9 29	1020	1136	..	..	13 5	1316	1614	1825	..	23 9
Savona	2 21	5 11	6 4	8 6	9 30	1015	1113	1224	..	..	1343	1434	1658	1914	2115	0 0
Loano	3 27	6 5	7 15	8 39	1015		1145	..	..	..		1539	..	20 0		0 54
Albenga	3 45	6 26	7 36	8 51	1029	R	1157	13 7	..	..	A	1558	1740	2013	x	1 9
Alassio.........	3 55	6 38	7 49	9 0	1038	11 5	12 6	1318		..	1435	1610	1750	2022	2156	1 19
Diano Marina ..	4 23	7 6	8 18	9 25	1053	C	1226	..	..	..	..	1638	..	2036	..	1 34
Oneglia	4 34	7 10	8 30	9 33	11 1		1235	1337	..		..	1648	18 9	2043	..	1 42
San Remo	5 32	8 15	9 20	1015	1140	1157	1314	1410	1552	1657	1522	1743	1842	2125	2236	3 18
Ospedaletti	5 41	8 24	9 27	1023	1147	12 4	1321	1419	16 0	17 4	1529	1751	1849	2134	2242	2 25
Bordighera	5 52	8 31	9 39	1032	1155	1214	1329	1433	16 9	1713	1539	18 2	1857	2144	2248	2 34
Vintimille .. arr.	6 0	8 39	9 48	1040	12 1	1220	1335	1440	1617	1720	1545	1810	19 3	2150	2254	2 40
												1 2 3				
Vintimille dep.	6 15		1025	1120	1315	.	15 6	1538	1655	18 5		1845	1935	2245	..	6 15
Mentone (Gn.tm) a	6 29	..	1037	1135	1328	1247	1519	1549	17 6	1817	16 8	1856	1946	23 0	..	6 29
Nice .... arr.	7 20	..	1118	1231	1411	1330	1559	1634	1746	19 1	1650	1942	2028	2355	..	7 20
Cannes .... ,,	8 12	..	1214	1341	1529	1412	1647	1714	1825	1953	1724	2035	21 9	0 51	..	8 12
Marseilles .. ,,	1117	..	1425	1715	1836	..	1959	2010	2117	..	..	2340	0 15	4 35	..	1117

A Cannes-Vienna Express, special running, see page 82 (Susp nded). **B** 1, 2 cl. Sleep. car Rome-Vintimille and *v.v.* **C** Riviera Express, special running, see page 81 (Suspended). **G** 1 & 2 cl. San Remo-Lausanne-Geneva. **R** Restaurant Car. **S** 1 and 2 cl. Sleep. car Nice-Berlin and *v.v.*
x Rapido Supplement payable.

(Turin), Chivasso, Aosta. [State Rly.

23	123	auto 23	123	Exp 123	123	auto 23	123	Mls.		23	123	23	123	auto 23	23	Exp 123
3 58	5 20	7 7	7 34	9 29	1348	1416	1928	0	dep. Turin (P.N.) .... arr	7 52	10 0	1347	1616	1824	21 2	2158
4 39	5 54	7 34	8 12	10 3	1434	1442	2018	18	arr. Chivasso ......dep	6 58	9 25	13 0	1544	1757	2010	2118
4 46	6 1	7 36	8*18	1010	1455	1443	2025	0	dep. Chivasso ...... arr	6 50	9 19	1223	15*18	1754	1942	2111
5 40	6 55	8 0	8 59	1051	1557	15 8	2126	22	arr. } Ivrea .... { dep	5 52	8 38	1132	1418	1729	1853	2030
5 45	6 59	8 1	..	1055	16 3	15 9	2133		dep. } Ivrea .... { arr	5 44	8a36	1127	1413	1728	8 49	2028
6 41	7 58	8 28	..	1140	17 6	1538	2219	38	Verres	5 5	8 0	1039	1322	17 4	1758	1953
7 50	9 2	9 14	..	1242	1818	1618	2315	62	arr. Aosta ....dep	4 17	7a7	9 45	12*20	1629	17 0	19 9
..		..			..			.	ar. Gt.St.Bernard (p.212) dp	..	..		..	..	..	
8 27	* 2 & 3 class	9a16	a July 1—Sept. 15	12*55	19*2	16a28	..	0	dep. Aosta .. .. arr	..	8 7		12*8		..	18*52
9 31		10 2		14*2	20*6	17a23		20	arr. Pre S. Didier ..dep	..	7 6	..	11*5		..	17*50
1010		..		1415	..	2030			arr. Courmayeur (p.212) dep	..	6 40	..	1040	..	..	1720
..		↓			..	..			ar. Lt.St.Bernard (p.212) dp	..	..			..		

(Turin) Alessandria, Piacenza (Bologna). [State Rly.

x Rapido.

123	2	123	123	23	123	2	123	Mls.	a 2nd and 3rd class.	123	2	123	123	2	123	23x
	x					x					x					
5 40	6 32	7 18	1218	1438	17 1	19 8	2115	..	dep. Turin (p. 301) .... arr.	9 22	1025	14 9	18 5	1857	2345	2353
		a	a		a	x					x		a	a		x
7 9	7 33	8 42	1343	1550	1829	20 8	2248	0	dep. **Alessandria** ...... arr.	7 41	9 20	1247	1618	1752	2214	2245
7 35	7 55	9 10	1415	..	1918	2035	2314	18	↓ Tortona (p. 302) .. ↑	7 14	9 4	1222	1544	1736	2149	2227
8 16	8 6	9 35	1443	1620	1948	2051	2346	24	Voghera (p. 302) ..	6 54	8 43	12 3	1518	1717	2133	2212
8 49	.	1013	1523	1644	2027	..	0 23	40	Stradella	6 7	..	1130	1435		2058	2147
9 26	8 43	1059	1514	1721	2119	2133	1 0	60	arr. **Piacenza** ....dep.	5 17	8 4	1058	1346	1639	2023	2120
—	—	—	123	123	12	—	—		(p. 303)	—		—	123r	—	—	12x
1150	1017	1354	1810	1933	0 32	2310	3 40		arr. Bologna ....dep.	2 43	6 30	8 40	1030	15 4	18 7	1043

Turin—Asti—Acqui—Genoa. [State Rly.

	23	2 *	23	23 *	123	23	Mls.		23	123	123	123	123	
* 1st cl. also Turin to Asti and v.v.	5 46	6 32	7 52	1213	17 5	1858	0	dep. Turin (p. 301) .. arr.	3 20	9 50	a	1748	0 3	a 2nd cl. Asti-Turin.
	7 0	7 9	9 7	13 5	1750	2016	35	arr. } Asti (p. 301) { dep.	7 28	8 58		1627	2218	
	7 17	Rap pp. a	9 19	1321	18 2	2031		dep. } Asti (p. 301) { arr.	7 15	8 47		1557	22 4	
	8 26		1043	1430	19 2	2159	64	arr. Acqui ....dep.	5 59	7 27		1443	2039	
	8 42		1217	1710	1924	..		dep. Acqui ....arr.	..	7 5	9 36	14 6	2012	
	1030		14 2	19 2	2123			arr. Genoa (P.P.) ....dep.		5 10	7 41	1222	1815	

Alessandria—Acqui—Savona. [State Rly.

	123	123	123	123	123	123	Mls.		123	123	123	23	123	123
a 2 & 3 cl.	5 10	7 28	1141	15 6	18 7	2258	0	dep. Alessandria (p.301) ar.	6 51	8 15	1146	1413	1614	2111
	5 54	8 32	1232	1558	19 6	2347	21	arr. Acqui ....dep.	5 56	7 22	1056	1318	1524	2021
	7 45	11a4	1421	1742	2110			arr. Savona (p. 209)..dep.		5 30	9 19	1114	1328	1826

Milan (Parma), Spezia (Pisa, Rome). [State Rly.

o Mixed Classes.

	23	23	o	23	123	23	123	Mls.		123	123	123	12	23	123	123	
a Rapido Supp. payable.	..	0 25	6 50	6 50	8 35	1250	1650	0	dep. Milan (p. 303) arr.	1035	1340	1340	1830	21 0	2310	..	a July 1—Sept. 30. r Rest. Car.
		o			o							o	r o				
	..	5 0	8 33	9 40	1226	1545	2015	14	dep. **Parma** .... arr.	8 18	9 57	1138	1446	18 1	21 7	22 6	
	..	5 36	8 59	1013	1255	1620	2045	80	dep. Fornovo .... arr.	7 35	9 20	11 7	1415	1725	2032	2138	
	..	7 44	1040	1159	1424	1824	2222	123	arr. St. Stefano di M. dep.	5 30	7 18	9 31	1241	1523	1825	20 0	
		8 2	1034	1214	1437	1845	2235	..	arr. **Spezia** ....dep.	5 10	7 0	9 15	1225	15 5	18 5	1945	
		123		o		o				o	o	o	o	o	o		
	6 40	x	↓ a	12 5	1430	1829	2230	..	dep. St. Stefano ...... arr.	5 19	7 9	..	1234	15 9	1814	..	
	6 49	..	↓	1214	1439	1838	2239	137	arr. Sarzana ....dep.	5 10	6 56	8 44	12 7	1429	1745	..	
	8 36	9 22	1213	1345	1642	2010	0 8	174	,, Pisa } (p. 301) { ,,	3 28	5 30	7 30	1055	1312	1622	..	
	..	1310	1630	1840	2045		6 40	386	arr. **Rome** } (p. 301) { dep.	23 0	2350	0 30	..	8 25	8 35		

Vesuvius Railway.

1st class only. *a* Subject to alteration.

						Mls.							
7 0	9 30	9 42	1330	14 0	1430		dep. Naples .... arr.	10 0	1438	1515	1737	18 6	1914
8 0	9 52	1025	14 0	1433	15 6	0	dep. **Pugliano** .... arr.	9 39	1357	1430	1713	1746	1819
8 24	10 9	1042	1417	1450	1523	2¼	dep. Centrale ....dep.	9 25	1341	1416	1659	1732	18 5
8 40	1025	1058	1433	15 6	1539	3¾	arr. **Eremo** .... ,,	9 12	1314	1423	1646	1718	1752
8 41	1026	1059	1434	15 7	1540		dep. Hotel Restaurant arr.	9 9	12 1	1234	1511	1641	1717
8 53	1038	1111	1446	1519	1552	5	arr. **Funicolare** Inf. ..dep.	8 58	1150	1223	16 0	1633	17 6
..	..	a	a		a	6	arr. ,, Sup...dep.	..	..	a	a	..	..

The times on the LEFT are to be read DOWNWARDS, those on the RIGHT UPWARDS.

Turin (Milan), Genoa, Pisa, Rome.

[State Rly.

Mls.	Thro' Services, see also pp. 118, 123, &c.	Rap 1 2 3	1 2 3	1 cl.	1 2 3	luxe 1 2	Exp 1 2 3	Rap 1 2 3	Exp 1 2 3	Exp 1 2 3	Rap 1 cl.	Exp 1 2 3	2 3	Exp 1 2 3	Exp 1 2	Exp 1 2 3
	From Paris, p. 265.	x		x	P	L		x			A x			r	Z	H
0	**Turin** (P.N.) b ..dep.	..	3 40	6 55	7 10	7 3	8 52	1210	1218	..	1655	17 1	1854	20 0	2140	2210
35	Asti b (p. 300)	..	4 29		..	..	9 49	r	13 7	..	↓	1754	2018	2054		23 1
56	**Alessandria** b (p. 300) arr.	..	4 56	A	8 20	..	1020	1319	1334	..	↓	1824	21 3	2124	2253	2332
	dep.	..	5 18		8 22	..	1022	1320	1336	1620		1836	2157	2126	2255	2335
58	**Milan** (p.302) dep.	..	4 ‡0	..	..	..	7 55	..	12‡0	1145		..	17 7	17 7	..	2125
70	Novi b	..	5 40		..	..	1047	P	1357	1655		1857	2241	2147	..	2356
101	Genoa (Samp.) b arr.	..	6 36	..	..	..	12 1	..	1448	1741	↓	2012	0 18	2239	.	0 44
104	**Genoa** (P. Prin.) b arr.	..	6 45	8 38	9 28	9 15	12 9	1424	1454	1752	1838	2020	0 35	22r47	0 2	0 50
				r		r							a		S	
	dep.	7 0	7 10	8 40	9 35	9 21	1240	1431	15 9	1810	1840	2037	1 10	23 9	0 20	1 1
111	Genoa (Nervi b	r	7 28		..	..	13 3	r	1528	1827	↓	2056	1 46	2328	..	1 20
121	S. Margherita b....		7 53		10 5	9 47	1335	..	1546	19 6	↓	2117	2 25	2345	-	1 37
122	Rapallo b..........	..	7 59	..	1010	9 52	1341	15 0	1552	1912	↓	2122	2 32	2351	..	1 43
128	Chiavari b	..	8 11	..	..	..	1354	..	16 2	1925	↓	2132	2 48	0 1		1 53
132	Sestri Levante b ..	..	8 21	..	..	..	1427	..	1612	1938	↓	2142	3 10	0 11	..	2 2
147	Levanto b	..	8 50	..	..	..	1438	..	1637	2002	↓	22 9	3 54	0 34	..	2 23
160	Spezia (p. 300) b ..	8 14	9 7	..	11 2	1039	1458	1547	17 1	2022	↓	2237	4 40	0 54	1 47	2 49
170	Sarzana (p.300) b ..		9 23		..	..	1517	..	1720	2050	↓	2255	5 19	1 11	..	
194	Viareggio b	8 57	1032		1148	1129	16 7	1630	18 2	2146	↓	2341	6 19	1 50	2 38	3 38
207	**Pisa** b .... arr.	9 22	1053	1026	1213	1146	1642	1654	1829	2220	2026	0 8	6 45	2 17	3 5	4 4
257	Florence (p.309) a.	1038	13 9	1146	1534	1457	1840	1840	2010	0 32	2244	2 17	8 53	5 27	5 27	6 20
..	**Pisa** b ....dep.	9 23	11 0	1027	1217	1147	17 3	1655	1837	2230	2027	0 21	7 10	2 23	3 9	4 16
216	Leghorn b	9 41	1118	1047	1236	12 4	1722	1713	1855	2249	2047	0 45	7 36	2 48	3 27	4 34
237	Cecina b		..		..	..	arr.	..	1925	..	↓	1 18	8 54	..	..	5 1
396	Grosseto b	..	.	..	14 9	..	..	..	2042	..	↓	2 50	1044	4 30	5 10	6 23
319	Orbetello b	..	..		..	..	..	..	2112	..	↓	3 43	12 1	..		6 52
341	Montalto b	..	..	..			..	..	r	..	↓	4 35	13 5			7 20
363	Civitavecchia b	..	..	..	1521		..	1941	22 2	..	↓	5 13	1336	5 45	6 34	7 49
413	**Rome** (Ter.) b ..arr.	1310	..	1350	1630	1530	..	2045	2320	..	2350	6 40	1520	6 55	8 0	9 5
569	NAPLES C (p. 310) ar.	18 7	..	18 7	1957	18b7	..	0 3	3 8	..	3 8	9 52	18 6	9 52	1247	1247
..	NAPLES M. (p.310) a.	1756	..	1756	2010	1756	..	..	..	..	..	1018	1756	1018	1248	1248

X 1 & 2 cl. Sleep. Cars Turin-Genoa-Rome, 1 & 2cl. Cars Paris-Rome. Z 1 & 2 cl. Sleep. Car Turin-Rome. a 1st cl. also from Pisa. b Piazza Garibaldi. r Rest. Car. x Supplement payable for travel by Rap. trains. † 1 and 2 cl. only. ‡ Connect at Genoa.

	1 2 3	1 cl.	1 2 3	2 3	1 2 3	1 2 3	1 2	1 cl.	1 2 3	1 2 3	1 2 3	1 2 3	1 2 3	1 2 3
NAPLES Merg. dep.	..	3 49	3 49	..	3 49	10 2	7 27	1525	1525	1525	1819	20 0	20 0	2135
NAPLES C .... ,,	..	3 53	3 53	..	4 38	9 52	8 15	1515	1515	1515	1835	1948	2035	2124
			Exp	..	PT	r x	L		x	H	VG	Exp	C	N
Rome (Termini) dep.	..	7 25	7 40	..	8 25	1220	1230	1725	18 0	19 5	2215	23 0	2350	0 30
Civitavecchia b	..	A x	8 49	..	9 28	..	..	r	..	2011	..	0 6	0 59	2 23
Montalto b	..	↓	..	..		..	..		..	2042	..	C		3 2
Orbetello b	..	↓	9 42	..	r	..	..	x	..	21 7	..	0 54	.	3 37
Grosseto b..........	..	↓	1018	..	1046	..	..	A	20 1	2143	0 33	1 23	2 21	4 40
Cecina b	..	↓	1140	..	..	..	..	..	..	23 2	.		3 37	6 9
Leghorn b..........	..	1031	1216	1138	1225	1548	1558	2031	2132	2339	2 17	3 6	4 14	7 2
Pisa b.......... arr.	..	1047	1235	12 1	1244	16 5	1615	2047	2149	2358	2 36	3 25	4 33	7 21
Florence (309) dep.	8 25		1115	10 5	1115	1425	1345	1838	1848	2150	0 40	0 40	..	5 10
Pisa b..........dep.	1055	1048	1312	1215	1256	16 6	1616	2048	2126	0 14	2 48	3 28	4 40	7 3
Viareggio b	1120	↓	1341	1247	1322	1630	1634	..	2152	0 41	3 14	3 54	5 8	7 58
Sarzana b	12 7	↓	1429	1335	..	..	r	..	..	1 23	..	4 35	5 57	44
Spezia b	1228	↓	1452	15 3	1415	1714	1726	..	2239	1 40	4 5	4 55	6 25	9 1
Levanto b	1253	↓	1518	1539	r	..	See p. LI.	x	..	..	..		6 53	9 29
Sestri Levante b	1314	↓	1545	1615	..	..		..	..	..	..	5 34	7 1	9 50
Chiavari b..........	1326	↓	1556	1627	15 0			..	..	2 26	4 50	5 45	7 29	10 1
Rapallo b	1338	↓	16 7	1640	1510		1817	..		..	..	5 56	7 40	1012
S. Margherita b	1344	↓	1613	1644	1515	18 7	1822	..	2333	..	..	6 2	7 46	1018
Genoa (Nervi) b	14 1	↓	1630	17 6	1531		..	..		..	..	6 18	8 3	1040
Genoa (P.P.) b ....arr.	1420	1236	1654	1736	1546	18 2	1847	2236	24 0	3 15	5 35	6 36	8 25	11 1
											1 2			
....dep.	1455	1238	1710	18 5	1555	1839	1854	2238	..	3 28	5 45	7 9	8 40	1130
Genoa (Samp.) b....	15 1	↓	1717	1814	..	..	..	..	..	3 36		7 16	8 47	..
Novi b	1614	↓	1825	1954	..	..	..	..	..	4 35	6 38	8 9	9 47	1219
Milan (p. 302)	2016	↓	..	2314	2016	..	..	..	..	8 10	9 35	1125	15 0	r
Alessandria b (p. 300). arr.	1639	↓	1846	2021	17 8	1943	..	..	..	4 55	6 59	8 29	1012	1238
dep.	1642	↓	1850	2127	1710	1944	..	..	..	4 59	7 1	8 31	1014	1255
Asti b (p. 300)	1714	↓	1922	2218	1737	..	..	..	..	5 31	7 28	8 58	1041	1320
Turin (P.N.) b arr	18 5	1425	2015	0 3	1830	21 0	2115	0 25	..	6 25	8 20	9 50	1135	14 9

A Aerodynamic service. B 1 & 2 cl. Cars Rome-Paris-Boulogne and v.v. C 1 & 2 cl. Sleep. Car, Rome-Genoa. G 1 & 2 cl. Slp. Cars Rome-Turin, Naples (Cent.) Milan. H 1 & 2 cl Sleep. Car Rome Milan and v.v to Aug. 31. L Rome Express, Sleeping Cars only. N 1 & 2 cl. Rome-Amsterdam. O 1 & 2 cl. Sleep. Cars Rome-Milan and 1 cl. Sleep. Car Rome-Domodossola only. P 1 and 2 cl. Cars Paris-Rome and v.v. S 1 & 2 cl. Sleep. Car Turin-Rome, and v.v. T 3 cl. Paris-Rome and v v. V 1 & 2 cl. Sleep. Cars Rome-Vintimille and v.v.

Via Alessandria, see below]

Milan, Pavia, Voghera, Genoa. (95 miles).

[State Rly.

r Rest. Car.	123	23	123	12	123	123	12	13	123	123	123	123	1 cl.	123	123
	D		Z a				A	r				Rap	Rap	r	
Milan (Cen.)............dep.	0 30	4 0	6 25	7 10	8 20	9 35	1037	12 0	1334	15 5	1712	1754	18 55	20 0	2125
Pavia .... ,,	1 13	4 35	7 1	7 45	8 57	..	..	1236		1542	1746	x	x	2037	22 0
Voghera (p. 300) .... arr.	1 42	4 59	7 28	8 15	9 26	1032	..	13 3	1430	16 9	1811	1844	|	21 4	2226
Voghera (p. 300) .... dep.	1 50	5 5	7 36	8 25	9 36	1048	..	1312	1436	1618	1821	1852	|	2114	2234
Tortona (p. 300) ....arr.	2 9	5 21	7 53	8 41	9 53	..	..	1329	..	1634	1840	r	↓	2130	2250
GENOA (P. Prin)(p.299/301) ,,	3 39	6 29	9 10	9 45	11 0	1156	1242	1435	1545	1752	1947	20 0	2025	2235	2357

x Rapido Supp. payable.	23	123	123	123	1 cl.	123	12	123	123	123	12	12	123	123	123
			D		Rap		r	r	Rap		A	Rap		Y r	P
GENOA (P.Prin.) (p.299/301) d.	1 4	5 0	6 0	7 1	7 33	9 0	1140	1243	1433	15 5	1625	1745	18 0	1946	2115
Tortona (p. 300) ....arr.	3 21	6 22	..	8 3	x	10 9		1357	..	1611	..		1911	2053	2222
Voghera (p. 300) ...... arr.	3 49	6 42	7 15	8 20	|	1026	1254	1414	1537	1628	..	1849	1928	2110	2239
Voghera (p. 300) ...... dep.	3 57	6 48	7 21	8 30	|	1032	13 0	1420	1542	1636	..	1855	1934	2116	2245
Pavia .... arr.	4 33	7 21		8 55	↓	1059	..	1447	x	17 2		..	1959	2145	2314
Milan (Cen.)............ ,,	5 34	8 10	8 23	9 40	9 5	1145	14 2	1526	1634	1745	1840	1950	2040	2230	2357

A Vienna-Cannes Exp. odd dates. See special running, *page* 82. **P** Slp. Car Genoa-Trieste, Genoa-Zurich. **D** Slp. Car Nice-Berlin and *v.v.* **Z** Slp. Car Bale-Genoa, ex Bale odd days. For Riviera Exp. see p, 81. **Y** Slp. Car Genoa-Bale, even dates.

Luino, Novara, (Milan), Alessandria, (Genoa).

[State Rly.

23	123	23	123	23	23	Mls.		123	23	12	123	123	23	12	23
..	0 5	0 5	8 54	1040	..	0	dep.Lucerne .. (p.287) arr.	1242	..	..	1827	2028	4 39	..	..
..	3 35	3 35	12 4	1433	..	102	,, Bellinzona ,,	9 38	..	..	1433	17 4	23 4	.	..
	23		23					23			3 cl.	123	23		
..	5 25	8 20	13 0	17 5	18a5	0	dep.**Luino** ...... arr.	8 16	1034	.	1255	1556	2059	..	..
.	7 2	9 46	1448	1859	19a44	42	arr. **Novara** ....dep.	6 34	9 3	..	1132	1416	1912	..	..
..	9 7	12 0	1736	2212	2212	.	arr. Turin (p.298) d.	3 40	7 15	..	9 10	12 0	1457		..
5 4	7 14	1229	..	18 3	2013		dep.**Novara** ....arr.	7 2	8 58	..	1035	1359	19 0	..	2216
5 40	7 35	13 9	..	1834	2048	57	arr. Mortara ....dep.	6 22	8 20	..	10 7	1322	1827	..	2138
	123		23	123	123	Mls.						23	123		
4 6	7 55	1145	1350	17 7	1920	frm	dep. **Milan** (Cen.) ar.	7§26	9 35	..	..	15 0	2016	..	2357
5 16	8 56	1258	15 3	1815	2036	Mil.	dep. Vigevano ..	6 38	8 27	..	..	1345	19 1	..	..
5 34	9 11	1316	1522	1831	2055	32	arr. Mortara ..dp.	6 19	8 12	..	..	1325	1840	.	2133
5 46	7 36	1326	..	1839	21 0	32	dep.Mortara .... arr.	6 11	8 * 8	..	10 5	1314	1822	..	2131
6 46	8 26	1429	..	1938	2152	59	arr. **Alessandria** dep.	5 9	7*10	⏟	9 25	12 6	1726	⏟	2029
7*0	8 37	1620	*	2126	2335	..	dep. Alessandria ar.	4 55	6 30	6 59	8 29	1012	1639	17 8	2021
8*28	9 52	1752	*	2247	0 50	106	arr. GENOA (p.301) dp.	3*28	4 10	5 45	7 4	8*40	1455	1555	18 5

a 3rd class. * 1st class also. § Porta Genova Sta.

Domodossola, Arona, Milan, Turin.

[State Rly.

From Paris & Berne, *see p.* 288. From Paris & Lausanne *see p.* 280.

123	123	23	12	123	123	23	123	123	123		123	123	123	123	123	123	12	23	123
	S		L	R	ZR		Exp	R				R	ExR	Exp	XR		L		S
1148	3 30	7 20	9 53	1022	1217	1432	1518	1752	2140	d.Domodossola a.	9 30	1219	1330	1651	1912	1937	2138	2249	2 40
1219	3 56	7 59	..	1048	1250	1522	1549	1824	22 5	,,Pallanza†d	8 56	1143	1249	1619	1842	1858	..	22 7	2 10
1227	4 4	8 9	1025	1056	1259	1532	1559	1833	2213	,,Baveno d.	8 49	1134	1242	1612	1834	1850	21 0	2156	2 2
1238	4 11	8 17	1033	11 3	13 5	1539	16 8	1845	2221	,,Stresa.. ,,	8 42	1126	1236	16 6	1825	1843	2054	2150	1 56
13 0	4 29	8 44	1053	1125	1323	1612	1625	19 5	2239	a. **Arona** d.	8 20	11 0	1214	1544	18 5	1823	2033	2120	1 37
13 4	4 31	8 46	1057	1127	1325	1652	1627	19 8	2241	d. **Arona** a.	8 18	1055	1210	1538	18 2	1821	2031	2118	1 35
1343	5 11	9 32	|	12 7	14 1	1745	17 2	1945	2316	d.Gallarate d	7 40	1024	1132	15 6	1730	1748	..	2038	1 3
|	5 42	8 53	|	1238	1624	1819	1744	2013	0 25	a. Varese d.	7 22	8 15	9 39	13 0	1548	1722	↑	2012	2315
|	6 28	9 14	|	..	1650	1850	1816	2040	..	,, P.C'r'sio,,	6 53	7 45	9 20	1241	1525	1656	|	1936	..
↓	7 50	1030	↓	..	18 5		..	..	..	,, Lugano ,,		..	8 30	1120	14 5	..	|	1825	
1432	5 55	1020	1215	1250	1448	1847	1744	2028	24 0	a.**Milan** ..d.	6 50	9 35	1045	1420	1645	17 0	1910	19a48	0 15
..	5 30	..	..	1154	1338	..	16*48	1916	..	d.ARONA..a.	8 13	1024	..	1530	..	1530	19 2	2113	
..	8 36	..	..	1450	1616	..	19*52	2212	..	a.TURIN..d.	5 20	7 23	..	1312	..	1312	14*57	1838	
	23			23			23				23					23			
..	6 55	..	..	1139	..	..	1648	1913	..	d.**Arona**..a.	8 33	..	..	1538	..	19 2	..	2113	* via Novara.
..	8 4	..	..	1224	..		1745	20 8	..	a.**Novara** d.	7 28	..	..	1416	..	18 4	..	2029	
..	1259	..	..	1752	..	..	2247	0 50	..	a.**Genoa**..d.	3 28	..	..	8 40	..	..	..	1455	

L Simplon Orient Exp. *see p.* 83. **R** Restaurant Car. **S** 1 & 2 Sleep. Car. Venice-Lausanne-Paris and *v.v.* **X** 1 and 2 cl. cars Milan-Berne-Calais, *see page* 124, and Milan-Berne-Paris daily. **Z** Through 1 & 2 cl. Boulogne-Berne-Brindisi (Mar.), *see p.* 123, also Paris-Berne-Milan daily (1, 2 & 3 cl.).
† Electric train service down to the Lake in 20 minutes. *a* Milan Porta Nuova

Milan (Verona), Bologna, Florence Rome. (393 Mls.). [State Rly.

	Rap 1 cl.	Rap 1 2 3	Exp 1 2 3	1 2 3	Exp 1 2 3	Rap 1cl.	Exp 1 2 3	Rap 1 2	Exp 1 2 3	fast 1 2 3	Exp 1cl.	Exp 1 2 3	Rap 1 2	Exp 1 2 3	Exp 1 2 3	Exp 1 2 2	Exp 1 2	Exp 1 2 3
			r	r	r	r					x	A r	r	D			S	
Milan (Cen.) .. dep.	7 45	6 50	8 35	1110	1250	1350	14 0	1520	1530	1620	18 0	1845	1940	2120	22 0	2250	2310	..
Piacenza ...... arr.	x	7 42	9 28	12 1	1336	..	15 6	x	1618	1725	..	1936	x	2222	2250	2348	0 8	..
Turin (*p.* 300) dep.		..	5 40	..	..	..	8 52		1218	1438	r	1438		.	1836	..	..	..
Alessandria . ,,		..	7 9	..	..	..	12 3		1343	1550	..	..		1812	2013	..	..	..
Piacenza ...... dep.		7 44	9 39	12 3	1338	..	1514		1621	1730	..	1938		2225	2258	2350	0 10	..
Fidenza		8 10	1012	1237	14 4	..	1545		1646	18 2	..	20 4		2258	2327	0 19	..	..
Parma (*p.* 300) dep.		8 28	1032	1255	1422	x	16 7		17 4	1821	..	2022		2318	2346	0 39	..	..
Modena ..... ,,		9 9	1119	1339	15 3	..	1651		1745	19 6		21 3		0 5	0 31	1 26	..	..
Bologna (*p.* 313) arr.	9 45	9 36	1150	14 6	1530	1543	1718	1733	1810	1933	1953	2130	2140	0 32	0 58	1 57	2 10	..
Venice (*p.* 308) dep.	7 50	7 0	9 10	1130	..	1130	1432	1535	..	1758	1758	2010	..	..	2255	..	..	2338 W
Verona (*p* 307) dep.	6 20	8 33	8 33	1040	..	1410	1550	1550	..	..	..	2057	2 3 1840	..	G	..	0 24	0 24
			r				r	P										
Bologna .... dep.	9 47	1030	1212	1430	..	1546	1753	1745	..	20 5	1956	2325	2152	0 55	1 55	2 7	2 27	2 47
Prato (Pisa, *p* 309) d.	.		1317	1535	..	..	1857	r	..	2134	..	0 28	2241	2 0	G	3 12	..	
Florence (Piaz Sta. Mar. Nov.) ar.	1045	1140	1330	1549	..	1638	1910	1855	..	2150	2048	0 45	2253	2 13	3 10	3 25	3 42	4 2
de.	1050	1145	1337	1555	..	1643	1916	19 0	..	..	2053	0 55	..	2 25	3 16	3 32	3 50	4 9
Arezzo		..	1444	17 4		Milan-Naples	2032		..	..	..	2 37	..	3 48	4 29	4 46	..	5 18
Terontola (*p.* 309) a.	r	x	15 9	1731			21 0	..	..	..	..	3 15	..	X X	.	5 13	..	5 45
Chiusi (*p.* 309) arr.		..	1531	1754	..		2122	2049	..	..	..	3 48		4 35	5 19	5 39	..	6 10
dep.		..	1533	18 7	..		2123	2050	..	..	..	3 56	..	4 37	5 22	5 42	..	6 11
Orvieto		r	16 5	1836	..	x	2152	r	..	..	..	4 26	..	..	5 51	6 12		6 40
Orte (*p.* 309)			1637	19 8	..		2224		..	..		5 2	..	5 36	6 35	6 44	..	7 15
Rome (Termini) arr.	1415	1530	1750	2020	..	1950	2310	2255	..	..	24 0	6 30	..	6 50	7 50	8 0	8 10	8 25
Naples C (*p* 310) a.	1559	18 7	2053	0 3		2159	3 8	3 8	..	..	3 8	9 52	..	9 52	1247	1247	1247	1247
Naples Merg. arr.	1549	17‡56	2110		..	21†49	..		..	..		1018	..	1018	1248	1248	1248	1248

	Exp 1 2 3	Rap 1cl.	1 2 3	Rap 1 2 3	Rap 1cl.	Exp 1 2 3	Exp 1 2 3	Rap 1 2	Exp 2 3	Rap 1 cl.	Exp 1 2 3	Exp 1 2 3	Exp 1 2 3	Exp 1 2 3	Exp 1 2	Exp 1 2 3	Exp 1 2 3	Ep 1 2 3
Naples Merg. dep.	3 49	3 49	5 8	5 8	1052	8 15	11 1	1128	1525	1525	1525	1445	1819	20 0	20 0	20 0		2135
Naples C (*p.* 310) ,,	3 53	3 53	6 16	6 16	11 1	7 27	1052	1117	1515	1515	1515	1610	1835	1948	1948	1948		2124
		x	x	r	x	r		x			r	r			S		D	
Rome (Ter.) .. dep.	7 10	7 5	9 15	9 30	13 0	1210	13 7	1425	1730	1725	18 5	1910	2140	2245	2310	2325	2350	0 5
Orte	8 16	..	P	1039	..	1318	1417		1830	..	1917	2016	2247	2352	E	G	..	1 34
Orvieto	8 50	..	..	1118	..	1353	1455	.	19 0	Naples-Mian	1955	2051	..	..	..	..	..	2 14
Chiusi ...... arr.	9 22	..	..	1150	..	1425	1530	1627	1928		2028	2123	..	1 0	..	..	2 2	2 58
dep.	9 23	..	..	1152		1427	1532	1628	1930		2030	2124	..	1 1	..	..	2 3	3 1
Terontola ...... ,,	9 48	.	..		..	15 3	1557	..	1949		21 0	2145	.		..	..		3 25
Arezzo .... ,,	1015	x	..	1240	.	1531	1624		2013		2131	2212	0 37	..	..	2 24	2 50	4 2
Florence (Piaz. Sta. Maria Novella) ar.	1120	1030	1258	1348	16 7	1637	1739	1814	2111	2032	2255	2317	1 45	2 52	3 15	3 34	4 2	5 30
		r	r			r		r					W					
.. dp.	1126	1035	13 4	1355	1611	1643	1745	1820	2115	2036	23 1	2323	1 51	3 0	3 22	3 40	4 5	5 45
Prato .... dep.	1147	..	..	1410	..	1657	1759	..	2128		2322	2337	2 5	3 15			4 20	6 0
Bologna ...... arr.	1248	1131	1414	1513	17 2	18 0	1912	1930	2220	2127	0 25	0 40	3 6	4 21	4 40	4 54	5 23	7 5
Venice ...... arr.	1555	..	1630	1749	1858	21 0	2215	2215	..	2340	4 40	4 40	6 10			8 0	10 0	1033
Verona (*p.* 307) a.	1452	..	1745		1837	2039	2140	2140	Exp 1 2 3	..	..	2 36	5 6		8 20	8 20	8 20	..
													A			1 2		
Bologna ...... dep.	1310	1133	1421	1531	17 5	1817	1955	1943	2 43	2130	1 25	..	5 4	4 36	4 50	7 15	5 38	7 30
Modena ...... arr.	1335	..	..	1555		1842	2020		3 12		1 55		5 32	5 1	..	x	6 7	7 55
Parma .... ,,	1421	..	..	1636		1924	21 5	x	4 4		2 48		6 15	5 44			7 4	8 41
Fidenza* .... ,,	1440	..	..	1654		1943	2126		4 29		3 17		6 32	6 2	..		7 24	8 59
Piacenza ...... arr.	1510	..	..	1724		2012	2159	2110	5 5		3 51		6 59	6 35	6 45		7 53	9 20
Alessandria .. arr.	..	..	..	2214		2214	6 33	2245	7 41		7 41	..	..	1030	1030		1030	1247
Turin ...... ,,		..	..	2345		2345	8 20	2353	9 22		9 22			1158	1158		1158	14 9
Piacenza ...... dep.	1513	..	..	1726		2025	22 3	2111	5 15		3 59		7 1	6 37	6 47		7 57	9 3
Milan (Cen.) .. arr.	1617	1335	1628	1830	19 0	2135	2310	22 0	6 22	2325	5 10		8 4	7 45	7 55	9 15	9 0	1035

A 1 & 2 Sleep. cars Paris Milan-Brindisi (Mar.) & *v.v.* *see p.* 313 **B** Sleep car Rome-Berlin & *v.v.* **C** Sleep. car Bologna-Rome, **D** Sleep car Milan-Naples **G** 1 & 2 Sleep. cars Venice-Rome & *v.v.* **J** Sleep. Car Rome-Padua. **P** 1 & 2 cl. car Paris-Lausanne-Rome & *v.v.* **S** Sleep. Car only Milan—Rome. **W** 1 & 2 Sleep. cars Trieste-Rome & *v.v.* **E** Sleep. car Bolzano-Rome & *v.v.* *r* Rest. Car. *x* Supp. payable for travel by Rap. trains. ‡ 1 & 2 cl. only. ‖ 2 & 3 cl. only. † 1 cl. only.

* **Salsomaggiore.**—Steam tram to and from Fidenza, 30 min. journey.

(All 1 & 3 class.) **Milan, Varese, Laveno.** [Nord-Milan Rly.

* Holidays				*																
		7 55	9 0	1043	1228	1312	1530	1740	1912	dp. **Milan** ar.	7 55	8 34	8 47	1018	1155	1354	1534	17 4	1835	21 2
		8 18	9 23	1114	1255	1325	16 3		1942	,, Saronno	7 32	8 11	8 25	9 55	1130	1325	1511	1651	1812	2032
		8 52	9 58	12 6	1350	1412	1641	1843	2036	,, Varese(N)	6 33	7 19	7 53	9 2	1051	13 0	1421	1616	1738	1940
		9 31	1027	1245	arr.	1451	1710	1921	2117	a. **Laveno** d.	5 45	6 30	7 11	8 19	10 4	1213	1340	1524	1713	19 4

(All 1 & 3 class.) **Laveno, Varese, Como.** [Nord-Milan Rly.

					a		Mls.			*			*			* Holidays
5 45	6 30	8 19	1213	1340	17 0	19 0	..	dep. Laveno (*above*) arr.	▲	8 18	9 31	1451	1721	1923	2115	
6 37	7 38	9 24	1257	1551	1826	2018	0	,, **Varese** (Nord) ,,	|	7 14	8 31	14 2	1539	1816	1956	
7 36	8 35	1019	1339	1629	1924	2111	18	arr. **Como** (Lake Sd.) d.	|	6 14	7 30	1317	15 0	1716	1856	
								a via Saronne								

(All 1 & 3 class.) **Milan, Como (via Saronno).** [Nord-Milan Rly.

									Mls.										
6 40	8 50	1043	13 8	14 0	17 0	1754	1824	1945	0	dp. **Milan** (Nord) a.	7 4	8 41	9 12	1221	1343	14 8	1833	1922	2152
7 7	9 11	11 7	1330	1420	1723	1818	..	20 5	13¾	,, Saronno dp.	6 40	8 19	..	12 2	1324	1347	1811		2130
7 49	9 40	1148	1259	1457	18 4	19 3	1912	2044	8¾	ar. **Como** (L. Sd.) d	5 49	7 50	8 30	1125	1245	1317	1732	1840	205.

Milan, Como, Chiasso (Lugano). [State Rly

Exp 123	Exp 123	Exp 123	Exp 123	Exp 123	Exp 123	Exp 123	123	Exp 123		Exp 123	123	Exp 123	Exp 12	Exp 123	Exp 123	Exp 123	Exp 123	123
	R			R									R					R
0 25	6 50	8 38	9 42	1220	1424	1710	1840	2253	d. **Milan** (Ct) a	5 58	8 24	10 6	13 7	1445	1645	1930	2230	0 15
0 43	7 10	8 54	..	1238	1442	..	19 0	2310	Monza	..	8 5	9 47	..	1425	1626	..	2211	..
..	..	9 9	..	1255	15 5	..	1916		Seregno ..	..	..	..		14 7	1614	.	2159	..
1 24	7 54	9 35	1038	1322	1522	18 6	1955	2350	a. **Como** ..d.	5 2	7 29	9 12	1215	1336	1543	1836	2127	2317
1 33	8 0	9 45	1043	1335	1538	1812	2010	2355	d. (S. Giov) a.	4 58	7 18	9 8	12 8	1331	1536	1832	2122	2313
1 43	8 10	9 55	1053	1345	1548	1822	2025	0 5	a. Chiasso d.	4 50	7 10	9 0	12 0	1323	1528	1824	2114	23 5
2 32	8 59	11 6	1140	1436	1637	1914	2130	1 4	a. Lugano } d	3 49	..	7 59	1115	1236	1430	1730	2023	2223
6 44	1242	..	1514	1827	2028	2219	..	4 39	a. Lucerne } d	0 5	..	..	8 10	8 54	1040	1344	1627	1858
									(*p.* 287).									

R Rest. Car Milan-Bale and *v.v.*

Milan, Lecco, Colico, Sondrio (Chiavenna). [State Rly.

23	123	123	23	123	123	23	23		123	23	23	123	23	123	23	123
4 55	7 0	8a44	1550	1435	17 0	1852	2047	dp. **Milan** (Ct.) ar.	9 6	1117	1138	1436	1829	19a57	2219	2330
5 22	7 18	9 4	16 2	1454	1722	1916	21 6	Monza	8 44	1051	1124	1415	18 7	1935	2151	23 8
6 35	8 12	9 54	1635	1554	1811	2010	2214	ar. } Lecco .. { d.	7 55	9 40	1049	1324	17 7	1841	2046	2219
6 58	8 15	9 57	1636	1556	1814	2013	2217	dp. } (*below*) { a.	7 50	9 31	1047	1322	17 3	1836	2036	2216
7 42	8 47	1026	..	1629	1848	2051	2248	Perledo-Varenna	7 19	8 49	..	1252	1629	18 4	1956	2145
8 16	9 18	1053	1713	1656	1916	2126	2313	arr. **Colico** ..dep.	6 48	8 8	1011	1224	1559	1736	1921	2114
9 20	10 3	1137	1752	1739	2018	2225	0 10	,, Sondrio ,,	6 4	7 3	9 30	1142	15 0	1648	1821	2031
..	10 9	11‖45	1753	1753	2028	..	7 37	dep. Sondrio arr.	5 55	5 55	9 14	1135	1450	..	1815	2023
..	1051	12‖37	1821	1821	21 8	..	8 19	arr. Tirano ..dep.	5 15	5 15	8 30	1059	14 7	..	1733	1947
		a						(*page* 289).						a		
8 26	9†26	1114	..	1718	1925	2131	..	dep. Colico .. arr.	6 24	..	10 6	12 8	1449	..	19 9	21 4
9 10	10 6	12 0	..	18 2	20 9	2215	..	ar. Chiavenna dp.	5 40	..	9 23	11†30	14 5	..	1825	2030

a July 1–Sept. 30.

Colico-Chiavenna *v.v.*, 2 & 3 cl. only, except trains marked † where 1, 2 & 3.

Como, Lecco, Bergamo, Brescia. [State Rly.

23	23	23	23	23	3	23	Mls.		3	23	23	23	23	23
..	4 50	7 0	13 0	..	..	1852	0	dep. **Como** (S. Gio.)* ar.	8 42	.	1427	1738	2010	
..	6 31	8 9	1420	..	..	20 0	26	arr. Lecco (*above*)* d.	7 15		13 0	1630	1842	
..	6 46	8 35	1334	1733	19 5	..	..	dep. Lecco .... arr.	7 6	..	9 44	1543	..	21 5
..	7 47	9 24	1430	1829	1951	..	46	arr. } Bergamo { dep.	6 20		8 50	1450	..	2010
5 30	8 3	9 45	1454	1857	2015	..	..	dep. } (*below*) { arr.	..	6 45	8 44	1432	..	20 3
6 29	9 5	1027	1547	1958	2056	..	66	arr. Rovato ...... dep.	..	5 50	7 50	1338	..	19 5
6 53	9 30	1043	1619	2021	2125		77	arr. **Brescia** (*p.* 305) dp.		5 22	7 27	1313	..	1843

† Treviglio (West). **Milan, Bergamo.** [State Rly.

	23	123	23	23	123	23	23		23	123	23	123	23	123
1337	7 23	9 11	1015	1510	1718	1858	2257	dep. **Milan** (Cen.) arr.	8 7	9 56	1343	1512	1958	2125
1416	8†11	9†43	11†22	16†5	17†50	19†30	23†50	,, Treviglio (*p.* 305) ,,	7†24	9†20	13†8	14†40	1915	20†52
1445	8 40	1010	1138	1632	1817	1957	0 17	arr. **Bergamo** ..dep.	7 2	8 57	1245	1419	1834	2030

The times on the LEFT are to be read DOWNWARDS, those on the RIGHT UPWARDS.

Mls.		123	123	23	123	123	2cl.	123	12	123	123		123	123	12	123	123
					Exp		Rap		luxe		Exp			Rap	luxe		Exp
..	Turin (p. 298)..dep.	2114	2114	..	..	..	6x31	7 17		8 55	11x32	..	12 0	15 8	A	15 8	..
			S				123		O	r	¶					r ¶	
0	**Milan** (Cent.) ....dep.	0 16	0 35	..	6 17	6 54	8 50	9r52	1222	1228	1330	..	1545	18 5	1854	1813	20 8
20	Treviglio .... ,,	..	1 10	..	¶	7 31	x	1024	..	13 2	..	..	..	r	|	1844	
40	Rovato (p. 304) .. ,,	..	1 47	..		8 10	..	11 3	..	1334	..		1649	..	|	1915	21 1
51	Brescia ....arr.	1 28	2 8		7 25	8 28	..	1121	..	1351	1437	..	17 5	x	|	1931	2116
68	Desenzano ......dep.	1 58	2 39		7 52	9 0	..	1152	..	1420	15 9		1736	..	|	20 2	..
77	Peschiera ......dep.		..	..	..	9 13		12 5	..	1434	..	..	1749	..	|	2015	..
92	**Verona** P.N.).. arr.	2 32	3 20		8 27	9 38	1028	1232	1425	1459	1544	..	1815	1948	2052	2041	2214
	(p. 307). dep.	3 48	3 28	7 10	8 34	9 45	1031	1238	1431	15 5	1550		1821	1951	2059	2053	2220
124	Vicenza .... ,,	3 30	4 15	8 15	9 18	1031		1326	..	1551	1635	..	19 7	..	|	2146	23 0
143	Padua (p. 308) .. ,,	3 56	4 45	8 49	9 47	11 1	1121	1355	1531	1619	17 3	..	1935	2041	|	2216	2325
160	Venice Mestre arr.	4 20	5 10	9 17	1012	1126	1142	1420	..	1644	1728	..	20 0	..	↓	2241	2346
	dep.	4§28	5 14	9 22	1014	1129	1143	1422	..	1646	1730	..	20 2	..	▼	2244	2349
166	**Venice** (S.L.) arr.	4§40	5 25	9 34	1025	1140	1153	1432	16 0	1656	1740	Rap	2012	2110	2232	2255	2359
	(p. 308)		T			23§						2 cl.		2cl.		23	
	dep	●●	5 47	7 27	1137	1222		1439	16 7	..	18 2	1910	2030	2212		0 15	..
..	Venice Mestre ..dep.	4 35	6 8	7 48	1155	1239	..	1455	|	..	1816		2046	2220		0 35	..
..	Portogruaro .... ,,	5 27	7 3	8 32	1243	1359	..	1552	|	..	1910	..	2141	x		2 4	..
209	Cervignano ...... ,,	6 15	7 44	9 10	1321	15 9	..	1640	|	..	1950	2020	2229	23 0		3 16	..
236	Monfalcone...... ,,	6 33	7 59	9 24	1336	1540	..	1655	|	..	20 5	2032	2243			3 42	..
246	Bivio Aurisina .. arr.	..	8 12	9 37	1350	16 0	..		▼		2018	..	..	2342		4 2	..
264	**Trieste** .... arr.	7 0	8 28	9 55	14 5	1623	..	1722	1822	..	2034	2055	2310	2355		4 25	..
			Exp		23								23			..	..
	dp.	7a25	9 37	1313	1555	2015	..	..	..	..	21 3	..	4 55	..		..	..
	Aurisina .... ,,	7 39	10 4	1332	1612	2035	.	..	..	..	2121	..	5 10	..		..	..
291	Divaccia (p. 307) ,,	8 6	1032	14 2	1639	2111	..	..	..	..	2149		5 41	..		..	..
306	St. Pietro del Carso a.	8a27	1057	1427	17 0	2140		..	..	..	2314	..	6 6	..		..	..
					23								23				
	,, (p. 307) ....dep.	8 31	11 3	1430	17 3	2220	..	..	..	..	..	..	6 11	..		..	..
335	Abbazia ....arr.	9 20	1151	1514	1748	2312	..	..	..	..	..	..	6 59	..		..	..
344	**Fiume** .... ,,	9 31	12 2	1524	1759	2224	.	..		..	..	..	7 14	..		..	

A Vienna-Cannes Exp. special running, see page 82.

Mls.		123	23	12	123	123	123	23	123	luxe	23	123	2e.	2 cl.	123	123
		¶		luxe			Rap		Exp	O		Rap		Rap		Exp
0	**Fiume** ....dep.	..	..	A	..	..	x	5 0	6a55	..	7 50	x	..	..	1355	1832
9	Abbazia .... ,,	..	..	..	..	..	..	5 9	7 4	..	7 59	..	..	..	14 7	1844
38	St. Pietro del Carso a	..	..	..	..	..	..	5 53	7 44	..	8 50	..	..	..	15 6	1944
..	,, (p. 307) ....dep.	..	..	..		..	..	5 58	7 47	..	8 53	..	..	..	1510	1948
58	Divaccia .... ,,	..	..	..	..	..	..	6 21	..	..	9 17	..	..	..	1538	2021
..	Aurisina ....arr	..	..	..	..	..	..	6 49	..	..	9 47	..	..	..	1612	2052
80	**Trieste**........ arr.	..	..	..	..	..	..	7 9	8a45	..	10 8	..	..		1635	2110
								123			123		r		Exp	S
	dep.	2225	0 5	..	..	..	6 0	9 30	..	1225	12r5	..	1343	16 5	1645	2135
	Bivio Aurisina .. ,,	2243	0 31	..	..	..	6 16		..	|		..	1358	..	..	2151
98	Monfalcone...... ,,	2257	0 48	..	..	..	6 30	9 56	..	|	1231	..	x	1629	1711	22 4
108	Cervignano ...... ,,	2317	1 17	..	..	..	6 49	1014	..	|	1250	..	1418	1643	1730	2223
135	Portogruaro .... ,,	2358	2 12	..	..		7 22	1047	..	▼	1333	..	..		1814	23 0
	Venice Mestre .. arr	0 51	3 19	..	..	..	8 9	1131	..	..	1426	..	1520		19 7	2350
178	**Venice** (S.L.) arr	1 5	3 35	..	..	..	8 20	1147	..	1448	14r39		1528	1753	1920	0§12
	(p. 308)		123					Exp			123	x	123		123	T
	dep.	1 25	5 2	..	6 30	8 40	1055	12 7	1345	1457	1510	1815	1820	..	19r38	0 1
	Venice Mestre ..dep.	1 39	5 14	6 37	..	8 53	11 6	..	1359	..	1524		1834	..	1950	0 22
201	Padua .... ,,	2 6	5 38	..	7 2	9 19	1128	1240	1427	1528	1549	1842	19 2	..	2018	0 52
220	Vicenza .... ,,	2 35	6 2	..	7 25	9 43		13 4	1456	..	1612	..	1934	..	2047	1 21
252	**Verona** (P.N.).. arr.	3 24	6 47	8 12	8 9	1027	1219	1318	1546	1633	1653	1933	2038	..	2135	2 9
	(p. 307) dep.	3 40	6 53	8 24	8 15	1033	1223	1354	1553	1639	1659	1936	2046	..	2147	2 25
267	Peschiera........ ,,	4 6	7 16	..	..	1050		r	1619	..	..	x	2118	..	..	2 55
276	Desenzano ...... ,,	4 24	7 33	..	..	1118		1431	1635	..	1738	r	2136	..	2223	3 16
293	Brescia.......... ,,	4 59	8 3	..	9 18	1153	..	15 2	17 7	..	18 8	|	2213	..	2252	3 58
304	Rovato (p. 304) .. ,,	..	8 19	..		r	.	..	..	..	r	|	2232	..	r	4 20
324	Treviglio .... ,,	5 54	8 44	..		..	..	..	..	..	..	▼	23 8		..	4 59
344	**Milan** (Cent.).... arr.	6 33	9 15	1030	1024	1310	14 5	16 8	1815	1855	1913	2115	2345	..	2355	5 40
		2cl							2cl.			2cl.				
..	Turin (p. 298).. arr.	9x14		..	13x45	13x45	18 4	1950	20x11	..	2210	x40	..			9 6

T Sleep. Car Trieste-Rome & v.v.

A Vienna-Nice-Cannes Express, suspended. **O** Simplon Orient Express, see p. 83.
S 1 & 2 cl. Sleep. Car Genoa-Trieste, and v.v. *a* 2 & 3 cl, *r* Restaurant Car. § Connect at Mestre.
x Supplement payable for travel by Rap. trains.
¶ 3rd class passengers cannot travel locally between Milan-Verona or between Verona-Venice.

a Mixed classes.

Venice, Treviso (Padua) Calalzo.

123	a	23	a	23		23	a	23	a	
5 40	1010	1445	1828	2037	dep. **Venice** (S. Lucia) .... arr.	7 0	12 0	14 2	1838	2040
6 32	1054	1530	1857	2125	,, Treviso (*p.* 808) .... ,,	6 11	11 3	1322	18 3	2011
7 17	1128	16 5	1912	2157	arr. Montebelluna ......dep.	5 45	1039	1257	1742	1952
3 20	7 36	13 8	1530	1815	dep. Bologna (*p.* 308) .. arr.	9 25	1415	1720	1947	23 2
5 43	1020	1457	1820	2049	,, Padua.. .... ,,	6 37	1143	1359	1816	2046
7 2	1123	16 1	1920	2159	arr. Montebelluna ......dep.	5 41	1044	1252	1739	1950
7 15	1134	1612	1923	22 5	dep. Montebelluna ...... arr.	5 39	1034	1247	1737	1945
9 5	1318	1759	2058	2341	arr. Belluno .... dep.	4 20	9 15	1115	1638	1814
9 12	1325	1812	21 4	..	dep. Belluno arr.	..	9 9	1110	1637	18 9
1046	1455	1945	2230	..	arr. **Calalzo** (Pieve di Cadore). ....dep.	..	7 58	9 56	1550	1658

(Dolomites Line). Calalzo, Dobbiaco.

13	13	13	13	13	13	13		13	13	13	13	13	13
6 15	8 40	9 53	1115	1455	1712	20 5	dep. **Calalzo** (F.S.) ...... arr.	1118	1524	1750	1917	20 0	..
..	..	..	1127	15 7	..	2016	,, Tai ....dep.	11 7	1512	1738	19 5	..	..
7 9	..	1038	12 3	1544	1752	2049	,, Borca .... ,,	1040	1434	17 2	1829	..	..
7 18	9 23	1044	1210	1551	1757	21 0	,, San Vito di Cadore .. ,,	1031	1427	1655	1822	1917	..
7 42		..	1231	1613		..	arr. Miramonti .... ,,		14 9	1634	1759	..	..
7 43	9 45	11 8	1235	1617	1818	2120	arr. Cortina.......... dep.	10 8	14 3	1630	1755	1855	..
8 25	..	..	1335	1730	1853	..	dep. Cortina arr.	9 55	1250	..	17 5	..	2140
8 58	..	..	1355	18 3	19 2	..	,, Carbonin (Misurina).. ,,	9 25	1217	..	1632	..	2110
9 28	..	..	1435	1830	1929	..	arr. **Dobbiaco** (Toblach) *p*198 d	9 0	1150	..	16 5	..	2045

Trento, Male.

[Italian State Rlys. (Electric Rly.)

13	13	13	13	13	13	13		13	13	13	13	13	13
7 21	9 17	1112	1310	1651	1831	1944	dep. **Trento** (T.V.) (*p.* 307) arr.	8 29	10 2	1138	16 0	1917	2138
6 3	9 59	1155	1352	1736	1913	2026	,, San Michele .... ,,	7 49	9 23	1058	1519	1837	2058
6 9	10 5	12 1	1358	1742	1919	2032	arr. Mezzocorona .... ,,	7 43	9 17	1152	1513	1831	2052
7 17	1110	1313	15 5	1851	2023	2132	arr. Dermulo ....dep.	6 49	8 21	9 56	1416	1738	1954
8 40	..	..	1515	..	2115	..	dep. Dermulo .... arr.	..	6 56	..	1411	..	..
9 31	..	..	16 6	..	22 6	..	arr. Fondo ....dep.	..	6 5	..	1320	..	..
7 18	1111	1314	15 6	1852	2024	1 33	dep. Dermulo .... arr.	6 48	8 20	9 55	1415	1737	1953
8 19	1212	1415	16 5	1951	2123	2231	arr. **Male** (*p.* 212) ....dep.	5 5	7 23	8 56	1318	1640	1855

Trento, Roncegno, Bassano, (Padua), Venice.

23	23	23	23	23	23	Mls.		23	23	23	23	23	23
..	5 10	8 0	1245	1845	1947	0	dep. Trento (above)........arr.	7 30	10 5	1125	1618	1840	2310
..	6 3	9 20	1343	1927	2044	20	,, Levico ....dep.	6 35	9 2	1041	1540	1743	2220
..	6 20	9 43	14 0	1939	21 2	25	,, Roncegno........... ,,	6 18	8 49	1028	1528	1727	2227
..	7 3	1048	1441	..	2146	40	,, Tezze................ ,,	5 36	8 4	..	..	1643	
..	7 5	1136	1454	2014	2154	42½	,, Primolano .... ,,	5 30	7 57	9 45	1451	1636	2124
..	7 47	12 8	1533	2039	2233	60½	arr. Bassano ....dep.	..	7 3	9 4	1423	1548	2040
	8 2	1312	1744	2045		0	dep. Bassano............arr.	..	..	8 59	14 0	1528	2034
	8 50	1421	1834	2131		30	arr. Padua (*p.* 305)......dep.	..	..	8 5	1251	1438	1920
5 42	7 49	1225	1546	2043	2239	60½	dep. Bassano ....arr.	..	7 1	9 2	1422	1545	2036
6 55	8 55	1318	1652	2125	2338	93⅛	,, Venice-Mestre........ ,,	..	5 47	7 53	1344	1440	1938
7 5	9 5	1325	17 4	2132	2348	98⅜	arr. Venice ....dep.	..	5 33	7 40	1335	1425	1927

Bolzano, Merano, Malles (Mals).

[Italian State Rlys.

	23	23	23	123	23	23	123	123	23	123	23	123	23
Bolzano-Gries (*p.* 307) ..dep.	6 5	7 5	7 32	9 20	1215	1227	1317	1425	1728	1840	1936	2045	2230
Merano .... arr.	6 42	8 2	8 28	10 9	1252	1324	14 3	15 9	18 4	1939	2026	2127	2320
Merano dep.	6 44	8 11	..		1254		..	..	..	19†50	..		..
Spondigna-Prato (*p.* 212) ,,	8 10	1043	..	..	1414	..	..	..	..	2148	..	*b*	..
Malles (Mals) .... arr.	8 24	11 6	..		1429	..	..	..	..	22 6	..	..	..

	23	23	123	123	23	123	23	123	23	23	123	23	23	123
Malles (Mals) ....dep.	..	6 0	..	..	10 0	..	..	..	13 0	1515	..	..	1844	..
Spondigna-Prato .... ,,	..	6 16	*b*	.	1012	..	..	..	1318	1527	..	..	1859	..
Merano .... arr.		8 0	..	..	1123	..	..	..	1538	1631	..	..	2036	..
Merano dep.	6 53	–	8 7	1030	1125	1216	1338	1544	⁀	1633	1650	1830	2045	2335
Bolzano .... arr.	7 49	..	8 59	1116	12 1	13 6	1423	1630	..	17 9	1745	1920	2142	0 18

b June 25 Sept. 24. † 2nd and 3rd cl, only.

The times on the LEFT are to be read DOWNWARDS, those on the RIGHT UPWARDS.

(Innsbruck), Brennero, Verona, Bologna, (Rome).

Exp 123	Rap 2cl	23	23	Rap 123	Exp 123C	Exp 123	123	Exp 123		Exp 123	Exp 123	23	123	Rap 12	2cl.	Exp 123	
			d	*b*	Fr. San Candido	GB	..				B	*a*	*	A *e*	*a*		
2 40	..	5 15	7 0	1028		1410	1840	2131	dep. Innsbruck (*p.*198) ar.	8 57	1551	2146		2035	*	3 48	
4 5	..	6 30	8 20	1143		1550	1823	2252	d. Brennero (Brenner) a.	7 23	1422	1850	1021	1920	2311	2 29	
4 25	..	6 57	8 44	12 3		1611	1844	2313	,, Colle Isarco ......d.	7 3	14 1	1839	9 50	1849	2247	2 9	
4 54	..	7 37	9 17	1230	1141	1643	1916	2345	a. Fortezza .... d.	6 30	1325	1754	0 4	1824	22 8	1 39	
4 55	..	7 41	9 23	1233	1148	1646	1917	2347	d. (Franzensfeste) a.	6 25	1321	1747	8 56	1821	22 3	1 38	
5 9	..	7 57	9 36	1245	12 3	17 0	1932	0 2	d. Bressanone ......a.	6 11	13 7	1733	8 40	18 7	2148	1 24	
5 20	..	8 16	9 47	1255	1216	1713	1947	0 16	d. Chiusa ....a.	5 56	1242	1718	8 19	1755	2132	1 12	
5 55	..	9 1	1025	1329	1252	1749	2023	0 50	a. Bolzano ....d.	5 22	1213	1640	7 30	1721	2050	1 38	
6 42		10 9	1252	1437	14 3	1939	2127	..	a. Merano (*p.* 306) d.	..	11 0	16 0	1835	16 0	1835	..	
..	7c18	8 7	..	1216	1338	1650	..	..	d. Merano (*p.* 306) a.	6 47	1245	1931	2337	193	2044	..	
6 3	8 45	9 15	1041	1341	14*46	1810	..	1 1	d. Bolzano .. ....a.	5 13	1143	1631	6 41	17 5	2018	0 31	
6 33	..	9 50	..	‡	1531	1847	..		d, Mezzocorona (*p.*306) d.	..	11 5	1545	6 4	*x*	*x*	0 15	
6 50	9 19	10 5	1119	1420	1548	19 3	..	1 48	a. Trento (*p.* 306).. d.	4 33	1048	1526	5 47	1621	1944	2338	
6 56	9 20	1013	1135	1426	1556	1911	..	1 55	d. Trento (*p.* 306).. a.	4 26	1041	1516	5 40	1621	1943	2331	
7 14	9 34	1037	1144	‡ *x*	1630	1932		2 16	a. Rovereto (*p.* 308) d.	4 5	1028	1441	5 19	..	1928	2310	
7 15	9 35	1038	1213		1632	1933	..	2 17	d. Rovereto (*p.* 308) a.	4 4	1018	1438	5 18		1927	23 9	
8 5	1017	1143	1337	1532	18 7	2035	..	3 15	a. Verona P.N. .....d.	2 55	9 0	1250	4 10	1511	1845	22 3	
1024	1310	14 5	16 8	1815	2115	2355		6 33	a. MILAN (*p.* 305) ....d.	0 16	6 17	9 52	0 42	1228	1545	..	
	23		2cl.		23						*r*						
8 33	1040	..	14x10	1550	1840	2057	..	3 30	d. Verona P.N. ....a.	2 36	8 20	1215	3 52	1452	1837	2140	
8 57	1118	..	*x*	A	1923	2131	..	..	a. Nogara ....d.	..	7 39	1117	..	*x*	*x*	..	
9 21	12 2	..	..		20 6	2158	..	..	a. Poggio Rusco ....d.	..	7 9	1040				2047	
1015	1337	..	1535	1725	2134	23 8	..	5 14	a. Bologna ....d.	1 0	6 0	9 20	2 10	13 5	1720	1950	
		..	Rap												Rap	Rap	
1140	1549	..	1638	1855	2253	0 45	..	7 4	a. Florence (*p.*303) d.	23‡23	3 40	7 10	0 40	11‡28	16‡11	1820	‡..
1530	1950	..	1950	2255	6 30	6 30	..	1125	a. ROME (*p.*303) d.	19‡10	2325	0 5	2 15	7‡10	13 0	1425	‡..

B Sleep. Car, 1 and 2 cl. Bolzano-Rome and *v.v.* **C** Sleep. Car Vienna-Merano, and *v.v.*, Weds., Fris. and Suns. only and 1, 2, 3 cl. Merano-Vienna and *v.v.* **G** Rest. Car Brennero-Verona and *v.v.*

a Also 1 cl. from Bolzano. *b* Rapido from Bolzano. *c* June 25—Sept. 24. *d* 2 cl. Rap Bolzano-Bologna. *e* Also 3 cl. from Bolzano. *x* Supplement payable for travel by Rapido trains.

* 2 and 3 cl. from Bolzano. ‡ 1 and 2 cl. only. **A** Sleep. car Rome-Berlin and *v.v.*

(Rome), (Venice), Trieste, Postumia, (Budapest).

x Rapidi trains with supplement.

123	123	12	123	12		123	123	12	12	12
	D	luxe	B			A	B	..	D	E
2140	0 5	..	9 30	1210	dep. Rome (*p.* 303) .. arr.	1750	2020	..	6 30	9 55
1 51	5 45	..	1355	1643	dep. Florence ...... arr.	1330	1549	..	0 45	6 1
3 20	7 36	..	1530	1815	dep. Bologna ...... arr.	1156	1415		23 2	4 52
5 55	1016	..	1656	2026	arr. Venice-Mestre ..dep.	9 20	1150	luxe	2026	0 13
5 47	1137	1557	18 2	2030	dep. Venice .... arr.	8 20	1147	1448	1920	1 5
6 8	1155	..	1816	2046	dep. Venice-Mestre .. arr.	8 9	1131	..	19 7	0 51
..	1350		2015	..	arr. Biv. Aurisina ..dep.	6 16	9 56	..	*	2242
8 28	14 5	1815	2034	2310	arr. Trieste .... dep.	6 0	9 30	1225	1645	2225
9 37	1520	1840	21 3	0 30	dep. Trieste .... arr.	5 20	9 4	1145	1329	2010
10 4	1538	↓	2121	0 51	dep. Aurisina ...... arr.	4 57	8 45	↑	13 7	1951
1031	1612	↓	2148	1 25	arr. Divaccia ......dep.	4 25		↑	1236	1924
7 36	1245	↓	1742	..	dep. Pola .... arr.	8 23		↑	1724	0 16
1032	1613	↓	2149	1 26	dep. Divaccia ...... arr.	4 24	..	↑	1235	1023
1057	1638	↓	2214	1 51	arr. St. Pietro del Carso dep.	4 0	7 58	1039	1212	1858
1059	1643	↓	2215	1 56	dep. St. Pietro del Carso arr.	3 59	7 54	1038	1211	1856
1113	17 0	1955	2228	2 10	arr. Postùmia *p.*332) dep.	3 45	7 40	1025	1155	1842
1134	..	..	2246	..	dep. Postùmia ...... arr.	..	7 22	..	..	1820
2145	..		9 45	..	arr. Budapest (S.) (*p.*201 d.	..	2015	..	..	8 10

A 1 and 2 cl. car Bucarest-Vintimille. 3 cl. car Belgrade-Trieste. All *v.v.*
B Sleep. Car Budapest-Venice and Vienna-Trieste. 1, 2 cl. cars Budapest-Rome. 3 cl. car Budapest-Venice. All *v.v.* **D** 1, 2 cl. car Sofia-Belgrade-Milan, 3 cl. car Loubljana-Trieste. All *v.v.*
E 1, 2, 3 cl. car Budapest-Vintimille, Budapest-Rome and Vienna-Trieste. 2, 3 cl. car Praha-Trieste.
‡ 1 and 2 cl. only. * 3 cl. to Trieste also. † 2nd and 3rd cl. to Trieste.

(Rome, Florence), Bologna, Venice, Udine, Tarvisio, etc. [State Rly.

Mls.	Station													
			1 2 3	1 2 3	1 2 3	1 2 3	1 2 3	1 2 3	1 2 3	1 2 3	2 cl.	1 2 3	1 2 3	2 3
					ExZ	Exp					Rap			
..	Rome (p. 808)	dep.	1910	2140	2325	0 5	0 5	7§10	9 15	9 30	13 0	1425	1210	1425
..	Florence (p. 808)	dep.	2323	1 51	3 40	5 45	8 48	1126	13 4	1355	611	1820	1643	1820
..	Bologna (p. 808)	arr.	0 45	3 5	5 0	7 8	1020	1245	1410	15‖5	17 0	19§30	18 0	1930
							r	r x	2cl x	S	x	r		2cl x
0	**Bologna**	dep.	1 5	3 20	5 10	7 36	1025	13 8	1440	1530	1710	1948	1815	2148
30	Ferrara (p. 809)	dep.	2 2	4 4	5 54	8 21	11 8	1353	1511	16 7	1741	2029	1853	2219
50	Rovigo	dep.	2 40	4 35	6 25	8 52	1139	1423	1533	1635	18 3	2058	1954	2241
77	Padua (p. 305)	arr.	3 34	5 27	7 12	9 54	1230	1516	16 4	1715	1832	2139	2010	2314
		dep.	3 39	5 30	7 14	9 56	1233	1518	16 5	1716	1833	2141	2012	2315
99	Venice (Mestre)	arr.	4 9	5 55	7 39	1021	1258	1543	1622	1738	1850	22 3	2037	2332
		dep.	4 28	5 58	7 47	1023	13 1	1544	1623	1739	1851	22 4	2049	2333
100	**Venice**	arr.	4 40	6 10	7 58	1033	1312	1555	1630	1749	1858	2215	21 0	2340
			2 3		*		2 3		..	1 2 3		1 2 3		
		dep.	6 1	..	8 47	1010	1252	..	1738	1840	19 0	2155	2240	..
101	Venice (Mestre)	arr.	6 12	..	8 57	1022	13 4	..	1750	1851	1911	22 6		..
		dep.	6 23	..	8 59	1026	1310	..	1752	1855	1921	22 9	A	..
119	Treviso	arr.	6 46		9 18	1058	1340	..	1814	..	1949	2228	..	..
..	Belluno	arr.	1318	..	1318	..	1759	‡..	2058	..	..	..	..	..
..	Calalzo (p. 806)	arr.	1455	..	1455	..	1945	‡..	2230	..	..	..	..	..
..	Treviso	dep.	6 51	..	9 20	1053	1347		1816	p	1954	2230	..	..
185	Conegliano	dep.	7 37	..	9 47	1127	1430	..	1851	..	2048	2258	..	..
185	**Udine**	arr.	9 34	..	11 7	1258	1625		2025	2044	2233	0 21	0 34	..
..	Trieste	dep.	..	..	9 47	..	17 0			19 0	..	..	..	..
..	Gorizia	arr.	..	..	1035	..	1743	..	..	1955	..	..	..	..
..	Udine	arr.	..	..	11 3	..	18 8	..	..	2033	..	..		..
..	Udine	dep.	..	..	1117	13‡35	1853	..	..	2059	..	..	0 39	..
245	**Tarvisio**	arr.	..	..	13 9	16‡15	2140		..	2250	..	..	2 15	
.	Vienna (p. 199)	arr.		..	2153	b	..		..	8 0		..	9 50	

Mls.	Station													
			1 2 3	2 3	2 3	1 2 3	1 2 3	2 3	2 3l.	2 cl	2 3	1 2 3	1 2 3	1 2 3
						ExS						ExZ		
..	Vienna	dep.	1510	..	..	22 0	..		..	..		9 0	..	
..	**Tarvisio**	dep.	3 10	..	5 50	7 10	..	1225	..	..	..	1815	..	
..	Udine	arr.	4 37		8 2	8 56	..	1455	..	..		20 0	..	
..	Udine	dep	..	..	7 19	9 11	..	1616	b..	.	..	2015	..	
..	Gorizia	dep.	..	..	7 49	10 3	..	1643	..	..	..	2044	..	
..	Trieste	arr.	..	..	8 36	10 8	..	1735	b..	..	..	2138	..	
								1 2 3						
..	Udine	dep.	4 43	6 48	8 42	9 10	1210	15 5	..	..	..	20 8	..	
..	Conegliano	dep.	..	8 6	1028	Via Portogruaro	1340	1628	..	..	..	2130	..	
..	Treviso	arr.	..	8 30	11 4		14 9	1659		..	..	2155	..	
..	Calalzo (p. 806)	dep.	A	..	7 58		9 56	9 56	..	..	..	1658	‡..	
..	Belluno	dep.		4 20	9 15		1115	1115	..	..	..	1814	‡..	
..	Treviso	dep.	..	8 32	1114		1411	17 1	..		..	2157	..	
..	Venice (Mestre)	arr.		8 53	1146	1050	1434	1721	..		..	2215	..	
		dep.	6 24	8 55	1148	1051	1444	1723	..	..	..	2217	..	
..	**Venice**	arr.	..	9 5	12 0	11 1	1455	1733	..	..	..	2227	..	
			—	1 2 3	..	r				x			X	r
		dep.	7 0	9 10	..	1130	1432		1535	1758	1832	2255	23‡38	2010
..	Venice (Mestre)	arr.	7 12	9 21	..	1141	1443	..	x	18 5	1845	23 0	23‡48	2022
		dep.	7 14	9 24	..	1152	1445	..		18 6	1850	2311	2358	2026
..	Padua	arr.	7 39	9 49	..	1217	1510		1558	1823	1933	2339	0 23	2051
		dep.	7 41	9 55	..	1219	1515		16 0	1824	1940	2341	0 25	2053
..	Rovigo	dep.	8 55	1035		1256	1556	..	1628	1851	2047	0 22	1 10	2136
..	Ferrara (p. 809)	dep.	9 26	11 7	..	1326	1630	..	1653	1914	2139	0 56	1 44	22 9
..	**Bologna**	arr.	1015	1156	..	1415	1720	..	1730	1947	2258	1 48	2 35	23 2
			Rap				1 2		1 2			V		
..	Bologna	dep.	1020	12 8	..	1425	1740	..	1740	20 0	..	1 56	2 40	2310
..	Florence	arr.	1140	1330	..	1549	1855	..	1855	2150	..	3 10	4 2	0 45
..	Rome	arr.	1530	1750	..	2020	2255	..	2255	6 30		7 50	8 25	6 30

Rovereto, Mori and Riva.

Auto	1 3	1 3	1 3	Mls.	Station		1 3	1 3	1 3
6 55	1012	1430	2018	0	dep. Rovereto (p. 807)	arr.	6 50	1330	1915
7 5	1022	1440	2028	..	„ Mori Station	„	6 40	1320	19 5
7 45	1118	1536	2135	12½	„ Arco	dep.	5 44	1224	18 6
7 55	1130	1548	2137	15⅝	arr. Riva	dep.	5 30	1210	1755

‖ 1 cl. only. * Local 3 cl. excluded. § 1 & 2 class only. ‡ 2 & 3 class.
A 1 and 2 cl. only Cannes-Vienna Express suspended. See spec. running p. 82, Winter only.
S 1 & 2 cl. Sleeping Cars, & 1 & 2 cl. Rome-Vienna and *v.v.* **V** Sleep. Car Rome-Venice and *v.v.*
X Sleep. Car. Trieste-Rome. **Z** 1 & 2 cl Sleep. Cars Rome-Prague, Wed., Fri. and Sun., Through Cars Rome-Warsaw daily and *v.v.* *a* 2 & 3 cl. only from Padua to Bologna. *b* From June 15,
r Restaurant Car. *p* Via Portogruaro. *x* Supplement payable for travel by Rapido trains.

Florence, Empoli, Pisa, Leghorn. (60 miles.) [State Rly.

23	23	123	2	123	23	123	123	123		123	23	123	123	123	2cl.	23	123
			¶								x			a	¶		
0 40	5 10	7 15	8 10	1115	1245	1425	1840	2150	dp. **Florence** PSMN ar	9 6	1146	1534	1840	2010	21 0	0 32	2 17
1 32	6 9	7 54	..	1153	1339	15 3	1921	2245	,, Empoli (*below*) d.	8 26	1114	1447	18 0	1928	x	2338	1 31
2 37	7 19	8 50	9 10	1243	1445	1554	2015	2351	a. **Pisa** (*to Genoa*, 301) d.	7 37	1040	1355	17 5	1840	20 2	2232	0 28
2 50	7 32	8 58	9 13	1252	1455	16 5	2030	0 5	dep. Pisa .... arr.	7 29	1033	1344	1652	1828	20 0	2222	0 13
3 8	7 55	9 15	9x30	1312	1516	1625	2048	0 25	arr. **Leghorn** ....dep.	7 10	1015	1325	1634	18 5	1943	22 3	2355

x Rapid Supp. payable. ¶ Motor Rail Car. r Restaurant Car. a 1st cl. from Pisa.

Empoli, Siena, Chiusi, (Rome). [State Rly.

23	23	23	23	23	23	23		23	23	23	23	23	23	23
				¶										
4 20	6 47	7 50	10 5	1410	1445	19 3	dep. **Florence** (*abv.*) a.	7 3	1025	1132	1534	19 7	..	2310
5 7	7 36	8 33	1118	1451	1619	20 5	dep. Empoli .... arr.	6 0	9 13	1037	1435	18 9	..	2224
6 50	9 7	9 48	1253	1552	1756	2145	arr. **Siena** dep.	4 30	7 50	9 15	1310	1635	.	21 6
6 59	9 12	..	1315	1555	1820	2210	dep. **Siena** arr.	..	7 28	9 9	13 4	1617	1845	21 3
7 50	9 50	..	14 3	1628	19 7	2247	,, Asciano ....dep.	..	6 45	8 38	1222	1540	18 0	2021
9 3	1057	..	1516	1726	2025	2348	arr. **Chiusi** ......dep.	..	5 24	7 32	1110	1435	1645	19 5
1125	1425	..	1750	2020	2255	5 55	arr. Rome (*p.* 303) dp.	..	0 5	..	7 35	1210	1425	1513

‡ 3 cl. only. ¶ Motor Rail Car.

Florence, Pistoia, Pisa, Leghorn. (75 miles). [State Rly.

23	23	23	23	23	123	23		23	23	23	123	123	23	23	23
											a				
4 20	6 12	8 33	13 9	1650	17 5	1828	dep. **Florence** .... arr.	7 4	8 25	9 45	1252	1621	18 5	21 4	2 5
4 53	6 39	8 58	1333	1711	1722	1843	,, Prato (*p.* 303) ,,	6 43	8 3	9 32	1239	16 2	1741	2038	1 49
5 32	7 3	9 22	1358	1725	1742	19 5	dep. Pistoia ...... ,,	6 16	7 41	9 10	1217	1537	1713	2014	1 34
5 55	7 24	9 42	1416	arr.	1758	1920	,, Montecatini dep.	5 56	7 20	8 51	1159	1516	1652	1950	1 20
6 57	8 18	1050	1640	..	19 0	2014	,, Lucca ...... ,,	5 5	6 30	8 12	1118	1420	1558	1855	0 50
arr.	8 48	1123	1724	..	1931	2040	arr. Pisa (*p.* 301) ,,	4 28	5 45	7 37	1042	1330	1520	1815	0 20
..	9 15	1312	1740	..	1957	2140	arr. **Leghorn** ....dep.	3 50	4 55	7 10	1015	1216	1442	1733	2355

‖ 3rd cl. Leghorn-Pisa. a 2 and 3 cl. Pisa-Lucca.

(Florence) Terontola, Perugia, Foligno, Orte, Rome. [State Rly.

23	123	23	23	123	23	23		23	23	23	2cl.	123	3cl.	123
											Rap x			
0 55	7 11	9 25	1337	1555	1730	1916	dep. **Florence** (*p.* 303) a.	9 25	12 3	1435		1637	2023	2255
3 35	9 0	1130	1515	1740	1955	21 8	dep. **Terontola** .. arr.	6 52	8 34	1047	..	1450	1721	2049
4 12	9 51	1214	1559	1834	2040	2146	arr. Perugia dep.	5 53	7 38	10 5	..	1350	1631	1958
										¶‡				
4 48	9 58	1242	16 4	1840	2050	2147	dep. Perugia arr.	4 47	7 34	9 56	1148	1335	1628	1952
5 20	1029	1317	1633	1913	2118	2210	Assisi	4 8	6 57	9 33	1128	13 3	16 0	1914
5 40	1050	1340	1650	1932	2134	2225	ar. Foligno (*p.* 312) dp.	3 47	6 37	9 20	1126	1245	1544	1852
				123	2x					2 x				
5 47	1117	1350	17 0	1944	2143	3 35	dp. Foligno ar.	2 10	6 10	9 15	1115	..	..	1842
7 25	1251	1535	1910	2125	2237	5 23	,, Terni ....dep.	0 38	4 33	8 15	1036	..	..	17 9
8 10	1335	1617	1957	22 6	23 9	6 10	arr. **Orte** ....dep.	2348	..	7 45	9 44	..	..	1620
9 40	15 0	1750	2115	2320	0 10	7 30	arr. Rome *p.* 303 dp.	2230	..	6 40	8 40	..	..	15 5

* 1 & 2 cl. only. ‡ 3 cl. only. x Rapids Supplement. ¶ Auto Rail.

Ferrara, Ravenna, Rimini. (77 miles.)

* 1 and 2 class. † 1 2 and 3 class. ‖ 3rd class.

3 cl.	123	123	23	123		23	23	123	23	123
1 32	3 55	6 42	1130	1758	dep. Venice (*p.* 305) ar.	1033	1312	1547	1749	23 5
5 0	7 29	8 55	1339	1922	dep. Ferrara ...... arr.	8 ‖ 6	9 47	12 7	1558	2046
6 15	9 1	1019	15 5	2050	arr. Ravenna .. dep.	6 40	8 14	1022	1413	1920
6 35	9 36	1023	1510	2056	dep. Ravenna .. arr.	6 32	8 9	10 2	1355	1916
7 41	1010	1124	1612	2159	arr. Rimini (*p.* 313) dep.	5‖43	7 5	8 42	1240	1811
9 32	1345	13 2	1912	2350	arr. Ancona (*p.* 313) dep.	1 45	..	6 53	9 25	1625

Rimini—San Marino

1 & 3 cl. Journey 1 hour.

dep. Rimini Stato 7.25, 10.12, 13.48, 18.24.
dep. San Marino 7.10, 9.57, 13.33, 18.20.

The times on the LEFT are to be read DOWNWARDS, those on the RIGHT UPWARDS.

Rome, Formia, (Aversa), Naples.

Mls.		123 r	123 Exp	123 r	12 x	123 Exp	123 Rap	123 fast	123 a	123 a	12 Exp	123 Rap	1 cl. Rap	123 Exp	123	12 Exp	123
0	ROME (Termini) ..dep.	7 10	7 25	9 50	1115	1235	1545	1552	1652	18 5	1850	1918	20 0	2023	2115	2155	0 40
89	Littoria .... ,,		8 11	1039	..	1324	x	1637	1741	1851	..	r		2110	22 4	..	..
80	Formia .. .. ,,		9 6	1138	..	1421	..	1729	1836	1944	..			22 4	2256	..	..
112	Villa Literno .. arr.		9 44	1213	..	r	..	18 4	1927	2022	r	..		2238		..	..
	Villa Literno .. ...dep.		9 52	1222	..		..	1810	1932	2030	..	..				..	..
126	Pozzuoli Solfatara .. arr.		1010	1239	..			1828	1957	2059	A	..	↓			B	..
131	Naples (Mergellina) ,,		1018	1248	1326		1756	1836	2010	2119		2129	2149				..
135	,, (P. Garibaldi) ,,		1030	..	1337	↓	18 7	..	2022	2122	..	2141	2159	↓	↓	..	..
	Villa Literno ......dep.		9 47	1217	..	..		18 5	1928	2023	..	..	..	2239		..	..
122	Aversa } below { arr.		9 59	1229	..	15 8	..	1817	1940	2035	21 8	..	..	2251	2342	..	..
	Aversa } below { dep.	↓	10 1	1230	..	1513	..	1821	1941	2036	2111	..	..	2253	2346	..	..
134	Naples (Central) .. arr.	9 52	1018	1247	..	1530	..	1838	1957	2 53	2128	..	..	2310	0 3	0 30	3 8
138	,, (Maritt.) .... ,,	..	..	..	..	..	..	..	..	..	..	..	..		..		..

NOTE.—Supplement charged for all "Rapido" trains. **A** 1 & 2 cl. Sleeping Car Rome-Syracuse also Rome-Palermo (from Oct. 14). **B** 1 & 2 cl. Sleeping Car, Rome-Syracuse and Rome-Reggio. *r* Rest. Car Rome-Naples. *a* 1 & 3 cl. from Villa Literno to Naples (Mergellina).

Naples (Aversa), Formia, Rome.

Mls.	*a* 1 & 3 cl. Naples—Villa Literno.	123 fast	123 Exp	23	12 Exp	123	123	12 fast	1 cl. Rap	123	123 Rap	123 Exp	12 Rap	123 Exp	123 fast	123 fast	123 Rap
0	Naples (Maritt.) ... dep.	C	S	a	A			B	..	r	r		X	a	r	r	
4	,, (Central) .. ,,	3 53		5 5	6 16	6 55	7 22	8 15	..	1140	..	1720	..	1835	..	2035	..
12	Aversa } below { arr.	..	a	5 32			7 39	..	..	1157	..	1737	..	1852	..	2052	..
	Aversa } below { dep.	..	..	5 39			7 41	..	..	12 0	..	1750	..	1853	..	21 2	..
21	Villa Literno .. arr.	..	..	5 56			7 53	..	..	1212		18 2	..	19 5	..	..	..
0	Naples (P. Garibaldi) dep.		3 38	4 55			..	..	1052	1117	13 5		1718	18 5	1948		2124
4	,, (Mergellina) ,,		3 49	5 8			7 22	..	11 1	1128	1316	1713	1730	1819	20 0		2135
9	Pozzuoli Solfatara . ,,		4 4	5 20			7 32	..	r	1140	..	1723	..	1826	..		..
22	Villa Literno arr.	↓	4 23	5 49			7 49	..		1157	..	1740	..	1956	2023	↓	
	Villa Literno ..... dep.	..	4 30	5 57	↓	↓	7 59	..	..	1218	..	18 6	..	19 7	2025	..	
54	Formia .... ,,	5 3	5 15	6 53	7 24	8 2	8 43	..	..	13 8	..	1853	..	1950	..	2153	
95	Littoria .... ,,	..	6 6	8 1	8 16	..	9 34	..	..	14 9	..	1944	..	2041	..	2249	↓
134	Rome (Termini) .. arr.	6 45	7 0	9 25	9 6	9 40	1025	1055	1252	15 5	1530	2035	1945	2135	2238	2340	2350

NOTE.—Supplement charged for all "Rapido" trains. **A** 1 & 2 cl. Sleeping Car Syracuse-Rome. **B** 1 & 2 cl. Sleeping Car, Syracuse-Rome also Palermo-Rome (from Oct. 15). **C** Sleeping Car Reggio-Rome. *r* Rest. Car Naples-Rome. **S** 1 & 2 cl. Sleep. Car Brindisi-Rome. **X** 1 & 2 cl. Sleep. Car Naples-Milan. *b* 2 & 3 cl. Naples—Villa Literno.

Naples (Rome), Foggia (Taranto), Brindisi.

123	123 fast	23	123 Exp	123	123	123 fast	12 Rap	123 Exp	Mls		123	23	23	123 Exp	123 Exp	123	123	123 Exp	12 Rap
5 17	9 28	1235	1455	1815	2042	2311	1752	a	0	d. Naples (Cen.) a.	8 10	1158	1549	1757	2042	2342	6 10	S	1226
5 44	9 55	13 2	1511	1842	21 9	2339	x	S	12	a. Aversa ...... d.	7 44	1130	1523	1730	2022	2316	5 41		b x
	7 25	9 50	1235	1552	1850	2115	b	0 25	..	d. Rome (above) a.	1025	15 5	1855	2035	2340	..	9 25	7 0	14 0
..	9 59	1229	15 8	1817	21 8	2342			.	a Aversa . d	7 41	12 0	1628	1750	21 2	..	5 39	..	..
5 48	10 5	13 3	1521	1848	2121	2354	↓	..		d. Aversa ..... a.	7 34	1124	1519	1724	2017	2314	5 33	..	..
6 11	1021	1326	1538	1913	2144	0 11	1821	2 56	22	a. Caserta . d.	7 15	11 3	1457	17 8	20 1	2254	5 15	4 7	1158
0 32		8 20		13 3	..	1845	1622	..		d. Rome (p. 310) a	1040	1635	2050	2355	..	7 0	12 5	..	.
6 20	1025	1330	1542	1922	2149	0 17	832	3 8	..	d. Caserta a.	7 11	1056	1452	17 1	1956	2248	4 58	4 3	1146
7 47	1134	15 0	1650	2046	2250	1 15	1924	4 13	60	d. Benevento .. a.	5 49	9 25	1325	1534	1842	2118	3 29	2 49	1050
9 58	1338	1715	1830	2252	0 20	3 0	2047	5 47	124	a. Foggia } (p. d.	3 42	7 13	1110	1353	1640	1857	1 20	1 6	9 25
1040	1356	arr.	1838	..	0 32	3 25	2055	6 3	..	d. Foggia } 313) a.	..	6 50	9 15	1341	1630	19 5	2349	0 10	9 15
1255	1618	..	2047	..	2 37	5 28	2213	7 53	201	a. Bari (p. 313) d.	.	4 12	7 57	1118	1415	1715	2115	2225	7 57
13 8	1711	..	2223	..	4 15	5 35	..	8‖25	.	d. Bari .... a.	..	..	7‖48	1053	14 9	16 5	2035	22 8	7‖30
1545	1943	..	2355	..	6 48	7 49		10‖28	278	a. Taranto .... d.	..	..	6‖13	8 25	1151	1332	1810	1957	4‖38
1310	1629	..	2057	..	4 5	5 45	2215	8 6		d. Bari .. ... a.	..	..	..	11 8	1357	1657	2049	22 5	7‖50
1531	1859	..	23 4		6 21	7 59	2341	9 58	270	a. Brindisi ... d.	..	..	..	8 57	1146	15 5	1829	2022	6‖24
		..	..			8 25	c	1022	271	a. Brindisi (Mar.) d		..	..			1438		1951	..

a Connection from Naples (Central at 23.55 via Cancello. *c* Bari–Brindisi 2 & 3 cl. Rapido only. † 1 & 2 cl. only. * 3rd class only. ‖ 2 & 3 cl. only. **S** 1 & cl. Sleeping Car Rome–Brindisi (Mar.) and *v.v.* *x* Rapido Supplement payable. *b* 2 cl. only Naples—Caserta and *v.v.*

The times on the LEFT are to be read DOWNWARDS, those on the RIGHT UPWARDS.

Rome, Naples, Metaponto, Brindisi.

[State Rlys.

		123	23	123	23		23	Mls	Through Services, see pp. 118, 119, 124, 301.	23	123	23	123	123	23	23	123
..	..	0 32	..	8 20	13 3	..	1655	0	dp. **Rome** (Ter.).. arr.	12 5	..	1040		1635	2050	2355	7 0
..	..	1 42	..	9 26	1430	..	1825	34	,, Segni .... ..dp.	1050		..	..	1518	1940	2245	5 25
..	..	3 12	..	11 8	1627	..	2045	86	,, Cassino ...... ,,	8 30	..	8 53		1312	1737	2044	3 0
..	..	4 54	..	1257	1813	..	2235	128	,, Capua .... .. ,,	6 33		7 57	.	1117	1558	1835	1 6
..	..	5 10	..	1313	1829	..	2252	185	a. } **Caserta** .... { ,,	6 16	..	7 47		11 0	1542	1817	0 50
..	..	5 16	..	1316	1836	..	23 0	..	d. } **Caserta** .... { ar.	6 9	..	7 46		1053	1533	1813	0 44
..	..	5 39	..	1336	1853	..	2317	142	,, Cancello .... ,,	5 50	..	7 37		1034	1513	1753	0 25
.	..	6 13	..	14 8	1924	..	2348	155	ar. Naples (C.) ..dp.	5 20	..	7 18	..	10 4	1442	1719	2355
12	123	123	23	23	123	123	12					12	12	..	..	123	123
0 42	0 50	10 5	1345	16 0	1858	2020	2148	0	dp. Naples (C.).... ar.	..	5 53	6 5	8 2	..	.	1558	2338
..	1 20	1024	1417	1637	1917	2042	..	15	,, T. Annunziata ,,	..	5 30	5 46	..		..	1538	23 6
..	1 26	1030	1425	1645	..	2048	..	16	,, Pompei ...... dep.	..	..		..	.	..	1534	23 2
1 41	2 24	1118	1523	1748	20 7	2150	2248	34	dp. Salerno ..... ,,	..	4 48	4 59	7 2		..	1448	22 6
2 0	2 58	1153	1555	1821	A	2226	23 5	46	,, Battipaglia.... ,,	..	4 21	4 39	6 40			1427	2137
To Sicily	3 7	12 2	16 4	1830		2235	To Sicily.	50	,, Eboli .... ,,	..	4 5	↑ From Sicily.	From Sicily.	..	.	1412	2122
	6 1	1451	1850	arr.	2224	1 38		104	,, Potenza .... ,,	..	1 48			..	.	1155	1855
	8 18	1655	2055		2350	3 29		170	ar. Metaponto .... ,,	..	23 1			..	.	9 6	1556
	9 25	1747	2155	..	0 24	4 25		197	,, Taranto ...... ,,	..	22 4			..	..	8 3	1450
	1135	20 4	..	..	..	6 34		241	ar. **Brindisi** .... dp.	..	2014			..	..	5 34	1235

A Rapido Train 2nd class only Salerno, Taranto.

r Restaurant Car. 1 & 2 cl. Sleep Cars *via* Foggia, *see p.* 310.

Rome, Pescara, Brindisi.

[State Rlys.

123	23	123	23	123	123	Mls			123	123	123	23	23	123	123
6 50	8 45	1243	1433	1742	2220	0	dep.	Rome (Termini) .. arr.	7 17	9 45		1429	1930	2029	0 18
7 37	9 50	1332	1536	1830	23 9	25	arr.	Tivoli ....dep.	6 14	8 58		1334	183[illegible]	1948	2337
9 11	1217	1518	1‖54	2039	0 51	68	dep.	Avezzano .... ,,	4 29	7 3	..	1122	1617	1820	22 5
1031	14 0	1639	1940	2210	2 5	108	,,	Sulmona ...... ,,	3 12	5 25		9 38	1429	17 6	2048
1151	1548	18 0	2125	2334	3 35	150	arr.	Pescara (P N.).. { dep.	1 25	3 39	a	7 23	1221	1513	1916
1229	1555	1845	2144	0 2	7 15		dep.	Pescara (P N.).. { arr.	2238	..	3 14	7‡0	1158	..	1812
1445	1724	21 6	2335	1 45	8 56	206	dep.	Termoli ....dep.	21 3	..	1 49	5‖20	9 21	..	16 0
1635	1833	2315	arr.	3 15	1028	293	arr.	Foggia (p. 313) { ,,	1920	—	0 25	..	7 14	..	14 0
1655	1838	0 32	..	3 25	1040		dep.	Foggia (p. 313) { arr.	19 5	2349	0 10	..	6 50	..	1341
1930	2047	2 37	..	5 28	1255	370	arr.	Bari .... dep.	1715	2115	2225	..	4 12	..	1118
23 4	23 4	6 21	.	7 59	1531	439	arr.	Brindisi ...... dep.	15 5	1829	2022	..	..	..	8 57

a Pescara Central. ‖ 3rd class only. ‡ 2 & 3 class only.

Brindisi (Bari), Metaponto, Reggio.

[State Rlys.

	23	123	23	123	Mls.		12*	123	23	123	23	123
..		5 34	1357	2014	0	dep. Brindisi...... ..arr.	1135	20 4	..	20 4	6 34	8†6
..		7 24	1543	2151	44	arr. Taranto........ dep.	9 40	1813		1813	4 42	6†15
	2223	5 35	13 8	1711		dep. Bari (p. 310) ....arr.	14 9	20†35	7 20	2035	7 20	1053
..	2355	7 49	1545	1943		arr. Taranto .. ....dep.	11†51	18 10	4 38	1810	4 38	8 25
..	2 35	8 3	1830	2015	44	dep. Taranto..........arr.	9 25	15†34	24 0	18 3	4 25	7 55
..	3 27	8 53	19 6	21 0	71	arr. Metaponto ......dep.	8 31	1437	23 5	1725	3 38	7 2
123	123	123	23	123			23	123	123	23	123	123
..	3 43	9 10	19 7	21 2		dep. Metaponto ......arr.	8 15	1430	2248	1724		6 59
	5 40	1120	2034	2225	121	arr. Sibari ....dep.	5 45	1230	2052	16 0	..	5 21
6†10	8†30	1430	2242	0 31	191	,, Crotone .... ,,	..	9 38	18†8	1352		3 6
7†18	1012	16†10	..	1 40	228	,, Catanzaro-Marina ,,		7†48	16†30	1240		1 50
7 40	1057	16†25	..	1 48		dep. Catanzaro Marina ar.	..	7†35	1620	12 7	22 2	1 43
9 16	1214	18 0	..	2 53	270	arr. Roccella Ionica ..dep.	..	6†15	1454	1020	2025	0 36
9 20	1220	18 5	.	2 55		dep. ,, ,, ..arr.	..	.	1452	1015	2021	0 34
1210	1442	21†4	.	5 10	336	arr. Reggio de Calabria dp.	..	..	1220	7 3	1733	2222
1218	..	..	..	6 44		dep. ,, ,, ... arr.	..	..	1216	6 53	1725	2216
1226	..	..	..	6 52	341	arr. ,, (Maritt) ....dep.	..	..	12 8	6 40	1716	22 8

† 2 & 3 class only. * 3 class only.

The times on the LEFT are to be read DOWNWARDS, those on the RIGHT UPWARDS.

Naples (V.S. Giovanni), Messina.

[State Rly.

1 2 3	1 2 3 r	1 2	1 2 3	1 2	1 2 3	1 2	Mls.		1 2 3 r	1 2	1 2 3	1 2 3	1 2	1 2 3	1 2
3 20	1040	1339	21 5	2148	2320	0 42	0	dep. **Naples** (C) .. arr.	2024	1716	3 33	4 25	6 5	7 10	8 2
4 41	1157	1435	2220	23 5	0 48	1 58	45	arr. Battipaglia ..dep.	1859	1617	2 18	2 56	4 39	5 35	6 40
4 43	1159	1436	2231	23 7	0 50	2 0	..	dep. Battipaglia .. arr.	1857	1616	2 15	2 53	4 38	5 33	6 38
..	1215	:	..	A	..	B r	58	Paestum	1836	..	A	..	B	..	A
8 30	1543	1751	1 57	2 30	4 15	5 20	106	Paola..	1456	1335	22 | 27	23 3	1 4	1 37	3 11
9 20	1635	..	2 49	3 24	5 7	6 6	206	arr. S. Euphemia	14 6	1251	2132	2213	0 8	0 35	2 23
1041	1754	..	4 7	4 44	6 45	C	252	dep. Nicotera	1244	x	C	2054	2247	2313	..
1114	1825	..	4 41	5 16	7 16		287	,, Palmi ......dep.	1211			2022	..	2239	..
1155	19 0	1928	5 20	5 48	7 54	8 18	..	arr. V. S. Giov. ..dep.	1132	1118	1930	1942	2153	22 3	0 22
1250	2020	2020	6 45	6 45	9 15	9 15	295	,, **Messina** (str.) ,,	1030	1030	1830	1830	2055	2055	2325
12 8	1915	1937	5 29	6 59	8 1	8 30	..	dep. V. S. Giov. .. arr.	11 2	1112	1914	1936	2136	2156	? 9
1232	1940	1950	5 57	6 14	8 25	8 45	295	arr. **Reggio** (Cala) dep.	1040	11 0	19 0	1910	2122	2130	2355

A Sleep. car Rome-Syracuse also Rome-Palermo (from Oct. 14) and *v.v.* **B** Sleep car Rome-Syracuse and *v.v.*
C Sleep. Car Reggio-Rome and *v.v.* *r* Rest. car. *x* Rapido supplement payable.

Electric Service.

Naples and Torre Gaveta.

Via Pozzuoli.

12½ miles, journey 45 mins.

From Naples 5.25, 6.40, 7.20, 7.50, 8.30, 9.10, 9.52, 10.50, 12.15, 13.0, 14.5, 14.35, 15.15, 16.0, 16.47, 17.10, 18.20, 19.0, 20.5, 21.0, 22.0, 23.5.

From Torre Gaveta 5.40, 6.22, 7.29, 8.5, 8.43, 9.25, 10.5, 11.5, 11.45, 13.10, 13.55, 14.53, 15.29, 16.15, 17.0, 17.52, 18.30, 19.15, 19.55, 21.10

Ancona, Foligno, Orte, Rome.

[State Rly.

2 3	2 auto	1 2 3	1 2 3	1 2 3 fast	2 x auto	1 2 3 Exp	Mls.		2 3	1 2 3	2 x auto	1 2 3	1 2 3	1 2 3 fast	2 auto	1 2 3 Exp
..	6 5	6 45	..	1540	1925	2350	0	dep. **Ancona** (Mar.).. arr.	..	2245	1125	1517	..	2245	0 36	6 4
..	6 14	7 5	1330	1610	1934	0 20	..	,, Ancona (*p.* 313) arr.	9 22	2220	1117	1452	2040	2220	0 28	5 38
..	6 22	7 17	1341	1621	1942	0 31	7	arr. Falconara (Mar.) dep.	9 9	22 7	11 7	1439	2026	22 7	0 19	5 25
..	x	5 45	1157	14 7	1717	2212	..	dep. Rimini ...... arr.	1129	0 25	1450	1638	2211	0 25	↑ x	7 49
..	6 23	7 22	1345	1619	1943	0 32	..	dep. Falconara (*p.* 313) arr.	9 6	22 3	11 6	1435	2022	22 3	0 18	5 22
..	7 18	9 8	1525	18 5	2041	2 8	45	,, Fabriano ..... dep.	7 48	2044	1015	1257	1852	2044	2328	4 7
..	8 14	1052	1654	1934	2142	3 26	87	arr. Foligno (*p.* 309) dep.	6 20	1855	9 17	1118	17 5	1855	2230	2 22
5 47	8 15	1117	17 0	1944	2143	3 35	..	dep. Foligno (*p.* 309) arr.	6 10	1842	9 15	11 2	1652	1842	2226	2 10
6 27	8 35	1155	1740	2022	22 4	4 17	97	,, Spoleto .... arr.	5 28	18 0	8 52	1023	1612	18 0	22 0	1 30
7 18	9 9	1246	1835	2116	2236	5 17	115	arr. Terni ...... dep.	4 33	17 9	8 16	9 31	1515	17 9	2126	0 38
7 25	9 10	1251	1910	2125	2237	5 23	..	dep. Terni ...... arr.	..	17 4	8 14	9 26	15 7	17 4	2125	0 30
8 10	9 37	1335	1957	22 8	23*a*9	6 10	184	arr. Orte (*p.* 309) dep.	..	1620	7 45	8 41	1425	1620	2055	2348
8 17	9 38	1341	20 3	2212	23*a*11	6 16	..	dep. Orte (*p.* 309) arr.	..	1614	7 43	8 35	1415	1614	2054	2340
9 40	1040	15 0	2115	2320	0 10	7 30	185	arr. **Rome** (*p.* 303) ..dep.	..	15 5	6 40	7 17	13 7	15 5	1955 r	2230

a Sets down only. *x* Rapido supp. payable. *r* Rest. car.

Ravenna—Faenza—Florence.

All trains between Ravenna and Faenza Auto Rail, 3rd class.

‖ 2 and 3 cl. Faenza-Florence.

3	3	3	‖ 3	2 3	‖ 3	2 3	Mls.		3	3	2 3	2 3	‖ 3	2 3	3
6 20	7 10	8 25	9 41	1250	1517	1743	0	dep. Ravenna ...... arr.	7 0	8 23	..	1135	1340	1930	22 0
6 50	8 4	9 13	1014	1320	1613	18 7	21	arr. Faenza (*p.* 313).. dep.	6 12	7 24		11 7	1250	19 0	21 5
7 24	..	..	1029	1325	17 0	1840		dep. Faenza (*p.* 313).. arr.	..	..	9 52	1044	1237	1839	2043
8 51	..	..	1146	1453	19 8	1956	63	arr. Borgo S. Lorenzo dep.	..	..	7 51	9 27	1115	1630	19 9
9 35	..	..	1225	1528	2019	2037	85	arr. Florence (*p.* 313) ..dep.	..	..	6 40	8 40	1032	1530	1823

Bologna, Ancona, Foggia, Brindisi, Lecce. [State Rlys.

Exp 1 2 3	Exp 1 2 3	1 2 3	Rap 1 2	1 2 3	1 2 3	Exp 1 2 3 B	2 3		Exp 1 2 3	Exp 1 2 3 M	1 2 3	1 2 3	Exp 1 2 3	1 2 3	Rap 1 2 x	1 2 3	1 2
1845	22 0	0 25	1225	6 50	8 35	1530	..	dep. Milan (*p.* 308) arr.	6 22	8 4	1628	x ..	1140	1353	1730	2135	22 0
..	1836	2115	..	x	5 40	1218	..	,, Turin (300) ,,	9 22	11 58	..	..	14 9	18 5	..	2345	x
1938	2258	1 43	..	7 44	9 39	1621	..	dep. Piacenza .... ,,	5 5	6 59	..	..	1050	1231	..	2012	2110
2130	0 58	3 40	1430	9 36	1150	1810	..	arr. Bologna ....dep.	2 43	5 4	1421	x ..	8 40	1030	1525	1817	1943
17c58	2010	2338	↓	7 c	9 10	1535	c	dep. Venice (*p.*308) ar.	6 10	7 58	1630	c	1312	1555	4 40	21 0	2215
19c47	23 2	2 35		1015	1156	1730	c	arr. Bologna ....dep.	3 20	5 10	1440	c ..	1025	13x8	1 5	1815	1948
				1 2 3						1 2 3	2 3		1 2 3				1 2 3
2145	1‡15	3 55	1435	1030	12 6	1820	7 12	dep. **Bologna** ...... arr.	2 12	4 ‡ 42	1347	..	8 28	1010	1522	1655	1925
..	..	..		..	1244	..	..	arr. Castel Bolognese d.	..	..	1258	..	..	..	..	1617	..
S	..	..		..	14d23	..	..	arr. Ravenna ..dep.	..	..	8d48	..	..	..	..	15d44	..
..	..	..	x	..	1245	..	..	dep. Castel Bolognese a.	..	..	1257	..	..	..	..	1616	..
..	1 54	4 35		11 2	1253	1854	7 44	arr. Faenza ......dep.	1 32	4 1	1249	..	..	9 30		16 8	..
..	..	..		8b40	10b25	15b30	..	dep. Florence (312) ar.	..	7 d 10	15d28	..	12b20	..	..	20b15	..
..	1 57	4 37		11 4	12 5	1856	7 46	dep. Faenza ...... arr.	1 30	3 59	1245	..	..	9 25	..	16 5	..
23 3	2 53	5 45		1157	14 7	1951	8 33	,, Rimini ......dep.	0 30	3 ‡ 9	1136	..	7 4	8 34	..	1457	18 2
..	3 58	7 18	↓	1334	16 1	‡	..	Falconara .... ,,	2259	1 56	9 41	..	..	7 7	..	1255	1636
0 15	4‡10	7 32	1635	1345	1615	21 7	9 42	ar. } **Ancona** .... { dp.	2245	1 45	9 25	..	5 48	6 55	1322	1245	1625
0 22	4‡17	7 50	1640	1355	1655	2115	9b55	dp. } **Ancona** .... { ar.	2217	1 35	9 5	..	5 40	6 44	13c17	1158	16 2
2 41	7 ‡ 4	1147	1830	1748	2052	2349	12b2	ar. } Pescara .. { dp.	1833	22 49	5 12	..	3 19	4 2	1128	8 10	1225
2 46	7 9	1222	1831	1838	2138	2354	1222	dp. } (Central) { ar.	1820	22 ‡ 44	1 2	..	3 14	3 57	1127	..	12 8
4 22	8 56	1445	..	21 6	2335	1 45	1445	dep. Termoli ......dep.	16 0	21 3	2246	..	1 49	2 10	..	..	9 21
5 44	1028	1635	2045	2315	arr.	3 15	1635	arr. **Foggia** ...... ,,	14 0	19 ‡ 20	2052	..	0 25	0 40	9 18	..	7 14
1158	1549	2043	6 10	6 10	..	8 14	2045	arr. Naples (*p.* 310) dep.	9 28	14 55	..		2042	2042	..	..	2355
1 2			1 2 3					(*From Naples, p.* 167).				1 2 3	F				
6 3	1040	1655	1838	0 32	..	3 25	..	dep. **Foggia** ...... arr.	1341	19 5	..	2349	0 10	..	9 15	..	6 50
F	1150	1820	1942	1 39	..	4 27	..	,, Barletta ......dep.	1224	..	..	2226	..	..	8 32	..	5 24
7 53	1255	1930	2047	2 37	..	5 28	..	arr. } Bari (*to Reg-* { dp.	1118	17 15	..	2115	2225	..	7c57	..	4b12
8 6	1310	2057	2057	4 5	..	5 45	..	dep. } *gio, p.* 311) { ar.	11 8	16 57	..	2049	22 5	..	7b50	..	..
9 58	1531	23 4	23 4	6 21	..	7 59	..	ar. **Brindisi** (Sta.) ..dp.	8 57	15 5	..	1829	2022	..	6 24	..	..
1022	..	..	..	..	..	8 25	..	,, ,, (Marit.) ,,	..	14 38	..	..	1951	..	..	..	..
1010	1544	23 8	23 8	6 42	..	8 12	..	dep. Brindisi (Sta.) arr.	8 49	14 52	..	1822	20 9	..	6 22	..	..
1046	1635	2352	2352	7 35	..	9 0	..	arr. Lecce ....dep.	8 0	14 20	..	1730	1935	..	5b45	..	..

B 1 & 2 cl. cars Boulogne-Berne-Milan-Brindisi (Mar.). **F** 1 & 2 cl. Sleepers Brindisi (Mar.)-Rome and *v.v.*
M 1 & 2 cl. Sleepers Brindisi (Mar.)-Milan-Paris. **S** 1 & 2 cl. Sleep. Cars Paris-Brindisi (Mar.).
a 1st, 2nd and 3rd cl. *b* 2 and 3 cl. only. *c* 2 cl. only Rapido. *d* 3 cl. only. *r* Rest. Car.
x Extra for Rapido trains.
* 1st and 2nd cl. only. ‡ Local 3rd cl. excluded.

Lecce—Gallipoli—Maglie—Otranto.

1 3	1 3	1 3	Mls.		1 3	1 3	1 3	1 3
6 30	7 48	1315	0	dep. Lecce (*above*) .. arr.	7 35	1250	1717	1852
7 3	8 20	1347	12	arr. Zollino ....dep.	7 5	1218	1645	1820
7 6	.	1350	..	dep. Zollino........ arr.	6 58	1214	1642	.
8 12	..	1456	34	arr. Gallipoli ......dep.	6 0	1111	1536	..
7 11	8 21	1352	..	dep. Zollino........ arr.	6 55	1213	1640	1816
7 29	8 39	1410	18	arr. Maglie ....dep.	6 36	1155	1617	1758
..	8 50	1420	..	dep. ,, ... arr.	6 31	1147	..	1750
..	9 24	1455	29	arr. **Otranto** ......dep.	6 0	1112	..	1715

Messina—Palermo.

[State Rly.

		A								Rap				A		
2 3	2 cl.	1 2	1 2	1 2 3	2 3	1 2 3	1 2 3	Mls.		1 2 3	1 2 3	2 cl.	1 2	1 2	2 cl.	1 2 3
..	Rap	1850	2155	0 40	..	..	7 10	..	dp. ROME (310) arr.	2340	6 45	6 45	9 6	1055	Rap	2340
..	..	2148	0 42	3 20	..	..	1040	..	,, Naples (312B) ,,	2024	3 33	3 33	6 5	8 2	*x*	20 8
..	..	6 45	9 15	1250	..	..	20 2	..	ar. Messina (P) dp.	1030	1830	1830	2055	2325	..	5 0
—	—	1 2 3	1 2 3	2 *x*	—	—	2 *x*	—	—	2 *x*	—	2 *x*	1 2 3	1 2 3	—	—
..	..	7 0	9 20	13 0	..	..	2025	..	dp. Messina (Mar) a.	1025	1815	1815	2040	2310	—	4 18
4 15	7 4	7 25	9 45	1310	1355	18 5	2044	0	,, Messina (Cen) a.	1012	1710	18 0	2010	2240	23 0	4 10
6 24	8 12	9 7	1113	1416	16 6	1929	2153	44	dp. Patti ......dp.	9 6	15 3	1658	1831	21 7	2154	2 8
7 31	8 48	9 48	12 2	1451	1730	2025	2224	67	,, S. Agata .. ,,	8 32	1356	1627	1747	2027	2121	1 10
8 57	9 38	1057	1316	1541	1858	2135	2310	..	,, Cefalu	7 42	1232	1539	1640	1924	2031	2357
9 42	10 1	1126	1352	16 4	1946	22 4	2333	122	ar. Termini ..dp.	7 16	1145	1512	16 9	1849	20 7	2317
1130	1032	1210	1435	1634	21 5	2245	24 0	146	ar. Palermo ..dp.	6 50	1037	1445	1530	1810	1940	22 5

A 1 & 2 cl. Sleeping Car Rome-Palermo and *v.v.* from Oct 14

x Supp. payable on Rapido trains.

Messina, Catania, Syracuse, &c.

[State Rly.

1 2 3	1 2 3	1 2 3	1 2 3	1 2 3	Mls.		1 2 3	2 3	1 2 3	1 2 3	1 2
18 5	1850	2155	0 40	7 10	..	dp. ROME (*p.*310) ar.	2340	*a*	6 45	9 6	1055
21 5	2148	0 42	3 20	1040		dp. Naples (312B) ar.	2024	*x*	3 33	6 5	8 2
6 45	6 45	9 15	1250	2020	..	ar. Messina (P.) ..dp.	1030	..	1830	2055	2325
2 cl.	1 2 3	1 2 3	—	2 *x*	—	—	2 cl.	—	—	B	1 2 3
Rap	7 0	9 20	13 0	2025	..	dp. Messina (Mar.) ar.	1025	..	1815	2040	2310
7 10	7 20	9 40	1320	2040	0	dp. Messina (Cen.) ar.	10 5	1435	1755	2016	2255
7 45	8 12	1031	1416	2115	30	ar. Taormina ....dp.	9 30	1344	1711	1932	2213
8 28	9 10	1133	1523	2159	56	ar. } Catania .. { dp.	8 39	13 0	1610	1824	21 7
8 34	9 18	1139	1537	22 1	..	dp. } Catania .. { ar.	8 20	1231	1548	1810	2055
x	9 29	..	1556	..	5	dp. Bicocca ......dp.	*x*	1222	..	..	B
9 44	1116	1318	1739	2317	114	ar. Syracuse (C.) ..dp.	7 7	1053	1354	1626	1915
..	1135	1332	1755	..	115	ar. Syracuse (P.) ..dp.	7 0	..	1340	16 6	19 0

B Sleeping Cars Rome-Syracuse and *v.v.* *x* Supp. payable on Rapido trains.
a Rapido train Catania-Messina, 2nd class only.

Catania—Palermo.

[State Rly.

2 3	2 3	2 cl.	1 2 3	2 3	2 3	2 cl.	Mls.		2 3	2 3	2 cl.	1 2 3	2 3	2 cl.
		x	Exp			*x*						Exp		*x*
..	6 0	8 42	1010	16 1	1750	1956		dp. Catania ......ar.	7 50	1149	1238	1556	2220	2345
..	6 13	..	1019	1613	18 1	..	2	ar. } Bicocca .. { dp.	7 38	1134	..	1548	22 9	..
..	6 14	..	1020	1614	18 4	..	..	dp. } Bicocca .. { ar.	7 37	1132	..	1545	22 7	..
..	9 19	1034	13 4	1918	2056	2149	72	ar. Caltanissetta- dp.	4 55	8 30	1041	1326	1825	2156
5 0	9 29	1043	1317	1928	..	2154		dp. Xirbi ar.	..	8 18	1037	13 9	1912	2153
											x			
6 28	1059	..	1437	2055	..	..	108	ar. Roccapalumba dp.	..	6 46		1150	1740	21 0
7 31	12 2	1212	1528	2153	..	2314	130	ar. Termini ..... dp.	..	5 21	8 59	1044	1618	2019
8 50	1325	1259	1620	2315	..	2342	152	ar. Palermo.. dp.	..	4 15	8 30	10 5	1455	1950

x Supp. payable on Rapido trains.

Caltanissetta—Xirbi, Agrigento.

Supp. on Rapido trains. *a* 2nd class. [State Rly.

	Rap				Rap				Rap				Rap	*a*
2 3	2 cl	2 3	1 2 3	1 2 3	2 cl.	Mls.		2 3	2 cl.	1 2 3	2 3	2 3	2 cl.	2 3
..	7 10	2055	7 20	1320	14 0		dp. Messina (Cen.) ar.	1425	1425	1755	..	2255	..	7 40
..	8 42	6 0	1010	16 1	1956	..	dp. Catania (*abv.*) ar.	1149	1238	1556	..	1940	..	2345
..	8 30	..	10 5	1455	1950		dp. Palermo (*abv.*) ar.	..	1239	1620	..	..	..	2342
dep.	1042	9 35	1331	1936	2158	0	dp. Caltanissetta-X. ar.	8 15	1033	13 0	arr.	17 7	arr	2147
5 50	1053	9 54	1350	1955	22 9	4	ar. Caltanissetta C. d.	8 5	1026	1250	1610	17 0	1842	2140
6 33	1124	1051	145[illegible]	2043	2243	22	ar. Canicatti......dp.	6 57	9 54	1140	1516	—	1810	2050
6 45	1127	1144	1510	2057	2246		dp. Canicatti.. .. ar.	6 43	9 52	11 0	1453	..	18 7	2040
7 40	1158	1245	1545	2152	2314	40	ar. } Aragona { dp.	5 41	9 16	10 9	1351	..	1725	1939
7 46	1159	1252	1549	2153	2315		dp. } Caldare.. { ar.	5 36	9 15	10 1	1344	..	1724	1931
8 1	..	1310	..	22 8	..	47	ar. Agrigento Bassa d.	5 14	..	9 43	1324	..	1710	1912
8 10	1214	1325	16 4	2215	2337	49	ar. Agrigento Cent. d.	5 5	8 55	9 35	1310	..	17 5	1855

a 2nd cl. Rapido train Canicatti-Calt. X

The times on the LEFT are to be read DOWNWARDS, those on the RIGHT UPWARDS.

Cook's Tourist Map
of
SOUTHERN ITALY

See Map. pages 298-299

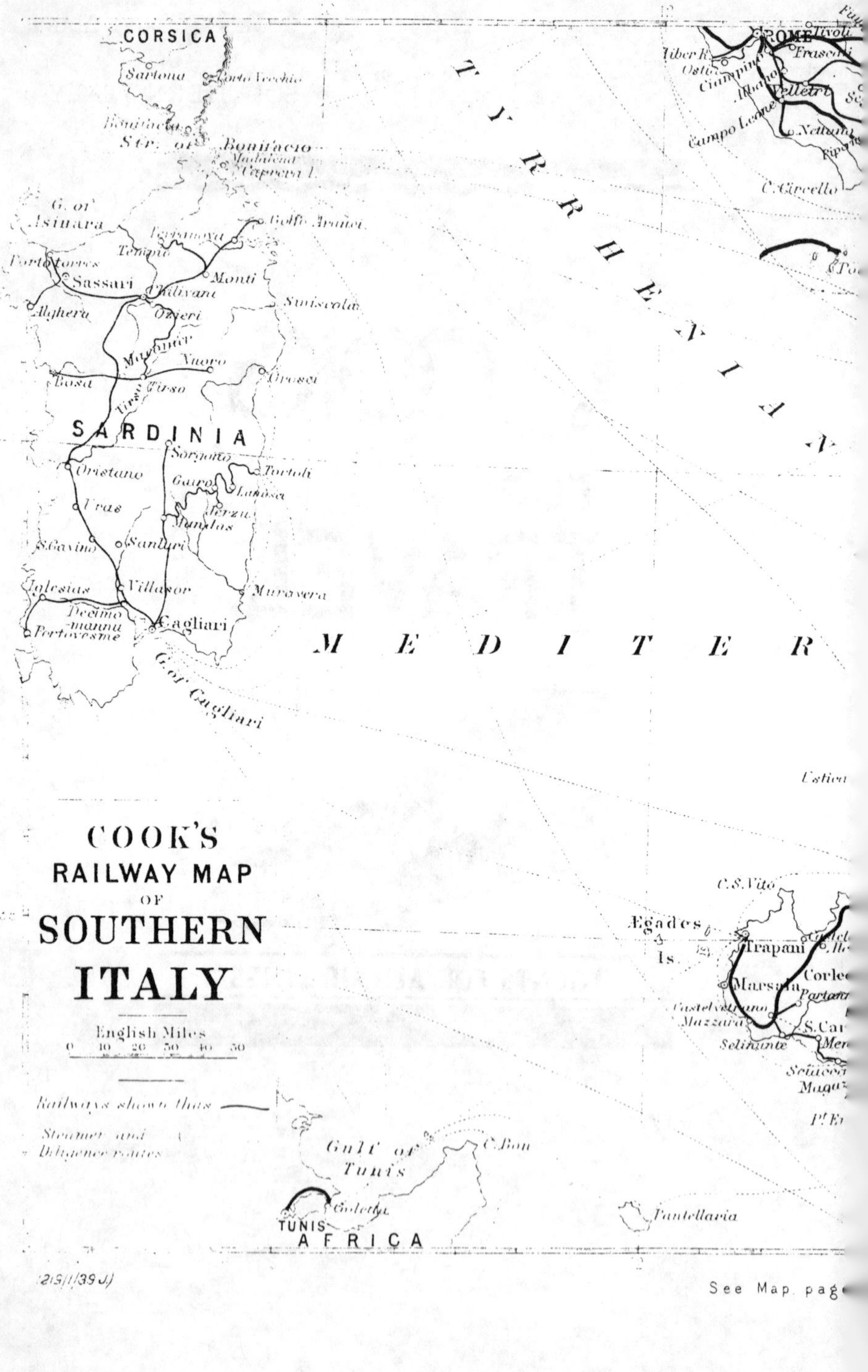

2.15(1/39 J.)

See Map. pag

14
16
18
Sora
Roccasecca
Isernia
Campobasso
San Severo
S. Marco
Manfredonia
Lucera
Foggia
Bojano
Presenzano
Teano
Capua
Caserta
Cancello
Benevento
Bovino
Ariano
Ascoli
Cerignola
Barletta
Trani
Corato
Bitonto
Molfetta
Giovinazzo
Bari
Mola
Monopoli
Fasano
Ostuni
Brindisi
Francavilla
Oria
Taranto
Manduria
Novoli
Lecce
Otranto
Maglie
Gallipoli
C. Leuca
ADRIATIC SEA
To Egypt
NAPLES
Vesuvius
Avellino
Rocchetta
Melfi
Rapolla
Rionero
Venosa
Spinazzola
Altamura
Gioja
Matera
Massafra
Pompeii
Nocera
Salerno
Sanseverino
Campagna
Potenza
Eboli
Ferrandina
Bay of Naples
Castellamare
Capri
G. of Salerno
Agropoli
Sala
Lagonegro
Foce del Basento
Metaponto
Policoro
Pisciotta
Policastro
Sapri
Rosceto
GULF OF TARANTO
Castrovillari
G. of Policastro
Sibari
Crati
Rossano
Cariati
Corigliano
Paola
Cosenza
Pietrafitta
Cotrone
C. Nau
S. Eufemia
C. Rizzuto
Catanzaro
G. of S. Eufemia
G. of Squillace
Squillace
Stromboli
Lipari Is.
Salina
Lipari
Vulcano
Pizzo
Nicotera
Gioja
C. Faro
Monasterace
Gerace
Bagnara
Villa S. Giovanni
Milazzo
Messina
Reggio
Bianco
C. Spartivento
Melito
Cefalu
Patti
Taormina
Nicosia
Mt. Etna
Bronte
Adernò
Giarre
Acireale
Leonforte
SICILY
Catania
Caltanisetta
Lentini
Augusta
Caltagirone
Terranova
Syracuse
Ragusa
Vittoria
Modica
Noto
C. Passaro
Str. of Messina
IONIAN SEA
To Greece & Turkey
To Alexandria
To Malta
38
40
of Greenwich
Entered at Stationers' Hall

Cook's Tourist Map

of

SOUTHERN ITALY

Roccapalumba—Agrigento—Porto Empedocle.

2 cl.	2 3	2 3	2 cl.	1 2 3	2 3	Mls.		2 3	2 cl.	1 2 3	2 cl.	2 3	2 3
Rap	..	4 15	7 47	10 5	1455	..	dep. Palermo (p. 314) arr.	8 50	9 56	1620	1756	2315	
..	..	6 52	↓	12 0	1745	0	dep. Roccapalumba .. arr.	6 25	↑	1433	↑	2050	
2311	..	8 44	↓	1346	1933	35	arr. Aragona Caldare dep	4 43	7 45	1250	x	19 4	
2315	7 40	8 46	Rap	1349	1939	..	dep. Aragona Caldare arr	4 41	7 44	1247	Rap	1859	1931
x	8 4	9 1	x	14 4	1954	41	arr. Agrigento Bassa dep.	4 23	x	1229	|	1841	1912
2331	8 10	9 10	1020	1413	20 2	43	arr. ,, (Cent.) .. dep	4 15	7 25	1220	1530	1825	1855
	8 10	9 46	..	1410	20 0	..	dep. Agrigento Bassa arr.	4 16	7 25	1223	..	1828	1858
	8 25	10 1	..	1425	2015	47	arr. Porto Empedocle dep.	3 55	7 5	12 0	..	18 5	1835

x Rapids supp. payable.

Catania, Caltagirone. (57 miles).

2 3	2 3	2 3	Mls		2 3	2 3	2 3
7 22	1352	19 0	0	d. Catania (abv) a	9 56	1322	1819
7 23	14 5	1919	15	d. Bicocca arr.	9 45	13 6	18 9
7 38	1431	1938		dp. Valsavoja a.	9 38	1251	1752
9 36	17 4	2131	57	ar. Calt'gironed.	7 47	1110	1620

Syracuse, Licata. (186 miles).

1 2 3	2 3	2 3	1 2 3	2 3		2 3	2 3	2 3	2 3
..	5 30	9 57	1135	1812	dp. Syracuse ar.	9 54	1320	1620	1836
..	6 10	1031	1222	1854	,, Noto....dp.	9 20	1141	1550	1754
5 30	8 14	1140	14 7	2011	,, Modica.. ,,	8 6	1027	1448	1620
7 41	1034	1258	1719	2135	ar. Vittoria ,,	6 35	9 2	1324	1420
9 19	1243	1411	1858	..	,, Licata .. ,,	..	7 44	1211	1249
11 0	1413	15 3	2025	..	ar. Canicatti d.	..	6 55	1130	1148

Palermo, Castelvetrano, Marsala, Trapani. [State Rly.

2 3	2 3	2 3	1 2 3	2 3	2 3	2 3	Mls.		2 3	2 3	2 cl.	2 3	1 2 3	2 cl.	2 3
..	4 10	6 40	1055	1425	1650	1725	0	dep. Palermo (Cent) arr.	7 57	9 15	9 52	1420	1710	17x44	2149
..	4 23	6 47	11 8	1435	1659	1737	4	,, Palermo (Lolli) ,,	7 47	9 3	9 45	14 9	1658	1736	2142
..	5 45	7 36	1216	1559	1744	1913	33	,, Partinico ....dep.	6 32	7 48	9 6	1235	16 2	1651	21 3
..	6 15	7 57	1248	1625	18 3	1945	46	,, Castellammare ,,	5 45	6 39	8 47	12 6	1523	1650	2040
	6 34	8 15	13 1	1645	1820	20 1	52	,, Alcamo-Calatafimi		6 27	8 28	1142	15 9	1629	2032
6 15	7 46	9 8	14 9	1754	1920	2114	75	,, Castelvetrano dep.		5 26	7 41	1040	1411	..	..
7 10	8 42	9 53	15 4	1850	20 4	22 7	102	arr. Marsala .... ,,		4 15	6 44	9 26	1314	a	a
7 14	8 47	9 55	15 9	1855	20 6	2212	.	dep. Marsala .... arr.		4 10	6 42	9 21	13 9	..	..
7 53	9 32	1027	1540	1935	2038	2253	122	arr. Trapani ....dep.		3 30	6 10	8 40	1242	1530	1943

a via Ummari. x Rapido Train

Palermo, Castelvetrano, Selinunte, Agrigento (Girgenti).

a 2 & 3 cl. b 1, 2, 3 cl.

1 3	1 3	1 3	1 3	Mls.		1 3	1 3	1 3	1 3
..	4a25	..	17a20	.	dp. Palermo (Cent.) abv. ar	14a20	17b10	2130	a
..	8 9	..	2055	..	arr. Castelvetrano .. dep	1040	1411	1750	
..	8 10	1425	1936	0	dep. Castelvetrano .. arr.	1019	135	1735	
..	8 46	1456	20 5	9	arr. Selinunte........dep.	9 45	1315	1651	
	1050	1638	2142	36	arr. Sciacca .....dep.	8 2	1135	1450	
3 30	12 0	1643	..	..	dep. Sciacca ....arr.		1 5	1434	2 40
7 0	1740	2016	..	77	arr. Porto Empedocle dep.		5 53	1015	2025
a 7 5	18a5	20a34	..	..	dep. Porto Empedocle arr.	..a	5 35	10 1	2015 a
a 7 25	1828	20a55	..	83	arr. Agrigento Bassa dep.	..a	5 17	9a46	20 0 a

Agrigento (Girgenti), Licata.

1 3	1 3	Mls.		1 3	1 3
10 0	1940	0	dep. Agrigento (Cent.)..arr.	7 40	2110
1147	2129	22½	arr. Margonia ....dep.	5 51	1926
1152	2134	..	dep. Margonia ....arr.	5 50	1925
14 0	2335	52½	arr. Licata ....dep.	3 45	1715

SARDINIA.

Cagliari—Chilivani—Terranova.

2 3	3 cl.	1 2 3	1 2 3	Rap 2 cl.		Rap 2 cl.	1 2 3	1 2 3	3 cl.	2 3	2 3
6 5	8 35	11 5	1524	17 0	dep. Cagliari.............. arr.	040	1240	1513	17 3	1955	24 0
6 49	9 29	1221	1618	18 8	,, San Gavino .... dep.	10 1	1146	14 5	16 8	19 2	2311
7 25	1012	1315	17 6	1840	,, Oristano .... ,,	9 28	11 1	1311	1529	1810	2232
9 55	13 1	1646	1959	2034	,, Chilivani .... ,,	7 37	8 35	10 1	13 0	1541	2 10
10†46	1351	1754	2053	..	,, Monti .... ,,		7 34	8 52	12 4	14†45	19 4
11†7	1412	1821	2115	2131	arr. Terranova ....dep	6 34	6 57	8 9	1135	14†15	1835
11†15	..	1840	2124	2135	,, ,, (Port) ..... ,,	6 30	6 50	8 0	..	..	..

† 3 class only.

ITALIAN LAKES—STEAMER, RAIL AND MOTOR SERVICES.

Lake of Lugano Steamers and Railways.

..	8 50	1150	1432	..	17 8	18†45	dep. **Menaggio** .... Rail arr.	1020	1310	1555	1824	..	..	..
..	9 25	1225	15 5	..	1742	19†20	arr. Porlezza ...... Rail dep.	9 45	12 15	1520	1750	..	..	..
						†	Steamer.						†	
..	9 40	1230	1520	..	1750	1925	dep. Porlezza ...... arr.	9 35	1225	1515	1740	..	1920	..
..	1029	1314	1554	..	1831	20 6	ar. S. Margherita dp.	8 53	1138	1433	1651	..	1838	..
..	1030	1315	1555	..	1832	20 7	dp. S. Margherita ar.	..	1137	1452	1650	..	1837	..
..	1058	1345	1625	..	19 0	2035	arr. **Lugano** .... dep.	8 25	11 5	14 5	1620	..	1810	..
8 30	1120	14 5	1630	1825	..	..	dep. (Central) arr.	7 50	1030	1250	1545	18 5	..	1850
8 35	1125	1410	1635	1815	1855	..	dep. (Paradiso) .. arr.	7 44	1025	1255	1539	18 0	..	1845
9 13	1230	1515	..	1930	arr.	..	arr. Porto-Ceresio dep.	6 40	9 20	12 5	1445	17 5	..	..
9 17	..	1520	..	..	..	..	dep. (*See p.*318/2) arr.	..	..	12 0	..	1655	..	1739
9 50	..	1555	1730	..		..	arr. **Ponte Tresa** .. dep.	..	..	1120	..	16 0	..	1735
9 55	..	16 0	1740	..	..	..	dep. Ponte Tresa .. Rail arr.	..	..	1125	..	1550	..	1730
1025	..	1635	1815	..	..	..	arr. **Luino** (Lake) .. Rail dep.	..	..	1050	..	1515	..	17 0

* Weekdays. † Sundays.

For services Lugano to Ponte Tresa by Electric Railway, *see p.* 290.

Belvedere—Lanzo Railway. (20 minutes)

Depart from Bevedere and Sta. Marguerita—9.15, 10.0, 10.35, 11.25, 12.15, 13.35, 15.58 16.25, etc.

Motor Service Lugano—Tremezzo.

See page 320.

9 20	14 0	1812	2030	dep. Lugano .... arr.	8 42	1325	18 0	20 5
1035	1515	1927	2145	arr. Tremezzo .... dep.	7 27	1210	1645	1850

Monte Generoso.

7 59	14 0	dep. Lugano (Central) .. arr.	1756	1951
8 17	1417	arr. Capolago Lake...... dep.	1738	1934
9 15	1410	dep. Capolago Lake .... arr.	1635	1835
9 25	1420	,, Capolago (sta.) .... ,,	1629	1831
1014	15 9	arr. Bellavista .... dep.	1540	1745
1040	1535	arr. Generoso-Vetta (Kulm) d.	1420	1720

Lake of Como Steamers.

	r	r		r					
7 10	9 50	1210	14 8	1845	dp. **Como** .... ar.	8 20	16 7	18 5	2015
7 25	10 1	1221	1422	1856	dp. Cernobbio .... dp.	..	1556	1751	1959
8 2	1017	1240	1441	1919	dp. Carate ...... dp.	7 52	1540	1735	1919
8 58	1045	1310	1512	1946	dp. Argegno...... dp.	7 26	1512	17 5	1849
9 47	11 4	1342	1538	20 4	dp. Lenno........ dp.	6 54	1453	1640	1754
9 54	1112	1350	1551	2016	Tremezzo .... ,,	6 41	1441	1632	1740
10 2	1128	1358	1558	2026	Cadenabbia .. ,,	..	1435	1622	..
1022	1132	14 8	1610	2038	Bellagio ...... ar.	6 30	1425	1612	1724
1039	1140	1418	1623	2040	ar. Menaggio dp.	6 20	1413	16 0	17 8
1043	1142	1420	1625	2050	dp. Menaggio ar.	6 17	1411	1558	17 5
11 0	1120	1436	1648	..	ar. Varenna.. dp.	6 7	14 0	1547	..
..	12 3	1438	1650	..	dp. Varenna.. ar.	6 5	1357	1545	..
..	14 0	1450	17 5	..	dp. Bellano ...... dp.	5 55	1345	1535	1652
	..	..	..	..	ar. **Colico**........ dp.	5 0	..		1510
	1010	1242	1358	1716	dep. Cadenabbia arr.	7 40	9 45	1242	1715
	1022	1232	14 8	1730	dep. Bellagio .. arr.	7 52	9 33	1229	1725
	1043	..	1420	..	dep. Menaggio .. dep.	7 25	9 17	1215	1658
	11 0	13 5	1436	1747	arr. Varenna .. dep.	7 8	9 0	12 0	1643
		..	1040	1547	dep. Varenna.... arr.	11 0	16 5	2150	
			1055	16 0	,, **Menaggio**.. dep.	1039	1548	2038	
		5 38	1110	1635	,, Cadenabbia ,,	1042	1533	2046	
		5 50	1122	1648	,, Bellagio.... ,,	1020	1515	2010	
		6 47	1219	1745	,, Mandello .. ,,	9 23	1418	1913	
		7 20	1250	1816	arr. **Lecco** ..... dep.	8 50	1345	1840	

r Restaurant on board.

† Infer Station.
* Weekdays.

ITALIAN LAKES—*continued.*

‡ Sup. Station.
‖ A tocar.
A Autocar Service,

Lake Maggiore Steamers.

	*	*	A						*	*	
5 35	7 30	8 55	..	1310	18‖5	dp. **Arona** .... ar.	1225	..	1830	2020	..
6 45	8 40	9 25	..	1340	1841	Stresa ...... ↑	1155	..	1715	1910	.
6 55	8 45	9 35	..	1355	..	Isola Bella ..	1145	..	1710	19 5	..
7 10	8 55	9 50	..	1410	1850	Baveno	1135	..	17 0	1845	.
7 25	..		1110		1915	Suna	..	..	..	..	..
7 35	9 10	10 5	1115	1425	19‖17	↓ Pallanza ..	1120	1431	1645	1830	..
7 50	9 30	1020	1116	1440	1920	ar. } Intra } dp.	..	1426	1630	1815	.
7 55	9 35	1021		1445	1925	dp. } Intra } ar.	..	1425	1625	1810	1915
8 10	..	1035	..	15 5	1940	ar. **Laveno** .. dp.	..		..	..	..
..			..	..	..	ar. Varese .. dp.	..	A	..	..	A
..		..	..		..	(*p.* 304).	..			..	
.			1045	1515	..	dp. Laveno .. ar.	.	15 5	1650	1845	1940
..	1030	..	1145	1625	.	dp. Cannero .. dp.	..	1355	1515	1720	1845
..	1045	..		1645	..	ar. } **Luino** } dp.	1030	..	1455	17 0	..
..	1050		..	1650	..	dp. } (*p.* 318) } ar.	1025	1420	1450	1630	..
..	11 5			17 5	..	dp. Maccagno† dp.	..		1435	1615	..
..	..	..	..	1715	..	dp. Maccagno‡ dp.	..	..	..	16 5	..
..	1120	..	12 0	1725	..	Cannobio .. ↑	..	1340	1420	1550	1830
..	1145	..	..			Brissago ..	9 30	..	..	1525	..
..				..	..	↓ Magadino ..	..	..	.	..	..
..	1135	.	..			ar. **Locarno** .. dp.	8 50	..	..	1430	..
..	1318		..	..		ar. Bellinzono dp.	8 31	..	..	..	..
..						(*p.* 287).					

Lake of Garda.

A Autocar.

A		A	A				A		A		A	A		A	
5 5	..	6 30	8 30	8 45	1135	1455	1825	dep. Riva Citta arr.	8 5	1040	8 5	1020	1430	1445	20 5
5 25		..	8 50	9 33	1212	..	1845	„ Limone		10 2	7 45	10 0	..	1355	1915
..	5 0	7 5		9 55	1235	1544	..	„ Malcesine .. arr.	7 30	9 40	.		1327	..	1153
..	..	..	..	..		..	..	„ Brenzone	7 15	..	.	..	..	..	..
								„ Castelletto							
..	5 45	7 20		1049		1629	..	di Brenz'ne ..	7 10	8 45	7 5	..	1240	..	..
6 5	6 10	7 24	9 30	1114	1331	1655	1925	dep. Gargnano	↑	8 20	7 0	9 20	1215	1315	1755
6 10	..		9 35	1121	1339	17 3	1930	dep. Bogliaco .... dep.		..	..	9 15	12 7	1310	1747
6 20	7 15		9 45	1149	14 7	1730	1940	Maderno .... ↑		7 15	6 50	9 5	1140	13 0	1720
6 25	7 23		9 50	1156	1414	1738	1945	Fasano Riv.		7 7	6 45	9 0	1132	1255	1712
6 30	7 33		9 55	12 6	1424	1748	1950	Gardone Riv.		6 57	6 40	8 55	1122	1250	17 2
6 40	7 47	↓	10 5	1220	1438	18 2	20 0	Salo		6 43	6 30	8 45	11 8	1240	1648
..	8 49	8 50		1323	1539	19 4		↓ Sirmione	5 45	5 41	..	..	10 6		1546
7 15	9 10	9 5	1040	1345	16 0	1925	2035	arr. Desenzano .. dep.	5 30	5 20	5 55	8 10	9 45	12 5	1525
..	..				..			dep. Maderno .. arr.	..	..	..	..	..	..	..
..	..	..	..	..	..	..	..	„ Garda	..	..	..	..	..	..	..
..	..	..		..	..		..	arr. Peschiera .. dep.	..	..	.	..	..	..	..

Lake of Orta.

1040	16 5	1840	dep. Omegna .... arr.	8 20	1430
11 4	1629	19 4	↓ Ronco ...... dep.	7 56	14 6
1126	1651	1926	Orta .... ↑	7 34	1344
1131	1656	1931	Isola	7 29	1339
1143	17 8	1943	Alzo	7 17	1327
1155	172	1955	↓ Isola	7 5	1315
12 0	1725	20 0	arr. Orta .... dep.	7 0	1310

Lake of Iseo.

a Hols.

				a		
5 0	1320	1440	dep. Lovere .... arr.	8 4	1128	2033
6 53	1452	1644	arr. Iseo .. .. dep.	6 25	9 30	1840
8 52		1957	arr. Brescia dep.	..	6 10	1720
6 55		1650	dep. Iseo ...... arr.	6 8	9 10	1823
7 28	..	1730	arr. Sarnico ... dep.	5 35	8 30	1750
..	..	..	arr. Bergamo dep.	..	..	..

Milan—Gallarate—Luino.

‡ Milan (P.N.) [State Rly. (Elec.)

	2 3	2 3	2 3	2 3	1 2 3	2 3		2 3	1 2 3	2 3	2 3	2 3
* Suns.	5 0	7‡48	10‡25	1320	1722	1854	dep. **Milan** (Cent.) arr.	8‡8	8‡40	14‡4	19 0	2226
excepted.	5 56	8 28	11 6	1416	18 2	1945	arr. Gallarate .. dep.	7 28	8 2	1325	18 0	2137
	7 42	9 52	1217	1534	1910	2048	arr. Luino ..... dep.	6 8	6 55	12 9	1642	20 4

Milan Varese Porto Ceresio.

(1 & 3 cl.) 1 State Rly. (Elec.)

Milan (P.N.) .... dep.	4*15	8 7	9*1	1120	1313	15*22	18 8	19 0	1953
Varese .... „	6 2	8 54	10 5	1220	14 7	1628	19 7	20 5	2047
Porto Ceresio .... arr.	6 32	9 14	1029	1240	1429	1650	1929	2034	2111
Porto Ceresio .... dep.	6 56	9 20	1245	1328	1543	1656	1938	2148	
Varese .... arr.	7 21	9 37	13 2	1353	16 6	1719	20 5	2215	
Milan (P.N.) .... „	8 18	1020	1345	1448	1716	18*25	2124	23*32	

* Milan (Cent.)

The times on the LEFT are to be read DOWNWARDS, those on the RIGHT UPWARDS.

REGULAR MOTOR COACH SERVICES IN THE DOLOMITES.

Societa Automobilistica Dolomiti.

Munich—Innsbruck—Bolzano.

b	a	b		b	a	b
..	..	8 35	dp. Munich ...... ar.	19 0	..	..
..	..	11 0	dp. Garmisch-P. ar.	1625	..	..
7 30	9 45	1415	dp. Innsbruck .... ar.	1310	1555	2050
9 20	1135	16 5	dp. Colle Isarco .. ar.	1125	14 0	1855
9 35	1150	1620	dp. Vipiteno ..... ar.	11 5	1230	1840
1055	1415	1735	dp. Giovo Pass .. ar.	1010	1135	..
14 0	1620	1930	dp. Merano ...... ar.	8 10	9 30	..
1445	..	2015	ar. Bolzano ..... dp.	7 15	..	16 0

a 15 June–30 Sept. *b* 1 July–15 Sept.

Landeck—Resiapass—Bolzano.

b	a		a	b
8 55	1450	dp. Landeck .... ar.	1150	1855
1115	1630	dp. Nauders ..... ar.	10 5	17 0
1145	17 0	dp. Resiapass ... ar.	9 25	1615
1245	1755	ar. Spondigna ... ar.	8 25	1515
17 0	1930	ar. Merano ..... ar.	..	8 30
18 0	2015	ar. Bolzano .... dp.	..	7 45

a July 5–Sept 5. *b* July 1–Sept. 10.

Bolzano—Dolomites—Venice.

a June 15–Sept. 15. *b* June 20–Sept. 20.

a	b	c	*c* July 15–Aug. 31.	c	b	a
7 30	9 20	15 0	dp. Bolzano .... ar.	1245	1730	2010
8 50	1055	1520	dp. Carezza ...... ar.	1140	16 5	19 5
10 0	1215	1725	dp. Canazei ..... ar.	1025	1440	1750
1055	1445	1815	dp. Pordoipass .. ar.	9 40	1215	1710
1245	17 5	20 5	ar. Cortina...... dp.	7 30	9 30	15 0
1520	..	..	dp. Cortina .... ar.	..		1235
1930		..	ar. Venice .... dp.			8 0

Bolzano—Brescia.

a	b		b	a
9 40	1515	dp. Bolzano ..... ar.	1110	1825
1140	1755	dp. Male .... ar.	8 45	1545
1430	19 0	dp. Madonna di C. dp.	7 45	1445
1710	..	dp. Riva ...... ar.	..	1040
1820	..	dp. Gardone R... dp.	..	9 40
1915	..	ar. Brescia ...... dp.	..	8 40

a July 10–Sept. 5. *b* June 23–Sept. 10.

Venice—Cortina—Grossglockner Salzburg—(Munich).

July 1–Sept. 15.

..	8 0	dp. Venice ...... arr.	..	1930
..	1530	dp. Cortina ...... ar.	..	1245
..	1640	dp. Misurina .... ar.	..	1135
—	1925	ar. Lienz .... dp.	—	8 45
7 55	..	dp. Lienz .... ar.	19 5	..
1435	..	dp. Zell a. See.... ar.	1110	..
16 0	..	dp. Lofer .... ar.	9 55	..
1730	..	ar. Salzburg .... dp.	8 20	..
16 0	..	dp. Lofer .... ar.	9 50	..
1855	..	ar. Munich ...... dp.	7 0	..

Bolzano—Merano.

a	b	c		c	b	a
7 45	1745	1915	dp. Bolzano ..... ar.	8 0	9 5	18 0
8 30	1830	20 0	ar. Merano ...... dp.	7 15	8 20	1715

a June 15–Sept. 30. *b* June 20–Sept. 20.
c July 5–Sept. 5.

Engadin—Stelviopass—Bolzano.

July 1–Sept. 10.

13 0	..	dp. Locarno ..... ar.	..	1255
1420	..	dp. Lugano ...... ar.	..	1142
1911	8 10	dp. S. Moritz..... ar.	1853	6 55
arr.	9 35	dp. Zernez .... ar.	1746	dep.
..	1420	dp. Stelviopass ... ar.	12 0	..
..	1550	dp. Spondigna ... ar.	9 55	..
..	1715	dp. Merano ...... ar.	8 30	..
..	18 0	ar. Bolzano ..... dp.	7 45	..

Davos—Munster—Bolzano.

June 15–Sept. 30.

7 40	dp. Davos .... ar.	1753
9 35	dp. Zernez. ...... ar.	1510
1440	dp. Munster ..... ar.	1120
1550	dp. Spondigna ... ar.	9 55
1715	dp. Merano ...... ar.	8 30
18 0	ar. Bolzano ..... dp.	7 45

Tirano—Stelviopass—Bolzano.

a	b		a	b
9 0	1320	dp. Tirano .... ar.	1545	1930
1019	1439	dp. Bormio Bagni ar.	1430	1815
1420	1635	dp. Stelviopass ... ar.	12 0	13 0
1510	1725	dp. Trafoi .... ar.	1040	1140
1550	1810	dp. Spondigna ... ar.	9 55	1055
1715	1930	dp. Merano ...... dp.	8 40	9 40
18 0	2015	ar. Bolzano .... dp.	7 45	7 45

a July 1–Sept. 10. *b* July 15–Aug. 31.

Bolzano—Gardena Valley—Cortina.

July 1–Sept 15.

8 30	dp. Bolzano ..... ar.	1650
9 55	dp. Ortisei. ...... ar.	1530
1445	dp. Pordoipass ... ar.	1215
17 5	ar. Cortina ...... dp.	9 30

Bolzano—S. Martino—Cortina.

c	a	b		c	b	a
..	8 15	1430	dp. Bolzano ..... ar.	..	11 0	19 0
..	9 50	16 5	dp. Carezza ...... ar.	..	9 40	1740
dep.	1020	1635	dp. Vigo di Fassa . ar.	..	8 50	1650
8 45	1230	1845	ar. S. Martino ... ar.	18 0	6 45	1450
17 5	..	..	ar. Cortina ...... dp.	9 30	dep.	dep.

a July 5–Sept. 5. *b* June 25–Sept. 15.

S. Martino—Feltre.

a	b	c		b	a	c
9 45	1445	1645	dp. S. Martino ... ar.	9 30	1435	1920
1130	1630	1830	arr. Feltre ...... dp.	7 40	1245	1730

a June 20–Sept. 15. *b* July 1–Sept. 10.
c July 15–Sept. 5.

Spondigna—Solda—Stelviopass.

July 10–Sept. 5

1830	..	dp. Spondigna ... ar.	..	8 5
20 0	8 5	dp. Solda .... ar.	1835	7 0
arr.	9 35	dp. Trafoi....... ar.	1720	dep.
..	11 0	ar. Stelviopass .. dp.	1635	..
..	1855	ar. Schuls ...... dp.	6 35	..

Cook's Tourist Map of
The MEDITERRANEAN and the LEVANT

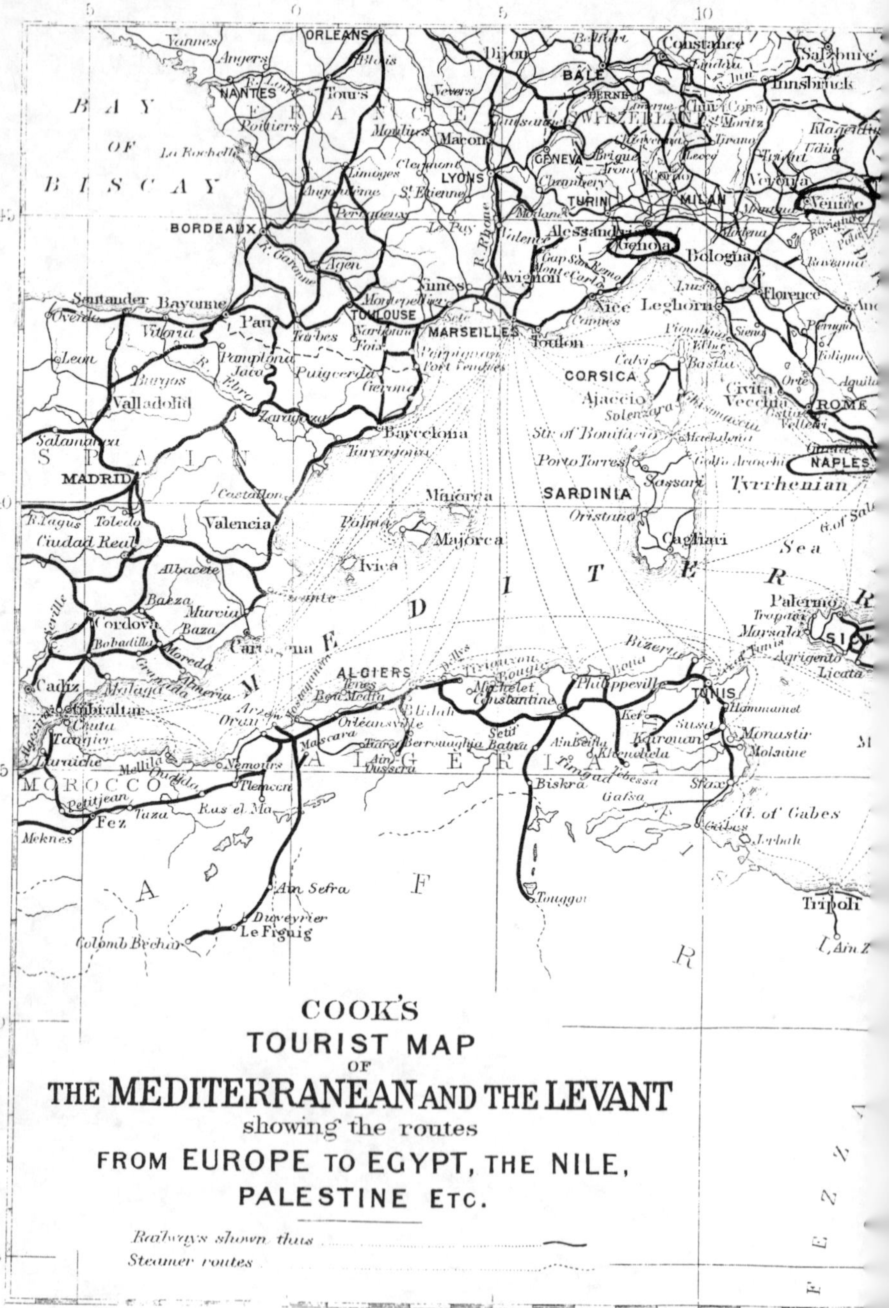

COOK'S TOURIST MAP OF THE MEDITERRANEAN AND THE LEVANT

showing the routes

FROM EUROPE TO EGYPT, THE NILE, PALESTINE ETC.

Railways shown thus

Steamer routes

W. & A.K. Johnston Ltd Edinr

(219/1/39 J.)

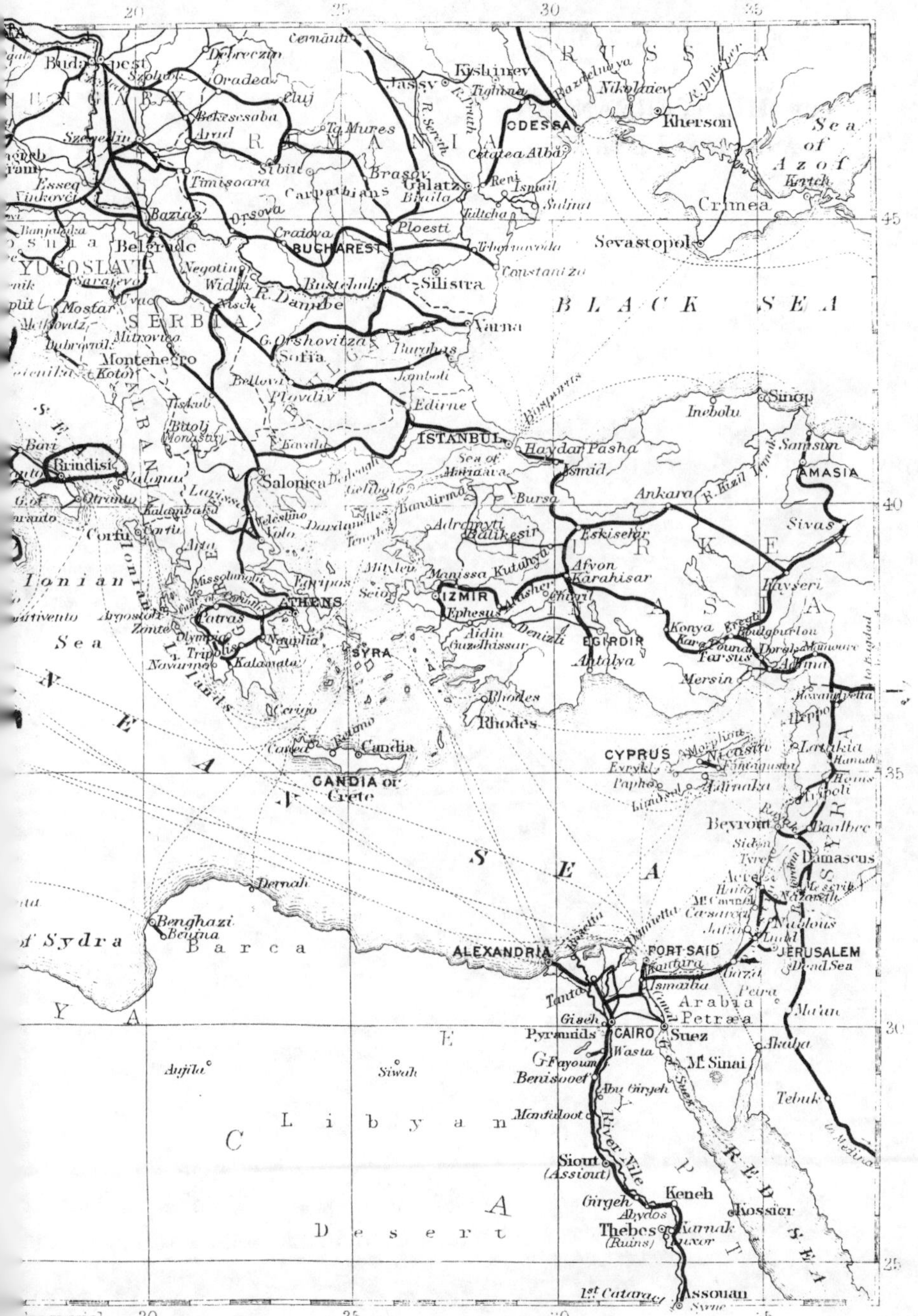

20
25
30
35
Budapest
Debreczin
Szolnok
Oradea
Cluj
Bekescsaba
Arad
Szegedin
Timisoara
Sibiu
Tg. Mures
Brasov
Carpathians
Galatz
Braila
Reni
Ismail
Sulina
Tultcha
Cernăuti
Jassy
R. Pruth
R. Sereth
Kishinev
Tighina
Cetatea Albă
ODESSA
Razdelnaya
Nikolaiev
R. Dnieper
Kherson
RUSSIA
Sea of Azof
Kertch
Crimea
Sevastopol
45
Esseg
Vinkovci
Bazias
Orsova
Craiova
BUCHAREST
Ploesti
Tchernavoda
Constantza
Silistra
Rustchuk
R. Danube
Belgrade
YUGOSLAVIA
Sarajevo
Banjaluka
Negotin
Widin
Nisch
Mostar
Split
SERBIA
Mitrovica
Dubrovnik
Montenegro
Kotor
G. Orshovitza
Sofia
BULGARIA
Varna
Burghas
Jamboli
Bellova
Plovdiv
Edirne
BLACK SEA
Bosporus
ISTANBUL
Haydar Pasha
Sea of Marmara
Ismid
Bursa
Inebolu
Sinop
Samsun
AMASIA
R. Kizil Irmak
Ankara
Sivas
40
Eskisehir
Balikesir
Bandirma
Dardanelles
Tenedos
Adramyti
Afyon Karahisar
Kutahya
Manissa
IZMIR
Ephesus
Aidin
Guzelhissar
Denizli
Chivril
EGIRDIR
Antalya
Konya
Eregli
Kayseri
TURKEY
ASIA
Adana
Tarsus
Mersin
Dorak
Alexandretta
Aleppo
Latakia
Hamah
Homs
Tripoli
Baalbec
Beyrout
Sidon
Tyre
Damascus
Acre
Haifa
Mt. Carmel
Caesarea
Jaffa
Nablous
Lydd
JERUSALEM
Dead Sea
Gaza
Petra
Ma'an
Akaba
Tebuk
to Medina
Üsküb
Bitolj
Monastir
Kavala
Salonica
Larissa
Kalambaka
Volo
Velestino
Corfu
Valona
Brindisi
Bari
Otranto
ALBANIA
Ionian Sea
Ionian Islands
Arta
Missolonghi
Egripos
ATHENS
Patras
Olympia
Nauplia
Tripolis
Kalamata
Navarino
Zante
Argostoli
Cerigo
SYRA
Scio
Mitylene
Rhodes
Canea
Retimo
Candia
CANDIA or Crete
CYPRUS
Morphou
Nicosia
Famagusta
Larnaka
Limassol
Papho
35
SEA
Derneh
Benghazi
Benina
Barca
of Sydra
ALEXANDRIA
Rosetta
Damietta
PORT SAID
Kantara
Ismailia
Tanta
Giseh
CAIRO
Suez
Pyramids
Arabia Petraea
30
Fayoum
Wasta
Benisoeef
Abu Girgeh
Mt. Sinai
Manfaloot
River Nile
Siout
(Assiout)
Girgeh
Abydos
Keneh
Kossier
Thebes
(Ruins)
Karnak
Luxor
RED SEA
EGYPT
1st Cataract
Assouan
Syene
25
Aujila
Siwah
Libyan Desert
Greenwich
20
25
30
35

Cook's Tourist Map
of
The MEDITERRANEAN
and the LEVANT

ITALIAN MOTOR COACH SERVICES—*continued.*

Ulzio—Sestrieres.

8 40	1510	dep. Ulzio .... arr.	1110	1835
9 40	1610	arr. Sestrieres ...... dep.	1010	1740

9 45	1410	2010	d. Pre St. Didier a. (*p.* 360)	6 50	1055	1740
10 5	1430	2030	a. Courmayour d.	6 30	1035	1720

1630	d. Aosta ...... a.	9 15
1745	a. St. Rhemy . . d.	8 0
..	a. Gr.S.Bernard d.	..

Como—Tremezzo—Menaggio.

7 52	10 2	1150	1620	1820	dep. Como .... arr.	7 42	9 2	1110	1510	1727
8 55	11 5	1253	1723	1923	dep. Lenno .... arr.	6 39	8 0	10 8	12 7	1625
9 5	1115	13 3	1733	1933	dep. Tremezzo ...... arr.	6 30	7 50	9 58	1358	1615
9 7	1117	13 5	1735	1935	dep. Cadenabbia .... arr.	6 27	7 47	9 55	1355	1612
9 17	1127	1315	1745	1945	arr. Menaggio ...... dep.	6 17	7 37	9 45	1345	16 2

Tremezzo—Lugano.

7 27	1210	1645	d. Tremezzo . a.	1035	1515	1927
7 27	1212	1647	d. Cadenabbia a	1033	1513	1925
7 35	1218	1653	d. Menaggio. a.	1027	15 7	1919
8 0	1243	1718	d. Porlezza . . a.	10 2	1442	1854
8 42	1325	18 0	a. Lugano . . d.	9 20	14 0	1812

Tirano—Stelvio. *a* July 5-Sept. 5

	a			*a*
9 0	1320	dp. Tirano .... ar.	1545	1930
9 35	1355	dp. Bolladore . ar.	1510	1855
1019	1439	dp. Bormio ... ar.	1430	1815
1140	16 0	ar. Stelvio ... dp.	1330	1715

Padua—Abano.

From Padua	7 55	1220	1410	1930
From Albano....	1120	1310	15 0	2015

Journey.

Florence—Fiesole.

1210	1830	19 0	dep. Florence .... arr.	8 45	1455	1525
1245	19 5	1935	arr. Fiesole ..... dep.	8 10	1420	1450

Rapallo—S. Margherita—Portofino Mare.

From Rapallo, 8.0, 9.0, 10.0, 16.0, 12.0, etc.
From Portofino, 8.0, 8.50, 10.10, 11.10, 11.40, 13.10, etc.

Journey, 15 mins.

8 20	17 0	d. Merano . . a.	7 30	1815
9 30	1820	a. S. L'on'do d.	6 15	1655

5 15	1450	d. Amalfi . . a.	1035	19 5
7 10	1645	a. Sorrento. d.	8 40	1710

8 20	1810	d. Amalfi . . . a.	9 40	1830
9 35	1925	a. Salerno . . d.	8 35	1715

Florence—Siena—S. Gimignano.

Daily in Sept.

Florence	dep.	8 0
Siena	arr.	1010
„	dep.	16 0
S. Gimignano	arr.	17 0
„	dep.	18 0
Florence	arr.	1930

Naples—Amalfi—Sorrento.

Daily.

Naples	dep.	8 35
Pompei	arr.	9 20
„	dep.	1130
Amalfi	arr.	13 0
„	dep.	1530
Positano	dep.	1645
Sorrento	arr.	1715
„	dep.	1745
Naples	arr.	1915

Rome—Perugia—Assisi—Siena—Florence.

Tues...	Rome	dep.	8 0
	Viterbo	arr.	1020
	„	dep.	1050
	Orvieto	arr.	12 0
	„	dep.	1430
	Todi	arr.	1550
	„	dep.	1620
	Perugia	arr.	1730
Wed...	Perugia	dep.	11 0
	Assisi	arr.	1130
	„	dep.	15 0
	Siena	arr.	1930
Thur...	Siena	dep.	16 0
	S. Gimignano	arr.	17 0
	„	dep.	1730
	Florence	arr.	19 0

Fri...	Florence	dep.	8 30
	S. Gimignano.. ..	arr.	1030
	„	dep.	11 0
	Siena	arr.	12 0
Sat...	Siena	dep.	8 30
	Perugia	arr.	12 0
	„	dep.	1630
	Assisi	arr.	17 0
	„	dep.	19 0
	Perugia	arr.	1930
Sun...	Perugia	dep.	10 0
	Todi	arr.	1120
	„	dep.	1140
	Orvieto	arr.	13 0
	„	dep.	1530
	Viterbo	arr.	1630
	„	dep.	17 0
	Rome	arr.	1920

SPAIN AND PORTUGAL.

IN SPAIN and PORTUGAL, Greenwich (W.E.) time. Thro' Services to Spain, *see pp.* 85,113,115,117,250,255

Irun, Burgos, Valladolid, Madrid.

902 miles. [Norte.

	1 2 3	1 2 3	luxe		luxe	
..	8 45	2050	1130	dep. PARIS (Orsay) arr.	2059	..
..	1648	4 29	1721	,, Bordeaux (*p.* 250).	1518	..
..	2017	8 26	2041	,, Hendaye ....dep.	12 0	..
		R	L		L	
..	..	..	..	Hendaye .... arr.	1135	..
8 0	..	..	2135	dep. **Irun** ...... ,,	1040	21 5
8 25	..	..	2150	arr. San Sebastian dp.	8 55	..
9 28	..	..	..	dep. Zumarraga..dep.	..	..
10 5	..	..	..	,, Alsasua .... ,,	..	..
1056	..	..	..	,, Vitoria...... ,,	..	..
1135	..	..	..	arr. } Miranda { ,,	..	..
1145	..	..	..	dep. } Miranda { arr.	..	..
1345	..	..	..	dep **Burgos** ....dep.	..	..
15 2	..	..	..	arr. } Venta-de- } ,,	..	..
15 7	..	..	..	dep. } Banos } arr	..	..
1557	..	..	..	,, **Valladolid** ..dep.	2 41	..
1637	..	..	5 40	ar. } Medina del Cam-	2 20	..
1645	..	..	..	dp. } po (*p.* 322) arr.	..	..
1830	..	..	..	dep. Avila ......dep.	..	..
2027	..	..	..	,, El Escorial.. ,,	..	..
2130	..	..	10 0	arr. **Madrid** (Nor.) dep.	22 0	8 15

L Sud Express daily Train de Luxe to Lisbon, *see p.* 85. **R** Rest. Car.

Hendaye—San Sebastian.

12¾ miles. All trains 1 cl. [S.E.F. y Tranvias

Amara Stat. to Norte Stat. ⅝th mile.

d. **Hendaye** (Electric) ..a.
d. Irun (Electric) ......a.
a S Sebastian (Amara) d.
a. S. Sebast. (Penaflorida) d.

San Sebastian—Bilbao—Santander.

Mls.	
0	d. S. Sebast. (Amara) a.
28	d. Deva .... d.
38	d. Malzaga...... d.
48	d. Durango...... d.
.	d. Azbarren .... d.
60	a. Bilbao (Achuri) d.
..	
.	d. ,, (Concor.) a.
103	d. MarrónAmpuero d.
135	a. Santander ...... d.

(Madrid) Venta de Banos, Vigo, Corunna.

[Norte.

		1 cl.	1 cl.	Mls.		1 cl.	1 cl.		
	r	*a*	*b*			*b*	*a*		*r*
..	8 0	1530	1530	0	dep. **Madrid** (*above*) a.	1130	1130	2145	..
..	8 56	1626	1626		arr. Villalba ....dep.	1045	1045	21 0	..
..	..	1850	1850	71	dep. Avila ...... ,,	8 25	1825	..	..
..	1345	2020	2020	..	,, Medina del Campo .. arr.	6 30	6 30	*r* 1610	..
r 5 0	1432	2110	2110	..	,, Valladolid ,,	5 30	5 30	1514	24 0
5 35	1512	2210	2210	175	,, **V. de Banos** ,,	4 45	4 45	1439	2325
5 55	1530	2227	2227	182	,, Palencia ..dep.	4 30	4 30	1420	2250
7 47	1720	0 30	0 30	259	arr. Leon ......dep.	2 25	2 25	1220	2055
8 0	1724	0 40	0 40		dep. Leon .... arr.	2 10	2 10	1210	2030
..	2150	..	..	361	arr. Gijon ....dep.	..	..	7 45	..
1355	..	5 55	5 55	407	arr. Monforte ..dep.	2025	2025	..	14 0
1435	..	6 15	6 20	.	dep. Monforte arr.	2012	2010	..	1325
..	..	..	..	..	,, Guillarey dep.	..	..	..	..
..	..	..	1014	. .	arr. **Vigo** .... ,,	16 5	..	..	..
20 0	..	1015	..	526	arr. **Corunna**....dep.	..	16 0	..	8 0

r Rest Car.

a Sl. car. Tues., Thurs., Sats., Suns.

b Sl. car. Mon., Wed. and Fri.

The times on the LEFT are to be read DOWNWARDS, those on the RIGHT UPWARDS.

Madrid—Santander.

Mls.		
0	dep. Madrid (Norte) ...... arr.	
24	arr. Villalba .... dep.	
125	dep. Medina del Campo. .. arr.	
148	arr. Valladolid (Norte).... dep.	
177½	arr. Palencia (Norte) .... dep.	
315	arr. Santander .... dep.	

Madrid—Bilbao.

1 2 A	Mls.		1 2 A
1910	0	d. Madrid (Norte) p321 ar.	12 0
20 6	24	arr. Villalba .... dep.	1115
2215	71	dep. Avila ...... ,,	9 20
2340	125	arr. Medina del dep.	7 30
24 0		dep. Campo (p. 321) a.	7 10
5 5	302	arr. Miranda de dep.	1 45
6 10	..	dep. Ebro .... arr.	0 45
..	323	dep. Orduna .... dep.	..
8 30	348	arr. **Bilbao** (Norte) d.	2215

A 1 & 2 cl. Sleeping Car Madrid - Bilbao and *v.v.*

(Irun) Medina (Madrid), Salamanca (Oporto) Lisbon, &c. [M., S., Fonteray.

luxe	Mls		1 2
1130	0	dep. PARIS (Quai d'Orsay) arr.	2059
2145	510	dep. Irun : Hendaye ...... dep.	12 0
S		(*pp.* 250 321)	S
5 56	780	dep. **Medina del Campo** .. arr.	2 26
7 29	828	arr. **Salamanca** .... dep.	0 52
..	0	dep. **Madrid** .... arr.	
..	71	,, Avila .... ,,	
	141	arr. Salamanca............ dep.	
7 41		dep. Salamanca ... . arr.	0 41
..	868½	arr. Fuente S. Esteban .... dep.	.
	..	dep. S. Esteban .... arr.	↑
	912½	arr. Barca d'A. .... dep.	
..	..	dep. Barca d'A. .... arr.	
..	1040	arr. **Oporto** (C) (*p.* 327) .. dep.	
	..	dep. Fuente S. Esteban.. arr.	..
1140	864	arr. Villa Formoso .... dep.	21 3
1850	1141	arr. LISBON (*p.* 327) .... dep.	1355

S Sud Express : Daily train de luxe Paris-Lisbon and *v.v.* EXTRA FARES, see *p.* 85.

† *Via* Pampilhosa. Saloon cars, 1st class only.

¶ 1 & 2 cl. thro' car Irun-Lisbon and *v.v.* EXTRA FARES.

(Irun) (Bilbao) Alsasua, Saragossa (Barcelona). [Norte.

			Mls.				
			0	dep. Irun .... arr.			
			64½	dep. **Alsasua** .... arr.			
			97	dep. Pamplona .... dep.			
			152	arr. Castejon .... dep.			
			0	dep. **Bilbao** .... arr.			
			65	dep. Miranda .... arr.			
			156	arr. Castejon .... dep.			
			..	dep. Castejon .... arr.			
			201	arr. Casetas .... dep.			
			..	dep. Casetas.............. arr.			
			209	arr. **Saragossa** (Sep.)...... dep.			
			424	,, Barcelona (Fran.) (*p.* 326) ,,			
				dep. Casetas.............. arr.			
			210	arr. Saragossa (Arrabal) .. dep.			
by train	1830	1755	..	dep ,, ,, .. arr.	1350	6 38	by train
	6 20	Sleep Car.	..	,, Lerida .... dep.	Sleep. Car.	20 0	
	7 0		325	dep. Lerida .... arr.		1830	
by bus	..		398	,, Manresa .... ,,		..	by bus
	13 0	6 30	439	arr. Barcelona (Norte).... dep.	24 0	1230	

U The times on the LEFT are to be read DOWNWARDS, those on the RIGHT UPWARDS.

Madrid, Badajoz (Seville), Lisbon. [Madr. Zarag. Alicante, & Portug. Rlys.

1 2	Mls.		1 2
S			S
21 0	0	dep. **Madrid** (Atocha) .... arr.	9 20
2219	38	dep. Algodor .... dep.	8 5
1 16	107	dep. Ciudad Real .... arr.	5 13
5 2	204	arr. Almorchon .... dep.	1 26
..	..	dep. Cordova .... arr.	..
..		(Cercadilla)	..
..	..	arr. } Belmez........ { dep.	..
..	..	dep. } Belmez { arr.	..
..	..	arr. Almorchon ...... dep.	
5 4		dep. Almorchon .... arr.	1 24
8 2	280	arr. Merida .... dep.	22 0
..	0	dep. **Seville** .... arr.	..
..	8	dep. San Jeronimo .... arr.	..
..	23	dep. Tocino .... dep.	..
..	108	dep. Zafra............ dep.	..
..	149	arr. Merida .... dep.	..
8 18	280	dep. Merida .... arr.	2145
9 25	317	arr. } **Badajoz** *c* ...... { dep.	2035
..	0	dep. } **Badajoz** *c* { arr.	..
..	10	dep. Elvas *c* .... dep.	..
..	66	arr. Torre das Vargens.... dep.	..
..	174	arr. LISBON (Rocio: *p.* 325..dp.	..

S 1 cl. Sleeping Car Madrid to Badajoz and *v.v.*

Madrid, Alcazar, Alicante, Cartagena (Valencia). [Mad, Zar., Alicante.

	1 2	Mls.		1 2	
r	A			A	*r*
9 0	2230	0	dep. **Madrid** (Atocha) .... arr.	7 45	19 0
..	..	30½	dep. Aranjuez .... dep.	..	..
..	..	40½	dep. Castillejo .... dep.	..	..
1121	0 49	93	arr. } **Alcazar** .... { dep.	5 28	1641
1128	0 5[illegible]		dep. } **Alcazar** { arr.	5 21	1635
1348	3 25	174¼	dep. Albacete .... dep.	3 58	1431
1410	3 50	186¼	arr. Chinchilla .... dep.	3 30	14 5
..	..	.	dep. Chinchilla ...... arr.	..	..
..	..	294	arr. } **Murcia** .... { dep.	..	..
..	..		dep. } **Murcia** { arr.	..	..
..	..	328	arr. **Cartagena** ...... dep.		..
1430	4 24	..	dep. Chinchilla .... arr.	3 11	1345
1557	5 57	235½	arr. La Encina .... dep.	1 21	1211
1615	6 20	.	dep. La Encina ...... arr.	0 45	1155
1845	9 0	306	arr. **Valencia** .... dep.	2145	9 0
..	..	..	dep. La Encina .... arr.	..	..
..	..	284½	arr. **Alicante** (*p.* 325) .... dep.	..	..

A 1 cl. Sleeping Car Madrid to Valencia and *v.v.* *r* Rest Car.

Alicante and Murcia.

Mls.	
0	dep. Alicante .... arr.
45	arr. Murcia.............. dep.

r	Mls.		*r*
9 10	0	dep. **Madrid**............. arr.	20 0
1030	38¾	arr. } Algodor .... { dep.	1829
1032		dep. } Algodor { arr.	1827
1045	57	arr. **Toledo**.............. dep.	1815

r Rest Car.

The times on the LEFT are to be read DOWNWARDS, those on the RIGHT UPWARDS.

Madrid—Granada (Almeria).

Mls.	*r* Rest. Car.
0	dp. **Madrid** (Atocha) ar.
197	arr. Baeza (*below*) dep.
	dep. Baeza .... arr.
271	arr. Moreda ...... dep.
	dp. Moreda ...... arr.
307	ar. Granada (And) dp.
	ar. Moreda .... arr.
280	dp. Guadix .... dep.
	dp. Guadix .... arr.
345½	ar. Almeria ...... dep.

Guadix—Alicante (Cartagena).

Mls.	
	dep Granada ... arr.
0	dep. Guadix .... arr.
33	arr. } Baza .. { dep.
	dep. } Baza .. { arr.
120	arr. Alcantrilla .. dep.
125	arr. Murcia .... dep.
	dep. Murcia ...... arr.
172	arr. Alicante .... dep.
	dep. Alcantrilla .. arr.
	dep Murcia .... dep.
166	arr. Cartagena .. dep.

Motor Omnibus: Madrid (Norte) to Madrid (Atocha)
Madrid (Atocha) to Madrid (Norte)

Medina, Salamanca, Seville, Cadiz.

[Madr., Zarag, Alicante

dep.	**Medina del Campo** (*p.* 321) arr.
arr.	**Salamanca** .... dep.
dep.	,, ... arr.
dep.	Plasencia .... dep.
dep	Arrayo .... dep.
arr.	Caceres .... dep.
dep.	,, ... arr.
arr.	Merida .... dep.
dep.	,, ... arr.
dep.	Zafra (P. de Armas) .... dep.
arr.	**Seville** .... dep.
arr.	} Seville (S. Bernardo) .... { dep.
dep.	} Seville (S. Bernardo) .... { arr.
dep.	Utrera .... dep.
dep	San Fernando .... dep.
arr.	**Cadiz** .... dep.

Cordova, Malaga and Granada.

Mls.	
0	dep. Cordova .... arr.
62	arr. La Roda .... dep.
0	dep. Espeluy (*above*) ...... arr.
20	dep. Jaen .... dep.
115	arr. La Roda .... dep.
62	dep. La Roda .... arr.
77	arr. Bobadilla .... dep.
	dep. Bobadilla .... arr
155	arr. **Granada** .... dep.
..	dep. Bobadilla .... arr.
..	dep. Alora .... dep.
120	arr. **Malaga** .... dep.

Madrid, Alcazar, Cordoba, Seville.

r Rest. Car
A 1 cl. Sleep. Car Madrid-Seville and *v. v.*

r	**A***r*				*r*	**A***r*
9 30	1845	dep	Madrid ..	arr.	2045	1145
1144	2220	arr.	} Alcazar {	dep.	1831	8 0
1150	2230	dep.	} Alcazar {	arr.	1824	7 0
1452	5 16	arr.	} Baeza {	dep.	1453	1 7
1455	5 46	dep.	} Baeza {	arr.	1450	0 32
1734	9 25	arr.	} Cordoba {	dp.	12 2	2045
1741	1016	dep.	} Cordoba {	arr.	1155	20 0
20 0	1355	arr.	Seville	dep.	9 30	1645

The times on the LEFT are to be read DOWNWARDS, those on the RIGHT UPWARDS.

Seville, La Roda (Granada, &c.)

				Andaluce.				
				dp. **Seville**.... ar.				
				ar. Utrera.... dp.				
				dp. Cadiz .. ar.				
				dp. Utrera .... ar.				
				,, Marchena .. dp.				
				ar. La Roda .. dp.				
				ar. Bobadilla .. dp.				
				dp. Bobadilla ar.				
				ar. Malaga .. dp.				
				dp Bobadilla .. ar.				
				ar. Granada .. dp.				
				dp. Bobadilla ar.				
				ar. Algeciras dp.				
				dp. Algeciras ar.				
				ar. Gibraltar dp.				

Madrid, Cordova, Algeciras (Gibraltar) and Malaga.

For full ferry Services, Algeciras-Gibraltar, *see p.* 371.

				Andaluce				
				dp. Madrid .. arr.				
				d. Cordova .... a				
				arr. **Bobadilla** dp.				
				dep. ,, arr.				
				arr. Malaga dep.				
				dp **Bobadilla** arr.				
				,, Ronda .... dp.				
				,, Jimera .. dp.				
				,, Almoraima dp.				
				ar. Algeciras† dp.				
				ar **Algeciras**‡ dp.				
				dp. ,, (stmr.) ar.				
				ar. **Gibraltar** dp.				

Madrid, Valencia, Lisbon.

M. C. & Port. & Port. Rlys.

			Mls.				
			0	dp. **Madrid** .. arr. (Delicias)			
			84	ar / dp } Talavera { dp / ar			
			205	arr. Arroyo .. dep.			
			..	,, Caceres .. ,,			
			..	dp. Arroyo .... ar.			
			250	ar **Valencia** d. / d. d'Alcantc a.			
			300	d. Torre das Varg.			
			342	a. Entrocamnto d.			
			..	d. Entrocamnto a.			
			412	a. **Lisbon** (*p.* 327)			

Cordova—Utrera (Cadiz).

				dep. Cordova (M.Z.A.)(*p.*324) a.			
				,, Marchena dp.			
				arr. Utrera .. ,,			
				,, Jerez .. ,,			
				,, Cadiz .. ,,			

(Barcelona) Tarragona, Valencia, Encina (Seville).

[Norte.

								Ms.										
								0	d. Barcelona (*p.*326) a.									
								57	dep. **Tarragona** .. arr.									
								110	dep. Tortosa .... dep									
								177	dep. Castellon .. dep.									
								230	arr. Valencia .... dep.									
									dep. Valencia .... arr.									
								255	dep. Carcagente dep.									
								300	arr La Encina .. dep									
									dep. La Encina .. arr.									
								442	dep. Alcazar .... dep.									
								546	arr. Baeza ...... dep.									
								656	arr. Granada(*p.*324) d.									
									dep. Baeza ...... arr.									
								627	arr. Cordova .... dep.									
								708	arr Seville ...... dep.									
									dep. La Encina .. arr.									
								349	arr. Alicante (323) dp.									

Narbonne, Barcelona (Tarragona), Saragossa, Madrid. [Madrid, Zarag., Alicante

1 2 3 Rest. Car ☞	1 2 With Sleep. Car 1 cl.	1 2 With Sleep. Car 1 cl.	Mls.		1 2 With Sleep. Car 1 cl.	1 2 With Sleep. Car 1 cl.	1 2 3 Rest. Car ☞
..	..			dp.Narbonne(p.255)ar.		..	..
..	..			,, Cerbere [Fr. tme.]		..	..
..	..			,, [Sp. tme.] ar.		..	..
4 10	..		0	dep.**Port Bou** ....arr.		..	2250
6 47	..		42	dep.Gerona ...... arr.		..	2015
7 27	..		60	arr.Emp.de Barona d.		..	1932
..			..	dep. Em.de Barc a.			..
..			85	arr. Arenys .... dp.			..
..			103	arr. Barcelona ,,			..
7 30			42	dep.Emp.de Barona a.			1929
..			83	arr. Granollers ..dep.			
8 50			106	a**B'rcel'na**(Termino)d			1810
		2025	0	d**B'rcel'na**(Termino)a	9 45		
		..	31	arr. Sitges ......dep.	..		
		2159	42	arr. San Vicente dep.	8 14		
		22 1		dep. San Vicente ar.	8 12		
		..	57	arr. **Tarragona** dp.			
	..	23 0		arr. Reus ....dep.	7 28	..	
..	..	..		dep. Tarragona arr.	..	..	..
..	..	..		arr. Reus......dep.	..	..	..
..	..	23 2	66	dep.Reus .... arr.	7 26	..	..
..	..	2 13	145	,, Caspe ......dep	4 7	..	..
..	..	4 31	215	arr. } **Saragossa** { dp.	1 43	..	..
..	22 0	4 43		dep. } (M.Z.A.) { ar.	1 33	6 10	.
..	..	..	223	dep. Casetas......dep.	..	..	..
..	8 35	1120	427	ar.**Madrid** (Atocha) d.	19 0	20 0	..

Canfranc to Saragossa.

Mls.	
0	dep **Canfranc** (p. 252)..arr.
15	dep.Jaca .... dep.
62	arr. Ayerbe ....dep.
85	arr. Huesca ....dep.
..	dep.Ayerbe ....arr.
92	ar } Zuera .... { dp.
..	dp } { ar.
108	arr. **Saragossa**(Arrabel)dep.
327	arr. Valencia (below) dep.

Saragossa—Teruel—Valencia.

Mls.	
0	dep. **Saragossa**(Arrabel) arr
2	,, ,, (Delicias) arr.
33	dep. Carinena ...... dep.
52	arr. Caminreal .. .. dep.
117	arr. } **Teruel** .... { dep.
—	dep. } { arr.
203	arr. Sagunto .... dep.
219	arr. **Valencia** (Aragon) dep

Barcelona—Montserrat. 29½ miles

dp.Barcelona (Catal.)a.
ar. Montserrat dep.
d. Barcelona(Pl.Esp.)a.
ar. Montserrat ....dep.

The times on the LEFT are to be read DOWNWARDS, those on the RIGHT UPWARDS.

Lisbon, Oporto, Valenca (Vigo).

[Portug. Rlys.

1 2¶	1 2 3	1 2¶	1 2 3	1 2 3	Mls.		1 2¶	1 2 3	1 2¶	1 2 3	1 2 3
Rap		Rap		S			Rap		Rap		S
8r40	10 0	18r6	2050	2210	0	dp. **Lisbon** (Rocio) ar	1413	20 0	2357	6†6	7 50
9 45	12 9	1912	2244	2349	50	dp Santarem dp.	1257	1729	2243	4 10	5 58
10 9	1254	1937	2323	0 18	70	ar. **Entronca-** dp.	1231	1640	2217	3 25	5 22
1011	1330	1940	2350	0 43		dp. **mento** ar.	1226	1555	2210	3 3	5 12
1158	1619	2129	2 54	3 35	141	ar CoimbraJnc dp.	1037	1243	2024	2350	2 8
12 0	1631	2131	3 8	3 45		dp CoimbraJnc ar	1034	1233	2021	2340	2 0
1217	1730	2149	3 51	4 26	150	dp. Pampilhosa .. dp.	1021	1214	20 9	2319	1 41
14 4	2018	2340	8 0	7 17	214	ar. Campanha.... dp.	8 35	8 47	1823	19 8	2221
14r18	2029	2350	..	7 37	..	ar. **Oporto** .. dep.	8r25	8 35	18r10	..	22 0
								1 2 3	1 2 3		
1425	..	..	10 0	7 37	..	d. **Oporto** ......arr.	..	2341	1750	..	20 4
1437	..	..	10 8	7 54	..	dp.Campanha ar.	..	2330	1740	..	1950
1636	..	..	1222	1011	.	a. Vianna doCastello a.	..	1926	1529	..	17 0
1745	..	..	1347	1140	301	ar. Valenca........dp.	..	18 4	1422	..	1538
1815	..	..		1430		dp. Valenca........ar.	..	1730	1345	..	..
1846	..	..	..	15 6	306	ar. Guillarey...... dp.	..	17 0	13 9	..	..
1856	..	..	..	16 4		dp. Guillarey ..... ar.	..	..	1259	..	..
1958	..	..		1710	329	ar. **Vigo** ...... dp.	..	..	1155		..

¶ Train with Super-Tax
r Rest. Car Lisbon-Oporto and *v.v.*
S 1 & 2 cl. Slp. Car Lisbon–Oporto and *v.v.*
† Lisbon P. Station.

(Irun) Barca d'Alba-Oporto

Mls.	
..	dep. Irun (*p.* 321) .. arr.
..	dep. Medina (*p.* 322) arr.
..	arr. **Barca d'Alba** *c* dep.
0	dep. **Barca d'Alba** arr.
..	
37	arr. Tua..........dep
87	arr. Marco ......dep.
120	arr. Ermezinde ..dep.
..	dep. Ermezinde .. arr.
125	arr. Campanha ..dep.
129	arr. **Oporto** .. ..dep.

(Irun), Medina, Villar-Formoso, Lisbon, Estoril.

1 2 3	1 2	1 2 3	Mls.		1 2	1 2
	luxe				luxe	
	2135		..	dp. Irun .... } *p.*322 ar.	1040	..
..	5 56	5 40	..	dp. **Medina** .. } *p.*322 ar.	2 26	2055
..	7 41	1220	..	dp. Salamanca } *p.*322 ar.	0 41	1746
..	1140	1617	..	arr. **Villar-Formoso** *c* dep.	21 3	1320
	S				S	
	1210	17 0	0	dep. **Villar-Formoso** .. arr.	2047	1223
dep.						
7 50	..	1820	29	arr. Guarda ....dep.	..	1055
1041	..	2149	105	arr. Santa Comba ....dep.	..	6 29
1150	1543	2250	126	arr. Pampilhosa ....dep.	1655	5 0
1214	1548	2319		dep. Pampilhosa .... arr	1650	4 8
1555	..	3 3	204	a. Entroncamento (*abv.*) d.	..	0 43
20 0	1850	6 6	275	a. **Lisbon** (Rocio) (*abv.*) d	1355	2210
			291	a. Estoril d.	..	

S Sud Express, see page 85. Extra fares.

r Rest. Car.

Lisbon—Seville via Villa Real and Huelva.

(1 & 2 cl.)

Wed. and Sat.	9 20	dep.	Lisbon (Terreiro de Paco pier) Steamer	arr.	23 36
	9 58	arr.	Barreiro (other side of the Tagus)	dep.	22 55
	10 1	dep.	,, by train } Rest. Car.	arr.	22r54
	16r40	arr.	Villa Real de Sao Antonio } Rest. Car.	dep.	16r5
	1650	dep.	,, ,, By Motor Boat	arr.	15 0
	17 0	arr.	Ayamonte, by Motor Boat	dep.	14 50
	1730	dep.	,, by Motor Bus	arr.	14 0
	19 0	arr.	Huelva	dep.	12 15
	1910	dep.	Huelva	arr.	11 30
	2145	arr.	Seville, by Motor Bus	dep.	9 30

Thurs. and Sun.

The times on the LEFT are to be read DOWNWARDS, those on the RIGHT UPWARDS.

Cook's Tourist Map

of

SPAIN AND PORTUGAL

See Map, pages 25

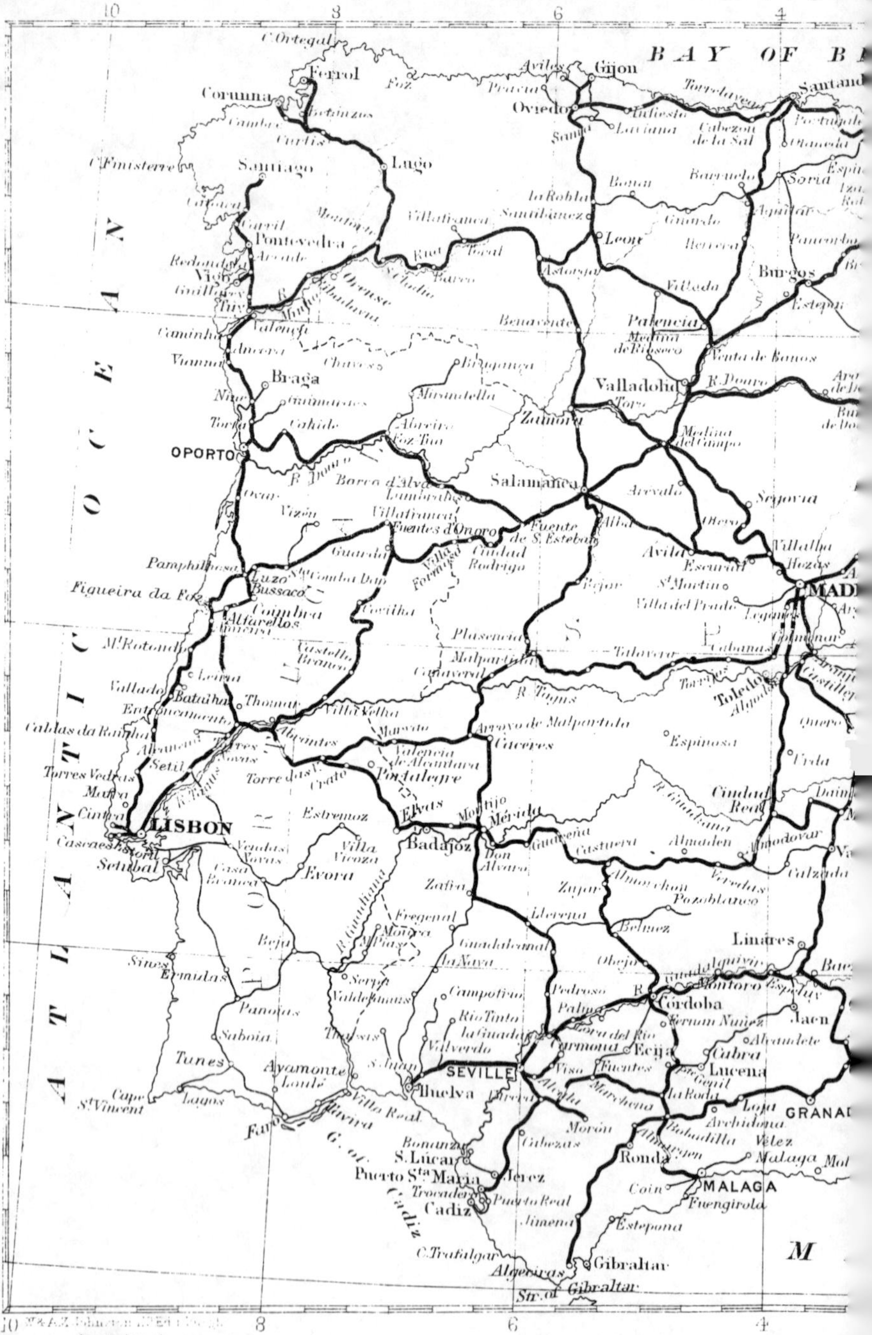

(219/1/39 J)

See Map, pages 338-339

Cook's Tourist Map

of

SPAIN AND PORTUGAL

Lisbon—Tunes (Faro)—Lagos.

1 2 A	1 2 3	1 2 3 W	1 2 3		1 2 3	1 2 3	1 2 B	1 2 3
9 20	9 20	1825	2115	dep. **Lisbon** (T. de Paco pier) steamer arr.	1225	1950	2336	7 40
10 1	10 6	19 7	22 0	dep. Barreiro (other side of Tagus) .. arr.	1143	19 7	2254	6 53
1014	1035	1929	2227	arr. Pinhal-Novo .... dep.	1121	1836	2240	6 26
1015	1040	1930	2230	dep. „ „ .... arr.	1120	1831	2239	6 21
..	1355	22 4	1 12	arr. Ermidas-Sado .... dep.	8 48	15 4	..	3 21
¶	14 0	22 9	1 14	dep. „ „ .... arr.	8 34	1459	¶	3 19
1325	1455	2254	2 0	arr. Funchiera .... dep.	7 50	14 5	1930	2 29
15 1	1849	..	4 55	arr. **Tunes** .... dep.	..		1751	2335
1548	1959		6 1[illegible]	arr. Faro .... dep.	..	..	17 6	2223
15§10	1917	..	5 15	dep. **Tunes** .... arr.	..	..	17§40	23 3
..	1924	..	5 25	arr. Algoz................ dep.	..	..	1733	2254
16 0	2018		6 41	arr. Portimao † .... dep.	..	..	1643	2145
16§26	2052	..	7 15	arr. **Lagos** .... dep.	..	..	15§58	21 0

A Weds. and Sats. only. **B** Thurs. and Sats only. **W** Weekdays only. § 1, 2 and 3 class.

¶ *Via* Casa Branca and Beja. † Motor Coach Services to Praia da Rocha.

MOTOR SERVICES IN SOUTHERN SPAIN.

La Linea (Gibraltar)—Malaga.

(Daily)

		dep. La Linea ...... arr.			
		arr. Malaga........ dep.			

Algeciras—Seville.

(Daily)

		dep. Algeciras arr.			
		arr. Seville dep.			

Algeciras—Cadiz.

(Daily)

		dep. Algeciras arr.			
		arr. Cadiz .... dep.			

Algeciras—Malaga.

(Daily).

		dep. Algeciras .. arr.			
		dep. San Roque .. arr.			
		arr. Marbella .... arr.			
		arr. Malaga .. dep.			

Granada—Malaga.

(Daily)

		dep. Granada ... arr.			
		arr. Malaga......dep.			

BALEARIC ISLANDS.

Palma—Arta (Felanitx), La Puebla.

Mls.	
0	dep. Palma .... arr.
9	arr. Santa Maria .... arr.
18	arr. Inca (for Pollensa) dp.
21¼	arr. Empalme........dep.
40	a. Manacor } for Porto dep.
..	d. Manacor } Cristo arr.
58¾	arr. Arta ....dep.
0	dep. Santa Maria arr.
36¼	arr. Felanitx ....dep.
0	dep. Empalme........ arr.
29½	arr. La Puebla (for Alcudia)......dep.

* Sundays and Holidays leave at 20.0.

Palma—Santany.

Mls.	
0	d. Palma ......ar.
34	a. Santany .... d.

† Thursdays only.

SOLLER RAILWAY.

1st & 2nd class. {Electric.

	Mls.
Palma ....dp.	0
Soller .... ar.	17
Soller ....dp.	0
Palma .... ar.	17

The times on the LEFT are to be read DOWNWARDS, those on the RIGHT UPWARDS.

ROUMANIA.

The trains run in Roumania according to East European time, which is two hours fast of normal Greenwich time, and one hour fast of Mid-European time.

Bucharest, Galatz, Iasi, Chisinau.

¶ *via* Tecuci. [Rouman. State Rys.

123 ExR	123	2 cl. A	123 Rap	123 Exp	123 Exp	123	12 P	123 Exp	123 Exp	123 Exp	123 Exp	123	R Rest Car / P Pullman Exp.
6 40	7 2	9 10	9 40	1343	1423	1635	1925	2110	2124	2245	0 3	0 10	d. **Bucharest** (N) a
7 43	8 32		1034	1446	1519	18 1	2021	2212	2225	2346	1 12	1 43	Ploesti Sud. d.
8 42	1015	1038	1127	1547	1613	1929	2117	2314	2326	0 46	2 17	3 21	arr. Buzau dep.
8 49	..	1040				1937	2120		..		..	3 28	dep. Buzau arr.
10 7	..	1145	Rest Car.	Rest. Car.	Rest. Car.	2149	2232	Sleep. Car.	..	Sleep. Car.	..	5 33	arr. Braila dep.
1055	..	1210				2250	2315		..		..	6 38	arr. **Galatz** dep.
	1024		1135	1554	1619			2320	2338	0 53	2 24		dep. Buzau arr.
	1233		1259	1731	..			..	1 11	..	3 58		,, Marasesci dep
	1612		15 8	20 6	¶	*via* Galatz	*via* Galatz	¶	3 40	¶	6 52	*via* Galatz	,, Roman .. ,,
	1719	..	1547	2048	..				4 23		7 47		arr. Pascani ,,
	1912	..	1912	0 26	2112			4 56	..	7 42	9 54	..	,, **Iasi** .. ,,
..	2252	..	2252	..	0 11	7 36	7 36	8 30	..	1218		16 0	,, Chisinau ,,
..	..	..		..		1128	1128	1128	..	1357	..	1735	,, Tighina (p230) d

R Rest Car / P Pullman Exp.	123 Exp	123	123 Exp	123 Exp	123	123 Exp	12 P	123	123 Exp	123 Rap	2 cl. A	123 ExR	123 Rap
d. **Bucharest** (N) a	6 0	6 33	6 56	7 25	8 55	9 5	9 52	1320	1615	2020	2030	2248	23 1
Ploesti Sud. d.	5 3	5 14	5 58	6 27	7 44	8 12	9 2	12 0	1525	1930	1948	2153	22 8
arr. Buzau dep.	3 53	3 4	4 45	5 17	6 10	7 6	8 1	1016	1425	1832	19 2	2046	21 4
dep. Buzau arr.		2 56			6 2		7 58	1012	..		19 0	2040	
arr. Braila dep.		0 40	Sleep Car.	Sleep. Car.	4 1	Rest. Car.	6 42	7 58		Rest. Car.	1755	1921	Rest. Car.
arr. **Galatz** dep.		2335			3 10		6 0	6 55			1730	1835	
dep. Buzau arr.	3 46		4 38	5 10		6 57		..	1415	1826			2057
,, Marasesci dep	2 7	..		..		5 34		..	1255	..			1936
,, Roman .. ,,	2315		¶	¶	*via* Galatz	3 9	Extra fares.		1048	¶	A Auto-Rapid.	*via* Galatz.	1710
arr. Pascani ,,	2217					2 26		.	10 6				1623
,, **Iasi** .. ,,	1852	..	2150	23 8		2332		.	8 2	1329			1353
,, Chisinau ,,	1415		..	1922	1810	1922	.	..	3 15	1050		9 25	8 50
,, Tighina (p230) d	1156			1737		1737	..	..		8 18		6 16	6 16

London, Paris, Vienna and Bucharest.

1 2	luxe 1 2	luxe 1 2	1 2			1 2	luxe 1 2	luxe 1 2	1 2
15 0	15 0	O	S	dep. LONDON	*see* p.128 a.	S	O	1620	1620
2120	2038	..	Mons., Wed. and Fri.	dep. Ostend	a.	..	..	1034	10 8
2246	2210	..		dep. BRUSSELS	a.	..	..	9 7	8 38
2 36	1 28	..		arr. COLOGNE	p. 188/9 dep.	..	..	5 26	4 19
6 46	4 34	..		dep. Frankfort	arr.	..	..	2 0	24 0
1510	11 4	..		dep. Passau	arr.	..	..	1923	15 8
1918	1520	..		arr. VIENNA (W.)	dep.	..	..	1514	1045
A	B	14 0	..	dep. LONDON	p. 112 arr	Sat., Mon. & Wed. from Bucharest.	1720	O	A
..	..	..	..	dep. Boulogne	arr		13 0	↑	↑
..	..	1725	..	dep. Calais	arr				
↓	↓	1955	..	dep. PARIS (Est.)	p. 274 arr		1012		
		2 11	..	dep. Strasbourg	arr		4 30		
		8 36	..	dep. Munich	arr.		2150		
↓	↓	1520	..	arr. VIENNA (W.)	dep.		1514		
1955	..	..	..	arr. VIENNA (E.)	dep.		..		6 42
..	↓	↓	1955	dep PARIS (Est) (*p*.336)	arr.	9 45	↑	..	..
..			14 0	dep London (*p*.123)	arr.	1720		..	..
..			2 48	dep Bale (*p* 269)	arr	2 54		..	..
..	↓	↓	9 0	dep Innsbruck (*p*.195)	arr.	2033		..	..
..	*	*	1715	arr. Vienna (W.)	dep.	1220	*	*	..
2350	1544	1544	17*28	dep. VIENNA (E.) *p*.200	arr	12*5	1429	1429	5 55
6 20	20 3	20 3	2120	arr. Budapest	d	8 15	1010	1010	2335
7 0	2034	2034	2355	dep. K.p.u. (East)	p.203 a.	6 26	9 41	9 41	22 5
1310	2 5	2 5	..	arr. Arad	dep	..	6 10	6 10	18 9
0 27	1230	1230	1955	arr. BUCHAREST	dep	13 5	1945	1945	6 55
..	17 5	17 5	..	arr. Constanza	dep	6 0	14 3	14 3	..

C Luxe Train Bucharest Ostend, Mn., W. & F.
S Arlberg-Orient Express, Sleeping Cars only, see pp. 123 and 124.
A 1 & 2 cl. Sleeping Car Ostend-Wurzburg and 1 & 2 cl. Car-Ostend-Vienna and *v.v.* daily. * Vienna (West).
B Luxe train from Ostend Tues. Th. and Sat. to Bucharest.
O Orient Exp. from Calais and Paris Tue., Thur. and Sat., from Constanza Mon., Wed. and Fri. See p. 84.

Bucharest—Belgrade

Roumania, and Yugo-Slavian Rys.

123	123			123	123	
10 5	1855	dep.	BUCHAREST (N)	¶	¶	¶ 1 and 2 cl. through cars Bucharest-Belgrade & *v.v.*
¶	¶		*p*. 331 arr.	2145	9 35	
14 6	0 23	,,	Craiova ,,	1740	4 27	
1922	6 50	arr.	Timisoara dep.	1222	22 0	
1950	7 35	dep.	Timisoara arr.	1132	2010	
2112	9 5	arr.	Stamora- (E.E.T.) dep.	10 8	1838	
2027	8 40	dep.	Moravicac (M.E.T.) arr.	8 29	1722	
2035	8 48	,,	Vatin dep.	8 21	1714	
2055	9 8	arr.	Vrsac dep.	8 1	1654	
2110	9 23	dep.	Vrsac arr.	7 34	1627	
22 8	1020	arr.	Alibunar dep.	6 39	1532	
2342	1155	arr.	BELGRADE dep.	4 53	1352	

(143 miles) Bucharest, Constanza

Roum. St. Ry.

123 R	123 Rap	123 Exp	12 P	123 S	¶ To Sept. 16th.	123	12 P	123 Exp	123 R	123 S
7 0	9 55	1340	1930	0 30	dp. **Bucharest** (N) a,	1213	9 50	1730	2324	5 45
..	..	A	..	1 5	,, ,, (Est.) ,,	1140		A	..	5 11
9 3	¶	1537	2120	4 47	,, Fetesti (*p*. 331) ,,	8 27	7 59	1534	2118	1 23
..	..	..	..	5 43	,, Saligny ....dep.	7 23	..	..	..	0 21
1040	1239	17 5	2246	7 4	arr. **Constanza** ,,	5 50	6 0	14 3	1927	2353
14†10	14†10	17†47			,, ,, (Port) ,,		..	13†5	15†30	..

A Limited train, seats must be reserved in advance.
R Rest. Car. **S** 1 & 2 cl. Sleep. Car. **P** 1 & 2 cl. Pullman Train.
† In connection steamer to and from Istanbul, *see page* 393.

The times on the LEFT are to be read DOWNWARDS, those on the RIGHT UPWARDS.

(Trieste)-Jimbolia-Bucharest.

[Roum. Rlys.

1 2 3	1 2 3	1 2 3	1 2 3	1 2 3	1 2 3	1 2	Mls.		1 2 3	1 2	1 2 3	1 2 3	1 2 3	1 2 3	1 2 3
		Exp	Exp		Exp	luxe				luxe	Exp	Exp		Exp	
	..	..	0 30	..	R	18 0	..	dep. Trieste .... arr.	..	1145	R	5 20	..	..	..
..	..	..	8 0	..	13 0	0 30	..	,, Zagreb .... ,,	..	5 25	1625	2150	..	..	..
..	..	..	1252		18 5	4 50	..	,, Vinkovci (p. 332A) .. ,,	..	0 54	1118	1629	..	..	
		..	1926		2 12	10 6	..	arr. Jimbolia ....M.E.T. dep.	..	1937	2 45	7 54	..	..	
	..	..	2050		4 40	1128	0	dep. Jimbolia......E.E.T. arr.		2015	2 30	8 34	1930	..	
	1350	..	22 0	..	7 55	1227	15	,, Timisoara .... ,,	..	1922	2310	6 50	1520		
..	20 0	..	1 54		11 4	1521	132	,, Orsova ....dep.	..	1618	1958	3 1	9 27	..	
..	2017	..	SR	..	..	..	135	,, Verciorova .... ,,	..	..	..	SR	9 12	arr.	
..	21 0	0 50	2 28	..	1132	1549	147	,, Turn Severin ...... ,,		1554	1934	2 34	8 49	6 7	..
	0 18	3 3	4 32	14 3	1328	1745	217	,, Craiova .... arr	1150	14 1	1738	0 16	5 14	3 39	
2258	1 40	4 0	5 29	1513	1426	1829	245	,, Piatra-Olt (*below*).... ,,	1053	1316	1650	2323	3 46	2 39	6 26
1 30	4 4	5 37	7 5	1719	1558	1954	293	,, Costesti ....dep.	9 13	1154	1525	2152	1 31	1 15	4 11
2 32	4 52	6 8	7 42	18 8	1627	2023	306	,, Pitesti .... ,,	8 42	1132	14 2	2123	0 38	0 53	3 16
5 45	7 30	8 3	9 35	21 0	1755	2145	374	arr. Bucharest (Nord) ....dep.	6 30	10 5	1327	1855	2130	2238	0 17

R Rest. Car

S Sleep. Car Bucharest to Timisoara and *v.v.*

Bucharest-Predeal-Lokoshaza (Budapest).

	1 2 3	1 2 3	1 2 3	1 2	1 2 3	1 2 3	1 2 3	† West Station. ‖ Kronstadt.	1 2 3	1 2 3	1 2 3	1 2 3	1 2	1 2 3	1 2 3
	Exp	ExR	RaR	luxe	Exp	Exp	S	R Rest. Car.	Ex.s	Exp	Ex s	Rap	luxe	Exp	Exp
	6 55	8 20	13 5	1945	1955	2050	2335	dep. Bucharest (Nord) .... arr.	0 27	8 10	9 24	1015	1230	1955	2358
	..		*	..	21 9	SR	0 46	,, Ploesti (Sud) .... dep.	..	7 12	8 15	SR	..	*	..
	7 50	9 25	14 2	2037	S	2157	..	,, Ploesti (West) ...... ,,	2336	..	..	9 22	1140	19 3	23 0
	9 56	1150	1621	2240	2347	0 40	3 12	,, Predeal .... ,,	22 8	4 49	6 5	7 15	9 58	17 3	2035
	1013	1243	1712	2323	0 35	1 30	4 6	,, Brasso‖ .... ,,	2114	3 53	5 8	6 21	9 2	16 7	1936
	..	17 8	2110	..	4 49		8 48	arr. Teius .... ,,	..	2254	0 19	..	..	1139	1440
	1759	↓	↓	6 8	..	9 48	..	,, Arad................ ,,	1316	↑		2123	2 7	↑	..
	1855			6 41	..	1059	..	dep. Curtici .... ,,	1233			2051	1 50		
	19 6	↓	↓	6 52	R	1110		arr. Lokoshaza .. E.E.T. dep	1214	↑	R	2013	1 24	↑	R
	22 5			9†41	..	1450		arr. Budapest (p. 203).... dep.	7 80	..	..	1445	20†34	R	..
	..	1710	2119	Mon., Wed and Fri	5 0		8 58	dep. Teius .... arr.		2243	0 10	..		1129	1430
	..	1948	2353		7 36	..	1135	,, Cluj (Klausenburg) .. dep.		1958	2126			8 46	1145
	..	2251	2 0		1036		1415	arr. Oradea dep.	..	1636	18 5	..		6 9	8 19
	..	..	2 7		1051	Sleep. Car	..	dep. (Grosswardein) arr.	..	1626	..		..	6 2	..
	..	..	3 3		1143		..	arr. Biharker- E.E.T. dep.	..	1540	..	..	..	5 5	..
	..	..	2 27		1113		..	dep. esztes M.E.T. arr.	..	1432	..	..	..	3 45	..
	..	..	6 26		1750		..	arr. Budapest (East)......dep.	..	7 48	..	..	..	2355	..

S 1, 2 & 3 cl Slp. Car Bucharest-Budapest and *v.v.* * Arlberg Exp. 1 & 2 cl. Sleepers to and from Paris 3 times weekly: *see p.* 83 *s* Sleep Car, 1 and 2 cl. Bucharest to Praha and *v.v.*

Buzau—Constanza.

1 2 3	1 2 3	1 2 3		1 2 3	1 2 3	1 2 3
	¶				¶	
8 6	1455	2120	dp. Buzau (p.204) ar.		9 43	2115
9 26	1532	22 0	dp. Faurei ....arr.	4 8	8 49	20 1
1135	1745	0 17	ar. Fetesci ......dp.	1 56	6 44	1757
14 5	1930	..	ar. Constanza ..dp.	2253	4 45	1540
14†10	20†0		ar. ,, (Port) dp.	..	..	15†30

¶ To Sept. 15.

Bucharest-Caineni-Sibiu.

1 2 3	1 2 3	1 2 3	1 2 3		1 2 3	1 2 3	2 3	1 2 3
								Exp
2353	10 5	1327	0 17	d. Bucharest ..a.	1755	2145	5 45	6 10
4 34	1321	17 5	6 38	,, Piatra-Olt(*ab*),,	1414	1642	2244	0 49
6 30	15 2	1913	8 58	,, Raureni ....,,	1155	1459	2035	23 6
8 13	1632	21 7	1040	d. Caineni......d.	10 1	1324	1853	2134
9 27	18 0	2240	1220	a. Sibiu ....,,	8 25	12 3	1715	2025

Bucharest, Giurgiu, Sofia.

Roum. St. Rly.

6 40	1340	dp Bucharest (N) a.	1535	2115
7 55	1453	Comana dep.	1424	20 0
8 45	1543	arr. Giurgiu	1325	1858
8 58	16 0	ar. Giurgiu (Port) d.	1225	1845
9 45	1630	dp. Giuriu (Str.) a.	1045	1815
10 0	1645	a. Rousse (Str) d.	1025	18 0
1130	1850	dp. Rousse arr.	9 45	1730
2050	7 42	ar. Sofia (p. 332B) dp.	22 5	8 35

Bucharest-Cernauti-Warsaw (Praha)—Vienna.

1 2 3	1 2 3	1 2 3	1 2 3	Mls.		1 2 3	1 2 3	1 2 3	1 2 3
Rap	ExZ	Ex¶	S			Ex *r*	ExS	Ex¶	RaZ
9*r*40	1348	2124	0 3	0	dep. Bucharest N. (p. 330) arr.	23 1	6 0	9 5	16*r*15
1135	1554	2338	2 24	80	,, Buzeu .... ,,	2057	3 46	6 57	1415
1554	2055	4 30	7 57	242	,, Pascani (p. 204) ....dep.	1623	2217	2 26	10 6
1840	0 27	7 55	13 6	337	,, Cernauti .... ,,	1312	1835	2316	7 16
19 0	0 50	8 20	1351	352	a. Oraseni.. E.E.T. ,,	1150	1753	2243	6*r*45
1840	0 20	8 5	14 0		d. Oraseni.. *c* M.E.T. a.	..	13 7	21 5	5 5
2252	5 40	1227	21 0	508	arr. Lwow .... dep.	..	7 20	17 6	0 20
2325	..	1520	..		dep. Lwow .... arr.	..	7 0	..	2343
7 42	.	2254	..	837	arr. Warsaw (p. 227)....dep.	..	2252	..	1544
2345	6 15	16 0		..	dep. Lwow .... arr.	..	..	1355	24 0
9 8	1510	0 30	..	..	arr. Bogumin ....dep.	..	..	5 47	1620
..	1644	2 51	..	..	,, Prerov (p. 203) .... ,,	..	..	3 18	1332
..	2119	6 53	..	..	,, Praha (Wil. Stn.) .. ,,	..	..	23 3	9 15
	2033	6 31	.	..	,, Vienna (East), p. 203 ,,	..	..	2320	9 50

S 1 & 2 cl. Sleeping Car Bucharest Cernauti and *v.v.*
Z 1 & 2 cl. Sleep. Cars daily Bucharest to Berlin and Ostend and *v.v.*, *see page* 204. † Nord Stn.

r Rest. Car Bucharest to Oraseni and *v v.* ¶ 1 & 2 Sleep. Car to Berlin, Rest. Car to Marasesci and *v.v.*

The times on the LEFT are to be read DOWNWARDS, those on the RIGHT UPWARDS.

The trains run in Yugo-Slavia according to Mid-European time which is one hour fast of Greenwich (West-European time). In Bulgaria the time is East-European, which is one hour fast of Mid-European and two hours fast of Greenwich.

Trieste, Belgrade, Nisch, Sofia, Edirne, Istanbul.

(Yugo Slav, Bulg. and Turkish State Railways).

2 3	1 2	1 2 3	1 2 3	1 2 3	1 2 3	1 2 3	1 2 3	Mls.		1 2 3	1 2 3	1 2 3	1 2 3	1 2	1 2 3	1 2 3
	luxe	A		Exp			S				A	Exp		luxe	S	
..	2220	2255	..	..	..	..	1620	0	dep. PARIS (p. 119/120) .... arr.	..	7 0	7 0	..	8 40	14 0	..
..	1840	0 30	..	..	..	..	1520	790	dep. TRIESTE .... arr.	..	5 20	5 20	..	1145	1329	2010
..	2029	2 54	..	..	..	..	1734	841	arr. Rakek .... dep.	..	3 0	3 0	..	9 46	1120	18 6
	O	1 2 3					B		[Yugo Slavia Railways.]		A			O	B	
..	2047	3 24	..		..	..	1756	846	dep. Rakek .... arr.	..	0 41	2 38	15 4	9 31	11 3	1756
..	2152	4 46	..	9 20	..	..	20 0	878	dep. Ljubljana .... arr.	..	2016	1 15	1322	8 17	9 23	1642
..	23 0	6 2	..	1031	..	..	2111	898	dep. Zidani Most .... arr.	..	19 4	2358	1055	7 6	8 12	14 3
..	0 20	7 3	..	12 0	..	..	2240	942	arr. } Zagreb .... { dep.	..	1740	2225	9 0	5 40	6 50	1250
..	0 30	8 0	8 20	1255	1835	2220	2316		dep. } Zagreb { arr.	1930	1625	2150	7 45	5 25	6 25	1140
..	..	9 18	1026	1414	2036	2355	..	987	dep. Sunja .... dep.	1724	15 8	2035	5 47	..	..	9 58
..	3 32	1133	1342	1635	2351	4 5	2 26	1069	arr. } Brod .... { dep.	1344	1247	1818	1 29	2 22	3 4	5 58
..	3 40	1141	1359	1643	0 9	4 22	2 34		dep. } Brod { arr.	1327	1239	1810	1 11	2 14	2 56	5 40
..	4 49	1249	1550	1748	1 41	6 23	3 19	1110	,, Vinkovci .... dep.	1151	1143	1714	2345	1 19	2 0	3 47
..	7 18	1517	20 5	2015	6 8	1025	6 20	1218	arr. Belgrade .... dep.	7 19	9 2	1423	1910	2220	2312	2333
2355	7 45	2330	22 0	2330	..	11 0	7 55		dep. Belgrade .... arr.	5 0	6 15	1334	1855	2149	2240	7 40
4 11	9 25	1 45	1 17	1 45	..	1344	9 51	1281	Lapovo	1 43	3 55	1032	16 6	..	2037	4 48
5 13	10 6	2 31	2 20	2 31	..	1440	1036	1305	Cuprija	0 29	2 56	9 10	15 9	1923	1956	3 53
6 51	..	3 51	4 31	3 51	..	16 9	1147	1349	Aleksinac	2238	1 26	7 27	1333	1815	1837	2 13
7 37	1130	4 22	5 20	4 22	..	1646	1215	1364	arr. } Nisch to Salon. { dep.	2150	0 53	6 37	1254	1748	18 9	1 35
1250	1140	4 40	6 0	..	.	..	1739		dep. } (p. 332A) .... { arr.	2112	0 32	5 41	12 5	1733	1715	..
1447	13 2	6 16	8 59	..	.	..	1937	1410	Pirot..	1815	23 8	3 55	1019	1616	1522	..
1525	1330	6 47	10 1	..			2015	1425	arr. Tzaribrod c	1620	2240	3 14	9 40	1550	1448	..
		R		Exp		Exp	1 2 3		[Bulgarian State Rly.]		R	Exp				Exp
1652	1447	8 20	..	1 2 3	..	1 2 3	2152		dep. Tzaribrod (E.E.ter.) arr.	..	2242	1 2 3	9 40	1620	1446	1 2 3
19 8	1628	1040	..	..	..	..	2332	1464	arr. } Sofia .... { dep.	..	2025	..	7 32	1441	1242	..
..	1642	12 0	..	2058	..	8 35	2355		dep. } Sofia { arr.	..	1745	6 40	5 10	1358		2115
..	1741	..	..	.		9 38	1 44	1490	Vakarel	..	17 0	6 7	4 53	1322	..	..
..	..		..		..	..	3 51	1529	Bellovo	..	15 7	4 31	2 2	..	..	1848
..	19 5	1445	..	2335	..	11 6	4 20	1535	dep. Saranevo .... arr.	..	1447	4 8	1 35	11 2	..	1831
..	.	15 7	..	2357		1126	4 56	1537	Pazardjik	..	1420	3 43	0 55	..	..	18 4
..	1957	1550		0 35	..	12 6	6 0	1550	arr. } Plovdiv { dep.	..	1330	3 2	2348	10 4		1712
..	20 8	16 4	..		..	..	8 25		dep. } (Phillippopolis) { arr.	..	1318		2130	9 52	..	..
..	..	1840	..			..	1122		Zlatidol	..	1048		1846	..		..
..	..	19 0	..		..	..	1146	1628	dep. Harmanli .... dep.	..	1026		1819	..	..	..
..	2257	1934	..			..	1222	1651	arr. Svilengrade .... dep.	..	9 50		1740	6 50		
									[Greek Railways.]							
..	2310	1955	..	To Burgaz with 1, 2 & 3 cl. Slp. Car.	.		..	1651	dep. Svilengrade (p. 333) c arr.	..	9 13	From Burgaz with 1 & 2 cl. Sleep. Car.	..	6 20	..	From Burgas.
..	0 4	2111	..		.	To Burgas.	..	1674	Edirne .... arr.	..	7 52		..	5 27	..	
..	0 52	2320	..		..		..	1696	arr. Pythion .... dep.	..	6 43		..	4 40	..	
									[Turkish Railways]							
..	1 0	2240	..		..		..	1696	dep. Pythion .... arr.	..	6 13		..	4 33	..	
..	7 20	6 40	..					1872	arr. Istanbul .... dep.	..	2235		..	22 0		

A 1 & 2 cl. Sleep. Cars Paris-Milan and *v.v.*, also Belgrade-Istanbul and *v.v.* daily. 1, 2 & 3 cl. cars Paris Istanbul and *v.a.* **B** 1 & 2 cl. Sleep. Car daily Ljubljana-Belgrade and *vice versa*.
O Simplon-Orient Exp. for days of running see page 83. **R** Rest. Car.
S 1 and 2 cl. Sleep. Car, Paris-Venice and *v.v.* daily. 3 cl. Car Paris-Belgrade and 1 & 2 cl. Car Milan-Belgrade-Sofia and *v.v.*

Belgrade—Sarajevo—Dubrovnik.

[Yugo Slav. Rly

Exp M	2 3	1 2 3	Exp 1 2 3	2 3	Mls.		1 2 3	Exp M	Exp 1 2 3	2 3
7 35	..	8 32	17 8	23 1	0	dep. Belgrade....arr.	2045	2217	[illegible] 27	1420
1112	1010	1427	2232	5 7	105	,, Cacak......dep.	15 2	1844	2 32	8 36
1236	1254	164[illegible]	0 28	7 29	147	,, Uzice...... ,,	1240	1718	0 3[illegible]	6 16
1645	1915	2315	6 14	1350	277	arr. Sarajevo .. ,,	6 18	13 5	18 [illegible]	0 5
M ¶	1 2 3		2 3				1 2 3	M ¶	2 3	1 2 3
17 0	1925	2350	7 44	..	.	dep Sarajevo .. arr.	5 35	1250	17 5	2320
2030	0 29	4 43	1313	..	374	arr. Mostar .... dep	0 30	9 18	1123	1738
24 0	5 45	9 40	1845	..	472	arr. Dubrovnik dep.	1945	5 46	6 0	12 5

¶ Sarajevo-Dubrovnik and *v.v.* June 15th to Sept. 15th only. See route *via* Brod, page 332B.
M 1 & 2 cl. Motor Train; Buffet Car; Limited accommodation; Extra fares.

The times on the LEFT are to be read DOWNWARDS, those on the RIGHT UPWARDS.

(Budapest) Kelebia—Belgrade—Nisch—Thessaloniki. [Yugoslav Rlys.

1 2 3	1 2 3	1 2 3	1 2 3	2 3	1 2 3	1 2 3	Mls.		Station	1 2 3	1 2 3	1 2 3	1 2 3	1 2 3	1 2 3	1 2 3	1 2 3
fast	ExA				Exp					fast			Exp				ExA
..	2348	..	..	8 2	1435	..	0	dep.	Budapest(E), *p*.200 a.	..	..	..	1456	1†15	..	..	6 2
..	3 16	..	..	1131	1736	..	102	dep.	Kelebia *c*.. .. dep.	..	..	..	1216		..	..	3 1
2344	3 55	4 8	7 46	1312	1822	1842	108	dep.	Subotica *c*.... arr.	6 59	1246	..	1115		1941	0 12	2 4
2 9	5 23	6 30	1022	1537	1955	21 6	172	arr.	Novi Sad...... dep.	4 7	9 49	..	9 40		17 9	2156	0 30
4 37	6 59	8 46	1222	1744	2133	2320	216	arr.	Zemun (Semlin) dep	0 20	6 2	..	8 10		1511	1953	23 0
4 48	7 8	8 55	1237	1753	2142	2329	219	arr.	Belgrade...... dep.	0 10	5 51	—	8 0		15 1	1942	2250
..	7 55	11 0	..	19 5	2330		..	dep.	Belgrade ..... arr.	..	5 0	7 40	6 15		1334	1855	2240
..	1224	17 1	..	1 14	4 50		374	dep.	Nisch .... dep.	..	2150	1 35	0 53		0 37	1254	18 9
..	1310	1810	..	2 18	5 42		402	dep.	Leskovac ..... dep.	..	..	2324	2355		..	1135	1649
..	..	20 6	..	4 12	7 30		451	dep.	Ristovac ..... dep.	..	..	2126	2213		..	9 37	..
..	1626	2219	..	6 20	9 21		095	arr.	Skoplje (Uskub) dep.	..	..	19 0	2010		..	7 10	1322
..	1642	2330	†..	6†45	9 50		..	dep.	Skoplje (Uskub) arr.	..	..	18†18	1947		..	4†50	1258
..	1746	1 2	..	7†58	11 6		542	arr.	Veles (*p*. 337) . dep.	..	..	17†1	1831		..	3 12	1152
..	..	2 7	..	..	1149		557	dep.	Gradsko ......dep.	..	..	..	1749		..	2 10	..
..	19 7	3 37	..	..	13 0		584	dep.	Demir Kapija ..dep.	..	..	..	1630		..	0 30	1019
..	20 0	5†1	..	..	14 6		612	arr.	Devdelija *c* ..dep.	..	..	..	1519		..	23†0	9 20
..	2120	6 25	..	..	16 0		..	dep.	Guevgheli *c*.....arr.	..	..	..	1525		..	2154	9 59
..	2255	9 8	..	..	1853		662	arr.	THESSALONIKI ..dep.	..	..	..	1253		..	19 3	8 20
..	1026	2329	..	..	..		980	arr.	Athens (*p*. 336) dep.	..	..	..	..		..	..	2045

A Sleep Car, 1 & 2 cl. Budapest-Athens and *v.v.*

† 2 and 3 class only.

Jesenice—Ljubljana—Zagreb (Belgrade). [Yugoslav Rlys.

2 3	1 2 3	2 3	2 3	2 3	1 2 3	2 3	Mls.		Station	1 2 3	1 2 3	1 2 3	2 3	2 3	2 3	1 2 3	2 3
	Exp				Exp	Exp					Exp	Exp				Exp	
5 40	7 45	1025	1422	1615	1825	10 8	0	dep.	Jesenice (*p*.199) arr.	9 10	9 22	1110	1345	1746	2142	2215	1 38
6 1	8 2	1050	1444	1634	1842	2027	8	arr.	Lesce Bled .....dep.	8 45	9 3	1051	1321	1722	2117	2155	1 13
7 30	9 5	1213	16 3	1758	1942	2133	40	arr.	Ljubljana .....dep.	7 5	7 50	9 40	1143	1540	1915	2038	2340
7 52	9 20	1340	..	1827	20 0	22 0		dep.	Ljubljana .....arr..	..	7 40	9 23	..	1322	1812	2016	2154
12 0	12 0	1657	..	22 5	2240	0 40	129	arr.	Zagreb (*p*. 332) dep.	..	4 45	6 50	..	9 0	1250	1740	1750
..	2015	6 8	..	..	6 20	8 40	400	arr.	Belgrade (*p*. 332) dp.	..	2058	2312	..	..	2333	9 2	..

Piedicolle—Bled—Jesenice. [Yugoslav Rlys.

2 3	2 3	1 2 3	2 3	2 3	2 3	1 2 3	Mls.		Station	2 3	1 2 3	2 3	2 3	2 3	2 3	1 2 3	2 3
		Exp				Exp					Exp						
..	..	1018	12 0	..	1610	22 0	..	dep.	Piedicolle *c* ......arr.	..	8 3	11 1	..	1531	..	19 6	..
4 40	6 55	1035	1244	1515	1713	2215	5	dep.	Bistrica *c*........arr.	6 45	7 46	1018	1226	1459	17 4	1854	23 7
5 7	7 23	11 1	1315	1543	1745	2241	20	arr.	Bled-Jezero .....dep.	6 20	7 22	9 52	12 9	1433	1638	1829	2242
5 25	7 40	1116	1335	16 0	18 5	2256	25	arr.	Jesenice *abv*. ....dep.	6 5	7 5	9 37	1145	1418	1623	1815	2220

Kotoriba—Pragersko—Rakek. [Yugoslav Rlys.

1 2 3	2 3	2 3	2 3	1 2 3	2 3	2 3	Mls.		Station	1 2 3	2 3	2 3	2 3	1 2 3	2 3	2 3
Exp				Exp						Exp				Exp		
1 17	1 34	5 42	9 35	1213	1515	17 8	0	dep.	Kotoriba (*p*. 201)arr.	4 47	8 43	..	1427	1744	1930	0 20
2 58	5 18	8 13	1328	1357	1752	2110	57	arr.	Pragersko .....dep.	3 8	6 5	..	1212	1558	1656	2149
3 20	5 41	9 47	1450	1412	1831	2129		dep.	Pragersko...... arr.	2 52	4 35	8 42	1113	1546	1646	2141
4 7	6 48	1052	1551	15 0	1935	2229	87	arr.	Celje ....dep.	2 5	3 26	7 39	10 9	1457	1542	2037
4 37	7 27	1131	1627	1531	2012	2335	102	arr.	Zidani Most....dep.	1 37	2 40	7 2	9 33	1426	15 6	20 0
5 48	9 2	1322	1812	1642	2154	1 15	142	arr.	Ljubljana .....dep.	0 21	0 45	5 30	7 52	1311	1340	1827
6 58	11 3	15 4	1950	1756	0 41	2 38	174	arr.	Rakek (*p*. 201)..dep.	2320	..	3 24	5 50	12 8	1217	..
9 4	1329	1853	..	2010	..	5 20		arr.	Trieste ....dep.	21 3	..	0 30	..	9 37	..	..

Vinkovci—Subotica—Jimbolia. [Yugoslav Rlys.

1 2 3	1 2 3	1 2 3	1 2 3	1 2 3		Station	2 3	1 2 3	1 2 3	1 2 3	1 2 3	1 2 3
	Exp											Exp
3 37	4 50	7 40	1252	18 5	dep.	Vinkovci (*p*.332) arr.	6 10	1118	1529	1629	2325	0 54
5 35	6 8	9 33	1441	20 5	dep.	Sombor ....dep.	4 12	9 32	1222	1438	2140	2339
7 2	7 13	11 1	16 3	2132	arr.	Subotica (*p*. 200)dep.	2 7	7 55	9 41	13 8	20 6	2242
2 3		2 3					2 3				2 3	
7 50	7 23	1250	1615	2153	dep.	Subotica ......arr.	1 55	6 55	..	1122	18 5	2228
8 55	8 9	1355	1714	23 2	dep.	Senta..........dep.	0 59	5 52	..	1019	17 2	2139
1031	..	1520	1824	0 30	dep.	Dragutinovo ...dep.	2350	4 42	..	9 11	1527	..
1058	9 28	1545	1846	1 1	arr.	Velika Kikinda *c* dep	2314	3 43	..	8 38	1425	2017
..	10 6	..	1926	2 12	arr.	Jimbolia *c* (*p*. 331) dp	..	2 45	..	7 54	..	1937

Vienna (Praha) Zagreb—Split. [Yugoslav Rlys.

1 2 3	1 2 3	1 2 3	1 2 3	1 2 3	Mls.			1 2 3	1 2 3	1 2 3	1 2 3	1 2 3
Exp	Exp	A	Exp					Exp	Exp		Exp	A
..	2120	8 0	9†30	..	0	dep.	Vienna (Sud) (*p.* 200) ..arr.	8 50	..	2210	..	2135
..	2 21	1316	1640	†..	195	arr.	Maribor *c* ....dep.	3 46	..	13†0	..	1632
..	B	2216	..	..		dep.	Praha (*p.* 196) ......arr.	B	..	..	..	6 20
..	2 48	1343	1758	†..	0	dep.	Maribor *c.* ....arr.	3 20	..	1144	†..	16 8
..	7 30	1710	22 5	†..	106	arr.	Zagreb ....dep.	2225	..	6†50	..	1240
6 37	8 50	1950	23 5	2330	..	dep.	Zagreb ....arr.	2025	2213	5 20	6 15	1120
8 51	1125	2218	1 1	2 18	171	dep.	Ostarije ....dep.	1743	2011	2 44	4 26	8 50
1243	1537	2 38	4 44	8 0	267	dep.	Gracac ....dep.	1349	1618	21 1	0 49	4 45
1549	1834	5 40	7 38	1141	341	arr.	Perkovic-Slivno ......dep.	1028	13 0	1639	2124	1 7
1732	1935	6 43	8 40	1247	355	arr.	Sibenik..............dep.	9 20	1024	15 7	2029	2338
1559	1840	5 46	7 46	1147	..	dep.	Perkovic-Slivno ......arr.	1022	1254	1629	2118	1 1
1725	20 5	7 10	9 5	1324	371	arr.	Split ....dep.	8 47	1120	1438	1950	2330

† 2 and 3 cl. only.

A Through 1, 2 and 3 cl. cars Vienna—Split, and 2 and 3 cl. Praha-Split and *v.v.*
B Sleep. Car, 1 & 2 cl. Vienna-Zagreb and *v.v.*

Zagreb (Belgrade) Brod—Sarajevo (Metkovic) Dubrovnik. [Yugoslav Rlys.

1 2 3	2 3		M	2 3	1 2 3	Mls.			1 2 3	M	2 3	2 3	1 2 3	
Exp		To Sept. 15.											Exp	To Sept. 15.
2310	2220		8 0	8 20	1255	0	dep.	Zagreb ......arr.	1517	1517	2150	7 45	6 25	
2 56	4 5		1133	1342	1635	127	arr.	Brod ....dep.	1247	1247	1818	1 29	3 4	
2312	2333		9 2	7 19	1423	0	dep.	Belgrade ......arr.	1517	1517	2015	6 8	6 20	
2 56	5 40		1239	1327	1810	140	arr.	Brod ....dep.	1141	1141	1643	0 9	2 34	
3 16	6 36		1250	1352	1917	0	dep.	Brod ....arr.	1042	1135	1638	2352	2 17	
6 21	1010		1452	1721	2256	59	dep.	Doboj ....dep.	7 20	9 34	1336	2048	2321	
10 6	1430		1728	2129	2 54	135	arr.	Lasva ....dep.	2 32	6 57	9 29	1638	1927	
12 3	1655		1840	2327	5 14	174	arr.	Sarajevo......dep.	0 17	5 45	7 7	1427	1730	
		M		1 2 3						1 2 3				M
1435	1923	17 0	..	2350	7 44	..	dep.	Sarajevo ......arr.	2320	5 35	..	1210	17 5	1250
20 0	0 29	2030	..	4 43	1313	271	arr.	Mostar ......dep.	1738	0 30	..	6 18	1123	9 18
..	1 53	2124	..	5 59	1449	294	arr.	Gabela ......dep.	1611	2311	..	..	9 46	8 24
..	2 21	2220	..	6 18	15 6	297	dep.	Metkovic ..dep.	1549	2250	..	..	9 20	7 54
..	2 0	2125	..	6 9	1452	..	dep.	Gabela ......arr.	16 1	23 9	..	..	9 42	8 23
..	4 31	2317	..	8 32	1738	348	arr.	Hum ....dep.	1322	2050	..	..	7 2	6 29
..	4 56	2332	..	8 57	18 3	354	arr.	Uskoplje......dep.	1253	2027	..	..	6 40	6 14
..	5 45	24 0	..	9 40	1845	369	arr.	Dubrovnik....dep.	12 5	1945	..	..	6 0	5 46
..	5 10	..	..	9 8	1822	..	dep.	Uskopje ......ped.	1239	2014	..	..	..	..
..	7 47	..	..	1134	21 8	401	arr.	Hercegnovi ..dep.	9 59	1750	..	..	..	..
..	8 15	..	..	12 0	2125	403	arr.	Zelenika ......arr.	9 30	1725	..	..	..	..

For services Belgrade to Dubrovnik via Cacak and Sarajevo, *see page* 332.

M 1 & 2 cl. Limited Motor Train; Extra Fares.

Gyekenyes—Zagreb—Susak. [Yugoslav Rlys.

1 2 3	1 2 3	1 2 3	1 2 3			1 2 3	1 2 3	1 2 3	1 2 3
Exp		Exp	Exp			Exp		Exp	Exp
4 1	7 24	1453	1955	dp.	Gyekenyes (*p.* 201) arr.	1452	2213	0 50	9 54
6 12	1050	17 0	2210	arr.	Zagreb dep.	1245	19 0	2242	7 46
8 10	1235	1730	0 0	dep.	Zagreb arr.	1220	1635	2135	4 40
..	1531	..	2 47	dep.	Ostarije dp.	..	1345	..	1 56
1018	1542	1935	3 0	dep.	Ogulin dep.	1019	1336	1934	1 42
1316	1912	2230	6 45	arr.	Skrljevo dp	7 7	9 26	1618	2154
1412	1953	2316	7 38	arr.	Bakar dep.	5 52	8 17	15 1	2041
1340	1952	2255	7 37	arr.	Fiume dep.	6 21	8 22	1539	2047
1318	1915	2232	7 0	dep.	Skrljevo ar.	6 59	9 16	1559	2139
1336	1945	2250	7 30	arr.	Susak dep.	6 30	8 32	1530	2057

Sofia—Plovdiv—Yambol—Burgaz. [Bulgarian Rlys.

2 3	1 2 3	123*s*			1 2 3	1 2 3	123*s*
	Exp	Exp			Exp		Exp
2355	8 35	2058	dp.	Sofia (*p* 332) a	2115	6 10	6 40
7 10	1222	0 51	dp.	Plovdiv . . ar.	17 0	2315	2 50
11 1	1530	3 56	dp.	Nova-Zagora	1348	1849	2347
12 0	1622	4 48	ar.	Yambol dp.	1254	1746	2253
12 8	1630	4 56	dp.	Yambol . . ar.	1246	1736	2245
15 0	1852	7 32	ar.	Burgaz (Pt) d.	1010	1418	20 0

s 1, 2 & 3 cl. Slp. Car Sofia-Burgaz and *v.v.*

Sofia—Varna (Bucharest). [Bulgarian Rlys.

Ex *r*		Ex **S**	Exp	¶				Ex *r*	¶	Ex **S**	Exp	
8 35	1410	20 0	21‡5	22 5	dep.	SOFIA	arr.	2050	7 42	8 15	9 36	1520
1240	1936	0 6	1 7	3 8	dep.	Pleven	arr.	1637	2 19	4 2	5 19	9 31
1435	2237	2 1	3 9	6 10	ar.	Gornia-Orehovitza	dp.	1442	2311	2 5	3 24	6 30
1453	23 5	2 18	3 26	6 35	dp.	Gornia-Orehovitza	ar.	1424	2251	1 48	3 6	6 5
1839	4 34	5 54	7 2	1119	dp.	Kaspichan	dep.	1051	18 8	2225	2342	1 14
20 8	6 50	7 25	8 28	1332	arr.	VARNA	dep.	9 14	1550	2050	22‡10	2240
1456	..	2 25	..	6 28	dp.	Gornia-Orehovitza	arr.	1423	2241	1 43	..	..
1730	..	5 15	..	9 52	arr.	Rousse	dep.	1150	1910	2255	..	..
2115	..	..	..	1535	arr.	Bucharest (*p.* 331)	dep.	6 40	1340	..	..	..

¶ 1, 2 & 3 cl. Sleep. Cars Sofia-Rousse with Rest. Car Gornia-Ore. Rousse and *v.v.* daily.

S 1, 2 & 3 cl. Sleep. Cars Sofia-Varna and *v.v.* daily.

r Rest. Car Sofia-Rousse and *v.v.*

‡ From July 1, with 1, 2 and 3 cl. Sleep. Car Sofia-Varna and *v.v.*

The trains run in Turkey according to EAST EUROPEAN time, which is one hour fast of Mid-European time, and two hours fast of Greenwich time.

(Paris) Svilengrade—Istanbul. [Turkish State Rly.

1 2 luxe	1 2 3 ExS	1 2 3			1 2 3	1 2 3 ExS	1 2 luxe
2220	2255	..	dep. Paris ...... (p. 332)	arr.	..	7 5	8 40
7 45	2330	..	dep. Belgrade.... (p. 332)	arr.	..	6 15	2149
1642	12 0	r	dep. Sofia ...... (p. 332)	arr.	r	1745	1358
2257	1934		arr. Svilengrade c.	dep.		9 50	6 50
2310	1955		dep. Svilengrade	arr.	..	9 13	6 20
2359	21 3		arr. Edirne ...... c.	dep.	..	8 0	5 30
0 4	2111	8 45	dep. Adrianople .. c.	arr.	1724	7 52	5 27
0 52	2220	9 33	arr. Pythion c.	dep.	1633	6 43	4 40
1 0	2240	9 35	dep. Pythion	arr.	1631	6 13	4 33
1 35	0 5	1011	dep. Uzunkopru	arr.	1555	5 22	3 58
2 49	1 23	1149	dep. Lulubourgas	dep.	1427	4 4	2 47
4 17	3 12	1342	arr. Cerkesköy	dep.	1235	2 15	1 19
4 25	3 20	1357	dep. Tcherkeskeny	arr.	1220	2 8	1 13
..	4 26	1458	dep. Kabakdca	dep.	..	0 56	.
5 37	4 44	521	dep. Catalca	dep.	1046	0 31	2350
6 44	6 0	1640	dep. Kutchuk-Cekmece ..	dep.	9 25	2315	2237
7 20	6 40	1725	arr. Istanbul	dep.	8 40	2235	22 0

r Rest. Car.

S 1 and 2 Sleep Car Belgrade to Istanbul and v.v.

Istanbul, Thessaloniki, Athens.

S r			S r
2235	dep. Istanbul	arr.	6 40
0 4	dep. Edirne	arr.	5 27
6 45	dep. Pythion	arr.	2228
8 49	arr. Alexandrople	dep.	2015
1022	dep. (Dedeagatch) ..	arr.	1913
2144	arr. Thessaloniki (p. 337)	dep.	8 40
2320	dep. Thessaloniki	arr.	7 50
1026	arr Athens (p. 336)	dep.	2045

r Rest. Car Salonica Alexandrople and v.v.

S Sleep. Car, Istanbul-Athens, Tues. and Sats.; Athens-Istanbul, Tues. and Sats.

Haydarpasa—Ankara. [Turkish Rlys.

	B	B	A								B	A	B
9 0	1422	1545	19 0	20 5	.	d.Haydarpasa	a.	10 6	1955	..	7 45	8 50	1150
1146	1810	1925	22 7	0 23	..	a.Arifiye ..	d.	5 50	17 7	..	4 18	5 33	8 3
1330	1820	1940	..	0 25		d. Arifiye ..	a.	5 45	..	..	4 0		7 45
1350	1840	20 0	..	0 45	..	a. Adapazari ..	d.	5 25	..	..	3 40		7 25
1148	1815	1927	22 9		dep.	d.Arifiye	a.	..	17 5	..	4 16	5 32	8 2
1616	2358	1 40	3 40	..	9 35	d.Eskisehir	a.	..	1310	1844	23 1	0 50	2 32
1924	4 23	5 47	7 10	..	14 3	a.Polath	d.	..	10 8	1418	1925	2133	1248
2110	6 55	8 10	9 10		1656	a.Ankara	d.		8 20	1115	17 0	1925	2020

A Anatolie Express daily with 1 and 2 cl. Sleep. Car, Rest. Car and 1, 2 and 3 cl. cars to Ankara and v.v. **B** 1 and 2 cl Sleep Car Haydarpasa-Ankara and Buffet Cars, daily.

Ankara.—Samsun. [Turkish Rlys.

S	X			X	S
9 25	2123	d.Ankara	a.	8 0	1910
1946	5 16	a.Bogazkopru	d.	2330	8 29
20 3	5 50	a.Kayseri (*side*)	d.	2255	8 10
2030	..	d Kayseri	a.	..	7 40
2 10	..	a.Sivas	d.	..	2 12
9 0	..	a Zile..................	d.	..	1937
1610		a.Samsun (Port)	d.	..	1130

S 1 and 2 cl. Sleep. Car, and Buffet Car Thur. and Sun. from Ankara; Tue. and Sat. from Samsun.

X Tauras Exp. Mon., Wed. and Fri. from Ankara; Wed., Fri. and Sun. from Kayseri.

Mersin, Tarsus, Adana.

1443	dep. Mersin ...	arr	1022
1547	dep. Tarsus ...	arr	9 36
1635	arr. Yenice ...	dep	9 0
1721	arr. Adana	dep.	7 55

Adana—Kayseri.

1330	1555	dep. Adana (p. 334)	arr.	1152	14 2
1440	1632	,, Yenice (p. 334)	dep.	1123	1315
1654	1818	,, Pozanti	,,	10 9	1057
2245	21 6	,, Nigde	,,	7 46	5 50
2 2	2358	arr. Kayseri (p. 333)	dep.	4 50	1 25

Izmir, Ephesus, &c

2250	dep. Izmir (the Point) ..	arr.	5 40
¶	arr. Ayassoulouk (Ephes)	dp.	†
3 35	,, Aydin (for Tralles)	,,	0 15
8 9	,, Gondjeli*	,,	1925
1340	,, Dinair	,,	1510
..	,, Egirdir	,,	..

* Station for Hierapolis & Laodices

¶ Sat., Mon., Wed., & Fri. from Izmir.
† Sun., Tue., Thur. & Sat. from Egirdir.

Alexandretta—Toprakkale.

	*			‡	
5 5	10 0	dep. Alexandretta	arr.	1715	1 20
6 58	1218	arr. Dortyol	dep.	1535	2333
7 0	1220	dep. Dortyol	arr.	1533	2331
7 52	1315	arr. Toprakkale (p. 334)	dep.	1435	2230

‡ Tue., Thur. and Sat.
* Mon., Wed. and Fri.

The times on the LEFT are to be read DOWNWARDS, those on the RIGHT UPWARDS.

Izmir-Afyon-Ankara.

		Mls.				
6S30	1640		d.Izmir a.	2045	1047	S Sleeping Car Suns., Weds. Fris.
8 38	1850	41	Manisa	1844	8 36	
1035	2042	..	Salihli	1655	6 55	
1154	2145	103	Alaschir	1550	5 50	
1620	..	177	Usak	12 0	..	
1950	..	201	a Afyon d	8 20	..	
8 10			a. Ankara d	20¶20	..	

¶ Sleeping Car Mons., Weds. and Fris.

Izmir—Soma—Bandirma.

			Mls.				
7†30	10¶5	..		d.Izmir ....a.	..	17¶10	22†1
9 20	12 7	19 5	41	d.Manisa....d.	8 25	1512	2021
1035	1339	2031	72	d.Ak-Hissar d.	7 15	1346	19 8
1140	15 1	2127	98	d.Soma *....d.	6 15	1233	18 8
1358	1755	arr.	155	d.Belikesir ..d.	..	9 42	1548
16†30	20¶50	..	218	a.Bandirma d.	..	6¶30	13†10

¶ Tue., Thu., Sat. & Sun. † Mon., Wed. & Fri. only.
* Station for Pergama (Motor 1¼ hours).

TAURUS EXPRESS. Haydarpasa—Adana—Aleppo (Cairo)—Mosul (Baghdad-Basra) Hamadan—Teheran.

Turkish Rlys., Sud Turkish Rly., Syrian and Baghdad Rly., and Irak Rlys.

Daily	9 0	dep.Haydarpasa .... arr.	20 0	Daily
	16 5	arr. Eskisehir .... dep.	1318	
	1620	dep. Eskisehir .... arr.	13 4	
Mo., We. & Fri.	21 3	arr. Ankara .... dep.	8 20	Th., Sa. & Mo.
	2118	dep. Ankara .... arr.	8 0	
	4 58	arr. Bogazkopru .... dep.	2334	
	5 6	dep. Bogazkopru .... arr.	2330	
	5 35	arr. Kayseri .... dep.	23 0	
	1147	arr. Yenice .. .. dep.	16 2	
	1223	arr. Adana (p. 333) .... dep	1527	
Tu., Thr. & Sat.	1245	dep.Adana .... arr.	15 3	We., Fri. & Su.
	1415	arr. Toprakkale (p. 333) ....dep.	1241	
	1434	dep.Toprakkale .... arr.	1239	
	1555	arr. Fevzipasa .... dep.	..	
	16 5	dep. Fevzipasa .... arr.	..	
	1945	arr. Mouslimie .... dep.	7 50	
	2012	arr. Aleppo (Baghdad) p. 335 dep.	7 25	
	2131	dep. Aleppo (Baghdad) ....arr.	6 14	
We., Fri. & Su.	6 39	arr. Tripoli (p. 335).. (By Motor) dep.	2028	Tu., Th. & Sat.
	7 0	dep. Tripoli (By Motor) arr.	2015	
	9 30	arr. Beyrout .... (By Motor) dep.	1745	
	14 0	dep. Beyrout (By Motor) arr.	1625	
	18 0	arr. Haifa .... (By Motor) dep.	1345	
Th., Sat. & Mo.	7 0	dep. Haifa (By Motor) arr.	1330	Mo. Wed. & Fri.
	2235	arr. CAIRO (p. 335) (by Rail) dp.	1730	
Tu., Thr. & Sat.	2046	dep.Aleppo (B.A.N.P.) .... arr.	6 59	Wed., Fr. & Su.
	21 8	dep.Mouslimie .... arr.	6 37	
Wed., Fr. & Sun	5 17	arr Derbesiye ....dep.	2235	Tu., Th. & Sat.
	5 50	dep.Derbesiye .... arr.	22 6	
	6 55	arr. Mardine ....dep.	21 5	
	5 31	dep Derbesiye .... arr.	2221	
	6 46	arr. Nusaybin .... dep.	21 5	
	9 45	dep.Tel Kotchek............dep.	1930	
	1615	arr. Mosul .... dep	1315	
Thr. Sa. & Mon.	1330	dep.Mosul (by Motor) ...... arr.	1245	
	1830	arr Kirkuk ,, ,, ...dep	7 45	
Thr., Sa& Mon.	2015	dep.Kirkuk (by Rail) ..... arr.	7 0	
Fri., Su.& Tue.	6 50	arr. Baghdad (Nord) .. dep.	21 0	Mon., Wed.& Fri.
Fri., Su.&Tues.	19 0	dep.Baghdad (West) .... .. arr.	8 2	Mon., Wed.& Fri.
Sat., Mo. &Wed	8 20	arr Basra .. .. dep.	1915	Sun., Tues. & Th.
Thur., Sat.& Mon	2015	dep.Kirkuk (by Rail) .. . arr.	7 0	Tue., Thr. & Sat
Fri., Su.& Tue.	6 15	arr. Khanikin .... dep.	2230	Mon., We.&Fr.
	7 0	dep.Khanikin (by Motor) ..arr	16 0	
	..	arr. Kermanshah....... dep	9 0	
	..	dep. Kermanshah....... arr.	21 0	Sun., Tu.& Thr
	20 0	arr.Hamadan .... dep.	..	
Sat., Mo.&Wed	8 0	dep.Hamadan .... arr.	..	
	19 0	arr.Teheran ....dep.	6 0	

TAURUS EXP. 1 & 2 cl. Sleeping Cars and Rest. Car Mon., Wed. and Fri. to Tripoli; Mon., Wed. and Fri. to Mosul; returning from Tripoli and Mosul, Tue., Thur. and Sat., 1, 2 and 3 cl. Cars Haydarpasa-Adana, Adana-Mardine and Derbesiye-Tel Kotchek and *v.v.*

Haydarpasa—Adana.

S		S
9 25	d. Haydarpasa ..a.	1855
1212	d. Izmit ....d.	16 0
1855	a. Eskisehir P. 333 d.	9 50
1925	d. Eskisehir P. 333 a.	9 3
0 19	a. Afyon .... d.	4 10
1 5	d. Afyon .... a.	3 17
7 55	a Konia .... d.	1940
8 25	d. Konia .... a.	19 0
1227	a. Eregli ......d.	1430
1712	a. Yenice .. d.	8 29
1740	d. Yenice .. a.	8 9
1818	a. Adana.........d	7 30

S Sleeping and Rest. Car Haydarpasa to Adana Tues. and Sat.; return Mon. and Thur.

Ankara—Diarbekir

S		S
9 25	d. Ankara ......a.	1910
1150	d. Irmak ....d.	1643
1530	a. Yerkoy ......d.	1244
20 3	a. Kayseri .. d.	8 10
2030	d. Kayseri .. a.	7 40
2 10	a. Sivas. .. d.	2 12
2 50	d. Sivas. .. a.	1 30
6 18	a. Cetinkaya....d.	22 5
1116	a. Malatya......d.	1630
1520	a. Yolcati ......d.	13 8
2025	arr.Diarbekir dep.	7 30

S Sleeping Car from Ankara Tues. and Sats. and fr. Diarbekir Mons. and Thurs.

Ankara–Zonguldak.

S		
1720	d. Ankara .... a.	1340
2335	d. Cankiri .... a.	7 50
6 30	d. Karabuk .. a.	0 29
9 46	d. Catalagzi .. d.	2038
1010	a. Zonguldak d.	20 5

S 1 and 2 cl. Sleep. Car, Thurs. and Suns. from Ankara; Mon. and Fri. from Zonguldak.

Cairo, Port Said, Kantara, Ludd, Haifa—(Jerusalem).

Sun., Mon., Wed. and Fri.	1 2 3 Tues., Thur. and Sat.	1 2 3		1 2 3		
		P		P		
		1730	dp. Cairo (*p.* 338) ar.	2235		
		2047	ar. Kantara (W) dp.	1927		
		2055	d. Port Said (*p.* 338) a.	1955		
		22 5	ar. Kantara (W) dp.	1855		
		A		B		
	Tues., Thur. and Sat.	0 15	dp. Kantara (E) arr.	18 0		
		5 15	dep. Rafa (below) d.	1424	Mon., Wed. and Fri.	
		6 40	arr. Gaza ...... dep.	1321		
		9 0	arr. Ludd ...... dep.	1115		
		..	dep. Ludd ...... arr.	..		
		..	arr. Jerusalem dep.	..		
11 0		9 30	dep. Ludd ...... arr.	1046	Daily	
1230		11 0	dep. Tulkeram .. dep.	9 18		
1438		13 7	arr. Haifa (Cent.) dp.	7 8		
1445		1315	arr. Haifa (East) dp.	7 0		

A Tues., Thurs. and Sats. from Kantara with Sleeping and Dining Car to Ludd.

B Mons., Weds. & Fris. fr. Ludd with Dining and Sleeping Car to Kantara.

P 1st cl. Pullman Cars Cairo-Kantara and *v.v.*, EXTRA FARES. R Restaurant Car.

NOTE—Passengers are conveyed across the Canal at Kantara by ferry (journey about 15 to 20 mins.)

Jerusalem, Ludd, Jaffa.

				d. Jerusal'm a.				
				arr. Ludd dp.				
				dep. Ludd arr.				
				arr. Jaffa dep.				

Beyrout, Rayak, Damascus, 92 miles

9 35	1412	2115	d. Beyrout (Port) a.	12 9	1831	..	6 55
1355	2021	3 29	a. Rayak *b* ...... d.	7 58	1415		1 38
1420	..	3 44	d. Rayak .... a.	..	1345	1956	1 2
1749	..	7 40	a. Damascus (Kanawat) .. d.	..	10 7	1532	2042

(Damascus) Rayak-Homs-Aleppo

10 7	1532	dep. Damascus ‡ .... arr	1749	1213
1410	2045	dep. Rayak .... arr	1359	7 18
1452	2130	arr. Baalbeck .. dep.	1325	6 44
1454	2132	dep. Baalbeck .. arr.	1322	6 42
1710	2359	arr. Homs .... dep.	1033	3 52
2035	6 14	arr. Aleppo (Bag.) .. dep.	7 10	2131

‡ Kanawat Station.

Rayak (Tripoli) Aleppo.

	¶			X
10 7	1532	d. Damascus .... a.	1749	1213
1410	2045	d. Rayak .... a	1359	7 18
1452	2130	a. Baalbek .. .. d.	1325	6 44
1710	2359	d. Homs .... d.	1033	3 52
1245	1745	d. Beyrout } Auto Car { .. a.	1455	9 25
15 0	20 0	a. Tripoli } Auto Car { .. d.	1240	7 10
1524	2028	d. Tripoli } rail { .... a.	12 4	6 39
1715	2357	a. Homs } rail { .... d.	1023	3 50
1350	↓	d. Damascus } Auto Car { a.	1355	↑
17 0	↓	a. Homs .... } Auto Car { d.	1040	↑
1720	0 22	d. Homs, rail .... a.	1012	3 32
1814	1 50	a. Hama .... d.	9 22	1 51
1816	2 12	d. Hama .... a.	9 14	1 36
2031	6 8	a. Aleppo (D.H.P.) .. d.	7 19	2137
2035	6 14	a. Aleppo (Baghdad) .. d.	7 0	2131

¶ 1 and 2 cl. Sleep. Car Tripoli-Aleppo daily; to Haydarpasa, Tue., Thur. and Sat, see *p.* 334.

X 1 and 2 cl. Sleep. Car Haydarpasa, to Tripoli, Tues., Thurs. and Sats., see *p.* 334, from Aleppo to Tripoli daily.

Haifa—Deraa—Damascus.

			1 2 3		1 2 3	3 cl.		3 cl.	1 2 3					
		..	..	..	8 45	14 0	dep. Haifa (East) .... arr.	9 50	17 35					
		..	..	..	11 28	16 43	arr. Samach .... dep.	7 0	14 45	..		..		
		A	A	A	1 2 3				1 2 3	A	A	A		
		..	..	..	12‡ 0	..	dep. Samach .... arr.		14‡15	..		..		
		..			14‡46	..	arr. Derra .... dep.	..	11‡30	..	..	..		
		6 50	11‡55	13†25	15‡15	..	dep. Deraa .... arr.	..	11‡ 4	11 50	15 ‡ 6	18†42		
		1020	15‡16	16†45	19‡12	..	arr. Damascus (Kanawat) dep.	..	7 ‡ 0	8 25	11‡50	15†25		

A Auto-Rail Car Service, 1st and 3rd cl. only. † Monday Wednesday, Friday and Sunday. ‡ Tuesday, Thursday and Saturday only.

Haifa—Jaffa.

7 35	dep. Haifa (East) .... arr.	1835
7 40	dep. Haifa (Cent) .. arr.	1832
9 8	arr. Ras El Ein .... dep.	17 0
9 13	dep. Ras El Ein .... arr.	1659
9 55	arr. Tel-Aviv ...... dep.	1615
9 59	dep. Tel-Aviv ...... arr.	1612
10 5	arr. Jaffa .... dep.	16 5

Damascus-Maan. [Hedjaz Rly.

	1 & 3		1 & 3	
Tue., Thur. and Sat.	1250	dep. Damascus ...... arr.	1545	Tue., Thur. and Sat.
	16 6	arr. Deraa *b* .... dep.	1227	
	8 45	dep. Haifa .... arr.	1735	
	1446	arr. Deraa .... dep.	1150	
Tu, Th & Sat.	16 0	dep. Deraa .... arr.	1045	Tu, Th & Sat.
	1930	arr. Amman .... dep.	7 0	
	3 cl.		3 cl.	
Wed.	8 0	dep. Amman .... arr.	1545	Fri.
	1130	dep. Katrani .... dep	12 5	
	1545	arr. Maan .... dep.	8 0	
	¶	arr. Tebouk .... dep.	¶	
	..	arr. Medina .... dep.	..	

¶ No service beyond Maan.

GREECE.

Trains run in Greece according to EAST EUROPEAN time, which is one hour fast of Mid-European time, and two hours fast of Greenwich time.

(Piræus) Athens—Larissa—Thessaloniki—Guevgeli.

R Rest. Car.

5 58	6 12	9 15	12 1	..	18 0	1956	..	dep. Piraeus .... arr.	22 7	0 9	9 14	1110	1622	2128	..
6 40	7 5	9 53	1245	..	1852	2045	..	,, Athens .... ,,	2119	2329	8 28	1026	1538	2044	..
8 30	8 48	1116	14 2	..	2041	2210	..	arr. Inoi (Skimatari) ,,	1930	22 6	6 38	8 52	1420	1856	..
..	9 33	..	1438	..	—	2247	..	,, Thebes .... dep.	1851	2133	—	8 18	..	—	..
..	1032	..	1530	..	..	2342	..	dep. Livadia .... ,,	1752	2045	..	7 26	..	..	..
..	1126	..	1615	..	..	0 27	..	arr. Amfiklia ...... ,,	1659	20 3	..	6 44	..	..	..
..	1151	..	1633	..	..	¶ S	..	,, Gravia (Delfi).... ,,	1634	1947	..	6 20	..	.	..
..	1245	..	1724	..	..	1 39	..	,, Lianokladi .... dep.	1520	1857		5 22	..	..	..
..	1520	..	1926	..	..	..	..	a. Ghephyra (Demerlie) d.	1228	1643	..	¶ S	..	..	
..	1626	..	2016	..	..	4 42	..	arr. } Larissa .... { dep.	1124	1550		2 25	..	..	..
..	1640	..	2025	..	..	4 50	9 32	dep. } (*above* { arr.	1115	1541	1938	2 17	..	..	..
..	173	..	R	..	..	..	1024	arr. Tempi .... dep.	1025	R	1848		..	..	..
..	1830	..		..	..	..	1121	,, Litochoron	9 16		1729	..	..	..	..
..	19 3	..	2157	..	7 20	6 22	12 3	dp Katerini ... arr.	8 57	14 7	17 4	0 43	..	..	2049
..	2112	..	2319	.	9 48	7 50	1410	arr. } Thessaloniki { dep.	7 0	1245	15 0	2320	..	..	1810
..	..	..	..	5 58	1253	8 20	19 3	, } (*p.* 337). { arr.	..	9 8	1517	2255		1853	..
..	..	..	..	9 35	1525	9 59	2154	arr. Guevgeli ...... dep.		6 25	1110	2120	..	16 0	..

S 3rd cl. Sleeper, Athens to Salonica and *v.v.*

¶ Simplon-Orient Exp. Athens-Paris with 1 & 2 cl. Sleep. cars, also to Berlin and to Paris *via* Vienna and *v.v.* r Rest. Car Athens—Livadia and Larissa, Salonica and *v.v.*

ATHENS AND PIRAEUS.—From Athens every 10 or 15 minutes from 5.0 to 1.0. From Piraeus to Athens every 10 or 15 minutes from 4.40 to 0.40.

(Piraeus) Athens, Patras.

r	A	A	Mls.	r Rest. Car.	A	r	A
5 20	13 0	19 1	0	dep. Piraeus .. arr.	1115	2045	0 40
5 45	1315	1916	5½	arr. Athens .. dep.	11 0	2020	0 25
6 5	1322	1921		dep. Athens .. arr.	1057	1057	0 15
7 6	..	..	23	arr. Eleusis .. dep.	..	1853	..
7 45	..	..	35	,, Megara .. ,,	..	1815	..
9 6	1522	2122	68	,, Corinth .. ,,	8 49	1651	2218
9 19	1526	2126		dep. Corinth .. arr.	8 44	1639	2217
1145	1645	..	102	arr. Akrata.... dep.	..	1411	2058
1147	1646	..		dep. Akrata.... arr.	..	14 8	2057
1215	17 3	23 0	110	arr. Diakofto .. dep.	7 19	1342	2040
1258	1721	2318	119	,, Æghion .. ,,	6 52	13 7	2022
1259	1722	2319	..	dep. Æghion .. arr.	6 51	13 6	2021
1435	1817	0 13	144	arr. Patras .... dep.	5 57	1125	1926

A 1 & 3 cl. Automobile Train.

Piraeus—Kalamata.

	r	A		r		A
..	6 10	1510	dep. Piraeus........ arr.	1940	..	2230
..	6 55	1532	,, Athens........ ,,	19 1	..	22 7
..	10 0	1732	arr. Corinth ...... dep.	1557	..	20 4
..	10 9	1737	dep. Corinth ...... arr.	1546	..	1955
..	12 5	..	,, Mycenae ...... dep.	14 6	..	..
..	1223	1847	arr. Argos .... ,,	1345	..	1847
..	1231	1849	dep. Argos .... arr.	1333		1842
..	13 2	..	,, Myli .... dep.	1317		..
..	14 1	..	,, Achladocampos ,,	1228	arr.	..
6 35	1550	2024	,, Tripolis ...... ,,	1126	1955	1718
8 30	1725	2123	arr. Bilali .... ,,	9 15	1750	1616
9 10	1730	2124	dep. Bilali .... arr.	9 10	1724	1615
1052	19 7	2223	arr. Zevgolatio .... dep.	7 15	1455	1518
1145	1914	2224	dep. Zevgolatio .... arr.	7 3	14 0	1517
1324	2010	..	arr. Asprochoma .. dep.	6 3	1237	1442
1326	2012	..	dep. Asprochoma .. arr.	6 0	1230	1441
1336	2022	23 5	arr. Kalamata...... dep.	5 50	1220	1434

r Rest. Car Athens to Argos and *v.v.*
A 1 & 3 cl. Automobile Train.

THESSALIAN RAILWAY.
Volo—Kalambaka.
(For the Monasteries of Meteora).

		Exp	(101 Miles.)	Exp		
6 10	9 34	17 7	dep. Volo .... arr.	1111	1510	1827
6 46	1022	1741	arr. } Velestino.. { dep.	1036	1425	1750
6 48	1034	1741	dep. } { arr.	1034	1420	174
8 38	1252	1934	arr. } Farsala .. { dep.	8 46	1158	1557
8 42	1311	1936	dep. } { arr.	8 42	1123	1555
9 59	1517	2054	arr. Karditza ...... dep.	7 17	9 8	1435
11 2	1647	2155	,, Trikala ...... ,,	6 16	7 33	1330
1140	1755	2244	arr. Kalambaka.... dep.	5 31	6 33	1251

Volo—Larissa.
(For the Valley of Tempe.)

Mls.					
0	Volo .... dep.	7 0	8 13	1315	1745
12	Velestino .... arr.	7 38	9 4	1357	1821
38	Larissa ..... arr.	8 48	033	15 0	1930

Mls.					
0	Larissa ...... dep.	7 12	12 5	1410	1741
26	Velestino ... dep.	8 25	1351	1522	1924
38	Volo.... ....arr.	8 57	1437	1554	2011

North West Railway.

7 0	1530	dep. Patras...... arr.	10 0	1820
		(Steamer.)		
8 0	1630	ar } Krionery .. { d.	9 0	1720
8 45	1720	d. } { ar	8 25	17 0
9 26	18 1	arr. Missolonghi dep.	7 44	1617
1125	20 0	arr. Agrinion .. dep.	6 0	1430

ATTICA RAILWAY.
Athens—Laurium.
(Cape Sunnium, Temple of Athena.)

		(40 Miles.)		
7 33	1625	dep. Athens .... arr.	9 25	1835
10 5	1857	arr. Laurium ...... dep.	7 0	1610

The times on the LEFT are to be read DOWNWARDS, those on the RIGHT UPWARDS.

Piraeus—Chalchis.

5 58	9 15	18 8	dep. Piraeus .... arr.	9 14	1622	2128
6 40	9 53	1852	,, Athens .... ,,	8 28	1538	2044
8 39	1117	2052	,, Inoi (Skinatari) ,,	6 31	1419	1851
9 2	..	2115	,, Vathy (Avlis) .. dep.	6 10	..	1830
9 24	1145	2137	arr. Chalchis ...... ,,	5 48	1350	18 5

Patras—Kalamata.

		A				A	
6 5	1450	1820	dep. Patras .... arr.	11 0	1955	1922	..
8 52	1733	1945	arr. Kavassila .. dep.	8 23	1655	1757	..
8 57	1738	1946	dep. Kavassila .. arr.	8 18	1650	1756	..
1021	19 4	2029	arr. Pyrgos .... dep.	6 55	1525	1713	..
1040	1920	..	dep. Pyrgos .... arr.	6 39	15 0	..	..
1054	1934	..	,, Alphios.... dep.	6 26	1447	..	..
[illegible]	2036	..	,, Zacharo .. ,,	5 21	1336	..	..
[illegible]	2120	..	arr. Kalonero .. ,,	4 33	1250	..	..
[illegible]	..	..	dep. Kalonero .. arr.	..	1237	..	2029
1417	..	..	arr. Zevgolatio dep.	..	1130	..	1915
1430	..	.	dep. Zevgolatio arr.	..	1114	..	1836
1543	..		arr. Kalamata .. dep.	..	10 0	..	17 0

A 1 & 3 cl. Automobile Train.

Diakofto—Kalavrita.

7 15	1350	dep. Diakofto ...... arr.	1150	1635
8 42	1517	dep. Megaspilion.... dep.	1045	1530
9 15	1550	arr. Kalavrita ...... dep.	1010	1450

Kalonero—Kyparissia.

Kalonero .... dep.	9 5	9 32	1310	2040	2130
Kyparissia .. arr.	9 18	9 45	1323	2052	2143
Kyparissia .. dep.	4 20	5 8	1215	1530	16 0
Kalonero .... arr.	4 32	5 20	1228	1542	1612

Kavassila—Killini.

9 10	19 5	dep. Kavassila .... arr.	5 58	1635
1020	2010	arr. Killini .... dep.	5 0	1525

Pyrgos—Catakolo.

Pyrgos .... dep.	6 5	9 45	1430	18 0
Catakolo .... arr.	6 41	1022	15 6	1836
Catakolo .... dep.	8 0	1145	1620	20 0
Pyrgos .... arr.	8 36	1221	1656	2036

Pyrgos—Olympia.

Pyrgos ...... dep.	8 0	1030	1910	2031
Alphios ...... ,,	8 14	1044	1924	2040
Olympia .... arr.	8 43	1113	1953	21 0
Olympia .... dep.	5 43	9 10	1330	1640
Alphios ...... ,,	6 10	9 37	1357	17 0
Pyrgos ...... arr.	6 23	9 50	1410	17 9

Kalamata—Messini (Nision).

Kalamata .. dep.	..	7 30	1140	1310	1517	1810	1957
Asprochoma dep.	6 6	8 41	1151	1327	1534	1822	2015
Messini .... arr.	6 15	8 50	12 0	1336	1543	1831	2022
Messini .... dep.	5 48	7 0	10 2	1216	1429	1658	1850
Asprochoma arr.	5 57	7 10	1015	1238	1443	1718	19 1
Kalamata .. arr.	..	7 22	1025	1250	1455	1730	1913

Bilali—Megalopolis.

9 16	1751	dep. Bilali ...... arr.	8 27	1717
9 31	18 6	arr. Megalopolis dep.	8 15	17 5

Lianokladi—Stylis.

6 40	13 5	1530	dep. Lianokladi arr.	1238	1458	20 8
6 58	1325	1550	arr. Lamia .... dep.	1223	1443	1953
7 50	..	1558	dep. ,, ... arr.	1214	..	1950
8 38	..	1643	arr. Stylis .... dep.	1124	..	19 0

Argos—Nauplia.

Argos .. dep.	7 0	9 10	1214	1225	1350	1850	2010	2121
Tirins .. dep.	7 16	9 26	1224	1241	14 6	19 6	2026	2131
Nauplia arr.	7 25	9 35	1238	1250	1415	1915	2035	2137
Nauplia dep.	6 15	6 37	8 30	9 45	13 0	1723	1728	1935
Tirins .. arr.	6 24	6 43	8 39	9 54	13 9	1729	1737	1944
Argos .. arr.	6 40	6 53	8 55	1010	1325	1739	1753	20 0

Thessaloniki—Alexandrople

6 40	8r40	1311	dep. Thessaloniki .. arr.	1558	2144	2228
1244	1223	19 2	arr. Serres .... dep.	9 52	1719	1618
1537	14 0	2137	,, Drama .... ,,	7 22	1538	14 1
1852	1633	..	,, Xanthi .... ,,	..	13 0	1037
2239	1913	..	arr. Alexandrople .. ,, (p. 333).	..	1022	6 32

r Restaurant Car Salonica-Drama & *v.v.*

Thessaloniki—Bitolj (Monastir)—Veles. [Greek & Yugoslav Rlys.

2 3	2 3	1 2 3	1 2 3	1 2 3	1 2 3	Mls.		1 2 3	1 2 3	1 2 3	2 3	2 3
..	..	..	7 20	1630	1843	0	dep. Thessaloniki ...... arr.	8 49	1310	1842	..	..
..	..	..	8 38	1711	1945	22	,, Plati .... ,,	7 40	1225	1735	..	..
..	..	..	1128	1915	2227	70	arr. Edessa .... dep.	5 7	1031	15 5	..	..
..	..	9 36	1437	2140	..	122	,, Florina Ville ...... ,,	..	8 6	1156	1714	..
..	..	10 5	1556	..	..	127	,, { Kenali } cE.E.T. ,,	..	..	1035	1635	..
..	10 0	..	1735	..	..		dep { Kremenica } c C.E.T. a.	..	..	9 0	1510	17 2
..	1023	..	18 5	..	..	137	arr. } Bitolj .... { dep.	..	..	8 34	1448	1640
7 12	1325	..	2150	..	..		dep. } Bitolj { arr.	..	..	6 33	1155	1628
8 26	1431	..	2322	..	..	165	arr. Prilep .... dep.	..	..	5 21	1059	1526
1051	1649	..	2 36	..	..	219	,, } Veles (p. 332A) .. { ,,	..	..	1 30	8 18	1215
1152	1832	..	3 12	..	..		dep. } Veles { arr.	..	..	1 2	7 58	11 6
2240	6 15	..	1855	..	..	541	,, Belgrade .... dep.	..	..	11 0	19 5	2330

The times on the LEFT are to be read DOWNWARDS, those on the RIGHT UPWARDS.

EGYPT.

Egyptian time is 2 hours in advance of Greenwich time.

ALEXANDRIA and CAIRO (130 miles).

123	P&2	123	123	123	123	1&2	123	123		P&2	123	123	123	123	123	1&2	123	123
Exp	Rap		Exp	Exp PR	Exp P	Rap P¶	Exp PR	S		Rap	Exp		Exp P	Exp PR	Exp	Rap P¶	Exp PR	S
6 25	7 20	7 50	9 0	12 0	15 0	1645	19 0	0 0	dep. **Alexandria** arr.	9 25	1020	1350	1240	1535	1845	1925	2245	5 30
7 26	..	9 21	9 56	1256	1556	..	1956	1 44	dep. Damanhour dep.	..	9 20	1123	1145	1440	1750	..	2150	3 49
8 29	8 56	1130	1054	1349	1659	1821	2054	3 23	dep. Tantah ....dep.	7 51	8 19	11 0	1049	1349	1649	1751	2049	2 13
9 7	..	1233	1132	1427	1737	..	2132	4 22	dep. Benha ....dep.	..	7 40	9 33	1010	1310	1610	..	2010	1 12
9 45	10 0	1330	1210	15 5	1815	1925	2210	5 30	arr. **Cairo** ......dep.	6 45	7 0	8 30	9 30	1230	1530	1645	1930	0 0
								S										S

P Pullman Cars on these trains: Supplement over 1st class fare.
R Restaurant Cars Alexandria-Cairo and *v.v.* S Sleeping Car Alexandria–Cairo and *v.v.*

On the Rapide trains headed "P & 2" first class passengers travel in the Pullman without extra charge except the Rapide Supplement. ¶ June 1st to Oct. 15, only.

NOTE.—Passengers travelling by Rapide trains are charged a Supplement of Pt. 5.

CAIRO, SUEZ, and PORT SAID. (148 miles).

	123	123	123	12	123	123		12	123	123	123	123	123
	Exp		Exp PR	Exp B		Exp PR		Exp B	fast	Exp PR		Exp PR	
Cairo ....dep.	7 10	9 30	11 0	1515	..	1730	**Port Said** ....dep.	7 10	8 5	1225	1510	1845	2055
Benha............dep.	7 52	1020	1143	1556	..	1813	Kantara (W.) ....dep.	..	8 56	13 6	1559	1927	22 5
Ismailia ....arr.	9 41	13 5	1335	1733		20 1	Ismailia.......... arr.	8 14	9 31	1335	1634	1956	2240
Ismailia ......dep.	10 5	..	1355	↓	..	2065	Suez (Pt. Taufiq) dep.	↓	7 10	1035	..	1720	..
Suez (Ville) ....arr.	1212	..	16 0	↓	..	2240	Suez (Ville) ....dep.	↓	7 20	1044	..	1730	..
Suez (Pt. Taufiq) arr.	1220	..	1610	↓	..	2250	Ismailia........ arr.	↓	9 22	1247	..	1935	..
Ismailia ....dep.	9 48	..	1342	1737	1815	2010	Ismailia ....dep.	8 19	9 37	1342	1639	20 1	..
Kantara (W.) ....dep.	1027	..	1416	..	1855	2047	Benha ....arr.	9 54	12 7	1532	1940	2151	..
Port Said ....arr.	1115	..	1455	1840	1955	2125	**Cairo** ....arr.	1035	1250	1615	2210	2235	..

B A supplement of Pt. 5 is payable on these trains.
P 1st cl. Pullman cars—EXTRA FARES. R Restaurant Car.

CAIRO–SUEZ. New Route.

23	23	23	Mls.		23	23	23
7 25	1520	1855	0	dep. Cairo (Pont Limoun) ......arr.	9 10	17 5	2145
9 35	1725	21 0	78	arr. Suez (Port Taufiq) ....dep.	6 50	1455	1930

NILE LINE. (556 miles).

123	123	123	123	123	123	123	123		123	123	123	123	123	123	123	123
	fast		Exp	fast	fast	Exp	Exp			fast		Exp	fast		Exp	Exp
..	6 15	6 55	8 20	1330	1540	1950	2250	dep. **Cairo** ....arr.	1250	1130	2030	1910	2145	..	6 10	8 40
..	6 55	7 55	..	14 9	1620	A	..	dep. Badrashein dp.	1152	..	1932	..	21 6	..	..	B
..	7 28	8 38	..	1442	1653		2344	dep. Ayat......dep.	11 9	1036	1849	..	2034	..	5 15	
6 25	8 4	9 50	9 40	1540	1729	2110	0 14	dep. Wasta ....dep.	1020	10 7	18 0	1750	1959		4 46	7 16
8 31	9 33	1156	11 2	1751	1859	2232	1 44	dep. Maghagha dep.	7 47	8 34	1522	1627	1827	arr.	3 13	5 56
1010	1045	1335	12 5	1925	2017	2335	2 54	dep. Minia ....dep.	6 10	7 18	1345	1525	1715	2140	2 5	4 55
13 5	arr.	1630	1411		2230	1 23	5 3	arr. **Assiut** dep.	—	5 0	8 0	1312	..	1845	2345	3 3
1315	—	18 0	1418	—	—	1 30	5 10	dep. **Assiut** arr.		—	7 50	13 5	..	1835	2335	2 55
1530	..	2015	16 5	..	..	3 3	7 4	dep. Sohag ....dep.	..	..	5 30	1125	..	1610	2122	1 17
arr.	..	—	1658	..	..	3 57	8 11	dep. Baliana ..dep.	..	..	..	1024	..	1350	2010	0 15
..	..	..	1749	..	..	4 37	9 5	dp. Nag-Hamadi dp.	..	..	..	9 45	..	13 0	1923	2338
..	..	..	2010	..	..	6 45	1155	arr. **Luxor** dep.	..	..	..	7 5	..	1015	1625	2130
..	..	..	—	..	8 0	6 55	1240	dep. **Luxor** arr.	..	..	..	—	—	10 0	1550	2115
..	..	..	..	..	1210	1025	1650	arr. **Assuan** dp.	..	..	..	..	..	5 40	1135	1745
..	6 45	9 0	..	1630	1220	1035	..	dep. **Assuan** ar.	7 45	..	..	1845	1355	..	1120	1730
..	7 0	9 15	..	1645	1230	1045	..	ar. Shellal *p.* 339 dp.	7 30	..	..	1830	1340	..	1110	1720

A Daily Service—Cairo–Shellal to Aug. 31. Sleep Car, Mon., Wed. and Thur.; Rest Car, Mon. and Thur. From Sept. 1 to Oct. 31, Sleep and Rest Car, Mon , Wed. and Sat. B Daily Service—Shellal–Cairo to Aug. 31. Sleep. Car, Tue., Thur. and Fri.; Rest Car, Tue. and Fri. From Sept. 1 to Oct. 31, Sleep and Rest Car, Tue., Thur., and Sun. ☞ For Sailings Cook's Nile Steamers, *see page* 370.

SUDAN RAILWAYS.

CAIRO—KHARTOUM.

Wed.	1950	Sat.	1950	dep. **Cairo** .... arr.	Wed.	8 40	Sat.	8 40
Thur.	6 55	Sun.	6 55	dep. Luxor .... dep.	Tue.	2130	Fri.	2130
,,	1035	,,	1035	dep. Assuan .... dep.	,,	1745	,,	1745
,,	1045	,,	1045	arr. Shellal .... dep.	,,	1720	,,	1720
,,	13 0	,,	13 0	dep. Shellal .... } Stea- arr.	,,	15 0	,,	15 0
Sat.	6 30	Tue.	6 30	arr. Wadi Halfa .... } mer dep.	Sun.	20 0	Wed.	20 0
,,	10 0	,,	10 0	dep. Wadi Halfa .... arr.	,,	1830	,,	1830
Sun.	2 10	Wed.	2 10	arr. Atbara .... dep.	,,	2 15	,,	2 15
,,	6 4	,,	6 4	arr. Shendi .... dep.	Sat.	2230	Tues.	2230
,,	1030	,,	1030	arr. **Khartoum** .... dep.	,,	1815	,,	1815

For Sleeping and Restaurant Car Services Cairo to Shellal and *v.v.* see *page* 338.
Sleeping and Restaurant Cars run from Wadi-Halfa to Khartoum and *v.v.*

KHARTOUM—PORT SUDAN (SUAKIN).
(Kassala—Gedaref—Sennar).

Sun. and Wed.	8 20	dep. **Khartoum** .... arr.	1745	Tue. and Sat.
,, ,,	18 0	dep. Atbara .... arr.	8 35	,, ,,
Mon. and Thur.	1 49	arr. Haiya Jnc. .... dep.	1 50	,, ,,
Mon. and Thur.	14 5	arr. Kassala .... dep.	9 30	Mon. and Fri.
Tue. and Fri.	2 50	arr. Gedaref .... dep.	22 0	Sun. and Thur.
,, ,,	1820	arr. Sennar Jnc. .... dep.	5 45	,, ,,
Mon. and Thur.	2 26	dep. Haiya Jnc. .... arr.	1 15	Tue. and Sat.
,, ,,	5 30	dep. Sinkat .... dep.	2248	Mon. and Fri.
,, ,,	8 25	arr. Sallom Jnc. .... dep.	18 7	,, ,,
Mon. and Thur.	1115	arr. Suakin .... dep.	14 0	Mon. and Fri.
Mon. and Thur.	8 35	dep. Sallom Jnc. .... arr.	18 2	Mon. and Fri.
,, ,,	9 20	arr. **Port Sudan** .... dep.	17 0	,, ,,

Sleeping and Restaurant Cars run between Khartoum and Port Sudan, with thro' 1 & 2 cl. coach to Gedaref and *v.v.*

OLD SENNAR—GEDAREF—KASSALA (Port Sudan).

Sat.	1730	Wed.	1730	dep. **Khartoum** .... arr.	4 45	Wed,	4 45	Sat.
Sun.	5 45	Thur.	5 45	dep. **Old Sennar Jnc.** ...... arr.	1820	Tue.	1820	Fri.
,,	6 1	,,	6 1	arr. } Sennar .... { dep.	18 5	,,	18 5	,,
,,	6 30	,,	6 30	dep. } Sennar .... { arr.	1745	,,	1745	,,
,,	1650	,,	1650	arr. } Gedaref .... { dep.	7 30	,,	7 30	,,
,,	22 0	,,	22 0	dep. } Gedaref .... { arr	2 50	,,	2 50	,,
Mon.	5 55	Fri.	5 55	arr. } Kassala .... { dep.	1830	Mon.	1830	Thur
,,	9 30	,,	9 30	dep. } Kassala .... { arr.	14 5	,,	14 5	,,
,,	2155	,,	2155	arr. Haiya Jnc. .... dep.	3 0	,,	3 0	,,
Tue.	3 28	Sat.	3 28	arr. Gebeit .... dep.	22 5	Sun.	22 5	Wed.
,,	7 0	,,	7 0	arr. **Port Sudan** .... dep.	17 0	,,	17 0	,,

KHARTOUM—EL OBEID.

Su., We. & Fr. 2015	Mo. Th. Sa. 8 30	dep. **Khartoum** .... arr.	Tue., Sa. & Su. 5 45	Sun., Tue. & Fri. 17 0
Mo., Th. & Sa. 1 50	,, ,, 15 0	dep. Wad-Medani .. dep.	,, ,, 0 40	,, ,, ,, 1110
,, ,, 4 35	,, ,, 18 9	arr. Old Sennar Jnc. dep.	Mo., Fri. & Sat. 2130	,, ,, ,, 7 25
— ..	,, ,, 1830	arr...Sennar Town.. dp.	— ..	,, ,, ,, 7 0
Mo., Th. & Sat. 5 0	—	dep. Old Sennar Jnc. arr.	Mo., Fri. & Sa. 2054	—
,, ,, 8 45	—	dep. Kosti .... arr.	,, ,, 1730	—
,, ,, 19 0	—	arr. **El Obeid** ...... dep.	,, ,, 7 20	—

Sleeping Car Khartoum—El Obeid Suns. and Weds. only; from Obeid on Mons. and Fris. only.

☞ **For Sailings of the Sudan Government Steamers on the White Nile, see page 370.**

CYPRUS.

Famagusta—Nicosia.

(Weekdays only).

		R	R†			R†	R	
Famagusta dp.	5 20	7 0	1430		Nicosia ..dep.	7 30	1425	1450
Prastion...dep.	6 13	7 44	15 9		Prastion..dep.	8 51	1544	1635
Nicosia .. arr.	8 30	8 55	1627		Famagusta arr.	9 25	1613	1722

R Rail Car—one class only. † Steam train on Mondays and Saturdays.

ALGERIA, MOROCCO AND TUNIS.

TIME.—Trains in ALGERIA and MOROCCO run by Greenwich (West European) time; in TUNIS by Central European time one hour in advance of Greenwich.

Algiers, Constantine, Tunis. [Alg. State Rlys.

A	Rap	A	A	A	A	Exp			A			A	A	Rap		Exp
6 0	7 50	9 8	1243	1652	1752	2130	2210	dep. **Algiers**......arr.	8 10	8 2	12 7	1414	1746	1946	20 5	6 43
6 27	8 5	9 22	1257	1710	18 6	2145	2232	dep. Maison Carrée	7 52	7 41	1149	14 1	1733	1929	1949	6 26
7 32	8 48	10 6	1343	18 8	1850	2225	2342	arr. Menerville dep.	6 55	6 26	1050	1314	1644	1836	1854	5 43
7 42	R	10 8	1345	..	1852	S	..	dep. Menerville .. arr.	6 53	..		1312	1642	R	1845	S
9 29	..	1112	1448	..	1955		..	arr. Tizi Ouzou ..dep.	5 52	..	..	1212	1541	.	17 4	
..	8 51	..	..	1811	..	2229	2352	dep. Menerville .. arr.	..	6 23	1046	..	..	1830	..	5 39
..	1019	..	..	1946	..	2350	1 25	arr. } Bouira.. { dep.	..	4 52	9 21	..	..	17 2	..	4 28
..	1024	..	..	1950		2356	1 35	dep. } { arr.	..	4 47	9 17	..	..	1657		4 23
..	1119	..	A	2044	A	0 41	2 36	arr. Beni-Mancour dep.	A	3 45	8 23	..	..	16 2	A	3 35
..	1421	..	7 13	2350	1653	4 2	..	dep. Sétif ..	9 38	..	5 43	..	..	1323	1926	0 56
..	1610	..	9 18	arr.	1842	6 38	..	El Guerrah	7 51	..	..	..	..	1144	1713	2227
..	1622	..	9 30	..	1854	6 52	..	Ouled Rhamoun	7 36	..	..	..	..	1129	1656	22 8
..	1636	..	9 46	..	19 8	7 6	..	arr. Kroubs dep.	7 21	..	..	..	..	1114	1639	2148
..	1659	..	10 9	..	1933	7 30		arr. **Constantine** dep.	6 57		..		..	1048	1613	2115
																‡
..	1623	..	..	..	..	6‡45	..	dep. **Constantine** arr.	..	..	..	..	..	11 3	..	22 2
..	1650	..	..	..	..	7 24	..	dep. Kroubs .. arr.	..	..	..	..	..	1038	..	2137
..	1844	..	..	..	..	9 20	..	Ham-Meskoutine	arr.	..	..	..	..	8 40	..	1936
..	1910	5 31	..	..	..	9 52	..	Guelma	7 38	..	..	..	..	8 18	..	1911
..	1958	6 26	..	..	..	1053	..	dep. Duvivier ....dep.	6 45	..	..	..	..	7 32	..	1826
..	21 2	7 39	..	..	..	12 3	..	arr. **Bona** ......dep.	..	..	..	..	..	6 20	..	17 4
..	A	4 36	1323	..	..	9 23	A	dep. **Bona** (p. 342) arr.	A	arr.	..	A	..	..	..	1937
..	1/23	6 30	1431	..	..	1049	1/23	dep. Duvivier arr.	1/23	6 16	..	1/23	..	..	..	1813
.	..	7 43	1541	..	..	12 2	..	a. Souk Ahras (p. 342) d	..	4 49	..	..	11 1	..	..	1657
..	..	..	..	..	..	1334		arr. Ghardimaou dep.		..	..		8 55	..	..	1510
..	5 16	..	..	..	..	15 5	1828	d. ¶ Ghardimaou arr.	10 3	..	..	2140	..	..	..	1531
..	6 58	..	..	..	..	1640	2028	Mastouta	8 38	..	..	2027	..	..	..	1359
..	8 48	..	..	..	..	19‡1	2236	arr. **Tunis** (Ville) dep.	6 28	..	..	18 0	..	..	..	11‡30

A Auto rail, Train. R Rest. Car. **S** 1 & 2 cl. Sleeping Car to Constantine, and *v.v.*
‡ Rest. cars Constantine and Tunis and *v.v.* ¶ Cent. European time Ghardimaou to Tunis.

Bougie Line. [Alg. State Rlys.

2210	..	7 50	..	dep. Algiers .... arr.	12 7	..	1946	6 43
3 40	5 24	1128	1630	dep. Beni-Mancour (ab.) arr.	8 6	1058	1545	0 30
5 45	8 36	1330	2028	arr. Bougie .... dep.	5 57	7 6	1340	21 2

r Rest. Car.

Philippeville Line. [Alg. State Rlys.

5†24	7 53	1343	1722	dep. Constantine (abv.) arr.	6 6	1025	15 0	2035
7†29	9 53	1544	1922	arr. Philippeville .... dep.	4 4	8 5	1244	1829

† To Sept. 30th.

ALGERIA.

Algiers, Djelfa.

[Alg. State Rlys.

¶	b		c		Mls.				¶	b
..	6 11	1030	..	1637	0	dep. Algiers (*below*) arr.	7 49	1152	..	1937
..	7 42	1250	..	1735	32	,, Blida .... ,,	6 44	1034	..	1815
..	9 31	1422	—	1917	63	,, Medea .... ,,	5 17	8 59	1412	1644
..	1040		1441	2020	84	arr. Berrouaghia ..dep.	..	7 46	1214	1531
6 11	1147	..	1642	2128	109	,, Boghari ...... ,,	..	6 26	9 48	1413
1241	15 8	..	..	..	206	arr. Djelfa ....dep.	..	..	4 15	1059

b Buffet Car, Boghari-Djelfa and *v.v.* *c* Not Fridays. ¶ Not Saturdays.

(Algiers) Constantine—Biskra

[Alg. State Rly.

123	123	123	123	Mls.		123	123	123	123
2130	..	7 50	..	0	dp. Algiers (*p.* 340) ar.	1722	..	1948	6 45
6 43	..	1543	..	285	ar. El Guerrah ....dep.	7 54	..	1216	2222
M 6 18	Weekdays to Sept. 15.	1444	1920	0	dp. Constantine ....arr. (*p.* 340)	7 6	To Sept. 15	12 9	M 2149
6 40		15 9	1940	10	arr. Kroubs ....dep.	6 44		1146	2132
6 42		1510	1941	..	dp. Kroubs ....arr.	6 41		1145	2131
7 10		1552	2011	24	,, El Guerrah ..dep.	6 16		1119	2110
8 23		1731	2142	74	arr. Batna ...... dp	4 41		9 44	1958
..	1213	1738	..	..	dep. Batna ...... ar.	4 36	1211	..	..
..	15 1	1855	..	91	,, El Kantara ..dep.	3 11	9 30	..	..
..	17 6	1959	..	126	arr. Biskra ....dep.	1 47	6 6	..	..

M Motor Rail Car.

Biskra—Touggourt.

A	M		B	C
2126	2234	dep. Biskra .... arr.	4 29	1 35
2217	23 5	Oumache ....dep.	3 33	0 57
3 30	1 57	arr. El Berd ...... ,,	21 8	2148
4 26	2 31	,, Djama .... ,,	2021	2117
4 57	2 49	,, Tamerna ...... ,,	1945	2057
6 30	3 52	arr. Touggourt ....dep.	1812	1955

A Suns. only to Sept. 15.
B Mons. only to Sept. 15.
C Tue., Thur. and Sats. to Sept. 15.
M Mons., Weds. and Fris. to Sept. 15.

Biskra—Tolga.

† Tues. & Sats. to Sept. 15. [State Rly.

4†40	dep. Biskra ...... arr.	11†36
5 17	,, Oumache ..	11 4
6†16	arr. Tolga ....dep.	9†54

Algiers—Oran (216 miles).

[P.L.M. Rly.

	Exp	Rap				b	Ex¶					b			Rap				Ex¶
6 11	..	8†39	1030	..	1637	18 0	2140	..	dep.	Algiers	arr.	1152	1350	..	18†15	1937	..	7 49	6 32
6 31	..	8 52	1047	..	1649	1820	2157	..	a.	Maison Carrée	d.	1132	1334	..	18 2	1918	..	7 33	6 11
6 32	..	8 53	1048	..	1650	1821	2158	..	d.	Maison Carrée	a.	1131	1333	..	18 1	1917	..	7 32	6 7
7 27	From Oudjda.	9 28	1135	..	1722	1916	2248	..	a.	Blidah (*above*)	d.	1042	1251	..	1729	1825	..	6 50	5 33
7 33		9 32	1139	..	—	1922	2253	..	d.	Blidah (*above*)	a.	1034	1245	..	1725	1818	..	..	5 27
7 57		9 49	12 0	..	..	1943	2321	..	dep.	Affroun	dep.	1011	1220	..	17 8	1755	..	..	5 1
8 23		R	arr.	..	..	20 9	..	..	,,	Bou Medfa	,,	9 45	—	..	R	1731	..	..	4 34
9 6		1044	—	..	..	2049	0 39	..	a.	Affreville	d.	9 7	..	..	1613	1653	..	—	3 47
9 14		1049		..	..	2054	0 51	..	d.	Affreville	a.	8 49	arr.	..	16 9	1647	..	..	3 39
1059		1214	From Oudjda.	..		2237	2 29	..	dep.	Orléansville	dep.	7 5	1045	..	1454	15 3	..	..	2 0
arr.	..	1321		..	From Oudjda.	arr.	3 53	..	a.	Relizane	d.	—	9 14	..	1338	—	..	..	0 29
—	..	1331		..			4 3	6 18	d.	Relizane	a.	Exp	9 7	Exp	1330	..	..	21 2	0 19
..	..	1414		..		..	5 0	7 9	a.	Perrégaux	d.	..	8 12	..	1251	..	..	2012	2324
..	..	1416		..		..	5 6	7 14	d.	Perrégaux	a.	..	8 7	..	1246	..	..	20 8	2317
7 8	8 54	15 7	1140	1858	2158	..	6 7	8 10	a.	St. B. du Tlélat	d.	6 50	7 12	11 1	12 3	1532	1745	1914	2217
7 9	9 2	1512	1145	19 6	22 3	..	6 14	8 11	d.	St. B. du Tlélat	a.	6 38	7 7	1059	1151	1520	1743	1911	22 5
7 37	9 30	1535	1218	1934	2236	..	6 50	8 41	arr.	Oran (*p.* 342)	dep.	6 7	6 37	1033	1130	1450	1717	1843	2130

¶ 1 & 2 cl. Sleep. car Algiers-Oran and *v.v.*, 1 & 2 cl. cars Algiers-Oujda also 1 cl. Couchettes Algiers-Sidi-bel-Abbes and *v.v.*, *see p.* 342. *b* Buffet Car. *r* Rest. car Algiers-Oran and *v.v.*

† 1 & 2 cl. cars Algiers-Casablanca and *v.v.*, *see p.* 342.

ALGERIA.

Oran, Perregaux, Tizi, Mascara, Bechar. [Alg. State Rlys

Mon., Wed. & Fri.				SR		Mls			Tues., Thurs & Sat.		SR		‡ Tues., Thurs. & Sat.
	..	6 4	Daily	1234	1641	0	dep. **Oran** (State) arr.	..		1029	1434	Daily	1848
	..	7 36		1351	1811	27	arr. Damesme....dep.	..		8 54	1311		17 7
	..	8 21		1420	1856	37	,, La Macta.... ,,	..		8 22	1247		1624
	..	9 30		15 6	1952	55	,, Perrégaux .. arr.	..		7 2	1159		1520
	..	1129		1653	22 1	87	,, Tizi (*below*) dep.	..		5 45	1032		1325
	..	1234		1732	2240	94	,, Mascara .. ,,	..		5 21	9 40		13 3
	..	1436		1852	24 0	180	arr. } Saida .. { dep.	—		4 4	8 48		1033
	5 23	—		19¶2	..	..	dep. } Saida .. { arr.	16 6		—	8‡39		..
..	12 6	..		0 22	..	244	,, Méchéria....dep.	10 0	arr.	..	4‡1		..
5 44	1543	..	Tues., Thurs. and Sats.	3 0	..	307	arr. Ain Sefra.... ,,	5 57	1747	..	1‡9	Mon., Wed. & Fris.	..
1128	..	..		7 34	—	399	,, Figuig ...... ,,	..	1135	..	2035		..
1337	..	..		9 4	..	436	,, Ben Zireg	..	9 5	..	19 8		—
1513	..	..		1010	..	468	arr. } Colomb { dep.	..	7 1	..	1746		..
..	..	7†40		12 0	..	.	dep. } Bechar { arr.	..	..	10c7	16*17		..
..	..	8†27		1247	..	482	arr. Kenadza ....dep.	..	..	9c20	15*30		..

R Rest. Car. S 1 & 2 cl. Sleep. car Oran-Colomb-Bechar and *v.v.*, Mon., Wed. and Fri. *c* Thurs. only.
¶ Dep. Mons., Weds. and Fris. † Mons., Weds., Thurs. and Fris. only. * Except Sats. and Suns.

(Algiers), Oran, Oudjda (Fez). (Alg. State & Moroccan Rlys.)

1 2 3	Exp	1 2 3	2 3	Exp	1 2 3	1 2 3	Mls.		2 3	1 2 3	Exp	2 3	1 2 3	Exp
..	2140	..		8 39	..	..	0	d. Algiers (*p.* 341) a.	..	..	1815	..	..	6 32
..	4 3	6 18	Not Saturdays.	1331	..	17 9	168	d. Relianze ...... a.	9 7	..	1330	..	21 2	0 19
..	6 7	8 10		15 7	..	1913	247	a. Ste. B. du Tlélat d.	7 12	..	12 3	..	1914	2217
..	6 7	1033		1450	1717	1920	0	d. Oran (*p.* 341) a	7 37	9 30	1218	..	1934	2236
..	6 38	1059		1520	1743	1946	22	a. Ste. B. du Tlélat d.	7 9	9 2	1145	..	19 6	22 3
..	6r50	11 1		1532	1745	1948	..	d. Ste. B. du Tlélat a.	7 8	8 54	1140	..	1858	2158
..	8 18	12 6		1647	1853	2051		a. } Sidi-bel- { d.	6 9	7 55	1042	..	1758	2058
..	8 28	1216		1657	19 0	..	54	d. } Abbès.... { a.	..	7 47	1031	..	1750	2053
..	9 0	1250		1730	1933		69	a. Tabia .... d.		7 14	10 3	..	1715	2022
..	9 22	↓	..	1754	↓		..	d. Tabia .... a.	..	..	..	..	1710	..
..	1231			20 2		..	112	a. Bedeau	..	..	..	..	1435	..
..	1248	↓	..	¶	↓		117	a. Ras-el-ma-Crampeld	..	..	r	..	14 8	..
..	9 1	1251	..	1731	1934	..	..	d. Tabia ....a.	..	7 13	10 2	..	1714	2021
6 55	1028	1415	1428	1858	21 0	..	109	a. Tlemcen ....d.	..	5 50	8¶41	1138	1554	19 2
7 43	1123		16 2	1955	r	..	127	a. Turenne ....d.	..	..	7 44	10 7	1459	18 8
8 28	12 7	..	1711	2036	..	..	146	a. Marnia..........d.	..	..	6 55	8 39	14 8	1722
9 3	1241	..	1822	2110	..	..	163	a. Oudjda .... d.	..	..	6 24	7 11	1334	1652
..	15 0	..	..	22 0	..	..	..	d. Oudjda ....a.	..	..	5 42	..	13 5	13 5
..	2140	..	..	5 0	..	..	244	a. Fez (*p.* 342A) .... d.	..	..	2330	..	6 30	6 30
..	6 5	..	..	11¶51	..	..	446	a. Casablanca (*p.* 342A) d.	..	..	17¶0	..	21 0	21 0

¶ 1 & 2 cl. Sleep. Car Tlemcen to Casablanca, also 1 and 2 cl. cars Algiers and Oran to Casablanca and *v.v.*: *see p.* 342A. *r* Rest. Car.

Tizi, Mascara. [Alg. State Rlys.

						Mls.							
6 10	1035	12 9	1343	17 0	2215	0	dep. Tizi (*above*) .. arr.	5 42	1015	1150	1324	1639	2151
6 42	11 0	1234	14 8	1732	2240	7½	arr. Mascara...... dep.	5 21	9 40	1129	13 3	16 4	2130

(Algiers), Oran, Ain Temouchent. [Alg. State Rlys.

			Mls				
..	..	8 39		dep. Algiers (*p.* 341) arr.	1815	..	6 32
6 47	1240	1748	0	dep. Oran ....arr.	8 13	14 6	1914
8 27	1420	1928	47	arr. Ain Temouchent dep.	6 37	1230	1738

(Bone), Souk, Ahras. Tebessa.

2 3	1 2 3	1 2 3	Mls.		1 2 3	1 2 3
..	9 23	1323	0	dep. Bone (*p.* 340).... arr.	..	1937
5 10	12 7	1551	67	,, Souk Ahras .... ,,	9 30	1637
6 55	14 7	1736	102	arr. } Oued-Kébérit { dep.	7 48	1453
7 10	1415	1741	..	dep. } Oued-Kébérit { arr.	7 40	1448
9 0	1646	1931	144	arr. Tebessa (*p.* 342B) dep.	5 48	1258

MOROCCO.

Tangier—Fez.

1 2 3	1 2 3	1 2 3	Mls		1 2 3	1 2 3	1 2 3
	From Casablanca	Exp ¶			To Casablanca		Exp ¶
..		..		dep. Tangier (Maritime) ..arr.		..	6a25
7 0		21 0	0	dep. Tangier .... arr.		15 5	6 10
9 15		2317	65	dep. Alcazarquivir ...... arr.		1345	4 0
1110		1 25	127	arr. Petitjean............ dep.		1145	2 13
1125	2051	2 18		dep. Petitjean............ arr.	8 5	11 4	0 58
13 0	22 5	3 58	161	arr. Meknés ....dep.	7 9	9 45	2353
1312	2210	4 10		dep. Meknés .... arr.	7 3	..	2338
1427	2318	5 46	197	arr. Fez ....dep.	6 0	..	2215
		¶					¶

¶ 1 & 2 cl. Sleeping Cars and ordinary cars Tangier to Casablanca, also 1 & 2 cl. Cars and Couchettes, 1 & 2 cl. Tangier to Fez and *v.v.* *a* Only on Sundays to Maritime Station.

Casablanca—Fez (Oudjda).

1 2 3	1 2 3	1 2 3	1 2 3	1 2 3	Mls.		1 2 3	1 2 3	1 2 3	1 2 3	1 2 3
		Exp ¶		fast				Exp ¶			fast
7 0	1335	17 0	1845	21 0	0	dep. Casablanca ....arr.	9 25	1151	15 5	2015	6 5
7 24	1357	1723	19 7	2126	15	dep. Fedala ....arr.	9 4	1129	1443	1954	5 42
8 34	15 2	1824	2013	2233	55	arr. Rabat (Ville) ....dep.	8 0	1027	1335	1850	4 35
8 40	15 5	1827	2015	2240		dep. Rabat (Ville) ....arr.	7 46	1024	1333	1848	4 31
9 27	1550	1914	21 0	2334	80	arr. Port Lyautey ....dep.	7 5	9 35	1244	18 5	3 37
9 44	..	1917	..	2339		dep. Port Lyautey ....arr.	..	9 32	1240	..	3 34
11 0	..	2037	..	1 10	138	arr. Petitjean ....dep.	..	8 13	1120		2 0
1125	..	2051	..	2 18		dep. Petitjean ....arr.	..	8 5	11 4	..	0 58
13 0	..	22 5	..	3 58	167	arr. Meknés ....dep.	..	7 9	9 45	..	2353
1312	..	2210	..	4 10		dep. Meknés ....arr.	..	7 3	..	..	2338
1427	..	2318	..	5 46	208	arr. Fez ....dep.	..	6 0	..	..	2215
	..	5 42	..	13 5	425	arr. Oudjda (p. 342)......dep.	..	22 0	..	..	15 0

¶ Rest. Car. Through 1 & 2 cl. cars Casablanca-Algiers and Casablanca-Oran, with 1 & 2 cl. Sleeping Car Casablanca-Tlemcen (p. 342) and *v.v.*

Tangier—Casablanca.

1 2 3	1 2 3	Mls.		1 2 3	1 2 3
R	fast ¶				fast ¶
..	..	0	d. Tangier (Maritime) a.	..	6a25
7 0	21 0	..	d. Tangier..........a.	16 5	6 10
9 15	2317	65	d. Alcazarquivir ....a.	1345	4 0
1110	1 25	127	a. Petitjean .... d.	1145	2 13
1120	2 0		d. Petitjean .... a.	11 0	1 10
1240	3 34	185	a. Port Lyautey d.	9 44	2339
1244	3 37		d. Port Lyautey a.	9 27	2335
1333	4 31	210	a. Rabat (Ville) d.	8 40	2240
1335	4 35		d. Rabat (Ville) a.	8 34	2233
1443	5 42	250	a. Fedala ....d.	7 24	2126
15 5	6 5	265	a. Casablanca ......d.	7 0	21 0
	¶				¶

¶ 1 & 2 cl. Sleeping Cars; also 1 & 2 cl. through cars Tangier to Casablanca and *v.v.* R Rest. Car Tangier-Petitjean. *a* Only on Sunday to Maritime Station.

Casablanca (Oued-Zem) Marrakech.

3 cl.	1 2 3	1 2 3	1 2 3		1 2 3	1 2 3	3 cl.	1 2 3
		¶				¶		
3 25	7 15	16 0	2045	d Casablanca a	1035	20 8	2219	6 33
4 59	8 3	1645	2221	a Berrechid d	9 51	1924	2040	5 4
5 12	↓	↓	..	d Berrechid a	..	..	2032	..
5 51	↓	↓	..	d Sidi-el-Aidi a	..	..	20 5	..
10 5	↓	↓	..	a Oued-Zem d	..	..	15 0	..
..	8 4	1646	2222	d Berrechid a	9 50	1923	..	5 3
..	8 19	17 7	23 0	d Sidi-el-Aidi a	9 36	19 9	..	4 36
..	1019	19 0	3 32	a Benguerir d	7 44	1713	..	0 7
..	1125	20 4	5 43	a Marrakech d	6 40	16 5	..	2148

¶ October 15th to May 31st.

Tetuan—Ceuta.

1 and 3 cl.

d. Tetuan.. a.
d. Castillejos a.
a. Ceuta d.
a. Ceuta Port d.

Fez—Oudjda.

1 2 3	1 2 3	Mls.		1 2 3	1 2 3
	Exp				Exp
6 30	2330	0	d. Fez ..... a.	2140	5 0
8 59	1 50	75	a. Taza .. d.	19 5	2 15
9 9	2 5		d. Taza .. a.	1855	1 44
1020	3 12	110	d. Guercif d.	1752	0 38
13 5	5 42	222	arr. Oudjda dep.	15 0	22 0

TUNISIA.

Tunis, Ghardimaou.

1/23	1 2 3	1/23	Mls.	A Auto-rail Cars.	1/23	1 2 3	1/23
A	Ex¶	A			A	Ex¶	A
6 28	1130	18 0	0	dp.Tunis ....arr.	8 48	19 1	2236
6 58	12 3	1829	15	dp.Djedeida dep	8 23	1833	22 6
8 38	1359	2027	69	dp.Mastouta dep.	6 58	1640	2028
10 3	1531	2140	174	ar. Ghardimaou d	5 16	15 5	1828
..	1937	..	..	arr.Bone(p.340)d.	..	9 23	..
	6 43	..	..	ar. Alg'rs(p.340)d		2130	..

¶ 1, 2 & 3 cl. Cars & Rest. Car Tunis-Constantine and *v.v.*

Tunis, Bizerta.

1/23	1/23	1/23	1 2 3		1/23	1/23	1/23	1/23
A*x*	A	A	A*x*		A*x*	A	A	A*x*
6 2	1030	1311	18 7	d.Tunis...a.	7 42	10 1	1452	1947
6 27	1055	1336	1832	d Djedeidad.	7 18	9 57	1427	1923
7 52	1213	1456	1952	a.Bizerta.d.	5 50	8 18	13 8	18 4

A Auto-rail Cars.
x Supplement payable.

Tunis, Tebessa.

1 2 3	1/23	1 2 3	Mls			1 2 3	1 2 3	1 2 3
R	A					A	R	
7 43	1820	1915	0	dep.	Tunis ....arr.	9 30	17 9	7 24
9 7	1935	2148	31	arr.	Depienne ....dep.	8 21	1554	4 53
9 8	1936	2149	..	dep.	Depienne ....arr.	8 20	1552	4 52
11 4	2120	1 0	75	arr.	Gafour ....dep.	6 35	14 3	1 11
1236	..	4 34	107	arr.	Les Salines ....dep.		1238	22 8
1345	..	6 57	129	arr.	Fedj-et-Tameur ......dep.	..	1141	2027
16 5	..	..	147	arr.	Slata ....dep.	..	..	17 5
1410	..	7 38	139	arr.	Oued-Sarrath ....dep.	..	11 6	19 3
1621	..	..	158	arr.	Kalaat-es-Senam ..dep.	..	8 45	..
1459	..	8 20	147	arr.	Kalaa-Djerda ....dep.		1026	1830
1732	..	..	176	arr.	Rhilane *c* (C.E.T.) ....dep.	..	8 25	..
17 2	..	..	..	dep.	Rhilane *c* (G.T.) ......arr.	..	7 5	..
18 3	..	..	185	arr.	Tebessa (p. 342) ......dep.	..	6 0	..

R Waggon-Bar Tunis to Tebessa and *v.v.*
A Auto rail Cars.

Tunis—Sousse—Sfax (Gabes).

1/23	1/23	1/23	Mls.		A Auto rail Cars.	1/23	1/23	1/23	1/23
A	A*x*	A*x*				A	A*x*	A	A*x*
6 35	7 25	17 0	0	dep.	Tunis ....arr.	8 4	9 50	19 7	2337
7 41	..	18 0	37	arr.	Bir-bou-Rekba ......dep.	6 59	8 50	18 4	2242
8 20		1845	48	arr.	Nabeul ....dep.	6 20	..	1720	R
7 43	R	18 3	..	dep.	Bir-bou-Rekba ......arr.	6 57	8 49	18 1	2241
8 16	..	1833	62	arr.	Enfidaville (*below*) ....dep.	6 25	8 17	1729	22 9
8 55	9 23	19 9	89	arr.	Kalaa-Srira ....dep.	5 48	7 42	1650	2132
8 56	9 23	1910		dep.	Kalaa-Srira ....arr.	5 47	7 42	1649	2132
9 3	9 30	1917	93	arr.	Sousse ....dep.	5 40	7 35	1642	2125
..	9 33	1927	..	dep.	Sousse ....arr.	..	7 32	..	2121
	1120	2115	174	arr.	Sfax ....dep.	..	5 45	..	1935
..	1125	..	..	dep.	Sfax................ arr.	..	..	..	1930
..	1325	..	264	arr.	Gabes ....dep.	..	..	..	1730

R Auto Rail-Bar Tunis-Gabes and *v.v.*
x Supplement payable.
a Motor connection to Kairouan.

Sousse—Kairouan. (Motor).

6 15	1250	1630	dep.	Sousse	arr.	8 12	9 50	1810
7 25	14 0	1740	arr.	Kaironan	dep.	7 2	8 40	17 0

Enfidaville—Kaironan. (Motor).

8 25	dep. Enfidaville ......arr.	17 12
9 47	arr. Kairouan........dep.	1550

Sousse (Kairouan) H.-Souatir (Tozeur)

1/23	1 2 3	Mls.		1 2 3	1 2 3	1/23
A	C			C		A
9 15	1955	0	dep.Sousse .. arr	7 25	..	1627
9 22	2012	4	ar.Kalaa-Srira dp	7 10	..	1620
7 25	17 0	..	dp.Tunis (*abv.*) ar	9 50	..	19 7
9 25	2013	..	dp.Kalaa-Srira ar	7 9	..	1619
1014	2130	80	a.Ain-Ghrasesia d	5 44	..	1530
10¶23	..	..	d.Ain-Ghrasesia a	..	10¶2	..
1050	..	88	ar. Kairouan dp	..	9¶35	..
1015	2131	..	d.Ain-Ghrasesia a	5 43	..	1529
1230	1 28	107	arr } Sbeitla { dp.	1 35	..	1315
1320	2 1	..	dp. } Sbeitla { arr	1 20	..	1215
1815	6 0	184	ar. } Henchir Souatir { dp	2035	..	6 20
..	6 25	..	dp } Henchir Souatir { ar	2015	..	..
..	1012	247	arr.Tozeur .. dep	1534	..	..

Sfax (Gabes) Tozeur.

1 2 3	1/23	1 2 3	A Rail Cars.	1 2 3	1/23	1 2 3
1025	1125	2130	dep. Sfax ...... arr.	1834	1930	5 30
1210	1223	2337	arr. Graiba .... dep.	1645	1832	3 21
..	1224	C	dep. Graiba .... arr.	..	1831	C
..	1325		arr. Gabes .... dep.	..	1730	
1227	A	2341	dep. Graiba .... arr.	1640	A	3 17
1759		6 11	arr. Gafsa .... dep.	1138		2114
19 4	..	7 24	a. { Metlaoui-Philippe-Thomas } d.	10 5		19 7
..	..	8 39	d. { Metlaoui-Philippe-Thomas } a.		..	1716
..		1012	arr. Tozeur .. dep.		.	1534

Henchir—Souatir—Metlaoui—Philippe-Thomas.

1 2 3	1 2 3	Mls.		1 2 3	1 2 3
6 25	..	0	dep.Henchir-Souatir arr.	..	2015
7 8	..	12	arr. } Tabeditt.... { dep.	..	1916
7 21	1659		dep. } Tabeditt.... { arr.	9 15	1912
C		29	arr. Metlaoui-Philippe-		C
8 24	1812		Thomas......dep.	7 50	1736

¶ Weekdays only. A Auto-rail Cars.

C 1, & 2 cl. couchettes Sousse-Henchir-Souatir, and Metlaoui and *v.v.*; also Sfax-Tozeur and *v.v.*

The times on the LEFT are to be read DOWNWARDS, those on the RIGHT UPWARDS.

LONDON AND MALTA.

(For 1st and 2nd class).

Subject to alteration or suspension without notice, owing to Quarantine, Strikes, etc.

SUMMARY OF OVERLAND THROUGH SERVICES.

I.—Via Paris, Marseilles and P. & O. (or British India) Steamer.

For details of Services, see pages 112, 113, 237, 259 and 366/7.

LONDON (Victoria)	dep.	11 0 Thu.
Calais	dep.	1450 ,,
Paris (Lyon)	arr.	1855 ,,
,, ,,	dep.	2050 ,,
Marseilles (St. Charles)	a.	7 53 Fri.

* P. & O. Steamers leave Marseilles, Aug. 5, 19, Sept. 2, 16*, approximately fortnightly, arr. MALTA the following day. British India Steamers dep. about 19.0, Aug. 26, Sept. 23.

P. & O. Steamers leave MALTA, Aug. 2, 16, 30, Sept. 13, arr. MARSEILLES two days later.

Marseilles (St. Charles)	d.	20 0
Paris (Lyon)	arr.	7 32
,, ,,	dep.	9 46
Boulogne	arr.	13 5
LONDON (Victoria)	arr.	1720

NOTE.—For particulars of P. & O. Express to & from Marseilles Docks (Sleep. Cars only), see page 31.

* Passengers must embark before midnight on Friday; steamers usually leave at 4.0 a.m. Saturday.

Luxe Service. II.—Via Rome.

1 & 2 cl. Sleep. Cars only Calais-Rome. 1 & 2 class sleepers Rome - Syracuse. Ordinary coaches, 1 & 2 class Rome-Syracuse and *v.v.*

For details of services see pages 82, 118, 265, 301, 310, 314 and 387.

LONDON—

(Victoria)	dep.	11 0	
Paris (Nord)	arr.	1740	
,, ,,	dep.	1753	
,, (Lyon)	arr.	1825	
,, ,,	dep.	1930	
Genoa	arr.	9 15	
Rome	arr.	1530	
,,	dep.	1850	
Syracuse (Port.)	ar.	1135	
Syracuse ,,	dp.	§14 0	Daily except Saturdays.
Malta	arr.	21 0	

§ Also on Wed. at 22 0, by Tirrenia Line, due Malta, Thur. 7.0.

†Malta	d.	0 0	Daily except Fris.
Syracuse	a.	7 0	2nd day.
,, (Port)	d.	19 0	,,
Rome	a.	1055	3rd day.
,,	d.	1230	,,
Paris (Lyon)	a.	9 10	4th day.
,, ,,	d.	9 57	,,
,, (Nord)	a.	..	,,
,, ,,	d.		,,
Victoria	a.	1720	,,

‡ Also on Thur. at 22.0, by Tirrenia Line, due Syracuse, Fri. at 6.0.

III.—Via Paris, Mont Cenis, Rome, Naples V.G. Giovanni, Messina, Syracuse.

For details of service see pages 112, 118, 265, 301, 310, 314 and 387.

1 and 2 class cars. Paris-Rome, Rome-Syracuse. 1 & 2 cl. sleeper Rome-Syracuse, Rapido Supp. Turin-Rome payable.

LONDON (Vic.)	dep.	9 0	
Paris (Nord)	arr.	1548	
Paris (Lyon)	arr.	..	Drive across
Paris (Lyon)	dep.	17 0	
Turin (P.N.)	arr.	6 30	
	dep.	7 10	
ROME (Ter)	arr.	1630	
	dep.	1850	
Syracuse	arr.	1135	
Syracuse (Port)	d.	§14 0	Daily except Saturdays.
Malta	arr.	21 0	

S 1 & 2 cl. Sleeping Cars Rome-Syracuse and *v.v.* § Also on Wed. at 22.0 by Tirrenia Line, due Malta, Thur. 7.0.

†Malta	d.	0 0	Daily except Fris.
Syracuse	a.	7 0	2nd day.
,, (Port)	d.	1340	,,
Rome	a.	6 45	3rd day.
,,	d.	8 0	,,
Turin	a.	1830	,,
	d.	1846	,,
Paris (Lyon)	a.	8 10	4th day.
	d.	9 35	,,
Paris (Nord)	a.	10 6	,,
	d.	1030	*via* Boulogne.
LONDON	a.	1720	,,

‡ Also on Thur. at 22.0, by Tirrenia Line, due Syracuse, Fri. at 6.0.

IV.—Steamer from Marseilles.

Pharaonic Mail Line.

For details of steamer services see page 386.

LONDON (Vic.)	dep.	Mon.	11 0	
Paris (Lyon)	dep.	,,	2050	
Marseilles	arr.	Tues.	7 53	
Marseilles	dep.	,,	12 0	Aug. 1, 8, 22, Sept. 5, 19
Malta	arr.	Thur.	7	

Malta dep. Sat. 9.0., Aug. 5, 19, 26, Sept. 2, 9, 16.

Marseilles	arr.	Mon.	7 0
Marseilles	dep.	,,	2015
Paris (Lyon)	arr.	Mon.	8 0
Paris (Lyon)	dep.	,,	9 35
Paris (Nord)	arr.	,,	10 6
Paris (Nord)	dep.	,,	1030
LONDON (Vict.)	arr.	,,	1720

GENERAL INFORMATION for PASSENGERS

THE TIME TABLES.

The following Time Tables are compiled from information supplied by the Steamship Companies, and the Editor cannot hold himself responsible for any delays or inconvenience caused by inaccuracies which occur herein. Every effort is made to render the information given correct, but changes are continually being made by the Companies, often without previous warning, and travellers are therefore recommended to compare these Tables with the Local Tables at every opportunity. Suggestions and corrections will be thankfully received and have due attention if addressed to the Editor, "Cook's Continental Time Tables Tourists' Handbook and Steamship Tables," Berkeley Street, Piccadilly, London, W.1.

THE FLEETS.

Where possible, a list of the fleet, with the gross tonnage of the various companies is given, but owing to the lack of space, it is impossible to include the fleets of the large companies such as the Peninsular and Oriental, Royal Mail Lines, Lloyd Triestino, Union-Castle Line, etc., etc. The Editor, however, has full information at hand and will be pleased to supply same upon application.

IMPORTANT EXPLANATIONS OF THE TABLES.

ONE LIST OF PORTS serves, in some of the tables, for both directions. In these cases the days and times on the LEFT of the names are to be read DOWNWARDS, but those on the RIGHT must be read UPWARDS, from the bottom to top. For instance, see page 372; *on the left* is the service *from* Trieste to the Black Sea or Danube ports, etc.; *on the right* those returning *from* the Black Sea or Danube ports, etc.

QUARANTINE, STRIKES, Etc.

The Time Tables given are in some cases those in force under normal conditions, but owing to Quarantine Regulations, Strikes, and other circumstances, the various companies give notice that their services are *liable to alteration or suspension without notice*. Prior to engaging passages or definitely arranging tours, enquiry should be made at one of COOK/WAGONS-LITS Offices. In the event of any steamer being detained in quarantine, the expense, whether on board or ashore, is invariably borne by the passenger, the charge being usually about ten shillings first class and five shillings second class per day.

PASSAGES.

During the respective seasons berths on the various steamship lines are usually booked a long while in advance, and it is recommended that passengers secure accommodation as early as possible. A deposit of half passage money is usually required before a berth is definitely booked. Passengers travelling to the Mediterranean ports by the Indian, Australasian, China and Japan steamers will frequently have difficulty in finding accommodation as the Companies can usually fill their vessels with "long distance" passengers. Any COOK/WAGONS-LITS Office will be pleased to apply for berths and issue passage tickets.

TRANSHIPMENT.

The cost of transhipment, either into a vessel of the same or a different line is usually borne by the passenger. Any COOK/WAGONS-LITS Office can make all arrangements for hotel accommodation, meeting passengers, etc.

BAGGAGE: CABIN TRUNKS.

A liberal allowance of free luggage is made by most steamship companies. Arrangements for forwarding heavy luggage can be made with THOS. COOK & SON, who also *insure* the baggage at very reasonable rates. Cabin trunks should not exceed 3 ft. in length, 1 ft. 8 in. or 2 ft. in breadth, and 1 ft. 3 in. in depth. Labels for the baggage should be asked for when passage has been booked.

LANDING AND EMBARKATION.

The expenses of landing, and in some cases of embarking, have to be borne by the passenger. Tickets at low rates, which provide for the landing or embarkation of the passenger with a reasonable quantity of luggage at Alexandria, Beyrout, Patras, Piræus, Port Said, Kantara, Tangier, etc., can be obtained at all COOK/WAGONS-LITS Offices.

THROUGH BOOKINGS.

Arrangements can be made with THOS. COOK & SON and WAGON-LITS COMPANY for the issue of Through Tickets in practically any part of the world.

PASSPORTS.

Full particulars on application. See also pages 34 to 37.

SECTION III.

STEAMSHIP SERVICES

FULL PARTICULARS OF ALL

THE CHIEF STEAMSHIP COMPANIES

FROM

The United Kingdom, The Continent, etc., to All Parts of the World.

WITH LOCAL EUROPEAN, AND EGYPTIAN SERVICES

ALSO USEFUL INFORMATION FOR PASSENGERS.

A Special Supplement (Part IVa.), shewing Steamer Services in Norwegian Fjords.

For Lake, River, and Canal Steamer Services, see Section II.

For further detailed information respecting Services in the Atlantic, Pacific, and the East, consult "COOK'S OCEAN SAILING LISTS," post free on application.

CONTENTS.

INFORMATION FOR PASSENGERS, page 344.

INDEX TO COMPANIES, pages 346 and 347.

TABLES OF DISTANCES between principal Ports in England and Scotland and the Continent and between principal Ports in the Mediterranean and the Black Sea, pages 348 and 349.

Summary of Services from ENGLAND to the MEDITERRANEAN, page 193.

	PORTS.	PAGE.	PORTS.	PAGE.	PORTS.	PAGE.
Summaries of Steamship Services from	Algiers	350	Haifa	353	Piræus	355
	Alexandria	351	Istanbul	353	Port Said	356
	Beyrout	351	Marseilles	354	Trieste	356
	Brindisi	352	Naples	354	Venice	356
	Genoa	352				

Summary of Services from the United Kingdom to Norway, Sweden, Denmark, etc. .. 401

TIME TABLES with full Itineraries, particulars of Fleet, Gross Tonnage, Passenger Accommodation, etc., in following order:

Part I.—Pages 357 to 369: United Kingdom and the Continent (Ports North of Gibraltar) to the Mediterranean, Black Sea, and Ports beyond via the Suez Canal.

Part II.—Pages 371 to 400: Services in the Mediterranean and Black Sea, and from the Mediterranean to Ports beyond via Suez Canal.

Part III.—Pages 402 to 412: United Kingdom to the Continent (Gibraltar and Ports North thereof) Norway, Denmark, Sweden and Russia.

Part IV.—Pages 413 to 430: Local Steamship Services between Continental Ports (North of Gibraltar) Norway, Denmark Sweden, Russia, etc.

Part IVa.—Pages 431 to 441: Special Supplement shewing Norwegian Fjord Summer Services.

Part V.—Pages 442 to 468: Services from the United Kingdom and Continent to Africa (*not* via Suez Canal), America (North and South), Australasia (via the Cape), Canada Canary Islands, etc., etc.

Part VI.—Pages 469 to 481: Miscellaneous Services.

INDEX TO STEAMSHIP COMPANIES.

PAGE

Aberdeen Line .. 442
Aberdeen and Commonwealth Line .. 357
"Adriatica," Soc. An. di Navigazione 371A, 371B, 372/374
Algeciras-Gibraltar Ferry Service .. 371
American Export Lines .. 443
American Mail Line .. 473
American Merchant Lines .. 459
American President Lines .. 473
Anchor Line (1935) Ltd. .. 357, 459
Anglo-Egyptian Mail Line .. 371
Argo Shipping Co. .. 402, 414
Arendal S.S. Co. .. 413
Asiatic S.N. Co., Ltd. .. 469
Associated Humber Lines, 402, 405, 406, 407, 410
Australian Oriental Line .. 469
Barber Line .. 447
Batavier Line .. 402
Berg'nske & N'rd'nfjeldske S.S.Co. 403, 414, 415, 444
Bibby Line .. 358, 403
Bland Line .. 374
Blue Funnel Line .. 358, 403, 442
" Western Australia Service 469
Blue Star Line .. 444
Bohuslanska Coast S.S. Co. .. 416
Booth Line .. 444
Bore S.S. Co. .. 416
Bornholm S.S. Co. (1866) .. 416
Braakman & Co.'s Steamers (Messrs. H.) .. 416
British India S.N. Co. .. 359, 471
Burns-Philp Line .. 470
Canadian Australasian Line .. 472
Canadian National Steamships .. 472
Canadian Pacific .. 403, 459, 472
Carregadores Acoreanos Line .. 403, 443
Cassar & Co. .. 387
Chargeurs Réunis .. 445
China Navigation Co., Ltd. 470
Commonwealth & Dominion Line Ltd. (see Port Line) .. —
Cowasjee, Dinshaw & Bros. Steamers 470
Cunard White Star Ltd. 404, 459, 481
Currie Line .. 360, 407
Dairen Kisen Kaisha .. 471
Denizbank .. 375
Deutsch Ost-Afrika Line .. 359, 446
Dodwell Castle Line (see Barber Line) .. 447
Donaldson Atlantic Line Ltd. .. 459
Dubrovačka Steamship Co. .. 374
East Asiatic Co., Ltd. (see Ostasiatiske Kompagni) .. 360, 460
East Bornholm S.S. Co. .. 418
Eastern and Australian S.S. Co. 473
Elder Dempster Lines .. 447, 472
Ellerman City & Hall Lines .. 361
Ellerman & Bucknall S.S. Co., Ltd. 448
Ellerman and Papayanni Lines .. 361, 410
Ellerman, Westcott & Laurance Line 361
Ellerman's Wilson Line .. 410
Empreza Insulana 448
Euphrates & Tigris Steam Nav. Co. .. 472
Fabre Line .. 448
Finland Line .. 404, 417
Finmark Fylkesrederis Skibe .. 419
Fiumana Soc. di Navigazione .. 375, 376
Fop Smit & Co. .. 419
Forenede S.S. Co. .. 404, 418/419
Fraissinet French Mail S.S. Co. .. 376, 448
Fred Olsen's S.S. Line 405, 423, 448
French Line (see Transatlantique)-(Cie Generale) —
Furness Line .. 360, 449, 459
Fyffes Line .. 449
Fylkesbaatene i sogn og Fjordane .. 434/438
Gdynia-Ameryka, Linje Zeglugowe S.A. 416, 449, 459
Do. (Palestine Service) .. 377
General S.N. Co. .. 405
Genovese di Navigazione a Vapore .. 377
German Africa Service (see Deutsch Ost.-Africa Line) .. —
Glen Line and Shire Line .. 360
Goteborg Frederikshavn Linjen Gothenburg Frederikshavn S.S. Co. .. 420
Gotha S.S. Co. .. 420
Gotland S.S. Co. .. 420
Grace Line .. 474
Guernsey, Alderney and Sark S.S. Co. .. 405
Halland Ångbats Åktiebolag .. 420
Hamburg America Line 362, 406, 417, 420, 450, 459
Hamburg-Bremer Afrika Line .. 359, 446
Hamburg South American Line .. 451
Handris S.S. Co. Ltd. .. 378
Hardanger Sunndhordlandske S.S. Co. 432/433
Harrison Line .. 452
Havraise Peninsulaire de Navigation a Vapeur 377
Helgelandske Dampskibsselskab .. 433
Hellenic Coast Lines .. 378
Henderson Line .. 362
Holland Australia Line .. 363
Holland Africa Line .. 363, 452
Holland America Line .. 406, 459, 462
Holland British India Line .. 363
Holland East Asia Line .. 363
Holland S.S. Co 406
Holland West Africa Line 452
Horn Line .. 453
Houlder Line .. 453
Hull and Netherlands S.S. Co., Ltd. 407
Iceland S.S. Co. .. 421
Indherreds S.S. Cos. .. 421, 440
Indian African Line .. 474
Indo-China Steam Nav. Co. .. 474
Indochinois, Societe les Affréteurs Maritime 475
Asiatique, Cie de Navigation, Haiphong .. 475
Interocean Line .. 453
Irrawaddy Flotilla Co., Ltd. 475
"Italia"—Soc. An. di Navigazione 454, 455
"Istria-Trieste" Societa di Navigazione a Vapore .. 381
Jadranska Line .. 379/381
Jamaica Banana Producers S.S. Co. Ltd. 455
Japan Mail Line (see Nippon Yusen Kaisha) —
Java, China, Japan Line .. 475
Jersey St. Malo Mail Service 409
John Hall Line (see Mac Andrews & Co. Ltd.) —
Johnson Line .. 456
Jugoslav Lloyd Line .. 381
Khedivial Mail S.S. and Graving Dock Co., Ltd. (See Pharaonic Mail Line)
Kitanihon Kisen Kaisha 477
Koninklijke Nederlandsche Stoomboot Maatschappij N V. .. 456
Koninklijke Paketvaart Maatschappij .. 476
Kosmos Line .. 450
Kristianssands S.S. Co. .. 416
Lamport and Holt Line .. 457

INDEX TO STEAMSHIP COMPANIES—continued.

PAGE

A/S Larvik-Frederikshavnferjen 420
Leith, Hull & Hamburg S.P. Co., Ltd. 360, 407
La Punta de Europa (Compañia de Vapores de) 371
Lloyd Triestino, Soc. An. Navigazione 456A, 382/385, 481
London Midland and Scottish Rly. 405
London & North Eastern Railway Co. .. 406
MacAndrews & Co. Ltd. 363
MacAndrew-Yeoward Service 468
Malta - Syracuse - Malta - Tunis Service (Cassar & Co.) 387
Mariehamn, S.S. Co. 421
Maritime Nationale Société 387
Matson Line .. 477
Messageries Maritimes de France .. 388/390, 457
Misr de Navigation Maritime (Societe) .. 387
Mixte (Compagnie de Navigation) 391
More Fylkes Rute Co. .. 439/440
Moss Hutchison Line Ltd. 407, 362
Næsoddens S.S. Co. 431
Namdalens Aktie-Dampsskibsselskap .. 421
Namsos S.S. Co. 422
Natal Line of Steamers 457
Navegacao (Companhia Colonial de) .. 457
Navegacao (Companhia Nacional de) .. 457
Netherlands Railways (s.s. Services) 422
North Atlantic Services 459
Nederland Line—Royal Dutch Mail 364
New Zealand Shipping Co., Ltd. 459
Nile Steamers 370
Nippon Yusen Kaisya .. 364, 407, 478
Nordenfjeldske & Bergenske S.S. Co. 408, 414/415
Norddeutscher Lloyd 365, 407, 417, 422, 458, 459
Nordmøre Fergeselskap A/S. 440
Normandy S.N. Co. 422
North Japan S.S. Co. Ltd. (see Kitanihou Kisen Kaisha .. .. —
Norwegian-America Line 459
Norwegian Fjord Steamers 431/441
Nouvelle Cie-Havraise Peninsulaire (see Havraise Peninsulaire de Nav.) .. .. —
Oceanic Steamship Company (Matson Line) 477
Ofotens Dampskibsselskap .. 415 & 424
Olsen (see under Fred Olsen Line) .. —
Oresund S.S. Co. 422
Orient Line 365
Osaka Syosen Kaisha 479
Ostasiatiske Kompagni 360, 460
Ozean Line 458
Pacific S.N. Co. 462
Palestine Maritime Lloyd 392
Paquet Line (Cie de N.) .. 392, 460
Partenopea Societe An. di Navigazione 391
Pärnu Rederi A-B, ... 423
Peninsular & Oriental S.N. Co. .. 366, 367
Pharaonic Mail Line 386, 477
Phillipine Inter-Island S.S. Co. .. 478
Polsko-Brytyiskie Tow. Okretowe S.A. (Polish British S.S. Co. Ltd.) 407
Port Line 460, 479
Prince Line 367, 480
Provinciale Stoombootdiénst op de Wester-Schelde 427
Red Star Line 402, 459
Rotterdam Lloyd Royal Mail Line 368
Royal Netherlands Steamship Co. (see Koninklijke Nederlandsche Stoomboot Maatschappij N.V.) .. .. —

PAGE

Royal Mail Lines, Ltd. 461/462
Royal Packet Steam Navigation Co. .. 476
Roumanian State Maritime Service 393
Rud-Christ Gribel .. 423
Saigonnaise Cie de Navigation et de Transport 480
Saltens S.S. Co. 424
Sandnaes S.S. Co. 425
Sartori & Berger's Steamers 424
Sark Motor Ships Ltd. 407
Seedienst Ostpreussen (Danzig and East Prussia Service) 417
Sergo & Co. 424
Shaw Savill Line 368, 442, 463
Skandinaviske Syd-Pacific Linje 463
Skipafelagid Føroyar (S.S. Co.) 427
Societe des Bateaux de la Côte d'Emeraude 426
Sondenfjelds Norske S.S. Co. 424
Sota and Aznar Line 368
Southern Rly. Co., Jersey-St. Malo .. 409
States Steamship Company 480
Stavanger S.S. Co. .. 418, 415, 425, 431
Stettiner Dampfschiffs-Gesellschaft J. F. Braeunlich, G.m.b.H. 417, 426
Straits Steamship Co. 480
Strick & Ellerman Lines 368
Sudan Railways White Nile Steamer Service 370
Sud-Americana de Vapores (Cia.) 463
Sud-Atlantique 445
Svea S.S. Co. 408, 425/426
Svenska Amerika Linjens Ostersjötrafik (Swedish America Line) .. 427
Svenska Lloyd (Swedish Lloyd) .. 408
Svenska Orient Linien (Swedish Orient Line) 369
Svenska Ostasiatiska Kompaniet (Swedish East Asiatic Co. Ltd.) 369
Swedish Lloyd (see Svenska Lloyd) .. .. —
Swedish-American Line .. 459
Terschellinger Stoomboot-Maatschappij .. 427
Texel's Own S.S. Co. .. 427
"Tirrenia," Societa An. di Navigazione 395/397, 397A
Tonsberg & Hortens S.S. Co. .. 431
Transatlantic S.S. Co. (Gothenburg) 463
Transatlantique (Cie Generale), 394, 404, 459, 466
Transports Maritimes à Vapeur (Societede) 398, 464
Trasatlantica Española 464
Trasmediterranea Compania 399, 465
Tyne Tees Steam Shipping Co., Ltd. 409
Troms Fylkes Dampskibsselskab .. 428, 440
Turkish Mail Line (Denizbank) .. 375
Union-Castle S.S. Co., Ltd. 369, 410/412, 467
United Baltic Corporation Ltd. 409
United Fruit Company 481
United Netherlands Nav. Co. 363, 452
United States Lines 409, 459
U.S.S.R. Steamers 393, 408
Vesteraalens S.S. Co. 415, 428
Villain and Fassio (Società di Navigazione) 398
Wasa North Sea S.S. Co. 428
Westfal-Larsen Co. Line 453
Wilh. Wilhelmsen Lines 369, 468
Woermann Line 359, 446
Ybarra y Cià, Seville 468
Yeoward Line (see MacAndrew-Yeoward Service)
Zetska, Plovidba A.D., Cetinje 398

Table of Approximate Distances between Principal Ports in ENGLAND AND SCOTLAND AND THE CONTINENT.

In Nautical Miles or Knots.

Dover to

	Nautical Miles
Calais	22
Ostend	68

Folkestone to

Boulogne	30

Goole to

Amsterdam	237
Antwerp	283
Boulogne	224
Ghent	265
Hamburg	413
Rotterdam	234

Grimsby to

Antwerp	220
Esbjerg	368
Gothenburg	502
Hamburg	360
Malmö	614
Rotterdam	197

Harwich to

Antwerp	140
Esbjerg	350
Flushing	90
Hamburg	340
Hook of Holland	101
Zeebrugge	88

Hull to

Amsterdam	223
Antwerp	263
Bergen	513
Christiansand	410

Hull to

	Nautical Miles
Christiansund	668
Copenhagen	612
Danzig	895
Ghent	253
Gibraltar	1501
Gothenburg	510
Hamburg	387
Leningrad	1307
Libau	938
Lisbon	1244
Malmö	627
Oslo	553
Reval	1130
Riga	1073
Rotterdam	230
Stavanger	413
Stettin	783
Stockholm	1233
Trondheim	756
Zeebrugge	200

Leith to

Amsterdam	375
Antwerp	470
Christiansand	385
Copenhagen	621
Dunkirk	394
Hamburg	489
Harlingen	356
Oslo	555
Reykjavik	880
Rotterdam	370
Stockholm	1093

Liverpool to

	Nautical Miles
Algiers	1665
Barcelona	1798
Bordeaux	690
Genoa	2144
Gibraltar	1260
Izmir	2870
La Pallice	605
Lisbon	983
Malta	2240
Marseilles	1964
Naples	2185
Oporto	796
Vigo	735

London to

Amsterdam Canal	188
Barcelona	1873
Boulogne	118
Bremen	405
Christiansand	511
Copenhagen	715
Gibraltar	1325
Gothenburg	609
Hamburg	435
Leningrad	1620
Lisbon	1027
Malta	2315
Marseilles	2030
Naples	2290
Oslo	656
Riga	1182
Rotterdam	183
Vigo	810

Newcastle (Shields) to

	Nautical Miles
Amsterdam	280
Antwerp	330
Arendal	400
Bergen	392
Christiansand	365
Copenhagen	586
Gothenburg	480
Hamburg	400
Malmö	592
Oslo	488
Rotterdam	300
Stavanger	342
Stockholm	998

Newhaven to

Dieppe	76

Plymouth to

Cherbourg	110
Gibraltar	1049

Southampton to

Antwerp	244
Cherbourg	83
Genoa	2022
Gibraltar	1172
Guernsey	104
Hamburg	520
Havre	104
St. Malo	151

Table of Approximate Distances between Principal Ports in the MEDITERRANEAN and BLACK SEA.

In Nautical Miles or Knots.

Ajaccio to

	Nautical Miles
Cagliari	250
Villefranche	140

Alexandria to

Barcelona	1465
Beyrout	340
Corfu	780
Danube	1080
Haifa	290
Istanbul	750
Izmir	540
Jaffa	267
Naples	1002
Odessa	1090
Piræus, The	512
Port Said	142
Suez	260
Syracuse	800

Alexandretta to

	Nautical Miles
Latakia	90

Algiers to

Ajaccio (Corsica)	390
Alicante	196
Almeria	271
Barcelona	283
Carthagena	180
Genoa	530
Gibraltar	420
Malta	575
Marseilles	410
Naples	584
Palermo	510
Villefranche	470

Almeria to

Naples	838

Ancona to

	Nautical Miles
Corfu	380
Trieste	140

Barcelona to

Naples	558

Batumi to

Sebastopol	415
Trebizond	95

Beyrout to

Haifa	72
Istanbul	840
Izmir	675
Jaffa	122
Larnaca	120
Tripoli (Syria)	45

Bourgas to

	Nautical Miles
Constanza	125
Sulina	190
Varna	53

Brindisi to

Alexandria	836
Corfu	135
Istanbul	845
Izmir	692
Malta	365
Marseilles	838
Patras	251
Piræus, The	482
Port Said	920
Trieste	426
Venice	395

Nautical Mile or Knot = 1·153 Statute Miles = 1,825 Metres.

Table of Approximate Distances between Principal Ports in the MEDITERRANEAN and BLACK SEA—continued.

Cagliari to

	Nautical Miles
Tunis	165

Candia to

	Nautical Miles
Kyrenia	397

Catacolo to

	Nautical Miles
Naples	464
Nauplia	220
Palermo	416

Catania to

	Nautical Miles
Messina	42

Civita Vecchia to

	Nautical Miles
Leghorn	120
Marseilles	357
Naples	160

Constanza to

	Nautical Miles
Gelibolou	320
Nicolaev	235
Sebastopol	218
Sulina	80
Varna	78

Corfu to

	Nautical Miles
Malta	335
Messina	300
Trieste	460

Genoa to

	Nautical Miles
Alexandria	1350
Barcelona	360
Bastia	144
Elba	110
Gibraltar	850
Istanbul	2046
Leghorn	82
Malta	650
Marseilles	215
Messina	498
Palermo	443
Piræus, The	990
Port Said	1485
Salonica	1548
Villefranche	85

Gibraltar to

	Nautical Miles
Algiers	442
Barcelona	525
Bona	650
Brindisi	1314
Carthagena	245
Elba	865
Istanbul	1765
Leghorn	880
Lisbon	304
Malaga	65
Malta	980
Messina	1020
Naples	960
Oran	230
Palermo	945
Port Said	1937
Tangier	33
Villefranche	760

Haifa to

	Nautical Miles
Jaffa	54

Istanbul to

	Nautical Miles
Batumi	585
Bourgas	129
Constanza	198
Gelibolou	120
Gireson	465
Izmir	283
Kherson	380
Malta	835
Odessa	320
Palermo	927
Piræus, The	356
Santorin	362
Sebastopol	300
Sinop	290
Sukhumi	550
Taganrog	590
Trebizond	490
Varna	140

Jaffa to

	Nautical Miles
Istanbul	860
Port Said	134

Kalamaki to

	Nautical Miles
Nauplia	115

Kyrenia to

	Nautical Miles
Beyrout	190

Leghorn to

	Nautical Miles
Marseilles	258

Malaga to

	Nautical Miles
Algiers	360
Cadiz	138
Marseilles	730

Malta to

	Nautical Miles
Alexandria	816
Marseilles	650
Messina	160
Naples	343
Nauplia	520
Palermo	240
Port Said	943
Tripoli	204
Tunis	225

Marseilles to

	Nautical Miles
Alexandria	1422
Gibraltar	694
Istanbul	1486
Piræus, The	1129
Port Said	1508
Syracuse	654
Taormina	608
Tunis	471

Messina to

	Nautical Miles
Naples	175
Palermo	120
Syracuse	80

Naples to

	Nautical Miles
Algiers	588
Genoa	336
Jaffa	1200
Marseilles	456
Patras	482
Port Said	1111
Syracuse	215
Trieste	815
Villefranche	360

Nauplia to

	Nautical Miles
Marseilles	1048
Messina	540
Syracuse	473

Odessa to

	Nautical Miles
Batum	570
Bourgas	285
Constanza	175
Gelibolou	460
Kherson	65
Sebastopol	163
Taganrog	500

Palermo to

	Nautical Miles
Candia	632
Naples	170
Suda Bay	581

Palma (Maj.) to

	Nautical Miles
Algiers	175
Marseilles	290
Villefranche	357

Patras to

	Nautical Miles
Corfu	105
Palermo	424
Trieste	610

Piræus, The, to

	Nautical Miles
Beyrout	695
Corfu, *round Morea* (Is.)	384
Gelibolou	260
Izmir	202
Jaffa	680
Kalamaki	88
Malta	525
Naples	656
Nauplia	92
Odessa	696
Palermo	610
Patras, *via Corinth Canal*	120
Sebastopol	660
Syracuse	490

Port Said to

	Nautical Miles
Beyrout	260
Ismailia	43
Suez	87

Rhodes to

	Nautical Miles
Kyrenia (Cyprus)	257

Santorin to

	Nautical Miles
Izmir	192
Rhodes	148
Suda Bay	86

Syracuse to

	Nautical Miles
Catania	30
Malta	90
Santorin	494

Tangier to

	Nautical Miles
Malaga	90
Palma (Majorca)	478

Taormina to

	Nautical Miles
Istanbul	807

Trieste to

	Nautical Miles
Alexandria	1200
Port Said	1295
Venice	67

Tripoli (Syria) to

	Nautical Miles
Latakia	60

Villefranche to

	Nautical Miles
Malta	683
Palermo	46
Syracuse	59

Nautical Mile or Knot = 1·153 Statute Miles = 1852 metres.

LINE.	PORTS OF CALL.	SAILING	PAGE.
	From LONDON.		
P. & O.	Tangier, Gibraltar, Marseilles, Malta (every 2 weeks), Port Said	Weekly	366
Do.	Gibraltar, Marseilles, Port Said	Fortnightly ..	366
Do.	(Gibraltar, Marseilles), Port Said	Fortnightly ..	367
Orient	Gibraltar, Toulon, Naples, Port Said	About fortnightly	365
Prince	Malta, Alexandria, Jaffa, Haifa, Beyrout (or Malta, Famagusta Haifa, etc.)	Every 3 weeks ..	367
British India	Malta, Port Said	Every 4 weeks ..	359
Do.	Marseilles, Malta, Pt. Said	Every 4 weeks ..	359
Nippon Yusen Kaisya ..	Gibraltar, Marseilles, Naples, Port Said ..	Fortnightly ..	364
Union-Castle	Tangier, Gibraltar, Marseilles, Genoa, Port Said	Every 4 weeks ..	369
Glen Line & Shire Line	Port Said	Fortnightly ..	360
Ellerman, Wescott and Laurance	Gibraltar, Malta, Alexandria	—	361
Do.	Gibraltar, Malta, Piraeus, Istanbul, etc. ..	—	361
Ellerman City and Hall ..	Marseilles (occasional), Port Said	Occasional ..	361
MacAndrew & Co. Ltd. (John Hall Line) ..	Gibraltar, Barcelona, etc.	—	363
Do. do.	Pasajes, Bilbao, Santander, Spanish Ports round to Barcelona	—	363
Do. do.	Lisbon, Gibraltar and Morocco Ports ..	Every 5 weeks ..	363
	From SOUTHAMPTON.		
P. & O.	Tangier (Gibraltar, Marseilles), Port Said ..	Fortnightly ..	366
Aberdeen & Commonw'lth	Malta, Port Said	Monthly ..	357
Rotterdam Lloyd ..	Lisbon, Tangier, Gibraltar, Marseilles, Port Said	Every 3 weeks ..	368
Nederland Line (Royal Dutch Mail)	Algiers, Villefranche (Nice), Genoa, Port Said	Every 3 weeks ..	364
East Asiatic Co.	Marseilles, Port Said	Occasional ..	360
German Africa Service	Lisbon, (Tangiers, Algiers, Villefranche), Genoa, Port Said	Every 3 or 4 weeks	359
Norddeutscher Lloyd ..	Genoa, Port Said	About monthly ..	365
	From LIVERPOOL.		
Bibby	Gibraltar, Marseilles, Port Said	Fortnightly ..	358
Blue Funnel	Marseilles, Port Said	Every 4 weeks ..	358
Anchor	Gibraltar, Marseilles, Port Said	Twice monthly ..	357
Ellerman's City and Hall Lines	Marseilles or direct to Port Said	Sev'l times m'thly	361
Henderson	Gibraltar, Marseilles, Port Said	Fortnightly ..	362
Ellerman & Papayanni Lines	Gibraltar, Malta, Alexandria, Jaffa, Haifa, Beyrout, etc.	Occasional ..	361
Do. do. ..	Piræus, Volo, Thessaloniki, Izmir, Istanbul, etc.	Occasional ..	361
Ellerman, Westcott and Laurance	Gibraltar, Malta, Alexandria and Cyprus ..	Every 3 weeks ..	361
Do. do. ..	Malta, Piræus, Thessaloniki, Istanbul, Izmir	Every 3 weeks ..	361
MacAndrew-Yeow'd Serv'e	Lisbon, (Casablanca occasionally), Madeira, etc.	Weekly	468
MacAndrew & Co. Ltd.	Barcelona, Valencia	Occasional ..	363
Do. do. ..	Pasajes, Bilbao, etc...	Occasional ..	363
Furness Line	Piræus, Volo, Thessaloniki, Izmir, Istanbul, etc	Every 3 weeks ..	360
	From MANCHESTER.		
Prince	Tunis, Malta, Alexandria, Jaffa, Haifa, Beyrout	About Fortnightly	368

SUMMARY of SAILINGS from ALGIERS to GREECE, EGYPT, Etc.

LINE.	PORTS OF CALL.	SAILING	PAGE.
Nederland Line (Royal Dutch Mail)	Villefranche (Nice), Genoa, Port Said ..	Fortnightly ..	364
Do. do. ..	Southampton	About fortnightly	364
Cie Transatlantique (French Line)	Marseilles	Four times w'kly	394
Cie. Mixte	Marseilles	Twice weekly ..	391
Do.	Port Vendres	Twice weekly ..	391
"Italia"	N'les, Palermo, Patras, Ragusa (Venice), Trieste	Occasional ..	455
Do.	Naples, Trieste	Occasional ..	455
Do.	Gibraltar (Lisbon)	Occasional ..	455
German Africa Service ..	Villefranche, Genoa, Port Said	Monthly	359
Do. do. ..	Tangier, Lisbon, Southampton, Antwerp or Rotterdam, Hamburg	Monthly	359

SUMMARY OF SAILINGS FROM ALEXANDRIA.

Subject to alteration in case of Quarantine, Strikes, etc.

LINE.	PORTS OF CALL.	SAILING.	PAGE.
American Export Lines	Jaffa, Beyrout	Fortnightly ..	443
Do. do. ..	Piræus, Naples, Genoa, Marseilles, etc. ..	Fortnightly ..	443
American President Lines	Naples, Genoa, Marseilles.. ..	Fortnightly ..	473
Pharaonic Mail Line ..	Pt. Said, Limassol, Famag'sta, Larnaca, Limassol	Weekly	386
Do.	Port Said, Jaffa, Haifa, Beyrout, etc.	Weekly	386
Do.	Naples, Genoa (or Malta), Marseilles	Fortnightly ..	386
Do.	Beyrout	Fort'tly in Sum.	386
"Adriatica"	Syracuse, Naples, Genoa (Grand Express) ..	Fortnightly ..	371A
Do.	Haifa (Grand Express)	Weekly	371A
Do.	Brindisi, Venice, Trieste (Grand Express) ..	Fortnightly ..	371A
Do.	Rhodes, Piræus, Brindisi, Venice, Trieste (Fast Line)	Fortnightly ..	371A
Do.	Rhodes, Piræus, Naples, Genoa	Fortnightly ..	371A
Do.	Port Said, Jaffa, Haifa, Beyrout, etc. (Line 56)	Fortnightly ..	371B
Do.	Port Said, Jaffa, Haifa, Beyrout, etc. (Commercial Line)	Fortnightly ..	371B
Do.	Candia (optional), Calamata (optional), Brindisi (optional), Venice, Trieste (Line 57)	Fortnightly ..	371B
Do.	Rhodes, Piræus, Brindisi, Bari, Trieste, Venice (Line 51)	Fortnightly ..	372
"Tirrenia"	Porto Bardia, Tobruk, Derna, Bengasi, Tripoli	Fortnightly ..	397
Messageries Maritimes ..	(Jaffa), Haifa, Beyrout	Weekly	388
Do. do. ..	Marseilles	Weekly	388
Roumanian	Piræus, Istanbul, Constanza	Fortnightly ..	393
Do.	Haifa, Beyrout, Piræus, Istanbul, Constanza ..	Fortnightly ..	393
Handris s.s. Co., Ltd. ..	.. ..	.. .. ..	378
Hellenic Coast Lines ..	Piræus	Weekly ..	378
Do do. ..	Piræus, Chalcis, Volo, Thessaloniki	Fortnightly ..	378
Do. do. ..	Port Said, Jaffa, Haifa, Beyrout, etc.	Fortnightly ..	378
Jugoslav Lloyd Line ..	Piræus, Dubrovnik 2, Venice, Trieste	Fortnightly ..	381
Soc. Misr de Nav. Maritime	Genoa, Marseilles	Fortnightly ..	387
Anglo-Egyptian Mail ..	Piræus, Marseilles	Fortnightly ..	371
Prince Line	Manchester, London, Hull, etc.	Every 12-14 days	368

SUMMARY OF SAILINGS FROM BEYROUT.

LINE.	PORTS OF CALL.	SAILING.	PAGE.
Pharaonic Mail Line ..	Tripoli (Lattakia fortnightly), Alexandretta, Mersin, etc.	Weekly	386
Do.	Larnaca, Haifa, Jaffa, P. Said, Alexandria ..	Weekly	386
Do.	Alexandria, Naples, Genoa, Marseilles ..	Fort'tly in Sum.	386
"Adriatica"	Alexandria, Syracuse, Naples, Genoa. (Grand Express)	Fortnightly ..	371A
Do.	Haifa, Larnaca, Brindisi, Trieste. (Palestine Fast Line)	Fortnightly ..	371A
Do.	Syrian Ports, Cyprus, Rhodes, Piræus, Candia, Brindisi, Venice, Trieste (Line 56)	Fortnightly ..	371B
Do.	Haifa, Jaffa, Port Said, Alexandria, Candia, (optional), Brindisi (optional), Venice, Trieste (Line 57)	Fortnightly ..	371B
Do.	Syrian Ports, Cyprus, Izmir, Naples, Marseilles, Genoa (Line 58)	Fortnightly ..	371B
Messageries Maritimes ..	Rhodes, Izmir, Ist'bul, Piræus, Naples, Mar'les	Every 4 weeks ..	388
Do. do. ..	Izmir, Istanbul, Piræus, Marseilles	Every 4 weeks ..	388
Do. do. ..	Haifa, Alexandria, Marseilles	Weekly	388
Do. do. ..	Larnaca or Tripoli or Alexandretta	Frequent	388
American Export Lines	Haifa, Alex'ndria, Piræus, Naples, Genoa, Mar'les	Fortnightly ..	443
Roumanian State ..	Haifa, Alexandria, Piræus, etc.	Fortnightly ..	393
Do. do. ..	Piræus, Istanbul, Constanza	Fortnightly ..	393
Hellenic Coast Line ..	Haifa, Jaffa, Port Said, Alexandria, Piræus, etc.	Fortnightly ..	378
Do. do. ..	Tripoli, Cyprus, Piræus, etc.	Fortnightly ..	378

SUMMARY OF SAILINGS FROM BRINDISI.

To Greece and Egypt, etc., etc.

Subject to alteration or suspension without notice, owing to Quarantine, Strikes, etc.

LINE.	PORTS OF CALL.	SAILING.	PAGE.
"Adriatica"	Alexandria, Haifa, (Grand Express)	Fortnightly ..	371A
Do.	Piræus, Rhodes, Alexandria (Fast Line)	Fortnightly ..	371A
Do.	Larnaca, Haifa, Beyrout	Fortnightly ..	371A
Do.	Piræus, Istanbul	Weekly ..	371B
Do.	Piræus, Alexandria, P. Said, Haifa, Beyrout, etc. (Line 56)	Fortnightly ..	371B
Do.	Patras, Calamata, Cyprus, Syrian Ports, Beyrout, etc. (Line 57)	Fortnightly ..	371B
Do	Piræus, Thessaloniki, C'alla, Ist'bul, etc. (Line 59)	Fortnightly ..	372
Do.	Santi Quaranta, Calamata, Piræus, Izmir, Mitylene, Thessaloniki, Istanbul, etc. (Line 60)	Fortnightly ..	372
Do.	Piræus, Rhodes, Alexandria (Line 51)	Fortnightly ..	372
Do.	Albanian and Dalmatian Ports Trieste. Venice	Weekly	373
Do.	St. Quaranta, Corfu, Piræus, Izmir, etc. (Line 43A)	Weekly	373
Do.	Albanian and Dalmatian Ports, Trieste, Venice	Weekly	373
Lloyd Triestino	Port Said (Grand Express)	Monthly	382
Handris s.s. Co., Ltd.	Piræus, Alexandria	Weekly	378
Hellenic Coast Lines Ltd.	Santi Quaranta, Corfu, Patras, Piræus, etc. ..	Twice weekly ..	378

SUMMARY OF SAILINGS FROM GENOA.

To the Adriatic, Egypt, Gibraltar, etc., etc.

Subject to alteration or suspension without notice, owing to Quarantine, Strikes, etc.

LINE.	PORTS OF CALL.	SAILING.	PAGE.
Union-Castle	Port Said	Every 4 weeks ..	369
Do.	Marseilles, Gibraltar, Tangier, London.. ..	Every 4 weeks ..	369
Nederland Line (Royal Dutch Mail)	Port Said	Every 3 weeks ..	364
Do.	Nice (Villefranche), Algiers, Southampton, Amsterdam	Every 3 weeks ..	364
"Adriatica"	Naples, Alex'dria, Haifa, Bey'ut (Grand Express)	Fortnightly	371A
Do.	Naples, Piræus, Rhodes, Alexandria	Fortnightly ..	371A
Do.	Naples, Sicily, Alexandria, Port Said, Jaffa, Haifa, Beyrout, etc.	Fortnightly ..	371B
Do.	Naples, Sicily, Piræus, Istanbul, etc. (Line 59 *bis*)	Fortnightly ..	372
Lloyd Triestino	Naples, Port Said. (Grand Express)	Monthly	382
Do. do.	Naples, Port Said (Australian Service)	Monthly	382
Do. do.	Naples, Messina, Port Said (Line B)	Fortnightly	383
Do. do.	Naples, Port Said (Line C)	Every 4 weeks ..	383
Do. do.	Naples, Port Said (Djibouti, Calcutta)	Monthly	385
Do. do.	Marseilles, Gibraltar	Monthly	456A
"Tirrenia"	Marseilles	Weekly	397A
Do.	Leghorn, Naples, Sicily, Fiume, Trieste ..	Weekly	397A
Do.	Cagliari, Tunis	Weekly	395
Do.	Palma, Tangier, Seville	Every 20 days	397A
German African Lines ..	Port Said	Every 3 or 4 weeks	359
Do. do. ..	Marseilles, (Algiers, Tangier, March-August) Lisbon, Southampton, Rotterdam, Hamburg	Monthly	359
Soc. Misr de Nav. Maritime	Alexandria	Every 4 weeks ..	386
Pharaonic Mail Line ..	Alexandria	Every 4 weeks ..	386
Do.	Marseilles		
Holland-Africa	Marseilles, (Tangier, Lisbon, Dover in Summer), Antwerp, Rotterdam, Hamburg	Monthly ..	363
East Asiatic Co.	Port Said, (Tangier, Lisbon, Southampton occasionally)	Monthly	360
Norddeutscher Lloyd ..	Port Said	About fortnightly	365
Do. do.	Southampton, Rotterdam, Bremen	Monthly	365
"Italia"	Naples	Occasional	454
Do.	Nice, Naples, Gibraltar	Several slgs. mthy	454
Do.	Nice, Barcelona	Occasional .	454
Cie Genovese	Naples, Sicily, Piræus, Istanbul & Danube Ports	Fortnightly	377
American Export Lines	Marseilles, etc.	Fortnightly ..	443
Villain-Fassio	Palma, Seville	Every 20 days ..	398

SUMMARY OF SAILINGS FROM HAIFA.

Subject to alteration owing to Quarantine, Strikes, etc.

LINE.	PORTS OF CALL.	SAILING.	PAGE.
"Adriatica"	Beyrout, Alexandria, Syracuse, Naples, Genoa (Grand Express)	Fortnightly ..	371A
Do.	Alexandria, Brindisi, Venice, Trieste (Grand Express).	Fortnightly ..	371A
Do.	Larnaca, Brindisi, Trieste (Palestine Fast Line)	Fortnightly ..	371A
Do.	Beyrout, Syrian Ports, Cyprus, Rhodes, Piræus, Brindisi, Venice, Trieste (Line 56)	Fortnightly ..	371B
Do.	Jaffa, Port Said, Alexandria, Candia (optional), Brindisi (optional), Venice, Trieste (Line 57)	Fortnightly ..	371B
Do.	Beyrout, Syrian Ports, Cyprus, Izmir, Naples, Marseilles, Genoa (Commercial Line 58)	Fortnightly ..	371B
Messageries Maritimes ..	Alexandria (Palermo occasionally), Marseilles	Fortnightly ..	388
Do. do. ..	Beyrout, Larnaca or Tripoli or Alexandretta ..	Weekly	388
Do. do. ..	Beyrout, Izmir, Istanbul, Piræus, Marseilles	Every 4 weeks	388
American Export Lines	Alexandria, Piræus, Naples, Leghorn, Genoa, Marseilles, Gibraltar, etc.	Fortnightly ..	448
Pharaonic Mail Line ..	Beyrout, Tripoli (Lattakia), Mersin, Alexandretta, etc.	Weekly	386
Do.	Jaffa, Port Said, Alexandria	Weekly	386
Roumanian State ..	Alexandria, Piræus, Istanbul, Constanza ..	Fortnightly ..	393
Do. do.	Beyrout, Piræus, Istanbul, Constanza	Fortnightly ..	393
Palestine Maritime Lloyd	(Beyrout or Port Said or Cyprus or Tripoli or Rhodes), Istanbul (optional), Constanza	About weekly ..	392
Jugoslav Lloyd Line ..	Alexandria, Piræus, Dubrovnik 2, Venice, Trieste	Fortnightly ..	381
Gdynia-America Line .. (Palestine Service)	Piræus, Istanbul, Constanza	Two or three times monthly	377
Hellenic Coast Lines ..	Jaffa, Port Said, Alexandria, Piræus, etc. ..	Fortnightly ..	378
Do. do. ..	Beyrout, Tripoli, Cyprus, Piræus	Fortnightly ..	378
U.S.S.R. Steamers ..	Port Said, Piræus, Istanbul, Odessa	Every 2–3 weeks	393

SUMMARY OF SAILINGS FROM ISTANBUL (CONSTANTINOPLE).

To Egypt, Syria, Greece, Italy, and France, etc., etc.

Subject to alteration owing to Quarantine, Strikes, etc.

LINE.	PORTS OF CALL.	SAILING.	PAGE.
Denizbank (Turkish Mail Line)	Izmir, Antalaya, Mersin (Payas)	Twice weekly ..	375
Do. do. ..	Izmir	Twice weekly ..	375
"Adriatica"	Piræus, Brindisi, Venice, Trieste	Weekly ..	371B
Do.	C'alla, Thessaloniki, Piræus, P'ras, St. Quaranta, Brindisi, Venice, Trieste (Line 59)	Fortnightly ..	372
Do.	Thessaloniki, Izmir, Calamata, Patras, Brindisi, Venice, Trieste (Line 60)	Fortnightly ..	372
Do.	Thessaloniki, Piræus, Naples, Marseilles, Genoa (Line 59 *bis*)	Fortnightly ..	372
Roumanian State ..	Piræus, Alexandria	Fortnightly ..	393
Do. do. ..	Piræus, Beyrout, Haifa, Alexandria	Fortnightly ..	393
Do. do. ..	Izmir, Piræus (optional), Malta, Naples, etc. ..	Occasional ..	393
Messageries Maritimes ..	Rhodes, Alexandretta, Beyrout	Every 4 weeks	388
Do. do. ..	Odessa, Constanza, Haifa. Beyrout	Every 4 weeks	388
Do. do. ..	Piræus, Naples (every 4 weeks), Marseilles ..	Fortnightly ..	388
Palestine Maritime Lloyd	(Optional) Haifa	Every 2–3 weeks	392
U.S.S.R.	Piræus, Haifa	Fortnightly ..	393
Gdynia-America Line .. (Palestine Service)	Jaffa, Haifa	Two or three sailings monthly	377
Genovese Cia.	Naples, Marseilles, Genoa	Fortnightly ..	377

LINE.	PORTS OF CALL.	SAILING.	PAGE
American Export Lines	Naples, Alexandria, Jaffa, Beyrout ..	Fortnightly ..	443
P. & O.	(Malta every two weeks), Port Said	Weekly	366/7
Do.	Gibraltar, Tangier, Plymouth, London ..	Weekly	366
British India	Malta, Port Said	Every 4 weeks ..	359
Orient Line (from Toulon)	To Naples, Port Said	About fortnightly	365
Do. do. ..	Gibraltar, Plymouth, London	About fortnightly	365
Bibby	Port Said	Fortnightly ..	358
Do.	Gibraltar, Plymouth, London	Fortnightly ..	358
Blue Funnel	Port Said	Every 4 weeks ..	358
Do.	London	Every 4 weeks ..	358
Henderson..	Port Said	Fortnightly ..	362
Do.	Gibraltar, U.K.	Fortnightly ..	362
Ellerman's & City Hall Lines	Port Said	Frequent sailings	361
Do. do. ..	Plymouth	About monthly	361
Union-Castle	Genoa, Port Said	Every 4 weeks ..	369
Do.	Gibraltar, Tangier, London	Every 4 weeks ..	369
German African Service	(Algiers, Tangier Mar.-Aug.) Lisbon, Southampton, Rott'dam, H'mburg	About monthly ..	359
Messageries Maritimes ..	(Naples, Ev. 4 weeks) Piræus, Istanbul, Rhodes, Alex'dretta or Odessa, Const'za, Haifa, B'rout	Fortnightly ..	388
Do. do. ..	Alexandria (Jaffa), Haifa, Beyrout	Weekly	388
Do. do. ..	Port Said	Frequent ..	389/90
East Asiatic Co.	Port Said	Abt. every 8 weeks	360
Nippon Yusen Kaisya ..	Naples Port Said	Fortnightly ..	364
Do. do. ..	Gibraltar, London	Fortnightly ..	364
Rotterdam Lloyd ..	Port Said	Every 3 weeks ..	368
Do. do. ..	Gibraltar, Tangier, Lisbon, S'th'pton, Rotterdam	Every 3 weeks ..	368
Anchor Line	Port Said	2-3 sailings m'thly	357
Soc. Maritime Nationale	Nice, Ajaccio, Tunis, Sousse, Sfax	Fortnightly ..	387
Norddeutscher Lloyd ..	Rotterdam, Hamburg	Frequent	365
Lloyd Triestino	Gibraltar (Dakar, etc.)	Monthly	456A
Chargeurs Reunis ..	Port Said	Monthly	374
Holland-Africa	(Tangier, Lisbon, Dover in Summer), Antwerp, Rotterdam, Hamburg	Monthly	363
Anglo-Egyptian Mail ..	Piræus, Alexandria	Fortnightly ..	371
Soc. Misr de Nav. Maritime	Genoa, Alexandria	Fortnightly ..	387
Pharaonic Mail Line ..	Genoa or Malta, Alexandria	Fortnightly ..	386
"Tirrenia"	Genoa, Leghorn, Naples, Sicily, Malta, Fiume, Trieste	Weekly	397A

SUMMARY OF SAILINGS FROM NAPLES. To the Adriatic, Istanbul, Syria. Egypt, &c.

Orient Line	Port Said	About fortnightly	365
Do.	(Villefranche), Toulon, Gibraltar, London ..	About fortnightly	365
Nippon Yusen Kaisya ..	Port Said	Fortnightly ..	364
Do. do. do. ..	Marseilles, Gibraltar, London	Fortnightly ..	364
Messageries Maritimes ..	Piræus, Istanbul, Rhodes, Alexandretta, Beyrout	Every 4 weeks ..	388
"Adriatica"	Alexandria, Haifa, Beyrout (Grand Express) ..	Fortnightly ..	371A
Do.	Piræus, Rhodes, Alexandria	Fortnightly ..	371A
Do.	Sicily, Piræus Istanbul, etc. (Line 59 *bis*) ..	Fortnightly ..	372
Do.	Sicily, Alex'dria, P't Said, Jaffa, Haifa, B'rout, etc	Fortnightly ..	371B
Lloyd Triestino	Port Said (Grand Express)	Monthly	382
Do. do.	Port Said (Australian Service)	Monthly	382
Do. do.	Port Said (Line A)	Weekly	383
Do. do.	Messina, Port Said (Line B)	Fortnightly ..	383
Do. do.	Port Said (Line C)	Every 4 weeks ..	383
Do. do.	Port Said (Djibouti, Calcutta)	Monthly	385
"Tirrenia"	Leghorn, Genoa, Marseilles	Weekly	397A
Do.	Sicily, Malta, Fiume, Trieste	Weekly	397A
Do.	Palermo, Tunis	Weekly	395
Do.	Syracuse, Malta, Tripoli	Weekly	396
Do.	Syracuse, Bengasi	Fortnightly ..	396
Do.	Palermo, Tripoli	Weekly	397
"Italia"	Genoa, Nice, Gibraltar | Gibraltar	Occasional ..	454
Do.	Patr's, Dubr'vnik (Rag'sa), (Venice occ'lly) Tri'ste	Occasional ..	455
Do.	Palermo, Algiers, Gibraltar, Lisbon	Occasional ..	455
Do.	Algiers, Gibraltar	Occasional ..	455
Do.	Trieste	Monthly	455
Genovese Cia	Sicily, Piræus, Istanbul & Danube Ports ..	Fortnightly ..	377
American Export Lines	Alexandria, Jaffa, Beyrout	Fortnightly ..	443
Do. do. ..	Leghorn, Genoa, Marseilles, etc.	Fortnightly ..	443
Pharaonic Mail Line ..	Alexandria	— ..	—
Do.	Genoa, Marseilles	— ..	386

Subject to alteration or suspension without notice owing to Quarantine, Strikes, etc.

SUMMARY OF SAILINGS FROM PIRÆUS (ATHENS).

To Istanbul, Syria, Egypt, the Adriatic, etc., etc.

NORMAL SERVICES.

LINE	PORTS OF CALL.	SAILING	PAGE.
"Adriatica"	Rhodes, Alexandria (Line 48)	Fortnightly ..	371A
Do.	Naples, Genoa (Line 48)	Fortnightly ..	371A
Do.	Istanbul (Fast Line)	Weekly	371B
Do.	Brindisi, Venice, Trieste (Line 54)	Weekly	371B
Do.	Al'andria, P. Said, Haifa, Beyrout, etc. (Line 56)	Fortnightly ..	371B
Do.	Candia, Brindisi, Venice, Trieste (Line 56) ..	Fortnightly ..	371B
Do.	Volo, Thessaloniki, Cavalla, Istanbul, etc. (Line 59).	Fortnightly ..	372
Do.	Patras, St. Quaranta, Brindisi, Venice, Trieste (Line 59)	Fortnightly ..	372
Do.	Izmir, Mitylene, Thessaloniki, Istanbul, etc. (Line 60)	Fortnightly ..	372
Do.	Calamata, Patras, Brindisi, Venice, Trieste (Line 60)	Fortnightly ..	372
Do.	Rhodes, Alexandria (Line 51)	Fortnightly ..	372
Do.	Brindisi, Bari, Trieste, Venice (Line 51) ..	Fortnightly ..	372
Do.	Izmir, Islands, Rhodes, (Line 43A)	Weekly	373
Do.	Corfu, Brindisi, Albanian and Dalmatian Ports (Line 43B)...	Weekly	373
Do.	Rhodes, Alexandria (Line 50)	Fortnightly ..	371A
Do.	Brindisi, Venice, Trieste (Line 50)	Fortnightly ..	371A
Do.	Istanbul, etc. (Line 59 *bis*)	Fortnightly ..	372
Do.	Naples, Marseilles, Genoa (Line 59 *bis*) ..	Fortnightly ..	372
Roumanian State ..	Istanbul, Constanza	Weekly ..	393
Do. do.	Alexandria	Fortnightly ..	393
Do. do.	Beyrout, Haifa, Alexandria	Fortnightly ..	393
Messageries Maritimes ..	Istanbul, Rhodes, Alexandretta or Odessa, Constanza, Haifa, Beyrout	Fortnightly ..	388
Do. do. ..	Naples (every 4 weeks), Marseilles	Fortnightly ..	388
Handris S.S. Co., Ltd. ..	Piræus, Alexandria, Piræus, Brindisi.. ..	Weekly	378
Hellenic Coast Lines Ltd.	Patras, Corfu, St. Quaranta, Brindisi	Weekly	378
Do. do. ..	Alexandria, Port Said	Weekly	378
Do. do. ..	Alexandria, Port Said, Jaffa, Haifa, Beyrout, etc	Fortnightly ..	378
Do do. ..	Cyprus, Beyrout, Haifa, Jaffa, Port Said, Alexandria	Fortnightly ..	378
"Jadranska" Line ..	Corfu, Dalmatian Coast Ports, Susak, Venice	Occasional ..	380
Do.	Patras, Corfu, Albanian and Dalmatian Coast. Trieste	Weekly	380
Anglo-Egyptian Mail ..	Alexandria	Fortnightly ..	371
Do. do. ..	Marseilles	Fortnightly ..	371
Jugoslav Lloyd Line ..	Haifa, Alexandria	———	381
Do. do.	Dubrovnik 2, Venice, Trieste	———	381
U.S.S.R Steamers.. ..	Haifa, Port Said	Every 2-3 weeks	393
Do.	Istanbul, Odessa	Every 2-3 weeks	393
Gdynia America Line (Palestine Service)	Istanbul, Constanza	Two to three times monthly	377
American Export Lines	Naples, Leghorn, Genoa, Marseilles, etc. ..	Fortnightly ..	443
Genovese Cia	Istanbul, Burgaz, Varna, Constanza and Danube Ports	Fortnightly ..	377

W **Subject to alteration or suspension without notice. owing to Quarantine, Strikes,**

To Palestine, Syria and Istanbul, etc.

LINE.	PORTS OF CALL.	SAILING	PAGE.
P. & O.	(Malta, every 2 weeks), Marseilles, Gibraltar, Tangier, Plymouth, London	Weekly	366
Orient Line	Naples, (Villefranche), Toulon, Gibraltar, London	Fortngly., mthly.	365
Anchor	Marseilles, Gibraltar, Liverpool	2/3 sailngs. mthly.	357
British India	Marseilles, Plymouth, London	Sevl. times mthly.	359
Bibby Line	Marseilles, Gibraltar, Plymouth, London	Fortnightly	358
Ellerman's City & Hall	(Marseilles), London, or Plymouth	Frequent	361
Henderson Line	Marseilles	Fortnightly	362
Nippon Yusen Kaishya	Naples, Marseilles, Gibraltar, London	Fortnightly	364
Nederland Line	Genoa, Nice (Villefranche), Algiers, Southampton, Amsterdam	Every 3 weeks	364
Norddeutscher Lloyd	Marseilles or Genoa (Southampton), Rotterdam, Hamburg	Occasional	363
Hamburg-America	Genoa (Barcelona), Rotterdam, Hamburg	Fortnightly	362
Rotterdam Lloyd	Marseilles, Gibraltar, Tangier, Lisbon, Southampton, Rotterdam	Every 3 weeks	368
Union-Castle	Genoa, Marseilles, Gibraltar, Tangier, London	Every 4 weeks	369
Dollar Line	Alexandria, Naples, Genoa, Marseilles	Fortnightly	473
Blue Funnel	Marseilles, London	Monthly	258
German African Service	Genoa, Marseilles, (Algiers and Tangier, Mar.-Aug.), Lisbon, S'hampton, R'terdam, H'burg.	Monthly	359
Holland-Africa	Genoa, Marseilles (Tangier, Lisbon, Dover in Summer), Antwerp, Rotterdam, Hamburg	Monthly	363
Pharaonic Mail Line	Limassol, Famagusta, Larnaca, Limassol, etc.	Weekly	386
Do.	Jaffa, Haifa, Beyrout, Tripoli, etc.	Weekly	386
"Adriatica"	Jaffa, Haifa, Beyrout, etc. (Line 56)	Fortnightly	371B
Do.	Jaffa, Haifa, Beyrout, etc. (Commercial Line 58)	Fortnightly	371B
Do.	Alexandria, Brindisi (optional), Venice, Trieste	Fortnightly	371B
Lloyd Triestino	Naples, Genoa (or Brindisi, Venice, Trieste) (Grand Express)	Monthly	382
Do. do.	Naples (Line A)	Weekly	383
Do. do.	Naples, Genoa (Line B)	Fortnightly	383
Do. do.	Naples, Genoa (Line C)	Every 4 weeks	383
Do. do.	Brindisi, Venice, Trieste. (Line D)	Fortnightly	383
Messageries Maritimes	Marseilles	Frequent	389/390
Hellenic Coast Lines	Alex'dria, Piræus, Chalcis, Volo, Thessaloniki, &c	Fortnightly	378
Do. do.	Jaffa, Haifa, Beyrout, Cyprus, Piræus, Thessaloniki, etc.	Fortnightly	378
Do. do.	Alexandria, Piræus	Weekly	378

SUMMARY OF SAILINGS FROM TRIESTE & VENICE. To Egypt, Palestine, Syria, etc.

LINE.	PORTS OF CALL.	SAILING	PAGE.
"Adriatica"	Brindisi, Alexandria, Haifa (Grand Exp.)	Fortnightly	371A
Do.	F'me, Bri'disi, Pi'us, Rh'des, Alex'dria (Fast Line)	Fortnightly	371A
Do.	(Fr Trieste only), Br'disi, Larnaca, Haifa, B'yrout	Fortnightly	371A
Do.	Brindisi, Piræus, Istanbul.	Weekly	371B
Do.	Brindisi, Piræus, Alexandria, Port Said, Haifa, Beyrout, etc. (Line 56)	Fortnightly	371B
Do.	Brindisi, Patras, Calamata, Cyprus, Syrian Ports, Beyrout, etc. (Line 57)	Fortnightly	371B
Do.	Brindisi, Piræus, Volo, Thessaloniki, Istanbul, &c	Fortnightly	372
Do.	Brindisi, Calamata, Piræus, Izmir, Mitylene, Thessaloniki, Istanbul, etc. (Line 60)	Fortnightly	372
Do.	Brindisi, Piræus, Rhodes, Alexandria (Line 51)	Fortnightly	372
Do.	Dalmatian and Albanian Ports, Brindisi, etc.	Weekly	373
Do.	Dalmatian & Albanian P'ts, Corfu, Piræus, Izmir	Weekly	373
Do.	(From Venice), Rhodes, Izmir, Piræus	Weekly	373
Lloyd Triestino	Brindisi, Port Said (Grand Express)	Monthly	382
Do. do.	Fiume, Messina, Port Said	Monthly	382
Do. do.	Brindisi, Port Said (Line D)	Fortnightly	383
Do. do.	Port Said (Djibouti, Calcutta)	Monthly	385
"Tirrenia"	(From Venice) Catania, Malta, Sicily, Naples, Genoa, Marseilles.	Weekly	397A
"Italia"	From Trieste to Ragusa, Patras, Naples, Palermo, Algiers, Gibraltar, Lisbon etc.	Occasional	455
Do.	From Trieste to Split, Naples, Algiers, Gibraltar	Occasional	455
"Jadranska" Line	From Venice to Dalmatian Coast Ports, Corfu, Itea, Piræus	Occasional	380
Do.	Dalmat'n & Alban'n Coast, Patras, Piræus, Izmir	Weekly	380
Jugoslav Lloyd Line	Split, Piræus, Haifa, Alexandria	—	381

Subject to alteration or suspension without notice, owing to Quarantine Strikes, etc.

PART 1.—TO THE MEDITERRANEAN

Services from the United Kingdom and the Continent (Ports North of Gibraltar) to the Mediterranean and Ports beyond, *via* Suez Canal.

	PAGE
Anchor Line Limited	357
Aberdeen and Commonwealth Line	357
Bibby Line	358
Blue Funnel Line	358
British India S.N. Co.	359
City Line ..	366
Deutsche Ost-Afrika Line	359
East Asiatic Co., Ltd. (see Ostasiatiske Kompagni)	
Ellerman City & Hall Lines ..	361
Ellerman and Papayanni Lines	361
Ellerman, Westcott & Laurance Line	361
Furness Line	360
German Africa Service (see Deutsch Ost-Afrika Line)	
Glen Line and Shire Line ..	360
Hamburg America Line	362
Henderson Line ..	362
Holland Australia Line ..	363
Holland Africa Line	363
Holland British India Line	363
Holland East Asia Line	363
John Hall Line (see Mac Andrews & Co. Ltd.)	—
Mac Andrews & Co. Ltd.	363
Moss Hutchison Line	362
Nederland Line—Royal Dutch Mail ..	364
Nippon Yusen Kaisya ..	364
Norddeutscher Lloyd ..	365
Orient Line	365
Ostasiatiske Kompagni	360
Peninsular and Oriental S.N. Co.	366/7
Prince Line ..	367
Rotterdam Lloyd Royal Mail Line	368
Shaw Savill Line	368
Sota & Aznar Line	368
Strick and Ellerman Lines	368
Svenska Orient Line	369
Svenska Ostasiatiska Kompaniet	369
Union-Castle Mail S.S. Co., Ltd.	369
United Netherlands Nav. Co.	363
Wilh. Wilhelmsen Lines	369

ANCHOR LINE LIMITED.

See also page 459.

Britannia 8800 tons, *California* 16792 tons, *Elysia* 6757 tons, *Castalia*, 6601 tons, *Circassia* 11200 tons, *Cilicia* 11200 tons.

Carrying Cabin Class only.

Liverpool to Gibraltar, Marseilles, Port Said, Suez, Bombay and Karachi.

SAILINGS. (Calling also at Suez).

Steamer.	L'pool. dep.	Gib'lt'r arr.	Mar-seilles.	P. Said arr.	Bmb'y arr.	Karachi dep.	Bmb'y dep.	P Said arr.	Marseilles arr.	Marseilles dep.	Gib'lt'r arr.	L'pool arr.
Castalia	Jun. 10	Jun. 15	Jun. 18	Jun. 23	July 5	July 22	—	Aug. 8	August 9	Aug. 10	Aug. 13	Aug 18
Cilicia ..	July 1	July 5	July 7	July 11	July 21	Aug. 2	Aug. 4	Aug 13	August 18	Aug. 18	Aug 20	Aug. 24
Britannia	Aug. 4	Aug. 9	Aug. 11	Aug 15	Aug 25	Sept. 6	Sept. 8	Sept 18	Sept. 23	Sept. 23	Sept. 25	Sep. 29
†*Circassia*	Aug. 19	Aug. 23	Aug. 25	Aug 29	Sept. 8	Sept. 20	Sep. 22	Sept 30	Oct. 5	Oct. 5	Oct. 7	Oct. 11
Elysia....	Aug 26	Aug. 31	ept. 3	ept 8	Sep. 20	Oct. 14	—	Oct 25	Oct. 31	Nov. 1	Nov. 4	Nov. 9
†*Cilicia* ..	Sept. 9	Sept. 13	Sept. 15	Sep. 19	Sep. 29	Oct. 11	Oct. 13	Oct. 21	ct. 26	Oct. 26	Oct. 28	Nov. 1
Castalia..	,, 27	Oct. 2	Oct. 5	Oct. 10	Oct. 23	Nov. 6	Nov. 8	Nov. 20	Nov. 26	Nov. 27	Nov. 30	Dec. 5

Dates at intermediate ports are only approximate. † Calls Karachi before Bombay.

ABERDEEN & COMMONWEALTH LINE.

Southampton to Malta, Port Said, Aden, Colombo, Fremantle, Adelaide, Melbourne, Sydney and Brisbane.

s.s. *Moreton Bay* (14145 tons); s.s. *Esperance Bay* (14176); s.s. *Jervis Bay* (14129); s.s. *Largs Bay* (14143). Carrying one class of passenger only.

OUTWARDS

Steamship.	Sou'pton dep.	Malta arr.	Pt. Said arr.	Aden	Colombo arr.	Frem'tle arr.	Adelaide arr.	Melb'rne arr.	Sydney arr.	Brisbane arr.
Jervis Bay ..	Sept. 6	Sept. 12	Sept. 15	Sep. 20	Sept. 26	Oct. 6	Oct. 11	Oct. 13	Oct. 16	Oct. 20
Largs Bay ..	Oct. 4	Oct. 10	Oct. 13	Oct. 18	Oct. 24	Nov. 3	Nov. 8	Nov. 10	Nov. 13	Nov. 17
Moreton Bay	Nov. 1	Nov. 7	Nov. 10	Nov. 15	Nov. 21	Dec. 1	Dec. 6	Dec. 8	Dec. 11	Dec. 15
EsperanceBay	Nov. 29	Dec. 5	Dec. 8	Dec. 13	Dec. 19	Dec. 29	Jan. 3	Jan. 5	Jan. 8	Jan. 12

HOMEWARDS

Steamship.	Brisbane dep.	Sydney dep.	Melb'rne dep.	Adelaide dep.	F'm'ntle dep.	Colombo	Aden	Pt. Said	Malta	Sou'pton arr.
Largs Bay ..	July 19	July 25	July 29	Aug. 2	Aug. 7	Aug. 16	Aug. 24	Aug. 29	Sept. 1	Sept. 7
Moreton Bay	Aug. 16	Aug. 22	Aug. 26	Aug. 30	Sept. 4	Sept. 13	Sept. 20	Sept. 25	Sept. 28	Oct. 4
EsperanceBay	Sept. 13	Sept. 19	Sept. 23	Sept. 27	Oct 2	Oct. 11	Oct. 18	Oct. 23	Oct. 26	Nov. 1
Jervis Bay ..	Oct. 24	Oct. 31	Nov. 4	Nov. 6	Nov. 11	Nov. 20	Nov. 27	Dec. 1	Dec. 4	Dec. 11
Largs Bay	Nov. 21	Nov. 28	Dec. 2	Dec. 4	Dec. 9	Dec. 18	Dec. 25	Dec. 29	Jan. 1	Jan. 8
Moreton Bay	Dec. 19	Jan. 2	Jan. 6	Jan. 8	Jan. 13	Jan. 22	Jan. 29	Feb. 2	Feb. 5	Feb. 12

BIBBY LINE.

See also page 403.

LIVERPOOL, GIBRALTAR, MARSEILLES, PORT SAID, PORT SUDAN, COCHIN, COLOMBO, and RANGOON. Fortnightly. First class only.

Outward Vessel.	Tons	Liverpool. dep.	Gibraltar. arr./dep	Marseilles. arr.	Marseilles. dep.	Port Said.	Port Sudan.	Cochin.	Colombo	Rangoon. arr.
Yorkshire	10184	Jly. 28	Aug. 2	Aug. 4	Aug. 5	Aug. 10	Aug. 13	Aug. 20	Aug. 21	Aug. 26
Derbyshire	11600	Aug 11	,, 16	,, 18	,, 19	,, 24	,, 27	Sept. 3	Sept. 4	Sept. 9
Shropshire	10560	,, 25	,, 30	Sept. 1	Sept. 2	Sept. 7	Sept. 10	,, 17	,, 18	,, 23
Staffordshire ..	10655	Sept. 8	Sept. 13	,, 15	,, 16	,, 21	,, 24	Oct. 1	Oct. 2	Oct. 7
Oxfordshire....	8646	,, 22	,, 27	,, 29	,, 30	Oct. 5	Oct. 8	,, 15	,, 16	,, 21
Worcestershire	11453	Oct. 6	Oct. 11	Oct. 13	Oct. 14	,, 19	,, 22	,, 29	,, 30	Nov. 4
Cheshire	10560	,, 20	,, 25	,, 27	,, 28	Nov. 2	Nov. 5	Nov. 12	Nov. 13	,, 18
Yorkshire	10184	Nov. 3	Nov. 8	Nov. 10	Nov. 11	,, 16	,, 19	,, 26	,, 27	Dec. 2
Derbyshire	11600	,, 17	,, 22	,, 24	,, 25	,, 30	Dec. 3	Dec. 10	Dec. 11	,, 16
Shropshire	10560	Dec. 1	Dec. 6	Dec. 8	Dec. 9	Dec. 14	,, 17	,, 24	,, 25	,, 30

Homeward Vessel.	Rangoon. dep.	Colombo dep.	Cochin. dep.	Port Sudan	Port Said. dep.	Marseilles. dep.	Gibraltar. arr. dep.	Plymouth. arr.	London. arr.a.m.
Staffordshire	Jly. 13	July 20	July 21	July 30	Aug. 2	Aug. 7	Aug. 9	Aug. 13	Aug. 14
Oxfordshire	,, 27	Aug. 3	—	Aug 13	,, 16	,, 21	,, 23	,, 27	,, 28
Worcestershire	Aug 10	,, 17	Aug. 18	,, 27	,, 30	Sept, 4	Sept. 6	Sept. 10	Sept. 11
Cheshire	,, 24	,, 30	,, 31	Sept. 9	Sep 12	,, 17	,, 19	,, 23	,, 24
Yorkshire	Sep. 7	Sept. 13	Sept. 14	,, 22	,, 25	,, 30	Oct. 2	Oct. 6	Oct. 7
Derbyshire	,, 21	,, 27	—	Oct. 6	Oct. 9	Oct. 14	,, 16	,, 20	,, 21
Shropshire	Oct. 5	Oct. 11	Oct. 12	,, 20	,, 23	,, 28	,, 30	Nov. 3	Nov. 4
Staffordshire	,, 19	,, 25	—	Nov 3	Nov 6	Nov. 11	Nov. 13	,, 17	,, 18
Oxfordshire ..	Nov. 2	Nov. 8	Nov. 9	,, 16	,, 19	,, 24	,, 26	,, 30	Dec. 1
Worcestershire	,, 16	,, 22	—	,, 30	Dec. 3	Dec. 8	Dec. 10	Dec 14	,, 15
Cheshire	,, 30	Dec. 6	Dec. 7	Dec 14	,, 17	,, 22	,, 24	,, 28	,, 29
Yorkshire	Dec 14	,, 20	—	,, 28	,, 31	Jan. 5	Jan. 7	Jan. 11	Jan. 12

BLUE FUNNEL LINE.

See also pages 403 and 442).

The Far East.—Via Suez Canal.

"A" class sailings, carrying 1st class passengers only.

Steamer.	Tons.	Liverpool dep.	Marseilles. dep.	Port Said. arr.	Colombo.	Penang. arr.	Singapore. arr.	Hong Kong. arr.	Shanghai ¶ arr.
Aeneas	10058	Aug. 5	Aug. 12	Aug. 17	Aug. 29	Sept. 3	Sept. 6	Sept. 13	Sept. 17
Sarpedon..	11231	Sept. 2	Sept. 8	Sept. 13	Sept. 24	,, 28	Oct. 2	Oct. 9	Oct. 13
Patroclus	11814	,, 30	Oct. 6	Oct. 11	Oct. 22	Oct. 26	,, 30	Nov. 6	Nov. 10
Antenor ..	11774	Oct. 28	Nov. 3	Nov. 8	Nov. 19	Nov. 23	Nov. 27	Dec. 4	Dec. 8
Hector ..	11198	Nov. 25	Dec. 1	Dec. 6	Dec. 17	Dec. 21	Dec. 25	,, 31	Jan. 5
Aeneas	10058	Dec. 23	,, 30	Jan. 4	Jan. 16	Jan. 21	Jan. 24	Jan. 31	Feb. 4
Sarpedon	11231	Jan. 20	Jan. 26	,, 31	Feb. 11	Feb. 15	Feb. 19	Feb. 25	Mar. 1

HOMEWARDS

Steamer.	Tons	Yokohama. dep.	Kobe. dep.	Shanghai. dep.	Hong Kong. dep.	Singapore. dep.	Penang dep.	Colombo dep.	Aden dep.	Port Said. dep.	Marseilles arr.	London. arr.
Patroclus	11814	July 14	July 18	July 22	July 26	Aug. 2	Aug. 4	Aug. 8	Aug. 15	Aug. 20	Aug. 25	Aug. 31
Antenor	11774	Aug. 11	Aug 15	Aug 19	Aug. 23	,, 30	Sept. 1	Sept. 5	Sept 11	Sept. 16	Sept. 21	Sept. 27
Hector ..	11198	Sept. 8	Sept 12	Sept 16	Sept 20	Sept. 27	,, 29	Oct. 3	Oct. 9	Oct. 14	Oct. 19	Oct. 25
Aeneas ..	10058	Oct. 6	Oct. 10	Oct. 13	Oct. 17	Oct. 25	Oct. 27	Nov. 1	Nov. 8	Nov. 13	Nov. 18	Nov. 25
Sarpedon	11231	Nov. 3	Nov. 7	Nov. 11	Nov. 15	Nov. 22	Nov. 24	,, 28	Dec. 4	Dec. 9	Dec. 14	Dec. 20
Patroclus	11814	Dec. 1	Dec. 5	Dec. 9	Dec. 13	Dec. 20	Dec. 22	Dec. 26	Jan. 1	Jan. 6	Jan. 11	Jan. 17
Antenor	11774	,, 29	Jan. 2	Jan. 6	Jan. 10	Jan. 17	Jan. 19	Jan. 23	,, 29	Feb. 3	Feb. 8	Feb. 14

"B" and "C" class sailings. "B" class carry 22 First Class passengers (no Stewardess).
"C" cl. vessels carry a few first cl. pass. with children or unaccompanied ladies in special circumstances.

SAILINGS:—From Liverpool, *via* Port Said to Batavia. From Liverpool, *via* Port Said to Colombo*, Penang, Singapore, Manila*, Hong Kong*, Shanghai*. Kobe, Yokohama. Sailings on application.
* Occasional.

¶ Continuing to Yokohama *via* North China ports.

See also p. 471.

BRITISH INDIA STEAM NAVIGATION CO.

London, Egypt, Colombo, Madras and Calcutta.

Cabin passengers carried.

Steamer.	Tons	From London.	Malta.	Pt. Said. arr.	Suez.	Aden. arr.	Colombo. arr.	Madras. arr.	arr. Calcutta.
Domala	8441	Aug. 12	Aug. 22	Aug. 26	Aug. 27	Sept. 1	Sept. 9	Sept. 13	Sept. 17
¶*Aska*	—	,, 22	—	Sept. 2	Sept. 3	,, 8	,, 14	,, 17	,, 20
¶*Modasa*	9070	Sept. 9	Sept. 18	,, 22	,, 23	,, 28	Oct. 6	Oct. 9	Oct. 13
¶*Mashobra* ..	8324	Oct. 7	Oct. 15	Oct. 19	Oct. 20	Oct. 25	Nov. 2	Nov. 5	Nov. 9
¶*Mulbera*	9100	Nov. 4	Nov. 12	Nov. 16	Nov. 17	Nov. 22	,, 30	Dec. 3	Dec. 7
Domala	8441	Dec. 2	Dec. 12	Dec. 16	Dec. 17	Dec. 22	Dec. 30	Jan. 3	Jan. 7
Dumana	8427	,, 16	,, 26	,, 30	,, 31	Jan. 5	Jan. 13	,, 17	,, 21

¶ Calling Cochin.

London—East Africa Service.

Sailing from London monthly, conveying "saloon" passengers only. Returning to England via same ports. For connecting services from Kilindini and Beira, see page 471. Next sailings:—

Steamer.	Tns.	London dep	Mar-seilles	Malta	Port Said arr.	Suez.	Port Sudan arr	Aden. arr.	Momb'sa Kili'dini arr.	Zanzi-bar.† arr.	Dar-es-Salaam †arr.	Beira. arr.
Matiana	9067	July 22	July 29	Aug. 1	Aug.5	Aug6	Aug. 10	Aug. 12	Aug. 18	Aug. 25	Aug. 26	Aug30
Mantola	9065	Aug. 19	Aug. 26	,, 29	Sep. 2	Sep.3	Sept. 7	Sept. 9	Sept. 15	Sept.22	Sept.28	Sep 27
Malda ..	9066	Sept. 16	Sept. 23	Sep 26	,, 30	Oct.1	Oct. 5	Oct. 7	Oct. 13	Oct. 20	Oct. 21	Oct.25
Madura ..	9032	Oct. 14	Oct. 21	Oct.24	Oct28	,, 29	Nov. 2	Nov. 4	Nov. 10	Nov. 17	Nov. 18	Nov22
Matiana	9045	Nov. 11	Nov. 18	Nov21	Nv.25	Nv26	,, 29	Dec. 2	Dec. 8	Dec. 15	Dec. 16	Dec 20

† By transhipping at Mombasa, arrive 3 or 4 days earlier.

Passengers are also booked by transhipment at Mombasa to Mozambique, Beira, Lourenco Marques & Durban.

Approximate Dates of Homeward Sailings from Egypt.

Steamers may be a day or two ahead or later than indicated.

Steamer.	Tons	P. Sudan dep.	Port Said	Marseilles arr.	Marseilles dep.*	Plymouth arr. about	London. arr.
†*Modasa*	9070	—	July 31	Aug. 6	Aug. 7	Aug. 14	Aug. 15
§*Malda*	9066	July 28	Aug. 1	,, 7	,, 8	,, 15	,, 16
†*Mashobra* ..	8324	—	,, 28	Sept. 2	Sept. 3	Sept. 9	Sept. 10
§*Madura*	9032	Aug. 25	,, 29	,, 4	,, 5	,, 12	,, 13
†*Mulbera*	9100	—	Sept. 23	,, 28	,, 29	Oct. 5	Oct. 6
§*Matiana*	9067	Sept. 22	,, 26	Oct. 2	Oct. 3	,, 10	,, 11
Domala	8441	—	Oct. 22	,, 28	,, 29	Nov. 6	Nov. 7
§*Mantola*	9065	Oct. 20	,, 24	,, 30	,, 31	,, 7	,, 8

§ Carrying "saloon" passengers only.

† Carrying "cabin class" only.

Steamers may call also at Malta if sufficient inducement.

*Departure date from Marseilles subject to confirmation.

DEUTSCHE OST-AFRIKA LINIE. GERMAN AFRICA LINES.

(See also page 446)

Combined Services of the WŒRMANN-LINIE A.G., DEUTSCHE OST-AFRIKA LINIE. HAMBURG-BREMER AFRIKA LINIE.

EASTERN ROUTE AROUND AFRICA. (For Homeward Sailings, see p.446).

s.s. *Watussi* .. 9521 tons July 22 | s.s. *Ubena* .. 9523 tons Sept. 23

s.s. *Usambara* .. 8690 tons Aug. 22 | s.s. *Watussi* .. 9521 tons Oct. 21

Calls also Suez, Port Sudan, Aden, Tanga, Zanzibar, Daressalaam, Port Amelia, Mozambique.

Hamburg dep.	Antwerp dep.	South-ampton dep	Lisbon. arr./dep.	Tangier.	Algiers.	Ville-franche.	Genoa. arr./dep.	Port Said arr.	Mombasa arr/dep.	Beira. arr.
July 22	July 26	July 27	July 30/31	Aug. 1	Aug. 3	Aug. 5	Aug. 6	Aug. 11	Aug.23/24	Sept. 4
Aug. 22	Aug. 26	Aug. 27	Aug.30/31	Sept. 1	Sept. 3	Sept. 5	Sept. 6	Sept.11	Sept 24/25	Oct. 5
Sept.23	Sept. 27	Sept. 28	Oct. 1/2	Oct. 3	Oct. 5	Oct. 7	Oct. 8	Oct. 13	Oct. 24/25	Nov. 4
Oct. 21	Oct. 25	Oct. 26	,, 29/30	—	—	—	Nov. 3	Nov. 8	Nov.19/20	,, 28

HOMEWARD SAILINGS, WESTERN ROUTE AROUND AFRICA (For Outward Sailings see p. 446).

s.s. *Ubena* .. 9523 tons July 22 | s.s. *Wangoni* .. 7782 tons Sept. 27

Beira dep.	Mombasa arr./dep.	Port Said	Genoa. arr./dep.	Marseilles arr./dep.	Algiers.	Tangier.	Lisbon arr./dp.	South-ampton	Antw'rp or Rotterdam arr./dep	Ham-burg.
July22	Aug. 1/2	Aug. 12	Au.16/17	Aug. 18/19	Aug. 21	Aug. 23	Aug. 24	Aug. 27	Aug. 28/29	Aug.31
Sep.27	Oct. 5/6	Oct. 16	Oct21/22	Oct. 23	—	—	Oct. 27	Oct. 31	Nov 1/2	Nov. 4

Calling also Mozambique, Port Amelia, Dar-es-Salaam, Zanzibar, Tanga, Mombassa, Aden, Port Sudan and Suez.

OSTASIATISKE KOMPAGNI. EAST ASIATIC LINE.

(See also page 460).

Motor Ship	Tons	Rotte'dm dep.	S'hampt'n dep.	Marseilles dep.	P. Said arr.	Colombo arr.	Penang	Port Swet'ham	Mal'cca	Singapore, ar.	Bangkok, ar
Selandia	8457	July 29	July 31	Aug. 8	Aug. 13	Aug. 25	Aug. 29	Aug. 30	Aug. 31	Sept. 1	Sept. 5
Boringia	5821	Aug. 19	Aug. 21	,, 29	Sept. 3	Sept. 15	Sept. 19	Sept. 20	Sept. 21	,, 22	,, 26
Lalandia	4913	Sept. 9	Sept. 11	Sept. 19	,, 24	Oct. 6	Oct 10	Oct. 11	Oct. 12	Oct 13	Oct. 17
Jutlandia	8457	,, 30	Oct. 2	Oct. 10	Oct. 15	,, 27	,, 31	Nov. 1	Nov. 2	Nov. 3	Nov. 7
Meonia ..	5214	Oct. 21	,, 23	,, 31	Nov 5	Nov. 17	Nov. 21	,, 22	,, 23	,, 24	,, 28
Alsia	5812	Nov. 11	Nov. 13	Nov. 21	,, 26	Dec. 8	Dec. 12	Dec. 13	Dec. 14	Dec. 15	Dec 19

China, Japan Line.

CARGO SERVICE with limited passenger accommodation to Yokohama, Kobe.

Motor Vessel.	Tons	Hamburg dep.	Genoa dep.	Port Said arr.	Singapore arr.	Manila arr.	Hong Kong arr.	Shanghai arr.	Japan
Kina......	9823	Aug. 15	Aug. 24	Aug. 29	Sept. 16	Sept. 22	Sept. 24	Sept. 28	Oct. 3
Java......	8681	Sept. 15	Sept 25	Sept 30	Oct. 19	Oct. 25	Oct. 29	Nov. 1	Nov. 6
——	—	Oct. 14	Oct. 23	Oct. 28	Nov. 14	Nov. 20	Nov. 23	,, 26	Dec. 1

FURNESS LINE.

(See also pages 449 and 459).

LIVERPOOL TO MEDITERRANEAN, BLACK SEA AND DANUBE PORTS.

s.s. *Dromore*, 4096 tons, s.s. *Jessmore*, 4099 tons s.s. *Aviemore*, 4098 tons, s.s. *Incemore*, 4098 tons. Cargo vessels carrying few Cabin class passengers, but not unaccompanied ladies. No doctor or stewardess.

Approximate days of arr./dep. shown in brackets.

SAILINGS:—About every 21 days from Liverpool *via* Piræus (12th day), Volo (16th day), Thessaloniki (17th day), Izmir (18/19 days), to Istanbul (24/25 days), Burgas (27th day), Varna (28th day), Constanza, (29/31 days), Sulina (32nd day), Galatz (arr. 32nd day). Depart Galatz (48th day), Sulina (48th day), Constanza (49th day), arr. Antwerp (63rd day).

GLEN LINE AND SHIRE LINE.

Subject to alteration without notice.

London to Port Said, Straits, China, Dairen and Japan.

Carrying 12 1 cl. passengers (s.s. Gleniffer 22/26 passengers; Glenfinlas 10: Radnorshire 8: Glenaffaric 5 and Flintshire 6. A Doctor is carried on all vessels and Stewardess on s.s. Gleniffer. The Glenaffaric and Flintshire do not carry Ladies, and Glenfinlas and Radnorshire do not carry unaccompanied Ladies.

OUTWARD SAILINGS

Dairen Service calling at North China Ports if inducement offers.

Vessel.	Tns	London dep.	P. Said arr.	Penang	Port Swet'ham	Singapore	Hong Kong	Shanghai	Taku Bar	Dairen	Yokohama	Kobe arr.
Denbighshire ..	—	Aug. 5	Dates at Intermediate Ports on application.									
Glenshiel	9414	,, 19										
Glenfinlas	7572	Sept. 2										
Glengarry	9459	,, 16										
Glenearn	–	,, 30										
Glenogle	9513	Oct. 14										

HOMEWARD SAILINGS

Calling also at Port Swettenham and Belawan alternate sailings.

Vessel.	Tns	Yokohama. dp	Shanghai dep.	Hong Kong.	Manila	Singapore. d.	Belawan, d.	Colombo	Port Said, dep	Casablana.	London. a.
Glenbeg	9460	—	Aug. 26	Dates at intermediate Ports on application.							Oct. 9
Breconshire ..	—	Sept. 1	—								,, 18
Glenapp	9503	—	Sept. 23								Nov. 6
Denbigshire	—	Sept. 29	—								,, 15
Glenshiel	9414	—	Oct. 21								Dec. 4
Glenfinlas	7572	Oct. 27	—								,, 16

CURRIE LINE (LEITH HULL & HAMBURG S.P. CO., LTD.)

(See also page 407.)

s.s. *Rutland*, 1433 tons, s.s. *Merkland*, 1360 tons, s.s. *Kirkland*, 1360 tons, s.s. *Lapland*, 1330 tons. Cargo steamer carrying a few passengers.

From LONDON to LISBON, MARSEILLES, GENOA, LEGHORN, NAPLES, SICILY and/or other ports. Round trip 5 to 6 weeks. Sailings at intervals of about 12 days.

ELLERMAN'S CITY & HALL LINES TO INDIA AND CEYLON.

CABIN CLASS ONLY. (See also page 410).

STEAMER.	Tons	Liver-pool. dep. abt.	Marseilles arr./dep.	Port Said. arr.	Port Sudan	Kar-achi.	Bombay. arr. abt.	Colombo arr. abt.	Madras	Calcutta arr. abt.
City of H'ngKong	9606	Sept. 14	Sept. 21	Sept. 26	—	Oct. 6	Oct. 8	—	—	—
City of Simla ..	10138	,, 23	,, 30	Oct. 5	—	,, 14	,, 16	—	—	—
City of Marseilles	8317	,, 23	—	,, 4	Oct. 7	—	—	Oct. 16	Oct. 18	Oct. 21
City of Cant'bury	8331	Oct. 5	Oct. 12	,, 17	—	,, 26	Oct. 28	—	—	—
City of Cairo ..	8034	,, 7	—	,, 19	,, 22	—	—	Nov. 1	Nov. 3	Nov. 6
City of Benares ..	10138	,, 21	,, 27	,, 31	—	Nov. 9	Nov. 11	—	—	—
City of Venice .	8762	Nov. 4	Nov. 11	Nov. 16	—	,, 25	,, 27	—	—	—
City of Baroda ..	7129	,, 4	—	,, 16	Nov. 19	—	—	,, 29	—	Dec. 4
City of H'ngKong	9606	Dec. 16	Dec. 23	Dec. 28	—	—	Jan. 8	—	—	—

HOMEWARD SAILINGS

STEAMER.	Tons	Calcutta dep.	Col-ombo dep.	Karachi dep.	Bombay dep.	Port Sudan	Port Said dep.	Mar-seilles arr.	Ply-mouth arr.	London arr.
City of Cant'bury	8331	—	—	Aug. 7	Aug. 9	Aug. 18	Aug. 21	Aug. 26	Sept. 2	—
City of Baroda ..	7129	Aug. 17	Aug. 23	—		—	Sept. 6	—	—	Sept. 18
City of Benares	11081	—	—	Aug. 30	Sept. 1	—	,, 11	Sept. 15	Sept. 21	—
City of Hong K'ng	9606	—	—	Oct. 26	Oct. 28	—	Nov. 8	Nov. 13	Nov. 20	—
City of Marseilles	8317	Nov. 5	Nov. 11	—	—	—	,, 23	—	—	Dec. 5
City of Simla .	11081	—	—	Nov. 6	—	—	,, 17	,, 22	,, 29	—
City of Cairo ..	8034	,, 16	,, 22	—	—	—	Dec. 4	—	—	,, 16
City of Cant'bury	8331	—	—	,, 18	Nov. 20	—	,, 1	Dec. 6	Dec. 13	—
City of Benares	11081	—	—	Dec. 1	Dec. 2	—	,, 12	,, 16	,, 22	—
City of Baroda ..	7129	Dec. 14*	Dec. 23	—	—	—	Jan. 5	—	—	Jan. 18

* Calls Madras Dec. 21.

ELLERMAN AND PAPAYANNI LINES LTD.

(See also page 410)

Destro ..	3554	*Andalusian* ..	3000	*Algerian* ..	2500	*Cressado* ..	1228
Dido ..	3554	*City of Oxford*	3000	*Lesbian* ..	2500	*Malvernian* ..	3133
Volturno ..	3424	*Assyrian* ..	3000	*Lisbon*	1965	*Belgravian* ..	3136
Flaminian ..	3300	*Egyptian* ..	2867	*Estrellano* ..	1963	**Ionian* ..	3144
City of Lancaster	3100	*Mardinian* ..	2800	*Palmella* ..	1569	**Corinthian* ..	—
Fabian ..	3060	*Oporto* ..	2800	*Darino* ..	1350		

* New Steamer.

Liverpool to Mediterranean and Syrian Coast Ports.

Sailings from Liverpool to:—Gibraltar, Malta, Alexandria, Jaffa, Tel-Aviv, Haifa, Beyrout, Tripoli*, Famagusta*. Limassol*, Average passage Gibraltar 6 days; to Malta 10 days, Alexandria 15 days. Round voyage about 7/8 weeks. Sailings on application.

Liverpool *via* Patras, Piræus, Volo, Thessaloniki, Izmir, Istanbul, Burgaz, Varna (and Contanza occasionally). Average passage to Piræus 14 days, Thessaloniki 16 days, Izmir 18 days, Istanbul 20 days. Round voyage 7/9 weeks. Sailings on application.

Liverpool *via* Genoa, Leghorn, Naples, Palermo*, Messina*, Catonia*, Bari, Dubrovnik†, Ancona*, Venice, Trieste, Fiume and Sušak. Round voyage 6/8 weeks. Sailings on application.

Most of the steamers operating above services have accommodation for a limited number of passengers. No surgeon or stewardess carried.

* If sufficient inducement offered. † With liberty to tranship.

ELLERMAN, WESTCOTT & LAURANCE LINE, LTD.

s.s. *Castilian*, 3066 tons s.s. *Egyptian*, 2867 tons; s.s. *Maronian*, 5086 tons; carrying 1st class passengers. Steward but no doctor carried.

FROM LONDON, W.I. DOCK for Gibraltar, Malta, Alexandria and Cyprus (Limassol, Larnaca, and Famagusta). Average passage to Malta 10 days, Alexandria 15 days. Round voyage about 6 weeks. Sailings on application.

From London (West India Dock) to Malta, Piræus, Thessaloniki, Istanbul, Izmir. Average passage to Piræus 14 days, Thessaloniki 16 days, Izmir, 18 days, Istanbul 20/21 days. Round voyage 9 weeks. Sailings on application. May call at other Mediterranean and Black Sea Ports.

HAMBURG-AMERICAN LINE.

See also pages 406 420, 450, 459.

Sailings from Hamburg to China and Japan as at present arranged :—

Ramses .. 8537 tons	July 1	*Duisberg* .. 7389 tons	Aug. 12
Kulmerland 7363 tons	July 15	*Sauerland* 7087 tons	Sept. 9

Vessels carry passengers "cabin" class, those indicated ‡ havidg limited cabin accommodation.

Hamburg dep.	Antwerp dep.	Rotterdam dep.	Genoa. dep.	Port Said arr.	Colombo arr.	Singa-pore.	Manila	Hong-Kong.	Shanghai. arr.
†*July 1	July 4	July 6	July 14	July 19	July 31	Aug. 7	Aug. 13	Aug. 16	Aug. 20
‡† ,, 15	,, 18	,, 20	,, 28	Aug. 3	Aug. 14	,, 20	—	,, 26	,, 30
†*Aug. 12	Aug 15	Aug. 17	Aug. 25	,, 30	Sept. 11	Sept. 17	—	Sept. 28	Sept. 27
†*Sept. 9	Sept. 12	Sept. 14	Sep. 22	Sept. 28	Oct. 10	Oct. 17	Oct. 23	Oct, 26	Oct, 30

* Calling also at Penang and Port Swettenham. † To Kobe, Yohohama. c To Dairen, Yohohama, Kobe.

†Homeward Sailings :

Kobe	Hong-Kong. dep.	Manila dep.	Singa-pore dep.	Colombo dep.	Port Said. arr.	Genoa arr.	Rotter-dam. arr.	Hamburg arr.

Sailings on application.

† Sailing dates from Dairen, Taku, Yokohama, Nagoya, Chefoo, Tsingtau, Cebu on application.

SERVICE TO EAST INDIES. * Carrying a limited number of cabin passengers.

Vessel.	Tons	Hamburg	Bremen. dep.	Rotterdam dep.	Antwerp dep.	
Freiburg	—	Aug. 15	—	Aug. 19	Aug. 23	Calling Sabang, Belawan, Deli, Padang, Batavia, Samarang, Sourabaya, Makassar.
Kurmark ..	—	Sep. 2	Sept. 6	—	—	
Menes	—	,, 26	—	Sept. 30	Oct. 4	
Uckermark ..	—	Oct. 14	Oct. 18	—	,, 25	
Essen ..	—	Nov. 7	—	Nov. 11	Nov. 15	
Heidelberg ..	—	,, 25	Nov. 29	—	—	

HENDERSON LINE.

Liverpool, Gibraltar, Marseilles, Egypt, Port Sudan and Rangoon—

(Fortnightly)

Steamers.	Tons.	Steamers.	Tons.	Steamers.	Tons.	Steamer	Tons.
Burma ..	7500	*Pegu*	7500	*Kemmendine* ..	7800	*Sagaing* ..	8000
Yoma ..	8200	*Salween* ..	7050	*Amarapoora* ..	8200	*Prome* ..	7043

The above steamers carry 1st cl passengers only. Sailings calling also at Suez out and home).

OUTWARDS Steamer	Liverpool dep.	Gibraltar	Marseilles dep.	Port Said arr.	Port Sudan arr.	Rangoon arr.
Pegu..........	Aug. 4	Aug. 9	Aug. 12	Aug. 17	Aug. 21	Sept. 5
Salween	,, 18	,, 23	,, 26	,, 31	Sept. 4	,, 19
Kemmendine ..	Sept. 1	Sept. 7	Sept. 9	Sept. 14	,, 18	Oct. 3
Yoma	,, 15	,, 20	,, 23	,, 28	Oct. 2	,, 17

HOMEWARDS Steamer	Rangoon dep.	Port Sudan dep.	Port Said dep.	Marseilles arr.	Gibraltar	U.K. arr.
Amarapoora ..	July 22	Aug. 8	Aug. 11	Aug. 17	Aug. 20	Aug *25
Prome	Aug. 5	,, 21	,, 24	,, 30	Sept. 2	Sept. ¶7
Burma........	,, 19	Sept. 4	Sept. 7	Sept. 13	,, 16	,, *21
Sagaing	Sept. 2	,, 18	,, 21	,, 27	,, 30	Oct. ¶5

* Calls London.
¶ Calls at Plymouth, or Bristol or Liverpool according to require-ments

MOSS HUTCHISON LINE.

(See also page 407.)

Steamer.	Tons.	Steamer.	Tons.	Steamer.	Tons.	Steamer.	Tons.
Hatasu ..	3198	*Kana* ..	2783	*Kantara* ..	3236	*Kufra* ..	2723
Heron ..	2374	*Kavak* ..	2781	*Kheti* ..	2734	*Meroe* ..	3831

Liverpool-Mediterranean Service by cargo steamers (with limited accommodation for passengers) No doctor or stewardess carried. Regular sailings every 10/14 days to Casablanca, Gibraltar, Malta, Alexandria (or direct), Limassol, Famagusta, Jaffa, Tel-Aviv, Haifa, Beyrout, Alexandretta. Mersin, Round voyage 7/8 weeks. Probable sailings: Aug. 9, 19, Sept. 2, 6, 13, 27.

UNITED NETHERLANDS NAVIGATION CO. (See also page 452).

m.v. *Aagtekerk*, 6811 tons | m.v. *Almkerk*, 6810 tons | m.v. *Arendskerk*, 7600 tons

Cargo vessels with accommodation for 10-12 passengers. No Doctor or Stewardess.

Other vessels *Talisse*, *Tanimbar* and *Tarakan*, occasionally chartered from Nederlands Line (*Djambi* from Rotterdam Lloyd).

SAILINGS: About monthly from Rotterdam and Antwerp *via* Port Said, Karachi, Bombay, to Fremantle, Adelaide, Melbourne, Sydney; homeward from Sydney *via* the Cape to Dunkerque, Antwerp and Bremen.

HOLLAND EAST ASIA LINE.

UNITED NETHERLANDS NAVIGATION CO. (See also page 452).

Steamer.	Tons.	Steamer	Tons.	Steamer.	Tons.
Gaasterkerk	6630	*Serooskerk*	6611	*Meerkerk*	7995
Grootekerk	6630	*Zuiderkerk* ..	6591		

Cargo steamers with accommodation for 12 passengers. No doctor or stewardess.

From Antwerp via Hamburg Rotterdam, Genoa, Port Said, Colombo (optional), Singapore, Manila, Hong Kong, Shanghai, Dairen, Yokohama.

HOMEWARD—Steamers leave Yokohama *via* Nagoya, Osaka, Kobe, Shanghai, Foochow (June-Oct.), Hong Kong, Manila, Singapore, Penang, Colombo, Aden, Port Said, Genoa, Antwerp, Rotterdam, Amsterdam and Hamburg. Monthly Sailings, details on application.

HOLLAND BRITISH INDIA LINE.

UNITED NETHERLANDS NAVIGATION CO. (See also page 452).

s.s. *Hoogkerk*, 5137 tons. s.s. *Streefkerk*, 6185 tons.

Cargo steamers with accommodation for 4 passengers only. No Doctor or Stewardess.

Sailings monthly from Hamburg, Rotterdam, Antwerp, Genoa *via* Port Said, Suez to Colombo, Madras and Calcutta. For sailings to Karachi and Bombay, see "Holland Australia" Line above.

HOLLAND AFRICA LINE.

UNITED NETHERLANDS NAVIGATION CO. (See also page 452).

SAILINGS OUTWARDS *via* SUEZ CANAL.

Vessel.	Tns	Ham-b'rg, d.	Amster-dam. d.	Ant-werp, d.	Mars'les dep.	P. Said arr.	Pt. Su-dan. a.	Mom-basa. a.	Zanzi-bar. a.	Beira arr.	L'renco Marques	Durban. arr.
†*Heemskerk*..	6516	Aug 8	Aug. 11	Aug. 14	Aug. 23	Aug 29	Sept. 2	Sept. 13	Sep. 16	Sep. 22	Sept. 27	Sept. 30
†*Randfontein*	5700	Sep. 9	Sept. 12	Sept 15	Sept. 24	Sep. 30	Oct. 4	Oct. 13	Oct. 16	Oct. 23	—	Oct. 26
‡*Nijkerk*	5766	Oct. 7	Oct. 10	Oct. 12	Oct. 21	Oct. 27	Oct. 31	Nov. 9	Nov 12	Nov 18	—	Nov. 21

Calling also at Suez, Aden, Tanga, Dar-es-Salaam, Port Amelia, Mozambique. Usually return *via* West Coast to Hamburg (*see page* 452). † One Class. ‡ Tourist Class only. § First and Steerage.

SAILINGS HOMEWARD *via* SUEZ CANAL. (See page 452 for outward sailings *via* West Coast to Cape Town, Mossel Bay, Port Elizabeth, East London to Beia).

Vessel	Durban dep.	Mom-basa. dp.	P. Said dep.	Genoa arr./dep.	Marseilles arr./dep.	Tan-gier.	Lis-bon.	Dover	Antwerp arr.	Rotter-dam. ar.	Ha'b'rg arr.
Boschfontein	June 28	July 15	July 24	July 28	July 29/31	Aug. 2	Aug. 3	Aug. 6	Aug. 7	Aug. 9	Aug. 11
§*Jagersfontein*	July 26	Aug. 12	Aug. 21	Aug 25	Aug. 26/28	,, 30	,, 31	Sept. 3	Sept. 4	Sept. 6	Sept. 8
†*Meliskerk* ..	Aug. 9	,, 26	Sept. 7	Sept. 12	Sept. 13/14	—	—	—	,, 22	,, 24	,, 27

Calling also Lourenco Marques, Beira, Mozambique, Port Amelia, Dar-es-Salaam, Zanzibar, Tanga, Suez.

MAC ANDREWS & CO. LTD.

(All services subject to confirmation.)

Cargo steamers not carrying Doctor or Stewardess.

☞ ***The normal Itineraries as follows may be altered owing to the political situation in Spain. Passengers for Spanish Ports will be advised on application as to available accommodation.***

LONDON—GIBRALTAR—BARCELONA SERVICE. m.v. *Pelayo*, (1375 tons) and m.v. *Ponzano* (1375 tons) from London Dock every 14 days to Gibraltar, Barcelona, Tarragona, Valencia and possibly other ports. Round trip occupies 25/28 days.

From Liverpool (Alexandra Dock) every 7/14 days by m.v. *Palacio*, m.v. *Pinto*, m.v. *Pacheo* (1346 tons) to Barcelona, Valencia and district. Round trip 17 days.

LONDON—SPANISH PORTS ROUTE SERVICE. From London Dock about every 14 days by steamers of 1800 tons to Pasajes, Bilbao, Santander, and principal Spanish ports round to Barcelona, returning *via* Southern Spanish and occasionally Portuguese ports.

Similar service from Glasgow, Liverpool (Alexandra Dock) and Swansea every fortnight by steamers of 1800 tons. (Passengers embark at Swansea and disembark at Liverpool). Round trip occupies five to six weeks.

LONDON—LISBON—GIBRALTAR—MOROCCO SERVICE. From London Dock, about every five weeks to Lisbon, Gibraltar and Morocco ports, (usually Tangier, Larache, Rabat, Casablanca, Mazagan, Mogador and Saffi), may also call at one or two Spanish and/or Portuguese ports homeward. Round trip occupies about 30 days. † Service of JOHN GLYNN & SONS LTD.

†LIVERPOOL and FOWEY to Genoa, Leghorn, Naples, Catania, Messina, Palermo, etc. (Passengers embark at Fowey and disembark at Liverpool). Round trip 5/6 weeks. Sailings every 14 days.

Amsterdam and Southampton via Algiers, Villefranche (Nice), Genoa, Port Said, Suez, Colombo, Sabang, Belawan Deli and Singapore to Batavia (Samarang Sourabaya).

Sailings from Amsterdam:— *Services subject to alteration.*

Motor Vessel Twin-screw)	Tons.	Date.	Motor Vessel (Twin-screw)	Tons.	Date.
M. Van St. Aldegonde	19000	.. July 26	*J. V. Oldenbarnevelt*	19429	.. Sept. 27
Chr. Huygens	15704	.. Aug. 16	*M. Van St. Aldegonde*	19000	.. Oct. 18
Oranje	20000	.. Sept. 6			

Above steamers carry 1, 2 and 3rd cl. passengers.

OUTWARD SAILINGS.

Amsterdam*.	Southampton. arr./dep.	Algiers	Nice (Villefranche)	Genoa* dep.	Port Said	Colombo.	Sabang	Belawan-Deli.	Singapore.	Batavia.
July 26	July 28	Aug. 1	Aug. 3	Aug. 4	Aug. 8	Aug. 17	Aug. 20	Aug. 21	Aug. 22	Aug. 24
Aug. 16	Aug. 18	,, 22	,, 24	,, 25	,, 29	Sept. 7	Sept. 10	Sept. 11	Sept. 12	Sept. 14
Sept. 6	Sept. 8	Sept. 12	Sept. 14	Sept. 15	Sept. 18	,, 27	,, 30	Oct. 1	Oct. 2	Oct. 4
,, 27	,, 29	Oct. 3	Oct. 5	Oct. 6	Oct. 10	Oct. 19	Oct. 22	,, 23	, 24	,, 26
Oct. 18	Oct. 20	,, 24	,, 26	,, 27	,, 31	Nov. 9	Nov. 12	Nov. 13	Nov. 14	Nov. 16

HOMEWARD SAILINGS from Batavia.

J. V. Oldenbarnevelt ..	19429 tons	July 26	*Chr. Huygens*	15704 tons	.. Sept. 27
Johan de Witt ..	10474 tons	.. Aug. 16	*Oranje*	20000 tons	.. Oct 18
M. Van St. Aldegonde ..	19000 tons	.. Sept. 6			

Batavia. dep. 12.0	Singapore. dep.	Bel'wan Deli. dep.	Sabang.	Colombo.	Port Said	Genoa*. arr./dep.	Nice (Villefranche)	Algiers	Southhampton	Amsterdam. arr.*
July 26	July 28	July 29	July 30	Aug. 2	Aug. 12	Aug. 16	Aug. 16	Aug. 18	Aug. 22	Aug. 23
Aug. 16	Aug. 18	Aug. 19	Aug. 20	—	Sept. 3	Sept. 7	Sept. 7	Sept. 9	Sept. 13	Sept. 14
Sept. 6	Sept. 8	Sept. 9	Sept 10	Sept. 13	,, 22	,, 26	,, 26	,, 28	Oct. 2	Oct. 3
,, 27	,, 29	,, 30	Oct. 1	Oct. 4	Oct. 13	Oct. 17	Oct. 17	Oct. 19	,, 23	,, 24
Oct. 18	Oct. 20	Oct. 21	,, 22	,, 24	Nov. 2	Nov. 5	Nov. 5	Nov. † 7	Nov. 11	Nov. 12

*SPECIAL BOAT TRAIN FROM HOLLAND. From The Hague a special train to and from Genoa runs in connection with the outward and homeward mailships. From London the Rome Express Train de luxe on the day before mailships leave Genoa is a guaranteed connection.

CARGO MOTOR MAIL VESSELS (9000 tons). Dep. Amsterdam, *Poelau Bras*, July 21. Dep. Amsterdam on date indicated direct for Genoa, Port Said, Sabang, Belawan-Deli, Singapore and Batavia. Doctor carried, but no stewardess. † Calling Lisbon, Nov. 9.

NIPPON YUSEN KAISYA.

JAPAN MAIL LINE.

[See also page 478.

London, Gibraltar, Marseilles, Naples to Port Said, Suez, Colombo, Singapore. Hong Kong, Shanghai, Kobe and Yokohama. (Fortnightly)

(Subject to alteration).

Twin-screw Steamers. † Motor Vessel.	Tons.	London dep.	Gibraltar.	Marseilles. ar.& d.	Napl's	Port Said arr.	Colombo arr.	Singapore arr.	Hong-Kong. arr.	Shanghai. arr.	Kobe. arr.	Yokohama arr
Hakusan Maru	10380	Aug 5	Aug. 9	Au. 11/12	Aug 14	Aug 18	Aug. 29	Sept. 3	Sept. 9	Sep. 12	Sep 15	Sept. 19
Haruna Maru	10421	,, 18	,, 22	,, 24/25	,, 27	,, 31	Sept. 11	,, 16	,, 22	,, 25	,, 29	Oct. 2
Hasukuni Maru	11930	Sept 8	Sept. 11	Se. 13/14	Sep. 16	Sep. 19	Oct. 1	Oct. 5	Oct. 10	Oct. 13	Oct. 16	,, 20
Kasima Maru ..	9908	,, 29	Oct. 3	Oct. 5/6	Oct. 8	Oct. 12	,, 24	,, 29	Nov. 4	Nov. 7	Nov 11	Nov. 14
Hakone Maru ..	10420	Oct. 13	,, 17	,, 19/20	,, 22	,, 26	Nov. 6	Nov 11	,, 17	,, 20	,, 24	,, 27
Husimi Maru ..	10936	,, 27	,, 31	Nov. 2/3	Nov. 5	Nov. 9	,, 21	,, 26	Dec. 2	Dec. 5	Dec. 9	Dec. 12
Hakozaki Maru	10413	Nov 10	Nov. 14	,, 16/17	,, 19	,, 23	Dec. 4	Dec. 9	,, 15	,, 18	,, 22	,, 25
Suwa Maru ..	10672	,, 24	,, 28	,, 30/D 1	Dec. 3	Dec. 7	,, 19	,, 24	,, 30	Jan. 2	Jan. 9	Jan. 9

HOMEWARD SAILINGS Calling also at Nagoya, Osaka, Moji, Keelung (occasionally), Penang and Suez.

Twin-Screw Steamers. † Motor Vessel	Yokohama dep.	Kobe. dep.	Shanghia. dep.	Hong-Kong dep.	Singapore dep.	Colombo dep.	Aden. arr./dep.	Port Said dep.	Naples	Marseilles. ar.&dp.	Gibraltar dep.	London arr.
Kasima Maru	Jly. 16	July 20	July 25	July 29	Aug. 3	Aug. 9	Aug. 17	Aug 22	Au. 26	Au. 28/29	Aug 31	Sept. 5
Hakone Maru	,, 29	Aug. 3	Aug 8	Aug 12	,, 17	,, 23	,, 30	Sept. 5	Sep. 8	Sep 10/11	Sep. 13	,, 25
Husimi Maru ..	Aug 13	,, 17	,, 22	, 26	,, 31	Sept. 6	Sept. 14	,, 19	,, 23	,, 25/26	,, 28	Oct. 3
Hakozaki M'ru	,, 27	,, 31	Sept. 5	Sept. 9	Sep. 14	, 20	,, 27	Oct. 3	Oct. 6	Oct. 8/9	Oct. 11	,, 15
Suwa Maru ..	Sep. 10	Sept. 14	,, 19	,, 23	,, 28	Oct. 4	Oct. 11	,, 16	,, 20	,, 22/23	,, 25	,, 30
Terukun Maru	,, 24	,, 29	Oct. 3	Oct. 6	Oct. 11	,, 16	,, 22	,, 27	,, 30	Nov. 1/2	Nov. 4	Nov. 8
Hakusan Maru	Oct. 8	Oct. 12	,, 17	,, 21	,, 26	Nov. 1	Nov. 7/8	Nov 13	Nv. 16	,, 18/19	,, 21	,, 25

Hamburg, Bremen, Antwerp, Rotterdam and Southampton to the Far East.

s.s. *Potsdam*	1,528 tons	Aug. 21	s.s. *Potsdam*	17528 tons	Nov. 3
s.s. *Gneisenau*	18160 tons	Sept. 4	s.s. *Gneisenau*	18160 tons	Nov. 27
s.s. *Scharnhorst*	18184 tons	Oct. 2			

The Express steamers *Scharnhorst*, *Potsdam* and *Gneisenau* carry First Class and Tourist Class. Particulars of vessels carrying a limited number of passengers on application.

Bremen	Rotterdam dep.	South-ampt'n	Genoa dep.	Port Said.d	Colom-bo. arr	Singa-pore. a.	Man-ila ar.	Hong Kong. a.	Shang-hai. arr.	Yoko-hama a	Kobe. arr.
Aug. 21	Aug. 23	Aug 24	Au. 29	Sep. 1	Sept. 9	Sept.13	—	Sept. 16	—	—	Sept.20
Sept. 4	Sept. 6	Sept. 7	Sep.12	,, 15	,, 23	,, 27	Oct. 1	Oct. 3	Oct. 5	Oct. 9	Oct. 11
Oct. 2	Oct. 4	Oct. 5	Oct.10	Oct.13	Oct. 21	Oct. 25	,, 29	,, 31	Nov. 2	Nov. 6	Nov. 8
—	Nov. 3	Nov. 4	Nov. 9	Nov12	Nov.20	Nov. 24	Nov 28	Nov. 30	Dec. 2	Dec. 6	Dec. 8
Nov. 27	,, 29	,, 30	Dec. 5	Dec. 8	Dec. 16	Dec. 20	Dec 24	Dec. 26	,, 28	Jan. 1	Jan. 8

HOMEWARD SAILINGS. Dates of call at Penang and Belawan on application.

s.s. *Gneisenau* ..	18160 tons	July 22	s.s. *Potsdam*	17528 tons	Sept. 22
s.s. *Scharnhorst*	18184 tons	Aug. 18	s.s *Gneisenau*	18160 tons	Oct. 13

Kobe dep.	Shang-hai. dep.	Hong Kong.d	Manila dep.	Singa-pore. d.	Colom-bo. dp.	Port Said. d	Genoa. arr.	Bar-cel'na,a.	South-'mpton	Rotter-dam.	Bremen. arr.
July 22	July 25	July 27	July 29	Aug. 2	Aug. 7	Aug.15	Aug. 18	Aug. 19	Aug. 22	Aug. 24	Aug. 25
Aug. 18	Aug. 21	Aug. 23	Aug 25	,, 29	Sept. 3	Sept.11	Sept. 14	Sept. 15	Sept.20	Sept. 21	Sept. 22
Sept.22	Sept. 25	Sept.27	Sept.29	Oct. 3	Oct. 8	Oct. 16	Oct. 19	Oct 20	Oct. 25	Oct. 26	Oct. 27
Oct. 13	Oct. 16	Oct. 18	Oct. 20	,, 24	,, 29	Nov 6	Nov. 9	Nov. 10	Nov. 15	Nov. 16	Nov. 17

From Bremen, Rotterdam and Antwerp *via* the Cape to Australia.

Freight steamers carrying a limited number of passengers. No doctor or stewardess carried.

Steamer.	Tons.	Bremen, d.	Rotterdam, d.	Antwerp, d.	
Neckar	8417	Aug. 24	Aug. 26	Aug. 29	To Adelaide, Melbourne, Sydney, Brisbane.
Oder	8516	Sept. 25	Sept. 27	Sept. 29	
Mosel	8428	Oct 26	Oct. 28	Oct. 31	
Lahn	8498	Nov. 27	Nov. 29	Dec. 1	

ORIENT LINE—TO AUSTRALIA MAIL SERVICE

Via the Mediterranean, Egypt, and Colombo.

SAILINGS from London (subject to alteration without no ice).

Steamer.	Tons.	Date.	Steamer.	Tons.	Date.	Steamer	Tons.	Date.	Steamer	Tons.	Date.
‡*Otranto*	20000	July 15	¶*Orion*	23500	Sept. 9	¶*Orford*	20000	Sep. 30	¶*Orcades*	23465	Oct. 7
†*Ormonde*	15000	Aug. 12	¶*Orontes*	20000	Sept.23	(Special Tour)			‡*Orama*	20000	Oct. 21
‡*Oronsay*	20000	Aug. 26							¶*Orford*	20000	Nov. 4

OUTWARD	‡*Otr'nto*	†*Ormonde*	‡*Oronsay*	¶*Orion*	¶*Orontes*	¶*Orcades*	‡ *Orama*	¶ *Orford*
London, d.	July 15	Aug. 12	Aug. 26	Sept. 9	Sept. 23	Oct. 7	Oct. 21	Nov. 4
Gibraltar	19	16	30	13	27	11	25	8
Toulon ..	21	18	Sept. 1	15	29	13	27	10
Naples ..	23	20	3	17	Oct, 1	15	29	12
Port Said	26	23	6	20	4	18	Nov. 1	15
Aden	30	27	10	24	8	22	5	19
Colombo	Aug. 5	Sept. 2	16	30	14	28	11	25
Fremantle	15	12	26	Oct. 10	24	Nov. 7	21	Dec. 5
Adelaide	19	16	30	14	28	11	25	9
Melbourne	21	18	Oct. 2	16	30	13	27	11
Burnie ..	—	—	—	—	—	—	28	—
Sydney, a.	23	21	5	18	Nov. 2	16	30	13
Brisbane	27	25	9	22	6	20	Dec. 4	17

HOMEWARD	¶*Orontes*	‡*Orama*	‡*Otranto*	†*Ormonde*	‡ *Oron'y*	¶*Orion*	¶*Orontes*	¶*Orcades*
Brisbane ..	July 3	July 31	Aug. 28	Sept. 28	Oct. 12	Oct. 28	Nov. 9	Nov. 23
Sydney dep.	15	Aug. 12	Sept. 9	Oct. 7	21	Nov. 4	18	30
Hobart	—	—	—	—	—	—	—	Dec. 2
Burnie	—	—	—	—	—	—	—	3
Melbourne ..	18	15	12	Oct. 10	24	7	21	5
Adelaide ..	20	17	14	12	26	9	23	7
Fremantle	24	21	18	16	30	13	27	11
Colombo ..	Aug. 2	30	27	25	Nov. 8	22	Dec. 6	20
Aden	8	Sept. 5	Oct. 3	31	14	28	12	26
Suez	12	9	7	Nov. 4	18	Dec. 2	16	30
Port Said ..	12	9	7	4	18	2	16	30
Naples	16	13	11	8	22	6	20	Jan. 3
Villefranche	—	—	—	—	—	—	21	4
Toulon d 14.0	18	15	13	10	24	8	22	5
Gibraltar ..	20	17	15	12	26	10	24	7
Plymouth ..	23	20	18	15	29	13	27	10
London, arr.	24	21	19	16	30	14	28	11

s.s. *Orford* ¶, depart Southampton, Sept. 30, arr. Malta Oct. 6, dep. Oct. 6; arr. Haifa, Oct. 10, dep. Oct. 10; Port Said, arr. Oct. 9, dep. Oct. 9, arr. London, Oct. 19.

† Tourist cl. only. ¶1st cl. & Tourist cl. ‡ 1st and Tourist cl. "B."

PENINSULAR & ORIENTAL S.N. COMPANY.

London—(*via* Marseilles and Port Said)—Bombay

**Ranchi*	17000	July 28	¶*Stratheden*	23500	Sept. 1	**Corfu*	15000	Sept. 22
**Cathay*	15000	Aug. 4	¶*Strathaird*	22500	Sept. 6	¶*Strathmore*	23500	Sept. 22
**Ranpura*	17000	Aug. 11	**Chitral*	15000	Sept. 8	¶*Strathallan*	23500	Sept. 29
¶*Maloja*	21000	Aug 18	¶*Mooltan*	21000	Sept. 15	**Canton*	16000	Oct. 6
**Rawalpindi*	17000	Aug. 25						

* Carries 1st and 2nd Class. ¶ Carries 1st and Tourist Class.

London ..dep.	Jly. 28	Aug. 4	Aug 11	Aug 18	Aug 25	Sept. 1	Sept. 6	Sept. 8	Sep. 15	Sep. 22	Sep. 22	Sep. 29	Oct. 6
S'thampton d.	29	—	12	—	26	—	—	9	—	23	—	—	7
Tangier......	Aug. 1	8	15	22	29	5	—	12	19	26	—	Obt. 3	10
Gibraltar arr.	1	8	15	22	29	5	—	12	19	26	—	3	10
Marseilles‡ d.	5	12	19	26	Sep. 2	9	11	16	23	30	28	7	14
Malta ....arr.	6	—	20	—	3	—	—	17	—	Oct. 1	—	—	15
Port Said arr.	9	16	23	30	6	‖13	14	20	27	4	Oct. 1	11	18
Aden .... ,,	13	20	27	Sep. 3	10	17	—	24	Oct. 1	8	—	15	22
Bombay .. ,,	17	24	31	7	14	21	22	28	5	12	9	19	26

Bombay dep.	Jly. 22	Jly. 29	Aug. 5	Aug 12	Aug 19	Aug 26	Sept. 2	Sept. 9	Sep. 16	Sep. 23	Sep. 30	Oct. 7	Oct 14
	**Rawalpindi*	¶*Strathaird*	**Chtral*	¶*Mooltan*	**Corfu.*	¶*Strathallan*	**Canton.*	¶*Narkunda.*	**Carthage.*	¶*Strathaird*	**Rajputana.*	**Comorin.*	¶*Strathmore*
Aden .... arr.	27	Aug. 3	10	17	24	31	6	13	20	27	Oct. 4	11	18
Port Said ,,	31	7	14	21	28	Sept. 4	10	17	24	Oct. 1	8	15	22
Malta .. ,,	Au. 2	—	16	—	30	—	13	—	27	—	11	—	—
Marseilles ,,	4	11	18	25	Sept. 1	8	15	22	29	6	13	20	27
Gibraltar ,,	7	14	21	28	4	11	18	25	Oct. 2	—	16	23	30
Tangier.. ,,	7	14	21	28	4	11	18	25	2	—	16	23	30
Plymouth ,,	10	17	24	31	7	14	21	28	5	—	19	26	Nv 2
London.. ,,	11	18	25	Sept. 1	8	15	22	29	6	11	20	27	3

‖ Calls also Port Sudan (*see below*).

London *via* Marseilles, Port Said and Colombo to Australia.

**Comorin*	15000 tons	Jly. 21	¶*Stratheden*	23500 tons	Sep. 1	¶*Strathaird*	22500 tons	Oct. 14
**Cathay*	15000 tons	Aug. 4	¶*Mooltan*	21000 tons	Sep. 15	¶*Narkunda*	17000 tons	Oct. 27
¶*Maloja*	21000 tons	Aug. 18	¶*Strathallan*	23500 tons	Sep. 29	¶*Strathmore*	23500 tons	Nov. 10

* Carries 1st and 2nd Class. ¶ Carries 1st Saloon and Tourist Class.

London ....dep.	July 21	Aug. 4	Aug. 18	Sept. 1	Sept. 15	Sept. 29	Oct. 14	Oct. 27	Nov. 10
Tangier .... ,,	25	8	22	5	19	Oct. 3	18	31	14
Gibraltar .... ,,	25	8	22	5	19	3	18	31	14
Marseilles‡ ...... ,,	29	12	26	9	23	7	21	Nov. 4	18
Port Said .... ,,	Aug. 2	16	30	13	27	11	22	8	22
Port Sudan ...... ,,	—	—	—	15/16	—	13/14	27/28	—	24/25
Aden .... arr.	6	20	Sept. 3	17	Oct. 1	15	29	12	26
Bombay .... ,,	10	24	7	21	5	19	Nov. 2	16	30
Colombo .... dep.	13	27	10	24	8	22	5	19	Dec. 3
Fremantle .... ,,	22	Sept. 5	19	Oct. 3	17	31	14	28	12
Adelaide.......... ,,	26	9	23	7	21	Nov. 4	18	Dec. 2	16
Melbourne........ ,,	28	11	25	9	23	6	20	4	18
Sydney .... ,,	31	14	28	11	26	8	23	7	20
Brisbane .... ,,	Sept. 4	18	Oct. 2	15	30	12	27	11	23

Brisbane..........dep.	June 27	July 12	July 25	Aug. 9	Aug. 22	Sept. 6	Sept. 20	Oct. 4	Oct. 17
	¶*Strathaird*	¶*Mooltan*	¶*Strathallan*	¶*Narkunda*	¶*Strathnaver*	**Comorin*	**Cathay*	¶*Maloja*	¶*Stratheden.*
Sydney............ ,,	July 8	21	Aug. 5	18	Sept. 2	15	29	13	28
Melbourne .... ,,	11	25	8	22	5	19	Oct. 3	17	31
Adelaide .... ,,	13	27	10	24	7	21	5	19	Nov. 2
Fremantle .... ,,	17	31	14	28	11	25	9	28	6
Colombo .... ,,	26	Aug. 9	23	Sept. 6	20	Oct. 4	18	Nov. 1	15
Bombay .... ,,	29	12	26	9	—	7	21	4	18
Aden .... ,,	Aug. 3	17	31	13	26	11	25	8	22
Port Sudan ...... ,,	4/5	—	—	—	—	—	—	—	—
Port Said .... ,,	7	21	Sept. 4	17	Oct. 1	15	29	12	26
Malta .... ,,	—	—	—	—	—	—	—	—	—
Marseilles .... ,,	11	25	8	22	6	20	Nov. 3	17	Dec. 1
Gibraltar .... ,,	14	28	11	25	9	23	6	20	4
Tangier .... ,,	14	28	11	25	9	23	6	20	4
Plymouth .... ,,	17	31	14	28	12	26	9	23	7
London .... ,,	18	Sept. 1	15	29	13	27	10	24	8

‡ Arrival time at Marseilles uncertain.

☞ N.B. Dates given at ports of call are liable to slight alteration.

(*P. & O. SAILINGS CONTINUED NEXT PAGE*)

PENINSULAR & ORIENTAL STEAM NAV. CO.—*cont.*

London--Marseilles—Ceylon—Straits—China and Japan.

Steamer.	Tons.	Date.	Steamer.	Tons.	Date.	Steamer.	Tons.	Date.
Rajputana	17000	July 14	*Chitral*	15000	Sept. 8	*Carthage*	15000	Oct. 20
Ranchi........	17000	July 28	*Corfu*	15000	Sept. 22	*Rajputana*....	17000	Nov. 3
Ranpura	17000	Aug. 11	*Canton*	16000	Oct. 6	*Ranchi*........	17000	Nov. 17
Rawalpindi ..	17060	Aug. 25						

All Steamers carry First and Second Class.

London ....dep.	Jly. 14	Jly. 28	Aug 11	Aug 25	Sept. 8	Sep 22	Oct. 6	Oct. 20	Nov. 3	Nov 17
Southampton	15	29	12	26	9	23	7	21	4	18
Tangier	18	Aug. 1	15	29	12	26	10	24	—	21
Gibraltar	18	1	15	29	12	26	10	24	—	21
Marseilles *	22	5	19	Sept. 2	16	30	14	28	10	25
Malta	23	6	20	3	17	Oct. 1	15	29	12	26
Port Said ....arr.	26	9	23	6	20	4	18	Nov. 1	14	29
Aden ....dep.	30	13	27	10	24	8	22	5	19	Dec. 3
Bombay	Aug. 3	17	31	14	‡28	‡12	26	‡9	*24	7
Colombo ....dep.	6	20	Sept. 3	17	Oct. 1	15	29	12	25	10
Penang ....arr.	10	24	7	21	5	19	Nov. 2	16	30	14
Singapore .... ,,	11	25	8	22	6	20	3	17	Dec. 1	15
Hong-Kong .... ,,	16	30	13	27	12	26	9	23	7	21
Shanghai .... ,,	20	Sept 3	17	Oct. 1	16	30	13	27	11	25
Kobe .... ,,	24	7	21	5	20	Nov. 3	17	Dec. 1	15	29
Yokohama	26	9	23	7	22	5	19	3	17	31

* Arrival time at Marseilles uncertain.
‡ Calls at Cochin two days after Bombay. * Cochin instead of Bombay.

Japan--China—Straits—Ceylon—Marseilles—London.

Yokohama ....dep.	Jne. 27	Jly. 11	Jly. 25	Aug. 8	Aug 22	Sep. 5	Sep. 19	Oct. 3	Oct. 17	Oct. 31
Kobe .... ,,	30	14	28	11	25	8	22	6	20	Nov. 3
Shanghai .... ,,	July 4	18	Aug. 1	15	29	12	26	10	24	7
Hong-Kong .... ,,	8	22	5	19	Sept. 2	16	30	14	28	11
Singapore..........arr.	14	28	11	25	8	22	Oct. 6	20	Nov. 3	17
Penang .... ,,	15	29	12	26	9	23	7	21	4	18
Colombo .... ,,	19	Aug. 2	16	30	13	27	11	25	8	22
Bombay	22	5	19	Sept. 2	16	30	—	—	—	25
Aden ....arr.	27	10	24	6	20	Oct. 4	17	31	14	29
Port Said .... ,,	31	14	28	10	24	8	22	Nov. 5	19	Dec. 3
Malta	Aug. 2	16	30	13	27	11	25	8	22	6
Marseilles ....arr.	4	18	Sept. 1	15	29	13	27	10	24	8
Gibraltar	7	21	4	18	Oct. 2	16	—	13	—	11
Tangier	7	21	4	18	2	16	—	13	—	11
Plymouth	10	24	7	21	5	19	—	16	—	14
London ....arr.	11	25	8	22	6	20	Nov. 3	17	Dec. 1	15
	Rawalpindi	*Canton*	*Corfu*	*Canton*	*Carthage*	*Rajputana*	*Ranchi*	*Ranpura*	*Rawalpindi*	*Chitral*

* Calling Port Sudan 2 or 3 days before arrival at Port Said. † Calling Cochin the day after Colombo.

(*See advertisement page* 516).

PRINCE LINE LTD.

(See also page 480).

MEDITERRANEAN SERVICE to EGYPT, PALESTINE and SYRIA.

PROPOSED SAILINGS. Subject to alteration without notice.

Port of Call.	*Palestinian Prince*	*Sardinian Prince*	*Cyprian Prince*	*Syrian Prince*
London ....dep.	—	Aug. 12	—	—
Manchester ....dep.	Aug. 5	—	Aug. 16	Aug. 30
Tunis..................	,, 13	—	,, 25	Sept. 7
Malta..................	,, 14	Aug. 22	,, 26	,, 8
Alexandria	—	,, 30	,, 30	—
Jaffa	—	Sept. 4	—	—
Tel Aviv	—	,, 5	—	—
Haifa	—	,, 6	—	—
Beyrout	—	,, 8	—	—
Famagusta	Aug. 18	—	—	Sept. 12
Beyrout................	,, 19	—	—	,, 13
Haifa..................	,, 19	—	—	,, 13
Jaffa..................	,, 20	—	—	,, 14
Alexandria ....arr./dep.	,, 21/31	Sept. 10/Oct. 1	—	,, 16
Jaffa ....dep.	—	—	Sept. 17	—
United Kingdom......arr.	Sept. 15	Oct. 16	Oct. 2	—

Steamers carry twelve 1st class passengers. Single and double cabins. No doctor or stewardess.

ROTTERDAM LLOYD ROYAL DUTCH MAIL.

Rotterdam, *via* Southampton, Lisbon, Tangier, Gibraltar, Marseilles, Port Said, Colombo, Sabang. Balawan Deli, Singapore and Java.

Steamer	Tons	Date	Steamer	Tons	Date	Steamer	Tons	Date
§*Baloeran*	17000	Aug. 2	§*Indrapoera*	12000	Oct. 4	§*Sibajak*	17000	Nov. 8
§*Sibajak* ..	17000	Aug. 23	§*Baloeran*	17000	Oct. 25	§*Dempo*	17000	Dec. 6
§*Dempo*....	17000	Sep. 13						

These steamers carry first, second and third class passengers.

OUTWARD SAILINGS. § Twin-screw Motor Vessel.

Rotter-dam. dep. 17.0	South-ampton. dep. 17.0	Lisbon. arr. a.m.	Tangier and Gibraltar. arr.	Marseilles. arr. a.m.	Marseilles. dp. 13¶o	Port Said. arr.	Colombo arr.	Sabang. arr.	Belawan arr.	Singa-pore. arr.	Batavia. ‡ arr.
Aug. 2	Aug. 4	Aug. 7	Aug. 8	Aug. 10	Aug. 11	Aug. 15	Aug 24	Aug. 27	Aug. 28	Aug. 29	Aug. 31
,, 23	,, 25	,, 28	,, 29	,, 31	Sept. 1	Sept. 5	Sept 14	Sept. 17	Sept 18	Sept 19	Sep. 21
Sep. 13	Sep. 15	Sep. 18	Sep. 19	Sep. 21	,, 22	,, 26	Oct. 5	Oct. 8	Oct. 9	Oct. 10	Oct. 12
Oct. 4	Oct. 6	Oct. 9	Oct. 10	Oct. 12	Oct 13	Oct. 17	,, 26	,, 28	,, 30	,, 31	Nov. 2
,, 25	,, 27	,, 30	,, 31	Nov. 2	Nov. 3	Nov. 7	Nov. 16	Nov. 19	Nov. 20	Nov. 21	,, 23
Nov. 8	Nov. 10	Nov. 13	Nov. 14	,, 16	,, 17	,, 21	,, 30	Dec. 3	Dec. 4	Dec. 5	Dec. 7
Dec. 6	Dec. 8	Dec. 11	Dec. 12	Dec. 14	Dec. 15	Dec. 19	Dec. 28	,, 31	Jan. 1	Jan. 2	Jan. 4

HOMEWARD SAILING.

s.s. *Slamat*	July 19	m.v. *Indrapoera*	Aug. 23	m.v. *Sibajak*	Oct. 4
m.v. *Dempo*	Aug. 2	m.v. *Baloeran*	Sep. 13	m.v. *Dempo*	Oct; 25

Batavia. dep.	Singa-pore. dep.	Belawan dep.	Sabang. dep.	Colombo dep.	Port Said. dep.	Marseilles. ar a.m ¶	Marseilles. dp. 15¶o	Gibr'ltar and † Tangier. dep.	Lisbon. dep.	South-ampton. arr.	Rotter-dam. arr.
July 19	July 21	July 22	July 23	July 26	Aug. 5	Aug. 9	Aug. 9	Aug 11	Aug. 12	Aug. 14	Aug. 15
Aug. 2	Aug. 4	Aug. 5	Aug. 6	Aug. 9	Aug. 19	Aug. 23	Aug. 23	Aug. 25	Aug. 26	Aug. 28	Aug. 29
Aug. 23	Aug. 25	Aug. 26	Aug. 27	Aug. 30	Sept. 9	Sep. 13	Sept 13	Sep. 15	Sept 16	Sep. 18	Sept. 19
Sep. 13	Sep. 15	Sep. 16	Sep. 17	Sep. 20	,, 29	Oct. 3	Oct. 3	Oct. 5	Oct. 6	Oct. 8	Oct. 9
Oct. 4	Oct. 6	Oct. 7	Oct. 8	Oct. 11	Oct. 20	Oct. 24	Oct. 24	Oct. 26	Oct. 27	Oct. 29	Oct. 30
,, 25	,, 27	,, 28	,, 29	Nov. 1	Nov. 10	Nov. 14	Nov. 14	Nov. 16	Nov. 17	Nov. 19	Nov. 20

¶ SPECIAL BOAT TRAIN.—A direct special boat train (1 & 2 cl. carriages, Restaurant and Sleeping Cars) runs from The Hague *via* Brussels, Paris and Marseilles and *vice versa* in connection with the steamers. ‡ Arrive Samarang two days and Sourabaya three days after leaving Batavia.

† Passengers landing at Gibraltar cannot re-embark for Tangier.

CARGO MOTOR VESSELS (limited passenger accommodation).

	Tons.		Tons.		Tons.		Tons.
Djambi ..	6983	*Kota Tjandi* ..	7309	*Kota Nopan* ..	7319	*Kota* —— ..	—

From Rotterdam and Genoa *via* Port Said, Sabang, Belawan, Singapore and Batavia.

(See also *page* 442)

SHAW SAVILL LINE. To AUSTRALIA *via* SUEZ.

Cargo steamers (via Suez) carrying a limited number of passengers in single and double cabins, calling usually at Port Said, Fremantle, Adelaide, Melbourne, Sydney and Brisbane.

SAILINGS ON APPLICATION

STRICK AND ELLERMAN LINES. DIRECT TO PERSIAN GULF.

Regular steamers from Glasgow and Manchester, London and Antwerp to Red Sea ports and ports in the Persian Gulf, and take goods on through Bs/Lading to Baghdad and Ahwaz.

SOTA and AZNAR LINE.

COMPAÑIA NAVIERA "SOTA Y AZNAR"

BILBAO—MALAGA and *vice versa via* COASTAL PORTS (Temporary Service).

m.v. *Altube Mendi*	2954 tons	m.v. *Arnabal Mendi*	2954 tons	m.v. *Aya Mendi*	2954 tons
m.v. *Anboto Mendi*	2954 ,,	m.v. *Artza Mendi*	2954 ,,	m.v. *Ayala Mendi*	2954 ,,
m.v. *Araya Mendi*	2954 ,,	m.v. *Axpe Mendi*	2954 ,,		

Itinerary: From Bilbao fortnightly on Thursdays *via*: Pasajes, Santander, Gijon-Musel, Ferrol, Coruna, Villagarcia, Vigo, Sevilla, Huelva, Cadiz, Ceuta, Melilla, Malaga, voyage 24 days.
Returning from Malaga fortnightly on Wednesdays, *via* Cadiz, Sevilla, Vigo, Villagarcia, Coruna, Ferrol, Gijon-Musel, Santander. Pasajes, Bilbao, voyage 18 days.

Cargo vessels with 3 cabins on deck and 4 under deck for maximum of 20 passengers.

SVENSKA ORIENT LINIEN

(SWEDISH ORIENT LINE.)

Vessels	Tons	Vessels	Tons	Vessels	Tons	Vessels	Tons
m.v. *Brageland*	3240	m.v. *Birkaland*	4760	m.v. *Vasaland*	4770	m.v. *Vikingland*	4275
m.v. *Bardaland*	4760	m.v. *Vingaland*	4755				

These ships are fast modern cargo vessels with accommodation for a few 1st class passengers but carry neither doctor nor stewardess.

SAILINGS:—Fortnightly from Gothenburg to Casablanca, Algiers, Alexandria, Jaffa/Haifa, Beyrout, Piræus, Istanbul and Black Sea Ports.

About twice monthly—From Alexandria, Jaffa/Haifa, Beyrout, Piræus, Istanbul and Black Sea Ports. To the Continent (Rotterdam, Hamburg) Scandinavia and Baltic Ports.

SVENSKA OSTASIATISKA KOMPANIET

(SWEDISH EAST ASIATIC CO., LTD.)

VESSEL.	Tons.	VESSEL.	Tons.	VESSEL.	Tons.	VESSEL.	Tons.
m.v. *Agra*	4569	m.v. *Formosa* ..	5554	m.v. *Ningpo* abt.	6100	m.v. *Shantung* ..	6527
m.v. *Canton*	5779	s.s. *Japan*	5235	m.v. *Nippon*	6095	s.s. *Sumatra*	5412
s.s. *Ceylon*	5235	m.v. *Nagara* ..	6525	m.v. *Peiping* ..	6390	m.v. *Tamara* ..	6390
m.v. *Delhi*	4571	m.v. *Nanking* ..	5931				

Services to and from India, respectively the Far East *via* Suez. These Cargo Vessels have limited accommodation for passengers but carry neither doctor nor stewardess.

From Oslo, Gothenburg, Antwerp, Rotterdam, Hamburg monthly departures *via* Port Said and Suez for Port Sudan, Colombo, Singapore, Manila, Hong Kong, Shanghai, Yokohama, Kobe, Moji, Dairen, and *v.v.*

From Oslo, Gothenburg, Hamburg, Antwerp and Rotterdam monthly departures *via* Port Said, Suez to Karachi, Bombay, Madras, Calcutta, Rangoon, and *v.v.*

UNION-CASTLE MAIL STEAMSHIP CO., LTD.

(See also pages 410 and 467).

Royal East African Service. *Via* Suez Canal.

From London *via* Tangier and Gibraltar, Marseilles, Genoa, Port Said, Suez, Port Sudan and Aden to Mombasa (Kilindini), Tanga, Zanzibar, Dar-es-Salaam, Port Amelia, Mozambique, Beira, Lourenço Marques and Durban, returning to England *via* South African Ports.

SAILINGS OUTWARD.	Tons.	London d	Tangier & Gibraltar.	Marseilles	Genoa arr./dep	Port Said	Port Sudan	Mombasa arr.
Llandovery Castle	10609	Aug. 3	Aug. 7	Aug. 10	Aug. 11/12	Aug. 17	Aug. 20	Aug. 28
Llandaff Castle ..	10786	,, 31	Sept. 4	Sept. 7	Sept. 8/9	Sept. 14	Sept. 17	Sept. 25
Llanstephan Castle	11299	Sept. 28	Oct. 2	Oct. 5	October 6/7	Oct. 12	Oct. 15	October 23
Llandovery Castle	10609	Oct. 26	,, 30	Nov. 2	Nov. 3/4	Nov. 9	Nov. 12	Nov. 20
Llandaff Castle ..	10786	Nov 23	Nov. 27	,, 30	Dec. 1/2	Dec. 7	Dec. 10	Dec. 18

† Thence *via* Tanga, Zanzibar, Dar-es-Salaam, Beira, etc. (see above), Cape Town, to London.

Vessels are also despatched from London *via* Teneriffe and Lobito, or Las Palmas, Ascension and St. Helena, to South and East African Ports, returning *via* Suez and Gibraltar, as under:

SAILINGS HOMEWARD.	London. dep	*Via* Cape Town, Natal, Mombassa	Mombasa dep.	Aden dep.	Port Sudan	Call Suez, Port Said. dep.	Genoa arr./dep.	Marseilles ar./dp.	Gibraltar and Tangier	London. arr.
Dunbar Castle	Jne. 16		July 26	Jly. 31	Aug. 2	Aug. 4/5	Aug. 9/10	Aug 11/12	Aug. 14	Aug. 18
Llangibby C.	Jly. 14		Aug. 23	Aug 28	,, 30	Sept. 1/2	Sept. 6/7	Sept. 8/9	Sept. 11	Sept. 15
Dunvegan C.	Aug 11		Sept. 20	Sep. 25	Sep. 27	Sept. 29/30	Oct. 4/5	Oct. 6/7	Oct. 9	Oct. 13
Dunbar Castle	Sep. 8		Oct. 18	Oct. 23	Oct. 25	Oct. 27/28	Nov. 1/2	Nov. 3/4	Nov. 6	Nov. 10
Llangibby C.	Oct. 6		Nov 15	Nov 20	Nov 22	Nov. 24/25	,, 29/30	Dec. 1/2	Dec. 4	Dec. 8
Dunvegan C.	Nov. 3		Dec. 13	Dec. 18	Dec 20	Dec. 22/23	Dec. 27/28	,, 29/30	Jan. 1	Jan. 5

WILHELMSEN LINES.

(See also page 468.)

The services are maintained by fast modern cargo liners, carrying mail with comfortable accommodation for passengers.

SAILINGS—**From Oslo, Gothenburg, Hamburg, Antwerp, Rotterdam, and Lisbon to India and Burmah**

Vessel.	Tons.	Oslo/Gothenburg. dep.	Hamburg dep.	Antwerp dep.	Rotterdam dep	Lisbon dep.	
s.s. *Rinda*	6029	Aug. 12	Aug. 16	Aug. 19	Aug 21	Aug. 26	Proceeding to Karachi, Bombay, Madras, Calcutta.
m.s. *Tigre*	5498	Sept. 13	Sept 16	Sept. 19	Sept. 21	Sept. 26	

SAILINGS—**From Hamburg, Lisbon, Barcelona and Marseilles to the Far East.**

Vessel.	Tons.	Hamburg. dep.	Lisbon. dep.	Marseilles. dep.	Port Said dep.	
m.s. *Talleyrand* ..	6732	July 29	Aug. 3	Aug. 7	Aug 12	Proceeding to Colombo, Singapore, Hong Kong, Shanghai, Japan.
m.s. *Toulouse*	7027	Aug. 30	Sept. 4	Sept. 8	Sept. 13	
m.s. *Temeraire* ..	6465	Sept. 30	Oct. 5	Oct. 9	Oct. 14	
m.s. *Triton*	6607	Oct. 30	Nov. 4	Nov. 8	Nov. 18	

COOK'S NILE STEAMER SAILINGS

(SEASON 1939-1940)

CAIRO TO ASYUT, LUXOR, ASWAN AND BACK

Steamer.	V'age No.	Leave Cairo 10 a.m.	Arrive Asyut morn.	Arrive Luxor morn.	Leave Luxor dawn.	Arrive Aswan aftn.	Leave Aswan dawn.	Arrive Luxor aftn.	Leave Luxor aftn.	Arrive Asyut morn.	Arrive Cairo morn.
		1939	1939	1939	1939	1939	1939	1939	1939	1939	1939
Arabia	1	Dec. 6	Dec. 9	Dec. 12	Dec. 14	Dec. 15	Dec. 17	Dec. 18	Dec. 20	Dec. 23	Dec. 26
Egypt	2	Dec. 13	Dec. 16	Dec. 19	Dec. 21	Dec. 22	Dec. 24	Dec. 25	Dec. 27	Dec. 30	1940 Jan. 2
Thebes	3	Dec. 20	Dec. 23	Dec. 26	Dec. 28	Dec. 29	—	—	—	—	—
Arabia	4	Dec. 27	Dec. 30	1940 Jan. 2	1940 Jan. 4	1940 Jan. 5	1940 Jan. 7	1940 Jan. 8	1940 Jan. 10	1940 Jan. 13	Jan. 16
Egypt	5	1940 Jan. 3	1940 Jan. 6	Jan. 9	Jan. 11	Jan. 12	Jan. 14	Jan. 15	Jan. 17	Jan. 20	Jan. 23
Sudan	6	Jan. 10	Jan. 13	Jan. 16	Jan. 18	Jan. 19	Jan. 21	Jan. 22	Jan. 24	Jan. 27	Jan. 30
Arabia	7	Jan. 17	Jan. 20	Jan. 23	Jan. 25	Jan. 26	Jan. 28	Jan. 29	Jan. 31	Feb. 3	Feb. 6
Egypt	8	Jan. 24	Jan. 27	Jan. 30	Feb. 1	Feb. 2	Feb. 4	Feb. 5	Feb. 7	Feb. 10	Feb. 13
Sudan	9	Jan. 31	Feb. 3	Feb. 6	Feb. 8	Feb. 9	Feb. 11	Feb. 12	Feb. 14	Feb. 17	Feb. 20
Arabia	10	Feb. 7	Feb. 10	Feb. 13	Feb. 15	Feb. 16	Feb. 18	Feb. 19	Feb. 21	Feb. 24	Feb. 27
Egypt	11	Feb. 14	Feb. 17	Feb. 20	Feb. 22	Feb. 23	Feb. 25	Feb. 26	Feb. 28	Mar. 2	Mar. 5
Sudan	12	Feb. 21	Feb. 24	Feb. 27	Feb. 29	Mar. 1	Mar. 3	Mar. 4	Mar. 6	Mar. 9	Mar. 12
Arabia	13	Feb. 28	Mar. 2	Mar. 5	Mar. 7	Mar. 8	Mar. 10	Mar. 11	Mar. 13	Mar. 16	Mar. 19
Egypt	14	Mar. 6	Mar. 9	Mar. 12	Mar. 14	Mar. 15	Mar. 17	Mar. 18	Mar. 20	Mar. 23	Mar. 26

ASWAN (Shellal) TO WADI HALFA AND BACK

Steamr.	Voyage No.	Leave Aswan (Shellal) 1 p.m.	Arrive Abu Simbel aftern'n.	Leave Abu Simbel morning.	Arrive Wadi Halfa morning*	Leave Wadi Halfa morning.	Arrive Abu Simbel aftern'n.	Leave Abu Simbel aftern'n.	Arrive Aswan (Shellal) evening.
		1939	1940	1940	1940	1940	1940	1940	1940
Thebes	1	Dec. 30	Jan. 1	Jan. 2	Jan. 2	Jan. 4	Jan. 4	Jan. 4	Jan. 5
		1940							
Thebes	2	Jan. 6	Jan. 8	Jan. 9	Jan. 9	Jan. 11	Jan. 11	Jan. 11	Jan. 12
Thebes	3	Jan. 13	Jan. 15	Jan. 16	Jan. 16	Jan. 18	Jan. 18	Jan. 18	Jan. 19
Thebes	4	Jan. 20	Jan. 22	Jan. 23	Jan. 23	Jan. 25	Jan. 25	Jan. 25	Jan. 26
Thebes	5	Jan. 27	Jan. 29	Jan. 30	Jan. 30	Feb. 1	Feb. 1	Feb. 1	Feb. 2
Thebes	6	Feb. 3	Feb. 5	Feb. 6	Feb. 6	Feb. 8	Feb. 8	Feb. 8	Feb. 9
Thebes	7	Feb. 10	Feb. 12	Feb. 13	Feb. 13	Feb. 15	Feb. 15	Feb. 15	Feb. 16
Thebes	8	Feb. 17	Feb. 19	Feb. 20	Feb. 20	Feb. 22	Feb. 22	Feb. 22	Feb. 23
Thebes	9	Feb. 24	Feb. 26	Feb. 27	Feb. 27	Feb. 29	Feb. 29	Feb. 29	Mar. 1
Thebes	10	Mar. 2	Mar. 4	Mar. 5	Mar. 5	Mar. 7	Mar. 7	Mar. 7	Mar. 8

* To connect with the 9.30 a.m. to Khartoum.

SUDAN GOVERNMENT WHITE NILE STEAMER SERVICES.

Connection between Khartoum and Juba† is maintained throughout the year by fortnightly sailings of Mail Steamers conveying 1st, 2nd and 3rd class passengers and cargo. Steamers depart from Khartoum at 5.0 on alternate Saturdays, Aug. 12, 26, etc., arriving in Juba† 13 days later, Aug. 25, Sept. 8, etc. From Juba leave on Sunday at 5.30, Aug. 13, 27, etc. and arrive in Khartoum on the second Monday following, viz., Aug. 21, Sept. 4, etc. Round trip of 21 days. † Connection at Juba with motor service to Nimule.

First-class south-bound passengers and their servants, also special second-class passengers, may join or leave the steamers at Kosti, travelling by Restaurant and Sleeping Car Train from Khartoum on Sunday. North-bound passengers also may disembark on Saturday at Kosti and travel by rail to Khartoum, arriving Sunday a.m.

WHITE NILE ROUTE.

TO KENYA, UGANDA, TANGANYIKA AND BELGIAN CONGO.

A fully-catered through service by train, river steamer and automobile is maintained throughout the year by a regular fortnightly service between Egyptian ports or Port Sudan, and Kenya and Uganda, Tanganyika and the Belgian Congo.

First-class through tickets, inclusive of catering and porterage, are issued by Thos. Cook and Son, Ltd., as agents for the Sudan Railways, for the journey between Shellal or Port Sudan and Juba or Nimule.

PART II.—MEDITERRANEAN AND BLACK SEA.

Services in the Mediterranean and Black Sea and from the Mediterranean to Ports beyond *via* Suez Canal.

	PAGE
"Adriatica" Soc. An. di Navigazione,	371A, 371B, 372/4
Algeciras-Gibraltar Ferry Service	371
American Export Lines (see page 443 in part V)	
Anglo-Egyptian Mail Line	371
Bland Line	374
Denizbank	375
Dollar Line (see page 473 in part VI)	
Dubrovacka Steamship Co.	374
Fiumana Soc. di Navigazione ..	375, 376
Fraissinet S.S. Co.	376
French Line, see Transatlantique (Cie Generale)	—
Gdynia Ameryca, Linje Zeglugowe A.G. (Palestine Services) ..	377
Genovese di Nav. a Vapore	377
Gdynia Amerika, Schiffahrtslinien A.G. (Palestine Line)	377
Havraise Peninsulaire de Navigation a Vapeur	377
Hellenic Coast Lines	378
"Istria-Trieste" Societa di Navigazione a Vapore	381
Jadranska Line	379/81
Jugoslav Line	381
Pharaonic Mail Line	386
La Punta de Europa (Compañia de Vapores)	371
Lloyd Triestino Soc. An. di Navigazione	382/85
Malta Syracuse-Malta-(Tunis) Service (Cassa & Co.)	387
Maritime Nationale Société	387
Messageries Maritimes de France ..	388/90
Misr de Navigation Maritime (Société) ..	387
Mixte (Cie de Navigation)	391
Palestine Maritime Lloyd	392
Paquet Line (Cie de N.)	392
Partenopea Societa Anonima di Navigazione	391
Roumanian State Maritime Service ..	393
"Tirrenia" Societa di Navigazione	395/7, 397A
Transatlantique (Compagnie Generale) ..	394
Trasmediterranea Compañia	399/400
Transport Maritimes à Vapeur (Soc. Gen. de)	98
Turkish Mail Line (Denizbank)	375
U.S.S.R. Steamers	393
Villain and Fassio (Societa di Navigazione)	398
Zetska Plovidba A.D., Cetinje	398

ALGECIRAS-GIBRALTAR FERRY SERVICE—Daily

COMPANIA DE VAPORES DE LA PUNTA DE EUROPA. p.s.'s *Margarita* 173 tons; *Aline* 216 tons

Liable to alteration. DAILY.

11 0	1830	dep. Gibraltar .... arr.	6 20	16 0
1130	19 0	arr. Algeciras .... dep.	5 50	1530

ANGLO-EGYPTIAN MAIL LINE.

MARSEILLES—PIRAEUS—ALEXANDRIA and *vice versa.* **(Fortnightly).**

s.s. *Cairo City*, 4792 tons (Oil Burner). Carrying 1 cl., 2 cl., Intermediate and 3 cl., passengers, Cabins de luxe and Semi-luxe cabins, 1 cl., with private bathrooms. Stewardess and Doctor carried.

From Marseilles, August 1.

From Alexandria, August 9.

	arr.	dep.		arr.	dep.
Marseilles	—	Tues. 1630	Alexandria	—	Wed. 15 0
Piræus ..	Sat. 6 0	Sat. 12 0	Piræus ..	Fri. 7 0	Fri. 12 0
Beyrout ..	Mon. 14 0	Mon. 22 0	Marseilles	Mon. 15 0	—
Haifa	Tues. 6 0	Tues. 11 0			
Alexandria	Wed. 9 0	—			

From Marseilles August 15, 29, Sept. 12, 26, Oct. 10, 24, Nov. 7.

From Beyrout August 22, Sept. 5, 19, Oct. 3. 17, 31, Nov. 14.

	arr.	dep.		arr.	dep.
Marseilles..	—	Tues. 11¶0	Beyrout......	—	Tues. 10 0
Piræus	Fri. 14 0	Fri. 19 0	Piræus	Thu. 12 0	Thu. 20 0
Alexandria	Sun. 9 0	Sun. 12 0	Marseilles....	Mon. 6 0	—
Haifa......	Mon. 12 0	Mon. 22 0			
Beyrout....	Tues. 6 0	—			

¶ Dept. 16.30 Aug. 15.

"ADRIATICA" Soc. An. di Navigazione.

All the steamers are fitted with Wireless Telegraphy, Electric Light, and have cabins for one, two, three, or more persons. A Surgeon and Stewardess carried on the principal Lines. Stewardess is carried on the Express Lines to Alexandria and Istanbul

The Company reserve the right to deviate from advertised routes and to change steamers.

GRAND WEEKLY EXPRESS SERVICE EUROPE-EGYPT.

LINE 47 from Genoa fortnightly. LINE 49 from Trieste, fortnightly.

LINE 47. GENOA—NAPLES—ALEXANDRIA—HAIFA—BEYROUT—GENOA

(Fortnightly) and *vice versa*.

s.s. *Esperia*, from Genoa, Aug. 5, 19, Sept. 2, 16, 30, Oct. 14, 28.
s.s. *Esperio*, from Alexandria, Aug. 12, 26, Sept. 9, 23, Oct. 7.

OUTWA'D.	s.s. *Esperia* —Aug. 5th only— arr.	dep.	Itiner'y: s.s. *Esperia* —From Aug. 19— arr.	dep.	H'MEW'RD	Itin'ry: s.s. *Esperia* arr.	dep.
Genoa ..	—	Sat. 15 0	—	Sat. 15 0	Alexandria	—	Sat. 12 0
Naples ..	Sun. 10 0	Sun. 17 0	Sun. 10 0	Sun. 17 0	Naples ..	Mon. 17 0	Mon. 20 0
Syracuse	Mon. 7 0	Mon. 10 0	Mon. 7 0	Mon. 10 0	Genoa ..	Tues. 15 0	—
Alexandria†	Wed. 7 0	Wed. 15 0	Wed. 7 0	Wed. 16 0			
Haifa ..	—	—	Thur. 9 0	Thu. 12 0			
Beyrout ..	Thur 10 0	Thur. 13 0	Thur. 17 0	Thu. 19 0			
Haifa	Thur. 17 30	Thur. 20 0	—	—			
Alexandria	Fri. 15 0	—	Fri. 16 0	—			

† Connecting with special trains from Gabbary Quai to Cairo.

LINE 49. TRIESTE—VENICE—BRINDISI—ALEXANDRIA—(HAIFA) Fortnightly.

s.s. *Marco Polo*, 12272 tons { Aug. 12, 26 from Trieste; Aug. 19. Sept. 2, from Alexandria.

OUTWARD.	arr.	dep.	HOMEWARDS	arr.	dep.
Trieste	—	Sa. 10 0	Al x'dria	—	Sat. 12 0
Venice	Sa. 15 0	,, 17 0	Brindisi	Mo. 11 0	Mo. 12 0
Brindisi ..	Su. 15	Su. 16 0	Venice	Tu. 11 0	Tu. 15 0
Alex'ndria †	Tu. 17 0	W. 12 0	Trieste	Tu. 19 30	—
Haifa......	Th 6 0	Th 0 0			
Beyrout ..	Th 15 0	Th 17 0			
Alexandria	Fri 14 0	—			

† Connecting with special trains from Gabbary Quai to Cairo.

LINE 55. ADRIATIC—CYPRUS—PALESTINE FAST LINE. (Weekly)

s.s. *Galilea*, 8,040 tons, Aug. 2, 23.
s.s. *Palestina*, 7,039 tons, Aug. 9.
s.s. *Gerusalemme* 8,052 tons, Aug. 16, 30.

arr.	dep.		arr.	dep.
—	We. 13 0	Trieste .. ↑	Mo. 14 0	—
Th. 16 0	Th. 17 0	Brindisi	Su. 8 0	Su. 9 0
Sat. 16 0	Sat. 17 0	Rhodes	Fri 10 0	Fri. 11 0
Su. 16 0	Su. 17 0	Larnaca	Th. 9 0	Th. 11 0
Mo. 6 30	Mo. 7 30	Jaffa....	—	—
—	—	Haifa ..	We. 15 0	We. 22 0
Mo. 8 0	Mo. 11 0	Tel-Aviv	We. 6 0	We. 10 0
Mo. 15 30	Mo. 24 0	Haifa	—	—
Tu. 7 0	—	↓ Beyrout	—	Tu. 20 0

Line 48. Genoa—Naples—Piræus—Rhodes—Alexandria. (Fortnightly).

m.v. *Egeo*, 3,202 tons. Via CAPE MATAPAN. s.s. *Adria*. July 30 and Aug. 13 only.

Au27,&c	Su. 11 0	Genoa .. ↑	Th. 11 0	—	July 30	Su. 11 0	Genoa ...	Fri 23 0	—
Mo. 10 0	Mo. 14 0	Naples ..	We. 10 0	We. 12 0	Mo. 13 0	Mo. 24 0	Naples ..	Th. 19 0	Th 21 0
We. 14 0	We. 18 0	Piræus ..	Mo. 8 0	Mo. 12 0	Th. 6 0	Th 11 0	Piræus ..	Tu. 13 0	Tu. 17 0
Th. 12 0	Th. 16 0	Rhodes ..	Su. 11 0	Su. 14 0	Fri 7 0	Fri 12 0	Rhodes .	Mo. 14 0	Mo. 17 0
Fri. 15 0	—	↓ Alexa'dria	Sep. 2&c.	Sat. 12 0	Sat. 14 0	—	Alexandria	Aug 6	Su. 12 0

LINE 50. ADRIATIC-EGYPT FAST LINE

(Fortnightly).

Via CAPE MATAPAN and RHODES.

m.s. *Calitea*, 4,013 tons.

arr.	dep.		arr.	dep.
Au. 5, etc	Sat. 10 0	Trieste ↑	Thu. 7 30	—
Sat. 15 30	Sat. 22 0	Venice	We. 19 0	Thu. 2 0
Sun. 7 0	Sun. 11 0	Fiume..	—	—
Mon. 9 0	Mon. 11‡0	Brindisi	Tue. 16 0	Tue. 17‡0
Tue. 20 0	Tue. 23 0	Piræus	Mon. 7 0	Mo. 9 0
Wed. 16 0	Wed. 18 0	Rhodes	Sun. 10 0	Sun. 14 0
Thur 16 0	—	↓ Al'x'dria	Au. 12, &c.	Sat. 12 0

‡ May leave earlier.

Line 54. Adriatic, Piraeus, Istanbul—Fast Line, *via* Cape Matapan. Weekly.

Sailings from Trieste, s.s. *Egitto*, 3220 tons, Aug 4, 18, Sept. 1, 15; s.s. *Rodi*, 3219 tons, Aug. 11, 25; Sept. 8, 22.

arr.	dep.		arr.	dep.
—	Fri. 11 0	Trieste ↓	Tue 21 0	—
Fri. 17 0	Fri. 21 0	Venice	Tu. 11 0	Tue 15 0
Sat. 24 0	Sun 1 0	Brindisi	Mon 6 0	Mon. 8 0
Mo. 10 0	Mo. 17 0	Piræus	Sat. 11 0	Sat 22 0
Tu. 18 0	—	Istanbul ↑	—	Fri. 10 0

Line 54. *bis.* Tyrrhenian—Piraeus—Istanbul—Fast Line. Fortnightly.

m.s. *Citta di Bari*, 3338 tons. *Via* Cape Matapan.

arr.	dep		arr.	dep.
Aug 6 &c	Su. 11 0	Genoa ↓	Fri. 8 0	—
—	—	Marseilles	Th. 7 0	Th. 17 0
Mo. 10 0	Mo. 14 0	Naples	Tue 15 0	Tu. 20 0
We. 14 0	We. 18 0	Piræus	Su. 13 0	Su. 17 0
Th. 9 0	Th. 17 0	Izmir	—	—
Fri. 12 0	—	Istanbul ↑	Aug 12 &c	Sat. 12 0

Line 56 Adriatic—Syria "A" Line. Fortnightly.

m.v. *Diana*, 3347 tons, Aug. 17, Sept. 14; s.s. *Quirinale*, 3779 tons, Aug. 3, 31.

	arr.	dep.
Trieste	Aug. 3, etc.	Thursday 22 0
Fiume	Friday 8 0	Friday 18 0
Venice	Saturday 8 0	Saturday 18 0
Ancona†	Sunday 7 0	Sunday 9 0
Bari†	Monday 6 0	Monday 8 0
Brindisi	Monday 15 0	Monday 17 0
Piræus	Wednesday 16 0	Wednesday 22 0
Candia†	Thursday 15 0	Thursday 18 0
Alexandria	Saturday 6 0	Saturday 16 0
Port Said	Sunday 7 0	Sunday 17 0
Tel-Aviv†	Monday 6 0	Monday 11 0
Haifa	Monday 17 0	Tuesday 23 0
Beyrout	Wednesday 7 0	—

Continued →

	arr.	dep.
Beyrout	Aug. 2, etc.	Wednesday 16 0
Alexandretta†	Thursday 9 0	Thursday 22 0
Mersina	Friday 6 0	Friday 20 0
Famagusta†	Saturday 7 0	Saturday 10 0
Larnaca†	Saturday 15 0	Saturday 24 0
Limassol†	Sunday 5 0	Sunday 11 0
Adalia	Monday 7 0	Monday 13 0
Rhodes	Tuesday 6 0	Tuesday 10 0
Piræus	Wednesday 11 0	Wednesday 16 0
Candia†	Thursday 9 0	Thursday 16 0
Brindisi	Saturday 15 0	Saturday 19 0
Venice	Monday 7 0	Monday 11 0
Trieste	Monday 19 0	—

May also call outward at Lixuri, Argostoli, Æghion, Nauplia, Canea, Rethymo and Jaffa, returning at Payas, Canea, Rethymo, Calamata, Izmir, Vathy, Carlovassi and Chios. † Optional.

Line 57. Adriatic Syrian Commercial "B" Line Fortnightly.

s.s. *Assiria*, 2755 tons, Aug. 10 Sept. 7. s.s. *Bolsena*, 2384 tons. Aug. 24, Sept. 7

Arrival and departure times may be earlier or later at all ports.

	arr.	dep.
Trieste	Aug. 10, etc.	Thursday 22 0
Fiume	Friday 8 0	Friday 18 0
Venice	Saturday 8 0	Saturday 18 0
Ancona†	Sunday 7 0	Sunday 11 0
Bari†	Monday 9 0	Monday 14 0
Brindisi	Monday 21 0	Monday 24 0
Patras	Wednesday 6 0	Wednesday 12 0
Æghion†	—	—
Limassol	Saturday 11 0	Saturday 22 0
Famagusta	Sunday 6 0	Sunday 17 0
Mersina	Monday 6 0	Monday 22 0
Alexandretta	Tuesday 7 0	Tuesday 15 0
Tripoli†	Wednesday 6 0	Wednesday 10 0
Beyrout	Wednesday 15 0	—

† Optional.

	arr.	dep.
Beyrout	Aug. 8, etc.	Wednesday 24 0
Haifa	Thursday 8 0	Thursday 24 0
Jaffa	Friday 6 0	Friday 15 0
Port Said	Saturday 6 0	Saturday 14 0
Alexandria	Sunday 7 0	Sunday 20 0
Candia†	Tuesday 10 0	Tuesday 18 0
Calamata†	Wednesday 14 0	Wednesday 22 0
Brindisi†	Friday 3 0	Friday 10 0
Bari†	Friday 17 0	Friday 22 0
Venice*	Sunday 8 0	Sunday 12 0
Trieste*	Sunday 20 0	—

* During the onion season may call at Trieste before Venice.

May also call Pola, Split, Argostoli, Zante, Catakolo, Canea outward or homeward, and at Gythion, Nauplia, Payas, Famagusta, Latakia, Rethymo and Ravenna on return.

Line 58. Tyrrhenian-Syrian Commercial Line. Every 10 days.

Carrying one class only at 2 cl. rates. s.s. *Snia Amba*, — tons, Aug. 5, Sept 5; m.v. *Cilicia*, 2747 tons, Aug 25, Sept. 25; m.v. *Caldea*, 2703 tons, Aug. 15 Sept 15.

Arrival and departure times may be earlier or later at all ports.

	arr.	dep.
Genoa	—	Aug 5 22 0
Leghorn†	Aug. 6 7 0	,, 6 24 0
Naples	,, 8 7 0	,, 8 16 0
Messina†	,, 9 8 0	,, 9 12 0
Catania	,, 9 17 0	,, 10 12 0
Alexandria	,, 13 12 0	,, 14 15 0
Port Said	,, 15 7 0	,, 15 17 0
Jaffa†	,, 16 6 0	,, 16 11 0
Haifa	,, 16 17 0	,, 17 23 0
Beyrout	,, 18 6 0	—

†Optional. *Continued* →

	arr.	dep.
Beyrout	—	Aug 18 11 0
Tripoli†	Aug. 18 16 0	,, 18 19 0
Alexandretta	,, 20 8 0	,, 20 22 0
Mersina‡	,, 21 7 0	,, 21 17 0
Larnaca	,, 22 7 0	,, 22 11 0
Limassol†	,, 22 16 0	,, 22 19 0
Candia	,, 24 8 0	,, 24 11 0
Canea†	,, 24 17 0	,, 24 19 0
Naples	,, 27 7 0	,, 27 12 0
Marseilles	,, 29 6 0	,, 29 18 0
Genoa	,, 30 12 0	—

Optional Calls also Rhodes, Candia, Piræus, Savona, Imperia, and other Tyrrhenian ports.

‡ May leave 24 hours later, in which case arr. and dep. at other ports will be postponed accordingly.

"ADRIATICA" Soc. An. di Navigazione—*continued.*

Danube Lines *via* Cape Matapan.

Line 59.

Adriatic Danube Commercial Line

Via Cape Matapan. Fortnightly.

s.s. *Abbazia*, 3706 tons, Aug. 5, Sept. 16.
s.s. *Vesta*, 3351 tons, Aug. 19, Sept. 30.
s.s. *Bosforo*, 3567 tons, Sept. 2, Oct. 14.

arr.	dep.		arr.	dep.
Aug. 5,	Sa. 19 0	Trieste ..	We. 7 0	—
Su. 6 0	Su 18 0	Fiume †	—	—
Mo. 7 0	Mo. 20 0	Venice	Tu. 7 0	Tu. 24 0
—	—	Ancona †	Mo. 6 0	Mo. 18 0
We. 6 0	We 11 0	Bari ...... ↑	—	—
W. 18 0	W. 21 0	Brindisi	Sa. 14 0	Sa. 24 0
—	—	St. Quaranta †	—	—
—	—	Patras	Fr. 6 0	Fr. 14 0
Fri. 21 0	Sat 19 0	↓ Piræus	We. 9 0	We. 24 0
Su 14 0	Su. 18 0	Volo †	Tu. 8 0	Tu. 14 0
Mo. 7† 0	Mo. 15 0	Thessaloniki	Su. 8 0	Mo. 19 0
Tu. 7† 0	Tu. 12† 0	Cavalla † ..	Sa. 6 0	Sat. 16 0
We. 12 0	Th. 20 0	Istanbul	Th 5 0	Th. 24 0
Fri. 9 0	Fri. 23 0	Burgas	We 6 0	We 17 0
Sat. 6† 0	Sat. 21. 0	Varna ..	Tu. 6 0	Tu. 23 0
Su. 6 0	Su. 21 0	Constanza	Su. 22 0	Mo. 21 0
Mo. 5 0	Mo. 6 30	Sulina	Su. 12 0	Su. 14 0
M. 16 0	—	Galatz-Braila	July30&c	Su. 4 0

† Optional.

Outward, may call at Corfu, Prevesa, Calcida and Stilida. On return may call at Corfu, Chios, Santi Quantara, Bari and Fiume.

Line 60.

Adriatic Black Sea Commercial Line

Via Cape Matapan. Fortnightly.

s.s. *Albano*, 2364 tons, carrying 4 saloon passengers, July 29, Sept. 9, Oct. 21.
s.s. *Spartivento*, —— tons, Aug. 12, Sept. 23, Nov. 4.
s.s. *Iseo*, 2366 tons, carrying 4 saloon passengers, Aug. 26, Oct. 7.

arr.	dep.		arr.	dep.
Jly29,&c	Sa. 19 0	Trieste......	Tu. 7 0	—
Su. 6 0	Su. 18 0	Fiume	—	—
Mo. 7 0	Mo. 17 0	Venice......	Mo. 8 0	Mo. 23 0
We. 5 0	We. 6 0	Brindisi	Sa. 14 0	Sa. 18 0
—	—	St. Quaranta †	—	—
—	—	Patras......	Fri. 11 0	Fri. 16 0
Th. 17 0	Th. 24 0	Calamata † ..	Th. 13 0	Th. 20 0
Fri. 18 0	Sat. 10 0	Piræus	We. 13 0	W. 20 0
Su. 8 0	Su. 23 0	Izmir †	Tu. 6 0	Tu. 16 0
Mo. 6 0	Mo. 8 0	Mitylene †	Mo. 15 0	Mo. 24 0
Tu. 6 † 0	Tu. 11† 0	Thessaloniki	Sa. 16 0	Su. 18 0
We. 6 0	We. 10 0	Alexandrople	—	—
Th. 6 0	Fri. 18 0	Istanbul	Th. 8 0	Th. 23 0
Sa. 7 0	Sa 24 0	Burgas	We. 6 0	We. 20 0
Su. 6 0	Su. 22 0	Varna	Tu. 7 0	Tu. 24 0
Mo. 6 0	Tu. 18 0	Constanza ..	—	—
Fri. 6 0	Fri. 20 0	Batumi	—	—
Sa. 6 0	Sa. 17 0	Trebizond ..	—	—
Su. 8 0	—	Samsun † ..	Au. 6,&c	Su. 17 0

† Optional.

Line 51.

Venice, Brindisi, Rhodes, Alexandria.

Via Cape Matapan. (Fortnightly).

s.s. *Barletta*, 1974 tons.

arr.	dep.		arr.	dep.
Aug. 2	We. 18 0	Venice......	We. 7 0	—
—	—	Trieste......	Mo. 9 0	Tue 24 0
Thu 18 0	Fri. 2 0	Bari........	Sat. 23 0	Sa. 10 0
Fri. 7 30	Fri. 11 0	Brindisi....	Sat. 15 0	Sat. 17 0
Sun 5 0	Sun 10 0	Leros	Thu 21 45	Thu 23 0
Sun 12 0	Sun 14 0	Calimno....	—	—
Sun 15 15	Sun 17 0	Cos	—	—
Sun 22 0	Mo. 14 0	Rhodes.....	Thu 12 30	Thu 14 30
Tue 14 30	—	Alexandria	Aug. 9	We. 12 0

Line 59 *bis.*

Tyrrhenian-Danube Line

(Fortnightly).

s.s. *Campidoglio*, 3702 tons (2 cl.) July 31, Sept. 11.
s.s. *Fenicia*, 2584 tons (carrying 12 saloon), Aug. 14, Sept. 25.
m.v. *Merano*, 3705 tons, Aug. 28, Oct. 9.

The itinerary may be varied (ports omitted or other ports called at) in accordance with requirements, also arrival and departure times may be earlier or later at all ports.

arr.	dep.	Ports. ↑	arr.	dep.
July 31	Mo. 22 0	Genoa	Su. 13 0	—
etc.	—	Marseilles ..	Fri. 12 0	Sa. 18 0
Tu. 7 0	Tu. 14 0	Leghorn † ..	—	—
We. 14 0	We. 20 0	Naples	We. 13 0	We. 19 0
Th. 13 0	Th. 24 0	Messina † ..	—	—
Fri. 6 0	Fri. 16 0	Catania	—	—
Su. 16 0	Su. 20 0	Piræus	Su. 12 0	Sun 18 0
—	—	Thessal'iki †	Sat. 6 0	Sa. 12 0
Tu. 9 0	We. 19 0	Istanbul....	Thu 5 0	Th. 18 0
Th. 9 † 0	Th. 24† 0	Burgas	We 6 0	We. 18 0
Fri. 7 † 0	Fri. 23† 0	Varna......	Tu. 6 0	Tu. 23 0
Sat. 7 0	Sat. 20 0	Constanza ..	Su. 22 0	Mo. 22 0
Sun. 5 0	Sun 6 30	Sulina	Su. 12 0	Sun 14 0
Sun 17 0	—	↓ Gal'tz/Braila	Aug. 6&c	Sun 4 0

† Call optional.

LINE 41. VENICE—DALMATIA—(GRAVOSA). (Bi-weekly).

m.v. *Francesco Morosini*, 2423 tons.

1st Voyage arr.	1st Voyage dep.	2nd Voyage arr.	2nd Voyage dep.	↓	1st Voyage arr.	1st Voyage dep.	2nd Voyage arr.	2nd Voyage dep. ↑
Au. 2, etc.	Wed. 6‡30	Au. 5 etc.	—	Venice	—	—	Mon. 2315	—
We. 1115	" 12 0	—	Sat. 12 0	Trieste	Fri. 18 0	—	" 18 0	Mon. 1830
	(See	note)		¶ Brioni		(See	note)	
" 1645	" 1715	Sat. 1645	" 1715	Pola	" 13 0	Fri. 1330	" 13 0	" 1330
" 2030	" 21 0	" 2030	" 21 0	Lussinpiccolo	" 9 30	" 10 0	" 9 30	" 10 0
Th. 0 30	Thur. 1 0	Sun. 0 30	Sun. 1 0	Zara	" 5 30	" 6 0	" 5 30	" 6 0
" 6 30	" 7 0	" 6 30	" 7 0	Spalato (Split)	Thur. 2330	Th. 24 0	Sun 2330	Sun. 24 0
" 1430	—	" 1430	—	Gravosa .... (Dubrovnik 2)	Au. 3, etc.	Th. 16 0	Au. 6, etc.	Sun. 16 0

¶ The m v. *Morosini* takes passengers for and from Brioni arriving half-hour before scheduled time of arrival Pola; in the reverse direction depart Brioni half-hour after departure Pola. Passengers for Brioni should inform the Ship's Captain of their destination.

‡ Pass. embark overnight on paying berth fee.

LINE 42. VENICE, DALMATIA. ALBANIA, BARI. (Weekly).

s.s. *Adriatico*, Aug. 1, 15, 29; s.s. *Monte Gargano*, Aug. 8, 22.

arr.	dep.	↓	arr.	dep. ↑
—	Tu. 24 0	Venice ..	Su. 7 0	—
We 7 0	We. 20 0	Trieste ..	Sa. 1230	Sa. 24 0
Th. 0 30	Th. 3 0	Pola .	Sa. 5 30	Sa. 7 30
Th. 6 0	Th. 6 30	Lussinpiccolo	Sa. 2 0	Sa. 2 30
Th. 10 0	Th. 12 0	Zara ..	Fri. 2030	Fri. 2230
Th. 1530	Th. 1630	Sebenico (Šibenik)	Fri. 16 0	Fri. 17 0
Th. 20 0	Th. 22 0	Spalato (Split)	Fri. 1130	Fri. 1230
—	—	Lagosta	Fri. 5 30	Fri. 7 0
Fri. 6 0	Fri. 8 0	Gravosa .. (Dubrovnik 2)	Th. 2030	Fri. 1 0
Fri. 1130	Fri. 1230	Kotor ...... (Cattaro)	Th. 16 0	Th. 17 0
Fri. 16 0	Fri. 17 0	Antivari....	Th. 1130	Th. 1230
Fri. 1930	Sa. 4 0	S Giov. di M.	Th. 5 0	Th. 9 0
Sa. 7 0	Sa. 12 0	Durazzo ..	We. 1530	Th. 2 0
Sa. 1630	Sa. 23 0	Valona‡	We. 7 0	We. 11 0
Su. 6 0	Su. 10 0	Brindisi ..	Tu. 1830	Tu. 24 0
—	—	Monopoli ..	Tu. 1230	Tu. 15 0
Su. 15 0	Mo. 2 30	Bari	—	—
Mo. 7 0	Mo. 8 30	Manfredonia	—	—
Mo. 1030	Mo. 1230	Barletta....	—	—
Mo. 15 0	—	Bari §	—	Tu. 10 0

‡ Calls at Saseno, outward and homeward.
§ May proceed to Molfetta and Bisceglie.

LINE 43. VENICE, TRIESTE, DALMATIA, ALBANIA, BRINDISI, PIRAEUS, IZMIR, RHODES, VENICE (Weekly).

m.v. *Lero*, Aug. 10, 31; m.v. *Brioni*, Aug. 3, 24; m.v. *Zara*, Aug. 17.

arr.	dep.	↓	arr.	dep. ↑
—	Thu. 24 0	Venice	Tue 7 0	—
Fri. 7 0	Fri. 22 0	Trieste..	Mo. 7 0	Mon. 24 0
Sat 7 0	Sat. 11 0	Fiume ..	Sun. 1730	Sun. 23 0
Sat. 1730	Sat. 21 0	Zara	Sun. 8 0	Sun. 11 0
Sun. 3 0	Sun. 5 0	Split	Sat 23 0	Sun 2 0
Sun 9 30	Sun. 1030	Lagosta	—	—
Sun. 15 0	Sun. 17 0	Gravosa (D'brov'k2)	Sat. 12 0	Sat. 15 0
Mo. 1 0	Mo. 5 0	Durazzo	Fri. 2330	Sat. 4 0
Mo. 9 30	Mo. 1230	Valona..	Fri. 1730	Fri. 19 0
Mo. 19 0	Mo. 21 0	Brindisi	Fri. 6 0	Fri. 11 0
Tu. 5 0	Tue. 8 0	S. Quaranta	Th. 2030	Th. 22 0
Tu. 11 0	Tue. 12 0	Corfu ..	Th. 18 0	Th. 1930
We. 15 0	We. 21 0	Piræus ..	Wed. 8 30	We. 15 0
Th. 13 0	Th. 19 0	Izmir ..	Mon. 8 0	Tue 17 0
Fri. 5 0	Fri. 6 0	Patmos..	—	—
Fri. 7 45	Fri. 16 0	Leros ..	Sun. 15 0	Sun. 21 0
Fri. 18 0	Fri. 21 0	Calimno	Sun. 1015	Sun. 13 0
Fri. 2215	Sat. 2 0	Cos ..	Sun. 7 0	Sun. 9 0
Sat. 7 0	—	Rhodes	—	Sun. 2 0

† May leave earlier.

LINE 61.
RHODES-PISCOPI-STAMPALIA. (Fortnightly).

s.s. *Fiume*, 654 tons.

arr.	dep.	↓	arr.	dep. ↑
Au. 9, &c	We. 13 0	Rhodes	Fri. 2030	—
Th 16 0	—	Stampalia..	Aug. 10	Th. 20 0

Calling at Simi, Cos, Calimno, Leros, Patmos (P. Lago).

LINE 62. RHODES—CASTELROSSO.

s.s. *Fiume*. (Weekly).

arr.	dep.	↓	arr.	dep. ↑
—	Fri. 24 0	Rhodes	Sat. 19 0	—
Sat. 7 0	—	Castelrosso ..	—	Sat. 12 0

LINE 44 *bis*. BARI—ALBANIA. (Weekly).

(See also Line 44).

m.v. *Loredan*, m.v. *Brioni*, s.s. *Duino*.

Bari	dep.	Sun. 15 0	Tues. 15 0
Brindisi	arr.	Sun. 21 0	Tues. 21 0
	dep.	Sun 24 0	Tues. 24 0
Valona	arr	Mon. 7 0	—
	dep	Mon. 17 0	
S. Quaranta	arr	—	Wed. 10 0
	dep.	—	Wed. 20 0
Brindisi	arr.	Mon. 24 0	Thur. 6 0
	dep.	Tue. 1 0	Thur. 8 0
Bari	arr	Tue. 7 0	Thur 14 0

"ADRIATICA" Soc. An. di Navigazione—*continued.*

LINE 45. VENICE—TRIESTE—FIUME—DALMATIA—BARI. (Weekly).
m.v. *Loredan*, 1367 tons, Aug. 7, 21; m.v. *Narenta*, 1361 tons, Aug. 14, 28.

—	dep. Mon. 24 0	Venice ↓ ↑	arr. Sun. 13 0	—
arr. Tue. 7 0	,, Tue. 22 0	Trieste	—	—
,, Wed. 6 0	,, Wed. 6 30	Cherso	—	—
,, Wed. 9 30	,, Wed. 12 0	Fiume	—	—
,, Wed. 20 0	,, Wed. 23 0	Zara	,, Sat. 19 30	dep. Sat. 23 0
—	—	Split	,, Sat. 12 0	,, Sat. 13 0
—	—	Lagosta	,, Sat. 6 0	,, Sat. 7 0
,, Thur. 13 0	,, Fri. 7 0	Metkovic	—	—
,, Fri. 16 0	,, Fri. 20 0	Gravosa (Dubrovnik 2)	,, Fri. 24 0	,, Sat. 3 0
,, Sat. 6 0	—	Bari	—	,, Fri. 14 0

LINE 44. BARI—DURAZZO.

		Daily	Suns. only.
Bari	dep.	23 0	10 0 ..
Durazzo	arr.	8 0	19 0 ..
	dep	21 0	.. 10 0
Bari	arr.	6 0	.. 19 0

LINE 63. RHODES—CASO. s.s. *Fiume*, 654 tons.
Fortnightly sailings for each service.

1st voyage. arr.	1st voyage. dep.	2nd voyage. arr.	2nd voyage. dep.		1st voyage. arr.	1st voyage. dep.	2nd voyage. arr.	2nd voyage. dep.
Aug. 8, etc.	Tues. 3 0	Jly. 31, etc.	Mon. 17 0	Rhodes	Wed. 7 0	—	Wed. 17 0	—
—	—	Mon. 1930	Mon. 2030	Symi	—	—	Wed. 1330	Wed. 1430
Tues 7 0	Tues. 7 30	Tues. 7 0	Tues. 7 30	Calchi	Wed. 2 30	Wed. 3 0	Wed. 2 30	Wed. 3 0
Tues. 1230	Tues. 1330	Tues. 1230	Tues. 1330	Scarpanto	Tues. 2030	Tues. 2130	Tues. 2030	Tues. 2130
Tues. 16 0	—	Tues 16 0	—	Caso	Aug. 8, etc.	Tues. 18 0	Au. 1, etc.	Tues. 18 0

BLAND LINE.

GIBRALTAR—TANGIER and *vice versa*, by s.s. *Gibel Dersa* (1225 tons).

Gibraltar Quay	dep. 13.0 Tu., Th. & Sa.
Tangier Quay	dep. 9.0 Mo., We. & Fr.

Passage under 3 hours.

DUBROVAČKA LINE.

s.s. *Kralj Aleksandar I.* 2500 tons, s.s. *Kumanovo*, 1500 tons, s.s. *Dedinie*, 1200 tons.

VENICE—SPLIT—DUBROVNIK—KOTOR.
to October 15.

Line 1.	Line 2.		Line 1.	Line 2.
Tu 24 0	Fr. 24 0	d. Venice ...... a.	Tu 17 0	Fr. 17 0
W. 1130	Sa. 1130	a. Susak ...... d.	,, 7 0	,, 7 0
,, 16 0	,, 16 0	d. Susak ...... a.	,, 6 0	,, 6 0
,, 1730	,, 1730	d. Crikvenica .. a.	—	—
,, 2045	,, 2045	d. Rab .... a.	Tu 2 45	Fr 2 45
Th 4 15	—	d. Sibenic .... a.	—	Th 20 5
,, 7 30	Su. 7 30	a. Split ...... d.	Mo 17 0	,, 17 0
,, 9 45	,, 9 45	d. Split ...... a.	,, 1630	,, 1630
,, 1145	—	d. Hvar .. a.	—	,, 1440
—	,, 12 5	d. Makarska .. a.	,, 1420	—
,, 1445	,, 1445	d. Korcula ... a.	,, 1150	,, 1150
,, 1830	,, 1850	a. Dubrovnik 2 d.	Mo 8 0	Th 8 0
Fri 8 0	—	d. Dubrovnik 2 a.	Fr. 22 0	—
,, 1040	—	d Hercegnovi a.	,, 1920	—
,, 12 0	—	a. Kotor .... d.	,, 18 0	—

TOURIST LINE 7 May 14-Sept. 30.

arr.	dep.		arr.	dep.
—	Su 22 0	Venice	Su 6 0	—
Mo 9 0	Mo 1030	Sušak	Sa. 1630	Sa. 1830
,, 12 0	,, 1230	Crikvenica	,, 13 0	,, 15 0
,, 16 0	,, 20 0	Rab......	,, 7 30	,, 9 30
Tu 6 0	Tu 11 0	Šibenic	—	—
,, 14 0	,, 1530	Trogir	—	—
,, 17 0	,, 21 0	Split	Fri 15 0	Fri 21 0
—	—	Hvar	,, 11 0	,, 13 0
—	—	Korčula	,, 6 30	,, 8 0
W. 6 0	W. 8 0	Dubrovnik 2	W. 22 0	,, 2 0
,, 1045	,, 1050	Hercegnovi	,, 1915	W. 1920
,, 1230	,, 13 0	Budva	—	—
,, 1545	—	Kotor	—	,, 18 0

FAST LINES.

SPLIT—DUBROVNIK 2, to OCTOBER 15.

Su. 21 0	W. 21 0	dep. Split ...... arr.	Sat. 7 30	Mon. 7 30
,, 23 0	,, 23 0	,, Hvar ...... ,,	,, 5 30	,, 5 30
Mo. 2 0	Th. 2 0	,, Korcula...... ,,	Sat. 2 30	Mon. 2 30
,, 6 0	,, 6 0	arr. Dubrovnik 2 dep.	Fri. 2230	Sun. 2230

Istanbul—Izmir (Weekly).

arr.	dep.		arr.	dep.
—	Sun. 11 0	Istanbul	Thur. 12 0	—
Mon. 10 0	—	Izmir	—	Wed. 12 0

Izmir–Piræus and v.v. (Weekly)

arr.	dep.		arr.	dep.
—	We 14 0	Izmir	Sat. 8 0	—
Th. 10 0	—	Piræus	—	Fri. 10 0

Istanbul-Alexandretta (1st Service) (Wkly.)

arr.	dep.		arr.	dep.
—	Tu. 10 0	Istanbul ..	Mo. 1130	—
—	—	Gelibolu ..	u. 2030	Su. 2130
Tu. 24 0	We. 0 30	Cannakale	Su. 16 0	Su. 18 0
We. 1630	Th. 10 0	Izmir	Sa. 1030	Sa. 22 0
Sa. 6 0	Sa. 10 0	Antalaya ..	Th. 9 0	Th. 1430
Sa. 1730	Sa. 19 0	Alanya....	We. 23 0	Th. 2 0
Su. 1 0	Su. 2 0	Anamur ..	We. 1515	We. 17 0
—	—	Kilindire ..	We. 1130	We. 1230
—	—	Tasucu ..	We. 6 30	We. 7 30
Su. 1430	Su. 23 0	Mersin ..	Tu. 8 0	Tu. 24 0
—	—	Dortyol ..	Mo. 2030	Mo. 2230
—	—	Payas ..	Mo. 15 0	Mo. 20 0
Mon. 8 0	—	†Iskender'n	—	Mo. 14 0

† Alexandretta

Istanbul—Mersin (2nd Service) (Weekly).

arr.	dep.		arr.	dep.
—	Fri. 10 0	Istanbul....	Sat. 1130	—
—	—	Gelibolu ..	Fri 2030	Fri. 2130
Fri. 24 0	Sat. 0 30	Canakkale .	Fri. 16 0	Fri. 18 0
Sat. 1630	Su. 12 0	Izmir ..	Th 1130	Th. 22 0
Th. 5 0	Th. 8 30	Antalaya ..	Su. 1430	Su. 2030
—	—	Alanya	Su. 4 30	Su. 6 30
Fri. 9 30	—	Mersin ...	—	Sa. 10 0

Calling at various other ports.

Istanbul—Trebizond.

Istanbul	..dep.	Tu. 12 0	Th. 12 0	Su. 16 0
Samsun	arr.	Th. 7 30	Sat. 7 0	Tu. 8 0
	dep.	Th 13 0	Sat. 13 0	Tu 13 0
Tr'bizond	arr.	Fri. 7 30	Su. 16 0	We. 1630
	dep.	Fri. 14 0	Su. 20 0	We. 18 0
Rize ..	arr.	Fri 18 0	Su. 24 0	We. 22 0
	dep	Fri. 24 0	Mo 2 0	—
Hopa ..	arr	Sat. 5 30	Mo. 7 0	—
	dep	Sat. 13 0	Mo 13 0	—
Rize ..	arr.	Sat. 20 0	Mo. 1730	—
	dep.	Sat. 24 0	Mo. 22 0	Thu6 0
Tr'bizond	arr.	Sun 8 0	Tu. 6 0	Thu9 30
	dep.	Sun16 0	Tu 20 0	Thu20 0
Samsun	arr.	Mo. 10 0	Th. 7 0	Sat. 7 0
	dep.	Mo 1630	Th. 163	Sat. 1630
Istanbul	.. arr.	We. 1430	Sat. 1230	Mo. 1230

Other ports of call (according to service) Zonguldak, Inebolu, Ayancik, Sinop, Ünye, Fatsa, Ordu, Grieson, Vakfikebir, Of, Akcaabad, Gerze, Tirebolu, Görele, Sürmene, Sinob, Pazar. Particulars on application.

Istanbul—Bandirma.

Istanbul dep. Mo., We., Fr. 8.15, Wed., Sat. 20.0
Bandirma arr. Mo., We., Fr. 1230, Thu., Sun. 5.0
Bandirma dep. Mo., We., Fr. 17.30, Th., Sun. 22.30
Istanbul arr. Mo., Wed., Fr. 22.15, Fri., Mo. 6.30

Istanbul—Imroz.

Istanbul dep. Sun. 9.0 Imroz dep. Mon. 12.30
Imroz arr. Mon. 9.30 Istanbul arr. Tue. 17.0

Istanbul—Mudanya. †

Mo.	We. Fri.	Sat.		Sun Mo.	Mo. We Fri.
13 0	8 45	13 0	dep. Istanbul arr.	1135	20 5
1545	1120	1615	arr. Mudanya dep.	8 30	17 0

† Connects with trains to Bursa.

Tu. Thu Sat.	Sun	Sun		Tue Th Sat.	Sun
8 45	8 45	20 0	dp. Istanbul ar.	2025	2215
11 0	11 0	—	ar Armudlu dp.	1750	1950
1115	1115	—	dp Armudlu ar.	1735	1935
1150	1150	2245	ar Mudanya dp	17 0	19 0
1230	1245	2315	dp Mudanya ar	1610	1640
1325	1340	0 10	ar. Gemlik dp.	1515	1545

Other Costal Services maintained, particulars on request.

FIUMANA Soc. di Navigazione.

FIUME—LAGOSTA—GRAVOSA

To Sept. 30th. (Line 141)

Thur. 23 0	dep Fiume .. arr.	Mon. 6 45
,, 24 0	dep Abbazia arr.	,, 5 45
Fri. 5 30	d. Lussinpiccolo a.	,, 0 30
,, 9 45	arr. Zara dp.	Sun. 1930
,, 12 0	dep. Zara arr.	,, 1830
,, 1545	ar. Sibenik d.	,, 1430
,, 1715	dp. Sibenik a.	,, 1330
,, 21 0	arr. Split dep.	,, 9 0
,, 23 0	dep Split arr.	,, 6 0
Sat. 5 30	dep. Lagosta arr.	Sat. 24 0
,, 11 0	arr. Gravoso dep.	,, 18 0

FIUME—TRIESTE—RAVENNA (Line 137)

Mon. 18 0	dep. Fiume.. arr.	Sun. 9 30
,, 19 0	dep. Abbazia arr.	,, 8 30
Tues. 1130	dep. Pola.... arr.	Sat. 1330
,, 1930	ar. Trieste dp.	,, 5 0
Wed. 20 0	dp. Trieste arr	Fri. 7 0
Thur. 7 0	arr. Ravenna dep.	Thur. 20 0

FIUME—ZARA (Line 140 B and C.)

Tues.	Fri.		Thur.	Sat.
7 30	1030	dep. Fiume ..arr.	1745	1730
1245	1530	dep. Arbe (Rab) ar.	1230	1245
1915	20 0	arr. Zara.... dep.	6 0	8 0

ANCONA {LUSSINO — POLA / POLA—ABBAZIA} FIUME

To Sept. 15. LINE 135.

Tue. 6 45	Fri. 0 45	Sat. 16 0	dep. Ancona ...... arr.	Mon. 9 30	Thu. 9 30	Sat. 5 0
—	,, 8 0	—	dep. Lussinpiccolo arr.	—	—	Fri. 22 0
,, 1130	—	,, 21 0	dep. Rimini ...... arr.	,, 5 0	,, 5 0	—
,, 18 0	,, 1130	—	arr. Pola .... dep.	—	Wed. 2230	,, 1830
,, 1830	,, 12 0	—	dep. ,, ,, arr.	—	,, 2130	,, 1730
,, 2315	—	Sun. 7 15	,, Abbazia ...... dep.	Sun. 1930	,, 17 0	—
,, 24 0	,, 1630	,, 8 0	arr. Fiume ...... dep.	,, 1830	,, 16 0	,, 13 0

ANCONA—ZARA *and vice versa.* (Daily). LINE 136.

†Ancona	dep. 10 0	Zara	dep. 21 30
Zara	arr. 17 30	†Ancona	arr. 5 0

† Coinciding with trains from and to Rome.

VENICE—(BRIONI)—POLA—FIUME.

To Sept. 15. LINE 134.

Mon. 9 30	Wed. 9 30	Sat. 18 0	dep. Venice ... arr.	Tues. 1930	Sat. 7 30	Mon. 8 30
,, 1530	,, 1530	Sun. 0 30	,, Brioni ...... ,,	,, 1350	,, 1 0	,, 2 0
,, 16 0	,, 16 0	,, 1 0	arr. Pola .... dep.	,, 13 0	,, 0 30	,, 1 30
,, 1630	,, 1630	,, 1 30	dep. ,, ... arr.	,, 1230	Fri. 24 0	,, 1 0
,, 21 0	,, 21 0	,, 6 30	arr. Abbazia .. dep.	,, 8 0	,, 19 0	Sun. 20 0
,, 2130	,, 2130	,, 6 45	dep. ,, ... arr.	,, 7 45	,, 1845	,, 1945
,, 22 0	,, 22 0	,, 7 30	arr. Fiume ... dep.	,, 7 0	,, 18 0	,, 19 0

FRAISSINET (FRENCH MAIL) STEAMSHIP CO. (See also page 448).

Steamers.	Tons.	Steamers.	Tons.	Steamers.	Tons.
†*Ile de Beauté*	2600	†*Cyrnos*	2405	†*Pascal Paoli*	3382
†*Ville d' Ajaccio* ..	2573	†*Gen'l. Bonaparte*	2796	*Sampiero Corso*	3823
†*Cap Corse*	2573				

First (de luxe, single, two-berth cabins), second and third class berths. † Stewardess carried.

DEPARTURES FROM CONTINENTAL PORTS TO CORSICA. Services to Oct. 14.

There are supplementary services during July-September—details on application.

Depart.			arr. Ile Rousse.	arr. Calvi.	arr. Ajaccio.	arr. Propriano.	arr. Bastia.
Marseilles ..	Mon.	1730	—	—	Tues. 6 15	Tues. 20 0	—
,, ..	Wed.	1515	—	—	—	—	Thur. 6 0
,, ..	Thur.	15 0	—	—	Fri. 6 15	Sat. 7 45(*a*)	—
,, ..	Fri.	12 0	Sat. 6 0	—	—	—	—
,, ..	Sat.	8 30	Sun. 1730	(s.s. *Ile de Beaute*, see below)		—	—
,, ..	Sun.	12 0	—	—	—	—	Mon. 6 15(*b*)
Toulon ..	Fri.	20 0	Sat. 6 0	—	—	—	—
Nice	Sun.	11 0	Sun. 1730	(s.s. *Ile de Beaute*, see below		—	—
,, ...	Tues.	12 0	—	Tues. 1915	—	—	—
,, ...	Wed.	11 0	—	Wed. 17 0	(s.s. *Ile de Beaute*, see below)		—
,, ...	Fri.	8 30	(s.s. *Ile de Beaute*, see below)		—	—	—
,, ...	Fri.	10 0	—	—	Fri. 1930	—	—
,, ...	Sat.	21 0	—	—	—	—	Sun. 6 0
Leghorn ..	Wed.	13 0	—	—	—	—	Wed. 19 0(*c*)

DEPARTURES FROM CORSICA FOR CONTINENT.

Depart.			arr. Nice.	arr. Toulon.	arr. Marseilles.	arr. Leghorn
Ajaccio	Tues.	1630	—	—	Wed. 8 15	—
,, ...	Wed.	2030	Thur. 6 0	—	—	—
,, ...	Sat.	19 0	—	—	Sun. 8 0	—
Bastia	Mon.	1630	—	—	Tues. 8 0	—
,, ...	Tues.	11 0	—	—	—	Tues. 17 0
,, ...	Thur.	1630	—	—	Fri. 9 30	—
,, ...	Fri.	21 0	Sat. 6 0	—	—	—
Calvi	Sun.	23 0	Mon. 6 15	—	—	—
,, ...	Thur.	12 0	Thur. 18 0	(s.s. *Ile de Beaute*, see below)		—
Ile Rousse ..	Mon.	12 0	Mon. 1830	(s.s. *Ile de Beaute*, see below)		—
,, ...	Wed.	20 0	—	Thur. 6 0	Thur. 1415	—

a Continuing to Bonifacio, Porto Vecchia & back. *b* Proceeding to Leghorn. *c* Proceeding to Marseilles.

ITINERARY OF LUXE SERVICE by s.s. "Ile de Beaute." To Sept. 29th.

arr.	dep.		arr.	dep.
—	Sat. 8 30	Marseilles	Fri. 1730	—
Sat. 1730	Sun. 11 0	Nice	—	Fri. 8 30
Sun. 1730	Mon. 12 0	Ile Rousse	—	—
Mon. 1830	Wed. 11 0	Nice	Thur. 18 0	—
Wed. 17 0	—	Calvi	—	Thur. 12 0

Also calls at Toulon, Porquerolles, Port-Cros, and St. Maxime Sats. out, Fris. home.

Cia. GENOVESE di NAVIGAZIONE A VAPORE.

GENOA—LEVANT AND DANUBE. Fortnightly carrying passengers, "Unica" class.

OUTWARD. Steamer	Tons.	Genoa. dep	Naples. dep.	Palermo	Piræus	Istanbul arr.	Burgaz & Varna (Optional)	Constanza. arr.	Sulina	Galatz or Braila. arr.
Capo Faro	5100	July 23	July 26	July 27	July 31	Aug 2	Aug. 3/4	Aug. 5	Aug. 6	Aug. 6
Capo Mele..	5400	Aug. 6	Aug. 9	Aug. 10	Aug. 14	,, 16	,, 17/18	,, 19	,, 20	,, 20
Capo Arma	—	,, 20	,, 23	,, 24	,, 28	,, 30	A 31/Se. 1	Sept. 2	Sept 3	Sept. 3
Capo Faro	5100	Sept. 3	Sept. 6	Sept. 7	Sept. 11	Sept. 13	Sept. 14/15	,, 16	,, 17	,, 17
Capo Mele..	5400	,, 17	,, 20	,, 21	,, 25	,, 27	,, 28/29	,, 30	Oct. 1	Oct. 1
Capo Arma	—	Oct. 1	Oct. 4	Oct. 5	Oct. 9	Oct. 11	Oct. 12/13	Oct. 14	,, 15	,, 15

Calling also at Leghorn, Messina, Catania.

DANUBE—NAPLES—MARSEILLES—GENOA.

HOMEWARD. Steamer	Tons.	Braila or Galatz dep.	Sulina	Samsun (Opti'al)	Ineboli (Opti'al)	Varna (Opti'al)	Burgaz (Opti'al)	Istanbul dep.	Naples	Marseilles dep.	Genoa arr.
Capo Arma	—	July 29	July 29	July 30	July 30	July 31	July 31	Aug 1	Aug. 5	Aug. 8	Aug. 10
Capo Faro	5100	Aug. 12	Aug. 12	Aug. 13	Aug. 13	Aug. 14	Aug. 14	,, 15	,, 19	,, 22	,, 24
Capo Mele	5400	,, 26	,, 26	,, 27	,, 27	,, 28	,, 28	,, 29	Sept. 2	Sept. 5	Sept. 7
Capo Arma	—	Sept. 9	Sept. 9	Sept. 10	Sept. 10	Sept. 11	Sept. 11	Sept 12	,, 16	,, 19	,, 21
Capo Faro	5100	,, 23	,, 23	,, 24	,, 24	,, 25	,, 25	,, 26	,, 30	Oct. 3	Oct. 5
Capo Mele	5400	Oct. 7	Oct. 7	Oct. 8	Oct. 8	Oct. 9	Oct. 9	Oct. 10	Oct. 1	,, 17	,, 19
Capo Arma	—	,, 21	,, 21	,, 22	,, 22	,, 23	,, 23	,, 24	,, 28	,, 31	Nov. 2

GDYNIA-AMERYKA LINJE ZEGLUGOWE S.A. See also pages 416, 449 & 459.

GDYNIA AMERICA SHIPPING LINES LTD.

(PALESTINE LINE).

s.s. *Polonia*, 7500 tons.

Accommodation in 1, 2, 3 and 4 berth Cabins, also Cabins De Luxe. Stewardess and Doctor carried.
Services (subject to alteration without notice) twice monthly.

Steamer.	Constanza dep 24 0	Istanbul arr. 16 0 dep. 19 0	Tel Aviv. arr. a.m. dep. a.m.	Haifa. arr. p.m.	Haifa. dep. 15 0	Piræus. arr 16 0	Piræus. dep 23 0	Istanbul arr 7 0 dep. 18 0	Constanza arr. 10 0
					Sailings	on appl	ication		

* Depart Haifa 10.0. ** Arrive Piræus 10.0.

NOUVELLE Cie HAVRAISE PENINSULAIRE de NAVIGATION.

FRANCE—MADAGASCAR.

Subject to alteration owing to Quarantine, Strikes, etc.

Steamers carry First Class Passengers. Two-berth Cabins amidships; on some steamers Luxe Cabins with two Beds. Steamers are fitted with Electric Light, but do not carry Stewardess or Doctor.

Steamer.	Tns. D.W	From Dunkerque	From Antwerp.	From Havre	From Bordeaux Pauillac)	From Oran.	From Algiers	From Marseilles	Port Said	Suez.	Djbouti	
Malagache	9000	Aug 17	—	—	Aug. 21	—	Aug 26	Sep. 1	Sep. 5	Sep. 6	Sep. 10	*
Ville de Rouen .	7150	Sep. 2	Sep. 4	Sep. 9	Sept. 12	Sep. 18	Sep 20	,, 27	Oct. 4	Oct. 5	Oct. 11	
Conde	9120	,, 2[illegible]	,, 25	,, 30	Oct. 3	Oct. 9	Oct 11	Oct. 18	,, 25	,, 26	Nov. 1	*
Ville de Reims ..	7240	Oct. 14	Oct. 16	Oct. 21	,, 24	,, 30	Nov. 1	Nov. 8	Nov 15	Nov 16	,, 22	*

* To Majunga, Nossi-Bé, Diego-Suarez, Sainte-Marie, Tamatave, Mananjary, Manakara, Port Louis, La Reunion, Fort Dauphin, Farafangana, Vatomandry. Ports of call after Djbouti on application.

Steamer	Ton	Steamer	Tons	Steamer	Tons	Steamer	Tons.
Andros	2068	*Lesbos*	1010	*Milos*	598	*Chios*	1121
Attiki	2560	*Athinai*	968	*Zakynthos* ..	968	*Paros*	969
Makedonia ..	1832	*Kephallinia* ..	1226	*Taraki*	1510	*Ionia*	2000
Hellas	2181	*Kerkyra* ..	1461	*Kriti*	1028	*Frinton*	1361
Skyros	683	*Ithaki*	680	*Syros*	1009	*Samos*	1208
Siphnos	814	*Lefkas*	379	*Psarra*	1002		

All steamers have (1st class) two, three and four berth cabins. s.s. *Hellas*, *Attiki*, *Makedonia*, *Chios*, *Lesbos*, single and two berth cabins also cabins de luxe. *Services subject to alteration without notice.*

Piræus—Egypt Line.

s.s. *Ionia*. Weekly service.

	arr.	dep.
Piræus ..	—	Tues. 16 0
Alexandria	Thu. 7 0	Thur. 17 0
Port Said	Fri. 6 0	Fri. 16 0
Alexandria	Sat. 6 0	Sat. 16 0
Piræus ..	Mon. 7 0	

Thessaloniki—Piræus { Cyprus-Syria-Palestine-Egypt (Fortnightly) or Egypt-Palestine-Syria-Cyprus-Piræus, etc. (Fortnightly),

s.s. *Taraki*, s.s. *Attiki*.

arr.	dep.		arr.	dep.
May 15	Mon. 18 0	Thessaloniki ↑	Mon. 7 0	—
Tues. 8 0	Tues. 11 0	Volo	Sun. 8 0	Sun. 11 0
Wed. 7 0	Wed. 16 0	Piræus	Fri. 20 0	Sat. 18 0
Fri. 17 0	Fri. 22 0	Limassol	Wed. 18 0	Wed. 22 0
Sat. 5 0	Sat. 10 0	Larnaca	Wed. 12 0	Wed. 15 0
,, 14 0	,, 18 0	Famagusta ..	Wed. 6 0	Wed. 9 0
—	—	Tripoli	Tues. 16 0	Tues. 18 0
Sun. 6 0	Sun. 12 0	Beyrout	Tues. 5 0	Tues. 12 0
,, 18 0	Mon. 10 0	Haifa	Mon. 16 0	Mon. 22 0
—	—	Tel-Aviv	Mon. 8 30	Mon. 11 0
Mon. 17 0	,, 22 0	Jaffa	Mon. 5 0	Mon. 8 0
Tue. 6 0	Tues. 18 0	Port Said ..	Sat. 7 0	Sun. 16 0
Wed. 8 0	Wed. 16 0	Alexandria ..	Fri. 14 0	Fri. 18 0
Fri. 19 0	Sat. 18 0	Piræus	Wed. 7 0	Wed. 16 0
Sun. 8 0	Sun. 11 0	Volo	Tues 8 0	Tues. 11 0
Mon. 7 0	—	Thessaloniki ↓	May 22, etc.	Mon. 18 0

Piræus—Chios—Mitylene Line Every Tuesday, Thursday and Saturday at 18.45.

Patras—Zante—Lixouri Argostoli. Every Wednesday at 19.0.

Piræus—Crete.

Dep. Piræus Wed. 19.0 Candia, Rethymno, Canea, Piræus. Dep. Piræus Fri. 19.0 for Canea, Rethymno, Candia, Chersonisso, Agios Nicolas, Pachia Ammo, Sitia.

Piræus-Chalcis-Ædipso-Volo-Thessaloniki.

Dep. Piræus at 18.0 on Mon., Tues., Wed., and Sat.

Coastal and Ægean Sea Services.

In addition to the above Services, the Company also maintain frequent services to ports in the Ionian Sea, Ægean Sea, etc., and information can be obtained on application.

BRINDISI—PIRÆUS.

By s.s. *Esperos*.

Dep. Brindisi, Mon. 17.0 (*via* Santi, Corfu).
Arr. Piræus, Wed. 7.0
Dep. Piræus, Sat. 19.0 (*via* Corfu, Santi—Quarants).
Arr. Brindisi, Mon. 7.0.
Also calls at Patras.

SERVICE TEMPORARILY SUSPENDED.

BRINDISI—PIRÆUS.

s.s. *Frinton*.

Dep. Brindisi, Wed. 17.0 (*via* Santi, Corfu, Ithaque, Patras).
Arr. Piræus, Fri 7.0.
Dep. Piræus, Mon. 19.0 (*via* Patras, Corfu, Santi).
Arr. Brindisi, Wed. 7.0.

HANDRIS S.S. CO. LTD.

ALEXANDRIA—PIRAEUS—BRINDISI and v.v. (Weekly).

s.s. *Patris*, from Piræus, Aug. 7, 14, 21, 28, Sept. 4, 11, 18, 25.

	arr.	dep.
Piræus	—	Mon. 20 0
Alexandria ..	Wed. 7 0	Wed. 17 0
Piræus	Fri. 6 0	Fri. 13 0
Patras	Sat. 8 0	Sat. 10 0
Corfu	Sat. 18 0	Sat. 20 0
Brindisi	Sun. 6 0	Sun. 10 0
Piræus .... ↓	Mon. 18 0	

JADRANSKA LINE.

Baška=Bescanuova.	Šušak, near Fiume	Korčula=Curzola	Omiš=Almissa	Krk=Veglia
Kraljevica=Portorè.	Šibenik=Sebenico	Hercegnovi=Castelnuovo	Dubrovnik 1=Ragusa	Rab=Arbe
Bar=Antivari.	Split=Spalato	Kotor=Cattaro	Dubrovnik 2=Gruz (Gravosa)	Trogir=Trau
Ulčinj=Dulcigno	Hvar=Lesina			Senj=Zengg

In addition to Ports mentioned Steamers call at many minor Ports, particulars on application.

Fast Lines Venice, Susak—Dubrovnik 2, Kotor.

s.s. *Prestolonaslednik Petar (Prince Peter)*, 1695 tons; s.s. *Karadjordje*, 1204 tons; s.s. *Jugoslavija*, 1275 tons.

		To October 15.				s.s. *Ljubljana*, Tourist Line, No. 59
	Line 1	Line 2	Line 3	Line 4	Line 5	May 18 to Sept. 28
Venice ....dep.	Sat. 24 0	Sun. 24 0	Mon. 24 0	Wed. 24 0	Thur. 24 0	Thur. 22 0
Sušak............arr	Sun. 11 0	Mon. 11 0	Tues. 11 0	Thur. 11 0	Fri. 11 0	Fri. 9 0
Sušak............dep.	Sun. 16 0	Mon. 16 0	Tues. 16 0	Thur. 16 0	Fri. 16 0	Fri. 1030
Crikvenica..........dep.	Sun. 1730	Mon. 1730	Tues. 1730	Thur. 1730	Fri. 1730	Fri. 1230
Rab..............arr.	Sun. 2015	Mon. 2015	Tues. 2015	Thur. 2015	Fri. 2015	Fri. 16 0
,, ...dep.	Sun. 2045	Mon. 2045	Tues. 2045	Thur. 2045	Fri. 2045	Fri. 20 0
Šibenik ....dep	—	—	Wed. 4 15	—	Sat. 4 15	†Sat. 6 0 (d. 11 0)
Split.............arr.	Mon. 7 30	Tues. 7 30	Wed. 7 30	Fri. 7 30	Sat. 7 30	Sat. 17 0
,, ...dep	Mon. 9 45	Tues. 9 45	Wed. 9 45	Fri. 9 45	Sat. 9 45	Sat. 21 0
Hvar ....dep.	—	Tues. 1145	—	Fri. 1145	Sat. 1145	—
Makarska ....dep.	Mon. 12 5	—	Wed. 12 5	—	—	—
Korcula ....dep.	Mon. 1445	Tues. 1445	Wed. 1445	Fri. 1445	Sat. 1445	—
Dubrovnik ....arr.	Mon. 1830	Tues. 1830	Wed. 1830	Fri. 1830	Sat. 1830	Sun. 6 0
,, ,, ...dep.	Mon. 19 0	—	—	—	—	Sun. 8 0
Herceg Novi.......dep	Mon. 2140	—	—	—	—	¶Sun. 1050
Kotor ....arr	Mon. 23 0	—	—	—	—	Sun. 1545
Kotor..............dep.	Tues. 3 45	—	—	—	—	Sun. 18 0
Herceg-Novi ....dep.	Tues. 5 0	—	—	—	—	Sun. 1920
Dubrovnik ....arr	Tues. 7 30	—	—	—	—	Sun. 22 0
,, ,, ...dep.	Tues. 8 0	Wed. 8 0	Fri. 8 0	Sat. 8 0	Sun. 8 0	Tues. 2 0
Korcula ....dep.	Tues. 1150	Wed. 1150	Fri. 1150	Sat. 1150	Sun. 1150	Tues. 8 0
Makarska ....dep.	Tues. 1420	—	Fri. 1420	—	—	—
Hvar ....dep.	—	Wed. 1440	—	Sat. 1440	Sun. 1440	Tues. 13 0
Split ....arr	Tues. 1630	Wed. 1630	Fri. 1630	Sat. 1630	Sun. 1630	Tues. 15 0
,, ...dep	Tues. 17 0	Wed. 17 0	Fri. 17 0	Sat. 17 0	Sun. 17 0	Tues. 21 0
Šibenik ....dep.	Tues. 20 5	—	—	—	Sun. 20 5	—
Rab ....arr.	—	—	—	—	—	Wed. 7 30
,, ...dep.	Wed. 2 45	Thur. 2 45	Sat. 2 45	Sun. 2 45	Mon. 2 45	Wed. 9 30
Crikvenica ....dep.	—	—	—	—	—	Wed. 15 0
Sušak..............arr	Wed. 6 0	Thur. 6 0	Sat. 6 0	Sun. 6 0	Mon 6 0	Wed. 1630
Sušak..............dep.	Wed. 7 0	Thur 7 0	Sat. 7 0	Sun. 7 0	Mon. 7 0	Wed. 1830
Venice.............arr.	Wed. 17 0	Thur. 17 0	Sat. 17 0	Sun. 17 0	Mon. 17 0	Thur. 6 0

† Calls Trogir, 14.0. ¶ Calls Budva, 12.30.

Tourist Line 6. (Weekly).

s.s. *Zagreb*, 896 tons.

Susak—Hvar—Makarska—Kotor.

arr.	dep.	↓	arr.	dep. ↑
	We 8 30	Sušak	Tu 6 0	—
We 9 50	We 1130	Crikvenica	Tu 4 30	Tu 4 40
We 1315	We 1415	Senj	—	—
We 17 0	We 23 0	Rab	Mo 1830	Tu 0 30
Th 7 20	Th 7 50	Šibenik	Mo 6 0	Mo 10 0
Th 14 0	Fr 5 0	Split	Su 1930	Mo 2 0
—	—	Makarska	Su 1330	Su 1530
Fri 11 5	Fri 1120	Korčula	Su 9 25	Su 1030
Fr 1615	Sat 7 0	Dubrovnik 2	Sat 2245	Su 4 30
Sat 12 0	—	Kotor	—	Sat 18 0

Other ports of call Preko, Biograd n/m, Trogir, Hvar, Orebic, Trstenik, Hercegnovi and Tivat.

Line 7.—Sušak, Kotor. (Weekly).

s.s. *Split*, 896 tons.

arr.	dep.	↓	arr.	dep. ↑
—	Su 8 30	Sušak	Sat 6 0	—
Su 1415	Su 1430	Rab	Sat 1 15	Sat 1 30
Su 24 0	Mo 2 0	Šibenik	Fri 15 0	Fri 1545
Mo 6 0	Mo 12 0	Split	Fri 8 0	Fri 11 0
Mo 1845	Mo 19 0	Hvar	Th 1945	Th. 20 0
Tu 8 15	Tu 8 30	Korčula	Th 9 15	Th 9 30
Tu 1430	We 5 0	Dubrovnik 2	We 2245	Th 4 30
We 6 0	We 8 0	Dubrovnik 1	—	—
We 1045	We 11 0	Hercegnovi	—	—
We 13 0	—	Kotor	—	We 18 0

Calling also outward and homeward at Krk, Preko, Biograd n/m, Jelsa Vis, Komiža, Velaluka, Prigradica Trstenik, Tivat: outward at Omišalj, Malinska, Silba, Omiš, Stari-Grad, Luka Sipanska, and homeward at Bol.

Line 9 —Sušak—Metkovic—Ulcinj.

s.s. *Vardar*, 550 tons; s.s. *Sosa*, 545 tons.
Calling at various other Ports. (Weekly).

arr.	dep.		arr.	dep.
—	Tu. 8 30	Sušak	Sa. 12 0	—
Tu. 1110	Tu. 1120	Crikvenica ..	Sa. 9 10	Sa. 9 25
Tu. 1240	Tu. 13 0	Senj	Sa. 7 25	Sa. 7 45
Tu. 2015	We. 5 0	Rab	Fri. 1630	Sa. 4 30
We. 1550	We. 16 5	Biograd n/m	Th. 1715	Fri. 4 0
We. 19 0	Th. 7 30	Šibenik	Th. 1215	Th. 14 0
Th. 14 0	Fri. 4 0	Split	We. 1615	Th. 6 0
Fri. 8 45	Fri. 9 10	Makarska ..	We. 9 45	We 1045
Fri. 1445	Sat 5 0	Metković ..	Tu. 1445	We. 5 0
Sat. 1045	Sat. 11 0	Korčula	Tu 7 15	Tu. 7 45
Sat. 1645	Su. 5 0	Dubrovnik 2	Mo. 1930	Tu. 0 45
Su. 6 0	Su. 8 0	„ 1	—	—
Su. 1215	Su. 1245	Budva	Mo. 7 10	—
Su. 15 0	Su. 1515	Bar (Antivari)	Su. 1830	Mo. 5 0
Su. 1640	—	Ulcinj	—	Su. 17 0

Lines 8, 10, 11, Split—Dubrovnik 2—Kotor.

s.s. *Kosovo*, 782 tons.

Split	Mon. 21 0	Thrs. 21 0	Fri. 21 0
Hvar	Mon. 23 0	Thrs. 23 0	—
Korcular	—	Fri. 2 0	—
Dubrovnik arr	Tues. 6 0	Fri. 6 0	Sat. 6 0
Dubrovnik dep.	Tues 8 0	—	Sat. 8 0
Herceg-Novi	Tues. 11 0	—	Sat. 11 0
Kotor	Tue. 1215	—	—
Budva .... arr.	—	—	Sat. 1245
Budva .... dep.	—	—	Sat. 1330
Kotor	Tues. 17 0	—	—
Herceg-Novi	Tues. 1820	—	Sat. 1530
Dubrovnik arr.	Tues. 21 0	—	Sat. 1830
Dubrovnik dep.	Tues. 2130	Fri. 10 0	Sat. 2130
Korcular	Wed. 1 40	—	—
Hvar	—	—	—
Split	Wed. 6 30	Fri. 19 0	Sun. 6 30

Line 12.—Sušak, Rab.

Daily.

14 0	d. Sušak .... a.	1050
1535	d. Crikvenica d.	9 20
1715	d. Senj ...... d.	7 40
20 0	a. Rab ...... d.	5 0

Line 18.—Aleksandrovo—Sušak.

s.s. *Slavija*, 234 tons. Daily.

4 0	dep. Aleksandrovo .... arr.	18 0
7 45	arr. Sušak .... dep.	14 0

Line 36. Metković.—Split.

s.s. *Bakar*, 133 tons

Daily.		Daily
6 50	dep. Metković ....arr.	1530
1030	„ Makarska .... „	1155
13 0	arr. Split ....dep.	9 25

Line 44. Velaluka Hvar—Split.

s.s. *Bosna*, 550 tons.

Daily except Tuesdays and Sundays	Tue.			Tue.
3 30	4 0	dep. Velaluka .. arr.	1830	1815
5 30	..	Hvar arr ... dep.	1630	..
5 45	..	Hvar dep. ... arr.	1620	..
8 15	8 15	arr. Split ...... dep	14 0	14 0

Daily except Tues. & Sun

Line 43. Stari Grad—Split.

s.s. *Neretva*, 160 tons.

	a	*b*
Stari Grad ...... dep.	4 0	4 30
Split .... arr.	7 40	7 40
„ .... dep.	14 0	14 0
Stari Grad ...... arr.	18 0	1725

a Mon., Tue., Thur., Fris. and Sats. *b* Weds. only.

Line 42. Komiža—Vis—Split.

s.s. *Sarajevo*, 559 tons; s.s. *Sumadija*, — tons.

Tues.	Dly. except Tuesdays		Dly. except Tuesdays	Tues.
15 0	dep. 15 0	Split	arr. 8 30	8 30
17 5	arr. —	Hvar	dep. —	6 20
1715	dep. —	Hvar	arr. —	6 10
1835	arr. 1730	Vis ..	dep. 6 0	5 0
1850	dep. 18 0	Vis ..	arr. 5 45	4 45
1950	arr. 19 0	Komiža	dep. 4 45	3 45

Line 56. —Trieste—Venice—Split—Metković.

(Weekly). s.s. *Bled*, 492 tons.

Wed. dep. 23 0	Venice ..	Wed. arr. 7 0
Thur. arr. 7 0	Trieste	Tue. dep. 23 0
„ dep. 18 0	Trieste	„ arr. 7 0
Fri. arr. 11 0	Šibenik	Mon. dep. 13 0
„ dep. 12 0	Šibenik	„ arr. 12 0
—	Trogir ..	Mon dep. 9 0
—	Trogir ..	„ arr. 8 30
Fri. arr. 16 0	Split ..	Mon. dep. 6 0
„ dep. 24 0	Split ..	Sun. arr. 15 0
—	Makarska	Sun. dep. 12 0
—	Makarska	„ arr. 1130
„ arr. 8 0	Metković	Sun. dep. 7 0

Line 58-Sušak, Trieste, Patras, Piræus, Izmir.

s.s. *Beograd*, 897 tons; s.s. *Srbin*, 982 tons (Weekly)

arr.	dep.		arr.	dep.
—	Fri. 17 0	Sušak	Th. 10 0	—
—	—	Fiume	(Optional)	
Sat. 7 0	Sat. 18 0	Trieste	We 7 0	We. 18 0
Su 15 0	Su. 24 0	Split	Tu. 7 30	Tu. 10 0
Mo. 10 0	Mo 13 0	Dubrovnik 2	Mo. 20 0	Mo. 2230
Mo. 1730	Mo 1830	Kotor	—	—
Mo. 2140	Mo. 2150	Budva	Mo. 1530	Mo. 1540
Mo 2330	Mo 24 0	Bar	Mo. 1330	Mo. 14 0
Tu. 7 0	Tu. 10 0	Durazzo	Mo. 6 30	Mo. 8 0
Tu. 16 0	Tu. 18 0	Valona	Su. 23 0	Mo. 0 30
Tu. 24 0	We 4 0	Sarande	Su. 1630	Su. 1730
We. 7 0	We. 8 0	Corfu	Su. 14 0	Su. 16 0
(Optional)		Prevesa	—	—
—	—	Leukas	Su. 6 0	Su. 8 0
(Optional)		Patras	Sat. 1230	Sat. 19 0
—	—	Vostizza....	Sat. 6 0	Sat. 10 0
Th. 8 0	—	Piræus	—	Fri. 22 0

Line 58a, Trieste—Sušak.

arr.	dep.		arr.	dep.
—	We. 18 0	Trieste	Sat. 7 0	—
(Optional)		Rijeka ... (Fiume)	Optional	
Th. 10 0	—	Sušak	—	Fri 17 0

Jadranska Line continued on next page.

JADRANSKA LINE —*continued*.

Line 48.—Drvenik—Trogir—Split.

s.s. *Brae*, 135 tons; s.s. *Kvarner*, 144 tons.

Mon., Wed., Fri.	Tue., Th., Sat.		Tue., Th., Sat.	Mon., Wed., Fri.
4 15	4 0	d. Maslinica d.	1710	17 0
5 0	4 45	d. Drvenik Otok a.	1625	1615
6 40	6 40	d. Trogir ..d.	1425	1425
7 40	7 40	a. Split ..d.	1315	1315

Line 49—Trogir—Split.

	Daily except Sunday.			Sunday.		
Trogir..... dep.	5 30	1045	16 0	5 30	1345	930
Split ...... arr.	7 30	12 0	1740	7 50	1545	1 0
Split ...... dep.	8 0	1315	20 0	9 30	16 0	23 0
Trogir ..... arr.	9 15	1515	2145	1150	1745	2345

Other Services maintained by the Jadranska S.S. Co., of which particulars will be given on application, are:

13. Sušak, Obrovac.
14. Sušak, Senj, Pag.
15. Sušak, Rab, Olib.
16. Vrbnik, Sušak.
17. Bakar Kraljevica
19. Baška-Crikvenica-Sušak.
20. Sušak Malinska.
21. Preko-Šibenik.
22. Olib, Šibenik.
23. Olib, Preko
24. Sali, Šibenik.
25. Sali, Preko.
26. Skradin, Šibenik.
27. Šibenik, Kaprije, Zirje.
28. Pirovac, Tijesno, Šibenik.
29. Rogoznica, Šibenik.
30. Šibenik, Pag, Obrovac.
31. Šibenik, Preko.
33. Olib, Preko, Biograd n/m
34. Šibenik-Obrovac.
37. Split, Brač, Metković.
38. Split, Sumartin.
39. Split, Jelsa, Metković.
40. Sumartin, Split.
41. Vrboska, Split.
45. Trpanj, Makarska.
46. Metković, Trpanj, Ston Mali.
47. Trpanj, Metković.
50. Split-Vis.
51. Sućurac Split (Poljud).
52. Omiš-Split.
53. Makarska, Split.
54. Split, Sutivan.
55. Velaluka, Metković.

"ISTRIA-TRIESTE" SOCIETÀ DI NAVIGAZIONE A VAPORE.

Trieste, Grado. (Weekdays)

16 0	dep. Trieste ....arr.	8 30
18 0	arr. Grado ......dep.	6 30

Trieste—Pirano—Portorose.

	Weekdays.			Suns. & Holidays.	
Trieste ... dep.	1145	1830		10 0	21 0
Pirano ... arr.	1310	1955		1125	2225
Pirano ....dep	1315	20 0		1130	—
Portorose . arr.	1335	2015	Daily	1150	—
Portorose . dep.	1535		2020	1215	—
Pirano . arr	1550	—	2035	1230	—
Pirano ....dep	1555	—	6 0	1235	—
Trieste .. arr.	1720	—	7 30	14 0	—

Calling at Isola.

Trieste—Monfalcone. (Weekdays).

		Sats.	
6 15	dep. Trieste......arr.	19 30	14 5
7 35	arr. Monfalcone dep.	18†15	12 45

† Not Saturdays.

Trieste—Parenzo. (Daily.)

1630	dep. Trieste.. arr	8 50
2040	arr. Parenzo..dep.	4 45

Calls at Isola, Pirano etc.

Trieste—Brioni—Pola Daily.

dep. 7 0	Trieste	arr.	14 30
arr. 7 55	Isola	dep.	13 30†
,, 8 0	Pirano	dep.	12 55
,, 11 10	Parenzo	dep.	10 15
,, 12 40	Rovigno	dep.	8 50
,, 14 12	Brioni	dep.	7 30
arr. 15 15	Pola	dep.	6 30

Calls also Salvore, Umago, Cittanova, Orsera, Fasana.
† On Suns. & Holidays omit Isola, arr. Trieste 14.5

Trieste, Brioni, Zara.

Tues., Fri.		Wed., Sat.
dp. 7 45	Trieste	ar. 1915
ar. 1110	Rovigno	dp. 1530
dp. 1227	Brioni	dp. 1430
dp. 13 0	Pola	dp. 14 0
dp. 1635	Lussinpiccolo ...	dp. 1040
ar. 2035	Zara	dp. 7 0

Calling also Pirano, Parenzo.

JUGOSLAV LLOYD.

Fortnightly.

Trieste—Piræus—Alexandria—Haifa.

By s.s. *Princesa Olga*, 8480 tons, carrying 1st, 2nd and 3rd class passengers. Doctor carried.

SERVICE TEMPORARILY SUSPENDED.

LLOYD TRIESTINO Soc. An. di Navigazione.

See also pages 456A, 481, *and Advertisement, page* 513. **LINE 163-164.**

GRAND EXPRESS—ITALY—INDIA—FAR EAST (Monthly)

s.s. *Victoria*, 13098 tons. s.s. *Conte Verde*, 18765 tons. s.s. *Conte Rosso*, 17879 tons.
s.s. *Conte Biancamano*, 24416 tons.

Giulio Cesare	*Conte Biancamano*	*Conte Verde*	*Victoria*	*Conte Rosso*	↓	↑	*Conte Rosso*	*Victoria*	*Giulio Cesare*	*Conte Biancamano.*	*Conte Verde*
Aug. 2	—	Aug. 30	—	Oct. 4	dep. Trieste	..arr.	Aug. 5	—	Sep. 26	—	Oct. 21
,, 2	—	,, 30	—	,, 4	,, Venice ..	,,	,, 5	—	,, 25	—	,, 21
,, 3	—	,, 31	—	,, 5	,, Brindisi	,,	,, 4	—	,, 24	—	,, 20
—	Aug. 16	—	Sept. 14	—	,, Genoa	,,	—	Sept. 4	—	Aug. 10	—
—	,, 17	—	,, 15	—	,, Naples	,,	—	,, 3	—	,, 9	—
,, 6	,, 20	Sept. 2	,, 17/18	,, 7	a/d. Port Said	a/d.	,, 2	Aug. 31	,, 21/22	,, 6	,, 18
—	,, 23	—	—	—	,, Massaua	,,	—	—	,, 18	,, 3	,, 15
—	—	—	—	—	,, Djibouti	,,	—	—	—	—	—
,, 10	,, 24	,, 6	,, 21	,, 11	,, Aden....	,,	—	,, 27	—	—	—
,, 14	,, 28	,, 11	,, 25	,, 16	,, Bombay	,,	Jly. 25	,, 23	,, 12/13	Sept. 28	,, 10
,, 17	,, 30/31	,, 13/14	,, 27/28	,, 18/19	,, Colombo	,,	,, 22	,, 21	,, 10	,, 25	,, 7
,, 21	Sept. 4	,, 18	Oct. 2	,, 23	,, Singapore	,,	,, 18	,, 17	,, 5	,, 21	,, 3
—	,, 8	—	,, 5	,, 27	,, Manila..	,,	—	,, 14	—	,, 18	—
,, 25	,, 10	,, 22	,, 7	,, 29	,, HongKong	,,	,, 14	,, 12	,, 1	,, 16	Sept. 29
,, 28	,, 12	,, 24	,, 9	,, 31	,, Shanghai	dp.	,, 12	,, 10	Aug 30	,, 14	,, 27

† Optional.

ITALY TO AUSTRALIA. LINE 170. (Monthly).

Motor Vessel.	Tons.	Genoa. dep.	Naples. dep.	Port Said. arr.	Melbourne arr.
Remo	9780	Aug. 5	Aug. 8	Aug. 13	Sept. 15
Esquilino	8657	Sept. 5	Sept. 8	Sept. 13	Oct. 16
Viminale	8657	Oct. 5	Oct. 8	Oct. 13	Nov. 15
Romolo	9780	Nov. 5	Nov. 8	Nov. 13	Dec.. 16

Calling also at Leghorn, Messina, Catania (optional), Suez, Mas-aua†, Colombo (optional), Fremantle, Adelaide (optional), Sydney and Brisbane.

† May also call Cochin and/or Aleppy.

HOMEWARD.

	Tons.	Brisbane. dep.	Sydney. dep.	Melbourne. dep.	Adel'ide (opt'nal) dep.	Port Said.	Al'xandria (optional)	Piræus. optional	Catania. (opt'nal)	Naples.	Genoa arr.
Esquilino	8657	June 24	July 4	July 8	July 11	Aug. 11	Aug. 12	Aug. 14	Aug. 16	Aug 17	Au. 19
Viminale	8657	July 26	Aug. 1	Aug. 5	Aug. 8	Sept. 8	Sept. 9	Sept. 11	Sept. 13	Sept. 14	Sep. 16
Romolo ..	9780	Aug. 26	Sept. 5	Sept. 9	Sept. 12	Oct. 13	Oct. 14	Oct. 16	Oct. 18	Oct. 19	Oct. 21
Remo ...	9780	Sept. 28	Oct. 3	Oct. 7	Oct. 10	Nov. 10	Nov. 11	Nov. 13	Nov. 15	Nov. 16	Nv. 18
Esquilino	8657	Oct. 25	Nov. 1	Nov. 4	Nov. 7	Dec. 8	Dec. 9	Dec. 11	Dec. 13	Dec. 14	Dec 16
Viminale	8657	Nov. 25	Dec. 5	Dec 9	Dec. 12	Jan. 12	Jan. 13	Jan. 15	Jan. 17	Jan. 18	Jan. 20

Calling also Fremantle, Colombo, Massaua (optional) and Suez.

ITALY—SOUTH AFRICA, Out *via* Suez, Home West Coast. (Monthly.) LINE 160.

Steamer.	Tons	Trieste.	Venice. dep.	Brindisi §	Messina	Port Said.	Mas'aua arr/dep	Mombasa	Durban. arr./dep.	Cape Town
Duchess d'Aosta	7872	July 18	July 21	July 23	July 24	July 29	Aug. 3/4	Aug. 17	Au. 30/Sp. 2	Sept. 7
Piave......	7565	Aug. 15	Aug. 18	Aug. 20	Aug. 21	Aug. 26	Ag31/Sp1	Sept. 14	Sept. 27/30	Oct. 5
Timavo....	7549	Sept. 12	Sept. 15	Sept. 17	Sept. 18	Sept. 23	Sep. 28/29	Oct. 12	Oct 25/28	Nov. 2

Calling also at Fiume, Catania, Suez§, Assab§, Aden, Dante, Mogadiscio, Merka§, Chisimaio§, Dar-es-Salaam, Mozambique, Beira, Lourenco Marques, East London, Port Elizabeth. § Optional.

HOMEWARD Steamer	Tons	Cape Town dep.	Walvis Bay	Pointe Noire	Lagos arr./dep.	Dakar	Marseilles arr./dep.	Genoa arr./dep	Venice	Trieste.
Timavo	7549	July 15	July 18	July 23	July 26/29	Aug. 5	Aug. 15/18	Au. 20/22	Aug. 31	Sept. 1
Rosandra	8034	Aug. 12	Aug. 15	Aug. 20	Aug. 23/26	Sept. 2	Sept. 12/15	Sep. 17/19	Spt. 28	Sept. 29
Duchess d'Aosta..	7872	Sept. 9	Sept. 12	Sept. 17	Sept. 20/23	Sept. 30	Oct. 10/13	Oct. 15/17	Oct. 26	Oct. 27
Piave ..	7565	Oct. 7	Oct. 10	Oct. 15	Oct. 18/21	Oct. 28	Nov. 7/10	Nov 12/14	Nov. 23	Nov. 24

Calling also at Grand Bassam, Casablanca§, Barcelona§, Sète, Leghorn§, Naples, Spalato. § Optional.

LLOYD TRIESTINO Soc. An. di Navigazione—*continued.*

NAPLES—MASSAUA—DJIBOUTI (Weekly). LINE 151.

SAILINGS.

Steamers.	Tons.		Steamers.	Tons.	
s.s. *Po*	.. 7156 ..	Aug. 8, 29.	s.s. *Tevere*	.. 8448 ..	Aug. 22, Sept. 12
s.s. *Arno*	.. 8380 ..	Aug. 15, Sept. 5.			

Itinerary.

arr.	dep.		arr.	dep
—	Tues. 18 0	Naples ↓↑	Fri. 14 0	—
Fri. 20 0	Fri. 24 0	Port Said	Tues. 8 0	Tues. 12 0
Sat 13 0	Sat. 14 0	Suez	Mon. 16 0	Mon. 18 0
Tues. 7 0	Wed. 16 0	Massaua	Fri. 10 0	Fri. 22 0
Thur. 9 0	—	Assab	—	Thur. 16 0

GENOA—MASSAUA—KISIMAJO (Fortnightly). LINE 152.

SAILINGS.

Steamers.	Tons.		Steamer.	Tons.	
s.s. *Vinci*	..7432	Aug. 9, Sept. 20.	s.s. *Crispi*	..7464	Sept. 6.
s.s. *Mazzini*	..7453	Aug. 23.			

Itinerary.

arr.	dep.		arr.	dep
etc.	Wed. 22 0	Genoa ↓↑	Thur. 13 0	—
Thur. 6 0	Thur. 15 0	Leghorn	—	—
Fri. 11 0	Fri 18 0	Naples	Wed. 7 0	Wed. 12 0
Sat. 7 0	Sat. 11 0	Messina	Tues. 15 0	Tues. 17 0
Tues. 9 0	Tues. 14 0	Port Said	Sat. 14 0	Sat. 18 0
Wed. 6 0	Wed. 7 0	Suez	Fri. 20 0	Fri. 22 0
Sat. 6 0	Sat. 24 0	Massaua	Tues. 6 0	Tues. 22 0
Mon. 5 0	Mon. 10 0	Djibouti	Sun. 15 0	Sun. 24 0
Mon. 20 0	Mon. 24 0	Aden	Sat. 23 0	Sun. 4 0
Wed. 13 0	Wed. 16 0	Dante	—	—
Fri. 15 0	Sun 12 0	Mogadiscio	Tues. 8 0	Wed. 10 0
Mon. 6 0	—	Kisimajo	etc.	Mon. 14 0

Optional call outward at Dante.

GENOA—MASSAUA—DJIBOUTI. LINE 153.

Subsidiary service every 4 weeks. s.s. *Colombo*, 11760 tons, Aug. 2, 30.

Itinerary.

	arr.	dep.		arr.	dep.
Genoa	Aug. 2, etc.	Wed. 12 0	Djibouti	Aug. 14, etc.	Mon. 20 0
Naples	Thur. 11 0	Thur. 21 0	Assab	Tues. 5 0	Tues. 11 0
Messina	Fri. 10 0	Fri. 16 0	Massaua	Wed. 5 0	Wed. 22 0
Port Said	Mon. 10 0	Tues. 17 0	Suez	Sat. 15 0	Sat. 17 0
Suez	Wed. 9 0	Wed. 10 0	Port Said	Sun. 9 0	Sun. 13 0
Massaua	Fri. 6 0	Sat. 22 0	Naples	Wed. 14 0	Wed. 19 0
Assab	Sun. 16 0	Sun. 20 0	Genoa	Thur. 18 0	—
Djibouti	Mon. 5 0	—			

TRIESTE—MASSAUA—DJIBOUTI (Fortnightly) LINE 154.

SAILINGS.

Steamer.	Tons.		Steamer.	Tons.	
s.s. *Palestina*.	7089	Aug. 4, Sept. 1, 29.	s.s. *Urania*,	7039	Aug. 18, Sept. 15.

Itinerary.

	arr.	dep.		arr.	dep.
Trieste	Aug. 4, etc.	Fri. 23 0	Djibouti	Aug 17, etc.	Thur. 21 0
Venice	Sat. 6 0	Sat 19 0	Massaua	Sat. 6 0	Sat. 12 0
†Fiume	Sun. 7 0	Sun. 12 0	Port Sudan	Sun. 14 0	Sun. 19 0
†Bari	Mon. 6 0	Mon 11 0	Suez	Wed. 6 0	Wed. 8 0
Brindisi	Mon. 17 0	Mon. 22 0	Port Said	Wed 24 0	Thur. 4 0
Port Said	Fri. 2 0	Fri. 6 0	Brindisi	Sun. 6 0	Sun. 8 0
Suez	Fri. 21 0	Fri. 22 0	Venice	Mon. 16 0	Mon. 24 0
Massaua	Tues. 6 0	Tues. 22 0	Trieste	Tues. 6 0	—
Djibouti	Thur. 6 0	—			

† From Fiume every 4 weeks, May 14, etc.; from Bari every 4 weeks, May 1, etc.

LLOYD TRIESTINO Soc. An. di Navigazione—*continued.*

LINE 155.

MASSAUA—KISIMAJO—MOMBASA (Fortnightly).

Prolonged from and to Naples every 4 weeks.

SAILINGS FROM NAPLES TO MASSAUA.

Steamer	Tons		Steamer	Tons	
s.s. *Dalmatia*	3254	Aug. 17	s.s. *Tripolittania*	2722	Oct. 12
s.s. *Eritrea*	2517	Sep. 14	s.s. *Somalia*	2699	Nov. 9

Every 4 weeks

Naples . . dep. 12 0	Au. 17	Sep. 14
Syracuse	19	16
Port Said	2[illegible]	20
Suez . . . . arr./dep.	24	21
Kosseir	25	22
Jeddah	27	24
Port Sudan	28	25
Massaua arr.	30	27

Fortnightly Service.

	arr.		dep.	
Massaua dep.	Aug. 18, etc.		Fri.	12 0
Hodeida	Sat.	a.m.	Sat.	p.m.
Assab	Sun.	a.m.	Sun.	p.m.
Djibouti	Mon.	a.m.	Mon.	p.m.
Aden	Tues.	a.m.	Tues.	p.m.
Berbera (opt'l)	Wed.	a.m.	Wed.	p.m.
Bender Kassim	Thur.	p.m.	Thur.	p.m.
Alula	Fri.	a.m.	Fri.	p.m.
Dante	Sat.	a.m.	Sat.	p.m.
Obbia	Mon.	a.m.	Mon.	p.m.
Mogadiscio	Wed.	a.m.	Thur.	p.m.
Merka	Friday	a.m.	Fri.	p.m.
Brava	Sat.	a.m.	Sat.	p.m.
Kisimajo	Sun.	a.m.	Sun.	p.m.
Mombasa	Tues.	a.m.	—	

Fortnightly Service.

	arr.		dep.	
Mombasa	Aug. 9, etc.		Wed.	p.m.
Kisimajo	Fri.	a.m.	Fri.	p.m.
Merka	Sat.	a.m.	Sat.	p.m.
Mogadiscio	Sun.	a.m.	Mon.	p.m.
Obbia	Wed.	a.m.	Wed.	p.m.
Dante	Fri.	a.m.	Fri.	p.m.
Alula	Sat.	a.m.	Sat.	p.m.
Bender Kassim	Sun.	a.m.	Sun.	12 0
Aden	Mon.	p.m.	Mon.	p.m.
Djibouti	Tues.	a.m.	Tues.	p.m.
Assab	Wed.	a.m.	Wed.	p.m.
Hodeida	Thur.	a.m.	Thur.	p.m.
Massaua arr.	Fri.	10 0	—	

Every 4 weeks

Massaua dep.	Aug 16	Sep. 13	Oct. 11
Port Sudan	18	15	13
Jeddah	19	16	14
Suez	22	19	17
Port Said	23	20	18
Naples	28	25	23

Commercial Line. GENOA—MASSAUA—MOGADISCIO (Monthly).

From Genoa, *via* Leghorn, Naples, Port Said, Suez, Port Sudan, Massaua, Djibouti, to Berbera (optional) and Mogadiscio.

Commercial Line. TRIESTE—MASSAUA—MOGADISCIO (Monthly).

From Trieste, *via* Fiume, Venice, Port Said, Suez, Port Sudan (optional), Massaua, Djibouti, Berbera (optional) to Mogadiscio.

Commercial Line. TYRRHENIAN—INDIA—SAIGON (Monthly).

From Genoa, *via* Leghorn, Naples, Palermo, Catania, Port Said, Suez, Massaua, Djibouti†, Berbera†, Karachi, Bombay¶, Singapore, Saigon; returning *via* Singapore†, Bombay†, Karachi†, Aden†, Massaua†, Suez, Port Said, Naples, Marseilles to Genoa.

¶ *May proceed to Bengal in lieu o Saigon—see Calcutta services below.*

May also call at Bangkok. † Optional.

Commercial Line. ADRIATIC—INDIA—PERSIAN GULF.

From Trieste, *via* Venice, Fiume, Ancona, Split, Brindisi, Port Said, Suez, Massaua, Aden§, Bombay, Karachi, Bender, Shahpour, Khoramshahr (Mohamerah), Basra, Karachi, Bombay, Suez, Port Said, Brindisi, Venice, Trieste. *After Bombay and Karachi, may proceed to Saigon in lieu of Persian Gulf—see itinerary above.*

§ Optional.

LLOYD TRIESTINO—Soc. An. di Navigazione—*continued.*

COMMERCIAL LINE.

ADRIATIC—INDIA—DUTCH EAST INDIES—FAR EAST FREIGHT LINE (Monthly). LINE 167.

SAILINGS OUTWARD.

Cargo Boats with limited Passenger accommodation "Saloon" class.

Vessel	Tons	Trieste dep.	Venice dep.	Fiume	Split §	Brindisi	To Port Said, Port Sudan, Massaua, Aden§, Karachi, Bombay, Colombo, Penang§, Singapore, Batavia, Samarang, Saigon, Hong Kong, Shanghai, Kobe.
—	—	Aug. 20	Aug. 21	Aug. 22	Aug. 23	Aug. 24	
—	—	Sept. 20	Sept. 21	Sept. 22	Sept. 23	Sept. 24	
—	—	Oct. 20	Oct. 21	Oct. 22	Oct. 23	Oct. 24	
—	—	Nov. 20	Nov. 21	Nov. 22	Nov. 23	Nov. 24	

§ Optional call.

GENOA—CALCUTTA (Monthly). LINE 168.

Steamer	Tons	Genoa dep.	Naples dep.	P. Said	Suez	Massaua arr.	Djibouti§ arr.	Bombay arr.	Calcutta arr.
—	—	Aug. 9	Aug. 15	Aug. 20	—	Aug. 25	Aug. 30	Sept. 6	Sept. 18
—	—	Sept. 9	Sept. 15	Sept. 20	—	Sept. 25	Sept. 30	Oct. 7	Oct. 19
—	—	Oct. 9	Oct. 15	Oct. 20	—	O t. 25	Oct. 30	Nov. 6	Nov. 18

Calling also at Leghorn, Catania, Madras.

Homeward from Calcutta *via* Rangoon, Madras, Colombo, Cochin§, Bombay§, Karachi§, Aden§, Suez, Port Said, Naples, Marseilles to Genoa. **§ Optional call.**

VENICE—CALCUTTA (Monthly).

Steamer	Tons	Venice dep.	Trieste dep.	P. Said	Suez	Massaua arr./dep.	Djibouti arr.	Calcutta arr.

Calling also at Split§, Fiume, Madras.

Homeward from Rangoon *via* Madras, Colombo, Bombay, Karachi, Suez, Port Said, Ancona§, Fiume§, Trieste to Venice. **§ Optional.**

PHARAONIC MAIL LINE. See also page 477.

(Subject to alteration without notice).

s.s. *Khedive Ismail*, 7289 tons. s.s. *Mohammed Ali El-Kebir*, 7289 tons.

Carrying 1st cl., 2nd cl., 3rd cl. Cabins with private bathrooms and cabins-de-luxe, 1st cl. Doctor and stewardess carried.

Marseilles (Genoa—Malta) Alexandria, *and vice versa.*

EASTWARDS			*Mohammed Ali El-Kebir*	*Khedive Ismail*	*Mohammed Ali El-Kebir*	*Khedive Ismail*	*Mohammed Ali El-Kebir*	*Khedive Ismail*	*Mohammed Ali El-Kebir*	*Khedive Ismail*	*Mohammed Ali El-Kebir*	*Khedive Ismail*	*Mohammed Ali El-Kebir*	*Khedive I-mail*	*Mohammed Ali El-Kebir*
	arr.	dep.	July	Aug.	Aug	Aug	Aug	Sep	Sep	Sep	Sept.	Oct.	Oct	Oct	Oct.
Marseilles	—	12 0	25	1	8	22	29	5	12	19	26	3	10	17	31
Genoa	7 0	14 0	—	—	—	—	30	—	13	—	27	—	11	—	—
Malta	12 0	16 0	27†	3†	10	24	—	7†	—	21†		5†	—	19	Nv2
Alexandria	8 0	—	29‡	5‡	13	27	Sp 3	9‡	17	23‡	Oct. 1	7‡	15	22	5
Alexandria	—	16 0	30	6	—	—	3	10	17	24	1	8	—	—	—
Beyrout	16 0	18 0	31	—	—	—	4	—	18	—	2	—	—	—	—
Limassol	11 0	15 0	—	7	—	—	—	11	—	25	—	9	—	—	—
Alexandria	10 0	—	—	8	—	—	—	12	—	26	—	10	—	—	—
Alexandria	18 0	—	Aug. 1	—	—	—	5	—	19	—	3	—	—	—	—
Alexandria	—	12 0	2	16	23	30	6	13	20	27	4	11	25	—	8
Malta	7 0	11 0	5	19	26	Sp 2	9	16	23	30	7	14	28	—	11
Genoa	12 0	16 0	—	—	—	—	—	—	—	—	—	—	—	—	—
Marseilles	7 0	—	7	21	28	4	11	18	25	Oc. 2	9	16	30	—	13

† arr. Malta 7.0, dep. 9.0. ‡ arr. 17.0.

Services to Cyprus and Palestine, Syria.

Fouadieh ..	1853 tons	*Talodi* ..	1585 tons	*Zaafaran* ..	1563 tons
Taif ..	1590 ,,	*Zamalek*	1566 ,,		

The above screw steamers carry 1st, 2nd, and 3rd class passengers and stewardess. (Doctor carried during Pilgrimage season). All vessels are fitted electric light, wireless telegraphy, cabins for 1, 2, 3 and **4 berths, bathrooms,** and saloons.

Egypt—Cyprus Mail Line.—Weekly.

s.s. *Fouadieh*, or other steamers.

July 4—October 24.

	arr.	dep.
Alexandria*	—	Tu. 12 0
Port Said‡	We. 6 0	We. 16 0
Limassol ...	Th. 10 0	Th. 12 0
Famagusta ..	Th. 18 0	Th. 24 0
Larnaca	Fr. 6 0	Fr. 11 0
Limassol ..	Fr. 15 0	Sa. 11 0
Port Said	Su. 9 0	Su. 15 0
Alexandria ..	Mo. 8 0	—

‡Connecting with P & O. Mail Steamers from and to Marseilles * Steamers call at Paphos fortnightly during the voyages from Alexandria, Aug. 1, 15, 29; Sept. 12 and 26 leaving Limassol homewards on Fri. at 24 0, due Paphos Sat. 6.0; dep. 11.0 for Port Said and Alexandria.

Egypt—Palestine—Syria Line.

(Weekly cargo service) carrying a few saloon passengers, and deck passengers.

s.s. *Zamalek* and s.s. *Zaafaran*.

arr.	dep.	↓ ↑	arr.	dep.
—	Sat. 16 0	Alexandria	Tu. 8 0	—
Su. 9 0	Mo 15 0	Port Said ..	We 10 0	We 16 0
Tu 6 0	Tu. 10 0	Jaffa	Tu. 15 0	Tu. 18 0
Tu. 11 0	Tu. 17 0	Tel Aviv ..	—	—
We. 6 0	We. 18 0	Haifa	Tu. 6 0	Tu. 10 0
Th. 6 0	Th. 12 0	Beyrout	Mo. 16 0	Mo 20 0
Th 16 0	Th 20 0	Tripoli	Mo. 8 0	Mo. 12 0
Fri. 8 0	Fri. 17 0	Lattakia (op)	—	—
Sat. 8 0	Sat. 16 0	Mersin	—	—
Su. 8 0	—	Alexandretta	—	Sun. 18 0

MALTA-SYRACUSE-MALTA SERVICE. Cassar Co. Ltd.

s.s. *Knight of Malta*, 1,600 tons, carrying 1st, 2nd, and 3rd class passengers. Cabins de Luxe.

SYRACUSE—dep. Daily (except Sat.)	14 0*	MALTA—dep. Daily (except Fri.)	,, 24 0
MALTA—arr. ,, ,, ,, ,,	21 0	SYRACUSE—arr. Daily (except Sat.)	7 0

* In connection with train from Rome due 13.32.

SOCIÉTÉ MARITIME NATIONALE MEDITERRANÉE

Marseilles—Corsica—Tunis—Sousse—Gabes—Sfax. (Fortnightly).

s.s. *Henri Estier*, 1908 tons, with Cabins de Luxe also carrying 1st, 2nd and 3rd class passengers.

	arr.	dep.		arr.	dep.
Marseilles	July 28th, etc.	Fri. 18 0	Sfax	Aug. 4th, etc.	Fri. 18 0
Ajaccio............	Sat. 12 0	Sat. 16 0	Sousse............	Sat. 12 0	Sat. 18 0
Tunis	Mon. 6 0	Mon. 16 0	Tunis	Sun. 6 0	Sun. 16 0
Sousse	Tues. 7 0	Tues. 12 0	Bastia	Tues. 7 0	Tues. 17 0
Gabes	Wed. 6 0	Wed. 24 0	Nice	Wed. 6 0	Wed. 17 0
Derba	Thur. 4 0	Thur. 12 0	Marseilles	Thur. 7 0	—
Sfax	Thur. 18 0	—			

Société MISR de NAVIGATION MARITIME.

EXPRESS SERVICE MARSEILLES-GENOA-ALEXANDRIA-GENOA-MARSEILLES an *vice versa* by s.s. *El Nil*, 7,667 tons, s.s. *Kawsar*, 7,952 tons, carrying 1st, 2nd and †3rd cl. (also deck) passengers. Cabines-de-luxe, single and two-berth cabins 1st class; two and three berth cabins, 2nd class; hot and cold running water in all cabins, 1st and 2nd class.

† 3rd class on s.s. *Kawsar* is in dormitories—no separate cabins or dining saloon.

Steamer.	Marseilles dep. 13.0.	Genoa. arr. 7.0. dep. 13.0.‡	Alexandria. arr. 16.0.	Alexandria. dep. 12.0.	Genoa. arr. 13.30. dep. 20.0.	Marseilles. arr. 13.0
Kawsar	July 26	July 27	July 31	Aug. 10	Aug. 14	Aug. 15
El Nil	Aug. 2	Aug. 3	Aug. 7	,, 24	,, 28	,, 29
Kawsar ..	,, 16	,, 17	,, 21	,, 31	Sept. 4	Sept. 5
El Nil	,, 30	,, 31	Sept. 4	Sept. 7	,, 11	,, 12
Kawsar	Sept. 6	Sept. 7	,, 11	,, 14	,, 18	,, 19
El Nil	,, 13	,, 14	,, 18	,, 21	,, 25	,, 26
Kawsar	,, 20	,, 21	,, 25	,, 28	Oct. 2	Oct. 3
El Nil	,, 27	,, 28	Oct. 2	Oct. 5	,, 9	,, 10
Kawsar	Oct. 4	Oct. 5	,, 9	,, 12	,, 16	,, 17
El Nil	,, 11	,, 12	,, 16	,, 19	,, 23	,, 24
Kawsar	,, 18	,, 19	,, 23	—	—	—
El Nil	,, 25	,, 26	,, 30	Nov. 2	Nov. 6	Nov. 7
El Nil	Nov. 8	Nov. 9	Nov. 13	,, 16	,, 20	,, 21
El Nil	,, 22	,, 23	,, 27	,, 30	Dec. 4	Dec. 5
El Nil	Dec. 6	Dec. 7	Dec. 11	Dce. 14	,, 18	,, 19
El Nil	,, 20	,, 21	,, 25	,, 28	Jan. 1	Jan. 2
El Nil	Jan. 3	Jan. 4	Jan. 8	—	—	—

‡ Connection with Rome Express from London and Paris, due Genoa 9.15.

Services Contractuels des MESSAGERIES MARITIMES.

See page 457.

MEDITERRANEAN SERVICES.

Steamer.	Tons.	Steamer.	Tons.	Steamer	Tons.
Felix Roussel (m.v.) ..	17083	*Theophile Gautier* ..	8194	*Sphinx*	11374
Mariette Pacha ..	12239	*Champollion*	12546	*Lamartine*	5110

Services subject to alteration with or without notice.

Steamers carry 1st, 2nd, and 2nd intermediate passengers. First class have cabins for one, two or more passengers, Bathrooms, Electric Light, etc. Passengers embark at Marseilles at the Mole de la Pinède.

Egypt—Palestine—Syria Line.

Steamer	SAILINGS FROM MARSEILLES.								
Mariette Pacha	July 27	Aug. 10	Aug. 24	Sept. 7	Sept. 21	Oct. 5	Oct. 19	Nov. 9	Nov. 23
Champollion ..	—	—	Aug. 31	Sept. 14	Sept. 28	Oct. 12	Oct. 26	—	—

ITINERARY

☞ *The following itineraries are given as information only, the Messageries Maritimes reserving the right to make therein, with or without notice, any alterations which may be deemed necessary.*

Marseilles dep. 12.0	Alexandria. arr.	Jaffa arr.	Tel-Aviv. arr.	Haifa. arr.	Beyrout. arr.	Beyrout. dep.	Tripoli. dep.	Haifa. dep.	Alexandria. dep.	Marseilles
July 27	July 31	—	—	Aug. 1	Aug. 2	Aug. 2	—	—	Aug. 4	Aug. 8
Aug. 10	Aug. 14	—	—	,, 15	,, 16	,, 16	—	—	,, 18	,, 22
,, 24	,, 28	—	—	,, 29	,, 30	,, 30	—	—	Sept. 1	Sept. 5
,, 31	Sept. 4	—	Sept. 5	—	Sept. 5	Sept. 6	—	Sept. 6	,, 8	,, 12
Sept. 7	,, 11	—	—	Sep. 12	,, 13	,, 13	—	—	,, 15	,, 19
,, 14	,, 18	—	Sept. 19	—	,, 19	,, 20	—	Sept. 20	,, 22	,, 26
,, 21	,, 25	—	—	Sep. 26	,, 27	,, 27	—	—	,, 29	Oct. 3
,, 28	Oct. 2	—	Oct. 3	—	Oct. 3	Oct. 4	—	Oct. 4	Oct. 6	,, 10
Oct. 5	,, 9	—	—	Oct 10	,, 11	,, 11	—	—	,, 13	,, 17
,, 12	,, 16	—	Oct. 17	—	,, 17	,, 18	—	Oct. 18	,, 20	,, 24
,, 19	,, 23	—	—	Oct. 24	,, 25	,, 25	—	—	,, 27	,, 31
,, 26	,, 30	—	Oct. 31	—	,, 31	Nov. 1	—	Nov. 1	Nov. 3	Nov. 7
Nov. 9	Nov. 13	—	Nov. 14	—	Nv. 14	,, 15	—	,, 15	,, 17	,, 21
,, 23	,, 27	—	,, 28	—	,, 28	,, 29	—	,, 29	Dec. 1	Dec. 5

North Mediterranean Line (Approx.) (Fortnightly).

MARSEILLES—PIRAEUS—ISTANBUL (BLACK SEA)—BEYROUT.

Steamer.	Marseilles. dep. 17.0	Naples. arr.	Piræus. arr.	Istanbul arr.	Odessa arr.	Consta'za arr.	Rhodes arr.	Alexandretta arr.	Haifa. arr.	Beyrout arr.
Theo. Gautier	Sept. 1	Sept. 3	Sept. 6	Sept. 8	—	—	Sept. 10	—	—	Sept. 12
Theo. Gautier	,, 29	Oct. 1	Oct. 4	Oct. 6	—	—	Oct. 8	Oct. 10	—	Oct. 11
Theo. Gautier	Oct. 27	,, 29	Nov. 1	Nov. 3	—	—	Nov. 5	Nov. 7	—	Nov. 8
Theo. Gautier	Dec. 15	Dec. 17	Dec. 20	Dec. 22	—	—	Dec. 24	Dec. 26	—	Dec. 27

BEYROUT—ISTANBUL—PIRAEUS—MARSEILLES.

Steamer.	Beyrout dep.	Tripoli dep.	Alexandretta	Rhodes dep.	Izmir dep.	Istanbul dep.	Piraeus dep.	Naples dep.	Marseilles arr.
Theo. Gautier	July 26	July 26	—	July 28	July 29	July 31	Aug. 2	Aug. 5	Aug. 7
Theo. Gautier	Sept. 12	Sept. 12	Sept. 13	Sept. 15	Sep. 16	Sept. 18	Sept. 20	Sept. 23	Sept. 25
Theo. Gautier	Oct. 11	Oct. 11	—	Oct. 13	Oct. 14	Oct. 16	Oct. 18	Oct. 21	Oct. 23
Theo. Gautier	Nov. 8	Nov. 8	—	Nov. 10	Nov 11	Nov. 13	Nov. 15	Nov. 18	Nov. 20
Theo. Gautier	Dec. 27	Dec. 27	—	Dec. 29	Dec 30	Jan. 1	Jan. 3	Jan. 6	Jan 8

Services Contractuels des MESSAGERIES MARITIMES—*cont.*

MAIN LINES.

For connecting Branch Lines, see page 390.

Marseilles, Port Said, Djibouti, Colombo, Singapore, Saigon, Hong-Kong and Shanghai.

Subject to alteration or cancellation without notice.

m.v. *Felix Roussel* .. 17083 tons.
m.v. *Jean Laborde* 11591 ,,
m.v. *Pres. Doumer* .. 11898 ,,
s.s. *Athos II.* .. 15275 tons.
s.s. *Andre Lebon* .. 13681 ,,
m.v. *Maréchal Joffre* 11782 ,,
m.v. *Aramis* .. 17536 tons
s.s. *Chenonceaux* .. 14825 ,,

Vessel.	Marseilles dp 12.0	Port Said, ar /dp.	Djibouti, arr.	Colombo arr.	Singapore, arr.	Saigon, arr.	Hong-Kong, arr.	Shanghai, arr	Kobe.
Aramis	July 21	July 25	July 29	Aug 4	Aug. 9	Aug. 11	Aug. 16	Aug. 18	Aug. 23
Jean Laborde ..	Aug. 4	Aug. 8	Aug. 12	Aug. 18	Aug. 23	Aug. 25	Aug. 30	Sept. 1	Sept. 6
Athos II	Aug. 18	Aug. 22	Aug. 26	Sept. 1	Sept. 6	Sept. 8	Sept. 13	Sept. 15	Sept. 20
Felix Roussel	Sept. 1	Sept. 5	Sept. 9	Sept. 15	Sept. 20	Sept 22	Sept 27	Sept 29	Oct. 4
Marechal Joffre	Sept. 15	Sept. 19	Sept. 23	Sept. 29	Oct 4	Oct. 6	Oct. 11	Oct. 13	Oct. 18
Pres. Doumer	Sept. 29	Oct. 3	Oct. 7	Oct. 13	Oct. 18	Oct. 20	Oct. 25	Oct. 27	Nov. 1
Aramis	Oct. 13	Oct. 17	Oct. 21	Oct. 27	Nov 1	Nov. 3	Nov. 8	Nov. 10	Nov. 15
Jean Laborde ..	Oct. 27	Oct. 31	Nov. 4	Nov. 10	Nov. 15	Nov. 17	Nov. 22	Nov. 24	Nov. 29
Athos II	Nov. 10	Nov. 14	Nov. 18	Nov. 24	Nov. 29	Dec. 1	Dec. 6	Dec. 8	Dec. 13
Chenonceaux	Nov. 24	Nov. 29	Dec. 4	Dec. 11	Dec. 16	Dec. 18	Dec. 23	Dec. 26	Dec. 31

Transhipping at Saigon for Haiphong (see page 390).

Vessel.	Kobe. dep.	Shanghai, dep.	Hong-Kong, dep.	Saigon. dep.	Singapore.	Colombo arr.	Djibouti, arr.	Suez.	Port Said. arr.	Marseilles, arr.
Felix Roussel	July 15	July 18	July 20	July 25	July 27	Aug. 1	Aug. 8	Aug. 11	Aug. 12	Aug. 16
Marechal Joffre..	July 29	Aug. 1	Aug. 3	Aug. 8	Aug. 10	Aug. 15	Aug. 22	Aug. 25	Aug. 26	Aug 30
Pres. Doumer....	Aug. 12	Aug. 15	Aug. 17	Aug. 22	Aug. 24	Aug. 29	Sept 5	Sept 8	Sept. 9	Sept. 13
Aramis..........	Aug. 26	Aug. 29	Aug. 3	Sept. 5	Sept. 7	Sept. 12	Sept. 19	Sept. 22	Sept. 23	Sept. 27
Jean Laborde ..	Sept. 9	Sept. 12	Sept. 14	Sept. 19	Sept. 21	Sept. 26	Oct. 3	Oct. 6	Oct. 7	Oct. 11
Athos II.........	Sept. 23	Sept. 26	Sept. 28	Oct. 3	Oct. 5	Oct. 10	Oct 17	Oct. 20	Oct. 21	Oct. 25
Felix Roussel	Oct. 7	Oct. 10	Oct. 12	Oct. 17	Oct. 19	Oct. 24	Oct. 30	Nov. 2	Nov. 3	Nov. 8
Marechal Joffre..	Oct. 21	Oct. 24	Oct. 26	Oct. 31	Nov. 2	Nov. 7	Nov. 13	Nov. 16	Nov. 17	Nov. 22

Marseilles—East Africa and Madagascar.

Subject to alteration or cancellation without notice.

s.s. *General Metzinger* .. 9312 tons.
s.s. *Explorateur Grandidier* 10267 ,,
s.s. *Bernardin de St. Pierre* .. 10085 ,,
s.s. *Gen. Metzinger*......... 9212 ,,
s.s. *Compiegne* .. .. 9986 tons
s.s. *Chantilly* .. .. 9986 ,,
s.s. *Ville de Verdun* .. 7006 ,,
s.s. *Porthos* .. .. .. 12692 ,,

Vessel	Marseilles dp 12.0	Port Said ar./dp.	Suez	Djibouti	Aden	Mombasa	Zanzibar.	Dar-es-Salaam	Tamatave	La Reunion arr.	Mauritius, arr.
Porthos	July 26	July 31	Aug 1	Aug. 5	—	Aug 12	Aug. 13	Aug. 18	Aug 21	Aug. 24	Aug 25
Compiegne....	Aug. 10	Aug 15	Aug 16	Aug 20	—	Aug 27	Aug. 28	Aug. 28	Sept. 4	Sept. 7	Sept. 8
Bernardin de St. Pierre	Aug. 24	Aug 29	Aug 30	Sep. 3	—	Sep. 10	Sept. 11	Sept. 11	Sep. 19	Sept. 22	Sep 23
Expl. Grandidier	Sept. 7	Sep 14	Sep. 13	Sep 17	—	Sep. 24	Sept. 25	Sept. 25	Oct. 2	Oct. 5	Oct. 6
Gen. Metzinger	Sept 21	Sep. 26	Sep. 27	Oct. 1	—	Oct. 8	Oct. 9	Oct. 9	Oct. 16	Oct. 19	Oct. 20
Chantilly	Oct. 5	Oct. 10	Oct. 11	Oct 15	—	Oct. 21	Oct. 22	Oct. 22	Oct. 30	Nov. 2	Nov. 3
Leconte de Lisle	Oct. 19	Oct. 24	Oct. 25	Oct. 29	—	Nov. 4	Nov. 5	Nov. 5	Nov 13	Nov. 16	Nov 17

Calling also regularly at Majunga, Nossi-Bé, Diego-Suarez and occasionally at Moheli, Moroni, Mutsamudu and Mayotte.

Vessel	Mauritius dep.	La Reunion dep.	Tamatave	Dar-es-Salaam	Zanzibar.	Mombasa.	Aden	Djibouti	Suez	Port Said	Marseilles. arr.
Gen. Metzinger	July 22	July 29	Aug. 1	Aug. 9	Aug 9	Aug. 10	Aug. 15	Aug 16	Aug. 20	Aug. 21	Aug 26
Chantilly	Aug. 12	Aug. 19	Aug 22	Aug. 30	Aug 30	Aug. 31	Sept. 5	Sept. 6	Sep. 10	Sept. 11	Sep. 16
Porthos....	Aug 26	Sept. 2	Sept. 5	Sept. 13	Sep. 13	Sep 14	Sep. 19	Sept 20	Sep. 24	Sept. 25	Sep. 30
Compeigne	Sept. 8	Sept. 15	Sep. 18	Sept. 26	Sep 26	Sep. 27	Oct. 2	Oct. 3	Oct. 7	Oct. 8	Oct. 14
Bernardin de St Pierre	Sep. 23	Sept 30	Oct. 3	Oct. 10	Oct. 10	Oct. 11	Oct. 16	Oct. 17	Oct. 21	Oct. 22	Oct. 28
Expl. Grandidier	Oct. 6	Oct 13	Oct. 16	Oct. 24	Oct. 24	Oct. 25	Oct. 31	Nov. 1	Nov. 5	Nov. 6	Nov 11
Gen. Metzinger	Oct. 20	Oct. 27	Oct. 30	Nov. 7	Nov. 7	Nov. 8	Nov 14	Nov 15	Nov 19	Nov. 20	Nov 25

Calling also at Diego-Suarez, Nossi-Bé, Majunga ; and occasionally at Mayotte, Mutsamudu, Meheli and Moroni.

Services Contractuels des MESSAGERIES MARITIMES—*cont.*

INDO—CHINA LINE.

Marseilles, Port Said, Djibouti, Colombo, Pondicherry, Madras, Singapore Saigon, Tourane, Haiphong.

STEAMERS	Tons	Marseilles dep 12.0	Port Said. arr.	Djibouti, arr	Aden. arr.	Colombo arr	Madras. arr	Pondicherry arr.	Singapore. arr.	Saigon, arr.	Tourane	Haiphong arr.
Andre Lebon..	13681	Aug. 9	Aug 14	Aug 18	—	Aug 25	Aug. 27	Aug 28	Sept. 2	Sept. 4	Sept. 8	Sept. 9
D'Artagnan ..	15105	Sept. 6	Sept 11	Sep 15	—	Sep. 22	Sept. 24	Sept. 25	,, 30	Oct. 2	Oct. 6	Oct. 7
Sphinx........	11374	Oct. 4	Oct. 9	Oct. 13	—	Oct. 20	Oct. 22	Oct. 23	Oct. 28	,, 30	Nov 3	Nov. 4
Andre Lebon ..	13681	Nov. 1	Nov. 6	Nov 10	—	Nov 17	Nov. 19	Nov. 20	Nov. 25	Nov 27	Dec. 1	Dec. 2
D'Artagnan ..	15105	,, 29	Dec. 4	Dec. 8	—	Dec 15	Dec. 17	Dec. 18	Dec. 24	Dec 26	Jan. 1	Jan. 3
Sphinx..... ..	11874	Dec. 27	Jan. 1	Jan. 5	—	Jan. 12	Jan. 14	Jan. 15	Jan. 20	Jan 22	,, 26	,, 27
					—							

STEAMERS	Tons	Haiphong / Tourane.	Saigon.	Singapore.	Madras.	Pondicherry.	Colombo.	Aden.	Djibouti.	Suez.	Port Said.	Marseilles arr.
Sphinx	11374	July 22/23	Jly. 27	July 29	Aug. 3	Aug. 5	Aug. 7	—	Aug 15	Aug 18	Aug. 19	Aug 24
Leconte de Lisle	9876	Aug. 22/23	Aug 27	Aug 29	Sept. 4	Sept. 5	Sept. 7	—	Sep 16	Sep. 20	Sept. 21	Sept. 26
Andre Lebon .	13681	Sept. 16/17	Sep. 21	Sep 23	,, 28	,, 30	Oct. 2	—	Oct. 10	Oct. 13	Oct. 14	Oct. 19
D'Artagnan ..	15105	Oct. 14/15	Oct. 19	Oct. 21	Oct. 26	Oct. 27	Oct. 30	—	Nov. 6	Nov. 9	Nov 10	Nov. 15
Sphinx ...	11874	Nov. 11/12	Nov 16	Nov 18	Nov 23	Nov. 24	Nov 27	—	Dec. 4	Dec. 7	Dec. 8	Dec. 13
Andre Lebon ..	13681	Dec. 9/10	Dec 14	Dec 16	Dec 21	Dec. 22	Dec 25	—	Jan. 1	Jan. 4	Jan. 5	Jan. 10
D'Artagnan	15105	Jan. 6/7	Jan 11	Jan 13	Jan 18	Jan. 19	Jan 22	—	Jan. 29	Feb. 1	Feb. 2	Feb. 7

BRANCH LINES IN CONNECTION WITH SERVICES SHOWN ON PAGES 389–390.

Via Quinhon and Tourane.

Saigon to Haiphong (in connection with China—Japan Mail Line, page 389). Sailing every 14 days.

Diego-Suarez to ports on Coasts of Madagascar: (*a*) West Coast—About every 31 days, Nossi-Bé, Ananalave, Majunga, Maintirano, Morundava, Morombe, Tulear.
(*b*) East Coast—About every 40 days, Vohemar, Sambava, Antalaha, Moroantsetra, Sainte Marie, Fenerive, Tamatave, Vatomandry, Mahanoro Mananjary, Manakara, Farafangana, Fort Dauphin.
Inter-insular service in the New Hebrides and voyages to the Wallis Islands.
Inter-insular service in Oceania.

AUSTRALIA—NEW HEBRIDES AND AUSTRALIA—INDO CHINA.

Steamer.	Sydney dep.	Noumea arr./dep.	Vila arr./dep.	Luganville	Saigon arr/dep.	Haiphong	Port Vila	Noumea arr./dep.	Sydney arr.

Details of Sailings on application.

a Calls Dart. *b* Calls Mare, Norsup, Port Sandwich.
c Calls Saku des Maskelynes. *d* Calls Mare.

NEW CALEDONIA *via* THE PANAMA CANAL.

(see page 457).

Compagnie de Navigation MIXTE (Cie. Touache).

El Djezair (Category A)	5800	*El Biar* (Category B) ..	4564	*Gouv. Genl. Lepine* (Cat. B)	3887
El Mansour Category A)	5800	*Gouv. Gen. Cambon* (Cat. B)	3737	*Djebel Aures* (Cat. D)......	—
El Kantara (Category A)	5100				

These Screw steamers, fitted with wireless telegraphy, carry first, second and third class passengers, and have in most cases cabins for one or two and more passengers, also family and "luxe" cabins. Smoking and dining room on deck, Bathroom. Passengers at Marseilles embark at Quai de la Joliette.

I.—Port Vendres, Algiers. (Mail Service)

RAPIDE, usually by s.s. *El Kantara.*

Tu., Fri.	10 0	dp. Port Vendres ar. ▲	ar.	15 0	Thu., Su.
We., Sat.	6 30	▼ ar. Algiers......	dp.	19 0	We., Sat.

II.—Port Vendres-Oran.

(Mail Service).

RAPIDE. Usually by s.s. *El Mansour.*

Wed., Su.	10 0	dp. Pt. Vendres ar ▲	ar	18 0	Tue. Fri
Thu., Mo.	9 30	▼ ar. Oran	dp.	16 0	Mo, Thu.

IV.-Marseilles-Bona-Philippeville.

Usually by s.s. *El Djezair.*

(dep. from and arr. Quai de la Joliette).

To Aug 17.		From Aug. 24.	
Marseilles, d.	Thu. 11 0	Marseilles, d.	Thu. 11 0
Bona......a.	Fri. 7 0	Phil'ville ..a	Fri 7 0
Bona......d.	Fri 15 0	Phi 'ville ..d.	Fri. 7 30
Phil'ville ..a.	Fri. 19 0	Bona.......a.	Fri. 1130
Phil'ville ..d.	Sat. 11 0	Bona..... d.	Fri. 17 0
Marseilles, a.	Sun. 8 0	Phil'ville . a	Fri. 21 0
		Phil'ville ..d.	Sat. 11 0
		Marseilles, a	Sun. 8 0

V.-Marseilles-Tunis.

Usually by s.s. *El Biar.*

(Depart from and arrive at Quai de la Joliette).

Marseilles	Tues. 11 0
Tunis	Wed. 15 0
Tunis	Thu. 10 0
Marseilles	Fri 14 0

III.—Marseilles—Algiers.

a By s.s. *El Djezair.* *b* By s.s. *G. G. Cambon.*

a	*b*		*a*	*b*
Mo. 11 0	We. 1130	dp. Marseilles ar.	We. 10 0	Sa. 1130
Tu. 7 0	Th. 1130	ar. Algiers.. dp.	Tu. 12 0	Fr. 10 0

PARTENOPEA Societa Anonima di Navigazione.

Steamers usually leave from the Molo Beverello. This should be confirmed in Naples.

(Line 91). CAPRI—NAPLES.

Daily.		Daily.
7 0	dep. Capri ...... arr. ▲	2015
7 25	arr. Mass'brense dep.	1950
7 30	dep. ,, arr.	1945
7 45	arr. Sorrento....dep.	1930
8 0	dep. ,, arr.	1915
9 15	▼ arr. Naples ....dep.	18 0

(Line 92) (Luxe). NAPLES-SORRENTO-CAPRI.

(Daily).

9 0	dep.	Naples	arr. ▲	19 5
1010	arr.	Sorrento	dep.	1755
1025	dep.	,, ...	arr.	1740
11 5 ▼	arr.	Capri	dep.	17 0

(Line 93). NAPLES—CAPRI—AMALFI.

(Daily except Holidays).

17 0	dep. Naples.. arr. ▲	9 20
1820	arr. Capri ..dep.	8 0
1835	dep. ,, .. arr.	7 40
1945	arr. Positano dp.	6 35
1950	dep. ,, arr.	6 30
2030 ▼	arr. Amalfi dep.	6 0

(Line 94). SALERNO—AMALFI (POSITANO).

Salerno dep. daily 13.15, *via* Maiori, Minori, Atrani, arr. Amalfi 14.35, Positano 15†30; dep. Positano 6†30, Amalfi 7.30, daily *via* same ports, due Salerno 8.50. † Between Amalfi and Positano April 15—Oct. 15 on Mons., Wed., and Sats. only.

PALESTINE MARITIME LLOYD.

s.s. *Har Zion*, 2493 tons, carrying 1st and 2nd class passengers.

HAIFA—ISTANBUL—CONSTANZA and *vice versa.* (Fortnightly).

Haifa. dep. 24.0	Port Sa'd, Beyrout, Tripoli, Cyprus, or Rhodes.*	Tel-Aviv. arr. 6.0 dep. 14.0	Constanza. arr. 7.0	Constanza. dep. 20.0	Istanbul. arr. dep. *	Tel-Aviv.** arr. 6.0	Tel-Aviv.** dep. 6.0	Haifa. arr. 18.0
Aug. 3	—	Aug. 4	Aug. 5*a*	Aug. 5*b*	—	—	—	Aug. 6*c*
,, 17	—	,, 18	,, 19*a*	,, 19*b*	—	—	—	,, 20*c*
,, 31	—	Sept. 1	Sept. 2*a*	Sept. 2*b*	—	—	—	Sept. 3*c*

a arr. 5.0. *b* dep. 14.0 *c* arr. 5.0.

* Optional calls. ** Weather permitting.

PAQUET LINE.

(COMPAGNIE DE NAVIGATION PAQUET).

See also page 460.

The steamers of this Company carry First and Second class passengers and are fitted with bath rooms, Wireless Telegraphy and Electric light. Stewardess and Surgeon are carried.

Marseilles and Morocco Ports. Express Service.

By s.s. *Chella*, 10800 tons, s.s. *Koutoubia*, 10800 tons, s.s. *Djenne*, 10800 tons, s.s. *Marechal Lyautey*, 10500 tons, s.s. *Medie II*, 8850 tons.

SAILINGS:

Steamers.	Marseilles. dep. 11.0	Tangier. arr. 9.0 dp. ab't 16.0	Casablanca. arr. 7.0	Casablanca. dep. 18.0	Tangier. arr. 6.0 & dp.	Marseilles. arr. 6.0-7.0
Djenne	July 29	July 31	Aug. 1	Aug. 5	Aug. 6	Aug. 8
Djenne	Aug. 12	Aug. 14	,, 15	,, 19	,, 20	,, 22
Koutoubia	,, 19	,, 21	,, 22	,, 26	,, 27	,, 29
Koutoubia	,, 30	Sept. 1	Sept. 2	Sept. 2	Sept. 3	Sept. 5
Djenne	Sept. 2	,, 4	,, 5	,, 5	,, 6	,, 8
Koutoubia	,, 6	,, 8	,, 9	,, 9	,, 10	,, 12
Djenne	,, 9	,, 11	,, 12	,, 12	,, 13	,, 15
Koutoubia	,, 13	,, 15	,, 16	,, 16	,, 17	,, 19
Djenne	,, 16	,, 18	,, 19	,, 19	,, 20	,, 22
Koutoubia	,, 20	,, 22	,, 23	,, 23	,, 24	,, 26
Djenne	,, 23	,, 25	,, 26	,, 26	,, 27	,, 29
Koutoubia	,, 27	,, 29	,, 30	,, 30	Oct. 1	Oct. 3
Djenne	,, 30	Oct. 2	Oct. 3	Oct. 3	,, 4	,, 6
Koutoubia	Oct. 4	,, 6	,, 7	,, 7	,, 8	,, 10

Boat Train Paris—Marseilles Quay. Special boat train leaves Paris (Gare de Lyon) at 21.15 on Friday, due Marseilles Quay at 9.10. Passengers embark by 9.0-10.0 at Mole A, Hanger 2.

South Morocco Service *via* Tangier to Casablanca, Saffi, Mogador, etc.

(Fortnightly)

s.s. *Le Rhin*, 4650 tons, Aug. 10, etc. s.s. *Oued Sebou II*, 5050 tons, Aug. 24, etc.

↓		↑
Thur.	Marseilles ..	Mon.
Fri.	Sete‡	—
Sun.	Oran§	Fri.
Mon.	Tangier	Thur.
Tues.	Mazagan ..	—
Wed.	Casablanca	Wed.
Thur./Fri.	Saffi	Mon./Tues.
Sat.	Mogador ..	—
Sun.	Agadir	Sun.

‡ From Sete to Morocco every 4 weeks, Aug. 11, etc.
§ From Oran to Morocco every 4 weeks, Aug. 13, etc.

m.s. *Basarabia* ..	6672 tons.	s.s. *Dacia*	3419 tons.	s.s. *Peles* ..	5700 tons.
m.s. *Transilvania*	6672 tons.	s.s. *Regele Carol I.*	2369 tons.	s.s. *Alba Julia* ..	5700 tons.
s.s. *Romania*	3151 tons.	s.s. *Ardeal*	5695 tons.	s.s. *Suceava*	5710 tons.

The above are twin screw steamers carrying 1, 2, & 3 cl. pass. Cabin accommodation consists of Cabins de Luxe, with 1 and 2 berths 1st class, Bathrooms, Smoking, Music and Reading Rooms in first Saloon. Electric Light. Wireless Telegraphy equipment. Stewards, Stewardess and Doctor carried. The *Dacia*, *Regele Carol I.* and *Romania* have also Gents' and Ladies' cabins with 3 berths.

Connection at Constanza with Bucharest for Simplon and Orient Expresses

All Services subject to alteration or annulment without notice.

Constanza—Istanbul—Piræus. {Alexandria—Haifa—Beyrout / Beyrout—Haifa—Alexandria} Piræus—Istanbul—Constanza.

m.s. *Transilvania*, Aug. 10, 24, Sept. 7, 21. m.s. *Basarabia*, Aug. 3, 17, 31, Sept. 14, 28.

Line I (Weekly).

arr.	dep.		arr.	dep.
Aug. 3, etc.	Thu. 21 0	Constanza .. ▲	Sun. 9 0	—
Fri. 8 0	Fri. 12 0	Istanbul	Sat. 18 0	Sat. 22 0
Sat. 8 0	Sat. 11 0	Piræus ..	Fri. 18 0	Fri. 22 0
Sun. 16 0	Mon. 16 0	Alexandria ..	Thu. 7 0	Th. 13 0
Tue. 7 0	Tue. 9 0	Tel Aviv ..	—	—
Tue. 12 0	Tue. 14 0	Haifa	—	—
Tues. 18 0	—	▼ Beyrout ..	Aug. 2, etc.	Wed. 12 0

Line II (Fortnightly).

s.s. *Dacia*, Aug. 7, Sept. 4, Oct. 2. s.s. *Romania*, Aug. 21, Sept. 18.

arr.	dep.		arr.	dep.
Aug. 7.	Mon. 21 0	Constanza.... ▲	Sat. 8 0	—
Tues. 13 0	Wed 9 0	Istanbul......	Fri. 12 0	Fri. 17 0
Thu 10 0	Thu. 18 0	Piræus	Thu. 7 0	Thu 11 0
Sat. 0	Sat. 17 0	Larnaca	Tues. 9 0	Tue 14 0
Sun. 7 0	Sun. 11 0	{Jaffa or Tel Aviv..}	—	—
Sun. 15 0	Sun. 24 0	Haifa	—	—
Mon. 6 0	—	▼ Beyrout	July 31.	Mon. 21 0

Danube—Mediterranean Line.

Passenger Service. Suspended until further notice.

s.s. *Alba Julia* and s.s. *Peles*. Steamers carry passengers "class unique" and "deck" only. From Galatz/Braila, ——— *via* Sulina, Constanza, Istanbul, Thessaloniki, Piræus, Izmir†, Malta, Tripoli or Tunis, Naples or Genoa†, Marseilles, Oran†, Algiers†, Malta†, Piræus, Istanbul, Constanza, Sulina, Galatz (Braila).

U.S.S.R. STEAMERS. (See also page 408).

Odessa—Istanbul—Piræus—Haifa and *vice versa* (Fortnightly).

☞ Subject to alteration without notice.

s.s. *Svanetia*, 5000 tons.

Odessa Dep. 16.0	Istanbul arr. 15.30 dep 10.0	Piræus arr. 10.15 dep. 18.0	Haifa arr. 14.30 dep 20.0	*Port Said arr. 8.0 dep. 18.0	Piræus arr. 11.0 dep. 17.0	Istanbul arr. 17.30 dep. 12.0	†Constanza arr. 1.30 dep. 6.30	Odessa arr. 11.30
July 25	Jly. 26/27	July 28	July 30	July 31	Aug. 2	Aug. 3/4	Aug. 5	Aug. 5
Aug. 8	Aug. 9/10	Aug. 11	Aug. 13	Aug. 14	,, 16	,, 17/18	,, 19	,, 19
,, 22	,, 23/24	,, 25	,, 27	,, 28	,, 30	,, 31/Sep. 1	Sept. 2	Sept. 2
Sept. 5	Sept. 6/7	Sept. 8	Sept. 10	Sept. 11	Sept. 13	Sep. 14/15	,, 16	,, 16
,, 19	,, 20/21	,, 22	,, 24	,, 25	,, 27	,, 28/29	,, 30	,, 30
Oct. 3	Oct. 4/5	Oct. 6	Oct. 8	Oct. 9	Oct. 11	Oct. 12/13	Oct. 14	Oct. 14
,, 17	,, 18/19	,, 20	,, 22	,, 23	,, 25	,, 26/27	,, 27	,, 28
,, 31	Nov. 1/2	Nov. 3	Nov. 5	Nov. 6	Nov. 8	Nov. 9/10	Nov. 11	Nov. 11

* Landing or embarking not allowed. † Optional call.

BLACK SEA SERVICE. ODESSA-BATUMI and *vice versa*.

s.s. *Armenia*, 6000 tons; s.s. *Gruzia*, 6000 tons, or other vessel.

Odessa dep.	22 0	Batumi dep.	19 0 1st day
2nd day Sevastopol dep.	1740	Yalta arr.	5 5 4th ,,
3rd ,, Yalta.. .. ,,	1 5	Sevastopol arr.	1230 4th ,,
5th day Batumi arr. at	1015	Odessa arr.	7 40 5th ,,

Calling also at Evpatoria, Feodosia, Novorossisk, Tuapse, Sochi, Gagri, Sukhumi and Poti.

From Odessa Aug. 2, 3, 5, 7, 9, 11, 12, 14, 16, 18, 20, 21, 23, 25, 27, 29, 30.

From Batumi Aug. 2, 4, 6, 7, 9, 11, 13, 15, 16, 18, 20, 22, 24, 25, 27, 29, 31.

Mediterranean Services.

See also pages 404, 459 and 466.

**Ville d'Oran*	9760	§*Gouverneur Gen. Grevy*	4865	§*Timgad*	5282
†*Ville d'Alger*	9760	§*Gouv. Gen. de Gueydon*	4513	§*Duc d'Aumale*	4452
†*De Grasse*	18435	§*Gouv. General Jonnart*	4513	§*Charles Roux*	4145
§*Gouverneur General Chanzy*	4384	§*Lamoriciere*	4713	§*Pres. Dal Piaz*	4900

These Steamers carry 1st, 2nd, 3rd and 4th class passengers. The *Ville d'Alger* has special single and two-berth cabins, also apartment de luxe, and the *De Grasse* single and deck cabins with bath. On the "Grande Rapides," luxe, demi-luxe, also special single and ten-berth cabins.

† Extra Rapide. § Grande "Rapides."

Services Marseilles (Quai de la Joliette), Algiers and *vice versa*. Subject to modification.

	s.s. *Ville d'Alger* and s.s. *Ville d'Oran*	Except s.s. *Ville d'Alger* and s.s. *Ville d'Oran*
Marseilles ....dep.	11 0	11 0
Algiers ....arr.	7 0	10 30 next day.

	s.s. *Ville d'Alger* and s.s. *Ville d'Oran* *Thur.*	*Sun.*	Except s.s. *Ville d'Alger* and s.s. *Ville d'Oran*
Algiers .....dep.	11 30	14 0	10 0
Marseilles ...arr.	8 0	10 30	10 30 next day

Sailings from Marseilles: s.s. *Ville d'Alger*, Aug. 1, 12, 15 26, 29, Sept 2. 5, 9, 12, 16, 19, 23, 26, 30; s.s. *G. G. Jonnart* Aug. 3, 10, 17, 24 31, Sept. 7, 14, 21, 25, 28; s.s. *Ville d'Oran*, Aug. 5, 8, 19, 22; s.s. *G.G. Chanzy*, Aug. 6, 20, Sept. 3, 17, 30; s.s. *G. G. Gueydon* Aug. 13, 27, Sept. 10, 24.

Sailings from Algiers: s.s *G G. Gueydon*, Aug. 1, 15, 29. Sept. 12, 26; s.s. *Ville d'Alger*, Aug. 3, 13, 17, 27, 31, Sept. 3, 7, 10, 14, 17 21, 24, 28; s.s. *G G. Jonnart*, Aug. 5, 12, 19, 26, Sept. 2, 9, 16, 23, 26, 30; s.s. *Ville d'Oran* Aug. 6, 10, 20, 24; s.s. *G. G. Chanzy*, Aug. 8, 22, Sept. 5, 19.

Marseilles, Oran. (Weekly).

Steamers start from and arrive at "C" Pier.

s.s. *Ville d'Oran.*

	arr.	dep.
Marseilles ..	—	Sun. 11 0
Oran	Mon. 1330	Tues. 14 0
Marseilles ..	Wed. 1730	—

Marseilles—Philippeville—Bone—Marseilles.

s.s. *G. G. Gueydon*, Aug. 8, 22; Sept. 5, 19.
s.s. *G. G. Chanzy*, Aug. 1, 15, 29; Sept. 12, 26.

	arr.	dep.
Marseilles	—	Tu 11 0
Philippeville..	We. 9 30	Th. 11 0
Marseilles	Fri. 1130	—

s.s. *G. G. Gueydon*, Aug. 4, 18; Sept 1, 15, 29.
s.s. *G. G. Chanzy*, Aug. 11; Sept. 8, 22.
s.s. *Lamoriciere*, Aug. 25.

	arr.	dep.
Marseilles	—	Fri 11 0
Bone	Sat. 1030	Su. 10 0
Marseilles	Mo. 1130	—

Marseilles—Tunis.

To July 29.
s.s. *Lamoriciere*, Aug. 5, 12, 19.
s.s. *Pres. Dal Piaz*, Aug. 26.
From Aug. 31, Thurs. and Sats.

Marseilles ....dep.	Sat. 11 0
Tunis .... arr.	Sun. 15 0
,, ...dep	Tues. 11 0
Marseilles ....arr.	Wed. 15 0

Marseilles—Bizerta—Tunis

Accelerated Service (Weekly).

s.s. *G. G. Grevy.*

	arr.	dep.
Marseilles	—	Wed. 11 0
Bizerta ¶	Thu. 1230	Thu. 24 0
Tunis ¶	Fri. 6 0	Fri. 24 0
Bizerta ¶	Sat. 5 0	Sat. 9 0
Marseilles	Sun. 1030	—

¶ In connection with arrivals at and departures from Bizerta, Motor Coaches run between Bizerta and Tunis, the journey occupying 60 minutes.

Boat Train Paris—Marseilles Quay. When the Tunis steamer leaves on same day as the Algiers steamer, passengers for Tunis can travel by the special train mentioned above.

Services subject to alteration or suspension owing to Strikes, etc.

"TIRRENIA" SOCIETA ANONIMA di NAVIGAZIONE.

Stewardess carried on all vessels.

Line 1. **NAPLES—PALERMO** and *vice versa.* (Daily).

By m.v. *C. of Tunisi*, 5418 tons, *C. of Palermo*, 5418 tons, *C of Genova*, 5418 tons, *C. of Napoli*, 5418 tons.

Naples	—	dep. 2230†¶	Palermo ..	—	dep. 19 0††
Palermo ..	arr. 9 25†	,, —	Naples ..	arr. 6 5	—

† The steamer from Naples on Wednesday proceeds to Tunis in Line 2. The steamer from Naples on Friday proceeds to Tripoli in Line 29. ¶ May be delayed 1 hr. to await arrival of Train R. 55, due Naples (Central), 21.55; 25 or 35 minutes to await Train 85 due Naples (Marittima), 22.0.

†† The steamer of Line 2 arriving from Tunis at Palermo on Saturday proceeds to Naples, and the steamer from Tripoli, Line 29, on Monday continues from Palermo to Naples in Line 1.

Line 2. **NAPLES—PALERMO—TUNIS** and *vice versa.* (Weekly).

By m.v. *C. of Tunisi*, 5418 tons, *C. of Palermo*, 5418 tons, *C. of Genova*, 5418 tons, *C. of Napoli*, 5418 tons.

—	dep. Wed. 2230	Naples .... ↑	arr. Sun. 6 5	—	* See note after Line 1.
arr. Thur. 9 25	,, Thur. 1830	Palermo....	,, Sat. 8 0	dep. Sat. 19 0	
,, Fri. 7 30	—	↓ Tunis	—	,, Fri. 19 0	

Daily. **Line 3.—Civitavecchia, Terranova.** s.s. *Olbia* or *Caralis.*

Civitavecchia......dep.	20 20	Terranova ....dep.	22 0
Terranova .... ..arr.	6 5	Civitavecchia ....arr.	7 45

Line 5.—Napoli—Cagliari.—Weekly.

C. of Bengasi, 2818 tons; *Citta di Tripoli*, 2933 tons.

—	dep. Tues. 8 0	Naples .... ↑	arr. Thur. 15 0	—
arr Wed. 7 0	—	↓ Cagliari	—	dep. Wed. 16 0

Line 8.—Genoa—Bastia—Porto Torres.—Weekly. m.v. *C. of Spezia*, 2474 tons.

—	dep. Fri. 22 0	Genoa .... ↑	arr. Thur. 7 0	dep. —	All departures may be delayed.
arr. Sat. 7 0	,, Sun. 0 30	Leghorn ..	,, Wed. 17 0	,, Wed. 22 0	
,, Sun. 7 30	,, Sun. 15 0	Bastia	,, Wed. 8 0	,, Wed. 11 0	
,, Mon. 7 0		↓ Porto Torres	—	,, Tues. 1730	

Line 15.—Genoa, Cagliari, Tunis.—Weekly.

m.v. *Arborea*, 4959 tons; s.s. *Garibaldi*, 5278 tons; s.s. *Praga*, 3741 tons; s.s. *Aventino*, 3781 tons.

—	dep. Wed. 24 0	Genoa.............. ↑	arr. Sun. 17 0	—
arr. Thur. 8 0	,, Thur. 20 0	Leghorn............	,, Sun. 6 0	dep. Sun. 10 0
,, Fri. 8 0	,, Fri. 12 0	Civitavecchia	,, Sat. 9 0	,, Sat. 18 0
,, Sat. 8 0	,, Sat. 20 0	Cagliari..........	,, Fri. 7 0	,, Fri. 13 0
,, Sun. 13 0	,, Sun. 1630	Trapani	—	—
,, Mon. 7 30	—	↓ Tunis	—	dep. Thur. 13 0

Proceeding to Malta and Tripoli in Line 26. Coming from Tripoli and Malta in Line 26.

Line 16. **PALERMO—TRAPANI—PANTELLERIA—TUNIS**—Fortnightly.

Aug. 4th, etc.	dep. Fri. 24 0	Palermo .. ↑	arr. Sat. 22 0†	—	Calling also at Mazzara del Vallo and Pantelleria. May also call at Castellammare Golfo.
arr. Sat. 7 0	,, Sat. 10 0	Trapani....	,, Sat. 12 0	dep. Sat. 15 0†	
,, Sat. 12 0	,, Sat. 16 0	Marsala....	,, Fri. 20 0	,, Sat. 10 0†	
,, Sun. 19 0	—	↓ Tunis	Aug. 10th, etc.	,, Thur. 1730	

Proceeding to Tripoli in Line 27. Coming from Tripoli in Line 27.

† May leave earlier.

Line 6. **GENOA-EAST SARDINIA-CAGLIARI-PALERMO**-(Fortnightly). By m.v. of 2480-2499 tns.

Aug. 7th, etc.	dep Mon. night†	Genoa .... ↑	arr. Mon. p.m	—	† May be delayed outward.
arr Tues. a.m.	,, Tues. a.m.	Spezia	,, Mon. a.m.	dep. Mon. a.m.	Calls also optionally at Siniscola, Orosei, Dorgali, Marsala and Castellammare del Golfo, Tortoli out and home.
,, Tues p.m.	,, Wed. night	Leghorn ..	,, Sun. p.m.	,, Sun. night	
,, Thur. a.m.	,, Thu.* p.m.	Portoferraio	,, Sun. a.m.	,, Sun. a.m.	
,, Fri. a m.	,, Fri. a.m.	Maddalena	,, Sat. p.m.	,, Sat. p.m.	
,, Fri. a.m.	,, Fri. a.m.	Palau	,, Sat. p.m.	,, Sat. p.m.	
,, Fri. p.m.	,, Fri.* p.m.	Terranova..	,, Fri. p.m.	,, Sat. noon	
,, Sun. a.m.	,, Tues. 13 0	Cagliari	,, Thur. 8 0	,, Thur* p.m.	
,, Wed. 6.30	,, Wed. a.m.	Trapani....	,, Wed a.m.	,, Wed. 1430	
,, Wed. p.m.	—	↓ Palermo ..	Aug. 7th, etc.	,, Mon. 23 0	* May leave earlier

N.B.—Steamers may leave later from all ports

Line 7. **GENOA—WEST SARDINIA—CAGLIARI—PALERMO**—(Fortnightly).

July 31st, etc.	dep Mon. night†	Genoa...... ↑	arr. Tues. p.m.	dep. —	† May be delayed outward
arr. Tues. a.m.	,, Tues. a.m.	Spezia	,, Tues. p.m.	,, Tues. p.m.	Calls at Capraia April-Sept.
,, Tues. p.m.	,, Wed. even'g	Leghorn....	,, Tues. a.m.	,, Tues. a.m.	Calls also optionally at S. Teresa di Gallura, Alghero, Bosa, Oristano, S. Antioco Castellammare del Golfo out and home.
,, Thur. a.m.	,, Thur. noon	Maddalena	,, Sun. a.m.	,, Mon. noon	
,, Thur. p m.	,, Thur. p.m.	Palau	,, Sun. a.m.	,, Sun. a.m.	
,, Thur. p m.	,, Fri.* night	Porto Torres	,, Sat. p.m.	,, Sat.* p.m.	
,, Sat. a m.	,, Sat. a.m.	Carloforte ..	,, Fri. a.m.	,, Fri.* p.m.	
,, Sat. even'g	,, Tues. 13 0	Cagliari	,, Thur. 8 0	,, Th.* night.	
,, Wed. 6.30	,, Wed. a.m.	Trapani	,, Wed. a.m.	,, Wed. 1430	
,, Wed. p m.	—	↓ Palermo....	July 31st, etc.	,, Mon. 23 0	

* May leave earlier. *N.B.—Steamers may leave later from all ports.*

Subject to alteration without notice owing to Quarantine, etc.

"TIRRENIA" Societa Anonima di Navigazione—*continued.*

Line 21.—Naples, Syracuse, Malta, Tripoli.—Every 2 weeks.

arr.	dep.		arr.	dep.
Aug. 8, etc.	Tues. 15 0†	Naples ↓ ↑	Sat. 10 0	—
Wed. 10 0	Wed. 13 30	Catania	Fri. 12 0	Fri. 15 0
Wed. 16 30	Wed. 22 0	Syracuse	Fri. 6 0	Fri. 9 0
Thur. 7 0	Thur. 14 0	Malta	Thur. 15 30	Thur. 22 0
Fri. 7 0	—	Tripoli	Aug. 2, etc.	Wed. 23 0

Line 22.—Naples—Messina—Syracuse—Malta—Tripoli.

Every 2 weeks.

arr.	dep.		arr.	dep.
Aug. 1, etc.	Tues. 15 0†	Naples	Sat. 9 0	—
Wed. 6 0	Wed. 10 30	Messina	Fri. 15 0	Fri. 18 0
,, 16 30	,, 22 0	Syracuse	Fri. 6 0	Fri. 9 0
Thur. 7 0	Thur. 14 0	Malta	Thur. 15 30	Thur. 22 0
Fri. 7 0	—	Tripoli	Aug. 9, etc.	Wed. 23 0

May call at Riposto. † May be delayed 1 hour.

Line 23.—Syracuse, Tripoli.—Weekly.

m.v. *Citta di Trieste*, 4658 tons.

arr.	dep.		arr.	dep.
—	Sun. 19 0*	Syracuse	Sun. 6 0	—
Mon. 17 30	—	Tripoli	—	Sat. 7 30

* May wait 35 minutes.

Line 24.—Naples, Syracuse, Bengasi.—Fortnightly.

s.s. *Citta di Bengasi*, 2813 tons. s.s. *Citta di Tripoli*, 2933 tons.

1st Voyage every 4 weeks.

arr.	dep.		arr.	dep.
Aug. 11, etc.	Fri. 15 0†	Naples	Mon. 10 0	—
Sat. 6 0	Sat. 10 30	Messina	—	—
—	—	Catania	Sun. 12 0	Sun. 15 0
Sat. 16 30	Sat. 21 0	Syracuse	Sun. 6 0	Sun. 9 0
Mon. 7 0	—	Bengasi	July 28, etc.	Fri. 18 0

2nd Voyage every 4 weeks.

arr.	dep.		arr.	dep.
July 28, etc.	Fri. 15 0†	Naples	Mon. 9 0	—
—	—	Messina	Sun. 15 0	Sun. 18 0
Sat. 10 0	Sat. 13 30	Catania	—	—
Sat. 16 30	Sat. 21 0	Syracuse	Sun. 6 0	Sun. 9 0
Mon. 7 0	—	Bengasi	Aug 11, etc.	Fri. 18 0

May proceed from Bengasi to Derna (arr. Wed. at 8.0 and dep. at 16.0). May also call Riposto.
† May be delayed 1 hour.

Line 25.—Syracuse, Bengasi.—Weekly.

Itinerary A.

Weekly. / *Fortnightly.*

arr.	dep.		arr.	dep.
—	Sat. 21 0	Syracuse	Sat. 6 0	Su. 6 0
Mo. 7 0	—	Bengasi	Th. 18 0	Fri. 18 0
			Aug 3, etc.	July 28 etc.

Itinerary B (Fortnightly).

arr.	dep.		arr.	dep.
Aug. 9	Wed. 21 0	Syracuse	Wed. 6 0	—
Fri. 7 0	—	Bengasi	July 31	Mo. 18 0

Line 26.—Tunis, Tripoli & *vice versa.*

(Coming from Genoa in Line 15). (Proceeding to Genoa in Line 15).

Itinerary A (Fortnightly).

arr.	dep.		arr.	dep.
July 31, &c.	Mo. 12 0	Tunis	Th. 8 0	—
Tue 10 0	Tu. 14 0	Malta	We. 8 0	We. 12 0
We. 7 0	—	Tripoli	Aug. 1	Tu‡ 13 0

Itinerary B (Fortnightly).

arr.	dep.		arr.	dep.
Aug 7, &c.	Mo. 12 0	Tunis	Th. 8 0	—
Tue 10 0	Tue 14 0	Malta	We. 8 0	We. 12 0
We. 7 0	Th. 23 0	Tripoli	Sun 6 0	Tu. 1‡30
Sat. 6 0	Sat. 16 0	Bengasi§	Mo. 8 § 0	Fri. 18§0
Sun 8 0	—	Derna	July 30	Su. 16 0

§ During stay at Bengasi, the steamer proceeds in Line 25. (Itinerary B to Syracuse and back.
May call Susa and/or Sfax. ‡ May leave earlier

Subject to alteration without notice, owing to Quarantine, &c.

"TIRRENIA" Societa An. di Navigazione—*cont.*

Subject to alteration or annulment without notice owing to Quarantine, &c.

See also page 481.

Line 27.—Tunis—Sfax—Tripoli—(Fortnightly).

The steamer may depart from or arrive earlier at all ports.

Coming from Palermo in Line 16. Continuing to Palermo in Line 16.

Aug. 7, etc.	dep. Mon. 1830	Tunis ...... ↑	arr. Thur. 8 0	—	* Optional call. If calling Zuara, arrival Tripoli on Friday a.m
arr. Tues. 11 0	„ Tues. 16 0	Susa	„ Wed. 8 0	dep. Wed. 16 0	
„ Wed. 12 0	„ Wed. 21 0	Sfax	„ Mon. 16 0	„ Tues. 12 0	
„ Thur. 3 0	„ Thur. 9 0	Gerba......	„ Mon. 8 0	„ Mon. 10 0	
„ Thur. *	„ Thur. —	Zuara	„ Sun. 6 0	„ Sun. 20 0	
„ Thur. 23 0	—	↓ Tripoli	Aug. 5, etc.	„ Sat. 22 0	
Proc'ds in Line 28				(Coming from Line 28).	

Line 28.—Tripoli—Bengasi—Tobruk—Alexandria—(Fortnightly).

Coming from Tunis in Line 27. Continuing to Tunis in Line 27.

July 29, etc.	dep. Sat. 22 0	Tripoli .... ↑	arr. Fri. 6 30	—	*N B.—Itinerary subject to variation according to requirements.*
arr. Sun 6 0	„ Sun. 12 0	Homs......	„ Thur. 18 0	dep. Thur 22 0	The ports of Zaira and Buerat may also be called at.
„ Sun. 1430	„ Mon. 4 0	Sliten......	„ Thur. 13 0	„ Thur. 15 0	† May dep. earlier.
„ Mon. 8 0	„ Mon. 20 0	Misurata ..	„ Thur 7 0	„ Thur 9 0	
„ Tues. 9 0	„ Tues. 16 0	Sirte	„ Wed. 13 0	„ Wed 20 0	
„ Wed. 12 0	„ Thur. 18 0	Bengasi	„ Mon. 8 0	„ Tues 16 0	
„ Fri. 7 0	„ Fri. 24 0†	Apollonia ..	„ Sun 16 0	„ Sun. 20 0	
„ Sat. 6 0	„ Sat. 21 0	Derna......	„ Sun. 9 0	„ Sun. 12 0	
„ Sun. 7 0	„ Sun. 22 0	Tobruk	„ Sat. 16 0	„ Sat. 24 0	
„ Mon. 6 0	„ Mon. 10 0	Port Bardia	„ Sat. 7 0	„ Sat. 9 0	
„ Tues. 11 0	—	↓ Alexandria	July 28, etc.	„ Fri. 6 0	

Line 29.—(Naples)—Palermo—Tripoli—(Weekly.)

m.v. *Citta di Tunisi*, 5418 tons. | m.v. *Citta di Genova*, 5413 tons. | m.v. *Citta di Palermo*, 5413 tons.

arr.	dep.		arr.	dep.	
	Fri. 22 30	Naples* .... ↑	Wed. 6 5	—	* See note after Line 1.
Sat. 9 25	Sat. 13 0	Palermo....	Tues. 13 15	Tues. 19 0	
Sun. 11 45		↓ Tripoli	—	Mon. 14 30	

"TIRRENIA" Societa Anonima di Navigazione—*continued.*

Line 32. Fiume—Genoa—Marseilles—Spain and *vice versa* Weekly.

m.v. *Puccini*, (2422 tons), m.v. *Rossini* (2425 tons), m.v. *Paganini* (2427 tons), m.v. *Verdi* (2428 tons), m.v. *Catalani* (2428 tons), m v *Donizetti* (2428 tons). The new motor vessels of this line have saloon accommodation for 28 passengers, but do not carry stewardess or doctor. Fitted with electric light.

Itinerary subject to alteration.)

arr.	dep.	↓	arr. ↑	dep.
—	Mon. 19 0	Fiume	Sat 6 0	—
Tues. 7 0	Wed. 18 0	Venice	—	—
—	—	Trieste	Wed. 6 0	Fri. 18 0
Thur. 6 0	Thur. 13 0	Ancona	—	—
—	—	Fiume	Tues 12 0	Tues. 20 0
Fri. 7 0	Fri. 20 0	Bari	Mon. 6 0	Mon 12 0
Sun. 6 0	Mon. 18 0	Catania	Fri. 5 0	Sat. 20 0
Tues 6 0	Tues. 17 0	Malta¶	Thur. 8 0	Thur. 18¶0
Wed. 14 0	Wed 18 0	Messina	Wed. 6 0	Wed 18 0
Thur. 6 0	Thur. 18 0	Palermo	Tues 7 0	Tues. 20 0
Fri. 8 0	Sat. 12 0	Naples	Sun. 20 0	Mon. 17 0
Sun. 10 0	Sun. 22 0	Leghorn	Sat. 6 0	Sat. 18 0
Mon. 6 0	Mon. 24 0	Genoa	Wed. 14 0	Fri. 22 0
—	—	Savona	Tues. 15 0	Wed. 12 0
Tue. 4 0	Tue. 14 0	Imperia	Tues. 8 0	Tues 12 0
Wed. 6 0	Wed. 12 0	Marseilles	Mon. 6 0	Mon. 18 0
Thur. 6 0	Thur. 20 0	Barcelona	—	—
Fri. 1 0	Fri. 18 0	Tarragona	—	—
Sat. 6 0	—	Valencia	—	Sat. 18 0

¶ After Malta, may call at Riposto.

LINE 9. TERRANOVA—LA MADDALENA (Daily).

	↓	↑
6 50 dep.	Terranova	arr. 2020
7 40 arr.	Golfo Aranci	dep. 1930
7 55 dep.	Golfo Aranci	arr 1915
‡1020 arr.	La Maddalena	—
1140 dep.	La Maddalena	—
1155 arr.	Palau	—
1225 arr.	La Maddalena	dep. 1650

‡ Coinciding with steamer to Bonifacio (Line 11).

LINE 11 and 11 bis. LA MADDALENA—PALAU. (Weekdays).

	↓	↑
*7 45 dep.	La Maddalena	arr. 1915*
*8 0 arr.	Palau	dep. 19 0*†
*8 15 dep.	Palau	arr. 18 0*§
*8 30 arr.	La Maddalena	dep. 1745*
1030†dep.	La Maddalena	arr. 1645
1045 arr.	Palau	dep. —
1325 arr.	Bonifacio	dep. 14 0

* Also Sundays, (Line 11 *bis*). † May be delayed.
§ Coinciding with Auto-Post to Terranova, etc.

LINE 12. CARLOFORTE—CALASETTA. Daily.

arr.	dep.	↓	arr. ↑	dep.
—	6 25	Carloforte	1130	—
6 55	7 20	Calasetta	1040	11 0
7 50	—	Carloforte	—	1010

LINE 13. CARLOFORTE—PORTOVESME. Daily.

		↓	↑	
—	8 10	Carloforte	1715	—
8 55	9 10	Porto Vesme	1545	1630
9 55	—	Carloforte	—	1500

Line 10. Genoa—Sardinia—Genoa. Fortnightly.

	arr.	dep.
Genoa	Aug. 10th, etc.	Thur. p.m.
La Maddalena	Fri. p.m.	Sat. a.m
Porto Torres	Sat. p.m.	p m.
Carloforte	Mon. a m.	Tues. a m.
Cagliari	Tues. p.m.	—

Calling a'so S. Teresa G., Castelsardo, Alghero, Bosa, Oristano, S. Antioco, Teulada (optional)

	arr.	dep.
Cagliari	Aug. 3rd, etc.	Thur. a.m.
Torrevecchia	Thur. a.m.	Thur. a.m.
Terranova P.	Fri. p.m.	Sat. a.m.
La Maddalena	Sat. a.m.	Sat. a.m.
Genoa	Wed. p.m.	—

Calling also Muravera, Tortoli, Dorgali, Orosei, Siniscola, Oneglia and Savona (optional)

Line 38. Genoa—Majorca—Spain.

s.s. *Firenze.* Service about Aug. 4 and every 20 days.

	arr.	dep.
Genoa	—	1st day at 17 0
Palma	3rd day at 8 30	3rd ,, ,, 18 0
Malaga	5th ,, ,, 6 0	5th ,, ,, 24 0
Ceuta	6th ,, ,, 6 0	6th ,, ,, 10 0
Tangiers	6th ,, ,, 13 0	6th ,, ,, 15 0
Cadiz	6th ,, ,, 19 0	7th ,, ,, 15 0
Seville	8th ,, ,, 6 0	—

	arr.	dep.
Seville	—	10th day at 18 0
Cadiz	11th day at 16 0	12th ,, ,, 8 0
Tangiers	12th ,, ,, 12 0	12th ,, ,, 15 0
Ceuta	12th ,, ,, 18 0	12th ,, ,, 23 0
Malaga	13th ,, ,, 6 0	13th ,, ,, 18 0
Palma	15th ,, ,, 12 0	16th ,, ,, 20 0
Genoa	18th ,, ,, 9 0	—

May call at Imperia and Ibiza.

TRANSPORTS MARITIMES À VAPEUR. (Société Générale De)

Passengers embark at Marseilles at the Quai de la Joliette, Mole J.3. [See also page 464]

FLEET—MEDITERRANEAN LINES.

Steamers.	Tons.	Steamers.	Tons.	Steamers.	Tons.	Steamers.	Tons.
Sidi-Mabrouk ..	3882	*Sidi-Bel-Abbes*	4500	*Gouvr. General Tirman* ..	3737	*Sidi-Aissa* ..	2600
Sidi-Brahim ..	2600	*Sidi-Okba* ..	2900			*Ipanéma* ..	4300

All the steamers are fitted with Electric Light. Cabins of two, three and four berths. s.s. *Sidi-Mabrouk* and s.s. *Sidi-Brahim* have also single and two berth "Priority" cabins with Toilette, two, three and four berth cabins.

Dep. Marseilles from Quai de la Joliette, Mole J. 3.

Marseilles—Oran. (Mail Service.)

s.s. *Sidi-Bel-Abbes* and s.s. *Sidi Brahim*.
(Category B). (Category D).
Twice Weekly.

Marseilles ..	dep.	Wed. 1730	Sat. 1730
Oran	arr.	Fri. 6 0	Mon. 6 0
,, ...	dep.	Sat. 17 0	Wed. 17 0
Marseilles ..	arr.	Mon. 6 0	Fri. 6 0

Marseilles—Algiers—Bougie.

s.s. *Gouvr. General Tirman* and s.s. *Sidi-Mabrouk*.
(Category B). (Category D).
Twice Weekly.

Marseilles ..	dep.	Wed. 1130	Sat. 1730
Algiers	arr.	Thur. 20 0	Sun. 20 0
,, ...	dep.	—	—
Bougie	arr.	Fri. 12 0	—
,, ...	dep.	Fri. 20 0	—
Algiers	arr.	—	—
,, ...	dep.	Sat. 17 0	Wed. 10 0
Marseilles ..	arr.	Mon. 6 0	Thur 13 0

Marseilles—Bona—Philippeville
Marseilles—Philippeville—Bona

s.s. *Ipanéma* (Weekly).

	arr.	dep.
Marseilles	—	Tues. 1730
Bona or Philippeville	Thur. 6 0	Thur. 20 0
Philippeville or Bona	Fri. 6 0	Sat. 8 30
Marseilles	Sun. 18 0	—

Marseilles—Sète—Oran or Mostaganem.

s.s. *Sidi-Okba* (Category D).
s.s. *Sidi Aissa* (Category D).

dep. Mon. 20 0 ↓	Marseilles	↑ Mon. 4 0
,, Tues. 15 0 ↓	Sète..........	—
arr. Thur. 7 0 ↓	Oran or Mostaganem..	Sat. 8 0

Subject to confirmation.

VILLAIN & FASSIO Steamship Navigation Co.

Genoa—Majorca—Seville Service. (Every 20 days.)

s.s. *Franca Fassio*, 2100 tons, fitted with Electric Light, Wireless Telegraphy, Stewardess.
Carrying 1st and 3rd class passengers. Cabins de luxe.

Genoa ....dep. about Aug. 14 and Sept 2.	Seville ....dep.
Palma (Majorca), arr.	Palma (Majorca), arr.
,, dep.	,, dep.
Seville.......... arr.	Genoa .... arr.

ZETSKA PLOVIDBA A.D., CETINJE.

s.s. *Lovcen*, from Susak, Aug. 26; from Constanza, Aug. 9, Sept. 6.

Calls also outward Vlone, Sarande.

arr.	dep	↓	arr.	dep.
—	Sat. 18 0	Sušak	*Sun. 18 0	—
Sun. 6 0	Sun. 13 0	Venice	Sun. 10 0	—
Mon. 8 0	Mon. 21 0	Sibenik	—	—
Tues. 7 0	Wed. 2 30	Split	Sat. 7 0	Sat. 12 0
Wed. 7 0	,, 10 0	Dubrovnik 2	Fri 9 30	Fri. 21 0
,, 1830	,, 20 0	Kotor	Thur. 1630	,, 5 0
Thur. 6 0	Thur. 12 0	Durazzo	,, 6 0	Thu. 7 0
Fri. 7 0	Fri. 10 0	Kerkyra (Corfu)	Wed. 6 0	Wed. 13 0
Sat. 9 0	Sat. 18 0	Piræus	Mon. 8 0	Mon. 19 0
Sun. 14 0	Sun. 17 0	Izmir	Sat. 18 0	Sun. 12 0
Mon. 20 0	Tues. 14 0	Istanbul	Fri. 7 0	Fri. 16 0
Wed. 9 0	—	Constanza .... ↑	—	Wed. 23 0

Calls also homeward Varna, Burgas, Izmir, Sarande, Vlone.

* Trieste, arrives Sušak, Saturday 6.0.

TRASMEDITERRANEA COMPANIA.

See also page 465.

Steamer.	Tons.	Steamer.	Tons.	Steamer.	Tons
s.s. *Rey Jaime I*	2800	s.s. *J. J. Sister*	—		

Steamers carry 1, 2 and 3 cl. passengers, and are fitted with Elec. Light. Stewardesses carried.

Line I—Malaga-Melilla, &c.

dep. Malaga,
dep. Melilla.

Line IV—Algeciras-Ceuta. (Passg. 1½ hrs.

Algeciras, dep.
Ceuta, dep
} Daily Service.

Almeria—Melilla. (Weekly)

Melilla—Ceuta. (Weekly)

Algeciras—Tangier. (Daily.)

Algeciras, dep.
Tangiers, dep.
} Suspended (Passage 3 hours.)

Valencia—Barcelona. Passage 11 hrs.

s.s. *J. J. Sister*.
From Valencia, Thurs., Sats. at 20.c.
From Barcelona, Tues., Fris .at 20.c.

Barcelona—Cartagena.

Barcelona, dep. Thurs. 6 c Cartagena, dep Sun 6 c.

Barcelona-Alicante-Oran-Ceuta.

(Weekly).

Barcelona		
Alicante		
Oran............		
Melilla		
Alhucemas		
Ceuta		
Alhucemas		
Melilla		
Almeria		
Melilla		
Oran............		
Alicante		
Barcelona		

† Passengers must call before 12 o noon at Co.'s Office with Passports.

B'rc'lona-Valencia-Gandia-B'rc'lona

Barcelona		
Valencia		
Gandia		
Barcelona		

Spain—Balearic Islands.

Screw Steamers.	Tons.	Screw Steamers.	Tons.	Screw Steamers.	Tons.
**Ciudad de B'rcelona* (m v.)†‡	4950	§*Balear*†	999	*Formentera*	112
**Ciudad de Palma* (m.v.) †‡	4950	§*Rey Jaime II.*†	1350	*Delfin*	625
§*Mallorca*†*	2300	§*Tintore*†*	1323	*Mahon*	636
§*Rey Jaime I.*†*	2300	*Ciudad de Alcudia*	173	*Monte Toro*	851
§*Bellver*†	1250	*Atlante* ..	1446		

First and Second class passengers carried. † Electric Light on these vessels. Two and four berthed cabins on all steamers. * One and two berthed cabins; twin screw. ‡ On these vessels, suites with sitting-room, berth, etc., also special cabins with bathroom, etc. § Fitted with Wireless Telegraphy.

s.s. *Rey Jaime I*.

Bar'lona—Palma (Rapide).	Palma—Bar'lona (Rapide)
Tues., Thurs., Sats. 20 c	Mons., Weds., Fris. 20 c
Passage, 11 hours.	Passage, 11 hours.

Barcelona—Mahon.

Barcelona, dep
Mahon, dep.
} Passage 13 hours.

Barcelona—Alcudia—Mahon.

arr.	dep.		arr.	dep.
		↓ Barcelona .. ↑		
		Alcudia		
		Mahon		

Ciudadela—Alcudia. (Passage 4 hours.)

Ciudadela, d. | Alcudia, d.

Palma—Ciudadela. Passage 11½ hours.)

Palma, dep. | Ciudadela, dep.

Valencia—Ibiza—Palma.

arr.	dep.		arr.	dep.
		↓ Valencia .. ↑		
		Ibiza		
		Palma		

Barcelona—Ibiza. (Passage 14½ hours.)

Barcelona, dep | Ibiza, dep.

Ibiza—Formentera. (Passage ½ hour.)

From Ibiza,
From Formentera,

Palma—Mahon. Passage 10 hours.

Palma, dep. | Mahon, dep.

Tarragona—Palma.

Tarragona, dep. | Palma, arr.
Palma dep. | Tarragona arr.

Palma—Cabrera.

From Palma,
From Cabrera,

Alicante—Ibiza—Palma.

arr.	dep.		arr.	dep.
		↓ Alicante.... ↑		
		Ibiza		
		Palma		

Valencia—Palma.

Valencia dep. | Palma arr.
Palma dep. | Valencia arr.

Services subject to alteration or suspension owing to Strikes, etc.

ALPHABETICAL SUMMARY OF SAILINGS from England and Scotland to Norway, Sweden. Denmark, Finland, Russia and Iceland Compiled from latest information to hand at time of going to press.

To	From	Departures	Duration	Company
Abo	Hull	Fortnightly (in summer)	4½ days	Finland Line
Bergen	Newcastle	Three sailings weekly.	26 to 33 hours	B & N. Line
Christiansand	Hull	Weekly	32 hours	Ellerman's Wilson Line
Copenhagen	Goole	Fridays	53 hours	Associated Humber Lines
,,	Hull	Weekly	50 hours	Ellerman's Wilson & Forenede Lines
,,	Leith	Weekly	56 hours	Currie Line
,,	Leith	See page 271	2½ days	Forenede Line
,, †	Newcastle	Weekly	50 hours	Ellerman's Wilson & Forenede Lines
,,	Hull	Weekly	Weekly	Finland Line
,,	London	Fortnightly	3 days	Ellerman's Wil. L (car. s.s.)
Danzig	London	Fortnightly	5 days	United Baltic Corporation
,,	Hull	Weekly	4 days	Polish British S. S. Co.
,,	London	Fortnightly	4 days	Polish-British S.S. Co.
Esbjerg	Harwich	W'days (daily Jly.-Aug.)	23 hours	Forenede Line
,,	Grimsby	Twice weekly	30 hours	Forenede Line
Gdynia	London	Fortnightly	4 days	United Baltic Corporation
Gothenburg	London	Two sailings weekly.	40/46 hours	Swedish Lloyd
,,	Newcastle	Weekly	—	Swedish Lloyd
,,	Hull	Weekly	—	Ellerman's Wilson Line
Helsingfors	Hull	Weekly	4½ days	Finland Line
,,	London	Weekly (Summer)	6 days	Finland Line
Leningrad	London	W'kly (except in Winter)	5 days	U.S.S.R. Steamers
Malmö	London	Fortnightly	5 days	Svea S S Co
,,	Hull	Fortnightly	2 days	Ellerman's Wilson Line
Memel	London	Fortnightly	5 days	United Baltic Corporation
Oslo	Hull	Weekly	6 days	Ellerman's Wilson Line
,,	Newcastle	Twice Weekly	48 hours	Fred Olsen Line
Reykjavik	Leith	See page 421	5 days	Iceland S S. Co.
Riga	London/Newc'sl	Fortnightly	4 days	United Baltic Corporation
Stavanger	Newcastle	Weekly	5 days	B. & N. Line
Stockholm	London	Fortnightly	4 days	Ellerman's Wilson Line
,,	London	Fortnightly	4 days	Svea Line.
,, *via* Rot'dam	London	Weekly	7 days	Svea Line
Tallinn (Reval)	London	Fortnightly	4 days	United Baltic Corporation

† Or other Danish port.

By TRANSATLANTIC LINES—ENGLAND TO CONTINENTAL PORTS.

To	From	Company.	Duration.	Page
Amsterdam	Southampton	Nederland Line—Royal Dutch Mail	22 hours	364
,,	Plymouth	Hamburg-American	—	450
,,	Plymouth	Royal Netherlands S.S. Co.		456
Antwerp	Southampton	Red Star	18 hours	402
Boulogne	London | Plymouth	Blue Star Line	—	444
,,	S'ampton or Plymouth	Hamburg-South America	12 hours	451
,,	London	Royal Mail Lines Ltd.	6/7 hours	461
,,	Plymouth	Holland-America	14 hours	406
,,	Southampton	Hamburg-American		450
Bremen	Southampton	Norddeutscher Lloyd	20 hours†	407
,,	Southampton	Hamburg-American	24 hours	406
Cherbourg	Southampton	Cunard White Star Ltd.	5 hours	404
,,	Southampton	Canadian Pacific	4½/5½/6½ hr.¶	403
,,	Southampton	Norddeutscher Lloyd	3½–4 hours¶	407
,,	Plymouth & S'hampt'n	Hamburg-American	—	406 and 450
,,	Southampton	Royal Mail Lines Ltd.	6 hours	461
Hamburg	Southampton	Hamburg-American	24 hours	406
,,	Plymouth	Hamburg-American	2 days	450
,,	Plymouth	United States Lines	2 days	409
,,	Plymouth or S'ampton	Hamburg-South America	34 hours	451
Havre	Plymouth	French Line (Cie Transatlantique)	7/8/9/10 hr.¶	404
,,	Southampton	French Line (Cie Transatlantique)	5 hours	404
,,	Plymouth	United States Lines	—	409
,,	Plymouth	Cunard White Star Ltd.	—	404
,,	London	Cunard White Star Ltd.	15 hours	404
,,	Southampton	Cunard White Star Ltd.	8½ hours	404
,,	Plymouth	Royal Netherlands S.S. Co.	—	456
Rotterdam	Southampton	Rotterdam Lloyd	17 hours	368
,,	Plymouth	Holland-America	Abt 26 hrs.	406
,,	Southampton	Norddeutscher Lloyd.	1 day	365

¶ Length of passage varies according to steamer. † By "cabin" steamer, a few hours longer.

CROSS CHANNEL and NORTH SEA SERVICES, &c., &c.

United Kingdom to Continental Ports (Gibraltar and Ports North thereof) Norway, Denmark, Sweden, U.S.S.R., &c.

Argo Shipping Co. .. .. .. PAGE 402
Associated Humber Lines, 402, 405, 406, 407, 410
Batavier Line 402
Bergenske & Nordenfjeldske S.S. Cos. .. 403
Bibby Line 403
Blue Funnel Line 403
Canadian Pacific 403
Carregadores Acoreanos Line 403
Cunard White Star Ltd. 404
Currie Line 407
Ellerman Line 410
Ellerman's Wilson Line 410
Finland Line 404
Forenede Line 404
Fred Olsen's S.S. Lines 405
French Line 404
General S.N. Co. 405
Guernsey, Alderney and Sark S.S. Co. .. 405
Hamburg America Line 406
Holland S.S. Co. 406
Holland America Line 406
Hull and Netherlands S.S. Co., Ltd. .. 407
Jersey St. Malo Mail Service 409
London, Midland & Scottish Railway PAGE 409
Leith, Hull & Hamburg S.P. Co., Ltd. .. 407
London & North Eastern Railway Co. .. 406
Moss Hutchison Line 407
Nippon Yusen Kaisya 407
Nordenfjeldske & Bergenske S.S. Cos. .. 403
Norddeutscher Lloyd 407
Olsen Line 405
Plymouth, C. Islands & Brittany S.S. Co. 407
Polsko-Brytyiskie Tow Okre Towe S.A. (Polish-British S.S. Co.) 407
Red Star Line 402
Sark Motor Ships Ltd. 407
Southern Rly. Co. (S.S. Service Jersey, St. Malo) 409
Svea S.S. Co. 408
Svenska Lloyd (Swedish Lloyd) 408
Transatlantique (Cie. Gle.) 404
Tyne Tees Steam Shipping Co. Ltd .. 409
U.S.S.R., London-Leningrad .. 408
Union-Castle Line 410/2
United Baltic Corporation, Ltd. 409
United States Lines 409

ARGO SHIPPING CO.

See also page 414.

s.s. *Albatross*, 1350 tons. s.s. *Adler*, 1500 tons. s.s. *Habicht*, 1500 tons. s.s. *Schwan*, 1500 tons. s.s. *Reiher*, 1500 tons.

From HULL (Wm. Wright Dock) to BREMEN every Tuesday and Friday at 17.0. From BREMEN to HULL every Tuesday and Saturday. Passage 32 hours.

HULL—HAMBURG. From Albert Dock, Hull, every Tues. and Sat.; from Hamburg on Weds. and Sats. Passage 32 hours.

LONDON—BREMEN. From London (Regents Canal Dock) every Sat. and Wed. From Bremen Hafen 1, Shed 2, Sats and Tues. passage 36 hours,

ASSOCIATED HUMBER LINES.

For Details of Services:—

From GOOLE (L.M.S.), see page 405. From HULL (Hull and Netherlands S.S. Co.), see page 407.
From GRIMSBY/HULL (L.N.E.R.), see p. 406. From HULL (Ellerman's Wilson Line), see p 410.

BATAVIER LINE.

Batavier II .. 1573 | *Batavier III*, .. 1700 | *Batavier IV* .. 1568 | *Batavier V* .. 1573

The above are Screw vessels carrying First and Second class passengers. They are fitted with Cabins of 1, 2 and 4 berths First class, separate Ladies' cabin, and Electric light. A Stewardess is carried.

The Steamers have glass-enclosed decks.

London to Rotterdam. (See page 136).

RED STAR LINE.

(See also page 459).

Cross Channel Sailings by Transatlantic Liners.

s.s. *Westernland* (16,500 tons); s.s. *Pennland* (16,322 tons).

Steamer.	Antwerp. dep.	Southampton.	Steamer.	Southampton.	Antwerp. arr.
Westernland	Aug. 5	Aug. 6	*Pennland*	Aug. 14	Aug. 15
Pennland	,, 19	,, 20	*Westernland*	,, 28	,, 29
Westernland........	Sept. 2	Sept. 3	*Pennland*	Sept. 11	Sept. 12
Pennland	,, 16	,, 17	*Westernland*	,, 25	,, 26
Westernland	,, 30	Oct. 1	*Pennland*	Oct. 9	Oct. 10
Pennland	Oct. 14	,, 15	*Westernland*	,, 23	,, 24
Westernland	,, 28	,, 29	*Pennland*	Nov. 6	Nov. 7

B. & N. LINE.

See also pages 414, 415 & 444.

B. BERGENSKE S.S. CO., Bergen.
N. NORDEN-FJELDSKE S.S. CO., Trondheim.

Service—Newcastle-on-Tyne to Bergen and *vice versa*.

m.v. *Vega*, 7287 tons. m.v. *Venus*, 5600 tons.

The above Vessels, fitted with Electric Light and usually run on the undermentioned lines. They carry first and second class passengers, have Bedstead cabins (first class), Bathroom, Ladies' cabins, etc., and carry Stewardesses. The m.v. *Vega* and m.v. *Venus* have also Suite de Luxe, Cabin with Bath. Wireless telegraphy.

Newcastle—Stavanger—Haugesund—Bergen. *Vega.*	*Venus.*				Bergen—Haugesund—Stavanger—Newcastle. *Vega.*	*Venus.*
Tues. & Sat. 1930	Mo. & Th. 1930	dep.	Newcastle .. (T.C. Quay)	arr.	Tue. & Fri. 8 0	Thu. & Sun. 1230
Wed. & Sun. 1330	—	arr.	Stavanger	dep.	—	Wed. & Sat. 18 0
,, ,, 14 0	—	dep.	,, ...	arr.	—	,, 1645
,, ,, 16 0	—	dep.	Haugesund ..	dep.	—	,, 15 0
,, ,, 2030	Tu. & Fri. 1630	arr.	Bergen..	dep.	Mon. & Thu. 11 0	,, 11 0

Passengers leave LONDON (King's Cross) Mons. at 13.5; Tues. at 13.5, Thurs. at 13.5; Sats. at 12.0 (13.5 from Sept. 16); due Tyne Commission Quay between 18.0 and 19.8.

From NEWCASTLE (T.C. Quay) Suns. at 13.40; Tues. and Fris. at 8.40 (also 10.0 "Silver Jubilee"—extra charge); Thurs. at 13.40.

BIBBY LINE. (See also page 357).

CONTINENTAL CRUISES, 1939.

Date	Dep. London Steamer	Tons	L'pool arr.	Date	Dep. London Steamer	Tons	L'pool arr.
Aug. 5 (b)	*Shropshire*	10560	Aug. 18				

(b) Hamburg and Antwerp.

Special Programme on application from all Cook/Wagons-Lits Offices.

COASTAL CRUISES— BLUE FUNNEL LINE. (See also pages 358, 442 and 481).

Steamer	Tons	London dep.	Rotterdam arr.	Rotterdam dep.	Glasgow arr.	Steamer.	Tons	London dep.	Rotterdam arr.	Rotterdam dep.	Glasgow arr.
Sarpedon	11321	Aug. 10	Aug. 11	Aug. 12	Aug. 16	*Antenor*	11174	Oct. 4	Oct. 5	Oct. 6	Oct. 10
Patroclus	11314	Sept. 7	Sept. 8	Sept. 9	Sept 13						

Special programmes on application from all Cook/Wagons-Lits Offices.

CANADIAN PACIFIC. (See also pp. 459 and 472).

CROSS-CHANNEL SERVICES BY TRANSATLANTIC LINERS.

Empress of Britain ..	42500	*Montcalm*	16400	*Montclare*	16400
Empress of Australia ..	21850	*Montrose*	16400	*Duchess af Richmond*	20022

All Sailings subject to alteration with or without notice.

Southampton—Cherbourg.

Steamer	Date
Empress of Britain..	Aug. 5
Empress of Australia	,, 12
Empress of Britain	,, 19
Empress of Australia	,, 26
Empress of Britain..	Sept. 2
Empress of Australia	,, 9
Empress of Britain..	,, 16
Montrose	,, 20
Empress of Australia	,, 23
Empress of Britain	,, 30

Cherbourg—Southampton.

Steamer	Date
Empress of Britain	Aug. 3
Empress of Australia	,, 10
Empress of Britain	,, 17
Empress of Britain	,, 31
Empress of Britain	Sept. 14
Empress of Britain	,, 28
Empress of Australia	Oct. 7
Empress of Britain ..	,, 12
Empress of Britain	,, 26

Havre—Southampton.

Steamer	Date
Montrose	Sept. 15
Montrose	Oct. 8
Montrose	Nov. 5

CARREGADORES ACOREANOS LINE. See also page 443).

s.s. *Pero d'Alenquer* (2593 tons), s.s. *Corte Real* (1972 tons). No Stewardess or Doctor carried.

From LONDON about every 14 days *via* ANTWERP, ROTTERDAM, to PORTUGAL (without guarantee)

Steamer.	London. dep.	Antwerp. arr./dep.	Rotterdam arr./dep.	Oporto. arr./dep.	Lisbon. arr./dep.	Oporto. arr./dep.	London. arr.
			Sailings	*on applic*	*ation.*		

Round Trip about 30 days.

See also pages 459 & 481)

CUNARD WHITE STAR LTD.

CROSS CHANNEL SAILINGS BY TRANSATLANTIC LINERS (Subject to change without notice).

Southampton to Cherbourg.

Queen Mary	81235	Aug. 2	*Queen Mary*	81235	Sept. 13
Aquitania	45647	,, 9	*Queen Mary*	81235	,, 27
Queen Mary	81235	,, 16	*Aquitania*	45647	Oct. 4
Aquitania	45647	,, 23	*Queen Mary*	81235	,, 11
Queen Mary	81235	,, 30	*Aquitania*	45647	,, 18
Aquitania	45647	Sept. 6			

Southampton to Havre.

Mauretania	34000	Aug. 5	*Mauretania*	34000	Sep. 30
Georgic	27759	,, 13	*Carinthia*	20277	Oct. 6
Britannic	26994	,, 27	*Georgic*	27759	,, 8
Mauretania	34000	Sept. 2	*Britannic*	26994	,, 22
Carinthia	26277	,, 11	*Mauretania*	34000	,, 28
Georgic	27759	,, 16	*Franconia*	20175	Nov. 5
Britannic	26994	,, 24	*Scythia*	19761	,, 19

Cherbourg to Southampton.

Aquitania	45647	Aug. 8	*Queen Mary*	81235	Sept. 11
Queen Mary	81235	,, 14	*Aquitania*	45647	,, 19
Aquitania	45647	,, 22	*Queen Mary*	81235	,, 25
Queen Mary	81235	,, 28	*Queen Mary*	81235	Oct. 9
Aquitania	45647	Sept 5	*Aquitania*	45647	,, 17

Havre to Southampton.

Britannic	26994	Aug. 4	*Aurania*	13984	Sept. 1
Aurania	13984	,, 4	*Mauretania*	34000	,, 8
Mauretania	34000	,, 11	*Ascania*	14018	,, 8
Ascania	14013	,, 11	*Carinthia*	26277	,, 15
Georgic	27759	,, 18	*Ausonia*	13912	,, 15
Ausonia	13912	,, 18	*Georgic*	27759	,, 20
Alaunia	14030	,, 25	*Alaunia*	14030	,, 22
Britannic	26994	Sept 1	*Britannic*	26994	,, 29

FINLAND LINE.

See also page 417.

s.s. *Arcturus*, 3510 tons. s.s. *Ilmatar*, 3560 tons. s.s. *Aallator*, 3800 tons.

1st and 3rd cl. Elec. Light. 1, 2, 3 and 4-berthed cabins, 1st cl. 2 and 4-berthed cabins, 3rd cl. Bathrooms. Smoke rooms. 1st cl. Ladies Boudoir, &c. Stewardess carried. Wireless Telegraphy.

Hull—Copenhagen—Helsingfors

[Weekly.

s.s. *Aallator*, 3800 tons, and s.s. *Ilmatar*, 3560 tons.

arr.	dep.		arr.	dep.
—	Sat. p.m.	↓ Hull (Alexandra Dock, Shed 23) .... ↑	Wed. noon	—
Mon. p.m.	Tues. 14 0	Copenhagen (Free Harbour)	Mon. 8 0	Mon. 10 30
Thurs. 9 0	—	Helsingfors (South Harbour)	—	Sat. 13 0

Fortnightly.

Hull—Copenhagen—Åbo.

arr.	dep.	s.s. *Arcturus*, 3510 tons	arr.	dep.
Aug. 9, etc.	Wed. —*	↓ Hull (Alex. Dock) .. ↑	Sun. a.m.	—
Fri. p.m.	Sat., 14.0	Copenhagen (Free H.)	Fri. 8.0	Fri. 10.30
Mon. 8.0	—	Åbo	Aug. 2, etc.	Wed. 19.30

* According to tide.

London—Helsingfors.

s.s. *Polaris*, 3200 tons (60 1st cl berths); s s. *Juno* and s.s. *Leo* (limited accommodation.)

§ Wed. p.m. dep.	↓ London (Surrey Docks) ..... ↑	arr	Thurs. a.m.
Mon. a.m. arr.	Helsingfors (South Harbour)	dep.	Sat. 11.0 ¶

¶ *Juno* and *Leo* leave from Kotka at noon.

§ *Polaris* { from London, Aug. 9, 30, Sept 20. ,, Helsingfors. Aug. 19, Sept. 9, 30.

FORENEDE LINE

(See also pages 136, 406, 418/9, 459.)

Hull to Copenhagen.

s.s. *Spero*, 1568 tons. s.s. *Hroar*, 1401 tons.

From HULL—Fridays p.m. | From COPENHAGEN. Thursdays, about 18.0

Newcastle—Copenhagen (or other Danish Port).

s.s. *Diana*, 942 tons. Service from Newcastle Mondays/Tuesdays. s.s. *Hebe*, 957 tons.

Passengers embark at Copenhagen Wharf, Quayside, Newcastle. Passage about 50 hours. From Copenhagen *via* Aalborg, Thursdays, about 18.0.

FRENCH LINE. CIE. GÉNÉRALE TRANSATLANTIQUE.

(See also pages 394, 459, 466).

CHANNEL SERVICE BY TRANSATLANTIC LINERS.

s.s. *Normandie* .. 82799	s.s. *Paris* .. 34569	s.s. *Champlain* 28094	s.s. *Colombie* 13390
s.s. *Ile de France* .. 43450	s.s. *De Grasse* .. 18435	s.s. *Cuba* .. 11336	

PLYMOUTH (SOUTHAMPTON)—HAVRE.

Aug.	5	*Champlain*	Sept.	13	*Champlain*
,,	7§	*Normandie*	,,	15	*Ile de France*
,,	14	*Ile de France*	,,	18§	*Normandie*
,,	21§	*Normandie*	,,	27	*De Grasse*
,,	26	*Champlain*	Oct	2§	*Normandie*
,,	30	*Ile de France*	,,	3	*Champlain*
Sept.	4§	*Normandie*	,,	28	*Ile de France*

§ From Southampton, not Plymouth.

HAVRE—SOUTHAMPTON.

Aug.	1	*Ile de France*	Sept.	6	*Normandie*
,,	9	*Normandie*	,,	9	*De Grasse*
,,	10	*Champlain*	,,	16	*Champlain*
,,	16	*Ile de France*	,,	20	*Normandie*
,,	18	*De Grasse*	,,	27	*Ile de France*
,,	23	*Normandie*	,,	30	*De Grasse*
,,	29	*Champlain*	Oct.	4	*Normandie*
Sept.	1	*Ile de France*	,,	11	*Champlain*

FRED OLSEN'S S.S. LINES.

See also pages 423 & 448.

Newcastle to Oslo and *vice versa.*

m.v. *Black Watch*, 5,200 tons and m.v. *Black Prince*, 5,200 tons, carrying 1 cl. and 2 cl. passengers.

Black Watch	*Black Prince*		*Black Prince*	*Black Watch*
Wed. 13.5	Sat. 13.5	dep. London (King's Cross) arr.	Thur. 13.15	Mon. 13.15
Wed. 18.22*	Sat. 18.18*	arr. Newcastle (Central) ..dep.	Thur. 8.15	Mon. 8.15
Wed. 20.0	Sat. 20.0	dep. Newcastle (Quay) ....arr.	Thur. 6.0	Mon. 6.0
Thur. 18.0	Sun. 18.0	arr. Christiansand ......dep.	Wed. 7.0	Sun. 7 0
Fri. 7.0	Mon. 7.0	arr. Oslo ....dep.	Tues. 20.0	Sat. 20.0

* Through carriages will be attached to the 13.5 train to TYNE COMMISSION QUAY (Oslo Wharf).

GENERAL STEAM NAVIGATION COMPANY, Ltd.

Adjutant	1931	*Gannet*	1336	*Laverock*	1199	*Peregrine*	933	*Swift* ..	936
Albatross	1943	*Groningen*	1205	*Leeuwarden*	1209	*Petrel* ..	1354	*Starling* ..	1320
Auk	1338	*Heron*	2374	*Mavis*	935	*Rook* ..	1041	*Teal*	1444
Cormorant	1220	*Hirondelle*	893	*Merel*	1038	*Seamew*	1332	*Woodcock*	1561
Crane (m v.)	785	*Lapwing*	1348	*Philomel*	2115	*Stork* (m.v.)	787	*Woodlark*	1501
Falcon	1025								

LONDON-BORDEAUX–Cargo services, limited accommodation for passengers, no Stewardess carried. Depart London (British and Foreign Wharf) weekly on Saturday p.m., due Bordeaux on Tuesday. Homeward: Leave Bordeaux on Sat., due Southampton Mon. and London on Tues. or Wed.

LONDON—HAMBURG.—Cargo services with limited accommodation for passengers. No stewardess carried Sailings two or three times weekly each way.

LONDON—BREMEN. - Cargo steamer every Monday from London; every Thursday from Bremen.

LONDON—HARLINGEN.—From London, on Wed. and Sun.; from Harlingen, Wed. and Sat. (Passage 22 hours).

LONDON—AMSTERDAM.—From London on Sat.; from Amsterdam, Tues. (Passage 18-20 hours).

LONDON—ROTTERDAM.—From London on Wed.; from Rotterdam on Sat. (Passage 18-20 hours).

LONDON—ANTWERP. - Two sailings weekly, each way, from London Wed. and Sat., returning from Antwerp Tues. and Sat.

GUERNSEY, ALDERNEY & SARK STEAMSHIP CO., LTD.

In conjunction with SARK MOTOR SHIPS Ltd. See *p.* 407.

s.s. *New Fawn* and s.s. *Courier* will leave (weather and circumstances permitting), Guernsey for St. Malo, weekly, Guernsey for Poole, Poole for Guernsey fortnightly, when sufficient cargo.

GUERNSEY to ST. MALO. (Passage 5 hours).				**ST. MALO to GUERNSEY.** (Passage 5 hours).			
Aug. 6 ..	.. 6 0	Sept. 2 ..	.. 24 0	Aug. 6	.. 22 0	Sept. 3 ..	.. 20 0
Aug. 12 ..	.. 24 0	Sept. 9 ..	.. 24 0	Aug. 13 ..	.. 19 0	Sept. 10 ..	.. 1730
Aug. 20 ..	.. 6 0	Sept. 17 ..	.. 6 0	Aug. 20 ..	.. 21 0	Sept. 17 ..	.. 22 0
Aug. 26 ..	.. 24 0			Aug. 27 ..	.. 19 0		

Guernsey-Sark.—Daily except Suns., from Guernsey at 10.0; from Sark at 17.0.

Guernsey-Alderney.—From Guernsey, Mon., Wed., Fri. at 9.0; from Alderney, Mon., Wed. at 16.0; Sats., 6.30.

Guernsey-Jersey.—

ASSOCIATED HUMBER LINES. L.M.& S. SERVICES VIA GOOLE

(See also pages 406, 407 & 410).

Steamers.	Tons.	Steamers.	Tons.	Steamer.	Tons.	Steamers.	Tons.	Steamers.	Tons.
Alt ..	.. 1004	*Dearne*	.. 1046	*Hodder*	.. 1016	*Mersey*	.. 1037	*Rother*	.. 986
Aire	.. 1108	*Don* ..	.. 1038	*Irwell*	.. 1040	*Ouse*	.. 1004	*Rye* ..	.. 1048
Blyth	,, 1108	*Hebble*	.. 1040						

The above are screw steamers and carry a limited number of saloon passengers. Electric light.

List of Sailings‡ from and to GOOLE (weather and other circumstances permitting).

‡ Steamers leave Goole according to tide. Passage (approx.) Embarkation time must be ascertained in advance.

To		Passage	From	
ANTWERP	Weds. and Sats.	24 hrs.	ANTWERP	Tues. and Sats.§
GHENT	.. Sats.	23 ,,	GHENT	Tues.§
ROTTERDAM	.. Sats.	21 ,,	ROTTERDAM	Tues.§
COPENHAGEN ..	.. Fridays	60 ,,	COPENHAGEN	.. Thursdays
HAMBURG ..	Weds. and Sats.	32 ,,	HAMBURG	Mons. and Fris.§

§ Calling at Hull on the inward journey with fruit and perishables at ship's option.

☞ All sailings are subject to change or cancellation.

Channel Services by Transatlantic Liners. (To and from U.S.A.)

Steamer.	Tons.	Steamer.	Tons.	Steamer.	Tons.	Steamer.	Tons.	Steamer.	Tons
Deutschland	21000	*Hamburg*	21000	*Hansa* ..	21000	*New York*	21500	*St. Louis* (m.v.)	17000

Vessel.	Cobh.	Cherbourg	Southampton.	Hamburg.
Hamburg	Aug. 2	Aug. 3	Aug. 3	Aug. 4
New York	,, 9	,, 10	,, 10	,, 11
Hansa	—	,, 17	,, 17	,, 18
Deutschland	,, 23	,, 24	,, 24	,, 25
Hamburg	—	,, 31	,, 31	Sept.1
New York	—	Sept.7	Sept.7	,, 8
Hansa	—	,, 14	,, 14	,, 15
Deutschland	—	,, 21	,, 21	,, 22
Hamburg	—	,, 28	,, 28	,, 29
New York	—	Oct. 5	Oct. 5	Oct. 6
Hansa	—	,, 12	,, 12	,, 13
Deutschland	Oct. 18	,, 19	,, 19	,, 20
Hamburg	,, 25	,, 26	,, 26	,, 27
New York	—	Nov. 2	Nov. 2	Nov. 3

Vessel.	Hamburg. ‡	Bremerhaven dep. ‡	Southampton. dep.	Cherbourg	Cobh.
Deutschland	Aug. 3	—	Aug. 4	Aug. 4	Aug. 5
Hamburg	,, 10	Aug10	,, 11	,, 11	—
New York	,, 17	—	,, 18	,, 18	—
Hansa	,, 24	—	,, 25	,, 25	—
Deutschland	,, 31	—	Sept.1	Sept.1	—
Hamburg	Sept.7	—	,, 8	,, 8	—
New York	,, 14	—	,, 15	,, 15	—
Hansa	,, 21	—	,, 22	,, 22	—
Deutschland	,, 28	—	,, 29	,, 29	—
Hamburg	Oct. 5	—	Oct 6	Oct. 6	Oct. 7
New York ..	,, 12	—	,, 13	,, 13	—
Hansa	,, 19	—	,, 20	,, 20	—
St. Louis	,, 26	Oct. 26	,, 27	—	—

* Galway, not Cobh. † Calls also at Galway.

‡ For all vessels which are listed to sail from both Hamburg and Bremen, embarkation will take place at Bremerhaven. Passengers from Hamburg will be conveyed by special trains or carriages on day of sailing to Bremerhaven.

HOLLAND AMERICAN LINE. (See also pages 459 and 462).

CHANNEL SERVICES BY TRANSATLANTIC LINERS. (*Subject to change without notice*).

Nieuw Amsterdam, 33,000 tons; *Rotterdam*, 24,150 tons; *Volendam*, 15,480 tons; *Statendam*, 30,000 tons, *Veendam*, 15,450 tons.

Steamer.	Plymouth dep. (approx.)	Boulogne. arr.	Rotterdam. arr.
Statendam	Aug. 11	Aug. 11	Aug. 12
Veendam	,, 21	,, 21	,, 22
Nieuw Amsterdam	,, 21	,, 22	,, 22
Statendam	,, 31	Sept. 1	Sept. 1
Nieuw Amsterdam	Sept. 11	,, 12	,, 12

Steamer.	Rotterdam. ‡ dep.	Boulogne. dep.	Southampton. arr.
Nieuw Amsterdam ..	Aug. 4	Aug. 4	Aug. 4
Volendam	,, 12	,, 12	,, 12
Statendam	,, 15	,, 15	,, 15
Nieuw Amsterdam	,, 25	,, 25	,, 25
Veendam	,, 26	,, 26	,, 26

‡ Embark previous night. Passage Boulogne—Southampton 6½ hours.

HOLLAND STEAMSHIP COMPANY.

(R.V. HOLLANDSCHE STOOMBOOT MAATSCHAPPIJ).

LONDON (Fennings' Wharf, London Bridge)-AMSTERDAM (Handelskade, 9), and *v.v.* throughout the year. From London dep. on Weds. according to tide; from Amsterdam, on Saturday p.m.

LIVERPOOL—MANCHESTER SERVICE. (All the year round.) Dep. Manchester for Amsterdam every alternate Fri. p.m. (3½ days), Aug. 11, etc. Dep. Amsterdam for Liverpool every alternate Thurs. p.m. (3 days), Aug. 3, etc. Steamers carry 1 cl. passengers (two-berth cabins).

ASSOCIATED HUMBER LINES.

L.N.E.R. SERVICES *via* **GRIMSBY/HULL.** (See also pages 405, 407 and 410)

Accrington 1650 tons | *Bury* .. .. 1691 tons | *Stockport* .. 1688 tons | *Macclesfield* 1100 tons
Dewsbury .. 1686 ,,

The Steamers in the Hamburg Service are provided with modern improvements for the convenience of passengers, including dining saloon, smoking room, 2, 3 and 4 berth cabins, etc., etc. All passenger steamers equipped with wireless. Special attention is paid to the catering on the steamers, an excellent cuisine being provided.

Sailing Dates subject to alteration.

GRIMSBY to HAMBURG (Royal Mail Route). s.s. *Bury*. Sailings every Saturday about 19.0 (after arrival of boat train due 18.18 at Grimsby Docks), due Hamburg (Sandthor Quay) Monday at 7.0. From Hamburg (Sandthor Quay) steamers leave Wednesday about 18.0, due Grimsby, Friday at 7.0.

HULL (Riverside Quay) to HAMBURG (Royal Mail Route). s.s. *Stockport*. Every Wednesday at 18.30; due Hamburg (Sandthor Quay) on Friday at 7.0. Dep. Hamburg (Sandthor Quay) on Saturday at 18.0, and arr. Hull (Riverside Quay) Monday at 7.0. (*See also page 410 for services by cargo steamers with limited passenger accommodation*).

GRIMSBY to ESBJERG. Forenede S.S. Co's (page 418) steamers (average passage 30 hours) Steamer Twice Weekly, about Mon. and Fri. a.m.; from Esbjerg on Fri. and Tues at 17.45.

ASSOCIATED HUMBER LINES. (See also pp. 405, 406 & 410)

HULL AND NETHERLANDS STEAMSHIP CO.'S SERVICES.

Two Sailings weekly in each direction between HULL and ROTTERDAM by the fast screw steamers, *Melrose Abbey*, 1900 tons, and *Dewsbury*, 1,690 tons, or other steamer carrying Saloon and Steerage passengers.

TO ROTTERDAM (Parkhaven)—The Steamers sail from HULL (Riverside Quay) at 18.30 ev. Wed. and Sat. Homeward from ROTTERDAM (Parkhaven) to HULL every Wed. and Sat. evening at 20.0. Average passage 17 hours (open sea 13 hours). Facilities for sleeping on board at Rotterdam.

CURRIE LINE (THE LEITH HULL & HAMBURG S.P. CO., LTD.).

See also page 360

s.s. *Courland*, 1325 tons | s.s. *Horsa*, 978 tons | s.s. *Hengist*, 984 tons | s.s. *Gothland*, 1286 tons

Two berthed cabins in saloon. Stewardess. Electric Light.

The above are Screw Steamers carrying 12 first class passengers.

LEITH (Victoria Dock) for COPENHAGEN. Sailings s.s. *Horsa* and s.s. *Hengist* weekly on Thurs. From Copenhagen, weekly on Thurs. (average passage 56/60 hours).

LEITH (Victoria Dock). s.s. *Gothland*, for HAMBURG (Hubener Quay), (average passage about 40 hrs.) From Leith, ——— HAMBURG to LEITH, ———

DUNDEE—HAMBURG, fortnightly.

GLASGOW, LIVERPOOL and MANCHESTER to HAMBURG and BREMEN. Sailings about every 10 days. Round voyage about 12 days from Glasgow, 15 days from Liverpool or Manchester.

MOSS HUTCHISON LINE LIMITED. (See also page 362)

LIVERPOOL—BORDEAUX and v.v. Small cargo steamers (with limited accommodation for passengers) leave Liverpool & Bordeaux ev. Fri. due Bordeaux & Liverpool respectively following Mon.

NIPPON YUSEN KAISYA. (See also pages 364 and 478).

COASTAL VOYAGES.

CONTINENTAL CRUISES.—LONDON to ANTWERP, ROTTERDAM and HAMBURG. August 25.

NORDDEUTSCHER LLOYD (See also pp. 365, 417, 422, 458, 459)

Channel Service by Transatlantic Liners.

s.s. *Bremen* .. 51731 tons | s.s. *Europa* .. 49746 tons | s.s. *Columbus* 32565 tons | s.s. *Berlin* .. 15286 tons

Steamer.	Galway	Cobh	Cherbourg	Southampton	Bremen	Steamer.	Bremen dep.	Southampton	Cherbourg	Cobh	Galway.
Europa	—	—	Aug. 7	Aug. 7	Aug. 8	*Bremen*	Aug. 4	Aug. 5	Aug. 5	—	—
Bremen	—	—	,, 17	,, 17	,, 18	*Europa*	,, 11	,, 12	,, 12	—	—
Europa	—	—	,, 28	,, 28	,, 29	*Bremen*	,, 22	,, 23	,, 23	—	—
Bremen	—	—	Sept. 4	Sept. 4	Sept. 5	*Europa*	Sept. 1	Sept. 2	Sept. 2	—	—
Europa	—	—	,, 14	,, 14	,, 15	*Bremen*	,, 8	,, 9	,, 9	—	—
Bremen	—	—	,, 21	,, 21	,, 22	*Europa*	,, 19	,, 20	,, 20	—	—
Europa	—	—	Oct. 5	Oct. 5	Oct. 6	*Bremen*	,, 26	,, 27	,, 27	—	—
Bremen	—	—	,, 12	,, 12	,, 13	*Europa*	Oct. 10	Oct. 11	Oct. 11	—	—
Europa	—	—	,, 29	,, 29	,, 30	*Bremen*	,, 24	,, 25	,, 25	—	—
Bremen	—	—	Nov. 9	Nov. 9	Nov. 10	*Europa*	Nov. 28	Nov. 29	Nov 29	—	—
Europa	—	—	,, 23	,, 23	,, 24	*Bremen*	Dec. 15	Dec. 16	Dec. 16	—	—
Bremen	—	—	Dec 14	Dec. 14	Dec. 15						
Columbus	—	—	,, 21	,, *21	,, 22						

* Calls at Plymouth instead of Southampton.

POLSKO—BRYTYISKIE TOW. OKRETOWE S.A.

(POLISH BRITISH STEAMSHIP CO. LTD.).

REGULAR LINES {LONDON / HULL}—**DANZIG—GDYNIA** and *vice versa*.

s.s. *Premjer*, 3540 tns., s.s. *Warszawa*, 2487 tns., s.s. *Lech*, 1568 tns., s.s. *Lublin*, 1409 ts., s.s. *Lwow* 1409 tns.

London (Mark Brown's Wharf) to Danzig, Gdynia.—Sailings fortnightly on Thursday p.m., Aug. 3, etc., returning from Gdynia fortnightly, Thursdays, Aug. 10, by s.s. *Lech*, 1,568 tons, carrying 2 cl. passengers only. No Stewardess.

Hull (Victoria Dock) to Danzig, Gdynia.—Every Thursday, s.s. *Lublin* and s.s. *Lwow* carrying 2nd class passengers only. Steamer from Gdynia to Hull every Thursday. Passage 3 days.

SARK MOTOR SHIPS LTD.

GUERNSEY—SARK and ***vice versa.*** Daily except Suns. Guernsey dep. 10.0; returning from Sark at 17.0.

GUERNSEY—ALDERNEY. From Guernsey on Mon., Wed. & Fri. at 9.0; returning Mon. & Wed. at 16.0; Sat. at 6.30.

All under Russian flag. *Subject to alteration.*

LONDON (Hays Wharf, London Bridge)—LENINGRAD and *v.v.*

m.v. *Andrei Zdanow* .. — | m.v. *Smolny* .. .. 3767 | m.v. *Cooperazia* .. 3767
m.v. *Maria Ulianova* .. — | m.v. *Felix Dzerjinsky* 3500

The new motor vessels have cabins with two bedsteads (1st class) on upper deck, four berth cabins (Tourist class) on main deck, and accommodation (Third class) in cabins with 4, 6 and 8 berths on the lower deck, and a limited number of two-berth cabins for married couples. First and Tourist class passengers share the same dining saloon. Third class passengers have a separate dining saloon. Otherwise, all passengers (irrespective of class) have the free use of all lounges, smoking rooms and decks. Each vessel carries a Doctor, and is fitted with Wireless Telegraphy.

SERVICES (*via* KIEL CANAL).

LONDON (Hays Wharf), dp. Saturday.
LENINGRAD .. arr. Thursday.
Aug. 5, 12, 19, Sept. 9, 16 Oct. 7, 28.

LENINGRAD .. .. dep. Tues.
LONDON (Hays Wharf) arr. Sun.
From Leningrad Aug. 1, 8, 29, Sept. 5, 26, Oct. 17.

SVEA S.S. CO.

(See also pages 417 and 425)

Cargo steamers with limited passenger accommodation, carrying stewardess and fitted with electric light.

LONDON—MALMÖ (*via* Rotterdam and Kiel Canal). s.s. *Gondul*, 1322 tons; s.s. *Gudur*, 1321 tons.—From London, Mark Brown's Wharf (or the wharf adjoining), every Wed. at p.m., due Rotterdam Thur. a.m., and dep. Sat. p.m., arriving Malmö Monday afternoon. From Malmö on Sat. at 17.0, due London on Tuesday a.m.

LONDON—STOCKHOLM, *via* Kiel Canal (Joint service with Ellerman's Wilson Line, see page 410). m.s. *Freja*, 2540 tons, m.s. *Fidra*, 2540 tons.

Fortnightly Service.

London (Millwall) dep. Aug. 2, etc., Wed. ¶ | Malmö (Nyhamen) dep. Aug. 3, etc. Thurs. ¶
Stockholm (Stads.) arr .. .. Sun. a.m. | Hull (Albert Dock) arr. .. .. Sun. a.m.

¶ Exact time of sailing given at time of booking.

LONDON-ROTTERDAM-LUBECK-STOCKHOLM-LONDON (*via* Kiel Canal). s.s. *Bele*, 1900 tons; s.s. *Brage*, 1900 tons; s.s. *Munin*. 1250 tons; s.s. *Ring*, 1922 tons.

arr.	dep.	↓	↑ arr.	dep.
—	Tues. p.m.	London (Millwall Dock)	Sun. p.m.	—
Wed. 12 0	Sat. p.m.	Rotterdam	—	—
Wed. a.m.	—	Stockholm	—	Wed. 17 0

SVENSKA LLOYD (Swedish Lloyd) Steamship Company.

s.s. *Britannia*, 4350 tons | s.s. *Suecia*, 4350 tons. | s.s. *Patricia*, 8854 tons

Regular passenger service GREAT BRITAIN—SWEDEN and *vice versa* with the above first class Royal Mail and passenger turbine steamers carrying 1st & 3rd class passengers (s.s. *Patricia* 1st, 2nd, and 3rd class). Single and double cabins. Lounge. Smoking Room. Verandah Cafe. Bath Rooms. Telephones. Wireless Telegraphy, etc. s.s. *Patricia* has also 1st class cabins with private bath.

Sailings London (Tilbury) to Gothenburg and *vice versa.*

Service liable to suspension or alteration owing to strikes, etc.

From LONDON (Tilbury) } Two sailings weekly. { Open sea voyage about 29 hours.
From GOTHENBURG }

☛ Timings for s.s. *Britannia* and s.s. *Suecia*. | ☛ Timings for s.s. *Britannia* and s.s. *Suecia*.

			↓	↑		
Wed.	Sat.	1728¶ dep.	London(St.P)	arr. 1020¶	Thur.	Mon.
,,	,,	1845 dep. (approx.)	Tilbury	arr. 7 30¶	,,	,,
Fri.	Mon.	7 0¶ arr.	Gothenburg	dep. 20 0¶	Tues.	Sat.

s.s. *Britannia*, Aug. 1, 5, 12 19, 26, Sept. 2.
s.s. *Suecia*, Aug. 3, 9, 16, 23, 30.

¶ For timings by s.s. *Patricia*, see below.

s.s. *Suecia*, Aug. 1, 5, 12, 19, 26, Sept. 2.
s.s. *Britannia*, Aug. 3, 8, 15, 22, 29.

☛ Sailings and Timings for s.s. *Patricia* (8854 tons).

From London, Aug. 4, 8, 12, 17, 21, 25, 29. | From Gothenburg, Aug. 2, 6, 10, 14, 19, 23, 27.

			↓	↑		
1st day	.. .. 16 13	dep.	London (Liverpool St.)	arr.	13 4	3rd day.
,,	.. .. .. —	arr.	Harwich	dep.	—	
,,	..approx. 18 30	dep.	,, ...	arr.	10 30	
3rd day	.. .. 11 0	arr.	Gothenburg	dep.	17 0	1st day.

NEWCASTLE—GOTHENBURG.—The s.s. *Northumbria*, 1500 tons (carrying 1st and 3rd class), and s.s. *Ingeborg*, 1200 tons (carrying cabin-class only).

From Newcastle (Newcastle Quay) s.s. *Northumbria* on alternate Sats. at 13.15, s.s. *Ingeborg* on alternate Fris. at 16.0. From Gothenburg every Friday at 17.0.

Newcastle dep.:
s.s. *Northumbria*, Aug. 5, 19, Sept. 2, 16.
s.s. *Ingeborg*, Aug. 11, 25, Sept. 8, 22.

Gothenburg dep.:
s.s. *Ingeborg*, Aug. 4, 18, Sept. 1, 15, 29.
s.s. *Northumbria*, Aug. 11, 25, Sept. 8, 22, Oct. 6.

Sea Passage 3 hours. s.s. *Brittany* (1445 tons) or other steamer.

JERSEY,	dep.	Times on application	Aug. 1, 2, 6, 7, 8, 10, 11, 13, 14, 15, 17, 20, 21, 22, 24, 25, 27, 28, 29, 31.
ST. MALO,	dep.		

TYNE TEES STEAM SHIPPING CO., LTD.

Sailings from Newcastle as follows:

To HAMBURG—s.s. *Craster*, 733 tons (or other steamer). From Newcastle on Tuesdays, returning from Hamburg on Fridays. Average passage 40 hours.

To ROTTERDAM—s.s. *Lindisfarne*, 969 tons. From Newcastle on Tuesdays, returning from Rotterdam Saturdays. Passage 24 hours.

UNITED BALTIC CORPORATION, LTD.

REGULAR MAIL, PASSENGER AND CARGO SERVICE.

s.s. *Baltrover*†, 4856 tons | s.s. *Baltallinn**, 1303 tons | s.s. *Balteako**, 1300 tons | s s. ‡*Baltonia*, 2017 tons
Stewardess carried on s.s *Baltrover*. No Stewardess on s.s. *Baltallinn* or s.s. *Balteako*. † Carrying cabin and 3rd class passengers only. ‡ Accommodation for 8 cabin class. * Accommodationfor 6 cabin class only.

London—Gdynia—Danzig—Gdynia—London Service Via KIEL CANAL (Fortnightly)

BALTIC CRUISES. Illustrated programmes can be obtained from all Cook-Wagons-Lits Offices.

	London.	Gdynia.		Danzig.		Gdynia.		London.
	Depart p.m	Arrive.	Depart.	Arrive.	Depart.	Arrive.	Depart.	Arrive a.m.
Baltrover	July 27	July 31	Aug. 1	Aug. 1	Aug. 2	Aug. 2	Aug. 3	Aug. 7
Baltrover	Aug. 10	Aug. 14	Aug. 15	Aug. 15	Aug. 16	Aug. 16	Aug. 17	Aug. 21
Baltrover	Aug. 24	Aug. 28	Aug. 29	Aug. 29	Aug. 30	Aug. 30	Aug. 31	Sept. 4
Baltrover	Sept. 7	Sept. 11	Sept. 12	Sept. 12	Sept. 13	Sept. 13	Sept. 14	Sept. 18
Baltrover	Sept. 21	Sept. 25	Sept. 26	Sept. 26	Sept. 27	Sept. 27	Sept. 28	Oct. 2

	London.	Memel.		London.		London	Memel.		London.
	Depart.	Arrive.	Depart.	Arrive.		Depart.	Arrive.	Depart.	Arrive.
Baltanglia	July 26	July 31	Aug. 3	Aug. 7	*Baltanglia*	Aug. 23	Aug. 28	Aug. 31	Sept. 4
Baltonia	Aug. 2	Aug. 7	Aug. 10	Aug. 14	*Baltonia*	Aug. 30	Sept. 4	Sept. 7	Sept. 11
Baltanglia	Aug. 9	Aug. 14	Aug. 17	Aug. 21	*Baltanglia*	Sept. 6	Sept. 11	Sept. 14	Sept. 18
Baltonia	Aug. 16	Aug. 21	Aug. 24	Aug. 28	*Baltonia*	Sept. 13	Sept. 18	Sept. 21	Sept. 25

	London.	Tallinn.		Hull.		London.
	Depart.	Arrive.	Depart.	Arrive.	Depart.	Arrive.
Baltavia	July 27	July 31	Aug. 2	Aug. 6	Aug. 7	Aug. 8
Baltallinn ..	Aug. 3	Aug. 7	Aug. 9	Aug. 13	Aug. 14	Aug. 15
Baltavia	Aug. 10	Aug. 14	Aug. 16	Aug. 20	Aug. 21	Aug. 22
Baltallinn ..	Aug. 17	Aug. 21	Aug. 23	Aug. 27	Aug. 28	Aug. 29
Baltavia	Aug. 24	Aug. 28	Aug. 30	Sept. 3	Sept. 4	Sept. 5
Baltallinn ..	Aug. 31	Sept. 4	Sept. 6	Sept. 10	Sept. 11	Sept. 12
Baltavia	Sept. 7	Sept. 11	Sept. 13	Sept. 17	Sept. 18	Sept. 19

	London.	Riga.		Liepaja.		London.
	Depart.	Arrive.	Depart.	Arrive.	Depart.	Arrive.
Balteako	July 28	Aug. 1	Aug. 4	Aug. 5	Aug. 5	Aug. 9
Steamer	Aug. 4	Aug. 8	Aug. 11	Aug. 12	Aug. 12	Aug. 16
Balteako	Aug. 11	Aug. 15	Aug. 18	Aug. 19	Aug. 19	Aug. 23
Steamer	Aug. 18	Aug. 22	Aug. 25	Aug. 26	Aug. 26	Aug. 30
Balteako	Aug. 25	Aug. 29	Sept. 1	Sept. 2	Sept. 2	Sept. 6
Steamer	Sept. 1	Sept. 5	Sept. 8	Sept. 9	Sept. 9	Sept. 13
Balteako	Sept. 8	Sept. 12	Sept. 15	Sept. 16	Sept. 16	Sept. 20

UNITED STATES LINES. Channel Services by Transatlantic Liners.

Services subject to confirmation. See also page 459.

s.s. *Pres. Harding*, 13,869 tons. s.s. *Manhattan*, 24,000 tons. s.s. *Pres. Roosevelt*, 13,869 tons.
s.s. *Washington*, 24,000 tons.

EASTBOUND. WESTBOUND.

Coming from N. York

Cobh (Qu'nstown) arr.	Plymouth arr.	Havre arr.	Hamburg arr.	Steamer.	Hamburg ‡ dep	Havre dep.	Southampton dep.	Cobh (Q'town) dep.
Aug. 1	Aug. 1	Aug 2	Aug 3	*Manhattan*	Aug. 9	Aug. 10	Aug. 11	Aug. 12
,, 9	,, 10*	,, 11	,, 12	*Pres. Harding*	,, 16	,, 17	,, 18	,, 19
,, 15	,, 15	,, 16	,, 17	*Washington*	,, 22	,, 24	,, 24	,, 25
,, 23	,, 24*	,, 25	,, 26	*Pres. Roosevelt*..	,, 30	,, 31	Sept. 1	Sept. 2
,, 29	,, 29	,, 30	,, 31	*Manhattan*	Sept. 5	Sept 7	,, 7	,, 8
Sept. 6	Sept. 7*	Sept. 8	Sept. 9	*Pres. Harding* ..	,, 13	,, 14	,, 15	,, 16
,, 12	,, 12	,, 13	,, 14	*Washington*.....	,, 20	,, 21	,, 22	,, 23
,, 20	,, 21*	,, 22	,, 23	*Pres Roosevelt*..	,, 27	,, 28	,, 29	,, 30
,, 26	,, 26	,, 27	,, 28	*Manhattan*	Oct. 4	Oct. 5	Oct. 6	Oct. 7
Oct. 4	Oct. 5*	Oct. 6	Oct. 7	*Pres. Harding* ..	,, 11	,, 12	,, 13	,, 14

Proceed'g to N. York

‡ Embark previous evening. * Southampton instead of Plymouth.

UNION-CASTLE MAIL S.S. CO., LTD. (See also pages 369 & 467)

CONTINENTAL CRUISES

To Antwerp, Rotterdam, Hamburg and back to London.

1st class Fare £12 12 0.

The Continental Cruises occupy from 11 to 12 days, and the fare includes meals and accommodation on board while at sea and in Continental Ports.

From London	Vessel		From London	Vessel	
Aug. 10	*Dunnottar Castle*	15007 tons	Oct. 5	*Pretoria Castle*	17000 tons.
Sept. 7	*Durban Castle*	17388 „			

☞ Special illustrated programme giving full particulars can be obtained from any of Cook's Offices.

ELLERMAN LINE. (See also page 361).

Cressado .. 1300 | *Darino* .. 1700 | *Palmella* .. 1800 | *Lisbon* .. 2000 | *Estrellano* .. 2000

The above are screw steamers with accommodation for a few passengers only.

Liverpool and/or Swansea, Lisbon and Oporto (May also call at Setubal).

Sailings on application. Average duration of voyage: To Lisbon, 5 days; to Oporto, 8/9 days. Round voyage, 17/21 days. Fare for the round voyage £16.

ELLERMAN'S WILSON LINE.

Albano ..1176	§*Carlo* ..1737	*Domino* ..2000	§*Gourko* ..2000	*Salerno* .. 870	*Teano* .. 672
§*Bassano*..7000	§*Consuelo*..7000	§*Draco* ..2018	§*Mourino* 1820	§*Spero* ..1568	*Volo* 2000
§*Borodino* 2000	§*Dago* 1757	§*Erato* ..1270	*Salmo* ..1880	*Tasso* 2000	

The above are screw steamers fitted with bathrooms and Electric Light. § These steamers are fitted with wireless telegraphy.

Hull to Christianssand and Oslo.—From Hull every Friday p.m., returning from Oslo every Friday p.m., except June, July, August. First class £5 single (victualling included).

Hull to Gothenburg.—From Hull every Friday p.m., returning from Gothenburg every Friday (Round voyage £12). £5 single (victualling included).

Hull to Copenhagen.—(In conjunction with the Forenede Line, see p. 404). Every Fri. at p.m., due Copenhagen, Mon. a.m., s.s. *Spero*, s.s. *Hroar*. Returning from Copenhagen Thur. at p.m., due Hull Sun. a.m. 1st class £5 10s., 3rd class £2 15s. single (victualling included).

(Round voyage—s.s. *Spero*, £12; s.s. *Hroar*, £11 5s.

London (via Kiel Canal) to Stockholm, Norrkoping, Halmstad, Malmo, Hull.—From London fortnightly by s.s. *Albano* and s.s. *Dago*. Round voyage (18 days), £18 Aug. 9, 23.

London to Copenhagen *via* The Skaw or Kiel Canal. s.s. *Cavallo*. From London, every Friday. Round trip, 10 days, £12.

London to Oslo and Christianssand. s.s. *Volo*. Round trip, £12. Aug. 11, 25.

Hull—Malmo—Hälsingborg—Halmstad—Hull. Fortnightly. From Hull, 10 days' round voyage, £10 10s. Sailings on application.

ASSOCIATED HUMBER LINES.

(See also pages 405, 406 and 407). Services of Ellerman's Wilson Line from Hull.

Limited accommodation for passengers.

Hull to Antwerp—Dunkerque to Hull.—From Hull on Sat., due Antwerp on Sun., returning from Dunkerque to Hull Wed. p.m. s.s. *Harrogate*.

Hull to Hamburg.—From Hull on Saturdays. From Hamburg Tuesdays. **Passage about 30 hours.** *For Royal Mail Route Hull-Hamburg and vice versa (see page 406).*

Arendal S.S. Co. .. .. PAGE 413
Argo Shipping Co. 414
Bergenske & Nordenfjeldske S.S. Co.'s 414/5
Bohuslanske S.S. Co. 416
Bore S.S. Co. 416
Bornholm S.S. Co. (1866) 416
Braakman & Co.'s Steamers (Messrs. H.) .. 416
East Bornholm S.S. Co. 418
Finmark Fylkesrederi Skibe 419
Finland Line 417
Fop Smit & Co. 419
Forenede Line 418/9
Fred Olsen's S.S. Line 423
Goteborg Frederikshavn Linjen (Gothenburg Frederikshavn S.S. Co.) 420
Gotha S.S. Co. 420
Gotland S.S. Co. 420
Gdynia Ameryka, Linje Zeglugowe S.A. .. 416
Hallands Ångbats Åktiebolag 420
Hamburg America 420
Iceland S.S. Co. 421
Indherreds S.S. Co. 421
Kristiansands S.S. Co. 416
Mariehamn S S. Co. 421
Namdalens Aktie Dampsskibsselskap .. 421
Namsos S.S. Co. 422
Netherlands Rlys. (S.S. Services) 422
Norden-Fjeldske S.S. Co. 414/5
Norddeutscher Lloyd 422
Nordlanske S.S. Co. 422
Normandy S. Nav. Co. .. .. .. PAGE 422
Ofotens Dampskibsselskap 415, 424
Olsen Line 423
Oresund S.S. Co. 422
Pärnu Rederi A—B 423
Provinciale Stoombootdienst op de Wester-Schelde 427
Rud-Christ-Gribel 423
Saltens S.S. Co. 424
Sandnaes S.S. Co. 425
Sartori & Berger's Steamers 424
Seedienst Ostpreussen (Danzig and East Prussian Service) 417
Sergo & Co. 424
Skipafelagid Føroyar (S.S. Co.) .. 427
Sociéte des Bateaux de la Côte d'Emeraude 426
Sondenfjelds Norske S.S. Co. 424
Stavanger S.S. Co. 413, 415, 425
Stettiner Dampfschiffs-Gesellschaft J. F. Braeunlich, G.m.b.H. 417
Svea S.S. Co. 425/6
Svenska Amerika Linjens Östersjötrafik (Swedish America Line) 427
Terschellinger Stoomboot Maatschappij .. 427
Troms Fylkes Dampskibsselskap 428
Texel's Own S.S. Co. 427
Vesteraalens S.S. Co. 415, 428/30
Wasa North Sea S.S. Co. 428

ARENDAL S.S. CO. and STAVANGER S.S. CO. §

*Oslo** .. Tons.	880	*Dronningen** Tons.	661	*Kong Oscar II.** T'ns	914	*Bergen* .. Tons	552
Christiania‡ ..	656	*Kronprinsesse Martha*‡	900	*Kong Haakon* ..	874	*Bjorgvin** ..	793

§ See also pages 415, 425 and 431. ‡ Stavanger s.s. Co.'s Steamers. * Arendal s.s. Co.'s Steamers.

The above are screw steamers carrying only 1st & 2nd cl. pass., the 1st cl. cabins accommodating 2 & 4 persons. The steamers have a separate ladies' saloon, carry stewardess, and fitted with electric light.

Oslo—Bergen *and vice versa.*

Weekdays from Bergen and Oslo.

June 1—August 31.

arr.	dep.	↓	arr. ↑	dep.
—	23 0	Oslo	22 0	—
—	6 30	Larvik	—	1515
1430	1530	Arendal	—	7 30
2015	2230	Christiansand	2345	1 30
—	7 0	Flekkefjord ..	—	1430
—	1030	Egersund	—	10 0
1530	19 0	Stavanger	2330	4 0
	23 0	Haugesund ..	—	20 0
5 30	—	Bergen	—	13 0

Calling also at Kragero, Risor, Lyngor, Grimstad, Kleven, Farsund, Rægefjord, Kopervik (details on application).

Oslo—Stavanger—Sandnæs. (Stavanger s.s. Co.)

s.s. *Rogaland*‡ 902 tons, s.s. *Ryfylke* .. 1200 tons
s.s. *Austri*‡ 491 ,, s.s *Vestri*‡ 491 ,,

Oslo	dp.	Mo. 21 0	Tu 21 0	We. 21 0	Th. 21 0	Sa. 21 0
Moss	dp.	—	,, 24 0	Th. 0 30	Fri. 0 30	,, 24 0
Arendal	dp.	Tu. 13 0	We. 8 0	,, 9 30	,, 9 30	Su. 8 0
Chris'sand	a.	—	,, 1130	,, —	—	,, 1130
,,	dp.	Tu. 18 0	,, 12 0	,, 1530	,, 1530	,, 12 0
Stavanger	a.	We. 8 0	,, 23 0	Fri. 6* 0	Sa. 6 0	,, 23 0
Sandnæs	a.	—	Th. 14 0	,, 13¶0	—	Mo. 14 0

¶ Proceeding to Stavanger, Sand, Saudesjoen, Sauda, Sand and Stavanger. * Dep. 12.0.

Sandnæs	dp.	Mo. 13 0	Tu. 16 0	We. 13 0	Th. 13 0	Sa. 13 0
Stavanger	dp.	,, 19 0	,, 20 0	,, 21 0	,, 20 0	,, 21 0
Egersund	dp.	Tu. 1 0	—	Th. 2 0	—	Su. 2 0
Chris'sand	ar.	—	—	,, 1030	—	,, 1030
,,	dp.	Tu. 1130	—	,, 1330	Fri. 12 0	,, 1330
Arendal	dp.	,, 16 0	—	,, 1730	,, 1630	,, 1730
Oslo	ar.	We. 5 0	Th. 3 0	Fri. 4 0	Sa. 4 0	Mo. 4 0

ARENDAL S.S. CO.

s.s. *Galtesund*, 623 tons; *Oslo*, 881 tons; *Kristiansund*, 473 tons.

a	*b*	*c*			↑	*a*	*b*	*d*
21 0	21 0	21 0	dep.	Oslo	arr.	7 30	7 30	7 30
8 0	8 0	7 30	arr.	Arendal	dep.	2030	2030	2030
9 0	9 0	7 45	dep.	,, ...	arr.	1930	..	1930
10 0	1015	..	dep.	Grimstad	dep.	..	..	..
13 0	1330	1115	arr.	Christiansand	dep.	1630	1630	1630

a Mons. and Thurs. *b* Tues., Weds. and Fris. *c* Sats. *d* Suns.

ARGO SHIPPING COMPANY.

(See also page 402).

(ARGO REEDEREI RICHARD ADLER & CO.).

BREMEN—FINLAND and *vice versa* by Steamers of about 1750 tons.

Bremen dep. ..	.. .. .. Thursday.	Helsingfors dep.	.. .. .. Tuesday.
Helsingfors arr.	.. .. Monday.	Kotka arr	.. .. Wednesday.
		Kotka dep.	.. .. Thursday.
		Bremen arr.	.. .. .. Monday.

BREMEN—WEST FINLAND by Steamers of about 1500 tons. Departures alternate weeks on Monday and Saturday respectively for Abo, Wasa, Mäntyluoto and Raumo.

B. & N. LINE.
ROYAL MAIL STEAMERS

B. BERGENSKE S.S. CO., Bergen.

N. NORDENFJELDSKE S.S. CO., Trondheim.

See also pages 403 and 444.

BERGENSKE FLEET.

See also page 403.

Steamer.	Tons.	Steamer.	Tons.	Steamer.	Tons.	Steamer.	Tons.
Ariadne ..	2048	*Delfinus* ..	1293	*Luna*	959	*Rigel*	3828
Ara	965	*Deneb*	856	*Lynx*	1474	*Saturnus* ..	955
Arcturus ..	1277	*Diana*	1154	*Lyra*	1366	*Sirius*	944
Brant County	5000	*Edna*	914	*Meteor*	3717	*Spica*	499
Canis (M.S.) ..	934	*Estrella* ..	3888	*Midnatsol* ..	978	*Titan* (tender)	42
Capella ..	877	*Iris*	1177	*Mira*	1152	*Uranus* ..	934
Castor	1682	*Irma*	1392	*Musca* (tender)	20	*Ursa*	957
Clio	556	*Jupiter* ..	2470	*Neptun* ..	1574	*Vega*	7287
Columba (M.S.)	1118	*Kora*	817	*Nova*	1381	*Vela*	1180
Cometa	3793	*Kem*	1705	*Nordstjernen* ..	1919	*Venus* (M.V. ..	5406
Corvus	1317	*Keret*	1718	*Pallas*	556	*Vesta*	1310
Crux	3828	*Leda*	2415	*Polarlys* ..	1069	*Vulcanus* (tender)	85
Cygnus ..	1333	*Leo*	1366	*Pollux*	1676		

NORDENFJELDSKE FLEET.

Kong Halfdan	1424	*Haakon Jarl* ..	899	*Sigurd Jarl* ..	884	*Tore Jarl* ..	1514
Prins Olav ..	2000	*Kong Erik* ..	940	*Sverre Sigurdsön*	932	*Atle Jarl*	1172
Prinsesse Ragnhild	1590	*Kong Magnus*	1410	*Tordenskjold* ..	921	*Rolf Jarl*	1846
		Kong Harald ..	1111	*Trondhjem* ..	607	*Arnfinn Jarl*	1172
Dronning Maud	1505	*Torfinn Jarl* ..	1481	*Henrik Wergeland*	488	*Bruse Jarl*	1847
Erling Jarl ..	737	*Einar Jarl*	1857	*Ottar Jarl*	1419	*Orm Jarl* ..	1847
Haakon Adelstein	710	*Roald Jarl* ..	1405	*Svein Jarl*	1908		

BERGENSKE S.S. CO. 1st & 3rd cl. pass. carried. Two-berthed Cabins amidships. Bath Rooms. Electric light. Stewardess.

ROTTERDAM—BERGEN—TRONDHEIM. Weekly service by s.s. *Ariadne*, s.s. *Jupiter*.

From Rotterdam		From Trondheim.	
s.s. *Jupiter* ..	Aug. 2, 16, 30, Sept. 13, 27.	s.s. *Ariadne* ..	Aug. 2, 16, 30, Sept. 13, 27.
s.s. *Ariadne* ..	.. Aug. 9, 23, Sept. 6, 20.	s.s. *Jupiter* ..	.. Aug. 9, 23, Sept. 6, 20.

arr.	dep.	↓	arr.	dep. ↑
—	Wed. 19.0	Rott'dam (Schieh'n)	Sun. 19.0	—
Fri. a.m.	Fri. 9.0	Stavanger	Sat. a.m.	Sat. 9.30
¶Fri. 17.0,	Sat. 21.30	Bergen	Fri. 4.30,	Fri. 22.0
—	Sun. 4.45	Floro	—	Th. 20.30
—	Sun. 7.0	Maaloy	—	Th. 17.30
Su. 11.0,	Su. 13.30	Aalesund	Th. 10.0,	Th. 12.0
—	Su. 17.0	Molde	—	Th. 7.0
Su. —	Su. 21 30	Christiansund	Th. 0.30,	Th. 2.0
Mo. 6.0,	—	Trondheim	—	Wed. 17.0

¶ Connection is made with steamer from Bergen on Friday to Trondheim — See page 415.

BERGEN—HAMBURG.

ITINERARY.
Weekly.
s.s. *Leda*.
(1st & 3rd class)

	arr.	dep.
Bergen	—	Tue. 22 0
Stavanger	We. 6 0	We. 9 30
Hamburg	Th. 15 0	Sat. 18 0
Stavanger	Su. 22 0	Sun. 24 0
Bergen	Mo. 7 0	—

May call also at Haugesund.

Express Service Bergen—Iceland. s.s. *Lyra* (Fortnightly)

		Aug	Aug	Aug
Bergen ....dep.	Thur. 22 0	3	17	31
Thorshavn dep	Sat. a.m.	5	19	Sp.2
Vestmanøy	Mon. —	7	21	4
Reykjavik arr.	Mon. p.m.	7	21	4
Reykjavik dep.	Thur. 19 0	10	24	7
Vestmanøy dep.	Fri. a.m.	11	25	8
Thorshavn dep.	Sat. p.m.	12	26	9
Bergen	Mon. a.m.	14	28	11

Bergen—Iceland.

(Aug. 7, Sept. 4, Oct. 2).
s.s. *Nova*.

From Oslo to Christiansand S., Stavanger, Bergen, Seydisfjord, Reykjavik, Seydisfjord, Bergen, Stavanger, Oslo.

Calling also at Faskrudsfjord, Reydarfjord, Eskefjord, Nordfjord, Husavik, Akureyri, Siglufjord, Isafjord.

Further details of dates on application.

B. & N. Services continued next page.

NORDENFJELDSKE S.S. CO.-*Continued.* **STAVANGER S.S. CO.** (See also pp. 413, 425 and 431). **VESTERAALENS S.S. CO.** (See also page 428). **OFOTENS S.S. CO.** (See also page 424).

EXPRESS SERVICES BERGEN, TRONDHEIM, NORTH CAPE, KIRKENES

and vice versa—(Daily).
(Calling at RØRVIK and various other minor ports).

							arr.	dep.		arr.	dep.							
—	—	—	—	—	—	Sun		9 0	Stavanger ...	21 0		—	—	—	—	—	Th.	—
—	—	—	—	—	—	—		12 0	Haugesund ..	..	18 0	—	—	—	—	—	Th.	—
Mo.	Tu.	We	Th.	Fri.	Sa*	Sun	18 0	2130	Bergen	4 30	11 0	Sat.	Sun	Mo.	Tu.	We	Th.	Fri.
Tu.	We.	Th.	Fri.	Sat	Sun	Mo.	..	4 45	Florö ...... ▲		2030	Fri	Sat.	Sun	Mo.	Tu.	We.	Th.
Tu.	We.	Th.	Fri.	Sat	Sun	Mo.	..	7 30	Maaloy	..	1730	Fri	Sat.	Sun	Mo.	Tu.	We.	Th.
Tu.	We.	Th.	Fri.	Sat	Sun	Mo.		1330	Aalesund.....	..	12 0	Fri	Sat.	Sun	Mo.	Tu.	We.	Th.
Tu.	We.	Th.	Fri.	Sat	Sun	Mo.		17 0	Molde	..	7 0	Fri	Sat	Sun	Mo.	Tu.	We.	Th.
Tu.	We.	Th.	Fri	Sat.	Sun	Mo.	..	2130	Christiansund	..	2 0	Fri	Sat	Sun	Mo.	Tu.	We.	Th.
We.	Th.	Fri	Sat	Sun	Mo.	Tu.	6 0	1115	Trondheim {	..	17 0	Th.	Fri.	Sat	Sun	Mo.	Tu.	We.*
										6 0	..	Th.	Fri	Sat	Sun	Mo.	Tu.	We.
Th.	Fri	Sat	Sun	Mo.	Tu.	We	..	1 0	Brønnøysund	..	1445	We	Th.	Fri	Sat.	Sun	Mo.	Tu.
Th.	Fri	Sat	Sun	Mo.	Tu.	We		4 15	Sandnessjoen	..	1515	We	Th.	Fri	Sat	Sun	Mo.	Tu.
Th.	Fri	Sat	Sun	Mo.	Tu.	We	12 g 30	13 g 30	Bodö	0 f 15	2 0	We	Th.	Fri.	Sat	Sun	Mo.	Tu.
—	—	—	—	—	—	Th.		0 30	Narvik§	1230	1315	—	We	—	—	—	—	—
Th.	Fri	Sat	Sun	Mo	Tu.	—	20 0	2130	Svolvaer	17 e 0	18 e 30	Tu.	—	Th.	Fri	Sat	Sun	Mo
—	Sat	—	—	Tu.	—	Th.		2 b 0	Lodingen	..	9 d 15	—	We	—	Fri	—	—	Mo
Fri	—	—	Mo	—	—	—		1 0	Stokmarknes	..	1345	Tu.	—	—	Fri	—	—	—
Fri	Sat	Sun	Mo	Tu.	We	Th.	6 i 30	7 i 30	Harstad	7 p 0	8 p 0	Tu.	We	Th.	Fri	Sat	Sun	Mo
Fri	Sat	Sun	Mo	Tu.	We	Th.		11 j 0	Finsnes	..	3 n 0	Tu.	We	Th.	Fri	Sat	Sun	Mo
Fri	Sat	Sun	Mo	Tu.	We	Th.	14 r 0	16 r 30	▼ Tromsö	21 m 0	24 m 0	Mo	Tu.	We	Th.	Fri	Sat	Sun
—	Sat	—	—	Tu.	—	Th.	..	2315	Øksfjord	..	1345	—	—	We	—	Fri	—	Sun
Sat	Sun	Mo	Tu.	We	Th.	Fri	2 30	4 0	Hammerfest	9 l 0	10 l 30	Mo	Tu.	We	Th.	Fri	Sat	Sun
Sat	Sun	Mo	Tu.	We	Th.	Fri		10 0	Honningsvaag		3 k 30	Mo	Tu.	We	Th.	Fri	Sat	Sun
Sat	Sun	Mo	Tu.	We	Th.	Fri	23 0	24 0	Vardö	12 0	1330	Sun	Mo	Tu.	We	Th.	Fri	Sat
—	Mo	—	We	Th.	—	Sat	3 30	4 0	Vadsö	8 0	8 30	Sun	—	Tu.	—	—	Fri	—
Sun	Mo	Tu.	We	Th.	Fri.	Sat	6 c 0	.	Kirkenes	..	6 h 0	Sun	Mo	Tu.	We	Th.	Fri	Sat

* From Bergen on Sat. to TRONDHEIM, and from TRONDHEIM on Wed. to BERGEN by steamer of Rotterdam Service—See page 414.
§ For other services from Bodö, Svolvaer and Lodingen to Narvik—See pages 424 and 440.
b Dep. 3.30 on Thurs. *c* Arr. 4.0 on Sun., Tues. and Fri. *d* Calls Lodingen 11.30 on Sat. and Wed. *e* On Fri. and Mon. arr. Svolvaer 14.30 and dep. 16.30. *f* On Wed., Thur., Fri. and Sun. arr. Bodö 1.15. *g* One hour later on Fri. and Tues. *h* Dep. 8.0 on Mon., Wed., Thur. and Sat. *i* Arr. 5.0 and dep. 6.30 on Sat. and Tues. *j* Dep. Finsnes 10.15 on Sat. and Tues. *k* Dep. 2.0 on Tues. *l* Arr. Hammerfest 7.30 and dep. 9.0 on Tues. *m* Arr. Tromsö 20.0 and dep. 22.30 on Tues. *n* Dep. Finsnes 1.45 on Wed. *p* Arr. Harstad 5.30 and dep. 6.0 on Wed. *r* Arr. 13.30 and dep. 16.0 Tromsö on Mons. and Fris.

SAILINGS.—For further details see Cook's programme for Norway, Sweden, Denmark, Iceland, Finland. (See page 428 for sailings of the Vesteraalen Co.)

Dep. Bergen for North Cape and Kirkenes

s.s. *Nordnorge*— Aug. 8, 22.

s.s. *Prins Olav*—Aug. 7, 21, Sept. 4.

s.s. *Irma*—Aug. 9, 23, Sept. 6.

s.s. *Dronning Maud*—Aug. 1, 15, 29.

s.s. *St. Svithun*—Aug. 11, 25.

s.s. *Nordstjernen*—Aug. 2, 16, 30, Sept. 13.

s.s. *Kong Harald*—Aug. 13, 26†.

s.s. *Prinsesse Ragnhild*—Aug. 4, 18, Sept. 1.

s.s. *Midnatsol*—Aug. 12†, 27, Sept. 9†.

s.s. *Polarlys*—Aug. 5‡, 20, Sept. 2‡.

s.s. *Sigurd Jarl*—Aug. 6, 19‡, Sept. 3.

†Between Bergen and Trondheim by s.s. *Ariadne* (see page 414).

‡Between Bergen and Trondheim by s.s. *Jupiter* (see page 414).

Extra Service
TRONDHEIM—HARSTAD and back
June 28 to July 23.

arr.	dep.		arr.	dep.
—	We. 23 0	Trondheim ▲	Su. 18 0	—
Fri. 2 30	Fri. 3 30	Bodö	Sat. 13 0	Sat. 14 0
Fri. 8 30	Fri. 9 30	Svolvaer ..	Sat. 7 0	Sat. 8 0
Fri. 19 0	—	▼ Harstad ..	—	Fri. 21 0

SPECIAL CHEAP TRIPS to North Cape. 12-Day Cheap Trips from Trondheim to North Cape by s.s. *Haakon Adalstein;* from Trondheim visiting Torghatten, Seven Sisters, Hestmanoya, Lofoten, Raftsund, Trollfjord, Fugleberget, Tromsö, Hammerfest and North Cape. (Also Bodö, Svolvær Harstad, Tromsö, Hammerfest.) Dep. Trondheim, on Thursdays.

BERGENSKE S.S. CO.'S SERVICE.
Cargo Steamers carrying a few passengers.
(Route 9A.)
s.s. *Lynx*, Aug. 24, Sept. 28, Nov. 2.
s.s. *Neptun*, Sept. 9, Oct. 12, Nov. 16.

Hamburg, dep. Thur.	Vadsö, dep. Mon.
Bergen, dep. Tues.	Trondheim, dep. Mon.
Trondheim, dep. Sat.	Bergen, dep. Fri.
For Vadsö.	Hamburg, arr. Mon.

Calls also at Christiansund and Mandal alternate weeks.

Services subject to alteration or suspension owing to Strikes, &c.

Mail Steamers.	Tons.	Mail Steamers.	Tons.	Mail Steamers.	Tons.
Goteborg†	429	*Valborg*	210	*Borgila*	168
R. Thorburn†	190	*Bohus*	221	*Byfjorden*	201
Uddevalla†	265	*Kung Rane*†	295	*Victor*	117
Oslo†	322	*Viken*	100	*Styrbjorn*	104

1st and 3rd cl. passengers carried. † Private cabins for one and two persons. Restaurant on board.

Gothenburg—Strömstad—Oslo and *vice versa*.

From Gothenburg, Suns., Weds. and Fris. at 8.0. From Oslo, Mons., Weds. and Sats. at 14.30. Steamers call at Lysekil, Gravarne, Hunnebostrand, Fjellbäcka, Grebbestad and Strömstad. Passage 29 hours.

Gothenburg—Uddevalla—Strömstad—Fredriksstad

From Gothenburg—Fredriksstad, Fris. at 6.0, calling at Uddevalla, Lysekil, Hunnebostrand, Strömstad.
From Fredriksstad Mons. at 12.0, calling at Strömstad, Hunnebostrand and Uddevalla. Passage 37 hrs.

Uddevalla—Gothenburg.

From Gothenburg, Suns. at 8.0, Mon. to Fri. at 10.0 | From Uddevalla Suns. at 15 0, Mon. to Fri at 7.30. Calling at intermediate stations.

BORE S.S. CO.

See also page 417.

STOCKHOLM—ABO (TURKU) and *vice versa*.

Passage 16½ hours.

In conjunction with Finland Line pp. 404 and 417, and Svea Line p. 425.
s.s. *Bore II*, s.s. *Wellamo*, s.s. *Brynhild*.

DAILY

17 0	dep.	Stockholm	arr.	10 0
8 0	arr.	Abo	dep.	2115

Also from June 17 to August 15, s.s. *Nordstjernan*—

Tues., Thur., Sun.,	9 0 dep.	Stockholm	arr.	22.30	Mon., Wed., Sat.
,, ,, ,,	16,30 arr.	Mariehamn	arr.	17.0	,, ,, ,,
,, ,, ,,	23.45 arr.	Abo........	dep.	9.45	,, ,, ,,

Train from Abo to Helsingfors, 9.12, 14.20 and 17.24. Train from Helsingfors to Abo at 9.0 and 15.0.

LÜBECK—ABO (Fortnightly.)

s.s. *Bore V* carrying 1st, and 3rd class passengers.

Lübeck, dep. Aug. 12, 26, etc. .. .. Sat. 16.0	Abo, dep. Aug. 5, 19, etc. .. .. Sat. 19.15
Abo, arr. Tues. 7.0	Lübeck, arr. Tues. 7.0

STOCKHOLM—MARIEHAMN.

The steamers from Stockholm on Tues., Thurs., Sat., from Abo on Tues., Thur., Sat., call at Mariehamn. Passengers Abo-Mariehamn and *vice versa* can only travel by the *Bore II* and *Wellamo*.
Also from June 23, s.s. *Bore I* and s.s. *Oihonna*—

Tues., Thur	13 0 dep.	Stockholm	arr.	Wed., Fri. 7.30
,, ,,	20 0 arr.	Mariehamn	dep.	,, ,, 1.0

BORNHOLM S.S. CO. (1866).

m.s. *Bornholm*, 1350 tons. m.s *Frem*, 999 tons. m.s. *Hammershus*† 935 tons.
The above Screw Steamers carry first and third class passengers. They are provided with two-berthed cabins, separate ladies' saloons and carry a Stewardess. † Electric Light on these vessels.

Copenhagen—Bornholm—Rönne. MAIL SERVICE.

From Copenhagen, 23 15 | From Rönne, 23.0. Average passage direct 8 hours.

N.V. EXPEDITIEDEDRYF v/h. H. BRAAKMAN & CO.

Telegraaf III, 250 tons. *Telegraaf IV*, 290 tons. First and second class passengers carried.

Rotterdam-Antwerp *via* Dordrecht, Zijpe, Wemeldinge, Hansweert, Walsoorden.

Rotterdam to Antwerp (passage 11 to 12 hours). From Rotterdam, From Antwerp,

KRISTIANSANDS S.S. CO.

m.v. *Skagerak*.

Kristiansand—Hirtshals and *vice versa*.

Mail steamer carrying "general" passengers. Passage 5 hours.

5 30	dep.	Kristiansand	arr.	2315
1030	arr.	Hirtshals	dep.	1815

† Connection with express trains to and from Copenhagen, Esbjerg and Hamburg, *see* p. 216.

GDYNIA AMERYKA LINJE ZEGLUGOWE S.A.

(*See also pp.* 377, 449 & 459)
(GDYNIA AMERICA SHIPPING LINES LTD.) m.v. *Batory*, 14400 tons; m.v. *Pilsudski*, 14400 tons.
COPENHAGEN—GDYNIA & *vice versa* by Transatlantic liners (to and from New York, *see p.* 459)
Gdynia dep. for Copenhagen Aug. 11, 24, Sept. 4, 18, 29, Oct. 13, Nov. 16, Dec. 28.
Copenhagen dep. for Gdynia, Aug. 13, 31, Sept. 14, 25, Oct. 9, 19, Nov. 2, Dec. 9.

Electric light on vessels. See also pages 404 & 416.

Oihonna .. 1096	*Baltic* .. 1086	*Norma* 1537	*Poseidon* .. 804	†*Polaris* 1614
†*Wellamo* .. 2047	*Capella* .. 1102	*Baltic* 1086	*Viola* 324	*Rigel* 1450
†*Ariadne* .. 2403	*Ilmatar* .. 2364	*V. Dobeln* .. 666	*Mira* 820	*Suomi* 659

Above are Screw Steamers carrying first, second, tourist, and 3 cl. passengers. († s.s. *Ariadne* and s.s. *Wellamo*, 1st and Tourist class, s.s. *Polaris* 1st and 3rd cl., s.s. *Rigel* carries 12 1st cl.) They have single and 2 berthed cabins, separate Ladies' Saloon, a Smoking Room, and carry Stewardesses.

Stockholm—Abo.

In conjunction with Bore S.S. Co. and Svea Co. (See page 416).

Stockholm-Helsingfors.

Combined Service with Svea S.S. Co., & Bore S.S. Co.

s.s. *Oihonna* (Finland Line), s.s. *Heimdall* (Svea S.S. Co.), s s. *Bore I* (Bore S.S. Co.)

Sun. 1030	Wed. 18¶0	Sat. 18¶0	dep. Stockholm .. arr.	Mon. 8 ¶ 0	Wed. 8¶ 0	Fri. 8 0
Mon. 9 0	Thur. 16 0	Sun. 16 0	arr. Helsingfors .. dep.	Sun. 1130	Tues. 1130	Thur. 1130

¶ Call Hango *en route*.

Helsingfors—Tallinn (Reval)

(Daily.) s.s. *Suomi*, *Ariadne* or *Aegna*.

Mon. to Fri.	Sat.		Sun.		Mon. to Thu.	Fri.		Sat.	Sun.
10 0	12 0	16 0	16 0	dep. Helsingfors .. arr.	1430	1330	2030	1430	2030
1430	1530	2030	2030	arr. Tallinn .... dep.	10 0	10 0	16 0	10 0	16 0

Lübeck—Helsingfors.

s.s. *Baltic* (1, 2 & 3 cl.) s.s. *Poseidon* (1 & 3 cl.)

Sat. 16.0 (Weekly)	dep.	↓ Lübeck ↑	arr.	Tues. 8 0
Tue. 8.0	arr.	Helsingfors	dep.	Sat., Aug. 12 (Fortnightly), at 14 0

Antwerp—Kiel/Holtenau—Helsingfors.

(Weekly.) *Via* Kiel Canal.

s.s. *Rigel*, s.s. *Hesperus* and s.s. *Norma*.

Wed. .. 16 0	dep. Antwerp (Bassin America 52)	arr.	Thurs. a.m.
Fri. .. 10 0	dep. Holtenau Lock	.. dep.	Tues. 5 0
Mon. .. a.m.	arr. Helsingfors (South Harbour)	.. dep.	Sat. .. 14 0

Stettin-Helsingfors.

s.s. *Ariadne*. (Weekly.)

See also p. 423 *re* Rud-Christ-Gribel Line.

Stettin	dep. Wed. 16 0	Helsingfors	dep. Sat. 12 0
Tallinn (Reval) ..	arr. Fri. 9.0 and dep. 10 0	Tallinn (Reval) ..	arr. Sat. 15.30 and dep. 1830
Helsingfors	arr. Fri. 1330	Stettin	arr. Mon. 9 0

Stockholm—Mariehamn.

See page 416. Passage 6-7 hours.

SEEDIENST OSTPREUSSEN. (DANZIG AND EAST PRUSSIAN SERVICE).

Norddeutscher Lloyd, Bremen Stettiner Dampfschiffs Gesellschaft F. F. Braeunlich, G.m.b.H. Stettin and Hamburg America Line, Seebäderdienst, Hamburg.

By m.v. *Hanesstadt Danzig*, m.v. *Preussen*, s.s. *Kaiser* and s.s. *Tannenberg*.

June 24—Aug. 31.

Kiel ....dep.	—	—	We. 6 0	—	—	Sa. 6 0	—
Travemünde..dep.	Mo. 8 20	—	—	—	Fri. 8 20	—	Sun 8 20
Swinemünde dep.	,, 19 0	Tu. 1830	,, 19 0	Th. 1830	,, 19 0	,, 19 0	,, 19 0
Zoppot........arr.	Tu. 8 0	We. 8 0	Thr 8 0	Fri. 8 0	Sat. 8 0	Sa. 8 0	Mo. 8 0
,, ...dep.	,, 8 15	,, 8 15	,, 8 15	,, 8 15	,, 8 15	,, 8 15	,, 8 15
Pillau........arr.	,, 1145	,, 1145	,, 1145	,, 1145	,, 1145	,, 1145	,, 1145
Memel........arr.	—	—	—	—	—	—	,, 19 0
Helsingfors ..arr.	We. 17 0	—	—	—	—	—	—
Helsingfors ..dep.	—	—	—	—	Thur. 22 0	—	—
Memel ......dep.	—	Tu. 6 0	—	—	—	—	—
Pillau........dep.	Mo. 1230	,, 1230	We. 1230	Th. 1230	Fri. 1230	Sat. 1230	Su. 1230
Zoppot ......arr.	,, 1550	,, 1550	,, 1550	,, 1550	,, 1550	,, 1550	,, 1550
,, ...dep.	,, 16 5	,, 16 5	,, 16 5	,, 16 5	,, 16 5	,, 16 5	,, 16 5
Swinemünde.. arr.	Tu. 6 0	We. 5 50	Th. 5 50	Fri. 5 50	Sat. 5 50	Su. 5 50	Mo. 5 50
,, ..dep.	—	—	,, 6 0	,, 6 0	,, 6 0	,, 6 0	,, 6 0
Travemünde.. arr.	—	—	,, 17 0	—	,, 17 0	,, 17 0	—
Kiel.........arr.	—	—	—	,, 1850	—	—	,, 1850

¶ June 15 and 22 only.

 (See also p. 404)

Vessels.	Tons.	Vessels.	Tons.	Vessels.	Tons.	Vessels.	Tons.
Aalborghus ..	1482	*Diana*	942	*Hebe*	957	*M. G. Melchior*	1029
Aarhus	1627	*Dronning Alexandrine*	1854	*Hroar*	1401	*Odin*	632
A. P. Bernstorff	2316	*Dronning Maud*	1779	*Jylland*	2762	*Parkeston* ..	2762
Bergenhus ..	1398	*England*	2767	*Kjobenhavn* ..	1670	*Sleipner* ..	1069
C. F. Tietgen ..	1850	*Esbjerg*	2761	*Kong Haakon*	1775	*Trondhjem* ..	1399
Cimbria	1056	*Frederikshavn* ..	1482	*Kronprins Olav*	3150	*Vistula*	1250
Dagmar	2471			*Margrethe* ..	2465	*Ydun*	644

UNDER ORDINARY CIRCUMSTANCES.

The Company also maintains services between Copenhagen and Bordeaux, La Rochelle, Havre and Dunkirk and to Copenhagen from Portugal, Spain, Italy, North Africa, and furthermore between Copenhagen and United States and South America. Details on application.

Sailings subject to suspension or alteration without notice.

Copenhagen to the Faroes and Iceland.

m.s. *Dronning Alexandrine*, 1854 tons.

‡ These screw vessels carry 1st and 2nd class passengers, and have Smoking Room, Ladies' Room, Bath Rooms, Electric Light, &c., and carry a Steward and Stewardess. The *Dron. Alexandrine* has cabins for two and four passengers.

m.s. *Dronning Alexandrine.*

	Aug	
Copenhag'n d.	9	Thence every 3 weeks.
Thorshavn (Faroes) d.	11	
Vestmanno d.	13	
Reykjavik a.	13	
Reykjavik d	14	
Isafjord .. d.	15	
Siglufjord d.	16	
Akureyri .. a.	16	

m.s. *Dronning Alexandrine.*

	July	Aug	
Akureyri d	28	18	Thence every 3 weeks.
Siglufjord d.	28	18	
Isafjord .. d	29	19	
Reykjavik a.	30	20	
Reykjavik d.	31	21	
Vestmanno d.	A. 1	22	
Thorshavn F.I. .. d.	2	23	
Copenhag'n d	5	26	

GERMANY—DENMARK—NORWAY *and vice versa.*

	m.s. *Kronprins Olav.*	s.s. *M. G. Melchior.*	s.s. *Odin.*	m.s. *Vistula.*
Stettin ...... dep	—	—	Sat. 1915	Tue., Fri., Sun. 1915
Copenhagen .. arr.	—	—	Sun. 9 0	We., Sat., Mon. 7 45
,, dep.	Mon., We., Sat. 1830	Fri., Wed. .. 20 0	Mon. 20 0	—
Frederikshavn arr.	—	Sat., Thur. .. 7 30	—	—
,, dep.	—	Sat. — .. 1830	—	—
Gothenburg .. arr.	—	—	Tues. 8 0	—
,, dep.	—	—	—	—
Horten ...... arr.	Tue., Thu., Sun. 6 0	Sunday .. a.m.	—	—
Oslo .... arr.	Tue , Thu., Sun. 1030	Sunday .. 8 30	—	—
	m.s. *Kronprins Olav.*	s.s. *M. G. Melchior.*	s.s. *Odin.*	m.s. *Vistula.*
Oslo .... dep	Tue., Fri., Sun. 18 0	Monday .. 21 0	—	—
Horten ...... de .	Tue., Fri., Sun. 20 0	Monday .. 2330	—	—
Gothenburg .. arr.	—	—	—	—
,, .. dep.	—	—	Wed. 18 0	—
Frederikshavn arr.	—	Tuesday .. 9 0	—	—
,, dep.	—	Tues., Thurs. 20 0	—	—
Copenhagen .. arr.	We., Sat., Mon. 10 0	Wed,, Fri. .. 7 30	Thur. 6 30	—
,, dep.	—	—	Thur. 16 0	We., Sat., Mon. 1730
Stettin ...... arr.	—	—	Fri. 6 0	Th., Sun,, Tues. 6 0

May 29 to Sept. 17.

Esbjerg—Antwerp—Dunkerque.

s.s. *A. P. Bernstorff.*

Esbjerg	dep.	Sat.	1730
Antwerp	arr.	Sun.	1830
,,	dep.	Mon.	14 0
Dunkerque	arr.	Mo. p.m. or Tues. a.m.	
,,	dep.	,,	13 0
Esbjerg	arr.	Wed.	1330

Copenhagen. West Norway.

s.s. *Bergenhus*, s.s. *Trondhjem.*

From Copenhagen every Friday 18.0, calling at Arendal*, Christianssand*, Stavanger, Haugesund, Bergen, Aalesund, Christiansund and Trondheim.

* Call uncertain southward direction.

Copenhagen—Tallinn (Reval).

Cargo steamer about every 14 days passengers carried occasionally by special arrangement.

EAST BORNHOLM S.S. CO.

s.s. *Ostbornholm*, 133 tons, s.s. *Nordbornholm*, 375 tons.

Copenhagen to Bornholm Island.

From **Copenhagen** (Havnegade) to **Bornholm** (Hasle, Allinge, Gudhjem, Svaneke and Nexö). June 11 to Aug. 18, from Copenhagen daily at 21.0. To **Copenhagen** from **Bornholm** (Nexö) every day.

Copenhagen—Riga.

s.s. *J. C. Jacobsen.*

(Fortnightly)

From Copenhagen............. July 28, etc.
From Riga .... Aug. 2, etc.

Ice conditions permitting.

Copenhagen—Danzig.

s.s. *Sleipner.*

Copenhagen	dep.	Tues.	16 0
Gdynia	dep.	*Wed.	p.m.
Danzig	arr.	Wed.	p.m.
„	dep.	*Sat.	p.m.
Copenhagen	arr.	*Sun.	p.m.

* No passengers accepted.

LOCAL SERVICES.

Copenhagen—Aarhus. Direct in 8 hrs.

s.s. *Aarhus* and s.s *Frederikshavn.*

Daily, July 1–Aug. 20.

Copenhagen, dep.		23 0
Aarhus	„	0 15

Copenhagen—Nykjobing M.

s.s *Limfjorden.*

Copenhagen, dep.	Wednesday	17 0
Nykjöbing M. „	Monday	a.m.

Copenhagen—Randers. 12½ hrs.

s.s. *Cimbria,*

Copenhagen, dep.	Mon., Thur.	20 0
Randers „	Wed., Sat.	18 0

Copenhagen—Horsens. 11¼ hrs.

s.s. *Ydun.*

Copenhagen dep.	Mons., Thurs.	20 0
Horsens „	Wed. Sats.	19 0

Copenhagen—Vejle. 13 hrs.

s.s. *Koldinghus.*

Copenhagen dep.	Mons., Thurs.	18 0
Vejle „	Weds., Sats.	17 0

Copenhagen–Fredericia–Middelfart–Kolding. m.s. *Fredericia.*

Copenhagen,	dep	Monday,	Thursday	18 0
Fredericia	arr.	Tuesday,	Friday (abt.)	6 0
Middelfart	„	„	„ „	10 0
Kolding,	„	„	„ „	14 0
Kolding,	dep.	Wednesday,	Saturday	11 30
Middelfart,	dep.	„	„	13 0
Fredericia,	„	„	„	18 0
Copenhagen,	arr.	Thursday,	Sunday (abt.)	6 0

Copenhagen–Odense. m.s. *Odense*

(No cabin).

Copenhagen, dep.	*Tues., *Thur., Sat.	18 0
Odense, arr.	Wed., †Fri., Sun.	8 30
Odense, dep.	*Mon., *Wed., Fri.	17 0
Copenhagen, arr.	Tues,, ‡Thur., Sat.	7 30

‡ arr. 6.30. * Calls also at Samso. † arr. 7.30

Copenhagen—Hobro.

s.s. *Benedikt.*

Copenhagen, dep.	Sunday	17 0
Hobro, dep.	Tuesday	11 30

Calls also at Hadsund and Mariager.

Copenhagen—Aalborg. Direct in 9¾ hrs.

m.s. *Aalborghus,* s.s. *Kjobenhavn.*

Daily, Sunday excepted. (Daily July 2-Aug. 20).

Copenhagen, dep.	21 0
Aalborg, dep.	22 0

Copenhagen—Assens - Faaborg—Svendborg

m.s. *Möen*

Copenhagen,	dep.	Sunday	15 0
Assens,	„	Monday	a.m.
Faaborg,	„	„	p.m.
Svendborg,	„	Tuesday	14 0
Copenhagen,	arr.	Wednesday	a.m.

Copenhagen—Svendborg.—Nakskov

m.s. *Möen.*

Copenhagen,	dep.	Wednesday	15 0
Svendborg,	„	Thursday	14 0
Nakskov,	„	Friday	16 0
Copenhagen	arr.	Saturday	5 0

Copenhagen—Nakskov.

s.s. *Bellona* or s.s. *Rota.*

Copenhagen dep.	Sunday	17 0
Nakshov arr.	Monday	8 0

Copenhagen—Nyborg—Rudkjöbing—Nykjöbing F.

s.s. *Benedikt.*

Copenhagen,	dep.	Wednesday	15 0
Nyborg,	„	Thursday	10 0
Rudkjöbing	„	„	p.m.
Nykjöbing, F.	arr.	Friday	a.m.
	dep.	„	p.m.
Copenhagen,	arr.	Saturday	1 0

Copenhagen—Sönderborg—Aabenraa—Haderslev.
Copenhagen—Haderslev—Aabenraa—Sönderborg.

s.s. *Falken,* s.s. *Sonder Jylland.*

		dep.			dep.
Copenhagen,	Sun.	12 0	Copenhagen,	We.	16 0
Sönderborg,	Mon.	a.m.	Haderslev,	Th.	a.m.
Aabenraa,	Mon.	12 0	Aabenraa,	Fri.	a.m.
Haderslev,	Tu.	12 0	Sönderborg,	Fri.	15 0
		arr.			arr.
Copenhagen,	Wed.	5 0	Copenhagen,	Sat.	8 0

FINMARK FYLKESREDERI SKIBE. Services on application.

HAMMERFEST—SKJERVÖY & *v.v.* **HAMMERFEST—ØKSFJORD** & *v.v.*

Hammerfest-Mehamn. Mehamn-Vardö. Vardö-Vadsö-Kirkenes.

Pop Smit & Co. S.S. Service—Rotterdam, Culemborg and *v.v.*

Summer Services.—Rotterdam to Culemborg and *v.v.* (4½ hours). Several services daily.

GÖTHA S.S. CO. Antwerp—Gothenburg and *v.v.* (Weekly Service).

s.s. *Belgia*, 1715 tons, s.s. *Burgundia* 1715 tons.
Accommodation for 1 cl. pass., also Single Berth Cabins.

s.s. *Belgia.*	s.s. *Burgundia.*		s.s. *Burgundia.*	s.s. *Belgia.*
Fri. 16 0	Fri. 16 0	Antwerp (Quay 124 Des Bassins) ▲	Mon. 19 0	Mon. 12 0
Sun. 13 0	Sun. 22 0	▼ Gothenburg (Masthuggskajen 30)	Sat. 10 0	Sat. 10 0

s.s. *Burgundia* from Antwerp, Aug. 11, 25, Sept. 8, 22, &c.; from Gothenburg, Aug. 5, 19, &c.
s.s. *Belgia* from Antwerp, Aug. 4, 18, Sept. 1, 15, 29; from Gothenburg, Aug. 12, 26, &c

GOTLAND S.S. CO.

m.v. *Gotland* .. 1800 tons | *Hansa* .. 552 tons | *Drotten* .. 852 tons | *Visby* .. 828 tons
The above are Screw Steamers, carrying 1st, 2nd and 3rd class passengers. Two-berthed Cabins in first-class, and electric light on all Steamers. Stewardess carried.

STOCKHOLM—VISBY *via* NYNASHAMN.

	Daily.		
Stockholm dep. (Central)	18.55	21.38	Rail.
Nynäshamn arr.	20.20	22.55	
Nynäshamn dep.	—	23.30	Steamer.
Visby .. arr.	—	6.45	

		Daily.
Steamer	Visby .. dep.	22.0
	Nynashamn arr.	5.15
Rail	Nynashamn dep.	6.10, 7.45
	Stockholm arr. (Central)	7.46, 9.10

STOCKHOLM—VISBY

Stockholm dep. Aug. 1, 3, 5, 8, 10, 12, 15, 17, 19, 22, 24, 26, 29.

Visby dep. Aug. 2, 4, 7, 9, 11, 14, 16, 18, 21, 23, 25, 28.

KALMAR—VISBY—KALMAR.

July 1 to Aug. 29.
From Kalmar, daily except Mons., at 23.10.
From Visby at 9.45, Fris., Sats. and Suns. at 20.0 Mons., Tues. and Weds.

VISBY-NORRKÖPING.

Visby dep. 20.0, every Thursday.
Norrköping dep. 21.0, every Friday.

Rederiaktiebolaget GOTEBORG—FREDERIKSHAVN-LINJEN (G.F.L.)

GOTHENBURG-FREDERIKSHAVN S.S. CO.

By M.s. *Kronprinsessan Ingrid.*

Gothenburg ....dep.	Daily	7 20	¶Frederikshavn ....dep.	daily	18 0
¶Frederikshavn ....arr.	,,	1050	Gothenburg ....arr.	,,	2130

¶ Direct connection at Frederikshavn with *Nordpilen* (Northern Arrow) to and from Hamburg.

HALLANDS ÅNGBÅTS AKTIEBOLAG (HALLAND LINE).

LÜBECK—COPENHAGEN—MALMÖ—GOTHENBURG.

Daily except Suns.	1730	dep. Lübeck ....arr. ▲	Daily except Suns.	7 0
	8 0	arr. Copenhagen....dep.		1630
Wed., Sat.	p.m.	dep. Copenhagen....arr.	Mon., Wed.	13 0
Wed.	p.m.	arr. Malmö ....dep.	Mon., Wed.	11 0
Thur.	1715	dep. Malmö ....arr.	Sun., Wed.	7 0
Fri., Sun.	7 30	▼arr. Gothenburg....dep.	Sat., Tues.	16 0

The steamer leaving Lübeck Fridays is going from Copenhagen *via* Helsingborg direct to Gothenburg.

HAMBURG-AMERICA LINE. See also pp. 362, 406, 450, 459.

SERVICES TO NORTH SEA RESORTS.

Daily to Sept. 15.

Hamburg, dep...7 30	Heligoland, dep. 1150
Cuxhaven, call 1130	Cuxhaven, call 1430
Heligoland, arr. 14 0	Hamburg, arr...1910

Timings vary according to day.
Heligoland dep. daily 14.30 for Hörnum (Sylt), Westerland, Norddorf (Amrum). In the reverse direction, dep. from Norddorf, Westerland, Hörnum daily, due Heligoland 11.10.

A/S LARVIK—FREDERIKSHAVNFERJEN—OSLO.

s.s. *Peter Wessel.* May 27 to Sept 10.

Daily.			Mon., Wed., Sat. and Sun.		
2145	▲dep. Frederikshavn ....arr.	19 5	8 15	dep. Fredrikstad............arr. ▲	8 0
5 15	arr. Larvik ....dep.▼	1140	11 0	▼arr. Larvik ....dep.	5 30

ICELAND S.S. CO., LTD., to Iceland.

Subject to alteration without notice.

s.s. *Gullfoss*, 1200 tons, *Lagarfoss*, 1500 tons, s.s. *Godafoss*, 2000 tons and s.s. *Bruarfoss*, 1500 tons, s.s. *Dettifoss*, 2000 tons. Fitted with wireless telegraphy and carrying 1 cl. & 2 cl. passengers.

	Gullfoss.	*Godafoss.*	*Bruarfoss.*	*Lagarfoss.*	*Dettifoss*	*Gullfoss.*	*Godafoss.*	*Bruarfoss.*	*Dettifoss.*	*Lagarfoss.*	*Gullfoss.*
Copenhagen dp.	July 18	—	Aug. 2	Aug. 8	—	Aug. 16	—	Sept. 2	—	Sep 15	Sep. 16
Hamburg . . dep.	—	July 25	—	—	Aug. 9	—	Aug. 25	—	Sept. 8	—	—
Hull . . . . . . dep.	—	,, 28	—	—	,, 12	—	,, 28	—	,, 11	—	—
Leith . . . . . . dep.	,, 21	—	,, 5	,, 12	—	,, 19	—	,, 5	—	,, 19	,, 19
Seydisfjord dep.	—	—	—	,, 18	—	—	—	—	—	,, 25	—
Akureyri ar./dp.	—	—	—	,, 23	—	—	—	—	—	Oct. 1	—
Siglufjord dep.	—	—	—	—	—	—	—	—	—	—	—
Isafjord . . dep.	—	—	—	—	—	—	—	—	—	—	—
Reykjavik arr.	,, 24	Aug. 1	,, 8	—	,, 16	,, 22	Sept. 1	,, 8	,, 15	—	,, 22
Reykjavik dep.	Jly. 27	Aug. 4	Aug. 11	—	Aug. 19	Aug. 25	Sept. 5	Sept. 14	Sept. 19	—	Sep. 26
Isafjord . . arr.	,, 30	,, 5	,, 12	—	,, 20	,, 28	,, 6	,, 15	,, 20	—	,, 29
Siglufjord	—	,, 6	,, 13	—	,, 21	—	,, 7	,, 16	,, 21	—	—
Akureyri ar./dp.	—	,, 6/8	,, 13/15	—	,, 21/23	—	,, 7/9	,, 16/18	, 21/22	—	—
Siglufjord		,, 8	,, 15	—	,, 23	—	,, 9	,, 18	,, 23	—	—
Isafjord dep.	—	,, 9	,, 16	—	,, 24	—	,, 10	,, 19	,, 24	—	—
Reykjavik arr.	Aug. 1	,, 10	,, 17	—	,, 25	,, 29	,, 11	,, 20	,, 25	—	Oct. 1
Reykjavik dep.	Aug. 4	Aug. 14	Aug. 21	—	Aug. 28	Sept. 4	Sept. 14	Sept. 26	Sept. 27	—	Oct. 4
Isafjord dep.	—	—	—	—	—	—	—	—	—	—	—
Siglufjord	—	—	—	—	—	—	—	To London *via* North a'r. Oct. 16	—	—	—
Akureyri ar./dp.	—	—	—	Aug. 31	—	—	—		—	Oct. 13	—
Seydisfjord	—	—	—	Sept. 1	—	—	—		—	,, 16	—
Leith . . dep.	,, 8	,, 18	—	—	—	,, 8	,, 18		—	—	—
Hull . . . . dep.	—	—		—	—		—		—	—	—
Grimsby . . dep.	—	—	,, 26	—	Sept. 2	—	—		Oct. 2	—	—
Hamburg . . arr.	—	,, 20	—	—	,, 4	—	,, 20		,, 4	—	—
Copenhagen arr.	,, 10	—	,, 28	,, 8	—	,, 10	—	—	—	,, 26	,, 9

Calling also at various other ports—Husavik, Vestmanno, etc.; details on application.

INDHERREDS S.S. CO.

(See also page 440).

s.s. *Namsos* 506, s.s. *Havda*, 678 tons, carry'g 1 & 3 cl. pass.; single & 2-berth cabins. Stewardess carried.

s.s. *Namsos.*	s.s. *Havda.*			s.s. *Namsos.*	s.s. *Havda.*
Wed. . . 17 0	Fri. . . 17 0	dep. Trondheim	arr. ↑	Tues. . . 7 0	Thur . . 8 0
Thur. . . 3 0	Sat. . . 3 0	dep. Christiansund	dep.	Mon. . . 21 0	Wed. . . 24 0
Thur. 8 0	Sat. 8 0	dep. Molde	dep.	Mon. . . 15 0	Wed. . . 18 0
Thur. . . 13 0	Sat. 13 0	dep. Aalesund	dep.	Mon. . . 11 0	Wed. . . 14 0
Fri. . . 6 0	Sun. 6 0	arr. Bergen	dep.	Sun. . . 17 0	Tues. . . 20 0
Fri. 17 0	Sun. . . 21 0	dep. Bergen	arr.	Sun. . . 1 0	Tues. . . 7 0
† —	Mon. . . 4 0	dep. Haugesund	dep.	— †	Mon. . . 24 0
Sat. . . 7 0	Mon. . . 8 0 ↓	arr. Stavanger	dep.	Sat. . . 15 0	Mon. . . 21 0

Steamers also call Maaloy. † *Via* Sandnes.

June 1-Sept. 1.

MARIEHAMN STEAMSHIP COMPANY.

(HÖYRYLAIVA O.Y., MARIEHAMN).

Stockholm—Mariehamn—Abo

By s.s. *Per Brahe*, 704 tons, carrying 1st, 2nd, Saloon cl. and 3rd cl. passengers. Stewardess carried

Mon., Wed., Fri. 1630	dep. Stockholm	arr. ↑	1230 Wed., Fri., Sun.
,, ,, ,, 2345	arr. Mariehamn	arr.	7 30 ,, ,, ,,
Tue., Thur., Sat. 8 0 ↓	arr. Åbo	dep.	2345 Tue., Thur., Sat.

NAMDALENS-AKTIE-DAMPSKIBSSELSKAP.

Summer Service May-Sept.

s.s. *Herlaug*, 250 tons, s.s. *Rollaug*, 222 tons, s.s. *Folla*, 250 tons, fitted with electric light.

	Mon	Tue.	Wed.	Thur.	Fri.	Sat.	
Namsos . . . . dep.	14 15	14 15	13 0	14 15	14 15	13 0	
Rorvik . . . . arr.	18 30	19 45	18 15	18 30	19 30	18 30	
	Sun.	**Tue.**	**Tue.**	**Wed.**	**Fri.**	**Sat.**	**Sat.**
Rorvik . . . . dep.	23 0	3 0	22 0	0 0	1 0	2 0	21 15
Namsos . . . . arr.	Mo 5.0	9 0	We. 7.0	Th. 7.0	7 0	9 15	Su. 1.15

NAMSOS S.S. CO.

s.s. *Aafjord*, 335 tons; s.s. *Kystea*, 299 tons; s.s. *Nauma*, 218 tons.

Trondheim dep.	Mo. 17 0	Tue. 22 30	Th. 22 30
Namsos, arr.	Tue. 16 0	Th. 9 30	Sat. 11 45
Namsos dep.	Tu. 20 30	Th. 20 30	Sat. 18 30
Trondheim, arr.	Th. 6 15	Fri. 19 45	Mon. 0 30

NETHERLANDS RAILWAYS. Enkhuizen—Stavoren (s.s. Service).

Passage 1 hr. 15 min.

Twin-screw steamers *R. van Hasselt*, *C. Bosman* and *Van der Wyck*, each of 500 tons, fitted with electric light; carrying 2000 passengers, luggage and autocars.

From Enkhuizen. Three services daily. | From Stavoren. Three services daily.

NORMANDY S.N. CO.

Steamers.	Tons.	Steamers.	Tons.	Steamers.	Tons.	Steamers.	Tons.
Augustin Normand	171	*La Touqques* ..	227	*Trouville* ..	293	*Adolphe de Prince*	348
Rapide	174	*Gazelle*	173	*Emile Deschamps*	348		

Timings vary according to tide. For definite information apply to Cook/Wagons-Lits Offices.

Havre—Trouville and *vice versa*. Passage 45 mins.

Two or three times daily to Aug. 31, hours of sailing upon application.

NORDDEUTSCHER LLOYD.

SERVICES TO NORTH SEA BATHING RESORTS.

BREMERHAVEN-HELIGOLAND and *vice versa*.
WILHELMSHAVEN—HELIGOLAND and *vice versa*.
NORDERNEY—HELIGOLAND and *vice versa*.
HELIGOLAND—NORDERNEY and *vice versa*.
BREMERHAVEN—WANGEROOGE and *vice versa*.
WANGEROOGE—BREMERHAVEN and *vice versa*.
WANGEROOGE—HELIGOLAND and *vice versa*.

Usually one or two Services daily during July and August.
Particulars on application.

ÖRESUND S.S. CO. (Copenhagen).

s.s. *Hven* .. 216 tons. | s.s. *Saltholm* 219 tons | s.s. *Oresund* .. 573 tons. | s.s. *Sverige* .. 849 tons. | s.s. *Hälsingborg* 670 tons. | s.s. *Malmo* .. 670 tons.

These steamers carry 1st and 2nd cl. pass. and have two-berthed cabins, etc.

COPENHAGEN—MALMO and *vice versa*. (Passage 1½ hrs.)

Services subject to alteration without notice.

From Copenhagen—8.0, 9.45, 11.5, 14.30, 17.15 20.0, 23.55.
From Malmo—8.15, 11.30, 13.15, 14.45, 18.0, 19.45, 23.55.

COPENHAGEN { **HELSINGBORG** / **MØLLE (KULLEN)** } Weekly Service in each direction.

Antwerp—Oslo and *vice versa*. SAILINGS (Weekly). Passage 48 hours.

m.v, *Bretagne*, 3200 tons. m.v. *Brabant*, 3200 tons.
The m.v. *Bretagne* and m.v. *Brabant* carry 1, 2 (and 3 cl. male passengers).
1, 2, 3 & 4-berth cabins, 1 cl. Electric light. Stewardess. Bathrooms. m.v. *Bretagne* has one two-berth cabin with bathroom, and m.v. *Brabant* has single and double cabins de luxe.

Sat. 17 0	‡ dep. Antwerp Quai 100/102 arr ▲	Mon. a.m.
Mon. 12 0	▼ arr. Oslo (Vippetangen) .. dep.	Sat. 10 0

‡ Connecting trains from Paris (Nord) at 8.0 and 9.15, due Antwerp (Est) 13.41 and 13.33 respectively. Special motor transport conveys the passengers from the railway station to the Quay at Antwerp

Rotterdam—Christianssand—Oslo and *vice versa*.

s.s. *Bali*, 2,500 tons, carrying 1 cl. and 3 cl. passengers; m.v. *Biarritz*, 2500 tons, carrying 1 cl. also 3 cl. (male) passengers.

Rotterdam	.. dep.	Fri. 19 0	Oslo	.. .. dep.	Fri. 18 0
Christianssand	.. arr.	Sun. 12 0	Christianssand	,,	Sat. 14 0
Oslo.. ..	.. arr.	Mon. 7 0	Rotterdam	.. arr.	Mon. 6 0

AMSTERDAM—EAST NORWAY (Oslo or other port(s) in Oslo Fjord) and *v.v.* Weekly service on Fridays in each direction.
s.s. *Akershus*, with berths for 6 passengers, Aug. 4, 18.
m.s. *Bomma* (new vessel) with berths for 12 passengers, Aug. 11, 25.

Oslo—Danzig. (Weekly). Passage about 60 hours.

Service by cargo steamers of 1500-2000 tons, with limited passenger accommodation. Dep. Oslo (or near port, *e.g.*, Sarpsborg, Fredrikstad, or Skien), on Fri. or Sat.; from Danzig Fri or Sat.

PÄRNU REDERI A-B. (Pärnu S.S. Co.)

Stockholm—Tallinn (Reval) or Pärnu and *vice versa*.

s.s. *Estonia* 1117 tons; s.s. *Vironia*, 2030 tons.
Carrying 1st and 2nd cl. (3rd cl. s.s. *Estonia* only), and deck passengers.

s.s. *Estonia*.	
Stockholm dep.	Sun. 14 0
Kuressare arr.	Mo. 11 0
,, dep.	,, 12 0
Pärnu ....arr.	,, 17 30
,, ...dep.	,, 21 0
Stockholm arr.	Tu. 21 0

a s.s. *Vironia*. *b* s.s. *Estonia*.

a	*b*	*a*			*a*	*a*	*b*
W. 16 0	Th. 13 0	Sat. 16 0	▼ dep. Stockholm	arr. ▲	Tu. 9 0	Fr. 9 0	Su. 12 0
Th 9 0	Fri. 9 0	Su 9 0	arr. Tallinn	.. dep.	Mo. 16 0	Th 16 0	Sat. 16 0

RUD-CHRIST-GRIBEL (STETTIN).

Stettin-Helsingfors, *via* Tallinn (Reval)

(Fortnightly). s.s. *Rugen*, 2000 tons.

arr.	dep.	ITINERARY.	arr.	dep.
Aug. 5, &c.	Sa. 16 0	Stettin .... ▲	Fri. 9 0	—
Mo. 9 0	Mo. 10 0	Tallinn (Rvl)	We. 14 0	We. 15 0
Mo. 14 0	—	▼ Helsingfors	Aug. 2, &c.	We. 10 0

See also service of Finland Line on page 417.
When Helsingfors is closed by ice, steamers proceed to and from Hangö or Abo.

Stettin—Riga. (Weekly)

s.s. *Regina*, 1500 tons. Passage 40 hours.

arr.	dep.		arr.	dep.
—	Tu. 15 15	Stettin .. ▲	Mo. 8 0	—
Th. 8 0	—	▼ Riga	—	Sa. 16 0

Stettin—Tallinn (Reval)—Kotka—Wiborg. (Weekly).

s.s. *Strassburg*, s.s. *Wartburg*.

arr.	dep.		arr.	dep.
—	Fri. 16 0	Stettin .. ▲	Su. p.m.†	—
Su. †p.m.	Mo. 16 0	Tallinn ..	Fri. a.m.	Fri. 18 0
Tu. a.m.	We. 18 0	Wiborg ..	—	—
Th. a.m.	—	▼ Kotka ..	—	Th. 18 0

† Or Monday a.m. Ice conditions permitting.

Stettin—Stockholm—Åbo.

Sailings from Stettin:—s.s. *Brandenburg*, Aug. 5, 19; Sept. 2, 16.

arr.	dep.		arr.
—	Sat. 15 0	Stettin .... ▲	Mon. p.m.
—	—	Norrkoping....	—
Tue. a.m.	Fri. 12 0	Stockholm	—
Sat. a.m.	—	▼ Åbo	Sat. 12 0

s.s. *Nordnorge*, 990 tons; s.s. *Baroy*, 424 tons; s.s. *Skogoy*, — tons; m.v. *Fykan*, — tons.

Narvik—Lodingen—Svolvær—Narvik

	Sun.	Mon.	Tues.	Wed.	Thur.	Fri.	Fri.	Sat.
Narvik ....dep.	7 30	14 0	9 0	—	9 0	6 0	1830	10 0
							Sat.	
Lodingen ... arr.	12 0	2330	13 0	—	13 0	1115	1 15	1345
Svolvær .. arr.	17 0	—	1730	—	1715	—	—	1745
	Sun.		Tues.		Thur.			Sat.
Svolvær .. dep.	2115	—	2115	—	2115	—	—	2115
	Mon.	Tues.	Wed.		Fri	Fri.	Sat.	Sun.
Lodingen .. dep.	1 45	2 0	1 30	—	2 0	12 0	2 0	1 45
Narvik .... arr.	7 45	8 30	8 30	—	8 15	1715	8 0	5 30

Bergen—Trondheim—Kirkenes—Bergen.

s.s. *Nordnorge*. See page 415.

SALTENS DAMPSKIBSSELSKAB.

Steamers: *Salten*, 350 tons; *Folden*, 303 tons; *Sivert Nielsen*, 281 tons; *Ofoten*, 301 tons; *Bodin*, 825 tons; *Osa*, 88 tons; *Tötta*, 40 tons; *Kunna*, 85 tons; *Hammerö*, 117 tons.

GOING NORTH.

	Mon.	Thur.	Sat.	Mon.	Thur.	Fri.
Bodo .. d.	17 0	18 0	16 0	—	—	—
	Tues.	Fri.				
Svolvær a	13 0	—	—	—	—	—
Svolvær d.	21 0	—	—	—	—	—
	Wed.		Sun.			
Lodingen a	4 0	10 0	8 0	—	—	—
Lodingen d	5 0	22 0	1130	1130	3 30	—
		Sat.				
Narvik ..a.	1230	7 30	2015	15 0	9 0	—

GOING SOUTH.

	Mo.	Mo.	Tu.	We.	Th.	Sat.	
Narvik ..d.	6 30	18 0	24 0	17 0	18 0	15 0	
		Tu.	We.	Th.	Fri.	Su.	
Lodingen a	1030	0 30	4 0	2 30	0 30	1 0	
				Th.	Fri.		Su.
Lodingen d	—	—	—	3 30	12 0	—	19 0
Svolvær a.	—	—	—	13 0	—	—	—
Svolvær d.	—	—	—	2130	—	—	—
				Fri.	Sat.		Mo.
Bodo.. a.	—	—	—	2015	8 30	—	12 0

Connecting at Bodo, Lodingen and Svolvær with the B. and N. Line. (Page 415).

SARTORI & BERGER, KIEL.

Screw steamers: first and second class passengers carried.

Kiel—Flensburg.
Kiel—Fehmarn.
Fehmarn—Kiel.
} Services on application.

(**Lübeck, Travemünde to Grömitz, Kellenhausen, Dahme and Burg-Fehmarn.** Services on application.

Cie. G. SERGO & KO.

Helsingfors - Tallinn and *v.v.*

s.s. *Aegna* and *Suomi*.

Daily Service in conjunction with Finland Line, see *p.* 417.

Copenhagen - Tallinn and *v.v.*

Every 10 days. s.s. *Ruhno*.

July 30	16 0	dep. Copenhagen arr.	Aug. 6	20 0
July 31	20 0	arr. Visby...... dep.	Aug. 5	17 0
,, ,,	21 0	dep. ,, ... arr.	,, ,,	16 0
Aug. 1	20 0	arr. Tallinn .... dep.	Aug. 4	16 0

SONDENFJELDS NORSKE S.S. CO.

†**Kong Ring* ..	1998 tons	†**Kong Trygve*¶ ..	2000 tons	†**Kong Sigurd*¶ ..	920 tons
†**Kong Dag* ..	1950 tons				

The above are electrically lighted screw steamers. † These vessels carry Stewardesses.
* Wireless. ¶ No 2nd class.

Hamburg—Kiel—Oslo and *vice versa*, *via* Kiel Canal.

WEEKLY. s.s. *Kong Dag* and s.s. *Kong Ring*. Passage Oslo-Kiel, 26 hours, only 6 hours open sea. From Hamburg (Strandquay, Schuppen 20), dep. Sat. 15.30; from Kiel (Nordhafen) (in connection with train from Hamburg) Sun 3.0 arr. Oslo (Tollbodbryggen) Mon. 7.0.
From Oslo (Tollbodbryggen) dep. Sat. 13.0, arr Kiel (Rly. Station Wharf), Sun. about 16.0 arr. Hamburg (Strandquay, Schuppen 20), Mon. 7.0.
FORTNIGHTLY —s.s. *Kong Trygve*¶ from Hamburg, Alt. Wed., Aug. 9, etc., at 15.30, calling Kiel, due Oslo (Tollbodbryggen) Friday about 9.0; return from Oslo (Tollbodbryggen), Wed., Aug. 2, etc., at 11.0, due Kiel (Rly. Station Wharf), Thursday, about 19.0 and Hamburg Friday 10.0.

HAMBURG—CHRISTIANSAND and *vice versa*

FORTNIGHTLY—s.s. *Kong Sigurd*¶ from Hamburg, 15.30, Thurs., Aug. 3, etc., due Christiansand Fri. evening. From Christiansand, 13.0 Sats. Aug. 12, etc.; due Hamburg, Sun. evening.

Screw Steamers *Sandnaes*, 678 tons, *Stavanger* I., 718 tons.
These steamers carry First and Second class passengers. They have first class cabins for two and four persons, separate ladies' saloon, carry a stewardess and fitted with electric light.

Stavanger–Bergen. Daily.

Stavanger, dep.	20 30	Bergen, dep.	22 0
Haugesund, dep.	0 30	Haugesund, dep.	5 30
Bergen, arr.	7 30	Stavanger, arr.	9 0

SVEA S.S. CO.

See also pp. 408-417.

Brynhild	1982	*Drottning Sophia*	730	*Odin*§	630	*Södra Sverige*	520
Heimdall	1313	*Egil*	730	*Ragne*§	1377	*Vesternorrland*	550
Æolus	870	*Hyperion*	600	*Regin*§	1377	*Angermanland*	650
Birger Jarl	840	*Konung Oscar*	740	*Rhea*	600	*Örnen*	750
Vesterbotten	590	*Lulea*	630	*Runeberg*	520	§ Twin Screw.	
Carl von Linné	410	*Njord*§	640				

The above are Screw Steamers carrying 1st, 2nd and 3rd class passengers. The steamers are provided with two-berthed cabins, both in 1st and 2nd class, and Electric Light. Stewardesses are carried.

Stockholm—Gothenburg.

June—August.

	Drott. Sophia or *Södra Sverige*	*Birger Jarl.*	*Ornen.*	*Runeberg.*	*Konung Oscar.*	*Ragne* or *Regin.*
Stockholm ..dep.	Sun. 10 0	Tues. 16 0	We.,Sa. 1530	Fri. 16 0	Sat. 16‡0	Sat. 18 0
Söd rtälje .. ,,	—	—	,, ,, 1745	—	—	—
Västervik .... ,,	—	—	—	—	—	—
Oscarshamn .. arr.	—	Wed. 7 30	Th.,Su. 5 30	Sat. 7 30	—	—
,, ..dep.	—	,, 8 30	,, ,, 5 45	,, 9 0	—	—
Borgholm .. arr.	—	,, 1115	Thur. 8 15	,, 1145	Sun. 9 30	—
,, .. dep.	—	,, 12 0	,, 9 0	,, 1230	—	—
Kalmar .... arr.	Mon. 6 30	,, 1330	,, 10.45 Su. 9.45	,, 1415	—	—
,, .. dep	,, 11 0	,, 1715	—	—	—	—
Karlskrona .. arr.	,, 1715	—	—	—	—	—
,, .. dep.	Tues. 11 0	—	—	—	—	—
Ronnebyredd arr.	,, 13 0	—	—	—	—	—
Karlshamn ar./dp.	—	—	—	—	—	—
Ystad	—	—	—	—	—	—
Malmö ...... arr.	Wed. 7 30	Thur. 9 15	—	—	—	Mon. 6 0
,, ... dep.	,, 12 0	,, 13 0	—	—	—	Tues. 17 0
Copenhagen arr.	—	—	—	—	—	,, 1830
Landskrona dep.	—	—	—	—	—	—
Halsingborg arr.	Wed. 15 0	Thur. 1530	—	—	—	—
,, ..dep.	,, 19 0	—	—	—	—	—
Gothenburg .. arr.	Thur. 7 0	—	—	—	—	—
Gothenburg dep.	Sun. 17 0	—	—	—	—	—
Hälsingborg arr.	Mon. 5 0	—	—	—	—	—
,, dep.	,, 10 0	Thur. 19 0	—	—	—	—
Landskrona ,,	—	—	—	—	—	—
Copenhagen ,,	—	—	—	—	—	Wed. 20 0
Malmö .. arr.	Mon. 1730	Thur. 2130	—	—	—	—
,, ...dep.	Tues. 17 0	Fri. 17 0	—	—	—	—
Karlshamn ar./dp.	—	—	—	—	—	—
Ronnebyredd ,,	Wed. 7 0	—	—	—	—	—
Karlskrona .. dep.	,, 20 0	—	—	—	—	—
Kalmar .. arr.	Thur. 3 0	Sat. 10 0	—	—	—	—
,, ...dep.	,, 1030	,, 1630	Fri.,Tu. 1155	Mon. 14 0	—	—
Borgholm .... arr.	—	,, 1815	,, ,, 1330	,, 1545	—	—
,, ...dep.	—	,, 1930	,, ,, 1430	,, 1645	Sun. 14 0	—
Oscarshamn ,,	—	—	—	—	—	—
Västervik .. ,,	—	—	—	—	—	—
Södertälje .. ,,	—	—	Sa.,We. 6 15	—	—	—
Stockholm .. arr.	Fri. 7 0	Sun. 1230	,, ,, 8 30	Tues. 1030	Mon. 7 30	Fri. 6 30

Ornen: June 4—Aug. 21. Mons. dep. Rönne 21.0, and ar. Kalmar, Tu. 7.30; Suns., dep. Kalmar 10.45, arr Rönne 21.0.

Konung Oscar: ‡dep. Friday, June 23 18 0, arr. Borgholm, Sat. 1130.

STOCKHOLM—NORRKOPING.

Stockholm dep. Mon. 16.0
Norrkoping arr. Tues. 6.0
Norrkoping dep. Tues. 18.0
Stockholm arr. Wed. 7.0

Weekly. STOCKHOLM—RIGA. Passage 24 hours.

s.s. *Æolus* June 4—August 25.

9 † 0	dep. Stockholm ..... arr.	↑	12 0
9 0	↓ arr. Riga ..... dep.		12 * 0

* Mon. and Fri. † Sun. and Wed.

STOCKHOLM—MARIEHAMN.—See page 416.

STOCKHOLM—ANTWERP—STOCKHOLM. (Via Kiel Canal. Fortnightly).

s.s. *Hugin*, and s.s. *Rane* (3 berth cabins). 1250 tons. Stockholm dep. every second Sat., 15.0, and arrive Antwerp Wed. a.m. From Antwerp every second Wednesday, arriving Stockholm on Sun. p.m. Steamers from Antwerp remain 12 days in Stockholm.

June—August. **Stockholm—Norrland.**

	Vester-botten.	*Ragne or Regin.*	*Konung Oscar*	*Njord*	*Odin*	*Runeberg.*	*Egil or Hyperion.*	*Rhea.*
Stockholm dep.	Su. 9 0	Su. 11 0	Tu. 11 0	Tu. 14 0	We. 11 0	Wed. 18 0	Thu. 11 0	Fri. 11 0
Gävle arr.	—	—	—	—	—	Thu. 6 0	—	—
„ dep.	—	—	—	—	—	—	—	—
Söderhamn arr.	—	—	—	Wd. 6 0	—	—	—	—
Hudiksvall ar.	—	—	—	Wd. 14 0	—	—	—	—
Sundsvall arr	—	Mo. 5 0	Wd. 7 0	Wd. 24 0	Th. 7 0	—	Fri. 8 0	Sat. 8 0
„ dep	—	Mo. 1130	We. 11 0	Th. 6 0	Th. 11 0	—	Fri. 12 0	Sat. 11 0
Wasa. ...... „	—	—	—	Th. 19 0	—	—	—	—
Härnösand arr	Mo. 6 30	—	We. 1430	—	Th. 1430	—	Fri. 15 0	Sat. 1430
dep	Mo. 1030	—	We. 16†30	—	Th. 18 0	—	Fri. 18 0	Sat. 17†0
Köpmanholmen	—	—	We. 2130	—	—	—		—
Örnsköldsvik arr	—	—	We. 23 0	—	—	—	Fri. 24 0	Sat 22 0
„ dep.	—	—	—	—	—	—	Sat. 9 0	Su. 0 30
Husum .. dep.	—	—	—	—	—	—	Sat. 12 0	—
Nordmaling dep.	—	—	—	—	—	—	—	Su 8 0
Holmsund arr	Mo 1930	—	—	—	—	—	Sat. 18 0	—
Umeå arr.	Mo. 2030	—	—	—	Fri. 5 30	—	—	—
Sikeå .. dep	—	—	—	—	—	—	—	—
Skelleftehamn a.	—	—	—	—	—	—	Sun. 3 0	Su. 18 0
„ dep.	—	—	—	—	—	—	Sun. 9 0	—
Byske .... dep.	—	—	—	—	—	—	—	—
Piteå.... ..arr.	—	—	—	—	—	—	Sun. 15 0	—
Luleå .. ar.	—	Tu. 8 0		—	—	—	Mon. 1330	—
Luleå dep.	—	We. 2040	—	—	—	—	Wed. 7 0	—
Skelleftehamn „	—	—	—	—	—	—	Wed. 18 0	Mo. 15 0
Umeå „	We. 7 30	—	—	—	Fri. 19 0	—	—	—
Holmsund „	We. 9 0	—	—	—	Fri. 23 0	—	—	—
Örnsköldsvik „	—	—	Fri. 7 30	—	Sat. 7 30	—	Thu. 8 30	—
Köpmanholmen	—	—	Fri. 9 0	—	—	—	—	—
Härnösand „	We. 1815	—	Fri. 12†30	—	Sat. 1330	—	Thu. 16 0	—
Wasa .... „	—	—	—	Th. 22 0	—	—	—	—
Sundsvall .. arr	—	Th. 1630	Fri. 1645	Fri. 9 0	Sat. 1645	—	—	Tu. 1030
„ dep.	—	„ 18 0	Fri. 1730	Fri. 1030	Sat. 18 0	—	—	Tu. 11 0
Hudiksvall „	—	—	—	Fri. 17 0	—	—	—	—
Söderhamn „	—	—	—	Fri. 22 0	—	—	—	—
Gävle ...... „	—	—	—	—	—	Thu. 18 0	—	—
Stockholm .. arr	Th 1345	Fri. 10 0	Sat. 1230	Sat. 13 0	Su. 13 0	Fri. 6 0	Fri. 14 0	We. 6 0

† Calls Ulvo Harbour (for Ulvön).

SOCIETE DES BATEAUX DE LA COTE D'EMERAUDE.

MOTOR LAUNCH (VIDETTES BLANCHES) SELVICE FROM ST. MALO.

SERVICES: From St. Malo to Dinard and *v.v.* every 15 minutes during May and June; every 10 minutes July, August and September.

Passenger Lines of Stettiner Dampfschiffs—Gesellschaft J. F. Braeunlich, G.m.b.H.

LINE I.—Stettin—Swinemunde—Island of Rugen (Sassnitz).

T.s.s. *Rugard*, 1200 tons, T.s.s. *Hertha*, 1200 tons, T.s.s. *Frigga*, 855 tons, and T.s.s. *Odin*, 1200 tons.

Stettin—Rügen.

Daily from June 18 to Aug. 20. (Weekdays only from Aug 21).

11 0	↓ dp. Stettin .. ar. ↑	15 0
1410	↓ dp. Swinemünde ar.	1145
1945	↓ ar. Sassnitz dep.	6 0
	Calling at Heringsdorf, Zinnowitz, Göhren, Sellin, Binz.	

EXCURSION LINES.

June 27–Aug. 19. **Swinemünde-Rügen.**

Rügen—Copenhagen. s.s. *Odin* or s.s. *Hertha* or s.s. *Rugard.*

Swinemünde - Heringsdorf - Zinnowitz - Bornholm (Rönne) and back, and **Island of Rügen-Bornholm (Rönne)** and back.

Kiel/Travemünde—Warnemünde—Binz—Swinemünde—Zoppot—Pillau—Memel—Helsingfors. (See page 417).

SVENSKA AMERIKA LINJENS ÖSTERSJÖTRAFIK.

(Baltic Service). **SWEDISH AMERICA LINE.** (See also page 459)

A s.s. *Marieholm*, 1200 tons. **B** s.s. *Kastelholm*, 800 tons.

Cabins for 2, 3 and 4 persons, 1st class; general saloons, Tourist class.

☞ Hours of departure and arrival given on application.

	Stockholm. dep.	Konigsberg. arr.	Memel. arr.	Kalmar. arr.	Zoppot. arr.	Gdynia. arr/dep.	Zoppot. dep	Pillau arr	Zoppot. arr/dep.	Pillau. arr.	Memel. arr.	Kalmar. arr.	Visby, arr.	Stockholm arr.
A	Aug. 2	—	Aug. 3	—	—		—	Aug. 8	Aug. 4/6	Aug 6	Avg. 7	—	—	Aug. 8
A	,, 11	—	,, 12	—	—	—	—	,, 12	,, 13/15	,, 15	,, 16	—	—	,, 17
B	,, 18	Aug 20	—	—	Aug 22	Au 24/25	Aug 25	,, 25	—	—	—	—	Aug 26	,, 27
A	,, 21	—	,, 22	—	—	—	—	,, 22	,, 23/25	—	,, 26	—	—	,, 27
A	,, 30	—	,, 31	—	—	—	—	,, 31	Sept. 1/3	Sept. 3	Sept. 4	—	—	Sept. 5
B	Sept. 2	—	—	—	Sept. 3	Sept. 5	Sept. 5	—	—	—	—	—	—	,, 7
A	,, 8	—	Sept. 9	—	—	—	—	Sept. 9	,, 10/12	—	,, 13	—	—	,, 14
A	,, 18	—	,, 19	—	,, 20	—	,, 21	—	—	—	,, 22	Sep. 23	—	,, 24
A	,, 27	—	,, 28	Sep. 29	,, 30	—	Oct. 2	—	—	—	Oct. 3	—	—	Oct. 4

SKIPAFELAGID FØROYAR. (FAROE ISLAND S.S. CO.)

s.s. *Tjaldur*, 1130 tons. Calling at various other ports.

FAROE ISLANDS—COPENHAGEN and *v.v.*

Thorshavn dep.						Copenhagen dep	23 0	Aug 16	Aug 24		
Copenhagen arr.						Thorshavn arr.	a.m.	,, 18	,, 27		

PROVINCIALE STOOMBOOTDIENST op de WESTER-SCHELDE

STEAMER SERVICES FLUSHING, BRESKENS OR TERNEUZEN, TO SEPTEMBER 17.

Particulars of Train and Auto Services from Breskens to Knocke and Maldeghem given on application.

Weekdays unless otherwise stated.

Flushing ..	dep.	6 30	7†45	9 0	0†15	1130	12 45	14 0	15†15	1630	17†45	19 0	..
Breskens	arr.	6 55	8†10	9 25	10†40	1155	13†10	1425	15†40	1655	18†10	1925	..
Breskens	dep.	7 0	8†15	9 30	10†45	12 0	13†15	1430	15†45	17 0	18 15	2010	21†45
Flushing	arr.	7 25	8†40	9 55	11†10	1225	13†40	1455	16†10	1725	18†37	2035	2210

† Also Sundays	Flushing ..	dep.	5 50	9 † 0	12 45	16 0	18‡0	‡ Sundays only
	Terneuzen ..	arr.	7 0	10†20	14 5	17 20	19‡20	
	Terneuzen	arr.	7 20	10†30	13 50	16 10	19‡20	
	Flushing	dep.	8 40	11†50	15 10	17 30	20‡40	

TEXEL'S OWN STEAMSHIP CO.

m.v. *Texel's Eigen* STOOMBOOT-ONDERNEMING. s.s. *Dokter Wagemaker* and s.s. *Marsdiep.*

Texel—Nieuwediep.

Average passage 45 minutes.

From Texel, Weekdays (Oude Schild) 5.50, 7.50, 11.20, 14.35, 17.35.
From Helder, Weekdays, 6.50, 10 0, 12.20, 16.20, 18.55.
From Texel, Sundays and Holidays, 7.50, 11.20, 17.20 (19.30, July 1-Sept. 1).
From Helder, Sundays and Holidays, 7.30, 12.20, 18.30 (21.15, July 1-Sept. 1).

} Subject to confirmation.

TERSCHELLINGER STOOMBOOT—MAATSCHAPPIJ.

Terschelling—Vlieland—Harlingen.

s.s. *Holland*, s.s. *Prinses Juliana*, s.s. *Minister Kraus*, s.s. *Storkemelk*, s.s. *Vlieland.*

Service to June 19, per s.s. *Minister Kraus*, leaving Terschelling and Vlieland daily 7.45 from Harlingen 13.30.

June 20th-Sept. 5th, twice a day, leaving Terschelling and Vlieland 7.45 and 17.30; from Harlingen 9.0 and 13.30. Also from July 15 to August 15, on weekdays, on the Island at 14.0, from Harlingen at 16.0

Terschelling-Vlieland, Texel-Helder and *vice versa* (July 15–Aug. 15)

Terschelling dep. Mon., Wed., Fri., 10.0 Helder dep. Tues., Thurs., Sats., 11.0

Subject to confirmation.

TROMS FYLKES DAMPSKIBSSELSKAP. (See also page 440).

s.s. *Lyngen*, 489 tons (Combined tourist steamer and icebreaker).

NORWAY—NORTH CAPE—BEAR ISLAND—SPITZBERGEN and back (1939).

From Tromsø, Aug. 5, 17, 29, at 18.0 ; calling at Hammerfest, North Cape (Bear Island), Long-year City, West and North West Coast, including the Bockfjord, returning to Tromsø 10 days later. Special programmes on application.

VESTERAALENS STEAMSHIP COMPANY STOKMARKNES.

(See also page 415).

Lofoten	1717	*Nordland*	725	*Mosken ca.* ..	350
Finmarken	1119	*Hestmanden* ..	979	*Rost* ..	350
Richard With	945	*Sortland*	638	*Hadsel*	302
Vesteraalen	618	*Vaagan*	687	*Risosund* ..	206
Andenæs	780	*Raftsund* ..	614	*Boroysund* ..	157

The above are screw Steamers carrying first and third class passengers. The accommodation consists of cabins for one and more passengers, and separate Ladies' saloon in most of them. A Stewardess is carried. Electric light on all steamers.

CHEAP TRIPS from TRONDHEIM to NORTH CAPE, Etc., per s.s. *Vesteraalen* or substitute.—To GLOMFJORD, LOFOTEN, RAFTSUND, TROLLFJORD, VESTERAALENS, LYNGENFJORD, ALTAFJORD, MALANGEN, NORTH CAPE (12 days). Fares from Kr. 175.00.

Express Mail Service.

Stavanger, Bergen, Trondheim, Tromsö, Vadsö, Kirkenes.

In summer season *via* North Cape.

Places of call.				
Bergen	Mo. 2130	Th. 2130		
Florö	Tu, 4 45	Fri. 4 45		
Maaløy	,, 7 30	,, 7 30		
Aalesund	,, 1330	,, 1330		
Molde	,, 17 0	,, 17 0		
Christianss'nd	,, 2130	,, 2130		
Trondheim ..	We. 6 0	Sat. 6 0		
Sandessjöen..	Th. 4 15	Sun 4 15		
Bodö	,, 1230	,, 1230		
Svolvær .	,, 2130	,, 2130		
Lödingen	—	—		
Stokmarknes..	Fri. 1 0	Mo. 1 0		
Harstad ..	,, 6 30	,, 6 30		
Tromsö......	,, 14 0	,, 14 0		
Hammerfest..	Sat. 4 0	Tu. 4 0		
Vardö	,, 24 0	,, 24 0		
Vadsö	—	We. 4 0		
Kirkenes	Sun 4 0	,, 6 0		

Places of call.				
Kirkenes	We. 8 0	Sun 6 0		
Vadsö ..	—	,, 8 30		
Vardö	,, 1330	,, 1330		
Hammerfest	Th. 1030	Mo. 1030		
Tromsö......	,, 24 0	,, 24 0		
Harstad	Fri. 8 0	Tu. 8 0		
Stokmarknes	—	—		
Lödingen	,, 1130	—		
Svolvær ..	,, 1630	,, 2030		
Bodö ..	Sat. 2 0	We. 2 0		
Sandessjöen	,, 1115	,, 1115		
Trondheim ..	Sun 17 0	Th. 17 0		
Christianss'nd	Mo. 2 0	Fri. 2 0		
Molde	,, 7 0	,, 7 0		
Aalesund	,, 12 0	,, 12 0		
Maaløy ..	,, 1730	,, 1730		
Florö ..	,, 2030	,, 2030		
Bergen	Tu. 4 30	Sat. 4 30		

SAILINGS (Summer, 1939) from Bergen in connection with which there are special tourist arrangements. See Cook's programme for Norway, Sweden, Denmark, Iceland and Finland.

s.s. *Lofoten*, Aug. 14, 28.
s.s. *Finmarken* Aug. 3, 17, 31.
s.s. *Richard With*, Aug. 10, 24.

VESTERAALENS STEAMSHIP COMPANY STOKMARKNES.

Svolvær—Lofoten—Svolvaer.

Svolvær..dep.	Sun. 2030	Tue. 21 0	Thu. 1830
Rost	Mon. 17 0	Wed. 17 0	Fri. 10 0
Bodo ....dep.	—	—	Sat. 14 0
Svolvær.. arr.	Tue. a.m.	Thu. a.m.	Sun. p.m.

Via Henningsvær, Stamsund, Leknæs, etc., etc. Rost, Værøy, Leknæs, Stamsund, Henningsvær, etc., etc.

Stokmarknes—Vesteraalen—Stokmarknes.

Stokmarknes d.	Mn 8*a*30	Tu 22*c*0	Wd 5*b*0	Fr. 1.30
Stokmarknes a.	Tu 7.0	Wd 24.0	Th 5.30	Sat. 2.0

a Circular Tour, Outer Vesteraalen.
b Circular Tour, Andoya Inner Vesteraalen.
c Circular Tour, Outer Vesteraalen.

Local Services.

Vesteraalen—From Stokmarknes, Monday, 8.30; Melbo, Wednesday, 5.0; Stokmarknes, Friday, 1.30
Lofoten—From Svolvær, Sunday 20.30, Tuesday 21.0, and Thursday 18.30.

WASA NORTH SEA S.S. CO., WASA, FINLAND.

Steamers:—*Bjarmia*, 1817 tons, *Lapponia*, 1172 tons; *Fennia*, 1197 tons. *Clio*, 996 tons, *Patria*, 695·61 tons; *Frej*, 561 tons: *Iris*, 446 tons. Motor Ship, *Njord*, 505 tons.

No Passenger service at present.

IN ALPHABETICAL ORDER OF FJORDS. **SUMMER SERVICES.**

INDEX TO STEAMSHIP COMPANIES.

Fylkesbaatene i Sogn og Fjordane	PAGE 434/8
Hardanger Sunndhordlandske S.S.Co.	432/3
Helgelandske Dampskibsselskab ..	.. 433
Indherreds S.S. Co.	440
More Fylkes Rute Co.	439/40
Næsoddens S.S. Co.	PAGE 431
Nordmore Fergeselskap A/S ..	440
Stavanger S.S. Co.	431
Tonsberg & Hortens S.S. Co.	.. 431
Troms & Fylkes Dampskibsselskab ..	.. 440

INDEX TO THE PRINCIPAL FJORDS.

Balsfjord ..	PAGE 440
Battensfjord	.. 439
Bukkenfjord	.. 431
Dalsfjord ..	.. 434
Eikefjord ..	.. 434
Fördefjord	.. 434
Hardangerfjord	432/3 and 437
Hjorundfjord	PAGE 440
Kvenangfjord	.. 440
Lyngenfjord	.. 440
Malangenfjord	.. 440
Maurangerfjord	.. —
Moldefjord ..	.. 439
Næerofjord ..	435/8
Nordalsfjord	PAGE 434
Nordfjord ..	.. 434
Oslo Fjord	.. 431
Romsdalfjord	.. 439
Ryfylke ..	.. 431
Saltdalen ..	424
Sognefjord	435/8
Söndmore ..	.. 439
Sunnfjord	PAGE 434
Sorfjord ..	.. 432
Sundalsfjord	.. 439
Trollfjord ..	424
Trondheim Fjord	440
Vaagsfjord	440
Vefsen ..	.. 433
Vetlefjord	.. 435

In addition to the stations mentioned, the Steamers call at a large number of intermediate stations. Full particulars will be supplied upon application.

OSLO FJORD.

The steamer services in the Oslo Fjord are too numerous to give in detail in this publication. Particulars can, however, be obtained of the Editor.

Oslo, Hankö, Fredriksstad. S.S. *Beta.*

Services on application.

The Næsoddens S.S. Co. Oslo—Drobak.

Steamers—*Dröbak, Fegerstrand I, Kronprins Olav, Spro* and *Tourist I, Nesodtangen.*

Services on application.

The Tönsberg & Hortens S.S. Co.

Oslo—Horten—Tönsberg.

Steamers—*Horten* and *Jarlsberg.*

Services on application

Stavangerske S.S. Co.

See also pages 413, 415, and 425.

Stavanger—Sand—Sauda (Ryfylke).

Steamers.	Tons.	Steamers.	Tons.	Steamers.	Tons.	Steamers.	Tons.
*Sand**	350	*Vestri*	331	*Suldal*	—	m.s. *Fjorddrott*	—

The above are screw steamers with accommodation for first and second class passengers. They have a separate ladies' saloon and carry a Stewardess. † Electric light.

June 15—Aug. 31. **Stavanger—Sand.—(Lake Suldal)** and ***vice versa.***

		Vestri.	*Sand.*	*Vestri.*	*Austri.*	*Fjorddrott.*
		Suns.	A	Fris.	Sats.	C
Stavanger	dep	9 0	1830	1830	1415	1630
Sand	arr	1230	2245	2215	1930	1910
	dep.	1245	2315	2230	1945	1930
Saudasjöen	dep.	14 0	0 30	2345	2045	2015
Sauda	arr.	1415	0 45	24 0	2115	2025
			B	Sats.		—
	dep.	1830	10 0	14 0	2130	7 0
Saudasjöen	dep.	1845	1015	1415	..	7 15
Sand	arr.	1950	1130	1530	..	7 55
	dep.	20 0	12 0	1545	..	8 10
Stavanger	arr.	2345	1630	1945	Sun. 2.30	1045

A Mon., Tues., Weds. and Thurs. **B** Mons. to Frids. **C** Daily, except Suns.

Lake Suldal

June 15-Sept.

a	*a*	*b*	*a*	*b*	*a*		*a*	*c*	*a*	*b*	*a*
7 30	13 0	14 0	1745	1830	2030	↓ dep. Solheimsvik † arr. ↑	6 30	10 0	17 0	18 0	20 0
8 30	14 0	15 0	1845	1930	2130	arr. Nesflaten ¶ dep.	5 30	9 0	16 0	17 0	19 0

a Except Suns.
b Suns. only.
c Daily.

† Motor services to Sand.
¶ Motor services to Odda.

The steamers in the above services call at other piers *en route.*

The Stavangerske Company also maintain frequent and regular services to all stations in the various Fjords, there being five or six departures daily. Full particulars will be supplied upon application.

HARDANGER FJORD. The Hardanger Sunnhordlandske S.S. Co.

See also pages 433 and 438

The Steamers in the undermentioned services call also at intermediate stations.

Hardangerfjord†*, 649 tns., *Vöringen*†*, 402 tns., *Ullensvang*†*, 469 tns., *Vikingen*†*, 421 tns., *Stord*†*, 464 tns., *Rosendal*†*, 358 tns., *Hardangeren*†*, 226 tns., *Hordaland* 148 tns., *Söndhordland**, 138 tns.

The above are Screw-Steamers carrying 1st and 2nd cl. pass. They have separate Ladies' and Smoking Saloons, and carry a Stewardess. Steamers marked † have private 2-berthed Cabins * Electric light.

Tourist Route I.

Granvin—Odda—Granvin.

June 1–Sept. 20. (DAILY).

Granvin (Eide) d.	8 15	Odda ...... dep.	13 0
Utne .... ,,	9‡15	Tyssedal .... ,,	13 30
Lofthus .... ,,	10 15	Lofthus .... ,,	18 † 0
Tyssedal .... ,,	11 45	Utne .... ,,	19 0
Odda ....arr.	12 15	Granvin (Eide) ar.	20 30

‡ Connection with Tourist Route II to Oystese & Norheimsund.

Receives at Utne from Tourist Route II from Norheimsund & Oystese

† Connection with car (*p.* 223) fr. Odda (dep. 16.30).

Tourist Route II.

Ulvik—Norheimsund—Ulvik. (DAILY)

From June 1st to Sept. 20th.

Ulvik ...... dep.	8 0	Norheimsund dep.	15 30
Eidfjord .... ,,	9 0	Oystese...... ,,	16 0
Ringoy‡.... ,,	10 15	Utne......... ,,	17§30
Utne ...... ,,	*11 0	Ringoy .... ,,	18‡15
Oystese...... ,,	13 0	Eidfjord.... ,,	19 15
Norheimsund arr.	13 30	Ulvik ...... arr.	20 30

* Connection from Tourist Route I from Granvin (Eide).

§ Del'vs to Tourist Route I to Granvin (Eide).

‡ Connection Auto from and to Odda (p. 223)

BERGEN—SUNNHORDLAND (Express).

June 19–Aug. 21.

Connections at Ølen with Autos to Sauda and Haugesund.

	I.	II.	III.	IV.	V.	VI.	VII.
Bergen ..dep.	Sun. 13 0	Mon. 13 0	Tues. 13 0	Wed. 13 0	Thur. 13 0	Fri. 13 0	Sat. 13 0
Lervik....arr.	,, 1715	,, 1715	,, 1715	,, 1715	,, 1715	,, 1715	,, 1715
,, dep.	,, 1745	,, 1745	,, 1745	,, 1745	,, 1745	,, 1745	,, 1745
Sunde....	,, 1830	—	—	—	,, 1830	—	—
Skanevik	,, 1930	—	,, 1930	,, 1945	,, 1930	—	,, 1930
Ølen	,, 2115	,, 2115	,, 2115	,, 2115	,, 2115	,, 2115	,, 2115
Skanevik	—	,, 2230	—	—	—	,, 2230	—
Sunde....	—	,, 2330	—	—	—	—	—
Lervik ..	Mon. 1 0	Tues. 1 0	Wed. 1 0	Thur. 1 0	Fri. 1 0	Sat. 1 0	Sun. 1 0
Bergen .. arr.	,, 6 30	,, 6 30	,, 6 30	,, 6 30	,, 6 30	,, 6 30	,, 6 30

Express Services Bergen—Hardanger—Bergen.

June 19–Aug. 21.

Bergen ....dep	Sun. *24 0	Mon. 20 0	Tue. 20 0	Wed. 20 0	Thur. 20 0	Fri. 20 0	Sat. 14 0
Bakke ...... ,,	—		—	—	Fri. 2 0	—	,, 20 0
Norheimsund ,,	Mon. 6 45	—	—	—	—	—	,, 23 0
Oystese .... ,,	,, 7 15	—	—	—	—	—	,, 2330
Utne ...... ,,	,, 9 15	Tu. 4 30	We. 4 30	Thur. 4 0	—	Sat. 4 30	Sun. 1 30
‡Lofthus .... ,,	,, 10 0	,, 5 30	,, 5 30	,, 5 0	,, 7 0	,, 5 30	,, 2 0
Tyssedal.... ,,	,, 11 0	,, 8 0	,, 8 0	,, 8 0	,, 9 0	,, 8 0	—
Odda ......arr.	,, 12 0	,, 9 0	,, 9 0	,, 9 0	,, 10 0	,, 9 0	,, 4 0

Odda ......dep.	Mon. 18 0	Tue. 18 0	Wed. 18 0	Thu. 18 0	Fri. 18 0	Sat. 17 0	Sun. 12 0
Tyssedal.... ,,	,, 1830	,, 1830	,, 1830	,, 1830	,, 1830	,, 1730	—
‡Lofthus .... ,,	,, 2030	,, 2030	,, 2030	,, 2030	,, 2030	,, 19 0	,, 15 0
Utne ...... ,,	,, 2130	,, 2130	,, 2130	,, 2130	,, 2130	,, 20 0	,, 17 0
Oystese .... ,,	—	,, 24 0	—	—	—	—	,, 1930
Norheimsund ,,	,, 24 0	—	—	,, 24 0	—	Sun. 22 0	,, 2030
Bakke...... ,,	—	—	Thu. 1 30	—	—	—	,, 23 0
Bergen ....arr.	Tue. 7 0	Wed. 7 0	,, 7 0	Fri. 7 0	Sa. 7 0	,, 5 30	Mon. 7 0

‡ For Auto Services to and from Odda, see page 223. * In connection with m.s. *Vega*.

Bergen—Hardanger—Bergen

I.	II.	III.	IV.	V.	VI.		I.	II.	III.	IV.	V.	VI.
Mo 17.0	Tu. 17.0	We 17.0	Fr. 17.0	Sa 15.30	Su. 8.0	d. BERGEN a.	M 22.30	W. 7.0	Fr. 7.30	Su 5.30	Su 21.45	Su 23 30
22.30	—	22.30	22.30	22.30	12.30	,, Rosendal d.	17.0	—	—	—	17.30	15.0
Tu. 1.0	We. 0.0	Th. 1.0	Sa. 0.30	Su. 0.30	14.15	Bakke	15.0	W 0.30	1.30	—	15.30	—
4.0	3.30	3.30	3.0	2.0	16.30	Norh'ms'nd	12.30	T. 22 0	Th 21.0	22.0	12.0	—
4.45	4.30	4.30	4.0	3.0	16.0	Oystese ..	13.0	21.0	20.0	—	11.30	—
7.30	7.30	7.30	7.15	—	—	a. Granvin dp.	—	17.0	—	—	8.0	—
8.30	8.15	8.30	8.15	—	—	d. (Eide) ar.	—	—	—	—	—	—
—	9.15	—	—	—	17.30	↓ Utne ↑	11.0	—	11.0	20.0	—	10.30
10.0	—	10.0	—	—	18.15	Ringøy	10.15	—	—	—	—	—
11.0	—	11.30	10.30	6.30	19.15	Eidfjord	9.0	11.0	9.0	10.30	—	6.30
12.30	—	14.0	12.0	7.30	20.30	↓ Ulvik ..	Mo. 8.0	Tu 12.30	Th 8.0	Sa 12.0	—	Su. 8.0
—	—	—	—	—	—	ar. Utne ..	—	—	—	—	—	—
—	10.15	—	16.30	—	—	,, Lofthus	—	—	—	—	—	—
—	—	—	—	—	—	,, Opedal ..	—	—	—	—	—	—
—	12.15	—	21.0	—	—	,, Odda .. dp.	—	—	—	—	—	—

Stavanger Hard nger.

	II.	IV.
Stavanger .. dep.	Wed. 13 0	Sat. 8 0
Haugesund .. ,,	,, 1730	,, 1230
Bakke ...... arr.	—	—
Norheimsund arr.	Thur. 5 30	Sun. 4 0
Oystese .... ,,	,, 6 30	,, 4 45
Granvin (Eide) dp.	,, 8 15	,, 7 0
Utne .... arr.	,, 8 0	—
Lofthus .... ,,	,, 1015	—
Odda .... ,,	,, 11 0	—
Ulvik	—	—
Eidfjord	—	—

Hardanger—Stavanger.

	I.	III.	IV.
Eidfjord	—	—	—
Ulvik	—	Wed 1330	—
Odda . .... dep.	Sat. 23 0	—	Thur. 1330
Lofthus ...... ,,	—	,, 18 0	—
Utne ...... ,,	—	,, 19 0	,, 19 0
Granvin .... dep	Sun. 8 15	—	,, 2030
Oystese ...... ,,	,, 1145	—	,, 2230
Norheimsund ,,	,, 13 0	,, 22 0	—
Bakke .... ,,	—	Thur. 2 0	Fri. 1 30
Haugesund .. ,,	Mon. 4 0	,, 1430	,, 1430
Stavanger .... arr.	,, 7 30	,, 18 0	,, 18 0

Bergen—Sundal—Bergen (Kvinnherad Route).

	I.	II.	III.	IV.	V.	VI
Bergen ...... dep.	Mon. 13 0	Tues. 13 0	Wed. 13 0	Thur. 13 0	Fri. 13 0	Sat. 1430
Gødøysund .. ,,	,, 1630	—	,, 1630	—	,, 1630	,, 1630
Sundal ...... ,,	—	,, 20 0	—	,, 2030	—	—
Rosendal .... ,,	Sun. 2230	,, 2230	,, 2230	,, 2230	,, 2230	,, 2330
Sundal ...... ,,	—	—	—	—	—	Sun. 2 0
Bergen ...... arr.	Mon. 9 0	Wed. 7 0	Thur. 7 0	Fri. 7 0	Sat. 7 0	,, 8 0

Stavanger—Bergen.

	I.	III.
Stavanger .... dep.	Mon. 13 0	Fri. 13 0
Haugesund ...... arr.	,, 1630	,, 1630
,, ... dep.	,, 17 0	,, 17 0
Lervik .... arr.	,, 1930	,, 1930
,, ... dep.	,, 20 0	,, 20 0
Rosendal	,, 2230	,, 2230
Bergen .... arr.	Tues. 7 30	Sat. 7 0

	II.
Bergen .... dep.	Tues. 1330
Sunde	,, 2230
Lervik .... arr.	,, 24 0
,, ... dep.	Wed. 1 0
Haugesund ...... arr.	,, 3 30
,, ... dep.	,, 4 0
Stavanger .... arr.	,, 7 30

HELGELANDSKE DAMPSKIBSSELSKAB.

To Vefsen.

s.s. *Ranen*, 462 tons, s.s. *Vefsen*, 296 tons, s s *Helgeland*, 242 tons, s.s. *Thorolf*, 225 tons, s.s. *Harek*, 165 tons, s.s. *Donna*, 79 tons.

Sandnessjoen . dep.	Mon. 12.30	Tu. 5.0	Wed. 7.0	Thur. 5.30	Sat. 5.30
Mosjoen ...... arr.	Mon. 17 0	Tu. 17.15	Wed. 11.0	Thur. 18.0	Sat. 9.30
,, ... dep.	Mon. 20.0	Tu. 20.0	Wed. 14.0	Thur. 21.0	Sat. 11.0
Sandnessjoen . arr.	Mon. 24.0	Tu. 24.0	Wed. 23.30	Fri. 1.0	Sun. 2.0

To Rana (Mo) Services on application.

TRONDHEIM—HARSTAD. s.s. *Ranen*.

arr.	dep.		arr.	dep.
—	Sat. 16.0	↓ Trondheim ..	Fri. 6.0	—
—	Sun. 5.0	Rorvik ...... ↑	—	Thur. 18.0
—	Su. 10.30	Bronnoysund	—	Thur. 13.0
—	Sun. 19.0	Mosjoen	—	—
Sun. 21.0	Sun. 24.0	Sandnessjoen	Thur. 7.30	Thur. 9 0
—	Mon. 16.0	Indre Kvaroy ..	—	Thur. 4.0
Mo. 22.30	Tues. 1.0	Bodo	Wed. 20.0	Wed. 21.0
Tue. 7.30	Tue. 10.0	↓ Svolvær	Wed. 13.0	We. 13.30
Tue. 21.0	—	Harstad	—	Wed. 2.0

NORDFJORD, SUNNFJORD & SOGNFEJORDS.

Fylkesbaatene i Sogn og Fjordane.

Steamer.	Tons.	Steamer.	Tons	Steamer.	Tons.	Motor Vessel.	Tons.
Fanaraaken †	590	*Kommandoren* †	543	*Stavenes* (Local)	182	*Vaagsoy*	—
Nordfjord I. †	572	*Alden* †	432	*Balder* (Local	100	*Svanoy*	—
Gudvangen †	575	*Hornelen* †	257	*Lardal* (Local)	66	*Maaloy*	—
Firda †	501	*Framnes* †	307	*Kvamsoy* (m.v.)	—	*Atloy*	—
Sogn †	383	*Gula*	264	*Floroy* (m.v.)	—	*Nesoy*	-
Fjalir †	245						

The above are Screw Steamers carrying first and second class passengers. Steamers marked † have private two berthed Cabins. All Steamers carry a Stewardess, and with the exception of the *G la*, *Balder* and *Laerdal* have a separate Ladies' Saloon.

NORDFJORD—1939.

The steamers call at intermediate Stations in addition to those shewn.

GOING.

	A1.	A2.	A3.	A4.
	June 19 to August 26, 1939.			
Bergen .... dp	Mo 2130	We 2130	Thu. 2130	Sa 16 0
Askvoll .... ,,	Tu 5 0	Th 5 0	Fri. 5 0	2215
Floro .... ,,	,, 8 30	,, 7 30	,, 8 30	Su 1 0
Nordfjordeid... ar.	,, 1945	,, 1430	,, 23 0	,, 7 30
Sandane ...... ,,	We 1 15	,, 1730	Sat. 7 30	,, 11 0
Sandane ...... dp.	,, 2 30	,, 1830	,, 9 0	,, 1215
Utvik .... ,,	,, 5 30	,, 2045	,, 1230	,, 1430
Stryn (Visnes).. ,,	,, 9 0	,, 2230	,, 16 0	,, 1745
Loen .... ,,	,, 10 0	,, 2315	,, 1645	,, 1830
Olden .... ar.	,, 1030	,, 2345	,, 17 0	,, 19 0

RETURNING.

	A1.	A2.	A3.	A4.
	June 21 to August 28, 1939.			
Olden .... dep.	We 13 0	Fr 8 0	Sun. 8 0	Mo 13 0
Loen .... ,,	,, 1330	,, 8 30	,, 8 30	,, 1330
Stryn (Visnes).. ,,	,, 15 0	,, 9 15	,, 9 15	,, 15 0
Utvik .... ,,	,, 1745	,, 1030	,, 1030	,, 1745
Sandane ...... ,,	,, 23 0	,, 13 0	,, 13 0	23 0
Nordfjordeid.. ,,	Th 6 45	,, 16 0	,, 16 0	Tu 7 0
Floro .... ,,	,, 2045	,, 23 0	,, 23 0	,, 2045
Askvoll ...... dep.	,, 2245	Sa 1 0	Mon. 1 0	2245
Bergen ...... arr.	Fri. 7 0	,, 7 30	,, 7 30	We 7 0

A5. Måløy—Sandane—Stryn.

June 21 to Aug. 27, 1939.

	I	II	III	IV	V	VI	VII
Måløy.......... dep.	—	Mo 7 30	We 7 30	Th. 1130	Fr 1930	Sa. 7 30	Sa 19 0
Nordfjordeid.... ,,	Su 8 45	,, 1245	,, 1245	—	,, 24 0	,, 1330	,, 24 0
Sandane........ arr.	—	,, 1730	,, 1730	—	—	,, 1815	—
Sandane........ dep.	—	—	,, 18 0	—	—	,, 1830	—
Utvik .... ,,	—	—	—	,, 22 0	—	,, 22 0	—
Stryn .... arr.	—	—	—	,, 24 0	—	,, 24 0	—

Stryn—Sandane—Måløy.

June 21 to Aug. 28, 1939.

	VIII	IX	X	XI	XII	XIII
Stryn.......... dep.	Su 3 0	—	—	—	Fri. 2 30	—
Utvik .... ,,	,, 4 30	—	—	—	,, 4 30	—
Sandane ...... arr.	,, 8 15	—	We 7 0	—	,, 8 15	—
Sandane........ dep.	,, 8 30	Mo 7 30	,, 7 30	—	,, 8 30	—
Nordfjordeid.... ,,	,, 13 0	,, 1245	,, 1245	—	,, 13 0	Sat 7 30
Måløy.......... arr.	,, 1845	,, 17 0	,, 1715	—	,, 1845	,, 1230

SUNNFJORD.

B1, B2, B3 = Fordefjord Service. **B7, B8, B9** = Dalsfjord Service. See dates opposite.

GOING.	B1.	B2.	B3.	B7.	B8.	B9.
	June 19—Aug. 25.			June 20—Aug. 26.		
Bergen d.	M. 19 0	W. 19 0	Fr 2130	Tu 19 0	Th. 19 0	Sa 15 0
Askvoll a.	Tu 2 15	Th 2 15	—	W. 3 30	F. 4 30	—
" d.	,, 3 30	,, 3 30	Sa 5 30	,, 4 0	,, 5 c 0	—
Floro.. ,,	,, 7 a 30	—	—	—	—	—
Askvol ,,	—	—	—	—	—	—
Forde arr.	,, 14 0	,, 12 0	Sa 1515	—	—	—
Bygstad ,,	—	—	—	,, 1145	,, 13 0	Su 3 45
Kvitenesset	—	—	—	—	—	,, 4 0

RET'RN'G.	B1.	B2.	B3.	B7.	B8.	B9.
	June 20—Aug. 27.			June 20—Aug. 27.		
Kvite'net d.	—		—	—	—	Su 1530
Bygstad ,,	—			W 1 0	F 1730	,, 1730
Forde .. ,,	Tu 16 0	Th 14 0	Su 12 c	—		—
Askvoll ,,	,, 24 c	—		—	—	—
Floro ,,	—	—	—	—		—
Askvoll ,,	—	,, 2330	Su 214'	,, 2230	,, 23 0	—
Bergen ar.	W 7 30	,, 7 15	M. 7 15	Th 7 15	Sa 7 15	M 7 15

a Connects with **A1** from Bergen. *c* Connection at **Askvoll**, with Route **A3** from Bergen.

Continued next page.

Fylkesbaatens i Sogn og Fjordane—*continued.*

B10 and B11 DALSFJORD.—June 20—Aug. 24.

Floro............dep.	Tue. 0 15	Th. 0 30
Askvoll...........arr.	,, *e*2 15	,, *f*3 0
Askvoll...........dep.	,, *e*5 0	,, *f*5 0
Bygstad ....arr.	,, 1230	,, 1230
Eidevik........ .. ,,	—	,, 13 0

Eidevik ....dep.	—	Th. 1315
Bygstad .... ,,	Tue. 1415	,, 1530
Askvoll ....arr.	,, 21 0	,, 2330
Askvoll...........dep,	,, *g*24 0	—
Floro.............arr.	Wed 2 15	Fri. 3 15

e Connects with **B1** from Bergen. *f* Connects with **B2** from Bergen.
g Connects with **B1** to Bergen. *h* Connects with **B2** to Bergen.

FORDEFJORD, B4, B5, B6.

June 21 to August 27, 1939.

Floro dep.	Wed. 1630	Sat. 4 0	Sun. 1 0
Forde arr.	,, 24 0	,, 1015	,, 7 0

June 20—August 26.

Forde dep.	Sat. 16 0	Sat 1930	We 3 45	—
Floro arr.	,, 24 0	,, 24 0	,, 1130	—

The s.s *Stavenes* & s.s. *Balder* & motorboat *Maaloy*, maintain a local service between the various stations in Kinn, Eikefjord, Dalsfjord, Bremanger, Selje, Fordefjord, Nordalsfjord Particulars on application.

SOGNEFJORD. June 18—August 27.

Bergen—Sogn.

See pages 437/8 for additional Services.

	D 1.	D 2.	D 3.	D 4.	D 5.	D 6.
Bergen ...... dep.	Mon. 2130	Tue. 2130	Wed. 2130	Thu. 2130	Fri. 2130	Sat. 19 0
Vadheim ......arr.	Tue. 8 15	Wed. 6 0	Thu. 8 0	Fri. 8 0	Sat. 7 0	Sun. 6 15
Vadheim ......dep.	Tue. 9 0	Wed. 7 0	Thu. 9 0	Fri. 9 0	Sat. 7 30	Sun. 7 0
Hoyanger ......arr.	Tue. 1045	Wed. 8 15	Thu. 11 0	Fri. 1045	Sat. 9 15	Sun. 8 30
Hoyanger .... dep.	Tue. 1230	Wed. 9 0	Thu. 12 0	Fri. 12 0	Sat. 1030	Sun. 9 30
Vik ....arr.	Tue. 16 0	Wed. 1130	Thu. 1530	Fri. 1530	Sat. 13 0	Sun. 1315
Balestrand ....arr.	Tue. 1730	Wed. 1245	Thu. 1645	Fri. 1645	Sat. 1430	Sun. 15 0
Leikanger ....dep.	Tue. 1930	Wed. 1345	Thu. 1815	Fri. 1930	Sat. 1545	Sun. 1730
Sogndal ....arr.	Tue. 2145	Wed. 1545	Thu. 2030	Fri. 2230	Sat. 1745	Sun. 2015
Sogndal ....dep.	Tue. 2230	Wed. 1615	Thu. 21 0	Fri. 2330	—	Sun. 21 0
Fronningan ..dep	—	—	Thu. 24 0	Sat. 3 15	—	Sun. 24 0
Aurland ......dep	Wed. 3 15	—	—	—	—	—
Flaam ....arr.	Wed. 3 45	—	—	—	—	—
Laerdal ....arr.	—	Wed. 1845	Fri. 1 30	Sat. 5 45	—	Mon. 2 30
Laerdal ......dep.	—	Wed. 1945	Fri. 2 0	Sat. 7 30	—	Mon. 3 0
Ardalstangen ..arr.	—	Wed. 2115	Fri. 4 0	Sat. 9 30	—	Mon. 5 0
Skjolden ......arr.	—	Thu. 1 45	—	Sat. 1815	—	Mon. 1315

Sogn—Bergen.

	D 1.	D 2.	D 3.	D 4.	D 5.	D 6.
Skjolden ......dep.	—	Thu. 2 30	—	Sat. 21 0	—	Mon. 1430
Ardalstangen ..dep.	—	Thu. 9 0	Fri. 4 0	Sun. 5 0	—	Mon. 22 0
Laerdal ....arr.	—	Thu. 1030	Fri. 6 15	Sun. 7 0	—	Mon. 24 0
Laerdal ......dep.	—	Thu. 11 0	Fri. 6 45	Sun. 8 0	—	Tue. 1 0
Gudvangen ....arr.	—	—	—	—	—	—
Gudvangen ....dep.	—	—	—	—	—	—
Flaam ....arr.	—	—	—	—	—	—
Flaam ....dep.	Wed. 5 0	—	—	—	Sun. 2330	—
Aurland ....dep.	—	—	—	—	Sun. 24 0	—
Sogndal ......arr.	Wed. 8 0	Thu. 1330	Fri. 9 45	Sun. 12 0	Mon. 3 30	Tue. 6 30
Sogndal ......dep.	Wed. 9 0	Thu. 14 0	Fri. 1015	Sun. 1230	Mon. 4 0	Tue. 9 0
Leikanger ....dep.	Wed. 12 0	Thu. 1615	Fri. 1245	Sun. 1445	Mon. 6 45	Tue. 1215
Balestrand ....dep.	Wed. 15 0	Thu. 1730	Fri. 15 0	Sun. 1615	Mon. 9 15	Tue. 15 0
Vik ....dep.	Wed. 1615	Thu. 1845	Fri. 1615	Sun. 1730	Mon. 1015	Tue. 1615
Hoyanger ......arr.	Wed. 1915	Thu. 2045	Fri. 1930	Sun. 2015	Mon. 1630	Tue. 1930
Hoyanger ....dep.	Wed. 20 0	Thu. 2115	Fri. 20 0	Sun. 2045	Mon. 1730	Tue. 20 0
Vadheim ......arr.	Wed. 2130	Thu. 2245	Fri. 2130	Sun. 2215	Mon. 19 0	Tue. 2130
Vadheim ......dep.	Wed. 22 0	Thu. 2330	Fri. 22 0	Sun. 2245	Mon. 1930	Tue. 22 0
Bergen ....arr.	Thu. 7 15	Fri. 7 15	Sat. 7 15	Mon. 7 15	Tue. 7 15	Wed. 7 15

G I. Local Service fr. Fjærland, Balestrand, Fjærland.

From June 19 to Sept. 3.

	a	*b*	*c*	*a*	*d*	*a*	*d*	*g*	*g*	*h*	*l*
Fjaerland ..dep.	7 0	7 30	8 0	—	—	11 0	12 0	—	1730	—	—
Vetlefjord dep.	—	—	—	—	—	1230	1330	—	—	—	—
Balestrand arr.	8 30	9 0	9 20	—	—	1330	1430	—	19 0	—	—
Balestrand dep.	8 45	—	—	8 45	9 30	—	—	1445	—	1930	1930
Vetlefjord ..dep.	9 30	—	—	9 30	1015	—	—	1530	—	—	2030
Fjaerland ..arr.	11 0	—	—	11 0	1145	—	—	17 0	—	21 0	2230

a Sats. only. *b* Mons. only. *c* Suns., Weds., Fris. *d* Daily, except Sats. *g* Daily.
h Fris. only. *l* Except Mons. and Weds

Fylkesbaatene i Sogn og Fjordane.—*continued.*

E. LOCAL STEAMERS.

From June 19 (Route I) to Sept. 3 (Route III).

BETWEEN LAERDAL and GUDVANGEN.

Corresponding with steamers to and from Flaam, Balestrand and Fjærland.

	Sun.	Mon.	Tues.	Wed.	Thur.	Fri.	Sat.
Lærdal ....dep.	8 30	8 30	8 30	8 30	8 30	8 30	8 30
Simlenes .... „	11 15*c*	11 15*c*	11 15*c*	11 15*c*	11 15*c*	11 15*c*	11 15*c*
Gudvangen ....arr.	12 30	12 30	12 30	12 30	12 30	12 30	12 30
Gudvangen ....dep.	16 30	16 30	16 30	16 30	16 30	16 30	16 30
Simlenes .... „	18 15*d*	18 15*d*	18 15*d*	18 15*d*	18 15*d*	18 15*d*	18 15*d*
Lærdal ....arr.	20 0	20 0	20 0	20 0	20 0	20 0	20 0
Lærdal ....dep.	—	—	22 30	—	—	—	—
Fronningan..........arr.	—	—	Wed. 0*e*	—	—	—	—
Lærdal ....dep	21 30	21 30	Wed. 3 0	21 30	—	21 30	—
Ardalstangen ....arr.	—	23 30	—	23 30	—	—	—
Ardalstangen ....dep.	23 30	—	„ 5 30	—	—	23 30	—
Solvorn .... „	Mon. 4 0	—	—	—	—	Sat. 4 0	—
Ardalstangen .... „	6 0	Tue. 6 0	—	Thur. 6 0	—	6 0	—
Lærdal ....arr.	8 0	8 0	Thur. 8 0	8 0	—	8 0	—

c Corresponding with Route F1 Flaam to Balestrand and F2 Gudvangen–Flaam.
d „ „ „ F1 Balestrand to Flaam and F2 Flaam–Gudvangen.
e „ „ „ D1 from Bergen to Flaam.

F1. LOCAL STEAMERS.

From June 19 (Route I) to Sept. 3 (Route III).

Between Flaam and Balestrand.

Corresponding with Steamers to and from Gudvangen, Lærdal, Fjærland, Vadheim, and Bergen (at Slinde with steamers to and from Sogndal).

	Sun.	Mon.	Tues.	Wed.	Thur.	Fri.	Sat.
Flaam ......dep.	9 30	9 30	9 30	9 30	9 30	9 30	9 30
Aurland ...... „	10 0	10 0	10 0	10 0	10 0	10 0	10 0
Simlenes .... „	1115*a*	1115*a*	1115*a*	1115*a*	1115*a*	1115*a*	11 0*a*
Slinde (*b*) .... „	1230	1230	1230	1230	1230	1230	1230
Balestrand ..arr.	1445*c*	1430*c*	1430*c*	1430*c*	1445*c*	1430*c*	1430*c*
Balestrand ..dep.	1530*d*	1530	1530	1530*d*	1530	1530	1530*d*
Slinde *b*) .... „	1715	1715	1715	1715	1715	1715	1715
Simlenes .... „	1815*g*	1815*g*	1815*g*	1815*g*	1815*g*	1815*g*	1815*g*
Aurland .... „	1915	1915	1915	1915	1915	1915	1915
Flaam ......arr.	20 0	20 0	20 0	20 0	20 0	20 0	20 0
Flaam ......dep	2030	Tu. 1 0	—	—	2015	22 0	—
Fresvik...... „	—	5 0*i*	—	—	2330*j*	Sa 2.30*m*	—
Fronningan.. „	Mo. 0 15	—	—	—	—	—	—
Aurland .... „	3 0	7 15	—	—	Fri. 2 0	5 0	—
Flaam ......arr.	3 30	7 45	—	—	2 30	5 30	—

a Corresponding with Steamer, Laerdal–Gudvangen Route E and Gudvangen–Flaam Route F2. *b* Connects with autos to and from Sogndal. *c* Connects with Route G to and from Fjærland; D4, D6, D1, D2, and D3 to Vadheim and Bergen. *d* Connects with D6 on Sunday (waiting until 16.0), D2 on Wednesday and D5 on Saturday. *g* Connection with Steamer, Route E. Gudvangen–Laerdal, and Flaam–Gudvangen, F2 *h* Connects with Route D6. *i* Connects with Route D6, Sogn–Bergen. *j* Connects with Route D3, Bergen–Sogn. *m* Connects with Route D4, Bergen–Sogn.

F2. Gudvangen—Flaam.

In correspondence with steamers from and to Lærdal, Balestrand, Fjærland, Vadheim and Bergen.

Daily	June 19–Sept. 3.	Daily
9 30	↓ dep. Gudvangen .. arr. ↑	20 0
1115*a*	„ Simlenes .... dep.	1815*b*
1215	„ Aurland .... „	17 0
13 0	arr. Flaam ...... „	1630

a Corresponds with steamer Route F1 from Flaam to Balestrand and Route E Lærdal to Gudvangen.
b Corresponds with steamer Route F1 Balestrand to Flaam and Route E Gudvangen to Lærdal.

FERRIES IN SOGNEFJORD.

Nordeide—Grinde.

June 19 to Sept. 3.

8 0	16 0	dep. Nordeide	arr.	1545	24 0
1045	1845	,, Balestrand¶	dep.	1315	22 0
1130	1930	arr. Grinde†	,,	1215	21 0

¶ Connects with Steamer to Fjaerland.
† Connects with Auto Service.

Balestrand—Vetlefjord.

June 19 to Sept. 3.

6 30	—	—	dep. Balestrand ..arr.	—	—	2115
8 0	1230	1745	,, Grinde ...dep.	1115	1715	—
9 30	14 0	1915	arr. Vetlefjord .. ,,	9 45	1545	2030

Laerdal—Gudvangen.

June 19 to Sept. 3.

Laerdal ......dep.	8 30	1215	1815	2015	2045	2315
Amlabukti ....arr.	9 30	1315	1915	2115	2145	0 15
,, ...dep.	9 45	1330	—	2130	—	—
Gudvangen ...arr.	1230	16 0	—	24 0	—	—
Gudvangen ...dep.	—	7 30	13 0	1630	—	—
Amlabukti ....arr.	—	1015	1545	—	—	—
,, ...dep.	7 0	1030	16 0	—	1930	22 0
Laerdal ......arr.	8 0	1130	17 0	20 0	2030	23 0

Brygga—Maaloy.

Mon., Tues., Wed. and Fris., June 19 to Sept. 1.

9 30	dep. Brygga ....arr.	1630
11 0	arr. Maaloy ....dep.	15 0

SPECIAL SERVICES FOR TRANSPORT OF MOTOR CARS AND PASSENGERS.

June 20th to August 31st.

Bergen ......dep.	Sun.	8 0	Sun.	2330*a*	Tues.	8 0	Thur.	8 0	Sat.	8 0		—
Leirvik ..... ,,	,,	1330		—		—		—		—		—
Vadheim .... ,,	,,	1545	Mon.	6 0	,,	1430	,,	1430	,,	1430		—
Vik .... ,,	,,	1845		—		—		—	,,	1730		—
Balestrand .. ,,	,,	1945	,,	9 15	,,	1745	,,	1745	,,	1830		—
¶Fjaerland ....arr.	,,	2230	,,	1145	,,	2230	,,	2230	,,	2230		—
Flam......... ,,	,,	2315	,,	20 0		—		—		—	Sat.	9 30
Laerdal .... ,,		—		—	,,	21 0	,,	21 0	,,	2145		—
Ardalstangen arr.		—		—	,,	2330	,,	2315	,,	24 0		—
Laerdal ......arr.		—		—	Wed.	2 0	Fri.	1 15	Sun.	2 0		—

June 21st to September 1st.

Laerdal .....dep.		—			Wed.	8 30	Fri.	8 30	Sun.	8 30		—
¶Fjaerland ... ,,	Mon.	7 30			,,	8 0	,,	8 0	,,	8 0	Sat.	1730
Balestrand .. ,,	,,	1145			,,	1145	,,	1145	,,	1145	,,	21 0
Vadheim .... ,,	,,	15 0			,,	15 0	,,	15 0	,,	15 0	,,	24 0
Bergen ...... arr.	,,	2130			,,	2130	,,	2130	,,	2130	Sun.	7 0

¶ Connection at Balestrand. *a* Connection with s.s. *Vega* from Newcastle.

FERRIES IN HARDANGERFJORD.

Kinsarvik—Alvik.

May 26 to Oct. 16.

Kinsarvik ....dep.	8 0	11 0	15 0	18 0
Alvik ....arr.	9 15	1215	1615	1915
Alvik ....dep.	9 30	1230	1630	1930
Kinsarvik ....arr.	1045	1345	1745	2045

Ulvik—Brimnes.

May 26 to Sept. 20.

9 0	13 0	16 0	dep. Ulvik .....arr.	1230	1530	1930
10 0	14 0	17 0	arr. Brimnes ..dep.	1130	1430	1830

Kyrping—Fjaera.

May 26 to Sept. 20.

7 15	1130	1630	dep. Kyrping arr.	11 0	1545	2130
9 0	1330	1830	arr. Fjaera ..dep.	9 15	14 0	1930

Skanevik—Utaker.

June 10 to Aug. 31.

8 0	1230	1730	dep. Skanevik ......arr.	10 0	1845
8 30	13 0	18 0	arr. Utaker ....dep	9 30	1815

Skanevik (Utaker)—Kyrping.

June 10 to August 31.

Skanevik ....dep.	10 0	—
Utaker .... „	—	13 0
Kyrping .... „	1115	1545
Skanevik ....arr.	1230	1730

THROUGH ROUTES HAUGESUND—OSLO.

Daily Service.

8 0	dep. motor	Haugesund ....arr.	1845
11 0	arr. „	Kyrping ....dep.	1550
1130	dep. ferry	„ ....arr.	1545
1330	arr. „	Fjaera ....dep.	14 0
14 0	dep. motor	„ ....arr.	1345
1515	arr. „	Odda ....dep.	1230

1630	dep. motor	Odda ....arr.	1215
1745	arr. „	Lofthus ....dep.	..
18 0	dep. steamer	„ ....arr.	..
2030	arr. „	Granvin ......dep.	8 15
2115	dep. train	„ .....arr.	7 40
22 0	arr. „	Voss ....dep.	6 55
2235	dep. „	„ ....arr.	6 30
7 5	arr. „	Oslo ....dep.	2230

8 0	1630	dep. motor	Odda .....arr.	1215	20 0
1045	19 0	arr. „	Eidfjord ..dep.	9 45	1730
12 0	20 0	dep. „	„ ......arr.	9 0	1655
1430	2320	arr. „	Haugastol dep.	6 0	1445
1444	1 30	dep. train	„ arr.	4 21	1438
2030	7 5	arr. „	Oslo .....dep.	2230	8 35

—	1915	dep. motor	Haugesund arr.	2250
—	21 0	arr. „	Olen .....dep.	2120
—	2115	dep. steamer	„ ..arr.	2115
—	6 30	arr. „	Bergen ...dep.	13 0
8 0	9 30	dep. train	„ ..arr.	9 0
1950	2030	arr. „	Oslo ......dep.	2230

NORDMORE-SONDMORE-ROMSDAL FJORD The More Fylkes RuteCo.

Steamer	Tons.	Steamer.	Tons.	Steamer.	Tons.	Steamer.	Tons.
†‡‖*Jotunheim* ..	342	†‖§*Erik Jarl* ..	213	*Moringen* ..	100	†‖*Str. Riddervold*	201
†‡‖*Romsdal* ..	138	*Gancer Rolf* ..	121	§*Nordmor* ..	180	‖*Smolen* ..	180
‡‖*Geiranger* .	201	§‖*Hanko*	242	†‖‡§*Nordalsfjord* ..	295	†*Solskjel*	198
Hjorundfjord ..	100	‖*Kvernes* ..	103	†‖*Nordfjord* ..	223	*Ternen*	58
§‖*Driva*	325	‖§*Morejarl*	—	*Rauma*	120	†‖*Tourist* ..	52
‖†*Eira*	132	‡ With three berth cabins.		§ With four berth cabins.		‖ Fittedwith electric light.	

The above are Screw Steamers, carrying first and second class passengers. Most of the steamers have a separate Ladies' saloon and carry a stewardess. † With two berth cabins.

For connecting Auto Services see page 221/3.

Tourist Services.

June 13—Sept. 11.

Tourist Route 15c.

Molde ...... dep.	6 45	12 30	16 0	19 30
Vestnæs(Helland) arr.	8 15	13 30	17 0	20 30
Vestnæs........ dep.	8 45	14 0	18 0	20 40
Molde .... arr.	9 45	15 0	19 30	21 40

Connections at Helland with auto services to and from Aalesund and Sjoholt.

Tourist Route 15d.

Molde.......... dep.	6 0	10 45	15 30
Afarnes.. .... arr.	7 30	12 15	17 0
,, ... dep.	8 15	12 30	17 30
Molde .... arr.	10 0	14 0	19 0

Connections at Afarnes with autos to Aandalsnæs and Valldal.

Route 12.

	Weekdays.	Sundays
Aalesund .... dep.	13 0	13 0
Molde...... arr.	1630	1630
Molde...... dep.	1645	1645
Vestnæs....	—	1730
Aandalsnaes arr.	19 0	1930
Aandalsnaes dep.	22 0	21 0
Molde .... arr.	0 15	2315
Molde .... dep.	1 0	24 0
Aalesund ....arr.	4 30	3 30

Tourist Route 10b.
Valldal-Geiranger.
Daily.

	a	b	b
Geiranger d.	8 30	8 0	1445
Hellsylt ..d.	9 30	9 0	1545
Stranda ..d.	1230	1030	—
Dyrkorn a.	1345	—	—
Dyrkorn d.	15 0	—	—
Valldal ..d.	1715	1130	1730
Stranda	—	—	1845
Hellsylt d.	19 0	1330	20 0
Geiranger a.	20 0	1430	21 0

a Jne. 10-23 & Au.21-Sep.10.
b June 24—Aug. 20.

Route 15b.—Molde—Romsdalen.

	Sun	Weekd'ys	
Aandalsnaes dep.	19 0	7 0	*Tues. 20 0
†Helland(Vestn's) d.	2225	9 30	*Wed. 2015
Molde........ arr.	2315	1040	*Thur. 1915
†Molde .... dep	2330	16 0	*Fri. 20 0
†Vestnaes .. ,,	M.015	1645	*Sat. 20 0
Aandalsnaes arr.	M.2 30	2015*	—

† Correspondence with auto services Orskog-Aalesund and at Molde with auto service to Gjemnes (Batnfjorden) or Angvik.

Tourist Route 10c.
Valldal-Dyrkorn.
Daily to August 20.

Valldal (*a*)...........dep.	11 30	18 15
Stranda	13 30	19 30
Dyrkorn ....arr.	15 0	20 30
,, (*b*) ....dep.	15 15	9 0
Stranda	16 15	10 0
Valldal (*a*)	17 45	11 0

(*a*) Connections with auto from and to Aandalsnæs.
(*b*) Connections with auto from Aalesund.

Route 24. Auto Ferry "Trygge."

Weekdays.					Sundays.				Sundays.			Weekdays.				
6 0	9 15	1430	1715	21 0	8 0	1430	21 0	dep. Christiansund arr.	12 0	2040	1 35	9 10	1145	1650	2040	2 35
7 5	1035	1535	1835	22 5	9 20	1535	22 5	arr. Gjemnes ....dep.	9 25	1545	0 30	7 10	1040	1545	1840	1 30

Connecting at Gjemnes with auto services to Molde, etc.

Route 36. Christiansund Trondheim.

	Tue.	Thur.	Sat.		Wed.	Fri.	Sun.
Christiansund dep.	4 0	4 0	4 0	Trondheim dep.	8 0	8 0	8 0
Trondheim arr.	16 0	1745	1515	Christiansund arr.	1830	20 0	19 0

Route 19. Christiansund—Romsdalen.

Mo. 6 0	Th. 6 0	d. Christiansund a. ↑	Tu. 1730	Fri. 1730
,, 1445	,, 1445	a. Molde ..... d.	,, 9 30	,, 9 30
,, 16 0	,, 16 0	d. Molde ...... a.	Mo. 24 0	—
,, 1830	,, 1830	↓ a. Aandalsnaes d.	,, 2130	—

Bergen—Aalesund—Molde—Christiansund—Trondheim.
Routes 38 & 39.

Sat. 22 0	Tues. 21 0	dep.	Bergen ....arr. ↑	Sun.	2330	Fr. 4 0
Mon.5 0	Wed. 22 0	arr.	Aalesund ....dep.	Sat.	23 0	We.20 0
,, 14 0	Thur. 4 0	dep.	,, ...arr.	,,	1930	We. 8 30
,, 2115	,, 7 30	arr.	Molde ....dep.	,,	16 0	We. 2 0
	,, 1030	dep.	,, ...arr.	,,	15 0	—
	,, 1530	arr.	Christiansund ....dep.	,,	10 0	—
	,, 21 0	dep.	,, ...arr.	,,	6 0	—
	Fri. 7 0	↓ arr.	Trondheim ....dep.	Fri.	20 0	—

MOREFYLKES RUTE CO.'S SERVICES—*continued.*

Route 10. AALESUND-ORSKOG-HELLESYLT-MEROK (GEIRANGER).

	Mn.	Tues.	Wd.	Thu	Fri	Sat.
†Aalesund dep.	15 0	9 30	1730	1130	1430	15 0
Aalesund ,,	12 0	8 0	16 0	8 0	12 0	12 0
Orskog .. ,,	1515	—	—	1145	1430	1515
Dyrkorn.. ,,	17 0	1130	1930	1330	1630	17 0
Stranda.. ,,	1845	13 0	21 0	15 0	18 0	1830
¶Valldal Sylte	2045	1415	2315	—	2030	1945
Hellesylt dep.	—	1745	—	1745	—	2230
Geiranger ar.	—	19 0	—	19 0	—	2330

	Sun.	Mo.	Tu.	Tu.	Thu	Thu	Fri.
Geiranger dp.	11 0	—	—	2030	—	2030	—
Hellesylt ,,	1215	—	—	2145	—	2145	—
¶Valldal Sylte	15 0	2 0	2 0	0W45	2 0	2 F 0	2315
Stranda ..dp.	1715	5 0	5 0	2 30	5 0	5 0	2 30
Dyrkorn.. ,,	1830	6 30	6 30	—	6 30	6 30	—
Orskog .. ,,	1930	—	—	5 15	—	7 45	—
Aalesund arr.	2230	9 15	9 15	7 15	9 15	9 45	6 45

† Connection by auto at Dyrkorn from or to Aalesund. ¶ Connection by auto Valldal—Aandalsnaes.

Route 8. AALESUND-BJERKE-(HJORUNDFJORD).

	Tue., Thur.,	Wed., Fri.	Sat.	Sun.
Aalesund ....dep.	16 0		17 0	8 0
Saebo .... ,,	19 15		1930	1030
Oie .... ,,	20 0		2015	1130
Bjerke .... arr.	21 45		22 0	13 0

	Daily ex. Sunday.	Sun.
Bjerke ....dep.	5 30	17 0
Oie .... ,,	7 30	19 0
Saebo .... ,,	8 15	1945
Aalesund .... arr.	1115	23 0

Connection at Oie with Auto Services to Hellesylt and Nord Fjord.

Routes 30 and 31. CHRISTIANSUND—SUNNDALSØRA—TODALSØRA.

	Mo.	Tu.	We.	Th.	Fri.	Sat.	Sun
Christiansund d.	13 0	13 0	16 0	13 0	13 0	17 0	—
Sunndalsora arr.	1930	—	22 0	—	1930	—	—
Surna ......d.	—	19 0	—	17 0	—	2145	—
Todalsöra ..arr.	—	21 0	—	1945	—		1 45

	Tue	We.	Th.	Fri.	Sat.	Sun
Todalsöra dep.	—	4 0	—	4 0	—	15 0
Surna ...... ,,	—	7 15	—	6 0	—	17 0
Sunndalsora ,,	4 0	—	5 0	—	4 0	—
Christiansund a.	10 0	1215	9 45	1030	1015	22 0

At Sunndalsora connections by auto for and from Opdal.

By s.s. Auto Carrier *Gaute.* **NORDMORE FERGESELSKAP AUTO SERVICE.** June 1 to Sept. 15.

	Daily.		Weekdays except Sats.			Saturday.			Sunday	
Christiansund dep.	8 0	1030	1315	16 0	1830	1430	17 0	1930	16 0	2045
Kvisvik .. .. arr.	9 15	1145	1430	1715	1945	1545	1815	2045	1715	22 0
,, ...dep.	9 15	1145	1430	1715	1945	1545	1815	2045	1930	22 0
Christiansund arr.	1015	1245	1530	1815	2045	1645	1915	2145	2030	23 0

Connecting auto services to Opdal, or Sunnadal, Trondheim.

TROMS FYLKES DAMPSKIBSSELSKAB. (See also page 428)

Lyngen	489	*Kvalö*	295	*Tromsö*	239
Dyröy	372	*Bjarköy*	286	*Salangen* (Diesel Motor Ship)	131
Skjærvö	331	*Malangen*	276	*Lavangen* ,, ,, about	100
Trondenes	305				

The above are Screw Steamers. They all carry only first and second class passengers. Cabins for one and two passengers. General Saloons each ship; also separate Ladies' and Smoking Rooms on the steamers. A Stewardess is carried. The vessels are fitted with Electric Light.

Harstad, Narvik.

Harstad dp.	Sun. 7 30	Tue. 7 30	Wd. 21 0	Th. 7 30
Lödingen,,	,, 1245	,, 1230	Thu. 4 † 0	—
Narvik ar.	,, 16 0	,, 1645	—	,, 1430
			† arr. 2.30	

Narvik dp.	Sun. 22 0	Tue. 20 0	—	Thu. 19 0
Lödingen,,	Mo. 2 0	„ 0 30	Thu. 3 30	—
Harstad ar.	,, a.m.	Wed. a.m.	8 30	Fri. a.m.
Tromso ar.	—	—	—	—

Tromsö, Harstad, Narvik.

TOURS INSIDE SENJA.—From Tromsö every Wed. 19.0, and Sat. at 18.0, due Harstad every Fri. a.m. and Sunday p.m. From Harstad every Mon. 20.0, and Sat. at 19.0, due Tromsö Wed. a.m. and Sun. p.m.

TOURS OUTSIDE SENJA—From Tromsö every Sun. at 22.0 and Thur. at 12.0, due Harstad every Tues. a m. and Fri. p.m.

From Harstad every Wed. at 14.0, due Tromsö Thur. p.m.

BALSFJORD **KVENANGFJORD** **VAAGSFJORD**
LYNGENFJORD **MALANGENFJORD** **ASTAFJORD** } *Services on application.*

Steamers: *Inherred* — tons; *Stenkjaer* 163 tons; *Kong Oscar*, 122 tons.

TRONDHEIM FJORD. Indherreds S.S. Co.

Trondheim—Indherred.

(See also p.421).

Mon.	Tu.	Tu.	We.	Th.	Fr.	Sat.	
11 0	8 0	16 0	8 0	15 0	8 0	15 0	Trondheim d. ▲
—	13 0	—	—	1930	13 0	—	Levanger dp.
21 0	—	2230	1530	2230	—	2130	Stenkjaer dp.
—	—	—	2030	—	—	—	▼ Hjellneset ..

Sunday.		Tu.	Tu.	Th.	Th.	Fr.
1930	18 0	9 30	23 0	19 0	9 30	14 0
—	14 0	—	1530	1430	—	10 0
14 0	—	4 0	—	8 0	4 0	5 0
—	—	—	—	5 0	—	—

PART V.—Services from the United Kingdom and the Continent to Africa (not *via* Suez Canal), America, Australia (*via* the Cape), Canada, Canary Islands, &c.

American Export Lines .. .. PAGE 443
Anchor Line 459
Barber Line 447
Bergenske S.S. Co. .. 444
Blue Funnel and Shaw Savill Line .. 442
Blue Star Line 444
Booth Line 444
Canadian Pacific 459
Carregadores Acoreanos Line 443
Chargeurs Béunis 445
Commonwealth & Dominion Line Ltd (see Port Line)
Cunard White Star, Ltd. 459
Deutsch Ost-Afrika Line 446
Donaldson Atlantic Line, Ltd. 459
East Asiatic Co., Ltd. (see Ostasiatiske Kompagni)
Elder, Dempster Lines 447
Ellerman & Bucknall S.S. Co., Ltd. .. 448
Empreza Insulana 448
Fabre Line 448
Fraissinet (French Mail) S.S. Co. 448
Fred Olsen Line 448
French Line (see Transatlantique Cié Generale)
Furness Line 449, 459
Fyffes Line.. 449
Gdynia Amerika Schiffahrtslinien, A.G. 449, 459
German Af'ca Service (see 'Deutsch Ost-Afrika Linie')
Hamburg America Line .. 450, 459
Hamburg-Bremer Afrika Line 446
Hamburg South American Line 451
Harrison Line 452
Holland Africa Line .. 452
Holland America Line 459, 462
Holland West Africa Line 452
Horn Line 453
Houlder Line 453
"Italia" Soc. An. di Navigazione 454/5
Interocean Line 453
Johnson Line 456
Jamaica Banana Producers S.S. Co., Ltd. 455
Koninklijke Nederlandsche Stoomboot Maatschappij, N.V. .. .. PAGE 456
Kosmos Line 450
Lamport and Holt Line .. 457
Lloyd Triestino, Soc. An. di Navigazione 456A
MacAndrew-Yeoward Service 468
Messageries Maritimes de France 457
Natal Line of Steamers 457
Navegacao (Companhia Colonial de) 457
Navegacao (Companhia Nacional de) .. 457
New Zealand Shipping Co., Ltd. .. 459
Norddeutscher Lloyd 458/9
Norwegian America Line 459
Ostasiatiske Kompagni 460
Pacific S N. Co... 462
Paquet Line 460
Port Line 460
Red Star Line 459
Royal Netherlands Steamship Co. (see Koninklijke Nederlandsche Stoomboot Maatschappij, N.V.)
Royal Mail Lines Ltd.. .. .. 461/2
Shaw Savill Line 442, 463
Skandinaviske Syd-Pacific Line 463
Sud Americana de Vapores 463
Sud-Atlantique Co. 445
Swedish American Line 459
Transatlantic S.S. Co., Ltd. (Gothenburg) 463
Transatlantique (Compagnie Generale) 459, 466
Transports Maritimes à Vapeur (Société Gen. 464
Trasatlantica Española (Compania) 464
Trasmediterranea Compania 465
Union Castle Mail S.S. Co., Ltd. .. 467
United Netherlands Nav. Co. 452
United States Lines 459
Westfal-Larsen Co. Line 458
Wilh Wilhelmsen Lines 468
Woermann Line 446
Ybarra y Cia, Seville .. 468
Yeoward Line (*see* MacAndrew-Yeoward Service)

BLUE FUNNEL AND SHAW SAVILL—Joint Service.

Blue Funnel steamers carry 1st class only. Shaw Savill steamers carry 1st, 1st and 3rd or cabin class, according to steamer. *Passengers embark/land Southampton. * First class only. † From London.

Steamer	Tons	Leaves Liverp'l	‡§Due Madeira or Teneriffe	Due Cape Town	Due Durb'n	Due Fremantle	Due Adelaide	Due Melbourne	Due Sydney	Due Brisbane
§*Domini'n Mon'rch**	27000	Aug. 4†	Aug. ‖ 7	Aug 18	Aug. 19	Aug. 30	—	Sept. 3	Sept. 5	Sept. 8¶
‡*Nestor*	14629	,, 12	,, 17	Sept 1	Sept. 4	Sept. 18	Sept. 23	,, 25	,, 28	Oct. 2
§*Ceramic*..........	18495	,, 26	,, 31	,, 13	,, 16	,, 29	Oct. 4	Oct. 6	Oct. 9	—
‡*Anchises*	10000	Sept. 23	Sept. 28	Oct. 13	—	Oct. 29	Nov. 4	Nov. 6	Nov. 9	Nov. 13
§*Themistocles*	11250	Oct. 7	Oct. 13	,, 27	—	Nov. 13	,, 18	,, 20	,, 23	,, 29
§*Domini'n Mon'rch**	27000	Nov. 23	Nov. 27	Dec. 7	Dec. 9	Dec. 19	—	Dec. 23	Dec. 25	ec. 28¶

§ Shaw Savill steamers call Teneriffe. ‡ Blue Funnel steamers call Madeira. ‖ Calls Madeira. ¶ New Zealand.

Steamer	Tons	Leaves Brisbane	Leaves Sydney	Leaves Melbourne	Leaves Adelaide	Leaves Fremantle	arr./dep. Durban	Dep. Cape Town	Due Maderia or Teneriffe	Due Liverpool
‡*Anchises*	10000	Jun. 28	July 8	July 12	July 15	July 21	Aug. 4/6	Aug. 9	Aug. 24	Aug. 29
‡ *Ulysses*	14652	July 26	Aug. 5	Aug. 9	Aug 12	Aug. 18	Sept. 1/3	Sept. 6	Sept. 21	Sept. 26
‡*Ascanius*	10048	Sept. 6	Sept. 16	Sept. 20	Sept. 23	Sept. 29	Oct 13/15	Oct. 18	Nov. 2	Nov. 7
**Domini'n Mon'ch*	27000	¶Oct. 3	Oct. 6	Oct. 8	—	Oct. 12	,, 22	,, 24	,, 3	,, 7*
‡*Nestor*	14629	,, 4	,, 14	,, 18	Oct. 21	,, 27	Nv. 10/12	Nov. 15	,, 30	Dec. 5

Syria—Palestine—Egypt—Greece—Italy—France—Boston—New York Service.

(Fortnightly throughout the year.)

Steamers carry a Doctor and Stewardess and carry "first-class" passengers only. Most of the 54 cabins are equipped with bath or shower. *Oil fuel, turbine engines.

*Steamer.	Tons.	*Steamer.	Tons.	*Steamer.	Tons.	Steamer.	Tons.
Excalibur	9300	*Excambion*	9300	*Exochorda*	9300	*Exeter*	9300

EASTBOUND.

Steamer.	New York. Sail 11 a.m. Sat. (o)	Marseilles. Arr.7 p.m. Tues. Sail midn. Wed.	Naples. Arr. 6 a.m. Fri. Sail 8 p.m. Fri.	Alexandria. Arrive noon Mon. Sail noon Wed.	Jaffa/ Tel Aviv. Arr.6 a.m. Thur. Sail 8 p.m. Thur.	Haifa. Arr.6 a.m. Fri. Sail midn. Fri.	Beirut. Arr.6 a.m. Sat. Sail midn. Sun.	Haifa. Arr.6 a.m. Mon. Sail noon Mon.
Exeter	July 8	July 18/19	July 21	July 24/26	July 27	July 28	July29/30	July 31
Excambion ..	„ 22	Aug. 1/2	Aug. 4	Aug. 7/9	Aug. 10	Aug. 11	Aug 12/13	Aug. 14
Exochorda ..	Aug. 5	„ 15/16	„ 18	„ 21/23	„ 24	„ 25	„ 26/27	„ 28
Excalibur ..	„ 19	„ 29/30	Sept. 1	Sept. 4/6	Sept. 7	Sept. 8	Sept. 9/10	Sept. 11
Exeter	Sept. 2	Sep. 12/13	„ 15	„ 18/20	„ 21	„ 22	„ 23/24	„ 25
Excambion ..	„ 16	„ 26/27	„ 29	Oct. 2/4	Oct. 5	Oct. 6	Oct. 7/8	Oct. 9
Exochorda ..	„ 30	Oct. 10/11	Oct. 13	„ 16/18	„ 19	„ 20	„ 21/22	„ 23
Excalibur ..	Oct. 14	„ 24/25	„ 27	„ 30/Nv. 1	Nov. 2	Nov. 3	Nov 4/5	Nov. 6
Exeter	„ 28	Nov. 7/8	Nov. 10	Nov. 13/15	„ 16	„ 17	„ 18/19	„ 20
Excambion ..	Nov. 11	„ 21/22	„ 24	„ 27/29	„ 30	Dec. 1	Dec. 2/3	Dec. 4
Exochorda ..	„ 25	Dec. 5/6	Dec. 8	Dec. 11/13	Dec. 14	„ 15	„ 16/17	„ 18
Excalibur ..	Dec. 9	„ 19/20	„ 22	„ 25/27	„ 28	„ 29	„ 30/31	Jan. 1

WESTBOUND.

Steamer.	Alexandria. Arr.6 a.m. Tues. Sail 6 p.m. Tues.	Piræus. Arr.6 a.m. Thur. Sail 5 p.m. Thur.	Naples. Arr.9 a.m. Sat. Sail 8 p.m. Sun.	Leghorn. Arr. noon. Mon Sail midn. Mon.	Genoa. Arr. 8 a.m. Tues. Sail 6 p.m. Wed.	Marseilles. Arr.8 a.m. Thur. Sail 5 p.m. Thur.	Boston. Arr. 8 a.m. Mon. Sail 9 a.m. Tues.	New York. Arrive. 10 a.m. Wed.
Exeter	Aug. 1	Aug. 3	Aug. 5/6	Aug. 7	Aug. 8/9	Aug. 10	Aug. 21/22	Aug. 23
Excambion ..	„ 15	„ 17	„ 19/20	„ 21	„ 22/23	„ 24	Sept. 4/5	Sept. 6
Exochorda ..	„ 29	„ 31	Sept. 2/3	Sept. 4	Sept. 5/6	Sept. 7	„ 18/19	„ 20
Excalibur ..	Sept. 12	Sept. 14	„ 16/17	„ 18	„ 19/20	„ 21	Oct. 2/3	Oct. 4
Exeter	„ 26	„ 28	„ 30/O. 1	Oct. 2	Oct. 3/4	Oct. 5	„ 16/17	„ 18
Excambion ..	Oct. 10	Oct. 12	Oct. 14/15	„ 16	„ 17/18	„ 19	„ 30/31	Nov. 1
Exochorda ..	„ 24	„ 26	„ 28/29	„ 30	„ 31/Nv. 1	Nov. 2	Nov. 13/14	„ 15
Excalibur ..	Nov. 7	Nov. 9	Nv. 11/12	Nov. 13	Nov. 14/15	„ 16	„ 27/28	„ 29
Exeter	„ 21	„ 23	„ 25/26	„ 27	„ 28/29	„ 30	Dec. 11/12	Dec. 13
Excambion ..	Dec. 5	Dec. 7	Dec. 9/10	Dec. 11	Dec. 12/13	Dec. 14	„ 25/26	„ 27
Exochorda ..	„ 19	„ 21	„ 23/24	„ 25	„ 26/27	„ 28	Jan. 8/9	Jan. 10
Excalibur ..	Jan. 2	Jan. 4	Jan. 6/7	Jan. 8	Jan. 9/10	Jan. 11	„ 22/23	„ 24

CARREGADORES ACOREANOS LINE.

LONDON—CONTINENT—PORTUGAL—AZORES.

(See also page 403)

s.s. *San Miguel* (2112 tons), s.s. *Villa Franca* (1998 tons) and s.s. *Goncalho Velho* (1595 tons).

Fortnightly via OPORTO, LISBON, MADEIRA, ST. MICHAEL'S (Azores), SOUTHAMPTON, HAVRE, HAMBURG, ROUND TRIP FIVE/SIX WEEKS.

No Stewardess or Doctor carried. SAILINGS (Without Guarantee).

Steamer.	St. Michael's dep.	Southampton arr./dep	Havre. arr./dep	Hamburg arr./dep.	Havre. arr./dep.	Oporto. arr./dep.	Lisbon. arr./dep.	Madeira. (Fu'chal)	St.Michael's. arr.

BERGENSKE S.S. CO. (See also pages 403 & 414/15.)

Norway—Brazil and River Plate. m.v. *Crux*, 6850 tons and s.s. *Cometa*, 6850 tons, Sailings from Christiansand or Oslo, about every three weeks, with limited accommodation. "cabin" class, for Bahia, Pernambuco, Rio de Janeiro, Santos, Monte Video and Buenos Aires.

BLUE STAR LINE. London—South America *via* Boulogne, Lisbon.

Steamer.	Tons.	Steamer.	Tons.	Steamer.	Tons.	Steamer.	Tons.
Arandora Star ..	16000	*Almeda Star* ..	15000	*Andalucia Star* ..	15000	*Avila Star* ..	15000

Steamers carry 1st class passengers only.

SAILINGS OUTWARD.	L'nd'n& B'ul'gne dep.	Lisbon	Madeira	Ten-eriffe.	Rio de Janeiro arr.	Rio de Janeiro dep.	Santos	Monte-video.	Buenos Aires arr.
Andalucia Star	Aug. 19	Aug. 22	Aug. 24	Aug. 25	Sept. 3	Sept. 4	Sept. 5	Sept. 8	Sept. 8
Almeda Star ..	Sept. 9	Sept. 9	Sept. 14	Sept. 15	,, 24	,, 25	,, 26	,, 29	,, 29
Avila Star	Oct. 7	Oct. 10	Oct. 12	Oct. 13	Oct. 22	Oct. 23	Oct. 24	Oct. 27	Oct. 27
Andalucia Star	,, 21	,, 24	,, 26	,, 27	Nov. 5	Nov. 6	Nov. 7	Nov. 10	Nov. 10
Almeda Star ..	Nov. 11	Nov. 14	Nov. 16	Nov. 17	,, 26	,, 27	,, 28	Dec. 1	Dec. 1
Avila Star	Dec. 9	Dec. 12	Dec. 14	Dec. 15	Dec 24	Dec. 25	Dec. 26	,, 29	,, 29

SAILINGS HOMEWARD.	Buenos Aires and Monte-video dep.	Santos	Rio de Janeiro arr.	Rio de Janeiro dep.	Ten-eriffe.	Madeira arr.	Lisbon.	Ply-mouth	Boulogne. & London
Almeda Star ..	August 1	Aug. 4	Aug. 6	Aug. 7	Aug. 17	Aug. 18	Aug. 20	Aug. 22	Aug. 23
Avila Star	,, 22	,, 25	,, 27	,, 28	Sept. 7	Sept. 8	Sept. 10	Sept. 12	Sept. 13
Andalucia Star	Sept. 19	Sept. 22	Sept. 24	Sept. 25	Oct. 5	Oct. 6	Oct. 8	Oct. 10	Oct. 11
Almeda Star ..	Oct. 10	Oct. 13	Oct. 15	Oct. 16	,, 26	,, 27	,, 29	,, 31	Nov. 1
Avila Star ..	Nov. 7	Nov. 10	Nov. 12	Nov. 13	Nov. 23	Nov. 24	Nov. 26	Nov. 28	,, 29
Andalucia Star	,, 21	,, 24	,, 26	,, 27	Dec. 7	Dec. 8	Dec. 10	Dec. 12	Dec. 13

South American Intermediate Service.

Regular Service about fortnightly by steamers of 10,000-12,000 tons and (m.v.) *Tuscan Star*, 11,449 tons, *Avelona Star*, 13,376 tons; s.s. *Sultan Star*, 12,306 tons, carrying a limited number of passengers. The vessels leave London and proceed *via* St. Vincent to Rio de Janeiro, Santos and Buenos Aires.

South Africa, Australia and New Zealand. Sailings on application.

These services are maintained by cargo ships of 8,000-12,300 tons carrying 12 passengers. A qualified surgeon is carried on each steamer.

The route between England and Australia and vice versa is *via* South Africa, with calls at Cape Town, Port Elizabeth, East London, Natal, Lourenco Marques and possibly Mossel Bay and Beira. Some vessels proceed direct *via* South Africa, but without calling.

The ports of call in Australia are usually Townsville and/or Port Alma, Brisbane, Sydney, Melbourne Adelaide (outward only) and Fremantle.

To New Zealand the route is usually *via* the Panama Canal, or South Africa.

BOOTH LINE. Liverpool to Oporto, Lisbon, Madeira, Para and Manaos.

Carrying 1st class passengers (also 3rd class on s.s. *Hilary* and s.s. *Anselm*).

Seven weeks' cruises 1,000 miles up the Amazon. A Doctor and Stewardess are carried in the passenger steamers.

OUTWARD SAILINGS.	Tons.	Liverpool sail	Leixões (Oporto) sail	Lisbon. sail	Madeira arr.	Ceará. arr.	Pará. arr.	Mánaos. arr.
Anselm	6000	Aug. 1	Aug. 4	Aug. 5	Aug. 7	—	Aug. 16	Aug. 24
Hilary	7500	Sept. 9	Sept. 12	Sept. 13	Sept. 15	—	Sept. 24	Oct. 1
Anselm	6000	Oct. 12	Oct. 15	Oct. 16	Oct. 18	Oct. 26	Nov. 1	—
Hilary	7500	Nov. 10	Nov. 13	Nov. 14	Nov. 16	—	Nov. 25	Dec. 3
Anselm	6000	Dec. 1	Dec. 4	Dec. 5	Dec. 7	—	Dec. 16	,, 24

HOMEWARD SAILINGS.	Tons.	Ceará. sail.	Manâos. sail	Pará. sail	Madeira sail	Lisbon sail	Leixões (Oporto) sail	Liverpool arrive.
Benedict	4949	—	July 13	July 20	—	Aug. 4	Aug. 6	Aug. 10
Hilary	7500	—	Aug. 9	Aug 15	Aug. 24	,, 26	,, 27	,, 30
Anselm	6000	—	,, 29	Sept. 5	Sept. 15	Sept. 17	Sept. 18	Sept. 21
Hilary	7500	—	Oct. 7	Oct. 13	Oct. 22	Oct. 24	Oct. 25	Oct. 28
Anselm	6000	—	—	Nov. 4	Nov. 14	Nov. 16	Nov. 17	Nov. 20

CHARGEURS REUNIS.

Indo-China Line.

From Bordeaux and Marseilles to Port Said, Djibouti, Colombo, Singapore, Saigon, Tourane and Haiphong. Sailings every 28 days.

s.s. *Cap St. Jacques*, *Cap Padaran*, *Cap Tourane*, *Cap Varella* (8,500 tons), *Desirade* (10,500 tons), "Single class" steamers with Cabins de Luxe and Cabins with two beds.

Steamer	Bordeaux dep.	Marseilles dep.	P. Said dep.	Djibouti dep.	Colombo dep.	Singapore arr.	Saigon arr	Tourane arr.	Haiphong arr.
**Cap Padaran*	Aug. 10	Aug. 25	Aug. 31	Sept. 5	Sept. 13	Sept. 19	Sept. 22	Sept. 26	Sept. 28
**Cap Tourane*	Sept. 7	Sept. 22	Sept. 28	Oct. 3	Oct. 12	Oct. 18	Oct. 21	Oct. 25	Oct. 27
Cap St. Jacques	Oct. 10	Oct. 20	Oct. 26	Oct. 31	Nov. 9	Nov. 15	Nov. 18	Nov. 22	Nov. 24
Cap Varella ..	Nov. 7	Nov. 17	Nov. 23	Nov. 28	Dec. 7	Dec. 13	Dec. 16	Dec. 20	Dec. 22
Cap Padaran ..	Dec. 5	Dec. 15	Dec. 21	Dec. 26	Jan. 4	Jan. 10	Jan. 13	Jan. 17	Jan. 19
Cap Tourane ..	Jan. 2	Jan. 12	Jan. 18	Jan. 23	Feb. 1	Feb. 7	Feb. 10	Feb. 14	Feb. 16

Through bookings to Penang, Bangkok, Batavia, Soerabaya, Samarang. *Calls Lisbon.

Bordeaux to the West Coast of Africa.

1st, 2nd, and 3rd class passengers.

m.v. *Brazza*, 11,100 tons, s.s. *Amerique*, 8,900 tons, s.s. *Asie*, 9,060 tons, s.s. *Foucauld*, 12,000 tons.

Steamer.	Bordeaux. dep	Madeira	Dakar	Conakry.	Port Bouet	Lome.	Cotonou.	Souellaba. (Douala)	Libreville.	Port Gentil.	Ponte Noire.
‡*Kerguelen* ..	Aug. 1	Aug. 5	Aug. 9	Au. 11	Au. 14	Au. 15	Au. 16	Aug. 18	Aug. 19	Aug. 19	Aug. 21
‡*Brazza*	,, 26	,, 30	Sep. 3	Sep. 5	Sep. 8	Sep. 9	Sep. 9	Sep. 11	Sep. 12	Sep. 12	Sep. 14
‡*Desivade* ..	Sept. 8	Sept. 13	,, 17	,, 19	,, 22	,, 23	,, 24	,, 26	,, 27	,, 27	,, 29
‡*Foucauld* ..	,, 20	,, 24	,, 28	,, 30	Oct. 3	Oct. 4	Oct. 4	Oct. 6	Oct. 7	Oct. 7	Oct. 9
†*Asie*	Oct. 6	Oct. 10	Oct. 14	Oct. 16	,, 19	,, 20	,, 20	,, 22	,, 23	,, 23	,, 25

† Calling also at Tabou. ‡ Calling at Sassandra.

River Plate and Brazil Services.

s.s. *Aurigny*, *Belle-Isle*, *Ceylan*, *Eubee*, *Formose*, *Groix*, *Jamaique*, *Kerguelen*, *Lipari*, 10,500 tons. 1st and 3rd class closed cabins (entrepont) passengers.

SAILINGS OUTWARD. (From Hamburg six days, Antwerp three days respectively before Havre).

Steamer.	Havre dep.	Bordeaux dep.	Corunna dep.	Vigo. dep.	Leixoes dep.	Lisbon. dep.	Casablanca.	Rio de Janeiro. arr.	Santos.	Monte Video.	Buenos Aires. arr.
Groix	Aug. 2	—	—	—	—	Aug. 6	Aug. 7	Aug. 22	Aug. 23	Aug. 27	Aug. 28
**Belle Isle*	,, 19	Au. 22	—	—	—	,, 25	—	Sep. 11	Sep. 13	Sep. 17	Sep. 18
Lipari ...	Sept. 5	—	—	—	—	Sept. 9	Sept. 10	,, 24	,, 25	,, 29	,, 30
Jamaique ...	,, 16	Sep 19	—	—	—	,, 22	—	Oct. 6	Oct. 8	Oct. 12	Oct. 13
Kerguelen ..	Oct. 4	—	—	—	—	Oct. 8	Oct. 9	,, 23	,, 24	,, 28	,, 29
**Formose*	,, 16	,, 21	—	—	—	,, 24	—	Nov. 10	Nov. 12	Nov. 16	Nov. 17

* Calls Pernambuco and Bahia.

COMPAGNIE DE NAVIGATION SUD ATLANTIQUE.

Brazil and River Plate Services. 1st, 2nd and 3rd class (closed cabin) passengers.

I.—Fast Service by s.s. *Pasteur* (30,000 tons), from Bordeaux to Vigo, Lisbon, Rio Santos, Montevideo and Buenos Aires.

SAILINGS.

Bordeaux. dep.	Vigo. dep.	Lisbon. dep.	Rio de Janeiro arr.	Santos. arr.	Montevideo and Buenos Aires. arr.	Montevideo and Buenos Aires. dep.	Santos. dep.	Rio de Janeiro dep.	Lisbon arr.	Vigo. arr.	Bordeaux. arr.
Sep. 14	—	Sep. 16	Sep. 23	Sep. 24	Sept. 26	S.30/O.1	Oct. 3	Oct. 4	Oct. 12	—	Oct. 14
Oct. 28	—	Oct. 30	Nov. 6	Nov. 7	Nov. 9	Nov. 15	Nov. 17	Nov. 18	Nov. 25	—	Nov. 27

GERMAN AFRICA LINES. (See also page 359.)
Combined Services of the Woermann-Linie/Deutsch Ost-Afrika Linie, and Hamburg-Bremer Afrika Linie.

OUTWARD SAILINGS: **SOUTH AFRICAN FAST SERVICE.** Calling also at Port Elizabeth and East London.

Steamer.	Tons.	Hamburg d	Rotterdam dp	South'mpton dep.	Las Palmas	Walfish Bay	Cape Town a/d	Durban arr/dep.	Lourenco Marques. arr.
Windhuk	17000	Jly. 21	July 22	July 23	July 27	Aug. 5	Aug. 7/8	Aug. 13/15	Aug. 16
Pretoria	17000	Aug25	Aug. 26	Aug. 27	Aug 31	Sept. 9	Sep.11/12	Sep. 17/19	Sept. 20
Windhuk	17000	Sep.22	Sept. 23	Sept. 24	Sep. 28	Oct. 7	Oct. 9/10	Oct. 15/17	Oct. 18
Pretoria	17000	Oct.27	Oct. 28	Oct. 29	Nov. 2	Nov. 11	Nv. 13/14	Nov. 19/21	Nov. 22

Calling also at East London and Port Elizabeth.

HOMEWARD SAILINGS:

Steamer.	Tons.	Lourenco Marques. dep.	Durban dep.	Cape Town dep.	Walfish Bay	Las Palmas	Southam'ton arr.	Antwerp or Rotterdam. arr.	Hamburg. arr.
Pretoria	17000	July 22	July 25	July 29	July 31	Aug. 9	Aug. 13	Aug. 14/15	Aug. 17
Windhuk	17000	Aug. 19	Aug. 22	Aug. 26	Aug. 28	Sept. 6	Sept. 10	Sept. 11/12	Sept. 14
Pretoria	17000	Sept. 23	Sept. 26	Sept. 30	Oct. 2	Oct. 11	Oct. 15	Oct. 16/17	Oct. 19
Windhuk	17000	Oct. 21	Oct. 24	Oct. 28	Oct. 30	Nov. 8	Nov. 12	Nov. 13/14	Nov. 16
Pretoria ..	17000	Nov 25	Nov. 28	Dec. 2	Dec. 4	Dec. 13	Dec. 17	Dec. 18	Dec. 21

OUTWARD SAILINGS: **WESTERN ROUTE AROUND AFRICA.** Returning *via* Suez (*See p.* 359)
Calling also at Antwerp, Walfish Bay, Luderitz Bay, Port Elizabeth, East London and Lourenco Marques.

Steamer.	Tons.	Hamburg. d.	Bremen dp	Rotterdam.	Southampt'n	Las Palmas	Luanda	Lobito.	Cape T'wn. arr./dep.	Durban arr.	Beira arr.
Wangoni	7782	Aug. 10	Aug. 12	Aug. 15	Aug. 18	Aug. 24	—	Sept. 5	Sept. 12/13	Se17/19	Sept 24
Ussukuma ..	7765	Sept. 8	—	Sep. 10	Sep. 11	Sep. 17	Sept. 29	—	Oct. 6/7	O.12/14	Oct. 19
A'fWœrmann	8577	Oct. 6	—	Oct. 8	Oct. 9	Oct. 15	—	Oct. 27	Nov. 3/4	N. 9/11	Nov. 16
Njassa	8754	Oct. 19	Oct. 21	—	Oct. 27	Nov. 2	Nov. 15	—	Nov. 22/23	N.27/29	Dec. 4

EASTERN ROUTE AROUND AFRICA (Outward via Suez, see page 359).
HOMEWARD SAILINGS: Calling also East London, Port Elizabeth, Luderitz Bay, Walfish Bay.

Steamer.	Beira dep.	Loure'co Marques arr./dep.	Durban dep.	Cape Town dep.	Lobito.	Las Palmas.	Southampton arr.	Antw'rp or Rotterdam arr.	Bremen arr.	Hamburg. arr.
A'fWœrmann	Aug. 7	Aug.9/11	Au 12/14	Au 18/19	Aug. 26	Sept. 7	Sept. 13	Sept. 14/15	—	Sept. 17
Watussi	Sept. 7	Sep. 9/12	Se. 13/14	Se. 18/19	—	Oct. 6	Oct. 11	Oct. 12/13	—	Oct. 15
Usambara ..	Oct. 8	Oc.10/13	Oc 14/16	Oc.21/22	Oct. 29	Nov. 10	Nov. 16	Nov. 17/18	Nov. 20	Nov. 21
Ubena	Nov. 7	Nv. 9/11	N. 12/14	Nv 20/21	—	Dec. 8	Dec. 13	Dec. 14/15	Dec. 17	Dec. 18
Watussi	Nov. 30	Dec. 2/4	Dec. 5/6	De.11/12	Dec. 19	Dec. 29	Jan. 4	Jan. 5/6	Jan. 8	Jan. 9

WEST COAST MAIN LINE—"A" Service.

Steamer.	H'mb'rg dep.	Rotterdam	Antwerp	Boulogne dep.	Southampton.	Madeira.	Teneriffe	Las Palmas	Freetown	Monrovia	Accra

Calls also made at Port Bouet, Takoradi, Lagos, Port Harcourt, Calabar, Victoria, Tiko, Isabel, Duala, Kribi, Pointe Noire, Luanda, Lobito.
Details of Ports called at on application.

"B" Service.

Steamer	Hamburg. dep.	Rot'rd'm. dep.	
			For Dakar, Bissao, Bubaque, Conakry, Freetown, †Sherbro, Sulima, Cape Mount, Monrovia, Marshall, Grand Bassa, River Cess, Sinoe, Grand Cess, Cape Palmas, Tabou, Sassandra, Lahou, Assinie, Keta, Lome. † If sufficient inducement.

"C" Service.

Steamer.	Hamburg dp.	Bremen dp	Antwerp dp	
				For Lisbon, Teneriffe, Las Palmas, Monrovia, Bata, Benito, Koko, Sao Thomé, Pointe Noire, Boma, Matadi. † To Teneriffe, Las Palmas, Praia, Monrovia, Ponte Noire, Matadi.

CONGO LINE—"D" Service.

Steamer	Hamburg. dep.	Bremen.	Antwerp. dep.	
				For Teneriffe, Las Palmas, Monrovia, Pointe Noire, Angola.

BARBER LINE.

New York *via* Panama to Los Angeles, Manila, Shanghai, Japan, Manila, Macassar, Sourabaya, Batavia, Singapore, Penang, New York.

The above service is maintained monthly by FAST NEW TWIN SCREW MOTOR VESSELS (with accommodation for a few passengers) equipped with every modern convenience. Some of the vessels have suites of rooms.

ELDER DEMPSTER LINES. (See also page 472

Liverpool *via* Madeira, Canary Islands to West Coast of Africa.

MAIL SERVICE. (Fortnightly).

Motor Ship.	Tons.	Date.	Motor Ship.	Tons.	Date.	Motor Ship.	Tons.	Date.
Adda	7816	Aug. 2	*Accra*	9336	Sept. 13	*Apapa*	9332	Oct. 4
Apapa	9332	Aug. 16	*Adda*	7816	Sept. 20	*Abosso*	11330	Oct. 18
Abosso	11330	Aug. 30	*Aba*	7937	Sept. 27	*Accra*	9336	Nov. 1

Modern twin screw vessels with short wave wireless installations and directional wireless finders. Doctor and Stewardesses carried on all mail ships. Suite rooms with baths, also single state rooms.

SAILINGS SOUTH BOUND.

Liverpool dep.	Madeira	Las Palmas.	Bathurst	Freetown	Mon-rovia.	Tak-oradi.	Accra.	¶ Lagos	Port Har-court.	Duala Victoria Calabar
Aug. 2	Aug. 7	—	—	Aug. 12	Aug. 13	Aug. 15	Aug. 16	Aug 17	—	Aug. 20/23
,, 16	,, 20	Aug. 21	Aug. 24	,, 26	—	,, 29	,, 30	,, 31	Sept.3	—
,, 30	Sept. 3	Sept. 4	—	Sept. 9	Sept. 10	Sept.12	Sept.13	Sep.14	—	Sept. 17/20
Sept. 13	,, 17	,, 18	Sept. 21	,, 23	—	,, 26	,, 27	,, 28	Oct. 1	—
,, 20	,, 25	—	—	,, 30	Oct. 1	Oct. 3	Oct. 4	Oct. 5	—	Oct. 8/11
,, 27	Oct. 2	—	—	Oct. 7	—	,, 10	,, 11	,, 12	—	—
Oct. 4	,, 8	Oct. 9	Oct. 12	,, 14	—	,, 17	,, 18	,, 19	Oct.22	—
,, 18	,, 22	,, 23	—	,, 28	,, 29	,, 31	Nov. 1	Nov. 2	—	Nov. 5/8
Nov. 1	Nov. 5	Nov. 6	Nov. 9	Nov. 11	—	Nov. 14	,, 15	,, 16	Nov19	—

¶ Connection at Lagos with m.v. *Calabar* for Forcados, Warri, Port Harcourt, Calabar, Victoria and Fernando Poo.

SAILINGS NORTH BOUND.

Calabar.	Port Harcourt	Lagos	Accra	Takoradi	Mon-rovia	Free-town	Bathurst	Las Palmas	Madeira	Ply-mouth arr.	L'pool
Aug. 1/2	—	Aug. 5	Aug. 6	Aug. 6	—	Aug. 9	—	Aug. 13	Aug. 14	Aug. 18	Aug. 19
—	Aug. 16	,, 19	,, 20	,, 20	Aug. 22	,, 23	Aug. 24	,, 27	,, 28	Sept. 1	Sept. 2
,, 22/23	—	,, 26	,, 27	,, 27	—	,, 30	—	Sept. 4	Sept. 5	,, 9	,, 10
—	Sept. 6	Sept. 9	Sept. 10	Sept. 10	Sept. 12	Sept. 13	Sept. 14	,, 17	,, 18	,, 22	,, 23
Se. 19/20	—	,, 23	,, 24	,, 24	—	,, 27	—	Oct. 1	Oct. 2	Oct. 6	Oct. 7
—	Oct. 4	Oct. 7	Oct. 8	Oct. 9	Oct. 11	Oct. 12	Oct. 13	,, 16	,, 17	,, 21	,, 22
Oc. 10/11	—	,, 14	,, 15	,, 16	—	,, 19	—	,, 24	,, 25	,, 29	,, 30
—	—	,, 19	,, 20	,, 20	—	,, 24	—	,, 28	—	—	Nov. 2
—	,, 25	,, 28	,, 29	,, 30	Nov. 1	Nov. 2	Nov. 3	Nov. 6	Nov. 7	Nov. 11	,, 12

LIVERPOOL CARGO SERVICES (Three Weekly).

With limited passenger accommodation, to Madeira, Teneriffe, Las Palmas, Dakar, Bathurst, Conakry, Freetown, Sherbro, Monrovia, Cape Palmas, Grand Bassam, Port Bouet, Gold Coast, Lome, Cotonou, Lagos, Apapa, Warri, Koko, Sapele, Port Harcourt, Duala and Kribi.

ANTWERP—HAMBURG—ROTTERDAM—DOVER—WEST AFRICAN SERVICE (Three Weekly).

With limited passenger accommodation to Madeira, Teneriffe, Las Palmas, Dakar, Freetown, Port Marshall, Grand Bassam, Port Bouet, Cape Coast, Lagos, Apapa (Warri, Koko, Sapele), Port Harcourt (Abonema, Opobo), Calabar, Ikang, Duala, Kribi. Alternate calls at Cape Palmas, Takoradi, Saltpond, Accra, Lome and Cotonou.

ELLERMAN & BUCKNALL STEAMSHIP CO., LTD.

London to South Africa

Steamer.	Tons	London dep.	Madeira	Cape Town	Lo'enco Marques arr.	Beira arr./dep	Lo'enco Marques dep.	Cape Town dep.	Madeira	U.K. ‡
City of Paris	10902	June 24	June 29	July 14	July 23	Jy.27/Au 1	Aug. 4	Aug. 15	Aug. 30	Sept. 4
City of Venice	8762	July 22	July 27	Aug. 11	Aug. 20	Aug. 24/29	Sept. 1	Sept. 12	Sept. 27	Oct. 2
City of London	8956	Aug. 19	Aug. 24	Sept. 8	Sept. 17	Sept. 21/26	,, 29	Oct. 10	Oct. 25	Oct. 30
City of Exeter	9654	S pt. 16	Sept. 21	Oct. 6	Oct. 16	Oct. 20/24	Oct. 27	Nov. 7	Nov. 22	Nov. 27

‡ London or Plymouth or other Port. Calling also at Port Elizabeth, East London & Durban.

EMPREZA INSULANA. Lisbon—Madeira—Azores.

s.s. *Lima*, 3865 tons, sails from Lisbon 8th of each month for Porto Santo (not July, Aug. & Sep.) Madeira, (10th), Santa Maria, St. Michael's, Terceira, Graciosa (Santa Cruz), St. Jorge (Calheta), Lages do Pico and arr. Fayal 16th. Returning from Fayal on 16/17th, Madeira on 22nd, arr. Lisbon 24th or 25th, calling also at other ports as outward.

s.s. *Carvalho Aranjo*, 4468 tons, sails from Lisbon 23rd of each month for Madeira (25th), St. Michael's, Terceira, Graciosa (Praia), St. Jorge (Velas), Caes do Pico, Fayal, (31/1), Corvo* and Flores. Returning from Fayal on 2nd (or 3rd†) *via* Caes do Pico, St. Jorge (Velas), Graciosa (Praia), Terceira, St. Michael's, Madeira, 6th (or 7th†), arr. Lisbon 8th (or 9th†). † These dates when preceding months has 30 days.

* Calls made at Corvo only in February, May, June, July, August and November.

FABRE AND FRAISSINET LINES.

"RAPIDE" SERVICE. West African Coast Service. (See also p. 376).

SAILINGS OUTWARD.

Steamer.	Tons.	Mars'il's dep.	Algiers.	Casa-blanca.	Dakar. arr.	Duala. arr.
†*Canada*	9684	Aug. 17	Aug. 19	Aug. 21	Aug. 25	Sept. 4
‡*Touareg* ...	5135	,, 29	,, 31	Sept. 2	Sept. 8	,, 18
†*Banfora* ..	9496	Sept. 12	Sept. 14	,, 16	,, 20	,, 30
‡*Hoggar*	5135	,, 26	,, 28	,, 30	Oct. 6	Oct. 16
†*Canada*	9684	Oct. 10	Oct. 10	Oct. 14	,, 18	,, 28

Calling also at Conakry, Freetown*, Tabou*, Sassandra*, Port Bouet, Accra, Lome Cotonou and Lagos*.

SAILINGS HOMEWARD.

Steamer.	Tns	Duala. dep.	Dakar.	Las Palmas. (optional)	Casa-blanca	Oran.	Algiers.	Mars'il's arr.
†*Banfora*	9496	July 30	Aug. 12	Aug. 15	Aug. 17	—	Aug. 19	Aug. 21
‡*Hoggar*	5135	Aug. 20	,, 31	Sept. 4	Sept. 6	Sept. 8	Sept. 9	Sept. 11
†*Canada*	9684	Sept. 8	Sept. 21	,, 24	,, 26	—	,, 28	,, 30
‡*Touareg*	5135	,, 20	Oct. 1	Oct. 5	Oct. 7	Oct. 9	Oct. 10	Oct. 12
†*Banfora*	9496	Oct. 3	,, 16	,, 19	,, 21	—	,, 23	,, 25

Calling also at Lagos*, Cotonou, Lome, Accra*, Takoradi*, Port Bouet, Sassandra*, Tabou*, Freetown*, Conakry.

† Fabre Line. ‡ Fraissinet Line. * Occasional.

"Mixte" Service by Cargo Steamers.

Steamer.	Tons.	Marseilles dep.	Casa-blanca.	Dakar.

Proceeding to Bathurst, Conakry, Sierra Leone, Monrovia*, Tabou, Sassandra, Grand Lahou, Port Bouet, Grand Bassam, Assinie, Gold Coast, Lome, Cotonou, Forcados, Bonny, Port Harcourt, Calabar, Douala, Spanish Guinea, Gaboon Congo.

HOMEWARD.—*via* Lagos, Cotonou, Lome, Accra, Gold Coast, Takoradi, Ivory Coast, Port Bouet, Sassandra, Tabou, Sierra Leone, Conakry, Dakar, Casablanca, Valencia and/or Barcelona, Genoa, Marseilles.

FRED OLSEN LINE. (See also pages 405 and 423)

LONDON—CANARY ISLANDS SERVICE.

m.v. *Brenas*, 2700 tons. m.v. *Betancuria*, 2700 tons. m.v. *Bajamar*, 2700 tons.

Cargo Vessels, with single and two berth cabins for 12 passengers.

From London weekly on Thursdays. † Duration of round voyage 12 to 14 days.

† Subject to confirmation.

SCANDINAVIA—CENTRAL AMERICA—NORTH PACIFIC SERVICE.

Steamer	Tons.	Steamer.	Tons.	Steamer.	Tons
m.v. *Abraham Lincoln* ..	5784	m.v. *Benjamin Franklin* ..	8518	m.v. *Knute Nelson* ..	7468
m.v. *Laurits Swenson*	5725				

On these vessels stewardess carried but no doctor. Regular sailings approximately monthly from Oslo *via* Antwerp, Panama Canal to San Pedro, San Francisco, Vancouver. Homewards *via* Seattle, Por and, San Francisco, San Pedro, Panama to Liverpool, London and Oslo.

FYFFES LINE.

ELDERS & FYFFES, Ltd.

DIRECT SERVICES TO BERMUDA AND JAMAICA.

These steamers are from 6,500 to 7,000 tons, and carry First class passengers only.

Steamer ..	*Carare.*	*Camito*	*Bayano*	*Arigu'ni*	*Cavina*	*Carare*	*Bayano*	*Camito*	*Ariguani*
Tons ..	7000	6500	6500	7000	7000	7000	6500	6500	7000
Bristol ¶ ...... dep.	July 31	Aug. 7	Aug. 14	Aug. 21	Aug. 28	Sept. 4	Sept. 18	Sept. 25	Oct. 2
Kingston, Jamaica ar.	Aug. 13	,, 20	,, 27	Sept. 3	Sept. 10	,, 17	Oct. 1	Oct. 8	,, 15
,, ...dep.	,, 15	,, 22	,, 29	,, 5	,, 12	,, 19	,, 3	,, 10	,, 17
Bristol ¶ .... arr.	,, 28	Sept. 4	Sept. 11	,, 18	,, 25	Oct. 2	,, 16	,, 28	,, 30

Also frequent sailings by "B" type of steamer (with accommodation for twelve passengers), from Liverpool, Avonmouth, Swansea to Jamaica, Colombia, Honduras and Guatemala. Dates of sailings and further particulars on application.

FURNESS LINE.

(See also pages 360 & 459)

United Kingdom *via* Panama Canal to North Pacific Ports.

The vessels carry a limited number of cabin passengers.

SAILINGS.

Vessel	Tons	Date.	Vessel.	Tons	Date.
Pacific Grove	7114	Aug. 11	*Pacific Ranger*	6866	Oct. 6
Pacific President	7114	Sept. 8	*Pacific Reliance*	6717	Oct. 20
Pacific Exporter	6723	Sept. 22	*Pacific Enterprise*	6722	Nov. 3

Thence every fortnight for Colon, Balboa, Guayaquil, Los Angeles, San Francisco, Victoria and Vancouver, B.C.

New York—Bermuda.

Sailings every three or four days by Turbo Electric vessel *Monarch of Bermuda*, 22424 tons and *Queen of Bermuda*, 22575 tons.

FURNESS RED CROSS LINE.

New York—Halifax, N.S.—St. John's, N.F.

Sailings from New York and St. John's. N.F. Weekly in Summer. Fortnightly in Winter.

New York—Trinidad **calling at St. Thomas, St. Croix, St. Kitts, Antigua, Montserrat, Guadeloupe, Dominica, Martinique, St. Lucia, Barbados, Trinidad. Returning via same ports, also Grenada and St. Vincent.**

Approximately monthly sailings by s.s. *Nerissa*, 5600 tons.

GDYNIA-AMERYKA LINJE ZEGLUGOWE, S.A.

(GDYNIA AMERICA SHIPPING LINES LTD.)

(See also pages 377, 416 and 459). **(South America Line).**

GDYNIA TO BRAZIL, URUGUAY AND ARGENTINA. **T.s.s. *Pulaski*, 6354 tons,**

T.s.s. *Kosciuszko*, 6522 tons.

Services subject to change without notice.

Dep. Gdynia, *via* Kiel-Holtenau, Rio de Janeiro, Santos, Montevideo for Buenos Aires.

Dep. Buenos Aires calling at the same ports and Boulogne sur Mer.

Passage about 23 days outwards; 24 days homewards.

m.v. *Iberia*, 9800 tons. **HAMBURG-CUBA-MEXICO.** m.v. *Orinoco*, 9660 tons.

Motor Vessel	Hamburg. dep.	Antwerp. dep.	South'mp-ton.	Cherbourg	Lisbon	Havana. arr.	Vera Cruz. arr	Tampico.
Orinoco	July 29	Aug. 1	Aug. 2	Aug. 2	Aug. 5	Aug. 16	Aug. 20	Aug. 26
Ibeira	Aug. 26	,, 29	,, 30	,, 30	Sept. 2	Sept. 13	Sept. 17	Sept. 23
Orinoco	Sept. 27	Sept. 30	Oct. 1	Oct. 1	Oct. 4	Oct. 15	Oct. 19	Oct. 25
Iberia ..	Oct. 28	Oct. 31	Nov. 1	Nov. 1	Nov. 4	Nov. 15	Nov. 19	Nov. 25
Orinoco	Nov. 25	Nov. 28	Nov. 29	Nov. 29	Dec. 2	Dec. 13	Dec. 17	Dec. 23

Motor Vessel	Tampico.	Porto Mexico	Vera Cruz.	Havana.	Lisbon.	S'uth'mt'n	Boulogne.	Hamburg
Iberia ..	July 31	—	Aug. 1	Aug. 4	Aug. 15	Aug. 18	Aug. 18	Aug. 20
Orinoco	Aug. 31	—	Sept. 1	Sept. 4	Sept. 15	Sept. 18	Sept. 18	Sept. 20
Iberia ..	Sept. 29	—	,, 30	Oct. 3	Oct. 14	Oct. 17	Oct. 17	Oct. 19
Orinoco	Oct. 30	—	Oct. 31	Nov. 3	Nov. 14	Nov. 17	Nov. 17	Nov. 19
Iberia ..	Nov. 30	Nov. 30	Dec. 1	Dec. 4	Dec. 15	Dec. 18	Dec. 18	Dec. 20
Orinoco	Dec. 28	Dec. 30	Dec. 29	Jan. 2	Jan. 13	Jan. 16	Jan. 16	Jan. 18

WEST-INDIAN CENTRAL AMERICAN SERVICE.

Motor Vessel.	Tons	Ham-burg. d.	Ijmui-den	Antwerp.	Boulogne & Dover d.	Bar-bados	Trinidad	Port Limon	Pto. Barrios Livingston
Caribia	12050	Aug. 26	Aug. 27	Aug. 28/29	Aug. 30	Sept 9	Sept. 10	Sept. 19	Sept. 21
Cordillera	12050	Sept. 23	Sept. 24	Sept. 25/26	Sept. 27	Oct. 7	Oct. 8	Oct. 17	Oct. 19
Caribia	12050	Oct. 21	Oct. 22	Oct. 23/24	Oct. 25	Nov. 4	Nov. 5	Nov. 14	Nov. 16
Cordillera	12050	Nov. 18	Nov. 19	Nov. 20/21	Nov. 22	Dec. 2	Dec. 3	Dec. 12	Dec. 14
Caribia	12050	Dec. 16	Dec. 17	Dec. 18/19	Dec. 20	Dec 30	Dec. 31	Jan. 9	Jan. 11

Calling also at La Guaira, Pt. Cabello, Curacao, Pt. Colombia, Cartagena Cristobal.

HOMEWARD. Motor Vessel.	Tons.	Pt.Barrios Liv'gt'n d.	Port Limon dp.	Trinidad	Bar-bados.	Ply'th & Cherb'g arr.	Ijmuiden or Amster-dam arr.	Hamburg arr.
Caribia	12050	July 28	July 30	Aug. 7	Aug. 8	Aug. 17	Aug. 18	Aug. 19
Cordillera ..	12050	Aug. 25	Aug. 27	Sept. 4	Sept. 5	Sept. 14	Sept. 15	Sept. 16
Caribia	12050	Sept. 22	Sept. 24	Oct. 2	Oct. 3	Oct. 12	Oct. 13	Oct. 14
Cordillera	12050	Oct. 20	Oct. 22	,, 30	,, 31	Nov. 9	Nov. 10	Nov. 11
Caribia	12050	Nov. 18	Nov. 20	Nov. 28	Nov. 29	Dec. 8	Dec. 9	Dec. 10
Cordillera	12050	Dec. 16	Dec. 18	Dec. 26	Dec. 27	Jan. 5	Jan. 6	Jan. 7

Calling also at Cristobal, Cartagena, Puerto Colombia, Curacao, Puerto Cabello, La Guaira.

HAMBURG—SOUTH AMERICAN (WEST COAST).

Joint Service with Kosmos Lines. *Via* PANAMA CANAL.

Vessel.	Tons	Hamburg dep.	Bremen dep.	Antw'p dep.
Monserrate	5600	Aug. 3	Aug 5	Aug. 8
Roda	6780	,, 17	,, 19	,, 22
Patria	15000	Sept. 2	—	Sept. * 4
Huascaran	—	,, 14	Sept. 16	,, 19
Hermonthis........	4888	,, 28	,, 30	Oct. 3
Rhakotis	6753	Oct. 12	Oct. 14	,, 17
Osorno	6700	,, 19	,, 21	,, 24
Monserrate	5600	Nov. 2	Nov. 4	Nov. 7

For Cristobal, Buenaventura, Guayaquil, Callao, Mollendo, Arica, Antofagasta, Valparaiso.

*Southampton next day.

HAMBURG—NORTH PACIFIC *via* Panama Canal.

Vessel.	Tons.	Hamburg. dep.	Bremen.	Antwerp† dep.
s.s. *Vancouver* *.............	8250	Aug. 1	Aug. 3	Aug. 5
s.s. *Oakland*	6957	,, 24	,, 26	,, 29
m.v. *Seattle*	7369	Sept. 14	Sept. 16	Sept. 19
s.s. *Tacoma*	8268	,, 28	,, 30	Oct. 3

For Cristobal (Panama Canal), Los Angeles, San Francisco, Vancouver, Seattle, Tacoma, Portland.
Additional to above ports, calling also at ports numbered against name of vessel.

† Emigrants can only embark if cabin class. * Calls also at La Libertad. ¶ Calls also at San José de Guatemala.

HAMBURG—AUSTRALIA *via* Cape of Good Hope.

Vessel.	Tons.	Hamburg. dep.	Bremen. dep.	Rotterdam dep.	Antwerp. dep.
s.s. *Leuna*	6856	Aug. 12	Aug. 14	Aug. 16	Aug. 18
m.s. *Magdeburg*..	6128	Sept. 13	—	—	—

Thence to Adelaide, Melbourne, Sydney, Newcastle, Brisbane.

HAMBURG SOUTH AMERICAN LINE.

(Hamburg-Südamerikanische Dampschiffahrts Gesellschaft)

Steamer.	Tons.	Steamer.	Tons.	Steamer.	Tons.
s.s. *Cap Arcona*	27560	m.v. *General Osorio* ..	12000	m.v. *Monte Sarmiento** ..	14000
s.s. *Cap Norte*	14000	s.s. *General Artigas* ..	11500	m.v. *Monte Olivia** ..	14000
s.s. *General San Martin*	11500	s.s. *Madrid*	8753	m.v. *Monte Pascoal* ..	14000
s.s. *Antonio Delfino* ..	14000	m.v. *Monte Rosa*	14000		

s.s. *Cap Arcona*, 1, 2 (& 3 cl. from Continent). *Cap Norte* and *Antonio Delfino*, intermediate (and 3 cl. from Continent).

Gn. Osorio, Gn. S. Martin, Gn. Artigas, Monte Rosa, Monte Pascoal & Madrid intermediate and 3 cl.

*These vessels carry 3 cl.pass. only.

SAILINGS (subject to alteration).

OUTWARD. Vessel.	Hamburg dep.	Bremerhaven dep.	Boulogne	Southampt'n	Lisbon arr./dp.	Madeira.	Teneriffe.	Rio de Janeiro arr	Santos	M'nt video	Bu'n. Aires arr.
Monte Pascoal (c)	Aug. 4	—	—	—	Aug. 9	—	—	Aug. 23	Aug24	Au 28	Aug 29
Antonio Delfino (a) (b)	,, 11	Aug. 12	Aug13	—	,, 16	Aug 18	—	,, 30	,, 31	Sep 3	Sept. 4
Madrid	,, 18	—	—	—	,, 24	,, 26	—	Sept. 9	Sep.11	,, 14	,, 15
Gen. Osorio	,, 25	—	,, 27	—	,, 30	Sept.1	—	,, 13	,, 14	,, 17	,, 18
Cap Arcona	,, 29	—	,, 30	Aug 30	Sept. 1	—	—	,, 11	,, 12	,, 14	,, 14
Monte Rosa (e)........	Sept 1	Sept. 2	—	—	,, 6	—	—	Sept.20	,, 21	,, 25	,, 26
Monte Sarmiento.....	,, 8	—	—	—	,, 13	—	—	,, 27	,, 28	Oct.2	Oct. 3
Gen. San Martin (e) ..	,, 15	—	Sep.17	—	,, 20	Sep.22	—	Oct. 4	Oct. 5	,, 9	,, 10
Cap. Norte (a).......	,, 29	,, 30	Oct. 1	—	Oct. 4	Oct. 6	—	,, 18	,, 19	,, 22	,, 23
Cap Olivia (c)	Oct. 6	—	—	—	,, 11	—	—	,, 25	,, 26	,, 30	,, 31
Cap Arcona	,, 10	—	,, 11	Oct. 11	,, 13	—	—	,, 23	,, 24	,, 26	,, 26
Gen. Artigas	,, 13	—	,, 15	—	,, 18	,, 20	—	Nov. 1	Nov. 2	Nov6	Nov. 7
Monte Pascoal (c)	,, 20	—	—	—	,, 25	—	—	,, 8	,, 9	,, 13	,, 14
Antonio Delfino	,, 27	Oct. 28	,, 29	—	Nov. 1	Nov. 3	—	,, 15	,, 16	,, 19	,, 20
Madrid	Nov. 3	—	—	—	,, 9	,, 11	—	,, 25	,, 27	,, 30	Dec. 1
Gen. Osorio (a) (b)	,, 10	—	Nov 12	—	,, 15	,, 17	—	,, 29	,, 30	Dec 3	,, 4
Monte Rosa (c)	,, 17	Nov. 18	—	—	,, 22	—	—	Dec. 6	Dec. 7	,, 11	,, 12

(*a*) Calls also Pernambuco. (*b*) Calls Bahia. (*c*) Calls Florianopolis and Rio Grande. (*d*) Calls Rio Grande.

NORTHBOUND.

HOMEWARD. Vessel.	Buenos Aires dep.	Monte Video dep.	Santos.	Rio de Janeiro	Teneriffe.	Madeira	Lisbon	Southamp'n	Boulogne	Bremerhaven	Hamburg arr.
Monte Rosa (d) (e)..	July 21	July 22	Jly26	July 27	—	—	Au 11	—	—	Aug. 15	Au.16
Monte Sarmiento (e)	,, 28	,, 29	Aug 1	Aug. 2	—	—	,, 18	—	—	—	,, 23
Gen. San Martin (f)	Aug. 4	Aug. 5	,, 8	,, 9	—	Au 23	,, 25	—	Aug 28	—	,, 30
Cap Arcona	,, 8	,, 9	,, 11	,, 12	—	—	,, 21	Au. 23	,, 24	—	,, 25
Cap Norte (e)	,, 18	,, 19	,, 22	,, 23	—	Sep.5	Sep.7	—	Sep.10	Sept. 11	Sep12
Monte Olivia (d) (e)	,, 25	,, 26	,, 30	,, 31	—	—	,, 16	—	—	—	,, 21
Gen. Artigas (e)....	Sept. 1	Sept. 2	Sep.5	Sept. 6	—	,, 20	,, 22	—	,, 25	,, 26	,, 27
Monte Pascoal (e)	,, 8	,, 9	,, 12	,, 13	—	—	,, 28	—	—	—	Oct. 3
AntonioDelfino(d)(f)	,, 15	,, 16	,, 20	,, 21	—	Oct.4	Oct.6	—	Oct. 9	Oct. 10	,, 11
Cap Arcona........	,, 16	,, 17	,, 19	,, 20	—	—	Sp.29	Oct. 1	,, 2	—	,, 3
Madrid . ..	,, 22	,, 23	,, 27	,, 29	—	,, 12	Oc.14	—	—	—	,, 19
Gen Osorio (e)	,, 29	,, 30	Oct.3	Oct. 4	—	,, 17	,, 19	—	,, 22	—	,, 24
Monte Rosa (d) (e)..	Oct. 6	Oct. 7	,, 11	,, 12	—	—	,, 27	—	—	Oct. 31	Nov.1
Monte Sarmiento (e)	,, 13	,, 14	,, 17	,, 18	—	—	Nov 3	—	—	—	,, 8
Gen. San Martin (f)	,, 20	,, 21	,, 24	,, 25	—	Nov 8	,, 10	—	Nov 13	—	,, 15
Cap. Arcona	,, 28	,, 29	,, 31	Nov. 1	—	—	,, 10	Nov12	,, 13	—	,, 14

(*d*) Calling also at Rio Grande and Florianopolis. (*e*) Calls Bahia.

(*f*) Calls Bahia and Pernambuco.

HARRISON LINE.

London to West Indies and British Guiana.

s.s. *Inanda*, 6,000 tons, s.s. *Ingoma*, 5,700 tons, s.s. *Inkosi*, 6,700 tons (carrying 1st class passengers only).

Steamer.	London. dep.	Antigua. arr.	St. Kitts. arr.	Barbados. arr.	Grenada. arr.	Trinidad. arr.	Demerara. arr.
Inkosi	Aug. 11	Aug. 23	—	Aug. 25	Aug. 26	Aug. 27	Aug. 30
Inanda	Sept. 9	—	Sept. 20	Sept. 22	Sept. 23	Sept. 24	Sept. 27
Inkosi	Oct. 7	Oct. 18	—	Oct. 20	Oct. 21	Oct. 22	Oct. 25

Calls at Windward and Leeward Islands as may be arranged. Connecting steamers to Nevis, Montserrat, Dominica, St. Lucia or St. Vincent, advised on application.

HOLLAND WEST AFRICA LINE.

United Netherlands Navigation Co.

(See also page 363 and below.)

Services subject to alteration.

s.s. *Amstelkerk* and s.s. *Maaskerk*, 3920 tons. Cargo "Express" Steamers with "cabin" class accommodation for 60 passengers.

Steamer.	Ha'burg dep.	Amst'rd'm dep.	Bordeaux (LeVerd'n) dep.	Dakar	Monrovia.	Port Bouet	Takoradi	Accra	Lagos/ Apapa.	Duala arr.

Freetown, Lome, Cotonou, Port Harcourt, Calabar, Victoria, Santa Isabel, and from Duala proceeds to Kribi.

Cargo service from Hamburg and Amsterdam, calling Dakar, Bathurst, Conakry, Freetown, Sherbro, Liberia, Tabou, Sassandra, Grand Lahou, Assinie, Gold Coast. Details of sailings on application.

HOLLAND-AFRICA LINE.

United Netherlands Navigation Co.

(See also page 363 and above)

REGULAR AND FREQUENT SERVICES

between European and South and East African Ports.

Outward *via* WEST COAST to THE CAPE, etc.

Steamer.	Tons.	Steamer.	Tons.	Steamer.	Tons.	Steamer.	Tons.	m.v. *Bloemfontein* 9800 Tns.
Meliskerk ..	5918	*Nijkerk*	5766	*Klipfontein*	. 5544	*Randfontein* .	5059	,, *Boschfontein* 7000 ,,
Heemskerk ..	6516	*Springfontein*	7342	*Streefkerk* ..	6185			,, *Jagersfontein* 9800 ,,

Doctor carried on all the "*Fontein*" steamers.

Vessel.	Amsterdam. dep.	Rotterdam. dep.	Antwerp. dep.	Hamburg. dep.	Ijm'iden. dep.	Dover. dep.	Capetown. arr.	Durban. arr.	Lourenco Marques. arr.	Beira. arr.
Bloemfontein	July 24	July 25	July 29	Aug. 3	Aug. 4	Aug. 5	Aug. 21	Aug. 28	Aug. 31	Sept. 3
Klipfontein ..	Aug. 7	Aug. 8	Aug. 12	,, 17	,, 18	,, 19	Sept. 4	Sept. 10	Sep. 13	,, 16
Boschfontein	,, 21	,, 22	,, 26	,, 31	Sept. 1	Sept. 2	,, 18	,, 25	,, 28	Oct. 1
Springf'ntein	Sept. 4	Sept. 5	Sept. 9	Sept. 14	—	,, 16	Oct. 10	Oct. 18	Oct. 22	,, 25

Calling at Mossel Bay (alternate sailings), Port Elizabeth, East London, Durban, Lourenco Marques. Return by same route (or *via* Suez Canal—see page 363).

HOMEWARD.

Vessel.	Beira. dep.	Durban. dep.	Capetown dep.	S'uthampton.	D'nkerque arr.	Antwerp. arr.	Rotterdam. arr.	Hamburg. arr.
Randfontein	July 22	July 31	Aug. 4	—	Aug. 28	Aug. 30	Sept. 1	Sept. 4
Nijkerk	Aug. 20	Aug. 29	Sept. 2	—	Sept. 26	Sept. 28	,, 30	Oct. 2
Heemskerk	Sept. 25	Oct. 4	Oct. 9	—	Nov. 2	Nov. 5	Nov. 7	Nov. 10
Jagersfontein‡	Oct. 31	Nov. 5	Nov. 11	Nov. 27	Nov. 28	Dec. 1	Dec. 3	Dec. 7

Calling also Lourenco Marques (occasionally), Durban, East London, Port Elizabeth.

† If sufficient inducement. ‡ Also calls Bremen.

HOLLAND AUSTRALIA LINE (*Via* THE CAPE.)

United Netherlands Navigation Co.

(See page 363.)

HOULDER LINE. United Kingdom to River Plate.

Regular Service of fast twin-screw steamers (8350-9500 tons) carrying First Class passengers only. Weekly sailings alternately from London and Liverpool for Monte Video and Buenos Aires. Many of the steamers have only single berth cabins (inter-communicating) with private bathrooms. Doctor and Stewardess carried on all vessels.

HORN LINE.

Hamburg, Antwerp and Dover to Trinidad, Venezuela, Curacao and Colombia.

Hamburg and Antwerp to Porto Rico, Dominican Republic, Jamaica and Haiti.

Motor vessels of 4,000-4,500 tons, fitted with wireless telegraphy. Cabines de Luxe with private bathroom or shower bath, also single and two-berth cabins. Stewardess and doctor carried on all vessels to Trinidad, etc., also on the m.v. *Claus Horn* and m.v. *Henry Horn* on the Porto Rico, etc. service.

SAILINGS OUTWARD TO TRINIDAD, VENEZUELA, CURACAO AND COLUMBIA.

Motor Vessel.	Hamburg dep.	Bremen. dep.	Antwerp dep.	Dover dep.
H.C. Horn	Aug. 5	Aug. 1	Aug. 8	Aug. 9
Frida Horn	,, 19	,, 21	,, 24	,, 25
Ingrid Horn....	Sept. 2	,, 29	Sept. 5	Sept. 6
Waldtraut Horn	,, 16	Sept. 18	,, 21	,, 22
Heinz Horn	,, 30	,, 26	Oct. 3	Oct. 4

For Port of Spain (Trinidad), La Guayra, Puerto Cabello, Curacao†, Puerto Colombia, Cartagena, Newport (Curacao).
† Connecting m.v. *Karibia* to Maracaibo.

HOMEWARD SAILINGS:

Motor Vessel.	Newport. (Curacao) dp	Cartagena	Havre.	Dover.	Hamburg. arr.
Waldtraut Horn	Aug. 5	Aug. 7	—	Aug. 29	Aug. 30
Heinz Horn	,, 15	,, 17	—	Sept. 8	Sept. 9
Mimi Horn ..	—	,, 26	—	,, 19	,, 20
H.C. Horn	Sept. 11	Sept. 13	—	Oct. 2	Oct. 3
Frida Horn ..	—	,, 28	—	,, 17	,, 19

Calling at Puerto Colombia, Willemstad, Puerto Cabello, La Guayra, Port of Spain. From Hamburg proceeds occasionally to Kotka—Hamburg.

SAILINGS TO PORTO RICO, DOMINICAN REPUBLIC JAMAICA AND HAITI.

Motor Vessel.	Hamburg dep.	Bremen dep.	Antwerp dep.
Claus Horn	Aug. 22	Aug. 23	Aug. 26
Steamer	Sept. 19	Sept 20	Sept. 23
Henry Horn	Oct. 17	Oct. 18	Oct. 21
Claus Horn	Nov. 14	Nov. 15	Nov. 18
Steamer	Dec. 12	Dec. 13	Dec. 16

For Ciudad Trujillo, Kingston, Port au Prince, Cape Haitien, Puerto Plata, San Juan, Curacao.
Homeward from Curacao *via* Ciudad Trujillo, Jacmel, Kingston, Port au Prince, Gonaives (St. Marc), Cape Haitien, Puerto Plata, Havre to Hamburg.

INTEROCEAN LINE.

WESTFAL-LARSEN COMPANY LINE.

Rotterdam, London and Panama to Vancouver, Seattle, Portland, Oakland, San Francisco, Los Angeles.

m.v. *Berganger*† ..	6826 tons	m.v. *Taranger* ..	4873 tons	m.v. *Brimanger* ..	4889 tons
m.v. *Moldanger*† ..	6827 tons	m.v. *Villanger* ..	4884 tons	m.v. *Hindanger* ..	4884 tons
m.v. *Trondanger*†..	6826 tons	m.v. *Heranger* ..	4877 tons		

Cargo vessels with accommodation for 12 passengers, fitted with wireless telegraphy. No doctor or stewardess carried. On vessels indicated † the cabins have private shower and toilet. Also there is one cabin de luxe.

Next Sailings:—

Vessel.	Rotterdam dep.	Vessel.	Rotterdam dep.
Heranger	Aug. 7	*Villanger*	Oct. 1
Berganger	,, 14	*Hindanger*	,, 3
Moldanger	,, 31	*Trondanger*	,, 8
Brimanger	Sept. 12	*Heranger*	,, 30
Taranger	,, 22		

From Vancouver, Seattle, Portland, San Francisco. Los Angeles to Montevideo and Buenos Aires.

Returning *via* Santos, Rio de Janeiro, (Bahia), Panama, Los Angeles, San Francisco, Portland, Seattle to Vancouver. Sailings on application.

"ITALIA." Soc. An. di Navigazione.

NORD AMERICA EXPRESS (OUTWARD).

Steamer.	Tons	Genoa dep.¶	Naples dep	Genoa arr./dep.	Nice dep.	Cannes.	Naples	Gibraltar arr./dep.	New York arr.
Rex	54000	—	—	Aug. 2	—	Aug. 2	Aug. 3	Aug. 4	Aug. 10
Conte di Savoia	48000	—	—	,, 24	—	,, 24	—	,, 25	,, 31
Rex	54000	—	—	Sept. 7	—	Sept. 7	—	Sept. 8	Sept. 14
Conte di Savoia	48000	—	—	,, 13	—	,, 13	Sept. 14	,, 15	,, 21
Rex	54000	—	—	,, 27	—	,, 27	,, 28	,, 29	Oct. 5
Conte di Savoia	48000	—	—	Oct. 12	—	Oct. 12	—	Oct. 13	,, 19
Rex	54000	—	—	,, 18	—	,, 18	Oct. 19	,, 20	,, 26
Conte di Savoia	48000	—	—	Nov. 1	—	Nov. 1	Nov. 2	Nov. 3	Nov. 9
Rex....	54000	—	—	,, 13	—	,, 13	,, 14	,, 15	,, 21
Conte di Savoia	48000	—	—	,, 22	—	,, 22	,, 23	,, 24	,, 30
Rex ..	54000	—	—	Dec. 4	—	Dec. 4	Dec. 5	Dec. 6	Dec. 12
Conte di Savoia	48000	—	—	Jan. 4	—	Jan. 4	—	Jan. 5	Jan. 11

¶ On these dates passengers accepted for Naples only.

NORD AMERICA EXPRESS (HOMEWARD).

Steamer	Tons	New York dep.	Mad-eira.	Casa-blanca	Gib-raltar.	Algiers.	Naples arr./dep.	Cannes.	Genoa. arr/dep.	Naples arr.
Conte di Savoia	48000	Aug. 5	—	—	Aug 10	—	—	Aug. 12	Aug. 12	Aug. 13
Rex	54000	,, 12	—	—	,, 17	—	—	,, 19	,, 19	,, 20
Conte di Savoia	48000	Sept. 2	—	—	Sept 7	—	Sept. 9	Sept. 10	Sept. 10	—
Rex	54000	,, 16	—	—	,, 21	—	,, 23	,, 24	,, 24	—
Conte di Savoia	48000	,, 23	—	—	,, 28	—	—	,, 30	, 30	Oct. 1
Rex	54000	Oct. 7	—	—	Oct. 12	—	Oct. 14	Oct. 15	Oct. 15	—
Conte di Savoia	48000	,, 21	—	—	,, 26	—	,, 28	,, 29	,, 29	—
Rex	54000	,, 28	—	—	Nov. 2	—	—	Nov. 4	Nov. 4	Nov. 5
Conte di Savoia	48000	Nov. 11	—	—	,, 16	—	Nov. 18	,, 19	,, 19	—
Rex	54000	,, 23	—	—	,, 28	—	,, 30	Dec. 1	Dec. 1	—
Conte di Savoia	48000	Dec. 2	—	—	Dec. 7	—	..	,, 9	,, 9	Dec. 10

TO SOUTH AMERICA (SUD AMERICA EXPRESS).

Steamer.	Tons	Genoa & Cannes dp	Barcelona dep.	Las Palmas	Pernam-buco.	Rio de Janeiro	Santos.	Monte Video.	Buenos Aires.
†*Conte Grande** ..	26000	Aug. 10	Aug. 10	A 13/14	Aug. 19	Aug. 22	Aug. 23	Aug. 25	Aug. 26
Augustus	34000	,, 24	,, 25	Aug. 28	—	Sept. 5	Sept. 6	Sept. 8	Sept. 29
‡*Conte Grande** ..	26000	Sept. 21	Sept. 22	S.24/25	Sept. 30	Oct. 3	Oct 4	Oct. 6	Oct. 7
Augustus	34000	Oct. 12	Oct. 13	Oct. 16	—	,, 24	,, 25	,, 27	,, 28
‡*Conte Grande** ..	26000	Nov. 9	Nov. 10	N 12/13	Nov. 18	Nov. 21	Nov. 22	Nov. 24	Nov. 25

†Calls also Bahia. * Calls Teneriffe (not Las Palmas).

FROM SOUTH AMERICA (SUD AMERICA EXPRESS).

Steamer.	Tons.	Buenos Aires dep.	Monte Video.	Santos	Rio de Janeiro.	Pernam-buco.	Dakar.	Barce-lona.	Cannes & Genoa arr.
Augustus	34000	Aug. 1	Aug. 2	Aug. 4	Aug. 5	—	Aug.* 13	Aug. 16	Aug. 17
‡*Conte Grande*....	26000	,, 29	,, 30	Sept. 1	Sept. 2	Sept. 5	Sept. 9	Sept. 14	Sept. 15
Augustus	34000	Sept. 12	Sept. 13	,, 15	,, 16	—	,, *24	,, 27	,, 28
‡*Conte Grande*....	26000	Oct. 10	Oct. 11	Oct. 13	Oct. 14	Oct. 17	Oct. 21	Oct. 26	Oct. 27
Augustus	34000	,, 31	Nov. 1	Nov. 3	Nov. 4	—	Nov.* 12	Nov. 15	Nov. 16

‡ Calls also Bahia. * Las Palmas.

TO CENTRAL AMERICA AND SOUTH PACIFIC *via* PANAMA,

Motor Vessel.	Tons.	Fr.Genoa	Mar-seilles	Bar-celona
Virgilio	11717	Sept. 2	Sept. 3	Sept. 4
Orozio	11670	Oct. 6	Oct. 7	Oct. 8
Virgilio	11717	Nov. 16	Nov 17	Nov 18

For Funchal and/or Las Palmas(optional), La Guayra, Puerto Colombia, Cristobal, Salinas, Callao, Mollendo, Arica, Iquique, Tocopilla (optional), Antofagasta, Valparaiso. § Optional call.

Italy—Central America—Pacific Coast.

Motor Vessel.	Trieste. dep.	Venice. dep.	§Split (Spalato) dep	Naples dep.	Leghorn. dep.	Genoa. dep.	Marseilles.	Barcelona §	Malaga §

To Colon Puntarenas, La Libertad, St. José di Guatemala, Los Angeles, San Francisco, Portland§ to Vancouver. Returning *via* same ports (except St. Jose, Malaga and Split); and also calling at Seattle§, Las Palmas.

Italy—Mexico.—From Genoa, monthly, *via* Leghorn, Marseilles, Cadiz, Las Palmas, San Jua de Portor§, Puerta Plata§, Havana, Vera Cruz, Tampico, New Orleans, Havana§, returning *via* Las Palmas, Barcelona§, Marseilles to Genoa. § Optional call.

"ITALIA." Soc. An. di Navigazione—*cont.*

TRIESTE—NEW YORK SERVICE.

OUTWARD :—

Motor Vessels Tine Screw.	Tons	Trieste dep	Ragusa. (D'bvnik)	Patras	Naples.	Pal-ermo.	Algiers	Gib-raltar.	Lisbon	Azores.	New York arr.
Vulcania ..	24000	Aug. 3	Aug. 4	Aug. 5	Aug. 6	Aug. 7	Aug. 8	Aug. 9	Aug. 10	Aug. 12	Aug. 17
Saturnia ..	24000	,, 24	,, 25	,, 26	,, 27	,, 28	,, 29	,, 30	,, 31	Sept. 2	Sept. 7
Vulcania ..	24000	Sept. 14	Sept. 15	Sept. 16	Sept. 17	Sep. 18	Sept. 19	Sept. 20	Sept. 21	,, 23	,, 28
Saturnia ..	24000	,, 28	,, 29	,, 30	Oct. 1	Oct. 2	Oct. 3	Oct. 4	Oct. 5	Oct. 7	Oct. 12
Vulcania ..	24000	Oct. 19	Oct. 20	Oct. 21	,, 22	,, 23	,, 24	,, 25	,, 26	,, 28	Dec. 2

HOMEWARD :—

T. S. Motor Vessels.	Tons	N. York dep.	Lis-bon.	Gib-raltar.	Algiers	Pal-ermo.	Naples.	Patras	Ragusa. (D'bvnik)	Venice. arr.	Trieste. arr.
**Saturnia*	24000	July 28	Aug. 6	Aug. 7	Aug. 8	Aug. 9	Aug. 10	Aug 11	Aug. 12	Aug. 13	Aug. 13
**Vulcania*	24000	Aug. 23	Sept. 1	Sept. 2	Sept. 3	Sept. 4	Sept. 5	Sept. 6	Sept. 7	Sept. 8	Sept. 8
**Saturnia*	24000	Sept. 8	,, 17	,, 18	,, 19	,, 20	,, 21	,, 22	,, 23	,, 24	,, 24
**Vulcania* ..	24000	,, 29	Oct. 8	Oct. 9	Oct. 10	Oct. 11	Oct. 12	Oct. 13	Oct. 14	—	Oct. 15
**Saturnia* ..	24000	Oct. 13	,, 22	,, 23	,, 24	,, 25	,, 26	,, 27	,, 28	—	,, 29
**Vulcania* ..	24000	Nov. 3	Nov 12	Nov 13	Nov. 14	Nov 15	Nov. 16	Nov 17	Nov. 18	—	Nov. 19

* Calls Boston and Azores and Vigo.

TRIESTE—SOUTH AMERICA SERVICE.

STEAMER.	Tons	Tr'ste dep.	Split (Sp'lato)	N'ples	Algiers	Gib-raltar.	Pernam-buco.	Bahia	Rio de Janeiro	Santos.	Monte Video.	Buenos Aires.
†*Neptunia*	21000	Aug. 2	Aug. 2	Aug. 4	Aug. 5	Aug. 6	Aug. 13	Aug 14	Aug. 16	Aug. 17	Aug. 19	Aug. 20
†*Oceania*	21000	Sept. 7	Sept. 7	Sept. 9	Sept. 10	Sep. 11	Sept. 18	Sep. 19	Sept. 21	Sept. 22	Sept. 24	Sept. 25
†*Neptunia*	21000	,, 28	,, 28	,, 30	Oct. 1	Oct. 2	Oct. 9	Oct. 10	Oct. 12	Oct, 13	Oct. 15	Oct. 16
†*Oceania*	21000	Oct. 25	Oct. 25	Oct. 27	,, 28	,, 29	Nov. 5	Nov. 6	Nov. 8	Nov. 9	Nov. 11	Nov. 12
†*Neptunia*	21000	Nov 15	Nov. 15	Nov 17	Nov. 18	No. 19	,, 26	,, 27	,, 29	,, 30	Dec. 2	Dec. 3

† Calls Rio Grande du Sul.

Steamer.	Tons.	B. Aires dep	Monte Video.	Santos	Rio de Janeiro	Bahia.	Pernam-buco.	Gib-raltar.	Algiers	Naples	Trieste.
‡*Oceania*	21000	Aug. 12	Aug. 13	Aug 16	Aug. 17	Aug. 19	Aug. 20	Aug. 27	Aug. 28	Aug. 30	Sept. 1
‡*Neptunia*	21000	,, 24	,, 26	,, 28	,, 29	,, 31	Sept. 1	Sept. 8	Sept. 9	Sept 11	,, 13*
‡*Oceania*	21000	Sept. 29	Sept. 30	Oct. 3	Oct. 4	Oct. 6	Oct. 7	Oct. 14	Oct. 15	Oct. 17	Oct. 19
‡*Neptunia*	21000	Oct. 20	Oct. 21	Oct. 24	,, 25	,, 27	Oct. 28	Nov. 4	Nov. 5	Nov. 7	Nov. 9
‡*Oceania*	21000	Nov. 16	Nov. 17	Nov 20	Nov. 21	Nov. 23	Nov. 24	Dec. 1	Dec. 2	Dec. 4	Dec. 6
‡*Neptunia*	21000	Dec. 6	Dec. 7	Dec 10	Dec. 11	Dec. 13	Dec. 14	,, 21	,, 22	,, 24	,, 26

‡ Calls also Rio Grande du Sul. * Calls at Bari.

GENOA, S. AMERICA POST. SERVICE (Calling at Gibraltar, Santos & Montevideo)

(3rd class only).

STEAMER.	Genoa dep.	N'ples	Gib-raltar	Tener-iffe.	Rio de Janeiro.	B. Aires. arr./dp.	Rio Jan'ro dep.	Tener-iffe.	Gib-altar	Naples. arr.	Genoa arr
P'ssa Giovanna	Jly. 19	Jly. 21	—	July 27	Aug. 7	Au. 12/21	Aug. 26	Sept. 7	—	Sep 13	Sep 14
P'ssa Maria ..	Au. 31	Sep. 2	—	Sept. 8	Sept. 19	Se24/O. 3	Oct. 8	Oct. 20	—	Oct. 26	Oct. 27
P'ssa Giovanna	Sep 30	Oct. 2	—	Oct. 8	Oct. 19	O. 24/N. 3	Nov. 8	Nov. 20	—	Nov 26	Nv. 27
P'ssa Maria ..	Nov 18	Nv. 20	—	Nov 26	Dec. 7	Dec 12/23	Dec. 27	Jan. 8	—	Jan. 14	Ja. 15

Calling also at Santos and Monte Video. Optional call at Barcelona on homeward journey.

JAMAICA BANANA PRODUCERS S/S CO. LTD.

London to Kingston—Jamaica Direct.

Carrying first class passengers with stewardess and doctor (except on m.v. *Pontos* and *Palime*).

Sailings—

Steamer.	Tons	Leave London	Arr. Kingston, Jamaica.	L've Kingston, Jamaica.	Arrive Rotterdam.	Arrive London.
Jamaica Planter ..	4098	Aug. 5	Aug. 18	Aug. 22	Sept. 4	Sept. 5
Jamaica Progress	5351	,, 12	,, 25	,, 29	,, 11	,, 12
Jamaica Pioneer ..	5349	,, 19	Sept. 1	Sept. 5	,, 18	,, 19
Pomona	3500	,, 26	,, 8	,, 12	,, 25	,, 26
Jamaica Producer	5825	Sept. 2	,, 15	,, 19	Oct. 2	Oct. 3
Jamaica Planter ..	4098	,, 9	,, 22	,, 26	,, 9	,, 10
Jamaica Progress	5351	,, 16	,, 29	Oct. 3	,, 16	,, 17
Jamaica Pioneer ..	5349	,, 23	Oct. 6	,, 10	,, 23	,, 24
Pomona	3500	,, 30	,, 13	,, 17	,, 30	,, 31

GOTHENBURG & ANTWERP *via* PANAMA TO WEST COAST PORTS OF NORTH AMERICA.

m.s. *Margaret Johnson*, 5200 tons; m.s. *Annie Johnson*, 5000 tons; m.s. *Axel Johnson*, 5000 tons; m.s. *Buenos Aires*, 5600 tons; m.s. *Canada*, 5500 tons; m.s. *Balboa*, 5500 tons.

Carrying 1st and 3rd class passengers. Fitted with bath, swimming-pool, electric light and electric fans. The m.s. *Margaret Johnson*, *Annie Johnson* and *Axel Johnson* carry Surgeon and Stewardess. All vessels have two berthed first-class cabins and two, three and four berth cabins in third class.

Monthly or three-weekly sailings from Gothenburg and Antwerp to Puerto Colombia, Panama, Central American ports, San Diego, Los Angeles, San Francisco and Vancouver. Occasional calls are also made at Punta Arenas, Corinto, La Union, San José de Guatemala Champerico and Seattle. Hawaiian Islands are called about every four months.

GOTHENBURG AND DOVER (occasionally) TO BRAZIL, URUGUAY AND ARGENTINE.

Monthly express service by m.s. *Brasil*, m.s. *Uruguay*, m.s. *Argentina* and m.s. *Nordstjernan*, of 5,300 tons. First-class only. Private bathroom to each cabin. Stewardess carried.

Fortnightly service of slower boats; m.s. *Santos* and similar. Tourist class only. Fitted with bath, swimming pool, electric light, etc. [at Pernambuco and Bahia.

Regular calls made at Rio de Janeiro, Santos, Montevideo and Buenos Aires. Occasional calls made

KONINKLIJKE NEDERLANDSCHE STOOMBOOT MAATSCHAPPIJ N.V.

ROYAL NETHERLANDS STEAMSHIP CO. COLON LINE.

‖*Colombia* (M.v.	10782	*Simon Bolivar*	7606	*Crijnssen*	4298
‖*Costa Rica* .	8672	‖*Venezuela*	6355	**Pericles* (m.v.) ..	3200

1st, 2nd and 3rd cl. passengers carried. Cabins de Luxe and Special Cabins with Private Bath Rooms and Shower Baths. Cabins with one, two, or more berths, Bath Rooms, Doctor and Stewardess carried.

OUTWARD. Vessel.	From Amsterdam.	From Boulogne and Dover.	Barbados.	Curacao.† arr./dep.	Kingston. arr./dep.	Puerto Limon arr.
‡*Pericles*	Aug. 4	Aug. 5	Aug. 18	Aug. 23/24	Aug. 30	Sept. 1
‡*Costa Rica*	,, 18	,, 19	,, 30	Sept. 3/4	Sept. 11/12	,, 14
‡*Simon Bolivar* ..	Sept. 1	Sept. 2	Sept. 14	,, 18/19	,, 26/27	,, 29
‡*Socrates* ...	,, 15	,, 16	,, 29	Oct. 4/5	Oct. 11	Oct. 13
‡*Colombia*	,, 29	,, 30	Oct. 11	,, 15/16	,, 23/24	,, 26
‡*Pericles*	Oct. 13	Oct. 14	,, 27	Nov. 1/2	Nov. 8	Nov. 10
Costa Rica	,, 27	,, 28	Nov. 8	,, 12/13	,, 20/21	,, 23

‡Calls Madeira.

Also calling at Trinidad, La Guaira, Pto, Cabello, Sta Marta, Puerto Colombia, Cartagena, Cristobal, (C.Z

†Connecting at Curacao with s.s. *El Libertador* to and from Aruba and Maracaibo and with the Co.'s coasting vessels to and from Jamaica, Haiti, Dominician Republic, Porto Rico, Bonaire, St. Thomas, St. Martin, Saba, St. Eustatius, St. Kitts. * Cargo vessel carrying 12 First class. ‖ Twin Screw.

HOMEWARD. Vessel.	Puerto Limon. dep.	Cristobal.	Curacao.†	Barbados‡	Plymouth arr.	Havre. arr.	Amsterdam arr.
Socrates	Aug. 4	Aug. 6	Aug. 10	Aug. 16	Aug. 28	Aug. 29	Aug. 30
Colombia	,, 18	,, 20	,, 24	,, 29	Sept. 8	Sept. 9	Sept. 10
Pericles	Sept. 1	Sept. 3	Sept. 7	Sept. 13	,, 25	,, 26	,, 27
Costa Rica	,, 15	,, 17	,, 21	,, 26	Oct. 6	Oct. 7	Oct. 8
Simon Bolivar	,, 29	Oct. 1	Oct. 5	Oct. 11	,, 22	,, 23	,, 24
Socrates	Oct. 13	,, 15	,, 19	,, 25	Nov. 6	Nov. 7	Nov. 8

Calling also at Cartagena, Pto. Columbia, Pto. Cabello, La Guaira, Trinidad. * Calls Madeira.

AMSTERDAM—SURINAM—NEW YORK LINE (Sailings every three weeks.)

Cottica 4000 tons, *Oranje Nassau* 3701 tons, *Van Rensselaer* 4300 tons, *Stuyvesant* 4203 tons, *Crijnssen* 4300 tons

First, second and third class pass. carried. Cabins de Luxe, Cabins with one, two or more berths Bath Rooms. Doctor and Stewardess carried.

Steamer.	Amsterdam. dep.	Dover dep.	Madeira arr./dep.	New York. arr.	New York. dep.	Madeira	Plymouth.	Havre.	Amsterdam.
Cottica	June 20	June 21	—	July 24	July 28	Aug. 28	Aug. 31	Sept. 1	Sept. 2
Stuyvesant	July 11	July 12	—	Aug. 14	Aug 18	Sept. 17	Sept. 21	Sept. 22	,, 23
Van Rensselaer	Aug. 1	Aug. 2	—	Sept. 4	Sept. 8	Oct. 8	Oct. 12	Oct. 13	Oct. 14
Crijnssen	,, 22	,, 23	—	,, 25	,, 29	,, 29	Nov. 2	Nov. 3	Nov. 4
Cottica	Sept. 12	Sept. 13	—	Oct. 16	Oct. 20	Nov. 20	,, 24	,, 25	,, 26

Calling out and home also at Paramaribo, Demerara, Trinidad, Carupano, Pampatar, Pto. Sucre (Cumana), Guanta, La Guaira, Curacao*, Port au Prince. In addition calls at Pto. Cabello homeward.

* See note above.

SOUTH PACIFIC LINE. (Fortnightly Service).

s.s. *Breda* .. May 19 | s.s. *Boskoop* .. .. June 2

Routing:—Amsterdam, Curacao, Cristobal Buenaventura, Manta, Guayaquil, Paita, Pimental, Salaverry†, Callao, Mollendo, Arica, Iquique, Antofagasta†, Coquimbo†, Valparaiso San Antonio, Talcahuano and Corral. Cargo steamers carrying a limited number of cabin, intermediate, and third class passengers only. s.s. *Baarn*, s.s. *Barneveld*, s.s. *Bodegraven* and s.s. *Boskoop* carry a doctor but no stewardess. The other steamers carry neither doctor nor stewardess.

† These ports are not always served direct.

GUATEMALA LINE (Fortnightly).

Amsterdam to Belize, Pto. Cortez, Pto. Barrios (subject to alteration). Cargo Steamers carrying a limited number of passengers, Tourist Class. Neither doctor or stewardess carried.

LLOYD TRIESTINO Soc. An. di Navigazione.

See also pages 382/5 and 481.

LINE 161.

AROUND AFRICA (OUT via CAPE, HOME via SUEZ).

Vessel.	Tons	*Genoa. dep.	Gibraltar. dep.	Dakar.	Cape Town arr./dep.	Port Elizabeth.	East London.	Durban. arr.
Sabbia ..	5788	July 25	July 29	Aug. 5	Aug. 21/23	Aug. 25	Aug. 26	Aug. 28
Sistiania	5827	Aug. 22	Aug. 26	Sept. 2	Sept. 18/20	Sept. 22	Sept. 23	Sept. 25
Perla ..	5741	Sept. 19	Sept. 23	,, 30	Oct. 16/18	Oct. 20	Oct. 21	Oct. 23
Edda ..	6107	Oct. 17	Oct. 21	Oct. 28	Nov. 13/15	Nov. 17	Nov. 18	Nov. 20
Sabbia ..	5788	Nov. 14	Nov. 18	Nov. 25	Dec. 11/13	Dec. 15	Dec. 16	Dec. 18
Sistiania	5827	Dec. 12	Dec. 16	Dec. 23	Jan. 8/10	Jan. 12	Jan. 13	Jan. 15

* Before Genoa calls at Trieste, Venice, Spalato, Messina, Naples, (optional), Leghorn, Marseilles.

HOMEWARD.

Vessel.	Tns	Durban. dep.	Beira. arr./dep.	Mombasa.	Massaua	Port Said.	Naples.	Marseilles. arr./dep.	Genoa. arr/dep.	Venice.	Trieste.
Perla ..	5741	July 5	Jly 10/13	July 19	July 30	Aug. 5	Aug. 10	Aug 12/16	Au 17/18	Aug. 23	Aug 24
Edda	6107	Aug. 2	Aug 7/10	Aug. 16	Aug. 27	Sept. 2	Sept. 7	Sept. 9/13	Sp. 14/15	Sept. 20	Sept. 21
Sabbia ..	5788	,, 30	Sept. 4/7	Sept. 13	Sept. 24	,, 30	Oct. 5	Oct. 7/11	Oc. 12/13	Oct. 18	Oct. 19
Sistiania	5827	Sep. 27	Oct. 2/5	Oct. 11	Oct. 22	Oct. 28	Nov. 2	Nov. 4/8	Nov 9/10	Nov. 15	Nov. 16
Perla ..	5741	Oct. 25	O. 30/N 2	Nov. 8	Nov. 19	Nov. 25	,, 30	Dec. 2/6	Dec. 7/8	Dec. 13	Dec. 14
Edda ..	6107	Nov 22	Nv. 27/30	Dec. 6	Dec. 17	Dec. 23	Dec. 28	D. 30/J. 3	Jan. 4/5	Jan. 10	Jan. 11
Sabbia ..	5788	Dec. 20	De. 25/28	Jan. 3	Jan. 14	Jan. 20	Jan. 25	Jan. 27/31	Feb. 1/2	Feb. 7	Feb. 8

Calling also at Lourenco Marques, Mozambique (optional), Dar-es-Salaam, Zanzibar, Merca, Mogadiscio, Dante, Port Sudan, Suez (optional.)

LINE 162.

ITALY—WEST AFRICA—CONGO LINE.

Monthly service from Trieste (on 30/31), *via* Venice, Fiume §, Spalato, Naples, Leghorn, Genoa, Marseilles, Gibraltar§, Casablanca§, Las Palmas§, Dakar, Conakry, Freetown, Port Bouet, Takoradi§, Accra, Lome§, Lagos, Douala, Libreville§, Pointe Noire, Matadi.

HOMEWARD:—Pointe Noire, Port Gentil, Oil Rivers§, Douala, Lagos, Accra§, Takoradi, Grand Bassam§, Grand Lahou§, Monrovia§, Freetown, Conakry, Bathurst§, Dakar, Gibraltar§, Marseilles, Genoa, Leghorn§, Naples§, Fiume§, Venice, Trieste.

ITALY—SOUTH AFRICA,

(Outward *via* Suez, *see page* 382).

LAMPORT & HOLT LINE.

Brazil and River Plate Services from Liverpool and London.

By modern cargo steamers (5332 to 7453 tons) with accommodation for saloon passengers.
From Liverpool depart monthly for Bahia, Rio de Janeiro, Santos and Rio Grande du Sul. May call at Peninsular ports.
From Liverpool monthly for Monte Video, Buenos Aires and Rosario.
From Middlesbrough, Antwerp and London to Monte Video, Buenos Aires and Rosario monthly.

Southampton—Lisbon—Madeira and back by T.s.s. *Vandyck* (13250 tons).
Suspended.

		Southampton ..			
		Lisbon			
		Madeira			

Services Contractuels des MESSAGERIES MARITIMES. See pp. 388/390.

New Caledonia *via* the Panama Canal. Marseilles, Papeete, Suva, Noumea.

Steamer.	Tons.	Marseilles dep.	Algiers	P'nte-a-Pit'e arr.	Fort-de-France arr.	Cristobal arr.	Papeete arr./dp	Raïatea arr. (Optl.)	Suva arr. (Optl.)	Port Vila	Noumea arr.
Eridon	9928	Aug. 21	Aug. 23	Sept. 5	Sept. 6	Sep. 11	Sp.27/28	Sept.29	—	Oct. 9	Oct.11
Sagittaire	—	Oct. 2	Oct. 4	Oct 16	Oct. 17	Oct. 21	Nov. 5/6	—	—	Nov15	Nov17
Ville d'Amiens....	6975	Nov. 13	Nov. 15	Nov 27	Nov.28	Dec. 2	Dc.17/18	—	Dec 25	Dec 27	Dec 29
Com. Ramel	10061	Dec. 25	Dec. 27	Jan. 8	Jan. 9	Jan. 13	Ja. 27/28	Jan. 29	Feb. 5	Feb. 7	Feb. 9

HOMEWARD.—From Noumea, Sept. 2, Oct. 18, Nov 24, Jan. 5, etc., *via* Port Vila, Raïatea, Papeete, Cristobal Curacao (occasionally), Fort-de-France, La Pointe-à-Pitre, Madeira to Marseilles.

NATAL LINE. London to Port Natal (direct.)

Taking 1st cl. passengers (only), for Cape Town, Natal (Durban), Lourenco Marques (Delagoa Bay), and Beira, calling en route at Las Palmas and Teneriffe alternately. Low fares. Sailings approx. every 3 weeks.

Steamer	Tons	Sailing	Steamer	Tons	Sailing	Steamer	Tons	Sailing	Steamer	Tons	Sailing
**Umvuma*	6730	Aug. 5	¶†*Umona*	5450	Sept. 9	†*Umtata*	8139	Oct. 14	†*Umvuma*	6730	Nov. 25
**Umtali*	8158	Aug. 19	**Umgeni*	8180	Sept. 30	**Umvoti*	7270	Nov. 4	**Umtali*	8158	Dec. 9

* Calls Las Palmas. ¶ Through steamer to Mauritius. † Calls Teneriffe.

COMPANHIA COLONIAL DE NAVEGACAO

s.s. *Mouzinho*, 8200 tons; s.s. *Colonial*, 7866 tons; s.s. *Joao Belo*, 7680 tons. 8309

Carrying 1, 2, and 3 class passengers. Stewardess and Surgeon carried.

East African Service. Lisbon dep. Aug. 12 and approx. monthly, for Funchal, S. Tomé, Pointe Noire, Sazaire, Loanda, Porto Amboim, Lobito, Mossamedes, Cape Town, Lourenco Marques, Mozambique, Beira, Lourenco Marques, Cape Town, Mossamedes, Lobito, Porto Amboim, Loanda, Sazaire, Pointe Noire, S. Tomé, Funchal, Lisbon.

s.s. *Guiné*, 3200 tons.

Guinea and Cape Verde Service. Lisbon dep. Aug. 8 and about every 6 weeks, etc., for Funchal, St. Vincent, Praia, Bolama, Bissau, Praia, St. Vincent, Funchal, Lisbon.

s.s. *Cassequel*. 7140 tons; s.s. *Ganda* 6810 tons; s.s. *Loanda*, 5910 tons; s.s. *Lobito* 4750 tons; Cargo vessels.

West African Service. Lisbon dep. Aug. 19 and monthly for St. Vincent, Praia, Principe, S. Tomé, Ambriz, Loanda, Porto Amboim, Novo Redondo, Lobito, Benguela, Mossamedes, returning *via* Benguela, Lobito, Novo Redondo, Porto Amboim, Loanda, Ambriz, S. Tomé, Principe to Lisbon (calling optionally on return at Praia, St. Vincent and Funchal).

COMPANHIA NACIONAL DE NAVEGACAO.

Nyassa ..	9000	**Congo* ..	5000	*L. Marques*	6400	*Chinde* ..	1382	*Ambriz* ..	858
Angola ..	8300	**Cubango* ..	8300	*Mocambique*	6000	*Ibo* ..	885	*Save* ..	763
Quanza	6500	**Cabo Verde*	6200	*Luabo* .	1385				

* Cargo vessels.

The above steamers carry 1, 2 and 3 cl. passengers. Stewardess and Doctor carried.

West Africa Service. Lisbon dep. Aug. 5 and approx. monthly for Funchal, St. Vincent, Praia, Fernando Poo†, Principe, S. Tomé, Cabinda, Sazaire, Ambriz, Loanda, Porto Amboim, Novo Rodondo, Lobito, Benguela, Porto Alexandre, Mossamedes, Benguela, Lobito, Novo Redondo, Porto Amboim, Loanda, Ambriz, Sazaire, Cabinda, S. Tomé, Principe, Fernando Poo†, Praia, St. Vincent, Funchal, Lisbon. May also call at Barra do Dande and Cuio. † Fernando Poo may be omitted. ¶ Omits Praia and St. Vincent on returning.

East Africa Service. Lisbon dep. Aug. 26 and approx. monthly, for East Africa (Mozambique), calling at Funchal, (Madeira), S. Tomé, Pointe Noire, Loanda, Porto Amboim, Lobito, Mossamedes, Cape Town, Lourenco Marques, Beira, Mozambique, Lourenco Marques, Cape Town, Mossamedes, Lobito, Porto Amboim, Loanda, Pointe Noire, S. Tomé, Funchal, Lisbon.

 See also pp. 365, 407, 417, 422, 459.

North Pacific Service, *via* Panama Canal.

Freight vessels, carrying limited number of passengers in the cabin class.
Doctor and Stewardess also carried except on *Schwaben* and *Este*.

Vessel.	Tons	Bremen, dep.	Antwerp, dep.	
Donau	9035	Aug. 12	Aug. 15	To Cristobal, La Libertad†, San José de Guatemala†, Los Angeles, S Francisco, Vancouver, Seattle, Tacoma, Portland.
Este..........	7915	Sept. 7	Sept. 9	

† Call optional.

South America (West Coast), *via* Panama Canal.

Cargo steamers with accommodation for about 20/28 passengers in cabin class.

Vessel.	Tons.	Bremen, dep.	Antwerp dep.	
Leipzig	5898	Aug. 12	Aug. 15	To Cristobal/Colon, Buenaventura, Guayaquil, Callao, Mollendo, Arica, Antofagasta, Valparaiso.
Nurnberg	5635	Aug. 26	Aug. 29	
Osnabruck	5095	Sept. 9	Sept. 12	
Hannover	5537	Sept. 23	Sept. 26	

South America (West Coast), *via* Straits of Magellan.

Cargo steamers with accommodation for a few intermediate passengers.

Vessel.	Tons.	Bremen, dep	Antwerp, dep.	
Koln	7881	Sept 9	Sept. 11	To Punta Arenas, Corral, Talcahuano, Valparaiso.

Bremen-Cuba-Mexico Service. (INCLUDING OZEAN LINE).

Cargo steamers with accommodation for a few cabin class.

Vessel.	Tons.	Bremen dep.	Antwerp.	Havana. arr.	Vera Cruz arr.	Tampico. arr.	Havana. dep.	Hamburg. arr.
Lech	3290	Aug. 12	Aug. 15	—	Sept. 1	Sept. 7	—	—
Memel	3183	Aug. 12	Aug. 15	Aug. 29	—	—	—	—
Iller	3290	Sept. 13	Sept. 16	—	Oct. 3	Oct. 10	—	—

North Brazil. Cargo steamers with accommodation for a few intermediate passengers.

Vessel.	Tons.	Hamburg, dep.	Antwerp dep.	
Steamer......	—	Aug. 4	—	Ceará, Parnahyba, Maranháo, Pará, Manaos.
Spree	2867	Aug. 17	Aug. 19	

Central America (West Coast) *via* Panama Canal.

Cargo steamers with accommodation for a few intermediate passengers.

Vessel.	Bremen dep.	Antwerp dep.	Cristobal arr.	Puntarenas arr.	Champerico arr.

South America—South Africa Service.

Cargo steamers with accommodation for a few intermediate passengers.

Steamer.	Tons.	Buenos Aires dep.	Rio de Janeiro. dep	Cape Town. dep.	Durban. arr./dep.	Buenos Aires. arr.
Minden	—	Aug. 12	Aug. 23	Sept. 5	Sept. 11/15	Oct.

Madeira and Canary Islands Service.

BREMEN—ANTWERP—MADEIRA—LAS PALMAS—TENERIFFE—ANTWERP—BREMEN fortnightly. Cabin class passengers only carried. Bathrooms. Doctor and Stewardess carried on both steamers. Round Trip Cruises 3 weeks. Single and return tickets also issued during low season.

Steamer.	Tons	Bremen dep.	Antwerp arr./dep.	Madeira arr /dep.	LasPalmas arr./dep	Teneriffe arr /dep.	Antwerp arr /dp.	Bremen arr.
Arucas	3369	Aug. 12	Aug. 14	Aug. 20	Aug. 21/22	Aug. 23/24	Aug. 31	Sept. 2
Orotava	3350	Aug. 26	Aug. 28	Sept. 3	Sept. 4/5	Sept. 6/7	Sept. 14	Sept. 16

Canary Islands Service.

HAMBURG—ANTWERP—LAS PALMAS—TENERIFFE—LA PALMA—TENERIFFE—LAS PALMAS HAMBURG, fortnightly. Cabin class passengers only carried. Bathrooms. Round Trip Cruises 3 weeks.

Vessel.	Tons.	Hamburg dep.	Antwerp arr./dep.	Las Palmas arr./dep.	Teneriffe. arr./dp.	Santa Cruz d La Palma arr./dep.	Teneriffe arr /dep.	Las Palmas arr./dep.	Hamburg arr.
Ems	3287	Aug. 5	Aug. 7/8	Aug. 16	—	Aug. 23	—	—	Aug. 29
Eider ..	3288	Aug. 19	Aug. 21/22	Aug. 30	—	Sept. 6	—	—	Sept. 12

After Las Palmas calls subject to confirmation.

Coastal Service—Panama Canal—Ecuador.

Cargo steamers with accommodation for a limited number of passengers.
Weekly service with the s.s. *Manizales*, *Cerigo* and *Durazzo*.
Ports of call:—Buenaventura, Tumaco, Esmeraldas, Bahia de C., Manta.

See also Cook's North Atlantic Sailing List, free on application.

ANCHOR LINE. (See also p. 357). Glasgow to New York and Boston, *via* Belfast/Moville or *via* Dublin.

CANADIAN PACIFIC.
(See also pages 403 and 47[illegible]).
Liverpool, Belfast, Glasgow or Southampton, Cherbourg to Quebec and Montreal (Summer); Liverpool, Belfast, Glasgow to Halifax, N.S. and St. John, N.B. (Winter).

CUNARD WHITE STAR LINE.
(See also pages 404 and 481).
Southampton, Cherbourg, New York; Liverpool, Cobh (Queenstown), Boston, New York; Liverpool, Belfast, Glasgow or Dublin, Galway to Boston and New York; Southampton, Quebec, Montreal, (Summer); Liv'pool, Greenock, Belfast, Quebec, Montreal (Summer), Southampton, Halifax, N.S (Wint'r); Liverpool, Belfast, Greenock, Halifax, N.S. (Wint'r)

DONALDSON ATLANTIC LINE LTD.
Glasgow to Quebec and Montreal (Summer). Glasgow to Halifax, N.S and St. John, N.B. (Winter).

FURNESS LINE.
(See also pages 360, 449).
Liverpool to St. John's N.F. Halifax (N.S.) and Boston

GDYNIA-AMERYKA LINJE ZEGLUGOWE S.A.
(See also pages 416, 449 and 459).
Gdynia and Copenhagen to Halifax, and New York.

HOLLAND AMERICA LINE.
(See also pages 406, 46[illegible]).
Rotterdam, Boulogne and Southampton to New York.

HAMBURG-AMERICAN LINE.
(See also pp. 362, 406, 420 450).
Hamburg. Bremen, Southampton and Cherbourg to New York; Hamburg or Bremen, Southampton and Cherbourg to New York; Hamburg, Southampton, Cherbourg, Cobh (Queenst'wn), New York; Hamburg, Southampton, Galway, Halifax, New York.

NORWEGIAN-AMERICAN LINE. Oslo *via* Stavenger and Bergen to New York.

NORDDEUTSCHER LLOYD
(See also pages 395, 407, 422, 458)
Bremen, Southampton and Cherbourg to New York
Bremen, Southampton, Cherbourg, Cobh (Queenstown) to New York.
Bremen, Southampton, Galway, Halifax. New York.

RED STAR LINE.
(See also page 402).
Antwerp to New York, and Southampton to New York.

SWEDISH-AMERICAN LINE.
(See also page 427).
Gothenburg to Halifax and New York.

CIE. GEN. TRANS-ATLANTIQUE. FRENCH LINE.
(See also pages 394, 404 466).
Havre & Southampton to New York

UNITED STATES LINES.
(See also page 409).
Hamburg, Havre, Southampton, and Cobb (Queenstown) to New York; Liverpool, Belfast, Boston, New York; London to New York, occasionally calling Boston.

NEW ZEALAND SHIPPING COMPANY LTD. (Incorporated in New Zealand).

LONDON TO NEW ZEALAND via PANAMA CANAL.

1st, Tourist and Tourist B passengers carried, except where otherwise stated.

T.-S. Vessel.	Tons	London dep.	Curacao arr.	Panama arr.	New Zealand. arr.	New Zealand. dep.	Panama arr.	Curacao arr.	London arr.
Rangitiki ..	16711	May 25	—	June 8	June 28W	July 27	Aug. 14	—	Aug. 29
Rangitata ..	16711	June 22	—	July 6	July 26WL	Aug. 24	Sept. 11	—	Sept. 26
**Remuera*¶ ..	11388	July 18	July 26	,, 28	Aug. 26WL	Sept. 28	Oct. 18	Oct. 21	Nov. 8
Rangitane ..	16711	,, 20	—	Aug. 3	,, 23A	,, 21	,, 9	—	Oct. 24
**Rimutaka*	17000	Aug. 17	Aug. 30	Sept. 1	Sept. 21W	Oct. 19	Nov. 6	Nov. 9	Nov. 22
**Rotorua* ..	12112	Sept. 9‡	Sept. 24	,, 27	Oct. 20A	Nov. 30	Dec. 22	Dec. 25	Jan. 9
Rangitiki ..	16711	,, 14	—	,, 28	,, 18W	,, 16	,, 4	—	Dec. 19
Rangitata	16711	Oct. 12	—	Oct. 26	Nov. 15W	Dec. 14	Jan. 1	—	Jan. 16
Rangitane	16711	Nov. 9	—	Nov. 23	Dec. 13A	Jan. 11	,, 29	†	Feb. 14
**Remuera*¶	11388	,, 16	Nov. 29	Dec. 1	,, 30WL	Feb. 1	Feb. 21	Feb. 24	Mar. 8

* Carrying Tourist class passengers only, ¶ *Via* Suva. (A) Auckland. (W) Wellington.
(PC) Port Chalmers. (L) Lyttleton, ‡ From Liverpool. † Calls Kingston (Jamaica).

Subject to alteration or cancellation without notice.

OSTASIATISKE KOMPAGNI.

EAST ASIATIC COMPANY, LTD.

See also page 360.

PACIFIC LINE *via* Panama Canal from SOUTHAMPTON.

Doctor and Stewardess carried.

SAILINGS:—

Motor Vessel.	Tons.	Copenhagen. dep.	Hull.	Southampton dep.	St. Thomas	Kingston. Jamaica	Pa'ma Canal	Los Angeles	San Francisco	Vancouver
Amerika ..	10218	Aug. 11	—	Aug. 14	Aug. 24	Aug. 26	Aug. 28	Sept. 7	Sept 9	Sept. 12
Europa ..	10400	Sept. 8	—	Sept. 11	Sept. 21	Sept. 23	Sep. 25	Oct. 5	Oct. 7	Oct. 10
Erria	9250	Sep 26	Oct. 7	Oct. 9	Oct. 19	Oct. 21	Oct. 23	Nov. 2	Nov. 4	Nov. 7
Canada ..	11100	Oct. 17	Oct. 28	Oct. 30	Nov. 9	Nov. 11	Nov 13	Nov. 23	Nov. 25	Nov. 28
Amerika ..	10218	Nov. 14	Nov. 25	Nov. 27	Dec. 8	Dec. 10	De. 12	Dec. 22	Dec. 24	Dec. 27

PAQUET LINE.

(See also page 392).

(CIE DE NAVIGATION PAQUET)

MARSEILLES SENEGAL SERVICE

Marseilles dep. *via* Tangier, Casablanca, for Dakar, returning *via* same Ports. Sailings:—

Steamers.	Tons.	Marseilles dep. 11.0	Tangier.	Casablanca	Dakar. arr	Dakar. dep.	Casablanca. arr./dep	Tangier.	Marseilles ar. 6.0
Mar. Lyautey ..	8256	Aug. 2	Aug. 4	Aug. 5	Aug. 9	Aug. 16	Aug. 21	Au. 22	Aug 24
Imerethie II ..	3713	Aug. 16	—	Aug. 19	Aug. 24	Aug. 30	Sept. 4	—	Sep. 7
Medie II	5078	Aug. 30	—	Sept. 2	Sept. 6	Sept. 13	Sept. 18	—	Sep. 21
Imerethie II .	3713	Sept. 13	—	Sept. 16	Sept. 21	Sept. 27	Oct. 2	—	Oct. 5
Medie II	5078	Sept. 27	—	Sept. 30	Oct. 4	Oct. 11	Oct. 16	—	Oct 19
Mar. Lyautey	8256	Oct. 11	—	Oct. 14	Oct. 18	Oct. 25	Oct. 30	Oct. 31	Nov. 2
Chella	8920	Oct. 25	—	Oct. 28	Nov. 1	Nov. 8	Nov. 13	Nov 14	Nov 16
Mar. Lyautey	8256	Nov. 8	Nov 10	Nov. 11	Nov. 15	Nov. 22	Nov. 27	Nov 28	Nov 30
Medie II	5078	Nov. 22	—	Nov. 25	Nov. 29	Dec. 6	Dec. 11	—	Dec. 14
Imerethie II ..	3713	Dec. 6	—	Dec. 9	Dec. 14	Dec. 20	Dec. 25	—	Dec. 28

PORT LINE.

COMMONWEALTH AND DOMINION LINE LTD. (See also page 479.)

LONDON TO NEW ZEALAND, via PANAMA CANAL.

Passenger accommodation limited to 12 saloon passengers in single and two-berth staterooms.

Usually carrying Doctor but not Stewardess.

Vessel.	Tons.	From	Sailing Date.	To:—
Port Alma	8400	London...	Aug. 24	Lyttleton, Dunedin
Port Huon	8432	Liverpool	Aug. 26	Auckland, Wellington, Lyttleton, Dunedin
Port Fairy	8337	London...	Oct. 26	Wellington, Auckland
Port Hunter	8802	Liverpool	Nov. 4	Auckland, Wellington, Lyttleton, Dunedin
Port —	—	London..	Dec. 6	Wellington, Lyttleton
Port —	—	London..	Dec. 28	Lyttleton, Dunedin

LONDON TO AUSTRALIA, via CAPE OF GOOD HOPE.

The motor vessels call at Cape Town.

Vessel.	Tons.	Date.	To:—
Port Brisbane	8739	Aug. 15	Melbourne, Sydney, Hobart
Port Chalmers	8535	Aug. 29	Melbourne, Sydney, Brisbane
Port Auckland	8789	Sept. 12	Melbourne, Sydney, Hobart
Port Dunedin	7441	Sept 26	Melbourne, Sydney, Brisbane
Port Campbell	8751	Oct. 10	Melbourne, Sydney, Hobart
Port Hardy	8897	Oct. 24	Melbourne, Sydney, Brisbane
Port Jackson	9687	Nov. 7	Melbourne, Sydney, Hobart
Port ——	—	Nov. 21	Melbourne, Sydney, Brisbane

NEW YORK TO AUSTRALASIA.

(See page 479).

ROYAL MAIL LINES, LIMITED.

MAIL AND PASSENGER SERVICES TO AND FROM BRAZIL, URUGUAY AND ARGENTINA.

SOUTHAMPTON SERVICE—SOUTH BOUND.

STEAMER. Tons.	*Almanzora* 15,531	*Alcantara* 22,151	*Asturias* 22,071	*Andes* 26,000	*Alcantara* 23,151	*Asturias* 22,071	*Andes* 26,000	*Alcantara* 22,151	*Asturias* 22,071	*Alcantara* 22,151	*Asturias* 22,071	*Alcantara* 22,151	*Asturias* 22,071
From	July	Aug.	Sept.	Sept,	Oct.	Oct.	Nov.	Nov.	Dec.	Jan.	Feb.	Mar.	Mar.
Southampton d.	22	11	1	26	13	20	7	24	20	19	16	8	29
Cherbourg	22	11	1	26	13	20	7	24	20	19	16	8	29
Corunna	—	—	—	—	—	—	—	—	—	—	—	—	—
Vigo	—	—	—	—	—	—	—	—	—	—	—	—	—
Lisbon ....dep.	25	14	4	28	16	23	9	27	22	21	18	10	31
Madeira	27	15	5	—	—	—	—	—	24	23	20	11	Apl. 1
St. Vincent C.V	30	—	—	—	—	—	—	—	—	—	—	12	2
Pernambuco ..	Aug. 4	22	12	—	24	31	—	Dec. 5	30	29	26	19	9
Bahia	5	23	13	—	25	Nov. 1	—	6	31	30	27	20	10
Rio de Janeiro	7	25	15	Oct. 7	27	3	18	8	Jan. 2	Feb. 1	29	22	12
Santos	8	26	16	8	28	4	19	9	3	2	Mar. 1	23	13
Montevideo....	11	28	18	10	30	6	21	11	6	5	4	25	15
Buenos Aires ar.	11	29	19	10	31	7	21	12	7	6	5	26	16
From	Aug.	Sept.	Sept.	Oct.	Nov.	Nov	Nov.	Dec.	Jan.	Feb.	Mar.	Mar.	Apl.
Buenos Aires d.	15	1	22	14	3	10	25	15	12	9	8	29	19
Montevideo ..	16	2	23	14	4	11	25	16	13	10	9	30	20
Santos	19	4	25	16	6	13	27	18	15	12	11	Apl. 1	22
Rio de Janeiro	20	5	26	17	7	14	28	19	16	13	12	2	23
Bahia	22	7	28	—	9	16	—	21	18	15	14	4	25
Pernambuco ..	24	8	29	—	10	17	—	22	19	—	15	5	26
St. Vincent C.V.	28	—	—	—	—	—	—	—	—	16	—	—	—
Madeira	31	—	—	—	—	—	—	28	25	22	21	11	May 2
Lisbon	Sept. 2	16	Oct. 7	26	18	25	Dec. 7	30	27	24	23	13	4
Vigo	—	—	—	—	—	—	—	—	—	—	—	—	—
Corunna	—	—	—	—	—	—	—	—	—	—	—	—	—
Cherbourg	5	18	9	28	20	27	9	Jan. 1	29	26	25	15	6
Southampton a.	5	18	9	28	20	27	9	1	29	26	25	15	6

LONDON SERVICE.

H'land Princess	14128	July 1	*H'land Chieftain*	14131	Aug. 26	*H'land Monarch*	14137	Oct. 21
H'land Brigade	14131	July 15	*H'land Princess*	14128	Sept. 9	*H'land Chieftain*	14131	Nov. 4
H'land Patriot	14128	July 29	*H'land Brigade*	14131	Sept. 23	*H'land Princess*	14128	Nov. 18
H'land Monarch	14137	Aug. 12	*H'land Patriot*	14128	Oct. 7			

South Bound.											
London (Tilbury) ..dep.	July 1	Jly. 15	July 29	Aug 12	Aug 26	Sept 9	Sep. 23	Oct. 7	Oct 21	Nov. 4	Nov 18
Boulogne .. dep.	,, 1	,, 15	,, 29	,, 12	,, 26	,, 9	,, 23	,, 7	,, 21	,, 4	,, 18
Corunna ....dep.	—	—	—	—	—	—	—	—	—	—	—
Vigo .. ..dep.	—	—	—	—	—	—	—	—	—	—	—
Lisbon .. dep.	,, 5	,, 19	Aug. 2	,, 16	,, 30	,, 13	,, 27	,, 11	,, 25	,, 8	,, 22
*Las Palmas.. arr. a.m.	,, 7	,, 21	,, 4	,, 18	Sept 1	,, 15	,, 29	,, 13	,, 27	,, 10	,, 24
Pernambuco	,, 14	,, 23	,, 11	—	,, 8	,, 22	Oct. 6	,, 20	Nov. 3	,, 17	Dec. 1
Rio de Janeiro .. dep	,, 17	,, 31	,, 14	,, 28	,, 11	,, 25	,, 9	,, 23	,, 6	,, 20	,, 4
Santos .. ..dep.	,, 18	Aug. 1	,, 15	,, 29	,, 12	,, 26	10	,, 24	,, 7	,, 21	,, 5
Monte Video ......arr.	,, 20	,, 3	,, 17	,, 31	,, 14	,, 28	,, 12	,, 26	,, 9	,, 23	,, 7
Buenos Aires arr.	,, 21	,, 4	,, 18	Sept. 1	,, 15	,, 29	,, 13	,, 27	, 10	, 24	,, 8
North Bound.											
Buenos Aires (La Plata) d	Aug. 3	Aug 17	Aug 31	Sept 14	Sept 28	Oct. 12	Oct. 26	Nov. 9	Nov 23	Dec. 7	Dec. 21
Monte Video ......dep.	,, 4	,, 18	Sept. 1	,, 15	,, 29	,, 13	,, 27	,, 10	,, 24	,, 8	,, 22
Santos .. ..dep.	,, 7	,, 21	,, 4	,, 18	Oct. 2	,, 16	,, 30	,, 13	,, 27	,, 11	,, 25
Rio de Janeiro ....dep.	,, 8	,, 22	,, 5	,, 19	,, 3	,, 17	,, 31	,, 14	,, 28	,, 12	,, 26
Pernambuco	,, 11	—	—	,, 22	,, 6	,, 20	Nov. 3	—	Dec. 1	,, 15	,, 29
Las Palmas ..dep. p.m.	,, 18	Sept. 1	,, 15	,, 29	,, 13	,, 27	,, 10	,, 24	,, 8	,, 22	Jan. 5
Lisbon .... dep.	,, 20	,, 3	,, 17	Oct. 1	,, 15	,, 29	,, 12	,, 26	,, 10	,, 24	,, 7
Vigo ....dep.	—	—	—	—	—	—	—	—	—	—	—
Boulogne .... dep.	,, 24	,, 7	,, 21	,, 5	,, 19	Nov. 2	,, 16	,, 30	,, 14	,, 28	,, 11
London .... arr.	,, 24	,, 7	,, 21	,, 5	,, 19	,, 2	,, 16	,, 30	,, 14	,, 28	,, 11

* Round Trips to Las Palmas can usually be made in 12 days.

ROYAL MAIL LINES, LIMITED (*continued.*)

LIVERPOOL SERVICE.

Cargo steamers having limited accommodation for Saloon Passengers (not carrying Doctor or Stewardess).

Steamer.				
Tons.				
From Liverpool ..dep.				
Rio Janeiro arr.				
Santos				
Monte Video				
Buenos Aires arr.				
Rosario .. arr.				

Steamer.				
Tons.				
Buenos Aires dp				
Montevideo ,,				
Santos				
Las Palmas				
Havre				
Liverpool arr...				

Joint Royal Mail and Holland America Line Service.

Rotterdam and London to Cristobal, San Francisco, Vancouver, Seattle. No Stewardess, but *Delftdyk* and *Damsterdyk* carry Doctors

SAILINGS (from Rotterdam 3 days before London):—

STEAMER.	Tons	London dep.	Swansea, dep.	STEAMER	Tons	London, dep.	Swansea dep.
‡*Loch Monar*..	9412	August 8	August 11	**Dinteldyk* ..	9 39	October 17	—
**Drechtdyk*....	9338	,, 22	—	‡*Lochavon*	9205	,, 31	Nov. 3
‡*Damsterdyk*	10155	Sept. 5	Sept. 8	¦*Loch Katrine*	9419	Nov. 14	—
**Loch Goil*...	9462	,, 19	—	‡*Loch Monar* ..	9412	,, 28	Dec. 1
‡*Delftdyk* ...	10220	October 3	October 6				

* Calls Bermuda and Kingston. ¦ Calls Guayaquil ‡ Calls Curacao

WEST INDIES SERVICE.

STEAMER.	Tons.	LONDON dep.

To Bermuda, Bahamas, Jamaica, Hayti. Cargo vessel with accomodation for about 12 passengers in two-berth cabins, not carrying Doctor or Stewardess.

PACIFIC STEAM NAVIGATION CO.

ENGLAND—(FRANCE—SPAIN)—BERMUDA—BAHAMAS—CUBA—JAMAICA—PANAMA CANAL—SOUTH AMERICA.

Steamer.	Tons.	Sailing.	Steamer.	Tons.	Sailing.
Orbita...................	15495	July 18	*Oropesa*	14057	Sept. 23
Reina del Pacifico	17707	Aug. 26	*Orbita*..	15495	Oct. 14
Orduna	15507	Sept. 7			

STEAMERS ..	*Orbita.*	*Reina del Pacifico*	*Orduna.*	*Oropesa.*	*Orbita.*
Liverpool sail	Jly. 13	Aug 26	Sept. 7	Sep. 23	Oct. 14
La Pallice....	15	28	9	25	16
Santander§	—	—	—	—	—
Corunna§	—	—	—	—	—
Vigo§	—	—	—	—	—
Bermuda	25	Sep. 5	19	Oct. 5	26
Nassau	28	7	22	—	29
Havana......	29	8	23	9	30
Kingston	31	10	25	11	Nov 1
Crist'bal a./d.	Au.1/2	11/12	27/28	13/14	3/4
Balboa	2	14	28	14	4
La Libertad..	4	14	30	16	6
Paita ..	5	16	Oct. 1	17	7
Callao	7	18	3	19	9
Mollendo	9	18	5	21	11
Arica	10	19	6	22	12
Iquique	10	20	6	22	12
Antofagasta	11	22	7	23	13
Valpar'iso arr.	13	—	9	25	15

§ The calls at Spanish Ports are subject to conditions prevailing at the time.

STEAMERS ..	*Oropesa.*	*Reina del Pacifico*	*Orbita.*	*Reina del Pacifico.*	*Orduna.*	*Oropesa.*
Valparaiso sail	July 4	July 18	Aug 22	Sep. 26	Oct 14	Oct. 31
Antofagasta	6	20	24	28	16	Nov. 2
Mejillones	7	20	25	28	17	3
Tocopilla ..	7	—	25	—	17	3
Iquique ...	8	21	26	29	18	4
Arica	8	21	26	29	18	4
Mollendo	9	22	27	30	19	5
Callao ar./dp.	10/11	24	28/29	Oct. 2	20/21	6/7
Balboa ar./dp	17/18	28	Sp.3/4	6	26/27	13/14
Cristobal ,, ,,	18	28	4	6	27	14
Kingston	—	30	6	—	—	—
Havana ,, ,,	21/22	Aug. 1	8/9	9	30/31	17/18
Nassau	—	2	10	10	Nov. 1	—
Bermuda	26	4	13	12	4	22
Vigo	Au.3/4	—	—	—	—	—
Corunna ...	—	—	—	—	—	—
Santander ..	—	—	—	—	—	—
La Pallice....	5	11	22	19	13	Dec. 2
Plymouth	—	12	—	—	—	—
Liverpool arr.	7	13	24	21	15	4

SHAW SAVILL LINE.

(See also p. 368)

Direct Line via Panama Canal between Southampton and New Zealand.

Carrying passengers "Cabin" and "Tourist" class according to steamer.

Sailings subject to alteration without notice. OUTWARD.

Steamer	Tons.	Southampton. dep.	Curacao.	Jamaica.	Panama Canal. arr.	New Zealand. arr.	First port in New Zealand.
†*Arawa*	14500	July 7	July 19	—	July 21	Aug. 10	Wellington
**Akaroa*	15128	Sept. 1	Sept. 13	—	Sept. 15	Oct. 5	Auckland
**Tamaroa*	12500	Sept. 29	Oct. 11	—	Oct. 13	Nov. 2	Auckland
**Mataroa*	12500	Oct. 27	Nov. 8	—	Nov. 10	Nov. 30	Wellington
†*Arawa*	14500	Dec. 22	Jan. 3	—	Jan. 5	Jan. 25	Auckland
**Akaroa*	15128	Jan. 19	Jan. 31	—	Feb. 2	Feb. 22	—

* Carrying "Cabin" class only. † Carrying Tourist class only.

HOMEWARD.

Steamer.	Tons.	New Zealand. dep.	Panama Canal dep.	Jamaica.	Curacao.	Southampton arr.
**Tamaroa*	12500	July 14	Aug. 2	—	Aug. 4	Aug. 16
**Mataroa*	12500	Aug. 11	Aug. 30	—	Sept. 1	Sept. 13
†*Arawa*	14500	Sept. 8	Sept. 27	—	Sept. 29	Oct. 11
**Akaroa*	15128	Nov. 3	Nov. 22	—	Nov. 24	Dec. 6
**Tamaroa*	12500	Dec. 1	Dec. 20	—	Dec. 22	Jan. 3

‖CARGO STEAMERS (see also page 368 *re* vessels *via* Suez) carrying a limited number of passengers, in single and double cabins. Details on application.

CIA SUD-AMERICANA DE VAPORES.

HAMBURG–ANTWERP–NEW YORK–PANAMA–VALPARAISO. Returning *via* Havana, Liverpool and Antwerp to Hamburg.

m.v. *Copiapo*, m.v. *Aconcagua*, m.v. *Imperial*, 10,500 tons displacement.

Sailings about every four weeks.

OUTWARDS.—Hamburg, Antwerp, New York, Cristobal, Buenaventura (optional), Guayaquil, Talara, Callao, Mollendo, Arica, Antofagasta, Valparaiso.

HOMEWARDS.—Valparaiso, Antofagasta, Mollendo, Callao, Cristobal, Havana, Liverpool, Antwerp, Hamburg.

TRANSATLANTIC STEAMSHIP CO., LTD. (GOTHENBURG).

m.v. *Klipparen* ..	3585 tons	m.v. *Eknaren* ..	5243 tons	m.v. *Yngaren* ..	5246 ton
m.v. *Kaaparen* ..	3386 ,,	m.v. *Mirrabooka* ..	5979 ,,	m.v. *Vaalaren* ..	3550 tons
m.v. *Hammaren* ..	3240 ,,	m.v. *Parrakoola* ..	5752 ,,	m.v. *Goonawarra*	5072 tons
m.v. *Tisnaren* ..	5748 ,,	m.v. *Bullaren* ..	5721 ,,	m.v. *Kanangoora*	5000 tons

Cargo vessels with accommodation for a limited number of passengers, first class. Stewardess carried, but No Doctor, unless circumstances make this desirable.

SAILINGS:—SOUTH AFRICA. From Oslo monthly to Cape Town, Algoa Bay, East London, Durban and Lourenco Marques.

AUSTRALIA, *via* The Cape. Monthly from Oslo to Fremantle, Adelaide, Melbourne and Sydney.

SKANDINAVISKE. SYD-PACIFIC LINJE.

(Scandinavian South Pacific Line). KNUT KNUTSEN O.A.S.

SCANDINAVIA—ANTWERP—WEST COAST SOUTH AMERICA.

m.v. *Emma Bakke*	4742	m.v. *Geisha* ..	5113	m.v. *Martin Bakke*
m.v. *Samuel Baake*	—	m.v. *Indra* ..	5041	m.v. *Vinland*

Modern cargo vessels, with accommodation for passengers, carry neither stewardess or doctor. Monthly sailings from Oslo, Gothenburg, Antwerp to Panama, Buena Ventura, Guayaquil, Callao, Mollendo, Arica, Tocopilla, Antofagasta, Valparaiso, San Antonio, Talcahuano, Corral.

Dakar, Brazil, and River Plate Services.

See also Mediterranean service, p. 398.

Steamer.	Tons.	Steamer.	Tons.	Steamer.	Tons.
Mendoza	8199	*Florida*	9149	‖*Campana*	15000
‖*Alsina*	8404			‖ Twin Screw.	

The steamers have cabins de luxe and also carry 1st, 2nd and 3rd class passengers.

Sailing from and Genoa Marseilles for Dakar, Rio Santos, Montevideo, and Buenos Aires.

Steamers.	Genoa	M'seilles	Bar-celona	Cadiz	Dakar.	Rio de-Janeiro.	Santos.	Monte-video.	Buenos Aires.
Alsina	Aug. 6	Aug. 7	—	—	Aug. 14	Aug. 22	Aug 23	Aug. 26	Aug. 25
Florida	,, 19	,, 20	—	—	,, 27	Sept. 4	Sept. 5	Sept. 8	Sept. 8
Mendoza	Sept. 6	Sept. 7	—	—	Sept. 14	,, 22	,, 23	,, 26	,, 26
Campana	,, 19	,, 20	—	—	,, 27	Oct. 5	Oct. 6	Oct. 9	Oct. 9
Alsina	Oct. 6	Oct. 7	—	—	Oct. 14	,, 22	,, 23	,, 26	,, 26
Florida	,, 19	,, 20	—	—	,, 27	Nov. 4	Nov. 5	Nov. 8	Nov. 8

Steamer.	Buenos Ayres dep.	Monte-video.	Santos	Rio-de-Janeiro	Dakar	Bar-celona.	Marseilles	Genoa arr.
†*Mendoza*	Aug. 1	Aug 2	Aug. 5	Aug. 6	Aug. 17	—	Aug. 25	Aug. 26
Campana	, 15	,, 16	,, 19	,, 20	,, 28	—	Sept. 4	Sept. 5
†*Alsina*	Sept. 1	Sept. 2	Sept. 5	Sept. 6	Sept. 17	—	,, 25	,, 26
Florida	,, 15	,, 16	,, 19	,, 20	,, 28	—	Oct. 5	Oct. 6
†*Mendoza*	Oct. 1	Oct. 2	Oct. 5	Oct. 6	Oct. 17	—	,, 25	,, 26
Campana	,, 15	,, 16	,, 19	,, 20	,, 28	—	Nov. 4	Nov. 5
†*Alsina*	Nov. 1	Nov. 2	Nov. 5	Nov. 6	Nov. 17	—	,, 25	,, 26

† Calls also Victoria, Bahia, Pernambuco, Casablanca, Gibraltar, Oran and Algiers.

Spanish Royal Mail Steamers.

COMPAÑIA TRASÁTLANTICA-ESPAÑOLA.

Services subject to alteration without notice.

Steamers.	Tons.	Steamers.	Tons.	Steamers.	Tons.	Steamers.	Tons.
Habana ..	10,552	*Argentina* ..	10,136	*Marques de Comillas*	9,690	*Manuel Calvo* ..	5,617
Cristobal Colon	10,833	*Juan S. Elcano* ..	9,690	*Manuel Arnus* ..	7,578	*Buenos Aires* ..	5,311
Uruguay ..	10,348	*Magallanes* ..	9,690	*Antonio Lopez* ..	5,975	*Montevideo*	5,20[illegible]

LINE I. NORTH OF SPAIN TO CUBA—MEXICO—NEW YORK. (Monthly).

Steamer.	Bilbao Santander dep.	Gijon	Cor-unna.	Vigo (opt.)	Havana arr./dp.	Vera Cruz ar /dp.	Havana arr./dep.	New York (opt)	Vigo	Cor-unna.	Gijon.	Santander Bilbao arr.

LINE III. MEDITERRANEAN—CUBA—MEXICO—NEW YORK.

Steamer.	Bar-celona dep.	Val-encia	Cadiz	Vigo	New York arr./dp.	Havana arr./dp.	Vera Cruz ar./dp.	Havana arr./dp.	New York arr./dp	Cadiz arr.	Bar-celona arr.	

‡ Calling also optionally at Tarragona, Alicante, Malaga, Corunna, Puerto Barrios.

LINE IV. MEDITERRANEAN—VENEZUELA—COLOMBIA.

Steamer.	Barce-lona dep.	Val-encia.	Malaga*	Cadiz dep	Las Palmas	Tene-riffe	Cris-tobal arr.

Calling also at San Juan Porto Rico, Ciudad Trujillo La Guayra.

* Optional.

HOMEWARD. Steamer.	Cristobal dep.	Teneriffe	Las Palmas	Cadiz	Barcelona

Calling also at Puerto Limon*, Puerto Colombia*, Curacao*, Puerto Cabello*, La Guayra, Ciudad Trujillo*, San Juan Porto Rico.

(See also page 399.)

TRASMEDITERRANEA COMPAÑIA.

Services subject to alteration or suspension owing to Strikes, &c.

m.v. *Ciudad de Sevilla* 10000 tons.	s.s. *Poeta Arolas* ..3525 tons.	s.s. *Fernando Poo* .. 10000 tons.
m.v. *Ciudad de Cadiz* 8000 tons.	s.s. *Legazpi* .. .. 4349 tons.	(see also below).
s.s. *Villa de Madrid* .. 10000 tons.	s.s. *Domine* ..10000 tons.	

1st, 2nd and 3rd class passengers carried. 1st and 2nd class berths in cabins for two and four. Ladies' saloon, Bath room, Smoking saloon, English library, Electric light, Wireless telegraphy.

Mediterranean to Fernando Poo.

Sailings on 17th of each month from Barcelona at 18.0, by s.s. *Ciudad de Cadiz* (8000 tons), s.s. *Domine* (10000 tons) and s.s. *Fernando Poo* (10000 tons); Valencia (18th), Cadiz (20th) for Arrecife, Las Palmas, Teneriffe, Santa Isabel (Fernando Poo). May proceed to San Carlos, Bata, Rio Benito, Kogo.

Subject to confirmation.

Barcelona—Africa—Canary Islands.

(Fortnightly).

s.s. *Isla Gran Canaria*, 5121 tons.
s.s. *Isla Tenerife*, 5121 tons.

	arr.	dep.
Barcelona		
Tarragona		
Valencia		
Alicante		
Cartagena		
Almeria		
Malaga		
Ceuta		
Cadiz		
La Palma		
Teneriffe		
Las Palmas		
Cadiz		
Alicante		
Valencia		
Barcelona		

Barcelona—Cadiz—Canary Islands

(Weekly). Rapide.

	arr.		dep.	
Barcelona..dep.	—		Sat.	noon
Cadiz .. „	Mon.	7 0	Mon.	15 0
Las Palmas „	Wed.	16 0	Thur.	24 0
Teneriffe .. „	Fri.	7 0	Fri.	24 0
Cadiz .... „	Mon.	9 0	Mon.	11 0
Barcelona.. arr.	Wed.	9 0	—	

Spain—Canary Islands.

Corunna
Villagarcia
Vigo
Cadiz
Las Palmas
Teneriffe
Cadiz
Vigo
Corunna

Southern Spain—Canary Islands.

Seville
Las Palmas
Teneriffe
Seville

INTERINSULAR SERVICES. (Subject to confirmation.)

Itinerary 1.—Dep. Teneriffe on Sat. at 22.0 for Santa Cruz de la Palma, San Sebastian*, Valverde, Santa Cruz de la Palma, Teneriffe, Las Palmas, Arrecife, Puerto Cabras, Gran Tarajal, Las Palmas, Teneriffe.

„ 2.—Dep. Las Palmas on Sun. at 22.0 *via* Gran Tarajal, Puerto Cabras, Arrecife, Las Palmas, Teneriffe, Santa Cruz de la Palma, Valverde, San Sebastian*, Teneriffe, Las Palmas.

„ 3.—Dep Teneriffe fortnightly Wed., to Santa Cruz de la Palma, Teneriffe, Las Palmas and fortnightly Mon., from Teneriffe *via* San Sebastian*, Hermigua, Agulo, Vallehermoso, Vallegranrey, Vallehermoso, Agulo, Hermigua, San Sebastian*, Santa Cruz de la Palma, Teneriffe, Las Palmas.

„ 4.—Dep. Las Palmas on Mon., at 12.0 to Teneriffe, Las Palmas, Teneriffe, Las Palmas and in the alternating weeks to Teneriffe, Las Nieves, San Nicolás, Mogán, San Nicolás, Las Nieves, Las Palmas, Teneriffe, Las Palmas, Teneriffe.

Spanish Sahara Line.—(Fortnightly). From Las Palmas on Sat. at 24.0 *via* Teneriffe¶, Las Palmas, for Las Palmas, Cabo Juby, Rio de Oro, Cabo Blanco, Rio de Oro, Cabo Juby, Las Palmas. *Canary Islands.
¶ May proceed *via* Santa Cruz de Teneriffe, Las Palmas, Carbo Juby, Las Palmas, Rio de Oro, etc.

Sailings subject to alteration or suspension.

FRENCH LINE.

See also pages 394, 404 and 459.

Havre—Plymouth—Panama—Port Limon Service. (Monthly.)

The Antilles, Venezuela, Curacao, Colombia and Costa Rica.

Steamer.	Tons	Havre. dep. 12.0	Southampton. 19.0	Fort-de-France.	Barbados	Trinidad.	Curacao	Cristobal	Puerto Limon†
Cuba	11336	Aug. 25	Aug. 25	Sept. 5	Sept. 6	Sept. 7	Sept. 9	Sept. 12	Sept. 13
Colombie	13718	Sept. 25	Sept. 25	Oct. 6	Oct. 7	Oct. 8	Oct. 10	Oct. 13	Oct. 14
Cuba	11336	Oct. 25	Oct. 25	Nov. 5	Nov. 6	Nov. 7	Nov. 9	Nov. 12	Nov. 13
Colombie	13718	Nov. 25	Nov. 25	Dec. 6	Dec. 7	Dec. 8	Dec. 10	Dec. 13	Dec. 14

Calling also at Pointe-a-Pitre, Basse-Terre, La Guayra, Puerto Colombia, Cartagena.

† Optional—June—November.

Homeward. Steamer.	Tons.	Cristobal. dep.	Trinidad.	Barbados.	Fort-de-France	Plymouth arr.	Havre. arr.
Flandre	8571	Aug. 18	Aug. 25	Aug. 26	Aug. 27	Sept. 7	Sept. 8
Cuba	11336	Sept. 16	Sept. 23	Sept. 24	Sept. 25	Oct. 6*	Oct. 6
Colombie	13718	Oct. 17	Oct. 24	Oct. 25	Oct. 26	Nov. 6	Nov. 6

Other ports of call, Cartagena, Puerto Colombia, Curacao, Puerto Cabello, La Guayra, Carupano, Basse-Terre, Pointe-a-Pitre. * Southampton.

St. Nazaire, Bordeaux to The Antilles, Venezuela and Colombia.

Connection at Fort de France with Cayenne Line, and at Pointe-a-Pitre for Haïti.

Steamer.	Tons.	St. Nazaire. dep.	Bordeaux. dep.	Vigo.	P'inte-a-Pit e& Basse-Terre (*a*)	Fort-de-Fra'ce (*b*)	Trinidad	
Bretagne ..	10108	August 8	Aug. 11	Aug. 13	Aug. 22	Aug. 23	Aug. 24	Calling also Carupano, La Guayra, Puerto Colombia, Cartagena and Cristobal.
De l Salle	8100	Sept. 10	Sept. 12	Sept. 14	Sept. 24	Sept. 25	Sept, 26	
Bretagne	10108	Oct. 8	Oct. 11	Oct. 12	Oct. 22	Oct. 23	Oct. 24	

Homeward.—From Cristobal, etc., *via* Cartagena, Puerto Colombia, Curacao, Puerto Cabello, La Guayra, Carupano, Trinidad, Fort-de-France (*b*), Basse Terre, Pointe-a-Pitre (*a*), Santander to Havre (St. Nazaire). *a* Connecting with Haiti Line (see below). *b* Connecting with Cayenne Line (see below).

Cayenne (Connecting Line.) By s.s. *Duc d'Aumale*

Connecting with arrivals and departures of above steamers at Fort-de-France to Sainte-Lucie, Barbados (optional), Trinidad, Demerara, Surinam, St. Laurent, and Cayenne.

Haiti (Connecting Line.) s.s *Saint Dominique* (3108 tons).

Connecting with arrivals and departures of above steamers at Fort-de-France for Pointe-a-Pitre, †St. Kitts, St. Barthelemy, Saint Martin, Saint Thomas, San Juan de Porto Rico, Ciudad Trujillo, Azua Barahona, Jacmel, †Les Cayes, Santiago de Cuba, Port-au-Prince and back *via* Cap Haitien, Puerto Plata, San Juan de Porto Rico, Saint Thomas, Saint Martin, St. Barthelemy, †St. Kitts, †Antigua, Pointe-a-Pitre to Fort-de-France. May also call Petit Goare, Saint Marc, Gonaives, and Port-de-Paix.

† Optional.

St. Nazaire—Cuba—Mexico Service.

Steamer	Tons	St. Nazaire dep	Sant'nder & Gijon.	Corunna and Vigo	Havana. arr./dep	Vera Cruz. arr. dep.	Havana. arr./dep.	Vigo¶ & Corunna	Gijon and Santa'der	St. Nazaire arr
Flandre	8571	Oct. 11	Oct. 12	Oct. 13	Oct. 24	Oct. 26/28	Oct. 31	Nov. 11	Nov. 12	Nov. 13
Flandre	8571	Nov. 18	Nov. 19	Nov. 20	Dec. 1	Dec. 4/6	Dec. 9	Dec. 20	Dec. 21	Dec. 22

¶ Optional call at Vigo.

North Pacific Line. (From Dunkerque and Antwerp.)

Vessel.	Tons	Havre. dep.	Cristobal.	La Libertad.	San Jose de Guatemala.	Los Angeles.	San Francisco	‡ Calls also at Puerto Colombia
s.s. *Wyoming* ..	8061	July 7	July 24	July 27	July 28	Aug. 3	Aug. 7	
s.s. *San Antonio*	6013	July 28	Aug. 14	Aug. 17	Aug. 18	Aug. 25	Aug. 28	

From San Francisco proceeds to Portland, Seattle and Vancouver.

Bordeaux—Morocco Service.

† From St. Nazaire. s.s. *Flandre*, 8571 tons. s.s. *Meknes* 6923 tons, s.s. *Marrakech*, 6178 tons.

Steamer.	Bordeaux, dep.	Casablanca. arr.	Casablanca, dep.	Bordeaux. arr.
Marrakech	Aug. 4 at 1830	Aug. 7 at 1730	Aug. 8 at 12 0	Aug. 11 at 13 0
Marrakech	,, 12 ,, 1330	,, 15 ,, 1230	,, 16 ,, 11 0	,, 19 ,, 12 0
Marrakech	,, 21 ,, 20 0	,, 24 ,, 19 0	,, 25 ,, 15 0	,, 28 ,, 16 0
Marrakech	,, 30 ,, 17 0	Sept. 2 ,, 16 0	Sept. 3 ,, 11 0	Sept. 6 ,, 12 0
Marrakech	Sept. 8 ,, 12 0	,, 11 ,, 11 0	,, 12 ,, 1630	,, 15 ,, 1730
Meknes	,, 13 ,, 16 0	,, 16 ,, 15 0	,, 17 ,, 11 0	,, 20 ,, 12 0
Flandre	,, 15 ,, 18 0	,, 18 ,, 15 0	,, 18 ,, 22 0	,, 21 ,, 23 0
Marrakech	,, 18 ,, 1930	,, 21 ,, 1830	,, 22 ,, 1330	,, 25 ,, 1430
Meknes	,, 21 ,, 12 0	,, 24 ,, 11 0	,, 25 ,, 1530	,, 28 ,, 1630
Flandre	,, 23 ,, 13 0	,, 26 ,, 10 0	,, 26 ,, 18 0	,, 29 ,, 1730
Marrakech	,, 26 ,, 15 0	,, 29 ,, 14 0	,, 30 ,, 11 0	Oct. 3 ,, 12 0
Flandre	,, 30 ,, 18 0	Oct. 3 ,, 15 0	—	—

UNION-CASTLE MAIL STEAMSHIP CO., LTD.

(See also pages 369 and 410.)

ROYAL MAIL SERVICE to SOUTH AFRICA. From SOUTHAMPTON conveying Mails and Passengers to MADEIRA, CAPETOWN, PORT ELIZABETH, EAST LONDON, and NATAL. Returning from NATAL via the same ports.

Vessel.	Tons.	Dep. Southampton.	Arr. Madeira.	Arr. Capetown.	Arr. Port Elizabeth.	Arr. East London.	Arr. Natal.
Athlone Castle	25564	Aug. 3	Aug. 6	Aug. 17	Aug. 19	Aug. 21	Aug. 22
Windsor Castle	19141	,, 10	,, 13	,, 24	,, 26	,, 28	,, 29
Capetown Castle	27000	,, 17	,, 20	,, 31	Sept. 2	Sept. 4	Sept. 5
Carnarvon Castle	20122	,, 24	,, 27	Sept. 7	,, 9	,, 11	,, 12
Winchester Castle	20109	,, 31	Sept. 3	,, 14	,, 16	,, 18	,, 19
Stirling Castle	25550	Sept. 7	,, 10	,, 21	,, 23	,, 25	,, 26
Arundel Castle	19029	,, 14	,, 17	,, 28	,, 30	Oct. 2	Oct. 3
Warwick Castle	27445	,, 21	,, 24	Oct. 5	Oct. 7	,, 9	,, 10
Athlone Castle	25564	,, 28	Oct. 1	,, 12	,, 14	,, 16	,, 17
Windsor Castle	19141	Oct. 5	,, 8	,, 19	,, 21	,, 23	,, 24
Capetown Castle	27000	,, 12	,, 15	,, 26	,, 28	,, 30	,, 31
Carnarvon Castle	20122	,, 19	,, 22	Nov. 2	Nov. 4	Nov. 6	Nov. 7
Winchester Castle	20109	,, 26	,, 29	,, 9	,, 11	,, 13	,, 14
Stirling Castle	25550	Nov. 2	Nov. 5	,, 16	,, 18	,, 20	,, 21
Arundel Castle	19029	,, 9	,, 12	,, 23	,, 25	,, 27	,, 28
Warwick Castle	27445	,, 16	,, 19	,, 30	Dec. 2	Dec. 4	Dec. 5
Athlone Castle	25564	,, 23	,, 26	Dec. 7	,, 9	,, 11	,, 12
Windsor Castle	19141	,, 30	Dec. 3	,, 14	,, 16	,, 18	,, 19
Capetown Castle	27000	Dec. 7	,, 10	,, 21	,, 23	,, 25	,, 26
Carnarvon Castle	20122	,, 14	,, 17	,, 28	,, 30	Jan. 1	Jan. 2
Winchester Castle	20109	,, 21	,, 24	Jan. 4	Jan. 6	,, 8	,, 9
Stirling Castle	25550	,, 28	,, 31	,, 11	,, 13	,, 15	,, 16

INTERMEDIATE SERVICES to SOUTH and EAST AFRICA. From LONDON (Tilbury).

Usually twice monthly *via* Canary Islands (Las Palmas or Teneriffe) to Capetown, Port Elizabeth, East London, Natal, Lourenco Marques and Beira without transhipment; also for Inhambane, Chinde, Quelimane and Mauritius. Monthly calls at Ascension and St. Helena.

Next departures as arranged at time of going to press:—

Dunvegan Castle ..	Aug. 11	..	*via* Las Palmas, Ascension. St. Helena.
Dunnottar Castle ..	,, 25	..	*via* Teneriffe and Lobito (due Sept. 8).
Dunbar Castle ..	Sept. 8	..	*via* Las Palmas, Ascension, St. Helena.
Durban Castle ..	,, 22	..	*via* Teneriffe and Lobito (due Oct. 6).
Llangibby Castle ..	Oct. 6	..	*via* Las Palmas, Ascension, St. Helena.
Pretoria Castle ..	,, 20	..	*via* Teneriffe and Lobito (due Nov. 3).
Dunvegan Castle ..	Nov. 3	..	*via* Las Palmas, Ascension, St. Helena.
Dunnottar Castle ..	,, 17	..	*via* Teneriffe and Lobito (due Dec. 1).
Dunbar Castle ..	Dec. 1	..	*via* Las Palmas, Ascension, St. Helena.
Durban Castle ..	,, 15	..	*via* Teneriffe and Lobito (due Dec. 29).
Llangibby Castle ..	,, 29	..	*via* Las Palmas, Ascension, St. Helena.

WILHELMSEN LINES.

(See also page 369).

The services are maintained by fast Cargo Liners, carrying mail, with comfortable accommodation for passengers.

From OSLO, HAMBURG, ROTTERDAM and ANTWERP to SOUTH AFRICA and AUSTRALIA.

SAILINGS.

Motor Vessel.	Tons	Oslo dep.	Hamburg dep	Rotterdam.	Antwerp dep.	Cape Town	Durban	
Titania	—	Aug. 15	Aug. 19	Aug. 21	Aug. 22	Sept. 11	—	Proceeding to Fremantle, Adelaide, Melbourne, and Sydney.
Tirranna	6704	,, 30	Sept. 2	Sept. 4	Sept. 5	,, 25	—	
Temeraire	6465	Sept. 15	,, 19	,, 21	,, 22	Oct. 11	Oct. 16	
Talisman	6701	,, 30	Oct. 3	Oct. 5	Oct. 6	,, 25	—	* From Gothenburg.
Tamesis	—	Oct. 14	,, 17	,, 19	,, 20	Nov. 8	—	
Taronga	7008	,, 31	Nov. 4	Nov. 6	Nov. 7	,, 27	Dec. 1	

From GDYNIA, GOTHENBURG, OSLO, AALESUND/CHRISTIANSUND to Savannah/Jacksonsville, Havana, Vera Cruz, Tampico and New Orleans.

SAILINGS.

Motor Vessel.	Tons.	Danzig, Gdynia.	Gothenburg dep.	Oslo dep.	West Norway dep.	
Kexholm	—	—	Aug. 17	—	Aug. 21	Proceeding to Savannah/Jacksonsville, Havana, Vera Cruz, and New Orleans.
Tauvis	4767	—		Aug. 28	—	
Tabor	4768	—	Sept. 18	—	Sept. 21	

Other services maintained by the Company are:—

From MANILA *via* HONG KONG, SHANGHAI, KOBE, YOKOHAMA to San Francisco, Los Angeles and New York.

From NORWAY (EAST and WEST NORWAY), to Boston, Philadelphia, Baltimore and Newport News.

From NEW YORK *via* NEWPORT NEWS and LOS ANGELES to Manila and Shanghai.

Sailings on application.

YBARRA Y CIA., S. en C., Seville.

Mediterranean—Brazil—Plata Service.

By motor vessels.

**Cabo San Augustin* ..	11868 tons	Carrying passengers 1st class, cabin class and 3rd class. Stewardess and Doctor on each vessel.
**Cabo Santo Tomé*....	11868 tons	
†*Cabo San Antonio* ..	11637 tons	

† Also luxe suite for 4 passengers. * Two luxe suites for 5 passengers each.

SAILINGS (*subject to confirmation and alteration*).

Vessel.	Genoa dep.	Marseilles	Barcelona and Tarragona†	Valencia and Alicante	Malaga	Cadiz	Santos	Monte Video	Buenos Aires arr.

	Buenos Aires dep.	Monte Video	Santos	La Palmas.	Cadiz	Barcelona	Marseilles	Genoa arr.

MACANDREW-YEOWARD SERVICE. Liverpool-Lisbon-Madeira-Azores

FLEET.—*Alca*, 4000 tons *Avoceta*, 3500 tons; *Alondra*, 3500 tons; *Aguila*, 3500 tons *Ardeola*, 3500 tons. 1st cl. passengers only carried. Bath rooms. Electric light. Cabines de Luxe. Stewardess and Doctor carried on all steamers.

Round Trip Cruises. Single and Return Tickets also issued.
Special Programmes on application to Cook/Wagons-Lits Offices.

Steamer *Round Trip*	*Alca.*	*Aguila.*	*Alca.*	*Aguila.*
Liverpool dep.	Aug. 5	Aug. 19	Sept. 2	Sept. 16
Lisbon	,, 10	,, 24	,, 7	,, 21
Casablanca....	,, 12	,, 26	,, 9	,, 23
Madeira	,, 15	,, 29	,, 12	,, 26
Santa Cruz....	,, 17	,, 31	,, 14	,, 28
Las Palmas ..	,, 18	Sept. 1	,, 15	,, 29
Orotava..	,, 19	,, 2	,, 16	,, 30
Azores	,, 22	,, 5	,, 19	Oct. 3
Liverpool arr.	,, 28	,, 11	,, 25	,, 9

PART VI.—MISCELLANEOUS STEAMSHIP SERVICES.

India, Ceylon, Strait Settlements, Dutch West Indies, Australia, China, Japan, America, &c.

	PAGE
American President Lines	473
Asiatic S.N. Co., Ltd...	469
Australian Oriental Line	469
Blue Funnel Line Western Australia Service	469
British India S.N. Co.	471
Burns-Philp Line	470
Canadian Australasian Line	472
Canadian National Steamships	472
Canadian Pacific	472
China Navigation Co., Ltd.	470
Cowasjee Dinshaw & Bros. Steamers ..	470
Cunard White Star Line	481
Dairen Kisen Kaisya	471
Eastern and Australian S.S. Co.	473
Elder Dempster Lines..	472
Euphrates and Tigris Steam Nav. Co. ..	472
Grace Line	474
Indian African Line	474
Indo-China Steam Navigation Co., Ltd. ..	474
Indochinois, Societe les Affréteurs Maritime	475
Indochinoise, Cie de Navigation, Haiphong	475
Asiatique Flotilla Co., Ltd.	475
Java-China-Japan Line	475
Kitanihon Kisen Kaisya	477
Pharaonic Mail Line	477
Koninklyke Paketvaart Maatschappy. (Royal Packet Steam Navigation Co.)	476
Lloyd Triestino Soc. An. di Navigazione..	481
Matson Line	477
Nippon Yusen Kaisya	478
North Japan S.S. Co., Ltd. (see Kitanihon Kisen Kaisya)	
Oceanic Steamship Co. (Matson Line) ..	477
Osaka Shosen Kaisya	479
Phillipine Inter-Island S.S. Co.	473
Port Line	479
Prince Line	480
Saigonnaise Cie de Navigation et de Transport	480
States Steamship Company	480
Straits Steamship Co...	480
United Fruit Company	481

ASIATIC STEAM NAVIGATION COMPANY, LTD.

(Incorporated in England).

The Steamers of this Line carry First Class and Deck passengers, and several Steamers Second Class. They are fitted with Electric Light, and have accommodation amidships.

The Andaman Stmrs. carry 1st, 2nd & deck pass., and are fitted with electric fans in cabins & saloon.

Regular fortnightly service Calcutta to Chittagong and Rangoon and back.
Regular fortnightly service Calcutta to Rangoon and Moulmein and back.
Regular fortnightly line Calcutta to Coast Ports and Bombay *via* Ceylon.
Regular service between India and Java Ports.
Regular Mail Service Calcutta, Rangoon and Madras to Port Blair (Andaman Islands) calling at Rangoon.

AUSTRALIAN ORIENTAL LINE.

s.s. *Changte* (4,324 tons) and s.s. *Taiping* (4,324 tons).

STEAMER.	Leave Melbourne	Leave Sydney	Leave Brisbane	Arr. Manila	Hong Kong arr.	Hong Kong dep.	Leave Manila.	Arr. Brisbane	Arr. Sydney	Arr. Melb'rn
Taiping ..	June 10	June 17	June 19	July 4	July 7	July 14	July 17	July 31	Aug. 2	Aug. 6
Changte ..	July 8	July 15	July 17	Aug. 1	Aug. 4	Aug. 12	Aug. 15	Aug. 29	,, 31	Sept. 4
Taiping ..	Aug. 8	Aug. 12	Aug. 15	,, 31	Sept. 3	Sept. 11	Sept. 14	Sept. 27	Sept. 29	Oct. 2
Changte ..	Sept. 6	Sept. 13	Sept. 15	Sept. 30	Oct. 3	Oct. 10	Oct. 13	Oct. 27	Oct. 29	Nov. 5†

Calling also at Townsville, Cairns, Thursday Island.

Calling also at Thursday Island, Cairns, Townsville. † *Via* Lord Howe Island.

BLUE FUNNEL LINE WESTERN AUSTRALIAN SERVICE.

(See also pages 358, 403 & 442).

Singapore—Australia and *vice versa.*

s.s. *Gorgon*, 3533 tns. s.s. *Centaur*, 3066 tns. s.s. *Charon*, 3600 tns. Doctor and Stewardess carried.

VESSEL.	Singapore. dep.	Batavia. dep.	Route.	Fremantle. arr.	Fremantle. dep.	Route.	Batavia.	Singapore.	Port Swettenham.	Penang.
Charon ..	July 6	July 8	1	July 20	July 26	9	Aug. 8	Aug. 10	—	—
Centaur ..	,, 22	,, 24	1	Aug. 7	Aug. 10	5	,, 24	,, 26	Aug. 29	Aug. 30
Gorgon ..	Aug. 5	Aug. 7	1	,, 18	,, 25	5*	Sept. 4	Sept. 6	—	—
Charon ..	,, 20	,, 22	3	Sept. 3	Sept. 8	8	,, 20	,, 22	Sept. 25	Sept. 26
Centaur ..	Sept. 5	Sept. 7	4	,, 19	,, 24	7	Oct. 6	Oct. 8	—	—

* Also calls Carnarvon. ‡ Also calls at Derby

ROUTE 1—*Via* Banjoewangi, Derby, Port Hedland, Point Samson
ROUTE 2—*Via* Banjoewangi, Derby, Port Hedland.
ROUTE 3—*Via* Banjoewangi, Derby and Carnarvon.
ROUTE 4—*Via* Banjoewangi, Onslow, Carnarvon.
ROUTE 5—*Via* Geraldton, Port Hedland, Broome, Sourabaya.
ROUTE 6—*Via* Geraldton, Carnarvon, Sourabaya.
ROUTE 7—*Via* Geraldton, Carnarvon, Port Hedland, Sourabaya.
ROUTE 8—*Via* Geraldton, Carnarvon, Port Hedland, Broome, Sourabaya.
ROUTE 9—*Via* Geraldton, Port Hedland, Derby, Sourabaya.

SOUTHWARDS. May also call at North Java Ports and Samarang, Denham and Geraldton.
NORTHWARDS. May also call at Denham, Samarang, and North Java Ports.

(Monthly). *All services subject to alteration and sailing dates from intermediate ports are approximate only.*

Leave Melbourne.	Leave Sydney.	Leave Brisbane.	Leave Batavia.	Arrive Singapore.	Steamers.	Leave Singapore.	Leave Batavia	Leave Brisbane.	Arrive Sydney.	Arrive Melbourne.
Aug. 1	Aug. 7	Aug. 9	Aug. 27	Aug. 29	*Merkur* ..	July 4	July 7	July 22	July 24	July 28
,, 31	Sept. 7	Sept. 9	Sept. 27	Sept. 29	*Marella* ..	Aug. 4	Aug. 7	Aug. 22	Aug. 24	Aug. 28

Calling also at Townsville (optional), Thursday Island, Darwin, Sourabaya, Samarang, Cheribon (optional). Steamers call at Java and Queensland ports as inducement offers.

(Tour 3) Sydney to Lord Howe Island, Norfolk Island, and New Hebrides.

s.s. *Morinda* leaves Sydney every 6 weeks, etc., calling at Lord Howe Island, Norfolk Island, Vila, and New Hebrides Group and return. Round trip occupies about 19 days.

SHORT CRUISE.—The s.s. *Morinda* leaves Sydney about every 6 weeks for Lord Howe Island and Norfolk Island. Duration of voyage 9 days.

Sydney-Queensland-Papua-New Guinea Service.

s.s. *Macdhui* and *Bulolo* leave Sydney every three weeks for Brisbane, Cairns, Port Moresby and New Guinea outports, and return. Round trip occupies about 35 days.

Sailings from Sydney, June 3. From Brisbane 2 days later.

Sydney-Queensland-Solomon Islands Service.

s.s. *Malaita* leaves Sydney every six weeks calling at Brisbane, Makambo, Tulagi, various outports of the Soloman Islands, etc., and return. Round trip occupies about 32 days.

Sailings from Sydney June 24. From Brisbane 2 days later.

CHINA NAVIGATION CO. LTD.

YANGTZE RIVER LINES.

Shanghai to Hankow via Principal Ports.—Daily sailings leaving French Bund, Shanghai, a midnight (Sundays excepted) by twin-screw vessels.

Shanghai to Ichang via Lower River Ports, Hankow and Shasi.—Regular weekly sailings, water conditions permitting, throughout the year.

Ichang to Wanhsien and Chungking, through the Yangtze Gorges. Services are maintained, water conditions permitting, by first-class passenger steamers, connections being made with the Shanghai and Hankow weekly sailing at Ichang.

Shanghai to Hankow and Changsha.—One sailing weekly from May to October. During the winter communication is maintained by means of tugs and lighters.

CHINA COAST LINES.

Shanghai to Tientsin via Tsingtao, Weihaiwei and Chefoo.—Two sailings weekly from French Bund, Shanghai, by express passenger steamers.

Shanghai to Newchwang and Dairen.—Occasional sailings. The port of Newchwang is closed to navigation from December to March.

Shanghai to Antung.—As inducement offers.

Shanghai to Ningpo.—S.S. *Hsin Peking* sails from French Bund, Shanghai, to Ningpo on Mondays, Wednesdays and Fridays at 5 p.m.

Shanghai to Foochow, Amoy, Swatow, Hongkong and Canton.—Five sailings weekly. Steamer via Amoy leaves on Wednesdays, via Swatow on Tuesday, Friday and Sunday, and via Foochow on Saturday.

Shanghai to Hoihow, Pakhoi and Haiphong, via Hongkong and Canton.—Weekly sailing leaving Shanghai on Fridays.

Canton and Hongkong to Tientsin via Swatow, Shanghai, Tsingtao and Chefoo.—Weekly sailings.

Canton and Hongkong to Tientsin via Swatow, Foochow, Tsingtao and Chefoo.—Weekly sailings.

Hongkong to Canton.—Daily sailings in conjunction with the Hongkong, Canton and Macao Steamboat Co.

OCEAN LINES.

Amoy to Manila.—Sailings every ten days.

Hongkong to Amoy, Swatow and Singapore.—Fortnightly sailings.

Hongkong to Bangkok via Swatow.—Sailing every ten days.

Hongkong to Hoihow and Singapore.—A three weekly service is maintained.

All Coast and Ocean Steamers are provided with Saloon accommodation and are equipped with wireless telegraphy.

COWASJEE DINSHAW & BROS. Aden—Somaliland.

s.s. *Ayamonte*, 844 tons; s.s. *Tuna*, 700 tons; s.s. *Velho*, 1100 tons; s.s. *Africa*, 500 tons.

Steamer leaves Aden for Berbera (Passage 14-16 hours) after arrival of English mail from London every week on Sunday evening, returning to Aden on Tuesday.

Weekly service on Thur. evening to Djibouti (arr. Fri. a.m.) returning on Saturday at noon, due Aden Sunday a.m.

Fortnightly service Aden to Perim, Hodeidah, Kamaran.

From Djibouti every alternate Saturday at 6.0 for Zeilah, returning to Aden on Sunday, a.m.

Service once or twice per month to Port Sudan and Jeddah, if sufficient inducement.

Fortnightly Service to Makalla and Sheher.

BRITISH INDIA STEAM NAVIGATION CO., LTD.

(INCORPORATED IN ENGLAND.) (See also page 359)

CALCUTTA—STRAITS—CHINA & JAPAN. Apcar Line Programme. Subject to alteration "S" (5,427-7,754 tons) and "T" (4,538-10,006 tons) class steamers. Twice monthly.

Calcutta dep.	Rangoon dep.	Singapore arr.	Hong Kong arr.	Shanghai arr.	Kobe arr.	Kobe dep.	Hong Kong dep.	Singapore dep.	Rangoon arr.	Calcutta arr.
July 13	—	July 25	Aug. 1	August 7	Aug 12	Aug. 14	Aug. 26	Sept. 2	Sept. 8	Sept. 12
Aug. 1	—	Aug. 9	,, 15	—	,, 24	,, 26	Sept. 9	,, 16	,, 22	,, 26
,, 10	Aug. 16	,, 22	,, 29	Sept. 4	Sept. 9	Sept. 11	,, 23	,, 30	Oct. 6	Oct. 10
,, 24	—	Sept. 5	Sep. 12	—	,, 21	,, 23	Oct. 7	Oct. 14	,, 20	,, 24
Sept. 7	Sept. 13	,, 19	,, 26	Oct. 2	Oct 7	Oct. 9	,, 21	,, 28	Nov. 3	Nov. 7
,, 21	,, 27	Oct. 3	Oct. 10	—	,, 19	,, 21	Nov. 4	Nov. 11	,, 17	,, 21
Oct. 5	Oct. 11	,, 17	,, 24	,, 30	Nov. 4	Nov. 6	,, 18	,, 25	Dec. 1	Dec. 5

Usually calling at Cocanada, Port Swettenham and Amoy. May omit calls at Rangoon and Shanghai outward or homeward as occasion demands,

CALCUTTA—AUSTRALIA.

Sailings monthly from Calcutta to Fremantle, Adelaide, Melbourne, Sydney returning *via* Melbourne, Adelaide, Fremantle, Colombo and Madras. Calling outward when inducement offers at Rangoon, Penang, Java ports or Colombo, and homeward at Hobart, Adelaide and Fremantle.

Occasional. **BOMBAY—SEYCHELLES, EAST & SOUTH AFRICA.** *Call every 4 weeks. "T" and "K" Class Steamers (7,933-9,891 tons).

BOMBAY.—Dep. fortnightly on Wednesday, via **Porebunder**†, **Marmagoa**†, **Seychelles***, for **Mombasa, Zanzibar, Dar-es-Salaam, Mozambique , Beira, Lourenco Marques, Durban,** returning from **Durban** fortnightly, on Snnday, via same ports.

EAST AFRICAN COAST. m.v. *Dumra*, 2,304 tons.

Northern.—Connecting with Main Line (see page 359) From **Kilindini** 2 or 3 times monthly, via **Tanga, Zanzibar, Dar-es-Salaam, Kilwa**†, **Lindi, Mikindani Ibo**†, **Mocimboa**†, **Lindi, Ruva Bay, Dar-es-Salaam, Zanzibar, Tanga** to **Kilindini.** †Occasional.

Southern.—Connection with Main Line (see page 359) at **Beira.** From **Lourenco Marques, Inhambane, Beira, Chinde, Quelimane, Angoche, Mozambique, Port Amelia** to **Ibo.** This service is being operated by the m.v. *Sofala*. Calls will be made at minor intermediate ports as inducement offers.

SINGAPORE—BANGKOK. *Non-Contract.*
m.v. *Kistna*, 1,465 tons ; m.v. *Kola*, 1,538 tons. Weekly service leaving **Singapore** on Sat., arr. Wed. ; leave **Bangkok** on Friday, arr. Tues.

CALCUTTA—RANGOON. *Bi-weekly.*
"E" Class Steamers and s.s. *Talamba*, 4,298-7,802 tons. **Calcutta** dep. weekly, on Sunday and Tuesday. From **Rangoon** on Thursday and Tuesday. Passage 2-2½ days.

CALCUTTA—COAST PORTS—BOMBAY AND KARACHI. Sailings on application.

RANGOON—MADRAS.
"E" Class Steamers, 5,108-5,574 tons. **RANGOON** dep. weekly, on Friday. From **Madras** on Friday. Passage 3 days.

RANGOON—COROMANDEL COAST PORTS. Sailings on application.

RANGOON-TAVOY RIVER & MERGUI.
Sailings on application.

MOULMEIN-TAVOY RIVER-MERGUI-VICTORIA POINT-PENANG. Fortnightly.

MADRAS—NEGAPATAM & STRAITS.
s.s. *Rajula*, 8,478 tons ; s.s. *Rohna*, 8,502 tons. **Madras** dep. fortnightly on Tuesday, calling at **Pondicherry, Cuddalore, Porto Novo, Karikal, Negapatam, Penang, Port Swettenham, Singapore,** returning fortnightly on Thursday.

CALCUTTA—RANGOON & STRAITS.
"K" Class Steamers.
Calcutta dep. weekly, on Friday, for **Rangoon, Penang** and **Singapore,** returning on Thursdays from Singapore. Outwards calls also at **Port Swettenham.**

CALCUTTA—BOMBAY & KARACHI.
Sailings on application. *Non-Contract.*

RANGOON, ARRACAN & CHITTAGONG.
Sailings on application

BOMBAY-KATHIAW'RCO'ST & KARACHI
Bombay dep. once weekly, on Saturday for **Cutch Mandvie, Port Okha** and **Karachi.** From mid-May to early Sept. the Kathitwar Ports are omitted.

Passage 12 days. **BOMBAY—KARACHI & PERSIAN GULF** (Fast Mail). †Call fortnightly.
s.s. *Varela*, 4,645 tons. s.s. *Varsova*, 4,691 tons. s.s. *Vasna*, 4,790 tons.

Bombay.—Dep. weekly, Thursday, for **Karachi, Bahrein, Khoramshahr** (Mohamerah) and **Basra,** due Thurs. **Basra.**—Dep. Sat. via same ports, due **Bombay** following Saturday.

SUBSIDIARY MAIL.—Bombay, dep. weekly, on Wed. via **Veraval, Mangrol, Karachi, Ormara**†, **Pasni**†, **Gwadur**†, **Charbar**†, **Muscat, Jask**†, **Bunder Abbas, Linga**†, **Sharja**†, **Dubai**†, **Bahrein, Bushire, Koweit**†, **Khoramshahr**† (Mohamerah) to **Basra.** Pass. 15 days. From **Basra,** dep. on ¶Fris., **Khoramshar**† on Fris., **Koweit** on Sats., **Bushire** on Sats./Suns., due **Bombay** following Thur. week. (Dates of call at intermediate ports given on application).
¶ May leave Basra on Thursday.

DAIREN KISEN KAISHA.

s.s. *Tsingtao Maru*, 4027 tons. s.s. *Hoten Maru*, 3975 tons. s.s. *Dairen Maru*, 3800 tons.

arr.		dep.	↑	arr.	dep.
Sailings every 2 or 3 days.	↓	Dairen		Sailings every 2 or 3 days.	
		Tsingtao			
		Shanghai			

Vancouver to Australasia via Honolulu and Fiji

Approximate schedule.

Calling also at Victoria. OUTWARD.						HOMEWARD. Calling also at Victoria.				
STEAMERS.	Van-co'ver. d	Hon'l'lu H.I. d.	Suva (Fiji) dp.	Auck-land ar.	Arrive Sydney	Depart Sydney	Depart A'ckl'nd	Suva (Fiji) dp	Depart Hon'l'lu	Arrive V'nc'ver
s.s. *Niagara* ..	July 5	July 12	July 21	July 24	July 29	Aug. 3	Aug. 8	Aug. 11	Aug. 18	Aug. 25
s.s. *Monowai*	Aug. 2	Aug. 9	Aug. 18	Aug. 21	Aug. 26	,, 31	S pt. 5	Sept. 8	Sept. 15	Sept. 22
s.s. *Aorangi* ..	,, 30	Sept. 6	Sept. 14	Sept. 17	Sept. 22	Sept. 28	Oct. 3	Oct. 6	Oct. 13	Oct. 20

CANADIAN NATIONAL STEAMSHIPS.

Canada—British West Indies (Western Group).

Sailings Montreal to Bermuda, Nassau, Kingston (Belize), July 6, 20.

Canada—British West Indies (Eastern Group).

From Halifax *via* Boston, Bermuda, St. Kitts, Nevis, Antigua, Montserrat, Dominica, St. Lucia, Barbados, St. Vincent, Grenada, Trinidad to Demerara, July 14, 28.

Vagabond Cruises from Montreal *via* Porto Rico, Barbados, Trinidad to Demerara, July 7.

CANADIAN PACIFIC. Vancouver to Japan, China and Manila.

(See also pp. 403 and 459). (Subject to change).

Westbound Steamships.	Tons.	Dp. Vancouver & Victoria	Arr. Honolulu.	Arrive Yokohama	Arrive Kobe.	Arrive Nagasaki.	Arrive Shanghai.	Arrive Hong Kong	Arrive Manila.
Empress of Japan..	26000	Aug. 5	Aug. 10	Aug. 19	Aug. 20	—	Aug. 22	Au. 25	Aug. 27
Empress of Asia	16900	Aug. 19	—	Aug. 30	Sept. 1	Sept. 3	Sept. 4	Sep. 7	Sept. 10
Empress of Canada	21500	Sept. 2	Sept. 7	Sept. 16	Sept. 17	—	Sept. 19	Sep 22	Sept. 24
Empress of Russia ..	16900	Sept. 16	—	Sept. 27	Sept. 29	Oct. 1	Oct. 2	Oct. 5	Oct. 7
Empress of Japan ..	26000	Sept. 30	Oct. 5	Oct. 14	Oct. 15	—	Oct. 17	Oct 20	Oct. 22
Empress of Asia	16900	Oct. 14	—	Oct. 26	Oct. 27	Oct. 29	Oct. 30	Nov. 2	Nov. 6
Empress of Canada	21500	Oct. 28	Nov. 2	Nov. 11	Nov. 12	—	Nov. 14	Nv. 17	Nov. 19
Empress of Russia ..	16900	Nov. 11	—	Nov. 23	Nov. 24	Nov. 26	Nov. 27	Nv. 30	Dec. 2
Empress of Japan..	26000	Nov. 25	Nov. 30	Dec. 9	Dec. 10	—	Dec. 12	Dec 15	Dec. 17
Empress of Asia ..	16900	Dec. 9	—	Dec. 21	Dec. 22	Dee. 24	Dec. 25	Dec 28	Dec. 30

China and Japan to Vancouver. (Subject to change.)

Eastbound Steamships.	Tons.	Dp H'ng Kong.	Dep Shanghai	Dep. Nagasaki.	Dep. Kobe.	Dp. Yokohama.	Dep. Honolulu.	Arrive Victoria and Vancouver
Empress of Canada	21500	Aug. 4	Aug. 6	—	Aug. 9	Aug. 11	Aug. 18	Aug. 23
Empress of Russia..	16900	Aug. 18	Aug. 20	Aug. 22	Aug. 24	Aug. 26	Sept. 3	Sept. 9
Empress of Japan..	26000	Sept. 1	Sept. 3	—	Sept. 6	Sept. 8	Sept. 14	Sept. 19
Empress of Asia ..	16900	Sept. 14	Sept. 16	Sept. 18	Sept. 20	Sept. 22	Sept. 29	Oct. 5
Empress of Canada	21500	Sept. 29	Oct. 1	—	Oct. 4	Oct. 6	Oct. 13	Oct. 18
Empress of Russia..	16900	Oct. 13	Oct. 15	Oct. 17	Oct. 19	Oct 21	—	Oct. 30
Empress of Japan..	26000	Oct. 27	Oct. 29	—	Nov. 1	Nov. 3	Nov. 9	Nov. 14
Empress of Asia ..	16900	Nov. 10	Nov. 12	Nov. 14	Nov. 16	Nov. 18	—	Nov. 27
Empress of Canada	21500	Nov. 24	Nov. 26	—	Nov. 29	Dec. 1	Dec. 8	Dec. 13
Empress of Russia..	16900	Dec. 8	Dec. 10	Dec. 12	Dec. 14	Dec. 16	—	Dec. 25

* If sufficient inducement.

ELDER DEMPSTER LINES

[See also page 447.

NEW YORK—WEST AFRICAN SERVICE (*via* CANARY ISLANDS). From New York, — to Madeira*, Teneriffe, Las Palmas, Dakar, Conakry, Freetown, Grand Bassam, Port Bouet, Takoradi, Cape Coast, Accra, Cotonou, Lagos, Apapa, Forcados, Burutu, Warri, Koko, Sapele.

CANADA—CAPE SERVICE. (Vessels have limited passenger accommodation.) From Montreal, — to Freetown (for Takoradi, Accra, Lagos, Apapa, Pt. Harcourt), Walfish Bay, Cape Town, Pt. Elizabeth, East London, Durban, Lourenco Marques and Beira.

EUPHRATES AND TIGRIS STEAM NAV. CO., LTD.

Tigris Service between Basra and Baghdad.—Paddle Steamers *Zenobia*, *Zobaida*, *Khalifah Malamir*, s.w. *El Kadri*, *Ihsan*.

Basra ....dep.	See note †	12 0	Baghdad ....dep.	See note †	12 0
Baghdad ....arr.	5 to 6 days later.		Basra .... arr.	3 to 4 days later.	

† No fixed sailing dates. Steamers run as near as possible in connection with arrival and departure of the British India S.N. Co.'s Mail Boats at Basra.

RIVER KARUN.—Service from Khoramshahr (Mohamerah) to Ahwaz weekly. (Deck pass. only.) Up journey 24 hours, downward journey 12 hours. Service from Ahwaz to Shuster indefinite.

Port.	*President Pierce,* 12,579 tons.		*President Coolidge,* 21,936 tons.	
Los Angeles	June 12	Aug. 6	June 26	Aug. 20
San Francisco	„ 13/16	„ 3/5	„ 27/30	„ 17/19
Honolulu	„ 21	July 28	July 5	„ 11/12
Yokohama	July 1	„ 20	„ 14	„ 4
Kobe	„ 2/3	„ 19	„ 15/16	„ 3
Shanghai	—	„ 16/17	„ 18/19	July 31/Aug. 1
Hong Kong	„ 6/7	„ 12/14	„ 21	„ 28/29
Manila	„ 8	„ 10	„ 23	„ 26

Port.	*President Taft,* 12,562 tons.		*President Cleveland,* 12,568 tons.		*President Pierce,* 12,579 tons.	
Los Angeles ..	July 10	Sept. 4	July 24	Sept. 18	Aug. 7	Oct. 1
San Francisco ..	„ 11/14	„ 1/3	„ 25/28	„ 15/17	„ 8/11	Sep. 28/30
Honolulu	„ 19	Aug. 26	Aug. 2	„ 9	„ 16	„ 22
Yokohama	„ 29	„ 18	„ 12	„ 1	„ 26	„ 14
Kobe	„ 30/31	„ 17	„ 13/14	Aug. 31	„ 27/28	„ 13
Shanghai	Aug. 2/3	„ 14/15	„ 16/17	„ 28/29	„ 30/31	—
Hong Kong	„ 5	„ 11/12	„ 19	„ 25/26	Sept. 2	„ 8/9
Manila	„ 7	„ 9	„ 21	„ 23	„ 4	„ 6

ROUND-THE-WORLD SERVICE.

DEPARTURES FROM NEW YORK.

Pres. Garfield, 10,495 tons, May 19, Sep. 8, Dec. 29 | *President Harrison*, 10,504 tons, July 14, Nov. 3.
President Adams, 10,516 tons, June 16, Oct. 6 | *President Polk*, 10,500 tons, Aug. 11, Dec. 1.

New York	May 19	June 16	July 14	Aug. 11	Sept. 8	Oct. 6	Nov. 3	Dec. 1	Dec. 29
Havana	„ 23	„ 20	„ 18	„ 15	„ 12	„ 10	„ 7	„ 5	Jan. 2
Panama	„ 27	„ 24	„ 22	„ 19	„ 16	„ 14	„ 11	„ 9	„ 6
Los Angeles	June 5/6	July 3/4	„ 31/A.1	„ 28/29	„ 25/26	„ 23/24	„ 20/21	„ 18/19	„ 15/16
San Francisco ..	„ 7/10	„ 5/8	Aug. 2/5	„ 30/S.2	„ 27/30	„ 25/28	„ 22/25	„ 20/23	„ 17/20
Honolulu	„ 17	„ 15	„ 12	Sept. 9	Oct. 7	Nov. 4	Dec. 2	„ 30	„ 27
Yokohama	„ 29	„ 27	„ 24	„ 21	„ 19	„ 16	„ 14	Jan. 11	Feb. 8
Kobe	July 1/2	„ 29/30	„ 26/27	„ 23/24	„ 21/22	„ 18/19	„ 16/17	„ 13/14	„ 10/11
Hong Kong	„ 6/7	Aug. 3/4	„ 31/S.1	„ 28/29	„ 26/27	„ 23/24	„ 21/22	„ 18/19	„ 15/16
Manila	„ 9/10	„ 6/7	Sept. 3/4	Oct. 1/2	„ 29/30	„ 26/27	„ 24/25	„ 21/22	„ 18/19
Singapore	„ 15/18	„ 12/15	„ 9/12	„ 7/10	Nov. 4/7	Dec. 2/5	„ 30/J.2	„ 27/30	„ 24/27
Penang	„ 19/20	„ 16/17	„ 13/14	„ 11/12	„ 8/9	„ 6/7	Jan. 3/4	„ 31/F.1	„ 28/29
Colombo	„ 24	„ 21	„ 18	„ 16	„ 13	„ 11	„ 8	Feb. 5	Mar. 4
Bombay	„ 27/29	„ 24/26	„ 21/23	„ 19/21	„ 16/18	„ 14/16	„ 11/13	„ 8/10	„ 7/9
Suez..........	Aug. 7	Sept. 4	Oct. 2	„ 30	„ 27	„ 25	„ 22	„ 19	„ 18
Port Said	„ 8	„ 5	„ 3	„ 31	„ 28	„ 26	„ 23	„ 20	„ 19
Alexandria	„ 9	„ 6	„ 4	Nov. 1	„ 29	„ 27	„ 24	„ 21	„ 20
Naples	„ 12	„ 9	„ 7	„ 4	Dec. 2	„ 30	„ 27	„ 24	„ 23
Genoa	„ 14/15	„ 11/12	„ 9/10	„ 6/7	„ 4/5	Jan. 1/2	„ 29/30	„ 26/27	„ 25/26
Marseilles	„ 16	„ 13	„ 11	„ 8	„ 6	„ 3	„ 31	„ 28	„ 27
New York	„ 29/S.2	„ 26/30	„ 24/28	„ 21/25	„ 19/23	„ 16/20	Feb13/17	Mar12/16	Apl. 9/13
Boston	Sept. 3	Oct. 1	„ 29	„ 26	„ 24	„ 21	„ 18	„ 17	„ 14

PHILLIPINE INTER-ISLAND S.S. CO. From Manila every Tuesday to Iloilo (Wed.), Zamboanga (Thurs.), Cebu (Fri.), Iloilo (Sat.), returning to Manila (Sun.).

EASTERN & AUSTRALIAN S.S. CO. LTD. Australia to China and Japan.

Subject to change without notice. Calling at Newc'tle, Townsville, Moji, Osaka and Nagoya/Yokkaichi (opt.)

Steamer.	Tons.	Melbo'rne dep.	Hobart.	Sydney. dep.	Brisb'ne dep.	Rabaul	Manila arr.	H'n-Kng arr	Shang-hai.	Kobe.	Yokoha-ma. arr.
Tanda	7000	July 5	July 7	July 15	July 17	July 23	Aug. 1	Aug. 4	Aug. 10	Aug 14	Aug. 19
Nankin ..	7055	Aug. 2	Aug. 4	Aug. 12	Aug. 14	Aug. 20	Aug. 29	Sept. 1	Sept 7	Sep.11	Sept. 16
Nellore ..	6583	Sept. 2	Sept. 4	Sept. 13	Sept. 15	Sept. 21	Sept. 30	Oct. 3	Oct. 9	Oct. 13	Oct. 18

Japan, China to Australia. Calling also at Nagoya and Mozi.

Steamer.	Tons.	Yokoh'ma dep	Kobe. dep.	Hong-Kong dep.	Manila.	Rabaul.	Brisbane arr.	Sydney. arr	M'l bo'rne arr.
Nellore ..	6583	July 22	July 26	Aug. 4	Aug. 7	Aug. 15	Aug. 2	Aug. 23	Aug. 28
Tanda ..	7000	Aug. 21	Aug. 25	Sept. 2	Sept. 5	Sept 13	Sept. 19	Sept. 21	Sept. 25
Nankin	7055	Sept. 18	Sept. 22	Sept. 80	Oct. 8	Oct. 11	Oct. 17	Oct. 19	Oct. 23
Nellore ..	6583	Oct. 21	Oct. 25	Nov. 3	Nov. 6	Nov. 14	Nov. 20	Nov. 22	Nov. 27

☞ Steamers call as requested at Pt. Adelaide, Pt. Pirie, Pt. Kembla, Pt. Alma, Cairns, Thursday Island, Darwin, Timor (Dilly) Ilo-Ilo, Kolambugan, Zamboanga Pt. Holland, Catabangan, Sandakan, Samarai.

GRACE LINE.

New York—West Coast South America.

Vessel.		Tons.	Vessel.		Tons.
*s.s. *Santa Lucia*	....	9135	*m.v. *Santa Barbara*	....	8060
*s.s. *Santa Clara*	..	8220	m.v. *Santa Rita*	....	4576
*m.v. *Santa Maria*	....	8060	m.v. *Santa Inez*	....	4576

*Through rates from Europe by North Atlantic Conference Lines *via* New York and Canada.

Vessel.	New York. Leave.	Cristobal. arr.	Balboa Canal dep.	Buena-ventura arr./dep.	Guay-aquil. arr./dep	Callao. arr./dep	Moll-endo. arr./dep.	Arica. arr/dep	Anto-fagasta. arr./dep.	Valpa-raiso. arr.
Santa Barbara	July 21	July 27	July 27	July 29	July 31	Aug. 2/3	Aug. 4	Aug. 5	Aug. 6	Aug. 8
Santa Inez....	,, 28	Aug. 4	Aug. 5	Aug. 7	—	,, 12	—	,, 14	,, 16	—
Santa Clara ..	Aug. 4	,, 9	,, 10	,, 11	Aug. 13	,, 16/17	,, 18	,, 19	,, 20	,, 22
Santa Maria..	,, 11	,, 17	,, 17	,, 19	,, 21	,, 23/24	,, 25	,, 26	,, 27	,, 29
Santa Rita	,, 18	,, 25	,, 26	,, 28	—	Sept. 2	—	Sept. 4	Sept. 6	—
Santa Lucia ..	,, 25	,, 30	,, 31	Sept. 1	Sept. 2	,, 6/7	Sept. 8	,, 9	,, 10	Sept. 12
Santa Barbara	Sept. 1	Sept. 7	Sept. 7	,, 9	,, 11	,, 13/14	,, 15	,, 16	,, 17	,, 19
Santa Inez ...	,, 8	,, 15	,, 16	,, 18	—	,, 23	—	,, 25	,, 27	—

Vessel.	Valpa-raiso. dep.	Anto-fagasta. arr./dep.	Moll-endo. arr./dep.	Callao. arr./dep	Guay-aquil. arr./dep.	Buena-ventura. arr./dep.	Balboa. arr.	Crist-obal. dep.	Havana.	New York.
Santa Maria ..	July 21	July 23	July 24	July 26	July 29	July 31	Aug. 2	Aug. 2	—	Aug. 8
Santa Rita ..	—	—	,, 29	,, 31	Aug. 3	Aug. 6	,, 7	,, 8	—	,, 15
Santa Lucia ..	Aug. 5	Aug. 7	Aug. 8	Aug 9/10	,, 12	,, 14	,, 16	,, 16	Aug. 19	,, 22
Santa Barbara	,, 11	,, 13	,, 14	,, 16	,, 19	,, 21	,, 23	,, 28	—	,, 29
Santa Inez....	—	—	,, 19	,, 21	,, 24	,, 27	,, 28	,, 29	—	Sept. 5
Santa Clara ..	,, 26	,, 28	,, 29	,, 30/31	Sept. 2	Sept. 4	Sept. 6	Sept. 6	Sept. 9	,, 12
Santa Maria	Sept. 1	Sept. 3	Sept. 4	Sept. 6	,, 9	,, 11	,, 13	,, 13	—	,, 19
Santa Rita ...		—	,, 9	,, 11	,, 14	,, 17	,, 18	,, 19	—	,, 26

Other ports of call according to sailing: Talara, Paita, Salaverry, Pisco, Tocopilla, Chanaral, Coquimbo outward, and Chanaral, Paita, Talara and Manta homeward.

CARIBBEAN SERVICE.—Sailings from New York every Friday to Curacao, La Guayra, Puerto Cabello, Puerto Colombia, Cartagena, Panama, Jamaica, Haiti.

INDIAN AFRICAN LINE.

CAPETOWN—EAST AFRICA—CEYLON—INDIA—BURMA and vice versa.

m.v. *Inchanga* 7069 tons | m.v. *Incomati* 7369 tons | m.v. *Isipingo* 7069 tons.

Carrying 1st, 2nd and deck passengers, cabins de luxe, single berth cabins, two berth cabins with private shower, etc., 1st class. Stewardess and Doctor carried.

Capetown dep.	Durban dep.	Calcutta arr./dep.	Rangoon arr.	Rangoon dep.	Calcutta dep.	Durban arr.	Capetown arr.
June 7	June 13	July 9/11	July 14	July 23	Aug. 4	Aug. 29	Sept. 6
July 7	July 13	Aug. 8/10	Aug. 13	Aug 23	Sept. 4	Sept. 29	Oct. 6
Aug. 7	Aug. 13	Sept. 8/10	Sept. 13	Sept. 23	Oct. 4	Oct. 29	Nov. 6

Outward calling also at Zanzibar, Mombasa, Colombo, Madras and homeward, calling also at Madras, Colombo, Mombasa, Zanzibar, Beira, Lourenco Marques, East London, Port Elizabeth, Mossel Bay.

INDO—CHINA STEAM NAVIGATION CO., LTD.

Calcutta and Japan Line.—Vessels leave Hongkong for Calcutta via Singapore, and Penang and for Japan approximately every fortnight. All steamers on this Line have excellent passenger accommodation, are fitted with wireless and carry a fully-qualified doctor.

***Hongkong-Shanghai Line.**—Sailings every Wednesday and Sunday from Hongkong to Tsingtau via Swatow and Shanghai. Returning via the same ports to Canton. Steamers on this Line are fitted with wireless and have good passenger accommodation.

Borneo Line.—A sailing about every 10 days to and from Sandakan by the two steamers *Hinsang* and *Mausang*. Both steamers have good passenger accommodation and are equipped with wireless.

***Hongkong-Tientsin Line.**—A regular weekly service is maintained between Hongkong and Tientsin, usually calling at Swatow, Foochow and Chefoo.

***Shanghai-Tientsin Line.**—The steamers *Fausang*, 2,256 tons, *Tingsang*, 2,256 tons, and *Leesang* leave Shanghai for Tientsin via Weihaiwei and Chefoo every Tuesday and Friday.

***Shanghai-Tsingtau Line.**—A bi-weekly service is maintained, steamers leaving Shanghai every Wednesday and Saturday.

*N.B.—These are the services operated in normal times, but at present are subject to various changes

INDOCHINOIS, SOCIÉTÉ les AFFRÉTEURS MARITIME. (S.A.)

SAIGON-SINGAPORE. Commercial Services, s.s. *Gouverneur Gen. Pasquier* 1933 tons. Sailing from Saigon every fortnight on Mondays, etc., from Singapore every fortnight on Mondays, calling at Poulo Condore.
SAIGON-SINGAPORE. Commercial Service by s.s. *Gouverneur Gen. Merlin*, 1543 tons. Sailing from Saigon every fortnight on Mondays, from Singapore every fortnight on Mondays.
SAIGON-NETHERLAND INDIES. Every 45 days, approximately by s.s. *Albert Sarraut*.
SAIGON-TONKIN. Every fortnight by s.s *Gouv. Gen Van Vollenhoven*, 691 tons

ASIATIQUE Cie de NAVIGATION, HAIPHONG.

Probable Services (subject to alteration).

HAIPHONG-HONGKONG. By s.s. *Gouv. Gen. Paul Doumer*, 784 tons, dep. Haiphong fortnightly on Wed from Hongkong fortnightly Passage 60 hours, calling at Fort Bayard.

HAIPHONG-HONGKONG. Direct by s.s. *Canton*, 976 tons. From Haiphong, dep. due Hongkong 2 days (44 hours) later. From Hongkong, dep.

IRRAWADDY FLOTILLA CO., LTD., BURMA.

Rangoon, Prome, Mandalay—Sailings from Rangoon twice weekly; from Mandalay twice weekly.
Prome, Mandalay—Daily each way in connection with trains to and from Prome.
Rangoon, Bassein - Daily. Passage about 17 hours. Mandalay Bhamo Express, calling at intermediate ports—from Mandalay once weekly; from Bhamo once weekly.
Mandalay Bhamo cargo with 1st and 2nd class accommodation—from Mandalay every alternate week from Bhamo every alternate week.
Katha-Bhamo.—Daily, in connection with mail train.

All the above services are maintained by fast Steamers, having comfortable accommodation for 1st and 2nd class passengers. Excellent messing, electric light, fans, etc.

IRRAWADDY FLOTILLA AND AIRWAYS LTD.

Regular Air Services are maintained between Rangoon and the Oilfields, and between Rangoon, Moulmein and Tavoy.

JAVA—CHINA—JAPAN LINE.

s.s. *Tjibadak* ..... 7803 tons	m.s. *Tjinegara* .... 9227 tons	s.s. *Tjisaroea* ...... 7089 tons
s.s. *Tjikarang* .... 9505 tons	s.s. *Tjisalak* .... 5787 tons	m.s. *Tjisadane* .. 9228 tons
s.s. *Tjikembang* .... 8013 tons	s.s. *Tjileboet* .... 5760 tons	*Tsimandek*...... 5620 tons
s.s. *Tjisondari* .... 8039 tons		

LINE 1.

Vessel.	Sourabaya dep.	Batavia dep.	Manila. arr.	Hong K'ng arr.	Shanghai. arr.	Shanghai. dep.	Hong K'ng dep.	Manila dep.	Bali. arr.	Sourabaya arr.
Tjitjalengka	Aug. 4	Aug. 8	Au.. 14	Aug. 16	Au. 21	ug 24	Aug 29	Aug. 31	Sept 7	Sept. 8
Tjinegara	,, 25	,, 29	Sept. 4	Sept. 6	Sep 11	Sep.14	Sept. 19	Sept. 21	, 28	,, 29
Tjitjalengka	Sept. 15	Sept. 19	,, 25	,, 27	Oct. 2	Oct. 5	Oct. 10	Oct. 12	Oct. 19	Oct. 20
Tjinegara ..	Oct. 6	Oct. 10	Oct. 16	Oct. 18	,, 23	,. 26	,, 31	Nov. 2	No . 9	Nov. 10
Tjitjalengka	,, 27	,, 31	Nov. 6	Nov. 8	Nov 13	No 16	Nov. 21	,, 23	,, 30	Dec. 1
Tjinegara ..	Nov. 17	Nov. 21	,, 27	,, 29	Dec. 4	Dec. 7	Dec. 12	Dec. 14	Dec 21	,, 22
Tjitjalengka	Dec. 8	Dec. 12	Dec. 18	Dec. 20	,, 25	,, 28	Jan. 2	Jan. 4	Jan 11	Jan. 12

Calling outward at Semarang, Cheribon, Amoy Homeward at Amoy, Cebu, Menado (alternate sailings) Macassar. Later Sailings and Itinerary on request.

LINE 2.

Vessel	Sourabaya dep.	Manila. arr.	Hong Kong. arr./dep.	Shanghai arr./dep.	Amoy.	Hong Kong. dep.	Batavia. arr.	Sourabaya arr.
Tjibadak ..	July 28	Aug. 6	ug. 8/11	Aug. 14/17	Aug. 19	Aug. 2	ug. 28	Sept. 1
Tjisadane ..	A g. 18	, 27	Aug. 29/Sp.1	Sept. 4 7	Sept. 9	Sept. 12	Sept. 18	., 22
Tji adak ..	Sept. 8	Sept. 17	Sept. 19/22	,, 25/28	,, 30	ct. 8	O t. 9	O t 12
Tjisadane	, 29	Oct. 9	Oct. 11 14	Oct. 17/19	O t. 21	,, 24	,, 30	N v. 2
Tjibadak ..	Oct. 20	,, 29	Oct.31/No .3	Nov. 6/9	N v. 11	No . 14	No . 20	,, 23
Tjisadane	No . 10	Nov. 19	Nov. 21/24	,, 27/30	Dec. 2	Dec. 5	Dec. 11	Dec. 14

Later sailings and Itinerary on request.

Calling outward at Macassar, Balik apan, Henado (occasional), Amoy. Homeward at Muntok, Cheribon, Samarang. * Calling if sufficient inducement offers.

LINE 4. Fortnightly sailings, Sourabaya, *via* Macassar, Balikpapan (occasional), Menado (occasional), to Kobe, retuning *via* Menado and Macassan to Sourabaya.

KONINKLIJKE PAKETVAART MAATSCHAPPIJ. (Royal Packet Navigation Co.)

SINGAPORE-JAVA-AUSTRALIA LINE OF THE K.P.M.

Calling at Samarang, Bali and Macassar (homeward only).

Steamer.	Tons.	dep. Singapore.	dep. Batavia.	dep. Soerabaja.	arr. Brisbane.	arr. Sydney.	arr. Melbourne.	arr. Adelaide.
Nieuw Zeeland	11066	Aug. 21	Aug. 24	Aug. 26	Sept. 6	Sept. 8	Sept. 11	Sept. 14
Nieuw Holland	11066	Sept. 19	Sept. 22	Sept. 24	Oct. 4	Oct. 6	Oct. 9	Oct. 12
Nieuw Zeeland	11066	Oct. 19	Oct. 22	Oct. 24	Nov. 4	Nov. 6	Nov. 9	Nov. 18

Steamer.	Tons	dep. Adelaide.	dep. Melbourne	dep. Sydney.	dep. Brisbane.	Soera-baja. ar.	Batavia. arr.	Singapore arr.
Nieuw Holland	11066	Aug. 10	Aug. 16	Aug. 21	Aug. 28	Sept. 3	Sept. 6	Sept. 9
Nieuw Zeeland	11066	Sept. 14	Sept. 20	Sept. 25	Sept. 27	Oct. 8	Oct. 11	Oct. 14
Nieuw Holland	11066	Oct. 12	Oct. 18	Oct. 23	Oct. 25	Nov. 5	Nov. 8	Nov. 11

ORIENT—JAVA—AFRICA LINE OF THE K.P.M.

Steamer.	Tons	H. Kong dep.	Manila. arr.	Bangk'k arr./dp.	Singapore arr.	Batavia arr./dp.	Mauritius arr./dep	Durban arr./dep	Capetown arr.
Tegelberg ..	15000	Aug. 3	Aug. 5	Au.12/14	Aug. 16	Au 18/21	Aug 29	Sept. 6/9	Sept. 11
Ruys	15000	Sept. 7	Sept. 9	Sep16/18	Sept. 20	Sp.22/25	Oct. 3	Oc.11/14	Oct. 16
Boissevain ..	15000	Oct. 5	Oct. 7	Oct14/16	Oct. 18	Oct20/23	Oct. 31	Nov.8/11	Nov. 13
Tegelberg ..	15000	Nov. 4	Nov. 6	Nv 13/15	Nov. 17	Nv 19/22	Nov. 30	Dec 8/11	Dec. 13

Steamer.	Tons.	Cape-town dep	Durban arr./dep	Mo'basa dep	Singa-pore arr./dp.	H. Kong arr./dep.	Shan-ghai arr./dp.	Hong Kong. arr
Ruys	15000	July 19	Jly23/25	Aug. 6	Au 18/19	Au.23/24	Au.26/28	Aug 30
Boissevain ..	15000	Aug. 16	Au.20/22	Sept. 3	Sp.15/16	Sp.20/21	Sp. 23/25	Sept. 27
Tegelberg ..	15000	Sept. 13	Sep17/19	Oct. 1	Oct13/14	Oct18/19	Oct21/23	Oct. 25
Ruys	15000	Oct. 18	Oct22, 24	Nov. 4	Nv.16/17	Nv21/22	Nv.24/26	Nov. 28

Other ports of call :—Saigon, Rodriguez, Réunion, Tamatave, Lourenco Marques, East London Port Elizabeth, Mossel Bay, Reunion, Tamatave, Zanzibar, Seychelles Belawan Deli, also at other Madagascar ports, Dar-es-Salaam and Tanga if sufficient inducement offers.

SINGAPORE—JAVA (Line 7).

arr.	dep.		arr.	dep.
—	Fri. 16 0	↓ Singapore ..	Mo.7 0	—
Su. 7 0	Su. 16 0	Batavia ..	Sat.7 0	Sat.16 0
Mo.9 0	Mo. 16 0	Samarang ..	Fri.7 0	Fri.13 0
Tu. 7 0	—	Sourabaya .. ↑	—	Th. 17 0

SINGAPORE—BATAVIA and *vice-versa*.

Line 7b, weekly.

	arr.	dep.
Singapore	—	Mon. 12 0
Batavia..	Wed noon	—
,,	—	Mon. 12 0
Singapore	Wed. a.m	—

SINGAPORE—HONG-KONG LINE OF THE K.P.M

m.s. *Cremer* and m.s. *Van Heutsz.* Fortnightly between Singapore and Hong-Kong. Passage 5 days. Dep. Singapore Thurs fortn'ghtly. From Hong-Kong, Thurs. fortnightly.

SINGAPORE-BELAWAN-DELI.—Dep Singapore Mon. 11.0 a.m., Belawan-Deli Tues. 12.0 dep Wednesday 5.0 p.m. arr. Singapore Fri. 7.0 a.m. Dep. Singapore Fri. p.m., Belawan-Deli Sun. a.m. Dep. Mon. p.m., arr. Belawan Deli Wed. a.m.

PENANG, BELAWAN—DELI, and *vice versa*

(Line3b). Penang dp. Sat. p.m., ar. Belawan-Deli Su. a.m.; Belawan-Deli dp. Thu. p.m ; ar. Penang Fri. a.m.

PALEMBANG SERVICES.

Wed.	dep. ↓	Singapore ↑	arr.	Mon.
Fri.	arr.	Palembang	dep.	Sat.

Wed.	dep. ↓	Batavia ↑	arr.	Mon.
Fri.	arr.	Palembang	dep.	Sat

PADANG SERVICE.

Alternately on Wed. or Thurs.	Line 1, South. (fortn.)	Line 3. South. (fortn.)
Batavia dep.	Thur.	Wed.
Padang arr.	Sun.	Sat.
,, dep.	Thur.	Sat.
Batavia arr.	Mon.	Tues.

BALI SERVICE.

Tues.	dep. ↓	Batavia ↑	arr. Wed.
Wed.	dep.	Samarang	arr. Tue.
Thur.	dep.	Sourabaya	arr. Mon.
Fri.	arr.	Boeleleng	dep. Sun.
Sat.	arr.	Macassar	dep. Sat.

SOUTH-PACIFIC LINE.

Calling also at Samarang, Sourabaya, Port Moresby, Port Vila and Noumea.

Vessel.	Tons	Saigon. dep	Singa-pore. dep.	Batavia. arr./dep	Auckland. arr./dep.	Welli'gton arr./dep.	Sydney. arr./dep.	Batavia. arr./dep.	Singa-pore arr.	Saigon arr.
Mætsuycker	4119	July 16	July 19	July 21/24	Aug. 13/—	Aug —/19	Aug. 23/25	Sept. 8/10	Sep. 12	Sept14
Tasman ..	4992	Aug. 16	Aug. 19	Aug. 21/23	Sep. 14/—	Sept.—/20	Sept. 25/27	Oct. 11/13	Oct. 15	Oct. 17
Mætsuycker	4119	Sep. 16	Sep. 19	Sept. 21/23	Oct. 13/—	Oct. —/20	Oct. 24/26	Nov. 9/11	Nov 13	Nov. 15
Tasman	4992	Oct. 18	Oct. 21	Oct. 23/25	Nov. 16/—	Nov. —/22	Nov. 27/29	Dec. 13/14	Dec 16	—

Calls also made according to steamer at Samarai, Rabaul, Port Vila and Noumea

Subject to modification without notice in the event of quarantine, &c.

Egypt-Jeddah-Sudan Mail Line.

ITINERARY of s.s. *Taif* (1590 tons) Fortnightly.

arr.	dep.	Ports.	arr.	dep.
Aug 9, &c	We. 17 0	Suez ↑	Su. 7 0	—
Sat. 8 0	Sat. 12 0	Yambo	Th. 10 0	Th. 12 0
Su. 8 0	Su. 12 0	Jeddah	We. 9 0	We. 12 0
Mo. 7 0	Mo. 9 0	Suakin	—	—
Mo 13 0	—	↓ Port Sudan	—	Tu. 12 0

† Optional.

ITINERARY of s.s. *Talodi* (1585 tons) Fortnightly.

arr.	dep.	Ports.	arr.	dep.
Aug 2, &c	We 17 0	Suez ↑	Su. 7 0	—
Th. 8 0	Th. 9 0	Tor	Sat. 11 0	Sat. 12 0
Fri. 8 0	Fri. 12 0	Wedj	Fri. 8 0	Fri. 12 0
Sat. 8 0	Sat. 12 0	Yambo	Th. 10 0	Th. 12 0
Su. 8 0	Su. 12 0	Jeddah	We. 9 0	We. 12 0
Mo. 7 0	—	↓ Port Sudan	—	Tu. 12 0

KITANIHON KISEN KAISHA S.S. CO. (North Japan S.S. Co., Ltd.)

Vladivostock-Tsuruga Service.

From Vladivostock 10th, 20th and 30th of each month. From Tsuruga 6th, 16th and 26th of each month.
By s.s. *Amakusa Maru.*

YUKI AND SEISHIN—TSURUGA and *v.v.* by s.s. *Manshi Maru.*
From Yuki 1st, 11th and 21st of each month. Details of sailings on application.

MATSON LINE. OCEANIC LINE.

Frequent Sailings from San Francisco and from Los Angeles for Honolulu, Hawaii.

s.s. *Matsonia* .. .. 17200 tons | s.s. *Lurline* .. .. 19000 tons

Steamer.	San F'ncisco dep. (Westbound)	Leave Los Angeles Harbor. (Westbound)	Honolulu. arr.	Honolulu. dep.	Arrive Los Angeles Harbor. (Eastbound)	San F'ncisco arr. (Eastbound)
Lurline ..	Aug. 3	Aug. 4	Aug. 9	Aug 11	Aug. 18	Aug. 16
Matsonia	,, 11	,, 10	,, 16	,, 17	,, 22	,, 24
Lurline	,, 17	,, 18	,, 23	,, 25	Sept. 1	,, 30
Matsonia .. .	,, 25	,, 24	,, 30	Sept. 1	,, 6	Sept. 8
Lurline	,, 31	Sept. 1	Sept. 6	,, 8	,, 15	,, 13
Matsonia	Sept. 8	,, 7	,, 13	,, 15	,, 20	,, 22
Lurline	,, 14	,, 15	,, 20	,, 21	,, 29	,, 26
Matsonia	,, 22	,, 21	,, 27	,, 29	Oct. 4	Oct. 6
Lurline	,, 28	,, 29	Oct. 4	Oct. 6	,, 13	,, 11
Matsonia	Oct. 6	Oct. 5	,, 11	,, 13	,, 18	,, 20
Lurline	,, 12	,, 13	,, 18	,, 20	,, 27	,, 25
Matsonia .. .	,, 20	,, 19	,, 25	,, 27	Nov. 1	Nov. 3
Lurline	,, 26	,, 27	Nov. 1	Nov. 3	,, 10	,, 8
Matsonia ..	Nov. 3	Nov. 2	,, 8	,, 10	,, 15	,, 17
Lurline	,, 9	,, 10	,, 15	,, 17	,, 24	,, 22
Matsonia	,, 17	,, 16	,, 22	,, 24	,, 29	Dec. 2
Lurliue	,, 23	,, 24	,, 29	—	—	—

OCEANIC STEAMSHIP COMPANY (Matson Line).

Sailings every 28 days for Australia and New Zealand *via* Hawaii, Samoa, Fiji.

s.s. *Mariposa*, 19000 tons, s.s. *Monterey*, 19000.

OUTWARD SAILINGS. Steamships	San Francisco leave	Los Angeles.	Honolulu. arr./dep.	Pago Pago. arr./dep.	Suva arr./dep.	Auckland.	Sydney. arrive	Melbourne. arr.
Mariposa ...	Aug. 15	Aug. 16	Aug. 21	Aug. 26	Aug. 29	Sept. 1	Sept. 4	Sept. 8
Monterey	Sept. 12	Sept. 13	Sept. 18	Sept. 23	Sept. 26	,, 30	Oct. 3	Oct 7
Mariposa	Oct 10	Oct. 11	Oct. 16	Oct. 21	Oct. 24	Oct. 27	,, 30	Nov. 3
Monterey	Nov. 7	Nov. 8	Nov. 13	Nov. 18	Nov. 21	Nov. 24	Nov. 27	Dec. 1
Mariposa	Dec. 5	Dec. 6	Dec. 11	Dec. 16	Dec. 19	Dec. 23	Dec. 26	,, 30

HOMEWARD SAILINGS. Steamships.	Melbourne. dep.	Leave Sydney.	Auckland.	Suva arr./dep.	Pago Pago arr./dep.	Honolulu. arr./dep.	Los Angeles. arr.	Arrive San Francisco.
Monterey	Aug 14	Aug. 18	Aug. 21	Aug. 24	Aug. 25	Aug. 30	Sept. 4	Sept. 5
Mariposa	Sept 11	Sept. 15	Sept. 18	Sept. 21	Sept. 22	Sept. 27	Oct. 2	Oct. 3
Monterey	Oct. 9	Oct. 13	Oct 16	Oct. 19	Oct 20	Oct. 25	Oct. 30	Oct 31
Mariposa	Nov. 6	Nov. 10	Nov. 13	Nov. 16	Nov. 17	Nov 22	Nov. 27	Nov. 28
Monterey	Dec. 4	Dec. 9	Dec. 12	Dec. 15	Dec. 16	Dec. 21	Dec. 26	Dec. 27

NIPPON YUSEN KAISYA. Seattle—Orient Service.

All sailings subject to alteration without notice. (See also page 364 & 407).

MOTOR VESSEL.	Tons	Seattle. dep.	Vanc'ver dep.	Yokohama. arr.	Yokohama. dep.	Kobe. arr.	Kobe. dep.	Osaka. arr./dep.	Kobe arr.
Heian Maru	11616	July 24	July 25	Aug. 7	Aug. 9	Aug. 10	Aug. 11	Aug. 11/12	Aug. 12
Hikawa Maru	11616	Aug. 11	Aug. 12	,, 25	,, 27	,, 28	,, 29	,, 29/30	,, 30
Hie Maru	11616	,, 25	,, 26	Sept. 8	Sept. 10	Sept. 11	Sept. 12	Sept. 12/13	Sept. 13
Heian Maru	11616	Sept. 8	Sept. 9	,, 22	,, 24	,, 25	,, 26	,, 26/27	,, 27

MOTOR VESSEL.	Tons	Kobe dep.	Nagoya.	Shimidzu.	Yokohama. arr.	Yokohama. dep.	Vanc'v'r arr.	Seattle. arr.
Hie Maru	11616	July 31	Aug. 1	Aug. 2	Aug. 2	Aug. 3	Aug. 14	Aug. 15
Heian Maru ..	11616	Aug. 15	,, 16	,, 17	,, 17	,, 18	,, 29	,, 30
Hikawa Maru	11616	Sept. 4	Sept. 5	Sept. 6	Sept. 6	Sept. 7	Sept. 18	Sept. 19
Hie Maru	11616	,, 18	,, 19	,, 20	,, 20	,, 21	Oct. 2	Oct. 3
Heian Maru	11616	Oct. 7	Oct. 8	Oct. 9	Oct. 9	Oct. 10	,, 21	,, 22

NIPPON YUSEN KAISYA. California—Orient Service *via* Honolulu

SAILINGS WESTBOUND Subject to alteration Vessel	Tons	Los Ang'les dep.	San Francisco dep.	Honolulu	Yokohama. arr.	Yokohama. dep.	Kobe. arr.	Kobe. dep.	Shanghai. arr.	Shanghai. dep.	Hong Kong arr.
Kamakura M. (m.v.)	17500	Aug. 14	Aug 17	Aug. 22	Aug 31	Sept. 1	Sept.2	Sept.7	Sept. 9	Sept. 10	Sept. 12
Taiyo Maru (m.v.)	14457	,, 31	Sept. 2	Sept. 8	Sept.19	,, 20	,, 21	—	—	—	—
Asama M'ru (m.v.)	17000	Sept. 6	,, 8	,, 13	,, 22	,, 23	,, 24	,, 29	Oct. 1	Oct. 2	Oct. 4
Tatuta M'ru (m.v.)	17000	,, 22	,, 25	,, 30	Oct. 9	Oct. 10	Oct.11	Oct.25	,, 27	—	—
Kamakura M (m.v.)	17500	Oct. 9	Oct. 12	Oct 17	,, 26	,, 27	,, 28	Nov 13	Nov. 15	Nov. 16	Nov. 18
Asama Maru (m.v.)	17000	,, 30	Nov. 2	Nov. 7	Nov. 16	Nov. 17	Nov18	,, 30	Dec. 2	Dec. 3	Dec. 5
Tatuta M'ru (m.v.)	17000	Nov. 20	,, 23	,, 28	Dec. 7	Dec. 8	Dec. 9	Dec 14	,, 16	,, 17	,, 19
Kamakura M. (mv.)	17500	Dec. 15	Dec. 18	Dec. 23	Jan. 2	Jan. 22	—	—	—	—	—
Asama M'ru (m.v.)	17000	Jan. 1	Jan. 4	Jan. 9	,, 19	Feb. 6	Feb. 7	Feb. 8	Feb. 10	Feb. 11	Feb. 13

SAILINGS EASTBOUND } subject to alteration Vessel.	Tons.	Hong Kong dep.	Shanghai. arr.	Shanghai. dep.	Kobe. arr.	Kobe. dep.	Yokohama arr./dep.	Honolulu arr./dep.	San Frn'cis'o arr.	Los Angeles. arr.
Taiyo Maru (m.v.)	14457	Aug. 4	Aug. 6	Aug 7	Aug. 9	Aug 10	Aug. 11/12	Aug. 21	Aug 27	Aug. 29
Asama Maru (m.v.)	17000	,, 11	,, 13	,, 14	,, 16	,, 17	,, 18/19	,, 27	Sept. 2	Sept. 4
Tatuta M'ru (m.v.)	17000	,, 27	,, 29	,, 30	Sept.1	Sept.2	Sept. 3/4	Sept. 12	,, 18	,, 20
Kamakura M. (m.v.)	17500	Sept.13	Sept. 15	Sept. 16	,, 18	,, 19	,, 20/21	,, 29	Oct. 5	Oct. 7
Asama Maru (m.v.)	17000	Oct. 6	Oct. 7	Oct. 7	Oct. 9	Oct.10	Oct. 11/12	Oct 20	,, 26	,, 28
Tatuta Maru (m.v.)	17000	—	—	,, 28	,, 30	,, 31	Nov. 1/2	Nov. 10	Nov. 26	Nov. 18
Kamakura M. (m.v.)	17500	Nov. 19	Nov. 22	Nov. 21	Nov24	Nov25	,, 26/27	Dec. 5	Dec. 11	Dec. 13
Asama Maru (m.v.)	17000	Dec. 6	Dec. 8	Dec. 9	Dec 11	Dec 12	Dec. 13/14	,, 22	,, 28	,, 30
Tatuta M'ru (m.v.)	17000	,, 20	,, 22	,, 23	,, 25	,, 26	,, 27/28	Jan. 5	Jan. 11	Jan. 13

NIPPON YUSEN KAISYA. Japan—Australia Service.

STEAMER.	Tons	Leave Yokohama	Leave Kobe	Leave Hong Kong	Dep. Manila.	Arrive Sydney	Arrive Melbo'rne	Leave Melbourne	Leave Sydney	Manila. arr.	Arrive Hong Kong.	Arr. Kobe.	Arrive Yokohama
Atuta Maru	7982	June 12	Jne 16	Jne.24	Jne.27	Jly. 13	July 17	July 22	July 29	Aug. 14	Aug17	Aug24	Aug.29
Kitano Maru	7952	July 17	July21	July29	Aug 1	Aug17	Aug. 21	Aug. 26	Sept. 2	Sept. 18	Sep.21	Sept28	Oct. 3
Kamo Maru	7955	Aug. 14	Aug18	Aug26	,, 29	Sep 14	Sept 18	Sept.23	,, 30	Oct. 16	Oct.19	Oct.26	,, 31
Atuta Maru	7982	Sept. 11	Sep.15	Sep.23	Sep.26	Oct.12	Oct. 16	Oct. 21	Oct. 28	Nov. 13	Nov16	Nov23	Nov.28

Steamers fr. Yokohama call also Nagoya, Osaka, Miike, Nagasaki Davao, Menado, Thurs. Island & Brisbane.
Steamers fr. Melbourne call also Brisbane, Thursday Island. Davao, Nagasaki, Osaka (opt. & Nagoya opt.)

NIPPON YUSEN KAISYA. China—Japan Rapid Express Service.

s.s. *Nagasaki Maru*, 5500 tons. s.s. *Shanghai Maru*, 5500 tons Sailings every 4 days in each direction.

arr.	dep.	↓ / ↑	arr.	dep.
—	1st day at 11 0	Kobe	3rd day at 15 0	
2nd day at 9 0	2nd ,, 13 0	Nagasaki ..	2nd ,, 12 0	2nd day at 17 0
3rd ,, 15 0	—	Shanghai ..	—	1st ,, 9 0

Japan—Bombay Line.

From Yokohama, *via* Kobe, Shanghai, Hong Kong, Singapore to Bombay (also calling at Nagoya Osaka, Moji, Karatsu, Penang, Colombo. From Bombay, *via* Colombo, Singapore, Hong Kong, Shanghai to Kobe. (Sailings on application).

SOUTH AMERICAN (West Coast) LINE.

Sailings on application.

From Hong Kong *via* Moji, Kobe, Yokkachi, Yokohama, Honolulu, Hilo, San Francisco, Los Angeles, Manzanillo (La Liberbad, occasionally), Balboa (Buena Ventura, occasionally), Callao, Pisco Mollendo, Arica, Iquique, Valparaiso. The vessels have 1st cl., 2nd cl., and Asiatic steerage accommodation.

Kobe-Mozi-Dairen Line. Twice weekly.

s.s. *Oryoku Maru*, 7363 tons; s.s. *Huso Maru*, 8199 tons; s.s. *Kokuryu Maru*, 7100 tons; s.s. *Nekka Maru*, 6784 tons; s.s. *Kiturin Maru*, 6783 tons; s.s. *Ussuri Maru*, 6886 tons; s.s. *Ural Maru*, 6375 tons. Sailings 4/5 times weekly, passage 3 days

Kobe—Tientsin.

m.v. *Tyozyo Maru* (2629 tons), m.v. *Tyoan Maru* (2632 tons), m.v. *Tyosyo Maru* (2611 tons). Depart Kobe three times fortnightly at 12.0, from Mozi 14.0 following day, due Tientsin 3rd day from Mozi.

Tsingtao Line. s.s. *Taizan Maru*, 3930 tons.

Seattle Maru (5773 tons), leaves Kobe 11.0 weekly, *via* Mozi, arrive Tsingtao about 3 days later. Leaves Tsingtao 11.0 weekly, *via* Mozi, due Kobe 3 days later.

Japan—Africa—South America Line (First Class.)

OUTWARD SAILINGS

Motor Vessel.	T'ns	Yokohama d.	Kobe dep.	Cape Town arr./dep.	Monte Video	Buenos Aires. a.
Santos Maru	7267	Aug. 5	Aug. 7	Sept. 7/8	Sept. 24	Sept. 25
La Plata Maru ..	7267	Sept. 28	Sept. 30	Oc.31/Nv 1	Nov. 17	Nov. 18
Buenos Aires Maru	9626	Oct. 24	Oct.26	Nov. 26/27	Dec. 13	Dec. 14
Argentina Maru	13000	Nov. 13	Nv. 17	Dec. 13/14	,, 27	,, 28

Also calling at Hong Kong, Singapore, Colombo, Durban, Rio de Janeiro, Santos. May also call at Shimidzu, Saigon, Port Elizabeth and East London.

HOMEWARD SAILINGS ¶

Motor Vessel.	Tons	Buenos Aires dep.	Los Angeles. arr./dep.	Yokohama. arr.	Kobe arr.
La Plata Maru	7267	July 11	Aug. 12/14	Sept. 1	Sept. 3
Buenos Aires Maru..	9626	Aug. 9	Sept. 11/13	,, 30	Oct. 2
Argentina Maru	13000	Sept. 3	Oct 1/3	Oct. 17	,, 19
Santos Maru	7267	Oct. 2	Nov. 3/5	Nov. 23	Nov. 25
La Plata Maru	7267	Nov 25	Dec. 27/29	Jan. 16	Jan. 18

Via Santos, Rio de Janeiro, (Belem occasionally), Cristobal. May also call at Montevideo, Rosario, La Plata, Victoria, (Brazil), Angra dos Reis, Bahia, Pernambuco and Havana.

Japan—Africa—South America Line. (Cabin Class.)

OUTWARD SAILINGS

Steamer.	Tons.	Kobe dep.	Mombasa, d.	Cape T'wn arr /dep.	Buenos Aires, arr.
Africa Maru .	9476	June 28	July 24	Aug. 10/11	Aug. 24
Hawaii Maru	9470	July 27	Aug. 22	Sept. 8/9	Sept. 22
Arizona Maru ..	9684	Aug. 2·	Sept. 24	Oct. 10/11	Oct. 24
Arabia Maru	9470	Sep. 28	Oct. 25	Nov. 10/11	Nov. 24

Also calling at Mozi, Hong Kong, Singapore, Colombo, Zanzibar, Dar-es-Salaam, Beira, Lourenco Marques Durban. May call at Saigon, Penang, Madras, Tanga, East London, Mossel Bay, Rio de Janeiro and Santos.

HOMEWARD SAILINGS

Steamer.	Tons	Buenos Aires, dep.	Mo'tevideo	Rio de Jan'ro dep	Cape Town arr/dep	Kobe arr.
Manila Maru	9486	July 29	Jul. 30	Aug. 6	Aug. 17/18	Sep 28
Africa Maru	9476	Aug. 30	Aug 31	Sept. 8	Sept. 19/20	Oct 31
Hawaii Maru	9470	Sept. 28	—	Oct. 6	Oct. 17/18	Nov 28
Arizona Maru	9684	Oct. 29	Oct.30	Nov. 5	Nov. 16/17	Dec 28
Arabia Maru	9470	Nov. 30	Dec. 1	Dec. 7	Dec. 18/19	Jan 31

Also calling at Santos, Mossel Bay, Port Elizabeth, East London, Durban, Lourenco Marques, Zanzibar, Mombasa, Singapore, Hongkong, Mozi. May call at Port Louis, Beira, Dar-es-Salaam, Tanga, Penang and Manila.

Other services by the *Osaka Syosen Kaisya* (particulars on application).

TAKAO—KEELUNG—SHANGHAI LINE.—From Takao 6th, 14th, 21st, 29th of each month, 8.0; from Shanghai 13th, 21st, 28th, 5/6 of each month.

BOMBAY LINE.—Yokohama, Nagoya, Yokkaichi, Osaka, Kobe, Mozi, Hong Kong, Singapore, Penang, Colombo, Bombay (Karachi).

CALCUTTA LINE.—Yokohama, Nagoya, Osaka, Kobe, Mozi, Hong Kong, Singapore, Penang, Belawan-Deli, Rangoon, Calcutta.

HONG KONG-HAIPHONG LINE.—From Hong Kong via Holkow, Pakhoi to Haiphong.

PHILIPPINES LINE.—Yokohama, Nagoya, Osaka, Kobe, Mozi, Nagasaki, Keelung, Takao, Manila, Cebu, Zamboanga to Davao.

SOUTH SEAS LINE.—Yokohama, Nagoya, Osaka, Kobe, Mozi, Keelung, Manila, Tawao to Sourabaya.

KOBE-KEELUNG LINE.—From Kobe via Mozi to Keelung.

SAIGON-BANGKOK.—From Yokohama via, Nagoya, Osaka, Kobe, Mozi, *Keelung, *Haiphong, *Saigon to Bangkok. Returning Bangkok, Saigon, Kobe, Osaka, Yokohama. * Optional.

PORT LINE (See also page 460).

COMMONWEALTH AND DOMINION LINE LTD.

New York to Australasia via Panama Canal.

Passenger accommodation limited to 12 saloon passengers in single and two-berth staterooms.

Vessel.	Tons.	Sailing Date.	To
Port Adelaide	84?2	Aug. 21	Brisbane, Sydney, Melbourne.
Port Bowen	8267	Oct. 1	Brisbane, Sydney, Melbourne.
Port —— ..	——	Nov 11	Brisbane, Sydney Melbourne.

PRINCE LINE (See also page 367).

ROUND THE WORLD EXPRESS SERVICE.
(Fast Motor Vessels).

ITINERARY.—New York, Hampton Roads, Savannah, Panama, Los Angeles, San Francisco, Manila, Shanghai, Hong-Kong, Manila, Cebu, Davao, Macassar, Sourabaya, Samarang, Batavia Telok, Betong, Singapore, Port Swettenham, Belawan, Penang, Colombo, Dakar, Halifax, Boston, New York.

All the vessels are twin-screw motor ships with excellent accommodation for up to 10 first class passengers in two-berth cabins amidships, bathrooms, electric light, fans, refrigerator, etc.

SAILINGS ON APPLICATION. } Through Bookings from the U.K. Round Voyage 130 days.

CIE SAIGONNAISE DE NAVIGATION ET DE TRANSPORT.

SERVICES SUSPENDED.

COCHIN CHINA and CAMBODGE LINES—From Saigon, at 21.0, via Mytho, due Pnom-Penh two days later. Return from Pnom-Penh due Saigon next day.
PNOM-PENH and KHONE—SUD via KRATIE.
KHONE—NORD and SAVANNAKEK via Kbong, Bassac, Pakse, Makeua, Naphone.
SAVANNAKEK,—VIENTIANE, via Thakkek, † Ban Sot, Paksane, Nong Keo. † Transfer for road to Vinh and Hue.

STATES STEAMSHIP COMPANY.

TRANS-PACIFIC SERVICES by "One Class Ships."

SERVICES SUSPENDED

STEAMER.	Tons.	Portland. dep.	Yoko-hama arr.	Kobe. dep.	Shanghai. arr./dep.	Hong Kong. arr.	Hong Kong. dep.	Manila. arr.

STEAMER.	Tons.	Manila. dep.	Hong Kong. arr./dep.	Shanghai. arr./dep.	Kobe. dep.	Yoko-hama dep.	San Francisco arr.	Portland. arr.

STRAITS STEAMSHIP COMPANY, LIMITED.

SINGAPORE—PENANG.—Weekly express service by s.s. *Kedah*, 2,498 tons, sailing on Thursday, journey occupies 19½ hours. Twice weekly service via Port Swettenham, on Mon. and Wed
SINGAPORE—BANGKOK.—s.s. *Kepong*, 1,874 tons; s.s. *Kudat*, 1,725 tons. Weekly express service sailing from Singapore on Wednesdays and frequent irregular sailings.
SINGAPORE to BRITISH NORTH BORNEO, Etc.—s.s. *Kajang*, 2,082 tons; s.s. *Darvel*, 1,929 tons, and m.v. *Marudu*, 1,926 tons. Weekly express service, dep. Singapore on Saturdays via Miri, Labuan, Jesselton, Kudat to Sandakan. Round trip 16 days.
SINGAPORE, MALACCA, PORT DICKSON, PORT SWETTENHAM, TELUK ANSON and PENANG.—Frequent sailings to all parts on the West Coast of Malaya.
SINGAPORE to KUANTAN.—Weekly service to intermediate East Coast Ports as far as Kuantan.
SINGAPORE to KELANTAN.—Sailings weekly in conjunction with Siam Steam Navigation Co. Ltd.
SINGAPORE to SUMATRA.—Weekly service to Belawan-Deli via Penang, sailing on Thursday.
PENANG to WEST SIAM and BURMA.—Sailing every 14 days to Siam and Burma Ports as far as Moulmein. Weekly express service to West Siam Ports, sailing on Saturdays.
PENANG to EAST COAST SUMATRA
PENANG to WEST COAST MALAYA } The Company maintains frequent sailings to these ports.

LLOYD TRIESTINO Societa Anonima di Navigazione

(See also pages 382/5 and 456A)

LINE 156.

Massaua, Suez. Sailings weekly.

s.s. *Tripolitana* 2722 tons. s.s. *Massaua* 1524 tons. s.s. *Eritrea* 2517 tons. s.s. *Adua* 3564 tons.

	arr.	dep.									
Massaua ..	—	Wed. 22 o	Aug 2	Aug. 9	Aug 16	Aug 23	Aug. 30	Sept. 6	Sept. 13	Sept. 20	Sep. 27
Port Sudan	Fri. 6 o	Fri. 15 o	,, 4	,, 11	,, 18	,, 25	Sept. 1	,, 8	,, 15	,, 22	,, 29
Jeddah ..	Sat. 8 o	Sat. 15 o	,, 5	,, 12	,, 19	,, 26	,, 2	,, 9	,, 16	,, 23	,, 30
Suez......	Tue. 8 o	—	,, 8	,, 15	,, 22	,, 29	,, 5	,, 12	,, 19	,, 26	Oct. 3
,,	—	Wed. 15 o	,, 9	,, 16	—	,, 30	,, 6	,, 13	—	,, 27	,, 4
,,	—	Thu. 15 o	—	—	,, 24	—	—	—	,, 21	—	—
Kossier ..	Thu. 17 o	Thu. 20 o	,, 10	—	—	—	,, 7	—		—	,, 5
,,	Fri. 17 o	Fri. 20 o	—	—	,, 25	—	—	—	,, 22	—	—
Jeddah ..	Sat. 8 o	Sat. 13 o	—	,, 19	—	Sept. 2	—	,, 16	—	,, 30	—
,,	Sat. 12 o	Sat. 16 o	,, 12	—	—	[illegible]	,, 9	—	—	—	,, 7
,,	Sun. 12 o	Sun. 16 o	—	—	,, 27	—	—	—	,, 24	—	—
Port Sudan	Sun. 6 o	Sun. 22 o	,, 13	,, 20	—	,, 3	,, 10	,, 17	—	Oct. 1	,, 8
,, ,,	Mon. 9 o	Mon. 22 o	—	—	,, 28	—	—	—	,, 25	—	—
Massaua ..	Tue. 7 o	—	,, 15	,, 22	—	,, 5	,, 12	,, 19	—	,, 3	,, 10
,,	Wed. 7 o	—	—	—	,, 30	—	—	—	,, 27	—	—

UNITED FRUIT COMPANY

SERVICE NO. 1. WEEKLY.—New York (Sat.), Havana (Tue./Wed.), Port Limon (Sat./Sun.), Cristobal (Mon)., Havana (Thur.), New York (Sun.).

SERVICE NO. 2. WEEKLY.—New York (Wed.), Kingston (Sun.), Barranquilla (Tues./Wed.), Cartagena (Wed.), Cristobal (Thur./Fri.), Kingston (Sun.), New York (Thur.).

SERVICE NO. 3. WEEKLY.—New York (Sat.), Santiago (alt. Weds.), Tela (alt. Thurs.), Puerto Barrios (Fri./Sat.), Puerto Cortes (Fri./Sat. and Sat./Sun.), New York (Thur.).

SERVICE NO. 4. WEEKLY.—New York (Fri.), Cristobal (Wed./Thur.), Santa Marta (Fri./Sat.), New York (Wed.).

SERVICE NO. 5. WEEKLY.—New Orleans (Sat.), Havana (Mon.), Panama (Fri./Sat.), Port Limon (Sun/Mon.), Tela (Wed.), Havana (Fri./Sat.), New Orleans (Mon.).

SERVICE NO. 6.—Aug. 15th and Sept. 26th. New Orleans (Tues.), Belize (Fri.), Puerto Barrios (Sat./Sun.), Puerto Cortes (Sun./Mon.), New Orleans (Thur.).

WEEKLY—Except Aug. 15th and Sept. 26th. New Orleans (Wed.), Puerto Barrios (Sat./Sun.), Tela (Sun./Mon.), New Orleans (Thur.).

SERVICE NO. 7. WEEKLY.—Philadelphia (Tues.), Puerto Barrios (Mon./Tues.), Philadelphia (Sun.).

Also regular Cruises from New York, Boston, Philadelphia, New Orleans.

Details on application.

EGYPT

When visiting
You cannot
do better than stay at the

VICTORIA HOTEL

SELECT AND REFINED.

CAIRO'S FIRST-CLASS AND MODERN HOTEL AT MODERATE RATES.

GARDEN, VERANDAHS, TERRACE, CENTRAL HEATING. NUMEROUS APARTMENTS WITH PRIVATE BATHS.

Three-colour signal light system for attendance, and telephone in every room. Two lifts. American Bar. English billiards. Experienced chef. Autobus to all trains. All steamers met.

Cook's Hotel Vouchers accepted.

J. VOCLES, Proprietor.

(1239)

All enquiries for Advertising Rates in

THE CONTINENTAL TIME TABLE

must be addressed to—

ADVERTISING DEPT.,

THOS. COOK & SON, LTD., BERKELEY STREET, Piccadilly, London, W. 1.

CALAIS.

TERMINUS HOTEL AND BUFFET

(GARE MARITIME)

The only one on Pier. Splendid view of sea and port. First class. Entirely renovated. Electric Lift and Light. Central Heating. Apartments with Bath. Renowned Cuisine and Cellar. Hall. Reading Room. Terrace. Bracing air.

Travellers have time for lunching at Buffet. Official notice is given of the departure of trains five minutes beforehand.

Cook's Hotel Vouchers accepted.

Under the management of the Cie International des Wagons-Lits, since June 15th, 1931. (T.C.)

NICE.

WESTMINSTER HOTEL

PROMENADE DES ANGLAIS.

150 rooms with private bath or running hot and cold water. Always open. Reduced terms. Telegrams : "Westminster, Nice."

(1039) **F. B. REBETEZ, Proprietor-Manager.**

NÜRNBERG.

HOTEL BAMBERGER HOF
AND
CENTRAL HOTEL

TWO SELECTED HOTELS NEAR THE MAIN STATION AND CITY.

(740)

NÜRNBERG

THE FAMOUS HOUSE WITH THE OLD REPUTATION

Cables: Grandhotel. Phone 22881

G. RICHERT & LOTZ
Managing Proprietors

(1039)

NUERNBERG.

HOTEL WUERTTEMBERGER HOF

(OPPOSITE THE STATION).

First-class hotel of old tradition and world reputation. Recently renovated. All modern comfort. Quiet position. 200 rooms. Mostly private bathrooms. Auto garage. Open air Restaurant in the nice hotel-garden. Near the Theatre and the most interesting points of the old city.

(4-939) **Proprietor : Cl. & W. GREISBACHER.**

OSTEND.

TERMINUS MARITIME

Hotel Buffet de la Gare Ostende-Quai

Under the Management of the International Wagons-Lits Company.

First-class hotel situated on the quay, adjoining station, so that direct access to it can be gained. All modern comforts. Lift. Electric light. Central heating. Bathrooms, hot and cold running water. Reading room. Smoking room.

Telephone No. 27. **Telegraphic Address.**

OSTEND.

FOR COMFORT TRY

"THE CARLTON"

RUE ROYALE 75

An up-to-date British private hotel. Ideal situation, two steps from best part of beach and Kursaal. 65 bedrooms with hot and cold running water. Bathrooms. Central heating. Lounge and smoke room. Nice restaurant with separate tables. All latest comfort. First-class cooking. Personal supervision. Moderate terms. Telephone 73964.

Cook's Hotel Vouchers accepted. **Proprietor: F. ROOSE.**

(5-1039)

OSTEND. *The LEADING HOTELS on the Sea Front.*

HOTEL SPLENDID — MAJESTIC PALACE

400 Beds. 250 Beds.

Open: March—October.

KURSAAL AND BEAU-SITE HOTEL

150 Beds.

First-class Hotels. Every modern comfort. Renowned Restaurants.

(140) Cook's Hotel Vouchers are accepted at all these Establishments.

OSTEND.

PACIFIC HOTEL

11, RUE DU JARDIN 11

BUILT IN 1929. PHONE 1728.

Sea view. Near Kursaal and Theatre. Every modern comfort. Lifts, central heating, bathrooms, etc. All bedrooms are provided with hot and cold running water and fireproof floors. First class Restaurant. Cook's Hotel Vouchers accepted. Managed by the Proprietor—

(5-1039) **R. VAN GLABBEKE.**

PARIS

HOTEL SAINTE MARIE

83, RUE DE RIVOLI—Ier ARR.

Telegram: Mariotel Paris 117.

Very central situation, 100 yards from the main entrance of the Louvre Museum. Metro station at the door to all directions. Renovated latest comfort. Moderate prices Special terms for long stay. Urban telephone in each room. Auto Garages next door.

(540) No obligations for guests to take meals in the hotel.

GEORGE V

THE PREMIER HOTEL

31, Avenue George V - PARIS

:: Télégram: Georgeotel-Paris ::

(See also announcement on Map, facing page 113).

WIESBADEN.

HOTEL NIZZA

(HOTEL DE NICE)

Best class hotel in residential part of town. H. and C. in all rooms. Thermal baths. Moderate terms. Patronised by English and American guests. R.A.C. and A.A. Hotel. Garage. Garden. Cook's Coupons accepted.

Manager-Prop., E. UPLEGGER.

(1139)

WIESBADEN.

TAUNUS HOTEL

160 beds. All comforts. Conference rooms. Restaurant. Café. Bar. Concert. Garage. Moderate terms. Best position. First-class family house.

Gg. PATZOLD, Proprietor.

(540)

ZERMATT for Winter Sports.
Altitude 5,315 ft. to 7,500 ft.

Stay at SEILER'S HOTELS

VICTORIA—MONT CERVIN—BEAU SITE

(450 Beds)

this winter and be sure of comfort and enjoyment. Central for all sports. Ski-ing, skating, curling and entertainments Managers in the Hotels. Two Orchestras. Free inclusive brochure from HOTELS SEILER, ZERMATT.

(1039)

ZERMATT (Switzerland).

SUMMER RESORT. WINTER SPORTS.

THE HOTELS SCHWEIZERHOF, NATIONAL TERMINUS AND BELLEVUE

Highly recommended. All comforts. First-class cuisine. Tea room. Tea gardens. Orchestra. Best position. Moderate terms. Cook's Hotel Vouchers accepted.

H. ZIMMERMANN, Managing Director.

(1239)

Carlton Elite Hotel

ZURICH.

Your real home in Zurich. Central situation. Rooms from frs. 6. Restaurant. Bar. Garage.

HUGO E. PRAGER, Proprietor.

(839)

See also facing page 218, and on page 408.

N·Y·K Line
TO THE FAR EAST
Fortnightly passenger services from London to Gibraltar, Marseilles, Naples, Port Said, Ceylon, Straits, China and Japan ● From Los Angeles and San Francisco via Honolulu to Japan and China ● From Seattle and Vancouver, B.C. to Japan and China ● Through bookings from Europe in connection with the above Pacific Services ● Round the world tours.
NIPPON YUSEN KAISYA
88 LEADENHALL STREET, LONDON, E.C.3 ● AVE. 1291
CUNARD WHITE STAR LTD., 26-7 COCKSPUR STREET, S.W.1
or any office of Thos. Cook & Son Ltd.